THE ROUTLEDGE CC
TO HERMENEU

Hermeneutics is a major theoretical and practical form of intellectual inquiry, central not only to philosophy but many other disciplines in the humanities and social sciences. With phenomenology and existentialism, it was also one of the twentieth century's most important philosophical movements and included major thinkers such as Heidegger, Gadamer and Ricoeur.

The Routledge Companion to Hermeneutics is an outstanding guide and reference source to the key philosophers, topics and themes of this exciting subject and is the first volume of its kind. Comprising over fifty chapters by a team of international contributors, the *Companion* is divided into five parts:

- main figures in the hermeneutical tradition movement, including Heidegger, Gadamer and Ricoeur;
- main topics in hermeneutics such as language, truth, relativism and history;
- the engagement of hermeneutics with central disciplines such as literature, religion, race and gender, and art;
- hermeneutics and world philosophies including Asian, Islamic and Judaic thought;
- hermeneutic challenges and debates, such as critical theory, structuralism and phenomenology.

Jeff Malpas is Distinguished Professor at the University of Tasmania, Australia and Visiting Distinguished Professor at LaTrobe University, Melbourne, Australia.

Hans-Helmuth Gander is Professor of Philosophy at Albert-Ludwigs-Universität Freiburg, Germany

ROUTLEDGE PHILOSOPHY COMPANIONS

Routledge Philosophy Companions offer thorough, high quality surveys and assessments of the major topics and periods in philosophy. Covering key problems, themes and thinkers, all entries are specially commissioned for each volume and written by leading scholars in the field. Clear, accessible and carefully edited and organised, *Routledge Philosophy Companions* are indispensable for anyone coming to a major topic or period in philosophy, as well as for the more advanced reader.

The Routledge Companion to Aesthetics, Third Edition
Edited by Berys Gaut and Dominic Lopes

The Routledge Companion to Philosophy of Science, Second Edition
Edited by Martin Curd and Stathis Psillos

The Routledge Companion to Philosophy of Religion, Second Edition
Edited by Chad Meister and Paul Copan

The Routledge Companion to Twentieth Century Philosophy
Edited by Dermot Moran

The Routledge Companion to Philosophy and Film
Edited by Paisley Livingston and Carl Plantinga

The Routledge Companion to Philosophy of Psychology
Edited by John Symons and Paco Calvo

The Routledge Companion to Metaphysics
Edited by Robin Le Poidevin, Peter Simons, Andrew McGonigal, and Ross Cameron

The Routledge Companion to Nineteenth Century Philosophy
Edited by Dean Moyar

The Routledge Companion to Ethics
Edited by John Skorupski

The Routledge Companion to Epistemology
Edited by Sven Bernecker and Duncan Pritchard

The Routledge Companion to Philosophy and Music
Edited by Theodore Gracyk and Andrew Kania

The Routledge Companion to Phenomenology
Edited by Søren Overgaard and Sebastian Luft

The Routledge Companion to Philosophy of Language
Edited by Gillian Russell and Delia Graff Fara

The Routledge Companion to Philosophy of Law
Edited by Andrei Marmor

The Routledge Companion to Social and Political Philosophy
Edited by Gerald Gaus and Fred D'Agostino

The Routledge Companion to Ancient Philosophy
Edited by Frisbee Sheffield and James Warren

The Routledge Companion to Eighteenth Century Philosophy
Edited by Aaron Garrett

Forthcoming:

The Routledge Companion to Seventeenth Century Philosophy
Edited by Dan Kaufman

The Routledge Companion to Islamic Philosophy
Edited by Richard C. Taylor and Luis Xavier López-Farjeat

The Routledge Companion to Philosophy of Literature
Edited by Noël Carroll and John Gibson

The Routledge Companion to Bioethics
Edited by John Arras, Rebecca Kukla, and Elizabeth Fenton

The Routledge Companion to Medieval Philosophy
Edited by J. T. Paasch and Richard Cross

The Routledge Companion to Thought Experiments
Edited by James Robert Brown, Yiftach Fehige, and Michael T. Stuart

PRAISE FOR THE SERIES

The Routledge Companion to Aesthetics

'This is an immensely useful book that belongs in every college library and on the bookshelves of all serious students of aesthetics.' – *Journal of Aesthetics and Art Criticism*

'The succinctness and clarity of the essays will make this a source that individuals not familiar with aesthetics will find extremely helpful.' – *The Philosophical Quarterly*

'An outstanding resource in aesthetics ... this text will not only serve as a handy reference source for students and faculty alike, but it could also be used as a text for a course in the philosophy of art.' – *Australasian Journal of Philosophy*

'Attests to the richness of modern aesthetics ... the essays in central topics – many of which are written by well-known figures – succeed in being informative, balanced and intelligent without being too difficult.' – *British Journal of Aesthetics*

'This handsome reference volume ... belongs in every library.' – **CHOICE**

'The *Routledge Companions* to Philosophy have proved to be a useful series of high quality surveys of major philosophical topics and this volume is worthy enough to sit with the others on a reference library shelf.' – *Philosophy and Religion*

The Routledge Companion to Philosophy of Religion

' ... a very valuable resource for libraries and serious scholars.' – **CHOICE**

'The work is sure to be an academic standard for years to come ... I shall heartily recommend *The Routledge Companion to Philosophy of Religion* to my students and colleagues and hope that libraries around the country add it to their collections.' – *Philosophia Christi*

The Routledge Companion to Philosophy of Science

A **CHOICE** Outstanding Academic Title 2008

'With a distinguished list of internationally renowned contributors, an excellent choice of topics in the field, and well-written, well-edited essays throughout, this compendium is an excellent resource. Highly recommended.' – **CHOICE**

'Highly recommended for history of science and philosophy collections.' – *Library Journal*

This well-conceived companion, which brings together an impressive collection of distinguished authors, will be invaluable to novices and experienced readers alike.' – *Metascience*

The Routledge Companion to Twentieth Century Philosophy

'To describe this volume as ambitious would be a serious understatement. ... full of scholarly rigor, including detailed notes and bibliographies of interest to professional philosophers. ... Summing up: Essential.' – **CHOICE**

The Routledge Companion to Philosophy and Film

'A fascinating, rich volume offering dazzling insights and incisive commentary on every page ... Every serious student of film will want this book ... Summing Up: Highly recommended.' – **CHOICE**

The Routledge Companion to Philosophy of Psychology

'This work should serve as the standard reference for those interested in gaining a reliable overview of the burgeoning field of philosophical psychology. Summing Up: Essential.' – **CHOICE**

The Routledge Companion to Metaphysics

'The *Routledge Philosophy Companions* series has a deserved reputation for impressive scope and scholarly value. This volume is no exception ... Summing Up: Highly recommended.' – **CHOICE**

The Routledge Companion to Nineteenth Century Philosophy

A **CHOICE** Outstanding Academic Title 2010

'This is a crucial resource for advanced undergraduates and faculty of any discipline who are interested in the 19th-century roots of contemporary philosophical problems. Summing Up: Essential.' – **CHOICE**

The Routledge Companion to Ethics

'This fine collection merits a place in every university, college, and high school library for its invaluable articles covering a very broad range of topics in ethics[.] ... With its remarkable clarity of writing and its very highly qualified contributors, this volume is must reading for anyone interested in the latest developments in these important areas of thought and practice. Summing Up: Highly recommended.' – **CHOICE**

The Routledge Companion to Philosophy and Music

'Comprehensive and authoritative ... readers will discover many excellent articles in this well-organized addition to a growing interdisciplinary field. Summing Up: Highly recommended.' – **CHOICE**

' ... succeeds well in catching the wide-ranging strands of musical theorising and thinking, and performance, and an understanding of the various contexts in which all this takes place.' – *Reference Reviews*

The Routledge Companion to Phenomenology

'Sebastian Luft and Søren Overgaard, with the help of over sixty contributors, have captured the excitement of this evolving patchwork named 'phenomenology'. The Routledge Companion to Phenomenology will serve as an invaluable reference volume for students, teachers, and scholars of phenomenology, as well as an accessible introduction to phenomenology for philosophers from other specialties or scholars from other disciplines.' – *International Journal of Philosophical Studies*

The Routledge Companion to Epistemology

A **CHOICE** Outstanding Academic Title 2011

'As a series, the *Routledge Philosophy Companions* has met with near universal acclaim. The expansive volume not only continues the trend but quite possibly sets a new standard. ... Indeed, this is a definitive resource that will continue to prove its value for a long time to come. Summing Up: Essential.' – **CHOICE**

THE ROUTLEDGE COMPANION TO HERMENEUTICS

Edited by
Jeff Malpas and Hans-Helmuth Gander

Routledge
Taylor & Francis Group

LONDON AND NEW YORK

First published 2015 by Routledge

2 Park Square, Milton Park, Abingdon, Oxfordshire OX14 4RN
711 Third Avenue, New York, NY 10017

Routledge is an imprint of the Taylor & Francis Group, an informa business

First issued in paperback 2017

British Library Cataloguing in Publication Data
A catalogue record for this book is available from the British Library

Library of Congress Cataloging-in-Publication Data
The Routledge companion to hermeneutics / edited by Jeff Malpas and Hans-Helmuth Gander.
pages cm. – (Routledge philosophy companions)
Includes bibliographical references and index.
1. Hermeneutics. I. Malpas, Jeff. II. Gander, Hans-Helmuth, 1954-
BD241.R68 2014
121'.686–dc23
2014018150

ISBN: 978-0-415-64458-7 (hbk)
ISBN: 978-1-138-57463-2 (pbk)

Typeset in Goudy
by Taylor & Francis Books

CONTENTS

CONTENTS

CONTENTS

CONTRIBUTORS

Leonardo Amoroso is Professor of Aesthetics at the University of Pisa. He received his PhD in 1983 from the Scuola Normale Superiore (Pisa) and was promoted Full Professor in 1995 at the University of Padua. His most recent books are *Ratio & Aesthetica. La nascita dell'estetica e la filosofia moderna* (2000, 2008²), *Scintille ebraiche. Spinoza, Vico and Benamozegh* (2004), *Per un'estetica della Bibbia* (2008), and *Introduzione alla 'Scienza Nuova' di Vico* (2011). He also translated into Italian Kant's *Kritik der Urteilskraft* and Heidegger's *Erläuterungen zu Hölderlins Dichtung*.

John Arthos is Associate Professor in the Department of Communication and Culture, at Indiana University Bloomington. He is the author of three books and over thirty peer reviewed journal articles. His research addresses the relationship between rhetoric and hermeneutics.

Babette Babich is Professor of Philosophy at Fordham University in New York City. Her most recent book is *The Hallelujah Effect: Philosophical Reflections on Music, Performance Practice and Technology* (2013) in which she discusses k.d. lang's cover of Leonard Cohen's *Hallelujah* and desire (male/female) in the context of phenomenological sociology and critical theory (Adorno), technological culture and music, from antiquity to Beethoven's liberation of dissonance (Nietzsche). In 1996, she founded the journal she currently edits, *New Nietzsche Studies*. She specialises in continental philosophy of science and technology, critical theory, the politics of academic philosophy, including women in philosophy, media aesthetics, ancient Greek music and tragedy as well as life-size ancient Greek bronzes.

Endre Begby (PhD, University of Pittsburgh) is Assistant Professor of Philosophy at Simon Fraser University. His publications include articles in *Journal of Philosophy*, *Philosophical Studies*, *Politics*, *Philosophy Compass* and *Thought*, as well as a major anthology, *The Ethics of War: Classic and Contemporary Readings* (with Gregory Reichberg and Henrik Syse; Blackwell 2006).

Fredrick Beiser is Professor of Philosophy at Syracuse University. He has been a major contributor to work on the history of modern philosophy, especially the history of German philosophy (Kant and German idealism) and the English Enlightenment. His book *The Fate of Reason: German Philosophy from Kant to Fichte* won the 1987 Thomas J. Wilson Prize for the Best First Book. He has won Thyssen and Humboldt research fellowships to study at the Free University of Berlin and was a 1994 Guggenheim Fellow. He received a 1999–2000 NEH Faculty Fellowship (at Indiana University).

Andrew Benjamin is Distinguished Professor of Philosophy and the Humanities at Kingston University, London and Professor of Philosophy and Jewish Thought in the Department of Philosophy and the Australian Centre for Jewish Civilization at Monash University, Melbourne. His main area of research specialisation is philosophical aesthetics. His most recent books include *Working with Walter Benjamin: recovering a political philosophy* (2013), *Of Jews and animals* (2010) and *Place, commonality and judgment: continental philosophy and the ancient Greeks* (2010).

Mauricio Beuchot received his PhD from the Universidad Iberoamericana de México. He is Professor and researcher in the Universidad Nacional Autónoma de México where he founded the Center of Hermeneutics within the Institute of Philology. His published works include *Tratado de hermenéutica analógica* ('Treatise of Analogical Hermeneutics') (1997); *La hermenéutica en la Edad Media* ('Hermeneutics in the Middle Ages') (2002); *Phrónesis, hermenéutica y analogía* (2004); and *Analogía y hermenéutica en la Edad media* (2013). He has developed a system of 'analogic hermeneutics' that is widely recognised in Latin America and Spain.

Tina Fernandes Botts is a Fellow in Law and Philosophy at the University of Michigan and previously an assistant professor of philosophy at the University of North Carolina at Charlotte. She has a PhD in philosophy from the University of Memphis and a law degree from Rutgers University – Camden. Her areas of specialisation are philosophy of law, philosophy of race, philosophical hermeneutics and feminist theory. Recent publications include 'Antidiscrimination Law and the Multiracial Experience' in the *Hastings Race and Poverty Law Journal* (Summer 2013) and co-authorship of the chapter entitled, 'Women of Color Feminisms' in the 4th edition of *Feminist Thought* by Rosemarie Tong (Westview, 2013).

Andrew Bowie is Professor of Philosophy and German at Royal Holloway, University of London. His research focuses on core issues in modern philosophy, especially as explored within the German tradition from Kant to the present, and he has written extensively about music and literature as well as philosophy. His many books include *Aesthetics and Subjectivity: from Kant to Nietzsche* (1990), *From Romanticism to Critical Theory. The Philosophy of German Literary Theory* (1997), *Music, Philosophy, and Modernity* (2007), *German Philosophy: A Very Short Introduction* (2010), *Adorno and the Ends of Philosophy* (2013).

Lee Braver is Associate Professor of Philosophy at the University of South Florida. He is the author of *A Thing of This World: A History of Continental Anti-Realism* (Northwestern, 2007), *Heidegger's Later Writings: A Reader's Guide* (Bloomsbury, 2009), *Groundless Grounds: A Study of Wittgenstein and Heidegger* (MIT, 2012), *Heidegger: Thinking of Being* (Polity, 2014) and editor of *Division III of Being and Time: Heidegger's Unanswered Question of Being* (MIT, forthcoming), as well as a number of articles and book chapters. He is also considered by many to be a Master Griller.

Philippe Cabestan is the author of *L'Etre et la conscience. Recherches sur la psychologie et l'ontologie sartriennes* (Ousia, 2004) and a dictionary about *Sartre* (Ellipses, 2009). He recently published (with Françoise Dastur), *Daseinsanalyse. Phénoménologie et psychiatrie* (Vrin, 2011). He is co-president of the Ecole Française de Daseinsanalyse.

Gaetano Chiurazzi is Associate Professor of Theoretical Philosophy at the University of Turin. He studied and worked as research fellow in the Universities of Torino,

Berlin, Heidelberg and Paris. His interests are especially concerned with French and German philosophy, in particular Derrida, Kant, Hegel, Husserl, Heidegger and Gadamer, as attested by his main publications: *Scrittura e tecnica. Derrida e la metafisica* (1992); *Hegel, Heidegger e la grammatica dell'essere* (1996); *Teorie del giudizio* (2005; Spanish translation: *Teorías del juicio*, 2008); *Modalità ed esistenza* (2001; German translation: *Modalität und Existenz*, 2006); *L'esperienza della verità* (2011). With Gianni Vattimo he is the co-editor of *Tropos. Rivista di ermeneutica e critica filosofica*.

Richard Coyne is Professor of Architectural Computing at the University of Edinburgh. He is author of several books on the philosophical implications of computers and digital media, particularly in the context of design. He co-authored the book *Interpretation in Architecture* (2006) and authored *Derrida for Architects* (2011) both with Routledge. He has authored four books with MIT Press, the most recent being *The Tuning of Place* (2010). He is currently Dean of Postgraduate Research in the College of Humanities and Social Science at the University of Edinburgh.

Fred D'Agostino is Professor of Humanities at The University of Queensland after a stint as Executive Dean of Arts. He has edited the journals *Politics, Philosophy and Economics* and *The Australasian Journal of Philosophy*, and recently co-edited the *Routledge Companion to Political and Social Philosophy*. He works at the intersection of political philosophy and epistemology and is currently working on a book titled *Disciplinarity and the Growth of Knowledge*.

Daniel Dahlstrom, Silber Professor of Philosophy at Boston University, is the author of *Das logische Vorurteil* (1994), *Heidegger's Concept of Truth* (2001), *Philosophical Legacies: Essays on the Thought of Kant, Hegel, and their Contemporaries* (2008) and *The Heidegger Dictionary* (2013). He has also produced a new translation of Husserl's *Ideas I* (2014) and edited *Interpreting Heidegger: New Essays* (2010).

Nicholas Davey was educated at the Universities of York, Sussex and Tübingen. He is presently Professor of Philosophy at the University of Dundee. His principal teaching and research interests are in aesthetics and hermeneutics. He has served as the President of the British Society for Phenomenology and on the Board of the British Society for Aesthetics. He is the author of *Unquiet Understanding: Gadamer and Philosophical Hermeneutics* (State University Press of New York, 2006) and *Unfinished Worlds: Hermeneutics, Aesthetics and Gadamer* (Edinburgh University Press, 2013).

Donatella Di Cesare is Professor of Philosophy at the Sapienza University of Rome. She is vice-president of the 'Martin Heidegger-Gesellschaft' and member of the scientific board of the 'Wittgenstein-Studien'. Her last publications are *Grammaire des temps messianiques* (2011), *Utopia of Understanding. Between Babel and Auschwitz* (2012), *Gadamer. A Philosophical Portrait* (2013).

Giuseppina D'Oro is Reader in Philosophy at Keele University. She is the author of *Collingwood and the Metaphysics of Experience* (Routledge, 2002) and of several articles which bring Collingwood's work to bear upon contemporary debates in metaphilosophy and the philosophy of mind and action. She is co-editor (with Constantine Sandis) of *Reasons and Causes: Causalism and Anti-Causalism in the*

Philosophy of Action (Palgrave, 2013) and (with James Connelly) of Collingwood's *An Essay on Philosophical Method* (Oxford University Press, 2005).

Robert Dostal is Rufus Jones Professor of Philosophy at Bryn Mawr College, Bryn Mawr, Pennsylvania. He is the editor of *The Cambridge Companion to Gadamer* (2002) and the co-editor of *Phenomenology on Kant, German Idealism, Hermeneutics, and Logic* (2000). He has published numerous papers on Kant, Husserl, Heidegger and Gadamer.

Paul Fairfield is Associate Professor in the Department of Philosophy at Queen's University in Kingston, ON Canada. His recent books include *Philosophical Hermeneutics Reinterpreted* (Bloomsbury, 2011) and *Education After Dewey* (Continuum, 2009). He is also editor of the volume *Education, Dialogue and Hermeneutics* (Continuum, 2010).

Ingo Farin is Lecturer in Philosophy at the University of Tasmania, Australia. He has translated (together with James G. Hart) Husserl's *Basic Problems of Phenomenology* (2006) and (together with Alex Skinner) Heidegger's *The Concept of Time* (2011). He has published papers on phenomenology and hermeneutics.

William Franke is Professor of Comparative Literature at Vanderbilt University (USA) and Professor of Philosophy and Religions at University of Macao (China). He is a research fellow of the Alexander von Humboldt-Stiftung and has been Fulbright Distinguished Chair in Intercultural Theology at the University of Salzburg. His books include *A Philosophy of the Unsayable* (2014); *Dante and the Sense of Transgression: 'The Trespass of the Sign'* (2013); *Poetry and Apocalypse* (2009); *On What Cannot Be Said* (2007) and *Dante's Interpretive Journey* (1996). Forthcoming in 2015 are *The Revelation of Imagination: From the Bible and Homer through Virgil and Augustine to Dante* and *Secular Scriptures: Theological Poetics and the Challenge of Modernity*.

Shaun Gallagher is the Lillian and Morrie Moss Professor of Excellence at Memphis University. His areas of research include phenomenology and the cognitive sciences, especially topics related to embodiment, self, agency and intersubjectivity, hermeneutics, and the philosophy of time. He also holds appointments at the University of Hertfordshire and the University of Wollongong, is Honorary Professor of Philosophy at both the University of Copenhagen and Durham University, and is Honorary Professor of Health Sciences at the University of Tromsø. He currently holds an Anneliese Maier Research Award from the Alexander Humboldt Foundation. His books include *Hermeneutics and Education* (1992), *How the Body Shapes the Mind* (2005), *Phenomenology* (2012) and (with Dan Zahavi), *The Phenomenological Mind* (2008). He is also the co-editor-in-chief of the journal *Phenomenology and the Cognitive Sciences*.

Hans-Helmuth Gander is Professor of Philosophy and Director of the Husserl-Archive at the Albert-Ludwigs-Universität Freiburg (Germany). His research focus is on Phenomenology, Hermeneutics and Political Philosophy. He is the author of *Selbstverständnis und Lebenswelt. Grundzüge einer phänomenologischen Hermeneutik im Ausgang von Husserl und Heidegger* (2006). He has been the editor of *Husserl-Lexikon* (2010) and *Martin Heidegger: Grundprobleme der Phänomenologie (1919/20)* (1993) and is the co-editor of *Resilienz in der offenen Gesellschaft* (2012).

Kristin Gjesdal is Associate Professor of Philosophy at Temple University. Her areas of specialisation include German Idealism, phenomenology and hermeneutics (from Herder and Schleiermacher to Gadamer, Davidson and beyond). Her work has appeared in journals such as *Journal of the History of Philosophy*, *British Journal of the History of Philosophy*, *History of Philosophy Quarterly*, *Kant-Studien* and *Hegel-Studien*. She is the author of *Gadamer and the Legacy of German Idealism* (Cambridge University Press, 2009) and the co-editor of the *Oxford Handbook of German Nineteenth Century Philosophy* (forthcoming with Oxford University Press).

Ambrosio Velasco Gómez is Professor of Philosophy of Science and Political Philosophy at the National Autonomous University of México. He received his PhD from the University of Minnesota. His published works include *Teoría política: Filosofía e historia. ¿Anacrónicos o anticuarios?* (1995), *Tradiciones naturalistas y hermenéuticas en la filosofía de las ciencias sociales* (1999), *Republicanismo y Multiculturalismo* (2006) and *La persistencia del humanismo republicano* (2009). He is co-editor of *Aproximaciones a la Filosofía política de la ciencia* (2013) and editor of the journal of philosophy *Theoría*.

Francisco Gonzalez is Professor of Philosophy at the University of Ottawa. In addition to publishing numerous articles in the areas of Ancient and Contemporary Continental Philosophy, he is the author of *Dialectic and Dialogue: Plato's Practice of Philosophical Inquiry* (Northwestern University Press, 1998) and *Plato and Heidegger: A Question of Dialogue* (Penn State Press, 2009).

Jean Greisch is currently the Guardini Professor at the Humboldt University in Berlin. He is one of the leading figures in contemporary hermeneutics and author of numerous books, translations and other works. His publications include: *Herméneutique et grammatologie* (1977); *L'Âge de la raison herméneutique* (1985); *La Parole Heureuse* (1987); *Hermeneutics and Metaphysics* (1993); *L'Arbre de vie et l'arbre du savoir* (2000); *Le Cogito herméneutique* (2000); *Paul Ricoeur L'Itinérance du sens* (2001); *Ontology et temporalité* (2002); *Entendre autre d'une oreille* (2006); *Qui sommes-nous?* (2009).

Jean Grondin is a professor of philosophy at the Université de Montréal. Author of important books in the fields of hermeneutics and metaphysics translated in fourteen languages, he was a pupil, friend and close collaborator of Hans-Georg Gadamer on whom he wrote a landmark biography (*Hans-Georg Gadamer: A Biography*, Yale UP, 2003). His other books include: *Introduction to Philosophical Hermeneutics*, Yale UP, 1994; *Introduction to Metaphysics*, Columbia UP 2004; *Paul Ricoeur* PUF, 2013; *Du sens des choses. L'Idée de la métaphysique*, PUF, 2013.

Paul Healy is Senior Lecturer in Philosophy at Swinburne University of Technology and Convenor of its Philosophy programme. His publications have focused primarily on the work of Gadamer, Habermas and Foucault, with particular emphasis on demonstrating the significance of philosophical hermeneutics for contemporary epistemology and sociopolitical thought.

Bruce Janz is Professor of Humanities and Director of the Center for Humanities and Digital Research at the University of Central Florida. He works on concepts of place and space across multiple disciplines, African philosophy, digital humanities and contemporary European philosophy. He has taught in the USA, Canada, Kenya and South Africa.

Hans-Herbert Kögler is Professor of Philosophy at the University of North Florida. He received his DPhil from Goethe Universität, Frankfurt, in 1991. His publications include *The Power of Dialogue: Critical Hermeneutics after Gadamer and Foucault* (1999), *Michel Foucault* (2004), *Kultura, Kritika, Dialog* (2006), the co-edited *Empathy & Agency: The Problem of Understanding in the Human Sciences* (2000), as well as recent essays on social theory, cosmopolitanism and hermeneutic ethics.

Arto Laitinen is Professor of Social and Political Philosophy at the University of Tampere, Finland. His interests include philosophical anthropology, ethics and social philosophy, and he has published for example on Charles Taylor, Hegel and theories of recognition.

Frederick G. Lawrence is an Associate Professor of Theology at Boston College. After studies at the Gregorian University, Rome (1963–66), doctoral work at the University of Basel (1966–71) culminated in the dissertation, *Believing to Understand: The Hermeneutic Circle in Gadamer and Lonergan* (1975). Since 1971, besides graduate and undergraduate teaching at Boston College, he has been Director of the annual Lonergan Workshops at BC and of Workshops in Rome, Toronto, Mainz, Jerusalem, editor of over twenty volumes of the Workshop journal, and translator of works by Gadamer, Habermas, Voegelin, Balthasar, et al. Author of more than a hundred articles in philosophy and theology, he has developed and taught in BC's CORE alternative, Perspectives in Western Culture.

Rudolf A. Makkreel is Charles Howard Candler Professor Emeritus of Philosophy at Emory University and author of *Dilthey, Philosopher of the Human Studies* and *Imagination and Interpretation in Kant: The Hermeneutical Import of the 'Critique of Judgment'*. He has co-edited five volumes of Dilthey's *Selected Works* and is completing a work entitled 'Judgment and Critique in an Orientational Hermeneutics'.

Jeff Malpas is Distinguished Professor at the University of Tasmania and Visiting Distinguished Professor at Latrobe University. He publishes across a number of disciplines, including philosophy, but also architecture, geography and the arts. His most recent book is *Heidegger and the Thinking of Place* (MIT, 2012).

Michael Marder is IKERBASQUE Research Professor in the Department of Philosophy at the University of the Basque Country (UPV-EHU), Vitoria-Gasteiz. His most recent books include *Phenomena–Critique–Logos: A Project of Critical Phenomenology* (2014); *The Philosopher's Plant: An Intellectual Herbarium* (2014); and *Pyropolitics: When the World Is Ablaze* (2015).

Ebrahim Moosa is Professor of Islamic Studies in the Department of History and in the Kroc Institute for the International Peace Studies at the University of Notre Dame. He is the author of the prize-winning book, *Ghazali and the Poetics of Imagination* and the forthcoming, *What is a Madrasa?* He has published extensively on Islamic law, ethics, theology and hermeneutics.

Eric S. Nelson is Associate Professor of Philosophy at the University of Massachusetts, Lowell. His research areas include hermeneutics, ethics and the philosophy of nature. He has published over sixty articles and book chapters on Asian and European philosophy. He is the co-editor with François Raffoul of the *Bloomsbury Companion to Heidegger* (2013) and *Rethinking Facticity* (2008). He has also co-edited with John Drabinski, *Between Levinas and Heidegger* (2014); with G. D'Anna and H. Johach, *Anthropologie und Geschichte. Studien zu Wilhelm Dilthey aus Anlass seines 100. Todestages* (2013); and with A. Kapust and K. Still, *Addressing Levinas* (2005).

William Outhwaite studied at the Universities of Oxford and Sussex, where he taught for many years, and is Professor of Sociology at Newcastle University. His books include *Understanding Social Life: The Method Called Verstehen* (1975); *Concept Formation in Social Science* (1983); *New Philosophies of Social Science: Realism, Hermeneutics and Critical Theory* (1987); *Habermas. A Critical Introduction* (1994); and *The Future of Society* (2006).

Ralf Poscher is Professor of Public Law and Director of the Institute for Staatswissenschaft and Philosophy of Law, in the Department of the Philosophy of Law at the Albert-Ludwigs University in Freiburg, Germany. His writings include a wide range of topics in public law and jurisprudence. His most recent writings in English cover jurisprudential topics such as a critique of the principles theory of Robert Alexy (*Ratio* Juris 2009, 425); the Hart–Dworkin debate, 'The Hand of Midas' (in Hage and von der Pfordten (eds), *Concepts in Law*, 2009, 99); and law and language, 'Ambiguity and Vagueness in Legal Interpretation' (in Lawrence Solan and Peter Tiersma (eds), *Oxford Handbook of Language and Law*, 2012, S. 128–44).

Bjørn Torgrim Ramberg (PhD, Queen's University 1988) is Professor of Philosophy and Core Group member of the Centre for the Study of Mind in Nature (CSMN) at the University of Oslo. He has published on pragmatism, and on interpretation and meaning, focusing mainly on Richard Rorty and Donald Davidson.

James Risser is Professor of Philosophy at Seattle University. He received his PhD from Duquesne University in 1978. His published works include *Hermeneutics and the Voice of the Other: Re-reading Gadamer's Philosophical Hermeneutics* (1997), and *The Life of Understanding* (2012). He is the editor of *Heidegger Toward the Turn: Essays on the Work of the 1930s* (1999), co-editor of *American Continental Philosophy* (2000) and Associate Editor of the journal, *Research in Phenomenology*.

Glenda Satne is a Marie Curie Experienced Researcher at the Center for Subjectivity Research, University of Copenhagen, Denmark and Assistant Researcher at the National Council for Scientific Research, Argentina. She is the author of *El argumento escéptico de Wittgenstein a Kripke* (2005) as well as of various articles and edited volumes on philosophy of mind, metaphilosophy and philosophy of language. Her current interests lie in normativity, the second person and shared intentionality.

Dennis J. Schmidt is Liberal Arts Research Professor of Philosophy, Comparative Literature and German at The Pennsylvania State University. He is the author of *Idiome der Wahrheit* (Klostermann, 2014); *Between Word and Image* (Indiana

University Press, 2012); *Lyrical and Ethical Subjects* (SUNY Press, 2005); *On Germans and Other Greeks* (Indiana University Press, 2001); and *The Ubiquity of the Finite* (MIT Press, 1989). He has co-edited *The Difficulties of Ethical Life* (Fordham University Press, 2008) and *Hermeneutische Wege* (Siebeck, 2000). He is also the editor of the SUNY Press *Series in Continental Philosophy*.

Gunter Scholtz completed his PhD in 1970 at the University of Münster. He is currently Professor of History and Theory of the Human Sciences in the Department of Philosophy at the Ruhr-Universität Bochum. He has published extensively on the history and theory of the *Geisteswissenschaften* and on philosophy of history, philosophy of religion and aesthetics. His primary focus is on the philosophy of the nineteenth and twentieth centuries, especially on Schleiermacher and Dilthey. He has been an editor of the *Archiv für Begriffsgeschichte* and the *Historisches Wörterbuch der Philosophie*.

Beata Sirowy is a postdoctoral fellow at the Department of Landscape Architecture and Spatial Planning, Norwegian University of Life Sciences. Her educational background consists of both philosophy and architecture, and her research interests lie at the intersection of these disciplines. She has published articles exploring different aspects of phenomenology and hermeneutics in relation to the built environment.

Nicholas H. Smith is Professor of Philosophy at Macquarie University, Sydney. He is the author of *Strong Hermeneutics: Contingency and Moral Identity* (Routledge, 1997) and *Charles Taylor: Meaning, Morals and Modernity* (Polity, 2002). He has edited several collections including *Reading McDowell: On Mind and World* (Routledge, 2002); *New Philosophies of Labour: Work and the Social Bond* (with Jean-Philippe Deranty, Brill, 2012); and *Recognition Theory as Social Research: Investigating the Dynamics of Social Conflict* (with Shane O'Neill, Palgrave Macmillan, 2012).

Fredrik Svenaeus is Professor at the Centre for Studies in Practical Knowledge, Södertörn University, Sweden. His main research areas are philosophy of medicine and psychiatry, bioethics, medical humanities and philosophical anthropology. He has worked mainly within the philosophical traditions of phenomenology and hermeneutics, attempting to show how these approaches are central to understanding subjects such as health and illness, medical practice and technology, the relationship between body and psyche and other philosophical issues of interest in medicine and health care.

Brian Treanor is currently Professor of Philosophy, Taylor Chair of Philosophy and Director of Environmental Studies at Loyola Marymount University. His research covers a wide variety of issues from a broadly hermeneutic perspective, focusing on the way in which philosophy can tap into the 'surplus of meaning' in texts and, by extension, other phenomena that solicit or require interpretation. His books include *Emplotting Virtue* (2014) and *Aspects of Alterity* (2006), and (as editor) *Interpreting Nature* (2013) and *A Passion for the Possible* (2010).

Gianni Vattimo is Emeritus Professor of Philosophy at the University of Turin and a former European Deputy. His most recent publications include *Della Realtà*

(2012), *Hermeneutic Communism* (2011, co-authored with S. Zabala) and *Farewell to Truth* (2011).

Georgia Warnke is Distinguished Professor in the Political Science Department at the University of California, Riverside and director of the university's Center for Ideas and Society. She is the author of five books including *Gadamer: Hermeneutics, Tradition and Reason* (1987) and *After Identity: Rethinking Race, Sex and Gender* (2007).

John E. Wilson is Professor Emeritus of Church History at Pittsburgh Theological Seminary. He has his PhD in hermeneutical theology from Claremont Graduate University (1975) and a habilitation in theology (theol. habil.) from the University of Basel, Switzerland (1983), where he was Privatdozent in Church History. His published works include *Schellings Mythologie* (1993), *Schelling und Nietzsche* (1996, and *Introduction to Modern Theology* (2007). He is the translator of *Franz Overbeck, On the Christianity of Theology* (2002) and *Early Preaching of Karl Barth* (2009).

Kathleen Wright, Professor of Philosophy at Haverford College (Haverford, Pennsylvania), is the editor of *Festivals of Interpretation* (1990) on Gadamer's hermeneutics. She has published papers in German and English critical of Heidegger's 'elucidations' of Hölderlin's poetry during and after the Third Reich. She has also published on Gadamer and Chinese philosophy and is presently working on the problem of modernity in the thought of the twentieth century New Confucian philosopher, Mou Zongsan.

Santiago Zabala is ICREA Research Professor of Philosophy at the University of Barcelona. He is the author of *The Hermeneutic Nature of Analytic Philosophy* (2008), *The Remains of Being* (2009) and *Hermeneutic Communism* (2011, co-authored with G. Vattimo); editor of *Nihilism and Emancipation* (2004), *The Future of Religion* (2005), *Weakening Philosophy* (2007) and *Art's Claim to Truth* (2008); and co-editor (with Jeff Malpas) of *Consequences of Hermeneutics* (2010) and (with Michael Marder) of *Being Shaken* (2013).

Catherine H. Zuckert and **Michael Zuckert** are both Nancy Reeves Dreux Professors of Political Science at the University of Notre Dame. Catherine is editor-in-chief of *The Review of Politics*, and Michael is editor-in-chief of *American Political Thought*. Catherine is the author of *Postmodern Platos: Nietzsche, Heidegger, Gadamer, Derrida, Strauss*. She and Michael have co-authored two books: *The Truth about Leo Strauss* (2006) and *Leo Strauss and the Problem of Political Philosophy* (2014).

ACKNOWLEDGEMENTS

Every edited volume is completely dependent on its contributors, without whom there would simply be nothing to edit. Consequently, our primary thanks go to all of the contributors to this volume for agreeing to be part of the project and for getting their contributions to us, for the most part, in good time. We are also grateful to Florian Spannagel, in Freiburg, who provided much needed administrative and editorial assistance without which the project would have been much harder, if not impossible, to complete. In addition, we would like to thank Tony Bruce and Adam Johnson, at Routledge, for giving their support to the project and helping deal with various hurdles along the way, and the anonymous reviewers who recommended that the project proceed and provided valuable feedback on the original proposal. Finally, we would like to acknowledge the Alexander von Humboldt Foundation whose support gave rise to the original collaboration out of which this project has grown.

INTRODUCTION: HERMENEUTICS AND PHILOSOPHY

Jeff Malpas

It is commonplace to refer to *hermeneutics* as 'the art or science of interpretation', or sometimes as the 'theory of interpretation'. In this sense, hermeneutics refers to any systematic approach to the questions of interpretation as those questions might arise in some particular domain – so one can speak of Talmudic or Biblical hermeneutics or of the hermeneutics of literature or the hermeneutics of social discourse. Something like this sense of hermeneutics was dominant for much of the early history of hermeneutics – especially prior to the twentieth century – and was also present, to some extent, in the development of hermeneutics in the late nineteenth and early twentieth centuries as a methodology for what are referred to, in German, as the *Geisteswissenschaften* (the term first being used in the German edition of John Stuart Mill's *Logic* as the translation of 'moral sciences' – see Mill 1974: 831ff),[1] particularly in the work of Wilhelm Dilthey (1833–1911) (on Dilthey see Chapter 6; see also Chapters 19, 33 and 39).

Although overlapping, to some extent, with the methodological conception of hermeneutics in the work of Dilthey and others, talk of *philosophical hermeneutics* is usually taken to indicate a more specific mode of hermeneutics that looks either to questions that arise regarding the understanding of interpretation as such (and so as they arise independently of any particular domain of interpretive practice) or else to questions of interpretation as they are seen to be central to philosophical inquiry. Often these latter sets of questions are taken to converge in a single enterprise that takes the inquiry into the nature of interpretation (and so also into various related concepts, including those of understanding, meaning and truth)[2] as by its very nature an inquiry into the questions that are basic to philosophy – philosophy is thus understood, on this account, as essentially interpretive or hermeneutical (see e.g. Figal 2010).

One might say, in fact, that hermeneutics *becomes philosophical* at the same time as philosophy itself comes to be seen *as hermeneutical*. It is within hermeneutics, and especially modern hermeneutics, that interpretation, and so too understanding, comes explicitly to be thematised as a *general* problem (and not merely as a problem from within some particular interpretive context). Understood in this way, the problem of hermeneutics converges with the problem of philosophy – that is, the question concerning the nature and possibility of interpretation converges with the problem concerning the interpretation of the world and our place within it.

When understood in this explicitly philosophical sense, hermeneutics inevitably takes on a *universal* character – as is most famously the case in the thought of Hans-Georg Gadamer (1900–2002) (see Gadamer 2007: 72–88) (on Gadamer see Chapter 11). On such an account, there is nothing that stands outside the hermeneutical – nothing that stands outside the interpretive – not philosophy, but also *not hermeneutics*. Hermeneutics thus comes to name a fundamental mode of interpretive reflexivity in which the very nature and possibility of interpretation, including the interpretive inquiry into interpretation – which is to say, hermeneutics itself – is the primary focus of interpretation. Moreover, the reflexivity at issue here necessarily extends to encompass both the interpreter and their interpretive situation, so that what comes to be at issue in hermeneutics is our own being *as interpreters* at the same time as that interpretive mode of being is taken to be fundamental to our being *as human*. To be human is thus to be an interpreter and not in any merely contingent sense, but essentially.

The idea of hermeneutics as the 'art', 'science' or 'theory' of interpretation suggests that hermeneutics is characterised by that which is its subject matter – by the way in which it is oriented to the question of interpretation. Yet although hermeneutics does indeed take up the question of interpretation, what should already be evident from the above considerations is that hermeneutics, and especially philosophical hermeneutics, cannot be understood merely in terms of what it is *about*. This is a point given particular emphasis by Martin Heidegger (1889–1976) (see Chapter 9) in a way that also connects with the idea of hermeneutics as having an essentially reflexive character.

In a lecture course from 1923 titled 'Ontology: the Hermeneutics of Facticity', Heidegger insists that hermeneutics is not *about* interpretation (which means it is not a *theory of* interpretation), but is rather a fundamental mode of *interpreting*. More specifically, Heidegger argues that hermeneutics is that mode of interpreting that takes what is in fact the interpreter's own being (what Heidegger calls *Dasein*) as that which is to be interpreted (Heidegger 1999: 11).[3] With Heidegger, hermeneutics thus appears explicitly as a mode of self-reflexive, interpretive, *ontological* inquiry – and it is this understanding of hermeneutics that has tended to be dominant within much twentieth-century philosophical hermeneutics, particularly in the work of Gadamer, as well as in the work of others such as Paul Ricoeur (1913–2005) (see Chapter 12) and Gianni Vattimo (1936–) (see Chapter 14). Moreover, the reflexivity that appears here is not peculiar to hermeneutics only in its philosophical instantiation, but to all hermeneutics – such reflexivity is a characteristic feature of interpretation ('all understanding is self-understanding', Gadamer 1976: 55).

Yet in characterising hermeneutics as a fundamental, and essentially reflexive, mode of interpreting – even in characterising it, in more traditional terms, as the 'art', 'science' or 'theory' of interpretation – what is meant by 'interpreting' and 'interpretation' remains obscure, and to that extent hermeneutics remains obscure also. What this means, however, is that there is no entry into the discussion of hermeneutics, or of interpretation, that is not already hermeneutical, not already interpretive – and here again the fundamental reflexivity, one might even say the *circularity*, of the hermeneutical and of the interpretive itself, reappears. One of the most basic, and most frequently cited, structures of interpretation is indeed the so-called circle of understanding – the 'hermeneutic circle' – first formulated as such by Friedrich Ast (1778–1841) in 1806[4] (on Ast see Chapter 5), and which appears in the work of many hermeneutic thinkers from Ast through to Gadamer. Such reflexivity or 'circularity' is an ineliminable feature of interpretation, and so also of hermeneutics, and it brings with it an ineliminable indeterminacy also. Interpretation never comes to an end – or, at least, any ending to which interpretation comes is always temporary, always contingent, always open to revision.[5] As hermeneutics is hermeneutical, so such indeterminacy applies to hermeneutics itself.

The very indeterminacy that characterises hermeneutics, and the reflexive and circular character of the hermeneutical from which it derives, seems likely to be one of the factors that has given rise to the somewhat indeterminate position of hermeneutics within contemporary philosophy, as well across the range of disciplines more broadly. For philosophers working in English, 'hermeneutics' is often seen as quite obscure, if it is known at all, connoting little beyond some connection to interpretation or the theory of interpretation, and as such, belonging as much to the disciplines of literature or rhetoric as to philosophy proper. Moreover, since the tendency within much so-called 'analytic' thought in English has been to disregard or downplay interpretation as a centrally philosophical issue (although the influence of Wittgenstein represents an important counter-tendency), so hermeneutics has been viewed as peripheral and often simply ignored. At the same time, however, hermeneutics is also seen by many, more commonly those working in languages other than English (especially Spanish and Italian), as indeed standing at the very heart of philosophy – and here, of course, philosophy is explicitly understood as an essentially interpretive project, not only in its engagement with texts, but in the very manner of its approach to the fundamental questions with which it deals.[6]

The indeterminacy (some would say the simple ambiguity) regarding the status accorded to hermeneutics within contemporary philosophy, and that is not entirely resolved by the reference to *philosophical* hermeneutics, is exacerbated by the way in which hermeneutics does indeed extend beyond philosophy alone into other disciplines and domains of inquiry – and not just those of literature or rhetoric (its strongest presence, in fact, is undoubtedly within theology and scriptural studies) – at the same time as it also brings with it a history that arguably extends back to the Greeks and a geographical spread that encompasses east and west, north and south. What the philosophical community might take hermeneutics to be, and how it might be seen to stand in relation to philosophy, is thus made especially complicated by its apparent intellectual, historical and geographic expansiveness.

This volume, as should be evident from the brief elaboration of the nature of hermeneutics already set out above – and as might be expected given the volume's focus – takes a stronger position on the nature and significance of hermeneutics than is dominant within most contemporary English-language philosophy. Not only in this Introduction, but also within many of the chapters contained here, there is a clear sense of hermeneutics as given over to philosophy by its very character as hermeneutical – so that one might view the very idea of 'philosophical hermeneutics' as pleonastic – and of philosophy as fundamentally hermeneutical. This is not to imply, however, that there is a single, unequivocal conception of hermeneutics that dominates throughout all of the pages that follow – that would certainly not be in accord with the hermeneutical character of hermeneutics that was noted above. Hermeneutics, by its very nature, is prone to multiple interpretations – although, at the same time, just how such multiplicity is to be understood is always, in its own turn, an interpretive question.

Inasmuch as this volume is committed both to a philosophical conception of hermeneutics, and to a hermeneutical conception of philosophy, so the volume can also be seen as more strongly aligned with contemporary philosophy as it currently exists outside English rather than within it. To some extent, this should be evident not only in the hermeneutical orientation of the volume, but also in the range of contributors that are included within its pages. It would, of course, have been possible to construct the volume so as to draw entirely on authors from within North America, the United Kingdom, Ireland, Southern Africa and Australasia. To have done so, however, would have been to construct the volume in a way that was not reflective of the linguistic and geographical configuration of contemporary hermeneutics.

Although philosophy has, since the end of the Second World War, tended to concentrate on work in English (something that itself reflects the economic and political dominance of English-language culture), that concentration is now, if still rather slowly, beginning to break down. Not only does that breakdown itself bring a set of hermeneutical issues to the fore, but it also suggests that a new orientation towards the hermeneutical may be required if there is indeed to be real engagement between English and non-English language philosophy as philosophy takes on a more genuinely multi-lingual and multi-geographical character. One might also argue that hermeneutics (together with phenomenology) is particularly well-placed as a ground on which such engagement can take place. In spite of the way in which hermeneutics has often been ignored, or even viewed antagonistically, by many within English-language philosophy (and this has also given rise to antagonism within hermeneutics), there are also many significant points of contact between the hermeneutical and the 'analytic' – as might be suggested by the assimilation, evident in this volume, of many English-language thinkers into the hermeneutic tradition, and the evident overlap of hermeneutic interests with those of, most obviously, analytic philosophy of language and philosophy of science (see, for instance, Chapters 16, 17, 18, 19, 21, 28, 33, 50).

This volume is ordered into five sections, plus the Introduction and Conclusion. The first section, 'Hermeneutic origins', focuses on what might be thought of as the 'proto-hermeneutic' tradition within Greek and medieval thought – although given the extent to which, as the authors make clear, hermeneutic problems and concepts figure so prominently here, it is debateable to what extent this is indeed *proto*-hermeneutical. Certainly, however, the sorts of issues that dominate here are more those of interpretation as applied to particular problems of textual interpretation than those that pertain to interpretation understood more philosophically. Nevertheless, especially in the medieval period, the issues at stake are not restricted merely to textual interpretation, but connect with more fundamental concerns about the understanding of the relation between, for instance, God and the world.

It is, however, only with the development of modern philosophy, and especially the philosophy of the nineteenth and twentieth centuries, that hermeneutics emerges as both a *sui generis* domain of inquiry and as having a more explicitly *philosophical* (rather than, for instance, *theological*) significance. Consequently, the focus of the chapters that make up Part II, 'Hermeneutic thinkers', is initially on Spinoza and Vico, but moves rapidly on to thinkers within the post-Kantian and idealist traditions, and then to a range of thinkers from the twentieth century up until the present – including thinkers from both the 'continental' and 'analytic' traditions. Together these chapters provide what is essentially a chronological account of the history of hermeneutics from the sixteenth century onwards through the key figures within that history – although it is also an account that follows both the central thread in the development of hermeneutics through Schleiermacher, Dilthey, Heidegger, Gadamer, Ricoeur and Vattimo, as well as dealing with figures such as Nietzsche, Strauss, Collingwood and Davidson, who might be viewed as standing somewhat independently of that development or as situated orthogonally to it. The historical account that is provided here is not intended, however, to be definitive or comprehensive. In fact, the reflexive character of hermeneutics, as well as the indeterminacy of interpretation, and the essential hermeneutical concern with the historical determination of understanding – which also means of the hermeneutical itself – has the inevitable consequence that hermeneutics' own history is even less amenable to interpretive consensus than is the case elsewhere in philosophy. What counts as belonging to the hermeneutic 'tradition', and how the history of hermeneutics should be configured, is thus itself a hermeneutic question.

A contemporary focus predominates across most of the thematic sections that follow on from the largely historical narrative that underpins Part II. Indeed, this contemporary focus can be said to be what underpins the majority of the volume – the intention is less to give an account of hermeneutics as a historical phenomenon (such an account is already available in many existing works – see e.g. Ormiston and Schrift 1990; Bruns 1992; Grondin 1994, 1995; Ramberg and Gjesdal 2013), and more to provide an overview of hermeneutics as a field of contemporary philosophical activity and engagement.

Part III, 'Hermeneutic questions', deals with core issues within the hermeneutic tradition – it is in this section that the reader will find discussion of key hermeneutic problems and concepts. These chapters inevitably overlap, however, since all remained centrally focused on the problems of interpretation and understanding, even though each chapter approaches those problems from its own perspective and with its own particular emphasis. Together these chapters can be seen to provide an overall view of the nature of hermeneutics that is nevertheless composed from the many different viewpoints that converge within it. Part IV, 'Hermeneutic engagements', extends the range of the discussion to encompass the interdisciplinary spread of hermeneutics and its connection to other fields and domains of inquiry. These chapters provide an indication of the way philosophical hermeneutics connects with other modes of hermeneutical inquiry, including what might be thought of as 'applied hermeneutics'. Part V, 'Hermeneutic challenges and dialogues', explores the various ways in which hermeneutics connects with other approaches and traditions. It also deals with the key critiques that have been advanced against hermeneutics from within domains such as feminism, critical theory and deconstruction.

The concluding chapter of the volume offers a set of thoughts on the future of hermeneutics from Gianni Vattimo – the thinker who is perhaps the last representative of the great twentieth-century tradition of hermeneutics. Vattimo's own approach to hermeneutics – based in Gadamer and Heidegger, but also Nietzsche and Marx – underpins his thinking here (see Chapter 14; see also Chapters 20 and 25), and the argument he offers as to the future of hermeneutics is a radical and provocative one. Whether or not one agrees with Vattimo's position in its entirety, it is nevertheless significant for the way in which it positions hermeneutics directly in relation to our contemporary situation and in relation to a radical politics.[7] For Vattimo, not only is philosophy essentially hermeneutical (which means that it is essentially given over both to interpretation and to conversation or dialogue), but so too is any mode of politics that refuses oppression and coercion. The task, then, is to realise the hermeneutical in relation to philosophy, but also to the political.

As with any such volume, there are omissions and inclusions here that will give rise to comment – inevitably so given the way hermeneutics puts its own character and history into question. Although there are preliminary chapters on Greek and medieval hermeneutics, there is no extended discussion of Stoic hermeneutics or of hermeneutic thinking as it might be thought to be present in the work of Latin authors such as Seneca and Cicero. Augustine and Luther are also largely omitted.[8] This principally reflects the modern focus of the volume, but in some cases it is also a result of the choices made by contributors.

The omission of both Kant and Hegel from the list of hermeneutic thinkers may be thought to represent a significant gap in the volume's modern coverage – although Kant figures prominently throughout many of the discussions below. Kant is, it might be argued, a figure who often stands in the background of modern hermeneutic thinking, especially as it develops in connection with neo-Kantianism in the late nineteenth century, even if he is not typically regarded as a hermeneutic thinker in his own right (though see Makkreel 1994 and Ameriks 2006 – see also Chapters 6 and 28). Hegel figures less prominently in these discussions, and that may be taken to indicate the more strongly Kantian orientation of much (though not all) contemporary hermeneutics. Yet Hegel is undoubtedly an important figure for Dilthey and Gadamer, as well as for thinkers such as Collingwood, Macintyre, Taylor and Brandom (see Chapters 15, 16, and 18). Michael Forster has argued that Hegel ought properly to be included within the hermeneutic tradition (see Forster 2008, 2011),[9] and indeed, Forster's reading of that tradition gives a much greater role to a range of figures who are dealt with only briefly if at all, in this volume (see Forster 2011) – figures such as Herder and Humboldt, as well as Hegel, but also Hamann, Schlegel and Ernesti. Forster also gives a significant place to J. L. Austin and Quentin Skinner, neither of whom are dealt with here – in spite of Forster's claim that they have 'made a far more important contribution to the development of hermeneutics than any made by Heidegger, Gadamer, or Derrida' (Forster 2011: 314). Austin and Skinner can certainly be read in ways that draw them into the hermeneutic fold (this is especially true of Skinner), but Forster's particular reading of their significance seems exaggerated at best.

It must also be acknowledged that the volume focuses almost exclusively on philosophical hermeneutics understood as a primarily 'Western' or European phenomenon. Although there is discussion of hermeneutics in connection with Islamic and Judaic thinking, there is only very limited engagement with, for instance, African, East Asian or South Asian traditions – there is one chapter that focuses on the relation between hermeneutics and Confucianism, and another chapter that takes up the broader issue of hermeneutics and intercultural understanding. Clearly there is a large body of material that could be addressed here – from hermeneutics within the various Buddhist traditions (see Lopez 1993) as well as in contemporary Chinese thought (see Pfister 2007; see also Ng 2008) to the hermeneutics of African philosophy as it engages both with its own indigenous traditions and the legacies of colonialism (see e.g. Serequeberhan 1994). Again, it is partly the focus on *philosophical* hermeneutics, rather than more textually oriented modes, that explains this restriction in the volume's compass – although it is also a result of the practical and publishing constraints, as well as the availability of contributors, that necessarily affect any such volume. There is certainly much more work to be done in both the elaboration of hermeneutic tendencies and trends in other cultures and traditions, and in the hermeneutic engagement with those tendencies and trends.

As already noted, this volume does not aim at presenting merely an account of the history of hermeneutics or of hermeneutics as it has developed through the key figures within the hermeneutical tradition. Indeed, while the volume does provide chapters on the history of hermeneutics and many of the key thinkers with that history, it does not attempt, in that regard, to provide a complete or comprehensive account. Instead, the aim has been to present hermeneutics, as far as possible, in its contemporary engagement with its own concepts and problems, with recent and contemporary philosophical problems and concerns, and with other disciplines and approaches. Such an aim is grounded in the idea that although there is an inevitable historical underpinning to understanding, it is always in relation to our current interests and concerns, and so ultimately to the future, that all understanding is oriented and towards which it is directed.

Notes

1 'Moral sciences' was then a common term in English for what we now think of as the historical and social sciences.

2 Of course, not every inquiry into such concepts is hermeneutical – what characterises the hermeneutical approach is precisely the treatment of these concepts as they stand *in relation to interpretation* – which is one reason why we might treat both Hans-Georg Gadamer and Donald Davidson as hermeneutical thinkers (see Chapters 11 and 17).

3 'In hermeneutics what is developed for Dasein is a possibility of its becoming and being for itself in the manner of an understanding of itself.'

4 Ast puts it in terms of the interdependence of part and whole: 'the particular can be understood only through the whole, and conversely, the whole, only through the particular' (Ast in Ormiston and Schrift 1990: 45; see also Ast 1808: 178), but it can also be seen in terms of the sort of interdependence within the structure of reflexivity that is indicated here or, as it is developed in the work of Heidegger and Gadamer, in terms of the 'projective' or 'pre-judgmental' character of understanding (see Chapters 9, 11 and also 28).

5 This does not mean that hermeneutics is therefore given over to 'relativism' (see Chapter 22) – indeterminacy operates against any such relativism no less than it operates against 'absolutism'. The indeterminacy of the hermeneutical is tied to a 'relationalist' or 'contextualist' (one might also say 'holist') conception of the nature of interpretation and

understanding – something that is explicit in many hermeneutic thinkers from Dilthey (see Chapter 6) to Rorty (see Chapter 17), and that can be seen to be expressed, in one especially clear form, in Gadamer's emphasis on 'dialogue' or 'conversation' (see Chapters 11, 26 and also 28).

6 One might say that it is only when philosophy is explicitly understood as an essentially interpretative enterprise that hermeneutics comes to prominence, but equally, it is only when hermeneutics comes to prominence that the interpretive character of philosophy becomes explicit.

7 This is in direct contrast to the tendency on the part of many critics of hermeneutics to see hermeneutics as inherently conservative – see Chapters 46 and 47, but also 25.

8 Jean Grondin provides and excellent general coverage of what he refers to as the 'prehistory' of hermeneutics, including Augustine, Luther and others (see Grondin 1994: Chap. 1); see also Ramberg and Gjesdal 2013.

9 In addition see Gallagher 1997 in which Hegel's relation to the hermeneutic tradition is also addressed. From a different perspective, Paul Redding has advanced a 'hermeneutical' reading of Hegel that focuses on the theory of recognition – see Redding 1996.

Bibliography

Ameriks, Karl (2006) *Kant and the Historical Turn: Philosophy as Critical Interpretation*, New York: Oxford University Press.

Ast, Friedrich (1808) *Grundlinien der Grammatik, Hermeneutik und Kritik*, Landshut: J. Thomann.

Bruns, Gerald (1992) *Hermeneutics. Ancient and Modern*. New Haven: Yale University Press.

Figal, G. (2010) *Objectivity: The Hermeneutical and Philosophy*, trans. T. D. George, Albany, NY: SUNY Press.

Forster, Michael (2008) 'Hegel and Hermeneutics', in *The Cambridge Companion to Hegel and Nineteenth Century Thought*, ed. Frederick C. Beiser, Cambridge: Cambridge University Press.

——(2011) *German Philosophy of Language: From Schlegel to Hegel and Beyond*, Oxford: Oxford University Press.

Gadamer, Hans-Georg (1976) *Philosophical Hermeneutics*, trans. David E. Linge, Berkeley: University of California Press.

——(2007) *The Gadamer Reader: A Bouquet of the Later Writings*, ed. Richard Palmer, Evanston, IL: Northwestern University Press.

Gallagher, Shaun (ed.) (1997) *Hegel, History and Interpretation*, Albany, NY: SUNY Press.

Grondin, Jean (1994) *Introduction to Philosophical Hermeneutics*, trans. Joel Weinsheimer, New Haven, CT: Yale University Press.

——(1995) *Sources of Hermeneutics*, New York: State University of New York Press.

Heidegger, Martin (1999) *Ontology: The Hermeneutics of Facticity*, trans. John van Buren, Bloomington: Indiana University Press.

Lopez, Donald S. (ed.) (1993) *Buddhist Hermeneutics*, Delhi: Kuroda Institute.

Makkreel, Rudolf A. (1994) *Imagination and Interpretation in Kant: The Hermeneutical Import of the Critique of Judgment*, Chicago, IL: University of Chicago Press.

Mill, John Stuart (1974) *The Collected Works of John Stuart Mill, Volume VIII – A System of Logic Ratiocinative and Inductive, Being a Connected View of the Principles of Evidence and the Methods of Scientific Investigation (Books IV–VI and Appendices)*, ed. John M. Robson, London: Routledge and Kegan Paul.

Ng, On-cho (ed.) (2008) *The Imperative of Understanding: Chinese Philosophy, Comparative Philosophy, and Onto-Hermeneutics*, Honolulu: University of Hawaii Press.

Ormiston, Gayle L. and Alan D. Schrift (eds) (1990) *The Hermeneutic Tradition: From Ast to Ricoeur*, Albany, NY: State University of New York Press.

Pfister, Lauren (ed.) (2007) *Hermeneutical Thinking in Chinese Philosophy*, London: Wiley-Blackwell.

Porter, Stanley E. and Jason C. Robinson (2011) *Hermeneutics: An Introduction to Interpretive Theory*, Grand Rapids, MI: Wm. B. Erdmans Publishing.

Ramberg, Bjørn and Kristin Gjesdal (2013) 'Hermeneutics', in *The Stanford Encyclopedia of Philosophy*, Edward N. Zalta (ed.), URL = http://plato.stanford.edu/archives/sum2013/entries/hermeneutics/.

Redding, Paul (1996) *Hegel's Hermeneutics*, Ithaca, NY: Cornell University Press.

Serequeberhan, Tsenay (1994) *The Hermeneutics of African Philosophy: Horizon and Discourse*, London: Routledge.

Further reading

Mueller-Vollmer, Kurt (1994) *The Hermeneutics Reader: Texts of the German Tradition from the Enlightenment to the Present*, New York: Continuum.

Ormiston, Gayle L. and Alan D. Schrift (eds) (1990) *Transforming the Hermeneutic Context: From Nietzsche to Nancy*, Albany, NY: SUNY Press.

Palmer, Richard E. (1969) *Hermeneutics. Interpretation Theory in Schleiermacher, Dilthey, Heidegger*, Evanston, IL: Northwestern University Press.

Schmidt, Lawrence K. (2006) *Understanding Hermeneutics*, London: Acumen Publishing.

Szondi, Peter (2003) *Introduction to Literary Hermeneutics*, trans. Martha Woodmansee, Cambridge: Cambridge University Press.

Thistleton, Anthony C. (2009) *Hermeneutics: An Introduction*, Grand Rapids, MI: Wm. B. Erdmans Publishing.

Part I
HERMENEUTIC ORIGINS

1
HERMENEUTICS IN GREEK PHILOSOPHY

Francisco Gonzalez

Our very term 'hermeneutics' comes from a family of Ancient Greek terms: *hermê-neuein* or *hermêneusai* and *hermêneia* to designate an activity, *hermênês* to designate the individual who carries out this activity, and *hermêneutikê* to designate a particular discipline associated with this activity. Given this ancient provenance of the word, it would seem not only that it makes sense to speak of an 'Ancient Hermeneutics', but that hermeneutics is something distinctively characteristic of Ancient Greek thought. But this seeming evidence quickly becomes problematic when we begin to reflect on what exactly the term *hermêneuein* and its cognates meant for the Greeks as distinct from what we have in mind today when we speak of 'hermeneutics'. How does the mediation of sense that the Greeks recognized and practised relate to what we today recognize as 'interpretation'? And to what extent is it possible to characterize Ancient Greek philosophy as 'hermeneutical' without gross misrepresentation and anachronism?

The 'hermeneutic' vocabulary of Plato

In pursuit of these questions, let us consider first the 'hermeneutic' vocabulary of Plato. In the *Cratylus* 407e, the term *hermênea* is connected etymologically to the name of the god Hermes. Whether this etymology is fanciful or has any historical basis, its significance is in identifying the task of the 'hermeneut' with that of the god: that of being a messenger (*angelos*) and, in particular, a messenger between gods and humans. It is precisely this meaning that one finds in the *Symposium* 202e3 where eros, being neither god nor human but a 'spirit' (*daemon*), is described as 'Hermê-neuon and transmitting to the gods the things from men and to men the things from the gods'. Here the verb translated as 'transmitting' (*diaporthmeuon*) is practically an explication of the verb *hermêneuein* that precedes it, as the latter can mean here only something like 'conveying' or 'communicating'. Indeed, the *hermêneuein* between gods and men is rephrased just a little later as a *dialektos*, that is, 'conversation', between gods and men (203a3).

It is in this context that we must consider the only occurrences in Plato's work of the substantive *herméneutiké* (*Statesman* 260d11 and *Epinomis* 975c6) where it is referred to as an art along with the 'mantic' art (*mantiké*), but with no further explanation. Given how we have seen the term *herméneuein* actually used in the context of the relation between gods and humans, and given that *mantiké* is the art that communicates the will of the gods to us (cf. *Epinomis* 984e2), *herméneutiké* is likely to be the art that directs us in how we are to communicate with the gods, rather than being, as Grondin (1995: 24) suggests, despite his finding no supporting evidence in the extant literature (22–3), an art of 'interpreting' what the gods reveal. Indeed, in the one other place in the Platonic corpus where the term *herméneutiké* is used, in the pseudo-Platonic *Definitions* (414d), it is associated with *dialektos*, though now in a context much broader than the communication between gods and mortals, that is, the context of all linguistic articulation as expressive.

In Plato's genuine works the term *herméneia* can indeed mean simply 'expression'. The clearest case of this is at *Theaetetus* 209a5 where an account (logos) is said to be the *herméneia* of the difference between the object it is about and other objects. At *Republic* 524b1 Socrates describes a case in which the *herméneiai* received from the senses are found strange (*atopoi*) by the soul and therefore in need of examination (*episkepsis*). What is called *herméneia* here is not the interpretation to which we subject the confusing message of the senses, but rather this confusing message itself. At *Theaetetus* 163c Socrates argues that while we see the shape and colour of written words and hear the sound of spoken words, what the *grammatistai* and *hermenes* teach us about them is something we neither see nor hear. Since writing is the special domain of the 'grammarian', we can assume that the *hermenes* is mentioned as dealing especially with spoken words and, specifically, with what spoken words express.

So far we have encountered no use of the word *herméneuein* to mean 'interpret'. One could of course argue that mediating between humans and gods involves 'translating' the divine into the human and vice versa. The word *hermenes* is indeed used in the context of human communication to refer to a 'translator' from a foreign language (*Philebus* 16a). But if we are inclined to believe that all translation is interpretation, we cannot simply assume that this was the case for the Ancient Greeks. The fact is, as Grondin has noted (1995: 25), that the Greeks gave no great significance to translation and took little interest in it. We must look to other uses of *herméneuein* if we want to find anything like our own concern with interpretation.

One passage that might appear promising in this regard is *Laws* 966b7 where we are told that with respect to the laws the guardians must be 'able in word' (*logoi te hikanous*) to *herméneuein*, where it is tempting to translate 'to interpret'. However, *herméneuein* is clearly here meant to be synonymous with a phrase used a couple of lines earlier in the same context: *tén endeixin tôi logôi endeiknusthai*, 'showing something forth' or 'expounding' it. What is at issue here is again expression or communication and not interpretation; this is why Clinias can remark that the inability to *herméneuein* would be the condition of a slave.

Another passage for which translators rarely resist the temptation of translating *herméneuein* as 'interpret' is *Republic* 453c9. Here, after Socrates presents the objection that their own previous claim that each person must do what properly belongs to him by nature contradicts their present claim that men and women should have the same jobs, Glaucon makes the following request: 'I ask you to *herméneusai* our argument, whatever it is.' If Glaucon were asking for an 'interpretation', he would need to be referring to the argument they have already given that different jobs must be assigned to different natures. But then it would make no sense for Glaucon to add, 'whatever it is'. The argument he is referring to, the one he cannot yet identify, must be the argument he and Socrates will proceed to make in reply to the objection. But then what Glaucon is asking is that Socrates 'expound' or 'present' it.

We can finally turn to the most important Platonic text in this context: the one seen by most as making a clear connection between the word *herméneuein* and our 'hermeneutics'. This text is the dialogue *Ion* where the relation between poets and gods and between poets and the rhapsodes who 'perform' their work is described with the word *herméneuein*. Specifically, at 530c3–4 we are told that 'The rhapsode should be the *herménea* of the thought of the poet to the listeners.' At 534e4 we are told that 'The poets are nothing other than *herménés* of the gods, each possessed by that god that possesses him', and at 535a5–6 that the rhapsodes are in turn *herménés* of *herménés*. An important and recent commentary on this dialogue (Capuccino 2005: 124–5) observes that all modern translators translate *herménés* and its cognates as 'interpret[ers]' (as does Grondin 1994: 22) and understand the word in the modern sense (though an important exception in English missed by Capuccino is Woodruff 1983 who translates 'present' and 'representatives'). Capuccino rightly counters that at 534e–535a the meaning is clearly that of passive medium or mouthpiece, not 'interpreter' (126). The point Socrates is trying to make is precisely that both the poet and the rhapsode do not know what they are talking about, but are only vehicles through which passes a message they cannot even understand, much less 'interpret'. We are here fully within the meaning of *herméneuein* noted in other passages, that is, that of conveying a message, communicating, expressing (as noted by Heidegger 1971: 29).

The passage at 530c3 might in contrast appear to demand the translation 'interpreter': what, after all, could it mean to be the *herménés* of the *thought* of the poet except to be the interpreter of the meaning of the poet's verses? Yet, as Capuccino notes (128, 131), the text itself proceeds to tell us what is meant: to 'utter many beautiful thoughts about Homer' (530d2–3) and 'get Homer well dressed up' (530d6–7). What is at issue here is therefore not anything we would call 'interpretation'. Capuccino goes on to note that what *Socrates*, though not *Ion*, insists on is that to be a *good* communicator of the thought of the poet one must *learn* and *understand* the thought of the poet. But even this does not imply that the task of the rhapsode as *herménés* is to *interpret* to his audience what the poet says (see Capuccino: 193).

The 'hermeneutic' vocabulary of Aristotle

If we turn now to Aristotle, we encounter *herméneia* used to mean 'expression' along the lines of what we find in the pseudo-Platonic *Definitions*. In the *Poetics* 1450b14, language (*lexis*) is defined as 'expression' (*herméneia*) through words. In the *Topics* 139b13–14, we are told that the person who seeks to define must employ 'the clearest form of expression' (*sophestaté téi hermêneiai*) instead of an unclear form of expression (*asaphei têi hermêneiai*), since he provides the definition for the sake of knowing. In what is apparently the only occurrence of the verb in Aristotle (*Sophist. el.* 166b11), we have described a statement (*lexis*) that can signify beyond its form when it signifies (*hermêneuêtai*) something that is not the same, for example, a man as a woman or a woman as a man.

It is in this context that the meaning of the title of Aristotle's work must be understood – *Peri hermêneias*, a work that it would be tempting to consider the first work of hermeneutics. Since the word *hermêneia* does not occur in the text itself, we must guess its meaning by considering what the work said to be on *hermêneia* is about, something Aristotle tells us in the very first sentence: it is about names, verbs, affirmations, negations, statements, and sentences. If all of these are to be understood as forms of *hermêneia*, the latter term must have the sense of 'expression' and certainly not the sense of 'interpretation'. This remains the case if we include in the sense of *hermêneia* the fundamental relations Aristotle goes on to describe between words and things: the affections of the soul 'express' the things outside the soul by being a natural likeness of them, not by 'interpreting' them; spoken words 'express' the affections of the soul, and written words 'express' spoken words, by being made to stand for them by convention (they are not 'images' but '*sumbola*'), not by 'interpreting' them. In short, the work that has been translated in English as *On Interpretation* has nothing to do with interpretation (contra Aubenque 2009: 107, and Palmer 1969: 20–1).

If modern readers tend nevertheless to read into Aristotle a notion of 'interpretation' that is simply not there, they also tend to ignore what would have been for him the obvious context of *hermêneia* understood as expression: *communication*. This context is made explicit in what are the most striking and revealing occurrences of the term *hermêneia* in Aristotle. In *De Anima* 420b20, Aristotle assigns the tongue two natural purposes: one dictated by necessity, which is taste, and one dictated by the pursuit of the good, which is *hermêneia* or *dialekton*, where the two terms are clearly being used synonymously. That it should be *the tongue* that serves *hermêneia* makes clear that the expressive communicative discourse intended here is *oral*. In *The Parts of Animals* 660a36 we are again told we use the tongue *pros hermêneian allêlois*, for communication with each other (see also *On Respiration* 476a19). We of course already saw in Plato the identification of *hermêneia* with 'dialogue' and we thus can surmise that we have here the primary sense of the term common to both philosophers.

The 'hermeneutic' vocabulary of poets and philosophers up to the Classical period

But do we find the vocabulary of hermeneutics associated with interpretation outside Plato and Aristotle? Though most of the occurrences of this vocabulary in poets and philosophers either contemporaneous with, or preceding them, have the meanings considered above, there are two important texts that refer to *hermênês* and have been almost universally taken to be about interpretation. The first is the second *Olympian Ode* of Pindar. On the usual translation the relevant text reads as follows:

'I have many swift arrows in the quiver under my arm, [85] arrows that speak to the initiated. But the masses need interpreters (*es to pan hermaneôn chatizei*)' (trans. Diane Arnson Svarlien). However, Most (1986a) demonstrated that this passage cannot be understood in this way. First of all, the Greek *es to pan* (literally, 'to the all') cannot mean 'the masses'; there is no occurrence of the phrase in the surviving literature of the period where it could have this meaning. Instead, Aeschylus uses the same phrase repeatedly to strongly affirm the word it accompanies and therefore as an equivalent of *pantôs* (307). In this case the above phrase would mean 'they (the arrows) *certainly* crave *hermaneis*' (308). If any reference to 'the many' is absent in the passage, then so is any contrast between the many and 'those who know' and therefore any suggestion that the former unlike the latter need 'interpreters'. But then what is the meaning of *hermênês* here? Arguing that in fifth-century literature the term 'never designates someone who performs literary interpretation or explanation, that is, someone who explains poetic utterances to the less intelligent masses' (308), Most argues that the relevant contrast in the passage is between the arrows hidden in the quiver and *their external expression*, so that the *hermênês* needed are those who '*express them aloud*', that is, *the poets themselves* (313). Note how in this case the meaning is the same as it is in Plato's *Ion* when the poets are characterized as *hermênês* and in neither case is the reference to 'interpreters' (Most translates: 'oracular announcers').

The other crucial text is Aeschylus' *Agamemnon*, line 616. Here, after Clytemnestra has boasted of her fidelity to her husband in his absence and the herald approves her speech, the Chorus says something that is most often taken to mean that 'clear interpreters' (*toroisin hermêneusin*) will be able to see through the false façade of Clytemnestra's speech. Making what they can of what is clearly a corrupt Greek text, Denniston and Page (1957) thus suggest the following translation: 'She spoke and you understood her thus, (but) to clear interpreters a fair-*seeming* utterance' (127). But the italics, so essential to the sense of this translation in stressing that the 'interpreter' will recognize the speech as *only seeming* fair, of course corresponds to nothing in the Greek which has simply the word *euprepôs*. Most (1986a) defends another reading of this passage that is more plausible in reading less into it: 'thus she has spoken to you who understand, a speech quite appropriate (*euprepôs*) for clear messengers' (310–11). The point could then be quite simple: whatever the truth, the message one wants to give to heralds who can proclaim it clearly is one that is worthy of the great and noble.

Conclusions to be drawn from the vocabulary of 'hermeneutics' in Ancient Greece

Two important conclusions can be reached from this survey: 1) Greek 'hermeneutics' during the Classical period is not about 'interpretation' but rather 'communication'. Against Grondin who insists, without evidence, that *hermêneuein* refers *both* to the movement outward we call 'expression' *and* to the movement inward we call 'interpretation' (1994: 20–1), we must therefore side with Capuccino who writes: 'It is clear that what we are dealing with here is *ex*-pression (vs. *in*-terpretation) or communication: the movement is outwards' (2005: 195). It is not, in other words, a matter of penetrating behind words in order to decide between possible meanings, much less to acknowledge a plurality of meanings, but rather of *conveying clearly* a thought or message, whether through one's own words or through mediating the words of others. 2) Greek 'hermeneutics' has nothing to do with the interpretation of texts. In all the cited cases, 'hermeneutics' is understood in the context of *oral communication*. It is a matter, as we would say, of my 'making myself clear' in a conversation and getting the other person to 'make himself clear' by asking him questions.

It must be admitted that the Greeks did recognize the possibility of words, especially the words of poetry and myth, having a *hidden meaning* and that this led to the practice of allegorical interpretation well before Plato who, as we will see, refers to this practice as something well known. The key word here was not *allégoria*, which is a much later term, but *huponoia* (see Pépin 1976: 85). In Xenophon's *Symposium*, for example, Socrates criticizes the rhapsodes for 'not knowing the hidden thoughts' (*huponoias*) in the *Iliad* and the *Odyssey* (III.6.3). Recall that Socrates characterizes the rhapsode Ion as a mere *hermênês* of a *hermênês* and therefore as not having any genuine knowledge of that of which he speaks. In other words, he does *not as a hermênês* know the hidden thoughts of Homer's poetry. Indeed, while we would consider the uncovering of hidden meanings in texts a paradigm case of 'interpretation', the word *huponoia* is nowhere in the extant literature associated with the word *hermêneia* and its cognates (something Grondin fails to note: 1994: 24; 1995: 30). Indeed, given what has been noted above, we must expect that the two words are even opposed in their signification. To *hermêneusai* is to communicate, to express a meaning, 'translating' it from one medium to another, whereas *huponoia* refers to a meaning that is kept hidden, not communicated, and that therefore can be arrived at only through some kind of inference.

If not associated with the 'hermeneutic' vocabulary, one therefore still finds in Ancient Greece the recognition that words can be ambiguous and therefore admit of both a surface reading and a deeper reading capable of uncovering the hidden thoughts: Isocrates in his *Panathenaicus* (240, 246–7, 251, 265) describes a student as making precisely this claim about his own speech (on which see Eden 1987: 60–2). The interpretation in question, however, is limited to the specific category of interpretation that can be called 'allegorical' in the literal sense: that is, where there is a clear surface meaning and a different meaning that is hidden. What is 'expounded' here is not the words, but what is *unsaid*. Secondly, it is not so clear how important allegory was to philosophers prior to Plato and Aristotle, given the fragments and second-hand testimony we have to deal with (see Tate 1927), but it was of no real importance to these last two philosophers. Plato recognized the possibility of hidden meanings in the poets: key texts here are *Republic* 378d5–7 and *Theaetetus* 180c8–d4. Yet as J. Tate, considering these texts and others, showed long ago in a couple of articles (1929, 1930), Plato considered the attempt to uncover these hidden meanings a complete waste of time, for reasons we will see below.

As for Aristotle, his insistence on the 'clearest *hermêneia*' left him with little interest in *huponoiai*. In Book 3 of the *Rhetoric*, at the beginning of chapter 2, Aristotle claims clarity (*saphê einai*) to be the virtue of *lexis* (as he also does at the beginning of ch. 22 of the *Poetics*), with the argument that a logos that did not make manifest (*dêloi*) would not perform its proper function. When the choice is between the foul language (*aischrologia*) of ancient comedies and the 'innuendo' (*huponoia*) of new comedies, Aristotle of course considers the latter form of laughter the more educated pleasure (*N.E.* 1128a20–25). He also rates metaphor very highly as a means of avoiding vulgarity in expression. However, even here clarity (*to saphes*) is the virtue (*Rhetoric* 3.2.8); the metaphor should draw from similarities and affinities so that as soon as it is uttered the affinity is made clear (*dêlon*, 3.2.12; 1405b). We seem quite far here from Paul Ricoeur's account of metaphor as an occasion for constructing meaning (see 1981: 175, 180). As Aristotle famously claims, to transfer well a meaning from one context to another, to both construct and understand a metaphor (*to eu metapherein*), is *to see the similarity* (*to homoion theôrein*, *Poetics* 59a7–8). In this regard Aristotle's poetics can be characterized as fundamentally anti-hermeneutical.

If the Classical Greeks 'lacked our hermeneutics to an astonishing degree', as Most (1986b: 236) concludes despite his attempt to find some trace of it in the sophist Protagoras (against which see below), this is not only in the sense of a theory or a discipline of interpretation that would reflect on and define specific rules and strategies for interpreting texts, but in a more fundamental sense. When modern hermeneutics claims that there is no understanding or truth without 'interpretation' (see Vattimo 1997: 4–5), this word appears to convey two main ideas: 1) that, from the side of the subject, all understanding is perspectival and is conditioned by certain presuppositions; 2) that, from the side of the object, there is both a surplus and an indeterminacy of meaning. Both of these ideas are foreign to Greek 'hermeneutics', as the use of the word *hermêneia* and its cognates makes clear. The key claim of Greek 'hermeneutics' is that all understanding is *communication*, understanding each other in conversation, expressing oneself clearly to others and understanding what they have to say; of this kind of understanding, the written text is only a very pale and distant reflection, as the critique of writing in Plato's *Phaedrus* insists (275d–e). Not only Ricoeur (1981: 62, 91, 139–40, 203–3), however, but even Gadamer (2004: 394–7), despite making dialogue his hermeneutical model, rejects the priority granted by the Greeks to orality (see also Palmer 1969: 244). One could argue that 'interpretation' has become a virtue for us because our 'understanding' is so completely focused on written texts where ambiguity, multiplicity of meanings, self-projection, creativity, and so on, can be seen as good things. But it should be obvious that these are definitely not virtues in an oral conversation where the focus must instead be on conveying clearly a particular meaning. A hermeneutics of orality is a hermeneutics that places all the emphasis on transparency (see Grondin 1995: 28).

Plato and Aristotle as 'interpreters'

To understand fully what kind of 'hermeneutics' one finds in Ancient Greek philosophy, and in Plato and Aristotle in particular, it is not sufficient to look at their vocabulary: one must also look at their practice. What one sees is that, rather than seeking to interpret the meaning of the texts of others, whether poets or philosophers, they instead seek to engage in debating *what these others likely wanted to say and therefore would say if one could converse with them.*

A good illustration is how both deal with Heraclitus, whose texts we recognize as especially ambiguous and needing interpretation. Plato notoriously reduces Heraclitus' philosophy to something Heraclitus never wrote: *that everything is in constant flux*. It is for Plato enough that such a view could be suggested by the fragment according to which it is impossible to step into the same river twice. Plato is not in the least interested in interpreting Heraclitus' text, but only in debating a view he always presents as shared by many others, including Homer! (See *Cratylus* 402a and *Theaetetus* 152e.) Ironically, in the one case in which we could say that a fragment by Heraclitus is 'interpreted', it is the character Eryximachus in the *Symposium* who dismisses Heraclitus' actual words as not well chosen, because they suggest that harmony comes from opposition, whereas Heraclitus *wished to say* the opposite (187a3)!

Aristotle too cannot take Heraclitus 'at his word' when it comes to the unity of opposites. In his critique of Heraclitus in the *Metaphysics* for purportedly denying the principle of non-contradiction, Aristotle is careful to say that this is what some take Heraclitus to be saying (1005b25). Indeed, Aristotle believes that if one had questioned Heraclitus himself, he would have been forced to agree that opposite statements cannot be true of the same subjects (1062a32). As it is, Heraclitus simply did not understand his own words (1062a35)!

That interpretation plays no essential role in their philosophical thought is not only shown by the practice of Plato and Aristotle (on which also see Tarrant 2000: 43, 50), but is a position explicitly argued for by Plato in a text of crucial importance that has led Most to characterize Plato's thought as 'essentially anti-hermeneutic' (1986b: 241; contrast Lhomme 2001). In a scene from the *Protagoras*, the sophist, unable to take advantage of the offer that he question Socrates as Socrates questioned him, instead turns to a poem of Simonides, not to interpret it, but to make Socrates look foolish by committing him to the excellence of the poem and then proceeding to show that two verses contradict each other: Socrates is thereby forced to eliminate the supposed contradiction by providing an interpretation of the poem. This interpretation is universally recognized as a violent one that twists Simonides' words and goes against their evident sense. But that the words are not what matter to Socrates is made clear when he concludes: 'This, Prodicus and Protagoras, I said, is what Simonides appears to me to have been thinking (*dianooumenos*) in composing this poem' (347a4). Socrates could thus be seen here as providing the kind of 'allegorical' interpretation described above. Yet Socrates proceeds to dismiss the very activity of interpretation as not only useless but fundamentally uneducated. It is useless because, unable to question the author, different people end up with different views on what the author had in mind with no possibility of deciding in favour of the one or the other (347e4–6). And even if we could determine this with certainty, we would still be left with the more important question of whether what the author believes is *true*. But then interpretation only distracts us from that genuine dialogue that would consist of *being together through ourselves*, mutually offering and examining our own accounts, thereby testing both the truth and ourselves (348a1–3; see also *Hippias Minor* 365d). Socrates therefore compares what we might today call 'the hermeneutical situation' to an uneducated symposium in which the symposiasts, unable through a lack of education to be together through their own voices (347c5–d1), must introduce the 'foreign voice' (347d2) of a flute player. What makes the interpretation of a written text the paradigm for modern hermeneutics, that is, that we have here discourse that is *alienated* from the context of conversation and therefore demands to be *reappropriated*, is precisely what for Socrates makes it comparable to the noise of a flute disrupting from without the genuine being-together of genuine dialogue. Far from recognizing the possibility of the kind of 'dialogical' interpretation of a text advocated by Gadamer (see 2004: 361–2, 389, 352; 1993: 6–7), Socrates presents interpretation and dialogue as irreconcilable (contra Cossutta's suggestion that Plato seeks an 'authentic hermeneutics' [2001: 148]; see Gundert 1952: 92–3). Most suggests that 'this disdainful and implacable closure will undermine the foundations of all hermeneutics for centuries to come' (1986b: 244).

Though in chapter 25 of the *Poetics* Aristotle, in setting forth criteria for judging a work of poetry (see Eden 1987: 69ff), provides criteria for dealing with seemingly contradictory statements, he also makes the testing of arguments in dialectical exchanges (*hoi en tois logois elenchois*) his model (1461b16–19) and does not elsewhere hesitate himself to cite a verse of Simonides' poem out of context for critique (*Metaphysics* 982b30). Furthermore, an interesting and illuminating parallel to how Socrates deals with Simonides' poem is to be found in Aristotle's comments in the *Rhetoric* 1407b14 on the opening lines of Heraclitus' book: 'Of the *logos* that is always uncomprehending are human beings, both before hearing it and hearing it for the first time.' Aristotle cites the passage here as an example of a badly formed *because unclear* discourse. Aristotle's objection is that the word order makes it impossible to determine whether the 'always' goes with 'is' or with 'uncomprehending'. This ambiguity violates what has been seen to be for Aristotle the natural function of language that even a metaphor must serve: *to make manifest*. While Aristotle is speaking here of a written text, it is striking that he regards it as no different from oral discourse and therefore as requiring the same clarity. What is written, he asserts, has to be not only easy to read (*euanagnôston*), but also easy to say (*euphraston*), since these *are the same thing* (*to auto*). This explains why Aristotle, unlike many modern interpreters, does not even consider the possibility that the mentioned ambiguity is intentional, is essential to the point Heraclitus is making, and that it is the virtue of a written text to be able to preserve such ambiguity. Indeed, one of the rules Aristotle presents in this same chapter is the avoidance of ambiguity (*mê amphibolois*, 3.5.4). Perhaps even more than Socrates' direct attack on hermeneutics in Plato's *Protagoras*, Aristotle's treatment of the opening lines of Heraclitus' book shows just how far the Ancient Greeks were from the modern emphasis on interpretation with the elevation of the written over the spoken word that it entails. Therefore a return to the Greeks, rather than merely legitimizing modern hermeneutics by providing it with a noble and ancient pedigree, provides us with something much more valuable: the opportunity to reflect on and question its most fundamental assumptions.

Bibliography

Aubenque, Pierre (2009) *Problèmes Aristotéliciens: Philosophique Théorique*, Paris: J. Vrin.

Capuccino, C. (2005) *Filosofi e Rapsodi: testo, traduzione e commento dello* Ione *platonico*, Bologna: CLUEB.

Cossutta, Frédéric (2001) 'La joute interprétative autour du poème de Simonide dans le Protagoras: herméneutique sophistique, herméneutique socratique?' in *La forme dialogue chez Platon*, eds F. Cossutta and M. Narcy, pp. 1119–54, Grenoble: Jérôme Millon.

Denniston, J. D., and D. Page (1957) *Aeschylus: Agamemnon*, Oxford: Clarendon Press.

Eden, Kathy (1987) 'Hermeneutics and the Ancient Rhetorical Tradition', *Rhetorica* 5, no. 1: 59–86.

Gadamer, H. G. (1993) *Wahrheit und Methode: Ergänzungen, Register, Gesammelte Werke 2*, Tübingen: J. C. B. Mohr [Paul Siebeck].

——(2004) *Truth and Method*, trans. rev. Joel Weinsheimer and Donald G. Marshall, second revised edition, London: Continuum.

Grondin, J. (1994) *Introduction to Philosophical Hermeneutics*, New Haven, CT: Yale University Press.

——(1995) *Sources of Hermeneutics*, Albany: State University of New York Press.

Gundert, Hermann (1952) 'Die Simonides-Interpretation in Platons Protagoras', in *Hermēneia: Festschrift Otto Regenbogen*, pp. 71–93, Heidelberg.

Heidegger, Martin (1971) *On the Way to Language*, trans. Peter D. Hertz, London: Harper and Row.

Lhomme, Alain (2001) 'Le fils d'Hermès', in *La forme dialogue chez Platon*, eds F. Cossutta and M. Narcy, pp. 155–87, Grenoble: Jérôme Millon.

Most, G. (1986a) 'Pindar, O. 2.83–90', *The Classical Quarterly* 36, no. 2: 304–16.

Most, G. (1986b) 'Sophistique et Herméneutique', in *Positions de la Sophistique*, ed. Barbara Cassin, pp. 233–45, Paris: J. Vrin.

Palmer, Richard E. (1969) *Hermeneutics*, Evanston, IL: Northwestern University Press.

Pépin, J. (1976) *Mythe et Allégorie: les origines grecques et les contestations judéo chrétiennes*, Paris: Études Augustiniennes.

Ricoeur, P. (1981) *Hermeneutics and the Human Sciences*, ed. and trans. John B. Thompson, Cambridge: Cambridge University Press.

Tarrant, H. (2000) *Plato's First Interpreters*, Ithaca, NY: Cornell University Press.

Tate, J. (1927) 'The Beginnings of Greek Allegory', *The Classical Review* 41, no. 6: 214–15.

——(1929) 'Plato and Allegorical Interpretation', *The Classical Quarterly* 23, no. 3/4: 142–54.

——(1930) 'Plato and Allegorical Interpretation (Continued)', *The Classical Quarterly* 24, no. 1: 1–10.

Vattimo, G. (1997) *Beyond Interpretation: The Meaning of Hermeneutics for Philosophy*, trans. David Webb, Redwood City, CA: Stanford University Press.

Woodruff, P., trans. (1983) *Plato. Two Comic Dialogues*: Ion *and* Hippias Major, Indianapolis: Hackett.

2

HERMENEUTICS IN MEDIEVAL THOUGHT

Mauricio Beuchot

English translation by Juan Tubert-Oklander

I. Introduction: the hermeneutic Middle Ages

Perhaps no other era has been as 'hermeneutic' as the Middle Ages – although this has not been widely acknowledged. The thought of the period was full of exegeses and commentaries, appearing in a wide variety of forms, and the Holy Scriptures were a focus for constant interpretation and re-interpretation. There is thus much that the era can teach us about hermeneutic practice.

I shall consider the Middle Ages as divided into the High Middle Ages, the Mature Middle Ages, and the Late Middle Ages. The High Middle Ages will be seen as preparatory to Scholasticism – the core of medieval thinking – the Mature Middle Ages as corresponding to its maturity, and the Late Middle Ages to its decadence. Yet although the scholastics dominate the thought of the Mature and Late Middle Ages, the High Middle Ages are ruled by the monastic, and this makes, as we shall see, for a profound difference.

I. The High Middle Ages: interpretation and monasticism

Johannes Scotus Eriugena

Following the Barbarian invasions, the recovery of Classical Culture took some centuries to accomplish. Well into the ninth century, Ireland was still subject to invasion by Vikings and Danes, leading many monks to migrate to France and other parts of Europe. In France, there was some revival of letters under Charlemagne. His successor, Charles the Bald, continued to favour scholarly work, and to his court came a monk called Johannes Scotus Eriugena – so called on account of his Irish origin (Eriugena means 'Ireland-born', and since 'Scottus' meant, at that time, 'Irish' or 'Gaelic', his name may be translated as 'John, the Irish-born Gael'). Eriugena translated Pseudo-Dionysus from Greek, commented on the Scriptures, and wrote a very complex work, called *Periphyseon* or *De divisione naturae*, circa 866. In the latter work, and drawing from Augustine and Pseudo-Dionysus, Eriugena constructs an interpretation of reality – a reading of the Book of Nature – in which there is a confluence of hermeneutics and ontology.

Eriugena engaged in two forms of hermeneutic activity: first, as the translator of Pseudo-Dionysus; second as a Biblical commentator or exegete. As a commentator, he uses the allegoric interpretation of the Scripture. He distinguishes between an *alegoria facti* – an allegory of facts, in which facts reveal mysteries, as in the narrative of the Eucharistic celebration – and an *alegoria dicti* – an allegory of words, as in parables, of things which have never actually happened. Factual allegories are mysteries and verbal allegories are symbols (Eriugena 1865a, I, 2, 136C).

Just like Augustine and Pseudo-Dionysus, Eriugena says that both the Bible and the world are texts (Eriugena 1865b, V, 3, 865D). In his Commentary to the Prologue of the *Gospel of John*, hermeneutics is said to be a mystagogy, since interpretation serves as an initiation to the Divine Mysteries. Here Eriugena draws upon Pseudo-Dionysus's negative theology, by which the interpretation of the Scriptures is developed in terms of the predominance of mystery over knowledge, and of the figurative over the literal.

Saint Anselm

Anselm was born in Aosta (circa 1033) and died in Canterbury (1109). He was a Benedictine monk, beginning his career in Bec, where he became abbot, and then going on to Canterbury as its bishop. He wrote philosophical works, such as the *Monologion* and the *Proslogion*, and also theological works. He developed his own version of Augustine's dictum, *credo ut intelligam* – "I believe in order that I may understand" – turning it into "*Fides quaerens intellectum*" – "faith looks for understanding" (Anselm 1952a: 685–87). Anselm was committed to the use of reason, and to dialectics or logic. Although charged with an excessive rationalism, his thinking not only followed reason, but it also remained true to authority – especially that of Augustine.

Anselm accepted that the Bible is polysemic, claiming that there are various meanings, and more than one probable interpretation, to be found in Scripture (Anselm 1952b, l. I, c. 18: 791–99). Yet in spite of such plurality, Anselm held that there is always one meaning or interpretation that is more strongly supported by evidence and argument. Hence, his preference for dialectics as his method of interpretation as the means to arrive at *ratio fideli* (in this, he went from monastic hermeneutics, based on rhetoric, to scholastic hermeneutics, based on logic). Yet Anselm extends the *ratio* to encompass many senses: ontological, logical, epistemological, and psychological. Moreover, he also admits joy as the proper aim of knowledge. Anselm's commentary on scripture aims at literality, and he makes only scant use of allegory – in this, he is already the precursor of scholasticism.

From the ninth to the twelfth centuries

The glosses on Scripture started to appear from the ninth century onwards, but they proliferated mainly in the twelfth. Little by little, this became the *Glossa Ordinaria*.

Glosses could be interlinear, marginal, or continuous. The *glosulae* or small glosses referred to a specific point, and they gradually became independent exegeses. Although without proper grounds, marginal glosses were attributed to Walahfrid Strabos (circa 808–49), and the interlinear glosses to Anselm of Laon (died 1117). There were others by Lanfranc, Berengario, and Drogo, and some were anonymous. Strabo summarized only those of his master, Rabano Mauro. Some used those of Saint Isidore (Beuchot 2002: 69–72).

Anselm of Laon intended to gloss the whole of Scripture, but was not able to accomplish this. Nonetheless, he wrote the gloss to Saint Paul and the Book of Psalms, and perhaps that of the Fourth Gospel. His brother Ralph compiled the gloss to Mathew, and Ralph's disciple Gilbert compiled that of the Pentateuch and the Major Prophets. The authorship of the gloss of the Minor Prophets remains doubtful. A disciple of Anselm of Laon, Gilbert de la Porrée, expanded his master's work, and this became known as the *Media Glosatura*. Peter Lombard expanded it even further, and it became the *Major* or *Magna Glosatura* (composed between 1135 and 1143). Peter used these glosses in his *Sentences*, written in 1152. This same *Glosa* was later commented upon by Peter Comestor, in his lectures on the Gospels (some time before 1168).

Hugh of Saint Victor

Born around 1097 and dying in 1141, Hugh of Saint Victor belonged to the School of Saint Victor, which privileged the allegoric and anagogic (mystical) exegesis over other forms. Literal interpretation was a support for spiritual interpretation. The aim of such an approach was to conjoin reason and passion with Neo-Platonic and Augustinian instruments. Following Augustine, the Victorines saw an excess in language – an allegory that surpassed literality. Influenced, through Eriugena, by Pseudo-Dionysus, theirs was a school hermeneutics, not only an individual one. It took the form of a dialectics of innovation and conservation.

The *lectio* ("reading") of the monks and canons precedes the *lectio* of the Scholastics. The former is *lectio divina* – sacred reading – including *meditatio* (meditation) and *oratio* (prayer); the latter takes the form of a scholarly lesson, with the *quaestio* and the *disputatio*. For the monks and canons of the *lectio divina*, the Scripture is conceived as a miraculous tree that is infinitely fruitful, and their primary focus was on the soul's relationship with God – which is why they commented so much on the *Song of Songs*. One of the best schools of exegesis was that of Saint Victor. The Victorines made use of allegorical meaning, but they also defended the literal, since without the latter, the former runs the risk of becoming arbitrary. Allegory itself was to be interpreted only in the light of doctrine.

In some of his *Annotations of the Scriptures and Sacred Writers*, Hugh speaks about the Bible having a triple sense (*triplex intelligentia*): it is both historical and allegorical, and he divides the allegorical into the proper and the anagogical (mystical). The historical sense is "that in which one considers the primary meaning of words in relation to the things in themselves to which they refer" (Hugh of Saint Victor, 1854a, 11D–12A). He says that Holy Scripture differs from other writings specifically in that it means some things that then become signs for other things. Allegorical sense occurs when the text "means something different, done in the past, the present, or the future" (Hugh of Saint Victor 1854a, 12AB), and this he subdivides into simple allegory and anagogy: "There is a simple allegory when a visible fact means an invisible one. Anagogy, that is, an uplifting, [occurs] when, through a visible fact, an invisible one is declared" (Hugh of Saint Victor 1854a, 12B). The anagogical corresponds to the higher, endless life – that of Heaven.

In his *magnum opus*, the *Didascalicon*, whose subtitle is *De studio legend* – "about the study, effort, or dedication to reading" – Hugh lists three points of focus in the approach of a text: *littera, sensus, sentential* (Hugh of Saint Victor, 1854b, VI, 4, 804). First, the letter (*littera*) or word, as it occurs at both the grammatical and the syntactic levels; second, the sense (*sensus*), that is, the things that are meant by the words, in the logic of discourse, or semantics; and finally, the content (*sententia*), which is the hidden lesson that should be extracted from word and sense, on a pragmatic level corresponding to the hermeneutical. Hugh invokes the idea of the double book – the Bible and the world – that is, Creation as a text, mirroring the text of Scripture (Hugh of Saint Victor 1854b, VIII, 2, 814). Hence, man, as a microcosmos, is a compendium of the world, a précis of the grand text of the Universe.

William of Saint-Thierry

Born in Liège, William of Saint-Thierry was a Benedictine monk who, in search of a greater rigour, went on, in Signy, to became a Cistercian. He was the abbot, from 1119 to 1135, of the monastery from which he takes his name. He died in 1148. Around 1145, William wrote an *Epistle to the Brethren of Mont-Dieu* – a veritable treatise on monastic life. In that work, he gave important indications on the interpretation of the Holy Scripture. He speaks of the *lectio divina* in terms of a hermeneutics of co-naturality developed by progressive sanctification (de Saint-Thierry 1940: 105), and admits allegorical or spiritual interpretation. He argues that one has to interpret through love, in a way that goes beyond knowledge. His commentary on the *Song of Songs* (*The Book of Solomon*), which he composed at the request of his friend Saint Bernard of Clairvaux, employs the spiritual or mystical interpretation that he favoured. Of the work, he wrote that it was for him "a sweet labour" interrupted by his fight with Peter Abelard in 1138.

William said that that his aim was to focus on the moral sense, which is common to everyone, without aspiring to the mystical one (de Saint-Thierry 1979: 26). Yet he also acknowledges the literal or historical sense, according to which the narrative is taken as a fable or parable, and even reaches towards the anagogical or mystical. William often resorted to etymologies – some of them forced – but always with the goal of turning the word towards the spirit, as the means to give it life.

Thierry of Chartres

Thierry, or Theodoric the Breton, belonged to the School of Chartres, of which he was the head from 1121 to 1134. He then taught in Paris until 1140, but he returned to Chartres the next year and succeeded Gilbert de la Porrée as its Chancellor. He taught Abelard, and then fought him, denouncing his theses as heretical. Among

other works, Thierry composed the *Eptateucon*, written before 1156, a text of ency-
clopaedic dimensions, which became, on account of its good pedagogy, a book used
in teaching during the twelfth century. He also commented on Cicero and Boeccio.
He died some time between 1150 and 1155.

This school had a humanist and Platonizing tendency, which can be seen both in
Thierry and in his disciple John of Salisbury. Thierry left, among his commentaries
on Cicero, one on *De inventione* and another on a piece falsely attributed to this
Latin orator, the *Rethorica ad Herennium*. The most striking feature in these two
works is that they contain, side by side with rhetoric doctrines, hermeneutic teachings. In the former, he speaks of doubts about the author's intention and intended
meaning – raising what is a highly hermeneutic question (de Chartres 1988: 82).
Meaning as derived from such authorial intention is seen as differing from and
adding to the literal meaning, but as having to be proven by means of dialectic
argumentation (de Chartres 1988: 202). He allows that one may appeal to custom
in interpreting, since custom compels use, and provides a pragmatic definition of
terms. One may also appeal to authority, both of the classics and of the person.
Thierry thus offers a psychological hermeneutics of intentions. In the case of interpretations that contradict a law, one is bound to show that one's own interpretation
is more useful than the other – and the written text must be used, not only to show
what is in it, but also what derives from it. Here Thierry shows himself as taking a
stand against ambiguity.

Joachim of Flora (Gioacchino da Fiore)

Joachim was born between 1130 and 1135 in Celico, Calabria, and died in 1202.
He was at the service of the Kingdom of Sicily and, circa 1160, he entered the Benedictine monastery of Corazzo, where he was professed and ordained as a priest. In
1177 he became its abbot. Towards 1182, he retired to the Casamari Abbey and
dedicated himself to writing. His main works are grouped in his grand trilogy, initiated in 1183, which comprises the *Liber Concordie novi ac veteris Testamenti*, the
Expositio in Apocalypsim, and the *Psalterium decem chordarum*. Although three pontiffs
(Lucius III, Urbanus III, and Clement III) had his writings examined, they encouraged him to proceed with them. In 1189, Joachim founded the first community of
his new Florens order in San Giovanni in Fiore. The Cistercian order declared him
to be a fugitive, but Pope Celestine III granted his approval of his new order. When
he died, in 1202, Joachim was preparing a new work – *Tractatus super quatuor Evan-
gelia* – which remained unfinished. In 1215, the IV Council of Letrán condemned his
doctrines on the Trinity, for being tri-theistic; in 1263, the Provincial Council of
Arles condemned all his works. He was well-meaning, but fell into heresy.

Joachim acknowledges traditional exegesis, in its four senses: literal, allegorical,
typological, and anagogical. His innovation was to apply biblical exegesis to historical evolution. He developed a theology of history. His exegetic method is based on
the spiritual or allegorical intelligence and on the typical or typological intelligence,
which have various degrees. Using allegory, he builds his conception of the history
of the world, with three ages that correspond to the three Divine Persons. His most
original interpretation is that of the mission of the Holy Ghost. He did not only see

Him as the fulfiller of Christ's teachings, but as someone who would bring about, before the end of time, the final form of interpretation and contemplative worship. He uses numerical, geometrical, zoological, and botanical symbols in order to explain and support this exegesis.

He considers anagogy to be a resemblance of the temporal and earthly with the mystical and heavenly (de Fiore, 1983, l. 2, p. 1, c. 3: 65). For him, there are three fundamental eras: that of the Father, that of the Son, and that of the Holy Ghost. For Joachim, literal interpretation, which belonged to the Old Testament, was that of the Father; allegorical interpretation, from the New Testament, was that of the Son; and anagogical or fully spiritual interpretation, from the era of monasticism, was that of the Holy Ghost.

II. The Mature Middle Ages: interpretation and scholasticism

The transition from the twelfth to the thirteenth century: glosses and sums

Up to the twelfth century there was of predominance of allegorical, symbolic, and spiritual hermeneutics, which was that of monks, monastic schools, and cathedral schools. With the emergence of universities and scholastics, hermeneutics becomes literal and historical. First there was a hermeneutics of sense, and then came another hermeneutics of reference; the former rejoiced in the multiple – practically infinite – connotations found by the monks, and the latter disciplined itself to find the proper denotation. Hermeneutics now became mainly literal, but without abandoning the allegorical. In the thirteenth century, the age of the University, there was a passage from rhetoric to dialectics or logic. There was an admixture of gloss (spiritual) and dispute (academic) (Beuchot 2002: 129 ff).

In this manner, some scholastic thinkers could write commentaries on the *Song of Solomon* while at the same time composing a *Summa Theologica* – as in the case of Thomas of Vercelli or Giles of Rome (Aegidius Romanus). Giles was a disciple of Thomas Aquinas, and combined rhetoric with dialectics, commentary with questioning. *Quaestio* itself has its origin in rhetoric. The many problems that emerged from the *lectio* determined the passage to the *disputatio*. In monastic and cathedral schools there was grammar and rhetoric for monks and canons; in the *stadium generale* and the university, dialectics or logic was added. There was a balance between glosses and sums. This was the Mature Middle Ages.

Saint Bonaventure

A good example of the balance between literal and allegorical meanings, commentary and dispute, is to be found in Bonaventure. He was a Franciscan, Professor at the University and, hence, a scholastic, but he was also a follower of Hugh of Saint Victor in the matter of symbolic reading. He was born Giovanni di Fidanza, near Viterbo, circa 1217–18. He studied in the University of Paris, from 1236 to 1242, the year in which he entered the Franciscan Order. He taught in this same University – although somewhat discontinuously on account of the opposition of certain secular teachers – but in 1257 was finally admitted as Master in Theology. That very same year he was elected Minister General of his order. In 1273, he was made Cardinal-Bishop, and as such he participated in the preparations and the discussions of the Second Council of Lyon, but died in 1274, before the Council concluded.

Bonaventure left many philosophical and theological works, but it is in his *Itinerarium mentis in Deum* that one can most clearly see the spirit of his reading. The work takes the form of an itinerary of the mind by creatures that are seeking the Divine Mind. That is, taking its point of departure from the creatures in their different grades (minerals, vegetables, animals, and man), the intellect seeks the vestiges of God. Bonaventure's hermeneutics is ontological, as well as poetical. All created things correspond to ideas in the Mind of the Creator. Interpretation demands some virtues from man. God expresses Himself and communicates through His creation. That is why one reads or interprets in search of Him. All things are the vestiges of God, His traces. They are signs in the grand Book of the World (Bonaventure, 1945a, cap. II, nn. 11–12: 588). They are words of the Word of God. Thus, in interpreting the world, one also uncovers its intentionality.

Saint Bonaventure expounds his hermeneutic scaffolding of the Bible in various writings, including the *Breviloquium* and the *Collationes in Hexameron*. Besides the literal meaning, he talks of allegorical, moral, and anagogical meanings (Bonaventure 1945b, pról., 4, 1: 183). Here he also refers to the idea of Creation as a book. Bonaventure privileges the figurative exposition of Scripture, which offers infinite readings (Bonaventure 1947, n. 2: 409). Yet although this means that Scripture allows an infinity of interpretations, such an infinity can only be encompassed by God – man is inadequate in the face of such infinity, and aided by the community in which, and for which, he interprets, his interpretive efforts must at some point simply come to a halt.

Bonaventure has two methodological procedures: *reductio* and *proportio*. *Reductio* is a logical method, already used by Plato and perfected by Eriugena. It is one of the parts of dialectics, which goes from the concrete to the abstract, as opposed to *division*, which goes from the abstract to the concrete. The *reductio in medio* tries to mediate between extremes, in a manner that resembles dialectics. But *reductio* is based on similarity or analogy. That is why he also uses *proportio*, since analogy is proportion. But this is not an analogy like that used in Thomism, but one which is more on the anagogic line, more dynamic and lively.

Saint Thomas Aquinas

Born in the castle of Roccasecca, near Aquino, Italy, in 1225, Thomas studied in Naples, where he entered the Dominican Order. He continued his studies in Paris and Cologne; he taught in Paris on two occasions (a rare privilege), as well as in the papal court. Thomas died in 1274, on his way to the Second Council of Lyon. He wrote commentaries on Aristotle, the Holy Scripture, Peter Lombard, and others. Thomas also produced some most remarkable works of his own, including the *Summa contra gentiles* and the *Summa Theologiae*.

In a prayer that is attributed to him, Thomas asks God to grant him skill in interpretation (*interpretandi subtilitas*), which is the hermeneut's virtue. In his own approach to interpretation, Aquinas looks first to the literal sense of the text, to which he devotes considerable labour, and then passes onto the other hidden or figurative senses. In his commentaries on Aristotle, he draws upon the literal sense, through the idea of the author's intention, the *intentio auctoris*, and in his reading of the Holy Scripture adds to this the figurative or spiritual sense.

Already in the *Summa Theologiae*, Thomas asks himself whether theology may use metaphors, and if a word may have several senses (Aquinas 1951, I, q. I, aa. 9 & 10). Since they speak about the spiritual through its similarity with the corporeal, Thomas argues that metaphor is acceptable, and he also acknowledges the existence of various meanings in Scripture, on the grounds that God, as its divine author, can make things, and not only voices, signify (Aquinas 1951, I, q. I, a. 10, c). Thomas then divides the spiritual sense in three: (i) *allegorical*, according to which what appears in the Old Testament are figures for the New; (ii) *moral*, according to which what Christ does is a sign of what we should do; and (iii) *anagogical*, according to which what appears in the New Testament are figures for those that occur in the Eternal Glory. These spiritual senses, taken together with the literal, make up the four senses to be found in Scripture.

Although Aquinas holds to the idea of literal sense, which he takes to correspond to the author's intention, he also holds that Scripture contains a variety of meanings and does so without falling into mere equivocation (Aquinas 1951, I, q. I, a. 10, AD 1m.) – this is because God, who understands everything by means of the divine intellect, is himself the author of Scripture (Aquinas 1951, I, q. I, a. 10, AD 1m.).

Thomas was bound to deal with the already established distinction between historical, aetiological, analogical, and allegorical meaning. For him, the historical, etiological, and analogical senses all belong to the same literal sense, since history is the simple narrating of events, aetiology is assigning a cause to events, and analogy enables us to see how the truth of one passage of Scripture does not, appearances to the contrary, undermine the truth of another (Aquinas 1951, I, q. I, a. 10, AD 2m.). What we call the parabolic sense is understood by Thomas to be contained in the literal (Aquinas 1951, I, q. I, a. 10, AD 3m.).

Following the custom of the University of Paris, Thomas's method in interpreting is first to make a *division* of the text, and then to make a declaration of its *sense* – the literal first and then the spiritual – according to authority, but also critically. He strives to find a central and guiding idea in the text in question – an idea or theme that he refers to as the *intentio libri*. The literal sense at issue here may be indeterminate and so compatible with more than one interpretation, and to it is added the spiritual sense.

In his commentaries to the *Sentences* of Peter Lombard, the great manual of theology, Thomas first makes the *divisio textus* and then the *expositio textus*, being fully conscious that dividing or classifying are already interpreting, while exposition is even more so. Although his commentaries on Aristotle look to the literal sense of the text, Thomas was no mere literalist – what he sought was the *intentio Aristotelis* beyond the *verba Aristotelis*. In order to achieve this, Thomas resorted to textual research and comparison, and undertook a painstaking form of exegesis which proceeded word by word. Studying not only the words of the Aristotelian text, but also their context, Thomas based his interpretive investigation on the *principia Aristotelis*, according to which each one of the Stagirite's texts must be related to the entire

Aristotelian *corpus*. Moreover, Thomas engages in a critical dialogue with Aristotle's commentators, writers such Averroes, as well as with Aristotle himself, thereby going beyond them. In this way, Thomas combined criticism with Aristotelian exegesis – *dubia circa litteram* (doubts about the text) and *Aristoteles sui interpretaes*. Thomas lets the author speak, recovers the author's intention, and then adds observations or reflections of his own, though always with much discretion.

Thomas followed the conventional medieval method according to which reading (*lectio*) came first, then meditation (*meditatio*), and finally questioning (*quaestio*). Questions were treated as glosses (interlinear or marginal) or as exposition. Exposition could be brief and in passing (*cursoria*) or more leisurely (*ordinaria*). One started with the letter of the text (*littera*), passed over to the sense (*sensus*), and ended in the content or opinion (*sententia*). The content was the deep meaning, enabling the true comprehension of the text. Questions were born from an ambiguous word, from two contrasting commentaries, or from the opposition of two authorities. The *quaestio* opened the way for the *disputatio*, the *quaestiones disputatae*, that is, controversy. This is why Thomas divides the Aristotelian text in *lectiones*, and then reserves the problems for the *quaestiones*, above all for the *quaestiones disputatae*. In everything, moreover, he paid attention to the context (*circumstantia litterae*), and frequently made use of distinction (*distinctio*) in order to clarify the meaning of texts.

Meister Eckhart

Born in Hochheim (Thuringia, Germany), circa 1260, Eckhart entered the Dominican Order of Friars Preachers, in Erfurt, around 1276. He studied in Strasbourg, was ordained in 1285, and then perfected his studies in theology in Cologne, from 1286 to 1288. In 1299 or 1300 he explained Peter Lombard's *Sentences* at the University of Paris. In 1302 Eckhart received the degree of Master in Holy Theology (*Magister in theologia*), and hence came to be known as *Meister* ("Master"). After holding some posts in his order, he went back to Paris to teach, in 1311. He then went to Strasbourg, in 1314, and there began his fame as a preacher. In 1320 Eckhart taught in Cologne, where he preached again, but being accused of heresy and processed, he publicly recanted. He went to Avignon, which was the seat of the pontiff's court at the time, in order for a papal commission to examine his works. Eckhart died before the final verdict was announced, and his death is placed, rather imprecisely, between 1327 and 1328. In accordance with the outcome of the commission, in 1329, Pope John XXII condemned twenty-eight of Eckhart's propositions. Recent criticism has shown, however, that rather than being heretical, they are simply ambiguous and unusual in their form.

Besides his commentary on the *Sentences* and his *Disputed Questions*, Eckhart has an *Opus Tripartitum*, with biblical exegeses and theological musings. But these are to be more properly found in his *Discourses on Distinction*, *The Book of the Divine Consolation*, and his sermons.

Eckhart's theology is highly influenced by Neo-Platonism, through Pseudo-Dionysius and Eriugena, and centres on the idea of the descent of creatures away from God and their ascent towards Him, most especially in the case of man, whose soul, in its ascent, moves towards union with the Holy Trinity. God is understood as absolutely transcendent from the world – which is why Eckhart sometimes adopts the language of negative theology, although he also uses the analogical discourse of affirmative theology. He uses the analogy of attribution, sometimes in a highly metaphorical manner, as, for instance, when he says that God is like the substance and creatures are like accidents – a claim that gave rise to the charge of pantheism. Eckhart took his use of analogy from the work of Aquinas (whom he called *Frater Thomas*). The main emphasis in Eckhart's thought is on the absolute distinction or difference between God and His creatures. God was understood as the Totally Other, only to be approached through the practice of self-annihilation and perfect humility.

When writing his commentary on the *Gospel of John*, Eckhart speaks of a double intentionality: the *intentio auctoris*, which is the author's, and the *intentio operis*, which is the text's (and which relates to the meanings of words in their correspondence to natural things and in their moral interpretation – Eckhart 1989, n. 3), as if they were two concordant intentions (as in Umberto Eco's *intentio operis* – Eco 1992: 29). He also identified an *intentio operantis*, which is that of the interpreter, combining all three in the *intentio operati*, which is the textual action carried out by interpretation (Eckhart 1989, n. 2). In addition, Eckhart makes use of metaphor and, hence, analogy, as well as the allegoric and the anagogic senses. Going beyond the idea of the world as a book, and Creation as a text, Eckhart claimed that all things are books, "since every creature is filled with God and is a book", and above all, every man is a book, which he himself writes in front of God, who allows him to write, to build, and to care for himself.

Raymond Lully (Ramon Lull or Raimundus Lullius)

Born in Palma of Mallorca in 1233, Lully died in 1316 while on his way from Bougie, in North Africa, to the Majorcan beaches. He died as a martyr, preaching in Muslim lands. In his approach to textual interpretation, Lully used a combinatory art which he claimed to have received through revelation when he was a hermit on Mount Randa in Mallorca. Nonetheless, various Arabic and Jewish precursors to this art have been identified. A combinatory reading method which Lully applied to the task of interpretation, Lully's *Ars Magna* contained a set of general rules concerning the relation between ideas that aimed at completeness and comprehensiveness. Taking from Eastern thought the device of the teaching story or parable, Lully deployed this, not only as a pedagogic resource, but also as an interpretative tool. It is a form of parabolic, symbolic, and allegorical interpretation.

In Lully's novel *The Book of Evast and Blanquerna*, one of the main characters, Blanquerna, who in the story becomes Pope, uses the Lullian method in order to meditate on the mysteries of Christianity and to interpret Holy Scripture. In another book, *Felix of the marvels*, Lully applies his combinatory method in exposition through parables. His main character, Felix, travels around the world marvelling at the prodigious things he meets, expressing himself in apologues, and thereby reading the Divine Order from the Book of Creatures. Reality itself appears to Felix as a grand parable of God, which he, Felix, has to interpret. Lully's method of combinatory exegesis provides a means to read both things and texts, and especially Holy Scripture. He finds the order of God in the reality of the world, and in the midst of intricate Cabalistic-like combinations.

III. The Late Middle Ages: reconciling monasticism and scholasticism

Jean Gerson

The fourteenth century corresponds to the Late Middle Ages, with the emergence of the nominalism of Ockham and his followers. Jean Charlier de Gerson (1363–1429) was known as Chancellor Gerson, because he occupied this position at the University of Paris for a considerable time (1395–1429). Gerson is usually considered to be a nominalist, but this not quite accurate. He did revere his nominalist teachers, even Ockham, and he defended some of the theses that are attributed to this school, but he also followed Aquinas and, above all, Bonaventure, both of whom were realists. Gerson was, more than anything else, a mystical-ascetic writer, but also a good logico-semantic philosopher. He was critical of realists, especially the Scotists, as well as the nominalists – the latter on account of their logicism – and sometimes he tried to reconcile them. Thus, Gerson mingled diverse currents of thought, and the result is complex. Following a certain disenchantment with, and even scepticism towards, the logicism of the nominalists, he sought refuge in a mystical attitude – a path not unlike that of Ludwig Wittgenstein.

In one of his mystical works, *De elucidatione scholastica theologiae mysticae* – a work that stands out from his others – Gerson tells us of his wish to conjoin mysticism and scholasticism. Among his exegetical works, most striking is his commentary on the *Song of Songs*, in which he appears as a scholastic who still keeps to the tradition of monastic exegesis. Gerson belongs to the mystical current of the *devotio moderna*, a renovative movement which was a forerunner of the Reformation. His hermeneutics can be seen in his commentary to *On the Celestial Hierarchy* of Pseudo-Dionysius, to which he adds some exegetic notes. In that work he draws upon allegorical and anagogical readings, and even considers the nature of symbolism. Showing a great appreciation for Richard of Saint Victor, Gerson draws together the monastic and the scholastic commentaries. Thus, when interpreting the notion of the divine idea, he follows Ockham, and distances himself from Saint Albert (Gerson 1940: 201–2).

Using allegory, Gerson compares the grades of Heaven with the grades of intelligence. The three heavens correspond to the grades of contemplation. Here, once again, he combines the scholastic with the monastic. Belonging to the University Gerson is scholastic, but he nevertheless recovers the symbolic hermeneutics of the monks. He even includes the anagogical sense in his interpretive approach, and reconciles intellect with affect (Gerson 1940: 266–67). Gerson touches on negative theology, but accepts the positive knowledge of God, even though not as He is in Himself – divine things are known through analogy (Gerson 1940: 326). In this manner, Gerson draws together all the senses displayed within medieval exegesis, thereby conjoining monastic hermeneutics with the scholastic.

V. Conclusion: towards analogism

The Middle Ages were hyper-textual, looking not only to the text of the Bible, but also to the text of the world. These two books, the Bible and the world, are both the creations of God, who is the author of both. God Himself is not a part of either text, since it was He who wrote each of them – and they are both His. Man, on the other hand, is a part of the text, but he is also, at one and the same time, its reader, and so is placed in a privileged position. Man's access to the divine text is by reading, and such reading relies upon four senses: the literal, the allegorical, the ethical or analogical, and the mystical or anagogic. In Christ, something very strange and special happens because, inasmuch as He is God, Christ is the author of the texts of the world and the Bible, but, inasmuch as he is a man, he is a part of the text and its reader. Christ is thus the conjunction of writing and reading; He is hermeneutics in itself, in its complete cycle; He the true microcosm. Both the image of God, but also the image of man – Christ is the ideal, the model.

As we have seen, in the High-Medieval or Patristic era, monastic hermeneutics, with its strongly allegorical orientation, predominated; on the other hand, in the Mature and Late Medieval period, scholastic hermeneutics took precedence, and so also did a literalist approach to interpretation. But many thinkers also strove to combine them, often arriving at a balance between the two. In this reconciliatory endeavour, analogy played an active part, and with it a mode of analogical interpretation – an analogical hermeneutics. Throughout the medieval trajectory, such an analogical hermeneutics, based on analogy and iconicity, appears at certain moments. Here Augustine, Bonaventure, Thomas Aquinas, and Meister Eckhart stand out as paradigmatic figures. All are part of an effort to go beyond the opposition between univocity and equivocity – an effort directed towards the achievement of analogism.

Bibliography

Anselm, Saint (1952a) *Epistula de incarnatione Verbi*, in *Obras completas*, Madrid: BAC.

——(1952b) *Cur Deus homo*, in *Obras completas*, Madrid: BAC.

Aquinas, Saint Thomas (1951) *Summa theologiae*, Madrid: BAC.

Beuchot, Mauricio (2002) *La hermenéutica en la Edad Media*, Mexico: Universidad Nacional Autónoma de México.

Bonaventure, Saint (1945a) *Itinerarium mentis in Deum*, in *Obras completas*, Madrid: BAC, vol. I.

——(1945b) *Breviloquium*, in *Obras completas*, Madrid: BAC, vol. I.

——(1947) *Collationes in hexaemeron*, in *Obras completas*, Madrid: BAC, vol. III.

de Chartres, Thierry (1988) *The Latin Rhetorical Commentaries by Thierry of Chartres*, ed. K. M. Fredborg (ed.), Toronto: Pontifical Institute of Medieval Studies.

de Fiore, Joachim (1983) *Liber de concordia Novi ac Veteris Testamenti*, E. Randolph Daniel (ed.), Philadelphia: The American Philosophical Society.

de Saint-Thierry, Guillaume (1940) *Un traité de la vie solitaire. Epistola ad fratres de Monte-Dei* [A treatise on solitary life: Epistle to the brethren of Mont-Dieu], M.-M. Davy (ed.), Paris: J. Vrin.

——(1979) *Comentario al Cantar de los Cantares* [Commentary on the Song of Songs], trans. M. R. Suárez, Buenos Aires: Monasterio Trapense de Ntra. Sra. De los Ángeles – Eds. Claretianas (Colección Padres Cistercienses, 6).

Eckhart, Johannes (1989) *Le commentaire de l'évangile selon Jean. Le prologue (chap. 1, 1–18)*, ed. A. de Libera, E. Wéber, E. Zum Brunn, en *L'oeuvre latine de Maître Eckhert*, Paris: Éds. du Cerf.

Eco, Umberto (1992) *Los límites de la interpretación*, Barcelona: Lumen. [Spanish translation of I limiti dell'interpretazione, Milan: Bompiani, 1990.]

Eriugena, Johannes Scotus (1865a) *Expositio super Hyerarchiam caelestem*, PL 122.
——(1865b) *De divisione naturae*, PL 122.
Gerson, Johannes (1940) *Notulae super quaedam verba Dionisij De Celesti Ierarchia*, in A. Combes, *Jean Gerson, commentateur dionysien*, Paris: Vrin.
Hugh of Saint Victor (1854a) *De scripturis et scriptoribus Sacris praenotatiunculae*, PL 175.
Hugh of Saint Victor (1854b) *Didascalicon*, PL 176.

Further reading

Copeland, Rita (1991) *Rhetoric, Hermeneutics, and Translation in the Middle Ages*, Cambridge: Cambridge University Press.
Fidora, A., and C. Serra (eds) (2011) *Ramon Llull: From the Ars Magna to Artificial Intelligence*, Barcelona: Artificial Intelligence Research Institute – Consejo Superior de Investigaciones Científicas.
Gallacher, Patrick J., and Helen Damico (eds) (1989) *Hermeneutics and Medieval Culture*, Albany, NY: SUNY Press.
Grondin, Jean (1994) *Introduction to Philosophcial hermeneutics*, trans. Joel Weinsheimer, Yale: Yale University Press – Chapter I.
Matkus, R. A. (1988) *Saeculum: History and Society in the Theology of St. Augustine*, Cambridge: Cambridge University Press.
Moran, D. (1990) *The Philosophy of John Scotus Eriugena. A Study of Idealism in the Middle Ages*, Cambridge: Cambridge University Press.
Shahan, W. and F. J. Kovach (eds) (1976) *Bonaventure and Aquinas. Enduring Philosophers*, Norman: University of Oklahoma Press.
Weisheipl, J. A. (ed.) (1980) *Albertus Magnus and the Sciences. Commemorative Essays*, Toronto: Pontifical Institute of Medieval Studies.
——(1984) *Friar Tommaso d'Aquino. His Life, Thought and Work*, Garden City, NY: Doubleday and Co.

Part II
HERMENEUTIC THINKERS

3
SPINOZA AND VICO: A NEW SCIENCE OF INTERPRETATION

Leonardo Amoroso

Translated by Aidan Butler

1. Hermeneutics as a new science

The cultural documents of pagan peoples (in particular Homeric poetry) and (even more so) the Bible are texts that have been, since the time of antiquity, the objects of very particular attention. They have, therefore, stimulated the birth of hermeneutics itself. At the outset of the modern age Humanism, promoting the study of classical antiquity, and the Reformation, promoting the principle of Biblical study for all within the Christian world, gave new and important impulses to the direction in which hermeneutics itself was to develop.

The hermeneutical thought of the two early modern authors whose works will be considered in this chapter developed through contact with these privileged documents: Spinoza proposed a method for interpreting the Bible; Vico a method for interpreting ancient culture (and Homeric poetry in particular). A decisive novelty applying to both of their bodies of work is the fact that by the time of Spinoza and Vico the inaugural event of modernity had already taken place: the birth of mathematical-experimental science. It was from this event that – in the 1700s, in the context of a general reordering of the sciences – hermeneutics was to be reborn as a general theory of interpretation, one with the claim, therefore, of being a science. But already in the cases of Spinoza and Vico – in the light of the relationships that their hermeneutics entertained with this crucial event – one can talk of a "science" or "new science" of interpretation. From this point of view both authors look, first and foremost, towards the experimental side of the new science. Indeed, there are undeniable analogies between textual interpretation itself and the study of the "book of nature": both texts and natural phenomena are data to be interpreted. Spinoza, as we shall see, affirms this analogy explicitly and, furthermore, presents his hermeneutic methodology in terms that recall, in certain respects, the works of Francis Bacon (Spinoza 1989:

140–4). Bacon is also an important point of reference for Vico, who wishes to apply to the world of men – or rather, to the documents and testimony that form the foundation of gentile civilization – the synthesis that Bacon, according to Vico's analysis (Vico 1994: 67–8), had applied to his studies of the natural world. Another father of modern science is of fundamental importance for Vico: Galileo, to whom he probably alludes in the title of the *New Science* itself (Vico 1994: 415).

2. Spinoza's biblical hermeneutics

Almost all of Spinoza's works (including his principal work, the *Ethics*) were published posthumously, in 1677, the year of his death. However the *Tractatus Theologico-Politicus* – the work that is of interest to us here, by virtue of the fact that it contains his biblical hermeneutics – was published (anonymously) in 1670. Spinoza had begun to write the work after his expulsion, in 1656, from the Jewish community of Amsterdam. This was the city where he had been born, in 1632, to a Marrano Jewish family who had escaped from the Iberian Peninsula. These events are noteworthy in part because Marranism constitutes one of the foundations of modern critical thought. It is accordingly no accident that Spinoza, a descendent of Marranos, was one of the initiators of the non-confessional approach to Biblical analysis. Beyond this, the *Tractatus Theologico-Politicus* is itself a "Marranian" work, insofar as it lends itself to multiple levels of reading, says things but does not say them and frequently suggests audacious (for the time) theses that it would have been impossible to set out explicitly. The results of this are that the work's apparent clarity of meaning is just that – apparent – and that scholars of the work continue to argue over the true meaning of the text today.

Notwithstanding all of this Spinoza, in the work's preface, declares its goal to be the following:

> When I pondered over these facts, that the light of reason is not only despised but it is condemned by many as a source of impiety, that merely human suppositions are regarded as divine doctrine and that credulity is looked upon as faith; and when I saw that the disputes of philosophers are raging with violent passion in Church and Court and are breeding bitter hatred and faction which readily turn men to sedition, together with other ills too numerous to recount here, I deliberately resolved to examine Scripture afresh, conscientiously and freely, and to admit nothing as its teaching which I did not most clearly derive from it.
>
> (Spinoza 1989: 53–4)

It is from here that the need for a scientific hermeneutics arises. The principles of this hermeneutics are established in the crucially important seventh chapter of the work (however, they are also applied in the earlier chapters, which are dedicated to certain aspects of the Jewish religion, namely prophesy, election, law, the function of religious ceremonies and the Biblical narratives, miracles, etc.). In this chapter, entitled *Of the Interpretation of Scripture*, Spinoza affirms that:

The method of interpreting Scripture is no different from the method of interpreting Nature, and is in fact in complete accord with it. For the method of interpreting Nature consists essentially in composing a detailed study of Nature from which, as being the source of our assured data, we can deduce the definitions of the things of Nature. Now it is exactly the same way the task of Scriptural interpretation requires us to make a straightforward study of Scripture, and from this, as the source of our fixed data and principles, to deduce by logical inference the meaning of the authors of Scripture.

(Spinoza 1989: 141)

For the scientific study of the Bible, just as for the scientific study of nature, it is necessary to begin by collecting materials and subsequently to deduce from these, by means of induction, certain general principles. First and foremost it is necessary to have a good knowledge of the languages in which the Bible was written, that is to say, of Hebrew and Greek. Spinoza is also quite insistent as to the importance of a knowledge of Hebrew for interpreting the New Testament, arguing that it was composed by men who – even when they wrote in Greek – thought in Hebrew. It should be recalled that Spinoza was himself the author of a (posthumously published) Hebrew grammar: an interesting aspect of which being the fact that Spinoza's grammatical categories recall those of his metaphysics (as elucidated in the first part of the *Ethics*, entitled *Of God*).

Once armed with this linguistic knowledge one should proceed to the classification of the propositions, noting in particular the most obscure among them. Spinoza affirms, with a decisive specification, that this obscurity can be identified "simply from linguistic usage" and not by reference to rational knowledge. Indeed, at least at this level of analysis, "the point at issue is merely the meaning of the texts, not their truth" (Spinoza 1989: 143). For example, the problem is not the truth of the statement "God is fire," but rather its compatibility with the statement according to which God is invisible. Yet the former statement might be taken as signifying that God is jealous and this metaphorical sense is the one in which it should be understood, despite the fact that, from a rational point of view, it is inadmissible to conceive of God as being affected by passions.

It is then also necessary to contextualize the texts historically and to study their transmission as this can, in some cases, help to clarify certain points and smooth out inconsistencies.

According to Spinoza one can proceed, on the basis of all this, to the tracing back of the teachings contained within the Biblical texts, beginning with those most universal. He states that it will be possible to gain far greater certainty regarding practical questions than regarding speculative ones (with which the Bible does not concern itself, with the exception of some very general truths; such as the existence of God).

Nevertheless, the essential importance of linguistic knowledge to Spinoza's method itself brings certain difficulties to light. The first difficulty arises from the fact that Hebrew, like other ancient languages, is a dead one: "The men of old who used the Hebrew language" – he observes – "have left to posterity no information concerning the basic principles and study of this language. At any rate, we possess nothing at all from them, neither dictionary nor grammar nor text-book of rhetoric" (Spinoza 1989: 149). Spinoza places particular stress on the fact that we lack a "phraseology" of Biblical Hebrew; that is to say, that we are often unable to understand "the idioms and the modes of speech" of the language. He stresses in particular that the language's "oriental" idioms ought to be taken for what they are: mere rhetorical forms. As early as Chapter I Spinoza argues that the *ruach Elohim* mentioned in Genesis 1:2 should not be interpreted as meaning the Spirit of God, but simply as a reference to a very strong wind. The point is made still more explicitly in Chapter IV, which deals with "miracles"; that is to say, with what are *considered* to be miracles, as for Spinoza it would be impossible for any event to occur outside of the necessary order of nature. Accordingly, the "miracles" spoken of in the Bible are – in reality – nothing other than unusual, but not supernatural, events that struck the imagination of those who described them in a poetical, rhetorical style.

Other causes of ambiguity in the interpretation of the Hebrew language are, according to Spinoza: the possible exchange of certain letters; the polysemy of certain conjunctions; the exchange of certain verbal forms; the absence of vowels and punctuation marks (the work of the medieval punctuators, carried out long after the original composition of the text, is, for Spinoza, unreliable).

There are also, Spinoza argues, more general philological difficulties that can be added to those listed above. For example, we do not know who the authors of many of the books were. Furthermore, we often lack knowledge of the context in which the texts were composed and of the literary genre to which they belong. To explain this last point (which is highly relevant to the correct interpretation of a text) Spinoza gives, amongst others, the following example: both the Biblical prophet Elijah and the eponymous protagonist of Ludovico Ariosto's poem *Orlando Furioso* are described as having flown. However, the texts in which these flights are recounted belong to different "literary genres": Ariosto's poem is – according to Spinoza – a work designed to entertain, while the Bible is a work designed to transmit moral teachings. Therefore, the meaning of a particular episode or image in one text can be completely different from the meaning of a similar image as described in the other.

The final cause of difficulty is the fact that certain Biblical texts have reached us only in translation. These include – according to Spinoza – the Gospel According to Matthew and the Epistle to the Hebrews, both of which would have originally been written in Hebrew.

Spinoza emphasizes the significance of all of these difficulties, going so far as to state that they are "so grave that I have no hesitation in affirming that in many instances we either do not know the true meaning of Scripture or we can do no more than make conjecture" (Spinoza 1989: 153). However, he argues that these difficulties do not apply to the interpretation of the moral principles contained in the Bible, which are expressed in the clearest of terms. Spinoza's aim here is evident: to limit the Bible's authority to precisely these areas. With regard to the political and social rules set out in the Old Testament, Spinoza argues that they have not been applicable since the fall of the Ancient State of Israel.

Having thus presented the principles of his method, Spinoza goes on to set out his polemical objectives. Firstly, he criticizes – not without irony – those who maintain that "a supernatural light" (Spinoza 1989: 155) is required for Biblical interpretation, arguing that it is unclear what exactly this might be (it would seem inadmissible for it to be faith, given that the intended recipients of the Bible are unbelievers). Secondly, he criticizes Maimonides (the great medieval Jewish philosopher and author of *The Guide for the Perplexed*) for falling victim to the opposite error, that of proposing to demonstrate programmatically the perfect compatibility of faith and reason, and in so doing – according to Spinoza – making misuse of allegorical interpretation and bending Scripture to the needs of philosophy. His third polemical objective is the position of those who support a tradition that would hold the keys of Scriptural interpretation. This tradition is represented in Judaism by Pharisees and in Catholicism by the Church of Rome. On the contrary, Spinoza argues that the interpretation of the Bible must be based only upon the texts themselves. Here Spinoza is – with regard to his support for the principle of *sola Scriptura*, "Scripture alone" – close to Luther; but the former's non-confessional goal is distant from that of the latter. Spinoza is thus able to conclude that:

> our method of Scriptural interpretation is the best. For since the supreme authority for the interpretation of Scripture is vested in each individual, the rule that governs interpretation must be nothing other than the natural light common to all, and not any supernatural right, nor any external authority. Nor must this rule be so difficult as not to be available to any but skilled philosophers; it must be suited to the natural and universal ability and capacity of mankind.
>
> (Spinoza 1989: 160)

Chapter VII is followed by four chapters (VIII to XI) in which the principles of this new biblical hermeneutics are applied to the *Pentateuch* and subsequently to other books. Here Spinoza argues, for example, that Moses could not have been the author of the *Pentateuch* and maintains that the editing of those books (and of others in the Bible) was postexilic and aimed at the refoundation of Israel. Notwithstanding this, Spinoza maintains that the editing was based on pre-existing sources.

The chapters succeeding these, from XII to XV, argue that the Bible is "sacred" and can be said to be the "word of God" only insofar as it provides moral teachings. More precisely, it provides these teachings not in philosophical form (which would be inaccessible to all but a few), but in poetic form. That is to say, by storytelling. As we have seen, reason serves an essentially important function in the interpretation of the Bible; however, that function must be an exclusively methodological one. With regard to content, the scope of reason must not be confused with that of faith. Scripture must not be subordinated to reason (here Spinoza takes up once again his critique of Maimonides) and nor must reason be subordinated to Scripture (here Spinoza cites Jehuda Alphakar, a critic of Maimonides).

The final five chapters of the work (XVI to XX) are of a markedly more political slant. They contain an apologia for a liberal state that Spinoza argues should, like his Biblical hermeneutics, have a scientific rather than confessional foundation.

3. Vico's hermeneutics of ancient gentile cultures

In his autobiography Giambattista Vico, who was by profession a teacher of rhetoric, presents himself as the paladin defender of a humanism menaced by the forces of Cartesian rationalism (cf. Vico 1963: 113 and 137–8). In his educational-cultural discourse *On the Study Methods of our Times* (1709) he maintains, for example, that it is an error to teach adolescents abstract subjects such as logic or algebra. This is because the study of these subjects requires the possession of a well-developed reasoning ability, an ability which Vico states is – in adolescents – secondary to fantasy and wit. Accordingly, he argues that the subjects most suitable for study by adolescents are history, literature and languages (cf. Vico 1963: 12–20). A similar point is made, at a phylogenetic level rather than at an ontogenetic one, in his principle work, the *New Science*, with regard to "the world's childhood" (Vico 1994: 71). The mode of thought of primitive peoples is in fact, according to Vico, akin to that of children: both poor in reason and rich in fantasy.

Vico's anti-Cartesian polemic acquires a metaphysical aspect in the text entitled *On the Most Ancient Wisdom of the Italians* (1710) where, amongst other things, he contrasts Descartes' mentalistic *cogito ergo sum* with another principle and criterion of truth: *verum ipsum factum* (cf. Vico 1988: 45–7). This principle reproposes the ancient ontological (and theological) conception of truth, but also rethinks it in a rather modern, pragmatic way: one can only know what one does. The principle is further developed in the *New Science* where this "do" is interpreted as a *poiein* or *poiesis*. That is to say, as the "poetry" or mytho-poetic creativity with which primitive peoples originally constructed their worlds (Vico 1963: 117).

Still more relevant for hermeneutics than these early writings (which were written in Latin) is Vico's principal work, the *New Science* (which was written in Italian). The first edition (1725) was entitled *Principles of a New Science concerning the Nature of the Nations, by which are found the Principles of Another System of the Natural Law of the Gentes*. The "another" system referred to in this title is that of Grotius and the doctrine of natural law. In the (shorter) title of the work's final edition – *Principles of New Science concerning the Common Nature of the Nations* (1744) – this polemical reference disappears, but the critique itself remains very much in evidence. Vico criticizes Grotius and the natural law theorists for reasons that are, in part, similar to those for which he criticizes Descartes; that is to say, for excess of rationalism. This defect is in this case all the graver because theirs is a subject that should give weight to history. Instead, they anachronistically project a rational, abstract model of law onto antiquity without taking into account the fact that primitive men did not construct their world by means of reason (something of which they had little), but through fantasy and myth.

There is a further important motive for the polemic: Vico, as paladin of Catholicism, criticizes the protestant doctrine of natural law for failing to take into account the role of divine providence in history and for failing to distinguish between sacred history (that of the Jews) and profane history (that of the gentiles).

From this it can be seen that the true object of the *New Science* is not the birth of the human world, but rather the rebirth of the gentile world. This becomes clear if we examine what we might call the "primal scene" of the *New Science*. Vico, a great interpreter of myths, proposes an original myth of his own (one which involves a liberal rethinking of biblical history, pagan mythology and physical evidence). It all begins a short time after the Great Flood, when the majority of mankind:

> without the religion of their father Noah, which they had repudiated … , were lost from one another by roving wild in the great forest of the earth, pursuing shy and indocile women, and fleeing from the wild animals with which the great ancient forest must have abounded. They were scattered further in search of pasture and water, and as the result of it all were reduced, at the end of a long period, to the condition of beasts. Then, on certain occasions ordained by divine providence … , shaken and aroused by a terrible fear, each of the particular Uranus and Jove he had feigned and believed in, some of them finally left off wandering and went into hiding in certain places. There, settled certain women, through fear of the apprehended divinity, in religious and chaste carnal unions they solemnized marriages under cover and begat certain children and so founded family. By long residence and burial of their dead they came to found and divide the first dominions of the earth.
>
> (Vico 1994: 9)

According to Vico's physical hypothesis, for a period of approximately two hundred years after the Flood there was neither thunder nor lightening. During this period, men became almost beast-like. When these meteorological events finally manifested themselves again the men were terrified by what were, for them, entirely new phenomena. They believed them to be signs from a god who was commanding them to bring an end to their unordered way of life. Thus arose religions, marriages and burials (which are, for Vico, the three fundamental anthropological principles (cf. Vico 1994: 96–9)). In this way, divine providence used even false religions for the benefit of humanity. (This contrasts starkly with the sacred history of the Jews, who have always preserved their conception of God, and have never fallen into superstition or become beast-like.)

Accordingly, Vico affirms that "the master key of this Science" is the "discovery … that the first gentile peoples, by a demonstrated necessity of nature, were poets who spoke in poetic characters." That is to say, in "images for the most part of animate substances, of gods or heroes, formed by their imagination" (cf. Vico 1994: 21–2). Thundering Jupiter is therefore no more than the first word of that first "language" (as Vico himself refers to it: cf. e.g. Vico 1994: 20–1) that is ancient mythology. These myths must on no account be interpreted as if they were the receptacles of sublime philosophical truths, but rather as documentation of the origins of (gentile) civilization. "By virtue of new principles of mythology herein disclosed as consequences of the new principles of poetry found herein, it is shown that the fables were true and trustworthy histories of the customs of the most ancient peoples of Greece" (cf. Vico 1994: 6). In the passage just cited Vico mentions Greece by name, because it is above all with Greek mythology that his investigations are concerned. This is especially the case for the work's second book, that is entitled *Poetic Wisdom*, follows on from a book entitled *Establishment of Principles* and does what its title would indicate. Yet Vico also makes reference, insofar as he is able to given the state of knowledge of the time, to the mythologies of other ancient peoples. He thereby attempts to make use of comparative mythology as an instrument of comparative anthropology.

The very brief third book of the *New Science* is dedicated to the *Discovery of the True Homer* and acts as a kind of appendix to the work's very ample second book. The solution that Vico offers to the Homeric question (so much debated since the time of ancient hermeneutics) is truly pioneering: "Homer was an idea or a heroic character of Grecian men insofar as they told their histories in song" (Vico 1994: 323). According to this argument Homer, the author of the *Iliad* and the *Odyssey*, is himself an "imaginative universal," like the gods and heroes who are the characters of his poems (Vico 1994: 310). In addition, Vico argues that the manner in which those poems are drafted suggests that they were the product of a long pre-existing oral-poetic tradition: that of the rhapsodes.

If, for Vico, it is the Homeric poems and the myths related within them that are the fundamental documents of Greek civilization it is the corpus of Roman law, starting with the Twelve Tables, that make up the fundamental documents of Roman civilization. Since both the poems and the laws are (like religious texts) privileged documents of interpretation, we can avail of this fact as a confirmation that Vico's *New Science* is, in part, a work of hermeneutics. Moreover, Vico affirms that there is a substantial affinity between the Homeric poems and the Roman laws: "All ancient Roman law was a serious poem, represented by the Romans in the forum, and ancient jurisprudence was a severe poetry" (Vico 1994: 390). This is the case because ancient law was not rational, despite what modern natural law theorists have claimed to the contrary.

All forms of ancient culture – religion, language, law and so on – were "poetic." First and foremost, this is the case because of their "fantastical" nature. However it is also true in a stricter sense, as Vico brilliantly and pioneeringly observes: prior to the birth of a written alphabet, in a society which must – of necessity – have an oral culture (such as that represented by Homer himself), all of the texts from which a human community draws its identity must take the form of verse, for the simple reason that it makes them easier to memorize: "It was by a necessity of nature that the first nations spoke in heroic verse ... so that their memories might be aided by meter and rhythm to preserve more easily the histories of their families and cities" (Vico 1994: 316; cf. 313–14).

The development of these ancient, fantastical cultures into more civilized, rational ones is described by Vico (taking up once again themes already dealt with at length in the preceding books) in the fourth book of the work, entitled *The Course the Nations Run*. However, he argues that this rationality can degenerate, during periods of decadence, into an abstract rationalism: a "barbarism of reflection" of civilized nations that is worse than the original "barbarism of sense." "Then providence" – states Vico – "for their extreme ill has its extreme remedy at hand" in which the hands of the clock of history are moved backwards, immersing humanity in a regenerative bath of "the primitive simplicity of the first world of peoples" (Vico 1994: 423–4). Vico defines this terminologically as "*recourse*." The (only) example of recourse given in the work is to be found in its fifth and final book, which contains an interpretation of the medieval period as *Recourse of the First Barbaric History* (Vico 1994: 397).

4. Spinoza's biblical prophets and Vico's "poet theologians"

In order to explore a comparison between Spinoza's hermeneutics and that of Vico a little more deeply, we can begin by referring, more generally, to their philosophy. That of Vico is dominated, in particular in the earlier works, by a polemic against Cartesian rationalism. He seeks to reaffirm the value of the humanistic disciplines and, simultaneously, to reaffirm the value of fantasy and wit in confrontation with reason. The importance of the role played by fantasy in the *New Science* itself (whose principal object of polemical attack is the rationalism of protestant natural law) is difficult to exaggerate. This is because it is with fantasy, not reason, that primitive peoples constructed their world of meaning. However, the practitioners of this new science by no means intend to descend, in an act of empathetic over-identification, into the fantasy world of those men. To do so would be a project destined to failure: "With our civilized natures we [moderns] cannot at all imagine and can understand only by great toil the poetic nature of these first men" (Vico 1994: 22; cf. 118). The – undoubtedly challenging – goal of the project is therefore that of elaborating a new science (rational, as all sciences must be) that is itself capable of comprehending fantasy.

When Vico's anti-Cartesianism is considered in this way – that is to say, not as a form of irrationalism, but as an elaborated form of reason all the more powerful by virtue of its ability to comprehend that which is not itself rational – it does not appear to be so very distant from the thinking of Spinoza, who was himself a Cartesian, but of a very particular kind. Spinoza was indeed the author of *The Principles of Cartesian Philosophy* (1663), and his principal work, the *Ethics*, can also be considered to be – in certain ways – a development of Descartes' own philosophy. However, that development is such as to constitute a truly radical transformation of Cartesian philosophy itself; one that can be understood from various points of view. One of these consists in the fact that Spinozan reason, unlike Cartesian reason, does not exclude imagination as such, but rather seeks to give (above all in the third and fourth books of the *Ethics*) an explanation of the mechanisms by which it functions.

The rational understanding of the imagination and its mechanisms that Spinoza puts forward in the *Ethics* is also an important presupposition of his hermeneutics, given that the Bible itself is a grandiose (and extremely influential) product of imagination. "The prophets" – Spinoza affirms – "were not endowed with a more perfect mind, but with a more vivid power of imagination." These two capacities exist, he adds soon afterwards, in an inversely proportional relationship: "Those with a more powerful imagination are less fitted for purely intellectual activity" (Spinoza 1989: 73). Vico himself affirms, analogously, that "Imagination is more robust in proportion as reasoning power is weak" (Vico 1994: 71). In the case of Vico, the men who are rich in imagination and poor in intellect are "theological poets," rather than biblical prophets (Vico 1994: 6 and passim). These "theological poets" are by no means poets who render rational theology into verse, but primitive men who imagine and interpret the presumed signs of the gods using their own "poetic" and "vulgar wisdom" (Vico 1994: 109–10 and 117–18). Somewhat analogously, for Spinoza a prophet is an "interpreter of God" working through the medium of imagination (Spinoza 1989: 59).

Before pointing out an important difference between the two philosophers, we will note one further analogy: that which exists between Spinoza's interpretation of the greatest prophet, Moses, and Vico's interpretation of the greatest poet, Homer. The analogy regards the question of whether the traditions attributing to them the foundational texts of their respective cultures is well founded. The responses of both Spinoza and Vico to these questions are, as we have seen, negative (and truly pioneering). Spinoza argues at length that Moses could not have been the author of the *Pentateuch*, or at least not of the text in its entirety, as the editing of the text was postexilical and carried out based on pre-existing sources (Spinoza 1989: 173–86). Vico argues at length that Homer is really nothing more than the personification of the mythopoeic creativity of the Greeks and that the *Iliad* and the *Odyssey*, as they have been transmitted to us, are the written formulation of a pre-existing oral tradition: that of the rhapsodes (Vico 1994: 301–28).

There is, however, at least one important difference between the two philosophers. Spinoza deals with Jewish culture, precisely the culture that Vico excludes from his *New Science*. On the one hand, several important scholars of Vico (such as, for example, Benedetto Croce) have maintained that this separation was motivated by religious scruples alone and that Vico could equally have applied to Moses the principles behind his discovery of the true Homer (for that matter, this discovery may have itself been inspired by the Moses of Spinoza). On the other hand, it can be observed that this very separation is an essential element of the complex strategy by which the Catholic Vico opposes the protestant doctrine of natural law (and also an indispensable element of his own peculiar kind of historicism). In any case, it is an interesting paradox that it was the Jew Spinoza – and not Vico – who denied the chosen nature of the Jewish people and therefore refused to grant any special hermeneutic status to the books of the Bible.

Bibliography

Spinoza, B. (1988) *The Principles of Cartesian Philosophy*, trans. by S. Shirley, Indianapolis: Hackett.

——(1989) *Tractatus Theologico-politicus*, trans. by S. Shirley, Leiden/New York/Copenhagen/Cologne: Brill.

——(2000) *Ethics*, trans. by G. H. R. Parkinson, Oxford-New York: Oxford University Press.

Vico, G. (1963) *The Autobiography*, trans. by T. G. Bergin and M. H. Frish, Ithaca: Cornell University Press.

——(1988) *On the Most Ancient Wisdom of the Italians*, trans. by L. M. Palmer, Ithaca: Cornell University Press.

——(1990) *On the Study Methods of Our Time*, trans. by Elio Gianturco, Ithaca: Cornell University Press.

——(1994) *The New Science*, trans. by T. G. Bergin and M. H. Frish, Ithaca: Cornell University Press.

Further reading

Amoroso, L. (2004) *Scintille ebraiche. Spinoza, Vico e Benamozegh*, Pisa: Edizioni ETS (includes a discussion of Spinoza's and Vico's relationships with Jewish civilization).

Croce, B. (2002) *The Philosophy of Giambattista Vico*, trans. by R. G. Collingwood, New Brunswick, NJ: Transaction Publishers (a very influential monograph on Vico).

Strauss, L. (1988) "How to Study Spinoza's *Theologico-Political Treatise*," in: Strauss, *Persecution and the Art of Writing*, Chicago: University of Chicago Press (discusses the willful ambiguity of the *Tractatus theologico-politicus*).

Verene, D. Ph. (1981) *Vico's Science of Imagination*, Ithaca: Cornell University Press (an exhaustive study of the works of Vico).

Zac, S. (1965) *Spinoza et l'interpretation de l'Écriture*, Paris: P.U.F. (an excellent presentation of Spinoza's biblical hermeneutics).

4

WOLFF, CHLADENIUS, MEIER: ENLIGHTENMENT AND HERMENEUTICS

Frederick Beiser

1. Christian Wolff in the history of hermeneutics

When we think of the history of hermeneutics the name Christian Wolff seldom comes to mind. We associate Wolff with the rationalist philosophy of the Enlightenment, which is (supposedly) the antithesis of the romantic philosophy of Friedrich Schlegel and Schleiermacher, which is often seen as the source of hermeneutics. It comes as no surprise, then, that neither Dilthey nor Wach, the first historians of hermeneutics, devote much attention to Wolff (see Wach 1926; Dilthey 1964).[1] It is time, however, that we lay aside these old prejudices. For it so happens that Wolff was a formative figure in the history of hermeneutics. In the eighteenth century the history of hermeneutics is either a reaction against or a development of Wolff's doctrines.

Wolff's so-called German logic, *Vernünftige Gedanken von den Kräften des menschliche Verstandes und ihrem richtigen Gebrauche in Erkenntnis der Wahrheit*, which was first published in 1713 (Wolff 2006),[2] contains several chapters on the interpretation and criticism of texts. This work was neither obscure nor forgotten. It appeared in no less than fourteen editions in Wolff's lifetime, and it was one of the most influential philosophical texts of the first half of the eighteenth century. Among those inspired by it were two major founders of hermeneutics in the eighteenth century: Johann Martin Chladenius (1710–59) and Hans Georg Meier (1718–77). Often critical of Wolff, neither Chladenius nor Meier were his mere disciples. Nevertheless, it is fair to describe them as Wolffians, because they adopt Wolff's basic logical and metaphysical doctrines, and because they follow his general programme of enlightenment. Most importantly, they developed Wolff's suggestions about interpretation and criticism into a systematic hermeneutics.

Our task here will be to consider one important chapter in the early modern history of hermeneutics, what we might well call its rationalist or Wolffian phase. We will examine the hermeneutics of Wolff and that of his two great successors, Chladenius and Meier. This means that we will cover the period from 1712, the publication of the first edition of Wolff's German logic, until 1757, the publication of Meier's *Auslegungskunst*. It is necessary to stress that this is only *one* chapter or phase of hermeneutics in the first half of the eighteenth century. We will not consider the development of hermeneutics in history, law and classical philology, each of which deserves a chapter on its own. We will also not treat developments in theology; we will therefore ignore the work of Siegmund Jakob Baumgarten (1706–57), Johann August Ernesti (1707–81) or Johann David Michaelis (1717–91), even though they made important contributions to hermeneutics, and even they too were Wolffians (see Hettner 1979: I, 349–73). Our focus will be entirely and solely upon those thinkers in the Wolffian tradition who formulated a *general* hermeneutics, one independent of any special discipline, such as history, law and theology.' We also will not venture beyond the 1750s. The 1760s, with the advent of Hamann and Herder, will bring a completely new chapter in the history of hermeneutics (on Hamann and Herder, see Forster 2010; and Schnur 1994).

2. Wolff's hermeneutics

Wolff never used the term "hermeneutics", even though it already had an established usage before him. He did think, however, that there are special parts of logic dealing with the interpretation and criticism of written texts. These are for Wolff parts of *applied* logic, or what he called "the exercise of logic" (*Ausübung der Logik*) or "the practice of logic" (*Praxis Logicae*). The task of applied logic is to get people to think logically or rationally in their ordinary lives and activities. Not the least of these activities, of course, is reading books. Wolff wants people to judge and criticize books well, that is, rationally. Hence chapter X of the German logic lays down rules for judging books, and chapter XI for "reading them fruitfully".

It was crucial and controversial that Wolff saw hermeneutics as a part of logic. Such an understanding of the discipline implies that logic alone is the chief instrument and criterion for understanding and judging books. That assumption was crucial for Wolff because his hermeneutics was an essential part of his programme of enlightenment, that is, the programme for removing prejudice, ignorance and superstition from the world and making it a rational place. Still, it was also a very controversial assumption – one that not only his enemies but even his friends would question. Baumgarten, Chladenius and Meier believed that logic alone is not sufficient for interpreting and understanding some texts; they held that there are some kinds of writings that require different kinds of rules than those of logic, for example, the rules for judging historical testimony or the beauty of works of art. Wolff's assumption later became the stone of offence to the *Sturm und Drang*. In the 1760s Hamann and Herder protested against the Wolffian logical straitjacket, which, they believed, would smother religious and aesthetic inspiration.

Beside his belief in the central role of logic, Wolff made another controversial assumption both fateful and influential for hermeneutics. Namely, Wolff thinks that to understand a text is to grasp the intention of the author (Wolff 2006: 10, §4; 11, §§3, 6). The reason for this assumption is his general view about the purpose of language: communication. The purpose of words, Wolff explains, is to communicate, that is, to reveal our thoughts so that others know them (Wolff 2006: 2, §1).

A speaker and listener, or a writer and reader, understand one another when the listener or reader has the same thought as the speaker or writer (Wolff 2006: 2, §2). With each word a certain concept is associated, which is its meaning (Wolff 2006: 2, §3); and so if speaker and listener, writer and reader, are to understand one another, they should associate the same concept with the same word (Wolff 2006: 11, §6). So understanding depends on grasping an author's or speaker's intention for the simple reason that this fulfills the purpose of language, which is communication. This assumption, as we shall soon see, also plays a central role in the hermeneutics of Chladenius and Meier. Gadamer has seen this assumption as a questionable part of romantic hermeneutics (Gadamer 1990: 188–201), but it is questionable whether it is questionable; and it is not characteristic of romantic hermeneutics, having a prehistory going back at least to Wolff.

Wolff tells us in chapter 10 that there are two kinds of books or writings, historical and dogmatic (Wolff 2006: 10, §1). The distinction, which reflects Wolff's general distinction between philosophical and historical truth (Wolff 1983a: 1, §7), is important because there are very different rules for judging each kind of writing. A dogmatic book contains a theory or doctrine about some non-historical subject matter, and makes a claim to philosophical or rational truth. An historical writing, as the name implies, is about events or actions that happened in the past, and it makes a claim to historical truth. These historical books can take two forms: natural history, which is about events in nature (Wolff 2006: 10, §5); and human history, which is about human actions (Wolff 2006: 10, §6).

Concerning dogmatic writings, Wolff lays down two basic rules: first, that we judge them according to the intention of the author; second, that we judge them according to their subject matter (Wolff 2006: 11, §1). We have to determine, in other words, whether the author achieves his aims, and whether his theory is correct about its subject matter. To understand the intention of the author, we have to make sure that we associate the same meaning with the words as the author himself (Wolff 2006: 11, §6). To judge his theory, we need to apply all the rules for determining "inventions" (*Erfindungen*, *Inventione*), that is, those rules that attempt to discover the unknown from inferences about the known (Wolff 2006: 11, §5).[4] For Wolff, these are the general rules of logic, whose application he describes in great detail (Wolff 2006: 4, §§1–29; 6, §§1–14). In applying these rules, we have to observe the following: (1) that we have clear and distinct concepts (Wolff 2006: 9, §4); (2) that we do not confuse real and verbal definitions (Wolff 2006: 9, §§2–3); (3) that we make sure that the propositions are correctly derived from true premises (Wolff 2006: 9, §6); (4) that we do not confuse theorems with principles (Wolff 2006: 9, §7); (5) that we determine whether the author's analysis of a task contains all necessary and sufficient factors for its fulfillment (Wolff 2006: 9, §§9–12).

Concerning historical writings, Wolff states, in a phrase worthy of Ranke, that everything depends on narrating the order and circumstances of an event "as it happened" (*wie es geschehen*) (Wolff 2006: 10, §2). There are three perfections of historical writing: truth, completeness and order (Wolff 2006: 10, §2). Regarding historical truth, Wolff says that it can be an object only of belief and not knowledge. We cannot *know* historical truth because we cannot demonstate it, demonstration being a necessary condition of all knowledge. Historical truths are about what happened; and since they are in the past and no longer exist, they are only a matter of belief (Wolff 2006: 7, §4). There are, however, important rules for belief, which Wolff lays down in chapter 7. Most of these rules concern the reliability of witnesses, namely, whether they were present when the event occurred, what interests they had in telling the truth, whether they were honourable and so on. Regarding historical completeness, Wolff explains that it has to be judged according to the intention of the author (Wolff 2006: 10, §4). We have to ask what the author intended to do, and whether he did everything necessary to achieve it: that is, whether he left out important facts, whether he added too many unnecessary to his ends. We must not demand more than the author intended, Wolff implies, because this would be to apply an external standard to his enterprise. Here Wolff anticipates a principle of much importance to later hermeneutics: that books have to be judged by their own standards. We should also judge an historical book, Wolff insists, according to "the conditions of its time", that is, according to what could have been known then (Wolff 2006: 10, §12). Regarding historical order, Wolff thinks that historical books should follow "the order of nature", which consists in showing how one thing inevitably led to another (Wolff 2006: 10, §22). He is critical of Arnauld and the Port Royal *Logique* for defining good order as bringing together in a single chapter everything under a single head or that belongs to a subject. This is the "Order of the Schools", which is organized more for the sake of memory than understanding.

It is striking that Wolff spends most of his effort elaborating rules for understanding historical books. For history had a deeply ambivalent status in Wolff's philosophy. Wolff understood science as the power of demonstration (see Wolff 2006: 2, §30; Wolff 1983b: 'Vorbericht', §2), so there is only as much science in a discipline as demonstrable content. But historical truths, Wolff realized and stressed, cannot be demonstrated (Wolff 2006: 7, §4). There could not be, then, in the strict sense of the word a science of history, still less a science for interpreting and criticizing historical books. The ambivalence runs even deeper. For Wolff understands that science also has to be based on experience, where experience, apart from the fleeting present, consists in history.[5] So history is both necessary to science and yet not a part of it. It was the task of Wolff's great successor, Chladenius, to resolve such a terrible tension.

3. The hermeneutics of Chladenius

The first major thinker to confront the problems, and to fulfill the promise, of Wolff's hermeneutics was Johann Martin Chladenius. In 1742 Chladenius published his *Einleitung zur richtigen Auslegung vernünfftige Reden und Schriften*, the first systematic treatise on hermeneutics in German (see Chladenius 1742).[6] Chladenius' other major claim to fame is his treatise on historiography, his 1752 *Allgemeine Geschichtswissenschaft* (see Chladenius 1752), which is generally regarded as the first major treatise on "historics" (the study of the logic of history). On the basis of both works, Chladenius gained a reputation as "the German Vico". Unfortunately, he suffered a similar fate to his Italian counterpart: he quickly lapsed into obscurity despite his genius. Fortunately, in the late nineteenth century he was rescued from oblivion (see Bernheim 1889, 6th edn 1914), and his star has been steadily rising ever since (see Szondi 1975; Henn 1976; Friedrich 1978).

It was Chladenius' great merit to address the tensions at the heart of Wolff's programme. The Wolffian conception of science was a challenge to him because it made a science of hermeneutics or history impossible. If historical facts are indemonstrable, and if science demands demonstration, then neither history nor hermeneutics, which deals with historical texts, can be a science. Chladenius' response to the problem, as we shall soon see, underwent some evolution, first in accepting the Wolffian conception of science but later in rejecting it in favour of a more pragmatic and pluralistic concept of science.

Chladenius' hermeneutics and historics are closely intertwined. The longest chapter of the *Einleitung* is devoted to the understanding of historical texts. The *Allgemeine Geschichtswissenschaft* therefore incorporates that part of Chladenius' hermeneutics dealing with historical texts. The concern of the *Einleitung* goes beyond history, however, because it deals not only with historical but also dogmatic texts. Its main interest is not with history *per se*, the past as such, but with the interpretation of texts, even non-historical ones.

As its title indicates, the *Einleitung* is meant to be an introduction to a theory of interpretation. This does not mean, however, that Chladenius' aims were primarily pedagogical (see Gadamer 1992: 182–3). His work is intended as an introduction in the sense that it lays down the basic principles for a *general* hermeneutics, that is, those necessary for the interpretation of all *texts*. It does not determine the rules required for the interpretation of *specific* kinds of texts. Hence Chladenius refuses to treat rules for the interpretation of poetry, law or the Bible, on the grounds that these texts require *special* principles for their interpretation (Chladenius 1752: b2–b4).

Chladenius informs us in the preface to the *Einleitung* that his aim in writing it is to make "the art of interpretation" (*Auslege-Kunst*) – or what he also calls "hermeneutics" (Chladenius 1742: §176, 96) – into a science (*Wissenschaft*) (Chladenius 1742: a2).[7] Each term has a precise meaning for him. *Interpretation* (*Auslegung*) means "bringing to bear all those concepts necessary for a complete understanding of a text" (Chladenius 1742: b1). The *art* of interpretation means the application of the rules necessary for such a complete understanding; and to make this art into a science means proving, explaining and systematizing such rules (Chladenius 1742: §176, 96). Chladenius, like most thinkers of his age, does not distinguish between art and science. He uses "art" in the broad traditional sense where it signifies the skill to produce anything. Science differs from art in that it does not make anything, and in that it is only a more self-conscious and systematic formulation of the rules involved in making things.

In his preface Chladenius declares that hermeneutics should be a science in its own right, having its own *sui generis* rules and structure. He complains that the rules of interpretation have become "an appendage" to logic (Chladenius 1742: a3). Though he mentions no names, he almost certainly has Wolff in mind. Silently taking issue with Wolff, Chladenius thinks that there are good reasons for making hermeneutics into a separate discipline. To be sure, the interpretation of texts is *partly* an application of logic; but it is also more than that, because it requires non-logical rules (see Chladenius 1742: §177, 96–7; §738, 584).

Chladenius begins his hermeneutics with an account of understanding (*Verstehen*), a theme later made famous by Schleiermacher and Dilthey. We understand someone, he explains, when we know from his words what he has thought (Chladenius 1742: §2, 2). What someone has thought is not only a matter of content but also of intention. Like Wolff, Chladenius is explicit that understanding comprises a grasp of the intention of the speaker or writer, not only the meaning of his or her sentences. His rationale for this position is the same as Wolff's: the purpose of speech or writing is communication, getting one person to know the thoughts of another. Chladenius realizes, however, that sometimes intention and meaning are at odds, that a person's words do not express or reveal what the author really wants to say (Chladenius 1742: §156, 86–7). Nevertheless, though intention and expression do not always coincide, Chladenius still thinks that the ideal or complete interpretation of a text is one that fully accords with the author's or speaker's intention; the reader must not think more or less than the author intended to say (Chladenius 1742: §696, 541–2).

Chladenius' theory of meaning follows from his general theory of understanding. Following Wolff, Chladenius defines the meaning (*Bedeutung*) of a word as the thought (*der Gedanke*) that we attempt to communicate to others (Chladenius 1742: §80, 39). A word is a sign for a thought, which gives it its meaning (Chladenius 1742: §740, 586–7). Chladenius has a simple psychological theory about the origin of meaning, according to which a word gets its meaning through association (Chladenius 1742: §81, 40). According to this theory, we associate words with thoughts through habit, imagination and memory. If in the past we hear a certain sound, or read a certain sign, in connection with a certain thought, we in the future continue to connect that sound or sign with that thought (Chladenius 1742: §81, 40).

Chladenius distinguishes four different forms of meaning: *proper* meaning (*eigentliche Bedeutung, significatio propria*), which is the ordinary and literal meaning of a word (Chladenius 1742: §82, 41); *figurative* (*verblümte*) meaning, namely, metaphors, similes, which consist in the attribution of a property to a thing that it possesses only partially (Chladenius 1742: §92, 46–7); *accidental* meaning (*zufällige*), which arises from context (Chladenius 1742: §129, 72); and finally *common* (*gemeine*) meaning, which is the general sense of a word, that which is defined in a dictionary (Chladenius 1742: §130, 72–3). Chladenius stresses that proper meaning is not the same as common (Chladenius 1742: §130, 72–3), because proper meaning is opposed to figurative only, whereas common is opposed to both figurative and accidental meaning (Chladenius 1742: §130; 72–3).

Chladenius' classificatory scheme seems to underplay the cultural and historical dimension of meaning (see Szondi 1975: 77). Since it makes context the source of only "accidental" meaning, it seems as if proper meaning is independent of social and historical context, as if it mysteriously stays the same even if its contexts change. These apparent implications are misleading, however, for Chladenius explicitly states that even the proper meaning of a word changes over time (Chladenius 1742: §84, 42). He indeed stresses that change of meaning is one of the main sources of difficulty in interpreting ancient writings. If we are not sensitive to how a word changes meaning, he warns, we find ancient texts incomprehensible (Chladenius 1742: §53, 22; §85, 42–3). Far from ignoring context, Chladenius emphasizes that the meaning of speech depends on its specific situation; that is, when, where and why something is said, and who says it (Chladenius 1742: §8, 4–5). His emphasis on the historical and cultural dimension of meaning is most explicit when he insists that the proper meanings of many words are unique, scarcely translatable from one language into others (Chladenius 1742: §77, 38).

Interpretation for Chladenius means the art of bringing to bear all the concepts necessary for a complete understanding of a text (Chladenius 1742: §169, 92–3). What does it mean to understand a text completely? "One understands a speech or writing completely", Chladenius replies, "when one thinks everything that the words, according to its reason and its rules, can stimulate as thoughts in our souls" (Chladenius 1742: §155 86). The complete understanding of a text, he later explains, involves three different levels of meaning or understanding (Chladenius 1742: §674, 519). First, the understanding of the immediate sense (*unmittelbarer Verstand*), which consists in the common meaning of its words. We grasp the immediate sense simply by having a mastery of a language, by understanding both its grammar and vocabulary. Second, the understanding of the mediate sense (*mittelbarer Verstand*), which arises from the application of a passage to our lives. This application Chladenius defines as "the activities our souls perform because we have read a certain book" (Chladenius 1742: §425, 308–9). It consists in "living knowledge", that is, knowledge insofar as it has an influence on our will and actions (Chladenius 1742: §474, 341; §616, 467). Finally, there is digression (*Ausschweifung*), which takes the words of the author as the occasion for saying something new or different not explicitly said by the author. While the immediate and mediate senses are bound by the rules of reason, digression works according to the imagination, and so is not bound by rules at all.

It is only at the close of his *Einleitung* that Chladenius confronts the general problem of how hermeneutics can be a science. To be a science it must be able to achieve certainty, not mere probablity. Science is the business of knowing, and knowing demands certainty. We establish certainty, Chladenius maintains like a good Wolffian, through demonstration, by inferring valid conclusions from true premises. Thus Chladenius formulates the concept of a "hermeneutical demonstration" that will prove the correct reading of a text (Chladenius 1742: §§752–3, 596–600). Such a proof states in its major premise a rule about the meaning of certain words; its minor premise states that a passage is an illustration of the rule; and the conclusion then infers what the particular passage ought to mean (Chladenius 1742: §§656–8, 503–4). Chladenius realizes that it would be tedious and pedantic to construct such syllogisms in all interpretations; the only reason he invokes them is to refute skepticism, to show that hermeneutics can, at least in principle, attain the certainty of science.

Chladenius is optimistic about the possibility of usually achieving certainty in interpretation. He thinks that the intersubjectivity of language, the existence of common rules about meaning, are sufficient in most cases for one person to understand another (Chladenius 1742: §737, 583; §741, 587; §§743–4, 589–90). He realizes fully, however, that there are many problems in determining the meaning of a text, namely, reconstructing an author's intention and context, translating foreign words that have no exact equivalent, resolving different and even conflicting interpretations. Well aware of these obstacles, he admits that in these cases certainty is unattainable, and that the interpreter has to resign himself to ignorance. Thus the concept of complete interpretation was for Chladenius an ideal, a goal that we could approach though never attain.

Despite his apparent obsession with rules, Chladenius never saw interpretation as a mechanical matter, as if its problems could be resolved simply by the application of rules. He saw interpretation as an ad hoc business where the reader struggled through texts whose meaning could not be resolved through rules. *Auslege-kunst* had no magic recipe for resolving obscurities (Chladenius 1742: §673, 517). We explain difficult or obscure passages in the same way in which we explain anything: by reasoning from the known to the unknown (Chladenius 1742: §673, 517). There is no a priori guarantee, however, that we will be able to resolve difficulties, so many passages will remain mysteries. Like all enquiry, interpretation proves to be, Chladenius concedes, a matter of luck and skill (Chladenius 1742: §673, 518).

It was probably because of these difficulties in achieving certainty of interpretation that Chladenius later changed his position about the foundation of hermeneutics. He dropped the ideal of hermeneutic demonstration because it demands too much: even if we construct a syllogism where the conclusion follows from the premises, the premises themselves are not incontrovertible, that is, it is possible to deny them without contradiction. The best we can achieve for the premises is a kind of probability. To address this difficulty, Chladenius stressed against Wolff that there are different ideals of certainty for different disciplines, and that we should measure this certainty in terms of the specific standards of each discipline (Chladenius 1742: pp. 280–353). This argument was developed in his 1748 work *Vernünftige Gedanken von dem Wahrscheinlichen und desselben gefährlichen Mißbrauche*. We should not demand one ideal of certainty that fits all disciplines, which was the fatal assumption behind the Wolffian programme.

4. Meier's hermeneutics

After Chladenius, the other major hermeneuticist of the Wolffian school was Georg Friedrich Meier. His major work on hermeneutics is his *Versuch einer allgemeinen Auslegungskunst* (see Meier 1757),[8] which appeared some fifteen years after Chladenius' *Einleitung*. Meier is better known for his work in aesthetics, from his *Anfangsgründe aller schönen Wissenschaften* (see Meier 1754), a popular exposition of Baumgarten's *Aesthetica*. But for years he had also laboured in the fledgling discipline of hermeneutics, giving lectures on the subject at the University of Frankfurt (Oder) since the early 1740s (see Meier 1757: "Vorrede", sheet 2). The *Versuch* was the culmination of these efforts.

In basic respects the *Versuch* follows the Wolffian tradition in hermeneutics. Meier not only borrows much from Wolff, but he seems to have learned from Chladenius too, even though he never cites him. Nevertheless, there are unique features to the *Versuch*, which are as interesting as they are novel. The most striking and distinctive feature is the significance that Meier ascribes to his new science. For Meier, hermeneutics is not subordinate to logic, as in Wolff, and it is not only independent of logic, as in Chladenius, but it is superordinate to logic, which falls under it. So much is clear from Meier's definitions of hermeneutics and logic. Meier conceives of hermeneutics as one part of characteristic, which, following Leibniz, he defines as the general science of signs (Meier 1757: §3, 2). Hermeneutics is that part of characteristic involved with the *interpretation* of signs, which is the activity of determining their meaning (Meier 1757: §3, 2; §8, 5). Logic for Meier is part of hermeneutics, since its tasks are creating and interpreting signs. There are two parts of logic: the art of logical designation (*Bezeichnungskunst*), which gives names to things; and the art of logical interpretation (*Auslegungskunst*), which is "the science of those rules from whose observation one can acquire theoretical knowledge from signs" (Meier 1752: §§484–5, 651–3).[9] Meier thus conceives of hermeneutics as the master science: the universal science of which all other sciences are only a part.

In the very beginning of the *Versuch* Meier lays down a set of definitions that determine the precise conceptual domain of his new science. He defines hermeneutics, or the art of interpretation (*Auslegekunst*), *in the broad sense*, as the science of those rules the following of which shows us how to determine meaning from signs (Meier 1757: §1, 1). *In the more narrow sense* hermeneutics is the science of those rules that show us how to determine meaning from speech (*Rede*) and how to communicate that meaning to others (Meier 1757: §1, 1). The *universal* art of interpretation (*hermeneutica universalis*) is the science of those rules that must be observed in the interpretation of all, or at least most, kinds of signs (Meier 1757: §2, 1–2); and the *special* art of interpretation (*hermeneutica particularis*) discusses those rules necessary to interpret a specific kind of sign or speech (Meier 1757: §2, 3).

The distinction between hermeneutics in the broad and narrow senses is one between a general science of signs and a more specific science of particular kinds of signs, namely, those involved in human speech or language. Meier defines a sign (*Zeichen, signum*) as the means by which the reality of something else can be recognized (Meier 1757: §7, 4). The sign might be natural or artificial (Meier 1757: §28, 14–15). A natural sign has a natural connection between the sign and thing signified (namely, smoke as a sign of fire, wet streets as a sign of rain), whereas an artificial sign creates that connection according to human choice and convention. Hermeneutics in the broad sense is therefore concerned with not only artificial but also natural signs. We normally think of hermeneutics as the interpretation of spoken or written language; but this would be only one half of hermeneutics for Meier, who also thinks that there is a particular hermeneutics of natural signs.

The second chapter of the *Versuch* is devoted entirely to this particular hermeneutics, the interpretation of natural signs. Meier begins with the general metaphysical principle, of Leibnizian provenance, that this is the best of all possible worlds (Meier 1757: §35, 18). This principle plays a crucial role in his hermeneutics. Because this world is the best possible, Meier thinks that there is the greatest possible connection between things (Meier 1757: §35, 18). Consequently, each part of this world is an immediate or mediate, close or distant, sign of every other part (Meier 1757: §36, 18). Because of the world's perfection, each natural sign is the best possible for another thing; hence that interpretation of the sign is best that shows the sign's perfection (§37, 19–20). It is from this metaphysics of perfection that Meier then derives his principle of "hermeneutical fairness" (*Billigkeit*). According to this principle, those interpretations are true that best reveal the perfection of the sign (Meier 1757: §9, 20). To reveal its perfection means to show its clarity (Meier 1757: §50, 26), its fruitfulness (Meier 1757: §41, 21), its sufficiency (Meier 1757: §43, 20) and its truthfulness (Meier 1757: §57, 30).

The scope of Meier's natural hermeneutics becomes plain when he expounds all the different kinds of natural signs. Each cause is a sign of its effect (Meier 1757: §68, 36); actions are signs of intentions, desires and passions (Meier 1757: §76, 40); the purpose is the sign of the means, and conversely (Meier 1757: §77, 40); a model is a sign of its copy, and conversely (Meier 1757: §78, 40). The net effect of Meier's natural hermeneutics is that disciplines like physics and psychology become parts of a hermeneutics. Rather than seeing hermeneutics as a human science distinct from the natural sciences, following the nineteenth century conception, Meier regards it as the universal science, of which the natural sciences themselves are only parts.

Although it might seem radical and modern, Meier's conception of a natural hermeneutics is really traditional and pre-modern. It is crucial to his natural hermeneutics that it ascribes *meaning* to things in nature. This conception goes back to the old medieval theory of nature as a *signum naturae*, a holy book where each thing serves as a sign of the divine wisdom. This old theory is never made explicit in the *Versuch*, but it is plain enough when Meier explains that signs are effects of their authors (Meier 1757: §23, 12), and that the author of a natural sign is God (Meier 1757: §39, 20). The principle of hermeneutic fairness derives from the fact that God is the ultimate author of each natural sign, which is an arbitrary or artificial sign for him (Meier 1757: §38, 19). It is part of our reverence toward God that we assume that each sign is the most perfect for the thing signified (Meier 1757: §39, 20).

Apart from the general significance it ascribes to hermeneutics, Meier's *Versuch* is very much in the Wolffian tradition. Its account of meaning, understanding and interpretation is indebted to Wolff and Chladenius. The meaning of a discourse consists in "that series of connected representations which the author wants to designate through his speech" (Meier 1757: §112, 62). Meier puts the same emphasis on intention as Wolff and Chladenius. Only what the author intends to say, Meier insists, belongs to the meaning of his discourse; what he *could* or *should* have said does not count as its meaning (Meier 1757: §112, 62). The interpreter must *take* the sense from the discourse, not *put* it into it (Meier 1757: §123, 67). The reader or listener understands the author or speaker when they are of one and the same mind (Meier 1757: §128, 69).

Following this emphasis on intention, Meier maintains that a wise and rational author knows, with the greatest certainty, the meaning of his own discourse (Meier 1757: §136, 74). No one knows his intentions better than himself; and hence the author is "the best interpreter of his own words" (Meier 1757: §136, 74–5). He would have disputed Schleiermacher's famous maxim that we can understand a writer better than he understands himself. Meier recognizes, however, that sometimes authors do not succeed, and that they do not always choose the best words to realize their intentions; and so he concedes that, at least in some cases, the interpreter can have a better knowledge of the sense of the writer than the author himself (Meier 1757: §129, 70).

The most distinctive feature of Meier's theory of meaning and understanding is his principle of fairness: what we would now call interpretive charity or sympathy. This principle demands that the listener or reader assume, at least as a working hypothesis, that the author or speaker is intelligent and that he or she chooses words appropriate for his or her purposes (Meier 1757: §89, 46). An interpreter should strive to find that meaning that corresponds best with the perfections of the author (Meier 1757: §95, 49; §100, 55). As we have seen, this principle has a metaphysical grounding in Meier's optimism; but, because he realizes that not all authors or speakers are perfect, Meier makes it more a *regulative* principle whose application has to be decided on a case by case basis.

Such, in crude summary, is the Wolffian tradition in hermeneutics. Doubtless, its ideas appear simplistic and crude to us today. But we should judge it by its standards, according to the principle of interpretive charity. In that light we will find that the many later criticisms of it have not entirely invalidated it. At the very least it is from the Wolffian tradition that we can measure how far we have, or have not, gone forward.

Notes

1 On the other hand, I am pleased to note that I am not alone in my appreciation of Wolff. Gadamer (1974: III, 1063), stresses the importance of Wolff's *Logik* for the first systematic formulations of hermeneutics. See also Mueller-Vollmer (1990: 4–5), who also assigns a central role to Wolff.

2 The edition cited here is the 1754 edition as reprinted in Wolff (2006). Citations in the text are to the chapter number, then the paragraph number, indicated by the '§' sign. All references to Wolff (2006), will be first to its "Abteilung", designated by a Roman numeral, and its volume, designated by an Arabic number.

3 This is not to say that the Wolffians were the first to formulate a general hermeneutics. There were important precedents even in the seventeenth century: J.K. Dannhauer (1642); J.H. Ernesti (1699); and J.G. Meiser (1693).

4 Wolff understands logic as an art of invention, where invention comes from inferring or discovering the unknown from the known. See Wolff 1983b 3, §362: "When one derives from known truths others that are not known, we say that we discover them. The skill of inferring the unknown from the known is the art of invention."

5 In *Discursis praeliminaris*, Wolff stresses the important role of history in philosophy (Wolff 1983a: 1, §§11–12). He even declares: "*Fundamentum ... cognitionis philosophicae est historica*" (ibid.: 1, §10).

6 This work will be cited first according to paragraph (§) and then page number.

7 References to the unpaginated preface are to sheets (letters) and parts of sheets (numbers).

8 This text will be cited first according to paragraph number (§) and then page number.

9 According to Geldsetzer (Meier 1757: xxvi), Meier was encouraged to subordinate logic to hermeneutics through the stimulus of Locke, who, in the final chapter of *An Essay Concerning Human Understanding*, made logic part of a general "Doctrine of Signs" (see Locke 1975: IV, xxi, §4).

Bibliography

Bernheim, E. (1889, 6th edn 1914) *Lehrbuch der historischen Methode*, Leipzig: Duncker & Humblot.

Chladenius, J.M. (1742) *Einleitung zur richtigen Auslegung vernünfftige Reden und Schriften*, Leipzig: Friedrich Lanckischens Erben.

——(1748) *Vernünftige Gedanken von dem Wahrscheinlichen und desselben gefährlichen Mißbrauche*, Greifswald: Weitbrecht.

——(1752) *Allgemeine Geschichtswissenschaft*, Leipzig: Friedrich Lanckischens Erben.

Dannhauer, J.K. (1642) *Idea boni interpretis*, Argentorati: Mulbius.

Dilthey, Wilhelm (1964) "Die Entstehung der Hermeneutik", in Georg Misch (ed.) *Gesammelte Schriften*, Göttingen: Vandenhoeck & Ruprecht.

Ernesti, J.H. (1699) *Compendium hermeneticae profane*, Leizpig: Lankisch.

Forster, Michael (2010) *After Herder: Philosophy of Language in the German Tradition*, Oxford: Oxford University Press

Friedrich, Christoph (1978) *Sprache und Geschichte: Untersuchungen zur Hermeneutik von Johann Martin Chladenius*, Meisenheim am Glan: Anton Hain.

Gadamer, H.G. (1990) *Wahrheit und Methode, Gesammelte Werke*, Vol. 1, Tübingen: Mohr.

——(1992) *Truth and Method*, London: Continuum.

Henn, C. (1976) "Sinnreiche Gedanken: Zur Hermeneutik des Chladenius", *Archiv für Geschichte der Philosophie* 58: 240–64.

Hettner, Hermann (1979) *Geschichte der deutschen Literatur im Achtzehnten Jahrhundert*, Berlin: Aufbau Verlag.

Locke, J. (1975) *An Essay Concerning Human Understanding*, ed. Peter H. Nidditch, Oxford: Clarendon Press.

Meier, G.F. (1752) *Vernunftlehre*, Halle: Johann Justinius Gebauer.

——(1754) *Anfangsgründe aller schönen Wissenschaften*, Vol. I–III, Halle: Carl Hermann Hemmerde.

——(1757) *Versuch einer allgemeinen Auslegungskunst*, intro. Lutz Geldsetzer, Halle: Carl Hermann Hemmerde.

Meiser, J.G. (1693) *Dissertatio de historica-philologica de insignibus conumque interpretation*, Leipzig: Wittgau.

Mueller-Vollmer, Kurt (1990) *The Hermeneutics Reader: Texts of the German Tradition from the Enlightenment to the Present*, New York: Continuum.

Schnur, Harald (1994) *Schleiermachers Hermeneutik und ihre Vorgeschichte im 18. Jahrhundert*, Stuttgart: Metzler.

Szondi, P. (1975) *Einführung in die literarische Hermeneutik*, Frankfurt: Suhrkamp.

Wach, Joachim (1926) *Das Verstehen*, Tübingen: Mohr.

Wolff, Christian (1983a) *Discursis prealiminaris de philosophia in genere*, in J. École and H.W. Arndt (eds) *Gesammelte Werke*, II. Abteilung, Vol. 1, 1, Hildesheim: Olms.

——(1983b) *Vernünftige Gedancken von Gott, der Welt und der Seele des Menschen, auch allen Dingen überhaupt*, in J. École and H.W. Arndt (eds) *Gesammelte Werke*, I. Abteilung, Vol. 2, Hildesheim: Olms.

——(2006 [1754]) *Vernünftige Gedanken von des Kräften des menschlichen Verstandes und ihrem richtigen Gebrauche in Erkenntnis der Wahrheit*, in J. École and H.W. Arndt (eds) *Gesammelte Werke*, I. Abteilung, Vol. 1, Hildesheim: Olms.

5

AST AND SCHLEIERMACHER: HERMENEUTICS AND CRITICAL PHILOSOPHY

Gunter Scholtz

1. The change to a new epoch

Friedrich Schleiermacher (1768–1834) and Friedrich Ast (1778–1841) belong to a new epoch of hermeneutics which is often referred to as "romantic hermeneutics". To be more precise, it should be spoken of as "neo-humanistic hermeneutics" because the conceptions of both authors were closely connected to their interpretation of ancient philosophy. Schleiermacher translated the Platonic dialogues into the German language, Ast edited Plato's writings in Latin and compiled his great Lexicon Platonicum, and both authors integrated elements of ancient thinking into their own philosophy. They espoused the ideal of humanity; Ast explicitly and Schleiermacher through his theological and philosophical thinking as a whole, his interpreters claim. For both (albeit in different ways), hermeneutics was part of a new type of philosophy. The transition to their theories of understanding and interpretation and presuppositions thereof can be traced back to the end of the eighteenth century, mainly to the works of J. G. Herder and to the writings and drafts of F. Schlegel (Patsch 1966; Rieger 1988; Schnur 1994). To understand Ast and Schleiermacher it is useful to note some important new tendencies in the eighteenth century.

The first and dominant requirement of the new hermeneutics at the beginning of the nineteenth century was the turn to history. The human world on the whole was seen from a historical point of view and scholars now pointed out the changes and differences of cultures – a process which was later called historicism. Since the famous *Querelle des Anciens et des Modernes* in the French Academy about 1700, that is, the discussion concerning ancient fine arts as leading paradigms for modern artists, an awareness of the different rules and ideals in epochs and cultures arose: they cannot be subjected to the same criteria of evaluation.

For hermeneutics the consequences were as follows: the close connection to logic ceased and hermeneutic theory came close to the philosophy of history, as one can see in the conceptions of F. Schlegel and Ast. Philosophical hermeneutics of the seventeenth and eighteenth centuries predominantly put author and reader at the same level, as contemporaries. J. G. Herder, though, stressed the gap between cultures and their individual characters and values (Herder 1984). From now on every theory of understanding and interpretation had to take into account that literary works can belong to completely different, foreign cultures. Therefore, hermeneutics no longer concentrated on difficult or "dark" passages of texts but considered the text as a whole and took its context into account. Also, the relation between interpreter and text changed. As a part of logic, philosophical hermeneutics in former times had to support the reading of scholarly literature to get valid truth. But with the upcoming cultural pluralism the application of the interpreted work was replaced by criticism – first by textual criticism, which verifies the sources, and secondly also by the assessment of form and content within the historical context. Whereas textual criticism was marginal in the philosophical interpretation theories of the Enlightenment, it became important in the new hermeneutics around 1800, as we can already see in the titles of the works of Ast (1808a) and Schleiermacher (2012).

With the new and sharper awareness of the diversities of cultures, the differences between languages became evident, too – and this is the second development. Following Aristotle, during the Enlightenment these differences were often based in the realm of signs only, while reason and thinking were looked upon as the same in all human beings; now the close connection between thinking and language was acknowledged and it was accepted that human reason can be active only within the plurality of individual languages. J. G. Hamann and J. G. Herder attacked Kant's *Critique of Pure Reason* with the help of their theory of language and the thesis: there is no *pure* reason but only *linguistically* thinking reason.

The consequence for hermeneutics was that philosophy of language became more important than logic and psychology. Hermeneutics now had to consider that depending on the language, thinking changes. Interpretation often crosses borders of languages and this situation had to be reflected and mastered. Under the title "grammar", Ast delineated his speculative theory of language and asserted that the true ideal and archetype is the classical Greek language, to which all other languages are related (Ast 1808a: 1–162). Schleiermacher developed his hermeneutics essentially from language and called the relation between languages irrational: no word in one language has an exact correspondent in one word of any other. Therefore, any translation can only approximate the sense of the original text.

The third development was that not only language in general but especially poetical language was closely considered. In 1750, A. G. Baumgarten published the first work entitled *Aesthetica* and the realm of beauty and fine arts gained increasing general interest. The relation to poetry changed: poetical works were not any longer defined as mere clothing for moral doctrines but as presenting a specific aesthetic truth, a *veritas aesthetica*.

The consequence of this was that philosophical hermeneutics was not only developed as a foundation for the interpretation of "rational languages and writings" as we read in the title of Chladenius' work on interpretation. At the centre of hermeneutic interest we now often see poetical texts and even religious works which could be appreciated for their aesthetic qualities. J. G. Hamann in his *Aesthetica in nuce* wrote: "Poetry is the mother tongue of the human race. ... The whole treasure of human knowledge and beatitude consists in pictures" (Hamann 1950: 197). J. G. Herder pronounced the Old Testament a great poetical work of art. Hermeneutic theory now explicitly considered form and the aesthetic character of texts. In this way the borderline to the incomprehensible was altered as well. During the Enlightenment texts were called incomprehensible if they seemed to be irrational or contradictory or if they belonged to the religious and transcendental sphere. According to F. Schlegel, every ingenious work of a great author contains something incomprehensible to which understanding can only approximate step after step (Zovko 1990: 140–90; Scholtz 2002: 25–53).

The final development to note is that in the eighteenth century there was a process of individualization, the liberation of individual cultural skills and the emancipation from old conventions. This also led to new forms of literature. The traditional rules of poetry and the doctrines of text genres handed down in rhetoric and poetics, lost their obligatory character. Only nature prescribes the rules to a genius, Kant stated. From now on unknown classical literature was also studied and the literature of the oriental cultures was acknowledged and appreciated. In this way individual freedom and historicism became closely connected.

As a result of this hermeneutics had to take into account that completely new sorts of texts could be objects of interpretation. The intention and the genres of texts had to be investigated and could not simply be supposed. One had to be prepared for the individuality and the differences of cultures as well as of writers. Inspired by the philosophy of Leibniz, M. Chladenius and Chr. A. Crusius attempted to find the point of view of an author and hypothetically to take his place. But now as Herder demanded to understand the "fineness" of an author (Herder 1967: 11), understanding of style had to be included, too. In 1753 Buffon uttered his famous statement: "Le style est l'homme meme." But only around 1800 was style an eminent subject of hermeneutical reflection. Now not only reason was required but also imagination. Herder formed the new word "Einfühlung", empathy, demanding that one should empathize in everything, by which he meant that activity of the imagination which may be able to complete given information and compose it into a complete image. For the reading of literary works especially of ancient times, for example, the *Odyssey*, Herder required *Divination*, a skill of divining for a complete and precise understanding: animated reading means to read in the mind of the author (Herder 1984: 611–12). Thus the new emphasis on feeling and imagination in hermeneutic theory was not a shift to irrationalism but to enable as exact an understanding as possible.

In conclusion, since the end of the eighteenth century the philosophical theory of interpretation was aiming at all forms of writing of all epochs; it constantly took into account that linguistic sources were eventually strange and incomprehensible and it gave the act of interpretation a higher rank at the same time: all texts and all spoken language should be understood in every minute detail (Schlegel 1975: 60). The new term coined for such precise understanding was "reconstruction", an expression which Schlegel traced back to geometry.

2. Friedrich Ast

Ast soon made a career and became a professor of classical philology in 1805. In his book *Grammatik, Hermeneutik und Kritik* of 1808 which completes his introduction to philology (Ast 1808b), hermeneutic theory covers only a small part; "grammar", his philosophy of language, is three times as long. The two parts are connected by his philosophy of spirit, the centre of his thinking. The human spirit expresses itself and becomes manifest in language, and is also the condition of all our understanding and cognition. Spirit even provides access to what, otherwise, seems to be completely strange, because spirit is the common base and the original unity behind the diversities of the world. Understanding would be impossible if there was no connection between the entities and us, provided by the original unity in the background of all things. Thus we are confronted with only relative foreign objects. The incomprehensible and the differences are merely caused by chance and belong to the superficialities only. It is the task of philology to reveal pure human nature.

To Ast philology is philology of classical antiquity and therefore his hermeneutics is directed at the interpretation of Greek and Roman literature. Every interpretation has to answer three questions. First: what is the subject, the content of the work? One has to identify the realm of the text: is it scientific, artistic or antiquarian? Ast calls the understanding achieved in this way "historical" for it is based on the knowledge of ancient life and culture. The second approach is "grammatical" and has to answer the question, what is the form?: how is the content embedded in language? The final question then is: what is the leading idea? This third and most important question aims at "spiritual understanding" and here the questions of subject and form have to be combined (Ast 1808a: 169). The idea alone creates the unity of the work, coins it, binds all parts together, reveals the "spirit" of the work. Thus, in Ast's theory the essential concept or idea does not mean a *mere* idea, but an "abundance of reality" (Ast 1808a: 169), thought and reality are inseparably joined in the idea. Ast, like Schelling before him, was apparently looking at the Platonic concept of idea as *paradeigma*, as archetype and productive force, and, therefore, knowledge of the idea of a text is the main key to understanding, especially unclear and dark passages. However, for the full understanding of that idea, on the other hand, the idea and the spirit of antiquity as a whole have to be conceived and considered. For epochs of cultures are manifestations of ideas too, and the whole world, too, embodies ideas – a theory which is explained in Schelling's philosophy.

Because idea and spirit interrelate the single parts, the words and sentences, to create a meaningful whole, Ast concentrates on the understanding of them and explains what became famous as the so called hermeneutic circle: "the fundamental law of all understanding and cognition is it, to find from the single parts the spirit of the whole and to understand the single aspects through the whole" (Ast 1808a: 178; Flashar 1979: 28–9). According to Ast this "circle" is neither an aporia nor a logical mistake, for it can be dissolved: the whole is not the sum of all single elements but is already present in the single element. Therefore, with the knowledge of one single element the complete whole may be divined and this intuition can, by stepping from element to element, be transformed to understanding and cognition of the whole. Because all single parts and the whole text have to be perceived at the same time, understanding is "synthetic", synoptic, on the one hand and "analytic", dissecting on the other (Ast 1808a: 178, 184–5). This twofold procedure has to be applied to the understanding of single texts as well as to the whole of the literature of antiquity. To explain the hermeneutic circle Ast could refer back to anterior ideas to be found in the history of philosophy. Aristotle had already claimed that the whole is the first (*proteron*) and earlier than the parts (the whole tree is included in the seed before roots, trunk and branches are growing). Kant, then, found a reciprocal relation between the single parts and the whole in organic nature: in living organisms the parts function as aims as well as a means of the whole, so that one cannot be recognized without the other. Therefore, for Ast and his contemporaries it was obvious that the cognition of interdependence as the outstanding principle of all understanding concerned entities of nature as well as of culture, including texts, above all, as Plato said – a good speech should have the shape of a living body.

In later hermeneutics J. G. Droysen and W. Dilthey stated an opposition between understanding and explaining which Ast did not make: for him explanation as explicit demonstration and communication is a further step of interpretation (Ast 1808a: 184). In such thinking, literary works are looked upon as organisms and so understanding and explaining both have to draw back to the act of creation and to firstly show how the idea of a work developed and emerged, generating more and more details. Only when all elements are finally extracted from the process of creation, the spirit and idea of the work can be perceived completely. In this way understanding and explaining a literary work become "true reproduction or recreation of the already produced" (Ast 1808a: 187). The same conception can be found in F. Schlegel, Schleiermacher and A. Boeckh. For all of them understanding has to reproduce; that is, it must try to retrace the genesis of a given work.

In analogy with the three questions making up understanding, Ast finally differentiates three forms of hermeneutics to be related. The "hermeneutic of the letter" provides explanations of single words and matters, the "hermeneutic of sense" is concerned with the explanation of parts within their context and the "hermeneutic of spirit" takes all aspects of the whole text into consideration (Ast 1808a: 191). But how in his theory understanding and criticism coincide is of greater interest. For a reconstruction of the predominant idea also involves an evaluation of the work in so far as it represents the matching realization of the idea in language. Like earlier in Herder, the idea immanent in a work functions as a first scale. But for complete understanding the work has to be related to other works and to the idea of antiquity, too, which provide further ideas and criteria for evaluation. As they are confined to certain epochs and nations those ideas allow only "relative judgements". Insight into the ideas of truth, good and beauty is necessary for an "absolute appreciation", the cognition of which can be realized only through philosophically educated philologists (Ast 1808a: 209–12).

Ast's hermeneutics is only a small though very important part of his philosophical philology and his historical philosophy. According to Ast philology has neither to confine itself to collecting historical facts – Ast calls this "materialism" – nor should philology be satisfied with the study of ancient languages, called "formalism": it permanently has to look for the "spirit" of antiquity which becomes most evident in the works of classical literature. Researching and realizing the spirit of antiquity is necessary because of the deficiencies and one-sidedness of the modern age which have to be corrected. Opposing the ancient and modern ages Ast accentuated what modern culture has to learn from a "true and vivid view and cognition of antiquity" (Ast 1808b: 6–11; 1805): in antiquity enthusiasm ruled – in the present time only reason is dominant. All ancient life was formative, "plastical"; it had a beautiful shape, as in its fine arts – modern life is inward-directed; it is "musical". Antique culture was poetic and realistic – modern culture is idealistic and intellectual. The ancient Greek world was a "beautifully shaped body" and every individual reflected the spirit of the whole – contemporary society is divided by individualism and self-love; public life is barbaric even if our sciences and fine arts are richer and more differentiated. Above all, the modern age has to regain the ancient sense of beauty, for beauty is the "highest of all vital forces and virtues". Not least because of this, Ast elaborated his philosophical aesthetics (1813). He widely shared Friedrich Schiller's point of view presented in his famous *Letters on Aesthetic Education* of 1795: ancient classical culture serves as a paradigm to reveal the deficiencies of the modern age, whereas idealization of antiquity and criticism of modernity are just two sides of the same concept. For Ast classical philology should become an important instrument for the reform of culture: modern culture has to be perfected by the reception and realization of the ancient paradigms – perfection by *Bildung*: this important concept in Ast's theory means self-education and the forming of character. Reception of antique humanity, encountering the "foreign beauty" of antiquity, can liberate one from "one-sidedness and subjectivity" (Ast 1805: 22).

Ast integrated the opposition of antiquity and modernity into his comprehensive philosophy of history, which also means into the elaboration and development of his philosophy of spirit. The history of mankind is conceived as a revelation of spirit and all historical epochs work as necessary steps of spiritual evolution. The underlying thought can be called dialectical progress: first an unfolded unity, then the spirit proceeds via a division to a new higher unity and totality. After the oriental epoch, in which religion and philosophy, or science, were still undivided, the original unity was dissolved in the classical Greek world with its beauty on the one side, and in Christianity with its subjectivity on the other. This started a connection or reconciliation of pagan Greek and Christian spirit in a fourth epoch of history and this new unity has to be forwarded. With the help of this historical construction Ast organized his *Universalgeschichte*, the world history (1810), and also in his history of philosophy – according to Ast the central part of world history – he arranged the epochs of thinking in proper order following that fundamental idea of spiritual progress and presented the structure in the form of a clear table (Ast 1807: 447). The turn back to Greek and Roman antiquity as blossom and youth of the human spirit appears as a requirement of world history to achieve a perfect culture. F. Schlegel presented this idea in a very similar way.

3. Friedrich Schleiermacher

Although Schleiermacher intended to publish his concept of hermeneutics and criticism, he only succeeded delivering his thoughts between 1805 and 1833 in his lectures and in 1829 in two speeches in the Prussian Academy. Nevertheless, today he appears to be one of the "classical authors" of hermeneutics. All his manuscripts are now published together with lecture notes of students within the new critical edition of his works, making a volume of more than a thousand pages (Schleiermacher 2012). Schleiermacher as a theologian developed his hermeneutical thinking from 1804 onwards, looking at the exegesis of the New Testament, especially of the Pauline letters. But he was also a philosopher and a philologist and so his hermeneutical theory is closely connected to the research of ancient philosophy, particularly to his translation of Plato's dialogues. We can find central elements of his hermeneutical conception as early as 1804 in his great introduction to his translation (Scholtz 2012). Schleiermacher developed a general, philosophically founded hermeneutics as a basis and integrated the application to special problems of theologian exegesis into nearly all of his lectures – and additionally showed that his conception can also be valid as a foundation of literary hermeneutics (Szondi 1975: 135–91). He refused Ast's reduction of hermeneutics to the literature of classical antiquity: a theory of interpretation should be valid for all linguistic utterances, even for newspaper articles and oral communication. Hermeneutic theory is particularly necessary as an instruction for a conscious, reflected procedure, if a strange aspect appears in a communication process. If everything is clear and understandable, hermeneutics is not needed. Likewise, if everything is strange and incomprehensible, hermeneutic theory is of no use; hermeneutics cannot build bridges if speaker and listener have not got anything in common. Hermeneutic theory of the Enlightenment was concentrated on dark and unclear passages which hindered fluent reading, Schleiermacher demands a much more precise procedure: threatened by misunderstanding at any time of reading, understanding has to be explicitly willed and sought for (Schleiermacher 2012: 127). However, according to Schleiermacher, hermeneutics will never enable one to understand everything of a really significant text. One has to be satisfied if understanding approximates the complete meaning since the inner life of the person will always be a secret. The same idea of the incomprehensible which remains in understanding can be found in the thoughts of F. Schlegel and W. von Humboldt.

From the beginning Schleiermacher tried to establish hermeneutic theory as a science: he intended to construct the discipline on correct and plausible principles, to form a "system", that is, a coherent theory as a doctrine for the art of interpretation in general. He found his principles in language, precisely in all uttered speech. This always springs from two sources: language and speaker. Language is the general element between the whole community of speakers, its universal aspect, whereas its user is the individual factor. Both influence and determine every utterance and text from opposing sides. Language coins the thought of authors – and authors use language in an individual way and so may alter linguistic tradition. All thinking, speaking and writing oscillate in a field of tension between a given language and the creative minds of individual speakers and writers. In his treatise on the problem of translation, Schleiermacher accentuates the power, even the force of both antipodes (Schleiermacher 2002c: 71–2). Some years later we can find the same expression in the writings of W. von Humboldt. The interpretation theory of the Enlightenment taught one to consider language and the individuality of authors as well, but only Schleiermacher understood them as opposing forces and constructed his hermeneutics completely on this foundation.

Two thoughts result from these different approaches to a text, two "interpretations", which form the skeletal structure of Schleiermacher's hermeneutics in all his drafts and lectures: the "grammatical interpretation", which starts from a comprehensive knowledge of the language tradition which was available for the author, and the "psychological interpretation", which proposes close intimacy with the thinking, character and life of the author. The expression "psychological" may provoke the assumption of a psychological theory and therefore modern psychologism was imputed to Schleiermacher. But Schleiermacher just took up the thread of the very old idea of style as a mirror of the soul, as already Cicero and other classical philosophers called it. Moreover, the psychological approach considers style, composition, that is, the way of thinking, and tone, that is, the character of the text which expresses the individuality of the author. The aesthetic aspect serves as a key to meaning; for example, whoever ignores the ironical tone in Socrates will misunderstand his statements. In his translations of Plato's works Schleiermacher reconducted the dialogue form to the philosophical content, and the link between form and content proved fertile for other interpretations, for example New Testament studies, as well. Even if we only have minor knowledge of biblical authors and ancient philosophers, we need a psychological interpretation for understanding their works. In such cases we become slowly acquainted with the authors while reading them and use the knowledge gained for further understanding – a slow procedure of approximation to the meaning. Considering the art of presentation, the *techne*, Schleiermacher calls this a "technical interpretation" sometimes. And from time to time, he drew a distinction between technical and psychological interpretation. The polarity, though, of language and the author as a corner stone was never given up, only blurred.

Additionally to the two ways of interpretation, Schleiermacher also distinguishes two methods: "comparison" and "divination", that is, precise guessing and intuitive understanding. Whereas comparison is a function of reason, divination derives from imagination and both methods are always closely related. There is a different focus on the methods: comparison dominates grammatical interpretation and for psychological interpretation mostly divining is important (Schleiermacher 2002d: 618–20). Thus Schleiermacher extracts the principles of his hermeneutic theory: firstly from the object of interpretation (language – author); secondly from the cognitive faculties (reason – imagination). In the process of understanding all activities have to cooperate. Whereas some scientists, however, deride divination as something irrational, Schleiermacher makes clear that only by activating the imagination can we learn to use language. His most important disciple in the realm of hermeneutics, the philologist A. Boeckh, soon seized the role of imagination but increased the role of the second element of hermeneutics, that of criticism. Inspired by Schleiermacher he develops a fully symmetrical system in which he opposes four hermeneutical and four critical aspects of interpretation which are prerequisites of each other. Hermeneutics has to consider the text in itself, criticism in its relation to others (Boeckh 1966, 1968). In the nineteenth century his conception had a great impact and was adapted much later, for example by E. D. Hirsch.

As for Ast, and according to Schleiermacher, as well, the understanding of the whole and the single parts are reciprocal prerequisites (Schleiermacher 2002d: 625–35). Schleiermacher avoids the term circle, though, and criticises Ast's thesis that we are able to form an immediate idea of the "spirit" of the whole by looking at one element only. The assumption of the essential unity of an age to him seems speculative and arbitrary. M. Chladenius already had noticed that sometimes a text may include more meaning than the author could have consciously intended, but the insight led to contradictions. F. Schlegel and Schleiermacher take it for granted because the interpreters, from their point of view, are able to perceive more and even different aspects from those the author had in mind. The result for Schleiermacher is the rule: first, we have to understand the utterances of an author as he understood them himself and secondly even better than himself (Schleiermacher 2012: 39, 128; 2002d: 618; Bauer 2011). For understanding an author better one has to look at the text from its seminal state to its perfection and, then, frame it with extended contexts, the background of earlier history, its history of reception and, thus, put it permanently into new light – a procedure which must necessarily stay unfinished.

Schleiermacher's philosophy set hermeneutics as a theory of interpretation in a central place. In his *Dialektik*, his theory of cognition and knowledge, he explains that real knowledge can be found only via dialogue and understanding of others. Science, thus, is a process of communication within the scientific community (*Erkenntnisgemeinschaft*) and productive science also has to tackle its own history to avoid one-sidedness. It is the aim of hermeneutics to make the thoughts of other persons and other epochs understandable which are all embedded in individually articulated languages. Schleiermacher calls this hermeneutical activity a form of "critical procedure" (Schleiermacher 2002b: 178–89, 190–1). Understanding other people's thoughts we are able to control, correct and widen our own knowledge.

The relation between hermeneutics and *ethics*, the most important philosophical discipline for Schleiermacher, is even closer. Ethics is based on these principles: the human being works as he creates symbols and he enfolds his individual abilities on the one hand, and his generally natural reason on the other. The understanding of symbols, therefore, constitutes culture as a whole and the tension between the individual and the universal can be found in all spheres of society, not only in language. Four equally entitled cultural areas show this tension in a different way: family/privacy, work/state, religion/fine arts/church and science/academy. In all of these understanding is required; however, religion, fine arts and science only exist through their symbol systems. In Schleiermacher's draft of a philosophical system hermeneutics belongs to the "technical disciplines" like politics and pedagogy, all of which can guide actions by reason (Schleiermacher [2]1927: 356). As political theory serves stately activities, hermeneutics should assist in the interpretation of texts. Within his theological system hermeneutics holds an important position as well: Christian theology has to reveal the essence of Christianity which can only be achieved by an understanding of its history, particularly of primeval Christianity. Therefore, Schleiermacher calls hermeneutics "the true centre of exegetical theology" (Schleiermacher 1998: 375–7; Scholtz 1995: 193–211).

In the group of philosophers belonging to so called German Idealism, Schleiermacher excels with his critical prudence: he explores nearly all philosophical disciplines – dialectics, ethics, aesthetics, politics, pedagogy, hermeneutics, anthropology and psychology, philosophy of religion, history of philosophy. But he looked at all systematic knowledge as being in permanent evolution because of the inherent one-sidedness and imperfection. To reform modern philosophy he postulated a constant look at the history of philosophy. To the academy of science he recommended a "critical and historical consideration of philosophy" which should try to understand all systems in the history of philosophy in detail to identify their one-sidedness and to make clear what may lead closer to truth (Schleiermacher 2002a: 6). According to him, philosophy is the corner stone of all scientific attempts and all practice in society. His whole thinking promotes the permanent reformation of society. He, like W. von Humboldt, was one of the leading figures of the Prussian Reforms.

Bibliography

Ast, F. (1805) *Ueber den Geist des Alterthums, und dessen Bedeutung für unser Zeitalter*, Landshut: Attenkofer'sche Buchhandlung.

——(1807) *Grundriss einer Geschichte der Philosophie*, Landshut: J. Thomann.

——(1808a) *Grundlinien der Grammatik, Hermeneutik und Kritik*, Landshut: J. Thomann.

——(1808b) *Grundriss der Philologie*, Landshut: Ph. Krüll.

——(1810) *Entwurf der Universalgeschichte. Zweite, vermehrte und verbesserte Auflage*, Landshut: J. Thomann.

——(1813) *Grundlinien der Aesthetik*, Landshut: Ph. Krüll.

——(1825) *Grundriss der Geschichte der Philosophie. Zweite, vermehrte und verbesserte, Auflage*, Landshut: J. Thomann.

Bauer, M. (2011) *Schlegel und Schleiermacher. Frühromantische Kunstkritik und Hermeneutik*, Paderborn, München, Wien: F. Schöningh.

Birus, H. (1982) "Zwischen den Zeiten. Friedrich Schleiermacher als Klassiker der neuzeitlichen Hermeneutik", in H. Birus (ed.) *Hermeneutische Positionen. Schleiermacher – Dilthey – Heidegger – Gadamer*, Göttingen: Vandenhoeck & Ruprecht, pp. 15–58.

Boeckh, A. (1966) *Enzyklopädie und Methodenlehre der philologischen Wissenschaften. Erster Hauptteil: Formale Theorie der philologischen Wissenschaft*, ed. E. Bratuschek, Darmstadt: Wissenschaftliche Buchgesellschaft.

——(1968) *On Interpretation and Criticism*, trans. J.P. Pritchard, Norman: University of Oklahoma Press.

Flashar, H. (1979) "Die methodisch-hermeneutischen Ansätze von Friedrich August Wolf und Friedrich Ast – Traditionelle und neue Begründungen", in H. Flashar, K. Gründer and A. Horstmann (eds) *Philologie und Hermeneutik im 19. Jahrhundert. Zur Geschichte und Methodologie der Geisteswissenschaften*, Göttingen: Vandenhoeck & Ruprecht, pp. 21–31.

Hamann, J. G. (1950) *Aesthetica in nuce* (1761), *Sämtliche Werke*, ed. J. Nadler, vol. 2: *Schriften über Philosophie / Phiolologie / Kritik*, Wien: Herder, pp. 195–217.

Herder, J. G. (1967) *Briefe, das Studium der Theologie betreffend* (1780/85), 1. Tl. *Sämtliche Werke*, ed. B. Suphan, vol. 10, Hildesheim: Georg Olms.

——(1984) *Auch eine Philosophie der Geschichte der Menschheit* (1774), *Johann Gottfried Werke*, in W. Pross (ed.) *Herder und der Sturm und Drang 1764–1774*, vol. 1, Darmstadt: Wissenschaftliche Buchgesellschaft, pp. 589–689.

Herz, A. (1997) "'Einfühlung'. Bemerkungen zum Divinationsaspekt in J. G. Herders Hermeneutik-Konzept", in H.-P. Ecker (ed.) *Methodisch reflektiertes Interpretieren. Festschrift für Hartmut Laufhütte zum 60. Geburtstag*, Passau: Rothe, pp. 215–52.

Patsch, H. (1966) "Friedrich Schlegels 'Philosophie der Philologie' und Schleiermachers frühe Entwürfe zur Hermeneutik", *Zeitschrift für Theologie und Kirche* 63: 434–72.

Rieger, R. (1988) *Interpretation und Wissen. Zur philosophischen Begründung der Hermeneutik Schleiermachers und ihrem geschichtlichen Hintergrund* (= Schleiermacher-Archiv vol. 6), Berlin, New York: W. de Gruyter.

Schlegel, F. (1975) "Lessings Gedanken und Meinungen" (1804), *Kritische Friedrich-Schlegel-Ausgabe* (= KFSA) vol. 3: *Charakteristiken und Kritiken (1802–29)*, ed. H. Eichner, München, Paderborn, Wien: F. Schöningh, pp. 46–102.

Schleiermacher, F.D.E. (²1927) *Entwürfe zu einem System der Sittenlehre, Werke* vol. 2, ed. O. Braun, Leipzig: Felix Meiner.

——(1998) *Kurze Darstellung des theologischen Studiums* (1830). *Kritische Gesamtausgabe* (= KGA) I, vol. 6, ed. D. Schmid, Berlin, New York: W. de Gruyter, pp. 317–446.

——(2002a) "Antrittsvortrag" (1810), KGA I, vol. 11, ed. M. Rössler, Berlin, New York: W. de Gruyter, pp. 1–7.

——(2002b) *Vorlesungen über die Dialektik*, KGA II, vol. 10.1, ed. A. Arndt, Berlin, New York: W. de Gruyter.

——(2002c) "Über die verschiedenen Methoden des Übersetzens" (1813), KGA I, vol. 11, ed. M. Rössler, Berlin, New York: W. de Gruyter, pp. 64–93.

——(2002d) "Über den Begriff der Hermeneutik, mit Bezug auf F. A. Wolfs Andeutungen und Asts Lehrbuch" [A. and B.] (1829), KGA I, vol. 11, ed. M. Rössler, Berlin, New York: W. de Gruyter, pp. 599–641.

——(2002e) "Über Begriff und Einteilung der philologischen Kritik" (1830), KGA I, vol. 11, ed. M. Rössler, Berlin, New York: W. de Gruyter, pp. 643–56.

——(2012) *Vorlesungen zur Hermeneutik und Kritik*, KGA II, vol. 4, ed. W. Virmond, Berlin, New York: W. de Gruyter.

Schnur, H. (1994) *Schleiermachers Hermeneutik und ihre Vorgeschichte im 18. Jahrhundert. Studien zur Bibelauslegung, zu Hamann, Herder und F. Schlegel*, Stuttgart, Weimar: J. B. Metzler.

Scholtz, G. (1995) *Ethik und Hermeneutik. Schleiermachers Grundlegung der Geisteswissenschaften*, Frankfurt am Main: Suhrkamp.

——(2002) "Das Unverständliche bei Chladenius und Friedrich Schlegel", in G. Kühne-Bertram, G. Scholtz (eds) *Grenzen des Verstehens. Philosophische und humanwissenschaftliche Perspektiven*, Göttingen: Vandenhoeck & Ruprecht, pp. 17–33.

——(2012) "Platonforschung und hermeneutische Reflexion bei Schleiermacher", in M. Erler and A. Neschke-Hentschke (eds) *Argumenta in Dialogos Platonis. Teil 2: Platoninterpretation und ihre Hermeneutik vom 19. bis zum 21. Jahrhundert*, Basel: Schwabe, pp. 81–101.

Szondi, P. (1975) *Einführung in die literarische Hermeneutik (Studienausgabe der Vorlesungen vol. 5)*, ed. J. Bollack and H. Stierlin, Frankfurt am Main: Suhrkamp, pp. 135–91.

Wach, J. (1926) *Das Verstehen. Grundzüge der hermeneutischen Theorie im 19. Jahrhundert, vol. 1: Die großen Systeme*, Tübingen: J.C.B. Mohr (Paul Siebeck).

Zovko, J. (1990) *Verstehen und Nichtverstehen bei Friedrich Schlegel. Zur Entstehung und Bedeutung seiner hermeneutischen Kritik*, Stuttgart-Bad Cannstatt: Frommann-holzboog.

Further reading

For the reception of Schleiermacher's hermeneutics D. Dilthey's essay "Die Entstehung der Hermeneutik" had the most important impact (*Gesammelte Schriften*, vol. 5, Göttingen: Vandenhoeck, ⁷1982, pp. 317–38). But more instructive is Dilthey's early treatise "Das hermeneutische System Schleiermachers in der Auseinandersetzung mit der älteren protestantischen Hermeneutik" (*Gesammelte Schriften* vol. 14,

Göttingen: Vandenhoeck, 1966, pp. 597–787). We find useful information in Dilthey's great work *Leben Schleiermachers* (*Gesammelte Schriften* vol. 13–14, ed. M. Redeker, Göttingen: Vandenhoeck, 1966–70). New research was integrated in K. Nowak: *Schleiermacher. Leben, Werk und Wirkung*, Göttigen: Vandenhoeck, ²2001. Concentrating on philosophy and considering the different interpretations in the reception, G. Scholtz (*Die Philosophie Schleiermachers*, Darmstadt: Wissenschaftliche Buchgesellschaft, 1984) presents an overview on all disciplines which Schleiermacher treated. A useful analysis of Schleiermacher's principles in his hermeneutical thinking we can find in D. Thouard, *Schleiermacher. Communauté, individualité, communication* (Paris: Vrin, 2007). L. Danneberg ("Schleiermacher und die Hermeneutik", in A. B. Baertschi and C. G. King (eds), *Die modernen Väter der Antike. Die Entwicklung der Altertumswissenschaften an Akademie und Universität im Berlin des 19. Jahrhunderts*, Berlin: de Gruyter, 2009, pp. 211–75) gives very useful commentaries to some important points of Schleiermacher's interpretation theory, seen in the historical contexts of hermeneutics. M. Frank (*Das individuelle Allgemeine. Textstrukturierung und -interpretation nach Schleiermacher*, Frankfurt am Main: Suhrkamp, 1977) shows the actuality of Schleiermacher's position in the context of poststructuralism. In 1966, T. Tice began to publish a bibliography, which contains the works of the author as well as literature: *Schleiermacher Bibliography. With Brief Introductions, Annotations, and Index*, Princeton, NJ: Theological Seminary, 1966. In 1985, 1989 and 1991, Tice completed the work by updatings. For a critical bibliography of all Schleiermacher's works see W. von Meding, *Bibliographie der Schriften Schriften Schleiermachers. Nebst einer Zusammenstellung und Datierung seiner gedruckten Predigten*, Berlin, New York: de Gruyter (= *Schleiermacher-Archiv*, vol. 5).

6
DILTHEY: HERMENEUTICS AND NEO-KANTIANISM

Rudolf A. Makkreel

Wilhelm Dilthey (1833–1911) conceived the task of hermeneutics in terms of a Critique of Historical Reason. Like his Neo-Kantian contemporaries, Dilthey took Kant's transcendental turn seriously. This becomes especially clear in his debate with Wilhelm Windelband (1848–1915) and Heinrich Rickert (1863–1936) about what distinguishes the human sciences from the natural sciences. In an essay published in 1894, Windelband launched this debate by attacking Dilthey's view that the natural sciences are primarily concerned with explaining outer experience and the human sciences with understanding inner experience and its relation to outer experience. Dilthey had argued that the kind of law-based explanations possible in physics have only a limited relevance to the experience considered by the human sciences. To understand human life we can make use of the interconnectedness of inner experience to find meaningful structures that situate us in our historical context. Windelband considered this explanation–understanding distinction to be overly focused on the content of experience and proposed that it be replaced with a more formal nomothetic–idiographic distinction to account for the differences between the natural and the historical/cultural sciences.

Dilthey in turn criticized the methodological approaches to history proposed by Windelband and developed by Rickert. More generally this exchange with these Baden School Neo-Kantians stimulated Dilthey to sharpen his own views about the human sciences. It also led him to revive his early interest in hermeneutics and realize that however much human understanding is rooted in experience, it needs to be refined by an analysis of different cognitive and reflective frameworks. In the final section, Dilthey's evolving views on hermeneutics will be related to the ways in which the Marburg Neo-Kantians Hermann Cohen (1842–1918) and Ernst Cassirer (1874–1945) interpreted history and culture.

1. Understanding and lived experience in Dilthey

In 1860 Dilthey submitted a long essay entitled "Schleiermacher's Hermeneutical System in Relation to Earlier Protestant Hermeneutics" to a prize committee of the

Schleiermacher Society. It won the prize, but Dilthey did not publish it, for at this stage of his philosophical development he still considered hermeneutics as a primarily religious discipline for interpreting biblical texts. The essay begins with the Reformation because it is regarded as setting exegesis free from the authority of tradition. Schleiermacher is claimed to have completed this process of liberation and despite the fact that many important philosophical influences on Schleiermacher's project are recognized, Dilthey himself would not explicitly formulate the philosophical relevance of hermeneutics until after his debate with the Neo-Kantians was launched more than thirty years later. Nevertheless, the early essay has more than theological interest and was published posthumously as part of the second volume of Dilthey's *Life of Schleiermacher*; it has also been translated into English (see Dilthey 1996: 33–227).

The way that theology had shaped hermeneutics as a doctrinal theory of exegesis led Dilthey to first direct his main philosophical interest elsewhere, namely, at the experiential roots of understanding and interpretation. The kind of understanding (*Verstehen*) needed for making sense of human life and its historical development is contrasted with the explanative faculty of understanding (*Verstand*) that Kant uses to ground the natural sciences. In Book One of his *Introduction to the Human Sciences* of 1883, Dilthey argues for the relative independence of the human sciences from the explanative methods of the natural sciences. Not all aspects of human behavior are causally determined by our bodily constitution and our physical circumstances. What we think and do is certainly conditioned by our physiology, but this should be conceived as a functional dependence that is more limited than strict causal determination.

Whereas the natural sciences of Dilthey's time examined outer experience and searched for the synthetic causal laws that connect natural events, the *Introduction to the Human Sciences* proposed that the human sciences start by describing and analyzing our inner experience. And in the *Ideas for a Descriptive and Analytic Psychology* of 1894, Dilthey goes on to claim that we possess an implicit but direct awareness of the overall connectedness of our consciousness. Whereas outer experience may be phenomenal in the Kantian sense, exposing us to things that appear to us piecemeal and which can only be unified by means of hypothetical explanations, human beings have a real access to the connectedness of their lives through their inner experience. This connectedness is non-hypothetical and can be directly understood as meaningful.

Dilthey's *Verstehen* involves a reflective understanding that explicates the whole of what is given through description and analysis. This supplements Kant's *Verstand* or purely intellectual understanding that proceeds discursively from part to part and looks for explanative connections. From now on we will just call *Verstand* the intellectual faculty that explains. In the *Ideas* Dilthey makes it clear in what way understanding is more encompassing than explanation: "We explain through purely intellectual processes, but we understand through the cooperation of all the powers of the mind activated by apprehension" (Dilthey 2010: 147). Human sciences such as a descriptive psychology should be concerned primarily with the understanding of the overall meaning-structures of human experience and only secondarily with explanations of details.

Up to now we have delineated the traditional opposition of inner and outer experience. But Dilthey came to prefer the term "lived experience" (*Erlebnis*) for its capacity to encompass both inner and outer sense. In the essay "The Origin of Our Belief in the Reality of the External World and Its Justification" of 1890, he argues that our original access to the external world is not based on an intellectual inference, but on a feeling of resistance to the will. The reality of the world is originally felt from within as restraining our intentions. Even the phenomenal objects of outer experience can have an inner meaning for us if they play a role in our lives. Thus Dilthey describes the perceived picture of Goethe in his study as an inner experience because he remembers that it used to hang in his father's house before he inherited it. To the extent that the picture has become part of his subjective life history, the awareness of it counts as a lived experience that has both inner and outer aspects.

2. Windelband and Rickert on history and Dilthey's response

Windelband and Rickert belonged to the Baden School of Neo-Kantians who were especially interested in the relation of the historical sciences to the natural sciences. Windelband delivered a lecture in 1894 on history and natural science, in which he questioned how Dilthey had made psychological descriptions of experience basic for the methodology of the human sciences. Psychology may belong to the human sciences in terms of its experiential subject matter, but methodologically it is a natural science, according to Windelband, because it looks for generalizations. Instead of distinguishing between natural and human sciences on the basis of explaining outer experience and understanding inner experience, Windelband distinguishes between natural sciences that are nomothetic and historical/cultural sciences that are idiographic. Psychology remains an explanative science and no place is made for Dilthey's descriptive psychology in the cultural sciences. It is interesting that this Neo-Kantian did not take note of the fact that Kant himself thought that psychology could only be descriptive and should be reconceived as an anthropology that can be pragmatic for human conduct. No doubt Windelband thought that the rise of experimental psychology gave new life to the explanative agenda. Whatever view is adopted about psychology, Dilthey's explanation–understanding distinction can be defended independently on hermeneutical grounds, for it can be shown to largely coincide with the philosophical distinction made by Kant between determinant and reflective judgment. Explanations can be explicated as determinant judgments that proceed from given universal concepts to particulars that can be subsumed under them. And the effort to understand can be shown to parallel reflective judgment in finding the appropriate universal for a given particular. Understanding and reflective judgment deal with phenomena for which there are no readymade concepts, and before new concepts can be found these phenomena will need to be properly situated in their own context.

Dilthey's own response to Windelband's nomothetic–idiographic distinction was twofold. First, he rejects the claim that the historical/cultural/human sciences can be defined as being idiographic. The understanding and interpretation of history necessitates relating the mere particulars of idiographic description with universals. To understand a historical figure or movement is not just a matter of specifying its uniqueness, but of seeing how it individuates a larger context. The human sciences must bring universals – whether they be law-based or structural patterns having a contextual origin – to bear on the particular subject matter. Secondly, there are natural sciences such as geography that could be considered just as idiographic as history. Thirdly, the human sciences include more than the humanities and the study of culture; they also encompass social sciences such as economics that aim at discovering lawlike generalizations and would therefore qualify as being nomothetic.

Rickert came to see the flaw in Windelband's distinction and agreed with Dilthey that both the natural and the cultural sciences make use of universals. He replaces the term "idiographic" with Dilthey's concern for "individuation." But whereas Dilthey saw individuation as a product of *judgment formation* that relates particulars and universals, Rickert defined individuation as a product of a special kind of *concept formation*. All the sciences use universals to select what is essential from what is unessential, according to Rickert, and these can be simple universals such as laws in the case of the natural sciences or a combination of universals such as values in the case of the cultural sciences. Universal concepts can be combined to form individual complexes that serve as values that guide historians in selecting what is important in history. Although this concept-based value theory comes closer to Dilthey's approach to history, it assigns values a transcendent status that Dilthey would reject.

Dilthey's judgment-based approach to historical understanding roots all values and evaluation in this life. Like Kant, he regards judgment formation as more fundamental than the kind of concept formation proposed by Rickert. Although Dilthey remained unconvinced by the counterproposals of Windelband and Rickert, he nevertheless decided to reevaluate his reliance on psychology for his theory of the human sciences. He came to recognize that inner experience is not a sufficient basis for historical understanding. In fact it is not even an adequate source for self-understanding.

We have already indicated that inner and outer sense can merge in one's own lived experience. But the problem of understanding history requires one to make sense of things that are outside one's own life. Here the outer is not just on the order of perceived objects like mountains and trees, nor is it a direct extension of my inner life as with the picture in Dilthey's study. To understand historical and cultural life requires me to discern in outer objects an inner sense that is not merely an extension of my subjective existence. In an essay of 1895–6 entitled "Contributions to the Study of Individuality" Dilthey suggests that the understanding of history involves apperceiving what is normally perceived as part of nature as also part of a human context. Here outer phenomena are not directly related to inner sense, but to the apperceptive overall "nexus of our facts of consciousness" (Dilthey 2010: 216). This apperceptive relation is called "transcendental" because it allows us to consider our experience in context and thereby reflect on our place in the "spiritual-cultural" world (Dilthey 2010: 216–17). Thus he adds to inner and outer experience, the notion of a reflective experience that makes sense of things in relation to the totality of our apperceptive awareness. This spiritual-cultural world is a shared historical world that is co-constituted. In doing so, we apperceive certain objects as more than external givens, namely, as objectifications of human activity. What outer experience perceives as an external object can under certain conditions be apperceived by reflective experience as expressing something about human history.

With this as a background, we can show that Dilthey's final hermeneutical position as developed in "The Rise of Hermeneutics" (1900) and in "The Understanding of

Other Persons and Their Life-Manifestations" (1910) places increasing emphasis on interpreting the objectifications of experience. To provide the cognitive basis for this shift, it will be useful to go back to the essay "Life and Cognition: A Draft for an Epistemic Logic and a Theory of Categories" (circa 1892–3). This essay, which was published posthumously in 1982, opens up what is meant by the givenness of things.

3. The contextual givenness of life

For Dilthey the given is not the sense-content of post-Kantian epistemology, but life as the context of all experience. In "Life and Cognition" he writes that:

> no matter how hard I struggle to obtain the pure experience of the given, there is no such thing. The given lies beyond my direct experience. ... Everything, absolutely everything that falls within my consciousness contains the given as ordered or distinguished or combined or related, that is, as interpreted in intellectual processes.
>
> (Dilthey 2010: 60)

The given is not immediately present for observation, but a mediated presence that needs to be interpreted in relation to life as what is always there in its *contextual givenness*.

Traditional epistemology has overlooked this contextual givenness of experience, but even more importantly it has ignored the self-givenness of consciousness. Even if consciousness is directed at so-called phenomenal objects, it possesses its own reality through a "reflexive awareness" (*Innewerden*) (Dilthey 1989: 6, 26, 202). The term "reflexive" here is to be contrasted with what is "reflective." Dilthey's reflexive awareness can be characterized as a pre-reflective *being with-itself* of consciousness. Whereas consciousness manifests an *aboutness* that can be directed at what is within or without, reflexive awareness is the self-givenness of consciousness. Dilthey describes reflexive awareness as:

> a consciousness that does not place a content over against the subject of consciousness (it does not re-present it); rather, a content is present in it without differentiation. That which constitutes its content is in no way distinguished from the act in which it occurs.
>
> (Dilthey 1989: 253–4)

Reflexive awareness is not representational, but it can access whatever is represented. It offers an implicit self-givenness that precedes an explicit sense of self. The felt self-givenness or with-itselfness of reflexive awareness is not to be confused with introspective observation attempted by the reflective self where willful acts of attention may disturb the natural course of experience.

Reflexive awareness as the being with-itself of consciousness provides a real sense of the connectedness of experience that lies at the origin of finding meaning. This connectedness can be articulated into cognitive, affective, and volitional structures, each of which provides its distinctive experiential nexus. But however much we may want to focus on one of these structures, we should never lose sight of the overall nexus of consciousness. Thus the cognitive ordering of experience cannot be fully isolated from the affective and the volitional. Cognition depends on inquisitive interest, which is a function of feeling; nor can it produce determinative results without attention, which is a function of willing.

4. Interpretation and reflective assessment

Although lived experience and reflexive awareness are real and indubitable for Dilthey, he begins to recognize that the meaning they ascribe to things is not necessarily reliable or objective. Reflexive awareness gives us access to meaning, but the contextual givenness of things is the essential framework for the proper understanding of meaning. Starting with the 1900 essay "The Rise of Hermeneutics," Dilthey comes to the realization that lived experience provides an intelligibility (*Verständlichkeit*) that is not yet an understanding (*Verstehen*).

Thus he writes that "even the apprehension of our own states can only be called understanding in a figurative sense" (Dilthey 1996: 236). The way we express ourselves, whether in communication or in action, becomes a necessary intermediary for self-understanding. Understanding must proceed through the interpretation of human objectifications to be reliable. Social engagement and the capacity to assess ourselves the way we observe and assess others is more important than introspection. Understanding is reconceived as "the process by which we recognize, behind signs given to our senses, that psychic reality of which they are the expression" (Dilthey 1996: 236). What we learn about ourselves from within must be tested by reflection on how we express what we feel and think and on how we act on our desires. Understanding is thus inseparable from interpretation. The study of hermeneutics which Dilthey had left behind since his early prize essay on religious hermeneutics is now given a new philosophical formulation.

Historical understanding must proceed through the medium of human objectifications and can attain universal validity only in relation to the most testable form of objectification, which is the written word. Dilthey concludes "The Rise of Hermeneutics" by asserting that the main purpose hermeneutics is:

> to preserve the universal validity of historical interpretation against the inroads of romantic caprice and skeptical subjectivity. ... Seen in relation to epistemology, logic, and the methodology of the human sciences, the theory of interpretation becomes an important connecting link between philosophy and the historical sciences, an essential component in the foundation of the human sciences.
>
> (Dilthey 1996: 250)

This formulation that relates hermeneutics to philosophical reflection about history through epistemology and methodology has come to define how Dilthey has been typed. However, it will become clear in Dilthey's *Formation of the Historical*

World in the Human Sciences of 1910 that there is more to the relation. In this final articulation of the Critique of Historical Reason, epistemology as the theory of cognition (*Erkenntnistheorie*) is incorporated into a more encompassing theory of knowing (*Theorie des Wissens*). Dilthey's term *Erkenntnis* applies to *cognition* that is discursive, conceptual, and scientific. But before the sciences cognize their respective worldly subdomains, we already possess a more direct *knowledge* (*Wissen*) of the surroundings in which we find ourselves. Whereas Hegel conceived this surrounding world as a universal sphere of objective spirit, Dilthey redefines it as a more local context of commonalities such as our native language and the customs of our region. The knowledge that is accumulated from the commonalities that we inherit from our local past produces a subjective certainty (*Gewissheit*) that is needed for everyday life. Both the human and natural sciences aim to replace this limited knowledge rooted in mere commonalities with conceptual cognition that represents the world in universal terms so that it can be tested for objective reliability (*Sicherheit*). But the success in developing scientific theories about human life and history comes at the price of fragmenting the historical world. It is not possible to find cognitive uniformities about history at large, only about particular histories focused on spheres such as political and economic life. Thus the understanding of human life and history that is the concern of the Critique of Historical Reason must go beyond the cognitive analysis of the human sciences. It must point "to all classes of knowledge: ... 1) the conceptual cognition of reality, 2) the positing of values, and 3) the determination of purposes and establishment of rules" (Dilthey 2002: 25).

The more encompassing knowledge needed for genuine historical understanding moves from the experience of commonalities to the formulation of universal cognitive theories and ends with a more comprehensive assessment that only individuals can make. Dilthey called the latter a "re-experiencing." This term is misleading, for he does not mean a psychological reliving of actual experiences from the past. Instead it is a re-creative articulation of an experiential nexus that involves an "appropriation of the world of human spirit" (Dilthey 2002: 235). Re-experiencing has a completing function that encompasses all three "classes of knowledge" cited above and can be considered a reflective assessment.

Dilthey's last essay on hermeneutics, entitled "The Understanding of Other Persons and Their Manifestations of Life," sums this up in terms of three levels of understanding: 1) the elementary understanding that derives from the commonalities that nurture us from birth; 2) the higher conceptual understanding contributed by the sciences; and 3) the highest understanding of re-experiencing as reflective assessment. Elementary understanding is locally shared and amounts to a direct kind of *common knowledge*. Higher understanding aims at *universal cognitive theories* that help us analyze the world at large. The overall assessment that completes the process of understanding results in what could be called "*reflective knowledge*." The interpretive task of hermeneutics is to mediate between these three levels of understanding and make sure that the respective insights of each level are not lost. Even if we no longer accept the standpoint of common sense and elementary understanding at face value, higher understanding must be able to account for why it made sense and explicate what its role was. Moreover some version of elementary understanding will continue to provide clues about life that the specialized cognition of the sciences may lose sight of and it is part of the task of "re-experiencing as reflective assessment" to re-appropriate those aspects. The fact that the discourses characteristic of these three levels of understanding are discrete and do not naturally merge introduces a certain tension into the hermeneutical circle that still has not been adequately recognized.

We saw that Dilthey moved beyond his initial assumptions that lived experience already amounts to self-understanding and that the understanding of others is merely a kind of extrapolation from the self. Increasingly Dilthey came to focus on the objectifications of human life as essential to historical understanding. While the human sciences analyze the ways in which we are conditioned by historical events, state institutions, and social customs, they also demonstrate how we can shape the world through our productive activities. Such objective achievements, Dilthey writes, "always contain, like man himself, a reference back from an outer sensory aspect to one that is withdrawn from the senses and therefore inner" (Dilthey 2002: 106). He then goes on to warn that it is a common error to equate this inner aspect with psychic life. Thus to understand the inner meaning of the laws of a state at a particular time one need not go back to the mental states of the legislators who voted for them. Historians must study the relevant legal documents of an age and the available records of court procedures as manifestations of the rules and norms that govern a system of jurisprudence. Understanding Roman law requires, not a reliving of the intentions of individual legislators or judges, but "a regress to a spiritual formation that has its own structure and lawfulness" (Dilthey 2002: 107).

The same is true for the understanding of individual human creations such as the work of a dramatic poet. What is to be understood in such a work "is not the inner processes in the poet; it is rather a nexus created in them but separable from them." This nexus of the work "consists in a distinctive relation of material, poetic mood, motif, plot, and means of representation" (Dilthey 2002: 107). The task is to grasp the inner structural meaning that holds these moments of the work together.

5. Relating hermeneutics to Cohen's legal philosophy and Cassirer's symbolic forms

So far we have related Dilthey to the Baden School Neo-Kantians Windelband and Rickert. But there was also a Marburg School whose best known representatives were Hermann Cohen and Ernst Cassirer.

Cohen was mostly interested in the natural sciences, but when he did reflect on the human sciences, he insisted that they find their basis in legal and ethical norms. In a work dealing with Kant's grounding of ethics published in 1877 and reissued in 1910, Cohen had argued that the philosophy of right must provide the same kind of *a priori* grounding for the human and cultural sciences that mathematics provides for the natural sciences. At its core, legal theory is conceived by Cohen as pure ethics applied reciprocally so that free wills can act on the basis of mutual respect. If this can be achieved, the model of finding lawful order can be preserved for all the sciences: in the natural sciences, we discover what laws of nature are at work; in the human sciences we establish laws in the normative sense.

Cohen's philosophy of right aims at more than external legality. Legitimacy and justice must be rooted in the same universal ideal of self-legislation that constitutes the ethical. If we conceive of the ethical as already involving "a community of purposes" (Cohen 1910: 413), then the reciprocity of justice at the heart of the philosophy of right will follow logically. Cohen focuses on the intelligible nature of the legal contract that allows a promise and its acceptance to coexist simultaneously and unite distinct individuals. Accordingly, Cohen interprets history, not as a political project of states, but as a social work project of all individuals. By means of contractual relations that lie at the heart of the theory of right according to Cohen, it is possible "to justly bind human workers to the ends of economic and social intercourse" (Cohen 1910: 505). This global contractual approach to history contrasts sharply with Dilthey's understanding of history which roots mutual human respect in feelings of solidarity and sympathy. While recognizing the importance that legal institutions play in channeling and transforming emotional bonds and in resolving human conflicts, Dilthey located such institutions in the medium of objective spirit, which remains centered in regional communities. No universal contractual relations can do justice to the complexity of the communal and cultural aspects of history. Nevertheless, legal theory should in principle be considered to shed light on the problem of legitimating interpretations.

Cassirer provides a more nuanced approach to history than his teacher Cohen. In the *Logic of the Humanities* (1942), Cassirer reflects on what it is that makes the historian Jacob Burckhardt's ideal type of a Renaissance man illuminating. It effectively coordinates some basic aspects of what was distinctive of the Italian Renaissance. Cassirer calls it a coordinative culture-concept that aims at the meaning of some particular region or period. It differs from nature-concepts that subordinate phenomena to universal laws. The ideal Renaissance man "is characterized by his delight in the senses ... his receptivity to the world of form, his individualism, his paganism, his amoralism" (Cassirer 1961: 137). Although it is admitted that no single historical person has been found who actually unites in himself all the traits mentioned by Burckhardt, Cassirer regards it as an important culture-concept.

In chapter 4 of the *Logic of the Humanities*, Cassirer locates this kind of concept formation as part of a hermeneutic. He acknowledges that:

> before we can write a cultural history ... we must have an overall view of the *achievements* of language, art and religion. ... It is necessary that we penetrate their *sense*; we must understand what it has to say to us. This understanding possesses its own method of interpretation (*Deutung*); an autonomous, most difficult and complex "hermeneutic."
>
> (Cassirer 1961: 173)

But for Cassirer this hermeneutic of cultural achievements only fulfills one of the tasks of the human or cultural sciences. Hermeneutics does not have the encompassing task that Dilthey assigned it. Because Cassirer geared hermeneutics to his ideal type cultural concepts, he regards it as an important but preliminary stage of analyzing *significance* that is to be followed by two more stages: the *analysis of form* and the *analysis of process*. The hermeneutics that analyzes the significance of human achievements must first be clarified by an analysis of their "basic forms" and "fixed orderings" (Cassirer 1961: 173). These are summed up in what Cassirer calls various "symbolic forms." Each of these cultural symbolic forms, whether it is mythical, linguistic, religious, or artistic, represents a systematic way of understanding the world. Each symbolic form is supposed to articulate a universal or ideal cultural function that goes beyond historical interpretation. This philosophical *formal analysis* can in turn be followed by a final stage of *process analysis* that attempts to find causal explanations for these cultural achievements. This seems to accord with the general Weberian postulate that some analytic philosophers such as Georg Henrik von Wright have accepted, namely, that understanding merely prepares the ground for explanation. But if we look closer, we see that Cassirer introduces cautions on this score. He points out that many attempts at explaining human language misconceive the sentential form as a mere aggregate of words that can be explained physiologically in terms of the utterance of sounds. The sentential function can only be understood through an analysis of the symbolic form of language. Symbolic forms are basic or irreducible phenomena (*Urphänomene*) that cannot be causally explained. Causal explanations can only be found for how aspects of human language acquisition come to be realized in time within the linguistic symbolic form.

Cassirer's limits on the role of causal explanation in the human and cultural sciences end up putting him closer to Dilthey's hermeneutical standpoint than is generally thought. It is often believed that Dilthey defined the human sciences purely in terms of the tasks of description, understanding, and interpretation, reserving explanation for the natural sciences. But in fact he claimed that the initial connectedness of the lived experience of ourselves and our relations to others allows us to describe a continuum that provides a holistic nexus of understanding that can be supplemented with explanations. But these will be explanations of detail like those that Cassirer argued for when discussing process analysis.

It is important to underscore that for Dilthey understanding in the human and cultural sciences is not a preliminary stage of awareness that is to be superseded by explanation. Explanations about human history and culture should always remain framed by reflective understanding, whose function is to define the appropriate meaning contexts for assessing them. Whereas Cassirer turns to a fixed set of overarching symbolic forms to frame the hermeneutics of culture, Dilthey thinks we should be open to introducing new systematic contexts that can bring history and culture into focus. The human sciences have the formative task of articulating organizational structures like the system of Roman jurisprudence discussed earlier. There are in principle many such institutional and functional systems that come about to organize the religious, cultural, intellectual, social, and economic life of human beings for periods of time. Dilthey considers these the productive organizational systems that converge on human life and shape its outcome. Hermeneutics has the task of negotiating among the distinctive discourses that serve to analyze the workings of these developing systems.

Bibliography

Cassirer, E. (1961) *The Logic of the Humanities*, trans. C.S. Howe, New Haven: Yale University Press.

Cohen, H. (1910) *Kants Begründung der Ethik: Nebst ihren Anwendungen auf Recht, Religion und Geschichte*, Berlin: Bruno Cassirer.

Dilthey, W. (1989) *Introduction to the Human Sciences, Selected Works*, vol. 1, eds. R. A. Makkreel and F. Rodi, Princeton: Princeton University Press.

——(1996) *Hermeneutics and the Study of History, Selected Works*, vol. 4, eds. R. A. Makkreel and F. Rodi, Princeton: Princeton University Press.

——(2002) *The Formation of the Historical World in the Human Sciences, Selected Works*, vol. 3, eds. R. A. Makkreel and F. Rodi, Princeton: Princeton University Press.

——(2010) *Understanding the Human World, Selected Works*, vol. 2, eds. R. A. Makkreel and F. Rodi, Princeton: Princeton University Press.

Rickert, H. (1962) *Science and History, A Critique of Positivist Epistemology*, trans. G. Reisman, Princeton: Van Nostrandt Co.

Windelband, W. (1924) "Geschichte und Naturwissenschaft," in *Präludien*, vol. 2, Tübingen: J.C.B. Mohr.

Further reading

Makkreel, R. (1992) *Dilthey, Philosopher of the Human Studies*, Princeton: Princeton University Press. (A comprehensive treatment of Dilthey's philosophy that more fully examines its response to the Kantian tradition and its relation to Husserl, Heidegger, and Gadamer.)

Mul, J. de (2004) *The Tragedy of Finitude: Dilthey's Hermeneutics of Life*, trans. T. Burrett, New Haven, CT: Yale University Press. (A detailed and lucid examination of Dilthey's philosophy that stresses the contingency of human life and its interpretive challenges.)

Wright, G. H. von (1971) *Explanation and Understanding*, Ithaca: Cornell University Press. (An attempt to conceive the understanding of human agency as a form of teleological explanation.)

7

NIETZSCHE AND THE UBIQUITY OF HERMENEUTICS

Babette Babich

Hermeneutics and interpretation in Nietzsche

To understand Nietzsche in the context of hermeneutics is to understand not only Nietzsche's philosophy of interpretation (Figl 1982a, 1984) but his perspective on perspective (Cox 1997) or "perspectivalism" (Babich 1994: 116f). In turn, given his background familiarity with hermeneutic methodology, this also corresponds to Nietzsche's own approach as an interpreter of texts and antiquity as of the life, culture, and history of ancient Greece (see the range of contributions to Jensen and Heit 2014 as well as Ugolini 2003; Figl 1984; and Pöschl 1979). And to do this, just to the extent that Nietzsche specifically reflects on interpretation as such, entails a hermeneutics of hermeneutics.

In this connection, although not otherwise concerned with hermeneutics, the analytically minded Hegel and Nietzsche scholar, Richard Schacht begins his reflections on "Nietzsche on Philosophy, Interpretation and Truth" by pointing out that not only would Nietzsche seemingly "reduce" all philosophy to the level of interpretation and hence merely *derivative* activity (here it is important to note that the defining claims about which the analytic-continental division continue to swirl have to do with anxieties regarding interpretation and influence as opposed to supposed or pretended "originality") but Nietzsche seems to characterize "his own philosophical activity as interpretive, even though this would appear to place his own position on a par with those he rejects and brands as 'lies,' 'errors,' and 'fictions'" (Schacht 1984: 75). As Nietzsche reflects: "Granted this too is only interpretation – and you will be eager enough to raise this objection? – well, so much the better" (Nietzsche 1973: 34). Very few of Nietzsche's predictions regarding the reception of his own work have had the same impact and analytic philosophers have been worriedly objecting to and thereby interpreting the same point for decades now.

But invoking Nietzsche's hermeneutics of hermeneutics remains elusive despite its obviousness. This may be due to the absence of the word hermeneutics, as Nietzsche does not focus specifically on the term itself but speaks in the broader conventional framework of the nineteenth century analyzing of the methods of philology (see Benne 2006; Babich 2010) and the terms Nietzsche uses include *interpretation, explication, exposition, explanation, poetizing*, and so on. Thus Nietzsche does not do anything so comfortably convenient for today's scholarship on hermeneutics as his predecessor Friedrich Schleiermacher (whom Nietzsche otherwise cites in connection with classical texts/theology, but for a discussion of Schleiermacher himself, see Hamacher 1990b). Defining hermeneutics as the "art of understanding," Schleiermacher carefully defers a complete or what he names a "perfect" definition of a "general hermeneutics" (Schleiermacher 1994: 73), speaking of a general hermeneutics a bit in the spirit of the fragment known as the "Oldest System Program." Now the authorship of this fragment continues to be disputed and this is to Nietzsche's mind the real meaning of a hermeneutic challenge, with claims of authorship for Hölderlin (of whom it would be convenient for philosophy to have him as its author and which attribution works very well simply because the text is included in an influential translation of his prose writings in English: Hölderlin 1988, where simply reading that citation here in the text seemingly settles the attribution) or Hegel in whose handwriting the text happened to have been written (and for which case, although Hegel is in no need of it to assure his philosophical credentials, the Hegelian Otto Pöggeler has argued very precisely – see Pöggeler 1965) or Schelling (it was certainly published for the first time in Schelling's name by Franz Rosenzweig in 1917; see also, Gordon 2005: 126) or else some other name history has not otherwise transmitted to us. The "Oldest System Program" is thus both an analogy to Schleiermacher's deferred definition of a "general" hermeneutics and an illustration of the durability of hermeneutic disputes with regard to matters of interpretation: the sheer fact that a text is written in author's own hand does not suffice to make the case for authorship (Hegel) nor indeed does the imprimatur of a publisher (nor yet the editorial attestation by Rosenzweig, a putatively neutral other) nor yet the easy accessibility of a translated conventionality (Pfau).

If Nietzsche by his profession is concerned with such textual points he goes further *as philosopher*, in Arthur Danto's title phrasing (1965) borrowed just a bit from the neo-Kantian expositor of both Kant and Nietzsche, Hans Vaihinger, *Nietzsche als Philosoph* (1902), and to this extent it is essential to speak in Nietzsche's case of the *ubiquity*, as it were, *of hermeneutics*. To invoke Cox's expression, interpretation for Nietzsche "goes all the way down and all the way up" (Cox 1999: 139). Nietzsche thus deploys hermeneutics as part and parcel and even as the motor of his philosophy, claiming that everything is interpretation, by which "everything" Nietzsche means *everything*: and he means the claim in its most logically articulated or consequent sense: to say that everything is interpretation entails that everything is interpreted and, to the extent that Nietzsche speaks against the fiction of the subject as a phantom of grammar (Gadamer picks up on just this point), Nietzsche also makes the object ontological claim that *everything* (including the text itself) is an interpreter. In this sense, the world itself, nature, the entire cosmos as such is for Nietzsche hermeneutic through and through.

In this empirically comprehensive and very literal sense, the ubiquity of hermeneutics in Nietzsche's thinking corresponds to the heart of Nietzsche's doctrine of the world "as" will to power. Hence, among the several subtitles Nietzsche gives to his provisional (and never completed) book project, *The Will to Power*, it is no coincidence that a prominent variant is an "attempt at," not, as is more commonly cited (and *pace* both Karl Löwith in an older tradition and Bernard Reginster more recently) "a Revaluation of Values" but "An Attempt at a New Explication [*Auslegung*] of all Events" (Nietzsche 1980: 11, 619; the formula recurs on 629 and again in Vols 12, 19 and 94, etc.). That Nietzsche intends to articulate this "new" schema of explication as literally or fundamentally as possible is manifest in the aphorism sketch immediately detailing the sense of his title with regard to the scientific explanation of nature itself: "The Explication of Nature: we introduce ourselves into it" (Nietzsche 1980: 622), a point Nietzsche was inclined to repeat throughout his work, reflecting on what he calls our tendency to "anthropomorphize nature" (Nietzsche 1980: 12, 16), a point to be considered in connection with his recommendation in his *The Gay Science* that "it will do to consider science as an attempt to humanize things as faithfully as possible" (Nietzsche 1974: 172–73) together with his even more explicit reflection there that "Mathematics is merely the means for general and ultimate knowledge of the human" (Nietzsche 1974: 215, trans. modified). For Nietzsche, the natural scientist is engaged in hermeneutic interpretation, interpreting nature after our own all-too human muster (and what other muster would be available to us?). Nietzsche continues to affirm, as if in the event that his point were not yet clear enough, that we have in all such cases to do with "world-interpretation, not world-explanation" (Nietzsche 1980: 12, 41). The point regarding the distinction Nietzsche repeatedly highlights between interpretation or description as opposed to explanation is important for Nietzsche. As he argues, the world for him, qua "chaos to all eternity" (Nietzsche 1974: 168) and in the most classic sense *chaos* (Babich 2006: 171f), entails that "there is no factual state [*Thatbestand*]." In other words: "everything is fluid, ungraspable, elusive; the most lasting things are just our opinions" (Nietzsche 1980: 12, 100), amounting to a tissue of new interpretations imposed over hardened versions of the same, all of them mere "cyphers" (Nietzsche 1980: 12, 100). Asking "What is the only thing that knowledge can be?" the response for Nietzsche is "Interpretation" (Nietzsche 1980: 104).

As Nietzsche explains:

> whatever exists, having somehow come into being, is again and again reinterpreted to new ends, taken over, transformed, and redirected by some power superior to it; all events in the organic world are a subduing, a becoming master, and all subduing and becoming master involves a new-interpreting, an adaptation through which any previous "meaning" and "purpose" are necessarily obscured or even obliterated.
>
> (Nietzsche 1967b: 77, trans. modified)

Nietzsche's claim for the ubiquity of interpretation recurs in his unpublished notes, restating the point made above that everything interprets and is interpreted in its turn, articulating:

> the world, seen as such and such, experienced, interpreted, such that organic life can sustain itself through this perspective of interpretation. The

human being is *not* only an individual but the ongoing life of organic totality in one specific lineage. In that [the human being] endures, is thereby demonstrated that a species of interpretation (if also always improved) has also come to stand, that the system of interpretation has not changed. "Adaptation" ["*Anpassung*"]

(Nietzsche 1980: 12, 251)

When Alexander Nehamas (1985) raises the question of interpretation as he does in the context of his reading of *Nietzsche: Life as Literature*, he contributes to (and further inspires) a debate on the range of possible interpretations. For analytic scholars in particular the question is a crucial one, although this issue is also a concern for the more metaphysically minded hermeneutic theorist Jean Grondin in his own discussion of Nietzsche and hermeneutics (Grondin 2010; see also Joisten 2004).

What is at stake here is truth and this is regarded as threatened by a range of possibilities (will they be infinite? can they be limited? etc.). Nietzsche himself says of textual interpretation: "The same text supports countless [*unzählige*] interpretations" (Nietzsche 1980: 12, 39). Much of the literature has turned upon the translation of *countless* as *infinite* but Nietzsche's point could not be clearer, as his claim is the careful assertion of interpretive modesty: "there is no 'correct' interpretation" (Nietzsche 1980: 12, 39).

However we read him, from a classically continental or an analytic or even a metaphysically intermediate perspective, Nietzsche is quintessentially a philosopher of interpretation and as such he is a hermeneutic thinker who takes up the task of a specific reflection on interpretation. There is no way to understand Nietzsche's philosophy apart from hermeneutics.

But within hermeneutics one must also have recourse to his thought. Without attending to Nietzsche's influence on the hermeneutic tradition one can risk not only failing to understand Heidegger's contribution to hermeneutics (Gadamer 1975: 228) but also, perhaps predictably given that Heidegger's hermeneutics is explicitly phenomenological (to wit, Heidegger 1988 and 1997), one can miss the growing attention recently paid to Nietzsche and phenomenology.[1]

Thus the scholar does well, in a hermeneutic context, to consider the traditional array of readings considering the relation between Nietzsche and hermeneutics. Here one might for comprehensive scope, focusing on the European context, begin with Hoffman's 1994 study of Nietzsche and the philosophical hermeneutic tradition where, just for the Anglophone reader seeking an overview, Gary Brent Madison's account of Nietzsche's influence on thinkers from Rorty to Derrida and Gadamer remains outstanding (Madison 2001) among a range of other scholarly studies focusing on Nietzsche and hermeneutics.[2]

The hermeneutic issue here is inevitably the problem of interpreting Nietzsche. Thus there is no end of dispute among authors who insist that they have got Nietzsche right (or what is the same, that others have got him wrong) and of course, and from a Nietzschean, as from one or other hermeneutic perspective (and there are many), this should go without saying (Allison 2001). In addition there is the problem already pointed to by noting Gadamer's reference to Nietzsche and Heidegger (and his own particular orientation to hermeneutics and phenomenology),

Dilthey's hermeneutics in addition to Gadamer's own, Ricoeur's hermeneutics, and also Vattimo's, and so on. Hermeneutics itself, as a discipline and like every discipline, requires a hermeneutic.

Understanding understanding in Nietzsche's hermeneutics

For Gadamer, understanding is inevitably understanding *otherwise*: "we understand in a different way if we understand at all" (Gadamer 1975: 264). Thus Gadamer articulates a Heideggerian recuperation of the creative impetus in Schleiermacher's own emphases upon the interpretive project of reading another: "understanding is not merely a reproductive, but a productive attitude as well" (Gadamer 1975: 264). Acts of understanding are themselves hermeneutic: creating new meaning in each case. This point recurs in Werner Hamacher's philologically attuned reading of what he calls the hermeneutic imperative between Immanuel Kant's philosophy of practical reason and Nietzsche's interpretive philology. Hamacher's own hermeneutic imperative is drawn from Schleiermacher's definition of hermeneutics, glossed as the "art" of "understanding correctly the speech of another, especially written speech" (Schleiermacher, cited in Hamacher 1990b: 19). In this way, "hermeneutics lives in fact off the collapse of its own project 'since each [soul] is in its individual existence the non-existence of the other' and therefore 'non-understanding refuses to dissolve itself completely'" (Hamacher 1990b: 19).

If Schleiermacher's goal was what he called "complete understanding," that is, to understand "the utterer better than he understands himself" (Schleiermacher 1998: 266), the directionality of this project goes in two directions inasmuch as it assumes that the original speaker (or author) may not understand everything that comes to expression in what is said. Here the full force of Gadamer's point becomes clear: understanding is not identical with what is understood, it does not simply reproduce it but comprehends the prior context for the original speaker's own understanding of what is said while at the same time anticipating and exceeding the one who interprets understandingly.

Ernst Behler, the Schlegel scholar and theorist of specifically literary hermeneutics offers a reflection between Nietzsche and Jacques Derrida (and Gilles Deleuze and thereby Heidegger). For Behler, Nietzsche's explicitly masked writing should compel our attention, as Nietzsche himself presents his own work as a "self-dissembling writing, groundless thought ... that brings all apodictic statements into question through the consideration of new possibilities" (Behler 1991: 20). Nietzsche's own esotericism remains elusive not only because one must come to terms with Nietzsche's reflections on the prime authors of political and philosophic esotericism and its tactics, namely Machiavelli and Descartes, including Catholicism (Nietzsche invokes the Jesuits) and Swiss Protestantism (Calvinism) as well as the preludes to political philosophy already at work in Nietzsche's classical philology, raising the complicated question of Nietzsche's Hellenism before turning to Nietzsche's reflections on truth and lie.

The ubiquity of hermeneutics begins at the outset with Nietzsche's own reading of Anaximander in his *Philosophy in the Tragic Age of the Greeks*. Writing as the first

Greek philosopher, Anaximander who was able to discern "in the multiplicity of things that have come-to-be a sum of injustices that must be atoned for, he grasped with bold fingers the tangle of the profoundest problem in ethics" (Nietzsche 1971: 48).

Philippe Lacoue-Labarthe's politico-historically modulated reflections on Nietzsche's *Untimely Meditations* on history are connected with "mimesis," that is, the hermeneutic effort to understand those who are historical and those who are not (let us take care to highlight, as Nietzsche reminds us, that the Greeks themselves are not "historical"). For Lacoue-Labarthe, "everything in fact is a problem of birth, that is to say of origin" (Lacoue-Labarthe 1990: 223).

But what are the origins of philosophy? How can we speak of a tradition that itself grows out of what is spoken (and is therefore eternally lost to us) and is steeped in a reflection (this is the force of Plato's *Phaedrus* as of his *Seventh Letter*) on that orality?[3] Far beyond scholarly debates on esoteric matters of the hermeneutics of antiquity (from Nietzsche himself to Ong and Illich) and the post-modern quivering of digital networks and the coded ideal of the imaginary hacker (Kittler) there is also the ontic fact of facticity, as the classicist Nietzsche always emphasized this. Thus as Kittler reminds us, citing Goethe's *Wilhelm Meisters Wanderjahre!*, "'Literature,' Goethe wrote, 'is the fragment of fragments; the least of what had happened and of what had been spoken was written down; of what had been written down, only the smallest fraction was preserved'" (Kittler 1987: 105). Inevitably, we know of the past no more than what has come down to us where the determination of that transmission is already a problem (see again the contributions to Jensen and Heit) whereby the parsing and evaluation of all such transmission is itself a matter of interpretation: hermeneutics and context.

Hermeneutics and the leavings of the past

Like Goethe cited above on the fragments of literature, the classicist philosopher, Frances MacDonald Cornford in his 1935 Oxford lecture, "The Unwritten Philosophy," emphasized the yet more literal fragmentary condition of philology inasmuch as:

> the literature, the history, the philosophy, we have inherited from the ancient world bear much the same relation to the total product in those fields that the contents of the Ashmolean bear to the cities and temples, theatres and houses, that once formed the complete and familiar scene of ancient life.
>
> (Cornford 1967: 28)

Catherine Osborne (1987) has reprised the force of the point Cornford makes regarding the circumspection required to approach the text *fragments* we happen to have. It has taken Pierre Hadot and Marcel Detienne (popularized for generalist theorists by Michel Foucault) for today's scholars to begin to understand Cornford's point, as indeed Osborne's point, which unfortunately does not mean that we shall all be going forth to deploy philology as Nietzsche recommended. Cornford's analogy as we cited it highlights the advantage of archeology as the physical happenstance for the bits we do have, the ruins of the past. The "monumental" point of the analogy, to use Nietzsche's terminology, contrasts Nietzsche's "antiquarian" philology with the "few potsherds" from which an expert can reconstitute an entire "krater of Euphronius" (Cornford 1967: 29). Today Cornford's example has a more dramatic illustration in the wake of the "monumental" 1962 discoveries in a complex of tombs at Derveni, including the Derveni Papyrus and the Derveni Krater (a volute krater, featuring glorious repoussé Dionysiac designs crafted in heretofore unknown bronze alloy). Down to its material constitution, the Derveni Krater remains a mystery, featuring maenads, satyrs, and a monosandalic figure (be it Pentheus or Jason as classically supposed or even, as I imagine, Empedocles) and with all its picture-book obviousness did not simplify the interpretation of the charred scroll, debates about which continue. Significantly, Anton Fackelmann, a papyrology librarian at the Vienna National Library who first unrolled the Derveni Papyrus managed to do so using an ingenious technique using plant fluids freshly crushed from living papyrus plants to reconstitute the carbonized substance of the text itself, literally offering "blood" to the vanished ghosts of the past (Fackelmann 1970, and see too Babich 2013b: 235). We do well to be mindful of the effects of such rehabilitations of the past, whereby in the interim, since Nietzsche's and Cornford's warnings if certainly not *because* of them, scholars otherwise decry the damage done by nineteenth and twentieth century reconstructions.

Nietzsche, who mixed his own metaphors of monumental and antiquarian philology, laments in his early philological *Nachlass* that "we stand in a field of shards" (cited in Babich 2006: 47). Not only have we only fragments, as Cornford and Osborne also emphasize and as dramatically illustrated by the task of reconstituting and then reconstructing so recent a find as the Derveni papyrus, of the bits we have, there is almost nothing that has not been "altered" (Nietzsche thought *damaged*) by the efforts of the same experts who create the "facts" of the past: "antiquity disintegrates under the hands of the philologists!" (Nietzsche 1980, 7: 353). But if Nietzsche began his career with a call for renewed hermeneutic solicitude in his own field and if in the 1970s this would at last inspire William Arrowsmith to feature Nietzsche's remonstrations to his fellow classicists in the journal *Arion*, beginning with his own translation of Nietzsche's notes for "We Philologists" (Nietzsche 1973–4), Nietzsche's hermeneutic recommendations, combining Apollonian rigor with Dionysian inspiration, could not describe a more difficult task. Despite Arrowsmith's efforts, scholarship has preferred the grey security of a Wilamowitz to the gaiety and light feet of a Nietzsche. The dancing philology Nietzsche recommended was, if anything, more arduous than the mechanical tread of the alternative path in the field of classics.

Like Heidegger, who arguably inspired today's philosophical (as opposed to theological or juridical) approach to hermeneutics with his 1927 *Being and Time*, we too may recall Leopold von Ranke's oft cited dictum "*wie es eigentlich gewesen.*" Read in context, Ranke articulates a methodologically reticent restriction, claiming less rather than more for his own project as he sought to contrast his efforts with the lofty ideals traditionally expected of history: "To history has been assigned the office of judging the past, of instructing the present for the benefit of future ages. To such high offices this work does not aspire: It wants only to show what actually happened (*wie es eingentlich gewesen*)" (Ranke 1824: vi). Ranke's modesty coheres with Nietzsche's critique of what he called the "educational institutions" of his own day and the same ideal of *Paideia* that would continue in classics and in history into our own times. Hence if Nietzsche emphasized, beginning with his own inaugural lecture at Basel, that it is common to pronounce a classical education indispensable for a civilized citizenry, the conviction tends to be undermined by the typically deficient character of that education: just how much culture does a citizen need in order to be an ideal citizen? In his *Daybreak*, Nietzsche proposes that we "point to the finest teachers at our grammar schools," and laugh at them, inviting us to make this question our own question in every case:

> are they the products of formal education? And if not, how can they teach it? And the classics! Did we learn anything of that which these same ancients taught their young people? Did we learn to speak or write as they did? Did we practice unceasingly the fencing-art of conversation, dialectics? Did we learn to move as beautifully and proudly as they did, to write, to throw, to box as they did? Did we learn anything of the asceticism practiced by all Greek philosophers? Were we trained in a single one of the antique virtues and in the manner in which the ancients practiced it? ... Did we learn even the ancient languages in the way we learn those of living nations – namely so as to speak them with ease and fluency? Not one real piece of ability, of new capacity out of years of effort!
>
> (Nietzsche 1982: 115–16)

Nietzsche's question here is even more timely in our era of austerity as this goes hand in glove with the wholesale redesigning of the university and the re-definition of philosophy as handmaiden to the natural sciences and no more.

If, historically, contextually, hermeneutically speaking, "the past is a foreign country," it is a country overrun not with tourists but colonialist archaeologists, each staking a particular national claim (thus French archaeology – and you know this if you have perhaps been to Delphi – differs from the German version with its concerns that likewise vary from the British, and nor are today's Greeks excluded from such scholarly imperialism). But where both Cornford and Nietzsche (Nietzsche here being the good student of the archaeological philologist Otto Jahn, as well as influenced by Semper, and other experts of the object remainders or ruins of the past) would have argued that while physical detritus gives us an abundance of information by comparison, the fragment that is the text, even a new text, tells us almost nothing.

We have already recalled Cornford's "The Unwritten Philosophy" and Platonists, especially of the Straussian kind, have borrowed the title of his lecture for their own, and Cornford's emphasis likewise resonates in Hans Joachim Krämer's reflections, *Plato and the Foundations of Metaphysics*.[4] However we need more than a reference to the Tübingen school or to Strauss in order to comprehend Nietzsche's notion of the esoteric. For that one must go back before such modern precipitates of a tradition shrouded in the metaphors of the obscure. John Hamilton (2003) approaches this without – this may be inevitable – framing the problem adequately and it goes without saying that he does not resolve it.

Nietzsche was enduringly concerned with the archaeology of knowledge of his own discipline, the "monumental" as opposed to the "antiquarian" legacies of traditional philology and both contra the "critical" philology he advocated for his own part. In the Alexandrian tradition, that is, the "antiquarian" legacy of scholarship to the current day, the past is inexorably translated into the present on the terms of the present. Pernicious for Nietzsche is the lack of any kind of self-awareness in this project, let alone self-doubt. Thus Nietzsche compares such Alexandrianism to the Romans as they appropriated their Etruscans (and their Greeks): "How deliberately and recklessly they brushed the dust off the wings of the butterfly that is called moment" (Nietzsche 1974. 137). Notoriously, in the case of the Romans, "Not only did one omit what was historical: one also added allusions to the present and above all, struck out the name of the poet and replaced it with one's own" (Nietzsche 1974: 137). Here, Nietzsche laments the danger to scholarship that is scholarship itself. Thus almost in Ranke's sense we read Nietzsche as he expresses the then-standard view, a perspective on scholarship that has not changed to this day: "Ought we not make new for ourselves what is old and find ourselves in it? Should we not have the right to breathe our own soul into this dead body?" (Nietzsche 1974: 137, trans. modified).

Nietzsche and hermeneutics today

Confounding the word-fetishism that is the consequence of today's digital scholarship – less reading than skimming and scanning or googling search results and then cobbling the results together as "scholarship" – Nietzsche uses the word "hermeneutic" rarely, and only in connection with critique and textual interpretation (specifically with reference to Schleiermacher's own usage and thus to Plato and religious texts). But Nietzsche articulated a hermeneutic or critically interpretive approach to texts as indeed to the discipline of classical philology, history as well as culture and politics, extending his interpretive approach to religion, not merely the received interpretation of the scriptural tradition of his day but beginning with his study of the religious service of the Greeks, including the tragic rites. Thus Nietzsche's *Untimely Meditations* begins with a critique of the methods of the modernist theologian, David Strauss, as well as a hermeneutic reflection on historical approaches for life as he expressed it in this same locus as well as institutional reflections on Schopenhauer as educator and so on. Nietzsche went on to write *Human, all too Human* in which he extended his hermeneutics of ancient and modern culture beyond religion to art, and philosophy and science, high and low culture, interpersonal or social interaction in addition to politics and a sustained reflection on the self (his later added volumes would be expanded with aphorisms on the same themes, specifically foregrounding cultural ones related to the arts but also interpretive reflections on first and final themes, life and death, with a final book entitled *The Wanderer and his Shadow*.) These reflections continued in *Daybreak* and *The Gay Science*, and, in a different voice, in his *Thus Spoke Zarathustra*, where he advances his doctrines of the world as will to power, the overhuman, and the eternal return of the self-same (for an interpretation of the reference to the wanderer and his shadow, eternal recurrence and death in Nietzsche's *Thus Spoke Zarathustra*, see Babich 2010 and 2013b; Loeb (2012) also foregrounds Nietzsche's classically mortal reflections).

And as to the wide range of his hermeneutic concerns, Nietzsche's non-traditional hermeneutics of logic and science remains a stumbling block (Babich 2010), as he writes that "natural philosophy is only a world-exposition and world-arrangement (according to us, if I may say so!) and *not* a world-explanation" (Nietzsche 1973: 27). A few aphorisms later, Nietzsche singles out physicists among other natural philosophers (or scientists) by taking them to task for their lack of philological or interpretive expertise, a deficient hermeneutic sense which Nietzsche challenged with methodological precision:

> Let me be pardoned, as an old philologist who cannot desist from the mischief of putting his finger on bad modes of interpretation, but "Nature's conformity to law," of which you physicists talk so proudly, as though – why, it exists only owing to your interpretation and bad "philology."
>
> (Nietzsche 1973: 34)

In this, the hermeneutic failure in question is neither to be parsed as interpretation for Nietzsche qua textual explication or articulation but, so he argues, qua attuned to the history of natural observation as to the textuality of theoretical accounts of "nature's conformity to law." Conforming to the high road of science, *philology* is hermeneutics in its most rigorous modality. Thus the Nietzsche who began his inaugural lecture in Basel by inverting Seneca at his conclusion, urging that philology *become* philosophy, would come as his thinking evolved to speak more and more of a "lack" of philology (*ein Mangel an Philologie*) (Nietzsche 1973: 59): a lack of hermeneutics. Only by keeping hermeneutics in the equation can we begin to understand ourselves as creative interpreters, as Nietzsche would say: the poets of our lives.

Notes

1 See the contributions to Boubil and Daigle 2013 and Rehberg 2011, including Rudolf Boehme's classic account of Nietzsche and Husserl (Boehme 1968, 1962), see also Babich 2013.

2 See Benne 2005, 2006; Figal 2000; Figl 1982b, 1984; Riedel 2001; as well as Schrift 1990; Bertman 1973; and many, many others.

3 See here the reflections of Walter J. Ong 1982 as well as Ivan Illich 1996 and Friedrich Kittler 1990

4 For a contextualization, see Nikulin 2012 and see Drury 1985 for the Straussian esoteric and for the Straussian convention of 'left' Nietzscheans – the reference here links Max Weber and Tracy Strong, see MacIntyre 1981; for "right" Nietzscheans, see Levine 1995 and Lambert 1997; for Strauss and hermeneutics, Cantor 1991.

Bibliography

Allison, David (2001) *Reading the New Nietzsche*. Lanham, MD: Rowman & Littlefield.

Babich, Babette (2014) "The Aesthetics of the Between: On Beauty and Artbooks – Museums and Artists." *Culture, Theory, Critique* 55, Iss. 1 (March): 1–28.

——(2013a) "Nietzsche's Performative Phenomenology: Philology and Music" in Élodie Boubil and Christine Daigle (eds.) *Nietzsche and Phenomenology: Power, Life, Subjectivity.* Bloomington: Indiana University Press. 117–40.

——(2013b) "Nietzsche's Zarathustra, Nietzsche's Empedocles: The Time of Kings" in Horst Hutter and Eli Friedlander (eds.) *Nietzsche's Therapeutic Teaching: For Individuals and Culture.* London: Continuum. 157–74.

——(2011) "Artisten Metaphysik und Welt-Spiel in Fink and Nietzsche" in Cathrin Nielsen and Hans Rainer Sepp (eds.) *Welt denken. Annäherung an die Kosmologie Eugen Finks.* Freiburg im Briesgau: Alber. 57–88.

——(2010) "Towards a Critical Philosophy of Science: Continental Beginnings and Bugbears, Whigs and Waterbears." *International Journal of the Philosophy of Science.* 24, No. 4 (December): 343–91.

——(2009) "'A Philosophical Shock': Foucault's Reading of Heidegger and Nietzsche" in Carlos G. Prado (ed.) *Foucault's Legacy.* London: Continuum. 19–41.

——(2006) *Words in Blood, Like Flowers: Philosophy and Poetry, Music and Eros in Hölderlin, Nietzsche, and Heidegger.* Albany: State University of New York Press.

——(1994) *Nietzsche's Philosophy of Science: Reflecting Science on the Ground of Art and Life.* Albany: State University of New York Press.

Behler, Ernst (1991) *Confrontations: Derrida/Heidegger/Nietzsche.* Steven Taubeneck (trans.) Stanford: Stanford University Press.

——(1983) "Ansätze zu einer literarischen Hermeneutik bei Friedrich Nietzsche" in Benjamin Bennett, Anton Kaes, and William J. Lillyman (eds.) *Probleme der Moderne: Studien zur deutschen Literatur von Nietzsche bis Brecht: Festschrift für Walter Sokel.* Tübingen: Neske. 15–32.

Benne, C. (2005) *Nietzsche und die historisch-kritische Philologie.* Berlin: de Gruyter.

——(2006) "Methodische Aspekte der Philologie im Denken Nietzsches" in Michael Knoche, Justus H. Ulbricht, and Jürgen Weber (eds.) *Zur unterirdischen Wirkung von Dynamit: vom Umgang Nietzsches mit Büchern.* Wiesbaden: Otto Harrassowitz Verlag. 15–33.

Bertman, Martin (1973) "Hermeneutic in Nietzsche." *Journal of Value Inquiry* 7: 254–60.

Boehme, Rudolf (1968) "Husserl und Nietzsche" in Boehme: *Vom Gesichtspunkt der Phänomenologie* (The Hague: Nijhoff), 217–37.

——(1962) "Deux points de vue: Husserl et Nietzsche." *Archivo di Filosofia* 3: 167–81.

Boubil, Élodie and Christine Daigle (eds.) (2013) *Nietzsche and Phenomenology: Power, Life, Subjectivity.* Bloomington: Indiana University Press.

Cantor, Paul A. (1991) "Leo Strauss and Contemporary Hermeneutics" in Alan Udoff (ed.) *Leo Strauss's Thought: Toward a Critical Engagement.* Boulder, CO: Lynne Rienner, 267–314.

Cox, Christoph (1999) *Nietzsche. Naturalism and Interpretation.* Berkeley: University of California Press.

——(1997) "The 'Subject' of Nietzsche's Perspectivism." *Journal of the History of Philosophy* 35, No. 2 (April): 269–329.

Cornford, Frances Macdonald (1967) *The Unwritten Philosophy and Other Essays.* Cambridge: Cambridge University Press.

Danto, Arthur (1965) *Nietzsche as Philosopher.* New York: Columbia University Press.

Drury, Shadia (1985) "The Esoteric Philosophy of Leo Strauss." *Political Theory* 13, No. 3 (August): 315–37.

Fackelmann, Anton (1970) "The Restoration of the Herculaneum Papyri and other Recent Finds." *Bulletin of the Institute of Classical Studies* 17, Iss. 1 (December): 144–47.

Figal, Günter (2000) "Nietzsches Philosophie der Interpretation." *Nietzsche-Studien* 29: 1–11.

Figl, Johann (1982a) *Interpretation als philosophisches Prinzip. Friedrich Nietzsches universale Theorie der Auslegung im späten Nachlass.* Berlin: Walter de Gruyter.

——(1982b) "Nietzsche und die philosophische Hermeneutik des 20. Jahrhunderts: mit besonderer Berücksichtigung Diltheys, Heideggers und Gadamers." *Nietzsche-Studien* 10/11: 408–30.

——(1984) "Hermeneutische Voraussetzungen der philologischen Kritik." *Nietzsche-Studien* 13: 111–28.

Gadamer, Hans-Georg (1975) *Truth and Method.* Garrett Barden (trans.) New York: Continuum.

——(1976) "The Universality of the Hermeneutic Problem (1966)" in: Gadamer, *Philosophical Hermeneutics*, David E. Linge (trans.) Berkeley: University of California Press. 3–17.

Gordon, Peter Eli (2005) *Rosenzweig and Heidegger: Between Judaism and German Philosophy.* Berkeley: University of California Press.

Grondin, Jean (2010) "Must Nietzsche be Incorporated into Hermeneutics? Some Reasons for a Little Resistance." *IRIS European Journal of Philosophy and Public Debate* (April): 105–22.

Hamacher, Werner (1990a) "The Promise of Interpretation: Reflections on the Hermeneutical Imperative in Kant and Nietzsche" in L. A. Rickels (ed.) *Looking after Nietzsche.* Albany: State University of New York Press. 19–48.

——(1990b) "Hermeneutical Ellipses: Writing the Hermeneutical Circle in Schleiermacher" in G. L. Ormiston and A. D. Schrift (eds.) *Transforming the Hermeneutic Context: From Nietzsche to Nancy.* Albany: State University of New York Press. 177–210.

Hamilton, John (2003) *Soliciting Darkness: Pindar, Obscurity, and the Classical Tradition.* Cambridge, MA: Harvard University Press.

Heidegger, Martin (1988) *Ontology – The Hermeneutics of Facticity.* John van Buren (trans.) Bloomington: Indiana University Press.

——(1997) *The Phenomenological Interpretation of Kant's Critique of Pure Reason.* Parvis Emad and Kenneth Maly (trans.) Bloomington: Indiana University Press.

Hoffman, Johann Nepomuk (1994) *Wahrheit, Perspektive, Interpretation: Nietzsche und die philosophische Hermeneutik.* Berlin: de Gruyter.

Hölderlin, Friedrich (1988) *Essays and Letters on Theory.* Thomas Pfau (trans.) Albany: State University of New York Press.

Illich, Ivan (1996) *In the Vineyard of the Text.* Chicago: University of Chicago Press.

Jensen, A. K. and H. Heit (eds.) (2014) *Nietzsche as a Scholar of Antiquity.* London: Bloomsbury.

Joisten, Karen (2004) "Wieviel Nietzsche verträgt der Interpret? oder Der Weg vom Verstehen über das Verstehen hinaus" in Volker Gerhardt and Renate Reschke (eds.) *Nietzscheforschung Bd. 11. Antike und Romantik bei Nietzsche.* Berlin: Akademie Verlag. 193–202.

Kittler, Friedrich (1990) *Discourse Networks 1800/1900.* Michael Metteer and Chris Cullens (trans.) Stanford: Stanford University Press.

——(1987) "Gramophone, Film, Typewriter." Dorothea von Mücke and Philippe L. Similon (trans.) *October* 41 (Summer): 101–18.

Krämer, Hans Joachim (1990) *Plato and the Foundations of Metaphysics: A Work on the Theory of the Principles and Unwritten Doctrines of Plato with a Collection of the Fundamental Documents.* Albany: State University of New York Press.

Lacoue-Labarthe, Philippe (1990) "History and Mimesis" in L. A. Rickels (ed.) *Looking after Nietzsche.* Albany: State University of New York Press. 209–31.

Lambert, Lawrence (1997) *Leo Strauss and Nietzsche.* Chicago: University of Chicago Press.

Levine, Peter (1995) *Nietzsche and the Modern Crisis of the Humanities.* Albany: State University of New York Press.

Loeb, Paul (2012) *Death of Nietzsche's Zarathustra.* Cambridge: Cambridge University Press.

MacIntyre, Alasdair (1981) *After Virtue.* Notre Dame, IN: University of Notre Dame Press.

Madison, Gary Brent (2001) "Coping with Nietzsche's Legacy: Rorty, Derrida, Gadamer" in: Madison, *The Politics of Postmodernity: Essays in Applied Hermeneutics*. Dordrecht: Springer. 13–36.

Nehamas, Alexander (1985) *Life as Literature*. Cambridge, MA: Harvard University Press.

Nietzsche, Friedrich (1986) *Human, all too Human: A Book for Free Spirits*. R. J. Hollingdale (trans.) Cambridge: Cambridge University Press.

——(1982) *Daybreak: Thoughts on the Prejudices of Morality*. R. J. Hollingdale (trans.) Cambridge: Cambridge University Press.

——(1980) *Kritische Studienausgabe*. G. Colli and M. Montinari (eds.) Berlin: de Gruyter.

(1974) *The Gay Science* W. Kaufmann (trans.) New York: Vintage.

——(1973–4) "Notes for 'We Philologists'." W. Arrowsmith (trans.) *Arion*, new ser. 1.2. 279–380.

——(1973) *Beyond Good and Evil*. R. J. Hollingdale (trans.) Harmondsworth: Penguin.

——(1971) *Philosophy in the Tragic Age of the Greeks*. Marianne Cowann (trans.) Chicago: Regnery.

——(1967a) *The Birth of Tragedy*. W. Kaufmann (trans.) New York: Vintage.

——(1967b) *On the Genealogy of Morals*. W. Kaufmann (trans.) New York: Vintage.

Nikulin, Dimitri (ed.) (2012) *The Other Plato: The Tübingen Interpretation of Plato's Inner-Academic Teachings*. Albany: State University of New York Press.

Ong, Walter J. (1982) *Orality and Literacy: The Technologizing of the Word*. London: Routledge.

Osborne, Catherine (1987) *Rethinking Early Greek Philosophy: Hippolytus of Rome and the Presocratics*. Ithaca, NY: Cornell University Press.

Pöggeler, Otto (1965) "Hegel als Verfasser des aeltesten Systemprogramms" in Georg Gadamer (ed.) *Hegel Tage in Urbino*. Bonn: Bouvier Verlag. 17–32.

Pöschl, Viktor (1979) "Nietzsche und die klassische Philologie" in Hellmut Flashar, Karlfried Gründer, and Axel Horstmann (eds.) *Philologie und Hermeneutik im 19. Jahrhundert: Zur Geschichte und Methodologie der Geisteswissenschaften*, Göttingen: Vandenhoeck und Ruprecht. 141–55.

Ranke, Leopold von (1824) *Geschichten der romanischen und germanischen Völker von 1494 bis 1535*. Leipzig: G. Reimer. Vol. 1.

Rehberg, Andrea (ed.) (2011) *Nietzsche and Phenomenology*. Cambridge: Cambridge Scholar's Press.

Ricoeur, Paul (1970) *Freud & Philosophy: An Essay on Interpretation*. Denis Savage (trans.) New Haven: Yale University Press.

Riedel, Manfred (2001) "Die Erfindung des Philologen: Friedrich August Wolf und Friedrich Nietzsche" in Riedel: *Kunst als "Auslegerin der Natur": Naturästhetik und Hermeneutik in der klassischen deutschen Dichtung und Philosophie*. Cologne: Böhlau. 97–118.

Rosenzweig, Franz (1917) *Das a?lteste Systemprogramm des deutschen Idealismus (von Friedrich Wilhelm Joseph Schelling) in Abschrift von Georg Wilhelm Friedrich Hegel: Ein handschriftlicher Fund*. Heidelberg: Heidelberger Akademie der Wissenschaften.

Schacht, Richard (1984) "Nietzsche on Philosophy, Interpretation and Truth." *Noûs* 18: 75–85.

Schleiermacher, Friedrich (1998) *Hermeneutics and Criticism and Other Writings*. Cambridge: Cambridge University Press.

——(1994) "General Hermeneutics" in Kurt Mueller-Vollmer (ed.) *The Hermeneutics Reader*. New York: Continuum. 73–86.

Schrift, Alan (1990) *Nietzsche and the Question of Interpretation: Between Hermeneutics and Deconstruction*. New York: Routledge.

Ugolini, Gherardo (2003) "'Philologus inter philologos'. Friedrich Nietzsche, die Klassische Philologie und die griechische Tragödie." *Philologus* 147: 316–42.

Vaihinger, Hans (1902) *Nietzsche als Philosoph*. Halle: Reuther & Reichard.

8

BARTH AND BULTMANN: THEOLOGICAL HERMENEUTICS

John E. Wilson

Karl Barth (1886–1968) and Rudolf Bultmann (1884–1976) have been the most influential Protestant hermeneutical theologians of the recent modern period. Barth, of the Swiss Reformed Church, began his teaching in Germany and was a leader in the Confessing Church movement until 1936, when the Nazi government removed him from his academic position. He returned to his native Switzerland and became professor of theology at Basel. Bultmann, a Lutheran, was professor of New Testament at Marburg. He too was a member of the Confessing Church but was able to remain in his position throughout the Nazi period. Barth initiated the new movement of "dialectical theology" with *The Epistle to the Romans* in its second edition of 1922. Bultmann joined the early group of theologians associated with Barth, but within a few years their differences made them theological opponents. Their teachers were largely the same leading figures in the dominant liberal theology and Neo-Kantian philosophy of the time, and for both prominent influences in the development of dialectic theology were Paul, Luther, Kierkegaard and the Basel church historian Franz Overbeck. A major issue during their student years was the method and use of historical criticism. Since the Enlightenment – and especially since D.F. Strauss' *Life of Jesus* (1835) – natural and historical science had questioned the objective validity of supernatural facts in the Bible and hence its religious authority. At the end of the nineteenth century the solution to the problem in liberal theology had been found in thought broadly in the tradition of Schleiermacher: the truth of religion was not in objective facts but subjectively experienced. Theology was most importantly reflection on religious experience as exemplified (or so one thought) in the religious life of Jesus. True understanding of Jesus was to be learned by being drawn through his teaching into his personal relationship with God. The disposition for this relationship was considered inherent in every human being. In the early careers of Barth and Bultmann, Ernst Troeltsch (1865–1923) named this root of religion the "religious a priori," which meant every person's subjective relation to a transcendent "Absolute" whose expressions were the religions of human history

(Troeltsch 1991: 36; Wilson 2007: 140–6). In this way of thinking, religion generally, and by means of value judgments Christianity in particular, could be validated while at the same time a way was provided to avoid dependence on problematic biblical facts and the dogmas that rested on them (Wilson 2007: 123–37). With religion supposedly subjectively secured, historical criticism was free to proceed without hindrance, although it largely produced results in conformity with liberal theology's anthropological point of view. Barth and Bultmann affirmed historical criticism, even as they sharply disagreed about its results. But both disallowed the "Absolute" and the "religious apriori." Such general religious concepts relativized God, making God subject to personal opinion, cultural custom and the changes of human history (Barth 1979: 8; 2004: I/1, 193; Bultmann 1960: 285–8; Robinson 1968: 317–25).

Karl Barth discovered something altogether different: "the strange new world within the Bible" (Barth 1957: 28–50). The dialectic of dialectic theology was essentially about the relationship of God and human being in the New Testament, that is, about God's affirming "Yes" to human being and God's "No" to its sinfulness and brokenness, the extent and depth of which humanity concealed from itself. According to Barth the same concealment was true of theologies that turned Christianity into mere "religion," something accommodated to their own mind and will, and it was typified in the presumptive confidence of both conservative and liberal theologies in the modern period. They failed to see how radical the uncovering of sin in the New Testament was and how much the failure affected concepts of God and faith – a critique Barth poignantly brought to bear on politics and social ethics (Hunsinger 1976). (It has often been pointed out that the rise of dialectic theology coincided with the collapse of an optimistic religious culture in the wake of World War I.) While God was the present and living center of reality, according to Barth no theology and no preaching of any stripe was capable of giving direct expression to God. God absolutely transcended human thought. Language "of" God, instead of abstract talk "about" God, was the prerogative of the Bible, where God miraculously speaks the "No" and the "Yes" in the time and space of the language, life, death and resurrection of Jesus, as witnessed in the New Testament writings. And this Word of God alone "possesses genuine transcendence" (Barth 1957: 62, 186, 199, 206f).

Barth's second edition of *Romans* is the most notable of all the works of dialectic theology. According to this book, "religion" is a subtle manipulation of behavior and thought to secure, not deny, sinful and broken human life (Barth 1933: 236f). God is "wholly other" than any and every humanly reasoned conception of God, and the "wisdom of death" is the wisdom of human limitation, especially in relationship to God. In the same way Kant's limitation of reason was an important concept. According to Barth, religion and metaphysical concepts in religious usage are but clever tools of subjectivist human thinking, such as when one speaks of the "infinite" and actually means only the obverse of the finite, while in truth God is completely other than our human conceptions (1933: 290, 303). Revelation in Christ is not a product of spiritual evolution, but God's own act, "vertical from above" (1933: 30). Apart from the revealed Word, God "speaks" only in eternal silence (1933: 98). Theology can only speak indirectly of God: dialectically, paradoxically, in parables and analogies, ever pointing beyond itself to the truth it cannot definitively and rationally possess. "It is vital that the possibility of an objective knowledge of

God should be wholly eradicated from our minds ... We must not forget that we are speaking in parables" (1933: 220f). "Men are not competent, even if they are gifted with tongues of fire, to speak of God other than in a parable" (1933: 333).

Barth understood himself as an orthodox theologian of the church, as reflected in the title of his definitive work, *Church Dogmatics*, the first volume of which was published in 1932. In the first volume, *The Doctrine of the Word of God*, he writes that the principle of general hermeneutics is to understand what a text is about: the text refers beyond itself to its subject matter. To stray from the text's intent is to miss its meaning altogether. Scripture is human word as witness to revelation, which is God in Christ and Christ's proclamation of the Kingdom of God (Barth 2004: I/2, 465–72, 723–40). Historical criticism in all its forms and in whatever it can bring to light regarding the situation and author of the text are indispensable to attentive listening to the text, but criticism by itself is not attentive listening (Barth 1960: 91). In the hermeneutical "reversal," the critic, who "grips" or masters the text in historical criticism, is "gripped" by the text (Barth 2004: I/2, 470). According to Barth this applies to the serious reading of any text, just as truly hearing a text means recognizing that form and content cannot be separated. In the particularity of biblical hermeneutics, the critic is grasped by the witness to revelation (2004: I/1, 340). According this witness, God is the sole agent of revelation, also in God's encounter with individual persons (2004: II/2, §32ff). It is emphatically God's freedom, not human freedom that is always uppermost in Barth's hermeneutics and in his theology generally. But the effect of God's freedom is human freedom from spiritual and, through social ethics and politics, physical enslavements. And this freedom must be found ever anew as human being is confronted by intellectual, social, economic and political situations that bind it to sinful reality. But God is ever present and working concretely against sinfulness to bring freedom to all of human life, to which Barth's doctrine of the angels eloquently speaks (2004: III/3, 441–520).

The hermeneutic of Barth's *Church Dogmatics* is characterized not only by dialectic but now also by analogy: the similarity within the dissimilarity in the relationship of God and human being (2004: III/2, 324; see also II/1, §27, and III/2, 45f). The change is largely due to dialogue with Catholic theology and signals a new appreciation of metaphysical thought. What was at issue was the question about the correspondence of the God of revelation and human knowledge of God in recognition of God's utter difference from human being. For Barth there can be no "analogy of being" in the relationship of God and human being, so that their beings might in some way share an identity or likeness (2004: II/1, 232, 262). He finds the solution in the biblical doctrine of Christ, the one true "image of God." Only God's creative Word spoken in and as the humanity of Christ, in which God affirms both himself, humanity and the world God has created, establishes similarity between God and humanity within their utter dissimilarity (2004: I/2, 34; III/1, 14, 30). Barth calls this an "analogy of relation" or an "analogy of faith." Christ's humanity is "only indirectly and not directly identical with God," for it "belongs intrinsically to the creaturely world." It reveals God in relation to the reality of the creature in its complete distinction from God (2004: III/2, 219f; II/1, 51–5; cf. I/1, 243f). Indeed, the human person of Christ is chosen by God before creation to "subsist" in the Word of God as the bearer of the revelation of who God is in relation to humanity (2004: II/2, §32f; see Jüngel 2001:

94ff). As God's Word "the humanity of Jesus is … the repetition and reflection of God Himself, no more and no less. It is the image of God." As the creaturely, human image of God and as the New Testament witnesses to him, the person of Christ is the point of reference for all speech about God and for understanding human being as existence before God. In believing and participating in revelation in Christ, the Word of God, the person of faith "corresponds" to God in prayerfully hearing God as "Father" and in speaking in and out of this relationship (2004: III/2, 188, 323; 1960: 52–61). The revelation of God is a miracle that "utterly transcends all our capacity, being and existence" (2004: II/1, 197f). It can only be understood within the miracle of the analogy of human being and human words: first in the humanity of Christ as Word of God and in the New Testament witness to him, then in the confession of the major creeds of the church, in important theologies of the past, and finally in theology's comprehension and proclamation of revelation in the language of contemporary humanity (2004: I/2, 729ff; II/1, 233ff). In Christ resides the truth about God and human being, and, as God is everywhere present and active for the truth, so also all persons exist within the one truth. "True words" are spoken outside the church, words whose truth is measured by the one truth as witnessed by Scripture (2004: IV/3, 110–53).

Although Barth does not speak of them as analogies, he describes the miracles of Jesus in a way similar to the way he describes the analogy of revelation, for here again the rule applies that "God is known only by God" (2004: II/1, 183). The miracles are real events accomplished "with a divine and unconditional freedom, and in this respect they are absolutely sovereign, alien, incomprehensible, and transcendent in relation to all the orders, forms and developments known to men" (2004: IV/2, 219). The miracle of Christ's resurrection "bursts through the framework of historical relation" (2004: III/1, 78f). But it is a real and in some mysterious sense a bodily event; otherwise it would be only a subjective invention of faith. The different stories about the resurrection are not in the form of an historical report but "are couched in the imaginative, poetic style of historical saga." They describe "an event beyond the reach of historical research or depiction" (2004: III/2, 452ff; see also I/1, 327; IV/2, 212–42).

Rudolf Bultmann's hermeneutical thought is expressed mainly in a series of essays that complement and often complete or clarify one another. He is best known for "demythologizing" the New Testament, with which he initiated a wide-ranging theological and philosophical debate (Bartsch 1948ff, 1972). Demythologizing generally means separating form and content, although not in such a way as to dispose of the form; and it is something that is caused first by God's action in history and only secondarily implemented by human acts. In the New Testament the "kerygma" – the Greek word for the proclamation of God's act in Christ – is couched in the form of myth that is now outdated; however myth is not to be eliminated, but interpreted. Myth for Bultmann is specifically the "world-view" or general understanding of the world that early Christians shared with the humanity of antiquity. To use Barth's term, one could say that for Bultmann God "grasps" human language in the kerygma, but not in myth (Jüngel 2001: 24). According to Bultmann myth in the New Testament is the "three story universe" of the ancient world: heaven above, the dark world below, earth in the middle. Powers beyond human understanding and control are depicted as objective supernatural figures: gods, angels and demons, which are in truth only human analogies. The miracle stories of the New Testament are like in kind to other miracles of the ancient world and are also given form by the mythical world-view (Bultmann 1989: 1–43, 95–130; 1958b: 11–21, 60–85). Myths generally are recognizable by their incompatibility with the modern scientific understanding of the world. Where they are objectively believed today, they require a sacrifice of the intellect, a belief that turns a blind eye to scientific explanations. "The course of history has refuted mythology" (1958b: 14; 1987: 247–61). Moreover naïve belief in myths conceals the sinful reality of human life the kerygma addresses. But myths are more than simply mistaken objectifications: they express the awareness that the world and human life "have their ground and their limits in a power which is beyond all that we can calculate or control" (1958b: 19; 1989: 9f, 98). In coping with this power modern humanity has its own means, those of its scientific world-view, which are used to secure imagined mastery of the world and of one's own life, with consequences that contradict the ethics of love in the kerygma. Modern thinking presupposes an observing subject over against and mentally distant from its object; where personal (or group) interest is involved, it involves calculation of advantage or disadvantage. This, according to Bultmann, is something love does not do, but love "cannot be observed by objective methods." With the methods of the modern scientific world-view love is not perceived as love but as a "psychological process" open to different interpretations. Similarly for Bultmann "God cannot be proved objectively," although the attempt is typically modern (1958b: 71f; 1989: 101f, 131–3).

Bultmann's essay, "The Problem of Hermeneutics" (1989: 64–94) begins with the statement that there must be some motivating "life relation" (an expression taken from Wilhelm Dilthey) to a given historical subject matter in order for any interest in it to arise. He names this life relation the historian's "preunderstanding" of the subject matter. The historical interest of preunderstandings can be highly varied; it may, for example, have nothing directly to do with the intention of the text, work of art or artifact it has in mind; and preunderstandings may change in the course of investigations. The problem with preunderstanding is that it is formed in terms of the current world-view, so that its results conform to it. What interests Bultmann most is the encounter in history with as yet unrecognized possibilities that involve one's own existence. When this happens, the historian is no longer a subject in distance from its object but is engaged existentially, and preunderstanding is questioned and transformed. This may be the case in investigations having to do with God, whom one's preunderstanding may recognize in some way as the mystery of the world and hence also of human existence (1989: 87).

During the time in the 1920s when Martin Heidegger wrote *Being and Time* Bultmann and Heidegger conducted seminars together at Marburg. In these seminars theological as well as philosophical texts were read, including the New Testament and especially Paul. Bultmann subsequently wrote that Heidegger's "existential analysis" of the "structures" of human existence was a "profane presentation of the New Testament view of who we are" (1989: 23; Schmithals 1968: 66f). Major concepts that Bultmann shares with *Being and Time* are anxiety and care, world, human existence as the freedom of possibility in the face of certain death, and authentic and inauthentic existence. Inauthentic existence for Bultmann means having one's being as possibility determined not in freedom, but by an already given understanding of human existence in a world-view: human possibility is predetermined by generalized forms of existence that come from the past. While "world" supposedly offers the benefit of a secure understanding of self, this security is actually a kind of bondage, for one's being as possibility is always already decided. Authenticity means to realize one's being in the freedom of possibility. In sharp disagreement with Heidegger however, inauthenticity for Bultmann is the sinfulness addressed in the kerygma, and authenticity means responding freely to God's word of love and ethical responsibility (1958b: 35–44; 1989: 15–23; 1987: 167–71). According to Bultmann, whenever and however one lives in obeisance to "world," one lives, in Paul's phrase, "according to the flesh" and in subjection to the "demonic" powers that hold sway within it – "demonic" now being not mythically but metaphorically understood (1958b: 21, 67f). For Bultmann, in *Being and Time* Heidegger makes the mistake of thinking authenticity means that, based only on oneself, one makes decisions about what one will make of one's freedom of possibility in confronting the nothingness of death and resolving to die. For Bultmann this radical *"Eigenmächtigkeit,"* assertion of one's own ultimate power over oneself, is but another presumption of human sinfulness. (The translator oddly translates "Eigenmächtigkeit" as "highhandedness," 1989: 28 – see the original German, Bartsch 1951: 37.)

Among other kerygmatic formulations of God's decisive act in the New Testament (e.g. in the Gospel of John, 1987: 165–83), Bultmann most appreciates the formulation of the kerygma in Paul. Paul's concept of "flesh" (e.g. Romans 8:13) is especially important. According to Bultmann it refers to the sphere of the visible, available and transient world. When human being makes it the foundation of life by living, in Paul's words, "according to the flesh," the "flesh" becomes a power over human being. This is true whether in the imprudent use of "alluring possibilities" or in the calculation of one's accomplishments in achieving something demonstrable, something with which one could approve of oneself (and disapprove of others). "We put confidence in the flesh" (Philippians 3:3f). The motivation for this is "care" that makes human being anxious to secure its life. But under the power of the "flesh" it loses its life (Bultmann 1989: 16f). Whether in the mythical world-view or in the modern or scientific world-view, human being tries to secure its life in what is objective, visible, available and temporal. Bultmann refers to 2 Corinthians 5:16: Paul no longer knows Christ "according to the flesh."

As the sphere of the visible and available world, the "flesh" is the sphere of objective history (1987: 217; 1951: 238). The distinction is important for the relationship between faith and historical science. If faith depends on what professors produce through objective historical research, it is lost (1987: 30f). In the kerygma the whole meaning of Christ – his person and work ending in God's decisive act in his death and resurrection – is one "eschatological event," the revelation of God and the truth of human being. Most importantly it is a present event in which human being is addressed by God. Where this address is heard, the "flesh" loses its power and the world is recognized wholly anew as God's world. "Like the doctrine of justification by faith, demythologizing destroys every longing for security" (1958b: 80, 84f).

God in Christ forgives the sins of the past, hence liberates from the past, and opens a genuine future free of the need for the security of "world." This can involve intensely meaningful existential experiences, experiences which the mythological world-view in its time projected into objectively factual miracles (1987: 252–9; 1989: 113). The truth of the resurrection of Christ is not that of an incredible objective historical event but that of faith's encounter with God, the grace of new life and the promise of a future beyond death (1951: 45, 349–52; 1989: 36–41; 1957: 152f; Schmithals 1968: 323). In faith's experience of the encounter with God every moment is alive with new possibility, openness to God's future for and with human being (1989: 115ff; 1987: 257ff).

God is for Bultmann non-objective, beyond all theoretical reach of human thought. Yet when the kerygma is heard, God is completely revealed in the living presence of personal encounter (1989: 50). As non-objective God is "hidden" (1958: 61ff; 1987: 252ff), but so also is human being as existential existence, which is the faith dimension of human life, the dimension of conscience and of freedom where God encounters human being, as in the command to love (1987: 136, 211). This also has consequences for theology. Since God cannot be objectively demonstrated, when theology reflects on the encounter with God it necessarily makes God (and itself) objective, and therefore it paradoxically steps outside of faith's direct relationship to God. But it does this only to reflect on the existential meaning of the kerygma, God and faith, not to comprehend God as an objective reality (1989: 54–8, 101). If God were an objective reality, available for metaphysics or a psychology of religious experience, God would have a place in the modern world-view, as God had such a place in the mythical world-view (1987: 53–65; 1989: 49–67; 1997: 50–75). God would no longer be God, but only an idea for reasoning manipulation and yet another means in human being's effort to secure its existence. According to Bultmann, the only way in which one may authentically speak of God in faith is by simple human analogy, as in the traditional word "father," a word that occurs in the Bible on two levels, mythological and existential (1958b: 66–70). Distinguishing them is not only the subject matter of demythologizing but also of what Bultmann calls "Sachkritik," which measures what is said by what is meant (Schmithals 1968: 245f).

Bultmann's concept of kerygmatic time and history is the existential "now" of being addressed by God and liberated from "world" (1989: 34f, 120; 1987: 302). Hearing the address of the kerygma is a recurring event that ever again overcomes sinful bondage to the past and opens to the future as a future owned by God. And the kerygma is not timeless, but spoken in different forms of speech within specific temporal situations (1987: 147, 218; 1989: 64f). Ordinary or objective history is completely different, as regards both life in time and historical method. While Bultmann's major theological works on the New Testament, *Theology of the New Testament* and *The Gospel of John*, involve in a certain sense the intersection of both times and histories, ordinary and kerygmatic, his classical work in "form criticism," *History of the Synoptic Tradition* (published in1921), which identifies layers or forms of tradition in the synoptic gospels, is purely objective. With this work Bultmann demonstrated that, as regards Jesus personally, only his teaching can be made available via critical research for historical investigation.

A few years later, in 1926, Bultmann published *Jesus and the Word*. In the Introduction he explains his method as an "encounter" with the prophetic Jesus of Jesus' teaching. But for Bultmann this encounter is not yet about the God who encounters human beings in the kerygmatic proclamation of the cross and resurrection of Jesus. It is through this God's singularly decisive act, whenever and wherever the kerygma is heard, that God judges and forgives human being and thereby (in Paul's words) divides the "old aeon" of the sinful world from the coming of the Kingdom of God, even though the person of faith who is freed from the world and for the Kingdom remains in the world (1957: 152). For Paul, the coming Kingdom was an immanent mythological event. But in the Gospel of John this has already been demythologized to the presence of eternal life already in this mortal life, as an interpretation of Jesus' death, resurrection and his gift of the Spirit. Here Bultmann follows John more than Paul in understanding the meaning of the kerygma as the radical existential openness of faith to the future given by God (1957: 38–55). A significant group of Bultmann's students argued that what Bultmann understands by the kerygma is already present, prior to the Easter event, in the teaching of Jesus in the synoptic gospels and in faith's encounter with this Jesus. They relied on critical methods learned from Bultmann, and they initiated what became known as "the new quest of the historical Jesus." Bultmann appreciated their historical work but never agreed with their thesis (Braaten and Harrisville 1964).

Bibliography

Barth, K. (1933) *The Epistle to the Romans*, trans. E.C. Hoskyns, London: Oxford University Press.

——(1957) *The Word of God and the Word of Man*, 1st English ed. 1928, New York: Harper and Row.

——(1960) *The Humanity of God*, trans. J.N. Thomas and T. Wieser, Richmond, VA: John Knox.

——(1979) *Evangelical Theology: an Introduction*, trans. G. Foley, Grand Rapids, MI: W.B. Eerdmans.

——(2004) *Church Dogmatics*, 4 vols, eds. G.W. Bromiley and T.F. Torrance, London and New York: T & T Clark International.

Bartsch, H.-W. (ed.) (1948ff) *Kerygma und Mythos*, Hamburg: Herbert Reich.

——(ed.) (1951) *Kerygma und Mythos*, 2nd unchanged edition, Hamburg-Volksdorf: Herbert Reich.

——(ed.) (1972) *Kerygma and Myth*, trans. R. Fuller, 2 vols. in one, London: S.P.C.K.

Braaten, C.E. and Harrisville, R.A. (eds) (1964) *The Historical Jesus and the Kerygmatic Christ*, New York and Nashville: Abington Press.

Bultmann, R. (1951) *Theology of the New Testament*, vol. I, trans. K. Grobel, New York: Charles Scribner's Sons.

——(1957) *History and Eschatology*, New York: Harper and Brothers.

——(1958a) *Jesus and the Word*, trans. L.P. Smith and E.H. Lantero, New York: Charles Scribner's Sons.

——(1958b) *Jesus Christ and Mythology*, New York: Charles Scribner's Sons.

——(1960) *Existence and Faith*, trans. S. Ogden, Cleveland and New York: Meridian Books.

——(1962ff) *Glauben und Verstehen*, 4 vols, Tübingen: Mohr-Siebeck.

——(1963) *History of the Synoptic Tradition*, trans. J. Marsh, New York: Harper and Row.

——(1971) *The Gospel of John*, trans. G. Beasley-Murray et al., Philadelphia: Westminster Press.

——(1987) *Faith and Understanding*, ed. R. Funk, trans. L.P. Smith, Philadelphia: Fortress Press.

——(1989) *New Testament and Mythology and Other Basic Writings*, ed. and trans. S. Ogden, Philadelphia: Fortress Press.

——(1997) *What is Theology?*, ed. E. Jüngel and K. Müller, trans. R. Harrisville, Minneapolis: Fortress Press.

Heidegger, M. (1962) *Being and Time*, trans. J. Macquarrie and E. Robinson, San Francisco: Harper & Row.

Hunsinger, G. (ed.) (1976) *Karl Barth and Radical Politics*, Philadelphia: Westminster Press.

Jüngel, E. (2001) *God's Being is in Becoming*, trans. J. Webster, Grand Rapids, MI: W.B. Eerdmans.

Robinson, J.R. (ed.) (1968) *The Beginnings of Dialectic Theology*, Richmond, VA: John Knox.

Schmithals, W. (1968) *An Introduction to the Theology of Rudolf Bultmann*, trans. J. Bowden, London: S.C.M.

Troeltsch, E. (1991) *Religion in History*, trans. J.L. Adams and W.F. Bense, Minneapolis: Fortress Press.

Wilson, J. (2007) *Introduction to Modern Theology: Trajectories in the German Tradition*, Louisville and London, Westminster: John Knox.

Further reading

Barth, K. (1962), *Anselm: Fides Quaerens Intellectum*, trans. I.W. Robertson, Cleveland and New York: Meridian Books, World Publishing Co.

Bultmann, R. (1955), *Essays Philosophical and Theological*, trans. C.G. Greig, New York: Macmillan.

——(1960) *This World and the Beyond. Marburg Sermons*, trans. H. Knight, New York: Scribners.

Busch, E. (1975) *Karl Barth: His Life from Letters and Autobigraphical Texts*, trans. J. Bowden, Philadelphia: Fortress Press.

——(2004) *The Great Passion, An Introduction to Karl Barth's Theology*, trans. G. Bromiley, Grand Rapids, MI: W.B. Eerdmans.

Hamann, K. (2012) *Rudolf Bultmann: A Biography*, trans. P.E. Devenish, Salem, OR: Polebridge.

Hunsinger, G. (2012) *Thy Word is Truth: Barth on Scripture*, Grand Rapids, MI: W.B. Eerdmans.

Jaspert, B. and Bromiley, G. (eds.) (1981) *Karl Barth–Rudolf Bultmann Letters, 1922–66*, Grand Rapids, MI: W.B. Eerdmans.

Jones, G. (1991) *Bultmann: Towards a Critical Theology*, Cambridge, UK: Polity Press.

Johnson, K. (2010) *Karl Barth and the Analogia Entis*, London: T & T Clark.

Labron, T. (2011) *Bultmann Unlocked*, Edinburgh: T & T Clark.

McCormack, B. (2008) *Orthodox and Modern: Studies in the Theology of Karl Barth*, Grand Rapids, MI: Baker Academic.

Oakes, K. (2012) *Karl Barth on Theology and Philosophy*, Oxford: Oxford University Press.

Perrin, N. (1969) *The Promise of Bultmann*, Philadelphia: Lippencott.

Ricoeur, P. (1974) "Preface to Bultmann," *Conflict of Interpretations*, Evanston: Northwestern University Press, 381–401.

Robinson, J.M. (2008) *Language, Hermeneutic and History: Theology after Barth and Bultmann*, Eugene, OR: Cascade Books.

9

HEIDEGGER: TRANSFORMATION OF HERMENEUTICS

Ingo Farin

Introduction

A concern with hermeneutics is present in many of Heidegger's works, albeit not in a selfsame and uniform manner. It appears in different configurations and with changing emphasis and is always embedded within Heidegger's other overarching philosophical projects. There are three distinct ways and phases in which hermeneutics figures in Heidegger's thought: (1) the initial breakthrough to a "hermeneutics of facticity" in the early Freiburg years (1919–24); (2) the argument for the foundational role of "understanding" in *Being and Time* (1927), which lays the groundwork for a hermeneutical ontology; (3) the idea that language and poets are the original interpreters in his later works after "the turn" in the 1930s. Heidegger's original and decisive hermeneutical impulses have greatly influenced many philosophers in the twentieth century, most notably Gadamer, Habermas, Ricoeur, Levinas, Derrida, Foucault, Rorty, and Vattimo.

1 The early Freiburg years: breakthrough to the hermeneutics of facticity

Against the so-called "fact of science" from which the neo-Kantians start, early Heidegger puts the "primacy of life" as his starting point for philosophy (2013: 105, 111).[1] It is in this context of *understanding life* that he develops four new hermeneutical ideas: (1) the hermeneutical exposition of lived experiences; (2) formal indication; (3) the hermeneutical situation and *Destruktion*; (4) the hermeneutics of facticity.

1.1 Hermeneutic exposition of lived experiences

Since early Heidegger holds that life is disclosed in and through lived experiences, everything hinges on the proper grasp of "lived experiences" (*Erlebnisse*). Heidegger contends that at their most basic level lived experiences are intrinsically holistic, historical, situational, worldly, and self-reflexively rebounding onto the experiencing personal self.[2] The experiencing "historical I" finds itself, to various degrees and intensities, involved, invested, and affected by what it experiences in its surrounding world. Heidegger calls lived experiences of this kind "*Umwelterlebnisse*" or lived experiences within a surrounding world; they have their own intelligibility, salience, significance, and meaning inscribed in them prior to all so-called theoretical and objective thematization of isolated and de-contextualized objects, properties, and so on. What is encountered in lived experiences is always already "meaningful" (*bedeutsam*). We directly understand what we encounter as bearing a message or intimation (*Kunde*), conveying good or bad tidings, as something which concerns us in one way or another, which challenges, warns, amuses us, and so on (2013: 42). This understanding is always rooted in a particular situation or opening towards the world, an ongoing "event" (*Ereignis*) in which one participates. The event is something *for* the experiencing self, which feels addressed by it, and which "ap-propriates" (*er-eignet*) the event by making it a part of its own self-understanding and life-story. Summarizing this view, Heidegger writes that living in a world that surrounds me, everything has meaning for me, everything is worldly: "It is everywhere the case that 'it worlds' [*es weltet*]" (2000b: 61). We are directly "immersed" in the world in which we live, without any cognitive "mediation" or filter.[3] Therefore, we do not encounter single, un-interpreted objects "outside" our minds to which we must build a bridge from our "inner" mental representations. Early Heidegger already decisively breaks with representationalism.

Heidegger claims that our experiences are structured and follow certain stabilized patterns along three interrelated axes: (1) the surrounding world or *Umwelt*, taken here in a narrower topological sense only, where it denotes the places where life is experienced and lived, such as "lands, regions, cities, and deserts"; (2) the with-world or *Mitwelt*, comprising other people encountered in these places, such as "parents, siblings, acquaintances, bosses, teachers, students," and so on; (3) the self-world or *Selbstwelt*, that is, the self as it appears and plays a more or less pronounced role in and through the engagements with the with-and surrounding-world (1993: 33 [2013: 27]). In addition, Heidegger notes that there are variously shaped, particular life-worlds, centered on religious, or political-economic, or scientific, or artistic concerns and interests (2013: 32), and he points to the inherent danger that one of these particular task worlds could gain tyrannical hegemony "over the whole of life," crowding out experiences prevalent in the other particular life-worlds (2013: 40). The threat of actual marginalization and suppression of experiences, as well as the danger of a scientifically impoverished and reductive concept of experience provides much of the driving impetus in early Heidegger's lecture courses.

In fact, Heidegger's account of lived experiences is an attempt to retrieve what he thinks has been occluded by the predominant but dogmatic supposition of a subject–object diremption and the resultant objectivism and theoretism in modern epistemology. As opposed to the dominant Cartesian picture where an independent, disembodied, and world-transcendent consciousness encounters a separate, un-interpreted "object" or "thing," Heidegger holds that there is a prior belonging together of "subject" and "object" within the encompassing, historical, surrounding world or worlding, where we live and move without Kantian glasses in "a sphere of understandings" (1993: 43 [2013: 35]). This direct, unmediated, historical understanding of world and self constitutes the primacy of the hermeneutical, relative to which the theoretical relation is derivative. Thus Heidegger effectively undercuts the legitimacy of epistemology and transcendental philosophy as first philosophy. More generally speaking, he challenges the pervasive intellectualism in philosophy, simply by exposing the unsurpassable ground level of world-embedded, historical, lived experiences beyond which one cannot go to some extra-mundane Archimedean point.

In his attempt to understand and explicate lived experiences, which is a task Heidegger takes over from Husserl as well as Dilthey, Heidegger consciously subjects these experiences to what is their very own *modus operandi*. In other words, the philosophical elucidation of lived experiences is not theoretical objectification, (transcendental) construction, or reconstruction, but, rather, the fruit of wakeful, lived experiences *about* them, that is, the explication, interpretation, communicating, and thus clarification of experiences by experiences. It is the self-clarification of lived experiences through themselves, a hermeneutical circle, which we cannot and should not avoid. It is on account of this inherent circularity that early Heidegger calls the investigation of lived experiences "hermeneutical" (2013: 43 n. 2, 213).

1.2 Formal indication

To avoid the resurfacing of reification and theoretism in the description of lived experiences, Heidegger proposes the method of "formal indication."[4] It prescribes a kind of "negative" discipline or precautionary stance according to which we must proceed with the greatest possible care in finding the proper foothold (*Ansatz*) for the explication of the phenomenon in question, that is, the character and feel of our lived experiences (2004b: 44). In contrast to the imperial gesture of a priori or "scientific" philosophy to provide absolutely secure and incorrigible knowledge, formal indication is content with modestly "pointing out" or "indicating" the direction or way towards the phenomenon under investigation, without prejudging the outcome or foreclosing the possibility of future clarifications and corrections.[5] In other words, formal indication does not dogmatically single out a particular description or angle as definitive for the way in which a phenomenon must be approached, leaving this, instead, "in abeyance" (*in der Schwebe*) (2004b: 44). Almost all of Heidegger's technical terms, including the ones from his later works, are best understood as formal indications, for instance, Dasein, facticity, world, earth, care, death, and so on.

In particular, formal indication makes no presumption that the theoretical-objective and/or matter-of-fact relation to a phenomenon (the de-contextualized "thing" outside the original historical experience in the "worlding" for a "historical I") is the default mode of our valid access to it. Put differently, formal indication warns against the confusion to take the very particular, disinterested theoretical stance for the one in which the phenomenon is originally disclosed within the environing world. By making a conscious and methodical effort not to narrow down or foreclose the access to the phenomenon in question, formal indication invites other inquirers to participate in the hermeneutic-phenomenological disclosure and to fill in and perform anew, from their perspective, what the indication points to in a first and preliminary fashion. Formal indication is an indirect communication of sorts by "showing" that we can authentically understand phenomena only by performing the intentional acts ourselves, instead of going by hearsay and second-hand opinion, or scientific and objective accounts for that matter. Formal indication is Socratic in its own way.

Folded within the method of formal indication we find Heidegger's general idea to merge Husserlian phenomenology and Diltheyean hermeneutics.[6] Heidegger goes out of his way to extol Husserl's "principle of all principles," that is to say, to take everything that presents itself to intuition for what it is, and he claims that this is not really an intellectual or "theoretical proposition" at all, because it simply takes cognizance of the normal procedure of all lived experiences (2000b: 92). Heidegger then argues that in explicating the phenomenon as given in intuition, unfolding its complete sense or meaning as it were, one articulates "the *logos* of the phenomena," where that "logos" must be understood "in the sense of '*verbum internum*,'" and not in the sense of logicizing (2004b: 43). In noting that phenomenology is not done with "just" seeing, but must find the words for what it sees and thus unfold intuition through understanding and interpretation, Heidegger consciously inserts the hermeneutical into phenomenology, transforming it into hermeneutical phenomenology, and it is for this reason that early Heidegger talks of "hermeneutical intuition" (2000b: 99). Thus Heidegger clearly breaks with the primacy of perception in phenomenology. But Heidegger does not abandon phenomenology as such. In fact, he attempts to inject the conceptual rigor of phenomenology into hermeneutics. For instance, the earlier mentioned conceptual determinations of the environing-, with-, and self-world, the concept of meaningfulness or intelligibility of lived experiences, and so on, all come to the fore through phenomenological-hermeneutical reflection and explication alone. They are not experienced straightforwardly in the immersion in the environing world, but gained and sharpened through the turning back onto experiences in the world. Hermeneutical philosophy is not opposed to conceptualization; it does not cultivate intellectual laziness, or what Heidegger calls "the uneasiness with concepts" (1984: 137). However, in following the method of formal indication, one can avoid conceptual dogmatism.

1.3 Hermeneutic situation and Destruktion

The extraordinary care and vigilance taken in formal indication does not aim at bracketing the historical, factical life whence it arises.[7] Quite to the contrary! Heidegger emphatically accepts the inescapable hermeneutical space in which all understanding as well as theoretical and philosophical interpretations take place. Since the world is not an aggregate of un-interpreted things, but a nexus of meaning, the world is disclosed through the articulation and communication of meaning in discourse and speech. This constitutes what Heidegger calls the "interpretedness of the world" (*Ausgelegtheit der Welt*) (2005: 354). As he puts it, "factical life" always finds itself within a "handed-down, re-worked, or newly established interpretedness" (2005: 354). The "hermeneutic situation," then, is nothing other than a particular, historical, interpretive space at a specific historical time, that is, the ensemble of past and present understandings, persuasions, interpretive strategies, discourse formations, available conceptualities, and paradigms, *insofar* as they constitute "the condition," or rather, possibility for new interpretive interventions or departures (2005: 347, n. 3). Therefore, whether it is pre-reflective or thematic, understanding or interpretation is never without presuppositions, that is, without the antecedent embedment within the historical hermeneutic situation. However, the hermeneutic situation is not something objectively given, let alone objectively determined. Instead, it is something to be "appropriated" and "shaped," namely by way of critically evaluating, correcting, seizing, and interpreting the inherited interpretedness, thus making the hermeneutical situation "transparent" (*durchsichtig*) to oneself (2005: 345).

For explicit and thematic interpretations, as for instance, philosophical interpretations and investigations, which themselves are shaped by inherited problems, concepts, theorems, questions, and so on, Heidegger phenomenologically differentiates between three distinct, interpretative aspects or moments (not to be misconstrued as technical rules), which underlie "every interpretation" and which need to be clarified and critically owned, if an interpretation is to be successful and transparent. The three distinctive constitutive moments of "every interpretation" are: (1) "the position of looking" (*Blickstand*); (2) "the scope of looking" (*Blickhabe*); (3) the "line of looking" (*Blickbahn*)[8] (2005: 346).[9] The *position of looking* refers to the actual "situation of life" whence the interpretation takes its starting-point; the *scope of looking* circumscribes the "as what" the thematic subject is taken preliminarily; and the *line of looking* delineates the region or "context" into which the interpreted subject is to be fitted. The three moments constitute the real conditions and presuppositions which govern any interpretation, whether pre-reflectively or reflectively. To the extent that they are self-consciously realized, fully present, and understood and integrated within the interpretation itself, the hermeneutic situation of the interpretation is transparent (2005: 346).[10]

Thus the hermeneutic situation is not automatically transparent, especially because the historically inherited interpretedness of the world has not been chosen by the interpreter. That is to say, the tradition has to be appropriated and made one's own, but not without critical scrutiny. For Heidegger argues that it is quite possible that the original motives and experiences, which once gave rise to the inherited interpretedness, have been forgotten, distorted, trivialized, or leveled off through routinization, carelessness, incompetence, or other corrupting influences in the tradition, such that it becomes necessary to critically peel back the obstructing layers of the tradition and lay bare these original motives again and appropriate them anew. Heidegger calls this critical review of the tradition and its possibly calcified content "*Destruktion*," dismantling or de-(con-)struction, and he goes out of his way to claim that "hermeneutics accomplishes its task only by way of *Destruktion*" (2005: 368).[11] Of course, these original experiences, simultaneously passed down and corrupted by the tradition, can only be formally indicated from within the hermeneutical situation of the present time. There is no God's eye point of view.

According to Heidegger, one can ignore the hermeneutic situation and the task of *Destruktion* only at the risk of continuing unquestioned historical tendencies. Because one can never engage an un-interpreted, "objective" world, independent of the interpretation in which it is handed down, it is in vain to try to escape the historical hermeneutical situation. But critical reflection or conscious appropriation of the hermeneutic situation allows for a better self-understanding of how one's own hermeneutical stance is reflected in one's interpretation and a better grasp of the historical realities that inform one's outlook. The emancipation from one's self-incurred historical blindness is thus facilitated.[12] Heidegger's hermeneutical stance is critical. It has nothing to do with the submission to anonymous forces of history, or the blind advocacy of relativism. The task of understanding one's own current philosophical hermeneutical situation comes with the critical insight that one cannot transcend one's historical situation. As Heidegger puts it, "philosophy is what it can be only as a philosophy of its 'time'" (1995a: 14). Historical-hermeneutical self-clarification of philosophy may thus help to cure philosophy of its fantastical mission "to take care of universal humanity" and "to release coming generations once and for all from care about questioning" (1995a: 14).

1.4 Hermeneutics of facticity

Early Heidegger's hermeneutical ideas culminate in his 1923 lecture course on the *Hermeneutics of Facticity* (1999b). Heidegger takes "factical life" or "facticity" as a formal indication, referring to the "character of being [*Seinscharakter*]" that is "'our' 'own' Dasein," in regard to its "being-there," being-involved with, and taking its while (1999b: 5). For Dasein its very own being is "at issue"; that is, Dasein is concerned about its own being. But what does "hermeneutics" mean in the context of a *hermeneutics of facticity*? Early Heidegger only gradually embraces the word "hermeneutics" to characterize his research. And when he does so, he goes back to the literal meaning of the original Greek *herméneuein*, which he translates as "to communicate" (*mitteilen*), that is, to put into words and share with others (1999b: 6). Thus, on Heidegger's reading, *hermeneutics* is not, *pace* Schleiermacher and the tradition, a second-order interpretation or general theory about the interpretation of pre-given texts, utterances, or expressions, but, rather, the first-order, original understanding, expression, dissemination, explication, and communication of meanings, messages, and intimations (1999b: 11). Early Heidegger also gives a more ontological reading of this understanding, according to which hermeneutics is the communication "and making known [of] a being [an entity] ... in its being in relation to – (me)" (1999b: 7). This early, unorthodox conception of hermeneutics is the one that Heidegger keeps as long as he avows a hermeneutical orientation (1971a: 29; 2010: 35).

But to come back to "the hermeneutics of facticity," it is nothing other than the attempt to understand factical life or Dasein, that is, to interpret it – for Dasein itself.[13] Heidegger emphatically distinguishes this "interpretation" or *Auslegung* of facticity from a mere description or "mere depicting," *Abschilderung*, noting that the latter usually mistakes the surface of what is commonly seen for the phenomenon as it is in itself (1999b: 60). Putting into words (*logoi*) the experiences and understandings of Dasein and thus explicating and clarifying them is the very possibility of speaking truth, which Heidegger reads in the Greek sense as *aletheuein*, to make accessible, to open up, and to present what formerly was concealed, and covered up (1999b: 8). Without the tendency of things "to hide," there would be no point in making them known in the first place. Not everything lies open in broad daylight.

Indeed, Dasein may misunderstand itself and make do with second-hand or traditional opinions about itself and the world in which it lives, which is why *Destruktion* is also called for in the case of interpreting Dasein. Without a doubt, early Heidegger here takes a leaf from Nietzsche's hermeneutics of suspicion.

Interpretation is not alien to Dasein, something imposed from outside. Since Dasein is concerned about itself, it cannot help but interpret itself. As Heidegger puts it, it is part of Dasein's being to exist in interpretation (1999b: 12). Hermeneutics of facticity, taken as a philosophical hermeneutics, is thus the attempt to develop and bring to clarity what is already at work in each factical life, that is, philosophical hermeneutics interprets and explicates the way Dasein understands or misunderstands itself. In fact, the traditional hermeneutic interest to fend off misunderstandings and facilitate understanding is also at play in Heidegger's philosophical hermeneutics.

Thus Heidegger claims that "in hermeneutics Dasein shapes its own possibility to become intelligible to itself and exist understandingly for itself," in part by confronting the "self-alienation with which it is afflicted" (1995a: 15 [1999b: 11]). The goal here is to enable each singular Dasein to become fully alert and awake to the possibilities of understanding itself, of finding itself, as it were. There is an unmistakably practical, emancipatory reform impulse here. As Heidegger puts it, rooted in factical life itself, philosophical hermeneutics "relentlessly pulls factical Dasein back to itself" in order to allow it to resolutely stand on its own ground (1995a: 18 [1999b: 14]).

By making the explication of self-understanding and self-misunderstanding in Dasein the focus of a hermeneutics of facticity, Heidegger effectively inverts the traditional hermeneutical outlook which used to be directed at the understanding of others, texts or people.[14] This Dasein-centric approach also determines Heidegger's discussion of the hermeneutical situation of his time. For in analyzing it in terms of the accomplishments and failings of contemporary philosophical and historical theorizing, he is primarily not interested in *what* they address (the content), but, rather, the way in which these writings manifest, reflect, or betray *how* Dasein itself is understood in and through these endeavors, in order then to interpret and critique this underlying self-understanding of Dasein (1999b: 28–52).

The foothold for this critique cannot be some scientific or objective truth. Rather, it is rooted in an original experience (*Grunderfahrung*) or self-understanding of the philosophizing Dasein, in which it encounters itself, wide awake for itself and its world (1999b: 12). But this cannot solidify into a full-blown doctrine because of the methodological restrictions of formal indication. It remains a suggestion or hint, outside the academic playground of proving theorems for this or for that. Hermeneutic explication makes do with evidence that remains "precarious," as Heidegger puts it (1995a: 16 [1999b: 12]). Nevertheless, philosophical hermeneutics takes its orientation from "philosophical wakefulness," which in turn is based on the original self-understanding that philosophy has given of itself, which of course requires an interpretation of its own (1999b: 14). All of this shows that although the hermeneutics of facticity is very much Dasein-centric and concerned about the self-clarification of Dasein, it is always embedded within the context of Dasein's historical belonging to a world and tradition which it shares and interprets through its hermeneutical experiences with others. Heidegger develops these themes in the new framework of *Being and Time* to which we turn now.

113

2 The foundational role of understanding in *Being and Time*

Heidegger's *magnum opus* is no longer concerned with the theme of life and lived experiences. Instead it is devoted to "the interpretation of the meaning of being" (2010: 20). Within this overall interpretive project Heidegger assigns a pivotal role to understanding (*Verstehen*), thereby inaugurating a new and entirely unprecedented *hermeneutical ontology*, comprising (1) the *hermeneutics of being* and (2) the *hermeneutics of Dasein*. In the pursuit of this new project Heidegger preserves, refines, and adjusts all of his earlier hermeneutical insights.

2.1 The hermeneutics of being

Heidegger claims that the question concerning the meaning of being is not only historically asked at the very beginning of Western philosophy, but is also *the* "fundamental question" taking precedence (*Vorrang*) over all other philosophical queries. Moreover, as human beings we always already live in an "average understanding of being" (*Seinsverständnis*) (2010: 4), because "whatever we talk about, intend, relate to in one way or another, as well as what and how we ourselves are" *is* or has being, that is, is an entity of sorts and thus has its own way of being, which we already understand, however clearly or obscurely (1977: 9 [2010: 5]). To the extent that philosophy takes on the task of clarifying the meaning of being, it is "nothing else than the radicalization" of the "pre-ontological understanding of being" that belongs to Dasein (2010: 13). Philosophy originates in and circles back to this "presupposition," making philosophy a thoroughly hermeneutic enterprise.

Drawing a sharp distinction between beings or entities (*Seiendes*) on the one hand and the being (*Sein*) of these entities on the other hand, Heidegger calls this the "ontological difference" (1982: 318–30, 17–24). Being is that which "determines" entities as entities, or, as Heidegger also puts it, it is that on the basis of which any entity whatsoever is "always already understood," "however it is discussed in detail" (1977: 8 [2010: 5]). Rejecting any hypostatization of being, Heidegger insists that "being is always the being of a being" or the being of an entity (2010: 8). Yet he also asserts that being is not a thing or mere entity (2010: 3), and, more importantly, that being always "transcends" entities (2010: 36). This is so, because being is the overarching horizon of intelligibility wherever human beings encounter, engage with, or talk about any entity whatsoever. As such, the meaning of being also governs and determines the more formal elaborations about the logical structure of entities in regional ontologies, and, *a fortiori*, ontic or empirical sciences and disciplines. Hence being circumscribes the "a priori condition of the possibility" of all comportments to entities, including all philosophical and empirical cognition, which is why Heidegger presents his inquiry into the meaning of being as "fundamental" ontology (2010: 10). Because Heidegger uses here an idiom that is somehow reminiscent of Kant's transcendental philosophy, he himself invites speculation about the transcendental or "hermeneutic-transcendental" character of *Being and Time* (1973: 15 [1997b: 378]), as he himself later put it.[15] Yet it is important to recognize that, in keeping with his earlier unambiguous, anti-transcendental stance (see Section 1.1), Heidegger empathically rules out "taking over ... the concept of the transcendental in Kant" and likewise rejects any invocation of a metaphysically construed being as such (1982: 23). He insists that while fundamental ontology "transcends entities, to reach being," it is precisely not reaching towards an entity "lying behind known entities as some afterworld [*Hinterwelt*]" (1997a: 23 [1982: 17]).

As a matter of fact, in *Being and Time* Heidegger does not talk about the transcendental "constitution" of beings through something called "being." Instead, in good hermeneutical fashion he states that there is no being as such in abstraction from the understanding of it (see 2010: 203). Put differently, "being reveals itself … in the understanding of being [*Seinsverständnis*]" only (1997a: 16; also 1984: 156). With this hermeneutical horizon in place, Heidegger then argues that the *question* concerning the meaning of being requires reflection on the *act of questioning* and, furthermore, the *entity which asks this question*. Questioning, however, is a "mode of being" of the kind of beings "we" are (2010: 7). And concerning "us" as inquirers, Heidegger states: "This entity which each of us is and which includes inquiring as one of the possibilities of its being, we shall denote by the term 'Dasein'" (1977: 10 [2010: 7]). He then concludes: "If we are to formulate our question concerning the meaning of being explicitly and transparently, we must first give a proper explication of this entity (Dasein) with regard to its being" as well as its understanding and questioning of being (1977: 10 [2010: 7]). This explication is the "analytics of Dasein," which is thus part and parcel of "fundamental ontology" (2010: 13).

The recourse to *Dasein*, through which *Sein* (being) is questioned and understood, might once again look similar to Kant and the Copernican turn to the transcendental subject. On reflection, however, it is clear that no such similarity can be asserted. First of all, Dasein is not narrowly conceived as an epistemic subject. Moreover, in keeping with the ontological line of inquiry, Heidegger thematizes Dasein's understanding as a "mode of its being." More importantly, for Heidegger Dasein's own existence, or the existence of anything else, for that matter, is not an object "constituted" in cognition. Second, even though Heidegger (1968a) in a letter to Husserl (sic!) speaks of Dasein's "transcendental constitution" of the world, he insists at the same time that Dasein is not a disembodied mind outside of space and time, but rather, exists in the world, albeit not "as a worldly real fact," that is, objectively defined as something present at hand.

The truth of the matter is that in contrast to any implicit or explicit transcendental framework, Heidegger characterizes the relationship between Dasein and *Sein* (or being) as a "circle," an *ontological* and *hermeneutical circle* to be precise (2010: 7, 147/48). Da-sein is the site (the "there" or "*Da-*") of the interpretation of entities and, their being (*Sein*), while at the same time this (interpreted) being (*Sein*) also affects and bears Da-sein, namely insofar as Dasein exists and relates to entities and therefore, has an understanding of being, in the midst of which it understands itself. Ontologically speaking we can say: there is no *Sein* without Da-sein, and no Da-sein without *Sein*.[16] Hermeneutically transposed it means the following: the understanding of being (in Dasein) and the being of understanding (within the world) are mutually implicated. The one is not divorced from the other. Put differently, the interpretation of the meaning of being is reflected in the being of Dasein itself and vice versa. Or, as Heidegger also puts it, "in all understanding of world" Dasein "is co-understood [*mitverstanden*] and vice versa" (1977: 202 [2010: 147]). That is to say, in stark contrast to the metaphysical tradition that often prioritized either world-understanding or self-understanding over its counterpart, Heidegger effectively suggests the necessary juxtaposition of both, where each one "presupposes" the other. This is not a "*circulus vitiosus*" or something that could be avoided. Rather, "what is decisive here is not to get out of this circle but to come into it in the right way" (2010: 148). But in contrast to the traditionally conceived hermeneutical circle of textual interpretation, this circle is an ontological one, where the understanding interprets not a text but being itself, starting with Dasein's own being and self-understanding and circling back to it through the understanding of entities and other human beings in the world, in the course of which the understanding of being has the chance to become more and more explicit, sophisticated, and transparent, in light of which Dasein then reinterprets itself. Of course, out of this process ontological treatises are generated as well, giving rise to an ontological tradition, which invests the understanding of being at any particular time. It is precisely for this reason that, in good hermeneutical fashion, Heidegger also projects a "*criticism*" or "*Destruktion*" of the "history of ontology" that is designed to lay bare the ontological *misunderstandings* arising from the neglect of the original, hermeneutical belonging of Dasein to being, which neglect has characterized not only traditional metaphysics, but also the more recent strands of scientism (2010: 19–25). The first task now is to investigate the being of Dasein as the first step towards an understanding of being.

2.2 The hermeneutics of Dasein

Heidegger states that the explication of Dasein "is hermeneutics in the original meaning of the term, according to which it denotes the business of interpretation," and not a theory about artful interpretation (1977: 50 [2010: 35]). Although he also enlists phenomenology for this task, it is clear that he reinterprets its meaning to fit his overall hermeneutical approach, for he claims, as in his earlier writings, that "the meaning of phenomenological description is *interpretation*" (2010: 35, emphasis added by Heidegger).

Heidegger's interpretation of Dasein is firmly centered on the idea that Dasein is neither a disembodied transcendental nor an empirically isolated subject building bridges from "inside" to an object "outside." Rather, Dasein is always already "outside" or "*draussen*" in the world (2010: 62), at some site or other, together with others, and engaged in various dealings and concerns with tools, things, and projects, all of which involves and reflects Dasein's own ability "to-be," or Dasein's care for its own being. *Being-in-the-world* is thus a key characteristic of Dasein's way of being (2010: 54). In being in the world, however, Dasein finds the world "there" as disclosed, opened up, intelligible, talked about, and interpreted. This disclosure of the world, which always encompasses the whole world with its entities, as well as Dasein itself and its being together with other Dasein, is part and parcel of being-in-the-world (2010: 84/85). Heidegger differentiates three "equiprimordial" aspects of Dasein's world-disclosure: (1) attunement (*Befindlichkeit*), (2) understanding (*Verstehen*), and (3) speech or discourse (*Rede*). These are interrelated moments in the unitary phenomenon of world disclosure; they cannot stand separately on their own (2010: 130 & 155).

2.2.1 Attunement

In attunement the world is disclosed as mattering for Dasein, affecting it in various ways as oppressive, threatening, burdensome, soothing, exciting, boring, and so on. Put differently, the world is felt as having a certain heaviness or lightness, importance, urgency, recalcitrance, blandness, and so on. In particular, Dasein is affected by the inescapable sentiment that – having being "thrown" into the world, without an intimation of the "whence" and "whither" – it is delivered over to itself. That is to say, Dasein finds itself confronted with the enigmatic facticity "that it is" and, moreover, that it "has to be" in a world it has not chosen, but which nevertheless constantly affects it and thus matters to it (2010: 131/32).

2.2.2 Understanding

Attunement constitutes the always present backdrop for the understanding (*Verstehen*). "Knowing" how it stands with Dasein as revealed by its attunement, the understanding projects future paths for Dasein's being-in-the-world, opening up, developing, and securing possibilities for engaging the world. Understanding is here taken as a certain competence in knowing one's way around in the world, of knowing how to proceed in the face of possibilities (2010: 138–43). In contradistinction to overly intellectualist conceptions of the understanding as, for example, the faculty of concepts, rational planning, or propositional knowledge, Heidegger likens understanding to *know-how*, "*etwas können*" (1977: 190 [2010: 139]), which can be exemplified in various practices.[17] However, this know-how is possible only on the basis of an antecedent "familiarity" (*Vertrautheit*) or acquaintance with the world as a whole (2010: 85), which is, therefore, part of the understanding, even though it may not be thematized in a particular instantiated practice.[18]

Like attunement, understanding discloses "the whole" of being-in-the world (2010: 140, 147, 133). That is to say, understanding is always holistic and historical. It ranges "equiprimordially" over "something like the 'world'," as well as "the entities" within the world, including other Dasein and one's own Dasein. Strictly speaking, there is no understanding at all unless its scope comprehends this entire "world-understanding" (*Weltverstehen*) (1977: 199, see also 202, 194/95, 18 [2010: 145, see also 147, 142, 12]). The "skipping over" the phenomenon of the world in modern ontology has also led to the neglect of world-understanding, which cannot be put together in piecemeal fashion by jumping from one "understood" and categorized "object" to the next.

More specifically, there is no isolated understanding directed exclusively at one's own Dasein, or the world alone, or other Dasein only. Understanding is always related to "the circle" of intelligibility as a whole, consisting of (1) the understanding of world and the entities in it, (2) one's own Dasein, and (3) other Dasein (*Mitdasein*) (1985b: 258). Going back and forth between "world," "Dasein," and other Dasein constitutes what Heidegger considers the ontological ground for the so-called "circle in understanding" (1985b: 258). Put differently, the three-way relation between self, others, and world is constitutive for understanding, according to Heidegger.[19] The primordial character of understanding must not blind us to its highly complex, dynamic, and hermeneutical nature. In fact, Heidegger claims that the back and forth movement of the understanding is possible only on the ground of temporality, the anticipation of future possibilities in light of the recollection of what has become. Since all understanding or interpretation is thus inevitably constituted in Dasein's temporality (2010: 343), Heidegger can claim that "the interpretation of time" also yields the ultimate horizon for posing the question concerning the meaning of being (2010: XXIX).

Understanding is a way of being in the world. It is not a particular type of ontic knowledge, standing in contrast to explanation, for example (2010: 138). Indeed, Heidegger claims that understanding is a necessary precondition for all higher-order, more specialized involvements with the world, including all varieties of thematic knowledge. This primordial and foundational character of understanding is further underlined when Heidegger, against all epistemologies inspired by Kant, holds that understanding constitutes the ontological root relative to which "intuition" (*Anschauung*) and "thought" (*Denken*) are just "remote derivatives" (2010: 143). This suggests that understanding is also the ground from which the contrasting poles of theory and praxis are first of all derived.[20] Hence it appears doubtful that Heidegger would *identify* understanding with a particular, ontic form of specifically practical coping within the environment.[21] Although Heidegger does indeed hold that understanding can disclose the world non-thematically and even pre-predicatively, he always argues that it does so by projecting new possibilities onto the world. The whole world is always opened up by the understanding and, in the words of Heidegger, "illuminated" as a "clearing" (*Lichtung*) (2010: 129), which may not require propositional knowledge, but certainly more than just a set of basic skills for some definitive tasks. In fact, every understanding is already interpretation, taking something *as* something, already employing what Heidegger calls the hermeneutical "as" (2010: 153). In short, in rejecting a narrow and rationalistic construal of the understanding, Heidegger does not throw out the baby with the bath water. He keeps and underlines the complex, disclosive power of the understanding – prior to the more specialized and restrictive applications of it in so-called theory *or* practice.

In fact, the understanding is not closed in on itself. Through "interpretation" (*Auslegung*) it can be explicated and articulated and, thereby, "come into its own" (1977: 197 [2010: 144]). "In interpretation understanding does not become something different, but rather itself" (2010: 144). According to Heidegger, the explication and articulation of the "hermeneutical as" is the specific task of interpretation. As already pointed out, it is important to note that already "pre-predicative," simple awareness takes something "as" something, that is, understands this something with regard to how it affords a foothold for Dasein's possible involvements in the world. In other words, the hermeneutical "as" pervades all understanding; it is not a miraculous surplus that all of a sudden springs into existence in interpretation (2010: 153). Interpretation merely brings out what is already contained in understanding. It follows that interpretation and understanding cannot be severed from one another. Put differently, all understanding is already interpretation, however inchoate and implicit it may be.

2.2.3 Speech

Articulate understanding or interpretation requires speech (*Rede*) or language (*Sprache*), the third "moment" in the structure of Dasein's world-disclosure.

Heidegger goes out of his way to underline the centrality of speech for Dasein, writing that speech is "constitutive" for Dasein (2010: 156); or that "*legein*, to talk, is the most fundamental characteristic [*Grundverfassung*] of human Dasein" (1992: 17 [2003a: 12]), or that "talking-with-one-another is in fact the fundamental way of being together with-one-another-in-the-world" (2011: 22). As in the case of interpretation, Heidegger sees speech originally anchored in and inseparable from understanding, without, however, being reducible to it. Speech is not a separate layer above understanding and interpretation: "Intelligibility is always already an articulate structure [*gegliedert*] even before the appropriation through interpretation. Speech is the expression [*Artikulation*] of intelligibility. Therefore speech underlies ... interpretation" (1977: 213/14 [2010: 155]). Consequently Heidegger rejects the view that we assign meanings to "word-things," arguing instead that to meanings laid out and preserved in understanding and interpretation "words accrue" (2010: 156).

Heidegger pursues the centrality of speech on two interrelated levels.

First, to the extent that understandings and interpretations are communicated and shared through speech and discourse, it follows that in sharing a language or discourse one also shares a certain "interpretedness" of the world (2010: 162). Moreover, if and when speech is merely absorbed, routinely and/or mindlessly passed on and applied at various appropriate and not so appropriate occasions, that is, without probing, testing, and renewing the underlying understanding itself, it can degenerate into mere talkativeness or *Gerede* (1977: 222–6 [2010: 161–3]). This is not some dubious or conservative form of cultural criticism,[22] but Heidegger's philosophical and critical reflection on the power of reified speech over Dasein, which is by no means restricted to popular culture, mass media, talk-shows, and so on. After all, whatever field, activity, or involvement with the world it may be, Dasein most often first encounters it as something talked about, without always having genuine *first-hand* understanding itself, thus making it more or less inevitable that Dasein, at least initially, relies on mere hearsay.

Second, Heidegger also points to another danger of reification, namely if and when interpretation is expressed in formal predicative statements or propositions (*Aussagen*). For with regard to predication, that is to say, formally determining something as something, which is nothing other than the fixation of the so-called apophantic "as," Heidegger does not only argue, as we have already seen, that the latter is "derived" from the original hermeneutical "as," but also points out that the thematic fixation of a "subject" vis-à-vis a "predicate" elides the originally situational character of interpretation and ignores the immersion of understanding in the world (2010: 149/50). Hence Heidegger warns against taking the apophantic "as" in propositions for the original and standard form of Dasein's understanding, a mistake often made in the philosophical tradition.[23] Such a one-sided view overlooks the whole gamut of linguistic forms in which interpretation is put in words, such as "narrations," personal "accounts," "situational reports," and so on, all of which keep closer to the original form of interpretation as disclosing the whole of being-in-the-world than mere propositions (1977: 210 [2010: 153]). This also underlies Heidegger's more general criticism that the scope of *logos* in the old definition of man as that being that has *logos* has been interpreted far too restrictively, as if to imply that formal logic or propositional attitudes defined the human being. In contradistinction to this restrictive reading,

Heidegger insists that the "basic meaning of *logos* is speech" – in all its varieties (1977: 43 [2010: 30]).

To conclude, in *Being and Time*, Heidegger makes world-disclosure, differentiated as attunement, understanding and interpretation, and speech, central not only for the analysis of human beings, but also the world, and indeed, being. If one identifies hermeneutics with the primacy of understanding and interpretation, then we can say that in *Being and Time* "philosophy itself becomes hermeneutic" in an unprecedented way (Hoy 1993: 172). While it is true that Dilthey (1957: 333) already envisaged "understanding" as the foundation for the human sciences, it is Heidegger who determines understanding or interpretation as *the* ontological cornerstone from which alone man's reality and his ontological relation to the world and being itself are disclosed. Frank's (1985: 14) view that Heidegger's hermeneutical work has had a truly "immeasurable impact" on subsequent philosophy is by no means an overstatement.

3 Hermeneutics after the turn

After "the turn" in the 1930s Heidegger distances himself from the explicit herme-neutical key in his earlier work. This is based on his self-critical assessment that "all hermeneutical-transcendental probing" in *Being and Time* is still too closely inter-twined with the traditional metaphysical language that evolved in the course of the forgetfulness of being (1973: 15 [1997b: 378]). Yet Heidegger does not simply disown hermeneutics.[24] In fact, even after the turn, Heidegger writes in *Contributions to Phi-losophy* that "Da-sein" can never be described like something present at hand, and can be elucidated only "hermeneutically" (2003b: 321 [1999c: 226]). Heidegger is not beholden to the idea that one can simply switch on or off a mode of thought. The debate whether or not his later philosophy neatly qualifies as "hermeneutics" is secondary compared to the task of understanding his train of thought in the first place.

On the one hand, Heidegger abandons thematic references to his own earlier conceptions of "understanding," "interpretation," "the hermeneutic 'as'," and, more importantly, extends and radicalizes his criticism of the subjectivism inherent in the hermeneutical recourse to so-called inner "lived experiences" that are outwardly "expressed," and so on (1999d: 25–9; 1971a: 34–6). But on the other hand, Heidegger now makes language (*Sprache*) the preeminent new locus for philosophy instead, holding that "language" is "the fundamental trait" in the "hermeneutic relation" of man to being, entities, and the ontological difference (1971a: 32; see also 2002: 261).

Heidegger's new focus on *language* and the *hermeneutical relationship* to the world (through speaking) keeps his late philosophy at the very least in the *neighborhood* of hermeneutics, especially if one is mindful of Schleiermacher's dictum that "what has to be presupposed in hermeneutics is nothing but language."[25] Moreover, since Heidegger complements his new shift towards language with an equally significant, albeit less often noticed or discussed, turn towards the problematic of thought (*Gedanke*) or thinking (*Denken*),[26] whereby he effectively puts the *discursiveness* of thought at center stage (again in opposition to "intuition" in phenomenology or neo-Kantianism), Heidegger is actually in agreement with Schleiermacher's (1977: 77) hermeneutic principle that "no one can think without words" and that "without words thought is not yet ready and clear."

Indeed, it is no exaggeration to say that the word or its disclosive power, especially in poetry, preoccupies Heidegger's later philosophy. In an interpretation of Stefan George's poem, entitled "Word," Heidegger ponders the far reaching idea that "without the word, no thing is" (1971a: 152). Words herald the presence and absence of things, and it is through words that we receive messages of what counts, is real, and determines our existence. Drawing on Hölderlin, Heidegger claims that "poetry" is "a saying" through which "guiding revelation comes to pass" for a people (1999d: 30). The essence of man is to stand in this open relationship of thinking, being, poetic language, and original saying.

In the "Letter on 'Humanism'" Heidegger writes:

> Thinking enacts the relation between being [*Sein*] and man's essence [*Wesen des Menschen*]. It does not make or cause this relation. Rather, thinking presents this relation to being solely as something handed over to thought from being itself. Such offering consists in the fact that in thinking being is articulated through language [*zur Sprache gebracht*]. Language is the house of being.[27] In this home human beings dwell. Thinkers and poets are the guardians of this home.
>
> (2004a: 313 [1998: 239])

This view clearly stands in contrast to Heidegger's earlier hermeneutical accentuation of the primacy of world-disclosive *everyday* understandings, especially when seen in terms of social practices. Later Heidegger sees humans as authentically dwelling in the *artful* language of poetry, which liberates from the humdrum and mindless monotony of the everyday work world (1999d: 22). Heidegger adopts Hölderlin's line: "Full of merit, yet poetically, man / Dwells on this earth" (1999d: 36).[28] It is the poet's elevated word, not the common word in everyday discourse, which measures the dimension between heaven and earth and thus locates man and provides guidance for his dwelling (1971b: 213–29).

This poetical guidance, however, has nothing to do with finding some unassailable master word for the epoch (as is characteristic of the imperial claim of philosophy since Plato). In demonstratively siding with the poets against Plato, Heidegger "indicates" and articulates a clear break with the philosophical justification of state violence – with obvious political implications at the time, as noted by Schmidt (2005). The same critical impulse is at work in Heidegger's hermeneutical criticism of what he calls "one-track thinking," or one-dimensional thought and its principle of "absolute univocity" (1968b: 26). In contesting this foreshortening of language – all too familiar today in the form of objective-bureaucratic nomenclature in politics, education, economy, and science – Heidegger defends nothing other than the liberating force of speaking outside bureaucratic forms and pre-fabricated phrases. As Heidegger argues, "saying" means "to show," "to let appear" (1971a: 122), which, in the words of Schmidt amounts to "naming what is repressive … , calling things by their real and possible names, revealing them for what they are, [and] discursively robbing them of their presumed constancy" (2005: 30).

Thus later Heidegger's hermeneutics remains true to his early commitment to interpreting, explicating, and clarifying the historical situation in which we live. This self-clarification takes place in the triadic structure of being, Dasein, and language, or as Heidegger puts it: "In its saying [*Sagen*], thinking merely puts into language the unspoken word of being" (2004a: 361 [1998: 274]). Indeed, when Heidegger provocatively states that "language speaks" and that "man speaks" insofar as "he responds to language" (1971b: 210), he is not reifying language as a super-subject, but rather attempting to keep at bay the instrumentalist view of language as a neutral tool to be used by supposedly autonomous subjects.[29] Even the seemingly extreme formulation, according to which "language *is* monologue" and that language "*alone* truly speaks," Heidegger puts in the appropriate perspective when he immediately adds that language is not without "relation," and that language "needs" its articulation through man (1985a: 254 [1971a: 134]).[30] Moreover, Heidegger clearly states that "the essential being of language cannot be anything linguistic" (1971a: 23/24). Language points beyond itself to being and man. In light of this, the charge of "linguistic idealism" seems mistaken.

Although Heidegger's path through hermeneutics is far from linear and straightforward, we can discern certain continuities. Whether he thematizes experience, or understanding, or thought and language, Heidegger is always driven by the worry that the full breadth and richness of man's dwelling on earth is given short shrift because of the fateful modern subject–object estrangement and its concomitant pathologies of objectivism and subjectivism. According to Heidegger, this "alienation" is the root cause for the ever increasing "homelessness" which is the "approaching destiny" of human beings in our world (1998: 260). The hermeneutical impetus is precisely to show the belonging of man and world through language and thought. This is always historical: "Each man is in each instance in dialogue with the forebears, and perhaps even more and in a hidden manner with those who will come after him" (1971a: 31).

Notes

1 Wherever possible and suitable I have used available English translations of Heidegger's texts. Where I use my own translation(s) instead, I refer to the German edition first, followed by a reference to the available English edition in square brackets.

2 See for this and the following characterization Heidegger (2000b: 53–79).

3 Out of this immersion in the event of "worlding" Heidegger develops the formal concept of "being-in-the-world" in *Being and Time*. For this theme, see Taylor (2013).

4 Groundbreaking discussions for this are in Dahlstrom (1994); Crowell (2001: 129–51); Burch (2011); Kisiel (2008).

5 In fact, later Heidegger understands the very nature of language as a kind of "showing" or "hinting," that is, pointing to: "*The essential being of language is Saying as Showing*" (1971a: 123).

6 Thus Heidegger writes that "the secret longing of his [Dilthey's] life" is now "being fulfilled [by phenomenology]" (2000b: 140).

7 See Bambach (1995: 187–273).

8 Heidegger's terminology taps into a semantic field that is somewhat reminiscent of Chladenius' "*Sehe-Punckt*." For Chladenius see Beiser (2011: 27–62).

9 An earlier version from 1919 lists these three moments under different names: "retentional grasp [*Rückgriff*]" or "motivation," proleptic or "protentional grasp [*Vorgriff*]" or "tendency," and "concept" (Begriff) (1999a: 116 [2000b: 98]). The Husserlian temporal structure

is clearly inscribed here, as the "concept" comes to stand between pretention and protention. It anticipates Heidegger's own view that the hermeneutical circle is ultimately founded upon Dasein's temporality. (See Section 2.2.2 below.)

10 Heidegger keeps this schema of interpretation also in *Being and Time* with the new titles of "fore-having" (*Vorhabe*), "fore-sight" (*Vorsicht*), and "fore-conception" (*Vorgriff*). He specifically notes there that "interpretation is never a presuppositionless grasping of something previously given" (2010: 146).

11 At one point, Heidegger even equates the two, writing that "hermeneutics is *Destruktion!*" (1999b: 81).

12 In fact, Heidegger holds that it is a misunderstanding and mere "prejudice" to strive after *Standpunktfreiheit* or the freedom from all standpoints, arguing that the real freedom would consist instead "in the explicit appropriation" and clarification of a standpoint, and he notes that this is "something historical, i.e., bound up with Dasein (responsibility, how Dasein stands regarding itself), and not a chimerical in-itself outside of time such" (1999b: 64).

13 The "hermeneutics of facticity" is what Heidegger calls "the hermeneutics" of "Dasein" in *Being and Time* (2010: 35).

14 See Gander (2006), as well as Figal (2006) and Tugendhat (1992: 458).

15 For a discussion of the latent transcendentalism in Heidegger see Crowell and Malpas (2007) and Lafont (2000; 2002; 2007: 265–84).

16 This inseparability of Sein and Dasein is emphasized by Sheehan (2001 and 2013).

17 This is very much emphasized by Dreyfus (1991: 184; 2005: 47–65). See also Schear (2013).

18 See Palmer (1984: 87).

19 Malpas (2002, 2012) has developed this thought in great detail, drawing also on Davidson.

20 In this I follow Gadamer (1990: 264) who writes about Heidegger's concept of understanding: "Before any differentiation of understanding into the various directions of pragmatic or theoretical interest, understanding is Dasein's mode of being, insofar as it is potentiality-for-being and 'possibility.'"

21 For a very perceptive discussion of this see Wrathall (2013).

22 See Jürgen Habermas (1992: 140).

23 For an extensive discussion of the hermeneutic "as," see Dahlstrom (2001: 175–210).

24 For an insightful discussion see Dreyfus (1984) who argues the case that later Heidegger gives up hermeneutical thought, and Palmer (1984) who argues the opposing view that Heidegger continues and even accentuates his hermeneutical orientation. See also Zaborowski (2011: 35–41).

25 This is the epigram Gadamer chose for the third part of *Wahrheit und Methode* (1990: 387 [1994: 381]). See also Grondin (1994: 68).

26 See Palmer (1988).

27 Later in the text Heidegger warns against taking the phrase of language as "the house of being" in a figurative sense only: "Talk of the house of being is not a transposition of the image 'house' onto being. Rather, from out of the properly conceived essence of being we may someday come to recognize what 'house' and 'dwelling' are" (2004a: 358 [1998: 272]). Incidentally, the striking phrase "house of being" can be found in Nietzsche's *Zarathustra* (1973: 463 [1966: 217]).

28 On Hölderlin and Heidegger, see Young (2001: 69–120).

29 See Matthew Abbott (2010).

30 On reflection, this view is not so different from Schleiermacher's more general claim that "each individual person is but the place where language appears" (1977: 78).

Bibliography

Abbott, Matthew, 2010, "The Poetic Experience of the World," in *International Journal of Philosophical Studies*, Vol. 18 (4), pp. 493–516.

Bambach, Charles R., 1995, *Heidegger, Dilthey, And The Crisis of Historicism*, Ithaca, Cornell University Press.

Beiser, Frederick C., 2011, *The German Historicist Tradition*, Oxford, Oxford University Press.

Burch, Matthew I., 2011, "The Existential Sources of Phenomenology: Heidegger on Formal Indication," in *European Journal of Philosophy*, Vol. 21 (2), pp. 258–78.

Crowell, Steven Galt, 2001, *Husserl, Heidegger, and the Space of Meaning: Paths Towards Transcendental Phenomenology*, Evanston, Northwestern University Press.

Crowell, Steven Galt, and Jeff Malpas, 2007, *Transcendental Heidegger*, Stanford, Stanford University Press.

Dahlstrom, Daniel O., 1994, "Heidegger's Method: Philosophical Concepts as Formal Indications," in *The Review of Metaphysics*, Vol. 47 (4), pp. 775–95.

——, 2001, *Heidegger's Concept of Truth*, Cambridge, Cambridge University Press.

Dilthey, Wilhelm, 1957, "*Die Entstehung der Hermeneutik*" (1900), in *Gesammelte Schriften*, Vol. 5, Stuttgart, B. G. Teubner Verlagsgesllschaft.

Dreyfus, Hubert L., 1984, "Beyond Hermeneutics: Interpretation in Late Heidegger and Recent Foucault," in *Hermeneutics: Questions and Prospects*, Ed. Gary Shapiro and Alan Sica, Amherst, The University of Massachusetts Press, pp. 66–84.

——, 1991, *Being-in-the-World: A Commentary on Heidegger's Being and Time, Division I*, Cambridge, MA, MIT Press.

——, 2005, "Overcoming the Myth of the Mental: How Philosophers Can Profit from the Phenomenology of Everyday Expertise," in *Proceedings and Addresses of the American Philosophical Association*, Vol. 79, pp. 47–65.

Figal, Günter, 2006, *Gegenständlichkeit*, Tübingen, Mohr Siebeck.

Frank, Manfred, 1985, *Das Individuelle Allgemeine*, Frankfurt, Suhrkamp.

Gadamer, Hans-Georg, 1990, *Gesammelte Werke*, Vol. I, *Wahrheit und Methode*, Tübingen, J.C.B. Mohr.

——, 1994, *Truth and Method*, New York, Continuum.

Gander, Hans-Helmuth, 2006, *Selbstverständnis und Lebenswelt*, Frankfurt, Vittorio Klostermann.

Grondin, Jean, 1994, *Introduction to Philosophical Hermeneutics*, New Haven, Yale University Press.

Habermas, Jürgen, 1992, *The Philosophical Discourse of Modernity*, Cambridge, MA, MIT Press.

Heidegger, Martin, 1962, *Being and Time*, Tr. John Macquarrie and Edward Robinson, Oxford, Blackwell.

——, 1968a, "Letter to Husserl," dated October 22, 1927, in Edmund Husserl, *Phänomenologische Psychologie*, Husserliana, Vol. IX, Ed. Walter Biemel, Den Haag, Martinus Nijhoff, pp. 601–2.

——, 1968b, *What is Called Thinking*, Tr. J. Glenn Gray, New York, Harper & Row.

——, 1971a, *On the Way to Language*, Tr. Peter D. Hertz, New York, Harper San Francisco.

——, 1971b, *Poetry, Language, Thought*, Tr. Albert Hofstadter, London, Harper & Row.

——, 1973, *The End of Philosophy*, Tr. Joan Stambough, New York, Harper & Row.

——, 1977, *Sein und Zeit*, Gesamtausgabe, Vol. 2, Frankfurt, Vittorio Klostermann.

——, 1982, *The Basic Problems of Phenomenology*, Tr. Albert Hofstadter, Indiana, Indiana University Press.

——, 1984, *The Metaphysical Foundations of Logic*, Tr. Michael Heim, Indiana, Indiana University Press.

——, 1985a, *Unterwegs zur Sprache*, Gesamtausgabe, Vol. 12, Frankfurt, Vittorio Klostermann.

——, 1985b, *History of the Concept of Time*, Tr. Theodore Kisiel, Indiana, Indiana University Press.

——, 1992, *Platon: Sophistes*, Gesamtausgabe, Vol. 19, Frankfurt, Vittorio Klostermann.

——, 1993, *Grundprobleme der Phänomenologie (1919/1920)*, Gesamtausgabe, Vol. 58, Frankfurt, Vittorio Klostermann.

———, 1994, *Prolegomena Zur Geschichte Des Zeitbegriffs*, Gesamtausgabe, Vol. 20, Frankfurt, Vittorio Klostermann.

———, 1995a, *Ontologie (Hermeneutik der Faktizität)*, Gesamtausgabe, Vol. 63, Frankfurt, Vittorio Klostermann.

———, 1995b, *Die Phänomenologie des Religiösen Lebens*, Gesamtausgabe, Vol. 60, Frankfurt, Vittorio Klostermann.

———, 1997a, *Die Grundprobleme der Phänomenologie*, Gesamtausgabe, Vol. 24, Frankfurt, Vittorio Klostermann.

———, 1997b, *Nietzsche: Zweiter Band*, Gesamtausgabe, Vol. 6.2, Frankfurt, Vittorio Klostermann.

———, 1998, *Pathmarks*, Ed. William McNeill, Cambridge, Cambridge University Press.

———, 1999a, *Zur Bestimmung der Philosophie*, Gesamtausgabe, Vol. 56/57, Frankfurt, Vittorio Klostermann.

———, 1999b, *Ontology – The Hermeneutics of Facticity*, Tr. John van Buren, Indiana, Indiana University Press.

———, 1999c, *Contributions to Philosophy*, Tr. Parvis Emad and Kenneth Maly, Indiana, Indiana University Press.

———, 1999d, *Hölderlin's Hymnen "Germanien" und "Der Rhein"*, Gesamtausgabe, Vol. 39, Frankfurt, Vittorio Klostermann.

———, 2000a, *Vorträge und Aufsätze*, Gesamtausgabe, Vol. 7, Frankfurt, Vittorio Klostermann.

———, 2000b, *Towards the Definition of Philosophy*, Tr. Ted Sadler, London, Athlone Press.

———, 2002, *Was Heisst Denken?*, Gesamtausgabe, Vol. 8, Frankfurt, Vittorio Klostermann.

———, 2003a, *Plato's Sophist*, Tr. Richard Rojcewicz and André Schuwer, Indiana, Indiana University Press.

———, 2003b, *Beiträge zur Philosophie (Vom Ereignis)*, Gesamtausgabe, Vol. 65. Frankfurt Vittorio Klostermann.

———, 2004a, *Wegmarken*, Gesamtausgabe, Vol. 9, Frankfurt, Vittorio Klostermann.

———, 2004b, *The Phenomenology of Religious Life*, Tr. Mathias Fritsch and Jennifer Anna Gosetti-Ferenci, Indiana, Indiana University Press.

———, 2005, *Phänomenologische Interpretationen Ausgewählter Abhandlungen Des Aristoteles Zur Ontologie Und Logik*, Gesamtausgabe, Vol. 62, Frankfurt, Vittorio Klostermann.

———, 2010 *Being and Time*, Tr. Joan Stambaugh, Revised and with a Foreword by Dennis J. Schmidt, Albany, State University of New York Press.

———, 2011, *The Concept of Time*, Tr. Ingo Farin and Alex Skinner, New York, Continuum.

———, 2013, *Basic Problems of Phenomenology*, Tr. Scott M. Campbell, New York, Bloomsbury.

Hoy, David Couzens, 1993, "Heidegger and the Hermeneutic Turn," in *The Cambridge Companion to Heidegger*, Ed. Charles Guignon, Cambridge, Cambridge University Press.

Kisiel, Theodore, 2008, "On the Genesis of Heidegger's Formally Indicative Hermeneutics of Facticity," in *Rethinking Facticity*, Ed. François Raffoul and Eric Sean Nelson, Albany, State University of New York Press, pp. 41–67.

Lafont, Christina, 2000, *Heidegger, Language, And World-Disclosure*, Cambridge, Cambridge University Press.

———, 2002, "Précis of Heidegger, Language, and World-disclosure," in *Inquiry*, 45, pp. 185–90.

———, 2007, "Hermeneutics," in *A Companion to Heidegger*, Ed. Hubert L. Dreyfus and Mark A. Wrathall, Oxford, Blackwell, pp. 265–84.

Malpas, Jeff, 2002, "Gadamer, Davidson, and the Ground of Understanding," in *Gadamer's Century: Essays in Honor of Hans-Georg Gadamer*, Ed. Jeff Malpas, Ulrich Arnswald, and Jens Kertscher, Cambridge, MA, MIT Press, pp. 195–215.

———, 2012, "Topology, Triangulation, and Truth," in Jeff Malpas, *Heidegger and the Thinking of Place*, Cambridge, MA, MIT Press, pp. 199–223.

Nietzsche, Friedrich, 1966, "Thus Spoke Zarathustra," Tr. Walter Kaufmann, New York, Penguin.

——, 1973, *Werke in Drei Bänden*, Ed. Karl Schlechta, Vol. II, München, Carl Hanser Verlag.

Palmer, Richard, 1984, "On the Transcendability of Hermeneutics," in *Hermeneutics: Questions and Prospects*, Ed. Gary Shapiro and Alan Sica, Amherst, The University of Massachusetts Press, pp. 84–95.

——, 1988, "Hints for/of Hermeneutics in *Was Heisst Denken?*" in *Hermeneutic Phenomenology: Lectures and Essays*, Ed. Joseph J. Kockelmans, Washington, Center for Advanced Research in Phenomenology and University Press of America.

Schear, Joseph K., 2013, *Mind Reason, and Being-in-the-World: The McDowell–Dreyfus Debate*, London, Routledge.

Schleiermacher, F.D.E., 1977, *Hermeneutik und Kritik*, Ed. Manfred Frank, Frankfurt, Suhrkamp.

Schmidt, Dennis J., 2005, "Wozu Hermeneutics," in Dennis J. Schmidt, *Lyrical and Ethical Subjects*, Albany, State University of New York Press.

Sheehan, Thomas, 2001, "A Paradigm Shift in Heidegger Research," in *Continental Philosophy Review*, 34, 183–202.

——, 2013, "What if Heidegger were a Phenomenologist?," in *The Cambridge Companion to Heidegger's* Being and Time, Ed. Mark A. Wrathall (Cambridge: Cambridge University Press), pp.381–401.

Taylor, Charles, 2013, "Retrieving Realism," in *Mind, Reason, And Being-in-the-World: The McDowell–Dreyfus Debate*, Ed. Joseph K. Schear, London, Routledge, pp. 61–90.

Tugendhat, Ernst, 1992, *Philosophische Aufsätze*, Frankfurt, Suhrkamp.

Wrathall, Mark A., 2013, "Heidegger on Human Understanding," in Mark A. Wrathall, *Heidegger's Being and Time*, pp. 177–200.

Young, Julian, 2001, *Heidegger's Philosophy of Art*, Cambridge, Cambridge University Press.

Zaborowski, Holger, 2011, "Heidegger's hermeneutic: towards a new practice of understanding," in *Interpreting Heidegger: Critical Essays*, Ed. Daniel O. Dahlstrom, Cambridge, Cambridge University Press.

Further reading

Dahlstrom, Daniel O., 2011, *Interpreting Heidegger*, Cambridge, Cambridge University Press.

Foucault, Michel, 2005, *The Hermeneutics of the Subject*, Tr. Graham Burchell, New York, Palgrave.

Figal, Günther, 2009, *Zu Heidegger: Antworten und Fragen*, Frankfurt, Vittorio Klostermann.

——, 2010, *Heidegger und die Literatur*, Frankfurt, Vittorio Klostermann.

Figal, Günther and Gander, Hans-Helmuth, 2005, *Dimensionen des Hermeneutischen*, Frankfurt, Vittorio Klostermann.

Malpas, Jeff, 2006, *Heidegger's Topology: Being, Place, World*, Cambridge, MA, MIT Press.

Risser, James, 2012, *The Life of Understanding: A Contemporary Hermeneutics*, Bloomington, Indiana University Press.

Schmidt, Dennis J., 2013, *Between Word and Image*, Bloomington, Indiana University Press.

Vattimo, Gianni and Zabala, Santiago, 2011, *Hermeneutic Communism: From Heidegger to Marx*, New York, Columbia University Press.

Wrathall, Mark A., 2011, *Heidegger and Unconcealment*, Cambridge, Cambridge University Press.

——, 2013, *Heidegger's Being and Time*, Cambridge, Cambridge University Press.

Zarader, Marlène, 2006, *The Untought Debt: Heidegger and the Hebraic Heritage*, Tr. Bettina Bergo, Stanford: Stanford University Press.

10
STRAUSS: HERMENEUTICS OR ESOTERICISM?

Catherine H. Zuckert and Michael Zuckert

Leo Strauss seldom used fancy words like "hermeneutics." He sought to return to the kind of philosophy practiced by the ancient Socratics, whose thought he tried to reclaim for the present. That thought was, as he sometimes put it, "common-sensical" in that it began from and was rooted in what was said in the market place and the assembly. Indeed, almost the only time the mature Strauss used the term "hermeneutic" was in an exchange with Hans Georg Gadamer in 1961 about the latter's *Wahrheit und Methode*. Gadamer was an old friend who had sent Strauss a copy of his book at its publication. The young Strauss had not only been Gadamer's friend, but he had also emerged from roughly the same philosophic circle that produced the great interest in hermeneutics that peaked in Gadamer's book.

Strauss was born in Hesse, Germany, in 1899, and had originally been attracted to the neo-Kantians under the leadership of Hermann Cohen. Cohen was especially interesting to the young Strauss, because both were Jews from observant backgrounds who pursued philosophy. Strauss earned his doctorate under Ernst Cassier, Cohen's successor as leader of the neo-Kantians, but Strauss's philosophic interests came to lie more strongly in the "new thinking" as practiced by Franz Rosenzweig and Martin Heidegger. He had an almost life-long interest in Nietzsche, and upon completing his doctorate went to Freiburg to study with Edmund Husserl. While in Freiburg he became acquainted with the teaching of Heidegger, an event that had a great impact on him.

For obvious reasons Strauss left Germany when he could and spent most of his career in the United States, first at the New School in New York, and then at the University of Chicago.

Strauss not only left Germany but, as he wrote to Gadamer in 1961, they had "marched from ... common ground in opposite directions." Gadamer went on to produce what Strauss called "the most important work by a Heideggerian" (Strauss and Gadamer 1978: 5); Strauss turned his interest away from Heidegger toward Socrates. His attempt to revive Socratic political philosophy became the center of his scholarly work. As a student of political philosophy he produced such works as *Natural Right and History* (1953), *Thoughts on Machiavelli* (1958), and *The City and Man* (1964), to mention only a few.

That march in the opposite direction from Gadamer, that is, away from Heidegger, had at its basis something Strauss had learned from Husserl and Heidegger: one must begin from the pre-scientific or pre-philosophic and understand science or philosophy to be a specific modification of the pre-scientific. Heidegger accused Husserl of not living up to his own standard, and in *Sein und Zeit* developed a more existential account of the pre-scientific than Husserl had. According to Heidegger, Husserl remained too theoretical. Strauss believed the same of Heidegger, as he thought was visible in the highly technical and abstract character of Heidegger's great work.

In his 1961 exchange of letters with Gadamer, Strauss denied that he had a hermeneutic in Gadamer's sense. In *Wahrheit und Methode* Gadamer claimed to be describing what he and all other human beings did when they tried to understand anything, not merely texts. But, Strauss observed, Gadamer's "theory of hermeneutic experience" did not correspond to his own experience as an interpreter of texts. Because it was intended to encompass all forms and instances of "interpretation," Gadamer's theory was necessarily universalistic. But, Strauss wrote, "the experience which I possess makes me doubtful whether a universal hermeneutic theory which is more than 'formal' or external is possible" (Strauss and Gadamer 1978: 5–6). Strauss rejects the notion of a "universal hermeneutic theory" because of his "feeling of the irretrievably 'occasional' character of every worthwhile interpretation." Strauss seems not to have meant by this claim what might appear most obvious: that the occasion for interpretation differs for each subject engaging in interpretation, with different questions and different purposes guiding the interpreting subject. Strauss speaks to this possible meaning of his concern with the "occasional" character of all interpretation when he observes that the "variety of hermeneutic situations" is not of decisive importance: "the difference of starting points and hence of the ascents does not lead to the consequence that the plateau which all interpretations as interpretation wish to reach is not one and the same." Strauss illustrates his point by imagining an economic historian seeking to understand Thucydides, who almost entirely ignores economic history. This historian is surely posing a different set of questions to Thucydides than Thucydides posed, or than the reader who approaches Thucydides as an "international relations theorist" would pose. Yet, Strauss says, the economic historian "must give an account of Thucydides' almost complete silence on economic subjects; ... he must answer the question of how economic things appear to Thucydides." The answer to that question "is nothing but a reproduction of Thucydides' thought on the human things in general"; that is, what Strauss has called "the plateau" at which all interpretations aim (Strauss and Gadamer 1978: 6).

So the occasional character of interpretation must lie not in the subject but in the object of interpretation, that is, the different kinds of communication sought to be understood. A conversation poses a task of understanding different from a literary text and different from a philosophic text. The universals involved across these different situations are "formal and external." Moreover, and perhaps most on Strauss's mind, is his well-known theory of the "art of writing." Different texts, even within one genre, are written quite differently. Some, for example, contain an exoteric exterior and an esoteric interior. The "hermeneutic" appropriate for the one is not appropriate for the other.

Despite his disavowals Strauss's philosophic efforts certainly give the appearance of being ventures in interpretation, for his corpus in the main consists of a series of studies in the history of philosophy; he was, it seems, above all an interpreter of historic philosophic texts. However, although he sometimes looked like an intellectual historian, his aspirations were clearly other: to revive and practice political philosophy. He was very clear in affirming that:

> political philosophy is not a historical discipline. The philosophic questions of the nature of political things and of the best, or the just, political order are fundamentally different from historical questions, which always concern individuals. ... In particular political philosophy is fundamentally different from the history of political philosophy itself. The question of the nature of political things and the answer to it cannot possibly be mistaken for the question of how this or that philosopher or all philosophers have approached, discussed or answered the philosophic question mentioned.
>
> (Strauss 1959: 56)

Strauss's philosophic practice, in contrast to his philosophic affirmation of the gulf between philosophy as such and the history of philosophy, brings us to our first thesis about Strauss and hermeneutics: for Strauss the practice of philosophy in our time is necessarily a hermeneutical, that is, historical, enterprise, despite the in-principle difference between philosophy and history. He argues that today "the philosophic effort and the historical effort have become completely fused" (Strauss 1959: 73). We identify two further hermeneutic claims embedded in Strauss's interpretive practices: first, the aim of all interpretive studies is "to understand the author as he understood himself." And, second, in interpreting the texts of past philosophers one must be alert to what he called "the art of writing."

The fusion of philosophy and history

Philosophy today must both fuse with history and remain distinct from it. That paradoxical combination tends to distinguish Strauss's work on the one side from historicists, such as Gadamer, who accept the idea of fusion, and analytic philosophers, who engage in political philosophy in almost complete independence from historical studies. Philosophy, Strauss thought, must begin with pre-philosophic opinion, but opinion in our post-Enlightenment age is thoroughly pervaded or infected by residues of earlier philosophy. For so many of today's political philosophers, for example, the question to be addressed is the nature of democracy or the effectuation of greater equality. These normative aims are taken to be, it seems, mere common sense or obvious political truisms, but they surely would not have been thought to be such by earlier thinkers. Strauss endorsed the Platonic image which suggests that we humans normally live in a cave defined by our opinions, the ascent from which constitutes the activity of philosophizing. But, Strauss thinks, we now live in a cave beneath the cave. Our cave is constituted by the layer upon layer of philosophically derived opinions that have become part of the atmosphere of thought that we breathe. In the face of our post-Enlightenment world, Strauss sees the need to follow a radical, yet slow and tentative path upward. We must begin with an effort to clarify the opinions constituting our cave, and that can be done only via studies in the history of political philosophy. Such studies aim to reconnect our dead or smoldering stubs and residues of philosophic thought with their sources so that these thoughts can live for us again. Such studies can awaken us to the alternatives that lie undigested and unintegrated in our common opinions. History of philosophy, as Strauss understands it, is merely propaedeutic to philosophy proper, but a necessary propaedeutic nonetheless.

But history is not a universally necessary propaedeutic. Philosophy must become a primarily interpretive activity in our day because of the particular character of our day, and the great barriers it poses to philosophy. Strauss thus agreed with Heidegger precisely where Gadamer did not. In order to avoid the obvious contradiction, Strauss argued, someone who affirms that all human understanding is historically bounded has to show why it is possible for human beings at this particular time to discover the transhistorical truth about the historical limitations of truth at all times. Gadamer claimed to be describing what human beings had, in fact, been doing at all times and places in trying to understand their world. But he had to admit that his own "hermeneutical" accounts of the work of art and language were not traditional; that is, they did not correspond to the self-understandings of the historical writers and artists he interpreted. Strauss concluded that "it is necessary to reflect on the situation which demands the new hermeneutics, i.e., on our situation"; and that "this reflection will necessarily bring to light a radical crisis." That crisis, as Strauss understood it, consisted in part in our existence in a cave beneath the cave, which demanded the fusion of history and philosophy now and for the time being, but not, as Gadamer would have it, as a universal.

Understanding a thinker as he understood himself

The second pillar of Strauss's hermeneutics, so far as we can attribute such to him, was the claim that the true or proper goal of interpretation is understanding a thinker as he understood himself. Just as Strauss's call for a fusion of philosophy and history shares much with Gadamer's hermeneutic, so his second thesis shares much with the Cambridge School of Quentin Skinner, who argued strenuously for this kind of understanding as the only kind that could qualify as authentic understanding. In making such a claim Strauss (and the Cambridge School writers) must affirm not only that such is the proper goal of interpretation but that this kind of understanding is possible. As Strauss pointed out in his correspondence with Gadamer, the Heideggerian Gadamer believes that "the finiteness of man as man necessitates the impossibility of adequate or complete or 'the true understanding'" (Strauss and Gadamer 1978: 6, citing Gadamer 1960: 355). There can be many different readings of a text, Strauss acknowledges, but they all implicitly, if not explicitly presuppose, and must be measured against the one understanding of the text held by its author (Strauss 1959: 67–8).

Gadamer sometimes put his case against this possibility in a way Strauss thought to be relevant. All understanding is implicitly understanding in terms of an answer to a question. The meaning of a text (or conversation) only exists within such a context of question and answer. But, according to Gadamer, "the logic of question and answer that [R.G.] Collingwood elaborated puts an end to talk about permanent *problems*. ... There is no such thing, in fact, as a point outside history from which the identity of a problem can be conceived within the vicissitudes of attempts to solve it" (Gadamer 1960: 375; cf. Strauss 1959: 25). Strauss had no difficulty accepting the notion of meaning as emerging from the question–answer nexus, but he found the conclusion that this insight led to the necessary denial of "permanent problems" to be quite unevident. Indeed, his philosophic, as well as hermeneutic position rests precisely on the claim that there are permanent problems and that they are accessible to us. (See Strauss 1959: 11, 39–40.) In the more strictly hermeneutic context this affirmation takes the form of the claim reported above, that the many different points of departure for historical inquiry do not preclude reaching the same plateau of understanding an author as he understood himself.

It is difficult to say how far Strauss believed actual attainment of this "authorial" understanding was possible. In his correspondence with Gadamer he conceded that "at least in the most important cases ... I have always seen that there remains in the text something of the utmost importance which I did not understand" (Strauss and Gadamer 1978: 6). Strauss, in other words, had not achieved his own goal. His unconditional affirmation of authorial understanding as the primary aim of all interpretation stands more clearly as a regulative methodological idea than as a realized attainment. The rejection of authorial understanding as goal is based on a too quick and unsubstantiated conclusion that there are no permanent problems; in light of this fact the authorial understanding is the best methodological basis of interpretation for it provides both a clear criterion of successful or correct interpretation and a sufficient motivation for understanding a text in the philosophically best way. Otherwise, as with the various historicist methodologies, we are always in danger of finding in a text more or less what we bring to it.

Strauss's rediscovery of a "forgotten kind of writing"

The task of understanding an author as he understood himself requires of the interpreter a certain point of view on a text. Unlike "reader response theory," for example, or various sorts of contextualizations, the interpreter must attempt to enter the mind of the author, must attempt to "think the thought" as the author thought it. The interpreter must also realize that the author in writing a text was not merely presenting a record of his best thinking, but was taking a public action in a particular context. The interpreter must, therefore, attempt to understand the context as the author did and to understand his public act of writing in that context. It may be, Strauss thought, that there was a conflict or tension between the thought of the author and the context such that the author might not express his thought in a straightforward manner. He might, for various reasons, practice an art of writing.

Strauss's discovery of the forgotten art of writing was to a degree a result of a certain biographical accident. As a Jew in Weimar Germany he sought an answer to "the Jewish problem," that is, to the problem of what the Jews, in a situation where the Enlightenment idea of assimilation appeared to be failing, should do. In search of a solution to "the Jewish problem," Strauss eventually turned to the writings of Maimonides. In his study of Maimonides, Strauss discovered a "forgotten kind of writing." He found that not only medieval Jewish and Arabic philosophers like Maimonides and his teacher, Alfarabi, but also ancient Greek poets, historians, and philosophers like Homer, Thucydides, and Plato employed an "art of writing" by virtue of which they "exoterically" appeared to accept the authoritative opinions of their respective societies, but, in fact, subjected those opinions "esoterically" to radical critiques that could be unearthed "between the lines" by a careful reader. Re-reading the canonical works of the history of Western philosophy in light of his re-discovery of the "art of writing," Strauss argued that philosophy does not consist primarily in the articulation of doctrines or arguments. As imaged in Plato's depiction of the life of Socrates and replicated in the works of later thinkers, philosophy consists in the investigation of perpetual problems. As such an on-going investigation, philosophy could not come to an end, as Nietzsche and Heidegger maintained that it had. On the contrary, philosophy continues to be the best and most satisfying way of life for a human being who is able to undertake it.

Strauss reported his revolutionary discoveries of the opposition between the exoteric surface or more conventional teaching and the esoteric philosophical challenge to it in the writings, first, of Maimonides, then of Plato, Herodotus, Hesiod, and other ancient Greek thinkers and poets, in correspondence with his friend Jacob Klein from January 1938 to November 1939.[1] He presented a more scholarly account of his discoveries in an article entitled "Persecution and the Art of Writing" that he first published in *Social Research* in 1941 and then made the opening chapter of a collection of essays under the same title. There he illustrated the exoteric art of writing as it occurred in several different medieval authors (Strauss 1952).

This art of writing had escaped the notice of recent historians of political thought, Strauss argued, for both political and scholarly reasons. First, these historians shared the presuppositions of their liberal societies. Taking "for granted the essential harmony between thought and society or between intellectual progress and social progress," these historians did not understand the conflict between philosophy and society that beset thinkers in the past, a conflict that encouraged them to develop an indirect mode of communicating their most radical thoughts. But for historians to develop accounts of the works of past authors on the basis of modern liberal assumptions is to commit a serious anachronism, an "unhistorical" error. Liberal societies are relatively rare and only recently developed. Most philosophers did not live or write in such societies. On the contrary, many past authors who openly disagreed with prevailing, officially endorsed opinions suffered penalties, ranging from social ostracism to torture and capital punishment.

The threat of persecution was only the first and most obvious reason, however, for past writers to practice the art of writing: questioning accepted opinions creates doubt about established moral norms and, therefore, some pre-modern authors concluded, a completely public presentation of the results of the philosophical search for truth is not compatible with the requirements of a stable political order. Attempting to act (or write) in a "socially responsible" manner, these authors sought to conceal their most radical questions and conclusions from all but their most careful and serious readers.

There was yet a further reason, moreover, that some authors chose to communicate their thoughts incompletely and indirectly. Truly philosophical authors write not so much to propagate doctrines as to encourage younger readers to follow them in a life of inquiry. Such authors artfully attempt to awaken the "young puppies," as Strauss used to say, by raising questions in the minds of their most attentive readers and then providing some hints concerning how those questions might be answered; but the philosophers leave their readers to think out the answers and the problems with these possible answers for themselves. Plato, who wrote only dialogues in which he presented conversations among others, was Strauss's model of such an author.

Strauss's ideas about concealed writing may have been controversial when he proposed them, but they were historically rather commonplace. For instance, Strauss notes, Maimonides spoke openly of concealed meaning in texts, and until the nineteenth century, many philosophers and theologians thought that Thomas Hobbes and Baruch Spinoza were really atheists who concealed their true views under misleading theological language.

Strauss's theory of esotericism was subtle and nuanced. He distinguished a modern variant from the classic version. Looking forward to the abolition of persecution as such, modern philosophers "concealed their views only far enough to protect themselves as well as possible." Older authors, however, were "convinced that philosophy as such is suspect to, and hated by, the majority of men" and thus concluded "that the public communication of the philosophic or scientific truth was impossible or undesirable, not only for the time being but for all times" (Strauss 1952: 33–4).

Strauss did not believe that all authors write esoterically. Indeed, he set up criteria that must be met before one has a right to posit esotericism in a text. Most importantly, one must read the text "on the lines" before one tries to read "between the lines." Only when problems – contradictions, noticeable gaps, and other anomalies – appear "on the lines" ought one to think of reading "between the lines." Moreover, Strauss's techniques of reading are not undisciplined or merely subjective as some critics assert. The scholar's calling, Strauss maintained, requires that one try to give an account of what was written "on the lines," that is, what an author literally wrote. If a coherent and accurate account of the content of any given text can be given on the basis of the author's explicit statements, the analysis ends there. But, if an obviously intelligent and knowledgeable author makes "such blunders as would shame an intelligent high school boy, it is reasonable to assume that they are intentional, especially if the author discusses, however incidentally, the possibility of intentional blunders in writing." One must also be sensitive to the literary form. "The views of the author of a drama or dialogue must not, without previous proof, be identified with the views expressed by one or more of his characters." Most controversially, he also held, "the real opinion of an author is not necessarily identical with that which he expresses in the largest number of passages" (Strauss 1952: 30).

In line with his comments to Gadamer, Strauss did not lay out a hermeneutical "method" to be applied to any or all texts, but he did suggest a few general strategies for reading such texts. According to classical rhetoricians, he noted, items placed in the middle are least exposed to superficial readers.[2] The observation that some topic or point comes in the middle of a list or text does not, of course, prove anything in itself. But it does give the reader a hint of where to look and what to think about. In all cases, an independent account of the significance of the central points must be provided (Strauss 1952: 13–14). Strauss also observes that we often learn how an author writes by observing how he reads another text. Explicating Maimonides' *Guide for the Perplexed*, Strauss pointed out "hints" provided by the author's own reading of the Torah that can help a careful reader decipher the "secrets" Maimonides claimed to be communicating only in intentionally disordered "chapter headings."[3] Strauss begins his essay "How to Study Spinoza's *Theologico-Political Treatise*," however, with a long and complex analysis of the reasons we cannot and should not try to read Spinoza the way he read the Bible or Euclid.[4]

Strauss's thesis about the "art of writing" has been met with skepticism on three issues. First, many citizens of modern liberal societies find it difficult to accept the special difficulties of writing in non-liberal societies. But surely it is possible that a thinker might have something to say that will be highly offensive to powerful figures in the community or to public opinion at large. Is it not plausible that a thinker might hesitate to run the risk of being completely open in public expression? A thinker also might come to conclusions that are at odds with claims important to the moral and political consensus and health of society. One example Strauss often used of such a conflict was the belief that just and unjust behavior was rewarded and punished in an after-life. But if a philosopher concluded that there is no reasonable evidence for such a belief, might he not have held his tongue in public, thinking that the belief supports moral order in society?

Second, some critics of Strauss's mode of reading fall back on historicist views about the relation of thought to its times. The only basis for the a priori and out of hand rejection of the possibilities outlined above is the dogmatic commitment to the view that philosophers never think outside the box of their time and place. But that stance is simply question-begging and too loaded with a priori elements to provide a reliable method for interpretation.

Third, critics object that Strauss's methods can never produce readings that satisfy "scientific" criteria for interpretation, including such things as easy replicability, interpersonal stability of interpretation, and ability to account univocally for all the "data" in a text.[5] This objection has more merit than the others; it points to a tension between Strauss's aims and his methods. The aim of his studies is to understand the philosophers exactly as they understood themselves. But if Strauss is correct about the way in which older writers wrote, then it becomes extremely difficult to establish a reading as *the* reading intended by the author. In *Persecution and the Art of Writing* Strauss in effect concedes that no incontestable reading of a philosopher allegedly engaging in esoteric writing can ever be established (Strauss 1952: 30). The very point of such writing was to make it difficult to prove that the thinker held views such as are produced in an esoteric reading. If there were a clear-cut and incontestable reading of an author who wrote in this way, the author would then have to be judged a failure at achieving what that mode of writing aimed to achieve: to establish at the very least "plausible deniability" for the doctrines not placed in the open.

The burden of establishing an esoteric reading is extremely heavy, Strauss admitted; and such reading can never be established to the satisfaction of all readers. However, given the undeniable possibility that some writers wrote that way, not to pursue the esoteric meaning even more definitively fails at the task of understanding the author as he understood himself. For if a writer did write esoterically, a reading that does not take that possibility into account necessarily closes the door to understanding the author much more decisively than Strauss's way of reading opens it to the possibility of error. Many of Strauss's critics fail to see that under-reading a text can be as much an error and often a much greater loss than the possibility of over-reading risked by Strauss's methods.

Notes

1 The contents of the letters are summarized in English by Lampert 2009: 63–76. The German originals can be found in Strauss 2001: 544–87.
2 Strauss 1952: 185, cites Cicero, *Orator* 15.50, *De oratore* 77.313.
3 Strauss thus begins his essay on "How to Begin to Study *The Guide of the Perplexed*" (Strauss 1968: xi–xiii) with an outline of the chapter headings that contrasts markedly with Maimonides' own explicit organization of the book.
4 On the basis of his suggestion that an author often reveals the way he himself writes in the way he reads the works of others, many commentators have concluded that Strauss himself writes exoterically, for example, Pangle 2006, Smith 2006, Drury 1988. As we see in the case of Spinoza, however, Strauss did not think that all authors should necessarily be read the same way they read others. Zuckert and Zuckert 2006: 115–54, argue that Strauss did not present a "secret teaching" although he did exercise "pedagogical reserve."
5 Consider Melzer 2006: 280: Strauss's claims about esotericism "open up a Pandora's box of interpretive difficulties."

Bibliography

Drury, S. (1988) *The Political Ideas of Leo Strauss*, New York: St. Martin's Press.

Gadamer, H. (1960) *Wahrheit und Methode*, Tübingen: Mohr, 1960.

——(1990) *Truth and Method*, trans. Joel Weinsheimer and Donald G. Marshall, New York: Crossroad.

Lampert, Laurence (2009) "Strauss's Recovery of Esotericism," in S. Smith (ed.) *The Cambridge Companion to Leo Strauss*, Cambridge: Cambridge University Press.

Melzer, A. (2006) "Esotericism and the Critique of Historicism," *American Political Science Review*, 100: 275–95.

Pangle, T. (2006) *Leo Strauss: An Introduction to His Thought and Intellectual Legacy*, Baltimore, MD: Johns Hopkins University Press.

Smith, S. (2006) *Reading Leo Strauss: Politics, Philosophy, Judaism*, Chicago: University of Chicago Press.

Strauss, L. (1952) *Persecution and the Art of Writing*, Chicago: University of Chicago Press.

——(1959) *What Is Political Philosophy? and Other Studies*, Glencoe, IL: The Free Press.

——(1968) "How to Begin to Study *The Guide of the Perplexed*," in Strauss, *Liberalism: Ancient and Modern*, New York: Basic Books.

——(2001) *Gesammelte Schriften*, ed. Heinrich Meier and Wiebke Meier, Stuttgart: J. B. Metzler.

Strauss, L. and Gadamer, H. (1978) "Correspondence Concerning *Wahrheit und Methode*," *Independent Journal of Philosophy*, 2: 5–12.

Zuckert, C. and M. Zuckert (2006) *The Truth about Leo Strauss*, Chicago: University of Chicago Press.

Further reading

Strauss L. (1952) *Persecution and the Art of Writing*, New York: The Free Press.

Strauss, L. (1959) "On a Forgotten Way of Writing," in *What Is Political Philosophy? and Other Studies*, New York: The Free Press.

Strauss, L. (1961) *On Tyranny*, Chicago: University of Chicago Press.

11

GADAMER: THE UNIVERSALITY OF HERMENEUTICS

Hans-Helmuth Gander

Hans-Georg Gadamer (1900–2002) is regarded as the founder of modern philosophical hermeneutics. He is considered one of the most important figures in twentieth century philosophy. Gadamer received this acknowledgement comparatively late, however, as the book establishing his worldwide fame appeared when he was already sixty years old. From today's perspective, it seems curious that, when Gadamer delivered the manuscript, the publisher accepted the term "hermeneutics" in the subtitle only ("Grundzüge einer philosophischen Hermeneutik" – "Outline of a philosophical hermeneutics"). As a result, Gadamer's work was released and read under the title *Wahrheit und Methode – Truth and Method* (2013) – especially in English, in which the subtitle has never appeared in the translation.[1] Following the publication of the book, soon acknowledged as the basis of modern hermeneutics, Gadamer had forty more productive years to further develop his conception of philosophical hermeneutics. The diversity and abundance of thematic extensions and new approaches in Gadamer's work is well documented since 1995 within the ten volumes of the *Gesammelte Werke* (*Collected Works*) (Gadamer 1986–95), underlining the open nature of his hermeneutics. Looking at Gadamer's work as a whole it is fair to say that *Truth and Method* is undeniably the systematic centre. For good reasons, then, Habermas counted it among the most significant philosophical works of the second half of the twentieth century (and he is in good company about this judgement). Drawing on *Truth and Method* and in constant relation to it, the subject matter of hermeneutics expanded in concentric circles, as it were. Gadamer's ongoing openness for dialogue initiated numerous thematic debates, for example with Habermas on the critique of ideology or with Derrida on the term "deconstruction," which sometimes led to mostly moderate revisions (see Malpas and Zabala 2010; Wischke and Hofer 2003; Hahn 1997). In line with the open agenda of Gadamer's hermeneutics, the goal of the following chapter is to highlight and portray some critical aspects of his work. I will argue that the question regarding human understanding is Gadamer's basic philosophical concern.

I.

Within Gadamer's hermeneutic approach, whenever we understand something (for example a text, machine or gesture), we simultaneously understand ourselves as well. Gadamer dismisses conceptions of hermeneutics as an art or methodology, associated with names like Wolff, Ast, Schleiermacher, Droysen or Dilthey, and in so doing he follows Heidegger's existential-ontological hermeneutics of human being-in-the-world. In light of its projective character, for Heidegger understanding is the distinctive way of being human that ontologically characterises a human being's sense of self and her relationship to the world as a whole.

Understanding is thus, for Heidegger, the original way of enacting human existence (*Dasein*). Gadamer repeatedly emphasised that he wanted to devote his own project to developing this aspect of the hermeneutic problem. Consequently, Gadamer holds that whoever understands does so in a way that involves "projecting oneself upon one's possibilities" (Gadamer 2013: 261), which is why "the accomplished understanding [as a way of knowing *one's* way around something] constitutes a state of new intellectual freedom" (Gadamer 2013: 261).

Like Heidegger, Gadamer conceives of the human being in accordance with the a priori existential character of that being as understandingly open towards itself and towards the world. Self-knowledge, in other words, unfolds only with world-knowledge, and so also our relation to the world shapes our relation to ourselves. However, if understanding in this sense is the ever-present enactment structure of human life, this simultaneously universalises the scope of hermeneutics with respect to knowledge of human existence (*Sein*). Understanding is no longer a kind of knowledge specific to the human sciences in contrast to, say, objective explanation. Rather, understanding is the very event of human existence, unlocking self and world, founding all kinds of cognition and their respective ways of knowing and acting. Going beyond Gadamer's own characterisation, Michael Steinmann sees this as the "transition into the philosophy of an advanced modernity: The self-liberation of philosophy from its ties to certain sciences and the search for an ownmost, genuine area of phenomena and knowledge" (Steinmann 2007: 101). Thus Gadamer's claim to universality of hermeneutics indicates "from this viewpoint nothing but the attempt to establish hermeneutics as a … radically modern epistemology … , no longer bound to certain historic conventions like 'cognition' or 'science' and instead established on a fundamental experience of meaning, which changes and perpetuates itself in a universal manner" (Steinmann 2007: 102).

For Gadamer, the experience of meaning is co-originary with language, the medium of hermeneutic experience. The "coming into language of meaning" (Gadamer 2013: 490) reveals language as a "universal ontological structure" (Gadamer 2013: 490); as "the basic nature of everything toward which understanding can be directed" (Gadamer 2013: 490). For Gadamer, to "come into language does not mean that a second being is acquired" (Gadamer 2013: 491). What comes into language portrays itself in it and "what something presents itself as [rather] belongs to its own being" (Gadamer 2013: 491). In a frequently quoted passage, Gadamer expresses the ontological shift of hermeneutics with the words: "*Being that can be understood is language*" (Gadamer 2013: 490), thereby identifying language as the horizon of a hermeneutical ontology. To clarify that what can be understood is language, he adds, "it is of such a nature that of itself it offers itself to be understood" (Gadamer 2013: 491). Accordingly, Gadamer conceives the meaning of a historical event, a text or the existence of an artwork, as nothing that exists for or in itself. Rather, everything "has its being in its presentation" (Gadamer 2013: 492). Everything is always already mediated in the universal medium of language as the determining factor of both the hermeneutical subject matter and the hermeneutical enactment. "[L]anguage that expresses meaning is not only art and history but everything insofar as it can be understood" (Gadamer 2013: 493). Accordingly "man's relation to the world is absolutely and fundamentally verbal in nature, and hence intelligible" (Gadamer 2013: 491). In this respect, Gadamer's hermeneutic position exemplifies what has been an increasingly prominent feature of philosophical discourse since the beginning of the twentieth century – the focus on the problem of language as a central topic of discussion. In the course of this so-called "linguistic turn," the methodology of the natural sciences has become something of a model for much analytic philosophy of language and logic. In contrast, Gadamer's ontological shift to language is not oriented towards a scientific ideal, but rather pays heed to "the hermeneutical archetypal phenomenon [*Urphänomen*] ... ," namely: "there is no possible statement that cannot be understood as the answer to a question and that [every possible statement] can only be understood in this way" (Gadamer 1986: 226).

In a decisive manner, Gadamer sets being (*Sein*), presentation, language and comprehensibility in a constitutive relation to each other, so that any particular entity achieves its being only in understanding: "The hermeneutical phenomenon here projects its own universality back onto the ontological constitution of what is understood, determining it in a universal sense as *language* and determining its own relation to beings as interpretation" (Gadamer 2013: 490). Thereby hermeneutics is "*a universal aspect of philosophy*, and not just the methodological basis of the so-called human sciences" (Gadamer 2013: 491). Insofar as all that Gadamer investigates in his many works – including the phenomena of art, culture, science, history or philosophy – comes to understanding only in the universal medium of language, so understanding as a basic hermeneutic experience gives rise to no methodological reduction or limitation as traditional hermeneutics (up to and including Dilthey) had assumed. "[L]anguage that expresses meaning is not only art and history but everything insofar as it can be understood" (Gadamer 2013: 493). This means that, for Gadamer, the "speculative character of being that is the ground of hermeneutics has the same universality as do reason and language" (Gadamer 2013: 493).

Gadamer does not take the universalisation of hermeneutic's claim of knowledge to lead to a final, absolute knowledge abstracting from all experience. This is evident in that the process of universalisation goes hand in hand with a historisation of the cognitive claim made by understanding. In this way finitude and relatedness to experience prove to be constitutive for all human (and therefore hermeneutic) knowledge. For Gadamer, the linguistic nature of understanding as universal medium underlines "the finitude of the verbal event in which understanding is always in the process of being concretised. The language that things have ... is the language that our finite, historical nature apprehends when we learn to speak. This is true of the language of the texts handed down to us in tradition ... . It is as true of the art as of the experience of history" (Gadamer 2013: 492). Both such language and such experience are "modes of understanding that emerge from the universal mode of hermeneutical being as forms of hermeneutic experience" (Gadamer 2013: 492). With this remark it becomes clear that Gadamer's preferred model in the development of his hermeneutic conception, that is, the model of text, does not imply any commitment to traditional hermeneutic positions. Rather, textual examples provide a high degree of structural intuitiveness when analysing hermeneutic experience and are thus of heuristic value. The concept of hermeneutic experience central to Gadamer's thought (in the German, Gadamer even speaks of the "dignity," *Würde*, of hermeneutical experience – see Gadamer 1990: 492) shows itself as "an encounter with something that asserts itself as truth" (Gadamer 2013: 504).

II.

Applied to understanding this means, in an insight crucial to Gadamer's conception of hermeneutics, that: "Someone who understands is always already drawn into an event through which meaning asserts itself" (Gadamer 2013: 506) – drawn, that is, into an event that speaks to us and tells us something. Viewed this way, human understanding never begins without presuppositions. The ontological structure of circularity characterising understanding manifestly demonstrates that this would be indeed impossible. Drawing on the ontologically positive sense of the circularity of human knowledge as Heidegger introduced it (see Heidegger 1996: §32) Gadamer develops his original reformulation of the hermeneutic circle, in terms drawn from the model of textual interpretation, so as to provide a new foundation for hermeneutics in the human sciences:

> A person who is trying to understand a text is always projecting. He projects a meaning for the text as a whole as soon as some initial meaning emerges in the text. Again, the initial meaning emerges only because he is reading the text with particular expectations in regard to a certain meaning. Working out the fore-projection, which is constantly revised in terms of what emerges as he penetrates into the meaning, is understanding what is there.
>
> (Gadamer 2013: 279)

The crucial point in Gadamer's approach is revealed by noticing how even when the text is present in the shape of an intended meaningful whole – it is always embedded in presuppositions preceding it and external to it, which remain largely implicit in the text itself. Thus the written always has a prehistory.

Although developed on the basis of a textual model, it is crucial for the hermeneutical scope of this insight that it is by no means restricted to texts alone. In fact, the point at issue holds for everything within the limits of possible human experience. On this basis, texts are themselves shown to be a part of the world of human experience. In a sense, they can be seen as its objectifications, in which the world of experience is accessible. In line with one of Dilthey's statements, texts can be conceived as "objectifications of historical life" (see Dilthey 2002). Once this is understood, it becomes clear why Gadamer was able to use the textual model to hermeneutically illustrate the existential pre-structure of understanding first introduced by Heidegger, and why also, contrary to occasional claims to the contrary, Gadamer by no means reduced the existential a priori scope of Heidegger's approach to a more traditionally oriented and purely *textual* hermeneutics. It is the idea of the text as precisely an objectification of historical life (and so as more than a "mere" text in the narrow sense of the term) that provides the model on which Gadamer bases his concrete analysis of Heidegger's formal indication of the pre-structure of understanding as viewed from the perspective of the one who understands in relation to what is understood.

For Gadamer, fore-knowledge is the starting point of every interpretation, which in turn determines the validity of all the fore-meanings directed at the text via the anticipated meaning. According to this model, validity (*Stichhaltigkeit*) names the kind of objectivity to be understood as *confirmation of the fore-meaning*. With respect to the adequateness of understanding, such validity amounts to a proof of the legitimacy of fore-meanings. Therefore, Gadamer's theory is not simply about the observation that humans, as understanding beings, can only understand by relying on fore-knowledge, that is, fore-meanings. Much rather, the hermeneutical task consists in illuminating what these fore-meanings are structurally like. This means that by way of reflecting on the fore-knowledge of the interpreter, Gadamer succeeds in determining the space or distance between text and interpreter in such a way that on both sides, that is, with regard to both text and interpreter, the respective fore-meanings are revealed as constitutive structural components for meaning-adequate understanding. In this sense, Gadamer distinguishes between two kinds of fore-meanings. Either fore-meanings relate to *language usage*[2] or they are the "fore-meanings concerning content with which we read texts, and which make up our fore-understanding" (Gadamer 2013: 281). These latter, however, must be distinguished from the fore-meanings pertaining to the text or author. Such fore-meanings "I have to take note of without necessarily having to share [them]" (Gadamer 2013: 281).

These two kinds of fore-meanings, those relating to "language usage" and to "content," determine the constitutive conditions under which a reader aiming at adequate understanding approaches something to be interpreted. Since the phenomenal matter articulated in both dimensions is irreducible, fore-meanings can never be eliminated. With respect to this fundamental hermeneutical fact, Gadamer argues that in order to do justice to the fore-structure of understanding concretised in the fore-meanings it is necessary to shed light on the interpreter's own dispositions. A first step in this direction "includes our situating the other meaning in relation to the whole of our own meanings or ourselves in relation to it" (Gadamer 2013: 281). To "remain open to the meaning of the other person or the text" (Gadamer 2013: 281) is thus made evident as a minimal standard of hermeneutic experience. As a result, Gadamer puts the basic methodological postulate of hermeneutics as follows:

> a person trying to understand a text is prepared for it to tell him something. That is why a hermeneutically trained consciousness must be, from the start, sensitive to the text's alterity. But this kind of sensitivity involves neither "neutrality" with respect to content nor the extinction of one's self,

but the foregrounding and appropriation of one's own fore-meanings and prejudices.

(Gadamer 2013: 282)

Consequently, that one must begin with oneself is unavoidable for Gadamer, as one can never approach a text neutrally. So far as a meaning-adequate understanding of the tradition reaching us via texts is concerned, a neutrality that claims objectivity by pretending the subject is not involved, and is therefore distanced from itself, is purely fictional. Instead, one must "be aware of one's own bias, so that the text can present itself in all its otherness and thus assert its own truth against one's own fore-meanings" (Gadamer 2013: 282). Hence, the text's meaning does not exist in itself and entirely apart from the process of interpretation. The claim to truth in the understanding of a text (i.e. the adequate grasp of its meaning) can be maintained only within and with respect to a critically reflective understanding. From this perspective, the hermeneutical task of an understanding guided by methodological awareness involves the requirement "not merely to form anticipatory ideas, but to make them conscious, so as to check them and thus acquire right understanding from the things themselves" (Gadamer 2013: 282). It is only when his presuppositions are transparent that the reader achieves full clarity in relation to his own intentions. Out of this hermeneutical self-assurance, he is then able to explicitly position himself regarding the meanings inherent to the text to be interpreted.

III.

The difference in fore-meanings as they pertain to text and to interpreter, characterises the methodological starting point for the hermeneutical project within the human sciences. According to Gadamer this position attains its philosophical significance in its fundamental "recognition that all understanding inevitably involves some prejudice [*Vorurteil*]" (Gadamer 2013: 283).

Gadamer differentiates between two relevant kinds of prejudice. The first are *personal prejudices* which are usually recognised by the interpreter and others, and can actively be dealt with by them (they can be made an immediate focus of attention and affirmed, denied or revised). The second are *hidden prejudices* (Gadamer 2013: 282) – the kind of prejudices or fore-meanings really relevant to hermeneutics – which are effective in us through history and whose origin is no longer directly accessible. An example here would be metaphysical notions, formed long ago and prior to any philosophical speculation or hermeneutical reflection, and which have taken the form of, for instance, particular cultural, political, aesthetic, religious or ethical self-beliefs. Such hidden prejudices can appear, relative to the respective cultural sphere, in such a way that a universal significance is attributed to them. They often create the liveliest effects precisely where their historical origin is least known or understood. Gadamer articulates this in a key insight seminal to his hermeneutical concept: "Long before we understand ourselves through the process of self-examination, we understand ourselves in a self-evident way in the family, society, and state in which we live. ... *That is why the prejudices of the individual, far more than his judgments, constitute the historical reality of his being"* (Gadamer 2013: 289).

Shedding light on the unseen prejudices of historical consciousness requires an analysis geared towards recognising the prejudicial character of all understanding as itself a historically generated process. Part of the significance of this insight lies in the positivity that must therefore be attached to understanding in its prejudicial character. Gadamer argues this is due

> to the historical character of our existence that prejudices in the literal sense of the word form the pre-directedness of our entire experience aptness. They are biases of our openness to the world, which are really conditions for us to experience something and for our encounters to tell us something.
> (Gadamer 1986: 224)

Gadamer links three mutually intertwined goals to this analytical approach: first, the recognition of prejudices as conditions for understanding; second, the rehabilitation of the concept of authority; and third, the bringing about of a rehabilitation of tradition. The starting point of the analysis is a question concerning the contemporary usage of the word "prejudice." The preliminary finding is that "prejudice" usually has a negative connotation. But following on from this, the hermeneutical task is to investigate the process of the shift in meaning within the conceptual history that leads to this negative connotation. For Gadamer, the source of this shift in meaning lies historically and factually in the "the global demand of the Enlightenment" (Gadamer 2013: 288) to overcome all prejudices. This demand, and the shift to which it gives rise, is strengthened, according to Gadamer, by yet another "hidden prejudice," in his own words: "the fundamental prejudice of the Enlightenment is the prejudice against prejudice itself, which denies tradition its power" (Gadamer 2013: 283). The fact that Gadamer associates the alleged meaning shift to a "disempowerment of tradition" reveals the direction of his somewhat controversial critique of the Enlightenment. In truth, however, Gadamer's attempt "to fundamentally rehabilitate the concept of prejudice" (Gadamer 2013: 289) is not so much about the Enlightenment and its goals, as directed toward a clarification of the hermeneutical situation, in which fore-meanings or prejudices undeniably structure the human understanding of self and world. Therefore, the hermeneutical role of prejudice in leading us factually and shaping our fore-knowledge is connected to the "fundamental epistemological question ... : what is the ground of the legitimacy of prejudices? What distinguishes legitimate prejudices from the countless others which it is the undeniable task of critical reason to overcome?" (Gadamer 2013: 289).

Gadamer connects this latter question to the fundamental epistemological question concerning the rehabilitation of the concepts of authority and tradition – it is this that has encouraged the repeated tendency on the part of interpreters to treat his position as essentially conservative. If the goal is, contrary to such a stereotypical reading, to understand the real philosophical significance of Gadamer's trio, *prejudice, authority, tradition,* and so also to recognise the unusual provocation inherent in his fundamental epistemological question, then it is necessary to uncover something of the *conception of truth* that is also at issue here (see Grondin 1994). In fact, in order adequately to determine the work of understanding with an eye to fore-knowledge as its condition of possibility, the problem of truth has to be clarified. This is because for Gadamer, ontologically speaking, the understanding of truth possesses the same function that Heidegger ascribes to the understanding of being as that which comes prior to all of Dasein's active engagement in the world.

Since Aristotle, traditional conceptions have privileged judgement as the proper *locus* of truth, on the basis of the understanding of truth as the adequacy of thought and thing (*adaequatio intellectus et rei*). For Gadamer, however, things are only accessible to us in the universal medium of language by means of our "prejudices" or in the light of our fore-knowing. In order for a claim to truth to be substantiated, and so for a judgement to be shown to be true or false, the judgement has to be confirmed or corrected in relation to the mode of givenness of the thing in question, and in view of the way both kinds of prejudice influence the formation of opinion. Through this inherently dynamic process – a process that operates by means of a hermeneutic circularity that includes prejudice – judgement loses its privileged position. If the point of departure is the pre-structure of understanding, then the potential of our prejudices as opening up a relation to truth, even as enabling truth, becomes evident. This potential comes to light in that it is with prejudice (or better, with fore-knowledge as the constitutive condition for the possibility of understanding) that the dimension of meaning in which the human openness to self and world belongs is made explicit. "We are ... occupied with something and through the very thing we are occupied with we are open to the new, different, true" (Gadamer 1986: 225). However, to the extent that fore-knowledge, as a spectrum of possibilities, encompasses my own explicit understanding and precedes it, so any particular instance of something's "being true" is always based in a prior openness of meaning. In this way, truth can itself be interpreted as an event of meaning that approaches and encompasses human beings, and in the sway of which understanding is enacted in all its singular and concrete instances. Not least for this reason, did Gadamer consider, as the original title for his *magnum opus*, "Understanding and Happening" ("*Verstehen und Geschehen*"). That this is indeed appropriate to the hermeneutical question of truth pursued in the work is evident in the way the idea of truth appears, through the analysis of the prejudiced nature of understanding, as itself a happening of meaning. Moreover, this way of understanding truth, and the role of prejudice, implies a clear rejection of those positions that take meaning to be something independent of us – as something that stands apart from prejudice. Even the critical revision of prejudices by means of their falsification never leads to the abolition of prejudice, but always to new prejudices (if perhaps more adequate to the things in question). Understanding, understood in terms of the expectations of meaning that it intends, cannot be taken to be directed towards any ultimate meaning that is somehow finally and completely fulfilled.

For Gadamer, as for Heidegger, meaning as an existential structure is always meaning "in a certain direction" [*Richtungssinn*]. This is why Gadamer says of the hermeneutical task that it is "to expand the unity of the understood meaning centrifugally. The harmony of all the details with the whole is the criterion of correct understanding. The failure to achieve this harmony means that understanding has failed" (Gadamer 2013: 302). The hermeneutical criterion of successful understanding is thus to be found in the harmony between the understanding as conditioned by its pre-judices and the hermeneutical experience of the thing that is thereby made possible. Compared to the traditional model of correspondence or simple adequation so often associated with truth, Gadamer's position involves a crucial modification: the thing to be understood does not appear as something *merely given*, instead its very mode of givenness is itself constituted by the prejudices of the interpreter. There is, in other words, neither a pure appearance of the thing taken on its own nor a total elimination of prejudices in regard to the thing. Rather, in their tension, both elements belong to a dynamic and dialectical movement. Yet although Hegel may appear to be invoked, the dialectical dynamic at issue here does not result in any complete self-knowledge of consciousness as Gadamer sees it. Correspondence or adequation requires a constitutive openness that is prior to it, but this openness stands quite apart from all traditional ideals of certainty or epistemic completeness. The original hermeneutical contribution to the philosophical debate over truth is thus to be seen in the surpassing of the model of truth as some sort of "equivalence" between subject and object. That model is surpassed just inasmuch as the dynamic of prejudice and thing – and so the process of correspondence or adequation – is one in which each pole is always determined in relation to the other and responsive to the other. There is no one element that gives any final determination to the overall structure.

Within the dynamic that appears here, prejudices are revealed as always, in principle, revisable. Such revisability is only possible, however, if the structure of fore-knowledge is not autonomous, but adaptable to new experiences, and so open to the experience of *alterity* – to a genuine experience of otherness. We are not, as Gadamer vividly illustrates, "enclosed by a wall of prejudices, allowing only that to pass through the narrow gate which provides a permit saying: nothing new is said here. Instead, the guest is welcome to us who promises our curiosity something new" (Gadamer 1986: 224). Correspondingly, for Gadamer the task of hermeneutics is based in the "polarity of familiarity and strangeness" (Gadamer 2013: 306) which remains a never-ending challenge. In Gadamer's eyes, "our own prejudice is properly brought into play by being put at risk. Only by being given full play is it able to experience the other's claim to truth and make it possible for him to have full play himself" (Gadamer 2013: 310). Yet how can prejudice be brought into play in this fashion? That can be done only when prejudice is deprived of its hidden effectivity, when prejudice is, as Gadamer stresses, provoked. Moreover, what provokes prejudice, allowing us to become conscious of it, is an "encounter with a traditionary text" (Gadamer 2013: 310) – prejudice is opened up as prejudice only in the encounter with tradition.

IV.

It is among the central tasks of philosophical hermeneutics, as Gadamer understands it, namely as an exertion of critical reason, to sensitise our expectations of meaning and knowledge to tradition's superior claim to truth – all that is to be understood, text or whatever else, has an unquestionable authority "based on tradition" (Gadamer 2013: 292). Gadamer himself expressed this situation quite lucidly in conversation: "We are formed by traditions; whether we know these traditions or not, whether we are conscious of them or arrogant enough to assume we would start without prejudices – all this does not alter the way traditions effect us and our understanding" (Dutt 1993: 21). This is why, for Gadamer, the present, not only the past, is an integral part of tradition as it affects all efforts at understanding (see Gander 2010: 132–43). Hence, the hermeneutical achievement of understanding in the sense of a productive capability is to "always retain something of the splendid magic of a direct mirroring of the present in the past and the past in the present" (Gadamer 1986: 222). In hermeneutics, the interrelation between history and self-hood as a basic structure of all understanding efforts must always be acknowledged. Accordingly, a "hermeneutics adequate to the subject matter would have to demonstrate the reality and efficacy of history within understanding itself" (Gadamer 2013: 310). What is called for is what Gadamer designates as *effective history* (*Wirkungsgeschichte*); that is, that particular relation between past and present in which past tradition is constitutive of present orientation. Gadamer thus insists that genuine historical consciousness must involve the recognition that whenever we are "trying to understand a historical phenomenon from the historical distance … , we are always already affected by [effective] history" (Gadamer 2013: 311). At the same time, this also means: "*Understanding is, essentially, a historically effected event*" (Gadamer 2013: 310). Effective history is, in other words, the history that wholly permeates and determines the present. Understood in terms of effective history, attending to history means attending to the fact "that the huge horizon of the past, out of which our culture and present live, is effective in everything [and this is important] that we want with regard to the future" (Gadamer 1986: 224). Here Gadamer deliberately follows Heidegger, who as Gadamer sees it: "showed the primacy of the futurity for the possible memorizing and retaining and thereby for our history as a whole" (Gadamer 1986: 224). For Gadamer history is thus "coexistent and itself existent only in the light of our futurity" (Gadamer 1986: 224).

On this basis, Gadamer insists on the need for us "to become conscious of effective history" (Gadamer 2013: 312) – which means to proceed from a historic consciousness to a consciousness, as he puts it, of effective history. Gadamer emphasises that the consciousness of effective history is accomplished "in language" (Gadamer 1986: 228), because "understanding is bound to language" (Gadamer 1986: 228), and so to the worldly experience of humans. Language, for Gadamer, is no mere system of signals. Thought in terms of a living speech, it is rather an "infinity of language building and world experiencing conduct" (Gadamer 1986: 230), which "persists throughout our building the world in our own language wherever we wish to tell us something" (Gadamer 1986: 231). In the light of language as the universal medium of hermeneutic experience, in which the universal claim of hermeneutics is explicit, Gadamer argues that it would be "utterly wrong to conclude, because there are different languages, reason were split in itself" (Gadamer 1986: 230). Gadamer claims instead that: "The contrary is true. It is precisely via finitude, the particularity of our existence, observable also in the diversity of languages, that the infinite dialogue, which we are, opens towards truth" (Gadamer 1986: 230). It is out of this insight into the finitude of human existence (*Dasein*), which is also a challenge for hermeneutics, that the universal and unending task of understanding arises.

Notes

1 On Gadamer's biography, see Gadamer 1997; and also Grondin 2004. In his later years Gadamer reflected upon his own development and work in detailed discussions that also provide a multifaceted insight in the intellectual history of the twentieth century (see Gadamer 2001, 2004).

2 Rather, we regard our task as deriving our understanding of the text from the linguistic usage of the time or the author. ... generally we do so in the experience of being pulled up short by the text. Either it does not yield any meaning at all or its meaning is not compatible with what we expected. This is what brings us up short and alerts us to a possible difference in usage.

(Gadamer 2013: 280)

Bibliography

Dilthey, W. (2002) *The Formation of the Historical World in the Human Sciences*, in *Wilhelm Dilthey: Selected Works*, Vol. 3, ed. Rudolf A. Makkreel and Frithjof Rodi, Princeton, NJ: Princeton University Press.

Dutt, C. (1993) *Hermeneutik – Ästhetik – Praktische Philosophie. Hans-Georg Gadamer im Gespräch*, Heidelberg: C. Winter.

Gadamer, H-G. (1986) *Die Universalität des hermeneutischen Problems*, in *Hermeneutik II (Gesammelte Werke Vol. 2)*, Tübingen: J.C.B. Mohr, pp.219–31.

——(1986–95) *Gesammelte Werke*, Tübingen: J.C.B. Mohr.

——(1990) *Wahrheit und Methode (Gesammelte Werke Vol. 1)*, Tübingen: J.C.B. Mohr.

——(1997) *Reflections on my Philosophical Journey*, in *The Philosophy of Hans-Georg Gadamer*, ed. L.E. Hahn (The Library of Living Philosophers, Vol. 24), Chicago: Open Court, pp.1–63.

——(2001) *Gadamer in Conversation: Reflections and Commentary*, ed. R. Palmer, New Haven: Yale University Press.

——(2004) *A Century of Philosophy. A Conversation with Ricardo Dottori*, ed. R. Dottori, New York: Continuum.

——(2013) *Truth and Method*, rev. 2nd edn, trans. Joel Weinsheimer and Donald G. Marshall, London: Bloomsbury.

Gander, H-H. (2010) "In the Nets of Tradition: A Hermeneutic Analysis Concerning the History of Human Cognition", in *Consequences of Hermeneutics. Fifty Years after Gadamer's "Truth and Method"*, ed. J. Malpas and S. Zabala, Evanston, IL: Northwestern University Press, pp.132–43.

Grondin, J. (1994) *Hermeneutische Wahrheit? Zum Wahrheitsbegriff Hans-Georg Gadamers*, Weinheim: Beltz Athenäum.

——(2004) *Hans-Georg Gadamer: A Biography*, New Haven: Yale University Press.

Hahn, L.E. (ed.) (1997) *The Philosophy of Hans-Georg Gadamer* (The Library of Living Philosophers, Vol. 24), Chicago: Open Court.

Heidegger, M. (1996) *Being and Time*, trans. Joan Stambaugh, Albany: State University of New York Press.

Malpas, J. and S. Zabala (2010) *Consequences of Hermeneutics. Fifty Years after Gadamer's "Truth and Method"*, Evanston, IL: Northwestern University Press.

Steinmann, M. (2007) *Auf dem Weg zu einer modernen Epistemologie*, in *Hans-Georg Gadamer: Wahrheit und Methode*, ed. G.Figal, Berlin: Akademie Verlag, pp.87–103.

Wischke, M. and M. Hofer (2003) *Gadamer verstehen/Understanding Gadamer*, Darmstadt: Wissenschaftliche Buchgesellschaft.

Further reading

Code, L. (ed.) (2003) *The Feminist Interpretations of Hans-Georg Gadamer*, University Park: Pennsylvania State University Press.

Coltman, R. R. (1998) *The Language of Hermeneutics: Gadamer and Heidegger in Dialogue*, Albany, NY: SUNY Press.

Dostal, R. J. (ed.) (2002) *The Cambridge Companion to Gadamer*, Cambridge: Cambridge University Press.

Gadamer, H.-G (2007) *The Gadamer Reader: A Bouquet of the Later Writings*, ed. J. Grondin, trans. R. Palmer, Chicago: Northwestern University Press.

——(2008) *Philosophical Hermeneutics*, ed. and trans. David E. Linge, 30th Anniversary edn, Berkeley: University of California Press (includes English translation of Gadamer 1986).

Grondin, J. (2002) *The Philosophy of Gadamer*, trans. Kathryn Plant, New York: McGill-Queens University Press.

Krajewski, B. (ed.) (2003) *Gadamer's Repercussions: Reconsidering Philosophical Hermeneutics*, Berkeley: University of California Press.

Makita, E. (1995) *Gadamer-Bibliographie (1922–1994)*, New York: Peter Lang.

Michelfelder, D. P. and R. E. Palmer (eds) (1989) *Dialogue and Deconstruction: The Gadamer-Derrida Debate*, Albany, NY: SUNY Press.

Risser, J. (1997) *Hermeneutics and the Voice of the Other: Re-Reading Gadamer's Philosophical Hermeneutics*, Albany, NY: SUNY Press.

Scheibler, I. (2000) *Gadamer. Between Heidegger and Hermeneutics*, Lanham, MD: Rowman and Littlefield.

Schmidt, L. K. (1985) *The Epistemology of Hans-Georg Gadamer*, Frankfurt: Peter Lang.

Silverman, H. J. (ed.) (1991) *Gadamer and Hermeneutics*, New York: Routledge.

Sullivan, R. (1990) *Political Hermeneutics: The Early Thinking of Hans-Georg Gadamer*, University Park: Pennsylvania State University Press.

Wachterhauser, B. (1999) *Beyond Being: Gadamer's Post-Platonic Hermeneutic Ontology*, Evanston, IL: Northwestern University Press.

Warnke, G. (1987) *Gadamer: Hermeneutics, Tradition and Reason*, Stanford: Stanford University Press.

Weinsheimer, J. (1985) *Gadamer's Hermeneutics: A Reading of "Truth and Method"*, New Haven: Yale University Press.

Wright, K. (ed.) (1990) *Festivals of Interpretation: Essays on Hans-Georg Gadamer's Work*, Albany, NY: SUNY Press.

12

RICOEUR: THE LONG WAY OF HERMENEUTICS

Jean Grondin

When one thinks of Paul Ricoeur (1913–2005) and his way of doing hermeneutics, one is reminded of Frank Sinatra's famous song: he did it his way. An avid reader and interpreter himself, he was most cognizant of the various forms of hermeneutics, say, those of Schleiermacher, Dilthey, Heidegger or Gadamer. His way of practicing hermeneutics cannot be reduced to any of these emblematic forms, but he did not relinquish any one of them and incorporated them in his unique way of hermeneutics. Schleiermacher's hermeneutics appealed to him because it grew out of philological and theological concerns and wished to provide a methodical hermeneutics offering rules and guidelines that would help us avoid misunderstanding. Later hermeneuts such as Heidegger and Gadamer strove to overcome this methodical understanding, but in so doing, Ricoeur argued, they perhaps lost sight of the basic issues of validity and of the rootedness of hermeneutical theory in the actual practices of interpretation. Questions of method should never be discarded in philosophy, this son of the land of Descartes believed. For Dilthey, hermeneutics was an effort to account for the unique scientific significance of the humanities, in which methodology played a part but also the emergence of historical consciousness. What Ricoeur learned from him was that a hermeneutics that could serve as a basis for the humanities needed to engage with the forms of interpretation they practice and to address the issue of the objectivity of historical knowledge in light of the challenge of historical consciousness. Heidegger broadened the scope of hermeneutics when he viewed it as an ontology of existence and its historical condition. In Ricoeur's perspective, this "ontological hermeneutics" rightly stressed the interpretative nature of existence and its anticipatory nature, but it cut itself off from the dialogue with the actual sciences of interpretation and historical inquiry, often seeming to view them with disdain. It recentered the issue of hermeneutics on existential concerns, which were very dear to Ricoeur whose first two books, published in 1947, were devoted to Karl Jaspers and Gabriel Marcel, but Heidegger's in his eyes non-dialogical way of thinking failed to provide real clues as to how one ought to interpret oneself and deal with the basic ethical issues of human existence. Gadamer's own form of "ontological hermeneutics" had the virtue of starting off with the humanities and the

truth experience one can gain from art, history, practical wisdom and dialogue, culminating in a universal hermeneutics of the linguistic and historical nature of our
experience. For Ricoeur, it offered a hermeneutics of our "ontological" belongingness
to language, tradition and history, which was very sympathetic to him, but it too
neglected to account for the possibility of distance from tradition and history, which
is stressed by the more methodical forms of hermeneutics or by Gadamer critics such
as Habermas or Apel.[1]

Paul Ricoeur came relatively late to these debates and out of his own preoccupa-
tions and challenges, namely, in his earlier work, the daunting task of a proper
understanding of religious symbols in the secularized age of modernity (which
sparked his first entry into hermeneutics in his book of 1960, *Finitude and Culpability*)[2], and, later, the summons addressed to traditional ways of understanding
(including those favored by Dilthey, Heidegger or Gadamer) by the hermeneutics of
suspicion (Freud, structuralism, Nietzsche, Marx). His generous way of hermeneutics
did not discount any of the hermeneutic breakthroughs of his predecessors, from
Schleiermacher to Gadamer and Habermas, nor those of distrust; it incorporated
them into a vast "arc," as he termed it, which helps us understand better what it is to
interpret and to be human. He thus honored Heidegger's starting point in an ontology of our being, which Ricoeur has never ceased to pursue from the beginning to
the end of his trajectory: at the outset, in his first major systematic book published
in 1950, it was called a *Philosophy of the Will*, but in the end it had evolved into
a hermeneutics of the capable self. Unlike Heidegger he did not however jettison
Dilthey's Cartesian concern with methodological issues, which are essential if hermeneutics is to retain its critical function. Like Gadamer he stressed the historical
and linguistic nature of our understanding, without downgrading in this process the
possibilities of human reflection and initiative. His work is thus exemplary of what
hermeneutics can be in an age offering many competing forms of interpretation. For
him there is no short way, or any short cuts, in the field of hermeneutics. His way
was the long way.

This long way (*la voie longue*, he always said, alluding to Plato's distinction in the
Politicus, 265a, between the short and long way of dialectics), requires quite a bit of
patience on the part of Ricoeur's readers, but hermeneutics itself, the art of reading
carefully, is a school of patience, in all the senses of the word which require time
and some suffering, *patior*, but through which alone we can learn. This is the case
because Ricoeur presented his conception over a succession of momentous books
he steadfastly published between 1947 and 2004, which are themselves quite volu-
minous, since they strive to take into account (this is part of his long way) almost
everything meaningful that has been said on a given subject. This creates a situation
that is at the same time a drawback and an embarrassment of riches: unlike authors
such as Heidegger or Gadamer, there is no masterpiece of Ricoeur on hermeneutics,
one book that stands out and that one should definitely master to get a full grasp of
his hermeneutical thinking. There is no *Being and Time* or *Truth and Method*, but a
good dozen books (and one is only counting the most significant mileposts) that one
can read as masterpieces.

After his early and underrated books on Marcel and Jaspers (see Ricoeur and
Dufrenne 1947, and Ricoeur 1947),[3] two existentialist authors he preferred to the

more fashionable Sartre and Heidegger, Ricoeur embarked in 1950 on the vast project of a *Philosophy of the Will*, comprising in its original conception three volumes. The first programmatic and captivating volume appeared in 1950 under the title "The Voluntary and the Involuntary" (following a trend Ricoeur would heed in almost all of his books, it was in itself a trilogy, its three parts being devoted to the phenomenological study of the main components of Decision, Action and Consent). The second volume of this *Philosophy of the Will* came out in 1960 under the heading "Finitude and Culpability," in which he spoke for the first time of a hermeneutics. But he did so in a most emphatic and unusual way. His book dealt with the powerful symbols and myths through which the human experience of evil found expression, including the confession of sins. His idea was that evil was in itself incomprehensible and that one could only "understand" it by taking into consideration this phenomenology of confession (*phénoménologie de l'aveu*) and the "Symbolism of Evil" through which the religious traditions had come to terms with it. But did he not cross here the boundary between philosophy and religion?

The task of hermeneutics, he first argued, was therefore to provide "rules of deciphering" which would make it possible to translate the religious symbolism of evil into rational philosophical discourse. "The symbol leads us to think" (*le symbole donne à penser*), he bravely stated. This motto (borrowed from Kant) became the title of the closing chapter of the book,[4] but in this conclusion hermeneutics became imbued with a much more far-reaching task, that of overcoming modernity's "forgetfulness of the Sacred" and "the loss of man to the extent that he belongs to the Sacred" (Ricoeur 1960/1988: 480). With respect to the Sacred, this hermeneutics would have a "restorative" purpose. Ricoeur would later regret this idea of "restoration," which he clearly espoused in 1960, but it would haunt the reception of his hermeneutical thought: many would suspect his hermeneutics of having a secret religious agenda, which was not a winning proposition in the iconoclast climate that would soon engulf the 60s and that Ricoeur would sum up under the heading of a hermeneutics of radical distrust. Under these auspices, it is obvious that a receptive hermeneutics of religious symbols was difficult to defend. Ricoeur himself would soon come to realize this and his valiant engagement with the rabid critics of such a hermeneutical approach would lead to a new understanding of the hermeneutic way.

Finitude et culpabilité, the second part of the trilogy of the *Philosophy of the Will*, also promised to be a trilogy. In 1960 Ricoeur only published its first two parts, on "Fallible Man" and "The Symbolism of Evil" (with its hermeneutical bend). Its third part, announced Ricoeur, would take into account the import of all the human sciences on the issues of culpability and evil. It was never published, again perhaps owing to the age's hostility to a religious hermeneutics and the suddenly somewhat "outdated' nature of the issues of culpability, sin and evil which had preoccupied Ricoeur in 1960. He also did not publish the entire third volume of the *Philosophy of the Will* itself which was supposed to offer a *Poetics of the Will*. Two important pieces are thus missing of Ricoeur's early *Philosophy of the Will* of which we "only" have something like 1000 pages. Instead of publishing these two pieces, that is, the third part of the second volume and the entire third volume (it is a safe bet they would have been trilogies), Ricoeur published in 1965 a major treatise On *Interpretation*, which was mostly read through its subtitle that promised "An Essay on Freud." It was indeed a brilliant philosophical inquiry on Freud, but its important introduction set his reading in the broader spectrum of a general and forthcoming theory of interpretation and language, of which it was becoming increasingly clear that it was to be named a "hermeneutics," a term Gadamer had used in *Truth and Method* in 1960, but Ricoeur's work of 1965 contained no reference to his great contemporary. The following book of 1969, *The Conflict of Interpretations*, which also did not contain any direct reference to Gadamer,[5] offered substantial "Hermeneutic Studies" (according to its subtitle) which can be viewed as stepping stones toward this general hermeneutics. Hermeneutics continued to be related to "symbols," but the notion took on a larger meaning than was the case in 1960, where Ricoeur mostly thought of religious symbols. Symbols, he now argued, are all linguistic expressions with a double meaning: an obvious, literary sense and a derivative sense we come to understand through interpretation. Hermeneutics is thus rooted in language itself and deals with the manifold ways of coming to terms with this double sense. Among those ways there is that of linguistic "structuralism" which studies language as a system of signs with its own autonomous laws that is not dependent on human consciousness. A hermeneutical sensibility would appear to be opposed to such a structuralist, objectifying view, but Ricoeur heralded in it a scientific understanding of language that an honest hermeneutics of our linguistic experience could not afford to ignore.

In 1975, in a book strangely called *The Rule of Metaphor* in English (its French title spoke, quite on the contrary, one can argue, of *La métaphore vive*, "live" or "sudden" metaphor, which indeed doesn't sound very good in English), Ricoeur concentrated on a specific, yet also universal form of "double meaning," the refreshing linguistic innovation brought about by what happens in the audacity of a metaphor which broadens our view of the world. For the first time, the issue of religious symbols, which remained important in *On Interpretation* and *The Conflict of Interpretations*, did not appear to be a major concern of Ricoeur's way of hermeneutics. It is also a book that for the first time takes into consideration a wide range of studies on its subject from the field of analytic philosophy, with which Ricoeur acquainted himself as he began to teach regularly at the University of Chicago in the early 70s. His hermeneutics had fully embraced the "linguistic turn." Just as he had done with structuralism in 1969, Ricoeur appeared to incorporate analytic philosophy into hermeneutics.

From 1982 to 1985, Ricoeur published a trilogy on *Time and Narrative*, where the main issue of hermeneutics seemed to revolve around narrative, both in its historical and fictional forms, and the way both give expression to our temporal condition. Isn't it through narratives that we always understand ourselves? Ricoeur came to develop in this respect his crucial notion of our narrative identity. Ricoeur thus focused in *Time and Narrative* – or refocused since it was already a decisive topic of his *Philosophy of the Will* – on the issue of selfhood. It would become the central theme of his 1990 book, *Oneself as Another*, which came out of his Gifford lectures delivered in 1986. It unfolds a "small ethics," which also stands in the continuity of the *Philosophy of the Will* and a precious book of 1955 on *History and Truth*. Ricoeur would return to this ethical thread in many publications of the 90s, for instance in his two volumes on *The Just*. In 1995, Ricoeur, who was increasingly and justly recognized as one of the most distinguished philosophers of his time, brought out two highly instructive autobiographical pieces (*Critique and Conviction*, 1995, based on interviews, and the sketch of *An Autobiography*, 1995, which was uncharacteristically – or characteristically in light of his modesty – short). One could think that the productive hermeneut, who was now over 80 years old, was through with long books. Yet, he continued doing it his way: in 2000, he published yet another extensive trilogy on *Memory, History and Forgetting*, and in 2004, a few months before his passing, another, smaller one, on *The Course of Recognition*. Those books from 1947 to 2004 are just the major mileposts, to which one would have to add a host of indispensable essay collections on *Hermeneutics and the Human Sciences* (1981), quite a few volumes of *Readings* (*Lectures 1, 2, 3*), biblical interpretations (in the long run, true to his own self, he could never let go of those even if they became more discreet in his vast hermeneutic treatises) as well as lectures on ideology, utopia and imagination.

Viewed from the outside, this might raise the bewildering impression of dispersion, of a work disseminated in many directions and volumes.[6] Is there a common thread that binds together his scattered works? This is and no doubt will remain a central question of Ricoeur studies, all the more so since many threads do run through his works, some of which seem to disappear for some time, only to reemerge in later works. These threads coalesce around the issues of the will (decision, action and consent), of hermeneutics (interpretation, the human sciences, language, metaphor), time and history as it is told in narratives which shape our identity and fuel our imagination. All strive to understand man as a being of capacities, as a being who can know, who can act and hope, but also as one who can suffer, who can inflict evil, yet who can also pardon and make sense of his experience through understanding, narrative and symbols. In his endless exploration of these possibilities of what it is to be human, Ricoeur never loses sight of the basic issues of philosophy, of ethics and hope, as they are summed up in two of the three main questions of Kant (which hermeneuts too often seem to disregard): what should I do? And what can I hope for?

Kant's first question "what can I know?" is one Ricoeur would perhaps frame this way: how should I interpret? The issue of interpretation is paramount because we are basically beings of interpretation: we constantly interpret our world, ourselves and our traditions. This is repeatedly highlighted by the more "ontological" hermeneutics of Heidegger and Gadamer. But for Ricoeur it is not enough to stress this, that is, that we are interpreting beings, one also has to attend to the basic issues raised by the actual challenges of interpretation: how *should* I interpret (in this Ricoeur is indebted to the older hermeneutical tradition of Schleiermacher and Dilthey, while never disowning the existential widening of hermeneutics brought about by Heidegger and Gadamer)? Ricoeur also correctly believes interpretation – or its theory, hermeneutics, for that matter – is not an end in itself: it is practiced in order to lead to a better understanding of oneself and of the possibilities of our action in and on the world. Why else would I interpret in the first place? Ricoeur strongly holds that philosophy should not be content with itself and its own traditions. It provides a rich trove of wisdom, but philosophy must go beyond itself and learn lessons from the many disciplines that actually practice interpretation and offer methods for it. This is one of the precious insights of his long way: instead of focusing on what he calls the short way of a "direct" hermeneutics of existence (Heidegger), which states and restates that we are interpretive beings and dependent upon traditions (Gadamer), one should espouse the long way of hermeneutics and consider the many forms of interpretation to be found in the field of the human and less human sciences: in history, exegesis, literary theory, linguistics, psychoanalysis. Don't they have a thing or two to teach the philosopher about what interpretation actually is and how it unfolds?

In his long way of hermeneutics, Ricoeur, ever attentive to issues of method, very usefully distinguishes two basic strategies of interpretation: one can practice a hermeneutics of trust or distrust. The first takes meaning as it presents itself and follows its lead and what it opens up to understanding. This hermeneutics of trust is exemplified by biblical exegesis and phenomenology: in both instances one encounters meaning, meaningful texts or meaningful forms of consciousness, whose full meaning can only be unfolded by an interpretation that penetrates into them to get a better sense of the direction they offer understanding. This form of interpretation as an unfolding, recollection or "ex-plication" of meaning is however not the only one. Another form of hermeneutics distrusts meaning as it presents itself since it could be an illusion and the product of a hidden genealogy. In the hermeneutics of trust, the interpreter "collects" meaning and views it as the revelation of a profound truth, in that of suspicion this meaning is assumed to be a lie, a useful lie perhaps but "nothing but" the expression of a concealed structure of drives or power. The main protagonists of this hermeneutics of distrust are Freud (who, lest we forget, wrote a seminal work on "The Interpretation of Dreams," thus a hermeneutics), Nietzsche, Foucault, Marx and the critique of ideologies. Until Ricoeur, those critical and iconoclastic authors, who of course seldom used the term hermeneutics, were more often than not ignored in the field of hermeneutics. They did not really fit into the golden chain of Schleiermacher, Dilthey, Heidegger and Gadamer. But is it not a theory of interpretation, argues Ricoeur, hence a distinct form of hermeneutics that they have to offer? It was all the more difficult for Ricoeur to ignore them since they had become very fashionable in France in the early 60s, especially in the new current of structuralism, at a time when Ricoeur was still working on the third part of the second volume of his *Philosophy of the Will* and on the third volume on the *Poetics of the Will*. As we have seen, it was instead an essay *On Interpretation* and on Freud that he published, in 1965.

One would think that an author such as Ricoeur, who had himself been schooled in the traditions of phenomenology and biblical exegesis, would feel much closer to the hermeneutics of trust than he would to the school of suspicion. The great surprise in this epic *conflict of interpretations*, which would form the basic antinomy of his book of the same title of 1969, is that Ricoeur does not take sides in this debate, much to the dismay perhaps of the proponents of both schools: some of the hermeneuts of trust felt that Ricoeur sold his soul to the structuralists by taking it so seriously, whereas some structuralists might have been led to believe that Ricoeur's approach was basically defensive in that he wanted to reject structuralism in the name of a hermeneutics of trust (and a secret religious agenda). The genius of Ricoeur's approach lies in his view that both forms of hermeneutics are essential to a true understanding of hermeneutics and of the understanding and willing self in this process. "The more one explains, the better one understands" became his new motto. To be sure, the hermeneutics of suspicion is the other from the standpoint of a hermeneutics of trust, but another which helps us understand better. The hermeneutics of distrust values objectification, distance and challenges the evidences of the *ego*, most notably its instinctive claim of enjoying a privileged access to itself and inner feelings. It is not the case, argues the hermeneutics of suspicion: from a psychoanalytic perspective, the conscious motives of the *ego* are nothing but the expression of subliminal drives and for a structuralist approach, meaning is not produced by consciousness itself but by the autonomous system of signs that the linguist uncovers and studies objectively. The perspective of distrust offers quite a dispiriting (literally!) picture of consciousness and meaning in that it humiliates the ego and its possibilities of self-reflection. Ricoeur's insight is that this humiliation is beneficial in that it frees the "broken" subject from a false consciousness and leads it to a more accurate and humble understanding of itself. It is thus a reflective gain one can garner from the suspicions of distrust. Its fallacy would only consist in claiming that there is no such thing as a quest for understanding in the first place. There is, insists Ricoeur; this is the starting point of the hermeneutics of trust, but it has to be wary of its own delusions which the cold shower of distrust helps us uncover. It is a deflated and fragile self that comes out of it, but one that understands itself better and that does better justice to what we really are.

This philosophy of the self is hermeneutical in two very important ways, at the ontological and the methodological levels. On the ontological plain, it views the human Being as an *ens hermeneuticum*, that is, as a self that is in need of interpretation (and narratives) and that cannot but interpret itself (in that it is very close to Heidegger's hermeneutical understanding of existence). Philosophy grows out of this quest of understanding and self-understanding. But it is also hermeneutical, on the methodological level, in that it unfolds its "hermeneutical" understanding of the human Being by taking into consideration all the forms of interpretation that are available, even if they appear antithetical to many. Trust and distrust are both essential if one is to understand better.

Furthermore and no less importantly, interpretation is the *only* way through which one can reach proper self-understanding. Self-knowledge, the goal of philosophy and the task of every human being, does not occur through introspection or reflective self-awareness; it can only be achieved through the endless effort of interpretation, that is, the long way of understanding the configurations or "objectifications" of meaning as they have been handed down to us by myths and symbols (the focus of Ricoeur's first hermeneutic book in 1960, *Finitude et culpabilité*), history and culture, art, literature and science itself. They provide us with the great books and sources of meaning out of which we carve our own hermeneutical identity and self-awareness. In his numerous and very thick books, devoted to religious symbols and myth, to the teachings of metaphor, narrative, history, memory and recognition, Ricoeur provided a powerful illustration of the manner in which self-understanding comes about through this "recollection of meaning" which knows there is no other road to self-knowledge than this interpretation nourished by culture and history. This is also part of what the "long way" of hermeneutics is all about: it is only through the interpretation of these sources of meaning that one can reach a more appropriate understanding of oneself. The long way is thus a way that doesn't shun "detours," through the great testimonies of culture and history.

There is a Hegelian motive at play in Ricoeur's historical sense of understanding (to say nothing of his fondness for trilogies), which occurs through the patient recollection of the objectifications of meaning. But it is resolutely unhegelian in that for Ricoeur there is no end-point in this process. The detours of interpretation, through the ways of trust and distrust, never reach a final destination. There is thus a tragic dimension to the hermeneutical quest of understanding and its hermeneutical processes. But life itself is tragic and this insight sparks philosophy into existence.

It could be shown that Ricoeur had very good biographical reasons to believe life was tragic: he never knew his parents (his mother died shortly after his birth in 1913 and his father was sent to the front in 1914, where he fell in 1915), in the Second World War he spent five years in a Nazi prison camp, became one of the leading intellectual figures of France in the 60s only to be ignominiously booted out of its university system in the aftermath of "Mai 1968," even if he had sympathies with the student movement, and one of his sons would later commit suicide. A testimony of this tragic sense of life can be found at the end of one of his last books, *Memory, History, Forgetting*, a stocky treatise he published in 2000 at the age of 87 and which he clearly viewed as a testament of sorts. On the very last page of the book, after its Epilogue and last chapter, he added a small, separate and intriguing text that he himself viewed as a kind of epitaph,[7] of his life and work. It was printed on the middle of the page and read, in French:

> *Sous l'histoire, la mémoire et l'oubli.*
> *Sous la mémoire et l'oubli, la vie.*
> *Mais écrire la vie est une autre histoire.*
> *Inachèvement.*
> $\qquad\qquad$ Paul Ricoeur

One can translate it thus:

> Beneath history, memory and forgetting.
> Beneath memory and forgetting, life.
> But writing about life is another history.
> Incompleteness.
> $\qquad\qquad$ Paul Ricoeur

The name Paul Ricoeur stands below these lines as if the author wanted to confirm to the reader that this curious text was indeed from him, that is was thus signed by him and that he was apposing in this fashion his own personal signature on his final hermeneutical work. The word *"inachèvement"* is hard to translate: what is *"inachevé"* is what is unfinished, uncompleted, never rounded out, because life itself is "uncompletable" (I realize this is not idiomatic). Ricoeur appropriately completes his hermeneutical work with the sigh of "Incompleteness." His text suggests why this must be so. After having written a mammoth book on "History, Memory and Forgetting," which took a lot out of him, Ricoeur recognizes, in a self-critical way (which is not untypical of him at the end of his long books), that "beneath" all of them lies life itself, the life we all lead, but that more often than not leads us where it wills. Writing about it (*écrire la vie*, literally: writing life itself) is however another story altogether because life cannot be encompassed in any history or memory. But what is history and memory all about if not about life? It is, to be sure, about life, it revolves around it, but mostly, seems to suggest Ricoeur, it remains about history and memory, not about life.

Nonetheless, the hermeneutical way of history and memory, forgetting and forgiving, of narrative and texts, metaphors and symbols, is the way we understand and imagine ourselves in order to make sense of our lives. But hermeneutics, while stressing this hermeneutical nature of our experience, points to what lies beyond hermeneutics or beneath it: life, which cannot be exhausted in a single story or narrative.

Ricoeur's hermeneutics thus rests on a philosophy of life, of its endless possibilities and its "striving to be" (*effort d'être*). After all, it was basically two fundamental attitudes towards life Ricoeur singled out when he differentiated the hermeneutics of trust from that of distrust and emphasized their solidarity. In both of them he recognized the same effort of life to assert itself in its search for meaning, which takes on so many, innovative forms which hermeneutics has to bring to the fore. There is thus a strong, somewhat Spinozistic impulse in Ricoeur's thinking that seeks to affirm life not in spite of but through its tragic dimension. We should not see in the undeniably tragic dimension of life and its necessary incompleteness a limitation – it could only be viewed as such from a divine perspective, which is never ours – but the spark and spur of all understanding, willing and hoping.

Behind or beneath Ricoeur's hermeneutics there is thus an ontology of the human being, at which the French philosopher liked to hint at the end of his major hermeneutical treatises. He often modestly, too modestly, spoke of this ontology as a promised land which is never reached, but it is clear that this ontology views the human experience through its effort or striving to be. Philosophers such as Leibniz, Spinoza and Marcel were attuned to this essential dimension when they understood the human Being out of its *conatus*, its effort to be, or when Aristotle highlighted in the dual notion of possibility and actuality an essential meaning of Being. Throughout his work Ricoeur defended this approach of man through his *conatus* and capabilities, his valiant struggle to be, which testifies to the possibilities of understanding, acting and hoping – we recognize here anew the gist of Kant's three grand questions: What can I know? What ought I to do? What may I hope? – that distinguish the human experience. Yes, the human condition is tragic and finite; philosophers stressed this repeatedly in the twentieth century. This insight is however as ancient as philosophy and the Greek tragics – but what fascinates Ricoeur is man's ability to make something out of his condition, his capacity of dreaming and imagining new spaces which we can inhabit, of transforming his world through his actions and institutions, his capacity for solidarity, pardon and forgetfulness. What do we gain by harping on about the sheer mortality of all things human? From his early *Philosophy of the Will* to his later hermeneutics of the capable self, Ricoeur remained defiantly critical of the exaggerated insistence of existential (and hermeneutical) philosophers on the experience of death and anguish. Actually, he always contended, our death is never part of our experience. It is a non-event since when it happens we are never there. Nobody puts into question the sobering character of our mortality, but an obsession with death and human despair tends to conceal and down-play the possibilities the human being has of reconciling itself with its condition, of consenting to it and thereby reconquering a certain second naivety (a favorite expression of the early Ricoeur) in its efforts and powers to be. Here again he was following Spinoza: the free man doesn't think about death all the time, but about life. The only thing that should disconcert us is not death or finitude, it is evil. It is only evil that we never understand, but at least we can try to do something about it, that is, against it, as beings of understanding, action and hope. As beings of understanding, action and hope, we are also beings of initiative.

In the second volume of his *Philosophy of the Will* Ricoeur could thus state that "man is the Joy of the Yes in the sadness of the finite," *la joie du oui dans la tristesse du fini* (Ricoeur 1960/1988: 156). Despite its finite and tragic condition and through it all, human nature can learn to reconcile itself with its condition and to consent to its necessity. This basic affirmation of life, its effort to be and the infinite possibilities of our experience is for Ricoeur the way of hermeneutics. This is why the way of hermeneutics can only be the long way and without end.

Notes

1 Ricoeur acutely took into account the wide spectrum of critical reactions to Gadamer's universal hermeneutics, especially in his essay "Logique herméneutique?," now in Ricoeur 2010: 123–96. See also Ricoeur 1981. The extant correspondence between Gadamer and Ricoeur has recently been published – see Gadamer and Ricoeur 2013: esp. 41–83. For a critical comparison of the hermeneutical projects of Gadamer and Ricoeur, see Grondin 2008, and Mootz III and Taylor 2011.
2 On this motivation of Ricoeur's first foray into hermeneutics see Grondin 2013b.
3 For a complete bibliography of Ricoeur's work, see Vansina 2008.
4 It was also the title of an important related article – see Ricoeur 1959. Like many other precious texts it is also available on the outstanding, French and English site of the Fonds Ricoeur: http://www.fondsricoeur.fr. If hermeneutics is to be properly propagated on the Internet, this exemplary site shows the way to go.
5 No *direct* reference because one can suspect an indirect one at two places in its first, defining chapter on "Existence and Hermeneutics" (see Ricoeur 1969: 15, 19) where Ricoeur states that hermeneutics should resist the temptation to separate the *truth* that is characteristic of understanding from the *method* practiced by the exegetical disciplines. Ricoeur underlines the two terms of truth and method, but fails to name Gadamer or his work in this context or in his entire book for that matter. Is that a pure coincidence or a sign of Ricoeur's first and rather critical reception of Gadamer's opus which he will then have viewed as the work of a Heideggerian? – all the more so since the piece on "Existence and Hermeneutics" is basically a critical discussion of Heidegger. I would tend to favor this latter reading. Needless to say, Ricoeur, while still maintaining the outlines of this criticism, would later see what distinguished Gadamer's project from that of Heidegger.
6 For a unitary presentation of Ricoeur's work and his way into hermeneutics see Grondin 2013a.
7 See Grondin 2013a, pp. 8–9.

Bibliography

Gadamer, H.-G. and Ricoeur, P. (2013), "Correspondance / Briefwechsel 1964–2000," *Studia phaenomenologica*, 13: 41–83.
Grondin, J. (2013a) *Paul Ricoeur*, Paris: Presses Universitaires de France.

——(2013b) "Ricoeur a-t-il d'abord introduit l'herméneutique comme une variante de la phénoménologie?," *Studia phaenomenologica*, 13: 87–106.

——(2008) "De Gadamer à Ricoeur. Peut-on parler d'une conception commune de l'herméneutique?," in G. Fiasse (ed.) *Paul Ricœur: De l'homme faillible à l'homme capable*, Paris: Presses universitaires de France, 37–62.

Mootz III, F.J. and G. H. Taylor (2011) *Gadamer and Ricoeur. Critical Horizons for Contemporary Hermeneutics*, London: Bloomsbury.

Ricoeur, P. (2010) *Écrits et conférences 2: Herméneutique*, Paris: Seuil.

——(1981) *Hermeneutics and the Human Sciences: Essays on Language, Action and Interpretation*, Cambridge: Cambridge University Press.

——(1969) *Le Conflit des interprétations*, Paris: Seuil.

(1960/1988) *Philosophie de la volonté II. Finitude et culpabilité*, Paris: Aubier-Montaigne.

——(1959) "Le symbole donne à penser," *Esprit*, 27/7–8: 60–76.

——(1947) *Gabriel Marcel et Karl Jaspers. Philosophie du mystère et philosophie du paradoxe*, Paris: Éditions du Présent.

Ricoeur, P., and M. Dufrenne (1947) *Karl Jaspers et la philosophie de l'existence*, Paris: Seuil.

Vansina, F. D. (2008) *Paul Ricoeur: bibliographie première et secondaire 1935–2008*, Louvain: Peeters.

13

LONERGAN'S HERMENEUTICS

Frederick G. Lawrence

Being a scientist is just an aspect of being human, nor has any method been found that makes one authentically scientific without heading one into being authentically human.
(Lonergan 1985)

In this article, the term 'hermeneutics' is linked to the "revolution in reading" initiated by Martin Heidegger that inspired multiple initiatives whose fertility is rooted in Heidegger's fundamental confrontation with historical mindedness, which grappled with *Dasein*'s historicity in a way that not only took over but also overtook Husserlian phenomenology's reorientation of philosophy from neo-Kantianism by "starting with the foundations instead of the roof." Heidegger called Marx's 11th Thesis on Feuerbach into question by reminding us that *changing* history depends at root on how one *interprets* history. In *Wahrheit und Methode* Gadamer followed Heidegger's lead in a way that others failed to do as successfully, in my opinion, by facing the problem of how to deal with the relativity intrinsic to human historicality without succumbing to Historicism or to nihilism.

Like the young Heidegger, philosopher and theologian Bernard Lonergan (1904–84) had an experience not altogether unlike what Heidegger described in a 1919 letter when he said that "epistemological insights, groping toward a theory of historical knowing, ... made the system of Catholicism problematic and untenable – but not Christianity and metaphysics, yet these at least in a new sense" (Heidegger 1980, 541). The young Lonergan, too, was provoked by the dominant Roman Catholic intellectual climate of ahistorical orthodoxy. Although the scholastics implementing Leo XIII's hermeneutic slogan in *Aeterni Patris* of 1879 ("to increase and perfect the old with the new") sincerely meant to operate *ad mentem divi Thomae*, they fell short of discovering what the 'old' really were.

Again, as happened for Gadamer, Lonergan's approach to hermeneutics emerged gradually in the course of five decades of serious reading. From the time of his studies in the late 1930s and early 1940s of the development of Thomas Aquinas's thought until the remarkable culmination of his hermeneutic thought in *Method in Theology* (1972), Lonergan's work in hermeneutics intended to correct (1) Catholic ahistorical orthodoxy, (2) the post-Vatican II adoption of historicist or positivist versions of historical-critical study of theology's sources, and (3) idealist or relativist opinions adopted widely in reaction to the earlier dogmatic *fixisme*. To navigate between archaism and anachronism in theology, Lonergan spent his life combining careful and serious reading and writing in philosophy and theology with thorough-going and painstaking reflection on that performance – a type of hermeneutic reflection he later named 'foundational methodology' (Lonergan 2004).

Throughout his teaching career, then, Lonergan was convinced that "the problem of hermeneutics coincides with the problems of a Catholic theology" (Lonergan 2010, 210–11). The background of the question of hermeneutics and its theoretical basis "lies in cognitional theory." As he explained:

> [Hermeneutics] is a peculiar problem at the present time because of the emergence of historical consciousness, because of the significance of meaning in the *Geisteswissenschaften*, because of either the application of mistaken philosophies to hermeneutics or the desire to do it without any philosophy at all, with the result that one is guided largely by catch-phrases, and because of a wholesale reinterpretation of the past that has been conducted by the modern mind.

This chapter will trace how Lonergan's career prepared him to meet the 'peculiar problem' of hermeneutics at the present time.

Two types of hermeneutical concern with the world of explanatory theory

From the beginning of his scholarly work, one hallmark of Lonergan's hermeneutics was his engagement with the two sets of articles in the 1930s and 1940s that became *Grace and Freedom* and *Verbum*. This marked Lonergan with an indelible appreciation for the world of theory and scientific explanation.

It has been said that smart people are good at coming up with answers, but it takes genius to discover the questions. Lonergan's study of Thomas Aquinas's theology of grace and freedom (Lonergan 1940, 1941, 1942) traced Aquinas's questions about grace and freedom within the context of the exigencies of Aristotelian *episteme* as he gradually put the many questions needed to attain a satisfactory explanation of God's gracious initiative without violating but rather by liberating human freedom. He realized that in understanding the evolution of the thought of a thinker like Aquinas, one must pay attention to and understand every change in meaning, explain the reasons for the changes, and grasp the relationships among the changed meanings.[1] Thus, following upon the definition in 1230 of the general relationship between natural and supernatural orders of a unified creation, it took Aquinas years to shift from a descriptive to an explanatory viewpoint on a complex network of systematically interconnected issues. Lonergan could not have accomplished this without understanding the nuances of the movement from the commonsense, descriptive world concerned with the *priora quoad nos* to that of explanatory theory concerned with the *priora quoad se*.[2]

Such pivotal shifts from descriptive to explanatory perspectives entered impor-tantly into his Roman courses on the Trinity (Lonergan 2009, 2007), which traced the gradual rise of increasingly differentiated questions by writers who exercised what Lonergan named a second order mode of reflecting upon propositions in order to provide a 'control of meaning' analogous to the movement from *mythos* and *doxa* to the logical control (*logos*) of meaning in Greek philosophy.

Clearly, to present such a development Lonergan needed not just to understand the movement from description to explanation or theory by a single author on a specific problematic, but he would have had to move beyond both the *simple* devices of ordinary interpreters of texts and the *reflective* interpretation capable of accounting for changes in meaning accordingly as either a single author or many authors need to be correlated with their diverse audiences (vis-à-vis differences in space [societies] and time [cultures]). What was needed – and what he already elaborated in the originally unpublished introduction to his study of Aquinas on grace[3] – was an explanatory heuristic structure that could account for changes that are reducible not just to developmental stages but to dialectical oppositions that might arise due to oversights, blind spots, and biases. Lonergan's fuller account of such a structure was worked out in *Insight* (1992, 585–616) before going to teach in Rome. We first have to consider the historical work without whose findings *Insight* would not have been possible in order then to briefly examine that achievement.

Verbum: Word and Idea in Aquinas (Lonergan 1967, 1997): Lonergan's hermeneutics of cognitional interiority

Lonergan's work on *verbum* shares a hitherto virtually unremarked agreement with Gadamer's interpretation of the same topic in *Wahrheit und Methode* (Lonergan 1946, 1947, 1949, 1966, 1967, 1997).[4] The core of this agreement (independently attained) established that Thomas's explanation of the way concepts and judgments depend on pre-predicative acts of understanding or insight *did not* depend on the Stoic contrast between the outer words people utter to the inward reasoning the words express. Rather, as both thinkers noted, Thomas's approach was based on Augustine's articulation in *De trinitate* of the first fully spiritual (i.e., unconditioned by space and time) analogy for the procession of the Word in God by discovering "a third *verbum* that was neither the *verbum prolatum* of human speech nor the *verbum insitum* of man's native rationality but an intermediate *verbum intus prolatum*" (Lonergan 1997, 6).

Paul Ricoeur's famous observation that philosophical hermeneutics is a graft upon the tree of phenomenology is pertinent to Lonergan's statement that "as Augustine's discovery was part and parcel of his own mind's knowledge of itself, so he begged his readers to look within themselves and there to discover the speech of spirit within spirit, an inner *verbum* prior to any use of language, yet distinct both from the mind itself and from its memory or its present apprehension of objects" (Lonergan 1997, 6). Previously, the chief scholastic interpreters had entirely overlooked how Augustine actually *performed* a phenomenology of the subject. This is directly related to the slogan of phenomenology: Back to the things themselves! If it is the case that the more one understands what an author is talking about, the more likely one is to understand what the author means, it also is true that such a phenomenology is indispensable when the author is speaking about his acts of understanding.

The heart of Lonergan's interpretation of Thomas on the *verbum* became the starting point for his mature Trinitarian theology. He discovered that Thomas Aquinas learned from Augustine that understanding the process in ourselves by which understanding and conceiving, reflecting and judging actually occur provides the natural analogy for processions in God. Aquinas claimed, "The human soul understands itself through its act of understanding, which is its proper act, perfectly demonstrating its power and its nature."[5] As he distinguished within his own experience of human cognition Aquinas still used the available language of Aristotle's metaphysical categories to express what he learned from Augustine.

Augustine also helped Aquinas pinpoint the weakness in the epistemology implicit in Aristotle's metaphysical account of knowledge. While acknowledging the correctness of Aristotle's identity theorem (namely, that the sense in act is one with the sensible in act, and the intelligence in act is one with the intelligible in act), he realized that this perfection in knowing does not yet adequately explain how such intentional identity attains knowledge *of the other*. To go beyond Aristotle's account, Aquinas supplied an empirically accessible justification of rational reflection's knowledge of the truth that eliminated every vestige of Platonism from Augustine's metaphorical description in terms of a vision of eternal truth.[6]

Lonergan's reconstruction of Aquinas's explanation of knowing the truth began by noting that for Thomas the finality of judgment is attained in the achievement of assent; and in order to be rational, assent results from a *resolutio in principia* (reduction to principles). Rather than interpreting the phrase *resolutio in principia* in solely *logical* terms (i.e., in terms of coherent inferences from premises) as the Thomistic tradition had generally done, Lonergan indicated how for Aquinas reflective understanding grounds the judgment of reality when he summarized Thomas's position as follows:

> We may infer that the reflective activity of reason returning from the synthesis of intelligibilities to its origin in sense and in naturally known principles terminates in a reflective act of understanding, in a single synthetic apprehension of all the motives for judgment, whether intellectual or sensitive, in a grasp of their sufficiency as motives and so of the necessity of passing judgment or assenting. For no less than the first type of inner word, the second proceeds from an *intelligere* [an insight or act of understanding].[7] No less than the procession of the first type, the procession of the second is an *emanatio intelligibilis* [intelligible emanation or procession of the judgment from the understanding's grasp of the sufficiency of the warrants for affirming or denying the correctness of a guess or hypothesis].
>
> (Lonergan 1997, 77)

Lonergan's construal stressed that for Aquinas, when one knows the truth, one knows *by what one is*, and not by any vision or contact or confrontation with the other, however down-to-earth (as in sense perception) or lofty and sublime (as in ontologism's inner vision of truth in God) such a vision may be imagined to be. For Aquinas and Augustine, the ultimate ground of our knowing is God, the eternal Light; but for Aquinas *the proximate reason* why we know is the light of intelligence within us, operating as a relentless desire to know that is capable of discerning when it "gets things right." By it we can know because "the very intellectual light that is in us is nothing other than a participated similitude of the uncreated light" (Lonergan 1997, 85).[8] Our minds move from the identities both of the sensible with the act of sensation, and of the intelligible with the act of understanding to "valid concepts of essence and true affirmations of existence, because such procession is in virtue of our intellectual light, which is a participation of eternal Light" (Lonergan 1997, 85–6). And so Lonergan summarized his interpretation of Aquinas's account of the two processions on the levels of both intelligence and reasonableness:

> Inasmuch as the act of understanding grasps its own conditions as the understanding of this sort of thing, it abstracts from the irrelevant and expresses itself in a definition of essence. But inasmuch as the act of understanding grasps its own transcendence-in-immanence, its quality of intellectual light as a participation of the divine and uncreated Light, it expresses itself in judgment, in a positing of truth, in the affirmation or negation of reality.
>
> (Lonergan 1997, 94)

Lonergan demonstrated how Thomas Aquinas learned from Augustine that one must understand the *conversational structure* of listening and speaking and of asking and answering questions built into human consciousness.[9]

Allow me to make three remarks here. First, the emphasis on the crucial pre-predicative, and receptive role of *intelligere* – insight: direct and reflective understanding – shows that his interpretation of Aquinas on knowing is nothing less than a hermeneutics of cognitional interiority.

Second, by way of clarification by contrast, Gadamer told me that *Truth and Method* might just as well have been called *Insight and Method*. I suggest that this statement springs from Gadamer's global and compact elucidation of Heidegger's notion of *Verstehen*, which included but did not clearly distinguish between understanding and interpreting on the one hand, and judgment on the other. By way of contrast, Lonergan learned from Aquinas's distinction between the *verbum* as concept, definition, hypothesis and the *verbum complexum* of judgment (affirmation, assent) to discriminate between direct understanding and its formulation and indirect or reflective understanding and its judgment. In "*Insight*: Preface to a Discussion," Lonergan (1974e, 150) said: "If one asks for the cognitional reason justifying our claim to know existence, that reason is a true judgment of the type, This exists. For truth is the medium in which being is known; truth formally is found only in the judgment." This will become a crucial issue for *Insight* and beyond.

Third, the emphasis on the decisive pre-predicative and receptive role of *intelligere* – or the acts of direct and reflective understanding that were systematically overlooked by the Wölffian/Kantian accounts of judgment – bears a family resemblance to a centerpiece in Gadamer's elaboration of his philosophical hermeneutics, namely, his account of *phronesis* in Aristotle (Gadamer 1991, 312–24). Lonergan said that his ability to grasp Aquinas's achievement on reflection and judgment was indebted to Newman's appropriation of Aristotle's *phronesis* in *An Essay in Aid of a Grammar of Assent* to articulate the "illative sense" (Lonergan 1974e, 263).[10] Anticipating both Gadamer and Lonergan, Newman had proposed Aristotle's analysis of *phronesis* as a concrete mode of human knowing that takes into account "arguments too various for direct enumeration, too personal and deep for words, too powerful and concurrent for refutation" (Newman 1955, 379). This is pertinent not just to the realm of moral judgment but to all fields of human knowing. Gadamer (1991, 9–42) made analogous arguments in retrieving *Bildung, sensus communis*, taste, and judgment (*Urteilskraft*) from the Humanist tradition in the first part of *Truth and Method*, and in interpreting *phronesis* and *physei dikaion* in the second part. As Lonergan formulated the salient issue: "This process of judging ... is in fact found to be ... a cumulative convergence of direct and indirect confirmations any one of which by itself settles just nothing" (Lonergan 1974a, 31).[11] And so, for Lonergan, the success or failure of any judgment mainly depends on the measure of responsibility on the part of the one making the judgment, that is, an *existential* issue. In summary, therefore, the correct interpretation of Aquinas on knowing was nothing less than *a hermeneutics of cognitional interiority*. Here interiority refers to what Heidegger called a "totally determinate, existential, performative meaning" irreducible to "the metaphysics of things" (Heidegger 1995, 199).

Insight – a modern hermeneutics of cognitional interiority

Contemporary hermeneutic philosophy tends to understand modern science in accord with the Baconian and Cartesian account, which might be summarized as *verum et factum convertuntur* (truth and product are convertible).[12] As a result science is always regarded as a *Herrschaftswissen* that reduces what it knows to the realm of *Verfügbarkeit* or manipulative control.

In *Insight* Lonergan brought Augustine's and Aquinas's phenomenology of the subject into a modern world decisively affected by the achievements of modern science and of modern historical science or scholarship. Lonergan deconstructed the modern epistemologies of Anglo-Saxon empiricism and Cartesian rationalism, because "the question of human knowledge is not whether it exists but what precisely are its two diverse forms and what are the relations between them" (Lonergan 1992, 12). This boldness of approach yielded a startling result:

> [The appropriation of one's own rational self-consciousness] is a necessary beginning. For unless one breaks the duality in one's knowing, one doubts that understanding correctly is knowing. Under the pressure of that doubt, either one will sink into the bog of a knowing that is without understanding, or else one will cling to understanding but sacrifice knowing on the altar of an immanentism, an idealism, a relativism. From the horns of that dilemma one escapes only through the discovery (and one has not made it yet if one has no clear memory of its startling strangeness) that there are two quite different realisms, that there is an incoherent realism, half animal and half human, that poses as a half-way house between materialism and idealism and, on the other hand, that there is an intelligent and reasonable realism between which and materialism the half-way house is idealism.
>
> (Lonergan 1992, 12)

This distinction between realisms highlights the phenomenological core of hermeneutic philosophy's correlation between acts of understanding and knowing with the objects or realities known. This correlation is precisely relevant to the hermeneutic precept that statements in texts are answers to questions, and to understand the answers one has to understand the questions.

Whereas Gadamer and Heidegger conceive *Dasein* as an incarnate question about Being which exists as presence-to-the-world-as-worded, Lonergan held that being in its *Gelichtetheit* performs cognitional acts by asking and answering questions for understanding and judgment. The realities understood and known are *not* instances of the 'already-out-there-now real' made accessible by "taking a good look" – which are the fundamental components in what Gadamer called "the horizon of *Vorhandenheit*"[13] – but realities in "the world mediated by meaning" as distinct from "the world of immediacy."[14]

In *Insight* Lonergan's phenomenology of the subject is a generalized empirical method. Empirical method is conventionally understood as confining scientific inquiry to the external data (whether directly or indirectly accessible) of sense; empirical method is generalized by including the internal data of consciousness. He thus transposed Aquinas's gnoseology into a cognitional theory (Lonergan 1974a, 149–50) "sufficiently refined to do justice to the problems caused by symbolic logic, by mathematics" (2001, 3–166), by the probable principles employed in the natural sciences (1992, 304–15), and by the ontological argument for God's existence (360–71)."

Before inviting readers to appropriate intelligence at work in the sphere of common sense, Lonergan invited them to do so in the spheres of mathematics and the sciences of sub-human nature. After treating how intelligence operates in relation to classical and statistical intelligibilities, he considered the concrete interplay between these two types of intelligibility in aggregates of kinds of things and events under a category he developed to correct both the Aristotelian and the Darwinian world-views, namely, *emergent probability*. Contemporary interest in ecology has made us acutely aware of regular patterns of intermeshing of kinds of things in accord with probabilities of their occurrence or non-occurrence. Lonergan's term for this is "schemes of recurrence" – think of the interplay between hydrogen and nitrogen cycles. Recurrence schemes are subject to probable schedules of emergence and survival.[15] Extrapolating to the totality of the material universe from particular instances of probability schedules for the emergence and survival of recurrence schemes, one may suppose that the overall intelligibility of the universe as conditioned by space and time has the shape of emergent probability.

This is important for Lonergan's hermeneutics because emergent probability also provides a heuristic for the overall intelligibility of the emergence and survival of the meanings constitutive of human societies and cultures; these in turn furnish the remote and proximate contexts for understanding all artifacts in the world both mediated and constituted by meaning, including primarily, language, social institutions (family, state, law, technology, economy, polity, educational institutions), human cultures (art, science, literature, religion, philosophy, theology); and secondarily, such things as ruins, shards, monuments, tablets, coins, books, text-fragments, and so on. The role of probability as rooted ontologically in the potentiality of an indeterminate energy which is open to all the genera and species that differentiate things and events in the realms of physics, chemistry, biology (botany, zoology), human psychology, and history would account for all the indeterminacies, relativities, possibilities of change for better and for worse, and hence contingencies and uncertainties about which deconstructive and genealogical approaches to hermeneutics (of theorists such as Derrida, Rorty, Foucault, Deleuze, and Guattari) have correctly desired to take into account.

Lonergan's cognitional theoretic breakthrough to the affirmation of oneself as a person who attains knowledge by both understanding and judging (1992, 343–71) made it possible to encircle the scope of knowing *tout court* within what he named the *notion* (or *intention*) of being (n.b. *not knowledge* of being!) (1992, 372–98). *Insight* engaged the reader in answering the **epistemological** question by postponing the articulation of a valid reply to this question until the reader affirms a positive and verifiable response to the prior question of *cognitional theory*:[16] What am I doing when I think I am knowing? Only then may one responsibly answer the question, Why is doing *that* knowing? Again, only by being able to explain in an explicitly critical realist sense how human knowing attains objectivity (1992, 399–409) can one critically ground the metaphysics latent in the activity of human knowing and stating the truth.

On the basis of a methodically (or hermeneutically) grounded cognitional theory, epistemology, and metaphysics, Lonergan presented a comprehensive semantics[17] of whatever may be discovered by the classical, statistical, and genetic methods of explanatory natural science.[18] This is grounded *hermeneutically*, because it is not confined to but transcends the logical scope of *apophansis*. To underscore the hermeneutical nature of his general semantics, Lonergan explicated "the *protean* notion of being" (Lonergan 1992, 509, 545, 590, 609) because the openness of human awareness as the non-objectifiable *Gelichtetheit* of being is polymorphic, with a virtually infinite plasticity. In this way he could account for the range of performance originating from the unity-in-tension constituted by the human being's organism, psyche, and rational self-consciousness as it develops over time and within social and cultural interactions. This is Lonergan's initial working out of a 'hermeneutics of facticity' as the groundwork for *human* studies (scholarship), the sciences, philosophy, and theology.[19]

In *Insight* the 'universal viewpoint' (Lonergan 1992, 587–600; Coelho 2001) is correlative to the 'protean notion of being' underpinning human intelligence's plasticity. As a basic context for a kind of interpretation that goes beyond both the simple interpretation and the reflective interpretation that is explicitly aware of ever shifting hermeneutic contexts, the universal viewpoint thematizes "a potential totality of genetically and dialectically ordered viewpoints." Entailed is grasping what it means to understand thoroughly what understanding is. The *genetic* aspect of the universal viewpoint involves both insight into how multiple acts of understanding coalesce into viewpoints, and seeing how viewpoints set the conditions for the emergence of further, often higher viewpoints. The 'protean' (added to the phrase 'notion of being') refers also to the universal viewpoint's *dialectical* dimension due to the perturbations to which understanding may be subjected by blind-spots engendered by both bias and a person's disordered desires and fears, as well as the proliferation of oversights that result from them.

Here, too, Lonergan focused on the dimension of development in relation to the sources of meaning and the series of expressions of meaning to which the sources give rise over time. Such an explanatory approach to meaning provides an anticipatory grasp of all there is to be understood in the world mediated and constituted by meaning, thus overcoming dogmatic theology's penchant for short-circuiting hermeneutics and history.

Such foundations unequivocally reject all positivist, naive realist, idealist, or relativist accounts of interpretation. Lonergan's full-blown non-relativist rejection of 'the principle of the empty head' (1972a, 157–8, 204, 223) – based on the fundamentalist denial that interpretation is needed to make sense of realities mediated and constituted by meaning – is grounded in a basic context for integral hermeneutics that also undermines any rationalist hermeneutics of suspicion by providing a differentiated account of the critique of belief.[20] Moreover, it goes beyond the 'higher' fundamentalism of the interpreters and historians who suppose that they have no need of such higher-level controls as the universal viewpoint.

The integral hermeneutics of method in theology

A. Meaning

Heidegger and his followers stressed that from the time we learn our mother tongue we almost always operate in the world mediated by meaning and guided by value, a world constructed by our operations of understanding, judging, and evaluating. Hence, meaning is far more comprehensive than the relationship between a sign and that which it signifies that had prevailed in *Insight*. Here is one of Lonergan's relatively early acknowledgments of what was at stake for him in this expanded significance:

> I have been meeting the objection that meaning is a merely secondary affair, that what counts is the reality that is meant and not the mere meaning that refers to it. My answer has been that the functions of meaning are larger than the objection envisages. I would not dispute that, for the child learning to talk, his little world of immediacy comes first, and that the words he uses are only an added grace. But as the child develops into a man, the world of immediacy shrinks into an inconspicuous and not too important corner of the real world, which is a world we know only through the mediation of meaning. Further, there is man's transformation of his environment, a transformation that is effected through the intentional acts that envisage ends, select means, secure collaborators, direct operations. Finally, besides the transformations of nature, there is man's transformation of man himself; and in this transformation the role of meaning is not merely directive but also constitutive.
>
> (Lonergan 1984c, 234–5)

As he was composing *Method in Theology*, the constitutive function of meaning became absolutely central for Lonergan:

> For it is in the field where meaning is constitutive that man's freedom reaches its highest point. There too his responsibility is greatest. There there occurs

the emergence of the existential subject, finding out for himself that he has to decide for himself what he is to make of himself. It is there that individuals become alienated from community, that communities split into factions, that cultures flower and decline, that historical causality exerts its sway.

(1984c, 235)

B. The world as mediated and constituted by meaning

After his breakthrough to the category of meaning, Lonergan adapted the notion of mediation (2010, 55) from Henri Niel's discussion of Hegelian dialectic (Niel 1945; Lonergan 1996, 160–76), using insights from Jean Piaget to distinguish the world of immediacy, in which objects are immediately present to our operations, from the world mediated by meaning, in which we operate "in a compound manner; immediately with respect to image, word, symbol; mediately with respect to what is represented or signified in this fashion" (Lonergan 1972a, 28). After *Insight* he built on Piaget's use of an analogy based on group theory[21] in a genetic theory of the stages of human cognitive development (by differentiating operations and grouping operations) to articulate the empirically verifiable notion of differentiations of consciousness.[22] Thus, he was able to characterize the development as moving (*via* common-sense knowing) from global and compact world-views to more differentiated and specialized expressions in order to resolve apparently irreconcilable 'chasms' among different universes of discourse (e.g., between symbolic and mythic realms and theoretical, explanatory language) that have troubled theology in different ways throughout its development.[23]

The basis for the resolution of such dichotomies is the capacity of the unity of differentiated consciousness to discern accurately the respective strengths and limitations of the permanent role played in human living by relatively undifferentiated consciousness vis-à-vis the systematic, interior, transcendent, and methodological exigencies built into historically unfolding human nature. Because of this possibility, the unity of differentiated consciousness became the keystone of Lonergan's analysis of the control of meaning,[24] and the stages of meaning (1972a, 85–99), as well as of both cultural and doctrinal pluralism, and interreligious dialogue (1971a, 1972a, 295–333, 335–53). In relation to hermeneutics generally, Lonergan noted the importance of mutual mediation among a variety of differentiations:

[M]aturity is comprehensive. … As it does not deny propositional truth, so it does not disregard or belittle religious experience. On the contrary, it is quite ready to claim with Karl Rahner that a mystagogy will play a far more conspicuous role in the spirituality of the future, and it is fully aware that spiritual advance brings about in prayer the diminution and at times the disappearance of symbols and concepts of God. Still, this differentiation and specialization of consciousness does not abolish other, complementary differentiations and specializations, whether social, sexual, practical, aesthetic, scientific, philosophic, historical, or theological. Nor is this multiplicity in any way opposed to integration. For in each of such diverse patterns of consciousness operation is oneself in accord with some facet of one's being and some part of one's universe; and while one lives in only one pattern at a time in some cycle of recurrence, still the subject **is** over time, each pattern complements, reinforces, liberates the others, and there can develop a differentiation of consciousness to deal explicitly with differentiations of consciousness. That pattern is, of course, reflective subjectivity in philosophy and theology. It follows the Hellenic precept "Know thyself." It follows the example of Augustinian recall, scrutiny, penetration, judgment, evaluation, decision. It realizes the modern concern for the authenticity of one's existing without amputating one's own rational objectivity expressed in propositional truth.

(1974a, 29)

C. Feelings and the transcendental notion of value

In order to solve the problem of integrating history into doctrinal and systematic theology, Lonergan realized that he had to integrate Augustine's hermeneutics of love into his foundational methodology.[25] When in *Verbum* he wrote, "For Augustine, our hearts are restless until they rest in God; for Aquinas, not our hearts, but first and most our minds are restless until they rest in God" (Lonergan 1997, 100), he unknowingly indicated the radical change he himself would have to undergo. From *Grace and Freedom* through *Insight* Aquinas's intellectualist[26] orientation had so dominated Lonergan's thought that shifting to Augustine's horizon meant undergoing a multitude of changes that were then far from obvious to him. By relinquishing the last residues of faculty psychology he overcame the need to choose between the intellect and the will as the more important faculty, so that Lonergan could then let go of Aquinas's definition of the will as an intellectual appetite (which implied the unequivocal priority of intellect), and drop the scholastic dictum *nil amatum nisi prius cognitum*: nothing is loved unless it is first known.

A further issue involves the pivotal notion of "intellectual conversion" and the reframing of *Insight*'s breakthrough in the reader's self-affirmation as a knower by acknowledging that morality could no longer be thought of simply as maintaining consistency between one's knowledge of the truth and one's decisions and actions. When Joseph de Finance helped him to distinguish between horizontal and vertical exercises of liberty,[27] it became clear to him that the authenticity of one's self-affirmation would entail an explicitly conscious decision or commitment involving a vertical exercise of liberty tantamount to becoming a new self. Thus, the post-*Insight* notions of 'horizon' and 'conversion' as a radical change in one's overall orientation – amounting to entry into a new horizon – opened the way for him to return to the topics he had treated in *Grace and Freedom* from a metaphysical perspective, but – once he had appropriated in himself the massive role of feelings as intentional responses to values – in consistently existential terms. Such feelings come crucially into play on the fourth level of conscious intentionality in which we deliberate and understand courses of action or appreciate already existing goods inasmuch as we make judgments of value under the influence of our intentional responses to values.

He was grateful to two decidedly Augustinian phenomenologists, Max Scheler and Dietrich von Hildebrand, for aid in understanding the role of feelings as "the mass and momentum and power of [human] conscious living, the actuation of [human] affective capacities, dispositions, habits, the effective orientation of [human] living" (Lonergan 1972a, 65). To relinquish the assumptions (1) that intellect holds precedence over the will, and (2) that knowing ever precedes loving was to acknowledge also that the role played by feelings as intentional responses to value in value judgments could not fit into the structure of factual judgments (1972a, 30–3), where the reflective act of understanding's grasp of the sufficiency of the evidence rationally compels the Yes or No of judgment. In time, he formulated his change of position from *Insight* as follows:

> In *Insight* the good was the intelligent and the reasonable. In *Method* the good is a distinct notion. It is intended in questions for deliberation: Is this worthwhile? Is it truly or only apparently good? It is aspired to in the intentional response of feeling to values. It is known in judgments of value made by a virtuous or authentic person with a good conscience. It is brought about by deciding and living up to one's decisions. Just as intelligence sublates sense, just as reasonableness sublates intelligence, so deliberation sublates and thereby unifies knowing and feeling.
>
> (Lonergan 1974e, 277)

The impact of these changes from *Insight* is evident in *Method*'s treatment of the human good (1972a, 27–55), insofar as later breakthroughs related to the fourth level of conscious intentionality (on which deliberation, understanding of courses of action or appreciating already existing goods, and value judgments occur under the influence of feelings as intentional responses to feelings) transformed his account of its structure of the human good.

Method in theology's integral hermeneutics

In *Method* Lonergan had to face head-on the profound challenges Protestant theology had been handling since the eighteenth century (Wilson 2007; Pannenberg 1997). Post-reformation Catholic theology tried to meet the accusations of corruption and Hellenization by inventing a "dogmatic" theology, which "replaced the inquiry of the *quaestio* by the pedagogy of the thesis" and "gave basic and central significance to the certitudes of the faith, their presuppositions and their consequences" – a logically dominated approach whose penchant for anachronism violated virtually every precept of sound hermeneutics.[28]

Once he discarded the priority of knowledge and articulated the primacy of love, Lonergan turned away from the abstract, *de jure* articulation of the stages in the beginning of faith (*initium fidei*) (Lonergan 2002). In the earlier Thomistic *de jure* analysis, 'faith' meant assent to revealed truth based on prior grace-enabled judgments. *De facto*, however, faith refers to the affective knowledge acquired through the gift of religious conversion by which one falls in love with God. So Lonergan distinguished (and did not separate) faith from belief (1972a, 115–18, 118–24). *Faith* is "the eyes of being in love with God," the apprehension of transcendent value born of religious love. Belief as the reasonable and responsible assent to truths not personally verified by one's personal acts of understanding and verifying always occurs in the light of *faith* – the pressure exerted by God's love on human intelligence (1972a, 41–7). Then Lonergan began regularly to quote Paul on "God's gift of his love poured into our hearts by the Holy Spirit that is in us" (Rom 5:5) to characterize religious conversion as falling-in-love with God and being-in-love with God (1972a, 105; 1972b, 223–34).

That love plays *the* determinative role in personal orientation and authenticity is made clear by Augustine's radical teaching that "my weight is my love; by it I move wherever I move."[29] After Lonergan recognized the pivotal role of love (1972, 33, 36, 105–6, 122, 240), of conversion, and especially of religious conversion, it did not take long for him then to conceive the intelligible relationship between Jerusalem and Athens (or faith and reason) in terms of two vectors of human development:

> There is development from below upwards, from experience to growing understanding, from growing understanding to balanced judgment, from balanced judgment to fruitful courses of action, and from fruitful courses of action to the new situations that call forth further understanding, profounder judgment, richer courses of action. But there also is development from above downwards. There is the transformation of falling in love: the domestic love of the family; the human love of one's tribe, one's city, one's country, mankind; the divine love that orientates man in his cosmos and expresses itself in his worship. Where hatred only sees evil, love reveals value. At once it commands commitment and joyfully carries it out, no matter what the sacrifice involved. Where hatred reinforces bias, love dissolves it, whether it be the bias of unconscious motivation, the bias of individual or group egoism, or the bias of omni-competent, short-sighted common sense. Where hatred plods around in ever narrower circles, love breaks the bonds of psychological and social determinisms with the conviction of faith and the power of hope.
>
> (Lonergan 1985b, 106)

These two developmental vectors constitute *the ontological structure of the hermeneutic circle.*[30] Prior to all our actions is the way of heritage emphasized by Gadamer. It works through love's influence on one's decisions, judgments, insights, and experiential perceptions. By acknowledging the priority of the way from above downwards, Lonergan affirmed Gadamer's stress on the aspect relegated to oblivion by the Enlightenment's 'prejudice against prejudice,' namely, that intellectual development's rhythm of believing to understand and understanding to believe is both inevitable and reasonable since it is just how reason works.

Lonergan's hermeneutics – like his phenomenology of understanding – is more differentiated than Gadamer's. Going beyond Gadamer's self-imposed confinement to the strictures of Kant's transcendental dialectic, Lonergan's unabashed recognition of the primacy of love allowed him to argue that philosophy can only be a comprehensive reflection on the human condition, if (knowingly or not) it is grounded in being-in-love with God. In determining "the one thing needful" in this life, the greater is philosophy's fidelity to the interplay between believing to understand and understanding to believe (*scil.*, the concrete dynamism of the integral hermeneutic circle), the less it can avoid either the radical issues of good and evil (sin and redemption), or the *de facto* offers and rejections of grace in history.

Once he incorporated the "appropriation of one's own rational self-consciousness" as "intellectual conversion" into integral hermeneutics (Lonergan 1984b, 219), Lonergan then clarified how intellectual conversion is made possible by a prior, distinct, *moral* conversion from satisfactions to true values or the truly good (1972a, 240–3). Finally, as Augustine had dramatically demonstrated, moral conversion tends to be made possible by *religious* conversion (1972a, 240–3). This cluster of insights converged for Lonergan into a sublation of Gadamer's account of the hermeneutic circle.

In Lonergan's theology, God's universal salvific will implies the invisible mission of the Holy Spirit to *all* human beings, whose source (which needn't be expressly acknowledged to be efficacious)[31] is redemption in Christ (Lonergan 1974c). So the hermeneutic spiral from above downwards starts with the prior gift of God's love, so that first religious, then moral, and finally intellectual conversion become the foundations for the hermeneutics of love – a hermeneutics that transforms the Christian approach to interreligious dialogue.

Philosophical counter-positions regarding knowing, objectivity, and being have bedeviled theology and faith, especially since the eighteenth century. For Lonergan we can resolve such issues by intellectually, morally, and religiously converted dialectics and dialogue. As a result, the specialized discipline Lonergan named dialectic (1972a, 235–66), becomes integral for the contemporary and interreligious theological *lectio* (i.e., hearing the outward word of religious traditions) through the functional specialties of research, interpretation, and history (1972a, 149–234). For Lonergan, such a dialectical confrontation with scholarly and ordinary mediators of tradition would both clarify and depend upon hermeneutical foundations that make intellectual, moral, and religious conversion thematic (267–93).

The ultimate benefit of Lonergan's life-long project of bringing history into theology as a functionally specialized (1972a, 125–45) collaboration was to have reoriginated Augustine's hermeneutics of love. The specialty of foundations that thematizes the horizons of interpretation can be a transcultural basis for all the human interpretative sciences, including philosophy and theology, as operating the hermeneutic spiral from below upwards. Lonergan was convinced that the more radical and the more differentiated the specific discipline of theology becomes, the more it needs the help of a hermeneutic philosophy that can provide explanatory analogies that "open a window" on the mysteries of faith. Then the traditional disciplines of *disputatio*, and *praedicatio* may be organized into the ongoing, functionally specialized collaborative tasks of foundations, doctrines, systematics, and communications, to round out a more authentic hermeneutics of love (1972a, 295–368).

Notes

1   We cannot take the reconstruction of the question to which a given text is an answer simply as an achievement of historical method. The most important thing is the question that the text puts to us, our being perplexed by the traditionary word, so that understanding it must already include the task of the historical self-mediation between the present and tradition. Thus the relation of question and answer is reversed. The voice that speaks to us from the past – whether text, work, trace – itself poses a question and places our meaning in openness. In order to answer the question put to us, we the interrogated must ourselves begin to ask questions. We must attempt to reconstruct the question to which the traditionary text is the answer. ... Reconstructing the question to which the text is presumed to be the answer itself takes place within a process of questioning though which we try to answer the question that the text asks us.

(Gadamer 1991, 373–4).

2 That is, what is first for us, for Aristotle, *proton pros hemas*, in *Insight*, "things related to our senses"; and what is first in itself, for Aristotle, *proton pros physin*, in *Insight*, "things related to each other." See Lonergan 1985b, 142–52 at 143–4 on the distinction between the "first for us" as cognitional reasons and what is 'first from the perspective of the things themselves' as ontological causes.

3 "The Form of the Development" (Lonergan 2000, 162–92) characterized this as the construction of "an *a priori* scheme that is capable of synthesizing any possible set of historical data irrespective of their place and time" through "an analysis of the idea of development in speculative theology."

4 On Gadamer's understanding of Aquinas on the *verbum internum* vis-à-vis Lonergan's, see Lawrence 2009.

5 Thomas Aquinas, *Summa theologiae* I, q. 88, a. 2 AD 3m: *Anima humana intelligit seipsum per suum intelligere, quod est actus proprius eius, perfecte demonstrans virtutem eius et naturam.*

6 Thomas Aquinas, *Summa contra Gentiles*, 2, c. 98 AD fin: *secundum autem positionem Platonis, intelligere fit per contactum intellectus ad rem intelligibilem* ...

7 Lonergan adduces the following texts of Aquinas as warrants for this interpretation: *De veritate*, q. 3, a. 2 c.; *De potentia*, q. 8, a. 1 c.; q. 9, a. 5 c; *Quaestiones quodlibetales*, 5, a. 9 c.; *Super Ioannem*, 5, 1, lect. 1.

8 Citing Thomas Aquinas, *Summa theologiae*, I, q. 15, a. 2 c: *ipsum enim lumen intellectuale quod est in nobis, nihil est aliud quam quaedam participata similitudo luminis increati.*

9 This is the ultimate ground for Hölderlin's famous phrase in the poem, *Friedensfeuer*, "Seit ein Gespräch wir sind, und hören voneinander," so significant for Heidegger and Gadamer.

10 See Dunne 1993 on the parallel between Newman's elucidation and Gadamer's rehabilitation of prejudice.

11 On *phronesis* see Gadamer 1991, 312–24; 1976, 201–2; and 1986, 163–4.

12 Thus Kant's assertion (1933, B xiv) that reason gains knowledge of something it produces in nature "according to a plan of its own" (*selbst nach ihre Entwurfe*).

13 The "*Horizont der Vorhandenheit*" combines **perceptualism** (the teaching that the only way to the really real is through "taking a look" and an object that is "already-out-there-now"), **conceptualism** (that universal concepts are prior to insights and that judgments are just syntheses of concepts), and **abstract deductivism** (concentration on the rigorous use of terms or concepts, propositions or statements, and inferences as moving from implier through implication to the implied) to the complete neglect of tacit knowledge or *phronesis*.

14 The 'world of immediacy' indicates human conscious intentionality's direct awareness (though not necessarily focal or foregrounded) of the data of the senses or the data of consciousness; the 'world mediated by meaning' indicates human conscious intentionality's direct awareness of images, symbols, or words, and its mediate (or indirect) awareness (although, again, not necessarily in a thematized manner) of what the images, symbols, or words signify. Illustrative of this difference is the early Husserl's endeavor to isolate acts of "pure perception" versus

Heidegger's turn toward language (or linguistic phenomenology): while pure perception may occur rarely, normally human conscious intentionality is present to the world as 'languaged' or worded; thus the significance of the "as-structure" in hermeneutic phenomenology.

15 A common-sense example: Marine biologists' concern about the virtual extinction of seals along the New England seacoast were allayed because seals have been returning, and with the renewed seal populations, there has been a noticeable rise in the population of sharks due to interventions and shifting conditions.

16 Lonergan differentiated 'cognitional theory' (as the answer to the question, What happens when we know?) from 'epistemology' (as the answer to the question, Why does doing that achieve objective knowledge?), whereas the German word, *Erkenntnistheorie* (usually translated as epistemology) does not.

17 See the four chapters on metaphysics (Lonergan 1992, 410–617).

18 On the natural sciences, see "Heuristic Structures of Empirical Method," "The Canons of Empirical Method," "The Complementarity of Classical and Statistical Investigations," "Space and Time," and "Things" (Lonergan 1992, 57–195, and 270–95).

19 On the human, social, and cultural sciences, see "Common Sense and Its Subject" and "Common Sense as Object," and the chapter, "Metaphysics as Dialectic," especially section 3, The Truth of Interpretation (Lonergan 1992, 196–269, 585–617).

20 On "The Notion of Belief" and "The Critique of Belief," see Lonergan 1992, 709–40, 735–9.

21   The principal characteristic of the group of operations is that every operation in the group is matched by an opposite operation and every combination of operations is matched by an opposite combination. Hence, inasmuch as operations are grouped, the operator can always return to his starting-point and, when he can do so unhesitatingly, he has reached mastery at some level of development.

(Lonergan 1972a, 27–8)

22 During the years before *Method in Theology* (1972), Lonergan worked out the following key differentiations of consciousness: common-sense, theoretical or systematic (as in the exact sciences of nature), scholarly (as in history or the humanities), interiority (as in intentionality analysis or generalized empirical method), and religiously or transcendently differentiated awareness.

23 These issues were traced in Lonergan's seminar courses at Rome's Gregorian University before the publication of *Method in Theology* in 1972: *De intellectu et methodo*, 1958–9 (Lonergan 2013, 3–227); *De systemate et historia*, 1959–60 (Lonergan 2013, 231–313); and *De methodo theologiae*,1961–2 (Lonergan 2013, 359–589), in which he first applied Piaget's ideas.

24 "For if social and cultural changes are, at root, changes in the meanings that are grasped and accepted, changes in the control of meaning make up the great epochs in human history" (Lonergan 1984c, 232–45).

25 The phrase, 'hermeneutics of love' is borrowed from Fortin 1996, 1–19. Although perhaps none of the authors mentioned expressly used the phrase, I think that was ultimately the gravamen of their work.

26 For Lonergan the term 'intellectualist' both stresses the priority of questions for intelligence, reflection, and deliberation and their corresponding acts of understanding and distinguishes Aquinas's and his own approach to knowledge from the 'conceptualist's' forgetfulness of both questioning and the different acts of understanding.

27 Whereas in a horizontal exercise of liberty one chooses among courses of action within an already fixed horizon, in a vertical exercise of liberty one enters an entirely new horizon, or becomes a new self (Lonergan 1972a, 40, 122, 237–8, 240, 269).

28 The 'thesis method' of pre-Vatican II Catholic theology transposed Agricola's method of forensic rhetoric based on *topoi* or 'commonplaces' into the use of *'loci'* in order to "prove" doctrines (Lonergan 1974b, 55–67 at 57). See Lehmann 1970 for a treatment of the issues involved in the transition to a new way of doing systematic or dogmatic theology.

29 *Confessions*, 13. 9. 10: *pondus meum amor meus, eo feror, quocumque feror* (Augustine 1992).

30 "If interpretation must in any case already operate in that which is understood and if it must draw its nurture from this, how is it to bring any scientific results to maturity without

moving in a circle, especially if, moreover, the understanding which is presupposed still operates within our common information about man and world?" (Heidegger 1962, 194). As Gadamer noted, Heidegger's point was "not so much to prove that there is a circle as to show that this circle possesses an ontologically positive significance" (1991, 266).

31 "[T]here is a notable anonymity in the gift of the Spirit. Like the Johannine *pneuma*, it blows where it wills; you hear the sound of it, but you do not know where it comes from or where it is going (John 3: 8)" (Lonergan 1974d, 174).

Bibliography

Works by Lonergan

1940, *Gratia operans: a study of the speculative development in the writings of St. Thomas of Aquin*, PhD thesis, Pontifical Gregorian University.

1941, 'St. Thomas' thought on *gratia operans*,' *Theological Studies*, vol. 2, pp. 289–324.

1942, 'St. Thomas' thought on *gratia operans*,' *Theological Studies*, vol. 3, pp. 69–88, 375–402, 533–78.

1946, 'The concept of *verbum* in the writings of St. Thomas Aquinas,' *Theological Studies*, vol. 7, pp. 349–92.

1947, 'The concept of *verbum* in the writings of St. Thomas Aquinas,' *Theological Studies*, vol. 8, pp. 35–79, 404–44.

1949, 'The concept of *verbum* in the writings of St. Thomas Aquinas,' *Theological Studies*, vol. 10, pp. 3–40, 359–93.

1963, 'La notion de verbe dans les ecrits de Saint Thomas d'Aquin,' *Archives de philosophie*, vol. 26, pp. 163–203, 570–620.

1964, 'La notion de verbe dans les ecrits de Saint Thomas d'Aquin,' *Archives de philosophie*, vol. 27, pp. 238–85.

1965, 'La notion de verbe dans les ecrits de Saint Thomas d'Aquin,' *Archives de philosophie*, vol. 28, pp. 206–50, 510–62.

1966, *La notion de verbe dans les ecrits de Saint Thomas d'Aquin*, trans. of 'The Concept of Verbum ... ,' (trans.) Régnier, M, Beauchesne, Paris.

1967, *Verbum: word and idea in Aquinas*, Burrell DB (ed.) University of Notre Dame Press, Notre Dame.

1997, *Verbum: word and idea in Aquinas*, Collected Works of Bernard Lonergan, vol. 2, Crowe, FE and Doran RM, University of Toronto Press, Toronto.

1971a, *Doctrinal pluralism*, Marquette University Press, Milwaukee.

1971b, *Grace and freedom: operative grace in the thought of St. Thomas Aquinas*, Burns, JP (ed.) Herder & Herder, New York.

1972a, *Method in Theology*, Herder & Herder, New York.

1972b 'Bernard Lonergan Responds,' *Foundations of theology: papers from the international Lonergan congress 1970*, McShane, P (ed.) University of Notre Dame, South Bend.

1974a, 'Insight revisited,' *A Second Collection*, Ryan, WJ and Tyrrell, BJ (eds.) Darton, Longman & Todd, London, pp. 11–32.

1974b, 'The dehellenization of dogma,' *A Second Collection*, pp. 11–32.

1974c, 'Theology in its new context,' *A Second Collection*, pp. 55–67.

1974d, 'The response of the Jesuit as priest and apostle in the modern world,' *A Second Collection*, pp. 165–87.

1974e, 'The future of Christianity,' *Second Collection*, pp. 135–63.

1984a, 'Insight: preface to a discussion,' *Collection*, Collected Works of Bernard Lonergan, vol. 4, Crowe, FE and Doran, RM, University of Toronto Press, Toronto, pp. 142–52.

1984b, 'Cognitional structure,' *Collection*, pp. 205–21.

1984c, 'Dimensions of meaning,' *Collection*, pp. 232–45.

1985a, 'Method: trend and variations,' *A Third Collection. Papers by Bernard J. F. Lonergan, SJ*, Crowe, FE (ed.) Paulist Press, Mahwah, pp. 13–22.

1985b, 'Healing and creating in history,' *A Third Collection*, pp. 100–109.

1992, *Insight: a study of human understanding*, Collected Works of Bernard Lonergan vol. 3, Crowe, FE and Doran RM (eds.) University of Toronto Press, Toronto.

1996, 'The Mediation of Christ in Prayer,' *Philosophical and Theological Papers 1958–1964*, Collected Works of Bernard Lonergan, vol. 6, Croken, RC, Crowe, FE, and Doran RM, (eds.) University of Toronto Press, Toronto, pp. 160–82.

2000, *Grace and freedom: operative grace in the thought of St. Thomas Aquinas*, Collected Works of Bernard Lonergan, vol. 1, Crowe, FE and Doran, RM (eds.) University of Toronto Press, Toronto.

2001, *Phenomenology and logic: the Boston College lectures in mathematical logic and existentialism*, Collected Works of Bernard Lonergan, vol. 18, McShane, P (ed.) University of Toronto Press, Toronto.

2002, 'Analysis of faith,' METHOD: *Journal of Lonergan Studies*, vol. 20, pp. 125–54.

2004, 'Philosophy and the religious phenomenon,' *Philosophical and Theological Papers, 1965–1980*, Collected Works of Bernard Lonergan, vol. 17, Croken, R and Doran, RM (eds.) University of Toronto Press, Toronto, pp. 395, 174,176, 246 ff.

2007, *The triune god: systematics* (trans. 1964, *De deo trino: pars systematica*) Shields, MG, Collected Works of Bernard Lonergan, vol. 12, Doran, RM and Monsour, HD (eds.) University of Toronto Press, Toronto.

2009, *The triune god: doctrines* (trans. 1964, *De deo trino: pars dogmatica*) Shields, MG, Collected Works of Bernard Lonergan, vol. 11, Doran, RM and Monsour, HD (eds.) University of Toronto Press, Toronto.

2010, 'Hermeneutics,' section dated 1962–9 in *Early Works on Theological Method 1*, Collected Works of Bernard Lonergan, vol. 22, Doran, RM and Croken, RC (eds.) University of Toronto, Toronto.

2013, *Early works on theological method 3*, *Exercitatio* graduate seminar courses at Pontifical Gregorian University (original Latin and English trans.), in Collected Works of Bernard Lonergan, vol. 23, (trans.) Shields, MG, Doran, RM and Monsour, HD (eds.) University of Toronto Press, Toronto:

Understanding and method (*De intellectu et method*, 1958–9), documented in typed notes of Rossi de Gasperis, F and Cahill, PJ and in some of Lonergan's own notes, pp. 3–227.

System and History (*De systemate et historia*, 1959–60), documented in the handwritten notes of Rossi de Gasperis, F Francesco and in some of Lonergan's own notes, pp. 231–313.

The Method of Theology (*De methodo theologiae*, 1961–2), pp. 359–589.

Other works

Augustine, A (1992), *Confessions*, trans. H Chadwick, Oxford University Press, Oxford.

Aquinas, T——(1866), *Super Ioannem. Opera Omnia*, vol. 13, Parma edn., Typis Petri Fiaccadori, Parma.

——(1888–1906), *Summa theologiae, Opera Omnia*, vols. 4–10, Leonine edn., Ex Typographia Polyglotta, Rome.

——(1934), *Summa contra Gentiles, Opera Omnia*, vols. 13–15, Leonine manual edn., Apud Sedem Commissionis Lioninae, Rome.

——(1949), *Quaestiones disputatae de veritate, de potentia, de malo, de spiritualibus creaturis, de anima, de unione Verbi incarnati, de virtutibus in communi, de caritate, se spe. Quaestiones disputatae*, vol. 2., Bazzi, P, Calcaterra, M, Centi, TS, Odetto, E, and Pession, PM (eds.) Marietti, Turin.

——(1949), *Quaestiones quodlibetales*, Spiazzi, RM (ed.) Marietti, Turin.

Coelho, I (2001), *Hermeneutics and method: a study of the 'universal viewpoint' in Bernard Lonergan*, University of Toronto Press, Toronto.

Dunne, J (1993), *Back to the rough ground: practical judgment and the lure of technique*, University of Notre Dame, Notre Dame.

Fortin, E (1996), 'Augustine and the hermeneutics of love: some preliminary considerations,' *The birth of philosophic christianity. Studies in early christian and medieval thought*. Ernest L. Fortin: Collected Essays, Vol. 1, Benestad, B (ed.) Rowman and Littlefield, Lanham, pp. 1–19.

Gadamer, H-G (1976), 'Martin Heidegger and Marburg theology (1964),' *Philosophical hermeneutics*, (trans.) Linge, DE, University of California Press, Berkeley, pp. 198–212.

——(1986) *The idea of the good in Platonic-Aristotelian philosophy*, (trans.) Smith, PC, Yale University Press, New Haven, pp. 163–4.

——(1991), *Truth and method*, (rev. trans) Weinsheimer, J and Marshall, DG, Crossroads, New York.

Heidegger, M (1962), *Being and time*, (trans.) Macquarrie, J and Robinson, E, Harper & Rowe, New York.

——(1980), 'Brief an Engelbert Krebs,' cited in Bernhard Casper, 'Martin Heidegger und die Theologische Fakultät Freiburg 1909–23,' *Freiburger Diözesan-Archiv*, vol. 100.

——(1995), *Phänomenologie des religiösen Lebens*, Gesamtausgabe 60, Jung, M, Regehly, T, and Strube, C (eds.) Vittorio Klostermann, Frankfurt am Main.

Kant, I (1933), *Critique of Pure Reason*, (trans.) Smith, NK, Macmillan, London.

Lawrence, F (2009), 'Lonergan's retrieval of Thomas Aquinas's conception of the *imago dei*: the trinitarian analogy of intelligible emanations in God,' in *Contemporary Thomisms*, Hibbs, TS and Candler, Jr., PM (eds.) *American Catholic Philosophical Quarterley* vol. 83, no. 3, pp. 363–88.

Lehmann, K (1970), 'Die dogmatische Denkform als hermeneutisches Problem. Prologomena zu einer Kritik der dogmatischen Vernunft,' *Evangelische Theologie* vol. 30, no. 9, pp. 469–89.

Newman, JH (1955), *An essay in aid of a grammar of assent*, Doubleday & Co. Image Books, New York.

Pannenberg, W (1997), *Problemgeschichte der neueren evangelischen Theologie in Deutschland. Von Schleiermacher zu Barth*, Vandenhoeck & Ruprecht, Göttingen.

Niel, H (1945), *De la Médiation dans la philosophie de Hegel*, Aubier, Paris.

Wilson, JE (2007), *Introduction to modern theology: trajectories in the German tradition*, Westminster John Knox, Louisville.

14

PAREYSON AND VATTIMO: FROM TRUTH TO NIHILISM

Gaetano Chiurazzi

1. Pareyson: truth, interpretation, freedom

The name of Luigi Pareyson (1918–91) is linked to the introduction of philosophical existentialism and philosophical hermeneutics into the panorama of twentieth century Italian philosophy. In the early decades of this century, Italian philosophy was dominated by Hegelian idealism, the leading figures of which were Giovanni Gentile (1875–1944) and Benedetto Croce (1866–1952). In this context, Pareyson represents a genuine fracture: in fact, for him philosophical hermeneutics, because of its existential roots, constitutes a radical alternative to Hegelianism. This point marks also the originality of his philosophical perspective in respect to German philosophical hermeneutics: while for Gadamer philosophical hermeneutics is an outcome of the internal dissolution of Hegelianism, which, starting from Dilthey, gives up the need for the absolute spirit and turns into a philosophy of the objective spirit, for Pareyson it arises from a philosophical movement alternative to Hegelianism, represented by post-Hegelian authors such as Kierkegaard and Feuerbach, or pre-Hegelians such as Fichte and Schelling. To Pareyson, a philosophical hermeneutics that seeks its roots in Hegelian philosophy, even when deprived of the absolute spirit, does nothing but legitimate its own historicist and relativistic outcomes. Contrary to this, existentialism allows for an integral opposition to the Hegelian system without renouncing the demand for truth; a demand that hermeneutics should continue to assert.

In the Introduction to the second edition of *Esistenza e persona* (Pareyson 1985), Pareyson distinguished three phases in his philosophical thought:

a) an existentialistic phase, which culminates in the elaboration of an ontological personalism;
b) a hermeneutical phase, in which the theory of interpretation is tied to an ontology of the inexhaustible;
c) an ontological phase, in which existential hermeneutics becomes a hermeneutics of religious existence and leads to an ontology of freedom.

These three phases show a coherent development in Pareyson's thought, which, first implicit and then more explicit, has freedom as its conducting theme: in fact, on the existential level, freedom is what turns a human being into a person; on the hermeneutical level, it is what explains the multiplicity of interpretations; on the ontological level, it finally constitutes the abyssal ground of Being, which explains its radical contingency and the existence of Evil.

Pareyson's interest in existentialism, as his Master's thesis on Karl Jaspers from 1939 already shows (Pareyson 1940), is motivated by a search for an alternative to Hegelian philosophy. In this context, Feuerbach and Kierkegaard have contributed in different ways to disrupt Hegelianism, either by inverting (Feuerbach) or breaking (Kierkegaard) the Hegelian system (Pareyson 1985: 41–78). Both – moving from a radical criticism of the philosophy of the "abstract and conciliating thinker," who claims to be pure thought and theorizes his own insufficiency in the face of the absolute – have tried to "assimilate" Hegelianism to praxis. The claim that the alternative to Hegel is to be found in praxis is a very important point for Pareyson's subsequent thought:[1] in fact, praxis is the field where two of the fundamental questions of his philosophy – that of freedom and that of artistic creation – are rooted.

However, according to Pareyson even if Feuerbach inverts the Hegelian system, he still remains inside of it: the finite (the human being) becomes merely the ground of the infinite, and is conceived as its "opposite," namely as sensibility and matter. Kierkegaard, on the other hand, separates the finite from the infinite: this way he "crumbles" the Hegelian system into a series of unique singularities, opening an abyss between the finite and the infinite, the individual and the universal, the real and the possible. This notwithstanding, according to Pareyson, Kierkegaard maintains the Hegelian idea of the finite as negativity, and therefore he is not able to think positively its relationship to Being and to truth: truth is completely out of the individual's reach.

The contribution of these two thinkers to the philosophy of existence is then merely negative, since they confine themselves to dissolving Hegelianism. Feuerbach misses the possibility of conceiving of the human being as a "spiritual being," while Kierkegaard misses the possibility of thinking its positive relationship to Being. Both these circumstances, which in different ways define all of existentialism, are, according to Pareyson, positively balanced out by his concept of "person" (*persona*).

The person, unlike Kierkegaard's Single Individual and Feuerbach's finite being, must be considered in a concrete dialectic of unity and duality, singularity and universality, passivity and activity, definiteness and infinity (Pareyson 1985: 197–201). The person is at the same time, Pareyson writes, "self-relation and hetero-relation." Through this hendiadys he wishes to convey that the person is constitutively defined by a relation with Being in which both terms are *in* the relation (the finite cannot exist without a relationship to the infinite), but where one is so since it *posits* the relation, the other since it *is* the relation (Pareyson 1985: 16).

> In other words, on one hand Being is irrelative, namely, unobjectifiable; it cannot be reduced to or resolved into the relation, neither can it be raised to a cause or a principle external to the relation. Nevertheless, it is *present* in the relation, since – because of its unobjectifiability, only it can *constitute* the relation that with it can be established; on the other hand, the human being is *in* relation with Being, since it *is* constitutively this very relation: the human being does not have, but *is* relation to Being.
>
> (Pareyson 1985: 16)

This structure of the person as coincidence of self-relation and hetero-relation constitutes the ontological core of Pareyson's hermeneutical theory. It arises, as we saw, from the need to propose an alternative to the persistent Hegelian connotations of existentialism. Those (Feuerbach, Marx, Nietzsche, Freud, Dilthey) who tried overcoming Hegel's absolute knowledge by showing that all knowledge is conditioned, established historicist philosophies, which turned out to make philosophy itself impossible. However, although historical conditionality of thought arguably gives rise to a multiplicity of positions and perspectives, this ought not to jeopardize the possibility of philosophy as such, that is, the possibility of affirming the uniqueness of truth.

> Does the acknowledgment of an essential multiplicity of philosophy endanger the uniqueness of truth? Is a pluralistic but not relativistic conception of truth possible? What is the point of view from where a perspectivist claim, which succeeds in conciliating the uniqueness of truth with the multiplicity of its formulations, can effectively find its place?
>
> (Pareyson 1985: 10)

Pareyson answers these questions by affirming the interpretative nature of philosophy. Philosophy is always interpretation of truth and truth is only given as interpretation: "*of truth, there is only interpretation, and ... there is no interpretation, lest it be of truth*" (Pareyson 1971: 53 [2013: 47]).[2] Interpretation arises from a personal relation to truth, thus its structure reflects that of the person: it is a hetero-relation, namely relation to truth, and at the same time self-relation, because truth is not possible outside of this relation.

The hendiadys of self-relation and hetero-relation in interpretation (as in the person) means that they both have an expressive and a revelatory nature at the same time. Here "the 'object' reveals itself to the degree that the 'subject' expresses itself, and vice versa" (Pareyson 1971: 54 [2013: 48]). Historicist hermeneutics tends to reduce interpretation and philosophy to the expressive dimension only: for them, "every era has its philosophy, and ... the meaning of a philosophical thought resides in its adherence to its own time" (Pareyson 1971: 15 [2013: 13]). This kind of historicism – unlike the classical historicism, which intended history as a progressive revealing of truth – detaches any relation between philosophy and truth: it is an absolute historicism, which in effect makes genuine philosophy impossible. Conversely, in revelatory thought the relation to truth is preserved. What is more, it is also expressive, since it cannot discard its relation to its own time, that is, the personal experience of truth. Still, it does not confine itself to this unilateral bind:

> truth is accessible only by means of an irreplaceable personal relation and can be formulated only through the personal pathway to it. Thought that starts from this originary solidarity of person and truth is at the same time ontological and personal, and therefore at the same time revelatory and expressive. Such thought expresses the person in the act of revealing truth and reveals truth to the degree that it expresses the person, without one of the two aspects prevailing over the other.
>
> (Pareyson 1971: 17 [2013: 15])

Interpretation then is this particular relation which binds person and truth: in the very act of grasping truth it expresses a person, namely a determinate historical concreteness, and, at the same time, by expressing a person, it reveals the truth, as that toward which it is open. There are many interpretations of truth, because it is unobjectifiable, that is inexhaustible. In fact, in every interpretation remains a symbolic dimension that can never be made completely explicit.

This non-explicit is not due to a *quid* that always remains hidden, but to the very nature of truth. Being unobjectifiable, truth can never be completely identified with its specific objectifications: to the mysticism of the ineffable Pareyson opposes an ontology of the inexhaustible. In this way of conceiving the interpretative relation we find Pareyson's debt to Heidegger's notion of the ontological difference: like Being, truth does not happen except in its ontic determinations; nevertheless, it still remains different from these.

Pareyson's theory of interpretation can be explained through his aesthetical theory, which in fact constitutes its very paradigm (Pareyson 1954). The "theory of formativity" (*teoria della formatività*) – perhaps Pareyson's most famous theory – conceives of artistic activity as a doing, which does not consist in corresponding to a law but which invents its own way of doing. Formativity is then not only form (*forma formata*), that is, the result of a doing, it is also a dynamic process (*forma formante*), the very process of artistic creation: it is "a doing which does not confine itself to executing something already fixed or to apply an already pre-arranged technique, instead in the very act of doing it is also inventing 'the way of doing'" (Pareyson 1965: 80). The similarity of this aesthetic theory to the theory of interpretation is due to the fact that, according to Pareyson, the object of interpretation is just the "form," intended in this processual meaning, that is, as formativity: so, Pareyson writes, "interpreting is a certain form of knowledge in which, in one way, receptivity and activity are indivisible, and in another, the known is a form and the knower is a person" (Pareyson 2009: 83).

But formativity is a more general feature of human praxis: it does not confine itself to artistic creation, which is only its privileged field, but characterizes every human activity, from the ethical (where it is a question of inventing a way of doing suitable for a certain case) to the theoretical. In fact, even thought itself is a doing, a creation, an invention. Formativity is then the outcome, on the practical level, of the interpretative nature of truth, of its always being personal. In an essay from 1969, which was included in the second volume of *Wahrheit und Methode* (Gadamer 1993: 433),[3] Gadamer recognized the affinity between Pareyson's vindication of the truth-value of both art and interpretation with his own. The theory of formativity represents eventually the intersection of two requirements in Pareyson's philosophical thought: it achieves the dissolution of Hegelianism into praxis (the model of which is found in artistic creation), and makes explicit what Pareyson considers the problematic kernel of praxis: freedom.

In fact, the last period of Pareyson's thought is completely focused on the question of freedom. If in the previous phases the decisive inspiration first came from Kierkegaard and then from Heidegger, in this phase it is Schelling who takes center stage (Pareyson 1995: 385–437). The ontology of freedom is an attempt to move beyond truth, which – though presented in Plotinian terms as an inexhaustible source – could still appear as a *datum*, as a sort of undisputed substance. Even though truth does not coincide with its historical formations, what we still have not grasped is, according to Pareyson, its radical contingency.[4] Contingency is rooted in freedom, which then appears as the very ground of the real in the shape of the choice for Being rather than for not-Being. On this level, the philosophical problematic intertwines inextricably with the theological one, because the ontology of freedom is also to be conceived as a hermeneutics of religious existence. It is in fact the experience of Evil – to which religion gives voice – that drives thought towards the problem of freedom: it attests the possibility of not-Being, which, according to Pareyson, has been defeated in God *ab origine* thanks to His free choice in favor of Being. The Good thus has an ethical and ontological status, inasmuch as it arises from God's choice of being rather than of not-being.

Philosophy, according to Pareyson, has never addressed the question of Evil adequately, because it has only developed it from a logical point of view. Contrary to this, it has been more adequately developed in myths and in literature (above all, in Dostoyevsky), insofar as literature itself is myth, that is to say is a story which points to or means something further – a story that transcends itself. Myth shows the very structure of interpretation in relation to truth in the shape of the coincidence of expression and revelation and as an inexhaustible source of new and different interpretations.

2. Vattimo: nihilism, weak thought, emancipation

As a pupil of Luigi Pareyson at the University of Turin, Gianni Vattimo (1936) develops some of his master's topics, but he does so in a more Hegelian and nihilistic direction. Hegel brings Vattimo closer to Gadamer (the first translation of *Truth and Method* was by Vattimo and published in Italy in 1972) as well as to the themes of historical consciousness, of language, and of culture as the medium of political and social life. Compared to Pareyson, it is this greater attention to the historical dimension of philosophy and especially his particular interest in the philosophy of history that makes Vattimo one of the most original thinkers of the passage from modernity to postmodernity. Still, for him this accentuation of historicity takes on another significance, which cannot be understood through Pareyson's coupled expression–revelation: if it is true that Vattimo emphasizes the historical nature of interpretation in order to minimize its alleged revelatory import, this does not involve, however, a reduction of philosophy and of interpretation to a purely expressive level but aims at stressing the *critical* function of interpretation. Rather than revealing truth, interpretation contributes to the deconstruction of domination.

The influence of Nietzsche is clear on this account. Actually, more than any other philosopher in the hermeneutical tradition, Vattimo has tried to link Nietzsche's nihilism to Heidegger's criticism of metaphysics. Nietzsche, to whom Vattimo has devoted many of his writings (*Ipotesi su Nietzsche* 1967; *Il soggetto e la maschera* 1974; *Dialogo con Nietzsche* 2001 [2006]), showed that metaphysics is nothing but the production of morality. Consequently, the criticism of morality is to be conceived as a general criticism of metaphysics, which, like morality, is a fact of life and belongs to life (Vattimo 1974: 111). As a result, the criticism of metaphysics coincides with a process of liberation in the sense of emancipation from the "slave-morality" which metaphysics gave rise to. The ontological interpretation of nihilism is correlative to the ethical interpretation of it: not only the death of God, but also the doctrine of the Eternal Return, has a deep ethical meaning, consisting in the transformative process its acceptance inevitably entails. The Eternal Return, despite its seemingly deterministic content (everything returns exactly as it happened) calls for a decision, for a choice. Thus, it holds the potential of becoming the supreme instance interrupting the inexorability of its circularity. Emblematic of this is the shepherd, who, in the scene of *Zarathustra* called "The vision and the enigma," transforms his own life by biting off the head of the snake (Vattimo 1974: 195 ff).

The link between Nietzsche and Heidegger becomes explicit in the 1980s in texts such as *Le avventure della differenza* (1980) and *La fine della modernità* (1985), which makes Vattimo one of the most relevant theoreticians of philosophical postmodernism. Postmodernism is for Vattimo the epoch of a progressive taking leave from metaphysics in the shape of *Verwindung*, a term which Vattimo inherits from Heidegger and defines as a movement of "distortion" (from the German *winden*, "to twist"), as a "deviant alteration" (Vattimo 1985: 180 [1991: 173]),[5] which is not external but internal to metaphysics:

> The end of metaphysics ... is the outcome of the course of metaphysics itself: in the world of late modernity the ground loses its capacity of persuasion, foundational thought dissolves ... , and so the *verwindend* thought, the logic of provenance and of torsion, thrusts its way forward, as a unique (not reactive) possibility.
>
> (Vattimo 1988: 220)

Verwindung means also something like a convalescence (as in the German expression "*eine Krankheit verwinden*": to heal, to be cured of an illness): in this sense, metaphysics cannot "'be left behind us like a doctrine in which we no longer believe'; rather, it is something which stays in us as do the traces of an illness or a kind of pain to which we are resigned" (Vattimo 1985: 181 [1991: 173]).

Vattimo's most prolific way to express the meaning of postmodernity is captured in his best-known formula: "weak thought" (*pensiero debole*). With this expression (which refers to the title of a collective book published in 1983: Rovatti and Vattimo 1983), Vattimo means the "convalescent" condition of philosophical thought after the end of metaphysics, that is, in Nietzsche's words, after the death of God. In the postmodern epoch, Being or God no longer appear as necessary to thought, they can only appear in a weak form, as something absent, which accordingly is merely an object of remembrance (in the sense of the Heideggerian *Andenken*), historically deposited in our language and in our culture.

This weakening process is the outcome of two phenomena, which Vattimo considers as central to Western civilization and particularly to Christianity (Vattimo 2002a: 75–88 [2002b: 69–82]): secularization and nihilism. To Vattimo, Jesus marks the beginning of secularization: *kenosis* (the "emptying" of Logos through incarnation) is the paradigm of any emancipation, because it brings about the weakening of the law of the Old Testament and the humanization of God as He enters history. Likewise, nihilism involves a gradual process of consumption of the metaphysical concepts and impositions, as Nietzsche's story "History of an Error. How the True World Has Become a Fable," in *Twilight of the Idols*, clearly shows. We can say then that Vattimo conceives of a substantial link between nihilistic ontology and the *kenosis* of God (Vattimo 1994: 63 [1997: 49]): "Nihilism is so much 'like' *kenosis* for one to see this likeness as simply a coincidence, an association of ideas" (Vattimo 1994: 65 [1997: 52]).

This way, *kenosis* emerges as the central moment in Western civilization, so that hermeneutics too can be understood in the light of this event (Vattimo 2002a: 63–73 [2002b: 57–68]). Interpretation allows for thinking the relation between the multiplicity of perspectives and the uniqueness of truth in an alternative manner in relation to both the Aristotelian ontological pluralism (the *to on léghetai pollachôs*, that is, the *structural* multiplicity of Being) and the Hegelian dialectic teleology (the idea that in history it is always a matter of *Aufhebung*, overcoming and increasing). The former would consider multiplicity simply as a structural and metaphysical fact; the latter would consider it as a mere moment that can be overcome on the way towards the final auto-transparency and full re-appropriation into absolute knowledge. Contrary to this, *kenosis* allows us to conceive of multiplicity as a result of a historical process of liberation that is never definitively fulfilled and moves towards a weakening of its dogmatic structures and, at the end, towards a non-religious Christianity (Rorty and Vattimo 2005a [2005b]).

At the end of metaphysics, Being must be thought in a "weak" sense considering that it is only given in our discursive and symbolic practices, mediated by linguistic and historical formations, that is, by interpretations. It can only be "remembered" in its traces as these arouse our *pietas*, our respect, for what is no more (Vattimo 1989). According to Vattimo, the ethical outcome of this is essential to interpretation: the respect for the other is not motivated by metaphysical reasons, but by the historical conditions of our life. It entails the rehabilitation of a historical rationality like the one we find in Heidegger and Gadamer, but with a more radical nihilistic mark partly alien to these thinkers.

It is in this perspective we are to understand the particular nihilistic inflexion Vattimo gives to the sentence which summerizes Gadamer's linguistic ontology in the Third Section of *Truth and Method*: "Being that can be understood is language" (Gadamer 2004: 470). To Vattimo, this sentence means that Being is language. Language is not some accessory property of Being, which it can have or not (entailing that there can be Being which does not come to language and is accordingly not understood): it is its essential property. Vattimo shares this opinion with Rorty (See Bubner et al. 2001), who interpreted Gadamer's thought, as well as philosophical hermeneutics in general, in a very nominalistic manner; this is also against Gadamer's own intentions given that he made a very strong criticism of nominalism in the last Part of *Truth and Method*.

The identity of Being and language is the ontological presupposition for vindicating Nietzsche's sentence, which synthesizes Vattimo's entire hermeneutics: "there are no facts, only interpretations; and also this is an interpretation." In this sentence – in which Gadamer saw a "challenge to every positivism" – lies the hermeneutic-nihilistic issue of Nietzsche's radical criticism of metaphysics.

From a formal point of view, the thesis "there are no facts, only interpretations" is open to several objections reminiscent of the confutation Plato moves against Gorgias' thesis "every discourse is false." If actually everything were interpretation, even this sentence would be an interpretation; hence it cannot pretend to be true. This apparently negative outcome is, according to Vattimo, exactly what this sentence means: the end of the very concept of truth and its dissolution in interpretation (Vattimo 2009 [2011]). If, from a formal point of view, the logical circularity of this sentence appears as a defect, from the point of view of philosophical hermeneutics it is nothing but the inevitable logical form of the object of any hermeneutics, that is, existence, as Heidegger recognized in *Being and Time*.

Furthermore, to Vattimo the true meaning of Nietzsche's sentence is neither exclusively nor primarily ontological. As he qualified in several writings, above all from the 1990s, the meaning of the reduction of the real to interpretation is first of all ethical (Vattimo 1994 [1997]). Interpreting means being able to consider any fact as non-definitive: it means seeing the facts as a result of interpretations, in their turn still interpretable, that is transformable. This consideration of the real not to be a limit, an unsurpassable thing-in-itself, is of course an idealistic point, we can even say a Fichtean motive in Vattimo's philosophy (though Fichte does not appear in it as an explicit referent; yet he was so for Pareyson): the primacy of ethics, in Vattimo as in Fichte, has the sense of an unceasing dissolution of the real into the ideal, that is of the facts into interpretations. And, just like for Fichte, also for Vattimo the choice between realism and idealism or irrealism is basically ethical.

The idea of a nihilistic consumption of every strong metaphysical structure (a structure which, according to Nietzsche's reading, appears as a violent imposition), finds its legitimation in an ethical choice, as confirmed in the recent "La dissoluzione etica della realtà" (Vattimo 2012: 133–8). This means that the dissolution of the real does not so much have the sense of an ascertainment, but as that of an ought-to-be: it is something that we ought to pursue even more and to put into effect; it is like a *telos* open to the event of the death of God – an event that marks the very starting point for Vattimo towards the increasing process of secularization. This is also the meaning of the ontological difference: ontological difference does not designate some metaphysical structure but indicates a task to thought, the task of constantly keeping open the space of "irreality" against the violent imposition of reality. Interpretation is then the sign and the operator of a derealisation, which gives to hermeneutical ontology a nihilistic declination: a sign, since it shows the inevitably plural nature of truth; an operator, since this way it contributes to weakening its violent metaphysical nature. Here lies, eventually, the critical import of interpretation. The "ontological difference" appears however more as an "historical difference," in the sense that what opens its critical space is the *Andenken*, the thought of the provenance.

The substitution of facts with interpretations implies the passage from the (positive and a-temporal) ontology of metaphysics to the (negative and temporal) ontology of ethics, which can be thought only as "ontology of actuality." This expression is drawn from Foucault, who in *What is Enlightenment?* distinguishes the analytic of truth (the investigation of the conditions of knowledge) from the ontology of actuality (the genealogic investigation of what we are and how we became it: Foucault

1984). Through the ontology of actuality, according to Vattimo, philosophy aims at defining our collocation in the contemporary world (that's why it is hermeneutic). It is possible then only one way: not as a "science of Being as Being," nor as an investigation of the sense of Being in general, but as an attempt to understand the sense of our actual being. This involves – as was also Foucault's intention – a displacement of attention from the eternal structures of Being to the contingent, changeable and historical ones. Actuality, then, is not mere presence: it is presence understood – in an Hegelian and Nietzschean way – in relation to its becoming. In this philosophical project Vattimo carries out a transformation of Heidegger's ontological problem – which, from a transcendental analysis on the conditions of the sense of Being in general becomes, above all after the "Turn," an investigation of the historical sense of Being, of its receptions and changes – combining it with Nietzsche's genealogic investigation, aimed at grasping the "human, all too human" roots of the metaphysical constructions.

The ontology of actuality is an analysis of contemporary society, in which philosophical investigation is combined with sociological and political considerations. Vattimo describes contemporary postmodern society as a society of generalized communication, where the new digital technologies enable a multiplicity of voices that appears chaotic, but which exactly thanks to this multivocity defies the risk of homologation and conformism.

> What I am proposing is: (a) that the mass media play a decisive role in the birth of a postmodern society; (b) that they do not make this postmodern society more "transparent", but more complex, even chaotic; (c) that it is precisely in this relative "chaos" that our hopes of emancipation lie.
>
> (Vattimo 2000: 11 [1992: 4])

The postmodern society is therefore radically opposed to the model of a "transparent" society, fully conscious of itself, which Hegel or the theoreticians of the second generation of the Frankfurt School, such as Habermas or Apel, seem to dream of. The society of generalized communication is a thoroughly differentiated society: it makes possible the equal dignity of all its members, following the, for Vattimo strongly emancipative, principle that, "the maximum of equality is the possibility to be different." Accordingly, true emancipation does not consist in the accomplishment of an abstract identity of human beings, but in the re-evaluation and *liberation* of differences, in the possibility of affirming and tolerating diversity. Such a differentiation is also an outcome of the fact that by now Western civilization can no more consider itself the *center* of World history: thanks to the diffusion of the computer and information technologies, new subjects emerge in the world establishing new centers of history. This defines the positive contribution of the human sciences (sociology, anthropology, history and philosophy) to the history of emancipation in modernity: instead of promoting a unique model of a society – that of Western civilization – they have contributed to its dissolution and relativization promoting a pluralistic vision that, albeit chaotic, is more tolerant and open to the other. "In general, the intense development of the human sciences and the intensification of social communication do not seem to produce a growth in the self-transparency of society. Indeed, they seem to have the opposite effect" (Vattimo 2000: 35 [1992: 22]).[6]

Vattimo has devoted his most recent writings (*Ecce comu* 2007; *Hermeneutic Communism* 2011) to the political implications of weak thought. In these writings, the criticism of metaphysics is parallel to the criticism of the capitalist society. The characteristics of metaphysics are thus also intended as characteristics of this society: it is founded on the ascertainment of facts, on a "politics of description," which aims at preserving the *status quo* in the context of what is called "framed democracy." This is a democracy which does not question its own structural, political and economical conditions, but rather conceives them as natural, essential and unchangeable facts. Hence, just as metaphysics, the politics of capitalist society appears basically as realistic. Contrary to this, the "politics of interpretation" is a politics that aims at changing this situation: it is revolutionary, anarchic and anti-realistic in the sense that it aims at weakening the strong conditions of a framed capitalist democracy. Here weak thought becomes a thought of the weak:

> As the political alternative to the impositions of neoliberal capitalism and the philosophy of the interpretative nature of truth, communism and hermeneutics, more than revolutionary positions at the service of power, have become alternative responses for the losers of history, that is, the weak.
>
> (Vattimo and Zabala 2011: 2)

For the weak of history, the path to emancipation is not truth but interpretation in its nihilistic declination: this is the condition of every true democracy, if, according to Vattimo, "the farewell to truth is the commencement, and the very basis of democracy" (Vattimo 2009: 16 [2011: Introduction, xxxiv]).

Notes

1 The interest in praxis is also an early motive in Vattimo's thought, who under Pareyson's guidance wrote his "tesi di laurea" on the concept of praxis in Aristotle. See Vattimo 1961.
2 I give in brackets the references to the English translation.
3 To Gadamer Pareyson devoted an essay published in 1970 ("Originarietà dell'interpreta-zione") and contained in Pareyson 1971: 53–90 [2013: 47–78].
4 On this point, see Vattimo's considerations in the Preface to Pareyson 2013: xii ff.
5 In Vattimo 1987 and Vattimo 1988 the meaning of *Verwindung* parallels clearly the concept of "secularization," which, according to Vattimo, as we will see, is another way to describe the internal dissolution of metaphysics.
6 In the second edition of *The Transparent Society* Vattimo reconsiders more critically his early optimism regarding the emancipative potentiality of the media. See Vattimo 2000: 101–21.

Bibliography

Bubner, R. et al. 2001. *"Sein, das verstanden werden kann, ist Sprache". Hommage an Hans-Georg Gadamer*. Frankfurt a.M.: Suhrkamp.
Foucault, M. 1984. What is Enlightenment? In Rabinow P. (ed.), *The Foucault Reader*. New York: Pantheon Books.
Gadamer, H.-G. 1993. *Wahrheit und Methode. Ergänzungen*. Tubingen: Mohr.

———2004. *Truth and Method*. Eng. tr. by J. Weinsheimer and D.G. Marshall, London/New York: Continuum.

Pareyson, L. 1940. *La filosofia dell'esistenzialismo e Carlo Jaspers*. Napoli: Loffredo.

———1954. *Estetica. Teoria della formatività*. Torino: Edizioni di Filosofia (new edition 1988, Milano: Bompiani).

———1965. *Teoria dell'arte. Saggi di estetica*. Milano: Marzorati.

———1985. *Esistenza e persona*. Genova: il Melangolo (first edition: 1950).

———1971. *Verità e interpretazione*. Milano: Mursia.

———1995. *Ontologia della libertà. Il male e la sofferenza*. Torino: Einaudi.

———2009. *Existence, Interpretation, Freedom. Selected Writings*. Ed. by P. D. Bubbio, tr. by A. Mattei, Aurora, CO: The Davies Group Publishers.

———2013. *Truth and Interpretation*. Eng. tr. by R. Valgenti, Albany, NY: SUNY Press.

Rorty, R. and Vattimo, G. 2005a. *Il futuro della religione. Solidarietà, ironia, carità*. Ed. by S. Zabala, Milano: Garzanti.

———2005b. *The Future of Religion*. Ed. by S. Zabala, New York: Columbia University Press.

Rovatti, P. A. and Vattimo, G. 1983. *Il pensiero debole*. Milano: Feltrinelli.

Vattimo, G. 1961. *Il concetto di fare in Aristotele*. Torino: Giappichelli.

———1967. *Ipotesi su Nietzsche*. Torino: Giappichelli.

———1974. *Il soggetto e la maschera*. Milano: Bompiani.

———1980. *Le avventure della differenza*. Milano: Garzanti.

———1985. *La fine della modernità. Nichilismo ed ermeneutica nella cultura post-moderna*. Milano: Garzanti.

———1987. *Metafisica, violenza, secolarizzazione*. In Vattimo G. (ed.). *Filosofia '86*. Roma-Bari: Laterza.

———1988. *Ontologia dell'attualità*. In Vattimo G. (ed.). *Filosofia '87*. Roma-Bari: Laterza.

———1989. *Etica dell'interpretazione*. Torino: Rosenberg & Sellier.

———1991. *The End of Modernity: Nihilism and Hermeneutics in Post-modern Culture*. Eng. tr. by Jon R. Snyder, Baltimore, MD: Parallax.

———1992. *The Transparent Society*. Eng. tr. by D. Webb, Baltimore, MD: Johns Hopkins University Press.

———1994. *Oltre l'interpretazione*. Roma-Bari: Laterza.

———1997. *Beyond Interpretation* Eng. tr. by D. Webb, Stanford, CT: Stanford University Press.

———2000. *La società trasparente*. Milano: Garzanti (first edition: 1989).

———2001. *Dialogo con Nietzsche. Saggi 1961–2000*. Milano: Garzanti.

———2002a, *Dopo la cristianità. Per un cristianesimo non religioso*. Milano: Garzanti.

———2002b. *After Christianity*. Eng. tr. by L. D'Isanto, New York: Columbia University Press.

———2006. *Dialogue with Nietzsche*. Eng. tr. by W. McCuaig, New York: Columbia University Press.

———2007. *Ecce comu*. Roma: Fazi.

———2009. *Addio alla verità*. Roma: Meltemi.

———2011. *A Farewell to Truth*. Eng. tr. by W. McCuaig, New York: Columbia University Press.

———2012. *Della realtà. Fini della filosofia*. Milano: Garzanti.

Vattimo, G. and Zabala, S. 2011. *Hermeneutic Communism*. New York: Columbia University Press.

Further reading

Bagetto, L. (ed.) 2008. *L'apertura del presente. Sull'ontologia ermeneutica di Gianni Vattimo*. Roma: Aracne (special issue of *Tropos. Rivista di ermeneutica e critica filosofica*).

Benso, S. and Schroeder B. (eds.) 2010. *Between Nihilism and Politics. The Hermeneutics of Gianni Vattimo*. Albany, NY: SUNY Press.

Chiurazzi, G. (ed.) 2008. *Pensare l'attualità, cambiare il mondo. Confronto con Gianni Vattimo*. Milano: Bruno Mondadori.

Ghisleri, L. 2003, *Inizio e scelta. Il problema della libertà nel pensiero di Luigi Pareyson*. Torino: Trauben.

Giorgio, G. 2006. *Il pensiero di Gianni Vattimo. L'emancipazione dalla metafisica tra dialettica ed ermeneutica*. Milano: Franco Angeli.

Tomatis, F. 2003. *Pareyson. Vita, filosofia, bibliografia*. Brescia: Morcelliana.

Valgenti, R. 2005. The Primacy of Interpretation in Luigi Pareyson's Hermeneutics of Common Sense. *Philosophy Today* 49 (4): 333–41.

Zabala S. (ed.) 2007. *Weakening Philosophy. Essays in Honour of Gianni Vattimo*. McGill-Queen's University Press.

[KH1]xbib

15

COLLINGWOOD AND OAKESHOTT: HISTORY AND IDEALISM

Giuseppina D'Oro

The philosophy of time is a branch of metaphysics that is concerned with questions concerning the nature of time. Is time real? Are past, present and future real properties of events or are they relative properties that events have only in virtue of the "before/after" relation in which they stand to one another? Some idealist philosophers made an important contribution to the philosophy of time. McTaggart (1993: 23–34), and Bradley (Bradley 1893) before him, claimed that the ascription of temporal properties to events generates paradoxes that cannot be overcome and concluded that the passage of time is illusory; time is just the way in which *we* perceive reality. Time, they concluded, is not ontologically real. Unlike their idealist predecessors Collingwood and Oakeshott are philosophers of history, *not* philosophers of time. Their philosophical reflection on the past is born out of a concern with the nature of historical understanding and the method at work in the historical sciences, and belongs to the philosophy of science or social science rather than metaphysics, at least not to metaphysics as it is ordinarily understood. Their guiding concern was to defend the methodological autonomy of history from other forms of enquiry, not to establish ontological claims about the reality/unreality of time. They asked *not* "is the past real or unreal?" *but* "how must the past be understood if it is to be understood historically?" Nor were either Collingwood or Oakeshott intent on formulating a theory of knowledge that would assist historians in advancing claims about the past that could be proved to be true to the sceptic who doubts any such knowledge to be possible. Their goal was not to demonstrate *that* historical knowledge is possible against sceptically minded philosophers who doubted the possibility of knowing the past, but rather to show *how* historical understanding is possible by uncovering its postulates, heuristic principles and presuppositions. Their reflections on the nature of historical understanding belonged neither to metaphysics, as traditionally understood, that is, as that branch of philosophy concerned with what exists, nor to epistemology, understood as that branch of philosophy concerned with providing a justification for our beliefs. Collingwood's and Oakeshott's reflection on the nature of historical understanding was guided by a conceptual rather than an epistemological concern; they were primarily interested in explaining what it means to understand the past historically rather than devising a method that could vindicate the possibility of knowing the past in the manner in which Descartes sought to vindicate our beliefs in the external world against the sceptic. As Oakeshott put it: "I am concerned with what perhaps may be called the logic of historical enquiry, 'logic' being understood as a concern not with the truth of the conclusions but with the conditions in terms of which they may be recognised as conclusions" (Oakeshott 1999: 6).

This concern with the nature of historical understanding rather than the nature of time was in keeping with Collingwood's and Oakeshott's idealism, which was not causal or genetic (in the manner of Berkeley's) but conceptual because focussed primarily on establishing the logical conditions (postulates, presuppositions or heuristic principles) which govern the particular form of knowing that goes under the name of *historical* knowing. In so far as their concern was primarily conceptual and methodological rather than metaphysical, their account of the distinctive categories, postulates or heuristic principles which govern historical understanding may be seen as an attempt to defend a version of the *Erklären/Verstehen* distinction.

I. History as a mode of understanding

Collingwood's and Oakeshott's claim that history is a mode of understanding[1] is best understood in the context of their attempt to close the (epistemic) gap between reality as it is in itself and reality as it is known to us that had been left open by Kant's transcendental philosophy. Since for both Collingwood and Oakeshott the concept of reality is logically or conceptually dependent upon forms of understanding, there can be no epistemic gap between reality as it is in itself and reality as it is disclosed within a particular form of experience. In *An Essay on Metaphysics* (1998), for example, Collingwood argues that presuppositions are required in order for questions to be asked. Where there are no presuppositions there can be no questions and where there are no questions there can be no forms or lines of enquiry. Since there can be no lines of enquiry without presuppositions, there can be no presuppositionless knowing and thus no such thing as metaphysics traditionally understood, that is, as a science of pure being.[2] An important implication of the claim that there is no presuppositionless knowledge is that there is no form of experience which is *ontologically* basic.[3] Both history and natural science, for example, are forms of world disclosure and the objects which they study belong to the reality disclosed, given the presuppositions, postulates or principles which govern those forms of enquiries. Thus the subject matter of history is "actions" because the historian is concerned with what happens as an expression of thought. The subject matter of natural science is "events" because natural scientists are concerned with what happens as an instance of general empirical laws (see Collingwood 1993: 205–334). Knowing determines what is known: "events" and "actions" are the *explananda* of different forms of enquiry:

There are two questions to be asked whenever anyone inquires into the nature of any science: "what is it like?" and "what is it about?" ... What I shall try to show ... is not only that of these two questions the one I have put first must necessarily be asked before the one I have put second, but that when in due course we come to ask the second we can answer it only by a fresh and closer consideration of the first.

(Collingwood 1999: 9–10)

Oakeshott too was committed to the claim that there is an intimate relation between *how* one knows and *what* is known. Method, he claimed, determines subject matter and this applies to all forms of enquiry, including natural science.[4] An historical situation "is the conclusion of a procedure of inference" (Oakeshott 1999: 61). History is thus not a metaphysical enquiry into the past as it is in itself, but the past as disclosed through the postulates and principles of historical understanding, the "historically understood" past. Equally science too is a form of experience, a mode of understanding, *not* an enquiry into nature in itself. Nature, as he puts it, "is the correlative of scientific method; it is the product, not the datum, of scientific thought" (Oakeshott 1933: 190). Oakeshott was very critical of the myth of a raw given presupposed by empiricist epistemology with its stark separation between sensibility and understanding, a separation captured by the metaphor of the building blocks of knowledge and the inferential or judgmental cement which holds them together. The view that there is a sense of reality which is mind-independent follows from the assumption that it is possible to speak of an object or content of knowledge independently of the judgement in which it is lodged. He acknowledged that "the notion of reality as separate from experience is so ingrained in our ways of thinking that it is not easily thrown off" (Oakeshott 1933: 61) and that it lies at the basis of many of the questions which govern contemporary philosophical debates. But he objects that many of these questions, such as, for example, whether or not we can know a mind-independent reality, simply make no sense if one accepts the dictum that method determines subject matter: "The common terms of philosophic debate – What do we know of the external world? How are objects related to mind? – are not merely misleading, but, to me, nonsensical" (Oakeshott 1933: 59).

In so far as both Collingwood and Oakeshott are committed to the claim that knowledge determines what is known or that method determines subject matter they close the epistemic gap between things as they are in themselves and things as they are known by us which had been left open by Kant's transcendental philosophy. But Collingwood's and Oakeshott's idealism, unlike Kant's, is premised not on a form of epistemic humility but on the view that reality is transparent to the mind. If knowing determines what is known or if method determines subject matter, there can be no subject matter or object of knowledge which is beyond the reach of the mind. Since the gap between things as they are in themselves and things as they are known to us, which had been left open by Kant's transcendental philosophy, is closed by denying that it is meaningful to speak of a form of experience independently of a set of postulates or presuppositions – *not* by identifying what is real with what is immaterial (in the manner of Berkeley) – their idealism is strictly conceptual, not ontological.[5]

II. The autonomy of historical understanding

An important implication of the claim that history is a mode of understanding is that the adjective "historical" qualifies not the object known (the past) but the knowing itself. It is understanding that is historical, not the past as such, for the past is historical only if it is understood in a particular way. The past as such is not just an object of concern for historians. Palaeontologists, for example, study fossils to determine the structure and evolution of extinct animals and plants and yet they are hardly regarded as being historians. As Oakeshott puts it, the term

> "history" is ambiguous; it is commonly used in at least two different senses. In one it stands for the notional grand total of all that has happened ... In another meaning, "history" stands for a certain sort of enquiry into, and a certain sort of understanding of, some such passage of occurrences.
>
> (Oakeshott 1999: 1–2)

It is with this second sense of "history", as a form of understanding or mode of experience, that both Collingwood and Oakeshott are concerned. And it is because they regard history as a form of understanding that they identify historical knowledge not with a body of facts but rather with the form of inference through which those "facts" are known.

Historical enquiry, for Collingwood, is governed by different absolute presuppositions from those which govern natural science. The investigation of nature relies on the method of observation and inductive generalization and this method presupposes what Hume called the principle of the uniformity of nature. Whilst the principle of the uniformity of nature is a necessary heuristic device for scientific enquiry it is unsuited to historical enquiry. Historians cannot help themselves to such a principle because the assumption that belief systems are uniform across time can only lead to dismissing the actions of agents whose beliefs diverge from those of the interpreter as irrational. The principle of the uniformity of nature not only fails to aid historical enquiry, but it positively hinders it.[6] When historians seek to understand the doings of human agents they are concerned not merely with an extensional context of explanation (the bodily movements) but with an intensional context or what Collingwood calls (somewhat misleadingly) the "inside" of an event. The subject matter of history is "actions" because the historian seeks to understand human deeds within a context of thought, as expressions of reasons, not as mere mechanical movements that can be explained through the method of observation and inductive generalization. The guiding presupposition of history thus is not that reality is uniform but that it is amenable to rational investigation. It is in so far as historians presuppose reality to be rational that they can also hope to shed intelligibility upon the actions of historical agents by reconstructing practical arguments or rethinking the trains of thought of past agents. It is because history and natural science are governed by different presuppositions that historians and natural scientists ask different kinds of questions and consequently look for different kinds of causal or "becausal" answers:

> When a scientist asks "why did that piece of litmus paper turn pink?" he means "on what kind of occasions do pieces of litmus turn pink?" When an historian asks: "why did Brutus stab Caesar?" he means "what did Brutus think, which made him decide to stab Caesar?"
>
> (Collingwood 1993: 214)

For the natural scientist to explain an event is to understand it as an instance of a general empirical law. But explanation in history is re-enactive rather than law-like or nomological because to understand the action of a past agent is to make sense of it, to see it as meaningful even if only in the eyes of the agent who performed it. In a historical explanation the description of the consequent (the action) is not logically or conceptually independent of the antecedent (the motive) or what Collingwood calls the "cause" in the historical sense of the term. And this explains why "when a historian knows what happened, he already knows why it happened" (Collingwood 1993: 214). Historical explanations are different in kind rather than in degree from explanations in the natural sciences because they establish internal/conceptual connections between the antecedent and the consequent. Historical explanations are thus not defective nomological explanations with poor predictive power but complete explanations of their own (rational/hermeneutic) kind.[7]

This is not to say that historians never generalize, but that when they do so their generalizations are different in kind from those at work in the natural sciences. In natural science generalizations are based on empirical regularities, on the observation of what Hume called "constant conjunctions". In history, by contrast, generalizations are based on the assumption that instrumentally rational agents with similar epistemic and motivational premises will act on conclusions which are justified by what they believe and desire. The fact that historians may speak of patterns of behaviour which prevail in certain periods of time does not entail that explanations in history are nomological, for actions are understood historically only when they are explained (normatively) as the rational thing to do, not (empirically) as what routinely happens.

Oakeshott too held that the concept of historical reality (the historically understood past) is not logically or conceptually independent of historical enquiry. As he put it:

> A recorded past is no more than a bygone present composed of the footprints made by human beings actually going somewhere but not knowing (in any extended sense), and certainly not revealing to us, how they came to be afoot in these particular journeys. Certainly, these survivals constitute an historian's present and are the only past upon which he can lay his hand, although even here his knowledge is not direct or immediate; but they provide nothing he seeks. For what he seeks – an historically understood past – is of a wholly different character: it is a past which has not itself survived. Indeed it is a past which could not have survived because, not being composed of bygone utterances and artefacts, it was never itself present. It can neither be found nor dug up, nor retrieved, nor recollected, but only inferred. An historically understood past is, then, the conclusion of a critical enquiry of a certain sort; it is to be found nowhere but in a history book.
>
> (Oakeshott 1999: 36)

But how does the historian construct the narrative through which the historical past (unlike the past for the palaeontologist or the astronomer) is allowed to emerge? For Collingwood historical inference differs from inference in natural science because the explanation of action is a rational (normative), not a nomological (descriptive) matter. Oakeshott fully agrees with Collingwood that there is little or no room in history for nomological explanations of the Hempelian variety. He too sees the transposition of nomological explanation to historical enquiry as a form of methodological imperialism and rejects the positivist claim for methodological unity in the sciences (see Oakeshott 1999: 83 ff). But his main reason for denying the claim for methodological unity lies not with the view that the explanation of action has a normative element which is absent in nomological explanations, but with the claim that the historian reconstructs the past on the basis of survivals in the present and that nomological explanations have no part to play in this kind of (historical) reconstruction. Historical narrative has to establish a link between a present matter of fact (the survivals or traces of the past in the present) and an unobserved matter of fact. The connection between these is established neither inductively nor deductively. In determining which events play the role of antecedent conditions historians do not rely on the observations of constant conjunctions in order to infer a like cause from a like effect; nor is it the case that they can deduce (analytically speaking) the effect from the cause, in the manner in which a geometer deduces the theorem of Pythagoras from the concept of a triangle. Oakeshott illustrates the distinctive nature of historical inference through the analogy of a dry wall:

> When a historian assembles a passage of antecedent events to compose a subsequent he builds what in the countryside is called a "dry wall": the stones (that is, the antecedent events) which compose the wall (that is, the subsequent event) are joined and held together, not by mortar, but in terms of their shapes. And the wall here has no premeditated design; it is what its components, in touching, constitute.
>
> (Oakeshott 1999: 103)

The analogy of the dry wall contains a simultaneous criticism of both a rationalist (deductively based) and empiricist (inductively based) conception of causation. The rationalist conception of cause, according to which an effect is analytically contained in the cause (and is thus knowable a priori or by means of reflection), leads to the view that historical events are like monads which, in Leibniz's famous phrase, are "pregnant with the past and laden with the future", and that the task of the historian is to describe their necessary unfolding. But in constructing the wall the mason has no instructions of the kind which come along with the pieces of a jigsaw puzzle. There is no necessary "course" of history that is independent of the narrative and which the narrative merely describes. Oakeshott is also critical of the empiricist conception of cause (according to which a cause is an antecedent state of affairs which, in accordance with a general empirical law, inductively entails the effect). This inductively based concept of causation relies on the observation of constant conjunctions of events which are then used to make a projection from observed to unobserved matters of fact. Such a method is of no use in history because it presupposes that the *explanandum* has already been understood as an event of a particular kind and the task of the historian is merely to retrodict its occurrence. Yet it is precisely the goal of historical enquiry to determine the nature of an event which has not yet been understood: "A cause may be sought only for an already known and understood effect." The inductively based notion of causation thus "assumes to be already known what it is the purpose of historical enquiry to ascertain" (Oakeshott 1999: 88). Oakeshott's defence of the autonomy of history is a concerted effort to outline a form of inference which is neither empiricist (or inductive) nor rationalist (or deductive) and it is largely for this reason that he denies that the notion of causation has any applicability in history:

> The word "cause" in historical discourse is commonly a loose, insignificant expression employed, for the most part, either to emphasize an alleged circumstantially noteworthy condition, or when the enquiry is abridged to a concern to determine the "responsibility" of agents for the outcomes of their alleged action … But … When the word purports to stand for a significant relationship between antecedent events and a subsequent historical event all that properly (or even distantly) belongs to the notion of causality is necessarily denied or excluded.
>
> (Oakeshott 1999: 92)

When historians connect one event with another they do so by establishing that certain events are "noteworthy conditions"; and this is the only meaning that can be attached to the term "cause" in history. Either one has to allow that the term "cause" is supple and that its meaning varies in accordance with explanatory context or one must deny the term "cause" has any applicability to history. Where Collingwood sometimes speaks of different senses of the term "cause" to signal the presence of different forms of inference at work in different forms of inquiry Oakeshott denies the applicability of the term "cause" to historical enquiry. But terminological choices aside they agree that historical inference is not causal if by "causal" one means "nomological".

Whilst Collingwood's and Oakeshott's defences of the autonomy of historical understanding differ in many important respects, they converge on the view that history is a mode of understanding that is irreducible to (natural) science. They both deny the claim for methodological unity in the sciences on the grounds that explanation is relative to subject matter. Collingwood's and Oakeshott's conceptual idealism thus opens up a completely different way of viewing the relationship between the sciences, one which does not rely on the Lockean portrayal of the relation holding between primary and secondary qualities. Historical descriptions, within this (conceptual) idealist framework, do not supervene upon the primary and intrinsic qualities of objects precisely because even the description of objects as having primary properties is a description that belongs to a form of world disclosure.

III. Preserving the integrity of the past

As we have seen, both Collingwood and Oakeshott denied that historical knowledge is to be identified with a body of mere facts. Historical facts are historically understood facts. Interestingly, however, they shared none of the scepticism concerning the possibility of historical knowledge that has characterized the postmodern reaction to the rejection of the fact/value distinction implicit in the empiricist metaphor of the building blocks of knowledge and the judgmental cement that holds them. In postmodern philosophies of history the rejection of the fact/value distinction has led to the conclusion that if the past cannot be known as it is in itself because there are no ontological anchors by means of which historical narratives may be hooked to the facts, then such narratives may be judged only on the basis of how well they present the evidence in relation to the present concerns of the historian. The conclusion that since the past cannot be known as it is in itself it can only be known from the epistemic standpoint of the historian is completely absent in both Collingwood and Oakeshott. Whilst they both deny that the *explanandum* of history is a brute fact of the matter, they also reject the view that the past is a mere construction from the standpoint of the present: they argue instead that it is the task of the historian to protect the integrity of the historical past from any attempt to assimilate it to the present.

Collingwood acknowledges that the task of understanding past agents may be riddled with difficulties and that there may be periods of history which will remain unfathomable to the historian. But he rejects the implication that, since it is hard to understand some periods in history it is not possible to understand any as a *non sequitur*, and argues instead that there is no barrier, in principle, to understanding the world from an epistemic perspective that is radically different from that of the historian. He identifies two reasons as to why some philosophers may deny that it is in principle possible to understand the thoughts of past agents from their own epistemological perspective.

The first has to do with some mistaken assumptions about the nature of thought. If thought is identified with the act of thinking, then of course it would never be possible for a person to have the same thought as another, since acts of thought (unlike their propositional content) cannot be shared. But such a view, Collingwood claims, simply rests on conflating the criteria for the identity of thought with the criteria for the identity of material things. Material things (including brain processes) can be distinguished spatially but thought cannot, because it makes no sense to say of a thought that it is "here" or "there". Since the criteria for the identity of thought are purely qualitative, two people who have thoughts with the same propositional content have exactly the same thought, not two thoughts of a similar kind. When a historian rethinks or re-enacts the thoughts of historical agents the historian re-enacts a practical argument with certain premises and with a given conclusion. It is the argument which the historian re-enacts, not the act of thinking it.[8] And the argument, unlike the act of thinking it, is the very same as that of the historical agent. It is noteworthy that the account of re-enactive explanation that is found in Collingwood is in sharp contrast with more recent attempts to tackle the question of historical understanding, such as Quine's account of radical translation (see D'Oro 2013). Having rejected the notion of synonymy Quine denies that there can be any fact of the matter about the correct translation. It is not just that correct translation is hard to achieve, but rather that it is not an *achievable* goal because once the notion of identity of meaning is jettisoned, there can be no such thing as a criterion of success for correct translation. This is precisely what Collingwood denied. Whilst it may be hard to reconstruct the thoughts of historical agents, it is at least (in principle) possible to think the very same thoughts. And this is what historians achieve when they successfully re-enact the thought of other agents: if a historian succeeds in rationalizing an action, the historian has understood the agent from that agent's point of view, not from her (the historian's) own. Whilst the task of understanding past agents may be hard, and the path to understanding them littered with epistemic obstacles, there is no principled barrier to understanding the world from an epistemic perspective that is radically different from that of the historian. The historian can in principle entertain the very same thought as historical agents by rethinking or re-enacting their same thought. The view that no such identity can be achieved arises out of the mistaken identification of thought with the act of thinking.[9]

A second reason as to why philosophers may deny that it is in principle possible to view the past from the perspective of past agents has to do with a form of epistemic moralizing of which Collingwood is very critical:

> if the reason why it is hard for a man to cross the mountains is because he is frightened of the devils in them, it is folly for the historian, preaching at him across a gulf of centuries, to say "this is sheer superstition. There are no devils at all. Face facts, and realize that there are no dangers in the mountains except rocks and water and snow, wolves perhaps, and bad men perhaps, but no devils." The historian says that these are the facts because that is the way in which he has been taught to think. But the devil-fearer says that the presence of devils is a fact, because that is the way in which he has been taught to think. The historian thinks it a wrong way; but wrong ways of thinking are just as much historical facts as right ones, and, no less than they, determine the situation (always a thought situation) in which the man who shares them is placed. The hardness of the fact consists in the man's inability to think of his situation otherwise. The compulsion which the devil-haunted mountains exercise on the man who would cross them consists in the fact that he cannot help believing in the devils. Sheer superstition, no doubt: but this superstition is a fact, and the crucial fact in the situation we are considering.
>
> (Collingwood 1993: 317)

To allow the agent's point of view to emerge one must be careful *not* to assume that truth is a norm of (historical) understanding. The re-enactment of practical arguments with false epistemic premises does not require the historian to believe the premises from which the action ensues to be true but only to presuppose them for argument's sake in order to discover what practical conclusions follow from them. Truth is not a regulative idea of historical enquiry: the historian who interprets past agents does not need to believe what they believed in order to understand them. If historians had to believe what the agents believed, then they would also have to hold those beliefs to be true, for truth is a norm of belief. But they do not and should not. If historians are to preserve the integrity of the past they must refrain from importing investigative norms which are extraneous to historical enquiry in order to allow for the possibility that false beliefs may be explanatory of past agents' actions. Collingwood's account of re-enactment thus also sharply contrasts with later twentieth century attempts to account for the possibility of historical understanding which claims that interpretative charity requires presupposing that the agents whose actions the interpreter is trying to understand must hold true beliefs. Historians must assume agents to be instrumentally rational; they should not assume that *what* the agents believe is true.[10] Such a presupposition engenders the very kind of epistemic moralizing that hinders historical understanding.

Oakeshott too was very concerned with safeguarding the integrity of the past. He was very critical of what Butterfield called the "Whig" approach to history where the goal of the historical narrative "is to produce a story which is the ratification, if not the glorification of the present" (Butterfield 1965: v). When the past is constructed from the perspective of the concerns of the present it is a merely a "practical" past, not a historical past. The historical past is indeed "what the evidence obliges us to believe"; but there is no implication that what the evidence obliges us to believe is a mere ideological reflection of the historian's own views. The historian stands to the historically understood past like a dry stone waller stands to a dry wall. Without a dry stone waller there would be no dry wall. But the design of the wall is determined by the shapes of the stones as much as by the skill of the dry stone waller who cannot simply force a pattern onto the stones, as if the stones were standard bricks which could be laid in one direction or the other. The past is a historical construction in much the same sense as nature is a construction of natural science. Natural scientists cannot say any old thing they want about nature; they can only say what the *scientific* evidence obliges them to believe. Equally, historians are not at liberty to reinvent the past since they too are bound by what the *historical* evidence obliges them to believe. To say that the past is what the evidence obliges the historian to believe is just another way of saying that since explanation is relative to subject matter, the kind of evidence that is relevant to historians will be different from the kind of evidence that is relevant to natural scientists. And a commitment to the view that the kind of evidence which is relevant to historians is different from the kind of evidence that is relevant to natural scientists in no way entails the (altogether different) claim that practising historians are free to manipulate the evidence from their own standpoint in time. The statement that the historical past is "what the evidence obliges us to believe" is not meant to license the inference that the historically understood past could and should inevitably be rewritten from the constantly changing concerns of the present. Oakeshott would have condemned such a view as resting on the conflation of the historical with the practical past. His critique of the applicability of the rationalist conception of cause in history and of robust teleological grand-narratives thus did not lead him to take the view that since there is no necessary unfolding of events in history historical narratives may be rewritten in multiple and contradictory ways.[11]

Neither Collingwood's nor Oakeshott's commitment to the claim that historical knowledge is inferential rather than factual led them to conclude that the perspective of the present inevitably enjoys a form of epistemological priority over that of the past. They rejected *both* the separation of historical fact from historical inference as premised on an empiricist epistemology that would have been anathema to them *and* the priority that the perspective of the present enjoys in postmodern philosophies of history. There is, of course, much more that could be said about their philosophies of history, but a fuller discussion of the affinities and differences between their conceptions of the role and character of philosophical enquiry and of the nature of historical understanding would go beyond the scope of this chapter. What can safely be concluded from this discussion is that their interpretation of the *Verstehen/Erklären* distinction is underpinned by a conception of the relationship between the sciences which is very different from the one which prevails in contemporary philosophy of mind because their approach rejects the assumption that the methodological practices of the natural sciences enjoy a form of ontological priority over those of history. Their idealist philosophies of history also deny the implication that the rejection of the fact/value distinction presupposed by empiricist epistemology entails that it is not possible to understand past agents from their own point of view and that the historical past is a mere construction from the present which needs to be re-written from the standpoint of the moral and political concerns of the historian.

Notes

1 The most important sources for Collingwood's philosophy of history are Collingwood 1993 and 1999. The most important sources for Oakeshott's philosophy of history are Oakeshott 1933, 1975, 1991 and 1999.
2 On Collingwood's account of presuppositions see Collingwood 1998: 1–80.
3 There is much that could be said concerning the relation between, and *logical* ordering of, forms of experience and how Collingwood's and Oakeshott's thought on this question developed. Generally although their mature philosophies shed much of the earlier idealist language they tend to retain the key insights of the earlier texts. Here I have made many interpretative assumptions. I have presupposed that there is continuity in Collingwood's thought between An Essay on Philosophical Method and An Essay on Metaphysics and that Collingwood is not a historical relativist. On this see: D'Oro 2002 and 2010 and Connelly 2003. On the issue of continuity between Oakeshott's earlier and later thought see Boucher 2012. See also Boucher 1984, 1989, and 1993.
4 On Oakeshott's account of scientific knowledge see Kaldis 2012: 64–85.
5 There are some differences between Collingwood's and Oakeshott's conception of philosophy that should be noted. Collingwood denied the possibility of presuppositionless knowledge. This denial is explicit in An Essay on Metaphysics where he claims that there can be no such thing as a science of pure being, that is, a form of enquiry without any presuppositions or postulates. He saw the task of philosophy to be precisely that of uncovering the presuppositions or postulates of different forms of enquiry. By contrast in Experience and its Modes Oakeshott speaks of philosophy as experience without reservations and this seems to imply that there is at least one form of knowing that is unconditioned or presupposition free. The claim that philosophical knowledge is presupposition free or unconditioned is however either recessive or absent from Oakeshott's later work which is an analysis of the conditionality of knowledge rather than the attainment of a presupposition-free vantage point.
6 Collingwood refers disparagingly to the kind of historians who accept historical evidence only in so far as it tallies with their own beliefs and discard the rest as unreliable as "scissors-and-paste historians". On this see Collingwood 1993: 257 ff.
7 Much of W.H. Dray's work was devoted to clarifying the distinction between the explanation of action and the explanation of events by seeking to show that rational explanations are irreducible to nomological explanations. On this see Dray 1957 and 1963.
8 For Collingwood's account of the criteria for the identity of thought see Collingwood 1993: 282–302. Collingwood is often read as an empathy theorist, but his goal was not to

provide a method for the recovery of the thoughts of other agents but to make a conceptual claim about the criteria for the identity of thought. On this see D'Oro 2000, Van der Dussen 1995 and Saari 1989.

9 On Collingwood's anti-relativistic conclusions about the recovery of the thoughts of historical agents see also Kobayashi and Marion 2011.

10 On this see D'Oro 2004. See also Glock 2003: 166–99.

11 For a fuller account of Oakeshott's philosophy of history see O'Sullivan 2003.

Bibliography

Boucher, D. 1984. The Creation of the Past: British Idealism and Michael Oakeshott's Philosophy of History. *History and Theory: Studies in the Philosophy of History* 23: 193–214.

——1989. Autonomy and Overlap: The Different Worlds of Collingwood and Oakeshott. *Storia, Antropologia e Scienze del Linguaggio* 4: 69–89.

——1993. Human Conduct, History and Social Science in the Works of R.G. Collingwood and Michael Oakeshott. *New Literary History* 24: 697–717.

——2012. The Victim of Thought: The Idealist Inheritance. In P. Franco and L. Marsh (eds) *A Companion to Michael Oakeshott*. University Park, PA: Pennsylvania State University Press, pp.47–69.

Bradley, F.H. 1893. *Appearance and Reality*. London: Swan Sonnenschein (second edition, with an appendix, London: Swan Sonnenschein, 1897; ninth edition, corrected, Oxford: Clarendon Press, 1930).

Butterfield, H. 1965. *The Whig Interpretation of History*. New York: W.W. Norton.

Collingwood, R.G. 1993. *The Idea of History* (revised edition, with an introduction by J. Van der Dussen). Oxford: Oxford University Press (originally Oxford: Clarendon Press, 1946).

——1998. *An Essay on Metaphysics* (revised edition with an introduction by R. Martin). Oxford: Oxford University Press (originally Oxford: Clarendon Press, 1940).

——1999. *The Principles of History* (edited by W.H. Dray and J. Van der Dussen). Oxford: Oxford University Press.

Connelly, J. 2003. *Metaphysics, Method and Politics: The Political Philosophy of R.G. Collingwood*. Exeter: Imprint Academic.

D'Oro, G. 2000. Collingwood on Re-enactment and the Identity of Thought. *Journal of the History of Philosophy* 38 (1): 87–101.

——2002. *Collingwood and the Metaphysics of Experience*. London and New York: Routledge.

——2004. Re-enactment and Radical Interpretation. *History and Theory* 43: 198–208.

——2010. The Myth of Collingwood's Historicism. *Inquiry* 53 (6): 627–41.

——2013. Understanding Others: Cultural Anthropology with Collingwood and Quine. *Journal of the Philosophy of History* 7 (3): 326–45.

Dray, W.H. 1957. *Laws and Explanation in History*. London: Oxford University Press.

——1963. The Historical Explanation of Actions Reconsidered. In S. Hook (ed.) *Philosophy and History*. New York: New York University Press, pp.105–35.

Glock, H.J. 2003. *Quine and Davidson on Language, Thought and Reality*. Cambridge: Cambridge University Press.

Kaldis, B. 2012. Worlds of Experience: Science. In E. Podoksik (ed.) *The Cambridge Companion to Oakeshott*. Cambridge: Cambridge University Press, pp.64–85.

Kobayashi, C. and Marion, M. 2011. Gadamer and Collingwood on Temporal Distance and Understanding. *History and Theory* 50 (4): 81–103.

McTaggart, J.M.E. 1993. The Unreality of Time. In R. Le Poidevin and M. McBeath (eds) *The Philosophy of Time*. Oxford: Oxford University Press, pp.23–34. (Originally published in *Mind*, 1908, vol. 17, 456–73.)

Oakeshott, M. 1933. *Experience and its Modes*. Cambridge: Cambridge University Press.

——1975. *On Human Conduct*. Oxford: Oxford University Press.

——1991. The Experience of Being a Historian. In *Rationalism in Politics and other Essays*, London and New York: Liberty Fund.

——1999. *On History and Other Essays*. Indianapolis: Liberty Fund. (Originally Oxford: Blackwell, 1983.)

O'Sullivan, L. 2003. *Oakeshott on History*. Exeter: Imprint Academic.

Saari, H. 1989. R.G. Collingwood on the Identity of Thought. *Dialogue: Canadian Philosophical Review* 28: 77–89.

Van der Dussen, J. 1995. The Philosophical Context of Collingwood's Re-enactment Theory. *International Studies in Philosophy* 27 (2): 81–99.

I am very grateful to James Connelly, Davide Orsi and Stephen Leach for their comments on an earlier draft of this chapter and to David Boucher and the audiences at Gregynog Hall for their questions.

16
MACINTYRE AND TAYLOR: TRADITIONS, RATIONALITY, AND MODERNITY

Arto Laitinen

Introduction

This chapter discusses five closely intertwined aspects of the work of Alasdair MacIntyre and Charles Taylor that are relevant to the traditions of hermeneutics: (i) their fundamental philosophical anthropology, (ii) their views on explanation and understanding in the human sciences, (iii) their analysis of modernity and the nature of contemporary late modern Western cultures, (iv) ethics, and (v) the question of rationally comparing and assessing rival traditions or cultures.

Charles Taylor was born in 1931 in Montreal, as a son of French-speaking Catholic mother and English-speaking Anglican father, in what was then traditional Catholic French-speaking Quebec surrounded by Anglophone Canada. He grew to have a subtle understanding of cultural differences, and experienced how such understanding is first and foremost implicit awareness or even know-how rather than codified knowledge. It came to be characteristic of his philosophical outlook that he, in the spirit of Gadamer's idea of fusion of horizons, stresses the possibility of having sympathies towards incompatible horizons of meaning. In Taylor's view, we moderns are torn between sympathies towards the culture of Enlightenment and the culture of Romanticism, both of which have valid lessons to teach us. The title *Reconciling the Solitudes* expresses nicely Taylor's standard approach to antagonisms – the task for both parties is to try to understand and learn from each other. In this way, Taylor's approach stresses the dialogical aspect of hermeneutics.

Alasdair MacIntyre was born in 1929 in Glasgow, Scotland. He has recounted how some of the older people he knew came from the Gaelic oral culture stressing storytelling, particular loyalties, and ties to kinship and land, while other people he knew argued that he should not waste time in learning Gaelic. A later experience that is emblematic to MacIntyre's work concerned the absence of rationally acceptable criteria to settle disputes: "Many of those who rejected Stalinism did so by reinvoking the principles of that liberalism in the criticism of which Marxism originated. Since I continued, and continue, to accept much of the substance of that criticism, this answer was not available to me" (MacIntyre 2007: xvii). Experiences such as these are in line with MacIntyre's continuous search for ways to assess rival views without assuming any Archimedean point outside our traditions or language. The search for such moral resources guided MacIntyre to the Aristotelian tradition, ultimately Thomism, and with it to a radical rejection of many aspects of the modern ethos. For MacIntyre, the conflicting aspects in contemporary experience are a sign of our having inherited incoherent conceptual schemes, which do not deserve our continuing attachment. Thus, the title *Against the Self-Images of the Age* nicely captures much of MacIntyre's approach, which has a heavy dose of what Paul Ricoeur called a hermeneutics of suspicion (of Nietzsche, Marx, and Freud). According to MacIntyre (2007: ix), it is only possible to understand the dominant moral culture of advanced modernity adequately from a standpoint external to that culture.

Both MacIntyre and Taylor were educated in British universities and have made most of their career in North America (Taylor at McGill, Montreal, MacIntyre at Notre Dame, among other places). Taylor studied history at Montreal before studying Philosophy, Politics, and Economics at Oxford, and MacIntyre did his undergraduate studies in Latin and Greek philosophy, literature, and history. They both approach hermeneutics through a training in analytical and Wittgensteinian philosophy, while drawing both on the history of philosophy and continental philosophy (MacIntyre studied especially Gadamer in 1970s, whereas for Taylor it was Merleau-Ponty who originally drew him to philosophy, with Herder, Hegel, Heidegger, and Gadamer being central points of reference).

They both had an early interest in Marxism and Left-wing politics, contributing to the British journals *New Reasoner* and *New Left Review* in the 1950s and 1960s. MacIntyre ultimately ended up preferring Aristotle to Marx, and Taylor, in his own words, Tocqueville to Marx (Taylor 2002). MacIntyre was active in many Marxist parties in Britain, and Taylor served as Vice President of the New Democratic Party (NDP), and ran for parliament against Pierre Trudeau in 1965. He has also been influential in defending Quebec's special cultural position within Canada and giving it worldwide attention in his essay "Politics of Recognition" (1992). During the 1980s Taylor and MacIntyre were labeled "communitarians" opposing "liberals" (such as John Rawls), because they criticized the Universalist Kantian aspirations and the idea of neutrality in politics. However, they both rejected the label for partly opposing reasons: first of all, they both think there can be oppressive communities. But second, Taylor wants to preserve the main liberal values such as individual autonomy, rights, and justice as well as the goals of recognizing cultural difference, and sustaining solidarity and welfare, whereas MacIntyre thinks that communitarianism does not reject modern liberalism (or contemporary moral conservatism for that matter) radically enough.

Christianity has also played a central role in their lives. MacIntyre was baptized a Presbyterian, then lost his faith, and in the mature phase of his career turned to Thomist Catholicism. Taylor has said he didn't have biblical faith before 1950–2. Religion has become more central in his life and writings after his *Sources of the Self* in 1989. They both have written about theism, secularization, and atheism from a historical perspective, as part of their studies on the nature of the modern age.

Charles Taylor's major books are *Hegel* (1975), *Sources of the Self: The Making of the Modern Identity* (1989), and *A Secular Age* (2007); and equally important are four collections of his papers (Taylor 1985a, 1985b, 1995, 2011), as well as his *Explanation of Behaviour* (1964). MacIntyre's major books are *After Virtue* (2007), *Whose Justice? Which Rationality?* (1988), *Three Rival Versions of Moral Inquiry* (1990), and *Dependent Rational Animals* (1999). There are also important volumes of collected papers (MacIntyre 1971, 2006a, 2006b, and 1998).

(i) Philosophical anthropology

In their philosophical anthropology, Taylor and MacIntyre share the view that for humans, their own being is an interpretative issue: "The human subject is such that the question arises inescapably, which kind of being he is going to realize. He is not just de facto a certain kind of being, with certain given desires, but it is somehow 'up to' him what kind of being he is going to be" (Taylor 1976: 281). Both authors stress the meaning-laden nature of human perception as opposed to theory-free experience of uninterpreted facts, and the value-laden nature of human action as opposed to physically caused behavior. Human agents are essentially irreducible to naturalist, physicalist, or objectivist systems which would bypass the agents' own understandings and interpretations of their situation. These self-understandings also have a temporal structure and go beyond a "punctual self" (Taylor) to cover the narrative unity of life (MacIntyre). These interpretations and meaningful experiences draw on acculturation in one or other culture or tradition, and both Taylor and MacIntyre are careful to warn of the temptations to "ontologize" or "universalize" views that are in fact products of particular cultures, for example Western modernity.

In Taylor's (1985a: 45–76) words, we are "self-interpreting animals," whose identities are not pre-given. The human world is always also a moral world, a moral space in which we cannot but orient towards some good or other. We rely on "strong evaluations," which involve "discriminations of right and wrong, better or worse, higher or lower, which are not rendered valid by our own desires, inclinations, or choices, but rather stand independent of these and offer standards by which they can be judged" (1989: 4). Virtue terms are examples of such strongly evaluative distinctions. In Taylor's (1989: 3) theory "selfhood and the good, or in another way selfhood and morality, turn out to be inextricably intertwined themes." Taylor is happy to give transcendental arguments for the universal claim *that* we are strong evaluators and live in a moral space, whereas the issue of *what* strong evaluations we engage in varies historically. MacIntyre agrees in holding humans as dependent, rational animals that have a *telos* in a life in accordance with virtues.

(ii) Explanation and understanding in the human sciences

Taylor has been one of the most vocal defenders of the hermeneutical approaches in human sciences. His article "Interpretation and the sciences of man" from 1971 (reprinted in Taylor 1985b) was a central landmark in the "interpretive turn" in human sciences, going back to Dilthey's distinction between explanation and understanding. He has also defended the continuing relevance of Herder, Dilthey, and Gadamer in a number of essays. MacIntyre's writings on this topic include a number of important essays and book chapters (e.g. 7 and 8 in MacIntyre 2007). They both hold that human reality is to be understood and explained in a different manner from physical nature, because the "objects" of interpretation are already "subjects" capable of interpretations of their own.

Concerning human behavior the aim is to understand the meanings and significance of actions, and the intentions, purposes, and understandings in the light of which the agents act, whereas explanation by subsuming an event under a putative covering law is not available. (MacIntyre 2007 argues forcefully that the idea of "managerial expertise" would require knowledge which is even in principle impossible – making the idea of such expertise mere fiction). The distinction between natural and human sciences is not that natural science is free from interpretation: all observations, experiments and data must be interpreted from the viewpoint of theories, and different theories yield different understandings of the phenomenon. Theories are underdetermined by data. The crucial difference is that the participants in the human societies already have understandings concerning the societies and themselves. They may protest against certain classifications of them, on ethical grounds: in "politics of recognition," influentially theorized by Taylor 1992, cultural groups want their particular features to be taken into account. Social scientists need not, however, restrict their views to the self-understanding of the subjects – indeed, MacIntyre's central point is that the moral culture of late modernity, which is in a state of disorder unbeknownst to the participants, can *only* be properly understood from outside. Nonetheless the very "culture" consists of the interpretations by the participants, so to abstract from them is to lose the object of study from sight (Taylor 1985b).

The problem of understanding other cultures or traditions is central for Taylor and MacIntyre, and they both argue that non-ethnocentric understanding of other traditions is possible (see Taylor 1985b). MacIntyre (1988: ch.19) makes the point in terms of rendering the incommensurable traditions translatable. In the beginning of such a process, the traditions do not understand each other, but members of one tradition can learn the language of another tradition as a "second first language" and finally master the practices of the other tradition. Someone in this position can translate his or her understandings into the vocabulary of their "first first language." Some parts of this translation can be done with "same-saying," whereas some parts need conceptual innovation. Through these conceptual innovations, the limits of translatability can be broadened and also by the same token the former limits of the "first first language" can be stretched. The stretching of these limits and the gaining of understanding of other practices then make it possible to criticize both traditions and identify inadequacies in them or point out possible solutions to the identified ones.

(iii) The nature of modernity

Taylor and MacIntyre differ notably in their takes on modernity. While neither is a "booster" of modernity, MacIntyre (2007) is a "knocker" of modernity, whereas Taylor (1992) locates himself between these two extremes.

Alasdair MacIntyre's *After Virtue* starts with a "disquieting suggestion." He invites us to think of a world, where after an environmental catastrophe, sciences are being blamed and banned, books burned, and laboratories and equipment smashed into pieces. Science is gradually forgotten. After some time, a revival movement collects the remaining fragments of theories, and starts a new practice that would be called physics, chemistry, and biology. It is a mere disordered mélange of theories: adults debate about the good and bad sides of fragments of phlogiston theory and relativity theory, and children learn by heart the remaining parts of the table of elements. That practice would not be genuine natural science at all, but neither analytical philosophers nor phenomenologists would be able to reveal that. A debate would ensue where some would doubt that science is merely a matter of voicing one's preferences.

MacIntyre's disquieting suggestion is that the contemporary moral culture is precisely in that shape. What remain are fragments of substantive ethical precepts which were at home in an earlier context of social practices which has now been lost. As a result, disagreements over central moral issues (say, on abortion or justification of war) have become peculiarly unresolvable. All parties appeal to impartial justifications, which should be able to convince everyone independently of their background, but no such universal justifications can be found – as a result the use of ethical language has become mere expression of subjective opinion (which it would not be in the context of shared practices that would give point and justification to the ethical precepts).

In MacIntyre's view, the failure of the "Englightenment project" (of Kant, Hume, and other modern moral theorists) in finding such universal justifications has created this situation. The project had to fail, because it denies that ethics is based on a shared understanding of the *telos* of human nature. Without this understanding of what ethical rules are for, modern subjects remain in a disorderly state of on the one hand aiming at a neutral, universalist justification which is not forthcoming, and on the other hand using moral language in fact to express their subjective opinions. The "Enlightenment project" has also created useful moral fictions, such as "rights" or "utility" which are so abstract that people can appeal to them in defending any concrete proposal. Another fiction is "managerial expertise" in finding effective solutions and means to any ends. Such managerial expertise would only be possible if there were lawlike generalizations concerning human reality, which is not the case. MacIntyre links both the emotivist use of moral language, and the social respect enjoyed by managers to manipulative relationships between individuals. In MacIntyre's view, the philosopher who best understood that the Enlightenment project had failed decisively and that contemporary moral assertions had characteristically become a set of masks for unavowed purposes was Nietzsche, who had the courage to reject such false appeal to unfounded moral principles. But MacIntyre stresses that Nietzsche's criticism does not apply to Aristotelian philosophy and practice, and thus these two are the only compelling options of contemporary ethics. MacIntyre argues in favor of Aristotelian (and Thomist) virtue ethics and argues moreover that only a history of ethical theory and practice written from an Aristotelian rather than a Nietzschean standpoint enables us to comprehend the nature of the moral condition of modernity (MacIntyre 2007, 1998 [1984]).

Taylor has much more faith in modern ideals and institutions. He thinks there have been moral motivations underlying modernization and secularization. He has written three big books on the self-understandings of the modern age and modern individuals. *Hegel* (1975) focuses on one towering figure, and argues that Hegel's aspirations to overcome modern dualisms are still ours, but Hegelian philosophical speculation is not the way to do it. *Sources of the Self* (1989) runs the intellectual history from peak to peak, stressing the continuous presence of modern tensions and cross-pressures between Enlightenment and Romanticism. *A Secular Age* (2007) aims to cover the valleys as well, trying to explain how certain secular under-standings have come to existence and managed to spread themselves from the elites into the prevailing taken-for-granted background imaginaries.

In *Sources of the Self* Taylor characterizes "modern identity" by which he means contemporary understandings of what it is to be a human agent, or a person, or a self. Taylor traces first of all "the rise of certain understandings of inwardness," from Augustine to Cartesian ego and self-control on the one hand and Montaigne's "self-exploration" on the other hand. Second, Taylor stresses the Reformation which put great emphasis on "ordinary life," the life of work and the family, or production and reproduction, instead of saints or heroes, priests or kings, or even citizens in their public role. Third, building on the first two changes, Taylor traces what he calls "the expressivist revolution" which emphasized powers of the creative imagination and developed an understanding of nature as a source of meaning. "The goal of self-exploration now extends to the ideal of authenticity, against the back-ground of the Herderian idea that each individual (and also each people) has his/her own way of being human, and must be true to this original mode" (1994c: 195–6).

In *A Secular Age* Taylor distinguishes three senses of secularity. The first can be called "political," focusing on the separation of state and church, while the second one is "sociological," focusing on the statistics of religious belief and practice. The third one can perhaps be called "existential" and it seems to be harder to define. It concerns what Taylor calls broad background conditions of belief and spiritual searching: something like the general assumptions implicit in one's lived experience, social and cosmic ima-ginary, which make a difference to what form (if any) one's religious aspirations take. Taylor focuses on this third sense and asks what has changed in that respect between 1500 when lack of belief in God was unimaginable, and 2000, when belief is one option among many. Taylor's discussion proceeds in terms of the ethical or existential issue of "fullness" and meaning in one's life, and he argues that various ideals have motivated the historical developments, such as the modern expressivist understanding of nature as a source, or sources immanent to human life and capacities, such as reason, imagina-tion, natural benevolence, or the authentic "inner voice." Taylor traces the seculariza-tion process through various stages all the way to "the age of Authenticity," when pluralization of options for belief and unbelief has reached the masses in the modern West. As a result, one thing that is shared by everyone in the contemporary West is the self-understanding that one's spiritual view, whether theism or "exclusive humanism" in any version, is just one option among many.

(iv) Ethics

In their ethical theories, both Taylor and MacIntyre reject subjectivism, decisionism, and emotivism on the one hand (as they stress the shared social practices and understandings) and universal, neutral objectivism on the other (as they stress that people are located in different traditions). There is no "Archimedean standpoint" outside any language or tradition.

The three notions of a practice, narrative unity of life and tradition, are crucial for MacIntyre's ethics, providing the context within which evaluative and moral terms make sense. By a "practice" MacIntyre means:

> any coherent and complex form of socially established cooperative human activity through which goods internal to that form of activity are realised in the course of trying to achieve those standards of excellence which are appropriate to, and partially definitive of, that form of activity, with the result that human powers to achieve excellence, and human conceptions of the ends and goods involved, are systematically extended.
>
> (2007: 187)

Practices in this sense include for example the arts, sciences, sports, family life, and politics in the Aristotelian (but not in the modern) sense. Such practices are a shared context for individuals who pursue self-realization through participation in the practices. Both practices and individual life-stories are embedded in living traditions: "the unifying form of an individual human life, without which such lives could not have a *telos*, derives from its possessing some kind of narrative structure. Individual human lives however are only able to have the structures that they do because they are embedded within social traditions" (1998 [1984]: 71–2).

While in *After Virtue* MacIntyre eschews Aristotelian "metaphysical biology," he later defends both a metaphysical grounding for human nature (appealing to Aquinas), and a (contemporary) biological grounding by comparing humans to dolphins and other species (see MacIntyre 1999). He also stresses the Thomist virtues of "acknowledged dependence" in addition to the traditional Aristotelian list of virtues. MacIntyre states that he became a Thomist in part because Aquinas was in these respects a better Aristotelian than Aristotle.

Charles Taylor's ethical theory starts from a more personal framework of strong evaluation, and an answer to the inescapable question of what kind of human being to be. Taylor discusses Sartre's example of a young man who is torn between staying with his ailing mother and joining the Resistance. According to Taylor, this example cannot be made sense of within Sartre's doctrine claiming that ethical commitments are based on a choice. If the moral claims that the man faces were based on a choice, he could "do away with the dilemma at any moment by simply declaring one of the rival claims as dead and inoperative" (1985a: 29–30). In Taylor's view, people have "conceptions of good" that are not a matter of choice but rather of conviction. Importantly, these conceptions are typically not fully linguistically articulated but can be partly implicit in moral reactions and practices. The goods are plural and potentially in conflict and to some extent ordered by their relative worth. The framework of "goods" is based on some ontological vision concerning nature, human subjects, or God, the articulation of which makes sense of the goods or which forms a background to the goods. Taylor speaks of "constitutive goods" which stand for "features of the universe, or God, or human beings, (i) on which the life goods depend, (ii) which command our moral awe or allegiance, and (iii) the contemplation of or contact with which empowers us to be good" (1991b: 243).

An exchange in 1994 between Taylor and MacIntyre summarizes their differences nicely. MacIntyre (1994: 188–9) claims that Taylor's moral theorizing provides no criteria for telling which judgments about goods are mistaken, and no criteria for the choice between rival and incommensurable goods. He is worried about a kind of erosion of moral frameworks from within, because of "the multiplication of goods and alternative possibilities of realising different sets of goods in different types of life" which "gradually frees the self from commitment to any one such set or type of life and leaves it bereft of criteria, confronting a choice of type of life from an initial standpoint in which the self seems to be very much what Sartre took it to be." There are simply too many ways of making sense of our lives, too many goods.

Taylor (1994c: 206) by contrast states that "I find baffling MacIntyre's call for 'criteria.' Because it seems to me that, in one common sense of this term, these have no place here." Taylor thinks that in ethical issues one must ultimately rely on one's implicit understandings, on one's know-how in assessing different articulations and formulations, so that full codifiability can never be reached (Taylor 1995: 68–78). By contrast, MacIntyre thinks there should be an impartial criterion, especially in disagreements; otherwise there is a danger that one is merely voicing one's opinions. For MacIntyre these criteria can be explicitly articulated, as they derive from shared practices and communicable understandings. For Taylor, our tacit understandings (even concerning shared practices) can never be fully articulated, while they can guide our actions in a very precise way. For example, in portrait painting "we may be very inarticulate … but still be excellent and discriminating at the art" (Taylor 1994a: 29).

Second, Taylor argues that rival conceptions of the good can be criticized and compared pairwise, and writes that "the contemporary philosopher from whom I have learned most in this account is none other than Alasdair MacIntyre"(Taylor 1994c: 205). Indeed, Taylor has integrated into his theory of evaluative frameworks MacIntyre's account of comparative assessment of alternative traditions, to which we can turn next.

(v) Comparison across cultures and traditions

One of the main points that MacIntyre and Taylor have contributed to the herme-neutical tradition concerns their detailed response to the threat of relativism while remaining within the confines of plurality of traditions or frameworks – their account of comparative justification.

The basic unit in MacIntyre's theory of rational justification is a tradition of (moral or scientific) inquiry (MacIntyre 1988: 354–61). The core elements of a tradition of inquiry consists first of all of a set of empirical and ontological assumptions and beliefs. In relation to science these beliefs structure the questions we ask and the appropriateness of different kinds of answers. Another element is a set of virtues. The virtues of a scientist are the abilities to live up to the standards of inquiry which one must fulfil in order to count as a member of the scientific community.

Furthermore, there is a set of methods and theories of inquiry. These include the universally shared standards of logic, but outside that, standards of scientific and practical rationality and methods of enquiry are incommensurable and incompatible within rival traditions (ibid.: 358–9).

These core elements are embodied in different ways. They are implicit in the practices of a tradition. By participating in these, one gains tacit knowledge some of which is not linguistically articulated at all. Thus, they are embodied in the acquired understandings of persons, especially those who are "authoritative voices." But further, there are authoritative texts, and the central beliefs and standards are linguistically embodied. The limits of a language are the limits of this linguistic articulation. These limits can be overcome by conceptual innovations (for example in the context of translating insights from other traditions).

There are a further three kinds of elements, which are relevant for the rational justification of the tradition: (a) an agenda of identified, unsolved inadequacies and unanswered questions. The normal practice of inquiry consists in successfully overcoming these and in identifying unsuccessful attempts as "anomalies" as Thomas Kuhn calls them. The ability to meet challenges in this constant process forms what can be called the "dynamic" aspect of justification. (b) There is a defined area of agreement and disagreement with other traditions. This is the raw material for the "dialogical" aspect of justification, which is based on comparison with other traditions. (c) The tradition of inquiry normally construes a narrative account of the history of inquiry within one's own tradition and of its encounters with other traditions. This is a narrative, which tells how we have arrived at these conceptions and standards. This has happened as a result of conflicts and challenges, which have been successfully overcome. Here we have the raw material for comparison with the past stages of a tradition, which is the "historical" part of the justification of the tradition.

By comparison with Kuhn's purely cumulative normal science, MacIntyre's picture includes "minor revolutions" as well: authorities are replaced, texts reinterpreted, new beliefs introduced, standards and methods developed. All this takes place within an overall continuity of the tradition in question. This capacity to make "minor revolutions" forms the dynamic aspect of the justification. MacIntyre's counterpart for Kuhn's "science in crisis" is an "epistemological crisis" of a tradition. Such a crisis develops gradually after more and more inadequacies have been identified. When the tradition has lost its capacity to overcome the difficulties, it is in crisis (MacIntyre 1977; 1988: 362).

Overcoming a crisis requires a conceptual or theoretical innovation which fulfils two conditions: first, it provides a solution to the problems that have arisen; second, it is capable of explaining why the problems were not solved before and what it was that made the tradition incoherent or sterile. This innovation means that the tradition-before-the-crisis is not commensurable with the tradition-after-the-crisis. If the proposed solution fulfils a third condition as well – if it succeeds in maintaining fundamental continuity with the shared set of beliefs and assumptions, which had constituted the tradition up to this point – the tradition has passed through the crisis successfully (MacIntyre 1988: 362–5).

But there is also another option, which is crucial for MacIntyre's arguments against relativism. If a solution is not found within the original tradition, there is a possibility that a rival tradition offers both a solution to the problems and an explanation of why the tradition itself was unable to offer these solutions. If this is the case, the tradition has lost its claim to rational justification, and the only sensible thing to do – when sensibility is measured with its own standards – is to give up its own standards (MacIntyre 1988: 365; cf. Taylor 1993a: 216). From this we get an account of the rational justification of the beliefs, standards, and methods of a tradition. This justification is at once dialogical and historical; it is based on a dialogue with rival positions and the history of overcoming inadequacies (MacIntyre 1988: 360). Further, the dynamic dimension of justification is linked with the capacity of the tradition to overcome identified inadequacies, by finding solutions.

Together these aspects of justification mean that although there are many living traditions, and each has their standards, there is no relativism, because it can be distinguished what kind of changes in the standards count as progress and which as regress. This is the lesson from MacIntyre that Taylor has integrated to his own view of personal ethical frameworks. Even though there is no neutral, universal standpoint from which to assess all conceptions of good at one go, "one can sometimes arbitrate between positions by portraying *transitions* as gains and losses, even where what we normally understand as decision through criteria – *qua* externally defined standards – is impossible" (Taylor 1993a: 215). Thus, Taylor and MacIntyre agree that comparative assessment of rival views is in principle possible. It is just that Taylor is more willing to think of the ethical framework as a personal one, whereas MacIntyre thinks that without shared understandings, embodied in social practices, we are at a loss. They both stress that leading an ethical life is not a matter of mechanically applying principles, but a matter of interpretation in multiple senses: articulating one's implicit views in a faithful manner, aiming at better understanding of the goods, and interpreting concrete situations by attending to their significant features – relying on the hermeneutical virtue of *phronesis*, practical wisdom.

Bibliography

MacIntyre, A. (1971) *Against the Self-Images of the Age. Essays on Ideology and Philosophy*, London: Duckworth.

——(1977) "Epistemological Crises, Dramatic Narrative, and the Philosophy of Science," *The Monist*, 60, 453–72.

——(1988) *Whose Justice? Which Rationality?*, Notre Dame: University of Notre Dame Press.

——(1990) *Three Rival Versions of Moral Enquiry: Encyclopaedia, Genealogy, and Tradition*, Notre Dame: University of Notre Dame Press.

——(1994) "Critical Remarks on *The Sources of the Self* by Charles Taylor," *Philosophy and Phenomenological Research* 54, 187–90.

——(1998 [1984]) "The Claims of *After Virtue*," *Analyse & Kritik: Zeitschrift für Sozialwissenschaften* 6:1, 3–7, 1984, reprinted in Kelvin Knight, ed., *The MacIntyre Reader*, University of Notre Dame Press, 69–72.

——(1998) *The MacIntyre Reader*, edited by Kelvin Knight, Notre Dame: University of Notre Dame Press.

——(1999) *Dependent Rational Animals: Why Human Beings Need the Virtues*, Chicago: Open Court.

——(2006a) *Selected Essays, vol. 1: The Tasks of Philosophy*, Cambridge: Cambridge University Press.

——(2006b) *Selected Essays, vol. 2: Ethics and Politics*, Cambridge: Cambridge University Press.

——(2007): *After Virtue*, third edition, Notre Dame: University of Notre Dame Press.

Taylor, C. (1964) *Explanation of Behaviour*, London: Routledge.

——(1975) *Hegel*, Cambridge: Cambridge University Press.

——(1976) "Responsibility for Self," in Amélie Rorty, ed., *The Identities of Persons*, Berkeley: University of California Press, 281–99.

——(1985a) *Human Agency and Language: Philosophical Papers vol. 1*, Cambridge: Cambridge University Press.

——(1985b) *Philosophy and Human Sciences: Philosophical Papers vol. 2*, Cambridge: Cambridge University Press.

——(1989) *Sources of the Self: The Making of the Modern Identity*, Cambridge: Cambridge University Press.

——(1991a) *Ethics of Authenticity*, Cambridge, MA: Harvard University Press.

——(1991b) "Comments and Replies," *Inquiry* 34, 237–54.

——(1992) *Multiculturalism and "The Politics of Recognition"*, Amy Gutmann, ed., Princeton: Princeton University Press.

——(1993a) "Explanation and Practical Reason," in Martha Nussbaum and Amartya Sen, eds., *The Quality of Life*, Oxford: Clarendon Press, 208–31.

——(1993b) *Reconciling the Solitudes: Essays on Canadian Federalism and Nationalism*. Montreal: McGill-Queen's University Press.

——(1994a) "Justice After Virtue," in J. Horton and M. Mendus, eds., *After MacIntyre: Critical Perspectives on The Work of Alasdair MacIntyre*, Cambridge: Cambridge University Press, 16–43.

——(1994b) "Précis of *The Sources of the Self*," *Philosophy and Phenomenological Research* 54, 185–86.

——(1994c) "Reply to Commentators," *Philosophy and Phenomenological Research* 54, 203–13.

——(1995) *Philosophical Arguments*, Cambridge, MA: Harvard University Press.

——(2002) "On Identity, Alienation and Consequences of September 11th. An interview by Hartmut Rosa and Arto Laitinen," in A. Laitinen and N. Smith, eds., *Perspectives on the Philosophy of Charles Taylor*, Helsinki: Societas Philosophica Fennica.

——(2007) *A Secular Age*, Cambridge, MA: Harvard University Press.

——(2011) *Dilemmas and Connections: Selected Essays*, Cambridge, MA: Harvard University Press.

Further reading

Ruth Abbey's *Charles Taylor* (Guildford and King's Lynn: Acumen, 2000) is a very good overall introduction to Taylor's thinking. Nicholas H. Smith's *Charles Taylor: Meaning, Morals, Modernity* (Cambridge: Polity, 2002) together with his *Strong Hermeneutics: Contingency and Moral Identity* (London: Routledge, 1997), provide a convincing picture of Taylor as a hermeneutical thinker in ethics and social criticism. Hartmut Rosa's *Identität und kulturelle Praxis: politische Philosophie nach Charles Taylor* (Campus Verlag, 1998) is recommendable on Taylor's views on modernity; my *Strong Evaluation without Moral Sources* (Berlin, New York: De Gruyter, 2008) analyzes Taylor's views in philosophical anthropology and ethics.

Thomas D. D'Andrea's *Tradition, Rationality, and Virtue: the Thought of Alasdair MacIntyre* (Aldershot: Ashgate, 2006) is a comprehensive discussion of MacIntyre's work. *After MacIntyre: Critical Perspectives on The Work of Alasdair MacIntyre* (Cambridge: Cambridge University Press, 1994, edited by J. Horton and S. Mendus) collects critical essays with MacIntyre's response. *The MacIntyre Reader* edited by Kelvin Knight (Notre Dame: University of Notre Dame Press, 1998) collects texts that emphasize MacIntyre's Aristotelianism, including an insightful introduction and two interviews. See also a collection of MacIntyre's papers edited by Paul Blackledge and Neil Davidson, *Alasdair MacIntyre's Engagement with Marxism. Selected Writings 1953–1974* (Leiden: Brill, 2008) as well as an edited collection *Virtue and Politics: Alasdair MacIntyre's Revolutionary Aristotelianism*, edited by Paul Blackledge and Kelvin Knight (Notre Dame: Notre Dame University Press, 2011).

17

DAVIDSON AND RORTY: TRIANGULATION AND ANTI-FOUNDATIONALISM

Bjørn Torgrim Ramberg

1. Davidson and Rorty: the hermeneutical challenge

In the history of twentieth century philosophy Donald Davidson's work of the 1960s and 1970s stands out as a major, indeed paradigmatic, contribution to what is perhaps vaguely but still quite uncontroversially designated *analytic philosophy*.[1]

Yet our task here, now, is to consider Davidson as a hermeneutic thinker.[2] Richard Rorty, who is also one of the most perceptive and innovative readers of Davidson, presents a similarly troublesome case with respect to philosophical genre. Perhaps most famous for the deconstruction of the idea of philosophy as epistemology performed in *Philosophy and the Mirror of Nature* (Rorty 1979), and thus, unlike Davidson, often thought of in opposition to analytic philosophy, Rorty is at first blush a more plausible candidate for inclusion in the present volume than is Davidson. Rorty, after all, provocatively proposed *hermeneutics* as the name for the kind of activity philosophers should be engaging in once the epistemological paradigm was left behind (Rorty 1979: 315ff). However, Rorty's conception of hermeneutics appears to be idiosyncratic. A pragmatic naturalist whose most persistent aim has been to show what philosophy is like when it is no longer metaphysics but rather a genre of cultural politics, Rorty seems to be fundamentally at odds with basic features and aspirations of hermeneutic philosophy. After all, philosophical hermeneutics is explicitly ontological, and indisputably aspires, in its way, to universality.[3] Rorty, too, then, confronts us with a basic challenge; in just what sense is his thought a contribution to hermeneutic philosophy?

My response will be to suggest that there can be *genuine dialogue* between canonical expressions of hermeneutic philosophy, notably the work of Hans-Georg Gadamer, and the philosophical projects of Rorty and Davidson. But what is genuine dialogue? What is the significance of its possibility? These are indeed questions that point toward the main theme of this chapter. The matter at hand – what Gadamer calls "die Sache" – is in our case precisely the nature of dialogical understanding.[4] It is with respect to this basic hermeneutic theme that Davidson, Rorty and Gadamer can be – so I will claim – brought into enlightening and productive conversation, and in relation to which we may see them as engaged in working up a common dis-cursive ground. That, at least, will be our exegetical working hypothesis. Davidson and Rorty are both multifaceted thinkers, with oeuvres spanning five decades. With respect to such bodies of text, it is tempting to divide them into temporal chunks, taking chronologically limited segments to provide the natural units of interpreta-tion – such limited units tend to be more easily assimilated to prevailing categories and genres. Thus, in Davidson's case, early Davidson may be assimilated with ana-lytic philosophy, late Davidson with – perhaps – hermeneutics. As for Rorty, it is sometimes claimed that he started out as a bona-fide analytic philosopher, and then broke rank – turning to Heidegger and others to debunk the tradition of which he himself is a part. However, while there are examples of warranted application, there is a real danger that this strategy of temporal division filters out exactly what is most original in a thinker. While there certainly are transitions and dialectical shifts to be tracked, it is in the dynamic unity of their thinking that Davidson's and Rorty's most fundamental contributions to philosophy lie. This is just what a hermeneutic reading must strive to make evident. And the claim of this chapter is that for both Rorty and Davidson, the dynamic unity of their work in its various phases and aspects is captured by a question characteristic of philosophical hermeneutics: how can we conceive of communicative understanding as a task for temporal, limited, situated agents – as, that is to say, essentially an achievement of human finitude?

From here we go on as follows. Section 2 highlights relevant aspects of Davidson's early contributions to analytic philosophy, and then describes characteristic features of his account of linguistic competence specifically. Section 3 notes that the link between meaning and truth, between understanding and agreement, has striking affinities with Hans-Georg Gadamer's hermeneutic account of understanding as a fusion of horizons.[5] We do run a risk here of overhasty and misleading assimilation, but, I argue, Davidson's basic concern with understanding as a shared achievement of temporal, finite creatures actually aligns him in a decisive and illuminating way with Gadamer's hermeneutic ontology of understanding. The issue turns on the sort of agreement one takes Davidson to be envisaging, and on this matter we must look to his idea that the nature of communicative intelligibility may be characterized in terms of *triangulation*.

The connection between Davidson's project and philosophical hermeneutics is salient in Rorty's response, and responsiveness, to the hermeneutic developments in Davidson's thinking. Moreover, by taking a Davidsonian view of Rorty – that is, reading Rorty as committed to the Davidsonian idea of triangulation – we also bring into view Rorty's own genuine proximity to hermeneutic thought. I suggest in Sec-tion 4 that Rorty's *anti-foundationalist* view of philosophy is not simply a diagnosis of the failures of epistemological efforts to ground knowledge. Breaking fundamentally with the representationalist presuppositions of epistemology since Descartes and Locke, Rorty's notion of solidarity is an effort to advance the historicist approach to knowledge, understanding and philosophy that hermeneutics represents. Thus, in my reading both Rorty and Davidson offer interpretations of the hermeneutic theme of the historicity of understanding. Crucially, Rorty and Davidson allow us to see historicity as an essentially and literally *productive* feature of understanding, rather than as an encapsulating condition; they advance a conception of communicative understanding that takes us, to borrow from Richard Bernstein, beyond objectivism and relativism.[6] In Section 5 I briefly sum up the case I have presented, underscoring its character as a hermeneutical exercise.

2. Agency, interpretation, charity

In the standard picture of twentieth century Anglophone philosophy Davidson's first major contribution is his succinct presentation (Davidson 1963) of the idea that while human actions must be considered to be fully embedded in the natural causal web of worldly events, they are nevertheless distinguished by the fact that they are done for reasons, and by the fact, moreover, that the justifying considerations – the *primary reason* – for an action are also, in the standard case, its cause. Reasons, in short, may be naturalistic causes, and indeed they had better be, Davidson argues, if the standard pattern for our accounts of action is to have real explanatory power.[7] This thesis in the philosophy of action appears to respond to a worry generated by something like a physicalist – or at least a naturalistic – metaphysics; a concern that the world view warranted by science makes problematic the idea of agency as an exercise of freedom and a manifestation of reason. Already here, however, Davidson has set out in a direction that will shake this framework and break with key assumptions built into it, assumptions that drive what is often referred to as "placement problems."[8] A resolution to a metaphysical placement problem, like the question whether there really can be such things as actions done for reasons in a universe naturalistically conceived, will be solved when we have a convincing account of what can respectably count as truth-makers for the requisite class of statements. And indeed we might take Davidson on action as having made a case for the view that action statements are truth-apt because they are about – refer to – naturalistically respectable events. More, however, is going on, and to see this, it will be useful to glance briefly at Davidson's relation to his most direct and explicit influence, W.V. Quine.

Quine's behaviorist, third-person account of linguistic behavior (Quine 1960), though devastating in its effect on the standard mode of metaphysics as conceptual analysis, gives us a view of linguistic understanding that remains metaphysically conditioned, at least in that it is intended to be compatible with an austere physicalist ontology. This ontology Quine took to be mandated by naturalism; ideal physics provides a basic ontological constraint on philosophical explanation of any kind. Now, in his work on linguistic meaning and on the nature of the mental in the 1960s and 1970s Davidson certainly takes the Quinean third-person approach to meaning as a mandatory starting point. Davidson shares Quine's thought that to explain linguistic communication is to account for the way in which what is available for public observation can be regimented so as to support systematic characterization of the linguistic behavior of speakers. However, Davidson develops quite different views of how that target behavior is best described, and also of how what is public can be said to support a systematic description of that behavior. Invoking the notions of truth and of charity (of which more below), Davidson breaks with Quine's understanding of the naturalistic constraint on philosophical theory.

Concomitantly the ontological stance that Quine occupies – along with many of those who opposed him from within a physicalistic perspective – undergoes with Davidson a significant transformation. In fact, Davidson's essential move is evident already in the early work on action; here he makes the point that an event that is a naturalistic cause may *also* be reason, in so far as it enters into a requisite kind of *pattern* of events. Whether we take an event as a purely naturalistic cause or primarily as a justifying reason is a matter of the kind of pattern we are considering – the irreducible difference between the mental and the physical, between agency and mere causation, as Davidson argues most famously in "Mental Events" (1970), is the difference between a pattern of description that is sensitive to norms of rationality and one that is geared toward non-rational regularity. Thus, Davidson claims, "events are mental only as described" (Davidson 2001a: 215). Events conceived atomistically and in isolation have no determinate character, either as physical or as mental.[9]

As I have described it so far, this ontological *monism* may look like a cheap answer to the metaphysician's worry; for, we will want to know, what is it about events that makes it the case that these different kinds of predicate actually apply to them (when they do)? What assurance of the propriety of these concepts can be found in talk of different kinds of patterns that events may be a part of? Davidson's account of actions as well as his monistic, non-reductive construal of the relationship between the mental and the physical is frequently met with versions of this response.[10] However, neither "Actions, Reasons and Causes," nor "Mental Events" and related papers (Davidson 2001a) are actually in the business of giving direct answers to the metaphysical question that concerns the kind of naturalist who worries about how there can be reason and mind in the world as revealed by physics. Concluding "Mental Events," Davidson remarks:

> Mental events as a class cannot be explained by physical science; particular mental events can when we know particular identities. But the explanations of mental events in which we are typically interested relate them to other mental events and conditions.
>
> (Davidson 2001a: 225)

Davidson's concern was never with how predicates of agency and of mental states can be seen properly to represent worldly items. His concern is with the particular nature of the human interests that those vocabularies express. That vocabularies are also ways of addressing and of dealing with the world is such a fundamental part of Davidson's outlook that worries of the metaphysician's kind cannot seriously arise. To see this, however, we need to turn to Davidson's work on language. It is in Davidson's account of linguistic communication that his break with representationalist metaphysics (for that is what we have been talking about in the last paragraphs) is most apparent and explicit. And it is along this track that we find the dynamic developments in Davidson's thought most relevant for present purposes.

Taking off from Quine's idea of radical translation, which was a device for imposing behaviorist constraints on an account of linguistic communication, Davidson developed his own account of *radical interpretation*.[11] A *radical interpreter* is an interpreter with no specific assumptions about what a speaker means by the words she uses. By making a wide range of suitable observations of the speaker – of what she says when – and applying a tight bundle of general principles which constrain what *ought* in various circumstances to be said, the radical interpreter proceeds to construct a theory that assigns syntactic structure and semantic value to the language of the speaker. The radical interpreter's theory, Davidson argues, captures the extension of the truth-predicate for the observed speaker's language.[12] The fundamental thought here is that what we get when we get what some uttered indicative sentence literally means, is the way in which the words in that sentence interact to generate its truth conditions. Here, though, it is important to be careful. It is not that Davidson thinks that there are such things as truth-makers in the world, and that these, described the right way, turn out to be the meanings of sentences. Rather, the thought is that if we understand how the elements of a language systematically combine to determine truth-conditions for any possible indicative sentence of the language, then we have understood all there is to know about the semantics of that language. When we talk about linguistic meaning, this, Davidson argues, is all we can be talking about. Aspects of linguistic communication that cannot be accounted for in terms of truth-theoretic structure do not belong to semantics.

Two important lines of inquiry flow from Davidson's idea that we can understand meaning in terms of a semantic truth theory. One concerns the actual prospects for truth-conditional semantics, including the question of what it is that such a semantics is supposed to apply to; what is the proper object of a theory that systematically ascribes semantic properties? The other line of inquiry asks what the basic principles are that allow the radical interpreter to use observations of speech behavior as constraints on theory formation at all. Davidson's key idea is that the process of construing meaning can be modeled by the empirical construction of a truth-theory for a speaker only in so far as the process of radical interpretation is governed by the constraint of *charity*. In Davidson's early essays, the principle of charity was taken to be a matter of an interpreter's construing a speaker so as to maximize agreement between them. Since what you will sincerely assert in a given situation will depend on what you actually take to be the case, the interpreter must make some assumptions about your beliefs, if she is to be able to construct a theory that assigns meaning to your sentences. Charity, as Davidson puts it in the 1973 paper, "Radical Interpretation," is "intended to solve the problem of the interdependence of belief and meaning by holding belief constant as far as possible while solving for meaning" (Davidson 2001b: 137).

Davidson claimed that the requirement of charity in radical interpretation entails more than intersubjective alignment. Charity guarantees that both speaker and interpreter are largely correct in their beliefs.[13] On this score, however, Davidson received a great deal of resistance. Why should the intersubjective convergence of belief required for interpretation also indicate truth? Is not what the interpreter constructs for the speaker's language not a truth-theory, but rather an "agreement-theory"? Couldn't we achieve intersubjective alignment while being massively mistaken *together*? Moreover, isn't an account of linguistic meaning that requires great overlap of belief between subjects highly implausible, anyway? Do we want a theory of meaning that severely constrains the possibility of disagreement, of difference in outlook and in world view?

These reactions are natural responses from the point of view of a representation-alist view of meaning and interpretation. The meaningfulness of thought and language surely does not depend on an interpreter's activities – it is a *target* for that activity. And if it is, then why should our contingent ability to construe as intelligible other minds and languages have essential bearing on whether something *is* a mind and *uses* language at all?[14]

The Davidsonian response to these questions points toward a deep division between Davidson and the theorists of mind and meaning who operate within the metaphysical framework alluded to earlier. To make this clear, however, we need to return to the first of the two questions that Davidson's meta-semantical proposal opens up, the issue of the prospects for truth-conditional semantics. Davidson himself, along with a great number of other philosophers of language and theoretical linguists, took this to be a matter of determining the extent to which features of natural language could be reconstructed in terms of truth-functional operations on the *logical form* of utterance types.[15] For many of those engaged in this project, the question of what it is that a theory of meaning actually construes, what it applies to, was not prominent. For Davidson, however, this question of what a theory of truth for a language actually applies to soon became a principal focus of philosophical attention. And what he had to say about it was surprising, and for many highly counterintuitive. In a controversial paper from 1986, "A Nice Derangement of Epitaphs," Davidson surprisingly concludes that, "there is no such thing as a language"[16] (Davidson 2005: 107). Truth-theories, in so far as they illuminate what goes on in linguistic communication, do not apply to given linguistic structures – languages – with set meanings that we as users know and as learners and interpreters must figure out. Rather, the idealized radical interpreter targets, with her truth-theory, not a language that the speaker has come to possess, but the language that a speaker is producing at the moment – an idiolect. Furthermore, this target, this idiolect, is not a fixed object but something undergoing constant change. As an interpreter of linguistic behavior, then, the radical interpreter is engaged in an ongoing process of perpetual modification of truth-theories.[17] The radical interpreter is dynamically construing what a speaker is continuously *doing*, rather than decoding some thing, some fixed structure, that the speaker *has* or *possesses* and gives sequential expression to. And a speaker, for her part, making herself understood, is engaged in a process of constantly exploiting what she takes to be the interpreter's evolving understanding of what she is doing.

While Davidson does not back away from the idea that truth-theoretical semantics of natural languages is a worthwhile explanatory project, it is now clear that even if such a semantics were convincingly developed for some natural language, we could no longer take that to explain philosophically what it is that we achieve, and how it is that we achieve it, when we communicate with language. Given that there is no such *entity* as a language that bears the semantic properties in question, what we now want to know about is the nature of the abilities that go into that dynamic process of mutual accommodation which is linguistic understanding, and in relation to which truth-theoretic semantics can never be more than an idealized static model. To understand those abilities is also to understand the underlying affordances that allow us to deploy them, and it is as he increasingly attends to this issue that Davidson's break with the representationalist approach to meaning and mind becomes fully explicit. Moreover, as Davidson dispenses entirely with representationalist worries about verificationism and other sins, the themes that connect Davidson with hermeneutic thought become prominent, as we will now see.

3. Triangulation, temporality and semantic historicism

In an early (1974) but transitional paper of great significance for present purposes, "On the Very Idea of a Conceptual Scheme," Davidson not only draws some important consequences of the radical interpretation approach to meaning, he also gives us important hints as to the conception in which this approach is embedded. For many readers, Davidson's initial remarks on the principle of charity had raised the question of exactly what it was that supposedly needed to be shared between interpreter and speaker for interpretation to be possible. How extensive must the overlap be? What sorts of things – a priori structures, perceptual beliefs, general empirical beliefs, epistemic interests or perhaps norms of rationality – would provide the required common ground? One reader who saw right away that this was entirely the wrong sort of question to ask, was Richard Rorty. For Rorty, Davidson's attack on the third dogma of empiricism, the metaphor of scheme and content, epitomized the radical character of Davidson's break with a representationalist, epistemic notion of meaning precisely because it made it clear that charity ought not to be construed as a preexisting cognitive overlap of any kind at all. Far from fulfilling the goal of finally guaranteeing a shared frame, Davidson, in Rorty's narrative, does away with the entire ambition. Rorty writes:

> To construct an epistemology is to find the maximum amount of common ground with others. ... Within analytic philosophy, it has often been imagined to lie in language, which was supposed to supply the universal scheme for all possible content. To suggest that there is *no* such common ground seems to endanger rationality.
>
> (Rorty 1979: 316–17)

What is being endangered, in Rorty's view, is a specious sort of rationality, a philosopher's invention, tied to the idea that languages or conceptual schemes are possibly treacherous mediators of reality. This is the master idea of philosophy as a cultural overseer (Rorty 1979: 317), of the theory of knowledge charged with adjudicating the representational reliability or lack thereof of language in its various modes of operation. Davidson, Rorty thinks, takes analytic philosophy beyond its founding epistemic remit exactly because he allows us to leave behind the empiricist picture that makes us worry that possessing a language may be to suffer some form of containment. To give up that picture is to give up on the possibility that epistemology provides foundations. More importantly, it is to give up the idea that foundations are needed. Thereby, as Davidson remarks in conclusion, "we do not give up the world, but re-establish unmediated touch with the familiar objects whose antics make our sentences and opinions true or false" (Davidson 2001b: 198).

Moving away from representationalism – which for both Rorty and Davidson is just another word for conceptual-scheme epistemology – is also to change our perspective on linguistic intelligibility. A representationalist about meaning will take it that philosophical understanding of communication is achieved by way of an adequate theoretical model of a certain kind of knowledge that a subject is supposed to possess and apply. On such a model languages may indeed also be structures of confinement; what is interpretable will depend on the semantic knowledge possessed or available to the speaker – the *limits* and presuppositions of such knowledge become salient philosophical themes. By contrast, as Rorty clearly sees, for both Davidson and Gadamer language is a capacity for openness.

Another constructive and groundbreaking reader of both Gadamer and Davidson (and of Rorty), John McDowell, puts this point well in an essay comparing Davidson and Gadamer on relativism: "Davison's argument against relativism turns on the thought that – to put it in a way that emphasizes the correspondence with Gadamer – any linguistic practice is intelligible from the standpoint of any other" (McDowell 2002: 181).

And why is this? It is not because we have philosophical assurance that our schemes or practices share core beliefs, or conceptual structures, or whatever. Rather it is because to engage in linguistic interpretation, as both Gadamer and Davidson conceive of it, is to *make* new ground, new intelligibility, together. That is what dialogical understanding amounts to. This is what Rorty saw, and this is why he invokes both Davidson and hermeneutics in the chapter of *Philosophy and the Mirror of Nature* where he explicitly rejects the very ideal of a foundational vocabulary, or ideal linguistic practice, in which all genuine content can be made commensurable.

McDowell, however, after recognizing this point, goes on to criticize Davidson for not being attuned to the significance of sharing linguistic practices, thus foregoing insights that Gadamer brings to the fore in his hermeneutic account of understanding as a fusion of horizons, and underscores with his notion of the working of *tradition* in effective-historical consciousness. We may wonder, though, whether McDowell here really follows Davidson far enough in his movement away from the idea that to understand is to apply a knowledge already possessed. What Davidson argues against in favoring, as McDowell slightly tendentiously puts it, idiolect over shared languages (McDowell 2002: 181), is the thought that the kind of sharing that makes understanding possible comes into view if we attend to the semantic and syntactic patterns that are characteristic of an individual's or group's manner of using language. It is not Davidson's point that such patterns are uninteresting or without significance – they are worthy objects of scientists of language, of ethnographers and of social scientists, and so on, and we need not stop doing either semantics or investigations of languages as living social structures. However, what Davidson is after is the level and pattern of interaction that provides that very context in which it makes sense to think of patterns of language use *as* communicative exchange, whether these are diverging or converging, changing or not. And here no specific commonalities, whether semantic, syntactic or cultural, do any explanatory work.

It is in characterizing distinctively linguistic behavior and its success conditions that Davidson invokes charity, and here what is actually shared, as a presupposition of understanding, is, as we should now see, in fact no determinate thing at all.

Taking on board the lessons of Davidson's argument against conceptual schemes and against the very idea of a language we must conclude that charity simply does not refer back to a determinate antecedently held set of beliefs or attitudes or practices at all. To say that charity is an assumption of successful understanding indicates rather that a certain kind of forward-looking commitment is required for dialogue to occur. Jeff Malpas seems to me to get this exactly right in his clarifying discussion of various levels of agreement that might be taken to be at issue here, and the different senses in which they might be thought to be presupposed by understanding. Malpas ends his critical discussion affirmatively: "The agreement that enables understanding is precisely the agreement that consists in this *openness toward* the world, an agreement that can never be uniquely determined, since it is that on the basis of which any determination is possible" (Malpas 2011a: 276).

The principal hook that Davidson used for over two decades to elaborate this point is the idea of *triangulation*. The idea is deployed in many contexts and interpreted in different ways over several essays (Davidson 2001c). Late in his life, looking back, Davidson sums it up thus:

> [T]he objectivity which thought and language demand depends on the mutual and simultaneous responses of two or more creatures to common distal stimuli and to one another's responses. This three-way relation among two speakers and a common world I call "triangulation".
>
> (Davidson 2001c: xv)

Triangulation is a dynamic of two (or more) subjects in an interactive situation where both are participants. The abstraction of the pure observer characteristic of radical interpretation is gone. Still, it may be possible to conceive of triangulation as an abstract specification of the structure of content. It might then be assimilated to what is fundamentally an epistemological perspective on meaning – whether as contents of utterances or of thoughts. Triangulation then indicates only how content is to be conceived, while still being taken principally as an object of knowledge in representationalist terms. This, however, is not Davidson's view. As he goes on to say: "triangulation is not a matter of one person grasping a meaning already there, but a performance that (when fully fleshed out) bestows a content on language" (Davidson 2001c: xv). What Davidson brings into focus here is the *making* of intelligibility; communicating agents' coming-to-share intelligibility as a creative social act in particular circumstances and surroundings. When Davidson says that meaning presupposes actual communication – something for which he has been much criticized – this is what he has in mind. And when Davidson speaks of triangulation as a kind of performance, he aligns himself with philosophical hermeneutics. This is the import of the claim that philosophical hermeneutics is a project of ontology, advanced both by Heidegger and Gadamer as they break fundamentally and self-consciously with the epistemic approach to meaning.

Hermeneutic thought, however, also gives us reason to be cautious here, even if the convergence I have sketched is real. For one thing, Davidson and Gadamer themselves were not very successful in their attempt to enter into dialogue with one another.[18] Of course this is not in itself a very significant consideration, but it may be indicative of more worrying issues; it may be that the failure of dialogue is due less to contingent facts of circumstance and personality and more to differences in theoretical vocabulary, in proximal influences, framing of problems and styles of argumentation. This leads Davidson, for instance, to a seriously flawed diagnosis of Gadamer's idea of the kind of sharing that understanding requires, and so to mischaracterize the relation between their views.[19] But then, if factors such as these are very different, is not this simply to say that Gadamer and Davidson belong to different traditions? And is not philosophical hermeneutics exactly a tradition, in Gadamer's sense of that term? Even if we take it, as we surely should, that a tradition is not a closed structure of meaning but a continuously developing source of new meanings, we must take seriously the challenge that the question of tradition raises here.

If there is a way forward, it will lie in the recontextualization of his own investigations that Davidson brings about with the emphasis on triangulation as performance pertaining to the ontology of intelligibility. Any strain of hermeneutic thought at its core is an effort to grasp the consequences for human understanding of the fact that we are essentially historical beings. As readers of Davidson will know, this is hardly a prominent theme in any of his essays. Yet as he attempts to characterize the performance of triangulation, Davidson connects with a set of issues that in historical terms may be traced to Hegel's reaction to Kant, and Kant's to empiricism, and his contributions may be situated in terms of that larger history.[20] In such terms, then, it may not be far-fetched to look for commonalities that are indicative of tradition in the requisite sense.

It might help to have a way to characterize the stance that is common, in this larger context, to both explicitly historicist thinkers and Davidson. I suggest *semantic historicism*. The essence of the view is that intelligibility comes into being through the dialogical interaction of agents. Philosophical hermeneutics, particularly through Gadamer, emphasizes the historical situatedness that makes this possible. It shows us how the particular, contingent resources agents take to any encounter represent their belonging and beholdenness to tradition, while at the same time constituting the flexible resources of their creative semantic agency. Through what Gadamer calls effective-historical consciousness, meaning comes to be through the ongoing fusion of horizons that is a mutual making and remaking in language of past from the present and present from the past. This dynamic, however, can also be looked at from a different perspective – from close up, as it were. What, in concrete interpretation, is the structure of the dynamic that allows meaningful utterance to be made and taken? Davidson's triangulation may be regarded as an answer to this question. It abstracts away from the particulars of the historicity of subjects, bringing into view instead the way that particular subjects interacting in a common world are able to acquire differentiating perspectives on that world – able to acquire, that is to say, a horizon – at all.[21]

Taking seriously the ontological dimension – as we understand this term in the context of philosophical hermeneutics – of Davidson's triangulation, means that we can recognize in Davidson's view, also, an elaboration of key hermeneutic insight. The differentiation of particular subjects as well as any subject's participation in contexts of commonality are two sides of the same dialogical process; both what is individual and what is shared is an intersubjectively produced intelligibility of the world to subjects and of the subjects to themselves and to other subjects. In "Three Varieties of Knowledge" (1993) Davidson makes just this point:

> Until a base line has been established by communication with someone else, there is no point in saying one's own thought or words have propositional content. If this is so, then it is clear that knowledge of another mind is essential to all thought and all knowledge.
>
> (Davidson 2001c: 213)

Self-knowledge, knowledge of other minds and knowledge of the objective world are mutually interdependent. For this reason, it is clear to Davidson that all understanding is always also self-understanding. Indeed, Davidson, we can now see, offers a particular way to understand this claim. It is not merely that as we learn more truths about objects in the world or other people, we thereby also come to learn more truths about ourselves – maybe we do, maybe we don't. Rather, the point is that as we succeed in making the world and others more intelligible, the intelligibility of ourselves to ourselves is also enhanced. As Davidson remarks, "What is certain is that the clarity and effectiveness of our concepts grows with the growth of our understanding of others. There are no definite limits to how far dialogue can or will take us" (Davidson 2001c: 219).

4. Solidarity

Keeping in mind the hermeneutic dimension of Davidson's thinking, we see that this last remark is something more substantive than mere pious hope. It expresses the hermeneutic insight that any claim to be tracing alleged limits of dialogue, in other than purely practical and contingent senses,[22] is to fall back to an ahistoricist, ultimately Platonistic, conception of meaning.[23] Discursive creatures are always on the way to intelligibility. This is a point that David Vessey makes when he remarks that the "bottom line for Gadamer is that anything intelligible to anyone is potentially intelligible to everyone"[24] (Vessey 2011: 255). As we have seen, it applies equally and for the same basic reason, to Davidson. Of course, though, the "potentially" matters here; it makes the point that there is no guarantee in any particular case that dialogue will bring us into a common discursive space where "die Sache" and our respective views emerge as clear and mutually accessible. Occasional, perhaps frequent, failure to realize mutual understanding is indeed our experience. But this is our fate not qua linguistically confined creatures, but rather as finite, temporal ones; further discursive effort *may* bring us closer, always, if we are able to dialogically augment the intelligibility of what is being said. Through language, say both Gadamer and Davidson, any particular finitude may always get past its current particular state of self.

These qualifications, the *ifs* and the *mays*, are perhaps not prominent in the formulations of Gadamer and Davidson, but they may have been what mattered most to Rorty. As I have suggested, Rorty's reading of Davidson enabled him to articulate his historicist view of intelligibility. However, Rorty's fundamental concern is with articulating a view of philosophical activity that faces up to the responsibilities to which this view opens us. That this is so, illustrates how very badly read Rorty has been by those who dismissed him as irresponsible and cynical, as a pernicious relativist and a subjectivist. One can understand that Rorty's notion of philosophy as conversation (1979) left many shaking their head in wonder – what's the point of a conversation with no point except its own prolongation? And indeed, Rorty, too, came to see his efforts in the final section of *Philosophy and the Mirror of Nature* as feeble.[25] And while Heidegger continued to compel Rorty's imagination, hermeneutics, as a line of philosophical thought, did not.[26] Still, though his explicit invocation of hermeneutics was also in his own eyes something of a failure, Rorty never went back on the seriousness of his efforts to think constructively about the normative implications of historicism for philosophical reflection that he performs in the final third of *Philosophy and the Mirror of Nature*. And perhaps we are now in a position to make the idea that philosophy should go hermeneutical, that keeping up the *conversation* is the point of philosophizing, rather than the resolution of metaphysical puzzles, slightly less bland. Vessey points out that Gadamer's notion of dialogue – *Gespräch* – is a great deal more constraining than, on the face of it, the notion of dialogue or communication. Rather than mere exchange of information or points of view, it is "the collaborative act of seeking to articulate understanding of a subject matter ... It belongs to the category of activities Gadamer calls play" (Vessey 2012: 36). Playing, and particularly playing together in conversation, becomes in Gadamer's hands a pivotal hermeneutic idea.[27] It involves both a kind of submission, a surrender of control of the individual subject to the norms inherent in a joint venture, and at the same time – indeed, by the same token – a realization of the subject's freedom *to* be moved by reason, *to* be changed, *to* become more by understanding more. Playing this game is risky, because genuine participation is to place one's fate as interpreter beyond one's subjective control. As Gadamer remarks, "all playing is a being-played" (Gadamer 1991a: 106). Playing the game and being played by it, one depends, at the very least, on the good faith and will of co-players – without that, there can be no play, no game, at all. A chief demand, then, of discursive play – a very serious activity for interpreting self-interpreters – is courage; a virtue that in this context is mirrored by – and made possible by – a presumption of *solidarity. Solidarity* in dialogue is the positive affirmation of the inextricability of our fates as interpreting and self-interpreting subjects – one enters the game of hermeneutic dialogue under the presupposition of this form of discursive solidarity. Solidarity is what charity becomes when it is conceived in terms of semantic historicism and therefore as also future-directed and considered in terms of its practical implications, rather than as invoking some presumed already-shared structure, scheme or practice.

Rorty's invocation of hermeneutics as a context for his proposed norm for postrepresentationalist philosophy – "philosophers' moral concern should be with continuing the conversation of the West" (Rorty 1979: 394) – may then be taken as a gesture toward the idea that the development of interpretive understanding asks us, above all, to cultivate future-directed charity, forms of courageous solidarity. Reading Rorty along these lines, we see that the key opposition between epistemological philosophy and hermeneutic philosophy that he articulates is really between philosophy that attempts to mark out the limits of a given common ground and philosophy that strives to bring common ground into being. Conversation, for Rorty, is a morally loaded term: "Disagreements between disciplines and discourses are compromised or transcended in the course of the conversation" (Rorty 1979: 317). This normative notion of conversation, sketchily worked out in his 1979 critique of representationalism, is what Rorty tries to work out in explicitly moral and political terms in what remained his own favorite book (see Rorty 2007a), *Contingency, Irony, and Solidarity* (Rorty 1989). That this book makes no mention of hermeneutics is perhaps an irony, but one that does not compromise the fundamentally hermeneutic character of Rorty's project.

5. Dialogue and the formation of a hermeneutic horizon

Though neither Rorty nor Davidson engage Gadamer in particularly deep or revealing ways, both, I have claimed, belong with philosophical hermeneutics. Both break fundamentally with what I have called the representationalist view of interpretation, by making meaning – what is understood – not primarily an object of epistemic determination, but a product of successful, charitable interaction between participating, acting, transforming and self-transforming subjects in a shared world. In Rorty's terms, dialogical understanding is an achievement of solidarity. Rorty's emphasis encourages us to take responsibility for our interpretive agency, in conversation but also, equally, as readers of texts, as participants in the formation of effective histories. And so it is also with our central issue; that is, the question whether a point of view is available such that our protagonists can be seen as dialogically working up a common tradition. There is a real risk, as Dostal emphasizes, that we may be involving ourselves with a curious overlap in intellectual history, rather than participating in an advance in philosophical understanding, a genuine fusion of horizons. Still, provided we are not confounded either by false conceptual friends or by merely apparent disagreements, and provided we reify neither language, nor tradition, nor vocabulary, this treacherous terrain may be negotiated. Davidson, Rorty and Gadamer can be brought together precisely in the perspective they afford on this very issue; taking the particular shape of our linguistic repertoire at any given time to constitute an openness, as the nature of our access to a common process of transformation – a serious playing and being played – all insist, fundamentally, that continuing fusion of horizons always remains a possibility. And if such a possibility is realized, if fusion of horizons here were to occur, if it is indeed occurring – in spite of subjective limitations on mutual philosophical understanding and self-understanding, as our protagonists all clearly display – then it is because we, the readers of Gadamer, Heidegger, Rorty and Davidson, are up to the challenge of bringing into being a common discursive space. Less metaphorically, it is a matter of creating a sufficiently rich set of shared, conceptually and historically interlinked questions to which Rorty, Davidson and hermeneutic thinkers are all trying to respond. To achieve through dialogue a shared sense of the relative importance of various questions and of the relevance to them of various considerations – that is indeed what a fusion of intellectual horizons comes to. The notions of semantic historicism and of conversational solidarity are proposed in this spirit. Their purpose is to let us see the emphasis on process and dynamics and incompleteness in Davidson's gradually emerging account of dialogical understanding as springing from questions and concerns that are of a kind with those that give us Rorty's historicism of solidarity and the hermeneutic view of understanding as a fusion of horizons.

The decisive question, then, is this. Are we able to retrieve a richer understanding of dialogical understanding by bringing together Davidsonian triangulation, Rortyan solidarity and the commitments of philosophical hermeneutics in the way that I have sketched? Are we in fact illuminating a subject matter? That is the condition of success against which these interpretive suggestions must be gauged. Accordingly, I have tried to show that Davidson with his notion of triangulation delivers a version of semantic historicism that also provides an extension of the scope and power of the hermeneutic account of the historicity of understanding. This is so, I think, even if Davidson nowhere discusses the historical situatedness of understanding in Gadamer's sense. And I have attributed to Rorty an idea of conversational solidarity that is available only if one accepts the hermeneutic view of intelligibility as coming into being through dialogue. *Forward-directed charity*, as I have called Rorty's notion of solidarity, emphasizes the moral and political responsibility we all bear, not by metaphysical necessity, but as a consequence of the recognition of our finitude and our dependence as discursive beings on the contingencies of dialogue beyond our subjective mastery and control.

I have, moreover, tried to show that Davidson's philosophical thinking, and Rorty's deployment of it in his deconstructive narrative of representationalist epistemology, is ultimately a transformation of Davidson's own contributions to the dialectical sharpening of the problems of analytic philosophy as they appeared in the 1960s and 1970s. While these are contributions for which Davidson is justly esteemed, his work, taken hermeneutically in its full diachronic span, opens a perspective on the philosophical puzzles of metaphysical naturalism from which they appear as a particular – ingenious – set of instances of a broader, on-going effort of human understanding to articulate its own finitude, incompleteness and openness. So while Davidson was, by his own account, a problem-oriented philosopher, his way with those metaphysical problems produced, over time, a body of work that gives us something much more important than metaphysical solutions. Davidson teaches us something about how those problems – of meaning, of mind and of action in a natural world – *come to be* problems for creatures like us, and what it means to be facing them philosophically. This is something that in particular Rorty's reading of Davidson allows us to see. So perhaps, then, it is exactly in their relation to analytic philosophy, the tradition in terms of which much of their writing is carried out, that Rorty and Davidson most clearly display their contribution to philosophical hermeneutics. Over the course of Davidson's and Rorty's work, the philosophical problems that constitute the defining challenges for familiar strands of analytic philosophy are stripped of their autonomy as metaphysics, though not thereby to be dismissed or overcome, but rather restored to us as tasks of concrete historical human self-understanding; as tasks, that is to say, of *self-formation*. Through this performance, Davidson and Rorty provide core insights of philosophical hermeneutics with *applications* that they otherwise would not have had.[28]

Notes

1 These are the papers in philosophy of mind, philosophy of action and philosophy of language that are collected in volumes first published in 1980 (here cited as Davidson 2001a) and 1984 (here cited as Davidson 2001b). Davidson as regarded from the point of view of analytic philosophy is expounded and interrogated most extensively and systematically – and emblematically – in works by Ernest Lepore and Kirk Ludwig (Lepore and Ludwig 2005, 2007; Ludwig 2003). See also (Preyer 2012) for recent essays on Davidson critically engaging the Lepore–Ludwig reading largely on its own terms.

2 John McDowell, in *Mind and World* (McDowell 1996), has done more than any other thinker to place Davidson and Gadamer within the frame of the same philosophical narrative. Several essays in a recent volume edited by Jeff Malpas (Malpas 2011b) examine the relationship between Davidson and Gadamer: Braver 2011; Dostal 2011; Fultner 2011; Hoy and Durt 2011; Malpas 2011a. David Vessey helpfully lists a number of papers addressing the topic in recent decades (Vessey 2011: 257 fn9). I have made use of Vessey's list in the suggested further readings.

3 These are main themes of Hans-Georg Gadamer's *Truth and Method* (Gadamer 1991a). See also his slightly later (1966) essay, "The Universality of the Hermeneutical Problem" (Gadamer 1976). For Rorty's dim view of universality claims, see for instance his "Universality and Truth" (Rorty 2000).

4 Robert Dostal is illuminating and chastening on the significance of Gadamer's use of this term, "die Sache," and on the treacherousness of translations into English (Dostal 2011: 172).

5 In addition to McDowell's influential work (cf. note 2), several commentators have explored this connection in recent years. My own early enthusiasm may be observed in (Ramberg 1989), while (Ramberg 2003) underscores the distance between Davidson and Gadamer's understanding of common terms. Kristin Gjesdal, emphasizing the fundamental hermeneutic thought that all understanding is also self-understanding, is even more skeptical (Gjesdal 2010). David Hoy, on the other hand, is more positive, in view of the common break with Cartesian understanding of subjectivity, as are Hoy and Christop Durt (Hoy and Durt 2011). The papers mentioned above (n. 2) in the Malpas volume all perform useful calibrations. Thus, for instance, Barbara Fultner's excellent paper on incommensurability very effectively situates Davidson and Gadamer in relation to this idea. Fultner's analyses bring out Davidson's and Gadamer's common stance against reifying conceptions of language and understanding, but she also suggests, considering the relation between interpretation and translation, that there are important differences in their basic conception of what understanding is (Fultner 2011: 231).

6 In his *Beyond Objectivism and Relativism: Science, Hermeneutics, and Praxis* (Bernstein 1983), Bernstein very effectively makes this point about the hermeneutic conception of historicity, and argues that Rorty and Gadamer here are closer than their different vocabularies indicate. However, he remains critical of both for failing, in Bernstein's view, to integrate the dimension of praxis.

7 See in particular Davidson's seminal paper, "Actions, Reasons and Causes" (Davidson 1963), and other papers in (Davidson 2001a).

8 The worry is whether there can be anything in the world capable of making true statements about metaphysically problematic entities (values, seemings, norms, etc.).

9 In "Laws and Cause" from 1995 Davidson provides an account of the nature of the physical in terms of the constitutive interests expressed in the relevant vocabularies. I try to come to terms with Davidson's view in Ramberg (1999).

10 The debate about mental causation, specifically about the kind of supervenience of the mental on the physical that mental causation actually requires, will serve as an example of this. It illustrates also Davidson's own occasional difficulties in disentangling his position from the metaphysical assumptions framing debates in mainstream analytic philosophy of mind. See the essays in Part One of J. Heil and A. Mele's very instructive collection, *Mental Causation* (Heil and Mele 1995: 3–52).

11 See the essays collected in Davidson's *Truth and Interpretation* (Davidson 2001b).

12 Davidson here adapts to natural language the work that Alfred Tarski did on formal languages. Tarski showed how we can define a truth-predicate for a given axiomatized language (Tarski 1944). When we give such a truth-definition, we are *using* one language (the language of the theory, or the meta-language) to *describe* the structure of another language (the object language). A consistently characterized formal language does not contain its own truth-predicate, and this places constraints on the adaptation Davidson performs.

13 Davidson writes:

> If we cannot find a way to interpret the utterances and other behavior of a creature as revealing a set of beliefs largely consistent and true by our own standards, we have no reason to count that creature as rational, as having beliefs, or as saying anything at all.
>
> (Davidson 2001b: 137)

14 These worries are often expressed by way of accusations of verificationism, irrealism, or even linguistic idealism.

15 The iconic collection *Semantics of Natural Language* from 1972 (Davidson and Harman 2013) embodies both the spirit and the practice of this research program, all aspects of which were under lively critical discussion from the start. See Lepore and Ludwig (2007) for a comprehensive and thorough recent examination of the program.

16 Here is what Davidson writes:

> I conclude that there is no such thing as a language, not if a language is anything like what many philosophers and linguists have supposed. There is therefore no such thing to be learned, mastered, or born with. We must give up the idea of a clearly defined shared structure which language-users acquire and then apply to cases.
>
> (Davidson 2005: 107)

17 Davidson describes this in terms of a dynamic between prior and passing theories:

> For the hearer, the prior theory expresses how he is prepared in advance to interpret an utterance of the speaker, while the passing theory is how he *does* interpret the utterance. For the speaker, the prior theory is what he *believes* the interpreter's prior theory to be, while the passing theory is the theory that he *intends* the interpreter to use.
>
> (Davidson 2005: 101)

18 Lee Braver (2011) analyses Davidson's misreading of Gadamer (Davidson 1997) in Davidson's invited contribution in the Library of Living Philosophers volume on Gadamer (Hahn 1997). Davidson emphasizes their common ground and expresses his great admiration for Gadamer both as a reader of Plato and as a theorist of understanding. He adds to this, however, some points of divergence. But where such initial disagreement for a hermeneutic reader would be entry-points for exploration, Davidson simply notes them, and this, Braver argues, betrays precisely a lack of hermeneutic charity. In hermeneutic terms, the principle of charity cannot amount simply to the demand that we interpret others to agree with us. Rather, charity expresses the idea that interpretation proceeds as a movement towards coming into agreement. As Braver puts it: "The expectation that the other has something to teach us is Gadamer's version of charity, which forms the necessary beginning point for all interpretation" (Braver 2011: 158). Hermeneutically speaking, humility is the better part of charity.

19 Several writers have convincingly demonstrated the point (Braver 2011; Malpas 2002). Dostal sums it up nicely:

> The difference between Gadamer and Davidson about this is not great. What difference there is comes from accentuating differently one of the two sides of Davidson's triangulation. Davidson sees Gadamer insisting on working out first a common

language and then coming to an agreement (or disagreement) about the topic of conversation. Davidson objects that the language does not come first, but rather that "it is only in the presence of shared objects that understanding can come about." Gadamer should not accept Davidson's characterization of his view here, for Gadamer would deny that language could be worked out "first" without reference to life in a world. Neither side, language or world, is first. Davidson would agree.

(Dostal 2011: 178; the embedded quotation is from Davidson 1997: 432)

20 Dostal makes this point (Dostal 2011). The point may be underscored by considering Robert Brandom, a philosopher who is in something of the same line of work as Davidson, and who uses the vocabulary of analytic philosophy to address the dynamics of the emergence of intelligibility through interaction (Brandom 1994). Unlike Davidson, Brandom has devoted a great deal of effort to construing this larger tradition and to inserting his own analytic work into it (Brandom 2002).
21 I owe this way of thinking about the aspects of semantic historicism to remarks by Ramon del Castillo, who suggested that semantic historicism affords both a macro-perspective and a micro-perspective, and that we need not take these to be isomorphic.
22 Of course practical and contingent limits to dialogue are immensely important, though not in a particularly philosophical way.
23 We should note that Gadamer's Plato may not have been a Platonist about meaning in the sense I invoke here.
24 As Vessey also puts the point, in a Davidsonian key: "We are never in a position to conclude that a disagreement in dialogue is evidence of incommensurability" (Vessey 2011: 255).
25 "My invocation of Gadamerian hermeneutics," writes Rorty, looking back across the decades, "was feeble and unproductive" (Rorty 2007a: 13).
26 For Rorty's engagement with Heidegger, see the essays collected in Rorty 1991b. Regarding questions raised by Rorty's conspicuous lack of engagement with hermeneutics, see Ramberg 2011b.
27 In the subsection of *Truth and Method* entitled, "Play as the clue to ontological explanation" (Gadamer 1991a: 101–34), Gadamer provides an initial condensed exposition of a basic claim about the structure of dialogical understanding and the relation of subjectivity to tradition. The fundamental theme is, "the *primacy of play over the consciousness of the player*" (Gadamer 1991a: 104, italics in the original).
28 I have been greatly aided by conversations with Kristin Gjesdal on the topics I pursue in this chapter. Ramon del Castillo and Ángel Faerna, astutely responding to a presentation of the main ideas, helped me make them clearer. Endre Begby, through conversations also about more empirically oriented matters, has had a greater influence on the reading of Davidson offered here than he may realize. The reader may notice that I have learned much from Jeff Malpas' work on Davidson. In any case, his sound advice not only made this chapter more interesting and more readable than it would otherwise have been, but also, and most fundamentally, his patient persistence also coaxed it into being. My sincere thanks go to all.

This work was partly supported by the Research Council of Norway through its Centres of Excellence funding scheme, project number 179566/V20.

Bibliography

Bernstein, R.J. (1983) *Beyond Objectivism and Relativism: Science, Hermeneutics, and Praxis*, Philadelphia: University of Pennsylvania Press.
Brandom, Robert (1994) *Making it Explicit: Reasoning Representing, and Discursive Commitment*, Cambridge, Mass.: Harvard University Press.
——(2000) (ed.) *Rorty and his Critics*, Malden, Mass.: Blackwell Publishers Ltd.
——(2002) *Tales of the Mighty Dead: Historical Essays in the Metaphysics of Intentionality*, Cambridge, Mass.: Harvard University Press.

Braver, L. (2011) "Davidson's Reading of Gadamer: Triangulation, Conversation, and the Analytic Continental Divide," in *Dialogues with Davidson: Acting, Interpreting, Understanding*, ed. Jeff Malpas, Cambridge, Mass.: MIT Press.

Davidson, D. (1963) "Actions, Reasons, and Causes," *Journal of Philosophy*, 60 (23): 685–700. Reprinted in Davidson 2001a.

——(1970) "Mental Events," in *Experience and Theory*, ed. L. Foster and J.W. Swanson, Amherst: University of Massachusetts Press. Reprinted in Davidson 2001a.

——(1974) "On the Very Idea of a Conceptual Scheme," in *Proceedings and Addresses of the American Philosophical Association*, 47, Newark: American Philosophical Association. Reprinted in Davidson 2001b.

——(1993) "Three Varieties of Knowledge," in *A.J. Ayer Memorial Essays*, ed. A. Phillips Griffiths (Royal Institute of Philosophy Supplement, 30) Cambridge: Cambridge University Press. Reprinted in Davidson 2001c.

——(1997) "Gadamer and Plato's Philebus," in *The Philosophy of Hans-Georg Gadamer*, ed. L.E. Hahn (The Library of Living Philosophers, Vol. XXIV), Chicago: Open Court Publishing Company.

——(1999) "Intellectual Autobiography," in *The Philosophy of Donald Davidson*, ed. L.E. Hahn (The Library of Living Philosophers, Vol. XXVII), Chicago: Open Court Publishing Company.

——(2001a (1980)) *Essays on Actions and Events*, Oxford: Clarendon Press.

——(2001b (1984)) *Inquiries into Truth and Interpretation*, Oxford: Clarendon Press.

——(2001c) *Subjective, Intersubjective, Objective*, Oxford: Clarendon Press.

——(2004) *Problems of Rationality*, Oxford: Clarendon Press.

——(2005) *Truth, Language, and History*, Oxford: Clarendon Press.

Davidson, D., and Harman, G. (2013) *Semantics of Natural Language*, 2nd ed., Synthese Library, Dordrecht: Springer.

Dostal, R. (2011) "In Gadamer's Neighborhood," in *Dialogues with Davidson: Acting, Interpreting, Understanding*, ed. Jeff Malpas, Cambridge, Mass.: MIT Press.

Fultner, B. (2011) "Incommensurability in Davidson and Gadamer," in *Dialogues with Davidson: Acting, Interpreting, Understanding*, ed. Jeff Malpas, Cambridge, Mass.: MIT Press.

Gadamer, Hans-Georg (1976) "The Universality of the Hermeneutical Problem," in *Philosophical Hermeneutics*, ed. and trans. D.E. Linge, Berkeley: University of California Press.

——(1991a) *Truth and Method*, 2nd revised edition, trans. J. Weinsheimer and D.G. Marshall, New York: Continuum.

——(1991b) *Plato's Dialectical Ethics*, trans. R.M. Wallace, New Haven: Yale University Press.

Gjesdal, K. (2010) "Davidson and Gadamer on Plato's dialectical ethics," in *Interpretation: Ways of Thinking about the Sciences and the Arts*, ed. P. Machamer and G. Wolters, Pittsburgh: Pittsburgh University Press.

Hahn, L.E. (ed.) (1997) *The Philosophy of Hans-Georg Gadamer* (The Library of Living Philosophers, Vol. XXIV), Chicago: Open Court Publishing Company.

Heil, J. and Mele, A. (1995) *Mental Causation*, New York: Oxford University Press.

Hoy, D.C. (1997) "Post-Cartesian Interpretation: Hans-Georg Gadamer and Donald Davidson," in *The Philosophy of Hans-Georg Gadamer*, ed. L.E. Hahn (The Library of Living Philosophers, Vol. XXIV), Chicago: Open Court Publishing Company.

Hoy, D.C. and Durt, C. (2011) "What Subjectivity Isn't," in *Dialogues with Davidson: Acting, Interpreting, Understanding*, ed. Jeff Malpas, Cambridge Mass.: MIT Press.

Lepore, E. and Ludwig, K. (2005) *Donald Davidson: Meaning, Truth, Language, and Reality*, Oxford: Clarendon Press.

——(2007) *Donald Davidson's Truth-Theoretic Semantics*, Oxford: Clarendon Press.

Ludwig, K. (ed.) (2003) *Donald Davidson*, Cambridge: Cambridge University Press.

McDowell, J. (1996) *Mind and World*, Cambridge, Mass.: Harvard University Press.

——(2002) "Gadamer and Davidson on Understanding and Relativism," in *Gadamer's Century: Essays in Honor of Hans-Georg Gadamer*, ed. Jeff Malpas et al., Cambridge, Mass.: MIT Press.

Malpas, J. (1992) *Donald Davidson and the Mirror of Meaning*, Cambridge: Cambridge University Press.

——(2002) "Gadamer, Davidson, and the Ground of Understanding," in *Gadamer's Century: Essays in Honor of Hans-Georg Gadamer*, ed. Jeff Malpas, Cambridge, Mass.: MIT Press.

——(2008) "On Not Giving Up the World – Davidson and the Grounds of Belief," *International Journal of Philosophical Studies*, 16: 201–15.

——(2011a) "What is Common to All: Davidson on Agreement and Understanding," in *Dialogues with Davidson: Acting, Interpreting, Understanding*, Cambridge, Mass.: MIT Press.

——(ed.) (2011b) *Dialogues with Davidson: Acting, Interpreting, Understanding*, Cambridge, Mass.: MIT Press.

Malpas, J., Arnswald, U. and Kertscher, J. (2002) *Gadamer's Century: Essays in Honor of Hans-Georg Gadamer*, Cambridge, Mass.: MIT Press.

Preyer, G. (ed.) (2012) *Donald Davidson on Truth, Meaning, and the Mental*, Oxford: Oxford University Press.

Quine, V.W. (1960) *Word and Object*, Cambridge, Mass.: MIT Press.

Ramberg, B. (1989) *Donald Davidson's Philosophy of Language: An Introduction*, Oxford: Basil Blackwell.

——(1999) "The Significance of Charity," in *The Philosophy of Donald Davidson*, ed. L. E. Hahn (The Library of Living Philosophers, Vol. XXVII), Chicago: Open Court Publishing Company.

——(2003) "Illuminating Language: Interpretation and Understanding in Gadamer and Davidson," in *A House Divided: Comparing Analytic and Continental Philosophy*, ed. C.G. Prado, Amherst: Humanity Books.

——(2008) "Rorty, Davidson and the Future of Metaphysics in America," in *The Oxford Handbook of American Philosophy*, ed. C. Misak, New York: Oxford University Press.

——(2011a) "Method and Metaphysics. Pragmatist Doubts," in *Dialogues with Davidson: Acting, Interpreting, Understanding*, ed. Jeff Malpas, Cambridge, Mass.: MIT Press.

——(2011b) "Turning to Hermeneutics: On Pragmatism's Struggle with Subjectivity," in *Pragmatische Hermeneutic. Beiträge zu Richard Rortys Kulturpolitik*, ed. M. Buschmeier and E. Hammer, *Zeitschrift für Ästhetik und Allgemeine Kunstwissenschaft*, Sonderheft 11, Berlin: Felix Meiner Verlag.

Rorty, R. (1979) *Philosophy and the Mirror of Nature*, Princeton: Princeton University Press.

——(1989) *Contingency, Irony, and Solidarity*, Cambridge: Cambridge University Press.

——(1991a) "Inquiry as recontextualization: An anti-dualist account of interpretation," in *Objectivity, Relativism and Truth*, *Philosophical Papers Vol. 1*, Cambridge: Cambridge University Press.

——(1991b) *Essays on Heidegger and Others*, *Philosophical Papers Vol. 2*, Cambridge: Cambridge University Press.

——(2000) "Universality and Truth," in *Rorty and his Critics*, ed. R. Brandom, Malden, Mass.: Blackwell Publishers Ltd.

——(2007a) "Intellectual Autobiography of Richard Rorty," in *The Philosophy of Richard Rorty*, ed. R.E. Auxier and L.E. Hahn (The Library of Living Philosophers, Vol. XXXII), Chicago: Open Court Publishing Company.

——(2007b) "Analytic and conversational philosophy," in *Philosophy as Cultural Politics*, *Philosophical Papers*, Vol. 4, Cambridge: Cambridge University Press.

Tarski, A. (1944) "The Semantic Conception of truth: and the Foundation of Semantics," in *Philosophy and Phenomenological Research*, 4: 341–76.

Vessey, D. (2011) "Davidson, Gadamer, Incommensurability, and the Third Dogma of Empiricism," in *Dialogues with Davidson: Acting, Interpreting, Understanding*, ed. Jeff Malpas, Cambridge, Mass.: MIT Press.

——(2012) "Gadamer and Davidson on language and thought," *Philosophy Compass*, 7: 33–42.

Further reading

Alcott, L.M. (2003) "Gadamer's Feminist Epistemology," in *Feminist Interpretations of Hans-Georg Gadamer*, ed. L. Code, University Park: Pennsylvania State University Press.

Bubner, R. (1994) "On the Ground of Understanding," in *Hermeneutics and Truth*, ed. B. Wachterhouser, Evanston: Northwestern University Press.

Dreyfus, H. (1980) "Holism and Hermeneutics," *Review of Metaphysics*, 34: 3–23.

Taylor, C. (2002) "Understanding the Other: A Gadamerian View on Conceptual Schemes," in *Gadamer's Century: Essays in Honor of Hans-Georg Gadamer*, ed. Jeff Malpas et al., Cambridge, Mass.: MIT Press.

Stueber, K. (1994) "Understanding Truth and Objectivity: A Dialogue between Donald Davidson and Hans-Georg Gadamer," in *Hermeneutics and Truth*, ed. B. Wachterhauser, Evanston: Northwestern University Press.

Wachterhauser, B. (2002) "Getting It Right: Relativism, Realism, and Truth," in *The 'Cambridge Companion to Gadamer*, ed. R. Dostal, New York: Cambridge University Press.

Weinsheimer, J. (2005) "Charity Militant: Gadamer, Davidson, and Post-critical Hermeneutics," in *The Force of Tradition: Response and Resistance in Literature, Religion, and Cultural Studies*, ed. D. Marshall, Lanham: Rowman & Littlefield.

18
BRANDOM AND MCDOWELL: HERMENEUTICS AND NORMATIVITY

Glenda Satne

Robert Brandom (1950–) and John McDowell (1942–) represent – along with Wilfrid Sellars – what has been sometimes vaguely called "the Pittsburgh School" (Maher 2012). Even if speaking of a school may be an overstatement, there are indeed several common themes to these philosophers who developed most of their careers at the University of Pittsburgh: the importance they place on the history of philosophy, and especially on Kantian and Post-Kantian thought, usually ignored in contemporary analytic philosophy; the attack on what Sellars called the Myth of the Given; the importance of human practices as a starting point for philosophical reflection, among others. But perhaps the most important idea that they share is the idea that normativity is an essential trait of human thought and that properly accounting for it is a paramount task for philosophy. The way in which they approach normativity and to what extent such approach is properly hermeneutical will be the topic of this chapter.

Normativity and the space of reasons

Kant famously argued that humans are citizens of two worlds: the world of nature and the world of freedom. Humans are part of the natural world but, at the same time, human thought and action seem to go beyond the realm of pure causal relations, involving motives, responsibilities and accountability. This distinction is further elaborated in terms of the one between understanding and explanation that figures prominently in the work of some central authors of the hermeneutical tradition. The basic idea is the following: While the realm of nature can be approached through the method of the natural sciences which can yield an explanation of it, this does not hold for the realm of human action and thought, what has sometimes been called Spirit or Reason. Core to this distinction is the idea that human actions, speech, institutions and the like can only be understood properly in terms of their location within a space of meaning that is not to be conceived as constituted by bare empirical facts. Accordingly, their description requires a specific method. Such a method can be properly called hermeneutical in that it is characterized by the attempt to grasp the meaning of phenomena that are embedded in historical cultural situations that are lived through by historical situated agents whose conception of facts is at issue.

Sellars has articulated this distinction further in order to characterize the very content of human thoughts and mental states in general. He described it in terms of the difference between a logical space of nature and a logical space of reasons, governed by two different kinds of normativity: "in characterizing an episode or a state as that of knowing, we are not giving an empirical description of that episode or state; we are placing it in *the logical space of reasons, of justifying and being able to justify what one says*" (Sellars 1963: 169, my emphasis). According to Sellars, it would be mistaken to characterize states such as beliefs, or knowings, and their corresponding propositional contents, judgeables or believables, in terms of mere empirical descriptions. This would be "a mistake of a piece with the so-called 'naturalistic fallacy' in ethics" (Sellars 1963: 131). Such a fallacy, first introduced by G.E. Moore (2008), consists in defining moral properties, such as being good or right, in non-moral or natural terms, hence conflating two different dimensions: what is or occurs, and the appropriateness or goodness of something – the way it should be. Sellars argues that the same distinction should apply to epistemic facts and intentional states more generally. While the normativity of natural laws and nomological generalizations characterizes the realm of nature in the way science describes it, the normativity of reasons and rational principles is characteristic of human actions and performances, and of intentional states such as beliefs, desires and the like in particular, defining them in terms of their appropriateness or correctness conditions.

Accordingly, the logical space of reasons is not the space in which we describe the psychology of the acts of thinking, but the space in which the correction conditions of our thoughts and actions are at stake, where our justificatory credentials are at issue. Beliefs and other intentional states are defined as standings in the space of reasons and as such they are essentially related to other states with which they are rationally articulated. It is against the background of these other states and the rational norms that govern their relations that each individual state is to be understood. Hence, the space of reasons is a unitary whole defined by the relations among its parts that, in their turn, gain their content by being located within that whole.

Both Brandom and McDowell follow this central insight from Sellars, making of this demarcation an issue that concerns how to understand the rationality of mental states, including beliefs, desires and other intentional attitudes and the specific normativity that applies to them. In characterizing the space of reasons, both of them underline its linguistic character. The space of reasons is a space we inhabit as linguistic creatures (Brandom 2013: 7): while language comes with the possibility of making ourselves intelligible to others and others intelligible for us, it also underlies the possibility of self-understanding and of having a genuine conceptual engagement with the world. If "man's being-in-the-world is primarily linguistic" (Gadamer 1992: 443; McDowell 2009a: 144), it is at the same time historical, since articulations of what is a reason for what are inherited in and through language. Thus, the space of reasons is articulated along three mutually related yet irreducible dimensions: the subjective, the objective and the intersubjective that are conjoined in the unitary medium of language.

In sum, it is the peculiar normative status that characterizes intentional states that calls for an understanding of them as located in the space of reasons, a space where our relation to the world is to be understood in terms of the rational demands that are imposed on our ability to entertain thoughts about it, a space that we co-inhabit with others, a space in which we come to live in as far as we are introduced in a language and tradition. That notwithstanding, the answers both Brandom and McDowell provide to the questions about the source of the normative force of rational norms, their social dimension and their objectivity define some significant differences between their views.

In the following sections, we will explore their understanding of the subjective, the intersubjective and the objective character of the normative space of reasons as well the differences between their perspectives.

Brandom: normativity and interpretation

As in the case of rules and principles, meanings proper to claims and intentional states establish a difference between what accords with them and what does not. To say that 'Fido is a dog' would be correct just in case Fido is indeed a dog, something that crucially depends on the meanings of the terms establishing a criterion for applying them in practice. Something can be said to have meaning in so far as it can draw a distinction between what accords with it and what does not. If anything could count as a correct application of a term or a rule, then its meaning will fade away (Wittgenstein 2009: §201). In accounting for this trait of intentional states, Brandom's account of normativity aims to accommodate two conditions of adequacy.

On the one hand, norms that account for the distinction between correct and incorrect should not be understood in terms of the distinction between regular and irregular applications of concepts. Brandom (1994: 26–30) calls this alternative in which norms are thought to be mere regularities in action "regularism." If norms are understood as regularities, they will fail to sort performances into correct ones (those that accord with the regularity) and incorrect ones (irregular), because any course of behavior embodies indefinitely many regularities. There is no principled ground for selecting one as opposed to others by appealing only to regularity in behavior. Furthermore, this view fails to account for normativity as embodied in the subject's performance of following a rule because those subject to the rules will be acting merely according with them and not in the light of the demands that the norms issue on their actions. The first condition of adequacy is thus that the normativity of meaning requires the behavior subject to the norm to be *sensitive* to its requirements in a more substantive sense that just acting according to a regularity.

On the other hand, accounting for the normativity of meaning requires rejecting the idea that what one does when following a rule is to follow explicit contents that one has in mind. Brandom (1994: 18–26) labels this view that treats normative contents as prescriptive rules "regulism." Regulism conceives of any norm on the model of rules that explicitly specify the actions that accord with them. Brandom argues that this view will be subject to the regress of interpretations made famous by Wittgenstein (2009: §201). If rules were the only form of norms, then they would fail to sort actions into correct and incorrect ones, since applying a rule is something that can be done correctly or incorrectly and actions that were correct according to one interpretation of the rule, would be incorrect according to another. This asks for a way of determining the correctness of a given interpretation and thus for another rule that establishes so, but again this calls for an interpretation, leading to a regress. The second condition of adequacy is thus that the normativity of meaning requires modeling the subject being *sensitive* to the norm without presupposing that she has the content of the norm "before her mind."

In Brandom's view, following Wittgenstein (2009: §202) and Sellars (2007), meeting these two conditions of adequacy amounts to thinking of meaning and normativity from the point of view of social linguistic *practices* in which subjects act in the light of the norms implicit in the practice without having before their minds the contents to which they are responding. Only the assessing attitudes implicit in the practice of treating performances as correct or incorrect – not thought of as propositionally contentful states, but as *practical doings* – can do the required job. Semantic norms should then be thought of as *instituted* by those who acknowledge them in practice. This account of normativity would prevent the regress of interpretations that affects regulism, on the one hand, and avoid a regularity account with no normativity in place, on the other. When we think of normative linguistic practices, these assessing attitudes set up – as proper devices for interpreting behavior – linguistic norms: semantically contentful norms implicit in our practice of treating behavior as correct or incorrect.

This social perspective advocated by Brandom needs to be clearly distinguished from a communitarian account of the nature of norms (Kripke 1982; Wright 1980) according to which the correct way of using a word, that is, its meaning, coincides with what the community as a whole thinks is correct. One concern with this view is that it would reinstate the worries concerning regularism, especially if all that is meant by it is that the regular behavior of the community members establishes the criteria of correction for concepts and terms. Moreover, Brandom (1994: 38–9) points out that the communitarian approach, by attributing authority to what "the community" takes as correct, mystifies the nature of the authority of norms by modeling it in terms of the authority of a superperson. Being a member of a community and following communitarian norms are normative notions that have to be themselves elucidated through a social account of normativity.

Brandom aims to provide an alternative account by following Davidson's complaint that providing an elucidation of linguistic practices requires approaching the relation between linguistic utterances and meaning from the point of view of an interpreter (Davidson 2005; see also Brandom 2010: 33–4): we cannot make sense of linguistic meanings without acknowledging the perspectival character of meaning-attribution within human social practices. This is what Brandom (1994: 37–42, esp. 39) calls the I–Thou relation. It is only through the eyes of the interpreter that we can make sense of language as a game or practice in which human beings are engaged. The I–We relation can only be understood as deriving from the I–Thou.

Unlike the communitarian approach, understanding, according to Brandom, is not dependent on "the existence of any form of preexistent, determined, 'internalised' agreement" (Malpas 2011: 261). Rather, understanding depends on interpretation, on a hermeneutical holistic process where an utterance or action is located within its wider context. This context includes both (1) the situation in which interpreter and speaker are mutually engaged, and (2) an attributed set of interrelated intentional states (such as beliefs, desires and intentions) articulating the rationality of the speaker's behavior in such situation. In Brandom's view, the interpretative stance – what he calls, using a baseball metaphor, 'scorekeeping' – can be thought of as equivalent to an external, observational standpoint, the one someone adopts towards an alien community. Inverting the communitarian claim, Brandom (2010: 33–4) argues that understanding an alien community, one's own or a discursive fellow essentially involves the same fundamental tools.

In characterizing those tools, Brandom's account of normative linguistic practices combines (1) a normative pragmatics through which he characterizes the social dynamics of the game of giving and asking for reasons in terms of authority and responsibility and the deontic statuses of commitment and entitlement through which the interpersonal interpretative practice is to be understood and (2) an inferential semantics, according to which the primary unity of meaning is inference.

The game of giving and asking for reasons is constituted by linguistic moves, assertions, performances that can serve and stand for reasons. Judging hence is committing oneself, taking responsibility and claiming authority for one's claims, and it is also putting forward one's assertion for anyone to undertake it and thus attribute entitlement to it. This all happens in the eyes of the participants, who keep score on each other's entitlements and commitments. According to Brandom, it is this authority and corresponding responsibility together with the notion of challenge that gives its characteristic dynamics to the inferential practice (Brandom 2010: 26–7). The judgeables or believables – propositional contents – associated with assertions can serve both as premises and conclusions of inferences. Contents are thus to be understood in terms of their inferential articulation with other moves of the game. There are two basic sorts of inferential relations that articulate inferential contents:

1. committive inferences specifying what one is committed to when making an assertion: for example by asserting 'That ball is green' one is committed to 'That ball is colored';
2. permissive inferences, specifying what one is entitled to and hence accounting for permissible moves in the game: for example the move from 'Fido drools' to 'Fido is a dog' is permitted but it is not something to which the assertor is thereby committed;
3. incompatibility entailments, specifying the inferential interactions between entitlements and commitments: two commitments are incompatible just in case commitment to one precludes entitlement to the other (e.g. 'this is green' is incompatible with 'this is red').

Equally fundamental to the game, there are also entry and exit moves that specify causal relations with the environment in perception and action. Acknowledgment of doxastic commitments can be reliably differentially elicited as responses to the environment in situations of perception and acknowledgments of practical commitments can reliably differentially elicit performances as responses in action (Brandom 1994: 271). In these cases reasons can play both normative and causal roles.

But accounting for the normativity of assertion not only involves making sense of the justification a speaker might have for making a claim (her evidence or other reasons), but whether the claim is correct regarding how things stand regarding the objects the claim is about, whether it is *true*, independently of anyone's attitudes with respect to it. To ask about this aspect of the practice is to demand an account of the objectivity of our assertional practice. Brandom rejects the idea that truth has an explanatory use and embraces a deflationary account: to say that 'the grass is green' is true amounts to asserting (to undertake the commitment and vindicate entitlement) that the grass in green. Accordingly, he purports to account for the objectivity of claims in terms of the inferential semantics of commitments and entitlements. It is within the context of social practices articulating perspective differences where objectivity is to be grounded (Brandom 1994: ch. 8; 2000: ch. 6.). The very idea of objective purport is, according to Brandom, *implicit* in the participants of the game keeping score of each other's entitlements and commitments, and the incompatibilities that hold among them. He argues that when considering the meaning of claims of the form 'S is committed to the claim that the grass is green,' 'S is entitled to the claim that the grass is green' and 'the grass is green,' the set of incompatible claims that are associated with each claim are different, thus showing that the meaning of the claim that the grass is green has different assertibility conditions than any claim relating to what someone is committed or entitled to. This distinction, and thus the objective dimension of the game, is made *explicit* by the vocabulary of propositional attitudes in which the distinction between *what someone takes to be the case* – what someone believes or is entitled to believe – and *what is the case* – when contents 'swing free' from their association with attitudes – is articulated.

Given Brandom's deflationary account of truth, the criterion of correction for interpretations is their coherence with other interpretations given by other practitioners along the history of the concept and not a supposed confrontation between interpretations and the world: the world relates with meaning causally and not directly as that which justifies our claims. This does not mean, nevertheless, a relapse into some form of *genealogical* reduction of norms to purely factual and hence contingent descriptions of their origins dissolving the normative in a mere world of natural non-normative facts. Precisely to overcome this peril, Brandom (2013) invokes what he calls, following Hegel, a *hermeneutics of magnanimity* – a hermeneutics based on trust for what previous interpretations have put forward as our tradition and forgiveness for what they may have missed. Such hermeneutics, against genealogy, makes of contingence not a challenge to the validity of rational norms as such but the way in which the content of those norms is progressively determined by a community: "[W]e understand the process whereby concepts acquire and develop their determinate content as putting contingencies of their application into normative shape," by "turning a past into a history"

(Brandom 2013: 15), that is, by retrospectively acknowledging in a discursive practice the way in which its norms were progressively shaped and made explicit. Accordingly, history and tradition are as much the way in which we acknowledge the past of a practice as the one in which a community determines the content of norms through time. Interpretation is the indefinite historical process of conceiving the content of social norms in terms of more and more determined and integrated wholes.

McDowell: normativity and second nature

As we have said, both Brandom and McDowell share the hermeneutical tenet that "knowledge of the non mental around us, knowledge of the minds of others and knowledge of our minds are mutually irreducible but mutually interdependent" (McDowell 2009b: 152).

Despite sharing this background assumption, McDowell insists that the connection between self, other and the world should not be understood following the central lines of an interpretational-perspectival approach.

From the very beginning of his major work, *Mind and World*, McDowell acknowledges an idea he attributes to Sellars – but that can be traced back to the origins of hermeneutics in the nineteenth century – namely, that "we must sharply distinguish natural-scientific intelligibility from the kind of intelligibility something acquires when we situate it in the logical space of reasons" (McDowell 1996: xix). Nevertheless, McDowell warns us, we must be especially careful as to the implications of such a distinction. In particular, such distinction must be made avoiding the confusion that underlies its identification with "a dichotomy between the natural and the normative" (ibid.). Such identification is precisely what he finds in Davidson's, Sellars' and Brandom's insistence on the purely causal significance of experience. The main reason that led them to such a conclusion is the urge to abandon reductive naturalism, and especially the 'Myth of the Given.'

The Given can be simply defined as (1) "what stands apart from the conceptual" (McDowell 1996: 4) while at the same time (2) that which is relevant to the justification of or warrant for our beliefs. To put it otherwise, "the Given is the idea that the space of reasons ... extends more widely than the conceptual sphere" incorporating "non-conceptual impacts from the outside of the realm of thought" (McDowell 1996: 7). Avoiding the Myth entails, for Davidson, Sellars and Brandom, rejecting this latter assumption (2 above), hence concluding that "nothing can count as a reason for holding a belief except another belief" (Davidson 2001: 141), that is, a believable or judgeable in Sellars' and Brandom's preferred labels. By the same token they assume that experience itself can only play a causal role, as an impact on the space of reasons that lacks any epistemological significance. This is why in Brandom's picture reliable dispositional responses to the environment can only count as judgments in so far as they are inferentially articulated with other judgments (in the eyes of the of the individual and/or the scorekeeper).

Against this view McDowell wants to make room for the idea that experiences are not mere sensations and can be "themselves cases of our sensory capacities at work, as opposed to being merely caused by our sensory capacities" (McDowell 2009b: 158). According to McDowell we can understand the world's impact on belief-formation as belonging already to the conceptual sphere. Experiences are "like beliefs in being actualizations of our conceptual capacities and so able to be rationally and not merely causally relevant to our thinking" (ibid.). The outcome of this thought is the idea that causal relations need not be exhaustively described as the "domain of physical fact." Significantly, this thought has hermeneutical roots and McDowell refers it back to Gadamer himself according to whom "the truth that science states is itself relative to a particular world orientation and cannot at all claim to be the whole" (Gadamer 1992: 449). If experience is actually capable of playing such a role as a warrant of beliefs, this would avail McDowell to a truth-conditions semantic avoiding the need of coherentism and inferentialism. Conversely, if experience could not be granted a rational role in the formation of beliefs, then, as Kant warned us, we would be left with empty concepts; without intuitions concepts would be spinning in a void (McDowell 1996: 11). Against Brandom, McDowell holds that experience can give a subject an entitlement to a belief by its own right, without having to conceive of this possibility as given by a further network of inferences that transform that causal relation into a conceptual one (cf. McDowell 2009d). Furthermore, experience in McDowell's account entitles one to the formation of a belief without necessarily implying that a belief will be formed on the basis of this entitlement. One can see that something is red, without forming the belief that there is something red there, for example when one falsely believes that there are abnormal lighting conditions. In Brandom's view these two steps cannot be separated, since without the formation of a belief, the state caused by the world would not amount to knowledge or any other conceptual state. Contrary to this, McDowell emphasizes that the capacity to "step back" and consider the reasons one has for holding a belief is constitutive of rationality – to which the exercise of freedom belongs – and as such has a place in understanding how experience can be a reason, an entitlement, for belief.

This brings to the fore a central difference between McDowell's philosophy and the way in which the question concerning the role of the world was approached both by Davidson and Brandom. If the world only has a causal role in the constitution of beliefs, beliefs can only be about it as the result of a device capable of turning causal relations into propositional contents. Such a device is no other than interpretation, which brings the causal into the net of propositional articulated contents.

McDowell expresses skepticism about the possibility of the existence of I–Thou sociality, the kind of minimal sociality that interpretation envisages as an account of meaning, without assuming a shared language in the background, something that pertains to a we. The different perspectives characteristic of the I–Thou relation cannot stand as perspectives in their own right until they are related and consequently understood as perspectives on the world. The central worry is then how, just by being related, they can convert from merely differential responses to the world into proper rational responses to it, as Brandom pretends they do. This kind of perspectival approach is affected – McDowell claims – by an essentially related problem that concerns the account of how the individuals' states can constitute standings in the space of reasons: individuals in the interpretational view seem to be incapable of being subject to rational constraints in their own right. The "supervising of" others in keeping score cannot hope to overcome such a problem.

Furthermore, McDowell argues that the dynamics of I–Thou scorekeeping misdescribes the kind of engagement proper to a genuine assertional practice (McDowell 2009c: 296). What is in fact available for each individual – her individual scores and the scores on others – would be compatible with an understanding of the practice in which no contentful norms were in place. Such a practice could be intelligibly interpreted in the eyes of a member of an alien community – a Martian, for example – as one in which all the linguistic moves are like moves in a game such as chess, a game only played for fun, without the kind of interest and cooperativeness proper to a game in which the moves in the game are ways of having interest in things outside the game (McDowell 2009c: 296). Such a practice seems to lack the necessary friction with the things outside the game that is proper of an assertional practice, in which the things outside the game stand as criteria of correction for what is being asserted. The question of whether interpretations understood in this way can be contentful becomes pressing.

McDowell expresses these articulated worries stating that whereas self, other and world are concepts that are irreducible and yet interdependent, the interpretational understanding of their mutual relation privileges the intersubjective as that through which objectivity is to be understood (this is mostly salient in Brandom's pursue of making explicit objectivity after having unpacked the dynamics of perspectival interpretation that belongs to the scorekeeping practice). McDowell insists that these three concepts should be kept at the same level, refraining from the temptation of explaining one in terms of the others.

In McDowell's view, individuals are able to rationally respond to the world without supervision, without there being any perspectival articulation of their responses in the light of the responses of peers. Sociality thus enters into his picture in a very different way. What makes thought social is the fact that reasons belong to language and language is itself a complex of interrelated practices, linguistic and non-linguistic, a "form of life," in Wittgenstein's words (Wittgenstein 2009: §§ 7, 19, 241). This form of life is for humans what McDowell, referring back to Aristotle's account of practical reason and practical virtues, calls a "second nature", a nature into which we need to be introduced by others: "A rational animal could not have acquired the conceptual capacities in the possession of which its rationality consists except by being initiated in a social practice" (McDowell 2009d: 287).

The concept of "second nature" suggests a different kind of naturalism than the one recommended by the methodology of natural science and is McDowell's device to account for the specific normativity of human intentionality while resisting the naturalistic fallacy: "the notion of correctness that belongs to practical reason is not to be constructed out of facts that are available to natural science" (McDowell 1998a: 184). This does not amount to denying that "the impersonal stand of science is a methodological necessity for the achievement of a valuable model of understanding reality"; but is a way of resisting the idea that this model provides "the metaphysical insight into the notion of objectivity as such, so that the objective correctness in any mode of thought must be anchored in this kind of access to the real" (McDowell 1998a: 182). Furthermore, what this model of rationality provides is a way out of the supposed dualism between reasons and causes: the notion of correctness that belongs to practical reason is not to be constructed out of facts that are available to natural science nor in terms that are external to nature (McDowell 1998a: 184). The central idea is that human rational capacities depend for their exercise on an individual's being initiated in an understanding of the articulation of reasons that comes with her upbringing and that molds her thinking in a way analogous to how being educated in the habit of acting according to virtue does:

> The practical intellect's coming to be as it ought to be is the acquisition of a second nature, involving the moulding of motivational and evaluative propensities: a process that takes place in nature. One's formed practical intellect ... just is an aspect of one's nature as it has become.
>
> (McDowell 1998a: 185)

Understanding sociality in such a way, McDowell holds that communication is possible without sharing a substantial view of the world but not, *contra* Davidson, without having "spoken as anyone else does" (Davidson 2005: 115). What is key to the idea of second nature is the need to be introduced into a world-view that is inherited from tradition. It is in learning language that we become the rational beings that we are; we learn from others, from a 'we' we progressively become part of, how reasons stand together, and thereby a full fledged conception of what is a reason for what (McDowell 1996: 155). Community – the We – is thus prior to the I–Thou form of sociality in which we can, optionally, though frequently, get involved. These capacities, in the exercise of which we are introduced by others and that are actualized in receptivity, shaping experiences themselves, "transform their possessor into an individual who can achieve standings in the space of entitlements by her own efforts" (McDowell 2009d: 287).

What is then at issue in understanding a standing in the space of reasons is an individual's orientation towards reality, and this orientation is informed by familiarity with a natural language in which verbal forms and tradition, the articulation of a world-view, are inseparable. No supervision by others is required and the first person is both autonomous and rationally oriented towards a shared world.

As we saw above, Brandom conceives of the perspectival game of giving and asking for reasons as a response to the challenge of giving an account of normativity that meets two conditions of adequacy, avoiding regularism and regulism. Brandom's answer to the puzzle is to think of norms as practical doings instituted by those who acknowledge them in practice. He rejects the I–We picture of normativity, claiming that it mystifies the nature of norms by modeling the imposition of them in the authority of a superperson. McDowell dismisses this concern, conceiving it as a consequence of the personalization of the very idea of authority to which he thinks Brandom falls victim. Alternatively, he claims that it is language itself – conceived as a world-view that has the world in view – that gives its normative shape to the world. He also rejects the very idea of interpretation, which he takes to be the main target of Wittgenstein's observations on rule following: what is to act in accordance to a rule or against it is shown in actual cases or practices, without the need of any interpretation (Wittgenstein 2009: §§201, 202 and McDowell 1998b).

This leads him to assert that our capacity to understand others is our ability to "hear someone else's meaning in his words" (McDowell 1998b: 258) as opposed to interpret or otherwise calculate their meaning. The availability of those meanings comes from being initiated in a language where a world-view is transmitted.

Between I–Thou and I–We

The dialectics between Brandom's and McDowell's accounts of the normativity of the space of reasons shows a tension between two alternative ways of thinking about sociality, the world and the self, the I–Thou versus the I–We. But do we need to choose? McDowell's privileging of the I–We perspective over the I–Thou seems ungrounded. After all, second personal exchanges play an essential role in upbringing and hence in the way we acquire our second nature. Thus, McDowell's emphasis on the enculturation of individuals might require an account of how individuals are able to engage with each other in the first place, an account that incorporates a form of understanding that is not yet linguistic but already rational, in order to make learning of the rational articulations possible. This argument extends to adult forms of exchange: answerability to each other, proper of second personal exchanges, cannot be substituted by an account of our initiation into a We, though it can be complemented certainly. Moreover, second personal exchanges play an important role in understanding communication when there are significant differences in background beliefs. This might lead us to vindicate Brandom's account of perspectival interpretation in those cases. What seems to be required is an articulation of the communal and interpersonal dimensions of our linguistic and normative practices in which instead of competing accounts, they could be integrated into a richer understanding of the forms of collective normative intentionality that are at issue.

Bibliography

Brandom, R. (1994) *Making it Explicit. Reasoning, Representing and Discursive Commitment*, Cambridge, Mass./London: Harvard UP.

——(2000) *Articulating Reasons. An Introduction to Inferentialism*, Cambridge, Mass./London: Harvard UP.

——(2010) 'Conceptual Content and Discursive Practice' in *Grazer Philosophische Studien*, 81: 13–35.

——(2013) 'Reason, Genealogy, and the Hermeneutics of Magnanimity' online. Available at http://www.pitt.edu/~brandom/downloads/RGHM%20%2012-11-21%20a.docx (accessed April 10, 2014).

Davidson, D. (2001) 'A Coherence Theory of Truth and Knowledge,' in *Subjective, Intersubjective, Objective*, Oxford: Oxford UP.

——(2005) 'The Social Aspect of Language' in *Truth, Language and History*, Oxford: Oxford UP.

Gadamer, G. (1992) *Truth and Method*, trans. Joel Weinsheimer and Donald Marshall, New York: Crossroad.

Habermas, J. (2000) 'From Kant to Hegel: On Robert Brandom's Pragmatic Philosophy of Language' *European Journal of Philosophy*, 8: 322–55.

Haugeland, J. (1998) 'Understanding Natural Language' in *Having Thought. Essays on the Metaphysics of the Mind*, Cambridge, Mass./London: Harvard UP.

Kripke, S. (1982) *Wittgenstein on Rules and Private Language*, Cambridge, Mass.: Harvard UP.

Maher, Ch. (2012) *The Pittsburgh School of Philosophy*, Routledge: New York.

Malpas, J. (2011) 'What is Common to All: Davidson on Agreement and Understanding' in *Dialogues with Davidson: Acting, Interpreting, Understanding*, Cambridge, Mass.: MIT Press.

McDowell, J. (1996) *Mind and World*, 2nd Edition, Cambridge, Mass./London: Harvard UP.

——(1998a) 'Two Sorts of Naturalism' in *Mind, Value and Reality*, Cambridge, Mass./London: Harvard UP.

——(1998b) 'Wittgenstein on Following a Rule' in *Mind, Value and Reality*, Cambridge, Mass./London: Harvard UP.

——(2009a) 'Gadamer and Davidson on Understanding and Relativism' in *The Engaged Intellect*, Cambridge, Mass./London: Harvard UP.

——(2009b) 'Subjective, Intersubjective, Objective' in *The Engaged Intellect*, Cambridge, Mass./London: Harvard UP.

——(2009c) 'Motivating Inferentialism' in *The Engaged Intellect*, Cambridge, Mass./London: Harvard UP.

——(2009d) 'Knowledge and the Internal Revisited' in *The Engaged Intellect*, Cambridge, Mass./London: Harvard UP.

Moore, G.E. (2008) *Principia Ethica*, New York: Cambridge UP.

Sellars, W. (1949) 'Language, Rules and Behavior' in S. Hook (ed.), *John Dewey: Philosopher of Science and Freedom*, New York: Dial Press.

——(1963) 'Empiricism and Philosophy of Mind' in *Science, Perception and Reality*, London: Routledge & Kegan Paul.

——(2007) 'Some Reflections on Language Games' in R. Brandom and K. Scharp (eds), *In the Space of Reasons. Selected Essays of Wilfrid Sellars*, Cambridge, Mass./London: Harvard UP.

Wittgenstein, L. (2009) *Philosophical Investigations*, ed. J. Schulte and P. Hacker, trans. G.E.M Anscombe, P. Hacker and J. Schulte, revised 4th Edition, London: Wiley/Blackwell.

Wright, C. (1980) *Wittgenstein and the Foundations of Mathematics*, Cambridge, Mass./London: Harvard UP.

Part III

HERMENEUTIC QUESTIONS

19
RATIONALITY AND METHOD

Ambrosio Velasco Gómez

Introduction

Rationality is usually taken to be a positive quality of beliefs, decisions, actions, and even institutions, practices, and ways of social life. More specifically, we say that a belief or action is rational if we can give reasons to justify it, or more simply if we can articulate that belief, decision, action or institution in terms of some kind of reasoning. What counts as a good reason or correct reasoning has been a central philosophical problem from antiquity to the present. There are philosophical views that defend the existence of universal concepts or criteria of rationality, or at least cross-cultural standards of rationality, but there are also philosophical conceptions that deny such universal criteria, arguing instead that the rationality of actions, beliefs, and so forth depends always on particular criteria and specific cultural contexts. These views are usually associated with relativism and are opposed to universalist views of rationality (see Hollis and Lukes 1986).

Yet beyond the universalist–relativist debate, there are also strong philosophical controversies concerning different kinds of rationality, mainly theoretical and practical rationality. Within these controversies, one central question is whether or not there is a substantial distinction between rationality of knowledge and rationality of decisions and practices, and whether there is a hierarchy between them; another concerns the possible difference between the rationality associated with the knowledge of formal and natural objects and that associated with the knowledge of human actions and works.

Since the central topic of this chapter is hermeneutics and rationality, and hermeneutics has traditionally been seen as concerned with social sciences and humanities, the focus here will be firstly on problems of rationality of knowledge as they arise in the social and historical realm, and only secondarily on the natural sciences. To deal with these problems, the first section presents an historical overview contrasting Aristotelian and Renaissance pluralist views of rationality with the modern conception of rationality initiated by Descartes that reduced rationality to a rigorous methodology for formal and natural sciences. This reductionist Cartesian conception soon became dominant in the natural as well as the social sciences – a form of

251

"naturalism" dominating in both. The second section is devoted to the rise of modern hermeneutics as a methodological critique of naturalism. A schematic reconstruction is presented of the methodological proposals associated with the founding authors of contemporary methodological hermeneutics, Dilthey and Weber. Their approaches constitute a methodological critique of naturalism, but not a radical critique of modern methodological rationalism. The third section addresses the work of two philosophers of science, Duhem and Neurath, who strongly criticize the modern conception of rationality based on a rigorous demonstrative method. Their critique of Cartesian rationality represents a shift towards practical rationality in the core of natural sciences. The following section analyses two hermeneutic authors who each develop an historical understanding of rationality based in the concept of tradition. Popper and Gadamer, from different but convergent perspectives, offer not only a specific conception of rationality for the social sciences and humanities, but also a hermeneutic conception of rationality that can be extended to any discipline and practical realm, including the natural and social sciences, the humanities, the arts, ethics, and politics. The fifth section is devoted to a discussion of the political implications of hermeneutical rationality based on the Habermas–Gadamer debate. The sixth and final section reformulates a hermeneutical conception of rationality in the context of cultural diversity.

1. Old and modern rationality

Aristotle distinguished between theoretical sciences that explain natural reality and constitute true universal theories (*episteme*) and knowledge about historical processes, human actions, and social institutions that are always changeable and therefore cannot be explained by universal laws and theories. According to Aristotle, the latter can only be interpreted in relation to particular circumstances and from a practical point of view – understanding of these constitutes *phronesis*.

The old distinction proposed by Aristotle between practical and prudential knowledge, on one hand, and the theoretical and universal sciences, on the other, was questioned by Descartes along with other modern philosophers. For them there is only one kind of rationality based on a rigorous demonstrative method that can construct, with certainty, true universal theories – such theories being found mainly in the realms of mathematics and physics. Since Descartes this model of methodological rationality has steadily come to dominate over other conceptions.

Thomas Hobbes is perhaps the most important advocate to extend the methodology of rationality proper to the formal and natural sciences to the political realm. During the next two centuries, this model was further extended to all sciences, including social and historical sciences. Authors as different as Karl Marx, Auguste Comte, Émile Durkheim, and John Stuart Mill all accepted and developed this model of scientific rationality – a model originally intended for mathematical physics. According to this model, it is possible, by virtue of a rigorous method, conclusively to demonstrate the truth or falsity of any theory or hypothesis. Demonstrative methodological rationality became not only the dominant conception of scientific rationality, but the only acceptable conception of rationality *tout court*.

The modern conception of rationality over-rode other alternative conceptions based on practices taken from domains such as dialectics and rhetoric – the latter having been recognized, since Aristotle, as forms of rational process for the discussion of questions and resolution of doubts in human affairs. Such non-demonstrative, but rational modes of argument are characteristic of historical, political, and ethical inquiry, and of investigation in the humanities in general. During the Renaissance, humanists like Vives, Erasmus, Rodolfo Agricola, and Alonso de la Veracruz strongly defended non-demonstrative argumentation such as can be found in rhetoric and dialectical logic (topical logic) within human disciplines against the seemingly arrogant demonstrative logic of medieval scholasticism (see Beuchot 1989). The basic point behind the defence of rhetoric and dialectical logic as relevant to practical and human affairs is that the latter are always bound to specific cultural and historical contexts and therefore cannot be discussed by reference solely to universal concepts and premises as they figure in demonstrative argument. Attempting to impose universal concepts to practical matters would be a pseudo-rational argument – a fallacy of sorts.

Yet the end-result of the Cartesian and Hobbesian epistemic revolution was the reduction of the plurality of rational methods to the single model of demonstrative rationality found in geometry and physics. According to Stephen Toulmin, seventeenth century philosophers and scientists:

> Rather than expanding the scope of rational or reasonable debate ... narrowed it ... They limited rationality to theoretical arguments that achieve quasi-geometrical certainty or necessity ... Descartes and his successors hoped eventually to bring all subjects to the ambit of some formal theory. As a result, being impressed only by formally valid demonstrations, they ended by changing the very language of Reason.
>
> (Toulmin 1992: 20)

2. The rise of hermeneutics against methodological naturalism

The hegemony of the naturalistic model in social sciences and the methodological and demonstrative conception of rationality were both questioned by Vico's *New Science* around 1725. Vico opposed the Aristotelian and Ciceronian conception of practical reason and rhetorical argumentation to the theoretical and demonstrative rationality that had become dominant, and defended the idea that true knowledge is possible only through specific historical understanding. Such understanding is always bound to time, and has nothing to do with the explanations of eternal facts or universal laws. Rather, historical understanding requires comprehension of the specific *sensus communis* (common sense) of each particular society. Later on, in the nineteenth century, German humanists and historians developed Vico's notion of historical understanding to establish the foundations of modern hermeneutics. Droysen, Humboldt, and Herder considered that history, taken as an academic discipline, does not attempt to discover general laws to explain or predict historical facts and processes, but rather searches for more specific understanding of the unique and singular meaning of historical events and human actions.

In the last decades of the nineteenth century Wilhelm Dilthey systematized the arguments of German historians so as to formulate a comprehensive hermeneutic model for the human sciences (the *Geistenwissenshaften*). He opposed this model to the natural one, since the human sciences do not seek to subsume human actions, cultural works, or historical process under general laws, and thereby to "explain" them, but rather aim at interpreting the specific and concrete meaning of human expressions. The human or cultural sciences thus require a different methodology from the sciences of nature. Objectively to understand cultural expressions, Dilthey proposed a specific hermeneutical method consisting in the reconstruction of the cultural context (the "objective spirit") together with the empathic understanding or revival (*Verstehen*) of the experience of the human author or agent.

Dilthey's hermeneutical proposal opened up an intense debate between hermeneutical and naturalistic models in social sciences. Those who defended the universality of the model of the natural sciences, holding it as valid for the social sciences also, were commonly called "monist" or "naturalist", while the advocates of the hermeneutical model for the social sciences were called "dualist". Within the social sciences, Max Weber is one of the outstanding proponents of hermeneutical dualism.

Weber's interpretative approach is strongly critical of those naturalistic and positivistic approaches in social science that are based on nomological explanation through "facts". Although Weber does not exclude the possibility of explanations based on general laws, the achievement of such explanations does not constitute the main objective of the social sciences. On the contrary, unlike naturalistic approaches – one example of which is historical materialism which seeks to explain social change in terms of general social and economic laws – Max Weber gives priority to interpreting the specific meaning of social actions in their particular context.

The defining characteristic of social life, according to Weber "is that it is a rule governed communal life, consisting of reciprocal relationships governed by external rules" (Weber 1988a: 99). The rules to which social agents attach their actions are constitutive of their specific meaning and rationality. Thus, the objective understanding of an action depends on an actor's own social and cultural context involving beliefs, values, traditions, institutions, and, of course, common social rules. In the same way, the rational evaluation of social actions depends on those internal criteria, norms, and values, and not on any external standard. This means that social scientists should restrain from introducing their own values, norms, and criteria into the evaluation of the social actions of their subjects (Weber 1988b: 70). Even more, Weber considers that social science cannot justify the superiority of one moral or ideological system over another. In general, science cannot justify, nor can it criticize, ethical or political principles and goals.

Weber's interpretative methodology is very different from the empathic understanding proposed by Dilthey. Weber's approach depends not upon any empathic or psychological revival of the actor's experience, but rather on a rigorous process of theoretical modelling and empirical testing. As the means to arrive at objective interpretations, Weber develops a specific methodology based on a theory of "ideal types" – an approach that he takes to be specific to the social sciences and to differ greatly from the explanatory and predictive methodologies of the natural sciences (see Weber 1988c: 9).

Weber is the most influential author belonging to the hermeneutic tradition within the social sciences. From his work, two different hermeneutical trends develop in the twentieth century: an analytical approach exemplified by, among others, Karl Popper and Peter Winch, and a phenomenological approach of which Alfred Schütz, Peter Berger, and Clifford Geertz are the outstanding representatives.

The rise of hermeneutics as an alternative model for the human sciences represented an important step in the critique of the modern conception of methodological rationality proposing, as it did, a very different set of methods and epistemic aims than those characteristically associated with the natural sciences. Yet in the end, as Gadamer pointed out, the major figures within the hermeneutic approach to the social sciences, like Dilthey and Weber, remained committed to some version of methodological rationality. The more radical criticism of methodological rationality came, not from within the hermeneutical approach to the social sciences, but rather, in the first decades of the twentieth century, from the very core of the philosophy of the natural sciences.

3. Philosophy of science and the critique of modern methodological rationality

In *The Aim and Structure of Physical Theory*, first published in 1906 (see Duhem 1962), Pierre Duhem argued against the sufficiency of logic and methodology for evaluating scientific theories. Duhem reformulated the concept of scientific rationality in a way that drew on notions that had traditionally been placed in the context of moral judgements (from such as Bergson, Shaftesbury) or aesthetic judgements (from Kant). Duhem's central thesis was that scientific theories are empirical, logical, *and* methodologically underdetermined – the implication being that there is no method for conclusive verification or refutation of scientific theories.

Duhem offers two main arguments to support his thesis. The first refers to the theoretical dependence of observations according to which every observation, every experiment, presupposes a prior interpretative theory. The second argument relates to the holistic nature of the empirical testing of hypotheses such that one can never empirically test a single isolated hypothesis, but only a set of interconnected hypotheses:

> In sum, the physicist can never subject an isolated hypothesis to experimental test, but only a whole group of hypotheses; when the experiment is in dis-agreement with his predictions, what he learns is that at least one of the hypotheses constituting this group is unacceptable and ought to be modified; but the experiment does not designate which one should be changed.
>
> (Duhem 1962: 187)

Yet the fact that there are not logical or methodological rules that unequivocally identify which of a set of hypotheses is mistaken, does not mean that decisions about where the error might lie are arbitrary or irrational. Instead, scientific rationality has to be understood as going beyond the scope of logic and strict methodology, necessarily entering into the realm of prudential deliberation and practical reasoning:

> No absolute principle directs this inquiry, which different physicists may conduct in very different ways without having the right to accuse one another of illogicality ... That does not mean that we cannot very properly prefer the work of one of the two to that of the other. Pure logic is not the only rule for our judgments; certain opinions which do not fall under the hammer of the principle of contradiction are in any case perfectly unreasonable. These motives which do not proceed from logic and yet direct our choices, these "reasons which reason does not know" and which speak to the ample "mind of finesse" but not to the "geometric mind", constitute what is appropriately called good sense.
>
> (Duhem 1962: 216–17)

Duhem considers that "good sense" needs to be consciously cultivated by each scientist through pluralist, tolerant, and wise dialogue with members of the particular scientific community to which the scientist belongs. By virtue of this pluralistic and reasonable dialogue, "good sense" will eventually emerge, and the scientific dispute will be settled rationally.

Some years later, in 1913, Otto Neurath, one of the founding fathers of logical positivism, published an insightful essay criticizing the idea that science is a set of definitive, true theories, justified through demonstrative methods. He called this mistaken conception of science "pseudorationalism":

> Whoever adheres to the belief that he can accomplish everything with his insight, anticipates in a way that complete knowledge of the world that Descartes puts forward as a far-off aim of scientific development. This pseudorationalism leads partly to self-deception, partly to hypocrisy ... The pseudorationalists do to true rationalism a disservice if they pretend to have adequate insight exactly where strict rationalism excludes it on purely logical grounds.
>
> (Neurath 1983: 7–8)

According to Neurath, the founding father of modern pseudorationalism was Descartes, and the most prominent pseudorationalist of the twentieth century is Karl Popper. True rationalism is conscious of the limited scope of logic and methodology, and recognizes the need for practical considerations that Neurath calls "auxiliary motives" in order rationally to choose between rival hypotheses. The reasons that spring from auxiliary motives are determined by the values, attitudes, and beliefs of the specific historical traditions in which scientists and citizens are educated:

> The auxiliary motive is well suited to bring about a kind of rapprochement between tradition and rationalism ... The application of the auxiliary motive needs a prior high degree of organization; only if the procedure is more or less common to all will the collapse of human society be prevented.

The traditional uniformity of behavior has to be replaced by conscious cooperation.

(Neurath 1983: 10)

The cooperative behaviour of scientists and citizens requires a wide and intense programme of scientific education and communication, but it also requires that different existing interests and values are voiced, discussed, and taken into account in scientific inquiry and technological development. Such consideration is necessary if science and technology are genuinely to contribute to the welfare of society. The social and political values that constitute auxiliary motives are intrinsic to the rational deliberations and decisions of scientists. So while true rationalism acknowledges the limits to the logical and methodological evaluation of scientific theories, calling for consideration of ethical, social, and political values in any such evaluation, pseudorationalism remains blind to those limits, and consequently disregards any values and considerations that are not strictly theoretical and epistemological. This pseudorationalist conception of science is not only mistaken, according to Neurath, but also tends to converge with political authoritarianism, since it excludes the public engagement with science as itself proper to scientific inquiry – instead presenting an image of science as constituting, within its own terms, the only valid source of knowledge which society must accept unquestioningly. In this sense pseudorationalism is seen as promoting a form of ideological domination on the part of science.

In summary, Duhem and Neurath strongly criticized the modern conception of rationality, showing that no method can be conclusive and demonstrative in any scientific discipline, including physics. On their account, the dominant conception of rationality was false – it was a pseudorational conception. Both acknowledged the limits of methodology and reasserted the importance of practical rationality based on pluralist disputation and reasonable dialogue. Unfortunately these new conceptions of practical rationality were not further developed within the mainstream philosophy of science of the time. Rather, the restoration of practical rationality was carried out by defenders of hermeneutics, including Popper, and also Gadamer, from very different perspectives – the first, epistemological and methodological, and the second, ontological.

4. Rationality in contemporary hermeneutics

Popper is best known as an analytic philosopher of science who defended a deductive methodological view of rationality in opposition to positivism. Yet in his works on hermeneutics he offers a historical understanding of scientific rationality that we can properly call a hermeneutical conception of rationality that is presented as common to science, the humanities, and the arts. This led Popper radically to distance himself from the positivist conceptions of the social sciences, as well as from much mainstream philosophy of science. Unfortunately his contribution to hermeneutics has rarely been explored or even acknowledged.

Contrary to the positivist conception of sciences to be found in the work of such as J. S. Mill or Otto Neurath, Popper accepts that understanding is the proper goal of the social sciences and the humanities. Moreover, contrary to hermeneutic theorists of the social and historical sciences (such as Dilthey, Weber, and Collingwood), Popper holds that understanding is not exclusive to the social sciences or to the humanities: "I am prepared to accept the thesis that understanding is the aim of the humanities. But I doubt whether we should deny that it is the aim of natural sciences also" (Popper 1972: 85). Popper is thus radically hermeneutical in his approach. He is critical of both positivists for trying to impose a natural science model on social sciences and hermeneutic humanists for assuming that positivism offers an appropriate model for the natural sciences.

Popper put forward a set of hermeneutical theses that would subsequently be developed by post-positivist philosophers of science such as Kuhn, Hesse, Shapere, Toulmin, Lakatos, Hacking, and Laudan – theorists who, often unintentionally, have promoted a hermeneutical shift in the philosophy of science. Among the hermeneutical theses at issue is the idea that the rational development of scientific knowledge is conditioned by historically inherited theories, methods, criteria, and values that together constitute rational traditions. Popper opposes the modern rationalists who have regarded tradition as an obstacle to objective knowledge. Modern philosophers ignored the historical fact that "we cannot free ourselves entirely from the bonds of tradition" and that "the so-called freeing is really only a change from one tradition to another" (Popper 1963: 122). Popper points out two essential epistemological functions played by tradition. The first is to provide knowledge developed over centuries and millennia, while the second is to promote a critical attitude to tradition. "We must stand on the shoulders of our predecessors. We must carry on a certain tradition" (Popper 1963: 129), but at the same time we must be able to free ourselves from the prejudices and taboos of tradition. Such liberation may be achieved through a reflexive engagement with tradition that leads either to the reaffirmation of traditional claims to knowledge or their rejection and replacement.

Popper proposed "situational analysis" as a method for the objective understanding of the rational development of traditions. Such analysis involves reconstructing the "problem situation" of the scientist or, in general, of any agent whose works require understanding. The problem situation is set by the "background" or "cognitive framework" within which the problem and the attempts to resolve it are located:

> This background consists, at least, of the *language* which always incorporates many theories in the very structure of its usages and of many other theoretical assumptions, unchallenged at least for the time being. It is only against a background like this that a problem can arise.
>
> (Popper 1963: 165)

Popper highlights the important role of the agent in the maintenance and transformation of traditions. Although traditions define limits for formulating and solving problems, traditions are also objects of criticism by particular persons in specific situations who promote changes and innovations (both imperceptible and revolutionary) within the same traditions that are handed down to them.

The most distinctive feature of the new conception of scientific rationality proposed by Popper is its treatment of rationality as a process of the historical transformation of traditions. A central factor in the rational progress of scientific traditions is the heuristic force of hypotheses and theories to discover new aspects of reality (*aletheia*). The tension that arises between maintaining what is given in the tradition or background and allowing for innovative change cannot be solved solely by reference to methodological procedures of refutation or corroboration. The resolution of such tension requires prudential deliberations and decisions, in a way very similar to that also invoked by Duhem.

As we have seen, this historical understanding of the rationality of traditions requires a hermeneutic method, that is, situational analysis, and in acknowledging this, Popper also acknowledges that the philosophy of science is primarily a hermeneutic discipline – anticipating the conclusion that Thomas Kuhn would reach many years later in his own work on the history of science. What is more surprising, however, is that Popper's conception of science as it stands in relation to tradition is itself convergent with Gadamer's philosophical view of the role of tradition in rational development in the arts and humanities, as well as elsewhere. It is surprising because Gadamer's ontological hermeneutics radically differs from Popper's epistemological hermeneutics. In spite of their difference, the two approaches coincide in fundamental aspects and can even be seen as complementary to one another.

In *Truth and Method*, first published in 1960, Gadamer criticized the main stream of hermeneutics within social science, mainly Dilthey's hermeneutics, for being concerned excessively with methodological problems. Instead of looking to a methodology of interpretation, Gadamer proposed a philosophical hermeneutics based on the idea of pluralistic dialogue between different cultural horizons. Drawing on Heidegger's ontological hermeneutics, Vico's conception of common sense, and Aristotle's notion of *phronesis*, Gadamer developed his own ontological hermeneutics, according to which understanding is tied to the process of the historical development of human beings, rather than to a specific form of knowledge. This historical process is precisely a tradition.

For Gadamer, tradition, though fundamentally conservative, does not exclude change and transformation. What is transmitted by tradition can be criticized, corrected, and supplanted. Conversely, "in ages of revolution, far more of the old is preserved in the supposed transformation of everything than anyone knows, and it combines with the new to create a new value" (Gadamer 2004: 282–3). Thus, in a way convergent with Popper, conservation and change are integrated within the movement of tradition itself.

Gadamer also rejects the idea that traditions are monolithic and unambiguous. In contrast, the essence of tradition is "a variety of voices in which the echo of the past is heard" (Gadamer 2004: 285). This idea of the multiplicity of the voices of tradition suggests that, far from being an object, tradition is like a partner that can be present only if the interpreter is willing to listen.

Understanding occurs as a hermeneutic "fusion of horizons": the horizon of the past that conveys the tradition and the horizon of the present, defined by prejudices of the hermeneutical situation of the interpreter: although the interpreter's prejudices determine the understanding of tradition, the dialogue into which the interpreter enters, if it is a genuine dialogue, sets those prejudices in motion in such a way that it is possible rationally to criticize them:

a hermeneutical situation is determined by the prejudices that we bring with us. They constitute, then the horizon of a particular present, for they represent that beyond which it is impossible to see ... In fact the horizon of the present is continually in the process of being formed because we are continually having to test all our prejudices. An important part of this testing occurs in encountering the past and in understanding the tradition from which we come ... *understanding* is always the fusion of those horizons supposedly existing by themselves.

(Gadamer 2004: 304–5)

Thus, like Popper, Gadamer defends the rationality of traditions and, in opposition to the Enlightenment, also defends the traditional character of all rationality.

Both Gadamer and Popper offer an historical understanding of rationality as a continuous change of traditions. Both of them recognize that traditions determine the hermeneutical situation or background knowledge that defines and limits the possibilities for change and innovation – possibilities that must be realized by creative agents who are the interpreters of tradition. In the process of interpretation and hermeneutical engagement within a tradition, there is a dialectic, an essential tension, between refutation-innovation and conservation-corroboration in relation to the prejudices or background knowledge of that tradition – a tension between creative discovery (*aletheia*) and reaffirmation of the already known (empirical adequacy). These tensions need to be solved through pluralist dialogue and prudential deliberation if they are to promote progressive change of the tradition in its entirety. The rationality of tradition ultimately consists in this progressive movement.

5. Political critique of hermeneutical rationality

Gadamer's hermeneutical conception of rational progress of tradition was deeply questioned by Jürgen Habermas in the confrontation between philosophical hermeneutics and critical theory. Habermas acknowledges the important contributions of Gadamer to the philosophy of social sciences. In particular, he holds that Gadamer's hermeneutic conception of the progressive development of tradition represents an important advance towards overcoming what he regards as the parochial and closed conception of language-games and their corresponding forms of social life associated with Wittgenstein. Habermas also accepts that Gadamer's concept of tradition provides a valuable corrective to objectivism and scientistic rationality. But Habermas also advances significant criticisms in relation to what he views as the political implications of Gadamer's philosophical hermeneutics.

Habermas argues that the conservative tendency on the part of hermeneutics to give authority to tradition means that hermeneutics cannot critically evaluate the prejudices transmitted by tradition. Prejudice is thus given an illegitimate protection: "Gadamer's prejudice in favor of the legitimacy of prejudices (or prejudgments) validated by tradition is in conflict with the power of reflection, which proves itself in its ability to reject the claim of traditions" (Habermas 1989: 170). Habermas gives greater emphasis to the critical analysis of traditions, associating rationality, not with recognition of traditional authority, but on the contrary, with the criticism and rejection of such authority. According to Habermas, hermeneutics has no effective criteria to discriminate true prejudices from false prejudices that may be hidden by distorting mechanisms:

> Now we have learned from hermeneutics that so long as we have to do with natural language we are always interested participants and cannot escape from the role of the reflective playing partner. We thus have no universal criterion at our disposal which would tell us when we are caught up in the false consciousness of pseudonormal understanding and are viewing something merely as the kind of difficulty which hermeneutics can clarify, when in fact it requires systematic explanation.
>
> (Habermas 1988: 302–3)

For Habermas, it is necessary to resort to "critical theories" such as psychoanalysis or historical materialism in order to have access to external, explanatory, causal laws that will allow the distorting mechanisms of communication to be uncovered and disarticulated (Habermas 1988: 302–3).

In response, Gadamer holds that although hermeneutical reflection does not offer any criterion of truth or rationality, it nevertheless takes into account relations of power, and can indeed promote critical reflection and emancipation. Yet Gadamer does not, in any case, consider the hermeneutic lack of a relevant criterion to be a weakness or fault. On the contrary, he affirms that any universal criterion of truth or rationality postulated beyond and above public discourse and consensus is suspect (Gadamer 1990). In this respect, one might say that Gadamer presents Habermas' claim concerning the need for critical theory to be, in the terms Neurath employs, pseudorationalist.

The dispute thus seems to take the form of a dilemma: either we affirm the need for universalistic theories that provide reliable criteria of rationality, but involve a monopoly of truth that excludes public dialogue and consensus, or we recognize the importance of consensus based on public and free communication, but lacking universal principles of rationality and truth. Gadamer chooses the second of these two options, giving priority to a set of ethical and political considerations; Habermas opts for the first, given his own Enlightenment preferences for epistemic criteria, and for a set of political commitments that are associated with these. The pressing question is whether we can overcome the dilemma rather than being forced to choose between just one or other alternative.

In an attempt to solve the dilemma, Paul Ricoeur points out that it is a mistake to oppose critique with the understanding of tradition, since critique itself belongs to a tradition, and understanding the meaning of the contents of any tradition opens up new avenues to the world that imply some critical view on the given reality. Yet recognizing the traditional nature of critique and the critical dimension to the hermeneutical understanding of tradition does not mean that the two are therefore the same. The understanding of a tradition gives priority to a recovery of the past that constitutes a historical consensus for a community; the critique of tradition, however, questions the historical consensus anticipating other possibilities for the being of the community in the future. Hermeneutics and the critique of traditions are themselves two different traditions that dialectically interpenetrate one another:

> nothing is more deceptive than the alleged antinomy between an ontology of prior understanding and an eschatology of freedom. In sketching this dialectic of the recollection of tradition and the anticipation of freedom, I do not want to abolish the difference between hermeneutics and the critique of ideology. Each has a privileged place ... on the one hand, attention to the cultural heritages ... on the other hand a theory of institutions and of phenomena of domination. The moment these two interests become radically separated, then hermeneutics and critique will themselves be no more than ... ideologies!
>
> (Ricoeur 1985: 100)

6. Hermeneutics and rationality in cultural diversity

The controversy between Habermas and Gadamer over the critical potential of hermeneutical reflection is formulated in more dramatic and radical terms in the debate between Peter Winch and Alasdair MacIntyre over the epistemic and critical relation between "scientific" and "traditional" knowledge (where "traditional" knowledge is understood as the knowledge found in so-called "primitive" societies).

Against the prevailing empiricist naturalistic view in social science, Peter Winch published, in 1962, *The idea of a social science*. In this book, drawing on Weberian comprehensive sociology and Wittgensteinian philosophy of language, Winch defends a hermeneutical approach to the social sciences. According to Winch, understanding the meaning of social actions requires relating the observational behaviour of social agents to intersubjective rules that determine the rationale of an action. Most of these rules are tacit, and agents are not normally conscious of them; nevertheless common and specific social rules constitute the main points of reference on the basis of which to understand the meaning of actions in terms of their contextual rationality. From this hermeneutic perspective, understanding an action, and evaluating its rationality, must be done from the internal point of view of the community to which the agent belongs, and not on the basis of any external criteria.

In a critical review of Winch's book, Alasdair MacIntyre acknowledged the significance of Winch's criticism to empiricist social sciences and accepted that understanding social actions from the point of view of agents is a necessary if preliminary step in social research. According to MacIntyre, the main problem is that Winch treats that preliminary step as if it were the whole work of social inquiry. Yet a further critical explanation of social action is required in order to determine whether or not the self-interpretations of agents' actions are objective and rational. Otherwise social theory would lose its critical potential on social reality. To be critical, it is necessary to introduce external causal explanations to uncover and criticize false social consciousness: "Attention to intentions, motives and reasons must precede attention to causes; description in terms of the agent's concepts and beliefs must precede description in terms of our concepts and beliefs" (MacIntyre 1967: 107).

In his article "Understanding a primitive society", Peter Winch responds to MacIntyre's criticisms, and gives particular attention to the relevance of external explanations and criticisms to the understanding of beliefs and actions. According to Winch, the adoption of such "external" explanations and criticisms is unacceptable since it entails giving to the scientist a privileged role assessing the rationality of agents' beliefs and actions, and allowing such assessment to be decided on the basis of the scientist's culture and criteria – an approach which is both ethnocentric and without justification. "If our concept of rationality is a different one from his" writes Winch, "then it makes no sense to say that anything either does or does not appear rational to him in our sense" (Winch 1964: 316).

Winch rejects MacIntyre's assumption about the epistemic and political hierarchy that places the scientist's beliefs and attitudes, including their social scientific theories, above the beliefs, attitudes, and culture of the society that is the focus of the scientist's inquiries. The beliefs and actions of members of a "primitive" society are as objective and rational as those of scientists. Criticism of the social life of a given community should be a reflexive process involving members of that community, and it is not a function proper to the social sciences. Thus, the only kind of rational criticism that social sciences can offer pertains to scientists themselves and not to the societies they study: "What we may learn about studying other cultures are not merely possibilities of different ways of doing things, other techniques. More importantly we may learn different possibilities of making sense of human life" (Winch 1964: 321).

This debate is more dramatic and radical than the Gadamer–Habermas controversy since what is at issue is not the *sensus communis* of an enlightened western society versus scientific knowledge of that same society, but the common sense of indigenous peoples (in Winch's case, indigenous Africans) versus the knowledge of that people delivered from an external scientific perspective. Winch's denial of the prioritization of scientific over community-based traditional knowledge suggests a commitment to a principle of epistemic equity applicable to every culture, modern or "primitive". Such a principle of epistemic equity is essentially multiculturalist, and may even appear relativist, since it rejects any universal criteria or standard of rationality. Yet it has some important implications for the understanding of rationality that may help to solve the dilemma that exists between ethnocentric universalism and multicultural relativism. The central point of relevance here is that epistemic equity is not the same as epistemic equivalence, but instead means something very similar to Dewey's concept of equality that consists in commitment to equality of participation in dialogue: "Equality does not mean that kind of mathematical or physical equivalence in virtue of which any one element can be substituted for another. It denotes authentic regard for what is distinct and unique in each, irrespective of physical or psychological inequalities" (Dewey 1985: 150–1). The very concept of epistemic equity demands open and pluralistic dialogue in which every participant, every culture, every tradition, has the right to be heard by all others, but it also insists that each has the obligation to learn from the others and critically to reflect on their own tradition and culture.

Epistemic equity was a central problem in the debates about the legitimacy of the conquest of the New World. Those who defended the legitimacy of the conquest, like Gines de Sepulveda, argued that the indigenous people of the New World were not rational, as were Europeans, but were instead barbarians, on the grounds that the people of the New World had different religions, languages, institutions, knowledge, and practices. Being different from Europeans meant being barbarian. The alleged rational superiority of the European over the indigenous American justified political and cultural domination. On the opposite side, humanists such as Bartolome de las Casas and Alonso de la Veracruz made hermeneutical efforts to understand American indigenous peoples in their own terms, and with regard to their particular differences, concluding that they were as rational as Europeans, and had, therefore, a self-evident right to self-government. As a consequence, these thinkers viewed Spanish conquest and domination of the Americas as unjust and perverse. In the *Relectio* of the inaugural cathedra of the Real Universidad de México in 1553, Alonso de la Veracruz claimed that:

> Inhabitants of the New world are not children nor irrational, but rather they are rational their own way and some of them are really outstanding. This is manifest since before the arrival of Spaniards they had very adequate governments and laws ... therefore they were not like children or mindless to be unable of self-government.
>
> (Veracruz 2007: 148)

In the sixteenth century defenders of the imperialist project supported a universalist conception of rationality while opponents of that project were committed to a hermeneutical and pluralist conception of rationality. Today a hermeneutical conception of rationality based on understanding different cultures and on pluralistic dialogue appears best fitted to the confrontation with the authoritarian ideologies and ethnocentric conceptions of rationality that continue to operate, often in complicity with forms of colonialism and imperialist globalization.

Conclusion

Both Habermas and MacIntyre raise the question as to just how rational are the alleged contextual rationalities that are so often the focus of hermeneutical approaches. The challenge of the demand for universal criteria of rationality – a problem that lies at the heart of much of the recent history of the philosophical discussion of rationality – is what gives rise to the problematic dilemmas that appear in the Gadamer–Habermas and Winch–MacIntyre debates. On the one hand, if we reject universal or transcultural criteria of rationality we fall into sceptic relativism, and the social sciences lose their critical function in relation to social and political reality; on the other hand, if we accept universal criteria of rationality, specifically those criteria derived from scientific knowledge, we seem given over to ethnocentrism and pseudorationalism. The solution to this dilemma is surely best located in the model of pluralistic and prudential dialogue sketched above. This model requires the recognition of the principle of epistemic equity as the means to promote intercultural conversation and fair and prudential deliberation. In sum, intercultural dialogue is the mediating path by which the dilemma between ethnocentric universalism or sceptic relativism can be overcome.

Intercultural dialogical rationality is itself hermeneutically founded – since each participant needs to understand the speech and expressions of different and distant cultures in order to be able to learn from those other cultures, as well as reflexively to assess their own familiar culture and tradition. Which elements of tradition should, in the face of criticism, be preserved and which should be abandoned is a matter of prudential deliberation – deliberation to be undertaken in a fashion similar to that which Popper and Gadamer suggest is characteristic of the progressive movement of the scientific and humanist traditions.

This dialogical and intercultural model of rationality is an expansion of the ideas of scientific rationality proposed by Duhem and Neurath. In this expanded intercultural dialogue, the natural sciences, humanities, and the arts are all relevant, but none are exclusive of the others. Moreover, according to the principle of epistemic equity, one must also give recognition to other epistemic voices – including those of cultures or communities that have been wrongly discriminated against. Such a conception of rationality is convergent with other alternative recent and contemporary proposals such as Oakshott's idea of the "conversation of mankind" (Oakshott 1962), Rorty's notion of edification (Rorty 1980), MacIntyre's view of the rationality of traditions (MacIntyre 1988), or Santos' "diatopic hermeneutics" (Santos 2010). All these ideas of rationality are intrinsically pluralist, dialogical, and hermeneutical, and all rely on practical rationality as well as rhetorical and dialectical argumentation.

Bibliography

Beuchot, M., 1989, "Estudio introductorio" in Veracruz, A. *Tratado de los tópicos dialécticos*, México, Universidad Nacional Autónoma de México

Dewey, J., 1985, *The public and its problems*, Athens, Ohio, Swallow Press.

Duhem, P., 1962, *The Aim and Structure of Physical Theory*, New York, Atheneum.

Gadamer, H. G., 1990, "Reply to my critics" in Ormiston, G. and Schrift, A. (eds) *The hermeneutic tradition. From Ast to Ricoeur*, New York, State University of New York Press.

——2004, *Truth and method*, London, Continuum.

Habermas, J. 1988 "On hermeneutics' claim to universality" in Mueller-Vollmer, K. (ed.) *The Hermeneutics Reader*, New York, Continuum.

——1989, *On the logic of social sciences*, Cambridge, MA, MIT Press.

Hollis, M. and Lukes, S. (eds), 1986, *Rationality and relativism*, Cambridge, MA, MIT Press.

MacIntyre, A., 1967, "The Idea of a Social Science", *Proceedings of the Aristotelian Society*, Supplementary Volume 41, 95–114.

——1988, *Whose justice? Which rationality?* Notre Dame, Notre Dame University Press.

Neurath, O., 1983, "The Lost wanderers of Descartes and the auxiliary motives" in his *Philosophical papers 1913–1946*, Dordrecht, The Reidel Publishing Company.

Oakshott, M. 1962, *Rationalism in politics and other essays*, New York, Basic Books.

Popper, K. R., 1963, "Toward a Rational Theory of Tradition" in *Conjectures and Refutations. The Growth of Scientific Knowledge*, London, Routledge and Kegan Paul.

——1972, "On the theory of objective mind", in his *Objective Knowledge: An evolutionary approach*, Oxford, Oxford University Press.

Ricoeur, P., 1985, "Hermeneutics and critique of ideologies" in his *Hermeneutics and the human sciences*, edited, translated and introduced by Thompson, J., New York, Cambridge University Press.

Rorty, R., 1980, *Philosophy and the Mirror of nature*, Princeton, Princeton University Press.

Santos, B., 2010, *La refundación del estado en Amércia Latina. Perspectivas desde una epistemología del Sur*, México, Universidad de lso Andes-Siglo XXI Editores.

Toulmin, S., 1992, *Cosmopolis. The Hidden Agenda of Modernity*, Chicago, University of Chicago Press.

Veracruz, de la, A., 2007, *De dominio infidelium et iusto bello*, Latin-Spanish critical edition by Heredia, R., México, Universidad Nacional Autónoma de México.

Weber, M., 1988a, "The nature of social action" in *Weber's selections in translation* edited by Runciman, W. G., New York, Cambridge University Press.

——1988b "The concept of following a rule", in *Weber's selections in translation*, edited by Runciman, W. G., New York, Cambridge University Press.

——1988c, "Value judgment in social science" in *Weber's selections in translation*, edited by Runciman, W. G., New York, Cambridge University Press.

Winch, P., 1964, "Understanding a primitive society", *American Philosophical Quarterly*, Vol. 1, No. 4 (October), 307–24.

20
BEING AND METAPHYSICS
Santiago Zabala

As the fundamental question of metaphysics, we ask: "Why are there beings at all instead of nothing?" In this fundamental question there already resonates the prior question: "How is it going with Being?" ... Being now just counts as the sound of a word for us, a used-up term. If this is all we have left, then we must at least attempt to grasp this last resonant of a possession.

(Heidegger 1935)

Just as Nietzsche was not always considered a philosopher in the strict sense of the word, neither was hermeneutics always an established philosophical position such as phenomenology, pragmatism, or critical theory. Alfred Bäumler, Ludwig Klages, and Wilhelm Dilthey regarded Nietzsche as a political, biological, or psychological thinker; similarly, hermeneutics was considered a method at the service of jurisprudence, theology, and philology in order to find a technique for ensuring a correct understanding of texts. As Jeff Malpas explains in his introduction, all this changed with Martin Heidegger's ontological investigations in the early 1920s; the German master not only elevated Nietzsche to the rank of the great philosophers of the past but also stressed the ontological nature of hermeneutics. Although Heidegger did not consider Nietzsche among the first hermeneutic philosophers, as many after him have done, his interest in both should not be interpreted separately but rather as the first step to overcoming metaphysics. If interpretation for Heidegger cannot be at the service of other disciplines, it is because it is the most fundamental form of being in the world, a form where Being is not simply analyzed or retrieved but also worked out anew beyond metaphysics.

In order to understand the relation of hermeneutics to Being and metaphysics it is necessary to venture into three phases that constitute the current ontological nature interpretation. Although these phases are not necessarily chronological, they all respond to a tradition that has not only been deconstructed but also weakened to the point where Being, as Martin Heidegger says, "just counts as the sound of a word for us, a used-up term" (2000: 77). (As we will see the task of hermeneutic ontology today is to interpret these remnants of Being, that is, everything beyond metaphysics.) The first phase consists in the destruction of Being's metaphysical tradition, the second in the reformulation of the fundamental question of metaphysics, and the third in the different answers hermeneutic philosophers have given to this question. While Heidegger is the central figure of the first two phases, the third encompasses a number of hermeneutic philosophers (in particular Hans-Georg Gadamer and Gianni Vattimo) who contributed in a substantial way not only to our understanding of the relation between Being and metaphysics but also to making hermeneutics the *koiné* of the twenty-first century, as Gianni Vattimo suggests in the conclusion. The goal of my chapter is to venture into these three phases in order to understand the ontological question of hermeneutics after metaphysics.

According to Heidegger, Western civilization, in all its relations with beings, is in every aspect sustained by metaphysics because every age, every epoch of Western thought, however different it may be from others, is established in some metaphysics, thereby placed in a definite relationship to an understanding of Being. Even though philosophy has been defined, since the mid-seventeenth century, as "ontology," the study of being as such, its essence was, is, and will always be metaphysical. The term "metaphysics" was given by an early editor of Aristotle's works who collected under the name of "metaphysics" (*meta*: after/beyond, and *physics*: nature) all the works that came after his *Physics*. Despite the fact that metaphysics includes other branches (e.g., cosmology, psychology, and so forth), for Aristotle it was meant to be the *first* philosophy, the philosophy that studied being qua being; the problem here is that by limiting itself only to the one-sided, objective, present Being of beings, metaphysics has used beings as the only cause for truth, providing an answer to the question of the Being of beings for civilization at large. But in this way it has skillfully removed from the field of investigation the problem of existence, hence, of Being. As we can see, metaphysics is the history of the different formations of Being; in other words, it represents the constitutive essence of philosophy where Being has been left aside in order to concentrate on the (physical, technological, ethical, etc.) manipulation of beings. Those problems that have in common this ontological dimension are metaphysical because they look beyond beings and toward their grounds. But why is it necessary to deconstruct metaphysics?

In one of the most important passages of *Being and Time*, Heidegger explains that the ancient interpretation of the Being of beings was oriented toward the "world" in the broadest sense and that it gained its understanding of Being from time:

> The outward evidence of this is the determination of the meaning of Being as "*parousia*" or "*ousia*," which ontologically and temporally means "presence," "*Anwesenheit*." Beings are grasped in their Being as "presence"; that is to say, they are understood with regard to a definite mode of time, the *present*.
>
> (Heidegger 1996: 22–3)

The problem with this determination of Being is that Being was determined by time exclusively as presence, in other words, ignoring the ontological difference. But when the distinction of essence and existence arises it is always the first that prevails, the priority of essence over existence leads to an emphasis on beings, on essence as what factually exists here and now. In this way the original meaning of existence as *physis*, originating or arising, is lost, and Being is set up as the permanent nominal presence. Through this interpretation, metaphysics also becomes the history of the oblivion of

Being, that is, of what remains of Being. If the destruction of these layers that cover up the original nature of Being, the layers that metaphysical thinking has constructed, has been undertaken in terms of the history of Being, it is because what is present in its presence became the completion of the extreme possibilities of the oblivion of Being.

As we can see, philosophy must destroy all that covers up the sense of Being, the unproven concepts, the functional context, the structures piled on top of one another that make the sense of Being unrecognizable in order to reveal hitherto unnoticed possibilities. These structures can be found in the passages in which the question of existence, of the "Being in beings," is touched on or is unconsciously implicit. Heidegger wants to deconstruct these metaphysical categories in order to recognize their negative and positive features, compelling them back to their forgotten inception. It is from this inception that we learn how they dominate, through their grammatical third-person-singular, the configuration of Being. Heidegger, in his course from 1927 gave a very clear indication of the goal of deconstruction in relation to the problem of construction:

> Construction in philosophy is necessarily destruction, that is to say, a deconstructing of traditional concepts carried out in a historical recursion to the tradition. And this is not a negation of the tradition or a condemnation of it as worthless; quite the reverse, it signifies precisely a positive appropriation of tradition. Because destruction belongs to construction, philosophical cognition is essentially at the same time, in a certain sense, historical cognition.
>
> (Heidegger 1982b: 23)

As we can see, Heidegger undertook this deconstruction of the history of Being in order to destroy the sediment that covers up the original nature of Being, the layers that metaphysical thinking has constructed. This is why the "question of Being attains true concreteness only when we carry out the destructuring of the ontological tradition" (Heidegger 1996: 23). If "destructuring of the history of ontology essentially belongs to the formulation of the question of Being and is possible solely within such a formulation" (Heidegger 1996: 20), it is because the goal is to achieve clarity not only regarding the concept of Being but also regarding the question, hence, "to reach the point where we can come to terms with it in a controlled fashion" (Heidegger 1993: 23). But in order to reformulate the fundamental question of metaphysics it is important to remember that "it is constitutive of the being of Dasein to have, in its very Being, a relation of being to this Being" and how this "relation" must be a "hermeneutical relation" with "respect to bringing tidings, with respect to preserving a message" (Heidegger 1982a: 32). Although this message obviously is the Being of beings, which is what calls humanity to its essential Being, why did Heidegger emphasize that this relation had to be hermeneutical? It must also preserve a message, that is, appropriate Being after metaphysics has been deconstructed. But in what condition is Being after such destruction?

> For we lay claim to being everywhere, wherever and whenever we experience beings, deal with them and interrogate them, or merely leave them alone. We need being because we need it in all relations to beings. In this

constant and multiple use, Being is in a certain way expended. And yet we cannot say that Being is used up in this expenditure. Being remains constantly available to us. Would we wish to maintain, however, that this use of being, which we constantly rely upon, leaves Being so untouched? Is not Being at least consumed in use? Does not the indifference of the "is," which occurs in all saying, attest to the wornness of what we thus name? Being is certainly not grasped, but it is nevertheless worn-out and thus also "empty" and "common." Being is the most worn-out. Being stands everywhere and at each moment in our understanding as what is most self-understood. It is thus the most worn-out coin with which we constantly pay for every relation to beings, without which payment no relation to beings as beings would be allotted us.

(Heidegger 1993: 51–2)

Heidegger's weak determination of Being expresses both the objective and subjective genitive of Being because there is nothing to Being as such; Being is "worn-out" and "needs man for its revelation, preservation and formation" (Heidegger 2003a: 37). Given that "worn" is the participle of "wear," meaning "spent," affected," or "exhausted" by long use, "worn-out" becomes something that is being used to threadbareness, valuelessness, or uselessness. As we can see, the end of the destruction of metaphysics blends with the end of the search for Being because philosophy, after having retrieved the question of Being, recognizes how we are left only with the many different interpretations, descriptions, and remains of Being framed within metaphysics. Even though Dasein must be the "guardianship" of Being at all times, Heidegger emphasizes that Being is never "used up in this expenditure," giving Being priority over Dasein. This is also why in his response to Jean-Paul Sartre he stressed that "we are precisely in a situation where principally there is Being" (Heidegger 1998: 293, 251).

As we can see Heidegger's destruction of metaphysics did not leave it "worn-out to the point of complete exhaustion and disparagement" (Heidegger 1993: 52) but rather served to disclose its remnants. This is particularly significant because the twofold excluding option between Being and Nothingness in the fundamental question of metaphysics ("why are there beings at all instead of nothing?") ends by favoring Being since it is Being that first "lets every Being as such originate. Being first lets every Being be, that means to spring loose and away, to be a Being, and as such to be itself" (Heidegger 1993: 52). Philosophy, and now also hermeneutics, does not seek which side is correct but rather the condition, amount, or state of Being. In sum, in order to think Being independently of metaphysics, without beings, in its actual worn-out state, it is necessary to modify the fundamental metaphysical question in such a way to question Being after its destruction in terms of remnants. As surprising as this might seem, Heidegger elaborated this new question in *Introduction to Metaphysics*:

As the fundamental question of metaphysics, we ask: "Why are there beings at all instead of nothing?" In this fundamental question there already resonates the prior question: how is it going with Being? What do we mean by the words "to be," Being? In our attempt to answer, we run into difficulties.

We grasp at the un-graspable. Yet we are increasingly engaged by beings, related to beings, and we know about ourselves "as beings." Being now just counts as the sound of a word for us, a used-up term. If this is all we have left, then we must at least attempt to grasp this last remnant of a possession. This is why we asked: how is it going with the word Being?

(Heidegger 2000: 77)

If Heidegger has raised the prior question ("how is it going with Being?") out from the fundamental question of metaphysics ("Why are there beings at all instead of nothing?"), it is because Being is not a present-at-hand fact but "the fundamental happening, the only ground upon which historical Dasein is granted in the midst of beings that are opened up as a whole" (Heidegger 2000: 216). If this were not the case, then Being could be opposed to Nothing within the traditional metaphysical question, ignoring the history of Being. However, as we've seen above, Being cannot be opposed to something. Although it appears as an empty word with an evanescent meaning, it still proves to be the most worthy of questioning because it "is the most worn-out and at the same time the origin" (Heidegger 1993: 52). As an origin, Being is the power that still today sustains and dominates all our relations to beings, and it must be experienced anew in the full breadth of its possible essence if we want to set our historical Dasein to work; after all, the "essence of Being is intimately linked to the question of who the human being is" (Heidegger 2000: 219).

Before venturing into the different answers hermeneutic philosophers have given to this question it is important to emphasize how after its destruction we have to settle down within the language of metaphysics because it is something we cannot overcome in the sense of "*überwunden*," defeating and leaving it behind, but only in the sense of "*verwindung*," recovering, twisting, or incorporating. This is why Heidegger emphasized how "overcoming is worthy only when we think about incorporation" (Heidegger 2000: 91). Thus, to overcome metaphysics means to incorporate it, to appropriate it, but if metaphysics and its question become something we cannot eliminate by answering the question, then philosophy finally becomes an "appropriation," an appropriation of what remains from the destruction of the history of Being. This is why for Heidegger hermeneutics is not meant to take:

cognizance of something and having knowledge about it, but rather an existential knowing, i.e., a Being [*ein Sein*]. It speaks from out of interpretation and for the sake of it. ... As far as I am concerned, if this personal comment is permitted, I think that hermeneutics is not philosophy at all, but in fact something preliminary which runs in advance of it and has its own reasons for being: what is at issue in it, what it all comes to, is not to become finished with it as quickly as possible, but rather to hold out in it as long as possible. ... It wishes only to place an object which has fallen into forgetfulness before today's philosophers for their "well-disposed consideration."

(Heidegger 1999: 14–16)

If a regard for metaphysics still prevails even in the intention to overcome metaphysics, then hermeneutics is the correct candidate to "cease all overcoming, and leave metaphysics to itself" (Heidegger 2002: 24). In this way philosophy becomes a "happening that must at all times work out Being for itself anew" (Heidegger 2000: 90). Working out Being anew is the essential obligatory task of Dasein because if there were no indeterminate meaning of Being, or if we did not understand what this meaning signified, there would be no language at all. Dasein is distinguished by the fact that in its very Being, Being is an issue for it, and mostly because through its comprehension it becomes the manifestation of Being. It is always a matter of naming Being, which is not a thing but a verb. In other words, if "our essence would not stand within the power of language, then all beings would remain closed off to us – the beings that we ourselves are, no less than the beings that we are not" (Heidegger 2000: 86). The fact that Being by now just counts as "a used-up," "worn-out" term for us, that "this is all we have left," and that we must at least attempt to grasp this "last remnant of a possession," signifies that Being remains philosophy's main concern, especially after being destroyed, because it becomes unpresentable, indeterminable, and ungraspable. Heidegger's destruction did not destroy but set us free into the remains of Being.

There are a number of philosophers who have not only "work[ed] out Being for itself anew," (Heidegger 2000: 97) as Heidegger requested after his destruction of metaphysics, but also proposed weak conceptions. Although not all of them declare themselves hermeneutic philosophers, they all share the need to apply the new fundamental question – how is it going with Being? – in order to understand the way that Being occurs today. These worn-out interpretations of Being will indicate how metaphysics cannot be ignored or overcome but only twisted or surpassed. I will outline Gadamer's and Vattimo's remnants of Being in order to emphasize why Being's worn-out condition suggests a point of departure for hermeneutics rather than its point of arrival.

Gadamer, by following Heidegger, who "modified the overcoming (Überwindung) of metaphysics and replaced it with a coming to terms with (Verwindung) metaphysics" (Gadamer 1997a: 191), was able to emphasize how philosophy can never totally and completely cut loose from its historical heritage. This is why Gadamer believes "that there can never be 'philosophy' without metaphysics. And yet philosophy is perhaps only philosophy when it leaves metaphysical thinking and sentence logic behind it!" (Gadamer 2007: 382). Heidegger's destruction was not meant to point back to a mysterious origin, an arché, or to repudiate this history but to "recover" from metaphysics in order to set thought free because the goal of the destruction, according to Gadamer, was only "to let the concept speak again in its interwovenness in living language" and had "nothing to do with obscure talk of origins and of the original" (Gadamer 1989b: 100). This is why there is "no ultimate language of metaphysics" because language is not only "the house of Being," as Heidegger emphasized, but also "the house of the human being, a house where one lives, which one furnishes, and where one encounters oneself, or oneself in others" (Gadamer 1989c: 166–73). If for Gadamer Being is on the way to language it is because language's nature is conversational, and only through conversation can Being be understood since it comes into language in conversation, and not the other way around.

In order to understand Gadamer's remnant of Being it is important to clarify the difference between the English terms "dialogue" and "conversation." Even though, literally, the German words "*Gespräch*" should be translated as "discussion," "*Dialog*" as "dialogue," and "*Unterhaltung*" as "conversation," most translators of Gadamer's works have rightly translated "*Gespräch*" always as "conversation," because of a philosophical demand implicit in the meaning of "*Gespräch*." When Gadamer refers to the "*Gespräch*," he is not alluding to something programmed in advance under the direction of a subject matter where the interlocutors leave aside their particular points of view. Quite the contrary, a genuine "*Gespräch*" is never the one we wanted to conduct but the one we fall into and become involved in as it develops because we are led by it instead of being the leaders of it. As we can see, Gadamer's "*Gespräch*" is closer to what in English we call "conversation," not "dialogue," which is more a specialized kind of conversation dedicated to finding the truth about something, as in the Platonic dialogues. Despite the fact that conversations are always directed toward specific agreements, it is important to note that the German thinker is referring to an "agreement" not about content but rather about the maintenance of a common language of an endless conversation. This is why philosophizing "does not just start from zero but rather has to think further and speak further the language we speak" (Gadamer 1997b: 30). The point is not that everything is language but only that Being that can be understood, insofar as it can be understood, is language because what cannot be understood poses an endless task of finding the right word.

As we can see, Gadamer, following Heidegger's destruction of the nature of metaphysics, whose question about the "whatness of beings" has obscured the question of the "thereness of Being," goes further to consider the notion of conversation as the most adequate mode of Being on the way to language because it leaves behind the metaphysical subjectivity of the transcendental ego and especially the meaning-directed intention of the speaker. In sum, if the "conversation" is all we have left, then we can conclude from Gadamer's analysis that conversation, Being's remnant, defines itself precisely "in what aims at being said beyond all words sought after or found" because "in a conversation, it is *something*, that comes to language, not one or the other speaker" (Gadamer 1989b: 118, 122).

Vattimo has further radicalized the weak condition of Being after its destruction. According to the Italian philosopher, if we have not been able to answer the fundamental question of philosophy it's not "because of its force … but because of its weakness" (Vattimo 1988: 86). This is why "if Being had a strong reason to be, then metaphysics would have significance, would have strength. But as things are, Being … is historical and casual, happened and happening" (Vattimo 2002: 463). For these reasons Vattimo believes that philosophy is weak thought, an ontology of weakness where philosophical effort ought to focus on interpretation as a process of weakening the objective weight of the presence of Being rather than its destruction. Vattimo believes the new epoch of Being, after the destruction of metaphysics, will not depend on our decisions but rather on recognizing how we belong to this same destruction, that is, to "a philosophy of 'decline,' a philosophy which sees what is constitutive of Being not as the fact of its prevailing, but of the fact of its disappearing" (Vattimo 1993: 5).

Vattimo's starting point is the term "*Ereignis*" (event), used by Heidegger in *Contributions to Philosophy* to mark the new ontological approach that excludes all essentialist views of Being. Vattimo believes that "what is ahead of philosophy as its goal, after deconstructionism, is a labor of stitching things back together, of reassembly" (Vattimo 1997a: x). In this condition, Being becomes an event because philosophy no longer corresponds to the Platonic agenda of understanding Being through the Eternal but rather seeks to do so through its own history; that is, it redirects itself toward history. However, this is only possible if Being and event are fused together so that Being derives not from Being "as it is" but from Being viewed as the product of a history of formulations, deconstructions, and interpretations that "are 'givens' of destiny understood as a process of transmission. They are points of reference we keep encountering each time we engage in thinking here and now" (Vattimo 1984: 151). If Being for Vattimo consists in a transmission, in the forwarding and destiny ("*Ueber-lieferung*" and "*Ge-schick*") of a series of echoes, linguistic resonances, and messages coming from the past and from others in the form of events, why is hermeneutics the philosophical position that responds to this process?

Vattimo believes that hermeneutics presents itself as the most appropriate form to the "thinking that corresponds to Being as *event*" because it is a philosophical position that grasps Being's vocation of giving itself as the truth of human language (Vattimo 1993: 149). This is why the "eventual" nature of Being is nothing but "the disclosure of historico-linguistic horizons within which beings (things, men, etc.) come into presence" (Vattimo 1982: 88). In this manner Being never really *is* but sends itself, is on the way, transmits itself through language. Having said this, one might think with Gadamer that language is something bigger than or prior to Being, but, on the contrary, it is an event of Being itself, an "eventuality" that indicates how everything we see as a structure, essence, or theorem is an event, a historical aperture or disclosure of Being. In this way, Being presupposes this disclosure, which is not an object of philosophical research but rather that into which it is always-already thrown. As we can see, Being is not what endures, what is and cannot not be – as Parmenides, Plato, and Aristotle would have it – but only what becomes because it "becomes" from the ontological difference. What becomes comes to life and dies and for that reason has a history, a permanence of its own in its concatenated multiplicity of meanings and interpretations.

Even though Gadamer and Vattimo recognize that hermeneutics originally was a theory that legitimized its interpretations by demonstrating it could reconstruct the history of a certain number of events, as we have seen, they are more interested in indicating how it can also be an interpretation from within, that is, from what it always-already belongs to "since this belonging is the very condition for the possibility of receiving messages" (Vattimo 1997b: 105). However, as we have seen, this belonging is nothing else than the remains of Being, or in Gadamer's and Vattimo's words, the conversation and events of Being.

While there are a number of other philosophers who have responded to Heidegger's request to "work out Being for itself anew" in order "grasp its last remnant of a possession" through the "new fundamental question of philosophy" (Zabala 2009). Gadamer and Vattimo have given hermeneutics the necessary tools for future generations to take on this task. But this task will prevent philosophy from falling back into metaphysics and will also grant it access to history, that is, allow it to become futural, as Heidegger once said: "The possibility of access to history is grounded in the possibility according to which any specific present understands how to be futural. This is the first principle of all hermeneutics. It says something about the Being of Dasein, which is historicity itself" (Heidegger 1992: 20). As we can see, hermeneutic philosophy becomes the key for the future because interpretation is, in itself, a response to a message, an articulated response to the remains of Being, which are never a static essence but rather an event always in motion.

Bibliography

Bernstein, Richard. 1983. *Beyond Objectivism and Relativism: Science, Hermeneutics, and Praxis.* Philadelphia: University of Pennsylvania Press.

Derrida, Jacques. 1989a. "Biodegradables: Seven Diary Fragments." Trans. Peggy Kamuf, *Critical Inquiry* 15: 812–73.

——1989b. "Three Questions to Hans-Georg Gadamer." In *Dialogue and Deconstruction: The Gadamer–Derrida Encounter.* Eds. Diane Michelfelder and Richard Palmer. Albany: SUNY Press. 52–54.

——2005. *Rogues: Two Essays on Reason.* Trans. Michael Naas and Pascale-Anne Brault. Stanford: Stanford University Press.

Gadamer, Hans-Georg. 1976. *Philosophical Hermeneutics.* Trans. and Ed. David E. Linge. Berkeley and London: University of California Press.

——1989a. *Truth and Method.* Rev. Ed. Joel Weinsheimer and Donald Marshall. New York and London: Continuum.

——1989b. *Dialogue and Deconstruction: The Gadamer–Derrida Encounter.* Ed. D. P. Michelfelder and R. E. Palmer. Albany: State University of New York Press.

——1989c. *Das Erbe Europas.* Frankfurt: Suhrkamp.

——1997a. "Reply to Jean Grondin." In *The Philosophy of Hans-Georg Gadamer.* Ed. L. E. Hahn. Chicago: Open Court Press. 171–2.

——1997b. "Reflections on My Philosophical Journey." In *The Philosophy of Hans-Georg Gadamer.* Ed. L. E. Hahn. Chicago: Open Court Press. 3–63.

——2007. *The Gadamer Reader: A Bouquet of the Later Writings.* Ed. J. Grondin. Trans. R. E. Palmer. Evanston, Ill.: Northwestern University Press.

Heidegger, Martin. 1982a. *On the Way to Language.* Trans. Peter D. Hertz. New York: Harper & Row.

——1982b. *The Basic Problems of Phenomenology* Trans. A. Hofstadter. Bloomington: Indiana University Press.

——1988. *Hegel's Phenomenology of Spirit.* Trans. Parvis Emad and Kenneth Maly. Bloomington and Indianapolis: Indiana University Press.

——1992. *The Concept of Time.* Trans. W. McNeill. London: Wiley-Blackwell.

——1993. *Basic Concepts.* Trans. G. E. Aylesworth. Bloomington: Indiana University Press.

——1996. *Being and Time.* Trans. Joan Stambaugh. New York: State University of New York Press.

——1998. "Letter on 'Humanism'." In *Pathmarks.* Ed. W. McNeill. Cambridge: Cambridge University Press. 239–76.

——1999. *Ontology: The Hermeneutics of Facticity.* Trans. John van Buren. Bloomington: Indiana University Press.

——2000. *Introduction to Metaphysics.* Trans. G. Fried and R. Polt. New Haven, Conn.: Yale University Press.

——2002. "Time and Being." In Heidegger, *The End of Philosophy: On Time and Being.* Trans. J. Stambaugh. Chicago: University of Chicago Press. 1–24.

——2003a. "Only a God Can Save Us." In Heidegger, *Philosophical and Political Writings*. Ed. M. Stassen. New York: Continuum. 24–48.

——2003b. "Overcoming Metaphysics." In Heidegger, *The End of Philosophy: On Time and Being*. Trans. J. Stambaugh. Chicago: University of Chicago Press. 84–110.

Vattimo, Gianni. 1982. "Difference and Interference: On the Reduction of Hermeneutics to Anthropology," *Res 4*: 85–91.

——1984. "Dialectics, Difference, and Weak Thought." Trans. T. Harrison, *Graduate Faculty Philosophy Journal 10*: 151–63.

——1988. *The End of Modernity: Nihilism and Hermeneutics in Postmodern Culture*. Trans. J. R. Snyder. Baltimore, Md.: Johns Hopkins University Press.

——1993. *The Adventure of Difference: Philosophy After Nietzsche and Heidegger*. Trans. C. P. Blamires and T. Harrison. Cambridge: Polity Press.

——1997a. "Foreword" to F. D'Agostini, *Analitici e continentali. Guida alla filosofia degli ultimi trent'anni*. Milan: Cortina: xi–xv.

——1997b. *Beyond Interpretation: The meaning of hermeneutics for philosophy*. Trans. D. Webb. Cambridge: Polity Press.

——2002. "Weak Thought and the Reduction of Violence: A Dialogue with Gianni Vattimo by S. Zabala." Trans. Y. Mascetti, *Common Knowledge 3*: 425–63.

Vattimo, Gianni and Santiago Zabala. 2011. *Hermeneutic Communism: From Heidegger to Marx*. New York: Columbia University Press.

Zabala, Santiago. 2009. *The Remains of Being: Hermeneutic Ontology after Metaphysics*. New York: Columbia University Press.

——2017. *Striving for Existence: The Anarchy of Hermeneutics* (forthcoming).

Further reading

Polt, Richard. 2006. *The Emergency of Being*. Ithaca, N.Y.: Cornell University Press.

Romano, Claude, 2009. *Event and World*. Trans. Shane Mackinlay. New York: Fordham University Press.

Rorty, Richard. 2004. "Being That Can Be Understood is Language." In *Gadamer's Repercussion: Reconsidering Philosophical Hermeneutics*. Ed. B. Krajewski. Berkeley: University of California Press. 21–9.

Schürmann, Reiner. 1990. *Heidegger on Being and Acting: From Principles to Anarchy*. Bloomington and Indianapolis: Indiana University Press.

Vattimo, Gianni. 1997. *Beyond Interpretation: The Meaning of Hermeneutics for Philosophy*. Trans. D. Webb. Cambridge: Polity Press.

——2013. *Della Realtà*. Milan: Garzanti.

——2014. "Insuperable Contradictions and Events." In *Being Shaken: Ontology and the Event*. Eds. Michael Marder and Santiago Zabala. London: Palgrave Macmillan. 70–6.

Zabala, Santiago. 2007. "Pharmakon's of Onto-theology." In Weakening Philosophy. Essays in Honour of Gianni Vattimo. Ed. S. Zabala. McGill-Queen's University Press. 231–49.

——2009. "Weakening Ontology through Actuality: Foucault and Vattimo." In *Foucault's Legacy*. Ed. Carlos Prado. London: Continuum. 109–23.

——2010. "*Being is Conversation. Remains, Weak Thought, and Hermeneutics*." In *Consequences of Hermeneutics*. Eds. Jeff Malpas and Santiago Zabala. Evanston, Ill.: Northwestern University Press: 161–76.

——2011. "Truth Absence: The Hermeneutic Resistance to Phenomenology." In *Phenomenological Variations on Truths: The Hermeneutic Challenge*. Eds. Kevin Hermberg and Pol Vandevelde. New York and London: Continuum. 201–8.

21
LANGUAGE AND MEANING

Daniel Dahlstrom

As soon as we consider and, in effect, interpret the practice of interpretation, we engage in hermeneutics. Traditionally, this engagement takes its bearings from interpretations of the meanings of the written word. Even when hermeneutics casts a wider net (embracing phenomena that are not prima facie linguistic, e.g., paintings, sculpture, architecture, music, customs, haptic behaviors, working with tools, and so on), it generally expresses their meanings in words. The following chapter presents a sketch of modern hermeneutic approaches to language and meaning, with a view to suggesting reasons for adopting such an approach. The sketch is based upon the work of central German originators of modern hermeneutics, from Schleiermacher and Dilthey to Heidegger and Gadamer. As a means of giving the sketch definition, comparisons and contrasts are made occasionally with contemporary Anglo-American considerations of meaning.

The hermeneutical quadrangle

Whatever else language is, however else it may be defined, it is composed of sounds, images, and/or movements that serve as markers for the sake of communication. Communication takes place when we understand what someone is saying in the course of employing those markers. The expression 'what someone is saying' – like some onomatopoetic expressions such as 'Ugh!' or 'Arrgh!' – may also refer to the sounds themselves. However, 'meaning' in modern hermeneutics stands for this or that significance of the linguistic expressions in use. In other words, meaning is what sounds, images, and/or gestures say insofar as someone uses them to signify something else. As such, meaning can, but need not, coincide with why someone makes those sounds, images, or movements. So, too, the meaning communicated can, but need not, coincide with what someone intended to communicate. This last observation does not entail that the meaning of what is said is unsayable, whether in other words or in any words at all, that is, that it is ineffable.

Language and meaning have a bilateral character given their grounding in the bilateral character of communication – and vice versa. Communication "takes two," that is, someone speaking and someone to whom what is said says something. But communication also requires that something be communicated (meaning) and the means of communicating it (linguistic markers). These four factors – a speaker, a speech that says something, and someone listening (an audience) to whom it says something – make up, as it were, the four points, the four essential angles of a hermeneutical quadrangle. An author, the author's text, the text's meaning, and its readers also constitute such a quadrangle. The import of this hermeneutical quadrangle might be expressed more formally as follows. There is language if and only if there is meaning (i.e., if and only if linguistic markers – or what are taken to be linguistic markers – say something), but there is meaning in this linguistic sense if and only if it is communicated (i.e., what is expressed is understood). On this account, language, meaning (in the sense indicated), and communication are hardly identical, yet they are equivalent; in other words, you cannot have one without the other.

The hermeneutical predicament and "the hermeneutical situation"

The two parties to the hermeneutical quadrangle face a predicament when communication initially fails, that is, the meaning of what is said or written is not understood. In this predicament, speakers and writers must recalibrate their words if the situation permits; for example, if a dialogue is possible. As for listeners and readers, their only recourse is interpretation. There is, of course, a "pedestrian" use of linguistic expressions where interpretation is kept to a manageable minimum. Used in this way, those expressions have all the communicative (if anonymous) sophistication and efficiency of traffic signals. Consider, for example, a driver's effective use of a turn signal, with the supposition, backed by law, of other drivers' understanding of its significance. In similar fashion, the parties to the hermeneutic quadrangle in routine, everyday forms of communicating take for granted both the meanings of the linguistic markers and the common capacities of interlocutors to understand them. And they do so more or less successfully, since the measure of success is itself pedestrian.

Yet, even when the means of communicating are as commonplace and uniform as traffic signals, effective communication requires a capacity to put ourselves in others' shoes. This hermeneutic consciousness, as we might put it, resembles the sort of triangulation that Davidson deemed necessary for language (Davidson 2001, p.213). Language will not be a way of communicating, that is, it will not be language, unless I have some reason to believe that its markers mean for others at least a semblance of what they mean for me. Thus, speakers and writers gauge how listeners and readers are likely to take up one expression or the other. And yet that capacity to put ourselves in others' shoes, to gauge what someone has said or how someone will take up what we say, is limited and fallible. Indeed, sometimes we find ourselves at a loss of what to say, not because we do not understand others, but because we do not understand ourselves – a phenomenon that reveals just "how indispensable it is that we recognize that we live in conversation" (Gadamer 2007 [1968], p.371). Accordingly, even in pedestrian uses of language, communication has an inherent fragility; what counts as success or lack of success in communicating is highly variable.

The fragility of communication, thanks to our limited ability to appreciate how others will receive our words, is only one factor contributing to the hermeneutical predicament. The predicament can also arise from the non-equivalence of words and meaning (what they say) generally. Thus, the same words can mean different things in the same context, while different words can mean the same thing in different contexts. Further complicating matters is the fact that words with different meanings – for example, 'Morning Star' and 'Evening Star' – may refer to the same thing. So, too, the fact that the meanings of words change over time or differ across contexts, not allowing us to assume that their present meanings hold in the text before us, presents an ongoing challenge to understanding the text.

Still other factors contributing to the hermeneutic predicament are rooted in particularities of the parties involved or the context itself. A listener, especially one new to a language, may have difficulty coping with a speaker's heavy accent or dialect; a reader may not know a word used by the author or what it means in the context at hand; an author may use a word in a dissembling or cryptic manner or in a way that is unfamiliar to the point of being barely intelligible. Uses of irony, enthymemes, and various tropes further complicate matters. So, too, we may be suspicious that what is said is tendentious or misleading, given what we know about the speaker or writer.

The contextual and holistic character of the linguistic markers and meanings communicated can also lead to the hermeneutic predicament. What words mean cannot be read off them in the way that we "read off" the color of an object in normal light. Instead, the meaning of any linguistic unit (word, clause, sentence, paragraph, etc.) depends upon its placement and its relation to other such units and, ultimately, to the meaning of their unity as a whole. This time-honored hermeneutical principle has its counterpart in Frege's so-called "context-principle," that is, the notion that words have meaning by virtue of the meaning of sentences in which they occur (Frege 1980 [1884]). At the same time, that unity as a whole depends upon the meanings of its parts, that is, the same linguistic units that it encompasses. This staple of traditional hermeneutics, too, has a counterpart in the contemporary principle of compositionality, the notion that the meaning of a sentence depends upon the meaning of its immediate parts and how they are combined (Szabo 2000, p.3; Werning, Hinzen, and Machery 2012, p.82).

Typically, this mereological character demands that, at first reading, we have to anticipate – to guess, to offer an advance *interpretation* of – what the respective wholes mean, revised as needed as we move from part to part, from parts to the whole, and from whole back to the parts again. Re-reading and re-interpreting are musts, given this mereological character. Moreover, since what counts as a whole depends upon a context that is in one sense already formed but in another sense still unfolding, the meaning of each whole is, so to speak, a moving target, constantly presenting readers with new versions of the hermeneutical predicament. Dilthey who, like Heidegger after him, has his eyes on a hermeneutics of life's experiences itself, ties the category of meaning to the mereological structure of life:

> The category of meaning designates the relationship of parts of life to the
> whole as rooted in the nature of life … It is a relationship that is never

completely consummated ... We recognize this meaning, as we do that of words in a sentence, by virtue of memories and future possibilities.
(Dilthey 2002 [1904–9], p.253; see also Dilthey 1979 [1900], p.262)

Perhaps the most common source of the hermeneutical predicament is to be found in forms of discourse that in crucial respects preclude reliance upon ordinary ways of understanding what someone says or writes. Among the most patent forms of such discourse are the non-pedestrian languages of science, literature, law, religion, art, history, and philosophy. It is no accident that the oldest forms of hermeneutics are to be found in biblical and juridical contexts.

Because these non-pedestrian languages have histories of their own that intersect with the histories of vernaculars, they can yield a problem for understanding (a hermeneutical predicament) in two complex ways. On the one hand, as pedestrian uses of words give way to non-pedestrian uses and, indeed, to neologisms, we obviously cannot rely upon the cues of everyday discourse. We need some other way of understanding the meanings of such highly formalized or specially constructed languages. On the other hand, for a variety of reasons, neither the turnover from the pedestrian uses nor the historical development of these specialized languages is ever complete. One reason for this incompleteness is the fact that scientists are not born but educated to be scientists, an education that relies upon the scientist's pedestrian language – a process repeated with each subsequent generation. The specialist's understanding of her respective language never ceases to trade, moreover, on ordinary discourse of one sort of another, thereby blurring to some degree the lines between pedestrian and non-pedestrian languages. Ordinary language itself has a seemingly boundless capacity to incorporate terms originally drafted in the formal contexts of science and technology, art and religion. At the same time, while meanings of what is said in a non-pedestrian language are always more or less stipulated within a tradition-laden context, neither those stipulations nor that context exhaust the respective and historically ever-unfolding meanings – thereby opening the door to different understandings of what is said. We always say more than we mean, whether we are speaking as scientists or non-scientists.

A further factor contributing to the predicament of understanding deserves special mention because it makes understanding and interpretation possible at all. This factor, dubbed by Heidegger "the hermeneutical situation," is the fact – and recognition of the fact – that no understanding is devoid of presuppositions. What makes understanding possible at all is a foregoing, threefold structure on the part of the reader. Thus, insofar as what is written is understood, it is subject to the reader's preview (*Vorsicht*) and preconceptions (*Vorgriff*), finding a place in a context of meanings and intentions already in the reader's possession (*Vorhabe*) (Heidegger 2011 [1924], pp.74–9; Heidegger 2010 [1927] pp.222–3). The hermeneutical situation entails that understanding is ineluctably circular in one sense, indeed, even where we do not find what we have already tacitly projected. As this inevitable dependency upon our projections suggests, the hermeneutical situation goes hand-in-hand with the primacy of the future composed of these projections. Heidegger accordingly regards the capacity to understand the present in the light of some future as "the first principle of hermeneutics" (Heidegger 1992 [1924], p.20).

The hermeneutical situation, so construed, is empowering, humbling, and a source of responsibility. It entails the unavoidability but also the fertile exigency of presuppositions. Gadamer speaks accordingly of *'préjuges légitimes'* in a deliberately provocative rehabilitation of the frequently derided concept of presupposition (see Gadamer 2013 [1960], p.283; Gadamer 1976 [1966], p.9). Yet the hermeneutical situation also calls for constant vigilance, given our limited grasp of our presuppositions and our tendency to be content with inherited, ready-made interpretations. At the same time, it enables us to retrieve and take responsibility for our interpretations (Heidegger 2010 [1927], p.148).

Combinations of all the factors noted above – the fragility of communication, the non-equivalence of words and meanings, the construction of tradition-laden, non-pedestrian languages, the mereological character of meaning, and the "hermeneutical situation" – present readers with versions of the hermeneutical predicament, for which there is only one recourse: interpretation. But what precisely is or counts as an interpretation?

The hermeneutical task

In order to try to answer this last question, let us consider a rudimentary hermeneutical context, namely, the case of a mother hearing her infant's different cries. One cry may signal hunger; another a need for attention; yet another, pain. The hunger, the need for attention, the pain may explain why the infant cries in the one way or the other. We might say that they are the reasons why it cries in those ways, though the infant hardly knows that those are the reasons. Mothers often learn to understand the different sounds, just as they learn to read the infant's movements and facial expressions. But the understanding is not automatic; the mother has to take the infant's utterances, mien, or movements as signs and attempt, no doubt through trial and error, to determine what they signify.

This attempt to determine the meanings of the infant's utterances is the mother's hermeneutical task, the task of interpretation. From the mother's adult perspective where understanding is commonplace, she may interpret the infant's sounds as quasi-exhortatory expressions ("Feed me!" "Hold me!") or even quasi-indicative ones ("I want to be fed," "I need to be held") – where 'quasi' is a placeholder for the mystery of what, if anything, is going through the infant's mind. What the sounds, images, or gestures say is their meaning. Hence, the range of meanings and thereby hermeneutics itself is as wide as the range of sounds, images, or gestures that say something – and the distinctive ways that they say it.

Though the example of a mother interpreting her infant's expressions presents a truncated form of the hermeneutical quadrangle, it instructively underscores three features of interpretation.

The first feature concerns a staple of traditional hermeneutics, namely, interpretation's inevitable grounding in an understanding (Dilthey 2002 [1904–9], p.226, pp.238–9; Dilthey 1979 [1900], p.248, pp.260–1; Heidegger 2010 [1927], p.144; Gadamer 2007 [1968], p.62). Interpretation consists in making explicit, that is to say, in giving expression to an understanding that may otherwise remain implicit. Like the baby's cries, the expression need not be strictly linguistic. Although the infant need not have anything in mind when it cries, a mother hears the cry as a sign. That is to say, she interprets the cry because she wants to alleviate her baby's anguish or discomfort. Thanks to this purposeful context that she possesses from the outset, she already has a way of seeing and conceiving her baby's cries (thereby exemplifying the threefold forestructure of the hermeneutical situation, noted above). What counts as a successful interpretation, that is, some response on her part through which her baby is comforted and stops crying, is based upon her hermeneutical situation. That response depends upon understanding and interpreting a semiotic (sign-signified) relation.

The mother's hermeneutical task exemplifies a second basic feature of interpretation, namely, its beholdenness to the respective signs to be interpreted. The task of interpretation is to make explicit the meaning of what is said or written. Ordinarily, meaning is closely associated with the use of 'mean,' where the latter refers to some deliberate intention or purpose on the part of the speaker. We might say, somewhat euphemistically, that what the infant "meant" by crying was the directive to hold her. Yet for normal native speakers of a language, it is not a euphemism to maintain that, typically, they mean what they say or that they try to say what they mean. Of course, there are liars and fabricators, but these dark arts have purchase thanks to the fact that for the most part, people use language genuinely, that is, they use it to say what they hold to be the case.

Nevertheless, the task of interpretation is to make the meanings of what is written explicit. This second feature of interpretation addresses the traditional concern over an author's prerogatives. The grounding of language and meaning in communication and the dimensions of the hermeneutical quadrangle may be seen as reaffirming the *mens auctoris* (the mind of the author), that is, authoritative role that the author's intention (what the author meant, what she intended to say) plays for interpreting what she wrote. We already noted the non-equivalence of words and meanings. Yet if meanings are not equivalent to words that happen to be employed to signify them, that does not entail that the meanings themselves correspond to something outside language or some content entertained by a speaker or writer. In other words, meanings communicated need not correspond to anything consciously meant by the user of the supposed markers of meaning. They are also not separate from the hermeneutical situation; that is to say, they are not irreal entities having a status such as is sometimes ascribed to propositions in contrast to sentences.

In this regard the example of the mother's interpretation of her infant's cries is again instructive. Their meaning is not what the infant "means," if it means anything at all. Their meaning is rather what the infant's sounds communicate to the parent, just as, more generally, meaning corresponds to what linguistic markers convey to the reader or listener. While language and meaning are bilateral (because, as noted above, communication "takes two"), communication can take place where the understanding is unilateral or one-sided. In simpler terms, someone can unconsciously or unintentionally communicate; she can communicate without understanding that she is doing so, albeit only if someone else who hears her has the requisite understanding.

The exigencies of the hermeneutical situation may, of course, be such that the speaker's or writer's intentions are essential to the meaning of what is said.

Consider, for example, a lovers' quarrel, where they hang on each other's words, wondering whether commitment or rejection is meant by words of passion, addressed to one other and no one else. So, too, when we ask someone her opinion, the meaning that we are seeking is precisely what she means, that is, what she thinks. These contexts are not at arm's length, to be sure; they involve interlocutors who use the first and second person with one another. But even where a writer is dead or absent, the hermeneutical situation can require understanding what the writer meant. So, for example, studies of past writers or philosophers may profitably look to determine their general outlook or intentions. Even Heidegger's efforts to determine what a philosopher does not say or should say – to understand him better than he understands himself – turns on determining what he supposes the philosopher was intending to say (Heidegger 1997 [1927–8], pp.2–3; 1997 [1929], pp.137ff).

Yet these cases of associating meaning with *mens auctoris* derive their legitimacy from a foregoing understanding, the interpreter's hermeneutical situation. They are by no means the only way of interpreting what is said or written, since, as noted already, we always say more than we mean. Indeed, as in the case of the baby's cries, the meaning of what we express may not be something that we have in mind at all. In any case, given the excess of meaning over intention, given that what we say has more potential meanings than any one of us could envision, there is an inevitable disparity between an author's intention and a text's meaning. What a text means always exceeds anything that the author might have meant.

In addition to this disparity, there is the general issue of the relative inaccessibility of someone else's mental states. This inaccessibility provides additional motivation for disjoining a text's meaning from its author's intention. So, too, does the fact that performing artists interpret original compositions, rather than simply reproducing them (Gadamer 2007 [1968], pp.57–8). Moreover, even if we have some access to an author's original intention, our main access is the text itself. Poets do not generally write commentaries on their poems, since the poems, as it were, say it all. There is nothing that the poet might add. These hermeneutical considerations closely resemble reasons for characterizing the practice of reducing an artwork's meaning to the artist's intention an "intentional fallacy" and its reduction to its psychological effects on its readers an "affective fallacy" (Wimsatt and Beardsley 1954; Gadamer 2007 [1968], p.62).

But then what does an interpretation add? From a hermeneutical point of view, interpretation consists, as noted above, in making explicit the meanings of what is written. To the extent that such meanings are already explicit, interpretation may be a matter of making those meanings explicit from a different perspective, whether tacit or quite removed from what is already more or less understandable. In each case, the character of the interpretation and thereby the meanings involved depends upon the hermeneutical situation. The meanings themselves are not Platonic entities or abstract types, hovering over the situation in some transcendental fashion. Instead they are further elaborations of what is more or less already understood, elaborations rooted in – but not reducible to – the interpreter's hermeneutical situation. Interpretation makes meanings explicit by saying in other words what is already said and more or less understood.

Because a text relies for its meaning upon a semantic framework that precedes the author, its meanings can be distinguished from the author's intentions in creating it.

The old medieval saying "books have their own fates" expresses this independence that persists even if the author is still with us, ready to explain what she meant (Maurus 1993). Plato's infamous remarks about the perils of philosophical writing (as opposed to dialogue) may well be tongue in cheek, but they stem from the same insight (see Plato's *Phaedrus*, 275c–d and *Seventh Letter*, 344c).

To be sure, dislodging or disjoining texts' meanings from their authors' intentions may seem counterintuitive, particularly given the association of 'meaning' with the verb 'to mean,' and the fundamentally communicative character of the hermeneutic quadrangle. Nevertheless, this insight follows from the fact that language and meanings come about as an indexical expression of a social inheritance. This last observation is intended to underscore the obvious if easily overlooked fact that language, meaning, and communication are not fundamentally structures but forms of existence. They develop ("come about") only inasmuch as we concretely speak and listen to one another and to ourselves; we write for one another and for ourselves; we read what others have to say and what we have to say. In other words, language and meaning are fundamentally social phenomena, and yet that there is a no less fundamentally indexical, even existential character to their unfolding (Dahlstrom 2010, pp.45–6).

These features of language and meaning correspond to the distinction between meanings that depend for their meaning upon the specific context ("occasion meanings") and those that do not ("standing meanings") (Quine 1960, p.35f; Kaplan 1989, p.520; Recanati 2012, pp.179–87). Although I use a language to say *what I mean*, the language that I use is, nonetheless, socially inherited. I can only use it genuinely or non-genuinely, because a group of users of the language have already established ways in which it can be used to say what is the case. So even when what I say has an indexical character (i.e., where in a sense I alone mean what I say), the meaningfulness of what I say is never mine alone. Given this account, the originators of modern hermeneutics tend to be neither semantic minimalists – reducing context-dependent expressions to a few expressions, for example, indexicals, demonstratives, and adverbial or adjectival equivalents of them (Cappelen and Lepore 2005) – nor radical contextualists (Searle 1980).

The hermeneutical ideal

We may be leery of saying that the infant meant for us to hold her when she cried a certain way because we associate meaning with a level of consciousness or intentionality that we are not sure the infant possesses. But when we hear someone speak with the facility of a native speaker, we do not hesitate to presume that they meant to say something and that their utterances have meaning. Of course, it is one thing for a sign to signify something and quite another to use the sign to signify it (Lewis 1970, p.19). "What is the meaning of this?" we might ask in a prickly, unexpected situation, where 'meaning' has nothing to do with anything linguistic, but rather with the intentions of those who brought about the situation. So, too, when we read some quite cryptic remark, we might ask "What does it mean?" Yet the question is ambiguous or, rather, it combines two questions into one, namely, a question of what the remark is about and a question of what the author had in mind in making it. In this way, the word 'meaning' ambiguously and perhaps fruitfully ranges over these two questions.

Since these two questions are distinct, they have engendered two different approaches to theorizing about meaning, albeit generally outside hermeneutical traditions: a "semantic" approach that attempts to explain what linguistic markers mean and a "foundational" approach that attempts to explain what it is about those who use the markers that gives them the meanings they have. One key issue for semantic approaches (tracing back to the work of Frege and Russell) is whether sentences' meanings are to be identified with propositions; that is, entities paired with linguistic expressions. Given hermeneutics' emphasis on the historical and holistic character of language and meaning, it has more affinities with thinkers, such as Wittgenstein, who tend to oppose any construal of meanings as propositions in that sense. Given modern hermeneutics' detachment of a text's meaning from its author's intentions, it parts ways with the foundational approach, at least insofar as the latter looks to the mental states – intentions or beliefs – of those using the linguistic expressions to explain why they are meaningful (Grice 1989; Lewis 1975).

At the same time, modern hermeneutics by no means rejects the questions raised by these two contemporary approaches to meaning. However, given its concern with the interpretation of a specific text, it also moves beyond concerns with their complementarity. To appreciate this last point, it may be useful to consider how Schleiermacher, one of the founders of modern hermeneutics, anticipates each of these approaches to meaning. Insisting on both the radical universality and radical individuality of language use, he cites the need to approach a text both from the universal side of its grammar and from the particular side of the author's technical application. However, he also appreciates the fact that these two sides come together in the writing and the written work itself. Standing meanings are combined with occasional meanings, shared experiences with the author's personal experiences, conscious or not. Hence, Schleiermacher posits the need for divining that synthesis. This divination is the hermeneutical ideal that informs the practice of interpretation (Schleiermacher 1998 [1838], pp.9–11, pp.88, 94). Despite his differences with Schleiermacher, Gadamer sees a similar synthesis at work in interpretation, the fusion of the horizon of the interpreter with that of the author of the text interpreted (Gadamer 2013 [1960], p.317). Here, too, hermeneutics is motivated by real but inherently limited possibilities of understanding the meanings of what is said or written. What is distinctive and valuable about the hermeneutic tradition, what particularly recommends its understanding of language and meaning, is precisely this synthetic ideal.

Bibliography

Cappelen, H., and Lepore, E. (2005). *Insensitive Semantics: A Defence of Semantic Minimalism and Speech Act Pluralism*, Oxford: Blackwell Publishing.

Dahlstrom, D. (2010) "Towards an Explanation of Language," *Proceedings of the American Catholic Philosophical Association* 84: 33–46.

Davidson, D. (2001) *Subjective, Intersubjective, Objective*, Oxford: Clarendon Press.

Dilthey, W. (1979 [1900]) *Dilthey: Selected Writings*, edited by H. P. Rickman, Cambridge: Cambridge University Press.

——(2002 [1904–9]) *Dilthey: Selected Works, Volume III: The Formation of the Historical World in the Human Sciences*, edited by Rudolf Makkreel and Frithjof Rodi, Princeton: Princeton University Press.

Frege, G. (1980 [1884]) *The Foundations of Arithmetic*, Evanston, Ill.: Northwestern University Press.

Gadamer, H. G. (1976 [1966]) *Philosophical Hermeneutics*, translated and edited by David E. Linge, Berkeley: University of California Press.

——(2007 [1968]) *The Gadamer Reader: a bouquet of the later writings*, Evanston, Ill.: Northwestern University Press.

——(2013 [1960]) *Truth and Method*, translated by Joel Weinsheimer and Donald G. Marshall, London: Bloomsbury.

Grice, P. (1989) *Studies in the Way of Words*, Cambridge, Mass.: Harvard University Press.

Heidegger, M. (1992 [1924]) *The Concept of Time*, translated by William McNeill, Oxford: Blackwell.

——(1997 [1927–8]) *Phenomenological Interpretation of Kant's Critique of Pure Reason*, translated by Kenneth Maly and Parvis Emad, Bloomington: Indiana University Press.

——(1997 [1929]) *Kant and the Problem of Metaphysics*, translated by Richard Taft, Bloomington: Indiana University Press.

——(2010 [1927)] *Being and Time*, translated by Joan Stambaugh, revised edition, Albany: SUNY.

——(2011 [1924]) *The Concept of Time*, translated by Ingo Farin, London: Bloomsbury.

Kaplan, D. (1989) "Demonstratives," in J. Almog, J. Perry, and H. Wettstein (eds.), *Themes from Kaplan*, Oxford: Oxford University Press.

Lewis, D. (1970) "General Semantics," Synthese 22: 18–67.

——(1975) "Languages and Language," in K. Gunderson (ed.), *Language, Mind, and Knowledge*, Minneapolis: University of Minnesota Press.

Maurus, T. (1993) *De syllabis*, edited and translated by Jan-Wilhelm Beck, Göttingen: Vandenhoeck and Ruprecht.

Quine, W. V. O. (1960) *Word and Object*, Cambridge, Mass.: MIT Press.

Recanati, F. (2012) "Compositionality, flexibility, and context dependence," in M. Werning, W. Hinzen, and E. Machery (eds.), *The Oxford Handbook of Compositionality*, Oxford: Oxford University Press.

Schleiermacher, F. (1998 [1838]) *Hermeneutics and Criticism: And Other Writings*, edited by Andrew Bowie, Cambridge: Cambridge University Press.

Searle, J. (1980) "The background of meaning," in F. Kiefer and M. Bierwisch (eds.), *Speech-Act Theory and Pragmatics*, Dordrecht: Reidel.

Szabo, Z. G. (2000) *Problems of Compositionality*, New York: Garland.

Werning, M., Hinzen, W., and Machery, E. (2012) *The Oxford Handbook of Compositionality*, Oxford: Oxford University Press.

Wimsatt, W., and Beardsley, M. (1954) *The Verbal Icon*, Lexington: University of Kentucky Press.

22
TRUTH AND RELATIVISM

Paul Healy

The problem of truth has been central to philosophy since its inception, with the quest for truth frequently characterised as synonymous with philosophy itself. This chapter considers the implications of the hermeneutic reconceptualisation of truth, and its potential relativistic overtones.

The problem of relativism could be regarded as the flip-side of the truth problem. It arises once the possibility of different conceptual frameworks, or paradigms, indexed to different historical periods and/or cultures, comes into play. The major classical philosophers mostly circumvented this problem by insisting on the existence of an ahistorical frame of reference incorporating incontrovertible standards impervious to history or culture, as famously epitomised by Plato's Forms. In more recent times, however, philosophy has had to come to terms not just with the possibility but also with the reality of multiple competing frameworks, or paradigms, no one of which can self-evidently claim superiority or greater veracity. While rampant postmodernism, valorising the unqualified proliferation of difference, represents one pole in this debate, philosophical hermeneutics provides a much more defensible response. For while also valorising the existence of multiple perspectives, deriving from the inherent historicality and situatedness of human understanding, it can nonetheless provide a philosophically defensible account of how truth can be preserved and invidious relativism avoided. Even so, as soon becomes apparent, the articulation of a viable hermeneutic truth conception is not without its own complexities and challenges.

Given his indissoluble association with philosophical hermeneutics, the present chapter explores these issues primarily through engagement with Hans-Georg Gadamer's treatment of the truth problem. But since coming to terms with Gadamer's position presupposes an appreciation of his Heideggerian legacy, I begin with a brief overview and critical appraisal of the Heideggerian reappropriation of truth as unconcealment or disclosure, elaborating on its alleged relativistic threats and querying its potential to respond adequately to these. Thereafter, I contend that Gadamer's distinctive reappropriation of his Heideggerian legacy enables his work to support a conception of hermeneutic truth as dialogical closure, embodying the resources needed to respond to the challenge of critical justification that traditionally accrues to truth.

However, the primary aim here is not the unequivocal defence of this, somewhat controversial, assessment but rather to apprise readers of key issues in the hermeneutic debate about truth, so as to better position them to judge these for themselves in awareness of their contested status. This is all the more important since space limitations largely necessitate substituting summary appraisals for extended argumentation below.

As noted, we begin with a brief introduction to the Heideggerian reappropriation of truth as unconcealment or disclosure.

Heideggerian legacy: truth as unconcealment

What is truth? In challenging an entrenched philosophical tradition, Heidegger provides a potentially ground-breaking response to this enduring problem, aimed at laying bare its "ontological foundations" (1962: 257). He does so initially by questioning the correspondence definition which, while not unproblematic, has traditionally been widely endorsed.

As epitomised in its medieval formulation *adequatio rei et intellectus*, the correspondence definition essentially encapsulates the common intuition that a thought (or statement) is true only if it corresponds to an actual state of affairs. Thus, famously, "the cat is on the mat" is true if, and only if, the cat *is* on the mat; otherwise, it is false. More consequently, the same applies to such claims as "current climate change is primarily human-made," or "Lee Harvey Oswald, alone, killed JFK." Moreover, as these examples illustrate, the truth problem has traditionally embodied two dimensions: one definitional, the other concerning warrant, evidence, or justification. Notably, however, in reappropriating the truth problem ontologically, Heidegger foregrounds the definitional dimension to the virtual exclusion of the "epistemological" (here loosely construed as pertaining to supporting evidence or warrant). He develops his position in *Being and Time*, Section 44 by critically engaging with the correspondence conception, given its traditional influence.

Although intuitively plausible, the correspondence definition is by no means problem-free. In particular, it begs questions as to how an intangible thought (or statement) can actually *correspond* with a worldly state-of-affairs and likewise regarding the specific nature of this correspondence relation. But Heidegger's project entails dissolving rather than solving such problems, by radically challenging the underlying metaphysical presuppositions. Accordingly, he focuses on elucidating the *ontological* conditions of the possibility of truth as correspondence (or "correctness", as he terms it). Elaborating, Heidegger identifies unconcealment (*aletheia, Unverborgenheit*) or disclosure (*Erschlossenheit*) as the primary condition, contending that an ontologically prior event of unconcealment is necessary for the thing (state of affairs, or subject matter) to show itself as it is, and hence to enable its adequation (or otherwise) to become manifest. Maintaining that this qualifies it as the indispensable ontological condition of the possibility for truth as correspondence, Heidegger deems unconcealment to constitute truth in a more primary sense, affirming that "the *Being-true (truth)* of the assertion must be understood as *Being-uncovering*" (1962: 261). Moreover, in keeping with his resolute efforts to recover an *originary* meaning for key philosophical concepts, Heidegger further contends that pre-Socratic word usage reinforces the tenability of this reconceptualisation (1962: 265). Although, commensurate with his celebrated "turn," Heidegger later goes on to re-pose the truth question from the perspective of Being (see especially Heidegger 1977a, 1977b) rather than Dasein (as in *Being and Time*), his emphasis on the primarily disclosive character of truth remains pivotal and enduring.

Notwithstanding his continued endorsement of the traditional correspondence conception, Heidegger's ontological investigations potentially transform how we conceptualise truth, in that they effectively undermine the metaphysical presuppositions on which the truth relation has been based, starting with "the conception of the disengaged knowing subject" favoured by traditional epistemology (Guignon 2002: 265). This shift in emphasis away from the knowing subject to the disclosive truth event as such raises some perplexing questions regarding the interrelation of the epistemological and ontological dimensions of the truth problem, all the more so since Heidegger himself maintains a sharp focus on the ontological dimension and says correspondingly little about the epistemological implications. Consequently, it is commonly assumed that the Heideggerian valorisation of truth as unconcealment dispenses with epistemological concerns. For critics, however, the seeming absence of epistemological resources intensifies the perceived relativistic threats implicit in the Heideggerian stance. As elaborated briefly below, these threats derive not just from the equation of truth with disclosure, but also from the attributes with which Heidegger is perceived to imbue the disclosive truth event as he successively revisits the topic, especially in the absence of clearly specified epistemological constraints. In particular, these factors raise challenging questions about the interrelation between the ontological and epistemological dimensions of the hermeneutic truth conception, while querying the capacity of the Heideggerian "corpus" to resolve them.

Before elaborating, however, the reader is reminded that these issues remain much contested. For one thing, the very attribution of relativistic overtones tends to be seen by Heidegger scholars as entailing a significant misunderstanding of the import of Heidegger's ontological project. More generally, the mere foregrounding of epistemological issues in a Heideggerian context is frequently attributed to a failure to appreciate how the Heideggerian revolution renders such concerns irrelevant, if not distorting. Challenging such assessments, however, the present chapter presses the contention that the ontological recasting of the truth problem inevitably has significant epistemological implications, particularly as pertaining to issues of justification or warrant, to which the Heideggerian truth conception is not immune. But given their contested status, the reader is urged to engage firsthand with the relevant primary and secondary sources so as to better appraise these issues for him or herself.

Although widely acknowledged as ground breaking, the Heideggerian reconceptualisation of truth as unconcealment or disclosure is also widely perceived by critics as embodying significant relativistic threats. Most notably, these include the following.

Problematic, firstly, is truth's event-like character. While philosophers since Plato have portrayed the acquisition of truth as the product of a process of inquiry which tests the tenability of proffered truth claims, the (later) Heidegger tends to portray the dawning of truth as a sudden event-like occurrence, using vivid metaphors like "lighting" and "lightening" to epitomise its overwhelming disclosive force (Dostal 1994: 56–7). For critics, his correlative valorisation of the artwork and of poetry as primary truth disclosive "media" further reinforce the putative relativistic implications, given that these have traditionally been viewed as epito-mising subjectivity. Moreover, the relativistic overtones of such characterisations are even more pronounced if accompanied by connotations of overwhelming immediacy and self-warranting validity. The further problem is that the corpus does not manifestly embody the resources needed to contain or dispel these rela-tivistic overtones, particularly since (the later) Heidegger appears dismissive of truth-warranting (or more broadly epistemological) concerns.

Problematic also is truth's inherent historicity. As definitive Heideggerian hall-marks, temporarality, finitude, and fallibility also inevitably characterise Heidegger's reappropriation of truth, with Being and truth held to manifest themselves differently in different epochal "mittences". While liberating in their departure from philosophy's traditional valorisation of truth's ahistoricality and atemporality, often epitomised by an unchanging mathematical ideal, these attributes again embody the spectre of relativism which, by definition, threatens whenever understanding or knowledge is relativised to a historical (or indeed, cultural) framework of understanding, especially since the internal connections between such epochal truth manifestations remain uncertain. As before, it remains unclear to what extent the Heideggerian corpus embodies the resources needed to repudiate or dissolve these concerns.

Problematic, thirdly, is truth's characterisation as entailing concealment as well as unconcealment. Opposing what he castigates as a *metaphysics of presence*, Heidegger vigorously affirms not just that (truth as) unconcealment must be wrested from concealment, but also that such disclosure as can be achieved inevitably remains shrouded in concealment. But while complementing truth's inherent historicity and finitude by challenging the traditional emphasis on its finality and completeness, this theme embodies additional relativistic implications by setting limits to possible dis-closure. For it is clear that truth can be radically compromised by omissions and failures of *adequate* disclosure just as much as by falsehood. Hence, it needs to be established that the intertwinement of concealment/unconcealment is not such as to compromise adequacy of disclosure, a theme which will achieve prominence in our analysis of the Gadamerian truth conception.

Finally, the foregoing relativistic threats are compounded by Heidegger's unre-lenting commitment to rethinking the truth problem from the perspective of his concern with the question of Being, as he always does. As previously noted, Heidegger's seemingly univocal focus on the ontological dimension is widely per-ceived as marginalising, if not excluding, the epistemological, and in particular, a concern with justification. But although it is often assumed that raising such ques-tions in a Heideggerian context constitutes a misunderstanding, if not distortion, of Heidegger's core project, it remains the case that the truth question has long stand-ing epistemological implications, including adequacy of justificatory resources, which cannot easily be ignored or dismissed especially if threats of arbitrariness and relativism are to be avoided. Hence, the question inevitably arises as to whether Heidegger's redefinition of truth as unconcealment, disclosure, or "Being-uncover-ing" embodies some way of responding to such threats in the apparent absence of accompanying epistemological resources. This question is at the nub of the incisive Tugendhat critique, which Heidegger scholars acknowledge as constituting a sig-nificant critical challenge, while disputing its actual impact. The outline that follows is again necessarily very brief and selective, simply foregrounding Heidegger's alleged neglect of justificatory concerns (but see Smith 2007 for an extensive analysis, incorporating appraisal of recent Heideggerian responses; see too Malpas (2014) for a further innovative response).

Essentially, Tugendhat's contention is that the Heideggerian reappropriation of truth is untenable because, in valorising disclosure over correspondence in *Being and Time*, it fails to do justice to truth's necessary epistemological connotations, without which truth loses its meaning. In particular, Tugendhat's concern is that Heidegger ultimately valorises disclosure to the extent of excluding adequation to the things themselves as the indispensable hallmark of truth (1994: 87f.). Thus shorn of its "specific" (or distinctive) meaning – as entailing adequation to the things or subject matter – Heidegger's stipulative redefinition of truth as disclosure fails, essentially because it loses the capacity to differentiate between true and false disclosures (Tugendhat 1994: 91–3). Worse still, in sidelining the need for evidential appraisal – that is, for putting our (disclosive) truth claims "to the test" – the Heideggerian stance actually *impedes* the disclosure of truth (Tugendhat 1994: 95), again essentially because it deprives us of the means of differentiating between the true and the false. In concluding, Tugendhat goes on to attribute these problems to Heidegger's failure to engage systematically with the epistemological dimension of the truth question, and in particular, to meet "the Socratic challenge of a critical justification", namely to discharge the epistemic responsibility for justifying our truth claims (1994: 96–7). Moreover, for Tugendhat, Heidegger's later writings simply exacerbate this problem (Smith 2007: 177, n. 6; but see Dahlstrom 2010; Wrathall 2006 for an inherently Heideggerian representation of Heidegger's position).

Although typically contested by Heidegger scholars, on balance, I concur with Tugendhat's concluding assessment that the challenge of critical justification – centred on ensuring adequation to the "things themselves" – must remain integral to a viable hermeneutic truth conception, even if Heidegger's radical rethinking of truth could be expected to transform how we conceptualise this epistemic responsibility. Surprisingly, the later Heidegger himself seems to concede the limitations of equating unconcealment with truth, noting that, retrospectively, "one thing becomes clear: to raise the question of *aletheia*, of unconcealment as such, is not the same as raising the question of truth. For this reason, it was inadequate and misleading to call *aletheia* in the sense of opening, truth" (Heidegger 1977c: 389). But while this assessment seems to acknowledge that the truth problem has dimensions not adequately encapsulated by an exclusive focus on unconcealment or disclosure, it remains unclear whether, or to what extent, the Heideggerian corpus embodies the resources needed to discharge the relativistic threats and more broadly justificatory concerns accruing to it (Dostal 1994: 52). On the other hand, the publication of thoroughgoing studies on Heidegger and knowledge (e.g., Guignon 1983) and science (e.g., Kockelmans 1985) demonstrates that the Heideggerian corpus is not inherently antithetical to epistemological issues, even if justificatory concerns do not figure prominently in Heidegger's reflections on truth.

However, in next engaging with Gadamer I seek to establish that, although heir to the Heideggerian legacy, the Gadamerian corpus is more readily equipped to discharge the epistemic commitments traditionally accruing to truth and that this

enhances, rather than detracts from, its credentials as a viable, ontologically oriented, hermeneutic truth conception.

Gadamer's reappropriation: hermeneutic truth as dialogical disclosure

As the very title of his major work attests, the concept of truth is as central for
Gadamer as for Heidegger. Moreover, Gadamer readily acknowledges his debt to
Heidegger with regard to truth as with other aspects of his position (e.g., Gadamer
1997: 47). Not surprisingly, then, the Gadamerian truth conception incorporates key
hallmarks of the Heideggerian. Thus in addition to being inherently ontological, for
Gadamer too, truth is primarily an event of unconcealment or disclosure (Gadamer
1994: 36; Dostal 1994: 48). Moreover, it is imbued with an event-like immediacy and
the artwork is valorised as elucidating its disclosive impact. Likewise, truth, for
Gadamer, is inherently contextualised and situated, embodying the possibilities and
limitations characteristic of human finitude and fallibility. Initially, then, the Gadamerian truth conception might seem indistinguishable from the Heideggerian.

But the matter is considerably more complex. For although readily embracing his
Heideggerian legacy, Gadamer's own project actually differs significantly from
the Heideggerian, with inevitable implications for its truth conception (Dostal 1994:
48–9; cf. Grondin 1995: 14–17). Thus firstly, Gadamer's core concern is with elucidating the operation of hermeneutic understanding rather than with the question
of Being as such, with a view to defending the distinctive character of the human
sciences and vindicating the possibility of truth beyond method (Gadamer 1989:
Introduction). Correlatively, in appropriating his Heideggerian inheritance, Gadamer
engages very differently with the broader philosophical tradition in ways that significantly influence his truth conception. In particular, Gadamer eschews the viabi-
lity of pursuing a putatively originary understanding in favour of active engagement
with key representatives of the philosophical tradition (e.g., Gadamer 1997: 26–40).
Accordingly, his position on truth as on other core themes bears the marks of his
engagement with such major philosophers as Plato, Aristotle, and Hegel as well as
with more contemporary hermeneutic theorists, each of whom contributes to tem-
pering his position. Crucially too, as we shall see, Gadamer vigorously vindicates the
intrinsically *dialogical* character of human experience and understanding.

Significantly too, unlike Heidegger, Gadamer did not dedicate a series of texts to
the elucidation of his truth conception (a partially informative exception being
Gadamer 1994), but instead typically assimilated his remarks about truth to his
treatment of other core themes. Consequently, despite its centrality, Gadamer's
truth conception remains significantly underspecified (Bernstein 1983: 151–2).
Hence, a considerable interpretative challenge is involved in reconstructing Gadamer's stance on truth, leaving open the possibility of alternate interpretations.
Hence, in contending below that the Gadamerian corpus embodies the potential to
underwrite a viable hermeneutic truth conception in ways that extend beyond the
Heideggerian in terms of meeting the Tugendhat challenge of critical justification, I
again encourage the reader to judge for her or himself through firsthand acquaintance with the relevant sources.

What then is the Gadamerian truth conception? Since Gadamer differs from Heidegger while leaving his actual position on this pivotal topic underspecified, it is necessary to approach the issue more circuitously. In so doing, I seek to establish that the Gadamerian corpus can support an "epistemically robust" hermeneutic truth conception, capable not only of responding to the relativistic threats it inherits but also of meeting the Tugendhat challenge of critical justification in an appropriately hermeneutic way. Accordingly, I proceed below by challenging a series of misinterpretations which accrue to this hermeneutic truth conception in virtue of Gadamer's distinctive appropriation of his Heideggerian legacy, in the absence of his systematic textual specification of what is entailed. More specifically, through thus responding briefly to four interrelated misinterpretations (or potential objections), I seek to establish that the Gadamerian corpus embodies the resource to underwrite a conception of truth as dialogical disclosure capable of counteracting not only the relativistic threats which Gadamer inherits, but also those deriving from his own distinctive project; and to do so in a way that can meet Tugendhat's challenge of critical justification, while remaining true to his own ontological, and more broadly hermeneutic, commitments.

Firstly, then, it needs to be recognised that the mere intent to attribute to Gadamer an epistemically robust truth conception capable of meeting the Tugendhat challenge is *not* at odds with his core aims, as is often assumed to be the case given Gadamer's manifestly ontological orientation. In this, Gadamer again exhibits some notable differences from Heidegger. In particular, given Gadamer's avowed involvement with the human sciences, epistemological concerns are explicitly to the foreground in *Truth and Method*, Part II, and hence can hardly be deemed to constitute a distortion of his ontological project (Healy 2012). Indeed, far from being antithetical to his concerns, Gadamer explicitly deems the task of ascertaining "the ground of the legitimacy of prejudices" "the fundamental *epistemological* question for a truly historical hermeneutics" (1989: 277; emphasis added). Similarly, he deems the challenge of ensuring the adequation of what is contended with the "things themselves" an indispensable condition for truth (1989: 266–7). Furthermore, in deeming this the "undeniable task of critical reason", he identifies "the preponderance of reasons for the one and against the other possibility" (1989: 364) as the appropriate basis for its discharge. Nor can such passages be dismissed as incautious terminological lapses on Gadamer's part since, as we shall see, they dovetail cohesively with other aspects of his position. Hence, on balance, it seems more judicious to conclude, with Rockmore, that while Gadamer is certainly not an epistemologist in the traditional sense, "he does not flee the question of knowledge" but rather seeks to reappropriate it from a perspective informed by an acute awareness of "the finite, historical character of human experience" (Rockmore 1995: 59, 66; cf. Alcoff 1996: Chs 1–2).

A similar assessment applies with regard to Gadamer's alleged repudiation of Enlightenment thinking, together with its epistemological predilections. Thus notwithstanding the numerous challenges that Gadamerian hermeneutics poses to entrenched Enlightenment presuppositions (and in particular to the need for neutral, atemporal foundations), a closer reading indicates that Gadamer is intent not on repudiating epistemology but rather on critically reappropriating and, indeed, potentially transforming it, motivated by the recognition that inquiry must always "be understood as issuing from a standpoint within, or conditioned by, [a] culture and its history, rather than from an ahistorical, transcultural, utterly neutral and objective standpoint of pure reason" (Detmer 1997: 283). Additionally, far from constituting a distortion, the recognition that Gadamer does not valorise the onto-logical to the exclusion of the epistemological and its justificatory concerns in the way that Tugendhat found wanting in Heidegger is inherently more compatible with his "both/and" style of thinking. Furthermore, acknowledging this has the advantage of enabling philosophical hermeneutics to make a significant contribution to the development of a viable postfoundationalist epistemology rather than being deemed irrelevant to contemporary epistemological concerns (Healy 2005: Ch. 2).

But to realise this potential, it also needs to be established that Gadamer does not fall prey to the relativistic implications of the Heideggerian emphasis on the histori-cality and contextuality of human understanding, especially since at first sight it could seem that his reappropriation of the Heideggerian stance on historicality effectively intensifies its relativistic implications. Thus in particular, he devotes the central part of *Truth and Method* to valorising a cluster of inter-related constitutive features which, in underscoring the influence of inherited prejudgments and prejudices on the constitu-tion of our hermeneutic situation and correlative horizon of understanding, might seem to render understanding and truth purely relative to changing and contingent historical influences and correspondingly immune to critical appraisal from other contextualised vantage points. Notably, these include the "hermeneutic circle", "effec-tive-historical consciousness", the ineliminable influence of "prejudices", the phe-nomenon of "application", and the inherently interpretive character of hermeneutic understanding. Additionally, far from minimising such seemingly relativistic over-tones, Gadamer appears rather to celebrate them, famously proclaiming that we always "understand in a different way, if we understand at all" (1989: 297).

In response, what needs to be noted is that these attributes are characteristic of Gadamer's *perspectival realism*, not relativism. Thus, while relativism would entail that our distinctive hermeneutic horizons close us off from differently situated others, Gadamer is emphatic that notwithstanding their inevitable conditioning influence, we nonetheless share a world in common with others who occupy different hermeneutic vantage points, albeit viewing it from different perspectives (Wachterhauser 1994b: 154–5; cf. Fay 1996: Ch. 4). In this, Gadamer draws on the key Husserlian insight that while we inevitably experience the world perspectivally, the world itself is intended in each of these perspectival experiences, which, accordingly, are internally related and mutually permeable. Hence, on Gadamer's analysis, far from being self-sealing or self-warranting, our experiential world remains inherently connected, and correspondingly open, to that of differently situated others. Moreover, our understanding of this shared world invites dialectical expansion, even transformation (1989: 447–8). Correlatively, since hermeneutics is often mistakenly assumed to license the free construction of one's own experiential world, it is also noteworthy that Gadamer's position is inherently "realist" (Wachterhauser 1994b), as epitomised by his emphatic phenomenological commitment to the "things themselves". Likewise, Gadamer explicitly defends the need for engaging with, and learning from, differently situated others so as to overcome the limitations of our initial presuppositions. Indeed, his dialogical commitments effectively render the need to thus engage with differently situated others a precondition for truly understanding our experiential world in its multifaceted complexity.

Thirdly, then, notwithstanding his strong Heideggerian affinities, Gadamer does not rest content with affirming the event-like character of truth, but also foregrounds the need for the dialogical exploration and appraisal of truth claims.

Given the well-known Gadamerian dictum that "In understanding we are drawn into the event of truth and arrive, as it were, too late, if we want to know what we are supposed to believe" (1989: 490), it is often assumed that Gadamer's appropriation of truth's event-like character falls prey to relativistic threats similar to those allegedly deriving from Heidegger's usage of metaphors of "lighting" and "lightening" (e.g., Irwin 2001: 67), especially given Gadamer's seeming valorisation of "the enlightening" (*Einleuchtende*) as a truth criterion (1989: 485–6; cf. Schmidt 1995a, 1995b, 1996). Again, however, a closer reading shows that this is not actually the case. For Gadamer does not in fact equate "the enlightening" with truth as such, still less confer on it self-warranting status. Instead, he is explicit that what thus comes to light "has not been proved", but rather "asserts itself ... within the realm of the possible and probable", leaving open the question of how it is to be assessed and integrated. Accordingly, while the enlightening is "like a new light being turned on", expanding the range of what needs to be taken into consideration, the challenge of assessing its veracity "presents a special task of hermeneutical integration" (1989: 485–6). In effect, then, rather than constituting an incontrovertible truth disclosure, the enlightening, for Gadamer, has the status of a possible truth claim. Furthermore, it is not to the enlightening as such but rather to "a discipline of questioning and inquiring" that Gadamer attributes the capacity to underwrite or warrant truth (1989: 491). Moreover, when delineating the requisite path of inquiry, it is "the model of Platonic dialectic" (1989: 362f.) rather than the Heideggerian prototype that Gadamer endorses, contending not only that the thing or subject matter does not reveal itself "without our thinking being involved", but also that only a specifically dialectical mode of thinking is capable of unfolding the logic proper to the thing itself (1989: 464). As briefly elaborated below, in thus embracing a dialectical model, Gadamer foregrounds the indispensability of dialogical questioning and testing as necessary for adequate truth disclosure. Notably too, this dialogical dimension is no mere appendage to Gadamer's thinking, but instead, as built into the structure of hermeneutic experience (*Erfahrung*) itself, is integral from the outset (e.g. 1989: 36; cf. Smith 1991: 190–2).

For Gadamer, then, a disciplined dialectical process of questioning and testing what is assumed to be true of the subject matter, whatever the origin of such assumptions, has priority over the immediacy of the enlightening truth event (Dostal 1994: 49, 58–60; Wachterhauser 1994a: 13). Or better, it is the tension between the enlightening event of truth and its dialectic unfolding that most appropriately characterises the Gadamerian stance (Dostal 1994, 63–7; Healy 2012). As contended below, this recognition that the event-like dawning of truth is but a "moment" in an ongoing dialectical process oriented toward the attuned and adequate disclosure of the phenomena under consideration enables Gadamer to discharge the challenge of critical justification in appropriately hermeneutic terms beyond what the Heideggerian position would readily seem to allow for.

Accordingly, I contend that transcending correspondence and coherence, hermeneutic truth construed as dialogical disclosure can judiciously discharge the Tugendhat challenge of critical justification in a manner which not only eschews the spectre of relativism (by ensuring adequacy as well as adequation), but which also embodies transformative possibilities.

How, ultimately, are we to conceptualise the Gadamerian conception of truth disclosure? While commentators have tended to foreground the correspondence (Wachterhauser 1994b: e.g. 153) and coherence (Alcoff 1996) dimensions, it should be clear that, by themselves, these are not sufficient for hermeneutic truth. Given that truth can fail as much through distortion or inadequate disclosure as by manifest untruth, the *adequacy* of truth disclosure must also be ensured, as evidenced by Gadamer's valorisation of "completeness" as a regulative ideal (e.g., 1989: 266–7, 293–4) and, correlatively, of achieving a "higher universality" which overcomes an initial partiality of perspectives (1989: 305–7). As bearing all the requisite hallmarks of the "discipline of questioning and inquiring" to which Gadamer explicitly attributes the capacity to underwrite or warrant truth, it is to a "model of Platonic dialectic" that we must look to safeguard the adequacy as well as adequation of truth disclosure (Healy In press). Thus construed, as elaborated briefly below, the Gadamerian truth conception is capable of discharging the "Socratic challenge of a critical justification" in ways that preserve the hermeneutic emphasis on disclosure while eschewing the spectre of relativism. More specifically, it achieves this in virtue of embodying attributes capable of ensuring adequacy as well as adequation, while avoiding the "enframing" and related limitations that render method untenable as a medium of hermeneutic truth disclosure. Most notably, these include: genuine openness, ongoing, appropriately directed questioning, sustained attunement to the subject matter, consideration of opposing views, and assessment of supporting reasons (Gadamer 1989: 362f.). As evidenced in the Platonic model, such dialogical exploration is necessary to ensure that plausible but ultimately misleading, or otherwise inadequate, interpretations are transcended, so that the subject matter can adequately disclose itself in its truth. Importantly, far from constituting an external imposition, this process of dialectical appraisal allows the subject matter to show itself in its truth through the active participation of dialogue partners (and likewise through internal dialogue) who bring to light, and test, the possibilities inherent in the thing itself provided the requisite dialogical conditions are in place.

Thus, in particular, to counteract the conceptual closure induced by entrenched presuppositions or methodological "enframing", a stance of genuine openness and willingness to learn from others is indispensable. Equally important are a commitment to questioning along with the developed ability to ask the right questions – that is, to interrogate the subject matter in ways that will genuinely open up the topic and advance the inquiry instead of prematurely closing it off or distorting it. Likewise, the subject matter must be allowed to disclose itself in its own terms and according to its inner logic, in the process eliminating "arbitrary", or otherwise untenable, "fancies", whatever their origin (Gadamer 1989: 362f.). Notably too, this dialectical interplay supports a dynamic learning process whereby the subject matter discloses itself in increasingly more adequate ways. Indeed, the core desideratum is to facilitate, and remain responsive to, this dynamic unfolding, so that "what is said is continually transformed into the uttermost possibilities of its rightness and truth" (Gadamer 1989: 367). Moreover, while a process of testing and justifying is integral, in contrast to traditional justificatory models the dialectical template is primarily oriented toward the transformative advancement of understanding through a "fusion" of heretofore partial perspectives (or horizons) on the subject matter. Famously, this "fusion of horizons" can facilitate the emergence of a new, more comprehensive (and correspondingly more adequate) understanding of the subject matter which, in transcending the partiality of earlier, more limited, views, inherently transforms not only the way we understand it, but also our very selves as situated and engaged inquirers (Gadamer 1989: 379).

In sum, then, it is contended that in virtue of embodying resources such as the foregoing the Gadamerian truth conception can effectively meet the challenge of critical justification which traditionally accrues to truth without compromising its distinctive hermeneutic attributes. Correlatively, in underwriting the adequacy as well as adequation of truth disclosure, this truth conception not only provides a bulwark against the threats of relativism and subjectivism inherent in a commitment to truth as situated and historicised disclosure, but also ensures that philosophical hermeneutics can make a significant contribution to the development of a viable postfoundationalist epistemology.

Bibliography

Alcoff, L. M. (1996) *Real Knowing: New Versions of the Coherence Theory*; Ithaca, NY: Cornell University Press.

Bernstein, R. J. (1983) *Beyond Objectivism and Relativism: Science, Hermeneutics, and Praxis*; Philadelphia: University of Pennsylvania Press.

Dahlstrom, D. O. (2010) "Truth as *Aletheia* and the Clearing of Beyng", in B. W. Davis (ed.), *Martin Heidegger: Key Concepts*; Durham: Acumen, pp. 116–27.

Detmer, D. (1997) "Gadamer's Critique of the Enlightenment", in L. Hahn (ed.), *The Philosophy of Hans-Georg Gadamer*, Library of Living Philosophers; La Salle, IL: Open Court, pp. 275–86.

Dostal, R. J. (1994) "The Experience of Truth for Gadamer and Heidegger: Taking Time and Sudden Lightning", in B. Wachterhauser (ed.), *Hermeneutics and Truth*; Evanston, IL: Northwestern University Press, pp. 47–67.

Fay, B. (1996) *Contemporary Philosophy of Social Science*; Oxford: Blackwell.

Gadamer, H.-G. (1989) *Truth and Method*, trans. J. Weinsheimer and D. Marshall, 2nd edn; New York: Continuum.

——(1994) "What Is Truth?", in B. Wachterhauser (ed.), *Hermeneutics and Truth*; Evanston, IL: Northwestern University Press, pp. 33–46.

——(1997) "Reflections on My Philosophical Journey", in L. E. Hahn (ed.), *The Philosophy of Hans-Georg Gadamer*; La Salle, IL: Open Court, pp. 3–63.

Grondin, J. (1995) *Sources of Hermeneutics*; Albany, NY: SUNY.

Guignon, C. (1983) *Heidegger and the Problem of Knowledge*; Indianapolis, IN: Hackett.

——(2002) "Truth in Interpretation: A Hermeneutic Approach", in M. Krausz (ed.), *Is There a Single Right Interpretation?*; University Park, PA: Penn State University Press, pp. 264–84.

Healy, P. (2005) *Rationality, Hermeneutics and Dialogue*; Aldershot: Ashgate.

——(2012) "Hermeneutic Rationality: A Contradiction in Terms?", in M. L. Portocarrero, L. A. Umbelino, and A. Wiercinski (eds), *Hermeneutic Rationality/La rationalité herméneutique*, 3; Münster: LIT Verlag, pp. 57–68.

——(In press) "Hermeneutic Truth as Dialogical Disclosure", *XXXIII World Congress of Philosophy* (University of Athens, 4–10 August 2013).

Heidegger, M. (1962) *Being and Time*, trans. J. Macquarrie and E. Robinson; New York: Harper & Row.

——(1977a) "On the Essence of Truth", in D. Farrell Krell (ed.), *Martin Heidegger: Basic Writings*; New York: Harper & Row, pp. 117–41.

——(1977b) "The Origin of the Work of Art", in D. Farrell Krell (ed.), *Martin Heidegger: Basic Writings*; New York: Harper & Row, pp. 149–87.

——(1977c) "The End of Philosophy and the Task of Thinking", in D. Farrell Krell (ed.), *Martin Heidegger: Basic Writings*; New York: Harper & Row, pp. 373–92.

Irwin, W. (2001) "A Critique of Hermeneutic Truth As Disclosure", *International Studies in Philosophy*, 33 (4), 63–75.

Kockelmans, J. J. (1985) *Heidegger and Science*; Washington, DC: University Press of America.

Malpas, J. (In press) "The Twofold Character of Truth: Heidegger, Davidson, Tugendhat", in Babette Babich and Dimitri Ginev (eds.), *The Multidimensionality of Hermeneutic Phenomenology* (Dordrecht: Springer, 2014), pp.243–66.

Rockmore, T. (1995) "Gadamer's Hermeneutics and the Overcoming of Epistemology", in L. K. Schmidt (ed.), *The Specter of Relativism: Truth, Dialogue, and Phronesis in Philosophical Hermeneutics*; Evanston, IL: Northwestern University Press, pp. 56–71.

Schmidt, L. K. (1995a) "Introduction: Between Certainty and Relativism", in L. K. Schmidt (ed.), *The Specter of Relativism: Truth, Dialogue, and Phronesis in Philosophical Hermeneutics*; Evanston, IL: Northwestern University Press, pp. 1–19.

——(1995b) "Uncovering Hermeneutic Truth", in L. K. Schmidt (ed.), *The Specter of Relativism: Truth, Dialogue, and Phronesis in Philosophical Hermeneutics*; Evanston, IL: Northwestern University Press, pp. 72–83.

——(1996) "*Das Einleuchtende*: The Enlightening Aspect of the Subject Matter", *Phenomenology, Interpretation, and Community*; Albany, NY: SUNY, pp. 175–91.

Smith, P. C. (1991) *Hermeneutics and Human Finitude*; New York: Fordham University Press.

Smith, W. H. (2007) "Why Tugendhat's Critique of Heidegger's Concept of Truth Remains a Critical Problem", *Inquiry*, 50 (2), 156–79.

Tugendhat, E. (1994) "Heidegger's Idea of Truth", in B. Wachterhauser (ed.), *Hermeneutics and Truth*; Evanston, IL: Northwestern University Press, pp. 83–97.

Wachterhauser, B. (1994a) "Introduction: Is There Truth after Interpretation?", in B. Wachterhauser (ed.), *Hermeneutics and Truth*; Evanston, IL: Northwestern University Press, pp. 1–24.

——(1994b) "Gadamer's Realism: The 'Belongingness' of Word and Reality", in B. Wachterhauser (ed.), *Hermeneutics and Truth*; Evanston, IL: Northwestern University Press, pp. 148–71.

Wrathall, M. (2006) "Truth and the Essence of Truth in Heidegger's Thought", in C. Guignon (ed.), *The Cambridge Companion to Heidegger*, 2nd edn; Cambridge: Cambridge University Press, pp. 241–67.

Further reading

Dahlstrom, Daniel O. (2001) *Heidegger's Concept of Truth*. Cambridge: Cambridge University Press. (A detailed and systematic treatment of the topic from an inherently Heideggerian perspective.)

DiCenso, James. (1990) *Hermeneutics and the Disclosure of Truth*. Charlottesville, VA: University Press of Virginia. (An insightful introduction to both Heidegger's and Gadamer's treatment of truth as disclosure, with an emphasis on the disclosive dimension.)

Kockelmans, Joseph J. (1984) *On the Truth of Being*. Bloomington: Indiana University Press. (An extended treatment of the later Heidegger's philosophy, with considerable emphasis on the truth aspect.)

Warnke, Georgia. (1987) *Gadamer: Hermeneutics, Tradition and Reason*. Cambridge: Polity. (Ch. 3 provides a helpful introduction to, and appraisal of, the "problem of subjectivism" (and hence of relativism) in Gadamer's work.)

23

HISTORY AND HISTORICITY

Kristin Gjesdal

Questions related to history and historicity take a prominent place in modern hermeneutics. However, while these questions are central to the hermeneutic tradition, there are few, if any, attempts at providing a solid definition of the terms. For the purpose of this chapter, I assume that "history" signifies both historical events, actions, and expressions and the narratively structured understanding of the events, actions, and expressions of the past. "Historicity," in turn, refers to the fact that we, as finite human beings, lead lives that are spanned out in time and understand ourselves, consciously or subconsciously, in and through a language and a culture that have been passed down through tradition. The way in which a given philosopher understands the relationship between the two will, by and large, signify the position he or she takes within the landscape of modern hermeneutics. For the sake of clarity, I divide these positions into three constellations, associated with (but not limited to) the eighteenth, the nineteenth, and the twentieth centuries.

While there has been a tendency to present hermeneutics, for good or bad, as a reaction to the critical spirit of Enlightenment (Gadamer 1994; Habermas et al. 1977), I would like to suggest that philosophical hermeneutics develops from within this paradigm. In the second half of the eighteenth century, philosophers introduce an awareness of human historicity as constituting both an enabling condition for reason and understanding and, at the same time, a limitation of them. For Johann Gottfried Herder this results in an analysis of prejudice and the notion of philosophy as an on-going process of education (*Bildung*) to humanity. For Friedrich Schleiermacher, it leads to reflection on how tradition enables, but also closes off historical understanding and thus necessitates a reference to regulative standards in interpretation. G. W. F. Hegel, in turn, views history as the gradual unfolding of freedom and rational comprehension in the actual world.

Nineteenth-century hermeneutics is often associated with Wilhelm Dilthey's attempt to provide a scientific grounding of the humanities. However, in this period, philosophers not only sought to articulate a hermeneutic foundation for the human sciences, but also to frame the questions of history and historicity within a model of societal critique and suspicion. In different ways, Friedrich Nietzsche, Karl Marx, and Sigmund Freud view tradition (if not the entire field of knowledge) as vested with interests and ideologies.

In the twentieth century, Martin Heidegger, Hans-Georg Gadamer, and Paul Ricoeur shape the contours of another hermeneutic paradigm. With Heidegger's *Being and Time* (1927; English translation: Heidegger 1996), history and historicity are no longer viewed as arenas of ideological battles, but as the central dimensions in and through which human existence obtains meaning. This approach to history and historicity as disclosing meaning (rather than being, primarily, a source of knowledge) is maintained in the works of Gadamer and Ricoeur, though the latter also borrows from Freud and Marx. Further, Gadamer's work – especially his insistence on the linguistic mediation of experience and the possibility of education in history and culture (*Bildung*) – has been a source of inspiration for Anglophone philosophers like Richard Rorty, Donald Davidson, John McDowell, and Robert Brandom.

Each of these theory constellations, serving as a systematic as well as periodical point of orientation, will be spelled out in more detail below.

1. Prejudice and human self-formation

Philosophical hermeneutics grows out of the paradigm of Enlightenment thought, both in its French version (Voltaire, Rousseau, Diderot, D'Alembert, and others), its English-language expression (Shaftesbury, Hutcheson, Hume, and others), and its German variety (Mendelssohn, Lessing, and others). At stake is an attempt to furnish the commitment to rationality and reason-giving with a more balanced image of the human being as embodied, sensuous, and situated within a given historical and linguistic culture. This point is made particularly clear in Herder's early work. Though Herder draws on previous theories of interpretation (including Chladenius and Meier), he initiates a shift from an interest in hermeneutic techniques and methods to a question of why we, as finite, historical beings, should engage in interpretation in the first place.

In Herder's view, human thought is realized in and through language, and language, in turn, is diverse and historically changing. Thus hermeneutics should not only focus on the object of understanding, but must also seek to analyze the subjective conditions under which understanding can take place. With this move, conducted in the 1760s, interpretation is granted a central place in his philosophy. The problem of historicity, in turn, is that around which interpretation spans. Herder draws three consequences from this insight.

First, Herder does not believe there is a constitutive difference between understanding one's own tradition and understanding expressions from different cultures. Within as well as between cultures, we see a diversity of values, practices, and beliefs. In both cases, the interpreter faces the challenge of recognizing an other *as* other rather than projecting onto the other a set of values and conceptual markers that derive from his or her own horizon or pattern of practice. Herder addresses this as the problem of prejudice (see for instance Herder 2008).

Second, Herder discusses our inclination to misrecognize expressions we cannot make immediate sense of. Against this tendency, hermeneuticians should adopt a more reflective attitude and address our epistemic access to objects of interpretation. The interpreter must ask if he or she is dealing with a full or partial work and critically consider his or her knowledge about the culture in which it emerged. Further, the interpreter must critically scrutinize the value concepts through which a given event or expression is approached. The reflective interpreter asks, for instance, what is meant by "work," "culture," and "civilization," rather than taking the meaning of these terms for granted. Along these lines, Herder points out that his contemporaries' rejection of Egyptian culture as static and primitive does not represent a genuine attempt at understanding, but is, rather, an effort to demonstrate the sovereignty of the modern, Enlightened point of view (Herder 2004: 15).

Third and finally, Herder, as a result of his focus on cultural bias and prejudice, points to the implicit political nature of historical work. In his view, history is a venue of conflicting values and interests. The job of the interpreter and the philosopher, working hand in hand, is to uncover these values and interests so as to further cooperation and mutual understanding between individuals and cultures. Hence Herder's critique of slavery and colonialism is not added on to his hermeneutic position, but grows directly out of it (Herder 2004).

Herder's critical spirit is taken up by Friedrich Schleiermacher. While Herder suggests that we should treat the Old Testament as (Hebrew) poetry, Schleiermacher goes one step further in thematizing the shift from *hermeneutica specialis* (discussions of particular kinds of texts such as the Bible and ancient works) to the question of understanding as such, *hermeneutica generalis* (Schleiermacher 1998: 5; although Schleiermacher takes credit for this shift, it was anticipated by eighteenth-century philosophers and philologists of the rationalist school [Szondi 1995]). As such a general discipline, Schleiermacher's hermeneutics is developed in his work on culture, religion, and the dialectical nature of truth-oriented discourse.

Schleiermacher is critical of the tradition, which, in his view, not only passes on the works of the past, but also has a tendency to petrify their meaning (Schleiermacher 1988: 107–10). Historical interpretation must proceed by assessing the validity of the traditional mediation of a given work. The standards by which such assessment takes place cannot be derived from tradition itself. In his hermeneutics, Schleiermacher seeks to articulate a set of regulative ideals by reference to which critical understanding proceeds. His point is not that these ideals or standards – combining knowledge of historical and linguistic context (grammatical interpretation) with sensitivity to individual application of the available symbolic resources (technical interpretation) – can guarantee adequate understanding of a given text, as if historical distance could be abolished by reference to transhistorical criteria. Rather, Schleiermacher suggests that only by holding our interpretative efforts up to a critical norm (or set of norms) can we hope to shed invalid prejudices and keep the tradition from hardening. In this way, the difference between Herder and Schleiermacher (whom Dilthey views as closely related [Dilthey 1996: 33–100]) is not that Herder is a historical thinker and Schleiermacher is not. The difference, rather, is that Schleiermacher, in responding to human historicity as a condition of possibility for *and* a limitation of (historical) interpretation, seeks to answer the larger ethical commitments that Herder had staked out by developing a philosophical language through which our thinking about issues in interpretation can take the form of methodological reflection. Schleiermacher shares this project with friends and colleagues such as Friedrich and August Wilhelm Schlegel.

Hegel positions himself in opposition to the Romantic movement to which Schleiermacher belonged. In Hegel's philosophy, the question is no longer how we can interpret and make use of insights gleaned from past or different cultures, but, rather, how a historical community can account for its commitment to truth and freedom (Hegel 1977: 11–14). There is no transcendent or metaphysical force behind history. The rationality of the historical development rests with spirit's ongoing attempts, in history, at making sense of how it has reached a given form or articulation. Hegel argues that his own time, that of post-revolutionary Europe, represents a final stage in spirit's accumulation of insight. Having arrived at the view of the human being as free, we can at this point expect no fundamental changes in our historical self-understanding (even though the realization of the idea of freedom still leaves a lot to be desired).

Hegel's hermeneutic position gives rise to a number of different (and not necessarily compatible) claims. In his *Lectures on the Philosophy of World History*, Hegel emphasizes the need to understand a historical period as it was (Hegel 2002: 29; McCarney: 2000). In the same work, however, he also underlines how a culture can only account for the validity of its practices by providing a historical account – which implies that both the past and non-Western cultures are sometimes judged to their detriment (see for example Hegel 2002: 173–94).

From a standpoint like that of Herder, this represents a return to a Eurocentric and presentist paradigm. From the point of view of the Hegelians, however, it represents a new and radical interpretation of human historicity, and thus, by implication, sheds light on the potential problems of the Herder–Schleiermacher model and its ideal of historical reconstruction. For Hegel, history is not simply to be reconstructed (in its constitutive otherness), but also to be articulated as part of the present identity of the historian. Historical understanding always involves a dimension of self-understanding. Hegel defends what Gadamer has called a hermeneutics of integration (Gadamer 1994: 164–9). While this is a position that Gadamer will later adopt and develop – though he has reservations about Hegel's idea of the end-of-history (Gadamer 1994: 98) – later nineteenth-century philosophers question this aspect of Hegel's thought.

2. Historicity, contingency, and the critique of ideology

There are at least two ways to address the philosophical discussions of history and historicity that follow in the wake of Hegel. On the one hand, we see the positions worked out by Herder and Schleiermacher attain a full, systematic articulation in the historicist movement and, framed somewhat differently, the work of Dilthey. On the other hand, the nineteenth century sees an upsurge of approaches – Nietzsche, Marx, and Freud – that present history as an ideological battleground and historical work as an effort to uncover the interests and motivations by which our past and present practices have been understood.

Friedrich Meinecke's magisteral *Historicism: The Rise of a New Historical Outlook* was the first important discussion of the philosophical presuppositions for, and implications of, the historicist movement (1936; English translation: Meinecke 1972).

Meinecke, however, views historicism as a reaction to an ahistorical Enlightenment, an effort to bring life, individuality, and meaning back into human self-understanding. More recently, Frederick Beiser has sought to revive historicism by presenting it as an extension of the broader Enlightenment paradigm and its efforts to ground history as a field of potential truth, objectivity, and knowledge (Beiser 2011). As it develops in the works of Barthold Niebuhr, Friedrich Karl von Savigny, Leopold von Ranke, and others, historicism is born out of a realization of the fundamental historicity (thus also potential contingency) of human expressions, actions, customs, and institutions, be it of the past or of the interpreter seeking understanding. Thus, making sense of the past is not a matter of antiquarian interest, but an issue that concerns the present and the future. Yet the way in which we can make sense of the past, these thinkers claimed, cannot follow along the lines of Hegel's system (at least not in the way it was perceived by the Hegelians of the day). As students and affiliates of Schleiermacher, the first generation of historicists insisted that the historian should uncover the past as it really was and seek to bracket his or her cultural presuppositions. However, in turning to history (as an object of study), a finite, human being is all the same situated in history (as an epistemic condition). In seeking to reconstruct history, what matters is thus the attempt to retrieve the meaning of individual expressions and events rather than a large-scale overview or teleological narrative. Such an attempt, however, requires not only historical work (which, like any other empirical research, is fallible), but also second-order knowledge about what would count as historical knowledge in the first place (i.e., a philosophical undertaking). Historicist philosophy seeks to identify the criteria for historical knowledge, the path towards obtaining it, and reflect upon its use and relevance.

The historicist orientation towards epistemology has led to the misunderstanding that historicism introduces a positivist attitude in the human sciences. Historicism does not reject existential issues or reduce them to epistemological quandaries. What it suggests, rather, is that if our values and institutions are thoroughly historical – if they are, in this sense, emphatically human – then it follows that we ought to take responsibility for them as such. This responsibility, in turn, involves the realization that historical understanding must be empirically committed and geared towards the attempt at unraveling the meaning of the individual expressions, events, and actions of which a given tradition consists.

This strategy of reasoning also shapes the work of Wilhelm Dilthey, which combines a historicist commitment to reconstruction with a comprehensive philosophical ambition to produce, along the lines of neo-Kantianism, a critique of historical reason. Dilthey, too, was a student of Schleiermacher. Yet his reading of Schleiermacher differs from those of the historicists. In Dilthey's reading, Schleiermacher's contribution should be located in the junction between a Fichtean emphasis on human spontaneity and a Herderian interest in the diversity of life-forms.

Dilthey captures the historical dimension of our being – and the challenge of historical understanding – by an appeal to lived experience (*Erlebnis*). History, he proposes, should be understood by trying to grasp a particular feeling of life or outlook on the world as it manifests itself in symbolic expressions. Poetry, in his view, represents an intensified, and thus particularly valuable, example of this (Dilthey

1985: 29–185). Further, Dilthey emphasizes the importance of biographical work (Dilthey 1985: 235–385). In his view, human reflection on the historicity of our being is not enhanced by grandiose narratives, but rests with concrete encounters, engagement with individual texts and works that express a particular worldview and an individualized understanding of human life. For Dilthey, such encounters facilitate their own kind knowledge. Rather than leaning on the natural sciences, the humanities must anchor their epistemic justification in the human historical world. In turning to historical-human existence, the scholar deals with an object that is, in principle, comprehensible to him or her (Dilthey 1989: 72).

With Nietzsche, Marx, and Freud we see a shift of emphasis from a critique of historical reason to an understanding of history as a struggle for ideological power and domination. As these thinkers see it, the tradition precludes our access to the past and conveys ideological structures that bar us from fully realizing ourselves. Nietzsche, Marx, and Freud do in other words share with the historicists and Dilthey a sense of values being historically developed (and thus humanly created), but in their case, this does not only lead to a reflection on epistemic or meta-philosophical issues, but also triggers a critique of ideology. Nietzsche, Marx, and Freud are not typically labeled hermeneutic thinkers. Still, they have come to play a significant role in twentieth-century debates about the possibility of a hermeneutics that seeks to uncover structures of power and distorted patterns of communication. Thus a few words must be said about the relevance of their respective approaches to hermeneutics and, relatedly, about their own hermeneutic practice as it is expressive of a certain conception of history and historicity.

Nietzsche starts out as a historical thinker, yet, from the very beginning, places history in the service of the present and the future. In the *Birth of Tragedy*, he traces the essence and demise of Greek tragedy while, all the same, seeking to free contemporary audiences from the grip of subjective aesthetics so as to retrieve the power of art (1872; English translation: Nietzsche 1999). Later on, in "On the Uses and Disadvantages of History for Life," Nietzsche analyses the nature and problems of different types of history writing: monumental history (viewing the past as providing examples of human glory), antiquarian history (retrieving the past for the past's own sake), and critical history (judging history and approaching it in terms of present needs) (Nietzsche 2011: 67–72). His own alternative to these approaches is worked out in *On the Genealogy of Morality*, in which he insists that historians should contribute to the assessment of the values we have become accustomed to taking for granted (Nietzsche 1998: 5). For a finite human being, the challenge is not only to reconstruct history objectively, but also to approach it in the service of life. Historical work is associated with emancipation; it exposes the sources of our values and can thus facilitate changes in our moral outlook.

Marx, too, will assume a connection between history and social change, though his objective is different from that of Nietzsche. His field is political economy, and in his view, political economists have lacked a historical sense. In order, however, for philosophers and critics to understand social and economical relationships and their pervasive influence on human practice and self-understanding, historical knowledge is needed. In Marx's view, we should seek to understand the historical beginnings of our economical system (capitalism) so as better to usher in its end. History must not be idealistic (or, in Marx's eyes, Hegelian), but should disclose the structural patterns of class and economy (Marx 2006: 126). Only in this way can human spontaneity be retrieved from reified structures and we can uncover the possibility of meaningful human lives.

Freud critiques the social and cultural patterns of bourgeois society, though from the point of view of an economy of instincts. His emphasis on history is twofold: the repression of drives and instincts in modern society (though all culture, to some extent, requires that) and the psychological history of individual instincts, often repressed, that can be subject to psychoanalytic recovery (Freud 1986: 131–52). Further, Freud forays into the hermeneutics of myth and religious narratives. In his view, there is an analogy between dreams (understood as private mythology) and myths (as the waking dreams of a culture). Freud draws from this that literature and dreams should be interpreted in the same manner (Ricoeur 1970: 494–553).

Though there is a long way from the position of the early historicists to Freud's cultural criticism, nineteenth-century hermeneutics can be seen as a series of responses to the anxieties – and, with Dilthey, Nietzsche, Freud, and Marx, also the opportunities – that follow from the realization that human values are historical by nature, and thus can also be changed. This entails a particular kind of responsibility. Such responsibility is historically coded; it requires insight into the fundamental historicity of the cultural and social world and a realization that our access to this world involves some version of hermeneutic work. Hence, for these nineteenth-century thinkers, human historicity (at an existential level) and historical interpretation (at a scholarly level) are mutually related.

3. Historicity and the quest for meaning

In the twentieth century, Heidegger and Gadamer develop the insights articulated by Dilthey and Nietzsche, yet alter both the context in which these insights are shaped and the philosophical implications to be gleaned from them. For Heidegger and Gadamer, history, and by implication the historical sciences, can only be properly understood to the extent that they are grounded in human existence.

Heidegger's approach to history and historicity can be divided into three different phases (and corresponding problem areas). In his early lectures, predating *Being and Time*, Heidegger is concerned with problems handed down from Dilthey and the historicists. Dilthey's philosophy helps Heidegger get beyond what he took to be the ahistorical phenomenology of his teacher, Edmund Husserl. However, in turning to Dilthey, Heidegger realizes that he must expand the framework of traditional philosophy. Heidegger is worried that Dilthey and the historicists turn history into an object of scholarship and study rather than an existential condition.

While some of this criticism is carried on into *Being and Time*, Heidegger, from the mid 1920s onwards, is ready to offer his own, phenomenological model of historicity and hermeneutics. As he now puts it, the problem with Dilthey and the historicists is not simply that they objectify history, but that they fail to see that historicity (as an "existential problem") is prior to history as a science or a reflective activity in which we engage. Historicity, for Heidegger, is the ultimate horizon of our lives. From this point of view, Heidegger further develops the Nietzschean critique of historical research, leading the antiquarian, the critical, and the monumental approaches back to their shared roots in human historicity (Heidegger 1996: 396–8). However, if Nietzsche, in Heidegger's view, did not fully grasp the common source of these approaches, he nonetheless realized that history is not simply a thing of the past. For Heidegger, as for Nietzsche, history can only be properly grasped within the horizon of the present and, ultimately, the future. While Nietzsche addresses the usefulness of history from the perspective of life, Heidegger's analysis, in *Being and Time*, leads to his idea of an authentic historicity that is coupled with the destiny of a people (Heidegger 1996: 384).

A final phase in Heidegger's reflection on historicity can be found in the period after *Being and Time*. In works such as *The Origin of the Work of Art* (Heidegger 2002: 1–57), Heidegger's main concern is no longer the tendency of historical science to objectivize the past. Nor is it that of authentic and inauthentic historicity and their respective relationship to history as a science. History is, so to speak, situated beyond individual human practice and self-understanding, and viewed as a condition for the kind of situation into which an individual human being (Dasein) is thrown and the truth in light of which it lives (or fails to live) its life. In Heidegger's mytho-poetical language, art lends expression to a strife between world, as the field of a human-historical meaning, and earth, as an ahistorical, material dimension of reality. The idea of history as a sublime event is further pursued in *Contributions to Philosophy (From Enowning)* (written 1936–38; for English translation of this posthumously published text, see Heidegger 1999). The concept of *Seinsgeschichte* seeks to capture the deeper structures of meaning and intelligibility that enable human agency in history.

In taking over, but also significantly reworking Heidegger's notion of historicity, Gadamer combines elements from the various phases of Heidegger's work. His 1960 *Truth and Method* deals with the conditions of possibility for the human sciences, yet anchors these conditions in a more profound experience of the historicity of human life through engagement with the eminent works of the tradition (Gadamer 1994). Prior to *Truth and Method*, however, Gadamer had published an important study of Plato. He had sought to utilize the young Heidegger's approach to historical research – returning, as it were, to a direct encounter with the text as it is in itself – so as to get beyond the monumental ontological analysis of the late Heidegger and emphasize the dialogical structure of rationality (Gadamer 1991). Gadamer's emphasis on dialogue, which has later been taken up by Jürgen Habermas, Paul Ricoeur, and Charles Taylor, fundamentally informs his hermeneutic philosophy in *Truth and Method*. This work, though, is marked by a tension between a reflective-dialogical attitude to historical understanding and an emphasis on how tradition is ontologically prior to the individual interpreter. As they have been handed down by generations of interpreters, the eminent texts of the past have amassed a richness of meaning that is constitutive for a tradition that unifies work and interpreter, thus, in Gadamer's view, also enabling interpretation. While the interpreter contributes to this meaning by applying the truths of the work in ever new contexts, he or she must nonetheless ascribe priority to the work over against individual consciousness. Gadamer explains this point with reference to the structure of playing. In playing, the play is, as it were, given priority over against the moves and strategies of the individual player. That is, only to the extent that the individual player recognizes the priority of the play can he or she be part of it in the first place. This model informs Gadamer's version of the hermeneutic circle (a notion that is also present in *Being and Time*: Heidegger 1996). The circle of understanding, the mutual interplay between text and interpreter, is an enabling condition for interpretational work (and thus not, as it might first appear, a vicious circle), but ultimately also a precondition for historical existence *überhaupt*. With Gadamer's model, historical distance is no longer a problem to be overcome, but a condition for the kind of meaning we find in art, literature, and human expression more broadly speaking. Hermeneutics, in turn, is no method of understanding, but a philosophical effort to account for the process of historical mediation, the meaning it entails, and the way in which it shapes the conditions for intersubjective interaction.

In the aftermath of *Truth and Method*, there has been much discussion of this point. Habermas and Karl-Otto Apel have worried that Gadamer deprives the individual interpreter of a capacity for reflective deliberation on the validity of past practices and expressions (Habermas et al. 1977). In thinking about historical work, do we not need a language to address how tradition conveys not only a binding meaning, but also undesirable attitudes such as racism, imperialism, or misogyny? Encountering these objections, Gadamer has pointed out that his theory does not exclude a critical stance in interpretation (Habermas et al. 1977: 57–83 and Ormiston and Schrift 1990: 273–98).

While he draws on the Heideggerian-Gadamerian analysis of historicity, Paul Ricoeur has sought to formulate a model of interpretation that integrates the insights of Nietzsche, Marx, and Freud (Ricoeur 1981). Further, Ricoeur emphasizes the analogy between discourse and action, thus significantly extending the arena of hermeneutic philosophy. Strangely, Ricoeur's line of reception has only played a lesser role in the recent, Anglophone adaptation of Heidegger and Gadamer's work. While Heidegger, mainly on the basis of the first division of *Being and Time*, has been read as a pragmatist (Okrent 1991), Donald Davidson, John McDowell, and Robert Brandom have turned to Gadamer's work so as to expand the scope of Anglophone theory of language and interpretation. In Davidson's words, he and Gadamer found themselves in the same "intellectual neighborhood" (Davidson 1997: 421). Likewise Brandom suggests a return to Gadamerian theory of interpretation as a framework for talking more generally about meaning and understanding (Brandom 2002: 92–118). With McDowell, however, we see a more direct interest in bringing out Gadamer's orientation towards history and historicity so as to articulate a sustainable notion of self-formation in and through cultural practice (McDowell 1994: 124–6).

4. Conclusion

The hermeneutic tradition provides a variety of models for thinking about history, historicity, tradition, and the foundations of the historical sciences. In contemporary discussion, Gadamer's *Truth and Method* is often portrayed as representing hermeneutics as such. In this work, however, there is a tendency to depict the modern hermeneutic tradition as a teleological process leading up to Heidegger's ontological turn, not as a series of alternative conceptions of human history, historicity, and the relationship between them. This can easily leave us with an incomplete picture of the tradition of hermeneutics, but also with a weakened grasp of the systematic possibilities this tradition entails. Wishing to balance this picture, I have sought to outline a broader spectrum of hermeneutic positions. The hermeneutic paradigm is robust enough to accommodate – indeed, it can only thrive in and gain from – a discussion of different conceptions of history and historicity. This, indeed, is what keeps hermeneutics alive as a genuine philosophical discourse. And it is what will keep us, as philosophers, alive to the historicity of our existence, the tradition in which we stand, and the historical presuppositions for and ramifications of our work in the field of hermeneutics.

Bibliography

Beiser, Frederick (2011). *The German Historicist Tradition*. Oxford: Oxford University Press.

Brandom, Robert B. (2002). *Tales of the Mighty Dead: Historical Essays in the Metaphysics of Intentionality*. Cambridge, Mass.: Harvard University Press.

Davidson, Donald (1997). "Gadamer and Plato's *Philebus*," in *The Philosophy of Hans-Georg Gadamer*. Ed. Lewis E. Hahn. Chicago: Open Court, 421–33.

Dilthey, Wilhelm (1996). *Hermeneutics and the Study of History*. Ed. Rudolf Makkreel and Frithjof Rodi. Trans. Theordore Nordenhaug et al. Princeton: Princeton University Press.

——(1989). *Introduction to the Human Sciences*. Trans. Michael Neville et al. Ed. Rudolf A. Makkreel and Fridhjof Rodi. Princeton: Princeton University Press.

——(1985). *Poetry and Experience*. Ed. Rudolf A. Makkreel and Fridhjof Rodi. Trans. Louis Agosta, Rudolf Makkreel et al. Princeton: Princeton University Press.

Freud, Sigmund (1986). *Historical and Expository Works on Psychoanalysis*. The Penguin Freud Library, vol. 15. Trans. James Strachey. London: Penguin.

Gadamer, Hans-Georg (1994). *Truth and Method* (second, revised edn.). Trans. Joel Weinsheim and Donald G. Marshall. New York: Continuum.

——(1991). *Plato's Dialectical Ethics*. Trans. Robert Wallace. New Haven: Yale University Press.

Habermas, Jürgen et al. (eds.) (1977). *Hermeneutik und Ideologiekritik*. Frankfurt am Main: Suhrkamp.

Hegel, G. W. F. (2002). *Lectures on the Philosophy of World History: Introduction*. Trans. H. B. Nisbet. Cambridge: Cambridge University Press.

——(1977). *Phenomenology of Spirit*. Trans. A. V. Miller. Oxford: Oxford University Press.

Heidegger, Martin (2002). *Off the Beaten Track*. Ed. and trans. Julian Young and Kenneth Haynes. Cambridge: Cambridge University Press.

——(1999). *Contributions to Philosophy (From Enowning)*. Trans. Parvis Emad and Kenneth Maly. Bloomingdale: Indiana University Press.

——(1996). *Being and Time*. Trans. Joan Stambaugh. Albany: State University of New York Press.

Herder, Johann Gottfried (2008). *Shakespeare*. Trans. Gregory Moore. Princeton: Princeton University Press.

——(2004). *Another Philosophy of History and Selected Political Writings*. Trans. Ioannis D. Evrigenis and Daniel Pellerin. Cambridge: Hackett.

Marx, Karl (2006). *Early Political Writings*. Ed. Joseph O'Malley. Cambridge: Cambridge University Press.

McCarney, Joseph (2000). *Hegel on History*. London: Routledge.

McDowell, John (1994). *Mind and World*. Harvard: Harvard University Press.

Meinecke, Friedrich (1972). *Historicism: The Rise of a New Historical Outlook*. Trans. J. E. Anderson. London: Routledge.

Nietzsche, Friedrich (2011). *Untimely Meditations*. Ed. Daniel Breazeale. Trans. R. J. Hollingdale. Cambridge: Cambridge University Press.

——(1999). *The Birth of Tragedy and Other Writings*. Ed. Raymond Geuss and Ronald Speirs. Trans. Ronald Speirs. Cambridge: Cambridge University Press.

——(1998). *On the Genealogy of Morality: A Polemic*. Trans. Maudemarie Clark and Alan J. Swensen. Cambridge: Hackett.

Okrent, Mark (1991). *Heidegger's Pragmatism: Understanding, Being, and the Critique of Metaphysics*. Ithaca: Cornell University Press.

Ormiston, Gayle L. and Alan D. Schrift (eds.) (1990). *The Hermeneutic Tradition: From Ast to Ricoeur*. Albany: State University of New York Press.

Ricoeur, Paul (1970). *Freud and Philosophy: An Essay on Interpretation*. Trans. Denis Savage. New Haven: Yale University Press.

——(1981). *Hermeneutics and the Human Sciences*. Ed. and trans. John B. Thomson. Cambridge: Cambridge University Press.

Schleiermacher, Friedrich (1998). *Hermeneutics and Criticism: And Other Writings*. Ed. and trans. Andrew Bowie. Cambridge: Cambridge University Press.

——(1988). *On Religion: Speeches to its Cultured Despisers*. Trans. Richard Crouter. Cambridge: Cambridge University Press.

Szondi, Peter (1995). *Introduction to Literary Hermeneutics*. Trans. Martha Woodmansee. Cambridge: Cambridge University Press.

Further reading

Bernstein, Richard J. (1983). *Beyond Objectivism and Relativism: Science, Hermeneutics, and Praxis*. Philadelphia: The University of Pennsylvania Press.

Dostal, Robert J. (2002). *The Cambridge Companion to Gadamer*. Cambridge: Cambridge University Press.

Malpas, Jeff, Ulrich Arnswald, and Jens Kertscher (eds.) (2002). *Gadamer's Century: Essay in Honor of Hans-Georg Gadamer*. Cambridge, Mass.: The MIT Press.

Mueller-Vollmer, Kurt (ed.) (1989). *The Hermeneutics Reader: Texts of the German Tradition from the Enlightenment to the Present*. New York: Continuum.

Szondi, Peter (1986). *On Textual Understanding and Other Essays*. Trans. Harvey Mendelsohn. Minneapolis: University of Minnesota Press.

24
ETHICS AND COMMUNITY

Hans-Herbert Kögler

Hermeneutics is concerned with the grounds of understanding and interpretation – but what is its relevance for ethics? Is hermeneutics relevant for ethics? Is a *hermeneutic ethic* possible? This chapter probes the conceptual resources of hermeneutic thought for the development of a hermeneutic ethic. At the center of such an ethic would be, I suggest, the intrinsic connection between *the normative orientation towards the other*, who is granted primordial importance for ethics, and *the role of interpretive understanding*, which is here considered essential for the realization of ethics. The recognition of the other as an irreducible agent in dialogue, to whom I owe the openness to take her views seriously, articulates the normative infrastructure of dialogical interpretation. The grounding for a hermeneutic ethic is found in our essential community with others, in the intertwinedness of ethical agency with intersubjective relations. We will prepare the development of such a position by reconstructing concepts such as empathy, understanding, tradition, dialogue, dialogical community, ethical recognition, and social reflexivity, suggesting them as constructive building blocks for a hermeneutic ethic.

1. The limits of empathy

The idea of a hermeneutic ethic is intersubjectively oriented towards the other. The recognition of the self-understanding of the other is central. This ethic thus aims to realize the moral bond between agents through the mutual understanding of one another as human subjects, as co-subjects who share the essential features of humanity. The source of such an ethical understanding is therefore thought to be found in modes of understanding that uniquely express such a human bond, that display a form or process of understanding that specifically exists when humans understand one another. It is here that the role of empathy as an essential feature of a hermeneutic ethic belongs. Empathy is a complex concept that may be grounded in the intuition of a uniquely emotional, pre-linguistic sense that humans are able to share. Inasmuch as 'pure' emotional states may also be shared among humans and higher animals, it may quickly become obvious that the uniquely human form of empathy may indeed not be separated from its linguistic and cultural contexts, and rather belongs in a theory of human agency that entails the social contexts as well as its symbolic and linguistic mediations as essential building blocks (Kögler/Stueber 2000).

Nevertheless, the aspect of an emotional understanding of the other has been a source of grounding and explicating an ethical recognition of the other. In thinkers like Adam Smith or David Hume, the emotional constitution of humans is designated as the very source of morality as such. Since moral thought is supposed to guide human action, and the concept of action involves a motivational dimension that cannot be explained by mere reference to beliefs, the step toward designating emotional states as those that uniquely define the moral dimension of action seems reasonable. Furthermore, what drives humans to act morally, that is, to concern themselves actively about the well-being of others, seems grounded in feeling-states about those others. One is able to display moral concern, solicitude, and care because one actually does care, caring being a state that involves an understanding of the other's plight combined with a feeling that is shared by the one who cares (Hoffman 2000). Therefore, the emotional state of caring expresses the individual intersubjective capacity to understand the state of the other, that is, to feel like another does, or to put oneself emotionally in the other's shoes. At the same time, such a state expresses, by means of this sharing-an-emotional-state ability, the fact of a shared human nature. The emotional capacity for first-personal empathetic experience, in which I feel like another and therefore can come to care for the other, becomes the phenomenological warrant of a shared ontology of empathic ability which assures us of our common humanity.

The focus on a hermeneutic ethic forces us to consider *the relevance of empathy* for the recognition of the other. The crucial step is taken by Friedrich Schleiermacher ([1819] 1957) and Wilhelm Dilthey ([1883] 1959), even though their decision to make empathy central for a theory of understanding is not motivated by moral concerns, but rather grounded in the attempt to do justice to the object domain of the human sciences. Inasmuch as this object domain represents human history and culture, it express intentional human agency and thus requires an adequate mode of understanding. Even though the concern is epistemological, doing justice to *human expressions as human expressions* entails a methodologically relevant *ontological recognition* of the other as a human subject. For Schleiermacher, understanding human agency involves both the linguistic side of the medium of expression as well as the intentional or psychological side of the expressing subject. Empathetic transposition into the other via re-experience or divinatory stipulation of the others' thoughts and motives represents the culmination of a never-completed process of interpretive approximation to the other's thoughts. Dilthey sees the epistemological ground of inter-human understanding in the ability to relive, within one's own self-transparent mental states, the other's thought and lived experiences. As the 'object domain' of the human sciences consists of human agents who express themselves through texts and other cultural objectifications, the hermeneutic process is defined by the triad of experience, expression, and understanding (*Erlebnis*, *Ausdruck*, and *Verstehen*). The interpreter adequately approaches the other if he or she gets involved in a process of adopting the other's experiential stance such as to re-live or re-construct the meaning of her intentional statements and actions.

The epistemological lesson of the limits of empathy is relevant for the project of a hermeneutic ethic. Here the interpretive understanding is to entail or yield the *recognition* of the other. Now grounded in the general capacity for empathically shared emotional states, it all depends on how the process of empathetic transposition into the other (which should lead to the understanding of the other) is conceived. It became clear to the late Dilthey, and was also acknowledged by Schleiermacher's emphasis on linguistic cultural understanding, that the recourse to self-experienced emotional states is too thin a basis for intersubjective understanding, and thus cannot ground intersubjective recognition. The emotional as much as the cognitive core of the interpreter's mind, on the basis of which an empathetic transposition into the other is undertaken, is itself only given in an already culturally and historically mediated form (Dilthey [1910] 2004). To designate one's own response to an event or phenomenon as the bridgehead into the other's self-understanding may trigger a naïve and misguided assimilation of the other's experiences and meaning to one's own beliefs, assumptions, and cultural practices.

The problem consists in the conflation of empathy with pre-communal feeling-states that are experienced by the individual. This suggests that moral understanding is grounded in the empathetic-emotional identification of the self with the experiential states of the other. Yet the fact that the other experiences these states in a particular cultural and social setting, which defines the full experience of the other as a human being, is thereby ignored. The emotional bridge is taken to cross, as it were, the different contexts to establish a direct emotional community with the other.[1] Emotional empathy not only invites the aforementioned problem of assimilative understanding, but also reduces the other's experience to its pure a-contextual and a-cultural core. It thereby fails to live up to the true ethical recognition of the other, which has to include the other's particular cultural identity as much as the other's reflexive ability to transcend her contextual situatedness. To be sure, reflexive models of empathy may entail these considerations, but they can only do so by basing the concept of perspective-taking on a more complex conception of human understanding that entails context.

2. Understanding: from Being-in-the-World to tradition

An important step towards a hermeneutic ethic thus consists in showing that the constitution of ethical agents derives from the socially shared context. This agrees with the *ontological turn in hermeneutics*, in which the interest in the methodological question of the correct and true interpretation of texts and meanings gives way to the project to understand human existence as such. Human agency is now seen *in its core* to be defined by *understanding and interpretation*. Making sense of oneself, one's environment, and other agents is not 'added on' to our (emotionally or otherwise) pre-constituted being, but *understanding constitutes the human being*. Humans are always already in the world, and they only exist by understanding it. What Martin Heidegger calls a 'hermeneutics of facticity' designates the philosophical project to reconstruct this basic ontology of our interpretive being (Heidegger 1999). The realization that we are not self-related subjects as such, but embedded to our core in social and practical relations opens a whole new vision onto the ethical problematic.

Instead of having norms or values added onto an otherwise solitary subject that confronts a world of mute and neutral facts, we are intrinsically normative and ethical due to our social constitution. The social ontology to which we owe our existence, and which forms our understanding of it, is taken to entail an *ethical bond* that a reflexive ethic aims to articulate.[2]

Yet Heidegger's ontological turn only prepares the grounding of ethics in a prior ethical bond that precedes any conscious subjective ethic. It does so because the self is now defined as *Dasein* which is essentially *Being-in-the-World*, and as such is defined as a socially and practically grounded understanding (Heidegger [1927] 1962). Understanding does not mean the cognitive activity of a solitary subject, but the embedded, intuitive, socially and practically constituted as well as historically defined projection of meaning. Implicit understanding happens prior to explicit interpretation. A 'fore-structure of understanding' (Heidegger) defines that we see a house as a house, a city as (that) city, hear a noise as that of a specific car or train. We exist in an objective spirit of significance (Dilthey), a shared world of beliefs, assumptions, and practices that pre-structure our conscious and intentional activities and experiences. Yet Heidegger's own phenomenological analyses of our Being-in-the-World proved to be shaped by philosophy's prior focus on the sole agent. Heidegger resituates the mind of the individual thoroughly in a shared practical and social world, but the ethos that defines *Being and Time* is the existentialist one of freeing the falling inauthentic self from the anonymous dictatorship of social institutions. While the ontological grounding and the foundational nature of a hermeneutic pre-understanding are forever established, a sufficient and much-needed phenomenological focus on the *uniquely intersubjective relation*, the relation of Being-with-one-another, is suspiciously absent (Löwith [1928] 2013).

What is required is thus not only to ground the self ontologically in a prior practical and social world, but to bring out the *ethical nature of our social existence*. The ethical reformulation of Heidegger's hermeneutics of facticity takes place in Hans-Georg Gadamer's philosophical hermeneutics (Gadamer [1960] 1989). While Gadamer's approach owes an immense debt to both early and late Heidegger, the perspective is nevertheless fundamentally different, based on an entirely different vision of the social. The situated agent is, as in Heidegger, pre-defined in her self-understanding by a largely implicit, embodied, and contextual background. Yet this background is now understood to be *tradition*. *Tradition is the lived intersubjective context of cultural and social practices that define the shared understanding of agents about themselves, others, and the world*. Tradition culminates and objectifies itself in symbolic form, of which eminent texts – which are themselves embedded in an endless web of textual and practical interpretations – are the most prominent linguistic objectifications. Tradition does not merely consist of textual or cultural objectifications as such – the objectified *Überlieferung*. It rather expresses in spirit and practice the self-understanding of cultural contexts within which agents engage in its linguistic articulation. As such it embodies the place of a linguistically mediated yet objective spirit, which shapes the agents' self-understanding as its *effective history* (*Wirkungsgeschichte*), as the ever-renewed interpretations of the phenomena at stake. But because Gadamer now understands this condition of understanding as an essentially intersubjective background, the task of *reflexive self-interpretation* changes: It is not premised, as in

Heidegger, on the radical escape from an inauthentic social conformity and self-alienation. *The task of interpretation is now the dialogical re-discovery of the intentional meanings, expressed by cultural objectifications and practices, about the things at stake.* The task of understanding becomes the recognition of *the truth*, that is of the important and challenging perspectives and viewpoints expressed in culture and society.

3. The idea of a dialogical community

If we approach Gadamer's philosophical hermeneutics in this way, we are able to see its contribution to the grounding of ethics in a sophisticated conception of *dialogical community*. Community is here neither an encompassing social whole or totality that overwhelms the self and makes it one with all others; nor is it merely the aggregate notion of an assembly of distinct agents who contingently form bonds across the gap that allegedly separates their inescapably individual selves. Rather, the self is able to understand itself only because it is embedded in a background understanding that entails *an implicit recognition and pre-existing bond with the other.* The other, or better: the basic intersubjective relation with the other, is a presupposition for one's existence as well as one's cognitive capacity. The hermeneutic pre-understanding, which is the condition of possibility for the understanding and interpretation of anything, is derived from a context that can only exist intersubjectively. This entails the ontological priority of the intersubjective relation before any other world- or self-relation. But how can such a claim be substantiated? How can we show that there is this prior connectedness and bond with the other that sustains our existence and grounds community?

The hermeneutic answer to these questions is a phenomenology of understanding, and more specifically the claim that understanding is indisputably linguistic in nature. Human experience is essentially defined by *language* since it is this symbolic medium which grants us our uniquely embedded and yet distanced relationship to the world; it makes possible a reflexive self-understanding that is nevertheless emergent from our existence in the real world. Humans experience themselves in a 'world,' which means they are not merely behaving via dispositions in an environment. Rather, what they experience is capable of being defined and reflexively coped with, meaning that our understanding of *what is* depends on our ability to express it as such: "Being that can be understood is language" (Gadamer [1960] 1989: 474). Such an approach does not, of course, deny that the world consists of more than words or speech acts; that experiences often lack expressions and fail to be fully expressable; or that language itself depends on shared practices and contexts that stabilize and support it. However, what makes the difference in contrast to merely behavioral or physical relations is that the symbolic mediation allows for a synthetic and shared development of meanings in which all our experiences are expressed *as experiences.* These meanings transcend their context of origin and enable us to re-define and re-evaluate the mere facticity of the given.[3]

The explication of the language-ontological presupposition of all understanding allows us to see how hermeneutic experience, as happening in the medium of language, entails an *ethical recognition* due to the dialogical nature of language:

Hermeneutical experience is concerned with *tradition*. ... But tradition is not simply a process that experience teaches us to know and to govern; it is language – i.e., it expresses itself like a Thou. A Thou is not an object; it relates itself to us ... It is clear that the experience of the Thou must be special because the Thou is not an object but is in relationship with us.

(Gadamer [1960] 1989: 358)

Gadamer is quick to emphasize that this does not mean to take tradition as the expression of another agent in her psychological or biographical setting; rather language, as we saw, enables the transcendence from the immediacy of the empirical context that is to be maintained in the dialogical reconstruction of interpretation. Yet what emerges now is a new, somewhat linguistically mediated immediacy that consists in the openness to the other's claim with which she addresses us via a symbolic expression. If we reduce the other to nothing but an 'object' of understanding, disregarding the claim she makes about the subject matter that is addressed in her speech or text's meaning, "the Thou loses the immediacy with which it makes its claim" (Gadamer [1960] 1989: 359). Instead, what is required is to allow the tradition its claim to validity, which in turn "calls for a fundamental sort of openness" (Gadamer [1960] 1989: 361).

4. The ethical recognition of the other in dialogue

Gadamer's approach presents us with the suggestion that the adequate understanding of symbolic expressions has to address 'the claim' they make on us. This follows from the dialogical nature of language 'expressing itself like a Thou.' The dialogical nature of language involves a *reciprocal mutuality* between the involved subjects that entails the openness to the other's claims vis-à-vis one's own beliefs and assumptions about the subject matter. But the openness towards the other is itself fostered and supported by the reflexive insight into one's own cultural and historical situatedness.[4] Understanding that one is not free of prejudices, that one is thoroughly situated in a never fully transparent or complete background understanding, urges the subject to endorse the claim of the other, thereby renewing the moral bond with her.

A person who believes he is free of prejudices relying on the objectivity of his procedures and denying that he himself is conditioned by historical circumstances, experiences the power of the prejudices that unconsciously dominate him as a vis a tergo. A person who does not admit that he is dominated by prejudices will fail to see what manifests itself in their light. It is like the relation between I and Thou. *A person who reflects himself out of the mutuality of such a relation changes the relationship and destroys its moral bond. A person who reflects himself out of a living relationship to tradition destroys the true meaning of this tradition in the same way* ... I must allow tradition's claim to validity.

(Gadamer [1960] 1989: 360, 361)

This argument from hermeneutic finitude is based on a complex but plausible intertwinement of epistemic and ethical considerations that are ultimately referring back to our ontological constitution as human beings. Understanding the other is not a cognitive act that captures a self-sustained object in its pre-existing determination. To understand the other is rather the renewal of our social co-existence in which I am held to address and react to what another agent, as a rational and equal co-subject, expresses linguistically vis-à-vis a shared subject matter. To understand the other epistemically is thus to recognize the other as a rational partner in dialogue, and thus to also recognize the other ethically as equal.

Gadamer further explicates what he means by this 'moral bond' by analyzing ethically inadequate modes of interpretation in the human and social sciences, which he correlates with objectifying and unethical intersubjective attitudes.[5] Gadamer strongly rejects 'objectifying' modes of interpretation, in which the other is conceptualized either as the representative or exemplar of a class, race, gender, nation, profession, age, and so on (as in much of the social sciences), or in individualized terms as a unique historical being (as in much of the humanities). Gadamer relates these modes of academic interpretation back to either a generalizing knowledge that uses stereotypical knowledge to predict and control the other's future behavior, or to an individualized empathetic attention that focuses on the other's unique circumstances.[6] The crux is that both attitudes reflect themselves out of the true and mutual relationship with the other, thereby disallowing any real challenge of the other towards oneself. Importantly, Gadamer explains that such a reflective objectification contradicts the moral constitution of the human being: "From the moral point of view, this (objectifying) orientation toward the Thou contradicts the moral definition of man" (Gadamer [1960] 1989: 358).

The project of a hermeneutic ethic can now be formulated as follows: The Kantian idea of the human subject *as an end in itself* is to be *dialogically reconstructed* as the 'ethical imperative' to respect the other such that his or her claims vis-à-vis a subject matter are taken seriously. The respect vis-à-vis the other's authentic voice, vis-à-vis the other's truth claims as important and challenging perspectives about something, defines the moral core of the dialogical ethic. To never approach the other merely as something to be understood, as an object in terms of one's own interpretive beliefs and assumptions, but always as a subject that is herself a source of beliefs and assumptions – such is the ethical orientation that follows from hermeneutic thought. The dialogical recognition of the other's presence as an interpretive source amounts to the recognition of the other as a human co-subject, and thus fulfills the moral demand of respect for the other's humanity.

5. The social possibility of the ethical bond

The ethical bond with the other can only be maintained and renewed in the dialogical attitude of respect towards the other by taking her claims seriously. It is the intersubjective participant's perspective that alone guarantees the ethical bond that unites self and other. The linguistic mediation of self and other ensures that the other is not assimilated or objectified, but is to come to speak for herself – which is only possible if the self understands that such speaking is always mediated by the self's own prejudgments, is encountered by an itself situated self. Yet if the inter-subjective nature of understanding and interpretation is thus granted, and if a strong intersubjectivist ontology is put forth in its defense, we still need to establish how the dialogical recognition is able *to emerge* from the situated understanding in which an agent is already immersed in her social life. How can the dialogical ethos of recognition come to be realized in our social life-world? How are agents who are defined by social context and circumstance capable of orienting themselves towards the dialogical attitude towards others? How can the self overcome the everyday social perception of others as defined by stereotypical and socially acquired cate-gories, such as class, race, gender, age, and so on? How, if those factors play a role in shaping the pre-understanding of agents, should the agents' situatedness by social factors be taken into account? And if those pre-assumptions necessarily define the agents' background and self-understanding to some extent, how are agents to become aware of them, challenge and evaluate them, and ultimately recognize the other by transcending them?

The challenge of a hermeneutic ethic is akin to bringing out the ontological *possibility* of a true dialogical relation with the other amidst one's actual social power situation (Kögler 1999). To suggest the predominant ontological *reality* of dialogical relations based on recognition would be absurd; yet to assume the *impossibility* of ethical recognition would be defeatist and ignore the phenomenological evidence. Contributions to a hermeneutic phenomenology of intersubjective experience mark steps towards a full picture how we may conceive this ontology of dialogical possi-bility. The work in hermeneutic phenomenology is defined by a paradox: to unearth the social origin of all understanding as a source for the ethical recognition of the other, and yet to equally realize that the *existing social relations entail the objectification and reduction of the other*. At stake is an approach that shows how true dialogue is possible in contexts that suggest otherwise.

The phenomenological task must begin by reconstructing how we initially encounter the other. The basic assumption about the social nature of our shared pre-understanding must be specified by how the other is experienced in our daily interactions, how we encounter one another usually, how we usually interact (Löwith [1928] 2013; Heidegger [1927] 1962; Mead 1934). Such interactions happen in the context of the multifold practical contexts in which we pursue our tasks and projects. Others are thus encountered in terms of the roles they play as co-subjects in the pursuit of these projects and practices. Individuals appear first as persons who occupy certain roles, they appear and approach us as a partner, friend, mother, boss, professor, president, and so on. The challenge is how, from this role-typical inter-pretation of others, a uniquely intersubjective relation with the other can emerge and be experienced. The task is to define possible experiences or attitudes that break through this *stereotypical construction of the other* – such that the authentic other, who is both more than her social role and yet also defined by it, can show herself. The other is to emerge as a being-in-itself, as an end-in-itself that is not identified with its social identity, but understood in its situated autonomy. This requires that the other self is not perceived through one's own purposes and interests, but as an equal, as someone who deserves full recognition as self. And yet, "this voluntary 'respect' for the other as a fully equal 'end-in-itself' is not a priori given as duty, but rather the 'ethical' result of one's 'natural' life-experience" (Löwith [1928] 2013).

The dialogical recognition of the other as equal partner must emerge from the socially situated life-contexts. Its content consists in establishing an authentic relation of the other as a *You* – and thus not merely as a self unto herself, as suggested by Heidegger who merely opposes the troublesome solicitude with an approach that lets the other free to be herself. Akin to Gadamer, Löwith defines the core of recognition as the uptake of this relationship as such, as the challenge that the *You* is regarded as an irreducible I that is essentially related to me. What is demanded here is a form of recognition in which the other is not only experienced as an internal resistance, a counter-stance, an object (Gegenstand) that blocks and intercepts the self's interpretive scheme. Instead, at stake is an encounter with the other in which the other truly breaks the monopoly of one's own interpretative scheme, de-centers the self's view, and emerges as another center of understanding, as a source of world-experience in itself. What we need is a phenomenology that lets the other show herself in this vein by establishing how the other can be experienced as a *You* (Buber [1923] 2004).

And yet the social situation in which the relevant experiences may appear may be structurally constrained and thus hinder the development of a true dialogue, the relationship with a *You*. In situations of institutional or social non-equality between the involved subjects, the openness towards the other and thus the to-and-fro with regard to a subject matter may have practically become impossible; similarly, certain discursive settings preclude some topics and suggest others. Conceptual frameworks enable the thematization of specific aspects, the raising of questions, and the invocation of angles vis-à-vis a subject matter – and preclude others. Social contexts assign speakers specific roles with regard to what can be said about what, who can ask and who can answer, and who can redirect, stop, enhance, or advance an ongoing dialogue. Finally, the respective discursive settings are themselves located in larger social contexts and structures that have pre-determined not only the speaker–hearer roles within these settings, but also the agents' embodied cognitive capabilities with regard to these roles and discourses. In doing so, social power not only exercises an external and formal authority with regard to what can and cannot be said, but also equips the participants with the respective capabilities and skills to conform to its pervasive regimes.[7]

Now the fact that agents are essentially mediated by a linguistic understanding, as we saw with Gadamer, builds into the particular discursive contexts certain general capabilities that potentially enable the situated transcendence of these contexts (Gadamer [1960] 1989; see also Heidegger 1971; Taylor 1985; Harris 2000). The constitution of the discursive rules and contexts proves itself to be the emergent result of dialogical actions that involve the capacity to reflexively thematize oneself in the world, to take the positions of another vis-à-vis a shared issue or question, and to situate one's overall symbolic and cultural understanding of issues within a larger social context. Agents are thus *in principle* capable of thematizing their own subjective position vis-à-vis the world, taking up the position of another vis-à-vis something, and structurally representing beliefs and actions as situated in a framework that relates to the context as a whole. These basic capabilities of linguistic understanding precede and enable the concrete constructions of grammars, semantics, and pragmatics as they evolve with their specific discursive and practical rules. As they are operative in the construction of those contexts, they get nonetheless domesticated, channeled, structured, and situated in context-specific settings, and yet, their existence presents a *potential* from which true dialogue with the other may emerge.

6. Source and ethos of open dialogue

Yet what we now have to ask is this: How can the force of dialogue unfold within the discursive institutions that define much of our everyday as well as formalized conversations with one another? How can the openness towards the other be realized in settings that restrict, constrain, predetermine who can say what about which issue and how? How can the ethical recognition of the other as someone to whom I owe the respect of taking her view seriously be unleashed, be realized, be heeded in the social contexts which define our current cultural practices and fields? The answer can only consist, against the background of our discussion, in *the communal cultivation of a dialogical ethos* that entails the subject's disposition to open herself to the other and her challenge for the self. The normative recognition of the other's equality is here actualized in the endorsement of a dialogue about shared issues in which the mutual value of the involved views as potential truth is deemed basic. The hermeneutic recognition of the other is understood to be an ongoing project that finds its ethical realization in the actual openness to what the other has to say. This ethos entails the commitment to recognize the other's input and experience while also reflexively understanding the actual practices and powers that constrain and possibly undermine such recognition. Its normative force transcends the existing role contexts and social identities without naively ignoring or underestimating them. It rather understands the ethical challenge for the self to precisely consist in the unlikely and counter-factual effort to realize dialogue where discursive formations and social fields seemingly dominate the game.[8]

It is for this reason that a hermeneutic ethic incorporates the egalitarian recognition of the other without pronouncing this recognition itself to be a formal rule, a new categorical imperative, yet another universal structure to be endorsed. The hermeneutic insight into the insurmountability of one's historical situatedness reveals that the establishment of such a rule misses its own intent by side-stepping the thing that really matters: its actualization with regard to the recognized concrete other. How to respond to the other, how to address the other's claim is an ongoing effort that cannot be solved or accomplished by a magic formula. *The formulations of such an ethic only mean to point to actual dialogues in their possible openness.* Thus it is equally misleading to ground an immediate recognition of the other via some foundational phenomenon like the encounter with the other *as face* (Levinas 1969, 1998).[9] Levinas' emphasis on the face, if taken as an event breaking through the power-defined grids of social existence, would both claim too much and too little. Too much because 'the face' is always mediated with the manifold experiences of all the others' faces, some seen and some unseen, and cannot as such overcome how the concrete other is pre-understood in one's power-defined language games and social role-identities. Too little because the revelation of the other *as face* can be nothing but a first step, a hint, a beginning of the experience of the other, the recognition of whom must entail the other's cultural self-understanding. *The face is but a sign to take up the dialogue with the other.*

Levinas' emphasis on the face presents the other as infinitely independent: the other *as face* cannot be incorporated or objectified by the self. Where we need to go from here is to an ethical disposition that endorses the irreducibility of the other. We need to cultivate an intersubjective experience that allows us to encounter the presence of an irreducible other. G.H. Mead's reflections on self-constitution can guide a social ontology that anchors dialogical possibility in the heart of self-existence because they show the self to depend on the irreducible other for its own existence (Mead 1934; see also Sokol/Sugarman 2012). The source for authentic dialogue with the other can be found in the core of the self. The social role-identities define me as well as my experience with others. The development of the self via social identities is based on perspective-taking: I take the perspective of the other towards me, and thus become an object of self-understanding. Agents develop by means of taking the perspective of another, of assuming another's viewpoint through imaginary role-taking in play. They come to understand themselves as agents because they are able to take the perspective of the other towards themselves.

Therefore, the self emerges *as a self* by taking the role of the other towards herself. The social situation in which perspective-taking is operative is prior to reflexive self-constitution, yet the process of perspective-taking, in which I come to understand me as a self, requires that I assume the other's subject-position vis-à-vis myself. Yet this subject-position is necessarily other than me, as it is able to objectify me. It is therefore transcending me, both because it is beyond me, and also because I can only understand me if the other is a subject that can objectify me. But as such the other self cannot itself be an object; it cannot be merely another objectified identity. *What is therefore given in my self-identification through the other is a reference to a subject that is beyond objectification* – just as it is represented by the presence of the other as face. Yet instead of merely transcending me as absolute other, this other constitutes me. By reflexively constructing myself through the perspective of another subject, I insert an irreducible and transcending subjectivity into myself. My self is thus the fusion of an objectified and a transcending part: I exist as a social identity, as a me, and yet I am also beyond that precisely by being me. My I is the reflexive position from which I can experience myself which can never itself be objectified. Since I become myself through emerging from a social situation in which I take the perspective of the other towards myself, *I ultimately owe my self-existence to an irreducible other.*

Our discussion has reached its culmination since we now see that the other's irreducible self lies at the center of the interpreting self. This irreducible other defines the normative orientation of a hermeneutic ethic. The dialogical recognition of the other opens itself to the other's concrete claims in their situated substance and yet understands these to emanate from an irreducibly autonomous source. To treat the other's symbolic expressions as claims and challenges means to respect the other as both defined by, and as transcending, her particular cultural identity. The hermeneutic process that actualizes the dialogical respect for the other can be seen as bound by four pillars of understanding. First, it always entails the understanding of the pervasive constraints of social contexts that may subvert and pervert our ideal to openness; second, it entails the empathetic openness to the other as other that is not bound by particular forms of discourse, but that opens oneself to the concrete life-contexts and existential perspectives as challenges to one's own way of being; third, it recognizes that the dialogical other is present only as the absence of a complete determination, since the other is herself a source and center of understanding; and fourth, it knows that the emergence of dialogical capabilities needs to be fostered in social and cultural contexts since they can only emerge through dialogically defined selves. The potential of social reflexivity, dialogical perspective-taking, context-transcendence, and cultivation of dialogical capabilities is grounded in our being within language, which is always actualized in our concrete existence in the here and now. A hermeneutic ethic understands the other as situated in this way, and thereby recognizes the other's humanity in the dialogical practice of understanding and interpretation.

Notes

1 Such a direct correspondence of *emotional states* fails to identify *shared experiences* due to context difference. Imagine an American soldier who partakes in a rather violent raid of an Iraqi home. Amidst the group of heavily armed marines who stampede through the house, he spots in a corner the angst-ridden family including a mother holding a young girl. He takes out of his pocket a picture of his similarly aged daughter to create an empathetic bond, a transcending moment. But as we can easily see, this is not able to create the empathetic bond that transcends the violent surrounding; it does little to instill peace and trust due to the context in which such an act must appear as a well-intentioned but ill-conceived gesture of privilege or even arrogance. Thanks to Espen Hammer for a similarly vivid example.

2 The basic idea of a hermeneutic ethic derives from the insight that the intersubjective relation between two subjects is constitutive not only for this relation itself, but also for the subjects as they exist and live. Ethics is thus not grounded in a set of norms, values, or imperatives that address the individual as an agent in some solitary and independent mode, but rather in the *prior connectedness with others* that derives from the subjects' shared social and practical context. Not the individual, but the social situatedness of the individual is the ground of the normative demand and commitment to respect and recognize the other. For a perceptive analysis of this connection, see Healy 2000.

3 The ensuing objectifications of our experience in language enable us to have experiences in the first place. Language remains nevertheless grounded in the historical and temporal context; it remains defined by the ongoing effort at self-understanding in which we constantly reinterpret and redefine how we understand ourselves, others, and nature.

4 This means that the interpreter must forego the illusion of a standpoint-less standpoint and admit to being guided by contextual assumptions and contingent-situated beliefs. In human-scientific interpretation, the subject matter of the text shows itself to the interpreter only in light of a pre-understanding that she brings to the text. To acknowledge the influence of the prejudgments on her own understanding is a first and indispensable step towards an open dialogue in which a true reciprocity of both perspectives can emerge.

5 Gadamer's project in the context of the issue of human and social-scientific interpretation is in part to renew the ethical impact of interpretation in the humanities. Yet if objectifying modes in intersubjective relations are transferred to the human and social sciences – as

Gadamer claims they are in many disciplinary paradigms of those sciences – the capacity of the tradition to renew its own ethical substance is severely damaged.

6 Both modes, the typifying-predictive mode, and the empathetic-individualizing mode, distance the other as an object to be explained or understood, and subsequently allow for interventions in the other's life that bypass the open recognition and interaction with the other. What is missing is that the interpreting self puts itself in true reciprocity to be challenged and addressed by the other. In these modes, the interpreter interprets and observes from a hermeneutic safe-haven of invisibility and untouchability. It speaks from the – alleged and illusionary – basis of a neutral observer's position, instead of becoming a participant in an open dialogue with the other. By doing so, it misrecognizes the other as a human other by making her an object of one's interpretive scheme, without taking into account that the other is itself a source of interpretation.

7 These capabilities and skills derive from one's social and cultural background, and thereby extend social power and distribution of authority into the dialogical event *via the identities of the involved agents*. For classic and influential analyses in this vein see Foucault ([1975] 1979); Bourdieu (1990).

8 A hermeneutic ethic is an ethos, a practical relation of the self towards the other that is grounded in the reflexive appropriation of one's relatedness to the other. To develop such an ethic involves the task to explicate how the social background entails the uniquely normative structure of an intersubjective relation that suggests the respect and recognition of the other. The core of a hermeneutic ethic is defined as the ethos of a *dialogical recognition of the other* against the background of (shared as well as different) beliefs, assumptions and practices. *Dialogical openness* is the adequate mode to recognize the other. For the problem of grounding a hermeneutic ethic, see Kögler 2014.

9 For an instructive analysis relating Gadamer's and Levinas' approaches to one another see Ruchlak 2004.

Bibliography

Bourdieu, Pierre (1990) *The Logic of Practice*. Stanford: Stanford University Press.

Buber, Martin ([1923] 2004) *I and Thou*. New York: Continuum Publishing House.

Dilthey, Wilhelm ([1883] 1959) *Einleitung in die Geisteswissenschaften (Introduction to the Human Sciences)*. Ges. Schriften I. Stuttgart: Teubner.

———([1910] 2004) *The Construction of History in the Human Sciences*. Princeton: Princeton University Press.

Foucault, Michel ([1975] 1979) *Discipline and Punish*. New York: Pantheon Books.

Gadamer, Hans-Georg ([1960] 1989) *Truth and Method*. New York: Crossroads.

Harris, Paul (2000) *The Work of the Imagination*, Oxford: Blackwell.

Healy, Paul (2000) "Self–Other Relations and the Rationality of Cultures," *Philosophy & Social Criticism* 26: 79–101.

Heidegger, Martin (1999) *Ontology – The Hermeneutics of Facticity*, Bloomington and Indianapolis: Indiana University Press.

———(1971) *On the Way to Language*. San Francisco: HarperCollins.

———([1927] 1962) *Being and Time*. New York: Harper & Row.

Hoffman, Martin (2000) *Empathy and moral development. Implications for caring and justice*. Cambridge: Cambridge University Press.

Kögler, Hans-Herbert (2014) "The Crisis of a Hermeneutic Ethic," *Philosophy Today* 58 (1): 9–22.

———(1999) *The Power of Dialogue: Critical Hermeneutics After Gadamer and Foucault*. Cambridge, MA: MIT Press.

Kögler, Hans-Herbert and Stueber, Karsten (eds.) (2000) *Empathy and Agency: The Problem of Understanding in the Human Sciences*. Boulder, CO: Westview Press.

Levinas, E. (1969) *Totality and infinity. An essay on exteriority*. Pittsburgh: Duquesne University Press.

——(1998) *Otherwise than being. Or beyond essence*. Pittsburgh: Duquesne University Press.

Löwith, Karl ([1928] 2013) *Das Individuum in der Rolle des Mitmenschen*: Freiburg, München: Verlag Karl Alber.

Mead, George Herbert (1934) *Mind, Self, and Society*. Chicago: University of Chicago Press.

Ruchlak, Nicole (2004) *Das Gespräch mit dem Anderen*. Würzburg: Königshausen & Neumann

Schleiermacher, Friedrich ([1819] 1957) *Hermeneutics:The Handwritten Manuscripts*. The American Academy of Religion, Atlanta, GE: Scholars Press.

Sokol, Bryan and Sugarman, Jeff (eds.) (2012) "Human Agency and Development," *New Ideas in Psychology* 30 (1): 1–85.

Taylor, Charles (1985) *Human Agency and Language*. Cambridge: Cambridge University Press.

25
POLITICS AND CRITIQUE
Michael Marder

1. Hermeneutics: conservative or revolutionary?

All too often, hermeneutics has been accused of serving as a philosophical façade for an essentially conservative political ideology. The reasons behind this accusation are not mysterious, so long as one accepts that hermeneutics is only meant to make explicit what is already there in the text, ensuring a continuous tradition of interpretation. Quite influential in this regard is Martin Heidegger's theory of "pre-interpretation," elaborated in *Being and Time*, according to which "the 'world' which has already been understood comes to be interpreted" (1962, p. 189). Save for the laying bare of what has been known all along, nothing changes as a result of attaining explicit understanding. Whether hidden or disclosed, the same meaning is conserved before and after the work of interpretation is accomplished. The hermeneutic circle closes tight, because "[i]n interpretation, understanding does not become something different. It becomes itself" (Heidegger 1962, p. 188). The possibility of rupture, associated at the political level with revolutions, is precluded from the get-go in that understanding which feeds on itself, like a snake biting its own tail.

Heidegger is not the first philosopher to advance a conservative hermeneutics, from which he departs in his later work, having embraced the event of being instead of the earlier question concerning the meaning of being. Before him, in dealing with the sacred scriptures, theological hermeneutics aimed to decipher the eternal truths locked in the word of God, while Plato conceived of knowledge as *anamnesis* or remembrance. The Platonic hermeneutics in particular was philosophically or onto-logically conservative, in that it strove to preserve, to save, to shield from destruc-tion or degeneration what was already in existence. As Claudia Baracchi puts it, in the case of Plato, "[m]nemonic retention and the protection of the living seem to stem from the same source" (2001, p. 107).

In turn, other hermeneutical approaches in the twentieth and early twenty-first centuries have either broken with this conservative tradition or have reinterpreted it, with a view to unearthing the revolutionary rupture and discontinuity it covers over. Paul Ricoeur's "hermeneutics of suspicion," highly indebted to the Nietzschean, Marxist, and Freudian critiques of consciousness and of the status quo (Ricoeur 1977, pp. 32–3; Ricoeur 1974, p. 99); John Caputo's (1988) "radical hermeneutics," relying on the method of Jacques Derrida's deconstruction; Richard Rorty's hermeneutic pluralism; and, most recently, Gianni Vattimo and Santiago Zabala's (2011) "hermeneutic communism," re-vindicating the thought of Heidegger himself through a certain reading of Marx – all these form the revolutionary currents of a philosophy that seems to have been organized around a conservative core. It is safe to say that the future of hermeneutics lies with these refreshing variations on the restricted horizons of traditional interpretation.

The practitioners of revolutionary hermeneutics insist, by and large, on the kind of methodological freedom that verges on freedom *from* method. Rorty, for example, notes how hermeneutics demands that we "look askance at the idea of method" (1982, p. 9). Caputo wishes for a deconstructive hermeneutics that leaves enough space for a free play of meanings; "[t]he point," he writes, "is to keep play in play" (1988, p. 262). Zabala (2016) goes a step further, as he envisions an anarchic theory of interpretation consistent with the openness of human existence. Politically, the emphasis on play, the enabling absence of method, and, obviously, anarchy betoken a non- or an anti-authoritarian vein in the latest wave of hermeneutical thought. Still, in order to assess the complicated triangulation of interpretation, politics, and critique, it behooves us to devise a framework that would go well beyond the superficial distinction between conservative and revolutionary approaches. In addition to these general orientations, we must specify the roles of agreement and disagreement; the question of what or who (if anything or anyone at all) could be the final arbiter in the field of multiple interpretations; and the thesis of continuity *versus* rupture.

2. The argument

This chapter maps the political implications of hermeneutics along three main axes. First, I concentrate on the horizontal continuum that runs from absolute agreement to sheer disagreement and show its relevance to such crucial hermeneutical terms as "the fusion of horizons" and "the conflict of interpretations." Second, I draw the vertical line, which extends between arbitration and non-arbitration, exploring the limits of hermeneutical method. Third, I outline the diagonal axis of critique, which traverses the entire system of political hermeneutical coordinates and puts into question the contrived opposition between con-flict and conversation, as well as between epistemic and ethical considerations, and between decisive action and deliberative interpretation. The desired outcome is an analytical tool that would help us find our bearings in the midst of diverse political hermeneutical approaches, situated between two extremes: critical disagreement without a chance for arbitration, on the one hand, and uncritical arbitrated consensus, on the other.

3. Agreement/disagreement

In *Truth and Method*, Hans-Georg Gadamer coined the term "the fusion of horizons," *Horizontverschmelzung*, in the course of explaining the workings of understanding.

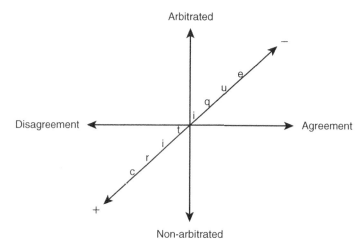

Figure 25.1 A system of coordinates for political hermeneutics

The "horizons" he invokes there are primarily temporal – that of the present, formed thanks to that of the past, which is carried on as a living tradition. According to Gadamer, "[t]here is no more an isolated horizon of the present in itself than there are historical horizons which have to be acquired. *Rather, understanding is always the fusion of these horizons supposedly existing by themselves*" (1989a, p. 306). Understanding is the sign of a profound agreement, if not consensus, between the past and its present emanation.

The fusion of horizons can also refer, more broadly, to the *sine qua non* of meaningful communication. Elsewhere, Gadamer puts forth the following view of human beings: "Each one is at first a kind of linguistic circle, and these linguistic circles come into contact with each other, merging more and more. ... That is the fundamental dimension of hermeneutics" (1976, p. 17). The merging of distinct linguistic circles in a growing community of understanding is a marker of agreement in the present, where dispersed perspectives are gathered together through *logos*, which is the Greek word for speech, language, or discourse, derived from the verb *legein*, "to gather." To address the other, to speak, is already to seek mutual understanding, which is why "every misunderstanding presupposes a 'deep common accord'" (Gadamer 1976, p. 7). For Gadamer, then, agreement is the default setting of human coexistence. And, on the contrary, disagreement is a deviation from – or, technically speaking, a negative modification of – the consensual basis for social and political life.

No doubt, a minimum of consensus is required for any polity, no matter how democratic, to function. When, however, a "deep common accord" is posited *a priori* and when the tendency toward the fusion of horizons and the merging of perspectives is unchecked, there is a heightened risk of instituting a totalizing and totalitarian political arrangement. In critical theory, Herbert Marcuse (1964) dubbed such an arrangement "one-dimensional society." In hermeneutics *proper* and with reference to global politics, Vattimo named it "*la pensée unique*," or "the

Washington consensus," in which he identified "a strong enemy of hermeneutics" (Vattimo & Zabala 2011, p. 63; Vattimo 2014, pp. 72–3). Accord is not just a matter of degree, but, rather, a key constituent of political ontology, built either on agreement or on disagreement. Opting for the latter, Jacques Rancière (who, to be sure, is usually not considered a hermeneutical philosopher) concludes that politics is predicated on "the incommensurable" and that one should not "lock oneself into false alternatives requiring a choice between the enlightenment of rational communication and the murkiness of inherent violence or irreducible difference" (2004, p. 43). Disagreement reflects the difference that underwrites politics, without automatically sliding into violence.

Throughout his body of work, Ricoeur, too, accentuates the significance of an ongoing contestation of meanings. Taken in the *epistemological* sense, this contestation is the condition of possibility for reflection: "we must ask not only why reflection requires interpretation but also why it requires conflicting interpretations" (Ricoeur 1974, p. 317). Tellingly, the fusion of horizons undermines the quality of reflection, even as it strengthens understanding (which is not surprising, since to reflect and, indeed, to think is to fail to understand). Taken in the *political* sense, hermeneutical contestation is the condition of possibility for democracy, seeing that:

> a democratic State is that State which does not propose to eliminate conflicts but to invent procedures allowing them to be expressed and to remain open to negotiation. A State of law, in this sense, is a State of organized free discussion.
>
> (Ricoeur 1991, p. 335)

Ricoeur's idea of a democratic state thus coincides with the Romantic ideal of "infinite conversation," hijacked, as Carl Schmitt complains, by liberal parliamentary democracies (2005, pp. 53–4). Even if, occasionally, mutual understanding may ensue, it is an organized conflict of multiple interpretations, rather than the emerging unity of consensus, that best describes the hermeneutical calling of democracy and of dialogic politics (Nikulin 2006, p. 211).

His complicated relation to hermeneutics notwithstanding, Jürgen Habermas concurs with the insight that conflicts of interpretation are ever-present in democracies. He writes: "[Constitutional] principles do not possess stable meanings beyond, and independent of, their application to concrete cases. Persisting conflicts of interpretation reveal conflicts about how to understand the underlying principles themselves" (Habermas 2003, p. 188). In other words, conflicts of interpretation percolate all the way down to the basic principles that, far from being self-evident, invite a plethora of readings. In the conclusion to his article "On Law and Disagreement," Habermas adds: "I do not see, at least not on this level of principled reasoning, any inevitable threat to the legitimacy of constitutional regimes arising from the unavoidability of endemic disagreement" (2003, p. 194). More than that, we might say that nothing but "endemic disagreement" makes constitutional democracies substantively legitimate.

4. Arbitration/non-arbitration

While in theological hermeneutics, God was the final arbiter of different interpretations, guaranteeing the truth of some amongst these, in modernity, reason has replaced God in the function of arbitration (McLean 2012, p. 65). God or reason is a higher authority that presides over, judges, and evaluates the merits and products of hermeneutical activity. Yet, the very need for arbitration betrays the persistence of disagreement and the open-endedness of interpretation. Although agreement is the outcome of a successful arbitration process, disagreements may endure even when clear guidelines for interpreting are in place. (In later Habermas, "endemic disagreements" are not incompatible with the rules for interpretation stemming from communicative rationality.) In contrast to the axis agreement/disagreement, which is relevant to hermeneutical ontology, then, the axis arbitration/non-arbitration pertains to hermeneutical methodology (or to a lack thereof). This distinction is strictly analytical, given that, in the actual practice of interpretation, the ontological and methodological dimensions tend to converge. It is, nonetheless, a distinction worth making, if only to reveal some of the main political themes in hermeneutics.

Arbitration alludes not only to the epistemic but also to the political authority to make decisions on the truth and legitimacy of interpretations. From Immanuel Kant onwards, Western philosophy transfers the task of such adjudication from an external and transcendent arbiter onto finite human reason, with its aptitude for self-critique. Critical reason can become its own arbiter in hermeneutics, as well, insofar as it "contributes a basis for arbitration between different interpretations by demanding that the extent to which an interpretation has clarified its own assumptions and scope ... be made a further test for the interpretation" (Hoy 1982, p. 130). Self-explication through self-critique would, as a consequence, impart Kantian autonomy to the hermeneutical method, which could turn into its own arbiter. Having eschewed the "objective," externally imposed criteria for truth, it would be a vehicle for political emancipation.

The problem with the attempt at critically clarifying the assumptions and scope of an interpretation is that it reaches its limit in the unconscious, which forecloses the self-transparency of the interpretation in question. In his exploration of the intersections between psychoanalysis and hermeneutics, Ricoeur problematized this direct application of enlightenment ideals to the task of interpretation. In fact, the analysis of the unconscious calls for a different kind of hermeneutics, since "I cannot understand the unconscious from what I know about consciousness" (1974, p. 100). Factoring this unknown into the hermeneutical equation breeds a vast array of muddled assumptions and magnifies the scope of interpretation beyond the grasp of self-critical reason.

From a pragmatic point of view, hermeneutical arbitration is contingent on the results it yields, which is to say that the arbiter is the one who understands and who can, thanks to correct understanding, effectively intervene in the world. Something of this idea resonates in Gadamerian hermeneutics, where "the text is a mere intermediate product [*Zwischenprodukt*], a phase in the event of understanding." "And the process of understanding a text," Gadamer continues, "tends to captivate and take the reader up into that which the text says, and in this fusion the text too drops away" (1989b, pp. 31, 41). In the event of a text's successful understanding, the mediate character of what is understood recedes to the background. The fusion of horizons, paradoxically productive of the illusion of immediacy, is the immanent standard of hermeneutical arbitration. It is this (perhaps necessary) illusion that prepares the transition from interpretation to *praxis*, as Richard Bernstein suggests in an echo of Ricoeur's "from text to action," arguing that "the implicit *telos* within philosophic hermeneutics requires us to move beyond hermeneutics itself" (Bernstein 1983, p. 113). But, while the pragmatic evaluation of interpretations stresses success stories, revolutionary hermeneutics dwells on failure and fallibility as the markers of "pure possibility," inherent in human finitude (Ricoeur 1986, p. 145). Worse yet, on the political level, successful understanding is the outcome of the "winner's history," within which the lived hermeneutics of the defeated and the oppressed presents itself in the shape of failure (Vattimo & Zabala 2011, p. 40).

So, if external arbitration is no longer plausible and if the internal (or immanent) self-arbitration of critical hermeneutical reason is fraught with difficulties, then what are the alternatives? Here, the critique of method in the revolutionary currents of hermeneutics holds the key. The anti-methodological stance – which admittedly, may be seen as a minimal or negative method – liberates the work of interpretation from authority, first and foremost, of tradition, of the past, and of a hierarchical criteriology. Rorty realizes that the rejection of a method will make hermeneutics itself unrecognizable as such, and he heartily endorses this "fantasy that the very idea of hermeneutics should disappear, in the way in which old general ideas do disappear when they lose polemical and contrastive force – when they begin to have universal applicability" (1990, p. 103). Similarly, Derrida (1989a) expressed the desire for his thinking to become "biodegradable," when deconstruction will have dissolved into the soil of culture and lost its identity there. By shedding its determinate outlines, a method gives up on its doctrinaire, prescriptive authority to pave, in advance, the path of thinking (the *hodos* of *methodos*). Letting go of its prerogative, it gives way to freedom. In Zabala's "anarchy of interpretation," the political meaning of this hermeneutical position is at its most unambiguous.

5. Continuity/discontinuity

The anarchic proliferation of meanings signals that hermeneutics has dispensed with the unitary principle (*arkhé*), governing its method and dictating the choices of suitable interpretations. In his original study of Heidegger, Reiner Schürmann observes that this an-archy is not only semantic but also ontological and, moreover, that it corresponds to the predicament of human existence as "life without why" (1990, p. 10). If there is no single cause that is able to explain multiple phenomena and their interpretations, then it is impossible to track this dispersed plurality, in an uninterrupted fashion, back to an authoritative common origin. Instead of a continuous tradition, flowing from the same source, we are faced with multiple points of departure. This situation is empowering, to the extent that it permits each person as an embodiment of existence "without why" to take charge of her life and to craft a unique interpretation out of it.

The Gadamer–Derrida encounter, which took place in Paris in 1981, brought the issue of discontinuity to the forefront of hermeneutics. In his reply to Gadamer's lecture at that event, Derrida suggested that a rupture underlies both understanding and misunderstanding: "Whether one speaks of consensus or of misunderstanding (as in Schleiermacher), one needs to ask whether the precondition for *Verstehen*, far from being the continuity of *rapport* (as it was described yesterday evening), is not rather the interruption of *rapport*, a certain *rapport* of interruption, the suspending of all mediation?" (1989b, p. 53). The argument that a rupture is "the precondition for *Verstehen*" means that there is no neutral "third" – be it a human arbiter, reason itself, or a set of predetermined procedures – that or who would facilitate the process of understanding the other. Following the philosophy of Emmanuel Levinas, which is behind the scenes of Derrida's question, the other who has been understood is not an other, but a part of the same. Not by chance, Levinas himself draws our attention to the irreducibility of anarchy (1998, pp. 100–1), which is, according to him, pre-ontological (i.e., ethical) and which maintains the space of separation between the I and the other.

Gadamer's response to Derrida highlights the way deconstruction invariably upsets the horizon of customary expectations; "[t]o him," Gadamer states, "any word appearing in written form is always already a breach" (1989c, p. 57). Caputo's radical hermeneutics confirms the view of deconstruction as the hermeneutics of a rupture. Contrasting what he calls "holy hermeneutics" to a "devilish hermeneutics," he writes: "Deconstruction is the affirmation – not the simple toleration or grudging admission – of discontinuity in the name of the coming of something unforeseeable. … Deconstruction is the advocate of the devil of discontinuity" (Caputo 2000, pp. 200–1). The political implications of vehemently affirming discontinuity in deconstructive hermeneutics are glaring: this mode of interpretation has nothing to do with the tame liberal desideratum of merely "tolerating" or "admitting" the other within the existing order. Rather, it amounts to a revolutionary politics of the event, "the coming of something unforeseeable," that may drastically disrupt the order, wherein it announces itself.

For Gadamer, conversely, discontinuity invalidates hermeneutics. In a supplement to *Truth and Method*, he takes issue with Schmitt's interpretation of Shakespeare's *Hamlet*, which pivots on the claim that "it is possible to recognize that fissure in the work through which contemporary reality shines and which reveals the contemporary function of the work" (Gadamer 1989a, p. 497). Gadamer's take on this is buried in the book's section on the ontology of the work of art: "A work of art belongs so closely to what it is related to that it enriches the being of that as if through a new event of Being" (1989a, p. 147). The event is not a sudden rupturing of the symbolic order by an element foreign to it, but the seamless supplementation of what is already in being with the work of art and with the subsequent history of its interpretation. It is this continuous hermeneutical tradition, encompassing "reality" itself, that constitutes the event for Gadamer, as opposed to the irruption of the unforeseeable or of the Real in Derrida and Schmitt, respectively.

The political relevance of the above disagreement can be hardly overestimated. Schmitt's "decisionism," symbolizing a purely arbitrary form of authority and sovereignty, has been misconstrued as a symptom of his profound allergy to the

work of interpretation, which, for example, mends the lacunae in the law by subsuming each new case under universal principles. Yet, one cannot make a decision
without interpreting the materials one decides upon, just as one cannot interpret
anything without making an unavoidably political choice in favor of one among
many contested interpretations (Marder 2010, Chapter 8). Complete legal hermeneutical dogmatism is as implausible as pure decisionism. As soon as we acknowledge the co-imbrication of continuity and discontinuity, interpretations and
decisions will finally find their rightful places in hermeneutics – the overarching
philosophical framework for the tradition *and* revolutionary events.

6. The role of critique

The preceding discussion of continuity and discontinuity has begun to elucidate the
role of critique in hermeneutics. The etymology of "critique" harkens back to the
Greek verb *krinein*, which means "to separate," "to distinguish," or "to discern" and
which is instrumental in the formation of the word "crisis." In light of the amplifi-
cation of its semantic scope, critique, like crisis, comes to denote a rupture, the
space of separation, and discontinuity that accommodates difference. Absent this
rupture that, at the origin, fissures the unity of the origin, there would not have been
anything or anyone separate, distinguishable, or discernable; indeed, there would
have been nothing but an undifferentiated blur. The plurality of interpretations,
some of them competing with others, is the comet tail of that originary crisis, which
is also the crisis of the origin and the beginning of anarchy. Although hermeneutical
critique may sift among various options and discern what, under the circumstances,
appears to be the best interpretation, it has no right to do away with the multiplicity
it is immersed in, hypostasizing one privileged meaning over all the others.

On the one hand, in disagreements over interpretations and in non-arbitrated
encounters with texts or human others, the critical drive is at its strongest, because
several hermeneutical alternatives remain sharply distinguished and separated. On the
other hand, when hermeneutical horizons begin to fuse and when a principle or an
authority figure imposes something that passes for the correct interpretation, critique
wanes, as differences are gathered into the unity of common understanding or into a
single source of truth. Politically speaking, anarchism, radical democracy, and new
varieties of communism are the regimes most conducive to hermeneutical critique, in
that they find themselves in a perpetual *crisis*, with sovereignty divided along spatial
and temporal lines (Derrida 2005). In other words, they preserve the spaces of
separation within the *body politic* and, refusing to impose the dominant version of
truth from above (Vattimo & Zabala 2011, p. 78), usher in an ethical politics, in which
the lived interpretations of *each* are indispensable to the flourishing of all.

The sense of separation and discernment was not foreign to Kant's enunciation of
critique, charged with the task of distinguishing between what could and what could
not be known by finite human reason. That, however, was a relatively crude discrimination, which inaugurated the master divide between the knowable phenomena
and the unknowable noumena. Compared to Kantian thought, critical hermeneutics
concerns itself with much more minute differences of interpretation that are highly

context-dependent. But, above all, the hermeneutical perspective on the relation between truth and critique is utterly dissimilar to that espoused in metaphysical philosophy.

From Gadamer to Rorty and Vattimo, hermeneutical philosophers have gravitated toward a non- or anti-representational paradigm of truth. Veracity is not a matter of correspondence between statements and external reality, but the "experience of truth" in "the *transformative* unfolding of dialogue" or in our "relation to Being" through a work of art (Risser 1997, p. 144). If this provisional definition of hermeneutical truth obtains, then the notion of critique must change accordingly. It is insufficient to put hermeneutics and criticism together around the ideal of "correctness," as Friedrich Schleiermacher does, with reference to hermeneutics, grasped in terms of "the art of understanding … correctly," and to criticism as "the art of judging correctly" (1998, p. 3). Nor is it enough, in the manner of Jean Grondin, to shift the burden of proof onto "self-understanding" that strives toward transparency and, subsequently, to stipulate that interpretation's "critical impulse lies in the effort to avoid self-misunderstanding as far as possible" (1997, p. 96). To hold onto the ideals of correctness and transparency is to pursue knowledge, in place of truth. Conversely, the "*transformative* unfolding of dialogue" implies that what undergoes constant transformation is correctness itself, both as a concept and as a label attached to some positions at the expense of others. In Hegel's phenomenology, "[c]onsciousness *verifies* to itself what it really is," such that "[i]n this verification," it "loses its initial truth, what it at first thought of itself" (Heidegger 1988, p. 22); in hermeneutics, my encounter with the other (person or text) divests my consciousness and self-consciousness of their self-contained, autonomous truth.

If engagement with the other is a necessary precondition for hermeneutics, then this basic ethical situation is already a concrete critique of the endeavor to deduce what is true in a purely epistemic mode from preexisting abstract principles. There are, actually, two types of critique in this engagement: external and internal. The first is a critique of everything that threatens to close the gap between distinct interpretations, thereby impoverishing ontologico-hermeneutical multiplicity. Insofar as absolute agreement erases the uniqueness of the I and the other, it verges on philosophical totalitarianism, which is the main target of external critique. The second is a critique of everything that stands in the way of the experience of truth and presents veracity as a *fait accompli*, independent of our capacity to undergo its transformative effects. I call this critique *internal* because it hinges on the phenomenological access to truth within a particular situation of my relation with the other. When a purportedly neutral "third" interferes in the function of an arbiter in this relation, the experiential dimension of truth is irretrievably lost. The political outcome of such arbitration in modernity is technocratic liberal proceduralism, which is still draining politics of meaningfulness and forestalling qualitative changes in the organization of human multiplicities.

Note that, in evoking "engagement with the other," I have not indicated whether this would be a collaborative or a conflictual relation; that is, whether the other is a friend or an enemy. In a combination of hermeneutical critique with Hegel's dialectics, it would be more opportune to demonstrate the speculative identity of *conflict* and *conversation*, each of them presupposing a being-with (*cum-*) the other. Only there where the spaces of critical separation are not sealed is political hermeneutics viable, prior to the formal distinction between friends and enemies. Far from rejecting the given, the role of critique is to safeguard the multiplicity of interpretations and to augment the sphere of givenness without settling for one standard of truth, accuracy, correctness, or methodological precision.

Bibliography

Baracchi, Claudia. 2001. *Of Myth, Life and War in Plato's Republic*. Bloomington & Indianapolis: Indiana University Press.

Bernstein, Richard. 1983. *Beyond Objectivism and Relativism: Science, Hermeneutics, and Praxis*. Philadelphia: University of Pennsylvania Press.

Caputo, John. 1988. *Radical Hermeneutics: Repetition, Deconstruction, and the Hermeneutic Project*. Bloomington & Indianapolis: Indiana University Press.

——. 2000. *More Radical Hermeneutics: On Not Knowing Who We Are*. Bloomington & Indianapolis: Indiana University Press.

Derrida, Jacques. 1989a. "Biodegradables: Seven Diary Fragments." Trans. Peggy Kamuf, *Critical Inquiry* 15: 812–73.

——. 1989b. "Three Questions to Hans-Georg Gadamer." In *Dialogue and Deconstruction: The Gadamer–Derrida Encounter*. Eds. Diane Michelfelder & Richard Palmer. Albany: SUNY Press.

——. 2005. *Rogues: Two Essays on Reason*. Trans. Michael Naas and Pascale-Anne Brault. Stanford: Stanford University Press.

Gadamer, Hans-Georg. 1976. *Philosophical Hermeneutics*. Trans. & Ed. David E. Linge. Berkeley & London: University of California Press.

——. 1989a. *Truth and Method*, rev. ed. Joel Weinsheimer & Donald Marshall. New York & London: Continuum.

——. 1989b. "Text and Interpretation." In *Dialogue and Deconstruction: The Gadamer–Derrida Encounter*. Eds. Diane Michelfelder & Richard Palmer. Albany: SUNY Press.

——. 1989c. "Reply to Jacques Derrida." In *Dialogue and Deconstruction: The Gadamer–Derrida Encounter*. Eds. Diane Michelfelder & Richard Palmer. Albany: SUNY Press.

Grondin, Jean. 1997. *Introduction to Philosophical Hermeneutics*. Trans. Joel Weinsheimer. New Haven: Yale University Press.

Habermas, Jürgen. 2003. "On Law and Disagreement: Some Comments on 'Interpretative Pluralism'." *Ratio Juris* 16: 187–94.

Heidegger, Martin. 1962. *Being and Time*. Trans. J. Macquarrie and E. Robinson. San Francisco: Harper Collins.

——. 1988. *Hegel's* Phenomenology of Spirit. Trans. Parvis Emad & Kenneth Maly. Bloomington & Indianapolis: Indiana University Press.

Hoy, David Couzens. 1982. *The Critical Circle: Literature, History, and Philosophical Hermeneutics*. Berkeley & London: University of California Press.

Levinas, Emmanuel. 1998. *Otherwise than Being, or Beyond Essence*. Trans. Alphonso Lingis. Pittsburgh: Duquesne University Press.

Marcuse, Herbert. 1964. *One-Dimensional Man: Studies in the Ideology of Advanced Industrial Society*. Boston: Beacon Press.

Marder, Michael. 2010. *Groundless Existence: The Political Ontology of Carl Schmitt*. London & New York: Continuum.

McLean, B.H. 2012. *Biblical Interpretation and Philosophical Hermeneutics*. Cambridge & London: Cambridge University Press.

Nikulin, Dmitri. 2006. *On Dialogue*. Lanham: Lexington Books.

Rancière, Jacques. 2004. *Disagreement: Politics and Philosophy*. Trans. Julie Rose. Minneapolis: University of Minnesota Press.

Ricoeur, Paul. 1974. *The Conflict of Interpretations: Essays in Hermeneutics*. Ed. Don Idhe. Evanston: Northwestern University Press.

———. 1977. *Freud and Philosophy: An Essay on Interpretation*. Trans. Denis Savage. New Haven: Yale University Press.

———. 1986. *Fallible Man*. Trans. Charles Kelbley. New York: Fordham University Press.

———. 1991. *From Text to Action: Essays in Hermeneutics*. Trans. Kathleen Blamey & John Thompson. Evanston: Northwestern University Press.

Risser, James. 1997. *Hermeneutics and the Voice of the Other: Re-Reading Gadamer's Philosophical Hermeneutics*. Albany: SUNY Press.

Rorty, Richard. 1982. "Hermeneutics, General Studies, and Teaching." In *Richard Rorty on General Studies and Teaching (with Replies and Applications)*. Fairfax, VA: George Mason University.

———. 1990. *Objectivity, Relativism, and Truth: Philosophical Papers, Volume 1*. Cambridge & London: Cambridge University Press.

Schleiermacher, Friedrich. 1998. *Hermeneutics and Criticism, and Other Writings*. Trans. Andrew Bowie. Cambridge & London: Cambridge University Press.

Schmitt, Carl. 2005. *Political Theology: Four Chapters on Sovereignty*. Trans. George Schwab. Chicago: University of Chicago Press.

Schürmann, Reiner. 1990. *Heidegger on Being and Acting: From Principles to Anarchy*. Bloomington & Indianapolis: Indiana University Press.

Vattimo, Gianni. 2014. "Insuperable Contradictions and Events." In *Being Shaken: Ontology and the Event*. Eds. Michael Marder & Santiago Zabala. London: Palgrave Macmillan.

Vattimo, Gianni & Santiago Zabala. 2011. *Hermeneutic Communism: From Heidegger to Marx*. New York: Columbia University Press.

Zabala, Santiago. 2016. *Striving for Existence: The Anarchy of Hermeneutics* (forthcoming).

26

DIALOGUE AND CONVERSATION

James Risser

The issue of dialogue and conversation is a concern in hermeneutics generally and a central concern in the philosophical hermeneutics of Hans-Georg Gadamer in particular. Dialogue and conversation are a concern for hermeneutics in general insofar as interpretation involves speech and human communication. In the hermeneutics of Friedrich Schleiermacher, the founder of modern hermeneutic theory, the idea of dialogue is implicit in the task of understanding an author's intention, which is expressed as an address to the reader in the original situation of discourse. When Martin Heidegger develops a hermeneutic phenomenology in *Being and Time*, in 1927, he gives hints of the importance of dialogue in the section on discourse, which immediately follows his analysis of understanding and interpretation (see Heidegger, 1962). For Heidegger, discourse is more than making statements; it is the significant structuring of the intelligibility of our being-in-the-world to which the phenomenon of being with others also belongs. Accordingly, discourse will always take the form of an "address" and is fundamentally oriented towards communication. In this capacity to make manifest and communicate, discourse constitutes the articulation of "being-with-one-another understandingly" in relation to which the phenomenon of listening becomes essential. In understanding through discourse, listening constitutes the primary and authentic openness of the human (*Dasein*) for its ownmost possibility of being and it is in listening to each other that the phenomenon of being-with is developed.

This idea of listening to an address becomes prominent in Heidegger's later philosophy in which he abandons the explicit hermeneutics of Dasein. In "A Dialogue on Language," a late text from 1953–4, Heidegger notes in response to a question from his Japanese interlocutor that his use of the word "hermeneutic" was initially intended as an attempt to think the nature of phenomenology in a more originary manner (Heidegger, 1971: 9). When his interlocutor asks what hermeneutics actually means, Heidegger responds by linking hermeneutics not to interpretation (*Auslegung*) but to the original meaning of the Greek word for hermeneutics which refers to "the bringing of the message and tidings." As he moves from his concern for the Being of Dasein to his later effort to think the event of Being itself,

Heidegger retains the character of the hermeneutical as the effort of bearing witness (*bekunden*) to the call of Being, and to a corresponding (*entsprechen*) to the call of Being. With this shift in hermeneutics from interpretative explication to corresponding Heidegger abandons the circular character of interpretation for the sake of what he calls "the originary experience of the hermeneutic relation [*hermenutischen Bezug*]" (Heidegger, 1971: 51).

He understands this relation to be a correspondence in the manner of a responding dialogue (*Entsprechen*) that would remain originally appropriated to the Saying (*Sage*) of Being. For such a responding dialogue, one must be able to listen and hear the Saying of Being that would set beings free from an event rather than a ground; for Heidegger "saying" is what grants beings and releases them into the open. "Saying" thus designates not the spoken word as such but the antecedent to such words whereby language "speaks." Thus for Heidegger a dialogue appropriated to "saying" would be one that responds to the non-representable event of Being in the call of language. Heidegger's interpretation of poetry in his later writings can be understood as his attempt to put into practice this idea of listening to language in a responding dialogue.

In contrast to Heidegger, Gadamer's idea of a dialogue with language seems to be quite different. For Gadamer dialogue takes the form of a real encounter. The importance of dialogue and conversation emerges early on in Gadamer's work as a result of his study of Plato (Gadamer, 1991 – a translation of Gadamer's second dissertation, this was originally published in 1931). From Plato Gadamer sees that dialogue is not just a literary device but a form of theoretical apprehension, and sees that this model of rationality can be used for hermeneutics where the rationality of modern science is not applicable. Dialogical discourse, when properly carried out, allows the knower to come to agreement and to see something in the unity of its aspects. To know something in this way is precisely what is at issue in interpreting texts, which has been the primary concern in hermeneutics. Gadamer also learns from Plato, perhaps in a deeper way than how this is acknowledged by Heidegger, that dialogue constitutes a specific possible way of being with another. Dialogue has a communal aspect that Gadamer will incorporate into his theory of dialogical understanding.

When Gadamer publishes much later his main work, *Truth and Method* (1960), he incorporates the issue of dialogue and conversation into his fully developed theory of language and the hermeneutics appropriate to it. Gadamer's main claim is not just that all understanding involves interpretation, but that "all interpretation takes place in the medium of language that allows the object to come into words and yet is at the same time the interpreter's own language" (Gadamer, 1989a: 389). For an object to come into words requires that language has the capacity to unfold meaning; it requires that language be pre-eminently "living language," which happens in the living speech of dialogue where words are summoned in relation to question and answer. But precisely how words are summoned has everything to do with the character of the encounter with what is to be understood.

Gadamer insists that in relation to historical life the traditionary object to be understood – that which is embedded in history and language – can only be understood when it is encountered as a "thou." Gadamer purposively uses this word to underscore the fact that the traditionary object is never a mere theoretical object for a knowing subject, but is the one pole of a relational encounter: I–thou. In his actual analysis he draws a distinction between three forms of an I–thou relation where it is only the third form that constitutes the appropriate relation for hermeneutic understanding. The first form of relating to an object reflects the character of relating in methodological historical research. The interpreter is an independent subject who is unattached and unrelated to the traditionary object standing over against the interpreter. It is a form of relating that attempts to master the traditionary object. The second form is implicitly a dialogical relation but only in the weakest sense. The interpreter regards the traditionary object as capable of making a claim on the interpreter, as if it is a form of intersubjective dialogue, but in the attempt to understand the object the interpreter still takes a distance from the object by reflecting him or herself out of the relational situation. In understanding an historical text, the interpreter still regards the otherness of the historical object as an ideal for an objective historical interpretation. The third form of relating is where the thou is truly experienced as a thou. In this form of relating the traditionary object makes a claim on the interpreter that cannot be overlooked; in this case the interpreter truly acknowledges that the traditionary object has something to say to the interpreter. It is only in this third form of relating that there can be a genuine dialogue for understanding, for it is only in this way of relating that the interpreter engages in listening. And with listening there can be openness to one another. Only with this openness can the distanced and foreign traditionary object "speak" and be understood. Ultimately for Gadamer dialogue takes place in order to hear what the other has to say.

The achievement of this openness is precisely what is enacted through a dialogue of question and answer. Questioning is the logical structure of openness, and the art of questioning is for Gadamer the art of questioning further as the art of thinking that takes place in dialogue. Gadamer astutely notes that in understanding through dialogue, questioning is not simply something produced by the inquiring interpreter. In interpreting an historical text it is the text that poses a question and places the interpreter's meaning in openness. For the interpreter to be able to answer the question, the interpreter must begin to ask questions. Moreover, questioning itself has an interesting dynamic. Every question provides a direction from which the answer can be given. Every question is related to an answer that is not yet settled, and in this regard asking a question brings about the undetermined possibilities of meaning as well as the testing of those very possibilities. Yet every question will have a limitation for it implies establishing of presuppositions. And, not unlike the nature of experience where one is surprised when one encounters something that does not meet one's expectations, questioning imposes itself on the interpreter in such a way that the interpreter must come to accept some things that go against what he or she initially believed.

Although the movement of question and answer generates the openness that is necessary for dialogical understanding, this movement is not by itself sufficient for dialogical conversation (*Gespräch*). There are two other features that Gadamer thinks are equally necessary. The first is the preliminary requirement for the communal basis of dialogue. To reach an understanding in conversation presupposes that the partners in dialogue are ready for it and have a good will to understand. This means, unlike a Platonic dialogue where the interlocutors often talk at cross purposes, a conversation aimed at understanding must "recognize the full value of what is alien and opposed to them" (Gadamer, 1989a: 387). Partners in genuine dialogue are not in fact arguing with each other, but they are engaged in an art of testing in relation to bringing out the real strength of what is being said. The second feature exhibits the real participatory character of dialogue. This art of testing amounts to letting the partners in dialogue be conducted by the subject matter. The idea expressed here is similar to what occurs in playing a game. To play a game successfully players must give themselves over to the actual playing of the game. The game has a life of its own independent of the players insofar as the players are taken up and absorbed in the playing of the game. So Gadamer will say that "the more genuine a conversation is the less its conduct lies within the will of either partner" (Gadamer, 1989a: 383). A genuine conversation has its own twists and turns so that one does not know in advance what will emerge from the conversation. It has a spirit of its own and is like an event that happens to conversational partners.

Gadamer understands dialogical conversation then as a process of coming to an understanding; it is a process that when successful the interpreter is able to hear what the other (thou) has to say. In several places Gadamer will say that the achievement of understanding through dialogue means to come to an agreement about what is said. This agreement is not so much the agreement between the two partners in dialogue, as if they have simply "hashed things out with each other," as it is the agreement over what the subject matter is saying. That agreement is possible is a function of the rationality that is carried by language itself. In speaking with one another, language is able to build up an aspect held in common, which is the subject matter being talked about. "The true reality of human communication is such that a conversation does not simply carry one person's opinion through against another's in argument, or simply add one opinion to another. Genuine conversation transforms the viewpoint of both" (Gadamer, 2007b: 96). Because of this transformation Gadamer is able to say that when we understand we understand differently if we understand at all. And because of the commonality reached in a successful conversation Gadamer is also able to say that the point is not that "I think this and you think that" but that there is an act of sharing of meaning.

Gadamer's description of genuine dialogue fits very well for actual conversation, but, for hermeneutics, dialogical understanding is not limited to an actual conversation between two people speaking to each other. The interpretation of historical and literary texts also occurs through dialogue. Obviously there is no actual dialogical partner when we read texts, but the act of reading as an act of interpreting what is written for the sake of understanding is faced with the same problem of understanding the other person who speaks. There is still the concern for the subject matter that is placed before the reader. The reader is trying to understand what the text is saying and this presents the reader with the real hermeneutical task. In performing a dialogue with a text what is fixed in writing is brought back into living speech; it is brought back into the living present of conversation where, from the authority of the text, the subject matter undergoes a similar kind of dialectic of question and answer. In all attempts at understanding written texts the interpreter must respond to what the text is trying to say; the interpreter finds the answer to the question of the text; the interpreter must find the right language if he or she wants to make the text speak to its reader.

The central importance of dialogue and conversation for Gadamer's hermeneutics is unmistakable. Understanding occurs within the dynamic of language in dialogical conversation.

The exact nature of dialogical conversation can be further clarified by looking at two issues that Gadamer treats in the presentation of his position. The first issue emerges when Gadamer associates the development of his ideas with those of Plato and Hegel. It is the issue of the dialectical character of dialogue and how dialogue differs from dialectic. The second issue emerges from Gadamer's writings after the publication of *Truth and Method* where he links conversation to a distinct form of being with others. This is the issue of the sociality of conversation.

Regarding the first issue, when Gadamer describes conversation as that which one speaks with others and to others, he characterizes the dynamics of language that takes place in speaking as a "dialectic of the word," which he explains with the Hegelian term "speculation." The dialectic of the word is the speculative dimension in language in which "the finite possibilities of the word are oriented toward the sense intended as toward the infinite" (Gadamer, 1989a: 469). In the dialectic of the word every word is related to the whole of language, causing the whole of language to resonate. In this sense "every word, as the event of a moment, carries with it the unsaid, to which it is related by responding and summoning" (Gadamer, 1989a: 258). In describing dialogical conversation in this way it is easy to confuse dialogue with dialectic, understood here as a progress to the whole in relation to identity and difference. Since Gadamer calls the movement of language dialectical, dialogue becomes a form of dialectics. In fact, Gadamer draws several distinctions to point to the difference between hermeneutic dialogue and the dialectical thinking found not only in the philosophy of Hegel, but also in that of Plato.

First, Gadamer draws a distinction between dialogue and dialectic in order to emphasize the non-methodological character of dialogical understanding. In his 1981 essay "Text and Interpretation," Gadamer writes:

[I]n full accord with Heidegger's critique of the concept of subject, whose hidden ground he revealed as substance, I tried to conceive the original phenomenon of language in dialogue. This effort entailed a hermeneutical reorientation of dialectic, which had been developed by German Idealism as the speculative method, toward the art of living dialogue in which the Socratic-Platonic movement of thought took place. This reorientation of dialectic was not intended to lead to a merely negative dialectic even though it was always conscious of the fundamental incompletability of the Greek dialectic. Rather, it represented a correction of the ideal of method that characterized modern dialectic as fulfilling itself in the idealism of the Absolute.

(Gadamer, 1989b: 23)

As a correction to the ideal of method, dialogue is not dialectic because every dialogue is to be a living dialogue, and presumably this means not only that it is a less formalized procedure in comparison with a Hegelian dialectic of contradiction, but also that it is not concerned with connecting the beginning and the end (the incompletability). But if dialogue is only understood in this way, it still remains in close proximity to dialectical thinking, for like dialectics dialogical understanding dissolves differences (overcomes opposition) in coming to agreement about what is said.

Second, Gadamer draws a distinction between dialogue and dialectic in order to emphasize the non-monological character of dialogical understanding. Gadamer is most direct about this distinction in his discussion of Hegel's dialectic in relation to ancient dialectic, since it is a key distinction separating Hegel from the ancients. Gadamer claims that Hegel's dialectic, which is a dialectic of the self-movement of the concept, is peculiar to him alone. Although he finds his model in Eleatic and Platonic dialectic, Hegel conceives of dialectical reason in terms of its ability to unify and become homogeneous. This homogeneity is the driving force in the resolution of the oppositions and differences, which arise from a reflection on thought's own content, into a higher unity. Gadamer does not think that this notion of an encompassing unity of reason can be found in ancient dialectic, despite Hegel's claim that he finds it there (Gadamer, 1976: 21). Gadamer, then, can still align his dialogical understanding with Hegelian dialectic only because, as he says elsewhere, he wants to save the honor of Hegel's "bad infinity." This phrase is used to signal the specific character of the dialectic in dialogical understanding: hermeneutic understanding is determined by the finitude of historical experience where what is to be understood is encountered as a foreign other, and language must be found to be able to hear what the other has to say. Thus for Gadamer the hermeneutic dialectic of the word is speculative in a different way than in Hegel's dialectic where at a formal level of the speculative proposition the subject term enters the predicate and continues in this self-development by internal necessity. Language is speculative for hermeneutics only in the sense that in it the subject matter enters into an interpretation through possibilities in language. In hermeneutic speculation "finite possibilities of the word are oriented to the sense intended as toward the infinite," where it can produce an understanding of an aspect of the subject matter but never a partial meaning of a self-same whole of meaning (Gadamer, 1989a: 469).

Third, Gadamer draws a further distinction between dialogue and dialectic based on this difference in the idea of dialectical speculation. As he presents the issue of dialectic in *Truth and Method*, Gadamer does not just want to separate himself from Hegel's dialectic, he also wants to separate himself from the formal dialectic of Plato that is exhibited in the late dialogues such as the *Sophist*. Taken together, both Hegel's and Plato's dialectic depend on subordinating language to the statement, but Gadamer thinks that "the concept of the statement, dialectically accentuated to the point of contradiction … is antithetical to the nature of hermeneutic experience and the verbal nature of the human experience of the world" (Gadamer, 1989a: 468). For Gadamer the event of speech is dialectical in the limited sense of finding the words to make oneself intelligible to the other. This is not to make statements but to hold what is said together with an infinity of what is not said in one unified meaning. And what is not said stands in relation to the motivations and intentions of meaning in speaking. Such meanings can never unfold in the manner of a logic of concepts that are presented through statements.

In what sense then is the dialogical encounter still dialectical? Certainly the dialogical encounter in hermeneutics is not Hegel's self-movement of the concept that comes to display the concept in its unity through the sublation of contradiction into a third. The hermeneutic dialogical encounter is dialectical only in the sense of a dialectic of question and answer which is always related to opening up possibilities of meaning. If there is any correspondence with Hegel's dialectic, it can be so only in the very general sense that "every interpretation must begin somewhere and seek to supercede the one-sidedness which that inevitably produces" (Gadamer, 1989a: 471). But Gadamer does not think that this is sufficient for a real correspondence with dialectics (see Gadamer, 1989a: 472). The one unified meaning produced in the dialogical encounter of conversation is always a different meaning in the event of understanding.

Regarding the second issue, when Gadamer discusses the importance of dialogue in his early writing on Plato, he emphasizes the ability of all speaking to be dialogical: all speaking is a speaking with someone and intends what it speaks about to be understood. This is true even when no one else is present to hear the speaker's words, for we think in a language which refers to possible others. In actual dialogue we seek the agreement of the other, but in doing so we express ourselves at the same time in moods and gestures, for example. When the other person responds not to what was said but to the speaker's self-expression, the shared understanding is only to enable the "participants themselves to become manifest to each other" (Gadamer 1991: 37). Plato's dialogues can be said to be unsuccessful because of this intrusion of the speaker's personality in the conversation. Most conversations in the dialogues of Plato are not ideal conversations where thinking would be devoted purely to the subject matter talked about. This situation of an impure conversation raises the question for Gadamer as to what constitutes a shared understanding and a real being-with-one-another in conversation. In this early text Gadamer is framing what he will later call in *Truth and Method* the second form of the I–thou relation in which the relation is inadequate for hermeneutic understanding precisely because it is reflective and not dialogical in its proper sense. In this second form of the I–thou relation a person reflects him or herself out of the mutuality of the relation, thus changing the relation and destroying the actual sharing. Despite the fact that this kind of conversation has the character of a "we" relation, it is actually a form of understanding that pushes the other away. A real conversation draws the speakers together when thinking is directed solely to the substantive intention of what is said; in a genuine conversation the distinction (and separation) between the partners in dialogue actually breaks down. It is only with this breaking down that there is a shared world (*Mitwelt*). For Gadamer, when a hermeneutic conversation between two people is successful it enacts a shared world.

This does not mean that Gadamer is opposed to self-reflection in dialogue. What he is opposed to is the way in which the reflexivity of reflection amounts to a "secondary phenomenon, compared to turning directly to the matter at issue" where the conversational partners lose themselves, so to speak (Gadamer, 2000a: 277–8). Gadamer wants to let the critical function achieved by reflection be carried out by the dynamics of question and response over the matter at issue in conversation. The distinction Gadamer is making about genuine conversation involving more than a reciprocal relating is an attempt to get at the enlarged sense that he gives to being-with-one-another through language and to the way in which the thou in the relation of one to another has priority. According to Gadamer, "who thinks language already moves beyond subjectivity" (Gadamer, 2000a: 286). When Gadamer speaks of this encounter in the language of I and thou, it is of critical importance for him that this relation not be taken as one of intersubjectivity. When asked in a 1993 interview whether his philosophy thematizes conversation as our capacity for rational inter-subjectivity, Gadamer quickly objects to the misleading concept of intersubjectivity, of a subjectivism doubled, as a way of characterizing a conversation with another person. A conversation is simply something one gets caught up in (Gadamer, 2001: 59). What Gadamer objects to is the framing of conversation in terms of the priority of a "subject," such that the very commonality that subtends subjectivity, namely, the shared common world of language to which we first belong as the condition for sharing, is lost.

Gadamer's reservation towards the idea of intersubjectivity is easily overlooked because of his use of the idea of the I–thou encounter in *Truth and Method*, as noted earlier. But the idea of the I–thou, which became prominent in the first part of the twentieth century with the publication of a book bearing the same title by Martin Buber (Buber 1958 – originally published 1923) was never understood to convey a simple idea of intersubjectivity. Gadamer realized this and that is why his account of the I–thou in *Truth and Method* is complex. As noted, it is only the third form of the I–thou that is the genuine form for hermeneutic conversation. It is the form that indicates how a historically effected consciousness operates in the interpretation of the historical tradition. Tradition expresses itself like a thou, but this does not mean that what is being understood is the opinion of another person. The I–thou indicates the partnership in which the interpreter situated in history is in relation to the his-torical object, as is the I with the thou. The relation amounts to a being in common in relation to which what is not understood can be understood. The opening to the thou is the necessary bond for the possibility of hearing the multifarious different voices in which historical tradition exists.

The priority of the thou is manifest in yet another way in conversation. This other way also reflects something essential that Gadamer takes from the Platonic dialogue, namely a version of Socratic humility. In another late essay, Gadamer remarks how it is that we live in conversation not just to understand the other person; we also need it "because our own concepts threaten to become rigid." His insight here is that the problem for understanding is not that we do not understand the other person, "but that we don't understand ourselves." For this reason when we attempt to understand the other "we must break down resistance in ourselves if we wish to hear the other as other" (Gadamer 2007a: 371). When we attend to the priority of the other in conversation we are able "to recognize in principle the limitation of one's own framework" and to allow "one to go beyond one's own possibilities"

(Gadamer, 2000a: 284). It is with this re-formulation of the dynamics of conversation that Gadamer would rather use the word "other" in place of the "thou." While Gadamer acknowledges the philosophical importance that the I–thou problem served in the 1920s, he also acknowledges that such speech "hides a mystifying substantiation" that blocks us from getting at the real problems. To say "the other" in place of "the thou" changes the perspective, for "every other is at the same time the other of the other" (Gadamer, 2000a: 282).

With this last idea, we have a better sense of the link that Gadamer wants to establish between conversation and a shared world. In another late essay, "Towards a Phenomenology of Ritual and Language," Gadamer remarks on how he began to conceive language differently after he learned from Heidegger how to break away from the traditional concept of language. He thinks that language exists only in "the with-one-another [Miteinander] of speaking and the to-one-another [Aufeinander] of listening" (Gadamer, 2000b: 22). The phrase "with-one-another" is used to indicate the distinctive way of sharing that allows humans to support one another. He contrasts this phrase with "together-with" (Mitsamt), which characterizes the life-world that dominates in the area of animal behavior. Gadamer finds this idea of with-one-another already in Aristotle's Rhetoric. Aristotle thinks that humans achieve a sense of community among themselves because they are capable of mutual understanding through speech (see Aristotle, 1967: 1253a15–18). Gadamer translates this basic idea into the linguisticality of understanding. The unity of meaning in a text or a conversation rests on this with-one-another. This is why Gadamer claims that hermeneutic understanding is always an act of communication. As he explains it, communication (Mitteilung) "involves the idea that we share [teilen] something with one another [Miteinander] that does not become less in the sharing but perhaps even grows" (Gadamer, 1983: 15). In sharing there is an opening, presumably between one and another, where the world becomes larger, not smaller. For Gadamer's hermeneutics dialogical conversation is this enactment of meaning through which the world becomes larger.

Bibliography

Aristotle (1967) Rhetoric, trans. J.H. Freese, Cambridge, MA: Harvard University Press.

Buber, Martin (1958) I and Thou, trans. Ronald Gregor Smith, Edinburgh: T. and T. Clark.

Gadamer, Hans-Georg (1976) "Hegel and the Dialectic of the Ancient Philosophers," in Hegel's Dialectic, trans. P. Christopher Smith, New Haven: Yale University Press.

——(1983) "Die Kultur und das Wort," in Lob der Theorie, Frankfurt: Suhrkamp.

——(1989a) Truth and Method, trans. Joel Weinsheimer and Donald Marshall, New York: Continuum.

——(1989b) "Text and Interpretation," trans. Dennis Schmidt and Richard Palmer, in Dialogue and Deconstruction, ed. Diane Michelfelder and Richard Palmer, Albany: SUNY Press.

——(1991) Plato's Dialectical Ethics, trans. Robert Wallace, New Haven: Yale University Press.

——(2000a) "Subjectivity and Intersubjectivity, Subject and Person," trans. Peter Adamson and David Vessey, Continental Philosophy Review, 33: 275–87.

——(2000b) "Towards a Phenomenology of Ritual and Language," trans. Lawrence K. Schmidt and Monika Reuss in Language and Linguisticality in Gadamer's Hermeneutics, ed. Lawrence K. Schmidt, Lanham: Lexington Books.

——(2001) *Gadamer in Conversation*, ed. and trans. Richard Palmer, New Haven: Yale University Press.

——(2007a) "Hermeneutics and the Ontological Difference," in *The Gadamer Reader*, ed. Richard Palmer, Evanston: Northwestern University Press.

——(2007b) "Language and Understanding," in *The Gadamer Reader*, ed. Richard Palmer, Evanston: Northwestern University Press.

Heidegger, Martin (1962) *Being and Time*, trans. J. Macquarrie and E. Robinson, New York: Harper & Row.

——(1971) *On the Way to Language*, trans. Peter Hertz, New York: Harper & Row.

Further reading

Gadamer, Hans-Georg (2006) "The Incapacity for Conversation," trans. David Vessey and Chris Blauwkamp, *Continental Philosophy Review*, 39: 351–9.

27

TEXT AND TRANSLATION

Dennis J. Schmidt

An attention to language is at the heart of hermeneutic theory. Indeed, it seems fair to say that to think language is the first and defining task of hermeneutics. This concern with language circumscribes the hermeneutic conception of experience and it forms the core of hermeneutic theory. One finds this conviction pointedly expressed by Hans-Georg Gadamer's celebrated remarks that "Being that can be understood is language" and that "language is the real medium of hermeneutic experience" (Gadamer 2004: 474). However, his remark about the great importance of language for hermeneutics is frequently misunderstood. Such misunderstanding arises when one presumes to know "what" language "is." The assumption that language is readily apparent and unproblematically available for our inspection is misleading. Against this assumption, philosophical hermeneutics begins with the recognition that language is poorest at articulating itself; consequently, if we are to think about language then we must first bring language forward. The problem, the obstacle to thinking the nature of language that is easily overlooked, is that language hides: we speak and pay attention to "what" words are "about" rather than hearing the words themselves. Language withdraws in order to serve up its message, in order to communicate, and so in speaking and writing, language is mostly silent about itself. Hermeneutics begins as the countermovement to this withdrawal of language; it sets out as the effort to bring language forward, to bring it to speak about itself, to bring language to our attention. This effort to slow the spontaneous flow of language, to become aware of what so easily hides despite its fundamental importance for us – for thinking, for our world, for our self-understanding – is difficult. Gadamer says simply: "this self-presentation of the word is not easy to grasp correctly" (Gadamer 1989: 47).

In order to take up this difficult task of thinking language, hermeneutics has long turned to those sites and experiences in which language more naturally asserts itself. That is why the long tradition of hermeneutics has roots in religious texts and juridical texts. In those texts the "wording" is paramount. More recently, poetic texts, works in which language itself is sounded out, have been the focus of hermeneutic investigation. But in the formulation of contemporary hermeneutic theory two sites of linguisticality have played especially important roles in this project of calling attention to language itself: the formation of texts and translation. One sees the almost unparalleled importance of these notions of text and translation for the formulation of a theory of hermeneutics in Gadamer's *Truth and Method*, which remains the most systematic and important articulation of a theory of philosophical hermeneutics. In the following remarks, my intention is to show why each of these ideas is centrally important for understanding philosophical hermeneutics and to clarify how the eminent character of the text and the special problems of translation expose something of the task of hermeneutic theory.

On texts

Philosophy began with a suspicion of and a deep concern about written texts. Plato expresses this in the *Phaedrus* (Plato 2014) when Socrates is presented with a written speech by the sophist Lysias. After the text is read to him, Socrates expresses a number of worries about what that text says, but then he expresses even greater worries about what happens to language when it is put into writing. His worries all point to a common concern about written texts; namely, he suggests that written texts can change us and how we think in ways that diminish our souls. When he explains this view Socrates contends that written words immobilize the movement of life, are incapable of answering any questions, and impair our memory. This is not the place to unpack this complex and important Platonic dialogue. However, it is worth noting that although these questions about the nature of texts and about the way they enter into and shape our understanding of the world stand at the beginning of philosophy, they are almost immediately lost in the long history that follows. The irony that Plato's worries about written texts are passed down through history as written texts is rather easy to see and is often noted, but what such written texts really mean for us and what sort of experience belongs to written texts is usually ignored. The most significant attempt to reconsider the importance of texts, to ask how they are formed and how they shape our understanding, is found in contemporary hermeneutics. Perhaps the most concise presentation of the notion of the text is found in the section entitled "Transformation into Structure and Total Mediation," in Gadamer's *Truth and Method* (Gadamer 2004: 110).[1] The intention of this section is to mark the moment in which the free play of human experience is transformed into the structure and stability of a text.

Gadamer emphasizes the immense significance of this transformation by saying that "a complete change takes place" and that this "transformation is a transformation into the true" (Gadamer 2004: 112). In becoming a text, in being brought into the structure and unity of a text, something like a new realm of the real is opened up, one that in a strange way is "more [the being of the real] than the original" (Gadamer 2004: 114). Such claims can seem rather extreme and yet it is precisely such conclusions that need to be understood and carefully developed. One needs then to ask how it is that the formation of a text *can be* "true" and even "more" "true" than that from which the text emerged.[2]

The roots of genuine texts, the source from which they emerge, are ultimately found in human experience. To be sure, not everything written or that claims to be a text is a text worthy of real attention; there are pseudo-texts, pre-texts, and failed texts, and the capacity to distinguish the real text from a mere pretext requires judgment. But those works that do deserve attention all trace themselves back to human experience insofar as the best texts always preserve something of the movement of life, they seem somehow "alive." This is what gives a genuine text its substance and meaning. The hermeneutic analysis of human experience is a complex matter, but its most important point is easy to identify: at its core, human experience is defined by *play*. While Gadamer's real intention is to let play serve as the defining trait of human experience, he begins by thinking about the widest sense of "playing." To this end, he speaks about the cat at play with a ball, the play of light, the play of water in a fountain, a child at play, playing music, playing a game, and playing a sport. The aim of all of these remarks is to let play serve as the "clue to the ontological explanation" of experience so that several features of experience might be made visible. Thus, once these remarks about play are brought to bear upon the broader analysis of experience one comes to see that experience, like play, is something open and freely moving. It is not however something random or simply a matter of disconnected moments; rather, like play, experience is a "to and fro movement" in which there is some sort of unity, some sense of wholeness and connectedness constantly being formed and reformed. In the end, all of this means that experience, like play, is something one can never master or complete, it is rather defined by being constantly *enacted* or *underway*. Experience, like play, is a *movement* and like play, experience absorbs us so that we are hardly ever really conscious of it.

The transformation of experience into a text is however a becoming conscious of experience. It is a transformation in which experience is articulated, structured, and woven together into a text.[3] Even more: in this transformation into the structure of a text something new appears insofar as the world that appears in the text is a "wholly transformed world" in which one interpretation, one way of structuring and rendering experience intelligible, is achieved. The text is precisely such an interpretation of experience, but by bringing the open, free, and unfinished movement of experience into a structure the text is a "raising up" ["*Aufhebung*"] of given experience – that which we normally call the "real world" – into its truth, its intelligibility so that it can be understood even better than it is in lived experience itself. This is why Gadamer writes that "Homer's Achilles is more ['true'] than the original" (Gadamer 2004: 114). In order to understand how this can be the case, two points need to be grasped. First that the highest form of a text is found in the work of art. Second, that such works are not copies of something that is drawn from experience and so to be considered as merely "secondary" or beholding to something that is more original, more "true."

To suggest that the work of art stands at the summit of the possibilities of the text is to say that in art the fullest achievement of the possibilities of texts are found. Above all, this means that in the work of art something of the movement of life, of its freedom and openness, is preserved. One sees this in the way in which works of art seem to be inexhaustibly rich and the way in which they seem to be alive. Understood hermeneutically, works of art are not to be approached or understood as objects, nor as finished products, but as a sort of movement, as an event. One might say that in its heart the work of art, like experience, is a matter of play, but *as a text* the artwork presents us with a unity, a structure, and thus an intelligibility that experience itself lacks. It is, in other words, an interpretation of experience in which we come to recognize something that is not able to be seen in experience by itself. This is why we can learn from works of art: "the world of the work of art, in which play expresses itself fully in the unity of the work, is in fact a wholly transformed world. In and through it everyone recognizes how things are" (Gadamer 2004: 113). The pleasure we take in works of art is the joy of the knowledge, the recognition in which the world and we ourselves are revealed, that is opened up by the work of art.

It should be clear from what has been said about the nature of texts and how they culminate in a work of art that texts can come in a variety of forms. Dance, music, sculpture, painting, poetry, literature, film – all of the ways in which texts can be formed – are all texts; they are all ways in which experience is transformed into structures that let us see and understand the world anew. To be understood each of these texts need to be "read" in the way appropriate to them. But while the notion of textuality is at the center of the hermeneutic understanding of works of art, it is also the case that hermeneutic theory invariably privileges the linguistic work of art. The poetic work, the literary text thus has a preeminence in hermeneutic theory and in the way in which texts are to be understood. Although he does acknowledge that "the difference between a literary work of art and any other text is not so fundamental," Gadamer also says that:

> nothing is so strange, and at the same time, so demanding, as the written word. ... the written word and what partakes of it – literature – is the intelligibility of mind transferred to the most alien medium. Nothing is so purely the trace of the mind as writing ... this is like nothing else that comes down to us from the past.
>
> (Gadamer 2004: 164)

We are beings of language. To speak and write is our great distinction, and texts that are structured by and woven together as language are texts that most bear the mark of our distinction. Such texts allow us to reach beyond the moment, indeed to reach and speak beyond the time of our own lives. They permit, as it were, a sort of conversation that is not fully bound by time, a conversation in which those living can enter into some sort of conversation with those who are dead. History becomes possible by virtue of such texts; it is a history that is not simply the record of events, but is rather a real to and fro, a real exchange in which we are able to reach – in some modest sense at least – beyond our own times and limitations.

Thus the written text, above all the poetic text, focuses the problem of the text and of language for hermeneutics in a special way. But there remains one final point that must be understood if the hermeneutic significance of the text is to be grasped. If it remains only scribbles on paper, the text does not achieve its promise; it must be *read*, it must be reanimated so that the movement of life, the play that is at its heart is set out once again. The text, any text, but above all the written text, was born of an interpretation, it came to be as a structure given to the dynamic of experience, but if it is to deliver its "truth" then it must be read, it must be interpreted again. Every text summons an interpretation, a reading, and in reading a new relation to time and history begins: "people who can read what has been handed down in writing produce and achieve the sheer presence of the past" (Gadamer 2004:

164). In reading one begins a new experience, one that is not restricted to the present or the limitations of a place. Reading a written text, one enters a world that is larger and different – a new world from which a new understanding can come to be. But no matter what "content" the text might "communicate," the linguistic text that has become a work of art – literature – shows most of all how language belongs to the world. In such texts, one is asked to *listen* not just to what is said, but how it is said. One listens to the text itself.

The text is at the beginning of the hermeneutic project. The transformation into the structure that is a text sets this project into motion. From out of a sensitivity to the text and to all that follows in its wake, the hermeneutic project of interpretation – of reading the world – begins anew. This beginning, the turn to the text, returns us to the question of language with a new force and a stronger sense of just what might be entailed in the effort to think language itself.

On translation

The effort to think language is sharpened by an awareness of the operations and significance of the text, but it is not completed by that awareness. Even though a keen sense of the nature of the text can help call attention to the being of language, the capacity of language to hide itself remains potent even when we make the effort to think about the nature of texts and so hermeneutic theory has a special interest, calling attention to other experiences of language in which language itself is front and center. One such experience is the experience of working and thinking between two different languages. In translation the friction and incommensurability that distinguish languages bring each language forward, calling attention to words themselves. In the struggle to translate what is said in one language to another, a struggle in which the differences between languages highlight something about the character of each language, one is compelled to think about language itself.

Every translator, everyone who has attempted to negotiate two languages in order to bring one language to say what is said in another language, knows that the task of the translator goes far beyond the attempt to find equivalent words in two languages. Dictionaries are of little help in translation if the translator does not understand both languages in the fullest, lived sense. Languages belong to cultures and worlds, they have histories and resonances that will never be fully commensurate with even the most kindred of other languages. When we enter into translation we move far beyond the technicalities of simply matching up words between languages.[4] In order to translate a text one needs to understand it, but even more: one needs to be able to hear and appreciate the nuances and particularities of the languages involved. In other words, one needs to attend to language itself. In this way, the experience of the translator is to be driven to listen to language itself. There is no translation possible without this listening.

But this experience of translation is not only one of the permeability of languages, of their kinship and connection. No listening to language, no matter how focused and intense, can resolve the profound experience of the difference between languages. Translation is always lodged in the particularities of language, in its concretion. In other words, translation requires a relation to language that is not able to be satisfied by generalities or abstractions about language. If one is to translate, then one must pay close attention to the reality of language itself. When one does this one discovers, among other things, just how deeply history has embedded itself into language.

Languages are the bearers of history and of memory. In what we say language carries into the present a residue of the past and how words have been understood and heard. Language also carries its own peculiar history in itself. It does this in the roots of words and in the way words come into being. Words arise out of other words and in response to the effort to say something. In short, no word is insulated from either its own or its culture's past. This means of course that languages are never innocent, but always mementoes of a culture and of a history that has been spoken and written. One of the more eloquent expressions of the way that language carries a history forward into every present comes from Heinrich Heine's comment about Martin Luther's translation of the Bible into German. Heine suggests that with this translation Luther stretched the syntax, grammar, and vocabulary of German to be able to say what had been inexpressible in German prior to this translation. In doing this Luther changed what could be said and thought in German, and so one must say that "he created the German language." Heine recognizes that Luther's translation of the Bible is not "simply" a linguistic achievement, but a political one that has left a long legacy in history: in this translation, Germans were presented with a language that united previously diverse linguistic groups. That is why Heine says that "when the political revolution takes place in Germany, it will result in the strange phenomenon that liberty will everywhere be able to speak, and its speech will be Biblical" (Heine 1986: 56). All language is a bearer of history, its own and its culture's; translations must confront this and cross the gap between the histories that different languages carry forward. In doing this, sometimes, as was the case with Luther's translation of the Bible, they create new possibilities and open new avenues to the future. But even translations that do not match Luther's great achievement find that they must confront the past.

One sees then how the translator must confront the largest dimensions of language and in this confrontation we are reminded of the full scope of language. A simple word can carry a large and long history. This means that to attend to language, to bring it forward – the first task of hermeneutic theory – is to wake up to the profound and inescapable force of history in language. A further consequence of this is that one realizes that different languages can belong to different histories and so historical frictions, as well as historical connections, enter into every translation. Here the great expanse that opens up with language becomes evident.

But translation also makes evident the way in which language is rooted in utter particularity and is localized in the body. This is more difficult to demonstrate, but it is something that those who speak a foreign language, even it is not a matter of translating it, can sense. I am referring to the real carnality of language, to the way in which the voice can seem different when one speaks another language. Accents are the most evident and audible result of this relation between language and the body. We have accents because our facial muscles are not practiced in certain movements required of different languages. Our faces are simply not able to produce some sounds because we have not exercised the muscles needed for those sounds.[5] This relation of language and the body, a kinship that cannot be severed, belongs to all language; however, it easily hides when one speaks one's native language. In speaking a foreign language, a language in which one becomes conscious of the sound of one's speech and of one's unshakeable accent, this carnality of all language becomes remarkably evident. In this way, the encounter with the foreign language serves yet again to bring language forward and to our attention.

So the experiences of and struggle with foreign languages bring language out of its hiddenness. In such experiences language comes to articulate itself and call attention to itself. In doing this we come to see both the enormous reach of language – the extension of each word into history – and the localized embodiment of language – the way it is written even on our faces and our accents. In each of these discoveries about the nature of language, we find the way in which language opens up and joins worlds and, at the same time, we find the way in which language shuts us out and limits us to our own histories, even our bodies. In the encounter with foreign languages, an encounter that is condensed in the work of the translator, one learns both about the transcendence and the materiality, the ideality and the stubborn resistance to a locality, that defines every language. In other words, one discovers with great intensity that every language lives in and with other languages, and that it is always at odds and in communication with other languages. One discovers as well that no language is seamless even within its own borders, but that every language is a sort of complex of forces and possibilities that are not always commensurate with one another.

Conclusion

At the outset of these remarks, I commented that hermeneutic theory is driven by the conviction that language articulates the world and us in such elemental ways that one can ultimately say "Being that can be understood is language." Hermeneutics does not end with its efforts to think the nature of language, but it does begin with these efforts. It also begins with the important recognition that language is not readily evident to us, but likes to hide. Indeed, this self-concealing character of language belongs to its nature and so it too needs to be understood. But if the nature of language is to be thought, then this self-concealing tendency of language needs to be confronted so that language can show itself. This is not an easy matter and so hermeneutics has long gravitated to those experiences in which language more readily calls attention to itself. The formation of texts and the experience of foreign languages, especially in translations, do this in different ways.

The transformation into the structure of a written text is one of the most significant ways in which language not only articulates a world, but can actually transform a world and render it "true". This coming to be of a text is, like language itself, something not readily apparent; in writing, one does not tend to think about the formation of the text, but of what needs to be said. Nonetheless, the meaning of the text and its transformative power is one of the most basic concerns in hermeneutics. In the text, language enacts one of its most far-reaching possibilities: it simultaneously gives a structure and new intelligibility to the world and it reaches beyond the present and into a future that is still unimaginable. And yet, the text arrives in need of something beyond itself, something it cannot satisfy of itself: it needs to be read. A text will always remain a mute inscription unless a reader reanimates it. In this neediness of the text, this absolute need of the reader, the text shows its own truth, namely, that it is a moment in a dialogue. The text is only a beginning and it is only this if it has the good fortune to be part of a dialogue.

The experience of translation – or more precisely, all of the forms in which a language encounters the "foreign" – plays a different, but no less significant role in hermeneutics. What is distinctive and hermeneutically interesting about this encounter is the way in which language announces itself and becomes evident. It is the friction between languages, and the incommensurability of their histories and bodily characters, that brings language itself to our attention. Above all, it is in the failure and limits of translation that language becomes ever more evident. This stubborn insistence of language remaining itself and not being converted into some other language is one of the most revealing ways in which language reveals itself.

Whereas the text is one of the ways in which language can be seen as constituting the world and as giving it a structure, translation is more significant as one of the ways in which language is able to be brought forward as language. Together the notions and experiences of the text and of translation, each in its own way, provide hermeneutic theory with a site in which language can be thought in its ownmost nature. Even a preliminary account of hermeneutic reflections upon texts and translation makes some of the characteristics of the nature of language clear. One sees, for instance, that although language likes to hide itself, it is not on that account without great power in the being of the world and in the shaping of our own natures. One sees the force of history emerging, one sees the plurality of languages engaging one another, one sees how a world can be structured and transfigured in writing, one senses the carnality of the word, and one finds that in engaging the nature of language one necessarily engages a world.

The largest aim of hermeneutic theory is "understanding." That aim is something different than "knowing." In knowing there is a strong grip on what is known, it is an effort to lay claim to a sense of truth as something stable and secure. Understanding, on the other hand, is a fundamental mode of our being in the world. It is, as Heidegger demonstrated in *Being and Time* (Heidegger 2010), how we find our way in the world and hence, unlike the cognitive task of knowing, the task of understanding is responsive and always underway, always unfinished. It is, one might say, an infinite task and in recognizing this, understanding recognizes its own finitude and the finitude of its "truth." This aim of hermeneutics – this goal of formulating and deepening our sense of understanding – necessarily engages the full dimensions of how we are in the world. However, hermeneutic theory begins with the recognition that language is the element of our being in the world and consequently that experience of language needs to be engaged and thought above all else. To this end of thinking the nature of language as the most far-reaching element of all understanding, the notion of the text and the experience of the foreign in translation play a privileged role.

Notes

1 In the strict sense, Gadamer is talking about a transformation of experience into a "structure" ["*Gebilde*"]; however, the sense of structure here is quite clearly the structure that defines a "text." See also Gadamer (1989). Also of great importance and clarity is Ricoeur (1977, 1984).

2 It is important to remember that Gadamer is not arguing that every text *will be* "true." In other words, not all writing comes to be a text in the fullest sense of the word.

3 The etymological connection between text and textile, a connection that reminds us that a "weaving" belongs to texts in much the same way as it does to textiles, should be noted.

4 This is one reason that computer generated "translations" will never be able to satisfy the demands of translation.

5 An interesting result of this relation of speech and the face is that our face is shaped by the language we speak everyday. The muscles and movements that give a face its definition are, in many ways, a consequence of the language we speak and practice daily.

Bibliography

Gadamer, H.-G. (2004) *Truth and Method.* Translated by Weinsheimer, J. and Marshall, D. New York: Continuum.

——(1989) "Text and Interpretation." Translated by Palmer, R. and Schmidt, D. in Palmer, R. and Mickelfelder, D. (Eds.) *Dialogue and Deconstruction.* Albany: SUNY Press.

Heidegger, M. (2010) *Being and Time.* Translated by Stambaugh, J. and Schmidt, D. Albany: SUNY Press.

Heine, H. (1986) *Religion and Philosophy in Germany.* Translated by Snodgrass, J. Albany: SUNY Press.

Plato (2014) *Phaedrus.* Translated by Scully, S. Newburyport, MA: Focus Publishing.

Ricoeur, P. (1977) *The Rule of Metaphor.* Translated by McLaughlin, K. and Pellauer, D. Toronto: University of Toronto Press.

——(1984) *Time and Narrative.* Translated by McLaughlin, K. and Pellauer, D. Chicago: University of Chicago Press.

Further reading

Walter Benjamin, "The Task of the Translator," translated by H. Zohn, in *The Translation Studies Reader,* edited by Lawrence Venuti, Routledge, London, 2000.

Antoine Berman, *The Experience of the Foreign: On Culture and Translation,* translated by S. Heyvaert, SUNY Press, New York, 1992.

Jacques Derrida, "Living On: Border Lines," translated by J. Hulbert, in *Deconstruction and Criticism,* Seabury Press, New York, 1979.

Jacques Derrida, "Plato's Pharmacy," translated by B. Johnson, in *Disseminations,* University of Chicago Press, Chicago, 1981.

William H. Gass, *Reading Rilke: Reflections on the Problems of Translation,* Knopf, New York, 1999.

Luigi Pareyson, *Truth and Interpretation,* translated by R. Valgenti, SUNY Press, New York, 2013.

Dennis Schmidt, "The Garden of Letters: Plato's *Phaedrus* on the Nature of Texts," in *Internationale Jahrbuch für Hermeneutik,* Bd. 12, 2013.

George Steiner, *After Babel: Aspects of Language and Translation,* Oxford University Press, Oxford, 1975.

Jesper Svenbro, *Phrasikleia: An Anthropology of Reading in Ancient Greece,* translated by J. Lloyd, Cornell University Press, Ithaca, 1993.

28
PLACE AND SITUATION
Jeff Malpas

Regardless of whether *herméneuein* (the Greek root from which the modern 'herme-neutics' comes) is actually derived from the name of the god Hermes, the nature of hermeneutics undoubtedly reflects the nature of the god. As the bearer of messages between heaven and earth, and also (along with Hestia) a god of the threshold (see Vernant 2006: 157–96), the nature of Hermes is bound to the 'between'. Herme-neutics too belongs to the 'between' – to the space between speaker and hearer, between reader and text, between interpreter and interpreted. It is the 'between' that names the proper place of hermeneutics – just as interpretation and understanding are also seen to be tied to place or situation. Understanding the significance of place and situation in relation to hermeneutic thinking is thus to understand something of the very essence of hermeneutics and the hermeneutical.

1. Hermeneutics, finitude and limit

The 'between' is not a boundless space, but one that is constituted precisely with respect to that which it both connects and separates. The 'between' is essentially bounded, essentially relational, essentially placed or situated. Indeed, to be situated or placed is to be 'between' just as it is also to be 'within'. It is its mode of being as a being 'between' that is characteristic of human being, and as such human being is also essentially situated or placed. Central to philosophical hermeneutics is the understanding of this being 'between' – this being placed or situated – as essentially *productive*.

There is a long tradition in philosophy that takes the fact of human being as always 'between' – always placed or situated, and so as always, in some sense, also in a state of dependence – as a primary obstacle to genuine knowledge and understanding. Phi-losophy has often aimed at finding a way to overcome such situatedness – to achieve what Thomas Nagel famously describes as a 'view from nowhere' (Nagel 1989).[1] One of the characteristic insights of hermeneutic thinking, however, has been that not only is this impossible to achieve, but that it is in any case unnecessary: far from being an obstacle to genuine knowledge and understanding, it is our very *situatedness* that makes these possible. The only view, then, is a view *from somewhere*, and it is in virtue of our being-somewhere – our *being-in-place* – that we can have a view at all.

As with the character of the 'between', the dependence of understanding on situatedness has been variously expressed within the hermeneutic tradition – although not always in terms of an explicit focus on situatedness or place as such.[2] The famous hermeneutic circle, whether understood in terms of the structure of part–whole dependence or the fore-structure of understanding, may seem not to invoke ideas of place or situation in any explicit fashion, and yet the circle is itself a 'topological' or spatial concept,[3] while the nature of the dependence that it articulates can be construed as indeed situational and orientational in character – what the circle suggests is that understanding is always a function of the manner and direction of approach to what is to be understood, or, as one might also put it, that understanding is always a *standing somewhere*, and it is this standing somewhere that underlies understanding itself.

Similarly, the hermeneutic focus on human *finitude*, and so on knowledge and understanding as belonging essentially to finite existence, and only to finite existence, may seem to involve no appeal to notions of situation or place in the first instance, and yet these notions are surely implicit, being brought directly into view as soon as any close attention is brought to bear on the idea of finitude as such. This point becomes all the more evident when one recognises that situation and place are directly implicated with the notions of bound or limit that are at the heart of the idea of finitude. Understood in terms of the Greek *topos*, place is itself directly tied to the idea of limit or boundary (see especially Aristotle 1983: 28 [212a5], but also Malpas 2012b: 233–5), while the explication of situation in terms of the idea of horizon (especially as developed in Gadamer) is indicative of the same connection. Moreover, what is also suggested, if it were not evident already, is that as *place* is at issue here, so too is *space*. Although place ought to be distinguished from space, the two are nevertheless closely bound together (see Malpas 2012b: 232–7; also Malpas 1999a: 34–43), and place brings with it an essential reference to spatiality in part through the idea of an essential *openness* that belongs to place (and perhaps also to situation) – an idea that becomes especially important in the later Heidegger (see Malpas 2006: 251–6).

Often, however, and especially within twentieth-century hermeneutics, the situatedness of understanding has been construed in terms of its primarily temporal or historical character, rather than in relation to the topographic or the spatial. This is most obviously the case in the early Heidegger (see Heidegger 1962; see also Malpas 2006: 65–146). Yet there is good reason to reject any reading of the temporal that does not already entail the spatial and the topographic (see Malpas 2012b: 235–7), while the very idea of situation is inseparable from the notion of place (so that even a temporal reading of situation would not stand apart from the notion of place, but would rather consist in imposing a temporal reading onto it – the latter being one way of construing Heidegger's project in *Being and Time*).[4] Moreover, although it may appear tempting (and is relatively commonplace), to treat the way in which place and space appear here as 'metaphorical' rather than 'literal', there is a real question to be addressed as to what such a distinction might mean in this context. What does it mean to talk of space or place – especially in relation to the structure of understanding – as being used 'metaphorically', or indeed, as being used 'literally'?[5]

Nowhere is this issue concerning the meaning of space and place more directly apparent than in Heidegger's famous assertion of language as the 'house' of being (Heidegger 1998: 239) – an assertion that invokes the spatial and topological, and yet does so in a way that cannot be dismissed as merely 'metaphorical'.[6] The dimensionality that Heidegger invokes here, a dimensionality that belongs to being and to language, is the most original mode of dimensionality, and perhaps the most primordial form of space (although it is not, Heidegger tells us, 'something spatial in the familiar sense' – see Heidegger 1998: 254). Language, one might say, gives place to being – being is thereby given the expansiveness that belongs essentially to it – and in so doing language also gives place, and so space, to understanding. Here the question concerning the role of place and situation in the event of understanding is brought together with the question of language and of being, and it is done in a way that brings to the fore the issue of the metaphoricity or literality of the language that is here deployed. The language of place and situation – and of space – seems a constant feature in the thinking of understanding, and perhaps in all thinking,[7] but how such language should be construed is a question all too quickly answered, if it is raised at all, by the supposition that such language is 'metaphorical'. What metaphor and literality might be, and their role in thinking, is thus a question that the very focus on place and situation itself provokes.

Even if the point is sometimes obscured, the essential insight of hermeneutic thinking is that knowledge and understanding are grounded in human situatedness – in the being of the human in place – and on this basis hermeneutics can be seen to consist precisely in the attempt to elucidate this fundamental situatedness. At the same time, as it does this, however, hermeneutics can also be seen as opening up a path into the understanding of the spatial (along with the temporal, since the two belong necessarily together) as well as the topological. Rather than belonging primarily to metaphysics, the understanding of these notions can now be seen as belonging properly to hermeneutics, just as hermeneutics emerges as more basic than any of the traditional forms of metaphysics. The focus on place and situation is thus an integral part of the transformation of hermeneutics into a mode of ontological inquiry – perhaps the most fundamental form of such inquiry – an inquiry that is both an inquiry into the being of place and the place of being, as well as an inquiry into the placed, situated, *finite* character of understanding.

2. Orientation and bound: Kant's rational geography

Although often absent from discussions of hermeneutics and its history (two notable exceptions are Makkreel 1994 and Ameriks 2006), Kant has an especially significant place in any discussion of the hermeneutical significance of place and situation. This is so for a number of reasons. First, because the transcendental framework that Kant develops and deploys, and which is crucial to hermeneutics understood as an inquiry into the *grounds* of understanding, is itself a framework that draws on a set of spatial and topological conceptions. Second, Kant is explicit in addressing questions concerning the structure of situatedness, not only in terms of bodily and mental *orientation*, but also through his focus on the necessary *bounds* of knowledge (those bounds being articulated using explicitly spatial and topological concepts). Third, in his arguments concerning the role of spatiality in relation to thought and to ideas of both objectivity and subjectivity, Kant shows how space and place might indeed play a fundamental ontological role in the very possibility of knowledge, understanding and also judgement.

There can be little doubt that, in its philosophical form, hermeneutics has an essentially transcendental character – a character it shares with phenomenology. In the terms in which Gadamer puts the matter, drawing directly on Kant, philosophical hermeneutics is centrally concerned with the question: 'how is understanding possible?' (Gadamer 1989: xxix). It thus looks to the grounds of understanding and it finds those grounds to be given in the very situatedness of understanding. Although the question of the nature of the transcendental remains a contentious one, there are good reasons for taking the transcendental to depend on a thoroughly topological mode of thinking, and the very implication of the transcendental with the issue of ground indicates as much. Kant famously construes the transcendental in legal terms – the *quid juris* as opposed to the *quid facti* (Kant 1998: A84/B116). Yet much of Kant's language elsewhere, and the language of others since, also associates the transcendental, and the larger project of the bounding and grounding of reason with which it is associated, with ideas of the spatial and topological – even though this fact is all too seldom reflected upon or acknowledged. Not only the language of ground is at issue here, but of turn and return, of movement backwards and forwards, of the unity of a region that is only discernable from within that region itself (see Malpas 1997). Significantly, the circularity that is often seen as a problem for transcendental argument, but is actually one of its underlying features, is itself associated with the spatial or topographical structure at issue here, at the same time as it also seems to mirror the circularity of the hermeneutical (see Malpas 1997).

The structure of spatiality and spatial awareness is something explicitly taken up by Kant in a number of his writings. Central to his thinking is a conception of spatiality as possessed of an orientation that belongs essentially to it. This is a point Kant demonstrates by reference to the phenomenon of so-called incongruent counterparts. Two things may be identical in terms of the spatial relations between their parts, as is the case with each of the gloves that make up a pair, and yet the spatial orientation of each may be quite different, so that a right-handed glove will not fit on the left hand nor will a left-handed glove fit on the right. To be oriented in space is to relate the differentiation present in space to a differentiation present in the self – more specifically, to a differentiation (between left and right, up and down, forward and back) that is given in one's own body and in one's bodily awareness (see e.g. Kant 1992: 364–72; see also Malpas and Zöller 2012). Although often taken to epitomise Kant's prioritisation of the subject (as it is by Heidegger, see Heidegger 1962: H109–10), this emphasis on the relation between spatial and bodily differentiation is better understood as indicating the mutual interconnection of subjective and objective within the structure of spatiality, and even of a certain form of relationality that belongs to subjectivity itself as well as to spatiality (see Malpas 2012a: 118–21). It also suggests the fundamental role of orientation, that is to say, of place or situation, in any engagement with world. Indeed, Kant will take spatial orientation as the starting point for understanding orientation in thinking as such (see Kant 1996: 1–18).

Kant provides one of the first sustained analyses of the structure of spatiality and spatial awareness. Not only does this include an account of the orientational character of spatiality, but also the unitary and bounded character of the spatial. To be in space is to find oneself within a single interconnected but differentiated domain. It is also to find oneself located within a certain horizon, that is, within certain *bounds* that allow that domain to appear as unitary and differentiated. This idea lies at the very heart of Kant's critical project – experience or knowledge is itself understood as just such a unitary but differentiated domain whose unity is established through the horizon within which it is also enclosed. The horizon – which is the proper bound of reason – is not merely restrictive of experience or knowledge, but rather operates (as the visual horizon operates in respect of the visual field) to make possible the experience or knowledge that arises within it. One might argue that it is this idea as it appears in Kant that represents the first appearance of that key hermeneutic insight according to which situatedness is the real ground for understanding.

Kant's account of orientation suggests that understanding – or knowledge or experience – is itself dependent on spatial locatedness. This is an idea reinforced by other aspects of Kant's analysis in the first *Critique*, including his account of space as the a priori condition for representation. The latter requires differentiation, and differentiation requires a notion of externality in which the differentiated elements can be grasped as standing apart from one another. Within the *Critique of Pure Reason*, this is a key element in the 'Refutation of Idealism' (Kant 1998: B274–9), and arguably also plays a part in the 'Transcendental Deduction' (Kant 1998: A84–130, B116–69), especially as developed in the B-edition (see Malpas 1999b). In the *Critique of Judgment*, the emphasis is not directly on spatiality, but on a notion of 'commonality' or 'publicness' as that which is presupposed by those judgements that aim at universality and objectivity (Kant 2001: §40). Such a notion of commonality seems to imply the idea of a shared space or place within which judgement is located (see Benjamin 2010: 31–4). The deployment of spatial and topological notions, whether implicit or explicit, is thus not restricted to the first *Critique*, but runs throughout Kant's thought.

Whether or not one regards Kant as genuinely a hermeneutic thinker, his position as the first thinker properly to open up the question of finitude as that which enables knowledge and understanding, together with the role played by spatiality, as well as notions of externality, commonality and publicness, in his thinking, nevertheless gives him an important place in the history of hermeneutics – especially with regard to the development of twentieth-century hermeneutics. Although Heidegger's own relationship with Kant is complex, Heidegger's ontologically oriented mode of hermeneutics is heavily indebted to Kant – and not least in the way in which it also gives attention to the spatial and topological.

3. Place and world: Heidegger and topology

In his lectures on the hermeneutics of facticity from 1923, Heidegger already speaks of the hermeneutical as that which is concerned with 'making something accessible as being there out in the open, as public' (Heidegger 1999: 8), thereby indicating the way in which hermeneutics might indeed be connected with a certain place or space of commonality. In both the 1923 lectures and in *Being and Time*, from 1927, Heidegger's use of the term *Dasein* as the focus for his investigations is also indicative of the centrality of the concept of situation, and implicitly of place, to his thinking (see Malpas 2006, 2012a – see also Fell 1979: 38–48). Inasmuch as *Being and Time* is itself a work of hermeneutical, as well as phenomenological, inquiry, so the concept of situation is at the heart of Heidegger's hermeneutical approach in that work. To a large extent, what *Being and Time* attempts is a working out of the idea of 'situation' as that given in the idea of the there/here that is the *Da* of *Dasein*.[8] Moreover, the situatedness at issue here is not to be construed in terms merely of a feature of some form of internalised subjectivity – as if it were a function of attitude, disposition or belief – but is rather a matter of Dasein's active engagement with others, with things and with itself, and so is worked out through Dasein's active engagement *in the world* (Malpas 2006: esp. ch. 3 – see also Dreyfus, 1991).[9] Heidegger can thus be seen as implicitly holding to an early form of what is now termed 'externalism' (see Malpas 2012a: 221–2), although that term also suggests a problematic opposition between the internal and external that is itself in tension with a genuinely topological approach.

One of the problems with which *Being and Time* grapples, not altogether successfully, is the extent to which the 'situation' at issue here is indeed to be construed in terms of notions of place or space (the two terms lacking any clear differentiation in Heidegger's early work).[10] As indicated in the introductory comments above, Heidegger's position as worked out in *Being and Time* takes *temporality* to be the key notion, and although Heidegger acknowledges the spatial connotations present in the idea of situation itself ('In the term Situation ... there is an overtone of a signification that is spatial. We shall not try to eliminate this from the existential conception, for such an overtone is also implied in the "there" of Dasein' (Heidegger 1962: H299)), he nevertheless argues for the grounding of spatiality in a more basic notion of temporality (see Heidegger 1962: H367–9). The attempt to prioritise temporality is not without its own problems, however, and arguably depends on treating the temporal as in some sense a mode of place (see Malpas 2006: 103). This is something Heidegger comes to recognise fairly quickly, abandoning the derivative treatment of existential spatiality (see Heidegger 1967: 16–17) and taking time and space to be intimately bound together within the single structure of what he terms 'time-space' (*Zeit-Raum*) (see e.g. Heidegger 2012: 293ff).

Regardless of exactly how the concepts of time and space, and the relation between them, are to be understood, there can be no doubt, however, that Heidegger views understanding (and indeed any sort of appearing or coming to presence), whether in his early or later thinking, as inextricably bound to situation. The event of understanding is, for Heidegger, always a happening that arises within a locality that is proper to it – it is an opening of and to the world that occurs in and through a certain singular and concrete placement in the world (such placement being an *openness* within *bounds*).[11] This is especially evident in Heidegger's development of the idea of truth as *aletheia* or unconcealment, and no more so than in the way this idea is elaborated and explored in 'The Origin of the Work of Art', from 1935–6. This essay, originally a series of lectures, is cited by Gadamer as the key text in his own philosophical development (Gadamer 1997: 47). In it Heidegger presents the art work as a dynamic event that is focussed in the work itself, and through which the work establishes and opens up a world (see Malpas 2006: 196–200; 2012a: 244–6). Truth is the concealing/revealing that occurs in the setting-in-place of the work that is also the opening up of world, and in which the possibility of any specific presence or absence, assertion or denial, 'truth' or 'falsity' is itself grounded.

Although the happening of truth as developed in 'The Origin of the Work of Art' cannot be simply identified with the situatedness of understanding as that is thematised in Heidegger's earlier work, a very similar structure is at work in both cases. Truth and understanding stand in an essential relation to world, but they nevertheless arise only in and through a certain happening of place. In this respect, the concept of the *Ereignis* – the Event – that appears in Heidegger's thinking from the mid-1930s onwards (see e.g. Heidegger 2012) is the idea of just such a happening of place that is also a happening of world; a gathering and belonging together of world and thing, of world and self, of world and other. It is this happening of place that lies at the heart of what Heidegger himself refers to as the 'topology of being' and to which he tells us all of his thinking belongs (Heidegger 2004: 47).

Although such a topology can indeed be seen at work in Heidegger's early thought as well as his later (and in the early thought it is present as much in the lectures on the hermeneutics of facticity from 1923 as it is in *Being and Time* from 1927), it is in the later thought that it is at its most explicit. This is especially true of his discussions of technology and dwelling in essays such as 'Building Dwelling Thinking', 'The Thing' (Heidegger 1971b: 141–84) and 'The Question Concerning Technology' (Heidegger 1977: 3–35). The idea of the Fourfold that appears in those essays is explicitly topological in character, presenting the very coming to presence of things as a gathering in and through place that also is itself the opening up of space (see Malpas 2006: 219–304). Such a topology is also evident in almost all of Heidegger's later inquiries into language, especially those in *On the Way to Language* (Heidegger 1971a – see also Malpas 2006: 263–6). In the 'Dialogue on Language' from that volume (Heidegger 1971a: 1–56) Heidegger explicitly addresses the issue of the hermeneutical in the context of a discussion of language that refers back to language as the house of being while also hinting at a further set of topological themes and implications relating not only to language, but to the dialogue itself (see Malpas forthcoming).

The 'Dialogue on Language' is unusual in its explicit thematisation of the hermeneutical, and although it also contains elements of the topological orientation that is evident elsewhere in Heidegger's thought, there is no direct exploration or explication in the 'Dialogue' of the relation between the hermeneutical and topological as such. Indeed, Heidegger almost nowhere addresses that relation in explicit terms. Yet as hermeneutic ideas and themes proliferate in Heidegger's thinking, and especially in his late thinking, just as do topological ideas and themes, so the two seem to stand in an implicit relation. Indeed, if hermeneutics is itself understood as implying an attentiveness always to the situated character of thinking and understanding, and so an attentiveness to the *place* and *placedness* of thinking, then hermeneutics must already be essentially bound to topology, as perhaps topology must also be bound to the hermeneutical. If there is anything close to an explicit indication of this in Heidegger, it is in the essay on Trakl that also figures in *On the Way to Language*

(Heidegger 1971a: 159–98). Heidegger titles this essay 'a discussion', but the term used is *Erörterung* – which also carries the sense of 'a placing' or 'situating' (from *Ort* meaning 'place'). Heidegger makes the connection to place here quite explicit at the same time as he also invokes the idea of the bounded character of place as that which preserves and releases – that which enables a genuine coming to presence.[12] Here the hermeneutical task, even if it is not named as such, and which in this essay takes the form of engagement with a poetic text, is understood unequivocally as taking the form of a certain topology – a placing, a heeding, a *saying* of place.

4. Horizon, dialogue and objectivity: Gadamer, Davidson, Figal

Although there is an explicit focus on the hermeneutical situation, there is in Gadamer no explicit thematisation of the spatial or the topological such as one finds in Heidegger. This is not because such notions are absent from Gadamerian hermeneutics (the topology present in Heidegger often seems to carry directly over to Gadamer's thought – Gadamer's deployment of the Heideggerian notion of truth as *aletheia* being an important instance of this). Instead it is as if Gadamer simply sees no need to take them up in any direct way in relation to his own hermeneutical project – when these ideas do appear in any direct way it is more often in Gadamer's discussion of Heidegger than in the course of development of his own thinking.

A key concept for Gadamer is that of the interpretive horizon. The notion is one also present in Heidegger, and has its origin in Husserl's analysis of the structure of intentionality. Gadamer says of the notion that it is essential to the concept of situation (Gadamer 1989: 302). The notion of horizon is itself a topological concept: the horizon is that always indeterminate bound within which is established an open space or region that makes possible appearance. Understood in this way, horizonality is clearly at work, even when it is not named as such, at many different points in Gadamer's work – as well as in Heidegger's. Not only does the idea of the horizon already incorporate the central Gadamerian notion concerning the pre-judgemental character of understanding[13] – our prejudgements are what open us to the world and so enable understanding – but the idea of the horizon brings with it the notion of that 'within' which shelters and sustains understanding, that gives it ground as well as 'room'. Moreover, the Gadamerian emphasis on the idea of understanding as essentially dialogical or conversational – and so as an engagement that occurs always in language, in the space between speakers, and in relation to some subject matter – itself opens up the idea of understanding as always occurring in an open space 'between'.[14]

In Gadamer, the explicitly *dialogical* character of understanding – its being in 'conversation' (*Gespräch*) – and the way such dialogue itself brings with it a conception of the situated or placed character of understanding (a placement that is not only with respect to history and tradition), is suggestive of parallels with Donald Davidson's account of the 'triangulative' structure that is determinative of content. Like Gadamer, Davidson takes understanding, and interpretation, to depend on the interaction between speaker and interlocutor as that occurs in relation to some thing – in Davidson's case to some 'common cause' that is also a common focus of action and intention (see Davidson 2001; also Malpas 2011). In spite of other differences in their approaches, both Gadamer and Davidson thus seem to share a conception of understanding as, in broad terms, grounded in the situated interaction between speakers as this occurs in an essential relation to language (see Malpas 2002). Taken together with his explicit focus on the interpretive context of thought and action, Davidson's topological approach to understanding provides grounds for reading him as a hermeneutical thinker in spite of his primarily analytic orientation (see Malpas 1999a, 2011, and 2012a: 199–224) – and even in spite of the mutual misreading that characterises the one published engagement between Davidson and Gadamer in the *Library of Living Philosophers* volume devoted to Gadamer's work (see Davidson and Gadamer 1997; see also Malpas 2002, 2011).

Concepts of place and situation figure significantly throughout hermeneutical thinking, and yet only occasionally are they directly taken up. In this respect, the way in which such concepts often seem to be taken for granted in Gadamer's thought reflects a more widespread tendency that extends across almost the entire field of hermeneutics, in both its historical and contemporary manifestations. Hermeneutics has thus seldom addressed the situational, spatial and topological ideas which it so frequently deploys and on which it often depends. Moreover, although Heidegger does address these questions, he tends to do so in a way that, for the most part, proceeds independently of any explicit connection to the hermeneutical – the idea of a 'topological hermeneutics' is thus something that may perhaps be attributed to Heidegger, but which he does not himself formulate in those terms. In this regard, the work of Günter Figal might be taken to constitute a notable exception within recent and contemporary hermeneutics, since Figal is himself quite explicit in the role he gives to what might be thought of as topological and certainly spatial elements within his phenomenologically oriented 'objective hermeneutics' (see Figal 2010).

Figal's emphasis on objectivity is intended to correct what Figal sees as an oversight in much previous hermeneutic thinking, and has similarities to Ricoeur's insistence (intended as a corrective to Gadamer) on the importance of *distanciation* as the essential counterpart to appropriation and as underpinning any genuinely critical interpretive stance (see Ricoeur 2008: 72–85). Like Ricoeur, Figal sees distance or remoteness as playing an essential role in interpretation. It is distance or remoteness that makes possible the experience of something as requiring interpretive engagement, and this distance or remoteness Figal understands in terms of objectivity. In hermeneutical experience, he writes, 'one is concerned with something that one himself is not, with something that stands over against [*entgegensteht*], and, because of this, places a demand. Hermeneutical experience is the experience of the objective [*das Gegenständliche*]' (Figal 2010: 2). The experience at issue here – the experience of something that presents itself in a way that originates from itself – is an experience that also occurs within the openness of what Figal refers to as 'hermeneutical space' (see Figal 2010: 121–53) whose structure is given in terms of three dimensions which Figal identifies as freedom, language and time (Figal 2010: 155ff, esp. 299–300).

There can be no doubt that Figal's position is unusual in its explicit connecting of the spatial and the hermeneutical. At the same time, however, Figal's approach seems to involve disconnecting the hermeneutical from some of the key elements in the ideas of place and situation. The primary emphasis in Figal's account is on *openness* as against *constraint* – as against bound or limit (Figal 2010: 129). Yet one of the characteristic insights of hermeneutics is surely the very dependence of openness on constraint – it is constraint or boundedness, from a hermeneutical perspective, that makes openness possible. Figal's hermeneutical space appears more akin to an elaboration of the homogenous *res extensa* of Descartes than to the heterogenous and bounded spatiality associated with place or situation or with the hermeneutical 'between'. Perhaps this is itself an indication of the extent to which Figal's approach does indeed privilege the phenomenological, or a certain mode of the phenomenological (one that is more strongly Husserlian), over the hermeneutical, and so too, over the topological and situational.

5. Conclusion: hermeneutics as philosophical topology

It is commonplace to talk of a turn towards space and place as a characteristic feature of much contemporary theory in the Humanities and Social Sciences. Just what such a turn might mean beyond the deployment of spatial and topographic terms and images is not always clear – often the turn appears more rhetorical and figurative than genuinely conceptual. Yet a turn towards the situational and the topological, as well as the spatial – a turn that is indeed at the level of the conceptual – has certainly been a feature of much hermeneutical thinking even if it has been less commonly acknowledged (Figal being a notable, if ambiguous, exception). If hermeneutics is understood, as I have suggested here it ought to be, as centred on the issue of the essential grounding of understanding in situation or place, then this implies that hermeneutics can also be seen as a form of 'philosophical topology' – where such a topology is itself seen as essentially hermeneutical in character. To understand place, then, is also to place understanding, and vice versa. Conceiving of hermeneutics in this fashion has implications in terms of clarifying the nature of a hermeneutical approach to thinking as well as of the proper focus for the thinking in which hermeneutics is engaged (see Malpas 2000, 2012a: 199–224). It returns us to the character of hermeneutics as indeed belonging to the 'between', and to the 'between' as belonging to the hermeneutical. It is this same 'between' that is also the proper place of the human.

Notes

1 In contrast, see Heidegger's critique of the idea of 'freedom from standpoints' in Heidegger, 1999: 63–4.
2 Although it is worth noting that the term *topos* figures within many forms of traditional rhetorical and hermeneutical practice to designate the 'place' of a discussion or approach, often in terms of the subject or 'topic' to which that discussion or approach is directed and within which it moves, and sometimes, as in Aristotle's *Topics* and in his *Rhetoric*, to mean a general argumentative type or form.
3 I use 'topological' here to mean 'pertaining to place', but one could as easily use the term 'topographic' (as I have elsewhere – see Malpas, 1999a). Heidegger tends towards the former usage referring to his work as a 'topology of being'. Note that the topological and

the spatial stand in an important relation – place implies space (as space also, I would argue, implies place) – but they cannot be simply identified, and neither, as I argue above, can the topological be construed as independent of time. If space is often emphasised in discussions of the topological, this is largely because the spatial is so frequently taken as secondary to the temporal.

4 Of course, one might say that in doing so, *Being and Time* also assumes a topographic understanding of time which it never properly makes explicit or explores – which is why the question of spatiality remains one of the great unresolved (and within the terms of *Being and Time*, unresolvable) problems of Heidegger's *magnum opus*.

5 All too often what space and place are is something assumed rather than put in question, and all too often the assumption is that a *physicalist* reading of these terms must come first, and that it is in such a reading that their 'literal' sense is to be found. Such assumptions deserve to be contested.

6 'Talk of the house of being is not a transposition of the image "house" onto being. Rather, from out of the properly conceived essence of being we may someday come to recognize what house and dwelling are' (Heidegger 1998: 272).

7 George Lakoff and Mark Johnson have argued that spatial and bodily metaphors underpin the structure of all thinking – see for example Lakoff and Johnson 1999 – although their account is much more oriented towards empirical psychology and biology than the sort of ontological-hermeneutical approach that is at issue here.

8 Although there is a tendency to insist that the 'Da' of Dasein has nothing to do with anything spatial, or presumably topological, such a view seems to depend on refusing exactly the direction of thought in which Heidegger himself moves in the period after *Being and Time* (and which is already implicit in that work even if in tension with other aspects of it), while also missing the spatial and topographic dimension that remains even when the 'Da' is interpreted in supposedly non-spatial or non-topological fashion – although often the substitution of other terms merely reinscribes the spatial or topological in a different way (as seems to be the case with Sheehan's insistence that the 'Da' does not mean 'there', but is rather to be understood in terms of 'the open' – see Sheehan 2001: 193). Not only the argument of *Being and Time*, but Heidegger's own rethinking of that argument in the period after 1927 indicates that the spatial and topographical connotations of the 'Da' cannot be ignored. To insist on a translation of Dasein that ignores those connotations is to refuse the very clue as to the elucidation of the being at issue here that the 'Da' of 'Dasein' already presents (see Malpas 2006: 47–51).

9 Although there are serious problems that attach to Dreyfus' pragmatist reading of Heidegger, it is certainly correct in its emphasis on the active and 'externalised' character of Dasein's being.

10 Although part of the shift to the later thinking may be seen as precisely a matter of the gradual separation of these two terms even while they also remain related.

11 Boundedness or limitation thus has to be understood as itself *productive* rather than merely *restrictive*. This is something Heidegger emphasises on a number of occasions (see especially Heidegger 1971b: 154), and the idea is central to his thinking, as it is also central to the thought of Kant as well as of Gadamer. It is an idea at the heart of any form of philosophical topology or topography (see Malpas 2012b), and underlies the hermeneutical emphasis on the enabling rather than disabling character of finitude.

12 'We use the word "discuss" here [*Erörterung*] to mean, first, to point out the proper place or site of something, to situate it, and second to heed that place or site ... The site, the gathering power, gathers in and preserves all it has gathered, not like an encapsulating shell, but rather by penetrating with its light all it has gathered, and only thus releasing it into its own nature' (Heidegger 1971a: 159–60).

13 In fact, Gadamer says that prejudgements 'constitute' the horizon – see Gadamer 1989: 306.

14 The ideas of the 'between' (*das Zwischen*) and of the 'open' (*die Offene*) address aspects of the same topological structure that is invoked by the idea of the horizon, and both ideas figure in Heidegger as well as in Gadamer.

Bibliography

Ameriks, Karl (2006) *Kant and the Historical Turn: Philosophy as Critical Interpretation*, New York: Oxford University Press.

Aristotle (1983) *Aristotle's Physics Books III and IV*, trans. Edward Hussey, Oxford: Clarendon Press.

Benjamin, Andrew (2010) *Place, Commonality and Judgment*, London: Continuum.

Davidson, Donald (2001) 'Three Varieties of Knowledge', in *Subjective, Intersubjective, Objective*, Oxford: Clarendon Press, pp.205–20.

Davidson, Donald and Hans-Georg Gadamer (1997) 'Gadamer and Plato's *Philebus*', and 'Reply to Donald Davidson', in *The Philosophy of Hans-Georg Gadamer*, ed. Lewis Edwin Hahn, Chicago: Open Court, pp.421–36.

Dreyfus, Hubert L. (1991) *Being-in-the-world: A Commentary on Heidegger's Being and Time, Division I*, Cambridge, Mass.: The MIT Press.

Fell, Joseph P. (1979) *Heidegger and Sartre: An Essay on Being and Place*, New York: Columbia University Press.

Figal, G. (2010) *Objectivity: The Hermeneutical and Philosophy*, trans. T. D. George, Albany, NY: SUNY Press.

Gadamer, Hans-Georg (1989) *Truth and Method*, 2nd rev. edn., trans. Joel Weinsheimer and Donald G. Marshall, New York: Crossroads.

——(1997) 'Reflections on My Philosophical Journey', in *The Philosophy of Hans-Georg Gadamer*, ed. Lewis Edwin Hahn, Chicago: Open Court, pp.3–63.

Heidegger, Martin (1962) *Being and Time*, trans. John Macquarie and Edward Robinson, New York: Harper and Row.

——(1967) *What is a Thing?*, trans. W. B. Barton Jr. and Vera Deutsch, Chicago: Henry Regnery.

——(1971a) *On the Way to Language*, trans Peter D. Hertz, New York: Harper and Row.

——(1971b) *Poetry, Language, Thought*, trans. Albert Hofstadter, New York: Harper and Row.

——(1977) 'The Question Concerning Technology', in *The Question Concerning Technology and Other Essays*, trans. William Lovitt, New York: Garland Publishing, pp.3–35.

——(1998) 'Letter on Humanism', trans. Frank A. Capuzzi, in *Pathmarks*, ed. William McNeill, Cambridge: Cambridge University Press, pp.239–76.

——(1999) *Ontology – The Hermeneutics of Facticity*, trans. John van Buren, Bloomington: Indiana University Press.

——(2004) *Four Seminars*, trans. Andrew Mitchell and François Raffoul, Bloomington: Indiana University Press.

——(2012) *Contributions to Philosophy (of the Event)*, trans. Richard Rojcewicz and Daniela Vallega-Neu, Bloomington: Indiana University press.

Kant, Immanuel (1992) 'Concerning the Ultimate Ground of the Differentiation of Directions in Space', in *Theoretical Philosophy, 1755–1770*, trans. and ed. David Walford in collaboration with Ralf Meerbote, Cambridge: Cambridge University Press, pp. 364–72.

——(1996) 'What does it mean to orient oneself in thinking?', trans. Allen W. Wood, in *Religion and Rational Theology*, The Cambridge Edition of the Works of Immanuel Kant, Cambridge: Cambridge University Press, pp.1–18.

——(1998) *Critique of Pure Reason*, trans. and ed. Paul Guyer and Alan Wood, The Cambridge Edition of the Works of Immanuel Kant, Cambridge: Cambridge University Press.

——(2001) *Critique of the Power of Judgment*, trans. P. Guyer and E. Matthews, Cambridge: Cambridge University Press.

Lakoff, George and Mark Johnson (1999) *Philosophy in the Flesh: The Embodied Mind and Its Challenge to Western Thought*, Cambridge, Mass.: The MIT Press.

Makkreel, Rudolf A. (1994) *Imagination and Interpretation in Kant: The Hermeneutical Import of the Critique of Judgment*, Chicago: University of Chicago Press.

Malpas, Jeff (1992) *Donald Davidson and the Mirror of Meaning*, Cambridge: Cambridge University Press.

——(1997) 'The transcendental circle', *Australasian Journal of Philosophy*, 75 (1): 1–20.

——(1999a) *Place and Experience: A Philosophical Topography*, Cambridge: Cambridge University Press.

——(1999b) 'The Constitution of the Mind: Kant and Davidson on the Unity of Consciousness', *International Journal of Philosophical Studies*, 7: 1–30.

——(2000) 'The Beginning of Understanding: Event, Place, Truth', in *Consequences of Hermeneutics: Fifty years After* Truth and Method, ed. J. Malpas and S. Zabala, Evanston, Ill.: Northwestern University Press, pp.261–80.

——(2002) 'Gadamer, Davidson, and the Ground of Understanding' in *Gadamer's Century: Essays in Honor of Hans-Georg Gadamer*, ed. Jeff Malpas, Ulrich von Arnswald and Jens Kertscher, Cambridge, Mass.: The MIT Press, pp.195–215.

——(2006) *Heidegger's Topology: Being, Place, World*, Cambridge, Mass.: The MIT Press.

——(2011) 'What is Common to All: Davidson on Agreement and Understanding', in *Dialogues with Davidson: Acting, Interpreting, Understanding*, ed. J. Malpas, Cambridge, Mass.: The MIT Press, pp.259–80.

——(2012a) *Heidegger and the Thinking of Place: Explorations in the Topology of Being*, Cambridge, Mass.: The MIT Press.

——(2012b) 'Putting Space in Place: Relational Geography and Philosophical Topography', *Planning and Environment D: Space and Society*, 30: 226–42.

——(forthcoming) 'The Beckoning of Language', available at: http://jeffmalpas.com/wp-content/uploads/2013/03/The-Beckoning-of-Language-Heidegger%C3%95s-H-ermeneutic-Transformation-of-Thinking.pdf (accessed May 2014).

Malpas, Jeff and Günter Zöller (2012) 'Reading Kant Geographically: From Critical Philosophy to Empirical Geography', in *Contemporary Kantian Metaphysics: New Essays on Space and Time*, ed. Roxana Baiasu, Graham Bird and A. W. Moore, London: Palgrave Macmillan, pp.146–66.

Nagel, Thomas (1989) *The View From Nowhere*, New York: Oxford University Press.

Ricoeur, Paul (2008) 'The hermeneutic function of distanciation', in *From Text to Action. Essays in Hermeneutics Vol 2*, trans. Kathleen Blamey and J. B. Thompson, London: Continuum, pp.72–85.

Sheehan, Thomas (2001) 'A Paradigm Shift in Heidegger Research', *Continental Philosophy Review* 34: 182–202.

Vernant, Jean-Pierre (2006) *Myth and Thought among the Greeks*, trans. Janet Lloyd with Jeff Fort, Cambridge, Mass.: The MIT Press.

29

SYMBOL AND ALLEGORY

William Franke

Two traditional forms of figuration

"Symbol" and "allegory" are among the most frequently used of all literary-theoretical terms, even in contexts far removed from literature and theory – notably in religion and anthropology – and they stand for two of the most pervasive and fundamental operations of figurative representation as such. Yet it is notoriously difficult to employ the terms "symbol" and "allegory" in any technically adequate, or even intuitively satisfying, way without finding oneself quickly enmeshed in quandaries and contradictions. Each term has a tendency to absorb all phenomena of figuration indiscriminately, and they have often been used interchangeably, for example, by Baudelaire. Indeed, in pre-modern tradition, they were most often considered as roughly equivalent terms (Eco 1987: chapter 6.2).

Are the West Wind or the Skylark (Shelley), or Rimbaud's Drunken Boat (*Batteau ivre*), or Hölderlin's Bread and Wine (*Brot und Wein*), or Wallace Stevens's Man with the Blue Guitar symbols or allegories? Efforts to define poetic expressions or styles in terms of one of these two types of figure founder when the other also turns out to be just as apt for describing the instance of language in question. Some critics conclude as a consequence that it is pointless to use either label.

Nevertheless, however confusing the terms may be, they continue to lend themselves to attempts to theorize the nature of figurative language, and in crucial ways both together are necessary to keep in focus the constitutive tensions which give rise to meaning especially (but not only) in poetry. The very contradictions and complexities attending their use afford an index of the richness of these terms and of their vital resources geared to the struggle to conceptualize the enigma of poetic creativity and of linguistic meaning generally in terms of the figurality of language. The problem of interpreting how verbal meaning is generated by figuration will be treated here as a core issue in the philosophical hermeneutics of language.

Such a philosophical perspective counsels us to avoid the ineluctable critical practice of attempting to assign instances of figurative language in poetic creations to either one or the other category. We are well advised, rather, to analyze symbol and allegory as aspects of one and the same thing, namely, what I am calling "figuration": figuration involves a connection between a unit of language and the meaning or reality that it stands for, but also a disjunction between them. Both symbol and allegory can thus be conceived of as operative in every instance of figuration. For every act of figuration involves both συμβάλλεῖν (*symballein*) – literally a throwing together of things into unity – and also speaking of one thing via another, or ἄλλος ἀγορευεῖν (*allos agoreuein*), literally "other speaking." Symbol and allegory are construed, accordingly, as intersecting axes or as reciprocally coordinated dimensions that are complementary but also in tension with one another. Together they exert pressure on the process of creation from which figurative language springs.

Such a distinction between axes or directions within figuration corresponds to a certain articulation in the nature of signification itself. If all language is figural, as thinkers such as Nietzsche and Vico maintain (and indeed the expression "literal" itself uses the letter as a figure for a type of language), then this theory applies to linguistic signification generally. In signifying something, whether figuratively or literally, in saying what it is, I am also, inevitably, modeling what it is not: my *saying* it is *not* what it is. When I am saying what something is, the saying articulates itself, whether implicitly or explicitly, as distinct from the being that is said. Signification has to get outside of a certain being, and differentiate itself from that being, in order to signify it. As soon as I talk about beings or being, I am not *simply* being: what I am doing is both more and less than being. It is rather *about* being. And whether this difference is dissembled or exposed determines whether we are primarily in a symbolic or rather an allegorical mode. It is characteristic of allegory to expose and foreground this structural difference between saying and being, while the symbol strives to dissemble or transcend it.

The evident difference, then – which, however, links symbol and allegory together as reciprocally defined and mutually conditioned – may be described, for the sake of a first approximation, as follows: allegory places into evidence its status as figural, while symbolism effaces its figurality in striving for total assimilation into the reality which it figures. Allegory presents itself as something constructed and manifestly distinct – even distant – from the imaginary or real things that it signifies, whether they are particular or abstract. The symbol, in contrast, strives to achieve synthesis with being, to actually *be* what it represents. In other words, the symbol, rather than tending to open up the gap between the figure and its meaning or interpretation, attempts to close it and thereby to eliminate interpretation through the immediate presence of meaning or of the real itself. The symbol endeavors to overcome its status as merely symbolic or figurative in order to become an unmediated presence.

The schematic distinction adumbrated here tallies in important ways with the histories to which these terms respectively belong. Allegory in fact begins, or rather first becomes theoretically self-conscious *qua* allegory, as an interpretive technique. Neoplatonic and especially Stoic commentaries on Homer in Hellenistic times began employing a method called *allegoresis* in order to expose narrative action and adventure as the surface of submerged philosophical and theological meanings. Allegorical interpretation typically attempted to revive myths of former civilizations by giving them new meaning and relevance in a later age. The miraculous deeds of gods and heroes, which could no longer be believed, were understood allegorically as imaginatively illustrating rational truths that *were* still eminently believable.

Techniques of allegorical interpretation were developed just as intensively in the Judeo-Christian tradition. Patristic exegesis of the Bible, for example, by Origen and

Clement, following Philo in the Alexandrian tradition and consequently influenced also by Rabbinic interpretation, produced a highly evolved hermeneutic method based on allegory. Interpretation of the Bible was variously systematized at many stages, for example, by Origen and Augustine, and led to the canonical four-fold method of allegorical exegesis famously expounded by Thomas Aquinas and adopted eventually by Dante (Pépin 1987).

The origin of allegory in interpretive techniques of *allegoresis* is key to its character even as a compositional technique. There is some consensus among scholars for considering Prudentius's *Psychomachia* in the fourth or fifth century AD to be the first allegorical narrative (Teskey 1990: 27). Of course, there are allegorical passages and tropes in more ancient literature, for instance, the song of the vineyard in Isaiah 7 and the personification of Rumor in Homer. But even as a compositional technique, allegory lends itself to being understood as a folding of interpretation back into description and narrative. A figure is allegorical precisely because it suggests and solicits its own interpretation. A giant named *Orgoglio* (Italian for "Pride") with a tiara on his head is a figure already interpreting itself as standing for the overweening pride of the papacy. Northrop Frye considered allegory to be a sort of internal commentary of a text upon itself, whereby the author "tries to indicate how a commentary on him should proceed" (Frye 1957: 89–90). Frye's views on allegory as an implicit principle of interpretation exerted by a theme in its control of a narrative by imposing an overarching sense on it were developed by Angus Fletcher (1964) and John Whitman (1987, 2003) and had wide influence, for example, on Morton Bloomfield, who fully identified allegory with "the interpretive process itself" (1972: 302).

The essentially interpretive character of allegory becomes a structural principle in allegorical narratives featuring a narrator together with his guide – like Dante and Virgil in the *Divine Comedy*, or "Geoffrey" and his eagle in Chaucer's *House of Fame*. Again, the Book of Revelation – the crucial archetype for Christian allegorical poems – announces itself as a revelation of God, who "sent and signified it by his angel unto his servant John" (1: 1). Such an authoritative figure within the narrative objectifies the self-conscious, interpretive mediation which lies at the heart of allegory.

The originally interpretive status of allegory builds into it a structure of secondariness. The allegorical narrative typically advertises itself as secondary to a meaning outside and beyond the text itself. Gordon Teskey writes of a "convention of secondariness wherein it is assumed that the allegorical text exists only to reach toward something outside its reach" (1990: 45). All that can actually be represented within the text amounts only to so many dark conceits or "shadowy prefaces" ("umbriferi prefazii"), as Dante puts it in *Paradiso* XXX.78. Teskey emphasizes that since, with allegory, real meaning is in extra-literary reality somewhere outside the structure of the artwork, allegorical quests are in principle open-ended and without any intrinsic principle of closure. Every new image fosters new traces for redefining and recommencing the search for a meaning that is never given as such within the terms of the allegorical quest.

This interminability is reflected in the standard rhetorical definition of allegory by Quintilian as "extended metaphor." The structure of extension, the continuous dimension of allegory, issues in temporal stretch and deferral rather than in the attainment of final meaning. The text moves at a tangent to its own meaning projected as an absolute existence, which, strictly speaking, is inexpressible. In allegory, representation and reality never meet or coincide. Temporality introduces an allegorical structure that prevents our ever arriving within a narrative at a final disclosure in the presence of truth. For rather than furnishing the signified in which all signifiers converge into identity, the structure of temporality makes truth itself just one more signifier in the series.

Temporality of figurative representation and its collapse

Just these aspects of allegory have found vigorous new theoretical advocacy in Walter Benjamin and – following in his wake – with literary thinkers such as Paul De Man. It is particularly the temporal structure of allegory – its encoding of the unsurpassable historicity of human experience – that has been brought to the fore by this revalorization. Benjamin (1963 [1928]) read history and its catastrophes as preserved even in being covered over by the natural landscape of Baroque tragedy, the *Trauerspiel*. He developed a radically original linguistic epistemology in which time was materially embodied in signs (most arrestingly, perhaps, in ruins) that objectified truth in an eschatological but always incomplete perspective that could never be comprehended by any subject, for it exceeded intentionality.

In this key, De Man (1971a) re-read the early Romantics, particularly Wordsworth and Rousseau, as privileging not the immediate synthesis of the symbol in subjective consciousness but rather a temporally mediated mode of conventional imagery. This was a radical revision of the view of modern lyric tradition as dominated by the symbol, a view fostered by the New Critical framework that De Man's reflections (1971b) fundamentally challenged.

This challenge breathed new life into the notion of allegory, which had been given up by many as quaint and antiquated. The rupture between sign and meaning that is characteristic of allegory has come to be viewed, particularly in post-structuralist milieus, as the fundamental statute of all representation, and any eliding or attenuation of the difference between them counts then as mystification based on blindness to the inescapable temporality of the human condition. Whatever is somehow fixed in form like a linguistic sign can never coincide fully with reality, which is always changing.

The ideal of the symbol, on the other hand, is total presence. The symbolic artwork is supposed to render present the reality that it symbolizes. The poem "should not mean but be," wrote Archibald MacLeish in "Ars Poetica," expressing a cardinal principle of the typically symbol-based poetics of modernist tradition. Of course, in a temporal world, presence is always fleeting and, in fact, is always already lost.

Often the symbol is taken to be inexhaustible and never-ending in its meanings. Yet these meanings are all in theory simultaneous. The interpretive time-span of writing and developing an insight or illumination, like the interpretive activity of reading and understanding it, does not belong properly to the symbol itself. In this perspective, the poem begins after its essential meaning has already taken place: the text is but the trace of what takes place or *is* before the temporality of interpretation begins. The symbolic poem aptly figures itself therefore as the foam left after a ship has vanished beneath the sea, as in Mallarmé's troping of the traditional topos of the "bark of genius" venturing upon perilous seas – borrowed from Dante (*Purgatorio* 1.2) and diffused by Petrarch into Renaissance tradition, where it is taken up by Sir Thomas Wyatt, et al. This paradigmatically modern symbolic imagination reverses a long tradition of allegorical poetry.

Dante, at the beginning of the *Paradiso* and at the last stage of his gnoseological quest, in which medieval allegorical tradition culminates, warns readers to turn back from dangerous seas exceeding their navigational capability – "O voi che siete in piccioletta barca, / Desiderosi d'ascoltar, sequiti / Tornate a riveder li vostri liti" ("O you who in a little boat, desirous to listen, have followed, return again to view your shores," *Paradiso* II.13–15) – lest they be lost ("smarriti" I.6), just as Dante himself was lost before being rescued by Virgil at the outset of the *Inferno* (I.3).

The symbolist poem, on the other hand, without warning, plunges headlong into shipwreck. Thus is its whole intent and purpose achieved. For shipwreck symbolizes a shattering of the confines of representation for the sake of full immersion in the sea of being. The "bark" of representation must be shattered. Such is the condition for the attainment of ultimate meaning in the symbolist conception. By rupturing the membrane between the sea and the self, the finite self is transcended – even at the price of self-destruction – and merges with the infinite sea. Whereas allegory floats on the sea of meaning and glides over a representational surface without ever plunging in, the symbol revels in collapsing representation and reality together. It brings about an apotheosis of the real in excess of all representation. Allegory respects the barrier between representation and reality, but symbolism shatters or suspends it.

Once the theoretical logic and motivation for the symbol have been brought into focus, we discover that images of shipwreck as figuring the bursting of the membrane between representation and reality turn up ubiquitously in Romantic and Symbolist poetry. Shelley's "Adonais," for example, ends with the conventional bark of the poet's genius propelled by overpowering storms of inspiration to the point of breaking in a cosmic cataclysm:

> The breath whose might I have invoked in song
> Descends on me; my spirit's bark is driven,
> Far from the shore, far from the trembling throng
> Whose sails were never to the tempest given;
> The massy earth and spherèd skies are riven!
> I am borne darkly, fearfully, afar;
> Whilst, burning through the inmost veil of Heaven,
> The soul of Adonais, like a star,
> Beacons from the abode where the Eternals are.

The immortality of Adonais attained by death and disaster uncannily prefigures Shelley's approaching fate in the Bay of Spezia, making this poem an especially poignant example of literature's exceeding its representational bounds to become real life or, in this case, real death. The poem turns out to be "symbolic" not only in its representational mode, but also as an autobio-thanato-graphical testament: it is a fulfilled prophecy in which representation and reality come to coincide.

Even more explicitly, Giacomo Leopardi's manifesto poem "L'infinito" imagines, with consummate simplicity, the merging of the poetic subject (the "io") with Infinity through the power of the symbol as, precisely, shipwreck: "and shipwreck is sweet to me in this sea" ("e il naufragar m'è dolce in questo mare"). This is the premise of the Romantic aesthetic that was to be radicalized into *Symbolisme*. The essence of art, and especially of poetry, as symbolic was taken to be the passage beyond the order of representation to a higher reality. In anthropological terms, the operative principle is the "efficaciousness of the symbol" (Lévi-Strauss 1949).

For the Symbolist poet, shipwreck symbolizes the attainment of ultimate meaning, for it is by a breakdown of all artifice, of figurality itself, transcending it into unity and being, that the symbol supposedly attains its goal. In allegorical literature, shipwreck sometimes threatens; however, averting it for the continuation of the voyage is imperative. Hence Dante's warning to those many who are not up to the arduous allegorical task he lays before them. And hence the labyrinthine elaboration and uncontainable expansion typical of allegorical narratives, paradigmatically of the medieval *Roman de la rose*.

Symbolist poetry, in contrast, eventually identifies itself wholly with the event of shipwreck. Rimbaud's Drunken Boat plunges him into the Poem of the Sea ("je me suis baigné dans le Poème / De la Mer"). Shipwreck subtends Mallarmé's *oeuvre* (to take the most eminent example) from beginning to end. The very first of his *Poésies*, "Salut," begins with the figure of a trace of foam equated with the poem itself: "Rien, cette écume, vierge vers … " ("Nothing, this foam, virgin verse … "). The maritime voyage the speaker proposes to take his readers on is situated in the wake of an event of shipwreck at the origin of symbolist meaning. The figure of sirens drowning "in reverse" ("Telle loin se noie une troupe / De sirènes à l'envers") suggests how poetry, as lyric or song, exists and can be temporally distended only by projection backwards to a moment before representation and therewith before the act of self-annihilation in which the poem consists. The verse is "virgin" only so long as it remains unmixed with representation, for representation adulterates it. As such, it is "nothing." The self-erasure of representation in the poem alludes to a hypothetical event of original rupture or catastrophe that sinks away from the grasp of consciousness.

Similar imagery at the other end of Mallarmé's collected poems, in "À la nue accablante tu," likewise constructs the poem as a trace of a shipwreck from beyond the threshold of representation. It refers hauntingly to a "sepulchral shipwreck" ("sépulcral naufrage") announced by "slave echoes" ("les échos esclaves") through a "trumpet without virtue" ("trompe sans vertu") and known only by the foam ("écume") that drivels ("baves") from the wreckage ("les épaves"). The event registers at all only in such traces, as again in the trailing white hair of a drowned siren youth (the virginity motif, once again), with which this untranslatable poem of traces ends. Only the "foam" matters in the wreckage ("suprême une entre les épaves"), not the mast or the vanished nymph. Just as there is no subject, there is no original sin, "furious fault" or "high perdition," but only the "vain" or empty "abyss" ("l'abîme vain") deployed in the wake of the drowning that "avariciously" ("avarement") leaves nothing else behind but this trace of emptiness – the poem.

Mallarmé's "Brise marine" tosses up on shore the same motifs in a register of longing for the freedom of the sea, for escape ("Fuir! là-bas fuir!"). It is driven by a desire to be mad like the birds ("des oiseaux sont ivres"), to be among the unknown foam and the heavens ("l'écume inconnue et les cieux!"). Romantic winds blow towards the fulfillment of shipwrecks ("naufrages") by storms ("orages") with unfurled lyric enchantment. The crest of this wave breaks in Mallarmé's *Un coup de dès* (*A Throw of the Dice*). Here hints of a shipwreck, which, however, cannot, in principle, crystallize explicitly as a theme, govern the imagery alike of sea and of stellar constellations, a cosmic explosion. Reference to "the original foamings" ("les écumes originelles"), turning foam into an origin rather than an effect, suggest how the origin of the poem is precisely the trace of an event that cannot properly be figured, since it transcends the representational order. Nevertheless, the suggestion of shipwreck serves to adumbrate the poem's destroying its own representational status so as to mingle with absolute being and nothingness.

The shipwreck motif, which is here proposed as a master figure of symbolism, is only a particularly dramatic instance of the fusion of representation and reality in the symbolist poem. Of course, poets exploring the resources of the symbol have used a great range of imagery, but the idea of language as achieving the status of a thing has been one of their characteristic obsessions. Such a word–thing identity images the break-down of the barrier between representation and reality. The submerged ideal is that of a return to the pre-lapsarian language of Eden, where words and things were not yet divided and disparate. The attempt of poetic language to achieve the status of a natural object is expressed, for example, in Hölderlin's "Brot und Wein" in the line "Now, now words for it must come into being like flowers" ("Nun, nun müssen dafür Worte wie Blümen entstehen," § 5).

The poet as Orphic interpreter of the language of being, to which animals and all nature spontaneously respond, is another governing paradigm throughout the vast current of culture funneled through the cult of the symbol. Representation exercises a kind of magical power over even brute reality – as when Amphion moves the stones by his music so as to raise the walls of Thebes. Symbolic are also the "correspondences" between various senses and sensations confused in the "profound unity" of the forest of symbols in Baudelaire's "Correspondances."

Favorite techniques of symbolist poetry include foregrounding the sound of words or even their iconic form as themselves meaningful. Independently of conventional meaning assigned semantically to words, these forms per se, taken for their sensuous qualities, are made to signify. The sub-semantic values of words, those inhering in the materiality of the signifier, become per se significant. So Roland Barthes (1953) generalizes on the attempt of "contemporary poetry" to turn form into sense. And Roman Jakobson (1960) defines the "poetic function" by its tendency to "render sense sensuous." The barriers between language and reality in these ways are broken down.

At the same time, it must be stressed that neither form of figurative language can finally articulate the real. In the symbol, ultimately the means of representation are destroyed, so that, just as in allegory, ultimate truth remains inexpressible. Allegory goes on expressing just this, the ineffability of its object, whereas symbol actually enacts the silencing of the poem and the suspension of language. While the allegorical poem tends to go on and on, the symbolic poem tends to brevity, as in Giuseppe Ungaretti's "Mattina" –

M'illumino
d'immenso
(I am illuminated
by immensity)

– and even, at the extreme, to total vanishing. Hence Günter Eich's: "Every poem is too long!" ("Jedes Gedicht ist zu lang!") and Eugene Gomringer's concrete poem consisting in nothing but the word "silence" ("Schweigen") repeated in stanzaic form around a void at the center of the page. Reality is revealed by such literature only as its own negation.

While allegory posits that the real and final meaning transcends its literary mediation, nevertheless the quest to attain final meaning in which the real would coincide with its literary expression, sustains the narrative's progress. The symbol, in contrast, endeavors through poetic language to attain reality in an experience that annihilates language. Yet, without language and its articulations, the real is nothing that can be grasped. Thus poetry and all its symbols for Mallarmé turn inevitably into allegories. He wrote to Villiers de l'Isle Adam on September 24, 1866 that he had discovered his life's work as a poet was to be a personal work called "Sumptuous Allegories of Nothingness" ("somptueuses allégories du néant"). Poetry in both traditions plays a role, according to its deep structure, as a kind of negative theology pointing to what words cannot express.

Within the broad compass of figurative expression, the energy of the symbol is self-transcending – aimed at spilling into the universe of being and so becoming infinite. The energy of allegory, in contrast, seeks to preserve itself from the flux and to signify what remains forever radically other to itself. In different ways, then, both are aimed at what exceeds interpretation and linguistic expression altogether.

Hermeneutic compenetration of symbol and allegory

We have been able to differentiate symbol and allegory in terms of a polarity at work in literary figuration in general between identification with the real versus distanciation from it. Both elements are necessary to any instance of figuration, since figuration attempts concretely to convey and embody the object that is being figured, even while figuring it is not the same as simply being it but implies rather the mediation of artifice. The fascination of figuration lies in the enigma that the artifice of language somehow catalyzes an event of meaning that is not just artifice but actual creation of an original, new reality.

With Goethe, the term "symbol" became dominant: he declared that the true nature of poetry is symbol (1940: 325–6). Literature was beginning in his age to strive to supplant reality by the free creations of the imagination. The poet claimed to be the demiurgic creator of a new world. The idealistic philosophies of Kant, Fichte, Schelling, and Hegel variously construed the mind and its representations as constitutive of phenomenal reality. Consciousness was conceived as the creative source of reality, and this is what is supposed to become transparent in the symbol.

Coleridge adopted this perspective of German idealist philosophy and adapted it to English Romantic literary theory centered on the doctrine of the symbol. The symbolic conception of figurative language as conferring unity and transparency on experience was to reach a certain culmination in the "verbal icon" theorized by the New Critics.

However, "symbolic" can also bear a diametrically opposite meaning, assigning language merely conventional sense rather than creative, constitutive efficacy. Philosophers like Ernst Cassirer and linguists such as Julia Kristeva, building on the psycholinguistics of Lacan, employ the term "symbolic" in a technical sense as simply a substitution of one thing for another in a signifying relation. All signs thus become categorically "symbolic." In aesthetics, contrary to this usage, the symbol typically is distinguished by its signifying not through absence but rather through making its object present. The symbolic is not the generic category of all species of signs but rather that exceptional sort of sign which *participates* in the thing that it signifies.

Working between linguistics and poetics, Paul Ricoeur offers a construction of the symbolic that agrees with our ordinary usage of the word to say that works of imagination, religious practices, and dreams have "symbolic" significance. For Ricoeur, the symbolic consists of saying one thing while meaning another (just like allegory!). Ricoeur is careful to point out that this is not the same as the relation between a sign and its referent, since the sign is intended to mean nothing besides its referent. The symbol, by contrast, has another meaning that is activated by its immediate meaning: in other words, it has further meaning(s) in addition to the signifier–signified relation that constitutes it as sign. It is a sign for a sign, or a "double-meaning structure" (Ricoeur 1965, 1969).

Ricoeur's hermeneutic analysis of the symbol makes it a kind of allegory in that it signifies one thing by virtue of signifying something completely different, something that presents itself as alleatory and provisional, as being for the sake of the other, hence "other speaking." Both the emphasis on structurality and the originary duality, which cannot be effaced, are quintessentially allegorical features. At the same time, Ricoeur also stresses that the symbol opens and discovers a domain of experience which would otherwise remain inaccessible (1960). To this degree, language is recognized as constitutive of reality – of phenomena that can be experienced. Language is key to truth as disclosure of the real in a hermeneutic perspective. A real world of reference can be opened by semiotic events, as Ricoeur (1975) stresses also in his theory of metaphor.

This world-disclosing power of the symbol leads onto a terrain illuminated by theories of religious language such as Paul Tillich's. Symbols are distinguished from signs in that they participate in the reality and power of that which they designate. The symbol, indeed, has a different, more far-reaching function than the normally referential or representative function of the sign. It opens a level or dimension of reality that otherwise would remain inaccessible to us. In order that this realm of being be opened, it is necessary for an internal transformation to take place as well – for a new level of existence to be opened to the soul. A symbol is therefore unique and cannot be replaced with another equivalent, as is always possible with signs. Symbols have an uncontrollable life of their own. They are born and die. They die in the moment that their relation to the inner life of the community for which they are symbols ceases. The level of reality opened uniquely with the aid of the symbol is a depth dimension ("Tiefdimension"), the ground of Being itself, the final ground or power of being, the holy ("letzten Seinsgrund ... Heiligen," Tillich 1983: 86).

While religious symbols participate in the holy, they are not identical with it. The holy which they mediate nevertheless transcends them: "Religious symbols indicate something which transcends them all" ("Die religiösen Symbole weisen auf das hin, was sie alle transzendiert," 1983: 87). To this degree, Tillich's understanding of the symbol points it in the direction of a disjunctive, unattainable, allegorical meaning. Truth in a religious sense thus requires building an allegorical dimension into the symbol itself.

Throwing things together into unity and speaking otherwise (or speaking about one thing *by means of* another), constitute two basic directions in which the process of figuration works, respectively "symbol" and "allegory." Between these poles of identity and difference, the forms of representation and expression that we call literature can be intelligibly mapped, and the process of figuration per se can be described as a function of these two modes. However, the two poles are constantly in the act of collapsing together – or on the brink of flipping over each into its opposite. The attempts to separate symbol and allegory in operation rather than only in theory invariably lead to paradox. Our purpose has been rather to appreciate how fundamentally these two aspects of figuration condition each other mutually in their respective, antithetical approaches to signifying the real and revealing its truth. As such, they form complementary aspects of the enigma of figurative signification.

This topic turns out to be highly revealing of the current situation of philosophical hermeneutics inasmuch as it brings out, in the forms of allegory and symbol, the reciprocal dependence of interpretation and its Other, of mediation and incommensurability. The evolution of philosophical hermeneutics in recent years has rendered patent the crucial importance of the *beyond* of interpretation (Vattimo) – what hermeneuts like Blanchot and Derrida and, in another way, Benjamin call the "immediate." Just this dialectic between interpretation and its Other has been at work all through tradition, particularly in the interplay between the poles of allegory and symbol that operate eminently in the figurative language of poetry.

Bibliography

Note: All translations from foreign languages are my own and not those of the published translations referenced below for the convenience of readers.

Barthes, R (1953) *Le Degrée zéro de l'écriture*, Paris: Seuil. Trans. Annette Lavers and Jonathan Smith (1967) *Writing Degree Zero*. New York: Jonathan Cape Ltd.

Benjamin, W (1963 [1928]) *Ursprung des deutschen Trauerspiels*, Frankfurt: Suhrkamp. Trans. J. Osborne (1998) *The Origin of German Tragic Drama*, London: Verso.

Bloomfield, M (1972) "Allegory as Interpretation," *New Literary History* 3: 301–17.

Bruns, G (1992) *Hermeneutics: Ancient and Modern*, New Haven: Yale University Press.

Dante (1966–7) "Paradiso," *La Divina Commedia secondo l'antica vulgata*, ed. G. Petrocchi, 4 vols., Milan: Mondadori. Trans. C. Singleton (1991) *Paradiso*, Princeton: Princeton University Press.

De Man, P (1971a [1969]) "The Rhetoric of Temporality," in *Blindness and Insight: Essays in the Rhetoric of Contemporary Criticism*, New York: Oxford University Press.

——(1971b [1969]) "Lyric and Modernity," in *Blindness and Insight: Essays in the Rhetoric of Contemporary Criticism*, New York: Oxford University Press.

Eco, U (1987) *Arte e bellezza nella estetica medievale*, Milan: Bompiani. Trans. H. Bredin (1986) *Art and Beauty in the Middle Ages*, New Haven: Yale University Press.

Fletcher, A (1964) *Allegory: The Theory of a Symbolic Mode*, Ithaca: Cornell University Press.

Frye, N (1957) *Anatomy of Criticism: Four Essays*, Princeton: Princeton University Press.

Goethe, W (1940) *Sämtliche Werke, Jubiläumsausgabe*, ed. Eduard von der Hellen, Stuttgart: Cotta, vol. 35.

Gomringer, E (1972) *Konkrete poesie*, Stuttgart: Reclam.

Holy Bible (1611) Authorized King James Version, New York: American Bible Association.

Jakobson, R (1960) "Linguistics and Poetics: Closing Statement," in *Style in Language*, ed. T Sebeok. Cambridge: MIT Press.

Lévi-Strauss, C (1949) "L'efficacité symbolique," *Revue de l'histoire des religions* 135/1: 5–27. Trans. C Jacobson and B Grundfest Shoepf (1963) "The Effectiveness of Symbols," *Structural Anthropology*, vol. 1, New York: Basic, 186–205.

Mallarmé, S (1945) *Oeuvres complètes*, ed. G. Jean-Aubrey, Paris: Pleiade.

Pépin, J (1987) *La tradition de l'allégorie. De Philon d'Alexandrie à Dante*, Paris: Études Augustiniennes.

Ricoeur, P (1960) *La symbolique du mal*, Paris: Aubier. Trans. E. Buchanan (1967) *The Symbolism of Evil*, New York: Harper and Row.

——(1965) *De l'interprétation: Essai sur Freud*, Paris: Seuil. Trans. D. Savage (1970) *Freud and Philosophy: An Essay on Interpretation*, New Haven: Yale University Press.

——(1969) *Le conflit des interprétations: Essai sur l'herméneutique*, Paris: Seuil. Trans. W. Domingo et al. (1974) *The Conflict of Interpretations: Essays in Hermeneutics*, ed. Don Ihde, Evanston: Northwestern University Press.

——(1975) *La métaphore vive*, Paris: Seuil Trans. R. Czerny, et al. (1978) *The Rule of Metaphor: Multi-Disciplinary Studies in the Creation of Meaning in Language*, Toronto: University of Toronto Press.

Teskey, G (1990) *The Spenser Encyclopedia*, ed. A.C. Hamilton et al., Toronto: University of Toronto Press.

Tillich, P (1983) "Das Wesen der religiösen Sprache," ed. M. Kaempfert, *Probleme der religiösen Sprache*, Darmstadt: Wissenschatliche Buchgesellschaft: 82–93. Trans. and ed. F. Church (1987) "The Nature of Religious Language," *The Essential Tillich*, Chicago: University of Chicago Press: 44–56.

Vattimo, G (1994) *Oltre l'interpretazione*, Rome-Bari: Laterza. Trans. D Webb (1997) *Beyond Interpretation: The Meaning of Hermeneutics for Philosophy*, Stanford: Stanford University Press.

Whitman, J (1987) *Allegory: The Dynamics of an Ancient and Medieval Technique*, Cambridge: Harvard University Press.

——(2003) *Interpretation and Allegory: Antiquity to the Modern Age*. Leiden: Brill.

30
LIFE AND WORLD

Eric S. Nelson

1. Introduction

This chapter offers a systematically oriented and historically informed examination of the notions of "life," "world," and "worldview" as they are articulated in classical hermeneutical thinking, particularly in relation to its intellectual context in the works of Wilhelm Dilthey, Edmund Husserl, and Martin Heidegger. I focus on the contrast and tensions between life explained as a naturalistic physical and biological phenomenon, life as felt and intuited directly through the self, and life understood as an interpretive social-historical enactment; and between world as factically, empirically, and immediately given and world as constituted and generated through relational contexts of sense and meaning that call for indirect processes of explication and communication to be appropriately enacted and understood.

In addition to examining life and world in their own senses, I consider the interactions between life and world in hermeneutical and phenomenological conceptions of lived-experience (*Erlebnis*), worldview (*Weltanschauung*), lifeworld (*Lebenswelt*), world as horizon (*Welthorizont*), and truth as world-givenness, world-formation, and world-disclosure. These interpretive conceptions are central from earlier hermeneutical thought to the contemporary situation and task of hermeneutics in the early twenty-first century. Such conceptions and the experiences they address help illuminate epistemic and ontological questions of the subjectivity, shared intersubjectivity, and objectivity of life and world that serve as orienting questions for this survey.

2. Life as natural, socially mediated, and subjective

The ordinary German words for life (*Leben*) and world (*Welt*), much like their English equivalents, have taken on an equivocal range of meanings that are not altogether compatible. This dissonance of sense is evident in their intellectual uses and interpretations of life and world.

In the case of world, for instance, discussants accentuate either the naturalness of the world, which Husserl described as the "naïve" acceptance of the world as given in the "natural concept of the world" (*natürlicher Weltbegriff*), or the constituted and mediated formation and sedimentation of meanings into a world, which the later Husserl called "lifeworld" (*Lebenswelt*).[1] World can be identified with the worlds of natural, social, and subjective life, as in the early Heidegger's distinction between self-(*selbst-*), with-(*mit-*), and environing-(*um-*) worlds.

Life likewise can refer to the factuality of an objectively explainable natural bio-logical process (e.g. "the life of amoeba") or to a symbolically and socially mediated form or way of life of a biographical individual (e.g. "the life of Goethe") or group of humans (e.g. "the life of the German working class"). There is a third more sub-jective personal sense of life, disseminated in individualistic forms of nineteenth-century Romanticism, life-philosophy, and existentialism, in which my or another's life appears to be so singular and unique that a life transcends the general conditions and features of natural and social life such as – perhaps most radically – in Søren Kierkegaard's indirect communications concerning a "non-numerical" and irre-ducibly singular individual in its interiority.[2]

In the writings of the nineteenth-century hermeneutical philosopher Dilthey, who plays a crucial role in the history of the concepts of life and world in hermeneutics and phenomenology, one finds side by side multiple senses of life in discussions of organic and bodily life, cultural, historical, and national life, and a personal life too complex to be reduced to its physical and social conditions. The dictum of Dilthey's incomplete multivolume biography of Friedrich Schleiermacher running into thou-sands of pages is accordingly "the individual is ineffable."[3] Dilthey's inexpressible individual diverges, however, from a transcendent incomprehensibility or irrational singularity: "each life has its own sense."[4] Immanent ineffability points toward the complex and infinite task of tracing and interpreting the mediations of natural and social life in an individual life: "The infinite richness of life unfolds itself in indivi-dual existence because of its relations to its milieu, other humans and things. But every particular individual is also a crossing point of contexts which move through and beyond its particular life."[5]

"Life" is thoroughly relational and holistic in Schleiermacher and Dilthey. Dilthey rejected a model of holism that relied on the image of a self-identical biological organism due to his methodologically prioritizing individual persons. His structural relationality concerning the external organization of society did not presuppose the real existence of collective entities. Life is hermeneutical according to Dilthey: the practical effective nexus of life (*Lebenszusammenhang*) in its facticity is concurrently the point of departure, the medium, and the purpose of intersubjectively oriented understanding (*Verstehen*) and interpretation (*Interpretation* or *Auslegung*). Dilthey recommends interpreting the "lived-experience" (*Erlebnis*) and pre-theoretical reflexively felt and aware "feeling of life" (*Lebensgefühl*) of individuals through their expression (*Ausdruck*) and their products and artifacts. The modes of human life are explicated out of their own worldly comport-ments and from their "being-there-within life" (*Darinnensein im Leben*).[6]

Traditional hermeneutics focused on the clarification of the historical, linguistic, and psychological conditions of Biblical and classical sources. Understanding and interpretation are gradually more associated – to a lesser extent in Schleiermacher, and more overtly in Dilthey – with the autobiographical participant perspective of personally inflected lived-experience.[7] The first-person life-perspective informs and orients social-historical and epistemic reflectiveness (*Besinnung*) and those sciences that cannot bracket the triple hermeneutic of inquiry into the "human world." The human sciences (*Geisteswissenschaften*) remain empirically oriented, methodologically generated, and systematically structured even as they presuppose, utilize, and interpret a concrete nexus of life.

Informed by multiple senses of "life," modern central European intellectual traditions have explained life as a naturalistic physical and biological phenomenon, perceived life as vitally felt and directly intuitable in the living present, posited life as a historical realm to be transformed through praxis or as a higher realm of meaning, value, and validity, and understood life as an already interpretive social-historical reality. Dilthey approached life as an acquired relational nexus of signification reflexively felt and practically interpreted with reference to the first person autobiographical perspective. Dilthey's non-theistic personalism is evocative for the non-naturalistic discourses of life and lifeworld unfolded in subsequent hermeneutics, phenomenology, and critical social theory.

The language of life-philosophy was also significant for the logical positivism of the Vienna Circle when it described its wider concerns. Rudolf Carnap was concerned in the 1920s with defending a scientific lifestance (*Lebenshaltung*) and life-conception (*Lebensauffassung*) in the midst of the menacing growth of irrationality and totalitarianism.[8] In the life-philosophical conclusion to the program of the Ernst Mach Society (*Verein Ernst Mach*), jointly published in 1929 by Carnap, Hahn, and Neurath, and dedicated to Schlick in honor of his remaining in Vienna, science and life as well as knowledge and affectively rooted worldview are affirmed to be complementary forces in a scientific-oriented life-conception. The love of science is rooted in an emotional disposition toward knowing the world and furthering practical life: the scientific lifestance is dedicated to serving life and in response is taken up by life.[9]

3. World as given and as constituted

The German word for world (*Welt*) likewise has an ambiguous range of meanings. The world can signify this particular world or the singular-plural world as such; it can be the world in its facticity, givenness, and thereness or the world as it is "given to me" or "there for me" to use Dilthey's expressions. The world is not just any world; it is a "constituted" world in Husserl's phenomenology and "disclosed" in Heidegger's thinking of truth.

World-constitution need not entail the strong idealistic thesis that the world is mentally dependent or originated. Husserl's argument concerns instead the active and passive intentionality of a conscious and bodily subject and its constitution of meaning.

World is in a fundamental sense "my" experiential world within an intended universal world-horizon (Husserl's *Welthorizont*) or it is in each case "my own" (*jemeinig*) world disclosed through my way of "being-in-the-world" (Heidegger).[10] Husserl maintained that "my world is the opening in which all experience occurs."[11] The "I am" is the "primordial intentional foundation of my world" ("der intentionale Urgrund für meine Welt"); there is nothing that appears outside of the horizon of "my world" or the first person perspective of the "I am."[12] World is generated, constituted, and sedimented through relational contexts of sense and meaning that presuppose an "I." This is the transcendental dimension of the "I" or subjectivity of the first-person perspective that bodily and mentally orients and forms the world.

The word "*Lebenswelt*" has a long history prior to Husserl, who did not systematically use the expression until the late work *Crisis of the European Sciences* published in 1936.[13] Like the word *Umwelt* (environing world), earlier usage of the expression "lifeworld" referred to the environment. Both phrases referred to either a natural setting or a historical cultural milieu in the context of nineteenth-century German thought. But there is continuity between the two senses as both were interpreted as relational and interactive. The organism reacts to and acts on its environing lifeworld. It is the co-relational sense of the constitution and disclosure of the world to the intentional subject and being-there that Husserl and Heidegger in the 1920s are drawing upon. The fluctuation in the experience and concept of world is evident in the variations on "world" in hermeneutics and phenomenology such as in Dilthey's life-nexus, Husserl's lifeworld (*Lebenswelt*), and Heidegger's environing world (*Umwelt*).[14]

4. Life as world picturing

In the following sections, I will explore the problematic of world in the context of Dilthey's philosophy of worldviews.

"Worldview" (*Weltanschauung*) is a concept with roots in German Idealism. It functions in Fichte and Schelling as an organizing depiction of life.[15] A worldview is the formation of life through the perception or picturing (*anschauen*) of a world. The idealistic account of worldview is rejected by Dilthey in support of a hermeneutical one. A historically situated and self-reflexive life interpretively pictures and forms a world for itself and expresses and communicates this world in myriad ways throughout its life. This picturing of world (*Weltbild*) does not transpire through the self-intuition or self-assertion of a self or subject. Its world is formed in the self's interactive cogivenness with the exteriority of things and others revealed in phenomena such as resistance and misunderstanding. As others make the self-interpretation and individuation of my life possible through processes of learning and socialization, one's world is primarily a "human world" for Dilthey, understood through historically constituted "life-views" (*Lebensanschauungen*) that often attempt to transcend merely human perspectives.

A plurality of life- and world-perspectives emerge as humans are constituted in social-historical worlds shaped by natural forces, biological drives, practical interests, sedimented customs and traditions, the reproduction of powerful structures and institutions, normative-spiritual strivings, and communicative and self-reflection. Given their varied sources, the sciences of the human world need to be multifaceted. Unlike the natural sciences that abstract from and bracket their basis in human life, the human sciences cannot escape from their own reflexivity and the need to self-reflectively engage the human world in which they transpire, as knowledge of the human world occurs within that world.[16]

As worldly embodied life is molded by sentiments and habits, exteriority and facticity, self-understanding and interpretation cannot be purely conceptual processes.[17] They involve all dimensions and "faculties" – cognitive and affective – of human existence. The human sciences can modify but not abolish the passions and interests of human life that enter into the study of that life. The internally given world of the self to itself indicates the initial givenness from the first-person perspective of co-agents or participants of meaningful social-cultural structures and processes. The "inner world" refers to the first-person life-context, which is intrinsically bodily, perceptual, and worldly as well as social-historical, in which objects are pre-conceptually and conceptually understood. The "internal" human world is constituted through social-historically formed practical goods, interests, norms, purposes, and values.[18]

The "outer" or "external world" refers to the abstraction of objects from their life-nexus in the third-person perspective of observation and explanation characteristic of the modern natural sciences and associated with worldviews such as naturalism and materialism.[19] Such worldviews remain metaphysical in affirming one conclusive picture and truth about the world. Dilthey construes metaphysics as representing the world through a unified point projected beyond the world in order to theorize the world as a translucent organized whole.[20]

Metaphysical statements presuppose a perspective outside of any possible worldly perspective and conflict with modernity and its skepticism concerning cognizing the world through the transcendent. Dilthey articulates this claim from the conflict between the historical consciousness of the present, and its awareness of difference, with every metaphysics taken as science.[21] The aporia between reason and history is due to reason extending beyond itself and claiming definiteness about the indefinite, cognitive clarity about what is a product of an affective mood (*Stimmung*) and historical life nexus.

The historical consciousness of difference stimulates possibilities for skepticism and relativism. After the end of objective metaphysics, including positivistic programs of a unified science, to what extent can value, validity, and truth arise in the multiplicity and relativity of human experiences? Without the metaphysical integration of one world, which has fallen into paradox and aporia for Dilthey, we are confronted with myriad incommensurable sources. As Heidegger remarked, being (*Sein*) is absent in beings (*Seiende*); the world has vanished in a plurality of worlds, and the ontological difference disappears in interminable ontic differences.[22]

Dilthey described how ontic and empirical multiplicity cannot be joined into one fixed and stable world-picture or sublimated (*aufgehoben*) in one integrated external world.[23] Rather than avowing the ultimate coherence of the world and knowledge, Dilthey unfolded a non-reductive pluralistic empiricism and moderate life-oriented skepticism in relation to "one world."

The validity of relativism and skepticism rests in the therapeutic adjustment of overgeneralized perspectives that reify the established contemporary type of human being as the natural and universal standard of all forms of life.[24] Given the commonalities of human existence, understanding and interpretation are not random but conditional in the life-contexts which they respond to and transform. The individuality of things does not make any possible interpretation permissible, as it calls the interpreter to be experientially receptive and responsive to the other phenomenally and immanently from out of itself and in its own empirical situation. Insofar as we are concerned with universal validity and facticity, commonality and singularity, a morphological-comparative strategy that elucidates individuality in relation to its context and its others is methodologically appropriate. It requires an epistemic strategy that includes all ontic and empirical aspects of human existence, and above all psychology and history.[25]

5. Living within the historical world

It is erroneous to assert that "[f]or Dilthey, the task of human understanding is to liberate the social from the empirical" and, as if world-picturing and the empirical were disconnected categories, it is "an image of the world, a *Weltbild*, [that] determines the value of life."[26] Values are not superimposed on life from the outside, even though they can be coercively applied, since it is life immanently valuing itself that forms a world-picture, which in turn orients and disorients that life in the tension between value and facticity. A *Weltbild* is a dynamic experientially shaped understanding and picturing of a world rather than a static and immutable "cosmic picture."[27] Instead of being underway from a doctrinal principle, originary source, or self-evident intuition to the phenomena, experience and worldview interact and inform one another as particular and general between part and whole. Dilthey's consequently prioritizes the empirical (*Empirie*), including the appearance of the unexpected that fractures or reorients a world, while resisting reductive conceptions of empirical explanation.

Heidegger suspects that Dilthey's notion of subjectivity remains beholden to a modern conception of the epistemic and psychological subject that needs to be overcome.[28] This criticism should be seen in relation to Dilthey's thinking of subjectivity through embodied worldly life. Subjectivity cannot be isolated in a monadic interiority; it is bound up with feelings and cognitions responsive to its environing world and life-context. It consists of interpreting the self's contextual historicity, which permits and requires developmental and comparative strategies of description and analysis.

Dilthey introduces the notion of types in this context that he employs in his morphology of world-pictures. Types have a preliminary heuristic character that allows them to open up and articulate the singular in relation to its contexts.[29] Types are not irrevocable constructs or irreversible prejudices. Types are the researcher's hermeneutical anticipations that can be transformed through research just as the self's anticipations about the other should be revised in encountering the other.[30] This is not only a methodological issue, as a world-picture is rooted in and expresses a life.[31] Dilthey's comparative morphology of life- and world-pictures leads to the elucidation of their living nexus and experiential context.[32]

This comparative coordinating strategy also informs Dilthey's response to the question of relativism. The antinomies within a scientific world-picture and the contradictions between world-pictures are not resolvable by conceptual theorizing because they are expressions of human life in its diversity and perspectivity.[33] The self-interpretation of a world-picture leads Dilthey to judge metaphysical and cognitive-theoretical propositions to be an expression (*Ausdruck*) of life and lived-experience. Metaphysics, or "philosophy" including Dilthey's hermeneutical experientialism, cannot resolve the conflict of worlds; life and world stances and their conflict are constitutive of the dynamics and perspectives of life itself.[34] The resolution of the antinomy in a projected systematic totality is to suppress the differences constitutive of life.[35] Instead of a systematic totality that suppresses what is thought to be contingent, Dilthey appeals for an epistemic humility.[36] Dilthey identifies with the cultivation of a tragic sensibility that is an openness to the world and the irresolvable differences and conflicts of life.[37]

Dilthey affirms preserving key insights from German idealism while rejecting the idealist priority of consciousness over embodied worldly life. Life not only projects and forms a world out of its own consciousness, or self-existence, its world is always already there (*da*) for it.[38] The world is inevitably present and there as a whole for the self in one way or another.[39] The self is not constituted in self-reflection alone but in consciousness, and reflection is a response to its exteriority, facticity, and worldliness.[40] Life becomes a world through the irremovable experience of resistance and reversal.[41]

Georg Misch contrasted Dilthey's "thereness" in the midst of life and Heidegger's transcendental and impersonal "it worlds." Thereness is not a "worlding of the world" that absorbs the individual, but the formation of an individual reality and individuation of a world for a co-relational self.[42] This formation of a world for a life centers on the feeling, thought, and will of the individual and the relation of the body to its world rooted in the senses and the bodily feeling of life.[43] Dilthey describes here the traumatic emergence of the self through its differentiation from the world in resistance and the exposure to facticity of its receptive spontaneity and vitality.

Dilthey argued for the crucial role of receptive spontaneity in contrast to the dichotomy between active spontaneity and passive receptivity. Receptivity and spontaneity are a continuum, conditional, and presuppose each other.[44] Therefore, life is first there in the tension of non-identity, in the reflexive awareness of the self in its feeling of something exterior and resistant to itself.[45] Self-feeling and self-consciousness arise and presuppose resistance and the externality of an environing world.[46] The "internal" human world is accordingly not an ideational or spiritual construct. It is constituted through social-historically formed practical goods, interests, norms, purposes, and values.[47] A world is mediated through material, social, and symbolic relations. A world is felt and lived and not merely a conceptual, ideational, or representational object.[48] Life interestedly cares about and understands its own life from out of itself and in response to others. It is structured in part by human activities and purposiveness and yet Dilthey's "lifeworld" has no teleological determination in an unfolding of an ultimate end or purpose in his philosophy of history.[49]

History and biography are the most suitable means for expressing and provoking the self-reflection of life. All sciences have an element of art in being practices, but some are more thoroughly artistic, employing all of our spontaneity and responsiveness. Poetry and the other arts provide the most powerful and moving insights into life and the individual's formation of a world-picture. Art and literature are nearest and most expressive of the self-presentation of life in its fullness and complexity.[50] Art-works do not only express life, they amplify and enhance it and disclose its further possibilities that often remain unseen and unheard in the course of daily life. Art is the richest articulation of the forces of the imagination. It is the imagination that approaches the singular without eradicating it in a non-coercive juxtaposition of singulars.[51]

The worlds experienced in art, religion, and philosophy involve the transformation – through extension and intensification as well as abridgement and impoverishment – of the feeling of life. The "internal" feeling of life is confronted by exteriorities that resist, threaten, and undermine it, including the irreducible exteriority and facticity of death.[52] Endeavors to systematically comprehend and organize the world as a whole must lead to aporia because of the finite and horizon-bound character of human life. Dilthey concluded his philosophy of worldviews with the proposal that philosophy can only be personal and individual in the end even while expressing what seems impersonal and universal.[53] A world is not an organized system of abstract concepts; a world is formed and experienced through a fundamental mood (Grundstimmung) and disposition (Gemütsverfassung), which conceptualization and reflection can in turn effect.[54] Moods affectively orient the picturing the world as it is formed and individualized in its epochal and generational contexts.[55]

6. The plurality and conflict of worlds?

Another conception that emerged from Dilthey's hermeneutics is the idea that there is a fundamental conflict (Streit, Widerstreit) between worldviews, life-tendencies, and interpretive orientations. Heidegger maintains that Dilthey did not comprehend this conflict decisively enough. Heidegger expounded his most adamant critique of Dilthey in his lecture course Introduction to Philosophy. Heidegger here reasons against understanding the world and world-picturing through the multiplicity of ontic differences for the sake of a more originary ontological difference. He problematizes the ontic differences of the empirical expressed by Dilthey.[56] A worldview is not an observational interpretive response to multiplicity for Heidegger; it is primarily world-intuition (Welt-anschauen) and a factically gripped being-in-the-world.[57]

Observation and empirical inquiry presuppose encountering and confronting the world, but the encounter can repeat, miss, or be transformed in the encounter such that the empirical ontic dimension should not be dismissed. This encounter prior to inquiry is understood as intuition in traditional thought. Dilthey stressed the interpretive formation of worldviews, whereas Heidegger emphasized their being intuited. Heidegger returns to a phenomenological intuition quite different than Dilthey's empirical interpretive strategies. Heidegger describes intuition as deferred through not grasping rather than an immediate grasping.[58]

Heidegger contends that a worldview is not formed out of multiple and heterogeneous aspects and elements. It is not of "diverse provenance" but an originary unified phenomenon in the transcendence of Dasein in its nothingness and eccentric and ecstatic lack of bearing.[59] Dasein is in each case betrayed and threatened in its transcendence-in-the-world, or in "the each time of the facticity of transcendence."[60] Dasein does not primarily ontically observe and inquire, it is ontically involved because it primordially understands and "intuits the world."[61] Human existence, understood as being-there (Da-sein), is each time an intuiting of world. It is a having and not having of the world that it itself is. Worldview is often reified into something objectively present, as a fulfilled possessing of the world. Opposing popular tendencies to reify dynamic world picturings into static ideological "viewpoints," Heidegger shows how worldview expresses the lack of bearing of being-there. To have a world is equally to be decentered into the world.[62]

Worldview is further misinterpreted for Heidegger in the idea of a "natural worldview." There can be no one natural worldview upon which a historically formed worldview is then additionally grafted, as little as there can be a *Dasein* that would not be the *Dasein* of the self and thereby dispersed in relations of self and other (*Ich-Du*).[63] Heidegger's denial of a natural worldview extends beyond Dilthey's analysis, as Dilthey interprets naturalistic world-picturing to be an expression of life (*Lebensäußerung*). As the manifestation of a form of life, instead of a theoretical grasping of it, naturalism has its own cogency that cannot be disproved. Dilthey concluded that naturalism is one expressive possibility of life among others, even if there can be no one unified natural worldview shared by all humans. Naturalism is one expression and enactment of the truth and only untruthful when it overextends itself and takes on a dogmatic totalizing metaphysical form. A worldview is essentially historical for Dilthey and Heidegger, but for Dilthey this entails that it is irreducibly individual and worthy of recognition for itself.

The empirical ontic multiplicity of worldviews is pertinent to any given picturing of the world, which is confronted by and recognizes or disavows other ways of picturing the world. Dilthey noticed that the historicity of worldviews entails that there is no master worldview from which to neutrally rank others. Persons are confronted with the incommensurability, difference, and conflict of worldviews that make a unified thinking of being impossible and undesirable, because they are inevitably participants in and party to agonistic life. That is why, notwithstanding their affinity, Heidegger increasingly sided with the hermeneutic conservatism of Graf Paul Yorck von Wartenburg and his drive toward ontology against Dilthey's "liberal" and "tolerant" hermeneutics with its ontic pluralism born of interpretive humility and charity.[64]

7. Conclusion: a plural world

Heidegger interpreted modernity and globalization as a historical event of Being in "The Age of the World Picture" (1938). Modernity occurs as a questionable leveling and totalizing of a consolidating and enframing (*Ge-stell*) "world-picture." By contrast, Dilthey showed how there is inevitably indeterminacy in and resistance to the pre-determined and totalized. There is, he argues, no pre-given or pre-established determinate system or universal concept that can sublimate all individuals, affairs, and situations. There is no "one" or "the" world but a multiplicity of overlapping, intersecting, and conflicting worlds. A world-picture is not a constant self-same identity unmoved by experience and conflict, as feeling, experience, and encounter historically transform world-pictures in relation to each other. There can as a result neither be one beginning, teleology nor end of history.

It could be asked in conclusion: Can there be then a world-formation and world-cultivation (*Bilden, Bildung*), centered in the "already known" (*Erkannte*) of local traditions and cultures, and nonetheless creative and responsive to the new and alternate? Can there be a "global" transnational community – as a pluralistic and multicultural *sensus communis* or *Gemeinschaft* – originating from the interplay, conflicts, and reflection of particular forms of life and world-pictures that are open and responsive to one another? Is a formation of life possible that brings diverse individuals and communities affectively and reflectively into shared relations in which individuality and communities can flourish? Such questions cannot be adequately addressed here.[65] But it might well be the case that a thoroughgoing reconstruction of Dilthey's hermeneutics is more appropriate for encountering and engaging the diversity of life and plurality of worlds necessary in the contemporary world than the ontological hermeneutics that dominated the twentieth century.

Notes

1 See Moran, D. (2013). "From the Natural Attitude to the Life-World," in L. Embree and T. Nenon (eds.), *Husserl's Ideen*, Dordrecht: Springer, 105–24.

2 Kierkegaard, S. (1998). *'The Moment' and Late Writings*, trans. H. V. Hong and E. H. Hong, Princeton: Princeton University Press, 143.

3 Dilthey, W. (1970). *Leben Schleiermachers: Auf Grund des Textes der 1. Auflage von 1870 und der Zusätze aus dem Nachlaß*, ed. M. Redeker, Göttingen: Vandenhoeck und Ruprecht, GS 13/1: 1. References to Wilhelm Dilthey's works are to: *Gesammelte Schriften*, 28 vols. Göttingen: Vandenhoeck & Ruprecht, 1914–2011; English translations, when available, are from Makkreel, R. A. and Rodi F. (eds.), (1985f). *Wilhelm Dilthey, Selected Works*, Princeton University Press.

4 *Gesammelte Schriften* 7: 199 / *Selected Works* III: 221.

5 Dilthey, W. (1959). *Einleitung in die Geisteswissenschaften: Versuch einer Grundlegung für das Studium der Gesellschaft und der Geschichte*, ed. B. Groethuysen, 4th edition, Göttingen: Vandenhoeck und Ruprecht, *Gesammelte Schriften* 1: 51 / English Translation: Dilthey, W. (1989). *Introduction to the Human Sciences*, ed. R. A. Makkreel and F. Rodi, Princeton: Princeton University Press, *Selected Works* I: 101; Dilthey, W. (1957). *Die Geistige Welt: Einleitung in die Philosophie des Lebens. Erste Hälfte: Abhandlungen zur Grundlegung der Geisteswissenschaften*, ed. G. Misch, 2nd edition, Göttingen: Vandenhoeck und Ruprecht, *Gesammelte Schriften* 5: 60; Dilthey, W. (1956). *Der Aufbau der Geschichtlichen Welt in den Geisteswissenschaften*, ed. B. Groethuysen. 2nd edition, Göttingen: Vandenhoeck und Ruprecht, *Gesammelte Schriften* 7: 135.

6 Dilthey, W. (1960). *Weltanschauungslehre: Abhandlungen zur Philosophie der Philosophie*, ed. B. Groethuysen, 2nd edition, Göttingen: Vandenhoeck und Ruprecht, *Gesammelte Schriften* 8: 99.

7 *Gesammelte Schriften* 1: 65 / *Selected Works* I: 115. Compare Makkreel, R. A. (1985). "The Feeling of Life: Some Kantian Sources of Life-Philosophy," *Dilthey-Jahrbuch* 3: 83–104.

8 See Nelson, E. S. (2012). "Dilthey and Carnap: Empiricism, Life-Philosophy, and Overcoming Metaphysics," *Pli: Warwick Journal of Philosophy*, 23: 20–49; Nelson, E. S. (2013). "Heidegger and Carnap: Disagreeing about Nothing?" in F. Raffoul and E. S. Nelson (eds.), *Bloomsbury Companion to Heidegger*, London: Bloomsbury Press, 151–6.

9 Neurath, O., Carnap, R. et al. (2006). "Wissenschaftliche Weltauffassung," in M. Sto?ltzner (ed.), *Wiener Kreis Texte zur wissenschaftlichen Weltauffassung*, Hamburg: Meiner, 27.

10 Husserl, E. (1950). *Husserliana: Gesammelte Werke: Formale und transzendentale Logik*, Den Haag: M. Nijhoff, 243. Compare Gander, H.-H. (2006). *Selbstversta?ndnis und Lebenswelt: Grundzu?ge einer pha?nomenologischen Hermeneutik im Ausgang von Husserl und Heidegger*, Frankfurt am Main: Klostermann, 137.

11 Husserl, 1950, 243. Compare Lawlor, L. (2002). *Derrida and Husserl: The Basic Problem of Phenomenology*, Bloomington: Indiana University Press, 163.

12 Husserl, 1950, 243.

13 Føllesdal, D. (2009). "The Lebenswelt in Husserl," in D. Hyder and H.-J. Rheinberger (eds.), *Science and the Life-World: Essays on Husserl's Crisis of European Sciences*, Stanford: Stanford University Press, 27.

14 Makkreel, R. A. (1985) "Lebenswelt und Lebenszusammenhang," in E. W Orth (ed.), *Dilthey und Philosophie der Gegenwart*, Freiburg/Münich: Karl Alber, 381–413.

15 The following discussion draws on my more extensive discussion of world and world-view in Dilthey and Heidegger in Nelson, E. S. (2011). "The World Picture and its Conflict in Dilthey and Heidegger," *Humana Mente*, 18: 19–38. Also see Nelson, E. S. (2013). "Heidegger and Dilthey: A Difference in Interpretation," in François Raffoul and E. S. Nelson (eds.), *Bloomsbury Companion to Heidegger*, London: Bloomsbury Press, 129–34; and Nelson, E. S. (2013). "Dilthey, Heidegger und die Hermeneutik des faktischen Lebens," in G. Scholtz (ed.), *Diltheys Werk und seine Wirkung*, Göttingen: Vandenhoeck & Ruprecht, 97–110.

16 *Gesammelte Schriften* 1: xvii / *Selected Works* I: 50.

17 *Gesammelte Schriften* 1: xvii / *Selected Works* I: 50.

18 *Gesammelte Schriften* 1: 9 / *Selected Works* I: 61.

19 *Gesammelte Schriften* 1: 9–10, 15 / *Selected Works* I: 61–62, 67.

20 *Gesammelte Schriften* 8: 38, 96.

21 *Gesammelte Schriften* 8: 3.

22 Heidegger, M. (2001). *Einleitung in die Philosophie*, ed. Ina Saame-Speidel, *Gesamtausgabe* 27, 2nd edition, Frankfurt: Klostermann: 344–68.

23 *Gesammelte Schriften* 1: 9–12 / *Selected Works* I: 61–4.

24 *Gesammelte Schriften* 8: 5, 75.

25 *Gesammelte Schriften* 8: 9.

26 Horowitz, I. L. (1989). *Persuasions and Prejudices: An Informal Compendium of Modern Social Science, 1953–1988*, New Brunswick: Transaction Publishers, 28–9.

27 Naugle, D. K. (2002). *Worldview: The History of a Concept*, Grand Rapids: W. B. Eerdmans, 87.

28 *Gesamtausgabe* 27: 346–7.

29 *Gesammelte Schriften* 8: 86, 99.

30 *Gesammelte Schriften* 8: 99–100.

31 *Gesammelte Schriften* 8: 78.

32 *Gesammelte Schriften* 8: 8.

33 *Gesammelte Schriften* 8: 8. On human diversity, see Marom, A. (2013). "Universality, Particularity, and Potentiality: The Sources of Human Divergence as Arise from Wilhelm Dilthey's Writings," *Human Studies*, 36, 3: 1–13.

34 *Gesammelte Schriften* 8: 98.

35 *Gesammelte Schriften* 8: 24.

36 The idea of "epistemic humility" has been developed by Langton, R. (2001). *Kantian Humility: Our Ignorance of Things in Themselves*, Oxford: Oxford University Press. On Dilthey's hermeneutical reformulation of Kantian epistemic humility, see Nelson, E. S. (2014). "Language, Nature, and the Self: The Feeling of Life in Kant and Dilthey," in F. Schalow and R. Velkley (eds.), *The Linguistic Dimension of Kant's Thought: Historical and Critical Essays*. Evanston: Northwestern University Press, 263–287.

37 *Gesammelte Schriften* 8: 71.

38 *Gesammelte Schriften* 8: 16.

39 *Gesammelte Schriften* 8: 43.

40 *Gesammelte Schriften* 8: 39.

41 *Gesammelte Schriften* 8: 16–18.

42 Misch, G. (1931). *Lebensphilosophie und Phänomenologie: Eine Auseinandersetzung der Diltheyschen Richtung mit Heidegger und Husserl*, Leipzig: B.G. Teubner, 247; Compare *Gesammelte Schriften* 8: 79.

43 Dilthey, W. (1977). *Die Wissenschaften vom Menschen, der Gesellschaft und der Geschichte: Vorarbeiten zur Einleitung in die Geisteswissenschaften (1865–1880)*, ed. H. Johach and F. Rodi, Göttingen: Vandenhoeck und Ruprecht, *Gesammelte Schriften* 18: 175.

44 *Gesammelte Schriften* 5: 84; *Gesammelte Schriften* 18: 156.

45 *Gesammelte Schriften* 18: 157–8.

46 *Gesammelte Schriften* 18: 166.

47 *Gesammelte Schriften* 1: 9 / *Selected Works* I: 61.

48 *Gesammelte Schriften* 8: 17.

49 Compare Beiser, F. C. (2011). *The German Historicist Tradition*, Oxford: Oxford University Press, 356. Also compare Heidegger's quasi-teleological meta-narrative of the philosophy of history discussed in Nelson, E. S. (2014). "Heidegger, Levinas, and the Other of History," in J. E. Drabinski and E. S. Nelson (eds.), *Between Levinas and Heidegger*. Albany: State University of New York Press, 51–72.

50 *Gesammelte Schriften* 8: 26.

51 *Gesammelte Schriften* 8: 26–7. On the exemplary role of aesthetics for Dilthey, see Makkreel, R. A. (1986). "Tradition and Orientation in Hermeneutics," *Research in Phenomenology*, 16: 73–85.

52 *Gesammelte Schriften* 8: 45–6, 53, 79, 81.

53 *Gesammelte Schriften* 8: 32.

54 *Gesammelte Schriften* 8: 33.

55 *Gesammelte Schriften* 8: 35, 82.

56 Compare Friedman, M. (2000). *A Parting of Ways*, Chicago: Open Court, 140–2.

57 *Gesamtausgabe* 27: 344.

58 *Gesamtausgabe* 27: 344.

59 *Gesamtausgabe* 27: 354.

60 *Gesamtausgabe* 27: 358, 367.

61 *Gesamtausgabe* 27: 367–8, 382–90.

62 *Gesamtausgabe* 27: 344–5.

63 *Gesamtausgabe* 27: 344–5.

64 See Gadamer, H. G. (1995). *Hermeneutik in Rückblick*, Tübingen: Mohr Siebeck, 9 and 186.

65 I discuss such issues of intercultural hermeneutics in Nelson, E. S. (2012). "Heidegger, Misch, and the Origins of Philosophy," *Journal of Chinese Philosophy*, 39, Supplement: 10–30.

31
NATURE AND ENVIRONMENT

Brian Treanor

1. Introduction

It is, for a variety of reasons, difficult to get a clear view of the field of environmental hermeneutics. First, "hermeneutics" and "the environment" are contested terms, which are themselves the subject of analysis by thinkers working on these subjects (see, among many examples, Nash 1976, and Vogel 1996). Second, environmental hermeneutics is a relatively recent phenomenon, at least as a distinct and self-conscious area of study. This means that both "hermeneutics" and "the environment" have independent histories prior to coming together to form a distinct field of concern and study at the close of the twentieth century and the dawn of the twenty-first. It also means that scholars are still actively engaged with developing and describing the field, which is evolving at a pace that insures any precise definitions are likely to be obsolete before the print dries on the page. However, if we are to grasp the nature of environmental hermeneutics today, we must begin by covering some of the history by which it came to be.

While environmental hermeneutics is a dynamic and evolving area of scholarly activity, it is nevertheless possible to describe with some degree of accuracy its historical development, some common intellectual traditions that inform it, and a number of overlapping spheres of concern that together allow us to circumscribe the field. Self-consciously hermeneutic approaches such as those found in philosophy, theology or religious studies, and literature occupy the center of this field. However, other genres including memoir, poetry, design theory, and history are sites where the field gradually transitions, as it were, back into the woods of other disciplines.

It is difficult to pin down the origins of hermeneutics, because while philosophical hermeneutics is a relatively recent phenomenon, it can trace its lineage to hermeneutic operations at the very dawn of written traditions and cultures, allowing it to lay claim to a very long heritage of thinking. Indeed, hermeneutics is, arguably, as old as language, which has always been open to, and even required, interpretation. We might locate a more precise origin for hermeneutics with the development of the alphabet and the preservation of words in texts. This invention changed the character of language in a fundamental way. As Plato pointed out, when words are fixed in text rather than living in conversation, they escape the control of their author and are open to all sorts of interpretations, including interpretations that might run counter to the intention of the author. Thus, Plato was suspicious of written texts, which he argued were inferior to the "living speech" of dialogue precisely because the former were open to interpretation, both from those who understand and those who do not (Plato 1961). In contrast, however, there are traditions that highly value the written text and the open-ended process of interpretation it solicits. Perhaps the most well-known example of such a hermeneutic culture can be found in the rich traditions of Talmudic scholarship stemming from the codification of the *Tanakh* (the Hebrew Bible).

The interpretive traditions of Talmudic scholarship influenced the trajectory of hermeneutics at a deep level, and early traditions of interpretation remained largely a theological concern. *Philosophical* hermeneutics, however, is a more recent phenomenon, which – beginning with Friedrich Schleiermacher (1998) and William Dilthey (1996), and moving through the work of Martin Heidegger (1962), Hans-Georg Gadamer (2003), and Paul Ricoeur (1984, 1985, 1988) – follows the gradual expansion of interpretation from sacred texts to a wide range of written texts and, eventually, to "texts" conceived metaphorically to include identity, social groups, the world, and similar phenomena. The expanding scope of philosophical hermeneutics introduces another ambiguity into the field. Some people think of hermeneutics as an enterprise focused primarily, or exclusively, on actual written texts. Others think it applies to language more generally. Still others conceive of texts even more broadly, including things like the "story" of a life or the "book" of nature. At the limit of this trend we find those who think that hermeneutics is not only a matter of interpretation, intentional or unintentional, but that it characterizes consciousness and embodiment as such (Kearney 2011).

The environment is also a contested concept, something most evident in attempts to define "nature" or "wilderness" (Nash 1976, Cronon 1996, Vogel 1996, Cameron 2013). Although there are, of course, myriad ways to try and understand the human relationship to the more-than-human world – from Orphic cults, to Judeo-Christian theology, to Cartesian dualism, to pantheism – the vast majority of contemporary environmental thinking begins with a commitment to the fact that human beings are one kind of animal among many others, beings that developed in a manner similar to other beings and which were subject to the same sorts of evolutionary constraints. If, however, human beings and other beings (plants, animals, fungi, etc.) share the same origin and were subject to the same evolutionary processes, it becomes difficult to say where and how humans and their projects cease to be natural. If a beaver is a natural creature when it builds its dam and, in so doing, radically modifies its environment, why would we call modern cities, which come about through human modification of the environment, "unnatural"?

"Wilderness" is a similarly contested term, particularly in North American environmentalism (Callicot and Nelson 1998; Rolston 1991; Guha 1989). Roderick Nash gave voice to the complexities of the issue when he argued that "wilderness" is not so much an objective reality, a thing out there in the world, but rather a "state of mind" that takes different forms in different times and places (Nash 1976, p.5). In North America, where the relationship with wilderness has been particularly influential, people (i.e., European settlers) have gone from viewing the more-than-human world as a menacing, alien, and foreboding chaos that must be conquered, domesticated, and brought under the plow to recreate Eden on Earth, to viewing it as a sacred, uncorrupted, and healing environment worthy of the strictest preservation. We've gone from viewing wilderness as the abode of the devil to viewing it as the purity of divine handiwork prior to corruption by human abuse.

So both "hermeneutics" and "environment" or "nature" are complicated concepts, and, as a dynamic and developing field, environmental hermeneutics exacerbates that complexity and ambiguity through its ongoing evolution. Contemporary environmental hermeneutics is a big tent under which many philosophers have returned to a broad and inclusive view of "nature" and "the environment." Following an arc not unlike that of environmentalism in general, though on a substantially different timeline, environmental philosophy has evolved from (a) a general concern with "the environs," which might not even be recognized as "environmental," in work prior to the twentieth century, to (b) a more specific interest in non-human nature in the middle to late twentieth century, to (c) a very broad concern for environments of all sorts (wild and domestic, natural and cultural, global, local, and bodily ecosystems). This means that contemporary environmental hermeneutics occupies a very large field in which diverse interests intersect.

Because of this diversity, I suspect the most accurate way to get a sense of the rich and varied landscape of environmental hermeneutics is to take both components in a broad sense: "hermeneutics" to include the interpretation of "texts" including books, identities, social groups, landscapes, and the like, and "environment" to include everything from the wilderness to the built environment to the intimately local environment of our carnal bodies. In fact, this broad account of hermeneutics and the environment is consistent with the approach of recent scholarship (Clingerman et al. 2013) and, I'd wager, with the majority of scholars who self-designate as environmental hermeneuts. Thus, environmental hermeneutics encompasses projects from the interpretation of Thoreau's *Walden* to reading the palimpsest of the landscape, and from the aesthetic accounts of architecture and design to accounts of personal identity as it relates to the natural world.

2. Surveying the field

The diversity of environmental hermeneutics insures that any point at which we might begin a survey of the field is, in some measure, arbitrary. Therefore, in what follows I hope only to sketch out in rough detail some of the signposts in the historical development of the field, and to offer a general overview of some of the main currents and areas of concern. Any such account will necessarily be incomplete, but given the constraints of a single chapter a representative overview is more appropriate than an attempt to construct some sort of strict genetic hierarchy or to exhaustively catalogue sub-fields.

(a) Literature

Although it is generally not self-consciously hermeneutic in the contemporary sense, we might locate one of the major tributaries feeding the stream of environmental hermeneutics in environmental literature. Before, during, and after the development of environmental philosophy, poets, essayists, novelists, and other thinkers were authoring works that explored the various meanings of nature, the moral or ethical significance of other beings in nature, the human place in and relationship to the more-than-human world, and similar themes. These literary contributions have played an important role in environmental hermeneutics. Among the writers that come to mind one might include Henry David Thoreau (1971), John Muir (1997), Annie Dillard (1975), Aldo Leopold (1985), Wallace Stegner (2002), Gary Snyder (1990), Rachel Carson (2007), and Edward Abbey (1990). These thinkers, and many others like them, are generally not offering a deliberate or self-conscious hermeneutic account, but they nevertheless offer perspectives on the more-than-human world that views it as full of significance, requiring in us a cultivated sensitivity, an openness or "willingness to listen," and an appreciation for what Paul Ricoeur would call the "surplus of meaning." Importantly, they do so without reducing it to the mere play of language – thus many writers, and environmental hermeneuts, have a deep respect for ecology, or at least a general commitment to observation and science.

Perhaps the archetypal example of this sort of work is Henry David Thoreau's *Walden* (Thoreau 1971), which is one of the most well-known literary accounts of the human relationship with the more-than-human world. Throughout the work, Thoreau makes liberal use of hermeneutic analogies related to reading texts, landscapes, and human character. One of his main goals is to encourage his readers to see the world in a new way, that is to change their hermeneutic perspective. But Thoreau's love of the natural world, his openness to what it can teach us, and his poetic sensibility are far from unique. A wide variety of writers, from poets to scientists, affirm the inexhaustible richness of the natural world and the necessity of "listening" carefully to what it has to teach us. Thus, novelist and essayist Wallace Stegner famously referred to the American West as the "geography of hope," a landscape that has conditioned the American character at the most fundamental level, and which "to this day" both informs and is informed by our literature. Biologist Rachel Carson also made use of hermeneutic techniques in her first book, *Under the Sea Wind* (Carson 2007), in which she tells three stories from the perspective of a sanderling, a mackerel, and an eel. In composing the book she "decided that the author as a person or a human should never enter the story, but that it should be told as a simple narrative of the lives of certain animals of the sea. As far as possible, I wanted my readers to feel that they were, for a time, actually living the lives of sea creatures" (Carson 1998: 55–6).

(b) Religion

As noted above, there has long been a close relationship between hermeneutics and the interpretive methods of textual commentary associated with a number of religious traditions. Therefore, another significant tributary – the import of which depends to a large degree on what sort of hermeneutics one is doing – can be found in the environmental worldview of various religious traditions. Hinduism, Judaism, Christianity, and other religious traditions offer their adherents a comprehensive worldview, which includes an account of creation, doctrines regarding the meaning and value of the more-than-human world, and, often, an account of the *telos* or goal of the world and the beings in it.

For example, the Judeo-Christian-Islamic creation narrative in Genesis offers a story of how the world came to be, what sort of value it has, and the relationship between its various denizens. God creates a world in which everything created is "very good"; it is full of plants and animals God exhorts to multiply fruitfully, filling the earth and the seas. Humans are made in the "image" of God and therefore somehow distinct from other creatures, tasked to "subdue" or "watch over" the Earth – depending on how one understands the Hebrew *radah* and *kavash*. However, precisely because this account solicits a fairly wide variety of interpretations, each of which has significance for the way in which a reader would understand the relationship between humans and the more-than-human world, one finds theologians arguing for both a "creation care" ethic in which people shepherd or watch over the Earth (Delio et al. 2008) and "dominion" theology in which non-human nature exists merely as a well of resources for human well-being (Hendricks 2005). Today, one finds a variety of contemporary movements to "green" theology, all of which make use of hermeneutic resources and techniques to re-read, re-interpret, or retrieve understandings of scripture and tradition that subvert traditional ontologies of domination in favor of accounts that suggest a less imperious, or even a non-anthropocentric, view of things.

The import of these religious hermeneutics extends well beyond the readership of believers. Because a large number of environmental issues are related to some "commons" issue (Hardin 1968), religious hermeneutics exert a powerful influence in a world largely populated by religious believers. The significance of religious environmental hermeneutics is attested to not only in the scholarly traditions themselves, but also in the work of critics who argue that religious interpretations of the relationship between humans and the more-than-human world have, traditionally, been less than enlightened, even downright rapacious, with respect to the environment. The most famous of these critiques is Lynn White's oft-cited and oft-criticized "The Historical Roots of Our Ecological Crisis" (White 1967) which argues that the hermeneutic perspective of the Judeo-Christian tradition lionizes anthropocentrism and a view of the world as nothing more than a well of resources available to satisfy human wants.

(c) Philosophical hermeneutics

The traditions of environmental literature and environmental theology were significantly modified by their encounter with properly philosophical hermeneutics, a transformation that radically accelerated in the latter half of the twentieth century, influenced by the work of Edmund Husserl (1970), Martin Heidegger (1962), Hans-Georg Gadamer (2003), Paul Ricoeur (1984, 1985, 1988), and others.

Although the work of interpretation had long been a philosophical issue – in, for example, Aristotle (1938, 1997), Augustine (2008), Vico (2000), and others – philosophical hermeneutics properly speaking began when thinkers began to "attempt to extract a general problem from the activity of interpretation which is each time engaged in different texts" (Ricoeur 1991, p.55), that is to say when philosophers began to think not about interpreting, for example, the sacred texts, but rather about the nature of interpretation itself. This move from a particular to a general theory of interpretation initiates an important change, one that opens hermeneutics to fields beyond philology or Biblical exegesis to include the analysis of culture and history.

However, it is the work of Martin Heidegger that marks the truly decisive turn in contemporary philosophical hermeneutics (Heidegger 1962). Heidegger is not interested in hermeneutics as it applies to the interpretation of texts, or even as we might extend the idea of interpretation to analogical "texts" like culture, history, or the "book" of nature. For Heidegger, hermeneutics is an ontological condition of being human (*Dasein*). Therefore, hermeneutics is no longer something one does, as would be the case, for example, with swimming. Sometimes I am swimming; other times I am not swimming. In contrast, after Heidegger we must talk of hermeneutics as an ontological condition or a feature of human being itself. It is not something I do, but something that I am; it is constitutive of the way in which I am in the world. Gadamer (2003) picks up and develops the Heideggerian insights, arguing that we are naturally linguistic beings, that language is our way of being in the world. We are formed by the horizon or world of our tradition and culture and we can thus never treat them as mere objects. The only way to move beyond our prejudices is through understanding how our tradition addresses others, which may, eventually, result in a "fusion of horizons" through which we better understand both our own tradition and others.

Early explorations in environmental hermeneutics tended to take on environmental issues indirectly, to follow closely the work of one or more of the giants of the hermeneutical canon, or both. Some of these efforts have only been appreciated as environmental hermeneutics in retrospect or as their ideas were recognized, retrieved, and developed by more explicitly environmental philosophers. This means that it is hard to mark the origin of environmental hermeneutics as a distinct field of study with any kind of accuracy. Although there are important early texts, one can always find something like a proto-environmental hermeneutics or a proto-hermeneutical environmentalism in earlier work. Nevertheless, as modern environmentalism took root and grew, philosophers, like thinkers in other fields, increasingly came to address environmental issues more or less directly, and this has been true of hermeneutics as well.

In the wake of philosophers like Heidegger, Gadamer, and Ricoeur, the field of philosophical hermeneutics expanded to the degree that it is no longer possible to identify or discern its edges, no longer clear where phenomenology stops and hermeneutics begins, or where philosophical hermeneutics stops and literary criticism, deconstruction, or some other field begins. The encounter between philosophical hermeneutics and environmentalism is marked by this ambiguity, and its development follows a similar arc.

(d) Environmental hermeneutics

For the aforementioned reasons, it is impossible to offer a full account of the origin and development of environmental hermeneutics, which began with a number of minor emissions in very diverse scholarly works in Europe and North America during the late twentieth century, before bursting forth in what appears to be the beginning of a full-scale eruption in the early twenty-first century. The further we get from any putative "originary" environmental hermeneutics, the more difficult it is to clearly circumscribe the field due to the scope and diversity of the issues under consideration; and by the time a survey arrives at contemporary work it is difficult, in a chapter as brief as this, to do much more than offer a cursory list of some representative work. A brief overview is therefore woefully, if necessarily, incomplete in terms of citing all the relevant work in which hermeneutic concern for the environment is expressed. In good hermeneutic fashion, this chapter offers only one story of the development of the field, which could be told with a somewhat different chronology and with alternative landmark works. I encourage the interested reader to refer to the list of recommended reading at the end of this chapter.

One of the earliest attempts to blend something like continental philosophy with a broad environmental ethics is Henry Bugbee's remarkable 1958 memoir-cum-reflective journal *The Inward Morning* (Bugbee 1958). Written in the style of Gabriel Marcel's *Metaphysical Journal*, but crossed with Thoreau's *Walden*, *The Inward Morning* is a singular work, one quite different from mainstream academic philosophy; however, it does offer its readers a personal, poetic, and philosophical reflection that is, among other things, something like a hermeneutical phenomenology of wilderness and place. But while *The Inward Morning* is an important text, for reasons that are no doubt complex Bugbee's work has remained relatively unknown, even within the circle of environmental philosophers. Therefore, perhaps a better candidate for a "breakthrough" work on what one might call, retrospectively in this case, environmental hermeneutics can be found in Erazim Kohák's *The Embers and the Stars* (Kohák 1984). Kohák's work was deliberately phenomenological – influenced by Husserl, Heidegger, and Ricoeur – and deliberately environmental, inquiring into the significance of place and the moral sense of nature. In it he argues for a personalist understanding of nature, God, and ethics/morality that is deeply rooted in the goodness of being. The entire book, however, is a careful meditation on the inexhaustible mystery and meaning of place, nature, and wilderness.

But if Bugbee and Kohák began as lone voices in the wilderness, it was not long before others also gave voice to something like a hermeneutic concern for the more-than-human world. Schonherr (1987 and 1989), Cronon (1992), Trepl (1992), Dupré (1993), and others made contributions to early efforts in environmental hermeneutics. Soon others took up the cause of wedding hermeneutics to environmental issues in a more focused and determined way. Much of the early activity came from scholars working on various sorts of place-based and space-based analyses. Among the most influential of these thinkers are Edward Casey and Robert Mugerauer. The strength of Casey's and Mugerauer's work on place has, following the place-based work of Kohák, insured that space and place are an active area of scholarship in environmental hermeneutics, even as new areas are explored and developed.

Casey's groundbreaking *Getting Back Into Place* appeared in 1993, and it remains an influential work. In it, he argues persuasively for the primordial nature of place, which he develops as a *sine qua non* of being (Casey 1993, p.15), and develops an astonishingly wide-ranging number of illustrations and examples of implacement, displacement, embodiment, built places, wild places, homelessness, and homecoming, or getting back into place. Shortly thereafter, Mugerauer published *Interpretations on*

Behalf of Place (Mugerauer 1994) and *Interpreting Environments* (Mugerauer 1995), solidifying the importance of placed-based analyses for what we would today call environmental hermeneutics. Mugerauer's work deeply engaged with design and architecture – as well as philosophers such as Heidegger, Foucault, and Derrida – and has led to the establishment of a distinct and healthy sub-field of "architectural-environmental" phenomenology and hermeneutics, or a hermeneutics of the built environment. Mugerauer develops a number of theoretical possibilities associated with different conceptual foundations for planning, architecture, and design, plumbing the "*alternating integrations and exclusions* that characterize much of human thought and action and the encompassing *epochal disclosures and concealments* that unfold in the history of culture" (Mugerauer 1994, p.8).

Another significant early trend in environmental hermeneutics can be found in ecofeminist thinkers. Ecofeminism deserves a place under the rubric of environmental hermeneutics for the manner in which it proposes a connection between the domineering and exploitative view of the environment and the exploitation and domination of women, arguing that both are perpetuated by the same sorts of worldviews and standpoints. There are a number of different foci in ecofeminism, which is a wide-ranging discourse worthy of a full-length treatment in its own right; however, a few of the major thinkers in this tradition include Val Plumwood (1994), Vandana Shiva and Maria Mies (1993), Rosemary Radford Ruether (1994), and Katherine Keller (2003).

(e) The contemporary landscape

Environmental hermeneutics remained a relatively small and particular concern from its origins sometime in the mid-1980s through about the turn of the century. However, shortly after the start of the new millennium, something of an explosion took place and, relatively suddenly, there were a great many people working on a variety of different issues that could reasonably be called environmental hermeneutics.

Again, while it is difficult to point to singular works on which hinge the turning of the entire field, Brown and Toadvine's *Eco-Phenomenology* (2003) occupies an important place in the next phase of the evolution of environmental hermeneutics. It includes work by pioneering philosophers like Erazim Kohák, Ed Casey, David Wood, and others, and it sets the tone for engaging environmental issues through the lens of continental philosophy. *Eco-Phenomenology* helped to make the case that the careful philosophical attention to experience could help to move us beyond our traditional, reductive view of nature as a well of resources. Shortly thereafter, Bruce Foltz and Robert Frodeman published *Rethinking Nature* (2004), which also contained a number of significant essays that fall under the rubric of a broadly conceived environmental hermeneutics.

A decade after Brown and Toadvine announced eco-phenomenology as a distinct field of study, and largely drawing on the work taking place in the wake of their influential book, a more specifically hermeneutical collection, *Interpreting Nature* (Clingerman et al. 2013), made a direct argument for the significance of hermeneutics in environmental philosophy. This volume argues that environmental hermeneutics is now active enough and large enough to be considered a distinct area or sub-field of philosophy, rather than the idiosyncratic project of the relatively few (visionary) scholars of the previous century. Drawing on both senior scholars (Mugerauer, Van Buren, Wood) and newer voices (Drenthen, Cameron, Gerschwandtner, and others) the collection sought, following *Eco-Phenomenology*, to announce and establish environmental hermeneutics as a distinct, self-conscious, and timely field of environmental philosophy. The contributions to this collection reflect only part of the diversity of environmental hermeneutics but still touch on theological hermeneutics, ethical hermeneutics, narrative as applied to identity, narrative as applied to understanding the more-than-human world, the hermeneutics of landscape restoration, the interpretation of built places, wilderness preservation, environmental justice, and more.

The essays of this collection – and other, similar sources – encompass a wide variety of approaches, issues, themes, and foci. Any attempt at comprehensiveness is bound to be found wanting, and any scholars or texts offered as representative are mentioned in the context of others who, in a longer treatment, could also be named. With that in mind, we should begin by noting that both place-based hermeneutics and ecofeminism – along with smaller, isolated efforts to retrieve or extend the thought of canonical philosophers like Heidegger, Gadamer, Levinas, and so on – are the logical way to bridge the gap from early concerns in environmental hermeneutics to the more active and diverse contemporary field we find today.

Theology and religious studies draw on long hermeneutic traditions and new ecological sensibilities in shaping their contributions. Here one might point to Catherine Keller's ecological process theology (Keller 2003), Bruce Foltz's explication and development of the Orthodox Christian tradition (Foltz and Chryssavgis 2013), and Forrest Clingerman's work on place (Clingerman 2011) as representative of this sort of work. Keller also represents an important contemporary voice in ecofeminism, along with others already mentioned, as well as Greta Gaard (Gaard 1993, 1998) and a host of younger scholars (see Gaard 2013).

The philosophy of place – both "natural" and built – remains one of the most active and influential concerns of environmental hermeneutics. Pioneers like Casey and Mugerauer are still active scholars, with work focused on space, place, edges, transitions, and similar phenomena. These philosophies of place have implications for urban design, the protection of bioregions, the understanding of identity, and more. Other scholars extend or develop this work (for example, Seamon 1993 and Stefanovic and Scharper 2012).

The "transitional" foci of philosophy of religion and, especially, philosophy of place, point us toward other contemporary concerns in environmental hermeneutics. The hermeneutics of place is, for example, tied to a host of issues related to the distinction between nature and culture and the nature of landscape restoration. Can we coherently differentiate between "nature" and, supposedly "unnatural," culture (Vogel 1996; Cameron 2013)? What do we do when we attempt to restore a landscape, ecosystem, or nature itself (Katz 1996; Higgs 2003)? Environmental hermeneutics provides us with resources to clarify these issues and, on some accounts, to respond to or solve them. Take, for example, accounts that suggest restoration is mediated, at least in part, through a hermeneutic sensitivity to narrative, in which the "naturalness" of an object or place is connected to its origins and its story (Elliot 1982).

The narrative solutions offered with respect to landscape restoration point toward a broader concern with narrative, which is a core component of certain hermeneutic approaches (Ricoeur 1992; Kearney 2001). Work in environmental hermeneutics questions the role of narrative in accounts of our perception, experience, and understanding of the more-than-human world (Treanor 2013; Drenthen and Keulartz 2014) as well as, on one account, the cultivation of environmental virtues (Treanor 2014). Utsler (2009) points out the significance of this approach for environmental philosophy more broadly.

3. Conclusion

It's difficult, if not impossible, to single out defining characteristics of environmental hermeneutics that would be uncontested or which would not require some qualification or elaboration, making it highly unlikely that the field will ever enjoy a pithy rallying cry along the lines of phenomenology's *"Zu den Sachen selbst!"* Nevertheless, we can gesture toward some broad, overlapping commitments that mark "environmental hermeneutics." The diverse members of this multifaceted movement are characterized by (1) a belief in what Ricoeur would have called the "surplus of meaning" in phenomena, with (2) a special interest in phenomena related to the more-than-human world, ecosystems, landscapes, wilderness, the built environment, the elements, weather, carnal bodies, and anything else one might consider "environmental," and (3) the use of hermeneutic resources drawn from philosophy, theology, and literary criticism, psychology, and similar fields to unpack some of that meaning. Thus, "environmental hermeneutics" captures a wide variety of endeavors which are generally characterized by bringing the resources of philosophical hermeneutics to bear on issues related to the environment, both in the narrow sense of the non-human natural or wild world and in the more general sense of *any* environs, natural or built.

Bibliography

Abbey, E. (1990) *Desert Solitaire*, New York: Touchstone Press.

Aristotle (1938) *On Interpretation*, trans. H.P. Cooke, Cambridge, MA: Loeb.

——(1997) *Poetics*, trans. M. Heath, New York: Penguin.

Augustine (2008) *On Christian Teaching*, London: Oxford World Classics.

Brown, C. S. and T. Toadvine (2003) *Eco-Phenomenology: Back to the Earth Itself*, New York: SUNY Press.

——(2007) *Nature's Edge*, New York: SUNY Press.

Bugbee, H. (1958) *The Inward Morning: A Philosophical Exploration in Journal Form*, Athens, GA: University of Georgia Press.

Callicott, B. and M. Nelson (1998) *The Great New Wilderness Debate*, Athens, GA: University of Georgia Press.

Cameron, S. (2013) "Must Environmental Philosophy Relinquish the Concept of Nature?" in *Interpreting Nature*, New York: Fordham University Press.

Carson, R. (1962) *Silent Spring*, New York: Random House.

——(1998) "Memo to Mrs. Eales on *Under the Sea-Wind*" in *Lost Woods: The Discovered Writing of Rachel Carson*, ed. Linda Lear, Boston: Beacon Press.

——(2007) *Under the Sea Wind*, New York: Penguin Classics.

Casey, E. (1993) *Getting Back Into Place*, Bloomington, IN: Indiana University Press.

Clingerman, F. (2011) "Environmental Amnesia or the Memory of Place?" in *Religion and Ecology in the Public Sphere*, New York: Continuum.

Clingerman, F., B. Treanor, M. Drenthen, and D. Utsler (2013) *Interpreting Nature: The Emerging Field of Environmental Hermeneutics*, New York: Fordham University Press.

Cronon, W. (1992) "A Place for Stories: Nature, History, and Narrative" in *Journal of American History* 78: 1347–76.

——(1996) *Uncommon Ground: Rethinking the Human Place in Nature*, New York: WW Norton and Co.

Delio, I., K. Warner, and P. Wood (2008) *Care for Creation: A Franciscan Spirituality of the Earth*, Cincinnati, OH: St. Anthony Messenger Press.

Dillard, A. (1975) *Pilgrim at Tinker Creek*, New York: Bantam.

Dilthey, W. (1996) *Hermeneutics and the Study of History*, Princeton, NJ: Princeton University Press.

Drenthen, M. and J. Keulartz (2014) *Environmental Aesthetics: Crossing Divides and Breaking Ground*, New York: Fordham University Press.

Dupré, L. (1993) *Passage to Modernity: An Essay in the Hermeneutics of Nature and Culture*, New Haven, CT: Yale University Press.

Elliot, R. (1982) "Faking Nature" in *Inquiry* 25, March: 81–93.

Foltz, B. (2013) *The Noetics of Nature*, New York: Fordham University Press.

Foltz, B. and J. Chryssavgis (2013) *Toward an Ecology of Transfiguration*, New York: Fordham University Press.

Foltz, B. and R. Frodman (2004) *Rethinking Nature*, Bloomington: University of Indiana Press.

Gaard, G. (1993) *Ecofeminism*, Philadelphia, PA: Temple University Press.

——(1998) *Ecological Politics*, Philadelphia, PA: Temple University Press.

——(2013) *International Perspectives in Feminist Ecocriticism*, London: Routledge.

Gadamer, H-G. (2003) *Truth and Method*, trans. J. Weinsheimer and D. Marshall, London: Continuum.

Guha, R. (1989) "Radical American Environmentalism and Wilderness Preservation" in *Environmental Ethics*, 11 (1), Spring: 71–83.

Hardin, G. (1968) "The Tragedy of the Commons" in *Science* 162 (3859): 1243–8.

Heidegger, M. (1962) *Being and Time*, trans. J. Macquarrie and E. Robinson, San Francisco, CA: Harper.

Hendricks, S. (2005) *Divine Destruction*, Brooklyn and London: Melville House.

Higgs, E. (2003) *Nature by Design*, Cambridge, MA: MIT Press.

Husserl, E. (1970) *The Crisis of European Sciences and Transcendental Phenomenology*, trans. David Carr, Evanston, IL: Northwestern University Press.

Ihde, D. (1990) *Technology and the Lifeworld: From Garden to Earth*, Bloomington: University of Indiana Press.

Jonas, H. (1985) *The Imperative of Responsibility*, Chicago: University of Chicago Press.

Katz, E. (1996) "The Problem of Ecological Restoration" in *Environmental Ethics*, 18 (2), Summer: 222–4.

Kearney, R. (2001) *On Stories*, London: Routledge.

——(2011) "What is Diacritical Hermeneutics?" in *Journal of Applied Hermeneutics*, article 2.

Keller, K. (2003) *The Face of the Deep*, London: Routledge.

Kohák, E. (1984) *The Embers and the Stars: A Philosophical Inquiry into the Moral Sense of Nature*, Chicago: University of Chicago Press.

Leopold, A. (1985) *Sand County Almanac*, New York: Ballentine.

Macauley, D. (2010) *Elemental Philosophy*, Albany, NY: SUNY Press.

Mugerauer, R. (1994) *Interpretations on Behalf of Place*, Albany, NY: SUNY Press.

——(1995) *Interpreting Environments*, Austin: University of Texas Press.

Muir, J. (1997) *John Muir: Nature Writings*, New York: Library of America.

Nash, R. (1976) *Wilderness and the American Mind*, New Haven, CT: Yale University Press.

Plato (1961) *The Collected Dialogues of Plato*, Princeton, NJ: Princeton University Press.

Plumwood, V. (1994) *Feminism and the Mastery of Nature*, London: Routledge.

Ricoeur, P. (1984) *Time and Narrative*, vol. 1, trans. K. McLaughlin and D. Pellauer, Chicago: University of Chicago Press.

——(1985) *Time and Narrative*, vol. 2, trans. K. McLaughlin and D. Pellauer, Chicago: University of Chicago Press.

——(1988) *Time and Narrative*, vol. 3, trans. K. Blamey and D. Pellauer, Chicago: University of Chicago Press.

——(1991) *From Text to Action*, Evanston, IL: Northwestern University Press.

——(1992) *Oneself as Another*, trans. Kathleen Blamey, Chicago: University of Chicago Press.

Rolston, H. (1991) "The Wilderness Idea Reaffirmed" in *The Environmental Professional*, 13: 370–7.

Ruether, R. R. (1994) *Gaia and God*, New York: Harper.

Schleiermacher, F. (1998) *Hermeneutics and Criticism*, trans. Andrew Bowie, Cambridge: Cambridge University Press.

Schonherr, H-M. (1987) "Ökologie als Hermeneutik – Ein wissenschaftstheoretischer Versuch" [Ecology as Hermeneutics – a Scientific Attempt] in *Philosophia Naturalis* 24: 311–32.

——(1989) *Von der Schwierigkeit, Natur zu Verstehen. Entwurf einer negativen Ökologie* [The Difficulty of Understanding Nature: A Model for a Negative Ecology], Frankfurt am Main: Fischer-Verlag Reihe Perspektiven.

Seamon, D. (1993) *Dwelling, Seeing, and Designing*, New York: SUNY Press.

Shiva, V. and M. Mies (1993) *Ecofeminism*, London: Zed Books.

Snyder, G. (1990) *The Practice of the Wild*, Berkeley, CA: Counterpoint.

Stefanovic, I. and S. Scharper (2012) *The Natural City: Re-Envisioning the Built Environment*, Toronto: University of Toronto Press.

Stegner, W. (2002) *Where the Bluebird Sings to the Lemonade Springs*, New York: Modern Library.

Thoreau, H. D. (1971) *Walden*, Princeton, NJ: Princeton University Press.

Treanor, B.——(2013) "Narrative and Nature" in *Interpreting Nature: The Emerging Field of Environmental Hermeneutics*, eds. F. Clingerman, B. Treanor, M. Drenthen, and D. Utsler, New York: Fordham University Press.

——(2014) *Emplotting Virtue: A Narrative Approach to Environmental Virtue Ethics*, New York: SUNY Press.

Trepl (1992) "Stadtnatur – in ökologisch-funktionalistischer und hermeneutischer Betrachtung" in *Stadtökologie* [City Nature from a Functional-ecological and Hermeneutic Perspective], München: Akademie der Wissenschaften.

Utsler, D. (2009) "Paul Ricoeur's Hermeneutics as a Model for Environmental Philosophy" in *Philosophy Today* 53 (2): 174–9.

Vico, V. (2000) *New Science*, trans. D. Marsh, New York: Penguin Classics.

Vogel, S. (1996) *Against Nature*, Albany, NY: SUNY Press.

White, L. (1967) "The Historical Roots of our Ecological Crisis" in *Science* 10, March: 1203–7.

Further reading

Those interested in further reading in contemporary environmental hermeneutics would do well to begin by referencing the bibliographies found in *Eco-Phenomenology*, *Nature's Edge*, and *Interpreting Nature*; but the following list may also be of use.

Abram, D. (1996) *The Spell of the Sensuous*, New York: Vintage.

Brown, C. S. and T. Toadvine (2003) *Eco-Phenomenology: Back to the Earth Itself*, New York: SUNY Press.

Clingerman, F., B. Treanor, M. Drenthen, and D. Utsler (2013) *Interpreting Nature: The Emerging Field of Environmental Hermeneutics*, New York: Fordham University Press.

Clingerman, F. and M. Dixon (2011) *Placing Nature on the Borders of Religion, Philosophy and Ethics*, London: Ashgate.

Cronon, William (1992) "A Place for Stories: Nature, History, and Narrative" in *Journal of American History* 78: 1347–76.

Drenthen, M. and J. Keulartz (2014) *Environmental Aesthetics: Crossing Divides and Breaking Ground*, New York: Fordham University Press.

Gare, Arran (1998) "MacIntyre, Narratives, and Environmental Ethics." *Environmental Ethics* 20: 3–21.

Keller, K. (2003) *The Face of the Deep*, London: Routledge

Kohák, E. (1984) *The Embers and the Stars: A Philosophical Inquiry into the Moral Sense of Nature*, Chicago: University of Chicago Press.

Mugerauer, R. (1995) *Interpreting Environments*, Austin, TX: University of Texas Press

Plumwood, V. (1994) *Feminism and the Mastery of Nature*, London: Routledge

Treanor, Brian. *Emplotting Virtue: A Narrative Approach to Environmental Virtue Ethics*. New York: SUNY Press, 2014

Van Buren, John (1995) "Critical Environmental Hermeneutics." *Environmental Ethics* 17: 259–75.

Wood, D. (2006) "On the Way to Econstruction" in Environmental Philosophy, vol. 3, issue 1.

32

SELF AND NARRATIVE

Shaun Gallagher

Narratives don't exist in thin air. They are physical things (made up of written or spoken words, gestures, and/or images). Their meaning is grounded in events, and especially in the actions that are narrated. In this regard they have the character of intentionality – they are *about* something. They are originally tied to a person who acts as narrator, and if they survive they are embedded in some social or cultural context and/or practice. This means they depend for their continued physical existence on others who listen and/or repeat them. Their original and continued meaning also depends on persons other than the narrator who are not only capable of understanding narratives, but without whom narratives would not exist since the language and much of the semantics that go into narratives come from others who may be known to the narrator, although most of them remain anonymous. All of this is well known.

Setting aside narrative's physical aspects (which, nonetheless, are not unimportant), the relations between narrative, meaning, action, and various forms of intersubjectivity (including social practices) are intertwined in specific ways that can be characterized in terms of hermeneutics. MacIntyre (1981: 218), speaking of the relationship between narrative and self, suggests that they are related as "mutual presuppositions." This is true only if one understands the self in a specific way (among a number of different ways to understand the notion of self); and the same (with the same proviso) can be said about the other relations between narrative and meaning, action, and intersubjectivity. On the one hand, one might think that these things can exist without narrative (there is some minimal form of self that does not depend on narrative; there is meaning to be found in [non-narrative] explanations; actions may not be narrated; and there are some forms of intersubjectivity that do not require narrative), but that narrative cannot exist without them. On the other hand, narrative contributes to, and in some cases, constitutes these things. Meaning may be instituted in narrative; actions may be defined by (or in response to) narratives; intersubjective understanding may be established by narrative. In such cases, one can talk of mutual presuppositions. In this respect the claim about mutual presuppositions is limited, but nonetheless important.

In cases where we can speak of a narrative self, I want to claim that all of these other elements (meaning, action, intersubjectivity) come into play, and that the mutual presuppositions that exist among them are hermeneutical. What I mean is simply that the relations between these elements can be characterized in terms of interpretation. The self interprets itself (and gets interpreted by others) in narrative form; the meaning of a narrative or the narration of a meaningful event are subject to interpretation; actions may interpret narrative (and not only in theatrical perfor- mance), and are interpreted in narrative; and narrative often contributes to the interpretation of others, and vice versa. A hermeneutical ecology, so to speak, is built around narrative.

I want to show that this hermeneutical ecology places sufficient limits on the con- cept of a narrative self to address the objections that have been raised against such a concept (by, for example, Strawson 2004), but that it also enriches the concept to provide more than an abstract or fictional notion of self (as one finds in Dennett's [2001] concept of the center of narrative gravity). I'll draw on the work of MacIntyre and Ricoeur, among others in the hermeneutical tradition, to show this.

Narrative

We need a definition, or at the very least, a characterization of narrative to begin. Peter Lamarque's definition of narrative is a good contrastive starting point: "At least two events must be depicted in a narrative and there must be some more or less loose, albeit non-logical, relation between the events" (2004: 394). Non-logical might include the notion of historical, but as Anthony Rudd (2012: 177) points out, Lamarque's characterization fails to mention temporality. On a hermeneutical view, temporality is essential to narrative. This is, for example, Paul Ricoeur's (1992) view when he focuses on the notion of plot.

Narrative involves temporality in two ways. First, there is always a temporality that is internal to the narrative itself, a serial order in which one event follows another. This internal time frame allows for the composition of plot structure. Ricoeur characterizes this structure in terms of *concordance* and *discordance*. Although in some way each event in the narrative is something new and different (discordance), in another way each event is part of a series (concordance), deter- mined by what came before and constraining a sense of what is to come, allowing the story to advance (Ricoeur 1992: 141ff). There is no such thing as a synchronic plot; plot always depends upon an extended temporality. There is also, by necessity, an external temporality that defines the narrator's temporal relation to the events of the narrative. This relation may be left unspecified ("Once upon a time … "); none- theless, it is open to a specification that the narrated events happened in the past, or that they have not yet happened but will happen in the future, relative to the narra- tor's present. This is also the case for self-narrative. Even if the event in question never did happen (for example, an event falsely remembered) or never will happen (for example, a planned event that never comes to fruition), in self-narrative it is still set in a temporal relation to the narrator's present (Gallagher 2003).

The internal temporality is more or less objectively fixed since the narrated events maintain their serial order, and one event may be more or less remotely past or future relative to any other event. This is what McTaggart (1908) calls the B-series. The external temporality of the narrative is perspectival; it's defined relative to the narrator who exists in the present (McTaggart's A-series). In self-narrative it is always the case that the narrator is related to the narrated events in a perspectival way. The events recounted in the narrative are part of the narrator's immediate or remote past, or are projected to be part of the narrator's future, or are happening to the narrator in the present. Those who are incapable of maintaining a perspectival temporal frame of reference (for example, very young children, and subjects who suffer from specific kinds of pathologies such as dysnarrativia [encountered for example in Korsakoff's syndrome or Alzheimer's disease, and destructive for self-understanding generated in narrative (see Bruner 2002; Young and Saver 2001)]) are unable to generate a self-narrative properly specified in this dual temporal structure (Gallagher 2003, 2013a).

The internal temporality of narrative supports the plot structure. With regard to self-narratives, plot structure mirrors Dilthey's concept of the "connectedness of life" (Ricoeur 1992: 115). The connectedness across time is not a mere causal connectedness (although it can also be causal); it's a connectedness of meaning – a connectedness that *makes sense* of the events, as MacIntyre, Ricoeur, Rudd, and others agree. This idea of a sense-making connectedness is neither a causal connection nor a "real connexion" in Hume's sense (see Strawson 2013: 19, 103). This doesn't mean, however, that it is purely imaginative or fictional. Rather, it's interpretational or hermeneutical, as well as normative, and in most cases involves evaluative judgments and reasons for action.

Narrative is not limited to a description of actions, although actions are in a certain way the events that connect other events. If a loved one dies, this is not an action on her part, or an action on my part (excepting suicide or homicide), but it is an event that involves affect and value in my life. It calls for a response, so it may lead to action or a series of actions. The sun rises every day, and that too may call for (but not cause) some action on my part – getting up, going to work, and so on. Some events have more significance than others. Across the span of a lifetime, some events, including some actions, are connected by different threads of significance. Getting up and going to work every day can add up to a career even if every day is not as clearly significant as the end result, which contributes to defining my life. I don't invent the events or their significance; such things are not the product of my imagination. The affective significance of the death of a loved one is not invented; the social significance of working in a specific career is something that is at least partially imposed on me. Narrative itself is a response to events – an attempt to make sense out of things that have sense or significance – an attempt to interpret and understand. As such, narrative is selective; it doesn't include every event or action.

In sum, narrative is an interpretive account that selectively connects events across time on the basis of their significance or meaning to oneself and/or to others. It's possible that such a narrative is fictional if the events are fictional, or the connections are fictional, or the others involved are fictional. Literary narratives may be fictional in any of these ways. Real (non-fictional) narratives are interpretive accounts of events that actually happen to real people; the connections are real if they are based on the having of significance or the making of meaning, from the perspective of self or others. That narratives involve meaning, significance, actions, selves, and others all points to the assumed and obvious fact that narratives are by and about persons (or events that have significance for persons). One can narrate the adventures of an object or artifact only if one personifies it.

The narrative self

Recent debates about the narrative self have centered around questions concerning realism/fictionalism, and whether one can or should think of the self in a narrative way. To stake out a position on these issues, let me first distinguish between different conceptions of self. The notion of self is a complex one (Gallagher 2013b). One basic distinction can be made between a minimal self and a narrative self (Gallagher 2000), where minimal self signifies any entity that has a bodily experience of itself (as distinct from non-self) in the present. Bodily experience depends on afferent (e.g., proprioceptive, kinaesthetic) and efferent (or motor control) processes that generate a prereflective sense of ownership or "mineness" for one's experience, and a (minimal and prereflective) sense of agency for one's actions. Such aspects are intrinsic to embodied movement and action; they are basic aspects of experience that are closely tied to the fact that experience involves a first-person perspective. These aspects can also be disrupted in various ways in pathologies such as somatoparaphrenia (involving a disruption of body ownership) and schizophrenia (where delusions of control disrupt the sense of agency). The minimal self is characterized as synchronic; a sense of self that is established in the specious present or most minimal experiential unit of time. I characterize this minimal self in terms of embodiment; others, like Strawson (1997, 2011) characterize it as purely a mental event. One can ask whether the minimal self is purely formal (similar to a Kantian transcendental ego), an abstraction from a fuller experience; or is the real embodied subject of experience who becomes the narrator of her own story (see e.g. Zahavi 2010).

In contrast, the narrative self has a diachronic character. It extends over time and thereby involves the issue of identity over time, or personal identity. As such it is sometimes considered a way to account for a personal identity that accommodates change over time – what Ricoeur refers to as identity in the sense of *ipse*, ipseity, or self (1992: 2–3). The claim that we find in Ricoeur, MacIntyre, and other hermeneutical thinkers such as Charles Taylor, is that persons are self-interpreting beings and that such self-interpretation in the form of narrative is at least in part constitutive of the self. On this view, as Marya Schechtman puts it, selves are agents, and to be agents "we must be intelligible to ourselves and to others; our actions must be meaningful and significant in a way that cannot be captured in purely naturalistic terms, but requires that we interpret our behaviors in the context of a narrative" (2011: 395). This still leaves a question similar to the one that is asked about the minimal self: is the self, constituted by narrative, a formal or abstract entity (or non-entity), or is it a self with real flesh and blood and history?

The first view has been defended by Daniel Dennett in his naturalistic conception of the self as "center of narrative gravity." Just as the center of gravity "is a fiction that has a nicely defined, well delineated, and well behaved role within physics" (1991: 103), so the self as a center of narrative gravity is a fiction, an abstract point which shifts around center as different self-narratives, defined by different roles that we play in life (son, husband, father, factory worker, community organizer, etc.) develop and overlap by varying degrees. The self, on this view, is a pragmatic fiction generated in narratives, and the narratives are generated not by a real self, but by the brain. "Human brains are narrative-generating machines and selves are the protagonists of the narratives they generate" (Schechtman 2011: 397, summarizing Dennett). The narratives that Dennett has in mind are also rather thin accounts of the events that happen to the organism; they are light on intentionality, action, and evaluation in contrast to the more hermeneutical views that emphasize the role that narrative plays in planning our goals, providing reasons for our actions, providing a means for reflective or "strong" (ethical) evaluations (Taylor 1989). On this hermeneutical view, the self that is partially constituted in narrative is also partially constituted by its real actions and a richer (more than minimal) sense of agency that involves prospective and retrospective assessment (see Gallagher 2012). In the case of self-narrative, on this view, the narrator and the narrated are one and the same embodied person who not only occupies space in the material world, but is existentially "in-the-world," creating meaning through his or her actions and interactions with others.[1]

In this regard, the hermeneutical view of narrative self-constitution should not be viewed as an ontological claim that the self is nothing other than what narrative makes of it, or the claim that equates the self with the protagonistic content of the narrative (see Rudd 2012). It can rather be viewed as the claim that our narrative competency, our ability to see and understand our lives in narrative form, contributes something to that which makes us selves. This is consistent with, rather than in conflict with views often found in developmental and evolutionary psychology (cf. Schechtman 2011). The narrative self means the self who is capable of narrating its life and who by doing so gains a new level of understanding. Schechtman quotes Katherine Nelson in this regard: "This level of self-understanding integrates action and consciousness into a whole self, and establishes a self-history as unique to the self, differentiated from others' experiential histories" (Nelson 2003: 7).

Galen Strawson (2004) objects to narrative views of the self and argues against what he calls the "psychological narrativity thesis" (the descriptive claim that humans actually experience their lives in narrative form) and the "ethical narrativity thesis" (the prescriptive claim that it is good to experience one's life in a narrative way). Strawson himself defends a view of the self that is more minimal than even the minimal self described above. In contrast to an embodied agent, Strawson (1997) thinks the core or essential aspect of self is equivalent to the subject of (mental) experience, and he rules out diachronicity, agency, and character.[2] Obviously, if this is the way that he defines the self, then narrative, in its descriptive sense, which involves both diachronicity and agency, and in its prescriptive sense, which involves moral character, is excluded. Strawson, however, goes further than simply insisting on a particular definition. He describes his own experience as "episodic" – that is, as not having a narrative structure. In effect, he offers a phenomenological account of the self as something that does not, and need not, involve narrative in the sense of either the psychological or ethical claim.

Strawson takes the descriptive or psychological claim to be ontological in some sense. The examples he cites claim that the self just is the narrative:

"each of us constructs and lives a 'narrative' ... this narrative is us, our identities" (Oliver Sacks); "self is a perpetually rewritten story ... in the end, we become the autobiographical narratives by which we 'tell about' our lives" (Jerry Bruner); "we are all virtuoso novelists. ... We try to make all of our material cohere into a single good story. And that story is our auto-biography. The chief fictional character ... of that autobiography is one's self" (Dan Dennett).

(Strawson 2004: 428)

On the one hand, however, if, as indicated above, we take the hermeneutical view, not as an ontological claim about the self, but a characterization of what narrative com-petency can provide in terms of self-understanding, which itself, in turn, shapes our selves (by way of shaping our intention formations and actions), Strawson's objection seems to miss the mark. Indeed, as Schechtman (2011) points out, if we consider the interpretational nature of narrative in this regard, Strawson's own characterization of himself as episodic is a narrative that can provide some self-understanding. On the other hand, the hermeneutical view includes those features that Strawson wants to rule out as essential to self – diachronicity, agency, and character. Yet, as Strawson himself indicates, every person is more than a minimal self in this regard. Even if one is episodic, in Strawson's sense, and "has little or no sense that the self that one is was there in the (further) past and will be there in the future," still, as he admits, "one is perfectly well aware that one has long-term continuity considered as a whole human being" (2004: 430). Strawson is making a classic distinction between self and a whole human being (as in Locke's distinction between person and human being). In that case, where one is insisting on the stipulative definition of self as minimal, and where the hermeneutical view would continue to characterize the continuity of human life, taken as non-minimal, the difference would become merely definitional and in fact more or less consistent with the distinction between minimal self and narrative self. And Strawson is not claiming that he, "as a whole human being" is only a minimal self; he is simply saying that as a minimal self he is episodic (i.e., that he experiences himself in that way), without denying that he is also "well aware" of his long-term continuity. The latter may not be for him anything that counts experientially. But it's not clear that the hermeneutical view would insist that it should.

Strawson's objection, then, motivates a clarification. Even if we stay with a con-ceptual distinction between minimal self and narrative self, on the hermeneutical view one should not maintain an existential distinction between these two.[3] The minimal self must be regarded as the self who narrates – the one who engages in the act of narrating. The question is whether the minimal self is also the self to whom the self-narration refers – the narrated self. In one sense the answer must be no, not just because the distinction between minimal self and narrative self would collapse, but because the narrated self is by definition much more than the minimal self. On the hermeneutical view, the distinction is maintained by recognizing that there is a kind of distanciation (or narrative distance) between the narrating self and the nar-rated self. As Ricoeur suggests, the kind of identity that one might claim about the self is not *idem* (or sameness) but *ipse*, which allows for change and difference over time. Ipseity in this sense intrinsically involves narrative distance.

Narrative distance is a complex concept that goes back to Aristotle's *Poetics*. It's used in narrative theory to indicate how far removed the narrator is from the narrated events (Lothe 2000; Andringa 1996). This distance may be characterized on at least three scales. First, more or less distance exists between the narrator and the narrated events if the narration is done from the third person versus first person perspective, respectively. Second, narrative distance may also be measured in terms of the extent and the valence of the narrator's evaluation of the events. A negative evaluation correlates with more distance than a positive one, for example. Third, distance may be defined in temporal terms as the difference between the time when the narrator narrates and the time represented by the narrated events. This kind of distance, however, is not simply about difference in time. It concerns how different kinds of access to the narrated events can introduce limitations and biases into the recounting of the events. For example, if my narrative of a series of events is based on episodic memory over a long period, then the limitations imposed by my memory may introduce important discrepancies between what I narrate and what actually happened – a difference between narrated events and historical events (Bedwell et al. 2011). Both Gadamer (1989) and Ricoeur (1981) suggest that temporal distance is unavoidable – all narrative recounting is an interpretation, the veracity of which is measurable in degree, but is never one hundred percent.

The case of autobiographical (or self-) narrative shows that narrative distance is a structural feature of narrative practice, defining the distance between the self who narrates and the self who is narrated. When the narrator says, for example, "I had a great time on holiday," the "I" points in two directions. It points back to the narrating self – the person here and now who is telling the story, the narrator, and it signifies that the narrator means to say something about herself and to assert an identity between herself as narrator and herself as narrated. It also points to the person or character who the narrator *was* at some point in the past. The narrator asserts an identity between herself and the person (the whole human being) she is talking about. Yet, even in a positive, first-person, autobiographical narrative about events in the not so distant past, the person the narrator is here and now (bordering on the minimal self) is not necessarily the same as the person she narrates. In regard to *idem* identity (sameness or numerical identity) the narrator is talking about herself rather than about someone else. Ipseity, however, is a concept that allows for a difference between myself as the one I am describing at an earlier (or later) time, and myself as narrator in the present. Narrative (self-)identity, according to Ricoeur (1992), is the product of the dialectic of *idem* and *ipse*.

This suggests that, in narrative practice, there is an integration, but not strict identity, of minimal self (as engaged in the act of narrating) and narrative (narrated) self. If the distinction between minimal self and narrative self, and the narrative distance between them can help to accommodate the difference between Strawson and the narrative theorists, another distinction might provide further negotiating points. This is the distinction between an explicit reflective narrative practice and an implicit and non-reflective narrative practice. The hermeneutical approach may accept both of these practices as important aspects of human understanding; Strawson would clearly deny the idea of an implicit narrative practice – that is, the idea that one necessarily experiences their actions (and the actions of others) in a narrative framework, without anything like an explicit formation of a story. If a reflective, evaluative understanding, and clearly what Taylor (1989) calls a strong evaluative attitude, is a part of explicit narrative practice, in which we formulate the stories we tell about ourselves, or interpret the stories that others tell about us, this may be an occasional practice and part of what Strawson means by being "well aware" of his long-term continuity "as a whole human being."

> I'm well aware that my past is mine in so far as I am a human being, and I fully accept that there is a sense in which it has special relevance to me* [the minimal self] now. At the same time I have no sense that I* [the minimal self] was there in the past, and think it is obvious that I* was not there, as a matter of metaphysical fact.
>
> (2004: 429)

The idea of an implicit narrative practice, however, is what he would deny when he claims that he experiences his life episodically and does not experience it in a narrative way. Here it may be that some people are more episodic than others, and others more narratively attuned than some. The idea of an implicit narrative framework informing our understanding of actions can apply equally to our understanding of others (Gallagher and Hutto 2008), but in this case some people are surely better than others at perceiving the meaning of another's action.

Normative dimensions of the narrative self

This still leaves in question the idea of the ethical narrativity thesis. Hermeneutical approaches to the narrative self, as Schechtman (2011) indicates, emphasize the role of narrative in evaluating action. Thus, MacIntyre states:

> To be a subject of a narrative is to be accountable for the actions and experiences which compose a narratable life. It is, that is, to be open to being asked to give a certain kind of account of what one did or what happened to one.
>
> (1981: 103)

Narrative, by way of the notion of narrative distance, opens up the space of reasons and the possibility of strong evaluation, and thus allows us to make our actions intelligible. Daniel Hutto (2008) argues in this way as well, calling this "the narrative practice hypothesis":

> children normally achieve understanding by engaging in story-telling practices, with the support of others. The stories about those who act for reasons – i.e. folk psychological narratives – are the foci of this practice. Stories of this special kind provide the crucial training set needed for understanding reasons.
>
> (Hutto 2008: 53)

Insofar as we are exposed to narratives during our development and continuously throughout adult life, we are exposed to contexts in which people (and characters) provide reasons for their actions and are evaluated on those reasons. This is not just the case with children's stories, where we learn about motives and acceptable and inacceptable actions; it continues in our everyday personal and cultural narratives.

It's not that one decides to participate in this scheme of giving reasons for actions. Rather, we are drawn into this practice, as a cultural and rational practice, because we are immersed in a social context with others from the very beginning. The stories we hear as children are given to us by others, and often with commentary. Story telling is a form of natural pedagogy (Csibra and Gergely 2009) – that is, an explicit case of ostensive joint attention towards actions, the lessons of which tend to be generalized by the child. Since we develop in social contexts and normally acquire the capacity for narrative in those contexts, then the development of self-narrative obviously involves others. Katherine Nelson (2003) points out that "with respect to the child's own experience, which is forecast and rehearsed with him or her by parents," competency for self-narrative starts to emerge in two-year-olds. Self-narrative requires building on our experiences of others and their narratives, so "children of 2–4 years often 'appropriate' someone else's story as their own" (Nelson 2003). Furthermore, to carve out a self-position within a set of narratives requires a self that is aware of itself as having a point of view that is different from others. By the time infants are two years of age and well practiced in understanding things as other people understand them, the acquisition of language, plus the capacity to recognize their own image in the mirror, feeds a developing conceptual understanding of themselves that is essential to the onset of autobiographical memory (Howe 2000), which is one important aspect that shapes narrative competency – an ability to see things in a narrative framework. Along with a growing linguistic competency, and a developing conceptual sense of self, autobiographical memory helps to kick-start narrative abilities during the second year of life. Two-year-olds start this process by working more from a set of short behavioral scripts than from full-fledged narratives; and their autobiographical memories have to be elicited by questions and prompts (Howe 2000; Nelson 2003). From two to four years and beyond, children fine-tune their narrative abilities via further development of language ability, autobiographical memory, and a more stable objective sense of self.

In this process children learn how others behave in relation to each other and they start to learn a vocabulary of intentional attitudes and a psychological understanding of intentions and emotions that they begin to apply to themselves. Importantly, narrative allows the child to see these attitudes in a wider context so they learn how and why these attitudes matter not only to the story protagonists, but also, since these early narrative encounters are themselves interactive engagements with caregivers, to their caregivers and to themselves. Reasons for acting, in their great variety and complexity, are put on show in this way (Gallagher and Hutto 2008).

Narratives thus provide what we can call a normative landscape in which we can set our own actions, as well as the actions of others. The dynamics of how we are able to enter this normative landscape are important. It is not just, as MacIntyre (1981: 212) pointed out, "because we live out narratives in our lives and because we understand our own lives in terms of narratives that we live out, that the form of narrative is appropriate for understanding the actions of others"; it begins by going the other way: because we frame our understanding of the actions of others in narratives, the form of narrative is appropriate for understanding ourselves.

If one thinks of the self in a philosophically autistic way, that is, as something that develops in its own isolation, as a subject without intersubjectivity, then clearly it becomes difficult to explain how we gain moral understanding. Strawson's objection to the ethical narrativity thesis fits well with his conception of the self as minimal. In his analysis (Strawson 1997) of what he identifies as the "strong" characterization of self, his list of eight features includes the idea that the self is a "single" thing, "ontically distinct from all other things" – in effect an individual. There is no mention of anything intersubjective on his strong list. And his further definition of minimal self eliminates a number of these features without adding anything else. It's not that Strawson would deny that we are social beings; but he takes nothing from that fact into his analysis of the self. And it's not that Strawson denies that we are moral agents (see especially his response to Wilkes in Strawson 1999); but there is no way to explain how we are so from his analysis of self. For the purposes of Strawson's project of defining the necessary features of human self-experience, one might think that the elimination of intersubjectivity may not matter. After all, as he suggests, autistic subjects are still subjects; they are still selves with human self-experience (see 1999: 492 n28). Beyond that project, however, and specifically in regard to his critique of narrative theories of self, it is not clear how the importance of intersubjectivity can be avoided.

Indeed, it's not clear that intersubjectivity can be eliminated as a feature of the minimal self. As Heidegger (1962) indicated, being-with (*Mitsein*) is an existential feature of human existence – not something that can be set aside ontically or ontologically. And this is even clearer in accounts of human development.[4] Thus, Ulrich Neisser (1988), in explicating the important dimensions of selfhood, includes the interpersonal aspect from the very beginning, that is, at birth (evidenced, for example, by the inclination of the newborn infant to imitate the facial gestures of their caregivers [Meltzoff and Moore 1977; Gallagher and Meltzoff 1996]). The developmental psychologist, Colwyn Trevarthen (1979) likewise provides an account of primary intersubjectivity starting at birth. Accordingly, prior to the emergence of the narrative self, the human subject is always and already involved in interactions with others in a self-formative way. Such self-formative processes operative from the very beginning are precisely the ones that lead us into the interactions that constitute our first actions, of which, at some point, we are asked to give an account. Our self-narratives are born here, already shaped by others, in a landscape that is already normative, and there is no self-understanding to speak of that does not originate in such narratives.

Notes

1 Dilthey suggests that "No real blood flows in the veins of the knowing subject constructed by Locke, Hume, and Kant, but rather the diluted extract of reason as a mere activity of thought" (1991: 3); to his list we could easily add Dennett. We can also note that there are theories of the narrative self that stake out positions located between Dennett's naturalism and the hermeneutical views – for example, Schechtman (1996), who characterizes her position in this way, and Velleman (2006).

2 Strawson (2011: 254) remains consistent with this notion of minimal subject:

> Consider a subject of experience as it is present and alive in the living moment of experience. Consider its experience – where by the word "experience" I mean the experiential-qualitative character of experience, experiential "what-it's-likeness", and absolutely nothing else. Strip away in thought everything other than the being of this experience.

3 This contrasts with Rudd (2012) who denies any existential status to the minimal self. For him the self, at least in the adult human, is narrative all the way down.

4 Not something one finds in Heidegger, see Gallagher and Jacobson (2012).

The author received support for this research from the Humboldt Foundation's Anneliese Maier Research Award, and the Marie Curie Actions Netword, Towards an embodied science of intersubjectivity (TESIS).

Bibliography

Andringa, E. 1996. Effects of "narrative distance" on readers' emotional involvement and response. *Poetics* 23: 431–52.

Bedwell, J., Gallagher, S. Whitten, S. and Fiore, S. 2011. Linguistic correlates of self in deceptive oral autobiographical narratives. *Consciousness and Cognition* 20: 547–55.

Bruner, J. 2002. *Making Stories: Law, Literature, Life*. New York: Farrar, Straus and Giroux.

Csibra, G., and Gergely, G. 2009. Natural pedagogy. *Trends in Cognitive Sciences* 13: 148–53.

Dennett, D. 1991. *Consciousness Explained*. Boston: Little Brown & Co.

Dilthey, W. 1991. *Selected Works, Vol I: Introduction to the Human Sciences*. Princeton: Princeton University Press.

Gadamer, H-G. 1989. *Truth and Method* 2nd ed. London: Sheed and Ward.

Gallagher, S. 2000. Philosophical conceptions of the self: implications for cognitive science. *Trends in Cognitive Sciences* 4 (1): 14–21.

——2003. Self-narrative in schizophrenia. In A. S. David and T., Kircher (eds.), *The Self in Neuroscience and Psychiatry* (336–57). Cambridge: Cambridge University Press.

——2012. Multiple aspects of agency. *New Ideas in Psychology* 30: 15–31.

——2013a. Intersubjectivity and psychopathology. In Bill Fulford, Martin Davies, George Graham, John Sadler and Giovanni Stanghellini (eds.), *Oxford Handbook of Philosophy of Psychiatry* (258–74). Oxford: Oxford University Press.

——2013b. A pattern theory of self. *Frontiers in Human Neuroscience* 7 (443): 1–7.

Gallagher, S. and Hutto., D. 2008. Understanding others through primary interaction and narrative practice. In J. Zlatev, T. Racine, C. Sinha and E. Itkonen (eds), *The Shared Mind: Perspectives on Intersubjectivity* (17–38). Amsterdam: John Benjamins.

Gallagher, S. and Jacobson, R. 2012. Heidegger and social cognition. In J. Kiverstein and M. Wheeler (eds.), *Heidegger and Cognitive Science* (213–45). London: Palgrave-Macmillan.

Gallagher, S. and Meltzoff, A. 1996. The earliest sense of self and others: Merleau-Ponty and recent developmental studies. *Philosophical Psychology* 9: 213–36.

Heidegger, M. 1962. *Being and Time*. Trans. J. Macquarrie and E. Robinson. London: SCM Press.

Howe, Mark L. 2000. *The Fate of Early Memories: Developmental Science and the Retention of Childhood Experiences*. Cambridge, MA: MIT Press.

Hutto, D. 2008. *Folk-Psychological Narratives*. Cambridge, MA: MIT Press.

Lamarque, P. 2004. On not expecting too much from narrative. *Mind and Language* 9 (4): 393–408.

Lothe, J. 2000. *Narrative in Fiction and Film*. Oxford: Oxford University Press.

MacIntyre, A. 1981. *After Virtue*. Notre Dame: University of Notre Dame Press.

McTaggart, J. M. E. 1908. The Unreality of Time. *Mind* 17 (New Series, no. 68): 457–74.

Meltzoff, A. N. and Moore, M. K. 1977. Imitation of Facial and Manual Gestures by Human Neonates. *Science* 198: 75–78.

Neisser, U. 1988. Five kinds of self-knowledge. *Philosophical Psychology*, 1: 35–59.

Nelson, K. 2003. Narrative and the emergence of a consciousness of self. In G. D. Fireman, T. E. McVay, and O. J. Flanagan (eds.), *Narrative and Consciousness: Literature, Psychology, and the Brain* (17–36). New York: Oxford University Press.

Ricoeur, P. 1981. *Hermeneutics and the human sciences: essays on language, action, and interpretation*. Trans. J. B. Thompson. Cambridge: Cambridge University Press.

——1992. *Oneself as Another*. Trans. K. Blamey. Chicago: University of Chicago Press.

Rudd, A. 2012. *Self, Value and Narrative: A Kierkegaardian Approach*. Oxford: Oxford University Press.

Schechtman, M. 1996. *The Constitution of Selves*. Ithaca, NY: Cornell University Press.

——2011. The narrative self. In S. Gallagher (ed.), *Oxford Handbook of the Self* (394–416). Oxford: Oxford University Press.

Strawson, G. 1997. The self. *Journal of Consciousness Studies* 4 (5/6): 405–28.

——1999. The self and the SESMET. In S. Gallagher and J. Shear (eds.), *Models of the Self* (483–518). Exeter: Imprint Academic.

——2004. Against narrativity. *Ratio* 17 (4): 428–52.

——2011. The minimal subject. In S. Gallagher (ed.), *The Oxford Handbook of the Self* (253–78). Oxford: Oxford University Press.

——2013. *The Evident Connexion: Hume on Personal Identity*. Oxford: Oxford University Press.

Taylor, C. 1989. *Sources of the Self*. Cambridge: Cambridge University Press.

Trevarthen, C. 1979. Communication and cooperation in early infancy: A description of primary intersubjectivity. In M. Bullowa (ed.), *Before Speech: The Beginning of Interpersonal Communication* (321–47). Cambridge: Cambridge University Press.

Velleman, D. 2006. The self as narrator. In D. Velleman, *Self to Self: Selected Essays*. Cambridge: Cambridge University Press.

Young, K. and Saver, J. L. 2001. The neurology of narrative. *SubStance* 30 (1&2): 72–84.

Zahavi, D. 2010. Minimal self and narrative self: A distinction in need of refinement. In T. Fuchs, C. Sattel, and P. Henningsen (eds.), *The Embodied Self* (3–11). Stuttgart: Schattauer.

Part IV

HERMENEUTIC ENGAGEMENTS

33

HERMENEUTICS, EPISTEMOLOGY, AND SCIENCE

Fred D'Agostino

1. Introduction

How are we to understand the relations among science, epistemology, and hermeneutics? There is, first of all, a difficult question about the relation between hermeneutics and epistemology. Are they distinctive and perhaps even opposed approaches to human knowledge formation or does one encompass the other as a special case (and, if so, which is encompassed, which encompassing)? We consider these issues in Section 2.

There is, secondly, a question about the possibility of a hermeneutical approach to science, with, again, a variety of views. According to some scholars, hermeneutics is an apt approach for the human, but not for the natural sciences. Other scholars disagree, either rejecting any difference in applicability, or seeing distinctive realms of application for the two approaches, but allocating these realms in quite a different way. These issues are taken up in Section 3.

In Section 4 we consider perhaps the most subtle discussion of the relation of hermeneutics to science, that by Gyorgy Markus, and consider his notion (Markus 1987: 8) that the 'hermeneutic naivete' of the natural sciences 'works' and, hence, that 'the natural sciences, in practice, seem to have no need of a hermeneutics', a conclusion that seems, at first glance anyway, to be in some tension with the assertion, as Joseph Kockelmans put it, that '[t]he hermeneutic nature of the entire [scientific] enterprise should by now have become obvious' (Kockelmans 1997: 312).

Section 5 is devoted to an examination of the work of Thomas Kuhn and, in particular, to what an interpretation of Kuhn's general approach might imply about our understanding in the most general terms of a hermeneutical approach to enquiry.

2. 'Two continental enterprises'

The anthropologist Clifford Geertz provides an elegant entrée to the issue of the relation between hermeneutics and epistemology (though, in context, he is also engaged with the relation between the social and the natural sciences, to which we will return in Section 3). He refers to 'the Taylor-Dilthey conception of two continental enterprises', and particularizes these enterprises as follows:

> [O]ne driven by the ideal of a disengaged consciousness looking out with cognitive assurance upon an absolute world of ascertainable fact, the other by that of an engaged self struggling uncertainly with signs and expressions to make readable sense of intentional action.
>
> (Geertz 2000: 150)

The project which encompasses 'disengaged consciousness' and 'ascertainable fact' is, traditionally, that of (classical) epistemology and that which takes in 'an engaged self' and works with the notion of 'readable sense' is, naturally, that of hermeneutics.

It is the burden of much contemporary discussion, as indeed it is of Geertz's account, that the contrast is radically overdrawn between these 'two continental enterprises'. Nevertheless the contrast has been drawn and both by those who associate themselves with hermeneutics and by those who examine the claims of classical epistemology. So, for example, Thomas Nagel has notoriously conjured the phrase 'the view from nowhere' to express the idea that we might have an understanding of the world that is more objective in being less tied than others to the specifics of an individual's characteristics or their situation (Nagel 1986: 5). While Nagel's own treatment of 'the view from nowhere' is nuanced, that very phrase serves well to indicate the aspirations of a particular form of epistemology which understands its mission as the discovery of such facts as are insensitive to the vicissitudes of everyday life and the fallibilities of humanity.

Bernard Williams, elucidating the philosophy of René Descartes, refers, less picturesquely, to 'the absolute conception of reality', 'the reality which is there "anyway", the object of any representation which is knowledge' (Williams 1978: 49). Richard Rorty, polemically engaged with the forms of classical epistemology being explored by Nagel and Williams, held that there is 'no description of how things are from a God's-eye point of view, no skyhook provided by some contemporary or yet-to-be-developed science, [that] is going to free us from the contingency of having been acculturated as we were'. He continued: 'Our acculturation is what makes certain options live, or momentous, or forced, while leaving others dead, or trivial, or optional' (Rorty 1991: 13).

All this is in stark contrast with the self-understanding of hermeneutics, which, in effect, sees 'the contingency of having been acculturated as we were' as the ground of, not as an impediment to, understanding and knowledge. Our engagement with the world and with each other starts with precisely the specifics of our characteristics and situations and with the 'prejudices' or pre-conceptions which we inherit from our traditions. In the useful summary of Paolo Parrini, hermeneutics shows itself in an approach to its objects that:

> is guided by a preunderstanding and some prejudices linked to the histor-ical horizon of the interpreter ... [such that] the clashings of our

expectations with the empirical data ... may lead to some changes in our intrasystemic beliefs as well as in the assumptions that constitute the ... frame of reference.

(Parrini 2010: 45)

Utterly absent from such an account are the aspirations of classical epistemology, as catalogued by Nagel, Williams, and Rorty, to transcend the historical and cultural particularity and the boundedness of our circumstances of knowing and understanding. Knowledge is developed, where it can be, by a dialectical engagement with tradition and particularity, not by their transcendence.

These observations give rise to one account, then, of the relationship of epistemology and hermeneutics: they are in stark opposition and contrast. What one, as a preliminary to knowledge-making, strives to eliminate is, precisely, what the other sees as vital to such knowledge-making.

There are, however, other accounts of the relationship of hermeneutics and epistemology, two of which not only find room for both epistemology and hermeneutics, but, though they differ on the directionality, see one as a species of the other.

So, for example, according to Tom Rockmore, 'hermeneutics and epistemology are not polar opposites, but compatible, since epistemology is a form of hermeneutics' (Rockmore 1997: 119), whereas, according to Merold Westphal, '*hermeneutics is epistemology*, generically construed'. He continues:

[Hermeneutics] is a species diametrically opposed to foundationalist epistemologies, but it belongs to the same genus precisely because like them it is a metatheory about how we understand the cognitive claims of common sense, of the natural and social sciences, and even of metaphysics and theology.

(Westphal 1998: 2)

Of course, a reduction such as Rockmore refers to, of epistemology to hermeneutics, doesn't leave epistemology intact, at least in the foundationalist form that we have been considering under the heading of 'classical epistemology'. In fact, on some accounts, it is precisely science, which classical epistemology sought to reconstruct as its standard-bearer, that deconstructs epistemology so that it can be properly understood as a form of hermeneutics. (We consider this in Sections 3 and 4.)

To summarize, there are three primary understandings of the relation of epistemology and hermeneutics:

1. Epistemology and hermeneutics are in opposition to one another in relation to their accounts of the preconditions of human knowledge-making.
2. Hermeneutics is a form of epistemology in the sense that it is interested, as is classical, foundationalist epistemology, in how human beings come to understand and have knowledge of themselves and their situations.
3. Epistemology is subsumed within hermeneutics in the sense that and because all knowledge-making involves fundamental hermeneutical mechanisms.

3. 'The seemingly monstrous hybrid'

It has been customary to align differences of approach (epistemology versus hermeneutics) with differences of subject-matter (natural versus social phenomena).
According to Georgia Warnke, 'the traditional distinction [is] between epistemology
as an inquiry into the grounds of science and hermeneutics as the ground of the
Geisteswissenschaften' (Warnke 2003: 105). Or, as Richard Rorty put it, 'The usual
way of treating the relation between hermeneutics and epistemology is to suggest
that they should divide up culture between them' (Rorty 1979: 319 – for a representative teaching text, see Hollis 1994). This is one approach, then, to the matter of
the allocation of responsibility as between epistemology and hermeneutics. Hermeneutics is fit to superintend the problem of understanding vis-à-vis the realm of
human meaning, whereas epistemology oversees the problem of explaining 'the reality which is there "anyway"'.

While Rorty has some interesting observations about how else we might demar-
cate the spheres appropriate to hermeneutics and to epistemology, and while we will
return to these observations, the idea that there is any effective demarcation has been
attacked, if you will, from two different but complementary angles.

First of all, hermeneutics has (in some, but not all, manifestations) asserted its own
universality and thus its applicability both to the natural and to the social or human.
Richard Bernstein provides a useful summary:

> Hermeneutics is no longer conceived of as a subdiscipline of humanistic
> studies or even as the characteristic method of the *Geisteswissenschaften*,
> but rather as pertaining to questions concerning what human beings are ...
> [U]nderstanding is not one type of activity, to be contrasted with other
> human activities. ... Understanding is universal and may properly be said to
> underlie and pervade all activities.
>
> (Bernstein 1983: 113–14)

Secondly, recent work in philosophy of the natural sciences seems increasingly and
in a variety of ways to show the specific ways in which 'understanding ... underlie[s]
and pervade[s]' the activities and outcomes of natural scientific enquiries, thus vali-
dating the otherwise programmatic and seemingly imperialistic claims of hermeneuticists, and giving rise to what Theodore Kisiel referred to as 'the seemingly
monstrous hybrid of a hermeneutics of the natural sciences, a crossbreeding and a
crossing of the sacred divide between the two alien cultures of the "hard" sciences
and the "soft" humanities' (Kisiel 1997: 329).

Perhaps ironically (in view of the discussion of Section 4), Markus provides a
useful account of developments, in our understanding of the natural sciences, often,
ironically, mediated by positivist enquiries, that discloses or uncovers what has been
there all along, namely, the centrality to the ways of science of some key elements of
the hermeneutical approach. He says:

> The [works] that directly address themselves to a hermeneutics of the nat-
> ural sciences have no difficulty in demonstrating that several fundamental

hermeneutical concepts and ideas can be fruitfully applied ... The role of a hermeneutics logic of *question and answer* in scientific inquiry has already been indicated by Popper ... The presuppositional character of scientific knowledge, entailed by ... Kuhn's concept of the paradigm ... can be treated as a case ... of those historically inherited '*prejudices*' (i.e., pre-judgements) which in hermeneutics constitute the precondition of any understanding. Similarly, the relationship between theory and observation can be analyzed in an enlightening way with the use of the idea of the *hermeneutic circle*.

(Markus 1987: 7–8)

Parrini provides a complementary account, touching on some of the same key points:

The recovery of Duhem's holism, the focusing on the implicit and tacit components present in the cognitive process, Quine's rejection of the dogmas of analyticity and reductionism, Sellars's criticism of the myth of the datum, the overcoming of the distinction between theoretical and observational language, all these elements together led to the emergence of theses in the philosophy of natural sciences similar to those supported in the field of hermeneutics about the hermeneutic circle, preunderstanding, and prejudices.
(Parrini 2010: 44–5 – see also Rickman 1990: 310 and Kockelmans 1997: 312)

These developments sit behind Bernstein's claim that 'the hermeneutic dimension of science has been recovered' and that 'we find [in mainstream philosophy of science] claims and arguments that are consonant with those that have been at the very heart of hermeneutics' (Bernstein 1983: 31). As Gianni Vattimo puts it, '[i]t is modern science, heir and completion of metaphysics, that turns the world into a place where there are no (longer) facts, only interpretations' (Vattimo 1997: 26). Or, anyway, it is modern philosophers of science, attending to the realities of natural scientific activities, who have brought us from a situation, documented by Patrick Heelan (1989: 484), where hermeneutics could be cast in 'dialectical opposition to science' or as involving a 'rejection of science' to one in which, as Kockelmans put it, '[t]he hermeneutic nature of the entire enterprise should by now have become obvious' (1997: 312).

There are, then, two broad approaches to the question of the relation of the natural sciences to hermeneutics. On one approach, the natural sciences are not superintended by nor do they show the marks of the hermeneutical apparatus of prejudice, circularity, historicity, and the like. On the other, they are simply another, and in this case triumphant, example of the universality of hermeneutics as an account of human enquiry and understanding.

We considered, earlier, Rorty's understanding of the relation of hermeneutics to science. While Rorty does not think that hermeneutics and epistemology divide the domain of enquiry as between the social and the natural sciences, he does see some utility for a distinction between epistemology and hermeneutics and suggests, provocatively, that the alignment is not with distinctive domains of enquiry, but, rather, with different phases of enquiry.

Crudely, Rorty thinks that we can usefully 'draw the line between epistemology and hermeneutics ... as a contrast between discourse about normal and about abnormal discourse' (Rorty 1979: 346), where the former has and the latter lacks 'agreed-upon criteria for reaching agreement' (Rorty 1979: 11). As Rorty notes, this distinction 'does, at the moment, roughly coincide with the distinction between the fields of the *Geistes-* and the *Naturwissenschaften*' (Rorty 1979: 352), thus perhaps explaining why the traditional alignment of approaches to domains of enquiry has seemed so plausible. More charmingly, and more insightfully, we find this passage that gives flesh to the rather schematic distinction between epistemology and hermeneutics:

> [T]he view that epistemology, or some suitable successor-discipline, is necessary to culture confuses two roles which the philosopher might play. The first is that of the informed dilettante, the polypragmatic, Socratic intermediary between various discourses. In his salon, so to speak, hermetic thinkers are charmed out of their self-enclosed practices. Disagreements between disciplines and discourses are compromised or transcended in the course of the conversation. The second role is that of the cultural overseer who knows everyone's common ground – the Platonic philosopher-king who knows what everybody else is really doing whether *they* know it or not, because he knows about the ultimate context (the Forms, the Mind, Language) within which they are doing it. The first role is appropriate to hermeneutics, the second to epistemology.
>
> (Rorty 1979: 317)

It is, of course, an open question whether there are any domains in which the 'agreed-upon criteria for reaching agreement' are sufficiently stable to preclude the hermeneutical engagement with disagreement and the role of prejudice in its resolution. Certainly, there are granularities of description at which settled fields of scientific enquiry give this impression. And perhaps, as Markus suggests, and as we will now consider, there may be some point to maintaining, if only as an 'ideology', the illusion that there are such settled fields.

4. 'The hermeneutical naivete of the sciences'

While Markus could write, in 1987, that '[a] hermeneutics of the natural sciences ... does not exist today' (Markus 1987: 5), and while this observation seems to have been overtaken by subsequent events and, indeed, was perhaps already an exaggeration, his key point in the widely cited article 'Why Is There No Hermeneutics of Natural Sciences?' remains an interpretive challenge. For, according to Markus, 'there is ... something contrived and artificial in all these attempts which simply transpose the readily-taken ideas of a general philosophical hermeneutics to the cultural field of natural scientific activities' (Markus 1987: 8). Indeed, precisely the sorts of transpositions that were mentioned earlier (Popper's question and answer dialectic, etc.) and which Markus was happy enough to list as examples of 'all these attempts' to associate science and hermeneutics, are, in Markus's considered judgement, ill-conceived. He continues:

> The relationship between hermeneutics and natural science is not only strained from the hermeneutics viewpoint; it is equally problematic from the natural sciences' viewpoint. Bluntly put, the natural sciences, in practice, seem to be in *no need* of a hermeneutics – they succeed quite well without it.
>
> (Markus 1987: 8)

Markus is aware, of course, that the 'appearances' are against him. Nevertheless, he is insistent that 'despite all these criticisms, the "hermeneutical naivete" of the natural sciences persists, because it "works"' (Markus 1987: 9). He adds:

> [T]he 'ideology' (*if* it is mere ideology) of the natural sciences which regards any acceptable scientific text as totally self-sufficient as to its meaning ... does succeed because the *hermeneutical* consequences of a so conceived practice seem to confirm this belief. From the viewpoint of its actually realized *hermeneutical achievements* natural science seems to be very 'superior' to the hermeneutically very conscious humanities and 'soft' social sciences.
>
> (Markus 1987: 9)

A first, and easier, point is, of course, that there is no contradiction, despite what Markus seems to say, between the 'hermeneutical naivete' of practising scientists and there being a fruitful approach to their activities that uses the hermeneutic ideas of prejudice, circularity, and historicity. These ideas don't have to be current in the self-understandings of practitioners in order to be relevant to their practices. They might be, to use a term of art deployed in a related context by Geertz (1983: 57–8), 'experience-distant' concepts that the theorist of science uses to make sense of the doings of scientists who rely, in their own work, on an at least partially disjoint set of 'experience-near' concepts.

Of course, such an analysis suggests a certain 'alienation' of scientific practitioners from a full, and hence hermeneutical, understanding of their own activities. Like Molière's Monsieur Jourdain, scientists engage hermeneutically with the objects of enquiry without realizing that they are doing so; they lack the hermeneutical 'self-consciousness' that Markus, quoted earlier, attributes to the 'soft' sciences.

But Markus's account runs deeper than simple self-misunderstanding. Rather, it shows a complexity in what it means to understand that is relevant, perhaps, to the claims of hermeneutics as a general account of understanding. For what Markus holds, in effect, is that it can, to adapt a phrase of Kuhn's (1970: 186), 'serve functions essential to science' for scientists not to understand their activities in the same way as the analyst does. While it may be true, analytically, that scientists are engaged in the interpretation of the paradigm with which they work (Kuhn uses the term 'articulation' – Kuhn 1970: 74), it would be dysfunctional for them to see what they are doing in that particular way. And, indeed, this is Kuhn's own view. As he puts it:

In the natural sciences the practice of research does occasionally produce new paradigms, new ways of understanding nature, or reading its texts. But the people responsible for those changes were not looking for them. The reinterpretation that resulted from their work was involuntary, often the work of the next generation. The people responsible typically failed to recognize the nature of what they had done. Contrast that pattern with the one normal to [Charles] Taylor's social sciences. In the latter, new and deeper interpretations are the recognized object of the game.

(Kuhn 2000: 222)

Scientists, on this account, can function effectively as interpreters of their domains of enquiry only if they do not understand themselves as interpreters, but, instead, perhaps, as seekers equipped with precisely the tools and ideas that will give access to 'the absolute conception of reality'. As Markus puts it, science works on the basis of an ideology 'which regards any acceptable scientific text as totally self-sufficient as to its meaning' (Markus 1987: 9).

On this account, then, while Kockelmans might well be right to claim that '[t]he hermeneutic nature of the entire [scientific] enterprise should by now have become obvious', its obviousness is, as it were, 'lost on' most practitioners … and it is important that this be so.

5. 'United by civility'

According to Heelan, 'analytic philosophy of science was shorn of certain elements – historicality, community, technicity, and creativity – that were important to its founding fathers' (Heelan 1997: 271). Kuhn's work has (inadvertently) been important to and for science, and for the development of a hermeneutics of science, precisely because it reconnected philosophy of science with these crucial elements.[1] Where mid-twentieth-century analytic, positivist philosophy of science was concerned with logical (and probabilistic) relations between observation sentences and scientific theories … where it embodied, as Wolfgang Stegmüller put it, 'the statement view of theories' (Stegmüller 1975: 94), Kuhn, and before him Ludwig Fleck, saw, instead, a social enterprise in which a community of enquiry, oriented to a common set of assumptions and using a common set of tools, used these tools, dialectically, to articulate the assumptions to produce an understanding of the domain of enquiry.

Although Kuhn's work is better known and certainly has been more influential in relation to an emerging hermeneutics of science, we can usefully begin with Fleck, who makes all the key points about science that enable us to see it as belonging, fundamentally, to the domain of hermeneutics rather than (at least 'classical') epistemology.[2] Fleck almost seems to be addressing Stegmüller's 'statement view' in the following passage, where there are echoes, as well, of the hermeneutic circle, and, for our purposes even more importantly, of an idea that we can call 'shallow consensus', to which we will return:

In the history of scientific knowledge, no formal relation of logic exists between conceptions and evidence. Evidence conforms to conceptions just as often as conceptions conform to evidence. After all, conceptions are not logical systems, no matter how much they aspire to that status. They are stylized units which either develop or atrophy just as they are or merge with their proofs into others. Analogously to social structures, every age has its own dominant conceptions as well as remnants of past ones and rudiments of those of the future. It is one of the most important tasks in comparative epistemology to find out how conceptions and hazy ideas pass from one thought style to another, how they emerge as spontaneously generated pre-ideas, and how they are preserved as enduring, rigid structure owing to a kind of harmony of illusions.

(Fleck 1979: 27–8)

Next we find the crucial notion of prejudice, expressed by Fleck, in terms that anticipate Kuhn's notion of the 'paradigm':

In comparative epistemology, cognition must not be construed as only a dual relationship between the knowing subject and the object to be known. The existing fund of knowledge must be a third partner in this relation as a basic factor of all new knowledge. ... What is already known influences the particular method of cognition, and cognition, in turn, enlarges, reviews, and gives fresh meaning to what is already known. Cognition is therefore not an individual process of any theoretical 'particular consciousness.' Rather it is the result of a social activity, since the existing stock of knowledge exceeds the range available to any one individual.

(Fleck 1979: 38)

Here, with one crucial exception (namely his axiology), are all *the* key elements in the Kuhnian hermeneutics of science. We have, in particular:

- a rejection of the relevance to the understanding of science of logical notions (in Kuhn's time, confirmation or probability);
- the notion of a 'dominant conception' (during a particular period and in a particular domain) which, in Kuhnian terminology, is the 'paradigm';
- an understanding of cognition as an essentially social activity, which shows itself in Kuhn's work in relation to a particular dynamics in the community of enquiry.

Also evident is an important qualification about the object of shared commitment, which Fleck signals by use of the phrases 'hazy ideas' and 'harmony of illusions'. These ideas show themselves in Kuhn's work as well, indeed sit at the heart of it, and illuminate something about science but also about hermeneutics and its techniques and aspirations. Joseph Rouse provides a good summary of Kuhn's general approach that enables us to see more readily its resonances with Fleck's work:

Normal science is thus characterized by the use of the same paradigms. Sharing a paradigm leads to other common features found in the practice of normal science: shared concepts, symbolic generalization, experimental and mathematical techniques, even theoretical claims. But these other features may be more loosely agreed upon, and the agreement itself may be more problematic. Kuhn insists that scientists can 'agree in their identification of a paradigm without agreeing on or even attempting to produce, a full *inter-pretation* or *rationalization* of it. Lack of a standard interpretation or of an agreed reduction to rules will not prevent a paradigm from guiding research.'

(Rouse 1987: 30–1)

Notice, first of all, that Kuhn, on this account, does not fail to recognize the importance of community and historicality to the workings of science. It is a community of scientists, working through the implications of a shared set of commitments during a period of time, that produces scientific knowledge. The process is neither individualized nor de-historicized. Notice, secondly, that Kuhn recognizes, indeed insists on the fact, that what is shared by the community of practitioners is not a particular (fine-grained) interpretation, but, rather, a commitment to the process of interpretation.

Each member of a scientific community, on Kuhn's account, shares a commitment to work with a particular set of tools and ideas, embodied in the paradigm or, latterly, the 'disciplinary matrix', which, as Rorty, quoted earlier, put it, 'makes certain options live, or momentous, or forced, while leaving others dead, or trivial, or optional'. Since the paradigm is a concrete achievement (Kuhn 1970: 11, 208), it both admits of and requires what Kuhn calls 'articulation' (Kuhn 1970: 23) in order to be useful in the specific experimental, computational, or theoretical contexts in which the particular scientist is using it. But since anything which requires articulation ipso facto permits different specific articulations, it cannot be precluded and indeed may be valuable that different individuals, committed to the same paradigm, will articulate it in different ways. As Kuhn insists, '[l]ack of a standard interpretation or of an agreed reduction to rules will not prevent a paradigm from guiding research' (Kuhn 1970: 44). Indeed, the fact that there need be and hence typically is no 'standard interpretation' may, as Kuhn puts it, serve functions essential to the advance of science (Kuhn 1970: 186).

In particular, the fact that different members of the community differently 'articulate' the shared paradigm means that they pursue slightly different investigative projects even as, because of what they share, they remain oriented to one another. And this means that they 'spread the risk' of an overhasty commitment to notions which may not survive sustained scrutiny if indeed they are subjected to it (see D'Agostino 2010.) In Kuhn's terminology, the 'essential tension' at the heart of science's success as a mode of engagement with the world lies precisely in the balance which such a shallow consensus affords between conservative (tradition-preserving) articulations of the interpretanda and innovative and hence disruptive articulations. The community doesn't remain trapped by its paradigm commitments nor does it scatter itself willy-nilly across the landscape of possibilities.

In other words, Kuhn's philosophy of science is hermeneutical in its explicit introduction of the scientific community and of the communicative issues faced by its members, sometimes talking past one another, as Kuhn puts it (1970: 109), when they stand on opposite sides of a paradigm shift, but always potentially meaning something at least slightly different even when they do seem to engage with one another because of the shallow consensus, about the paradigm, about the values which superintend scientific enquiry, and about theories and concepts which they share. But while the mutuality of shallow consensus is imperfect, it does mean that each member of the community of enquiry remains oriented to the others – while they interpret the paradigm or the values differently, at finer granularities, they share an interpretative approach, at coarser granularities, and hence can recognize one another as being engaged in the same enterprise, and, indeed, in a shared enterprise in which paying attention to one another is important.

This account seems to justify Bernstein's claim that 'without being completely aware of what he is doing, Kuhn is appealing to a conception of rationality that has been at the core of the tradition of practical philosophy that Gadamer seeks to disclose and revive' (Bernstein 1983: 41), and hence to Crease's judgement that '[t]he days are gone when it could be seriously debated whether a hermeneutical perspective on the natural sciences exists' (Crease 1997: 261). It exists, in particular, in *The Structure of Scientific Revolutions*, which describes, in Rorty's terms, a community which is 'united by civility' in their common pursuits differently pursued (Rorty 1979: 318).

Notes

1 Bernstein nevertheless reminds us – and the reminder is salutary – that '[i]t would be a mistake to think that postempiricist philosophers of science [such as Kuhn] have been directly influenced by hermeneutics. In the main ... they have been virtually ignorant of the hermeneutical tradition' (Bernstein 1983: 33).
2 Kuhn acknowledges Fleck's work in the Preface to *The Structure of Scientific Revolutions* (Kuhn 1970: vi–vii).

Bibliography

Bernstein, R. (1983) *Beyond Objectivism and Relativism*, Oxford: Basil Blackwell.

Crease, R.P. (1997) 'Hermeneutics and the natural science: Introduction', *Man and World*, 30: 259–70.

D'Agostino, F. (2010) *Naturalizing Epistemology*, London: Palgrave.

Fleck, L. (1979) *The Genesis and Development of a Scientific Fact*, trans. T.J. Trenn and R. K. Merton, Chicago: University of Chicago Press.

Geertz, C. (1983) '"From the Native's Point of View": On the Nature of Anthropological Understanding', reprinted in *Local Knowledge*, New York: Basic Books.

——(2000) 'The Strange Estrangement: Charles Taylor and the Natural Sciences', in *The Availability of Light: Anthropological Reflections on Philosophical Topics*, Princeton: Princeton University Press.

Heelan, P.A. (1989) 'Yes! There Is a Hermeneutics of Natural Science: A Rejoinder to Markus', *Science in Context*, 3: 477–88.

——(1997) 'Why a hermeneutical philosophy of the natural sciences?', *Man and World*, 30: 271–98.

Hollis, M. (1994) *Philosophy of Social Science: An Introduction* (revised and updated), Cambridge: Cambridge University Press.

Kisiel, T. (1997) 'A hermeneutics of the natural sciences? The debate updated', *Man and World*, 30: 329–41.

Kockelmans, J.J. (1997) 'On the hermeneutical nature of modern natural science', *Man and World*, 30: 299–313.

Kuhn, T.S. (1970) *The Structure of Scientific Revolutions*, Chicago: University of Chicago Press.

——(2000) 'The Natural and the Human Sciences', in J. Conant and J. Haugeland (eds), *The Road Since Structure*, Chicago: University of Chicago Press.

Markus, G. (1987) 'Why Is There No Hermeneutics of Natural Sciences? Some Preliminary Theses', *Science in Context*, 1: 5–51.

Nagel, T. (1986) *The View from Nowhere*, New York: Oxford University Press.

Parrini, P. (2010) 'Hermeneutics and Epistemology', in G. Wolters and P. Machamer (eds), *Interpretation*, Pittsburgh: University of Pittsburgh Press.

Rickman, H.P. (1990) 'Science and Hermeneutics', *Philosophy of the Social Sciences*, 20: 295–316.

Rockmore, T. (1997) 'Gadamer, Rorty and Epistemology as Hermeneutics', *Laval theologique et philosophique*, 53: 119–30.

Rorty, R. (1979) *Philosophy and the Mirror of Nature*, Princeton: Princeton University Press.

——(1991) *Objectivity, Relativism and Truth: Philosophical Papers Volume 1*, Cambridge: Cambridge University Press.

Rouse, J. (1987) *Knowledge and Power*, Ithaca: Cornell University Press.

Stegmüller, W. (1975) 'Structure and Dynamics of Theories', *Erkenntnis*, 9: 75–100.

Vattimo, G. (1997) *Beyond Interpretation*, Stanford: Stanford University Press.

Warnke, G. (2003) 'Rorty's Democratic Hermeneutics', in C. Guignon and D.R. Hiley (eds), *Richard Rorty*, Cambridge: Cambridge University Press.

Westphal, M. (1998) 'Hermeneutics as Epistemology', in J. Greco and E. Sosa (eds), *The Blackwell Guide to Epistemology*, Oxford: Blackwell < 10.1111/b.9780631202912.1998.00020.x >, accessed 16 December 2013.

Williams, B. (1978) *Descartes: The Project of Pure Enquiry*, London: Pelican.

Further reading

Byers, W. (2011) *The Blind Spot: Science and the Crisis of Uncertainty*, Princeton: Princeton University Press.

Crease, R. (ed.) (1997) *Hermeneutics and the Natural Sciences*, Dordrecht: Kluwer.

Feher, M., O. Kiss and L. Ropolyi (eds) (1999) *Hermeneutics and Science*, Dordrecht: Reidel.

Ginev, D. (1997) *Essays in the Hermeneutics of Science*, Avebury: Ashgate Publishing.

34

HERMENEUTICS AND LITERATURE

Andrew Bowie

The right-wing Secretary of State for Education in England, Michael Gove, cited the work of E.D. Hirsch on 'core knowledge' and 'cultural literacy' as the basis for his recent ill-conceived reforms of early school education. The idea here is that giving children a series of supposedly canonical pieces of information and literary texts is the route to them improving their academic performance. (See http://www.tes.co.uk/article.aspx?storycode=6061320; for criticisms, by distinguished children's author, Michael Rosen, see http://michaelrosenblog.blogspot.co.uk/2012/10/o-gawd-here-comes-cultural-literacy.html.) Hirsch's ideas derive from his work on hermeneutics, whose essential direction is summed up by the blurb of his *Validity in Interpretation*: 'By demonstrating the uniformity and universality of the principles of valid interpretation of verbal texts of any sort, this closely reasoned examination provides a theoretical foundation for a discipline that is fundamental to virtually all humanistic studies.' This claim seems to make hermeneutics akin to a natural science, involving uniform, universal principles for establishing validity (though establishing what such universal principles could be, even for the natural sciences, has proved to be beyond epistemology: see, e.g., Kitcher 2013). Hirsch assumes that there is a stable, unchanging object of investigation in interpretation, which is the author's 'meaning', as opposed to what Hirsch terms the changing 'significance' of the text as a part of a changing world.

This example shows how theoretical claims about interpretation can feed into concrete political and cultural questions connected to the understanding of scientific claims in relation to other ways of responding to the world. The perceived relationship between scientific claims and interpretation in other spheres has evident effects on politics, as Gove's use of Hirsch shows. Consideration of that fact allows one to gain some purchase on why thinking about the notion of literature in a philosophically fruitful manner may have important practical consequences. The connection of literature to hermeneutics that is decisive here lies, as we shall see, in the idea that the rise of modern hermeneutics and of a workable notion of literature are inextricably connected.

Consider a case where finding out the author's meaning in a text in a manner related to what Hirsch claims would be a valid aim. The debate over what Hitler actually ordered with respect to the annihilation of the Jews continues to preoccupy historians, and the lack of decisive written documents makes knowing what Hitler intended very difficult. Were a document concerning the genocide of the Jews to emerge which was written by Hitler it would be vital for the understanding of events in the period to try to establish its meaning in terms of its relation to the known actions of Hitler and the Nazis. This would involve assessing its performative status in the relevant contexts, and it could then be that a broad consensus on the objective meaning of the document would emerge. In this case the meaning can be convincingly articulated because it is inextricably linked to ascertainable political aims, and is inseparable from a notion of intention relating to action. However, it is also clear that such a case cannot furnish a general method for interpretation.

If we take the case of a 'literary' text, like Franz Kafka's 'Metamorphosis', the criteria for establishing its meaning will not be most effectively derived from the text's connection to public action. What Kafka intended in a performative sense by writing it does little to elucidate its meaning qua literature. The very notion of what the text means is, though, as its reception history can demonstrate, essentially contested. Is it about Kafka's complex relationship to his own body, or generally about the impositions on the body of the alienated world of work in capitalism, as Gregor Samsa's concern that his new insect body will make him late for work suggests? However, the fact that the meaning is so contested need not be seen as a methodological problem to be obviated by use of the correct general principles for establishing interpretative validity. It is the questionable notion of objectivity involved in Hirsch's position which leads to political consequences, because it reifies the notion of textual meaning in ways which are echoed in other philosophical approaches which can affect how educational and cultural aims are implemented.

The meaning of a literary text can be thought of precisely in terms of the *absence* of something objective which would give validity to a specific interpretation, consisting rather in the opening up of space for the reader to make diverse connections between the text and differing ways in which they understand their world. This approach does not, as is too often claimed, open the way to an interpretative free for all. The fact that one reader's connections might be rejected as aberrant by other readers introduces the perspective of intersubjective validation of the 'meaning' of Kafka's text, for which evidence can be adduced from the text. This need not, though, fix the possible ways in which it is read, and could actually increase the number of interpretative possibilities, even as some are rejected as making no sense. If a view like the one just outlined is apposite the perspective of 'core knowledge' is problematic with respect to the role of literary texts in education, because, in the name of a questionable assumed cultural consensus, it can exclude the ways in which texts, readers, and contexts can always interact to make new sense, rather than being repositories of received meanings.

These two examples can suggest some parameters for seeing how the connection of hermeneutics to literature might be understood. There are crucial differentiations to be made with respect to how texts relate to readers and agents in the world, and to the status of 'meaning' in differing forms of communication. However, rather than trying to map out a theory defining the nature of these differentiations, which vary widely in significance in differing contexts, it makes more sense to look at how they arise historically and have developed in relation to philosophical concern with interpretation. The decisive historical factor here is the relationship of interpretation to the diminishing role of theology in Europe from the mid eighteenth century onwards, a relationship which is closely connected to the emergence of modern notions of literature.

A characteristic modern notion of literature as something that demands specific kinds of understanding probably first emerges in an articulated form in the early German Romanticism of Novalis and Friedrich Schlegel (see Bowie 1997), who see literary texts as generating 'infinite reflection' on what they present, rather than mimetically representing it (see Athenaeum Fragment 116 in Schlegel 1988, and Benjamin, 'Der Begriff der Kunstkritik in der deutschen Romantik' in Benjamin 1980). Such a view of a work as not complete in itself but as always developing new significance is only possible when a shift occurs in how the relationship of language to the world is manifest. This can crudely be characterised as a move from language being a means of representing a ready-made objective world, to language playing a productive role in the way the world is constituted. The changing aims of hermeneutics testify to this: in an increasingly dynamic historical world, the mediaeval concern to sustain the authority of Scripture is largely abandoned. For Martin Luther the individual reader had been subjected to the authority of the Scripture, because they freely accepted that it was based on a higher truth than they, qua individual, were capable of attaining. When the dogmatic assumptions of divine authority are undermined in the Enlightenment by the empirical sciences and by philosophers such as Hume and Kant, the sources of interpretative authority become a crucial philosophical problem.

If, as in some aspects of pre-modern theology, like the 'doctrine of signatures', the world is a text written by God, the notion of truth depends on the authoritativeness of its source. Once that source comes into question, the essence of truth is, as Heidegger contends, also put in question, because what grounds truth is no longer unquestionably given. The fact that Heidegger will come to see art, including literature, as a 'happening of truth' that makes things 'unhidden' which otherwise would not be manifest means that what is at issue here is not confined to more narrowly conceived versions of hermeneutics and aesthetics, but goes to the heart of the aims of modern philosophy, where disagreements about truth remain perennial. The debates about the origin of language that are characteristic of the second half of the eighteenth century are an evident sign of the shift with respect to the understanding of language in modernity, from the assumption of a divinely grounded symbolic order to one where the ground of language itself becomes a central philosophical concern. The simultaneous changes in the understanding of music, which go as far as elevating it into a higher form of language than verbal language, further indicate a profound shift in assumptions about meaning and understanding (see Bowie 2007). Modern hermeneutics is one response to the new situation, and another is precisely the new sense of the importance of the creative or world-disclosive potential of language that is germane to the notion of 'literature'.

At the same time, the spectacular success of the modern natural sciences in giving warrantable law-governed accounts of the functioning of nature make the issue of interpretation inherently contentious. The status of the validity claims made about interpreting texts will haunt modern hermeneutics, as Hirsch's attempt to revive what is a kind of early Enlightenment hermeneutics illustrates. Georg Friedrich Meier's 'Attempt at a Universal Art of Explication' of 1757, for example, sought to control meaning by a 'science of rules, via the observation of which meanings can be recognised by their signs' (in Schleiermacher 1977: 14–15), and Meier, directly presaging Hirsch, claims the meaning of an utterance is 'the sequence of linked ideas (*Vorstellungen*) which the author wishes to designate via the utterance' (in Birus 1982: 24).

When this kind of model breaks down the issue of hermeneutics is determined by the instability of the relationship between the notionally subjective and the notionally objective. As the objective truths generated by the sciences come to dominate, the role of the individual subject's understanding of the world comes into question, even as the subject liberates itself from traditional theological and feudal ties and seeks new forms of expression and new ways of manipulating the world. That liberation can also be understood, however, as it will be by Heidegger, Adorno, Gadamer, and others, to be connected to the way the subject dominates nature by the application of scientific method. The subject's self-empowerment, is, though, also put in question by its dependence on a language it does not invent, relying on what Lacan will call the 'discourse of the other' to realise itself. In modern theories of interpretation the text consequently often shifts between being seen as the product of the individual subject, and being seen as the result of the subject being in some sense 'spoken' by the language into which they are socialised, which suggests that meaning has some kind of objective status.

However, as disputes about semantics and its relationship to pragmatics show, it is not clear exactly how this objectivity is to be conceived, and this leads back to the social and political aspects of interpretation and to the questions raised by the idea of literature. The origin of the notion of ideology can be located here: how is the 'real meaning' of an utterance that is in some measure determined by a person's location in a system of relations constituted by the exercise of power to be established? Is it what they intend as they say it, or is it the concrete working of the utterance in a social context, which is not the same as what the utterer intends? The commitment of a person to what they say can often be shown to be objectively caused by a social context and the pressures it involves. This situation relates closely to one of the canonical ideas about interpretation in modern hermeneutics.

In the *Critique of Pure Reason* of 1781 Kant says of Plato that one can sometimes understand a thinker 'better than he understood himself' (Kant 1968: B322). If this is the case the author can no longer be regarded as the definitive source of meaning: the question is what that source now is. In Kant's interpretation of a philosophical text the truth of what the text says takes it beyond what the author understood of the issue in question, and it is this truth that is to be sought. As such, there is no obvious 'source', in the sense of a ground of meaning that is the origin of that truth, the truth emerging instead from the reading of the text in a new context. F.D.E. Schleiermacher develops the consequences of such a position, which he sums up as follows:

> The task can also be put like this: 'to understand the utterance at first just as well as and then better than its author'. For because we have no immediate

knowledge of what is in him, we must seek to bring much to consciousness which can remain unconscious to him, except to the extent to which he reflexively becomes his own reader. On the objective side he as well has no other data here than we do [the data being the utterance in question].

(Schleiermacher 1977: 94)

This aspect of his approach, which Schleiermacher is describing as a method for interpreting the New Testament, but which he insists applies to all kinds of text, has no implications that are exclusive to the issue of literature.

However, Schleiermacher further argues that there are two sides to interpretation: 'grammatical' interpretation, in which 'the person ... disappears and only appears as organ of language', is distinguished from 'technical interpretation' (he also refers to 'psychological interpretation'), in which 'language with its determining power disappears and only appears as the organ of the person, in the service of their individuality' (Schleiermacher 1977: 171). The significance of literature is a result of the tension between these two aspects, between the application of general rules for establishing meaning, and grasping the particular sense of a specific text. 'Dichtung', which is not just 'poetry', relating to the Greek 'poiesis', which involves a more general sense of creative making and so means something like 'literature' in the sense at issue here, has to 'provide something that cannot really be given by language, for language only ever provides the general' (Schleiermacher 1842: 639). For Schleiermacher 'the poet ... is concerned with the truth and complete determinacy of the singular' (Schleiermacher 1842: 639), and the 'truth' of the singular cannot be based on conceptual identification and classification. The question is therefore how something singular is to be conveyed, and Schleiermacher's answer is by 'style', the particular manner of combination of words that enables the particularity both of things and of responses to things to become manifest despite the general nature of the words combined. Importantly, Schleiermacher maintains that 'there can be no concept of a style' (Schleiermacher 1977: 172), that is, a rule for identifying a style, because that would have to cover the infinity of kinds of possible verbal combinations. Wittgenstein will later talk in this respect of 'something which only these words in these positions express. (Understanding of a poem)' (Wittgenstein 1971: 227).

The underlying methodological question here was raised by Kant in the *Critique of Pure Reason*, in a discussion of judgement which has proved to be vital for philosophical discussion of language and interpretation (see Brandom 1994). Kant's argument is that the application of concepts, as rules for identifying objects, cannot itself be bound by rules, because that would lead to a regress of rules for rules, which would make judgement impossible. There is therefore a crucial dimension of understanding which has to be developed in ways which cannot rely on learning to apply rules. How does one learn a rule at all in the first place, given that even knowing that it is a rule cannot be based on a rule? The idea of style in Schleiermacher's sense links this issue to the idea of literature. The modern world can, on the one hand, be known and manipulated most effectively by bringing it under general rules; on the other hand, this can obscure the uniqueness and particularity of things (and people), as the concern in Romanticism about the disenchanting effects of the claims of natural science and the potential of art to compensate for these makes clear. Most crucially, in the present context, the subsuming of the world under general concepts is itself actually reliant on abilities, like judgement, which themselves cannot be so subsumed, as Kant realises. This means that issues often relegated, particularly in the analytical tradition, to the philosophically supposedly marginal area of aesthetics may turn out to be philosophically central.

These issues point to a paradigmatic alternative in modern philosophy, between the aim of extending the reach of what is rule-bound into every domain, and the revelation of how such an aim cannot ground itself because it relies on aspects of understanding that are not rule-bound and are themselves the ground of the very ability to explain in terms of rules. It will be in the work of Heidegger that the latter position is developed most extensively. One of the sources of Heidegger's insights is his realisation that a concern of much nineteenth century philosophy leads to a mistaken notion of what understanding is. The nineteenth century concern is to establish a methodological status for the human sciences which rids them of a widespread sense of inferiority in relation to the natural sciences. The work of Wilhelm Dilthey, whilst containing important insights, tends to be problematic, for instance, because his idea of a 'science of the experience of the human mind' (Dilthey 1990: 27), which deals precisely with things like literary texts, in contrast to a science of the human mind in the form of experimental psychology, is open in some respects to accusations of subjectivism. In a wider context the very word '*Literaturwissenschaft*' and its academic manifestations testify to the questionable nature of the enterprise, because its methodological status is never established in the way that the experimental method allows the natural sciences to subject claims to public experimental and observational validation. What underlies the problematic status of literature and the study of literature is the notion of truth with respect to the sciences and the arts.

Heidegger opposes more effectively than Dilthey and others the idea that truths about the arts must result from methods akin to those in the natural sciences. The truth that is manifest through art is not the same as true statements made about works of art. From a strictly semantic viewpoint this makes no sense, and a lot of the efforts in the semantic tradition are devoted to trying to show why, by regarding truth as being a property of propositions. The fact that this stance can lead to the position in some of the work of the Vienna Circle, where most of what anybody says is 'meaningless', because it is neither observation statement nor logical statement, and so is not truth-determinate, suggests the danger here. By limiting the scope of truth, crucial dimensions of our understanding are excluded. Schleiermacher already warned about such approaches:

> Language never begins to form itself through science, but via general communication/exchange (*Verkehr*); science comes to this only later, and only brings an expansion, not a new creation, in language. As science often takes the direction of beginning from the beginning, it must choose new expressions for new thoughts. Forming new root words would be of no help because these would in turn have to be explained by already existing ones.
>
> (Schleiermacher 1942: 511)

Scientific enterprises would not be intelligible without the background capabilities that are embodied in everyday language-use and everyday practices. In Heidegger's terms, research into entities relies on a prior understanding of being.

As we saw, Heidegger comes to relate this priority to what happens in art, and it is here that crucial aspects of hermeneutics' relationship to literature become apparent. If the essential nature of being is to be hidden, the differing ways in which the world becomes disclosed become a core theme for philosophy. In the 'Age of the World Picture' Heidegger characterises the way natural science works as 'research', where there is an initial frame, the 'mathematical', that determines the results which can emerge. The questions asked of nature presuppose that the answers will take the form of law-bound regularities expressible in mathematical terms. These answers enable an unprecedented degree of control of nature. However, the dominance of technological approaches also suggests how, even though the sciences exponentially increase the ability to predict and control the course of natural events, technology can also result in other aspects of our relations to the natural world being repressed. Disenchanted nature loses any sense of intrinsic value, becoming a resource for practical human ends, and the task Heidegger sees is to disclose things in ways which can reveal new kinds of sense, which he associates with the possibilities revealed in Dichtung, as a non-objectifying mode of world-disclosure. Heidegger's approaches to specific literary texts can be controversial, but much of the framework he offers can be employed independently of his more questionable interpretations.

An instructive tension is evident here, between the search for forms of articulation which uncover what is hidden by modern ways of 'subjectifying being' which lead to the forgetting of what is prior to forms of objectification, and the idea, present in modernist forms of art and in thinkers, like Adorno, who orient their ideas in terms of such art, of the need to produce new forms of sense which question the dominant modern forms of rationalisation. Hermeneutics is therefore always faced with the tension between recovering hidden meanings and disclosing new meanings. The more charitable construal of what Heidegger is seeking is that he thinks these two tasks go hand in hand, though his lack of substantial engagement with modern art suggests some possible limitations of his approach. However, the reflections in 'Origin of the Work of Art' on art, including literature, as a 'happening of truth' and on 'putting truth into the work' relate closely to the concern with disclosing the world in ways which are obscured by the dominant forms in modern society, that appears, for example, in Russian formalism's notion of *ostranenie*, and in Brecht's idea of 'alienation' in 'epic theatre', which make the apparently ordinary appear in a new light.

Heidegger's pupil, Hans-Georg Gadamer, sums up a key aspect of the questions here in the title of his magnum opus of 1960, *Truth and Method*. Like Heidegger, he sees the sciences as defined by the way they frame the world in a certain way, in terms of 'method'. He therefore wishes to 'seek out the experience of truth which exceeds [*übersteigt*] the realm of control of scientific method ... and to interrogate it as to its own legitimation' (Gadamer 1975: xxvii). This is because 'it is not right to separate the question of art from the question of truth and to deprive art of all the knowledge it can communicate to us' (Gadamer 1993: 203). His way of characterising such knowledge offers a challenge to received ideas about interpretation. Literary texts, as we saw, are open to multiple interpretations, and the ways they are interpreted can change radically with history, as, for example, the changing reception of Greek Tragedy in the modern period suggests. From the point of view of 'method', which sees the work as an object to be analysed, this lack of definitive interpretations points to an inherent subjectivism which excludes interpretation from truth-determinacy.

Gadamer rejects this perspective. In his view, the way in which such changes take place belongs to the very being of the work, because it is only in being understood that the work comes into being as a work of art at all. The pre-existing object which becomes the work does not become art by being endowed by the subject with some kind of extra properties. Indeed, without the world-disclosure made possible by works of art of all kinds, the subject would lack essential resources for making its own forms of sense. When we are overwhelmed by a great work of art, we are not just projecting ourselves into it, but are opening ourselves to being changed by the work as a manifestation of 'spirit', of sense that transcends the individual, including the individual creator of the work. The interaction between subject and work is dialectical: there is no way of achieving an extra-mundane stance in relation to understanding, which always entails a participatory aspect, in the form of a dialogical relationship to the other that is being interpreted. Gadamer talks of a 'fusion of horizons' that is the essence of understanding: rather than assimilating the other to oneself, one is changed by the engagement with the other.

Such a perspective opens up a strong sense of the way in which literature matters because it keeps open the possibility of always seeing the world differently, of combatting the kind of ethnocentrism that thinks truth is always just the product of rational argument, rather than being what happens when the world becomes unhidden in new ways. The objection to Gadamer's position is that it arguably gives no way of asserting that an interpretation is false. For Gadamer 'understanding is never a subjective relationship towards a given "object", but belongs rather to the effective history, and that means: to the being of that which is understood' (Gadamer 1975: xix). He therefore does not accept that one understanding of a work is better than another, and thinks 'it is enough to say that one understands differently, if one understands at all' (Gadamer 1975: 280).

Hirsch and others at this point raise the spectre of relativism, but the question is what the absolute is in relation to which interpretations are relative. There are always differing understandings and resolution of their incompatibility matters hugely in some contexts, but it does not matter at all in others. Indeed, as we saw, one conception of literature results precisely from valuing such conflicting construals as 'infinite reflection'. At the same time, avoidance of a crass relativism, in which the justified demand for critical evaluation is ignored in the name of a lazy tolerance of any interpretation, plays a significant role in effective aesthetic education. However, perhaps the most interesting point here is that the tension between seeing literature and art as themselves manifesting truth via their unconcealment of aspects of the world, which can lead to contradictory interpretations at different times and in different places, and the demand for critical assessment of such forms of world-disclosure, that can be couched in the form of assent to or rejection of propositionally articulated truth claims, underlies key disputes in contemporary philosophy, as well as informing political and social reflection on cultural goals.

Philosophy which is practised on the basis of theory-building that relies on truth-claims that can be accepted or rejected is confronted with the fact that such claims are inherently contested. The gap between radical eliminative materialists and neo-Hegelian idealists, for example, is huge. The form of many kinds of philosophy dictates that it is couched in propositions which make positive truth claims, but the result is actually anything but positive, and claims to truth of such a kind, unlike those in some areas of warranted natural science, generally do not constitute anything approaching useable knowledge. An analytical reliance on particular arguments about discrete issues generates contradictions, but the way we inhabit the world depends upon our ability to orient ourselves, despite the contradictions that arise both between different people's interpretations and between one's own interpretations of specific issues. The holistic approaches of hermeneutics are based on the sense that our understanding is dependent on being involved in contexts where such contradictions are unavoidable. When Heidegger says that mathematics is not stricter than history, because the existential foundations of history are so much wider (Heidegger 1979: 153), he points to the need for ways of making and grasping sense that are not essentially manifest in discrete propositions, but rather in connections between differing forms of expression and assertion, which he comes to see as manifest in literature and the other arts. Mikhail Bakhtin sees novels as 'polyphonic': they make us negotiate conflicts of perspective and realise that human existence is defined by living with differences which may never be finally resolved, but which can also enrich our relations to the world and each other. This negotiation can affect how we conceive of philosophy itself. Karl Ameriks talks of:

> understanding, in a non-subjectivistic way, how the writing of philosophy in a historical manner can be like a kind of 'art' as well, especially insofar as … such writing aims to incorporate a stylistically effective, as well as at least partially persuasive, interpretation of the (often tragic) 'play' of recent history of philosophy.
>
> (Ameriks 2013)

Heidegger says of the way his *Kant and the Problem of Metaphysics* can be seen as distorting the meaning of Kant's thought that it is 'an attempt to ponder the unsaid, instead of codifying what Kant said. What is said is meagre, what is not said is full of riches' (Heidegger 1973: 249). Given the illuminations Heidegger offers concerning Kant, philosophy itself may, then, as Rorty maintains, really be a kind of literature.

The key to a hermeneutic approach to philosophy and its connections to literature is the idea that philosophy, rather than predominantly seeking to increase knowledge, a job the modern sciences perform far more effectively, should open up ways of making new sense and of recovering lost sense. That is why the kind of attempts to regulate interpretation and 'cultural literacy' with which I began are so questionable. The false objectivism implicit in Hirsch's approaches can be questioned via Schleiermacher's expression of admiration for children's powers of language acquisition:

> it seems to me that we only smile at the wrong uses that children make of the elements of language they have acquired – which they not infrequently

make only via too much logical consistency – in order to console ourselves for or revenge ourselves on this preponderance of an energy which we ourselves no longer possess.

(Schleiermacher 1977: 327)

That energy for making new sense of the world is in danger of being lost if philosophical attention to interpretation remains, as it too often does in analytical philosophy, at the level of trying to establish the semantics of already well understood individual assertions. That is not to say that we learn nothing from such approaches, but the hermeneutic insistence on understanding the world, as a context of conflicting and multiple 'domains of sense' (Gabriel 2011), demands that we also cultivate ways of comprehending complex interrelations between different domains, of the kind that characterise significant literature.

Bibliography

Ameriks, K. (2013) 'History, Idealism, and Schelling', MS.

Benjamin, W. (1980) *Gesammelte Schriften* I.1, Frankfurt: Suhrkamp.

Birus, H. (1982) *Hermeneutische Positionen*, Göttingen: Vandenhoek and Ruprecht.

Bowie, A. (1997) *From Romanticism to Critical Theory*, London, New York: Routledge.

——(2007) *Music, Philosophy, and Modernity*, Cambridge: Cambridge University Press.

Brandom, Robert (1994) *Making it Explicit*, Cambridge Mass., and London: Harvard University Press.

Dilthey, Wilhelm (1990) *Die Geistige Welt. Einleitung in die Philosophie des Lebens*, Gesammelte Schriften Vol. 5, Stuttgart: Teubner.

Gabriel, M. (2011) *Transcendental Ontology. Studies in German Idealism*, London: Continuum. Kindle edition.

Gadamer, Hans-Georg (1975) *Wahrheit und Methode*, Tübingen: J.C.B. Mohr.

——(1993) *Ästhetik und Poetik I. Kunst als Aussage*, Tübingen: J.C.B. Mohr.

Heidegger, Martin (1973) *Kant und das Problem der Metaphysik*, Frankfurt: Klostermann.

——(1979) *Sein und Zeit*, Tübingen: Niemeyer.

Hirsch, E.D. (1967) *Validity in Interpretation*, New Haven: Yale University Press.

Kant, Immanuel (1968) *Kritik der reinen Vernunft* (CPR), Werkausgabe III and IV, Frankfurt: Suhrkamp.

Kitcher, P. (2013) *Preludes to Pragmatism*, Oxford: Oxford University Press.

Schlegel, Friedrich (1988) *Kritische Schriften und Fragmente 1–6*, Paderborn: Ferdinand Schöningh.

Schleiermacher, F.D.E. (1842) *Vorlesungen über die Ästhetik*, Berlin, Reimer.

——(1942) *Friedrich Schleiermachers Dialektik*, ed. Rudolf Odebrecht, Leipzig: Hinrichs.

——(1977) *Hermeneutik und Kritik*, ed. Manfred Frank, Frankfurt: Suhrkamp.

Wittgenstein, Ludwig (1971) *Philosophische Untersuchungen*, Frankfurt: Suhrkamp.

35

HERMENEUTICS, RELIGION, AND GOD

Jean Greisch

In the first of his *Speeches on Religion* (1799), Friedrich Schleiermacher, the father of philosophical hermeneutics, presents himself as a virtuoso interpreter of the religious soul, the only interpreter capable of understanding religion as it wants to be understood. Those who lack Schleiermacher's genius or his audacity and who want nevertheless to understand in which sense religion and its discourse about God is a core hermeneutical phenomenon, are well advised to consult the long history of hermeneutics covering two thousand years. Of course, the realm of hermeneutics must not be reduced to religion alone, for Hermes, who gave his name to "hermeneutics" is not only the messenger of the divine; he is also the god of travellers, diplomats, and outlaws.

For this inquiry, drawing on some of Heidegger's insights in his *Phenomenology of Religious Life*, I propose to focus on four themes: "inspiration", "sacred texts", historicity", and "traditionality". A draft stanza of Friedrich Hölderlin's *Friedensfeier* (1801) can serve to highlight the most pertinent issues:

> Humans have experienced much,
> and named many of the heavenly ones,
> since we are a dialogue
> and able to listen to one another.

If we take the word "experience" (*Erfahrung*) in its most genuine sense, experiences are not made, initiated, or controlled by ourselves, but they are events that we undergo and that *transform* us more or less radically. Taken in this hermeneutical and historical sense, our experiences of the divine, the world, others, and ourselves are manifold and impossible to reduce to the unity of a single discipline. The same is true of the names that humans have invented in order to speak of gods and the divine. Both the experiences and the names are deposited in *traditions* that we have inherited and that still determine our life-forms and ways of existing.

If language is not just one semiotic structure among others, but takes body as a "dialogue" (*Gespräch*), enabling us not just to receive and emit messages but to truly speak to each other, then far from being a mere instrument of communication, it constitutes our very being. It constitutes us as a community in converse with one another and with the divine. The last line of Hölderlin's stanza indicates that the capacity to speak is inseparable from the capacity to listen; indeed it suggests that listening comes before speaking. That makes sense from a hermeneutical point of view: there is no understanding without a prior listening.

I. Divinatory rationality and hermeneutical intelligence

The first philosopher to ponder the problems raised by the different skills of interpretation practised in his culture was Plato, who dedicated one of his dialogues, the *Ion*, to this question. Socrates submits Ion, who prides himself on being not only a genial reciter but also an incomparable commentator of the great poets, especially Homer, to a severe cross-examination. The interpreter's virtuosity is a "divine gift" (*theia moira*), but precisely for this reason, it must not be confused with a technique or a science (*episteme*).

Plato's critique of the poetic *hermeneia*, and the way he separates the voices of inspired poetry and of rational discourse (see Nancy 1984), applies also to "mantics", the art of divination practised in the temple of Apollo and elsewhere in Greece. In order to identify the opportune time (*kairos*) for engaging in risky ventures, for instance declaring a war or founding a new colony, one should "consult" the numinous powers that manifest themselves in oracles. This is a strategy for bringing chance under control as far as possible, an archaic form of *Kontingenzbewältigung* ("mastering contingency"), which according to Niklas Luhmann defines the social function of religion.

Gods are supposed to send signs and messages to the mortals. The understanding of these signs is never obvious. This explains why in one form or another divination has existed in all great civilizations. Oracles and prophecies play a fundamental role in many religions, and their interpretation becomes a complex science. The Delphic Pythia was allowed to divagate, but her ramblings were not considered as mere mumbo-jumbo. They were on the contrary submitted to a specially trained college of experts: the *hosioi* or "theologians". Even in Voodoo-cults at least one "theologian" is necessary in order to discern which god is riding the soul of the adept, when he or she falls into a trance. The techniques of interpretation that come along with "mantics" have prompted some anthropologists speak of "divinatory intelligence" (see Vernant et al. 1974), differently developed in Africa, China, and Greece.

Philosophical rationality that focuses on the questions "what?" and "why?" favours an understanding of reality in terms of cause–effect relationships. Knowing "how" to deal with events and situations (which is the primary meaning of the *Verstehen* that Heidegger and Gadamer put forward) is another way of addressing reality, akin to what ancient Chinese thinkers designated by the key-term *Dao*, the Way (see Cheng 1997). Divination, in this tradition, is "the daughter of religion and not of magic" (ibid., 48). The *Yijing*, or *Book of Changes* is a handbook of divinatory hermeneutics that has always been taken as a contribution to "philosophy". A philosophical hermeneutics that keeps in mind intercultural and interreligious horizons will ponder the wisdom that underlies its subtle understanding of universal change. Far from leading back to an opportunistic "anything goes", according to a commentator akin to Mencius it deals with the fact that everything has "roots and branches" and that events finish only to start again.

"The Lord whose is the oracle at Delphi neither utters nor hides his meaning (*oute legei, oute kryptei*), but shows it by a sign (*alla sémainei*)" says Heraclitus (Fr.93 – Kirk and Raven 2003: 211). In pointing to the "oracular" dimension of religion, Heraclitus, unlike many today, does not see religion as an instrument for generating meaning, but rather as a producer of signs that need to be interpreted. The fact that the Delphic oracle does not speak in rational discourse does not mean that it is mute; it simply belongs to another register of expressions than those of philosophy whose *organon* is the *logos*. Philosophers are strongly tempted to reject such a discourse as being cryptic, esoteric, or theosophical, with the effect that the corresponding hermeneutics is doomed to be hermetic.

Plato's attitude to the ancient mantic art of interpretation is not so rationalistic and dismissive. When he presents divination (*mantikê*) as a sort of madness (*manikê*), he might appear to urge the replacement of these archaic understandings by an entirely rational vision. But he does not class madness (*mania*) with mere ignorance (*amathia*); there are at least four varieties of madness that are "divine gifts": the art of divination (*mantikê*), the gift of Apollo; *telestic madness*, the gift of Dionysos, used in Orphic rites of purification and initiation; *poetic madness*, inspired by the Muses, whose "victims" are the poets and their interpreters; *erotic madness*, the gift of Aphrodite. In addition, philosophy itself is called a sort of madness.

In stating that the true poets do not know what they say, that their interpreters do not know what they do, and that their listeners do not know what they experience, Plato established for more than a millennium the boundaries between hermeneutics and philosophy. This does not mean however, that he intended to banish interpreters of all sorts from the city. He aimed rather to rationalize as far as possible the irrational that has its source in the realm of the divine and that never ceases to challenge the defenders of philosophical *logos*. This explains why some Neoplatonic philosophers took great interest in Chaldaic oracles and why Iamblichus envisioned in his *De mysteriis* ritual actions as a sort of "theurgy", that is, as actions whose true subject is the Divine itself.

II. Philosophical issues in scriptural interpretation

A second major field of investigation for studying the relationship between religion and hermeneutics is the existence of "sacred" texts that induce specific processes of reading and interpretation in the religious communities that acknowledge these texts as founding their own identity. Is there a rational basis for the authority of texts that believers read as the "Word of God" and that are supposed to be "inspired" by the Holy Spirit? Can the human and historical texture of the composition, reception, and interpretation of Scripture be reconciled with the claim that it is also the Word of God?

Historically, the full meaning of Scripture unfolded as it was embraced by the whole community, and the labour of interpreting it became coterminous with the deepest religious and philosophical questions of the community. Thus Emmanuel Levinas speaks of a "Judaism received from a living tradition and nourished by the reflection upon severe texts that are more living than life itself" (Levinas ³1979: 9). In modern times, as Paul Ricœur notes, there has been a reciprocal interplay between philosophical and biblical hermeneutics.

The concept of interpretation that underlies the traditional exegesis of the Bible works with five axioms or orientations that challenge us to find their equivalents under the conditions of modernity:

1. "The Great Code"

Paul's discourse to the citizens of Athens initiated a new age of hermeneutics. Hermes, who up to then was in charge of the ministry of "communication" now became the minister of truth. The task was no longer to reconstruct as accurately as possible the thoughts of the biblical writers, but rather to translate their message into the language of other periods and cultures with their new horizons of expectation.

Although each monotheistic religion has developed its own hermeneutics, they have in common the principle of a plural reading of the "Book of Books" in which Message and Law are inseparable. Adapting William Blake's dictum that "the Old and New Testaments are the great code of art", Northrop Frye recounts how the Bible became the ultimate key of all understanding, the book of life, an inexhaustible treasury of meaning, supplying an encompassing interpretation of the world and leaving out no aspect of human existence (see Frye 2002). The interpretation of such a book must aim at a comparable comprehensiveness and diversity.

Sacrae Scripturae interpretatio infinita est, Scotus Eriugena (1865b, II, 20, 560A) claimed. He established a correspondence between potential infinity of biblical interpretation and God's own infinity. The "anticipation of completeness" that according to Gadamer is presupposed in all understanding means in that case that even where the Scripture speaks of purely mundane matters, as in Leviticus or Proverbs, in the context of the Great Code these must have a deeper, hidden meaning. Even the most material details of the book (the graphic form of the Hebrew letters, the disposition of the text on the scroll, the repetition of a word or a series of numbers) may have a hidden meaning that becomes accessible if one uses the appropriate key of understanding. Some forms of exegesis, especially in the Kabbalah, read the slightest details as a mystical cipher reflecting the abysmal infinity of God.

2. "Rota in medio rotae"

The plural reading of the Scripture does not form a static hierarchy of meanings; it must be understood as a dynamic process. This explains why the major theoreticians of the fourfold meaning of the Scripture, such as Gregory the Great, link this process to the *perpetuum mobile* of the *Merkabah* envisioned by the prophet Ezekiel. The four living beings who draw the chariot represent the four levels of meaning, summarized in the famous distich: "*Littera* gesta docet, quid credas *allegoria / moralis* quid agas, quid speres *anagogia*" (The letter tells what was done, allegory what is to be believed, the moral what you should do, and anagogy what you may hope).

Similarly, in Talmudic tradition, the four rivers that bathe the Garden of Eden (Gen 2:10–14) signify the literal meaning (*pchat*), prolonged by the allusive meaning (*remez*), the interpretation (*drach*), and the hidden meaning (*sod*). The to-and-fro between different levels is an elaborate hermeneutical circle in which advance on one level of understanding prompts breakthroughs on other levels. In modern times, closer study of the literary historical sense has tended to undercut traditional allegories, but this generates the demand for a comprehensive theological vision of the sense of Scripture that might be a rough equivalent of what the ancient system provided.

3. "Scriptura cum legentibus crescit"

Pondering the vision of the *Merkabah*, Gregory the Great formulated another axiom of this hermeneutics: *Scriptura cum legentibus crescit*, "Scripture grows with its readers" (Bori 1991: 38–9). He imaged Scripture as a great river that sheep can cross without danger and in which elephants can bathe. This entails more than the scholastic axiom: *quidquid recipitur ad modum recipientis recipitur* (whatever is received is received in the manner of the receiver). Gregory suggests that there are several ages of understanding. The same text speaks differently to us according to our human and spiritual maturity. The infantilism of some readings is due not to the text itself, but to its readers.

While many would say that Scripture has shrunk with the advance of modern knowledge, it can also be seen as growing in new ways with its readers. Our greater sense of its historical, theological, and literary diversity, in its interconnections with ancient cultures, and our awareness of non-Christian sacred texts, has made reading Scripture a broader human adventure, which must lay the basis for a deeper spiritual vision as well.

4. God's two Books

Contrary to speculative mysticism, such as Eckhart's, that stresses the insurmountable limits of human language, traditional scriptural hermeneutics took creation itself to be the primary language through which God speaks to humans, and read Creation and Scripture as two sources of divine self-revelation, referring each to the other. Indeed the testimony of Scripture itself is what enabled its readers to understand Creation as a great theophany. In the Renaissance, a period that Michel Foucault characterized as the age of universal resemblance (see Foucault 1966: 32–91), various hermetic strategies enriched the interplay between the two Books, making it necessary to find safeguards that would prevent this hermeneutics from "going wild".

5. "Novum in Vetere latet, Vetus in Novo patet"

The Hebrew Bible is the fruit of a ceaseless rereading and reinterpretation of ancient traditions, producing new effects of meaning (for instance the Deuteronomistic reading of the Exodus, with its strong insistence upon the "today" of salvation). Christian hermeneutics relays this long and complex process of interpretation, but it gives it an entirely new turn. The New Testament scriptures would never have come into existence without the powerful impulse of the motif of the "fulfillment of the Scriptures". The coexistence of two Testaments was never evident. From Marcion to the "German Christians" at the time of Hitler, there were numerous attempts to get rid of the embarrassing inheritance of the Old Testament. The mainstream of orthodox Christianity has resisted these temptations, claiming with St Augustine: "The New is hidden in the Old, the Old is exposed in the New." This formula establishes a vital link not between two groups of texts, but between the old texts and a new event: the historical figure of Jesus Christ who is the ultimate key of understanding of the Scriptures. According to Martin Luther, the Christian understanding of the Scriptures must be Christocentric or it will miss its mark. In the prologue of the Gospel of John, the term "exegesis" (*exegêsato*) does not refer to the interpretation of a text. For humanity, the Word is the only truthful interpreter of the Father and his interpretation is contained in the circumstances of his life and his death.

Contrary to appearances, the "mystical mill" represented on a famous sculpture in Vézelay has not yet come to a standstill, either in Christianity or in other religious traditions. Rather than set up a competition between the traditional interpretations and the methods of modern historico-critical exegesis, we should ask whether these readings are just an obstacle for modern hermeneutical consciousness, or whether they can still prompt reflection. The tension between the letter and the spirit that has often marked the history of scriptural interpretation re-emerges today in the question whether the tribute that believers pay to historical consciousness condemns them to read the Bible as a book located only in the past, or whether the emphasis should be placed rather on how scriptural texts, appropriately selected, can speak to the worshiping community with authority and spiritual power.

Since the religious crisis of the sixteenth century, the founding text of Christian faith has become the field of a sometimes bloody "conflict of interpretations", a "confessional civil war" (O. Marquard). In 1512, Martin Luther entered a passionate plea for church reform through renouncing fables and focusing upon the pure Gospel and its interpretation. This led him progressively to denounce allegorical interpretations that overshadowed the literal meaning, the only source of life and consolation; though in his own massive Genesis commentary he indulges many allegorical readings. From the beginning to the end, the Bible speaks for itself and its understanding does not require the wormy crutches of tradition. Scripture is its own interpreter (*Scriptura sacra sui ipsius interpres*).

As Dilthey noted, this maxim does not indicate how the Scripture itself, the community of readers, and the inner light of understanding can be related to each other. In his *Clavis scripturae sacrae* (1567), Matthias Flacius Illyricus endeavoured to formulate secure criteria of interpretation allowing one to understand obscure or contentious verses without referring to the authority of tradition. His golden rule was the circle of the whole and the part and the consideration of the principal aim (*scopus*) of the text. Flacius thus draws our attention to the literary unity of the Bible, recently rediscovered by literary critics like Northrop Frye and emphasized by canonical critics such as Brevard Childs.

"I must bark against philosophy in order to foster the Holy Scripture", wrote Luther. Although there is greatness in his barkings, the caravan of modern philosophy, led by Descartes, pursued its way. In Descartes' caravan, we find not only

philosophers and scientists, but also victims of religious persecutions such as Soci-
nians and Arminians, eager to justify Christian faith confronted with the challenge
of modern rationality, summarized in the metaphor of the "light of natural reason",
a metaphor that tends to fuse with the idea of "natural religion".

Louis Meyer's famous book: *Philosophy as the interpreter of the Holy Scripture* (1666)
is the first important attempt to subject the Bible to the Cartesian idea of reason.
Asking that the interpreter make use of his reason in order to establish the true
meaning of a verse is not enough. He must also check whether this meaning is not
contradictory to the philosophical truths that the Cartesian rule of evidence helps us
to discover. If Luther's *Sola Scriptura* transformed the Bible into one great burning
bush, according to Meyer the clarity that we discover in Scripture cannot match that
of clear and distinct ideas. He knew that if philosophy and not theology is taken as
the only reliable guide for interpreting Scripture, Scripture itself risks becoming
increasingly superfluous, resembling a Spanish hostel where philosophical travellers
consume the picnic that they have brought along with them.

Baruch Spinoza (1632–77) found a better solution, showing what our salvation,
that is, our bliss and liberty consists in: a "constant and eternal love of God or
God's love for humans" (Spinoza 1999: V, 36sc.). Spinoza resisted the notion that
the only way of acceding to the light of Revelation was to hold in contempt reason
itself. But contrary to Meyer he endeavoured to clarify the relationship between two
complementary ways of salvation: religion and philosophy. Since everybody has the
right to read and to interpret the Bible, the only norm of its interpretation is the
natural light of reason common to all. In thus "naturalizing" the rules for interpreting the Bible Spinoza confronts all following generations, up to today, with a very
tricky problem: can a text that is scrutinized in the cold and clinical light of natural
reason still speak to us, or must we reject the very idea of a "Word of God" as being
the matrix of all superstition?

III. Religious and historical consciousness

At the beginning of the nineteenth century, hermeneutics understood as the art of
interpretation underwent a major paradigm shift (see Laks and Neschke-Hentschke
1991). In the writings of Friedrich August Wolf (1759–1824), Friedrich Ast (1778–
1841), Friedrich Schlegel (1722–1829), and above all of Friedrich Schleiermacher,
hermeneutics became the *art of understanding*. It acquired a new and universal
dimension, requiring thorough philosophical analysis of the experience of understanding and misunderstanding. This brought a new account of the relationship
between biblical hermeneutics and general hermeneutics. In his *Lessons on hermeneutics* Schleiermacher states clearly that we must not start with the principle that
"inspired" texts require specific rules of interpretation, for only if we understand
them correctly do we discover in what sense they are inspired.

The new paradigm gave birth to a genuine *philosophical hermeneutic* pioneered by
Wilhelm Dilthey (1833–1911). In the first half of the nineteenth century a new
epistemological continent emerged: the "human sciences", first of all history, followed by psychology, sociology, and the sciences of religion. Dilthey worked out a

"critique of historical reason" that sought a similar role to these sciences as that of Kant in regard to Newtonian physics. He saw the new sciences as sharing the method of understanding as opposed to the method of explanation proper to natural science. History, rather than natural science, opens onto the depths of human reality, and a philosophy that seeks to understand all expressions of life itself that manifest themselves in the historical world is a hermeneutical enterprise on the largest scale. From Leopold von Ranke he inherited the idea that the fundamental vocation of the historian is to understand the hidden intentions of divine Providence at work in history. Historical consciousness confronts us with the finitude of all historical phenomena, of all human and social affairs, and also with the relativity of all beliefs. Instead of viewing this as a mortal danger, Dilthey celebrates the liberation of life from abstract concepts and the spider's webs of dogmatic thinking.

Nor does historical consciousness endanger genuine religious feelings. On the contrary, like Schleiermacher, Dilthey holds that religious experience will forever constitute the most intimate secret of the human soul. The objects of understanding in the realm of religious consciousness are its objective manifestations such as texts, rites, customs, and life-forms. In his late writings, Dilthey focused on the productions of the collective spirit crystalized in language, myths, traditions, mores, laws, and institutions. But contrary to Hegel, who considered art, religion, and philosophy as manifestations of the absolute Spirit, Dilthey views them as the historical manifestations of the objective Spirit. Although he acknowledges that religion has a specific and central role in the realm of the objective Spirit, he never ceased to struggle with the difficulty of attuning his historical approach, vowed to a perpetual comparatism, with the dogmatic presuppositions of Christian faith.

The great problems that a hermeneutical approach of religion has to confront are those of the general value of religion as such, the relationships of historical religions, their truth-claims, and the religious future of humanity. In promoting a new understanding of religious experience, Dilthey was one of the creators of a new model of philosophy of religion that prevailed during the twentieth century (see Jung 1999: 19). Eager to understand life as it understands itself, he confronts us with the problem of the relationship between the facticity of life and the religious experience of the Absolute.

IV. Cultural and religious tradition

Since the Enlightenment the authority of all traditions has been weakened, and they are exposed to the suspicion of representing a heteronomy incompatible with the subject's right to self-determination. This critical dismissal is subjected to a metacritical cross-examination in Hans-Georg Gadamer's *Truth and Method*. Contrary to Dilthey's hermeneutics, which made too many concessions to historical consciousness, stressing perpetual changes and overlooking the continuity of the cultural traditions that constitute our true hermeneutical universe, Gadamer endeavours to discern in the realms of art, history, and language truth-experiences that vindicate the universality of philosophical hermeneutics.

Although he does not explicitly address the truth-claims of religion, his critique of an abstract aesthetic consciousness that severs works of art from everyday life, consigning them to the museum, can be prolonged in a similar critique of an abstract religious consciousness that focuses exclusively on the inner feelings of the religious subject, the *sensus numinis*, the "feeling of absolute dependency", and so on. If our experience of art cannot become a securely established knowledge that makes the encounter with the work of art superfluous, the same holds true for religious experience. In both cases, we are transformed by the experience that obliges us to ponder the mode of being of that which we encounter.

Religion plays an irreplaceable role in what Kant called the "great game of life" in which we all take part in some way or another. Thus liturgical action confronts the participants with a truth that has no common measure in the subjective performance of the celebrants. Speaking of a "genial" preacher or celebrant is absurd, because the cultic game is only meaningful for those who view it as a real encounter with the divine. Liturgical celebrations as well as kerygmatic proclamations confront us with the same fundamental hermeneutical problem: their understanding requires a "total mediation".

But is our historical consciousness compatible with the hypothesis of such mediations? Many things depend upon our understanding of historicity. Contrary to what some critics of Gadamer suspect, his rehabilitation of prejudgements and authority is not equivalent to a softer version of a traditionalism similar to that of Louis de Bonald or Joseph de Maistre in the nineteenth century. If our prejudgements much more than our judgements constitute our historical reality, history does not belong to us, but we belong to it.

Of course, the modes of this belonging are not the same in the case of cultural and religious traditions. But in both cases, we are confronted with the question of the *hermeneutical fecundity of temporal distance*. The simplistic opposition between two understandings of temporal distance, the one that puts forward an unbroken continuity guaranteed by the sameness of tradition and the other that is fascinated by the "awful abyss" of time that engulfs all continuity, must give way to the idea that an event needs time in order to reveal its true meaning. Instead of making us prisoners of our world-view, our hermeneutic awareness operates a permanent "fusion of horizons", in which the past and the present are integrated and in which our present experiences open out to new and forthcoming experiences.

Our cultural and religious memories confront us with a language that speaks to us, prior to our own speech. This does not mean that we have to subscribe blindly to what traditions tell us. Gadamer uses an image borrowed from Rilke: hermeneutical understanding is a game in which an "eternal Partner" throws a ball – the ball of truth – that we have to catch as skilfully as possible and that we are also able to throw back. In developing our capacity for religious understanding (see Ricœur 2013: 415–43), we do well, as Jean Nabert suggests, not to focus too narrowly upon the topic of "God", but to work out a "criteriology of the divine", inseparable from a hermeneutics of the testimonies of the Absolute that manifest themselves from time to time in the darkness of human history (see Nabert [2]1996).

Bibliography

Bori, P.C. (1991) *L'interprétation infinie. L'herméneutique chrétienne ancienne et ses transformations*, Paris: Cerf.

Cheng, A. (1997) *Histoire de la pensée chinoise*, Paris: Seuil.

Eriugena, Johannes Scotus (1865) *De divisione naturae*, PL 122.

Flacius, Matthias (1567) *Clavis scripturae sacrae*.

Foucault, M. (1966) *Les mots et les choses. Une archéologie des sciences humaines*, Paris: Gallimard.

Frye, N. (2002) *The Great Code. The Bible and Literature*, Boston, MA: Mariner Books.

Jung, M. (1999) *Erfahrung und Religion. Grundzüge einer hermeneutisch-pragmatischen Religionsphilosophie*, Freiburg: Alber.

Kirk, G.S. and Raven, J.E. (2003) *The Presocratic Philosophers*, Cambridge: Cambridge Univerity Press.

Laks, A. and Neschke-Hentschke, A. (eds) (1991) *La naissance du paradigme herméneutique. Schleiermacher, Humboldt, Boeckh, Droysen*, Lille: Presses universitaires de Lille.

Levinas, Emmanuel (^{3}1979) *Difficile liberté. Essais sur le judaïsme*. Paris: Livre de poche.

Meyer, L. (1988) *La philosophie interprète de l'Écriture Sainte*, trans. J. Lagrée and P.-F. Moreau, Paris: Intertextes Editeur.

Nancy, J.-L. (1984) *Le partage des voix*, Paris: Galilée.

Nabert, J. (^{2}1996) *Le désir de Dieu*, Paris: Cerf.

Ricœur, P. (2013) *Le destinataire de la religion: l'homme capable*, in *Anthropologie philosophique*, Paris: Seuil: 415–43.

Spinoza, B. (1999) *Œuvres III, Traité théologico-politique*, trans. J. Lagrée and P.-F. Moreau, Paris: Presses universitaires de France.

Vernant, J.-P. et al. (eds) (1974) *Divination et Rationalité*, Paris: Seuil.

Further reading

Beauchamp, P. (1976) *L'un et l'autre Testament*, vol. I: *Essais de lecture*, Paris: Seuil.

——(1990) *L'un et l'autre Testament*, vol. II: *Accomplir les Écritures*, Paris: Seuil.

Belaval, Y. and Bourel, D. (eds) (1986) *Le siècle des Lumières et la Bible*, Paris: Beauchêne.

Brinkmann, H. (1980) *Mittelalterliche Hermeneutik*, Darmstadt: Wissenschaftliche Buchgesellschaft.

Bühler, A. (ed.) (1994) *Unzeitgemässe Hermeneutik. Verstehen und Interpretation im Denken der Aufklärung*, Frankfurt: Klostermann.

Bühler, A. and Cataldi Madonna, L. (eds) (1994) *Hermeneutik der Aufklärung*, Hamburg: Meiner.

Chalier, C. (1996) *L'inspiration du philosophe. "L'amour de la sagesse" et sa source prophétique*, Paris: Albin Michel.

Childs, B.S. (1994) *Biblical Theology of the Old and New Testaments*, New York: Augsburg Fortress.

De Lubac, H. (1959–64) *Exégèse médiévale. Les quatre sens de l'Écriture*, 4 vols, Paris: Aubier.

De Saint-Victor, H. (1991) *L'Art de lire. Didascalicon*, Paris: Cerf.

Ebeling, G. (1942, 3rd edn 1993) *Evangelische Evangelienauslegung. Eine Untersuchung zu Luthers Hermeneutik*, Tübingen: Mohr.

——(1964) *Wort Gottes und Tradition. Studien zu einer Hermeneutik der Konfessionen*, Göttingen: Vandenhoeck & Ruprecht.

Eco, U. (1990) *The Limits of Interpretation*, Bloomington: Indiana University Press.

Frei, H. (1974) *The Eclipse of Biblical Narrative. A Study in 18th and 19th Century Hermeneutics*, New Haven, CT: Yale University Press.

Gadamer, H.G. (2004) *Truth and Method*, London: Continuum.

Greisch, J. (2002a) *Le Buisson ardent et les Lumières de la raison*, vol. I: *Héritages et héritiers du XIXe siècle*, Paris: Cerf.

——(2002b) *Le Buisson ardent et les Lumières de la raison*, vol. II: *Les approches phénoménologiques et analytiques*, Paris: Cerf.

——(2004) *Le Buisson ardent et les Lumières de la raison*, vol. III: *Vers un paradigme herméneutique*, Paris: Cerf.

——(2006) *Entendre d'une autre oreille. Les enjeux philosophiques de l'herméneutique biblique*, Paris: Bayard.

Grondin, J. (1993a) *L'universalité de l'herméneutique*, Paris: Presses Universitaires de France.

——(1993b) *L'horizon herméneutique de la pensée contemporaine*, Paris: Vrin.

——(1994) *Der Sinn für Hermeneutik*, Darmstadt: Wissenschaftliche Buchgesellschaft.

Heidegger, M. (2004) *The Phenomology of Religious Life*, Bloomington: Indiana University Press.

Hinske, N. (ed.) (1989) *Zentren der Aufklärung I: Halle – Aufklärung und Pietismus*, Heidelberg: Schneider.

Jullien, F. (1993) *Figures de l'immanence. Pour une lecture philosophique du Yi King, le classique du changement*, Paris: Grasset.

Kolakowski, L. (1969) *Chrétiens sans Eglise. La conscience religieuse et le lien confessionnel au XVIIe siècle*, Paris: Gallimard.

Lagrée, J. (1991) *La Raison ardente*, Paris: Vrin.

Lagrée, J. et al. (1992) *L'Écriture Sainte au temps de Spinoza et dans le système spinoziste* (*Travaux et documents du Groupe de Recherches Spinozistes*, n°4), Paris: Presses de l'Université Paris-Sorbonne.

Moretto, G. (1997) *La dimensione religiosa in Gadamer*, Brescia: Queriniana.

Neusner, J. (1981) *Judaism. The Evidence of the Mishnah*, Chicago, IL: The University of Chicago Press.

——(1985) *The Oral Torah. The Sacred Books of Judaism*, San Francisco, CA: Harper & Row.

——(1986) *Judaism in the Matrix of Christianity*, Philadelphia, PA: Fortress Press.

——(1987) *Christian Faith and the Bible of Judaism. The Judaic Encounter with Scripture*, Grand Rapids, MI: Eerdmans.

——(1991) *Jews and Christians. The Myth of a Common Tradition*, London: SCM Press.

Ohly, F. (1958, 2nd edn 1980), *Vom geistigen Sinn des Wortes im Mittelalter*, Darmstadt: Wissenschaftliche Buchgesellschaft.

Pelican, J. (1984) *The Vindication of Tradition*, New Haven, CT: Yale University Press.

Reventlow, H. (1990) *Epochen der Bibelauslegung*, vol. I: *Vom Alten Testament bis Origines*, Munich: C.H. Beck.

——(1994) *Epochen der Bibelauslegung*, vol. II: *Von der Spätantike bis zum ausgehenden Mittelalter*, Munich: C.H. Beck.

——(1997) *Epochen der Bibelauslegung*, vol. III: *Renaissance, Reformation, Humanismus*, Munich: C.H. Beck.

——(2001) *Epochen der Bibelauslegung*, vol. IV: *Von der Aufklärung bis zum 20. Jahrhundert*, Munich, C.H. Beck.

Risser, J. (1997) *Hermeneutics and the Voice of the Other. Re-reading Gadamer's Philosophical Hermeneutics*, Albany, NY: SUNY Press.

Scholder, K. (1966) *Ursprünge und Probleme der Bibelkritik im 17. Jahrhundert. Ein Beitrag zur Entstehung der historisch-kritischen Theologie*, Munich: Kaiser.

Scholz, O.R. (1999) *Verstehen und Rationalität. Untersuchungen zu den Grundlagen von Hermeneutik und Sprachphilosophie*, Frankfurt a.M.: Klostermann.

Strauss, L. (1930, 2nd edn 1981), *Die Religionskritik Spinozas als Grundlage seiner Bibelwissenschaft. Untersuchungen zu Spinozas Theologisch-Politischem Traktat,* Darmstadt: Wissenschaftliche Buchgesellschaft.

Voderholzer, R. (1998) *Die Einheit der Schrift und ihr geistlicher Sinn. Der Beitrag Henri de Lubacs zur Erforschung von Geschichte und Systematik christlicher Bibelhermeneneutik,* Einsiedeln: Johannes Verlag.

Warnke, G. (1987) *Gadamer. Hermeneutics, Tradition and Reason,* Cambridge: Blackwell.

Zac, S. (1965) *Spinoza. L'interprétation de l'Écriture,* Paris: Presses Universitaires de France.

36

HERMENEUTICS, JURISPRUDENCE AND LAW

Ralf Poscher

"Legal interpretation takes place in a field of pain and death." Robert Cover's opening sentence of "Violence and the Word" (Cover 1986) became the famous line that it is because it captures what is so distinctive about legal hermeneutics: Hermeneutics in law can be a matter of life and death, freedom and incarceration, the powers of presidents and parliaments, the validity of elections, exclusion and inclusion, discrimination and equality and any other question that is in need of an ultimate decision – and it is always backed by institutions that wield the ultimate physical power of the police and armed forces. Legal hermeneutics not only contributes to an ongoing debate, it also has immediate real world consequences beyond the text, thereby shaping not only individual lives but also societies and their self-understanding. The burden of legitimation that comes with these far-reaching immediate consequences outside the texts might explain why general questions about hermeneutics – its truth aptness, its scientific character, its methodological status – are so pressing for judges, lawyers and legal scholars. It might explain on the one hand the special sensitivity that legal hermeneutics has displayed throughout history towards grasping the different kinds of activities involved in it, and on the other its difficulties in accepting the different roles played by the interpreter. The following will give a brief overview of some historical and contemporary jurisprudential accounts of and controversies over the different activities involved in legal hermeneutics. It entertains the possibility that the distinctions central to discussions of legal hermeneutics might shed some light on hermeneutics in general.

Since the first modern reflections on legal hermeneutics, a distinction of which legal scholars have been acutely aware is that between legal interpretation and legal construction. Already in his 1809 lectures on legal methodology Carl Friedrich von Savigny distinguished between legal interpretation and "Fortbildung des Rechts" that is, the doctrinal development of the law (see Savigny 1993: 150; Savigny 1867: § 50). Three years before Savigny published his methodological teachings in 1840 (Savigny 1867), Francis Lieber's seminal essay "On Political Hermeneutics, or on Political Interpretation and Construction" appeared in the *American Jurist and Law Magazine* (Lieber 1837). Lieber, too, distinguished – even more sharply than

Savigny – between two hermeneutical activities, which he called legal interpretation and legal construction.

> Lawyers frequently call both construction; divines, on the other hand, use the word interpretation for both. It appears, however, that the distinction is founded in the nature of the subject … If we are desirous of avoiding confusion of ideas, let us avoid confusion of words.
>
> (Lieber 1837: 56)

Ever since then, we can see the hermeneutical debate in law as being organized around this distinction (e.g. for a contemporary discussion Whittington 1999; Solum 2010; Barnett 2011). It is thus worth considering each of its elements separately before attending to their complex interrelations.

1. Legal interpretation

Historically, one of the most stringent accounts of legal interpretation has been provided by Lieber. For Lieber, interpretation must aim at what he calls the "true meaning" of the law: "Interpretation … is the discovery and representation of the true meaning of any signs, used to convey certain ideas. The 'true meaning' of any signs is that meaning which those who used them were desirous of expressing" (Lieber 1837: 39 f.). With regard to law, interpretation must aim at the meaning the legal authority was desirous of expressing, even if it does not correspond to the standard meaning of the expression (Lieber 1837: 41). For Lieber, legal interpretation aims to reconstruct the intentions of the legislator. As a means for reconstructing the true meaning of the law, Lieber suggests eight rules of interpretation which center on the rule that interpretation must be carried out in good faith with respect to "what the utterer probably meant" (Lieber 1837: 72).

Like Lieber, Savigny is very much in accord with the Romantic hermeneutics developed at his time by Schlegel, Schleiermacher, Ast and others. In contrast to previous rationalistic approaches, which aimed at a timeless reason embedded in texts, Romantic hermeneutics centered on the individual and historical nature of texts and their authors. Understanding meant empathizing with the author and her time in order to reconstruct what she wanted to express (Savigny 1867: 171). In its structure, Savigny's historical account of the law and legal interpretation stays true to this central element of Romantic hermeneutics, but it is also closely connected to his systematic conception of legal institutions. For Savigny, the law is shaped by legal institutions that reside in the historical spirit of a people. These often implicit legal institutions are the object of study on the part of legal scholars, who bring them to light in a system of law. With their laws, legislators try to formalize some of the legal rules that constitute these legal institutions, but nevertheless rely – more or less consciously – on the legal institutions that legal scholarship can bring to light. Thus the systematic efforts of legal scholars help to make explicit the systematic meaning at which legislators aimed with their legislative acts (Savigny 1867: 37–3, 172 f.). Thus Savigny's interpretation, too, aims at the meaning that the legislator tried to convey with a legal act, but this meaning is enriched with the full systematic content of legal institutions. Despite this rich concept of legal interpretation, in his later writings Savigny accepted – under certain institutional preconditions – the legitimacy of legal construction, which goes beyond legal interpretation in cases where the law is dysfunctional due to inconsistencies or other indeterminacies (Savigny 1867 #1728: § 51).

The basic idea of Lieber's and Savigny's account of legal interpretation as being directed at the meaning that the legislator tried to convey remains a strong current in so-called intentionalist or subjectivist accounts of legal interpretation throughout the nineteenth and twentieth centuries. These accounts insist that the meaning of the law ultimately lies in the intentions of its author, with some accounts being closer to Lieber and some closer to Savigny in stressing the systematic ambitions underlying legislative intent. Given the burden of legitimation in legal hermeneutics, it is easy to see why conceiving it as a reconstruction of legislative intentions is so attractive. If judges – and lawyers in general – merely reconstruct predetermined legislative intentions, they can shift the burden onto the legislator. Especially under democratic auspices, this not only relieves the interpreter of responsibility, but also entails a stronger legitimation of the law.

In contemporary legal theory, intentionalist accounts of legal interpretation rely on the analytical connection between intention and meaning. Drawing on intentionalist accounts in literary theory, they insist that there is no meaning without the ascription of at least some intention. The letters "I love you" drawn in the sand by the ocean waves have no meaning (see Knapp and Benn Michaels 1982: 727). They only gain meaning if we imagine an author connecting an intention to them – like a couple on a romantic walk and one of them stating her or his affection. For intentionalists, the meaning connected with a legal utterance is determined by the communicative intentions of the authority that issued the act (e.g. Alexander and Prakash 2004; Fish 2011). Interpretation must thus aim at the communicative intentions of the legislator. In Gricean terms, intentionalists aim at the speakers' meaning or what in contemporary linguistics is often referred to as the pragmatic meaning of the law (for an explicitly Gricean intentionalist account of legal interpretation see Neale 2008).

Contemporary textualists, by contrast, do not focus on the legislator but on the addressees of the law. For rule of law reasons like the transparency and the predictability of the law they see the task of interpretation as being to establish the meaning that the addressees of the law are justified in connecting with a legal utterance. The addressees are usually justified in connecting the communicative intentions with utterance tokens that are commonly, usually or in standard cases connected with an utterance type. For textualists, interpretation aims at the semantic meaning of the law or at what Grice referred to as "sentence meaning." Due already to the indexical nature of many of our expressions, textualists cannot and do not rely on some kind of pure lexical meaning. Textualists too must rely on a contextually enriched semantic meaning (Goldsworthy 2005; Asgeirsson 2012). But this does not betray their normative cause as long as the relevant context is transparent for the addressees of the law.

In non-pathological cases, the semantic and pragmatic meaning of the law will not diverge. The legislator will usually rely on expressions to convey its intentions that an average speaker would have chosen in the same circumstances. If, however, the intentions of the legislator diverge from the meaning that an addressee of the law would be justified in assigning to it, textualist interpretation would privilege the addressee. For example, in contemporary constitutional law originalist textualists rely on the semantic meaning of the law at the time of its creation (Lawson 1992: 875; Scalia 1998: 21–38; on the different kinds of originalism, see Solum 2013).

One important fact that intentionalist accounts of interpretation bring to light is the empirical character of legal interpretation. Inferring the intentions of the legislator from the semantic meaning of the law and the context of the legislative act is at heart a purely empirical task. Whether the legislator connected a specific communicative intention with an utterance is an empirical question. Communicative interpretation in law and in general is an empirical enterprise.

> We thus need have no special sort of activity, distinct from the normal descriptive or explanatory activities of science, that requires justification. …
> The communicative model thus causes no ripples in the smooth waters of science. Moreover, the model no doubt accurately captures perhaps the most ordinary, most familiar usage of "interpretation".
>
> (Moore 1995: 5; see also Fish 2008: 1116)

Cum grano salis this also holds true for textualist accounts of legal interpretation. When textualists rely on the semantic meaning of the terms employed by the legislator, they rely on some average, core or standard kind of intentions connected with a given utterance type. The question of which kind of communicative intentions are standardly connected with an utterance type is again principally empirical in nature (see Fish 2008: 1123: "A dictionary is a statistical report") and is investigated by linguists with ever more sophisticated empirical means like computerized corpus analysis, which are increasingly taking the place of traditional lexicography. A normative element is only involved insofar as the exact determination of the reference class of language users, usage and the relevant quantities is concerned. However, these normative questions, due to their very general nature, are distinct from the normative questions typically raised by legal construction.

2. Legal construction and the doctrinal development of the law

There are many reasons why hermeneutics in law cannot be restricted to communicative interpretation – be it of the intentionalist or more textualist kind. The most fundamental reason is that communicative interpretation can fall short. The intentions an authority connected with a legal utterance might simply not include an intention applicable to the case at hand. The regulator that limited the surface of windows to 20 percent of the façade in Berlin-Mitte simply might not have considered glass brick elements; and for textualists the semantics of "window" are equally inconclusive due to vagueness. In a conversational or other setting that allows for dialogue, such issues are easily resolved by asking the speaker about her intentions with regard to the specific case. But – as hermeneutic scholars like Paul Ricœur have stressed (Ricœur 1973: 93–7) – in many contexts of written communication this kind of clarificatory dialogue is not possible. For historical texts there is no author alive to be asked or the author might even be unknown; for other texts, even if there is a contemporary author, she might be unavailable or reluctant to specify her intentions, because it may be precisely the point of some texts – as in literature – to engage the reader in developing his own constructions; for other texts as in law there are institutional limits. Although Enlightenment legislatures in France and Prussia attempted to force courts to refer cases of indeterminacy to special legislative bodies, the *référé législatif* proved to be an utter failure and would today even raise constitutional concerns with respect to the separation of powers.

The inability to establish the communicative meaning of a text with respect to a case at hand alone, however, would not explain the need to go beyond communicative interpretation. For many contexts, hermeneutics can take "No" for an answer. It would be a respectable result of a historical investigation into a text to find that its author did not connect any intentions regarding a certain state of affairs with it or that it can no longer be established whether the author did so or not. For law, however, this is not an option. As the famous Art. 4 of the Code Napoléon states: "Le juge qui refusera de juger, sous prétexte du silence, de l'obscurité ou de l'insuffisance de la loi, pourra être poursuivi comme coupable de déni de justice." Law generally operates under the prohibition of the denial of justice. Thus courts and judges must deliver a decision even in those cases where communicative interpretation leaves them empty-handed. They must thus engage in another kind of hermeneutical activity that in law falls under the heading of legal construction.

If in the above example of the Berlin bylaw a court had to decide on the legality of a façade consisting up to 40 percent of glass bricks, it would have to determine whether to apply the bylaw to glass bricks even if the intentions of the legislator and the textual meaning left them in limbo. The court would have to amend the bylaw with a determination for glass bricks in order to be able to decide the case. In legal construction, the law is developed doctrinally on a case-by-case basis to make it applicable to the case at hand. The law must be applied to circumstances that its creators did not or could not foresee.

Legal construction creates a kind of a double bind: On the one hand it seems inevitable for the law, and on the other hand it shifts the full burden of legitimation to the judge or whoever has to construct, that is, to amend, the law. So there has always been some unease about whether legal construction can be supported by a sufficiently strong legitimation given the wide-ranging effects of legal hermeneutics. In constitutional law, the question of legitimation is especially pressing, since the legislator, being bound by the constitution, does not even have a remedy against constitutional constructions, since he cannot overrule them by regular legislation. In constitutional construction, the legitimation of the courts is pitted against the legitimation of the legislature, which makes it especially sensitive in democracies. Yet it is precisely the constructive feature of legal hermeneutics that has drawn the interest of philosophical hermeneutics.

Hans Georg Gadamer famously referred to the law and its application as revealing a general feature of hermeneutics, which by the time of his *Truth and Method* had developed – following Martin Heidegger's lead – into a fundamental ontological concept. For Heidegger and Gadamer, our most fundamental relation with the world is hermeneutical. Heidegger insisted that we are ontologically situated in a world that is always already interpreted, that always already comes with a certain meaning. There are no uninterpreted objects, no objects as such (Heidegger 2010: § 32). A hammer is the object it is because we interpret it as such with respect to certain purposes and usages (see ibid.: § 18). Our understanding of the world is thus hermeneutical in the most fundamentally ontological way. One feature of this existential hermeneutics is what Heidegger called the "fore-structure of understanding" (ibid.: § 32), which Gadamer coined into the famous "fore-understanding" (Vorverständnis) of the hermeneutical subject (Gadamer 1989: 265–307). Our world is shaped by the hermeneutical fore-understanding with which we encounter it. We see a hammer as a hammer only if we already know about hammering, nails and so forth. The involvement of the hermeneutical subject, its situatedness in the present, its particular hermeneutical fore-understanding became a central theme for Gadamer. He rejected the concept of Romantic hermeneutics as developed by Schlegel, Schleiermacher, Ast and others and taken up in large part not only by legal methodology but also by nineteenth-century historiography. He rejected the idea that interpretation should aim to reconstruct the intentions or experiences of the author, since this did not take into account the importance of the situatedness and fore-understanding of the hermeneutical subject.

For Gadamer, the case in point for showing that understanding always involves situatedness and fore-understanding is law. The central task in law is the application of a – historical – text to a present case. Due to changing historical contexts, for Gadamer the application of a legal text to the present always requires that the normative content of the law be determined anew (Gadamer 1989: 327). The application of the law amounts to more than the historical or psychological reconstruction of legislative intentions. It requires the mindful and prudent adaption or "appropriation" (Ricœur 1981) of the law to present circumstances and cases. It not only requires technical legal skills but practical wisdom: Aristotelian *phronesis* not mere *techne* (Gadamer 1989: 317–24). For Gadamer, "legal hermeneutics is no special case but is, on the contrary, capable of restoring the hermeneutical problem to its full breadth and so re-establishing the former unity of hermeneutics" (Gadamer 1989: 328). In this perspective, legal hermeneutics brings the applicational element of any hermeneutics into the spotlight, which Gadamer sees at work in historical interpretation as well. First, a historian too cannot help but approach a historical text from the perspective of his contemporary understanding (Gadamer 1989: 327) and can – following Gadamer – only bridge the gap by a fusion of horizons (Gadamer 1989: 307). Second, Gadamer points to the fact that historiography is not interested in historical facts as such, but in their meaning in an emphatic sense, which can only be constructed by relating it to our present interests and concerns (Gadamer 1989: 328).

Gadamer's account of legal hermeneutics has been quite influential. Even critics of Gadamer's views on historical hermeneutics like Emilio Betti (Betti 1980/1990: 81–4) stress that legal hermeneutics show the specific constructive elements mediating between the historical horizon of the text and its present application. But unlike Gadamer, Betti regards legal hermeneutics as a special form of hermeneutics, which he describes as "value-oriented" or "normative":

> That the application of the law demands a legal interpretation that is related to the present and to contemporary society follows by necessity out of the function of the law as the ordering of co-existence in a human community. It is part of its essence, therefore, that it should achieve a concretion of the law; it should be practically relevant in that it is called upon to provide a legally adequate direction and directive for communal existence and behavior.
>
> (Betti 1980/1990: 83)

Already in the mid-1880s German legal scholars (Binding 1885: 454 passim; Wach 1885: 254 passim; Kohler 1886: 1 passim) had argued for an "objective" approach to legal hermeneutics. They insisted that the law can be more intelligent than the legislator and that the degree of systematic intention ascribed to the legislator by authors like Savigny only paid lip service to a misguided subjectivist methodology. Authors in this tradition, which is – in diverse and moderated forms, such as interest jurisprudence (Schoch 1948) – still influential today, felt emboldened by Gadamer, who provided them with a philosophical, even ontological basis against subjectivist accounts, especially of a positivistic provenance, which were centered on legislative intent. The preeminent work of this way of receiving Gadamer's œuvre is "Vorverständnis und Methodenwahl" by Josef Esser (Esser 1972), who claimed to show for contemporary civil law that its application depended on views about the "rightness" of the result and that the choice of legal methods was determined less by a methodological canon than by our fore-understandings of right outcomes (further influential hermeneutical approaches in German legal methodology include Larenz 1991: 206–8, 212–13; Kaufmann 1997: 44–6; see also Kaufmann 1963).

In Anglo-Saxon jurisprudence the most prominent reference to Gadamer's work has been made by Ronald Dworkin (see also the contributions in Leyh 1992; Mootz 1994). Like Gadamer, Dworkin develops his general hermeneutics by discussing the interpretation of art, and he begins to develop his account with Gadamer's notion of application: "We must first notice Gadamer's crucial point, that interpretation must *apply* an intention" (Dworkin 1986: 55 emphasis in original). Like Gadamer, he is at great pains to stress that interpretation is always constructive even if it only aims at the intentions of the author. "Once again I appeal to Gadamer, whose account of interpretation ... strikes the right note" (ibid.: 62). For Dworkin, interpretation is essentially constructive and his account of the law is interpretative through and through. Not only is the application of individual laws an act of constructive interpretation, but the law as a social practice in general must also be assessed by an act of constructive interpretation, which presents the practice in the best light. In his own constructive interpretation of the law he discards conventionalism and pragmatism and develops an integrity account of the law. "The adjudicative principle of integrity instructs judges to identify legal rights and duties ... on the assumption that they were all created by a single author – the community personified – expressing a coherent conception of justice and fairness" (ibid.: 225). Integrity is operationalized in the dimensions of fit and justice: the dimension of fit demands to find the principles that agree with the relevant past legal decisions; the dimension of justice selects among these principles that which shows the practice in the best light. Although Dworkin admits that there can be tradeoffs between the two dimensions – a better fitting principle may fall short in justification to a less fitting one – he famously insists that integrity will deliver single-right-answers in every case (ibid.: 260–75; see also Dworkin 1978).

For more than a century, critics – from the German Free-Law-Movement to the French Juristes Inquiets, to the Scandinavian and American legal realists, to Kelsen's Pure Theory of the Law, to Critical-Legal-Studies, and recent naturalistic approaches – have challenged the hermeneutical account of legal construction as a sham. If the law is indeterminate on an issue and in need of amendment to give an answer to the case at hand, in what sense can amending the law still be a hermeneutical activity? What could possibly distinguish legal construction from the mere exercise of political discretion akin to legislation? Many of these critical accounts regard the whole interpretative concept of legal construction to be window-dressing designed to disguise the exercise of political power by the courts.

The critics rightly stress that legal construction comes with the power to amend the law. But what makes legal construction a distinctly hermeneutical activity is its justificatory structure (see Moore 1995: 17). It follows the model of communicative interpretation. In communicative interpretation, we must justify our claims about the content of an utterance by delivering arguments that support our attribution of intentions to the speaker's utterance. Most commonly we can justify the attribution by pointing to the semantic meaning of the utterance, the context and to the lack of indications that the speaker wanted to use the utterance in a non-standard way. We justify our communicative interpretation of an utterance by referring to reasons that support the attribution of a certain communicative intention to the author of the utterance. The same justificatory scheme applies to legal construction. A legal construction must be justified as the attribution of a specific communicative intention to a text. Legal construction has to make the case that its content is an intention that an intentional subject could have connected to the text that the construction is a construction of – even though the real author of the text had no such intention in mind. Thus, unlike legislation, a legal construction cannot be justified by merely looking at outcomes. If the legislative intentions are indeterminate in a specific case, the case cannot be decided by relying on what would be best all things considered – as could be done were it a mere policy decision. Rather, the case must be decided on the basis of a constructed rule that can be defended as an intention connected to the legal text that applies to the case.

As the construction of a text, a construction cannot be justified by reference to any intention connected with a text but only with reference to a *communicative intention*. Just like communicative interpretation, construction relies on double level intentionality. Unlike communicative actions, communicative utterances like texts are not only intentional, but also have the communication of an intention as their object. Thus it does not suffice to point out that the legislation intended to pursue a certain goal with a text; it must be justified that this goal was pursued by a certain communicative intention that can be ascribed to the text. If the legislator intended to protect the environment with a law establishing a refund system for soft drinks and it was indeterminate whether the legislator wanted the system to be applied to milkshakes, milkshakes could not be ruled out as soft drinks in the sense of the law on the grounds that refunding had no environmental benefit. Rather, a case would have to be made that milkshakes are not soft drinks in some plausible communicative sense of the term. Legal construction must not simply construct intentions of any kind, but communicative intentions plausibly connected with the given text.

The structural affinity of legal construction to communicative interpretation explains some of the features stressed in the discussion of legal construction from the outset. Lieber, for instance, wanted to apply all methods of legal interpretation to construction (Lieber 1837: 81). The similarity in method is explained by the fact that legal construction must be justified in much the same way as legal interpretation. Thus a legal construction, too, is only justified if it respects – *cum grano salis* – the semantic meaning of the text it constructs, since for construction the same presupposition holds that utterances usually express the intentions that are typically expressed by them. It also explains the rationalizations often found in descriptions of "objective interpretation" which do not rely on the actual intentions of the legislator, but on the intentions of a sensible or rational legislator or even on the personification of the law as in Dworkin's integrity account, which suggests interpreting the law as if it were created by a "single author" (Dworkin 1986: 225, 242). If we do not or cannot rely on the actual intentions connected with an utterance, we must still justify our constructions as intentions that some intentional subject could plausibly have connected with them. Just as our interpretations of dreams have to be justified as messages from some personified unconscious self, conceived as an intentional subject.

Although legal interpretation and construction present the same justificatory structure, the material justificatory standards are strikingly different. Whereas legal interpretation relies on empirical epistemic justification, legal construction relies largely on evaluative and pragmatic normative considerations. (On three types of reason, see Skorupski 2010: 35–56). The point is no longer to find an actual, empirically instantiated intention, but to construe a communicative intention that a sensible, rational, legally knowledgeable and so on intentional subject could have connected with the legal text for the specific case at hand. The justification is no longer empirical, but rational in a normative sense. Thus legal construction is a normative hermeneutical activity in an evaluative and pragmatic sense by which new legal norms are created. It goes without saying that the normative standards considered appropriate as well as what is regarded as the text the construction supervenes upon – the concrete regulation, the statute in its entirety, the law as a whole including or excluding previous decisions by courts – is largely determined by the specific legal culture and object of intense debates. These debates are part of and share the evaluative and pragmatic normative nature of legal construction itself.

3. The relation

Many of the disputes in legal hermeneutics can be understood as debates about the relation between legal interpretation and construction. On one side are those who deny the theoretical possibility or at least the normative defensibility of communicative interpretation. The theoretical arguments are either general or local. There are three general theoretical arguments against communicative interpretation in law.

Often with reference to the interpretation of art (Gadamer, Dworkin), the first objection suggests that we are never able to fully bridge the historical gap between authors and their audience and thus will never be able to reconstruct the intention of the legislator. However these issues should be addressed in the case of art, it is highly implausible that we are incapable of entertaining sound epistemic hypotheses on the kind of communicative intentions connected with a legal utterance in mundane questions of law. At least for the easy cases which constitute the bulk of our legal practice it does not even seem remotely credible to suggest that we do not know what the legislator intended, for example when he set the speed limit at 55 mph. We know what kind of communicative intentions were connected to the law with respect to someone driving at 70 mph. This does not imply that even such clear cut regulations as speed limits cannot run into borderline cases for which it might not be possible to retrieve an actual historic intention. This, however, only entails that even seemingly clear cut rules might be in need of legal construction. It does not mean that the intentions, for paradigm cases at least, cannot be retrieved even across fairly extended timespans. As historical distance increases it might become more and more difficult. This accounts for our talk of degrees of understanding, which can diminish over time or become more and more uncertain, at least in non-standard cases. But this, too, only leads to a growing need for construction, not to the impossibility of communicative interpretation.

The second general argument stems from the idea of application. It maintains that the law is always in need of application and that the application of the law must always accommodate the intentions originally connected with it to the case at hand. This argument relies on an equivocation. Application can designate legal construction in cases where the intentions connected with a legal utterance by its author do not allow us to make a decision either due to original indeterminacy or to changing circumstances. Should a traffic regulation designed for horse-drawn carriages also apply to motorcars? The regulation might need adjustment by legal construction to apply it to new or unforeseen circumstances. It was this kind of construction that Gadamer drew attention to under the heading of application. There is, however, a different kind of application in the sense of mere rule-following, highlighted by Wittgenstein. This kind of application does not pertain to the adaptation of a rule to unforeseen circumstances, but to its application in paradigm cases. As Wittgenstein made clear with his regress argument, application in the sense of rule-following does not require interpretation (Wittgenstein 1953: § 201) let alone construction. Rather, rule-following is best understood as the exercise of an ability (Baker and Hacker 2009: 135–40; for an inversion of the relation between a rule and its application see Brandom 1994: Ch. 1). Just as the ability to swim is exercised in an ocean swim or the crossing of a river, the ability to follow a rule is exercised by applying it to standard cases. It is the exercise of a rule-following ability that bridges the gap between a rule and its application to standard cases – just as only the exercise of the ability to swim and no interpretation of the concept of swimming will save us from drowning. In standard cases covered by the intentions of the author of a regulation, only application in the sense of rule-following is needed. This kind of application, however, does not require the interpretation or construction that Gadamer rightly pointed to in cases where the law needs adjustment or emendation to make it applicable.

A third reason put forward by Gadamer turns on yet another equivocation already exposed by Betti (on the controversy see Hoy 1985: 140–7). Gadamer insisted that even a legal historian would never be interested in the pure reconstruction of a historical fact for its own sake and that any sensible form of historiography would always try to understand the meaning of a historical fact from the contemporary perspective. This argument, however, confuses meaning with significance (Betti (1980/1990: 173). The significance of a legal regulation might only be assessed from the ever-changing present perspective. But this does not automatically affect its meaning. A speed limit on certain roads does not change its meaning by the fact that it has become insignificant due to permanent heavy congestion. As Betti rightly insisted, meaning and significance must be kept separate. Legal hermeneutics is about the meaning of laws, not about their significance.

There is a last seemingly catch-all general argument that could be leveled against the possibility of a purely empirical concept of interpretation. It could entertain that the distinction between the empirical and the normative that the distinction between legal interpretation and construction builds upon is itself merely a hermeneutical construction. A purely hermeneutical philosophical account of metaphysics, ontology and epistemology might suggest that the empirical world is just one of our hermeneutical constructions. However such an account might be spelled out in detail, and however convincing it might prove, it could only be an adequate account were it to reconstruct the difference between the empirical and the normative within the overall hermeneutical theory. Thus, however, it would carry no weight against the distinction, which would then simply be a distinction internal to hermeneutics, but without losing any of its discriminating character on pain of being inadequate.

The most important local theoretical argument against communicative interpretation in law stems from the difficulties in giving an account of the collective intentions of large and complex legislative bodies (Hurd 1989; Waldron 2001). Without going into the details, there are, however, reductionist accounts of collective intentions (e.g. Bratman 2004: 109–30; Searle 1990: 401–15), which could in principle be applied to legislative bodies like parliaments (see Ekins 2012). They reconstruct collective intentions as interlocking individual intentions, thus making sense of our pervasive talk about collective actors and their intentions. However these accounts are spelled out, they set a fairly high epistemic bar for confidently asserting legislative intent. But again, in many mundane standard cases of the law, this bar can be lifted. It is simply that turning to legislative intent rarely delivers clear results in non-standard cases, where serious hermeneutical issues arise. There are, however, no theoretical reasons why that should always be the case.

Besides theoretical arguments, normative arguments are also leveled against communicative interpretation in law. Rule of law values like the transparency of the law, its predictability and reasons of fairness seem to argue against relying on the intent of the legislator in the last resort, since the common addressee of the law usually has no access to the intentions of the legislator. Again, however, we must distinguish between mundane and more complicated cases. In mundane instances of the law, the average addressee has epistemically sufficient means to grasp the intention of the legislator by relying on the semantic meaning of the legal text and its context. The average addressee of a speed limit knows perfectly well what the legislator intended. Rule of law values come to bear only when the legislator intended a regulation that is not suggested by the semantic meaning of the text in its context. In the more frequent cases of semantic vagueness, however, where rule of law values cannot be served by relying on the text due to its indeterminacy, a democratic argument can be made in favor of legislative intent. If there is a clear legislative intent in these cases – which there usually is not – they come down to a choice between the predetermined political decision of the legislator and a *post facto* legal construction by the courts. The stronger democratic legitimation of the legislator and the impartiality credentials of a predetermined decision then speak favorably of the latter.

However the normative argument about legislative intent plays out, it illustrates one sense in which the idea that legal hermeneutics is construction through and through is correct. Although legal interpretation and legal construction can be distinguished, the question of whether legal interpretation or some kind of construction will determine the law is normative and thus itself a legal construction. Whereas legislative intent can in principle be investigated by purely empirical means, there are no empirical means for deciding whether to privilege it over the textual meaning of the law or a construction. At least insofar as these questions of legal methodology are not reflexively regulated by the legislator – as they rarely are – legal hermeneutics always relies on legal construction at this basic methodological level.

The interrelations between legislative intentions and legal construction are further complicated by another twist in their dialectics. Externalist semantics have rightly highlighted the fact that in a certain sense the meaning of an utterance does not have to be in the head of the speaker. The less controversial aspect of the externalist picture of meaning can be found in the *deferential* structure that our meaning providing intentions often encompass (for a realist semantics in law see Moore 2007: 249 f.; for a neo-descriptivist see Nimtz 2007). In the externalist semantics of natural kind terms, speakers often defer to expert opinions about the true nature of the kind. When a speaker wants to buy "gold" for an investment, he refers to a chemist or the markets if he does not know whether "white gold" is really gold or just a special kind of silver. Even before he knows, he will insist that he only wanted to buy gold, whatever actually counts as gold.

In a similar way the legislator will often defer the determination of the law to the courts. As documented in numerous legislative materials, it sometimes even explicitly leaves some problematic cases for the courts to decide. When the legislator has deferential intentions with respect to legal constructions by the courts, legal construction and legislative intent become intricately intertwined. Given the legislator's knowledge that no regulation can be designed in such a way as to rule out the need for legal construction at least in fringe or unforeseen cases and given also his awareness of the whole institutional judicial framework of courts, lawyers and attorneys to deal with them, it does not even seem farfetched to assume a standing deferential intention of the legislator to legal constructions. Even if it were difficult to establish such a general deferential intention as an empirical interpretation, it would have considerable merit as a normative construction. The assumption of deferential intentions already lay at the heart of Savigny's concept of interpretation. It relied on the legislator basing his laws on not immediately visible legal institutions and deferring their disclosure to the systematic work of legal scholarship (Savigny 1867: 37–9, 172 f.).

The intricate relations between legal interpretation and construction are one factor that should caution against the other side in the debate between interpretationists and constructionists in legal hermeneutics. The interpretationists rightly insist on the possibility of legal interpretation but question in a more or less general fashion the legitimacy of legal contribution by the courts.

They aim to restrict the hermeneutics practiced by the courts to legal interpretation. In administrative law especially there is a widespread opinion that the construction of statutes should be left to administrative agencies. For example the Chevron doctrine of the US Supreme Court prohibits the court from imposing "its own *construction* on the statute" (467 U.S. 837 (1984) at 843 – emphasis added). Courts are only allowed to challenge an agency decision when they can rely on a clear legislative intent. Similarly, it is suggested for the US constitutional law that the Supreme Court should refrain from legal construction (Whittington 1999). As is to be expected, however, the case law on the Chevron doctrine is hardly intelligible and full of perplexities (for an overview, see Duffy and Herz 2005: Ch. 3). The close relations between legal interpretation and legal construction make them unsuitable for clear-cut distinctions. That they are so closely related also depends on the fact that they follow the same justificatory structure. This leads to the second reason why restricting legal hermeneutics in the courts to legal interpretation does not seem a promising approach. The courts are by all functional criteria – professional expertise, institutional structure and institutional tradition – the most appropriate branch of government to engage in approaching legal issues hermeneutically. It is the only branch of government that is not directly policy-driven. This does not suggest that policy does not play a role in legal hermeneutics, which can come with hermeneutical discretion especially in cases of legal construction. The discretion is, however, hermeneutical in nature and thus – to differing degrees depending on the specifics of the legal culture – distanced from mere policy choices.

For ages law upheld a sense for both insights into legal hermeneutics: that distinct activities are involved and that they are closely related to each other. In contemporary terms, the different activities involved can be distinguished as communicative interpretation, legal construction and rule-following. They are not only related, but even intertwined. Especially in the practice of legal hermeneutics, the analytical distinctions hardly ever play a role. Courts do not subdivide their decisions into sections pertaining to interpretation, construction and rule-following. In the practice of the law, the different aspects are merged and could – if at all – only be taken apart analytically *post facto*. In insisting on its complexity and on the interrelatedness of its composite parts, legal hermeneutics might vindicate the role that Gadamer once saw for it.

Bibliography

Alexander, L., and Prakash, S. (2004) "'Is That English You're Speaking?' Why Intention Free Interpretation is an Impossibility," *San Diego Law Review*, 41: 967–95.

Asgeirsson, H. (2012) *Textualism, Pragmatic Enrichment, and Objective Communicative Content*. Online. Available: papers.ssrn.com/sol3/papers.cfm?abstract_id = 2142266 (accessed January 22, 2014).

Baker, G. P. and Hacker, P. M. S. (2009) *An Analytical Commentary on the Philosophical Investigations, Volume 2 – Wittgenstein: Rules, Grammar and Necessity: Essays and Exegesis of §§ 185–242*, 2nd edn, Chichester: Wiley-Blackwell.

Barnett, R. E. (2011) "Interpretation and Construction," *Harvard Journal of Law & Public Policy*, 34: 65–72.

Betti, E. (1980) "Hermeneutics as the General Methodology of the Geisteswissenschaften," in J. Bleicher (ed.) *Contemporary Hermeneutics: Hermeneutics as Method, Philosophy and Critique*, London: Routledge, 51–94. Also published in G.L. Ormiston and A. D. Schrift (eds.) *The Hermeneutic Tradition: From Ast to Ricoeur* (1990), Albany: State University of New York Press, 159–97.

Binding, K. (1885) *Handbuch des Strafrechts*, vol. 1, Leipzig: Duncker & Humblot.

Brandom, R. (1994) *Making it Explicit: Reasoning Representing and Discursive Commitment*, Cambridge, Mass.: Harvard University Press.

Bratman, M. E. (2004) *Faces of Intention: Selected Essays on Intention and Agency*, Cambridge: Cambridge University Press.

Cover, R. M. (1986) "Violence and the Word," *Yale Law Journal*, 95(8): 1601–29.

Duffy, J. F. and Herz, M. (2005) *A Guide to Judicial and Political Review of Federal Agencies*, Chicago, Ill.: American Bar Association.

Dworkin, R. (1978) "No Right Answer?," *New York University Law Review*, 53(1): 1–32.

——(1986) *Law's Empire*, Oxford/Portland, Oreg.: Hart Publishing.

Ekins, R. (2012) *The Nature of Legislative Intent*, Oxford: Oxford University Press.

Esser, J. (1972) *Vorverständnis und Methodenwahl in der Rechtsfindung: Rationalitätsgrundlagen richterlicher Entscheidungspraxis*, Frankfurt a.M.: Athenäum Fischer Taschenbuch Verlag.

Fish, S. (2008) "Intention is all there is: A Critical Analysis of Aharon Barak's Purposive Interpretation in Law," *Cardozo Law Review*, 29: 1109–46.

——(2011) "The Intentionalist Thesis Once More," in G. Huscroft and B. W. Miller (eds.), *The Challenge of Originalism*, Cambridge: Cambridge University Press, 99–119.

Gadamer, H.-G. (1989) *Truth and Method*, 2nd edn, New York: Crossroad.

Goldsworthy, J. D. (2005) "Moderate versus Strong Intentionalism: Knapp and Michaels Revisited," *San Diego Law Review*, 42: 669–84.

Heidegger, M. (2010) *Being and Time*, Albany: State University of New York Press.

Hoy, D. C. (1985) "Interpreting the Law: Hermeneutical and Poststructuralist Perspectives," *Southern California Law Review*, 58: 135–76.

Hurd, H. M. (1989) "Sovereignty in Silence," *Yale Law Journal*, 99: 945–1028.

Kaufmann, A. (1963) "The Ontological Structure of Law," *Natural Law Review*, 8: 79–96.

——(1997) *Rechtsphilosophie*, 2nd edn, München: C.H. Beck.

Knapp, S. and Benn Michaels, W. (1982) "Against Theory," *Critical Inquiry*, 8(4): 723–42.

Kohler, J. (1886) "Ueber die Interpretation von Gesetzen," *Zeitschrift für das Privat-und Öffentliche Recht der Gegenwart (GrünhZ)*, 13: 1–61.

Larenz, K. (1991) *Methodenlehre der Rechtswissenschaft*, 6th edn, Berlin: Springer.

Lawson, G. (1992) "Proving the Law," *Northwestern University Law Review*, 86: 859–904.

Leyh, G. (ed.) (1992) *Legal Hermeneutics: History, Theorie and Practice*, Berkeley, Los Angeles, Oxford: University of California Press.

Lieber, F. (1837) "On Political Hermeneutics, or on Political Interpretation and Construction, and Also on Precedents," *American Jurist and Law Magazine*, 18: 37–101.

Moore, M. S. (1995) "Interpreting Interpretation," in A. Marmor (ed.), *Law and Interpretation: Essays in Legal Philosophy*, Oxford: Clarendon Press, 1–30.

——(2007) "Can Objectivity be Grounded in Semantics?," in E. Villanueva (ed.), *Law: Metaphysics, Meaning, and Objectivity*, Amsterdam, New York: Rodopi, 235–61.

Mootz, F. J. (1994) "The New Legal Hermeneutics," *Vanderbilt Law Review*, 47: 115–44.

Neale, S. (2008) *Textualism with Intent*, excerpt from Manuscript for Discussion at Oxford University, Law Faculty, November 18, 2008, Online. Available: http://www.ucl.ac.uk/laws/jurisprudence/docs/2008/08_coll_neale.pdf (accessed January 22, 2014).

Nimtz, C. (2007) "Kripke vs. Kripke: Eine bescheidene Verteidigung der Kennzeichnungstheorie," in A. Rami and H. Wansing (eds.), *Referenz und Realität*, Paderborn: mentis, 99–121.

Ricœur, P. (1973) "The Model of the Text: Meaningful Action Considered as a Text," *New Literary History*, 5(1): 91–117.

——(1981) "Appropriation," in J. B. Thompson (ed.), *Hermeneutics and the Human Sciences: Essays on Language, Action, and Interpretation*, Cambridge, New York, Paris: Cambridge University Press, 182–93.

Savigny, F. C. v. (1867) *System of the Modern Roman Law*, vol. 1, trans. W. Holloway, Madras: J. Higginbotham.

——(1993) "Methodologie (Vorlesungsnotizen)," in F. C. v. Savigny (ed.), *Vorlesungen über juristische Methodologie 1802–1842*, Frankfurt am Main: Vittorio Klostermann.

Scalia, A. (1998) *A Matter of Interpretation. Federal Courts and the Law*, 6th edn, Princeton, N.J.: Princeton University Press.

Schoch, M. (ed.) (1948) *The Jurisprudence of Interests: Selected Writings*, Cambridge, Mass.: Harvard University Press.

Searle, J. R. (1990) "Collective Intentions and Actions," in P. R. Cohen, J. Morgan and M. E. Pollack (eds.), *Intentions in Communication*, Cambridge, Mass., London: MIT Press, 401–15.

Skorupski, J. (2010) *The Domain of Reasons*, Oxford: Oxford University Press.

Solum, L. B. (2010) "The Interpretation–Construction Distinction," *Constitutional Commentary*, 27: 95–118.

——(2013) "Originalism and Constitutional Construction," *Fordham Law Review*, 82: 453–537.

Wach, A. (1885) *Handbuch des deutschen Civilprozessrechts*, vol. 1, Leipzig: Duncker & Humblot.

Waldron, J. (2001) "Legislators' Intentions and Unintentional Legislation," in J. Waldron (ed.), *Law and Disagreement*, Oxford, New York: Oxford University Press, 119–46.

Whittington, K. E. (1999) *Constitutional Interpretation: Textual Meaning, Original Intent and Judicial Review*, Lawrence, Kans.: University Press of Kansas.

Wittgenstein, L. (1953) *Philosophical Investigations*, Oxford: Blackwell.

Further reading

Betti, E. (1980) "Hermeneutics as the General Methodology of the Geisteswissenschaften," in J. Bleicher (ed.) *Contemporary Hermeneutics: Hermeneutics as Method, Philosophy and Critique*, London: Routledge, 51–94.

Gadamer, H.-G. (1989) *Truth and Method*, 2nd edn, New York: Crossroad, 305–35.

Leyh, G. (ed.) (1992) *Legal Hermeneutics: History, Theorie and Practice*, Berkeley, Los Angeles, Oxford: University of California Press.

Lieber, F. (1837) "On Political Hermeneutics, or on Political Interpretation and Construction, and Also on Precedents," *American Jurist and Law Magazine*, 18: 37–101.

Moore, M. S. (1995) "Interpreting Interpretation," in A. Marmor (ed.), *Law and Interpretation: Essays in Legal Philosophy*, Oxford: Clarendon Press, 1–30.

Mootz, F. J. (1994) "The New Legal Hermeneutics," *Vanderbilt Law Review*, 47: 115–44.

Whittington, K. E. (1999) *Constitutional Interpretation: Textual Meaning, Original Intent and Judicial Review*, Lawrence, Kans.: University Press of Kansas.

37
HERMENEUTICS AND RHETORIC

John Arthos

Crossing the Western firmament like two avatars of intellectual culture and education, ballasts for the profoundest sea-changes in our intellectual heritage, hibernating when necessary along subterranean channels in the ebb and flow of intellectual fashion, rhetoric and hermeneutics have slowly begun to understand the complex nature of their kinship as constitutional features of human discursivity. Hermeneutic insights were embedded in the educational programs of rhetorical paideia from its beginnings, since the productive competence of rhetoric had always oriented itself toward questions of reception. If rhetoric vied with philosophy throughout antiquity as the fount of a liberal education, hermeneutics emerged into a disciplinary identity only under the pressure of modernity. A hermeneutic discipline emerged out of the womb of the rhetorical tradition and borrowed its idioms and imperatives from its older sibling, but repaid the favor by developing an acutely reflective awareness of its shared discursive identity.

The emergence of the hermeneutic discipline from rhetoric had two watershed moments, the first being an immanent preparation or anticipation of the second. The shift to a reading culture energized by the Gutenberg revolution and the Protestant Reformation reversed the focus on discourse from the side of production to that of reception, as marked by Melanchthon's modeling of a new *ars bene legendi* on the shoulders of the old *ars bene dicendi*. Crucial to its later ontological forms, the hermeneutic canons of interpretation developed out of the Lutheran teaching that the Word is itself the historical emergence of the body of Christ in the life of the Church. The second constitutive moment came with the ontological mutation of hermeneutics as the discursive idiom of finite being. The epistemic turn of rhetoric in the twentieth century soon found affinities with this ontological turn, deepening the historical collaboration of the two disciplines and opening avenues for future synergies.

The Hebrew tradition of oral exegesis and interpretive commentary is still one of the unsurpassed exemplars of rhetorical-hermeneutic collaboration, prefiguring and modeling the ontologic character of the heritable word (Déaut 1982). Because holy scripture was what nurtured a coherent historical identity for the Israelites, hermeneutic practice found itself at the center of cultural practice, its rituals of teaching, argument, debate, and deliberation developed as a necessary corollary. Since scripture prescribed conduct for the community of the faithful, it required a judicial apparatus for mediating questions of application. Exegesis, preaching, and legal adjudication became part of the textual weave of Jewish identity. For the early Jewish communities scriptural interpretation developed in oral practice ("The Oral Law"), but as communities spread out, a written commentary tradition developed that produced texts requiring their own exegetic forms. As a result, the interpretation and application of covenant law from generation to generation developed hermeneutic methods of unparalleled richness and flexibility that not only arbitrated textual meanings but actively constituted the law over time.

A similar though less rigorous collaboration developed in the Hellenized political institutions of Roman culture. The cardinal hermeneutic principles of part–whole reciprocity, hermeneutic charity, and the standard of appropriateness emerged from the classical rhetorical canons. To be sure, hermeneutics did not develop during this period into a distinct discipline, and its green shoots were, as Dilthey put it, "an agglomeration without a connecting principle" remaining embedded in and nourished by the preceptive traditions of rhetoric (1996: 33). How closely married were oratory and textual interpretation can be gathered from Quintilian's instruction in the interpretation of literature (*enarratio auctorum*). Careful attention is given to the literary text's genre, style, and vocabulary, and how to handle "the different meanings which may be given to each word," how to read a text in its context. However, the very first piece of advice Quintilian gives for textual interpretation regards "when the student should take breath, at what point he should introduce a pause into a line, where the sense ends or begins" (1920: 147 [I. 8]). This advice relates to the fact that interpretation in classical antiquity was performative, instruction in production and reception being quite literally inseparable.

The early Church Fathers combined exegesis, evangelizing, and doctrinal formation by adapting the rhetorical offices to their own traditions. As church and state moved increasingly toward text-based forms, political, judicial, and religious institutions transposed rhetorical principles such as *decorum*, *equitas*, and *oeconomia* into interpretive canons of law. So as the growing Christian community expanded across vast geographies of cultural difference, testing the strictures of scriptural authority developed in a specific cultural context, the rhetorical ideal of *accomodatio*, the flexible adaptation of the speaker to the occasion, was enlisted for patristic jurisprudence of empire as the charitable application of rule to case (Eden 1997). It is notable that in the Christian appropriation of pagan culture, both the sequence and order of privilege for rhetoric and hermeneutics were reversed: "There are two things necessary to the treatment of the Scriptures: a way of discovering those things which are to be understood, and a way of teaching what we have learned" (Augustine 1958: 7).

By the Renaissance, with the impact that the recovery of ancient texts was having on the already complex processes of assimilation of pagan and Christian culture, education in the principles of speech production and textual interpretation intermingled in close proximity, so that Erasmus's advice to a teacher designates the tools of production and reception as identical: It would be advisable to "have at your fingertips the chief points of rhetoric, namely propositions, the grounds of proof, figures of speech, amplifications, and the rules governing transitions. For these are conducive not only to criticism but also to imitation" (1978: 670). Thus for instance the rhetorical principle of decorum can be applied to the interpretation of scriptural passages whose meaning depends on "what is said and to whom, at what time and occasion, with what words and what spirit, with what proceeds and what follows" (Erasmus 1933: 285).

The educational ideals of Renaissance humanism were nourished by principles of rhetorical instruction that continued as the staple of education for the priestly class and the burgeoning professional classes, and even as the age of reason got underway, the Reformation required training of a new pastorate to interpret the vernacular Bible and disseminate its teachings, and beyond this to establish a compulsory general education for the learning of catechisms (Gawthrop and Strauss 1984: 31–43). One of Luther's assistants, the humanist-trained Philip Melanchthon (1497–1560), wrote a textbook that adapted the rhetorical canons to this purpose. His 1531 *Elementorum Rhetorices* applies the productive principles of reasoning, argument, expository presentation, style, and arrangement to the receptive tasks of biblical exegesis and legal interpretation. The passage from *ars bene dicendi* to *ars bene legendi* is not marked in the text. Melanchthon's method marks the convergence of the liberal ideal of the cultivation of the citizen with the Lutheran focus on the individual's personal relationship to God, a potent confluence that secured the greater collaboration of rhetoric and hermeneutics going forward.

The Church's institutional assertion of authority over matters of faith at the Council of Trent (1545–63) only provoked greater literacy education efforts. Protestants saw the Church as living through its members, and the encounter with Scripture as "an experience that consists both of comprehending and living through the inner coherence of Scripture" (Dilthey 1996: 37). A good example of the intellectual resources mobilized for this purpose is the *Clavis Scripturae Sacrae* of Matthias Flacius Illyricus (1520–75), a guide to biblical interpretation for pastors and laity. The *Clavis* (1567) integrates rhetorical and hermeneutic principles into a theory of production and reception that starts from close textual analysis (*ars critica*) to oral exegesis (*ars praedicandi*) to assimilation of the Word into daily Christian life. To wrench the jealously guarded privilege of scriptural interpretation from its perch in the Church establishment and put it into the hands of the public, Flacius devised precepts of self-education and interpretive method that included straightforward techniques of textual analysis, transfer of understanding through sermonic eloquence, and concrete examples of scriptural application to daily life.

Using similar mirroring techniques to those of Melanchthon, Flacius adapted rhetorical canons to the functions of scriptural paraphrasing and outlining, but infused the moment of *subtilitas applicandi* into every stage of the method. So for instance, the interpreter identifies the genre of a scriptural passage from among "those various kinds of writings with which these arts deal, which are accustomed to occur in the life of men, in the treatment of things, and in human affairs ... whether judicial, deliberative, demonstrative, didactic, or some other form of writing." After seeking "out what kind of invention, arrangement, and elocution is present," you put "the writing into your own words, so that with your words, an anatomy of sorts having been performed, you delineate the flesh, that is, the adornment of amplifications, ornamentations, digressions, and similitudes, from the skeleton" of the text (Flacius Illyricus 2011: 111–12). Such a paraphrase technique aids the accurate understanding of the gospel for assimilation by "those who otherwise have a heart not perceiving, eyes not seeing, and ears not hearing" (89–90). The paraphrase is not intended "merely to establish a bare type or shadow, or set forth some sort of dream, but rather to establish His testament with the clearest and most specific words possible and fix His covenant unalterably" in the minds of the faithful (116).

Thus a rhetorical paideia infused with heightened hermeneutic features survived at the level of school instruction even as the imperatives of Enlightenment reason came to supplant learning at the university level. The last wave of protest against the demotion of the humanist tradition is heard in the career of the eighteenth century Italian humanist Giambattista Vico (1668–1744), who occupied the chair of rhetoric at the University of Naples in the early eighteenth century. Anticipating Hegel in the breathtaking originality of his vision, he attempted a wholly original synthesis of humanist learning with the new science, integrating the new forms of reason with rhetorical invention and judgment, and interpreting human knowledge as a manifestation of history, culture, and political community. Vico's theory of interpretation, which he dubbed "a new critical art," drew on classical rhetorical principles of legal and historical interpretation, but raised these principles to the status of an ontology:

> But when the facts are in doubt, they should be taken in accordance with laws, and when the laws are in doubt they should be interpreted in accordance with nature. … peoples in doubt must have acted in conformity with the forms of their governments, forms of governments in doubt must have suited the nature of the men governed, and the natures of men in doubt must have been governed in accordance with the nature of their locations.
>
> (2002: 67)

Initially of course Vico's imaginative reconstruction of *scientia* within a humanist framework fell on dry ground, and the status marginality of rhetoric only deepened. But the insight that knowledge is the content of its own historical development and that the poetic imagination is not ancillary to but the condition of critical reason fed subterranean channels of intellectual culture that eventually made their way to an intensified collaboration between rhetoric and hermeneutics.

If rhetoric's influence since the Enlightenment is a history of decline, hermeneutics flourishes over the same period, initially under the sway of the imperatives of Enlightenment rationalism, and then taking part in the reaction against it. Such hermeneutic luminaries as Joseph Konrad Dannhauer (1603–66), Christian Wolff (1679–1754), Johann Martin Chladni (a.k.a. Chladenius) (1710–59), and Georg Friedrich Meier (1718–77) took inspiration from the universalist rationalism of Leibniz in seeking a *hermeneutica generalis* predicated on scientific principles of demonstrable logic. So for instance Wolff's interpretive method followed a procedure of classification and subsumption:

> [W]e are to abstract each proposition in common plain terms from the context, and separate each from whatever is advanced with for illustration,

definition, or demonstration. And if we then perceive under what class the thing treated on comes, we must examine it in a proper manner … and then pass a rational judgment thereon.

(1770: 185–6)

Despite this rationalist orientation, the efflorescence of Enlightenment hermeneutics in the seventeenth century drank deeply at the well of rhetoric. Dannhauer produced an educational handbook, the *Epitome Rhetoricae* (1651), that organizes the collaborative responsibilities of grammar, logic, poetics, and rhetoric under a unified organon. Meier appropriated the classical rhetorical principle of *aequitas* as an interpretive rule (Grondin 1994: 57–8). Chladenius adapted the rhetorical principle of scopus (*Sehepunkt*) to assess the validity of historical accounts.

Biblical, philological, historical, and legal studies continued to nurture the growth of hermeneutics in the eighteenth century. Johann Jacob Rambach's (1693–1735) popular textbook on biblical exegesis, the *Institutiones Hermeneuticae Sacrae* (1725), interwove a humanist pedagogy of grammar, rhetoric, logic, and hermeneutics into a kind of manual of spiritual life. With the goal of developing students for evangelical ministry, it left no breathing space between the critical arts of interpreting, persuasive skills of preaching, and assimilation into the pious life. The goal of cultivating the Word in the lives of the faithful meant that the agency of the Word was active through all of these stages, the meanings derived from scripture necessarily "*in suos usus prudenter ac sincero advectu transferenda*," application being a kind of transduction from one mode of being to another (Rambach 1732: 820).

Chladenius taught rhetoric at the University of Erlangen and developed a *hermeneutica generalis* that, despite its Enlightenment underpinnings, applied the Pietist doctrine of the *Affektenlehre*, which theorizes how the arrangement of words affect the disposition of the speaker's audience, and in the reverse direction, how the interpreter decodes these affective strategies to understand a rhetorical text. Perfect understanding is achieved when words arouse thoughts in the receiver that correspond to the thoughts of the communicator: "A meaningful oration or written work is presented or written in order to cause a stirring in our souls" (2000: 56). The nexus between Paul's letters and sermons served as Chladni's exemplars for this application of rhetorical theory to interpretive practice.

It was because of the sharp turnabout of hermeneutics in the nineteenth and twentieth centuries from a committed ally to a determined foe of Enlightenment rationalism that Hasso E. Jaeger suggests that contemporary hermeneutics is "without tradition" (1974: 84). (My historical account may be regarded as a rejoinder to Jaeger's thesis, but without the least challenge to the importance of his magisterial work of research.) But as we have seen, rhetoric served quietly as a floor of continuity through this conflicted history. Although not strictly within the hermeneutic tradition, Wilhelm von Humboldt's (1767–1835) language theory had an enormous influence, and his contributions were deeply rooted in humanist principles of rhetorical education. He asserted that "language develops only in social intercourse, and humans understand themselves only having tested the comprehensibility of their words on others," echoing the humanist tradition of *multiplex disputandi* (2000: 101). Echoing the Italian humanists, he promoted a method of historical research that depended heavily on invention (*ingenium*) and cultivation (*Bildung*):

> The more deeply the historian is able to comprehend humanity and its activity through his genius and study, or the more humanly he is disposed by nature and circumstance, and the more purely he allows his humanity to reign, the more completely will he resolve the task of his enterprise.
>
> (2000: 107)

His influential theory of language development was an uncanny echo of Erasmus's instruction in the principle of *imitatio*, the creative application of models to new contexts: "[I]ts 'dead' part must always be regenerated in thinking, come to life in speech and understanding, and hence must pass over entirely into the subject" (Humboldt 1999: 62). Johann Droysen (1808–84) appropriated from preceptive rhetoric the reciprocity of part and whole for his theory of the relation of the individual and the spirit of history, and developed a topical system based on Aristotle's commonplace logic for a classification of interpretative methods. These humanist appropriations kept the rhetorical heritage of hermeneutics alive.

The practical integration of rhetoric and hermeneutics was eventually codified by Friedrich Schleiermacher (1768–1834), who saw a perfect symmetry between the two arts: "The belonging together of hermeneutics and rhetoric consists in the fact that every act of understanding is the inversion of a speech-act" (Schleiermacher 1998: 7). This parallel of the disciplinary functions corresponds to the competencies of speech and interpretation, speech acting as "the mediation of the communal nature of thought" in building a *sensus communis*, and interpretation tracing each utterance to "the knowledge of the whole of the historical life to which it belongs". Schleiermacher preserved the humanist impulse of hermeneutics by situating the competency of human studies in human judgment (1998: 7–8). Wilhelm Dilthey (1833–1911) embodied the conflicted heritage of hermeneutics as heir to the Enlightenment pursuit of knowledge and stepchild of humanist rhetoric. His 1867 lecture "On Understanding and Hermeneutics" carried over Droysen's disciplinary distinction between explanation and understanding to hermeneutics: "We want to understand human beings. Regarding all other objects there is an interest to explain" (Dilthey 1996: 229). In this schema hermeneutics is indebted to classical rhetoric as a course of study focused on the cultivation of the person. But Dilthey also believed the "main purpose" of hermeneutics was "to preserve the universal validity of historical interpretation against the inroads of romantic caprice and skeptical subjectivity, and to give a theoretical justification for such validity, upon which all the certainty of historical knowledge is founded," intensifying its schizophrenic identity in an increasingly polarized disciplinary universe (1996: 250).

Dilthey continued to think of hermeneutic understanding as the sympathetic re-creation of the original intent behind historical texts, "reconstructing the whole of inner life, so that something like a second self-consciousness of history is achieved," promoting the Schleiermachian sense of historical repetition rather than dialogue. It is important to recognize that this was eventually amended in Dilthey's exposition by an appeal to rhetorical models of social reasoning, and of their priority over institutional hierarchies of knowledge, thus anticipating Heidegger (1996: 234), who in the summer of 1924 lecture course proclaimed that "We are better off since we possess the Aristotelian *Rhetoric* rather than a philosophy of language. In the *Rhetoric* we have something before us that deals with speaking as a basic mode of the being of the being-with-one-another of human beings themselves" (2009: 80). These lectures are shot through with a rhetorical ethos, of "what one debates in life in a customary way, and the manner and mode of talking it through," of "occupying oneself with other human beings," "of being-with-and-toward-others" (2009: 84, 121, 83). Public discourse becomes the articulating structure and binding agent that organizes institutional forces, straddles temporal ruptures, and relays back and forth between identity and action – the discursive armature of being-in-the-world. Gadamer put this in disciplinary terms: "Heidegger's own new appropriation of Aristotle does not take its start from the *Metaphysics* but from the *Rhetoric*, and the *Ethics* as well" (2007: 379). Both Heidegger and Gadamer pushed to reverse the order of privilege between the knowledge production of the research paradigm and the rhetorical ideal of paideia, eclipsing the technique of the expert with the practical reason of the *idiota mente*. This advocacy recapitulates the counter-Enlightenment thrust against the siren song of science and for the humanist legacy expressed in the paradigm of rhetorical deliberation. If wisdom is formed out of and responsive to the needs and ends of a community as it confronts each particular occasion, philosophy sits now within a rhetorical framework.

The sensation caused by the publication of Gadamer's *Truth and Method* gave the concept of hermeneutics cultural currency at roughly the same time that rhetoric had regained a measure of intellectual prestige, resonating with the linguistic turn pursued by Heidegger, Wittgenstein, and others (Simons 1990). It is well known that Gadamer turned to rhetoric in the opening section of *Truth and Method* ("The Significance of the Humanist Tradition for the Human Sciences"), but just as important to a collaboration between hermeneutics and rhetoric are Gadamer's later papers and remarks on the subject, an emphasis which seems only to increase with urgency over time. Gadamer's most emphatic statements on the subject occur in a symposium with Ricardo Dottori, where he challenges the view that the art of persuasion is dependent on a prior ethical knowing: "Rhetoric is the starting point. The whole of ethics is rhetoric, and the idea that phronesis is rhetoric already occurs in Aristotle" (Gadamer 2000: 52–3). When Gadamer was asked at the age of 96 what remained for him to do in hermeneutics, he responded: "Could we perhaps go back to the ancient meaning of rhetoric?" (2000: 427).

Hermeneutics and rhetoric have not become fused as Heidegger had imagined or as Gadamer had urged, in part because of the durability of modern disciplinary divisions, and in part because hermeneutics has continued to manifest its conflicted identity as child of the Enlightenment and of classical humanism. With Ricoeur and Habermas, the hope that some form of Kantian reason might prevail in a hermeneutically inflected discourse theory suggested that rhetoric should keep its secondary status. In rhetoric studies, hermeneutics falls between stools, either because it is suspected of conservative leanings by critical rhetoric scholars, or is treated as one flavor among various continental perspectives in philosophy or critical studies (Hariman 2003: 290–1). But if history is any judge, the occasions for the two disciplinary competencies to be joined and support each other will continue.

Bibliography

Chladenius, J. M. (2000) "On the Interpretation of Historical Books and Accounts," in Mueller-Vollmer, K. (Ed.), *The Hermeneutics Reader*, New York: Continuum, pp. 64–71.

Déaut, R. (1982) *The Message of the New Testament and the Aramaic Bible (Targum)*, translated by Miletic, S. F., Rome: Biblical Institute Press.

Dilthey, W. (1996) *Selected Works*, Vol. 4, translated by Makkreel, R. A. and Rodi, F., Princeton: Princeton University Press.

Eden, Kathy (1997) *Hermeneutics and the Rhetorical Tradition*, New Haven: Yale University Press.

Erasmus, D. (1933) "Ratio seu Methodus Compendio Perveniendi ad Veram Theologiam," *Ausgewählte Werke*, edited by Holborn, H., Munich: C. H. Beck'ssche.

——(1978) *Collected Works of Erasmus*, Vol. 24, edited by Thompson, C. R., Toronto: University of Toronto Press.

Flacius Illyricus, Matthias (2011) *How to Understand the Sacred Scriptures from Clavis Scripturae sacrae*, translated by Johnston, Wade R., Saginaw, MI: Magdeburg Press.

Gadamer, H. G. (2007) "Hermeneutics Tracking the Trace [OnDerrrida]," in Palmer, R. (Ed.), *The Gadamer Reader*, Evanston, IL: Northwestern University Press, pp. 372–406.

——(2000) *A Century of Philosophy*, translated by Coltman, R., New York: Continuum Press.

Gawthrop, R. and Strauss, G. (1984) "Protestantism and Literacy in Early Modern Germany," *Past and Present*, Vol. 104, pp. 31–55.

Grondin, J. (1994) *Introduction to Philosophical Hermeneutics*, translated by Weinshiemer, J., New Haven: Yale University Press.

Hariman, R. (2003) "Prudence in the 21st Century," in Hariman, R. (Ed.), *Prudence: Classical Virtue, Postmodern Practice*, University Park: Pennsylvania State University Press.

Heidegger, M. (2009) *Basic Concepts of Aristotelian Philosophy*, translated by Metcalf, R. D. and Tanzer, M. B., Bloomington: Indiana University Press.

Humboldt, W. von (2000) "The Nature and Conformation of Language," in Mueller-Vollmer, K. (Ed.), *The Hermeneutics Reader*, New York: Continuum, pp. 99–104.

——(1999) *On Language*, edited by Losonsky, M., Cambridge: Cambridge University Press.

Jaeger, H.-E. H. (1974) "Studien zur Frühgeschichte der Hermeneutik," *Archiv für Begriffsgeschichte*, Vol. 18, pp. 35–84.

Quintilian, M. F. (1920) *Institutio Oratoria Books I–III*, translated by Butler, H. E., Cambridge, MA: Harvard University Press.

Rambach, J. J. (1732) *Institutiones Hermeneuticae Sacrae*, Jena: Hartungiana.

Saint Augustine (1958) *On Christian Doctrine*, translated by Roberston, Jr., D. W., Indianapolis: Bobbs-Merrill.

Schleiermacher, F. (1998) *Hermeneutics and Criticism and Other Writings*, edited by Bowie, A., Cambridge: Cambridge University Press.

Simons, H. W., ed. (1990) *The Rhetorical Turn: Invention and Persuasion in the Conduct of Inquiry*, Chicago: University of Chicago Press.

Vico, G. (2002) *The First New Science*, translated by Pompa, L., Cambridge: Cambridge University Press.

Wolff, C. F. von (1770) *Logic, or Rational Thoughts on the Powers of the Human Understanding*, translated by Wolfius, B., London: Hawes, Clarke and Collins.

38
HERMENEUTICS AND INTERCULTURAL UNDERSTANDING

Bruce Janz

If we want to think about the relationship between hermeneutics and intercultural understanding, it is worth thinking first about how intercultural understanding sometimes happens apart from hermeneutics. Historically, of course, intercultural understanding in the West often amounted to the projection of the self on the other. So, Europe in the colonial era "understood" the non-European world as the source of labor, resources, adventure stories, and as a missionary endeavor. It became a projection of European desire and fear, of paternalistic impulses and cautionary tales. For Hegel and subsequent "scientific" theorists of culture, the non-European world was the origin story in a tale of progress to modernity and civilization. Again, it was an actor in a European story, and as such was subsumed and consumed. It is at times also possible to find this kind of ethnocentrism and cultural superiority in other cultures' attitudes towards outsiders.

Clearly, whatever else this approach yielded, it was not intercultural understanding. And so, more recently others have emphasized cultural alterity, trying to resist the impulse to subsume other cultures under a European narrative. Some of these attempts are indirectly inspired by a Rousseauean romanticism which valorized difference without attempting to understand it, while others essentialized one or more aspects of cultural existence. In either case the impulse is to correct the self-serving assumptions of culturally superior approaches to others. Despite these good intentions, we find articles such as "Understanding Africans' Conceptualizations of Intercultural Competence" (Nwosu 2009), which generalizes on Africans' character, values, subjectivity, heritage, and so forth, in order to provide a ready guide to uninitiated non-Africans on how to interact with another culture. This sort of approach is intended as a rough guide to beginning conversation between (mainly) Westerners and (in this case) Africans, but even if such sweeping generalizations are sufficient for that purpose (and it is not clear that they will even get the casual visitor very far), they fall well short of anything like intercultural understanding in a philosophical sense.

There is a third approach, more limited in scope, which we can also identify. This occurs when specific cultural artifacts (these may be practices or they may be material objects or linguistic elements) are compared across cultures. In philosophy, for instance, one may ask about the concept of truth in various languages and cultures, and attempt to draw implications about other aspects of culture from these clues (Hall 2001; Wiredu 1996). This more modest approach does not aspire to characterize another culture in general terms (we hear nothing about what "Africans" are like, for instance), but instead focusses on specific items which bear both similarities and differences from a researcher's culture. So, the concept of "truth" clearly has a range of meanings in English, and the question then becomes, how is it used in another culture?

This has much to commend it, but it does have its limitations as well. What is the "it" that is being compared? Do we need to assume some underlying ontology that makes the most basic recognition possible? Many philosophers, from Quine to Derrida, would agree that the assumption of such an ontology is highly questionable at best. "Truth" can mean different things within a single language, depending on one's philosophical approach, and such variation is even more pronounced between languages and cultures. This does not necessarily mean that we are left with complete relativism, but that there must be another way to approach intercultural understanding at the conceptual level apart from assuming some prior ontological agreement.

Versions of these approaches to intercultural understanding exist to this day, but hermeneutics stands apart from all of them, or rather, stands as an answer to the forms of misunderstanding that each of these introduces. At the most basic level, philosophical hermeneutics shifts the primordial condition of understanding, from assuming that we currently lack understanding and therefore simply need new information and experience, to assuming that we currently misunderstand, and therefore need to have the sources and conditions of our own misunderstanding uncovered and examined so that a healthier and more productive interaction can take place. In other words, understanding is as much about oneself and one's own situatedness as it is about that which is being understood, or more precisely, it is an account of the experience of encounter itself. Some have argued that hermeneutics understood in these terms is useful for intercultural understanding (Pillay 2002), or even that cross-cultural interpretation makes historical interpretation possible (Lampert 1997).

Past this first step, though, intercultural hermeneutics can take many forms and have many goals. Hermeneutics in an intercultural setting has been variously understood as:

- A method for facilitating dialogue across cultures, with a view to accessing emic content (e.g., Michrina and Richards 1996; Geertz 2003);
- A way of comparing cultural traditions (Mall 2000);
- A way of analyzing cultural objects or practices by those within the culture (e.g., Madu 1992);
- A term for some forms of linguistic or semantic analysis (e.g., Odera Oruka's use of the term for Hallen and Sodipo's work; Bongmba 1998);

- A way of describing a cultural life-world – intra-cultural, rather than intercultural (Okere 1983);
- A way of accessing "non-philosophy" (Okere 1983);
- A way of uncovering modes of misunderstanding in cultural encounter (e.g., Serequeberhan 1994; Mbembe 2001; Mudimbe 1988);
- A method of establishing a philosophical tradition in a place that does not have some hallmark of philosophy (e.g., a textual corpus – Okere 1983; Owolabi 2001);
- A way for a non-European philosophy to characterize other cultural philosophies (Watsuji 1961);
- A way to create new philosophical questions that come from and resonate with a geographic and cultural place (Janz 2009).

Some of these approaches treat hermeneutics as a method, with a specific kind of understanding in mind as the goal or which describes some kind of encounter such as dialogue which itself has a further goal, while others hew closer to a Gadamerian approach and regard method as a step on the way to hermeneutic philosophy, that is, the uncovering one's *Vorurteile*, or prejudices, inclinations, and blind-spots while at the same time establishing the basis for reciprocal understanding. Not only is there a continuum between method and philosophy in hermeneutics, there also is between hermeneutics as explicitly intercultural, and as more or less intra-cultural. In other words, there are thinkers in a variety of cultures who see hermeneutics as a tool for encounter with other cultures, and there are others who see hermeneutics as a means for understanding elements of their own cultures, in order to uncover their own standing in relation to their own tradition. The "other" that is encountered may be another culture or it may be one's own history or tradition; it may be the untheorized aspects of one's own culture, or the practices of another.

The roots of hermeneutics in the West are, in part, in the analysis of religious texts, and in particular the attempt to bridge the gap between a simple exegesis of an historical text and the contemporary moral, spiritual, or practical applications of that text. Gadamer's use of *phronesis* comes in part from the need to bring an ever-receding historical text into relevance, as we think about what cultural competence actually means, and how those texts are formative in a culture. To that extent, intra-cultural hermeneutics can and does occur around the world. But hermeneutics is about more than just competence within one's own culture – it is about the understanding and constitution of the self, and the recognition that the self is a free actor that is nevertheless embedded in a constellation of meanings which shape every decision, and which require interpretation at every step of the way. "Culture" is a somewhat artificial shorthand for meaning-sets, or horizons, that are shared. But the artificiality comes when we realize that elements of those sets of meanings overlap in multiple ways with other cultures. There is not, after all, a single horizon that someone from French culture has, that differs from that which someone from Kenyan culture or Chinese culture has. The different forms of overlap are myriad, and any cultural ascription is therefore a shorthand, a snapshot of a moment, taken for specific purposes, solidifying a set of characteristics deemed significant by someone.

In other words, while the categories of "intra-cultural" and "intercultural" hermeneutics might seem to be fairly obvious and distinct, the boundaries are less clear the more that they are examined. Not only that, but the reasons for those bound-aries may well be caught up in the construction of self, culture, and nation. To whom is it of value to think of cultures as things that might be in dialogue (as opposed to people, for instance, or systems of thought)? At the beginning of this chapter, I pointed out that cultural interaction had several problematic forms. Clearly for someone like Kant, Hegel, or Hume, identifying cultures with clear and bright lines between them helped to justify the story about the advance of civiliza-tion to its pinnacle, which was, of course, European civilization. And yet, there is clearly difference in the world. Romanticism fetishized it, again rendering it an element in a European story, but the imperative to deal with difference remains.

This is why hermeneutics looks, at first glance, so important and useful. It at least attempts to offer a way of thinking difference that is not as uncritical as attempts in the past (and present). And this is also why the border between intra- and inter-cultural hermeneutics must remain blurry – to reify the notion of culture tends to undermine what is most important about hermeneutics – that it allows a self-critical and self-constitutive encounter with difference as embedded in an already meaningful life-world.

Possible hesitations concerning hermeneutics and intercultural understanding

Despite its seeming usefulness, there are some reasons for questioning the place of hermeneutics in intercultural understanding. Space permits consideration of only two of these, but they are crucial to this discussion.

1. Is hermeneutic philosophy really universal, or does it implicitly promote the West and devalue other cultures?

Gadamer's claim for philosophical hermeneutics is that it is universal (Gadamer 1989: 474ff), or more precisely, that it is a "universal aspect of philosophy." This claim has given pause to a number of European commentators, such as Habermas and Derrida. It has equally raised questions about the usefulness of her-meneutics in an intercultural situation. Thomas Ellis argues that Gadamer's herme-neutics is essentially a colonial project. "Gadamerian Bildung, with its undeniably conservative bent, reflects an attempt to reduce the other to the same" (Ellis 2009: 107). "[Jarava Lal] Mehta," he says, "suggests that philosophical hermeneutics may help the self understand the self, but it does not help the self understand the other" (Ellis 2009: 105). Ellis' argument is that Gadamerian hermeneutics in particular, despite attempting to avoid the limitations of the kinds of intercultural encounter that were outlined at the beginning of this chapter, nevertheless still falls prey to the fundamental problem, which is the reduction of the other to the self. In a critique reminiscent of Habermas, Ellis (using Mehta) argues that hermeneutics tends to maintain and build the self, rather than subject it to any thoroughgoing critique. The assumption of misunderstanding does not extend very far, and the other "becomes a constitutive moment in the enrichment of the self," which is the "heroic" nature of hermeneutics (Ellis 2009: 109). Ellis' call is not to abandon hermeneutics, but instead transform the image of the heroic odyssey into a pilgrimage. "[U]nlike the philosophical hero who returns only to an enriched home, [the pilgrim] recognizes, and is subsequently reconciled to, the death of its traditional identity, that is, its home" (Ellis 2009: 116).

The question about the usefulness of hermeneutics to intercultural understanding is at least partially addressed by making two distinctions. Kathleen Wright (2004) points out that it is true in one sense that any claim to universality invites suspicion. A Nietzschean impulse to unmask the will to power is appropriate. The claim of hermeneutics, though, is not to a universality of either perspective or method. Hermeneutics is a "universal aspect" of philosophy, which means that it is the impulse toward a shared understanding. The shared understanding is not presumed, but stands as a goal. It is a different basis for understanding from the approaches listed at the beginning of the chapter, because it does not depend on a universally held narrative, or method (such as science), or a shared ontology. In a sense, then, hermeneutics as a universal aspect of philosophy exists as the antithesis of the versions of intercultural understanding which look for some universally shared set of values, or even a universally expressible essence (the "African character" from before).

The second distinction is between hermeneutics as a universal aspect of philosophy, and hermeneutics as universal understanding. Gadamer clearly supports the first but not the second. There is no position, either in time or space, where understanding can be universal. All understanding exists in tradition and depends on *Vorurteile*. David Couzens Hoy (1991) argues that hermeneutics is pluralistic rather than ethnocentric because there is no convergence on a single language or a single interpretation. Armin Geertz speaks of "ethnohermeneutics" (2003) to reflect this pluralism (although, his report of the failure of a cross-cultural conference to establish research protocols of anthropologists among the Hopi suggests that the hermeneutics is mainly a method for uncovering data rather than a philosophy that raises questions about the self – 337ff).

None of this means that, in an intercultural situation, anyone's guard should be dropped. It is all too easy for the will to power to exert itself, and for a conversation which seems constructive to hide misunderstandings. But it is important to understand hermeneutics in this context as much to be about self-critique and self-understanding as anything else. If an intercultural encounter can make apparent that one's questions about another culture have been based on misunderstanding, that is as important as any piece of knowledge gained from interaction.

2. Which cultures do we have in mind, when we speak of hermeneutics and intercultural understanding?

The answer might seem obvious – any culture counts. But "culture," as already mentioned, is a kind of shorthand for a set of differences. It is a useful shorthand, but like any conceptual solidification, it can also be obscuring. This becomes clearer if we consider a debate often not seen as part of intercultural hermeneutics – the Gadamer–Derrida debate.

In the Gadamer–Derrida debates in April of 1981, we have an encounter that is usually seen as a kind of family squabble between the intellectual children of Heidegger, a dialogue (or in Gadamer's opinion, a lack of dialogue) between hermeneutics and deconstruction. It was also an encounter between generations, between languages, and between nations which, less than forty years earlier, had been at war. It was an encounter which has been analyzed and referenced, which has been seen as important in the history of the development of both hermeneutics and deconstruction (at least in the sense that it clarified the mission for these projects), and which occurred at the same time that others such as Paul Ricoeur and John Caputo were also thinking about the terms of an encounter between these two traditions.

And yet, we rarely if ever think of this philosophical encounter as intercultural. Why is that? Is it because it is a dialogue within European traditions, or between thinkers who can claim many of the same intellectual forebears? Is it because we don't really think of France and Germany as being different cultures, at least not intellectually? Does intercultural encounter in some way presume that at least one of the partners in the encounter is not European or in the European tradition? What of Latin American philosophy – it is clearly mostly within a European intellectual tradition, and yet is sometimes seen as intercultural? Does intercultural understanding deal with cultural particularities, and if so, which ones? And does the intellectual life rise above those particularities, or is it implicated by them? Or do we presume that in some cultures the intellectual rises above the cultural, while in others it does not?

This matters because it gets to the heart of what we think of as "self" and "other," at the level of culture. There is a tendency to group a set of cultures together as "the West," and another set as "traditional" cultures, or "developing countries," or something like that. We tend not to think of philosophy conducted in the West as having a place, much less many places, some which share languages (but not other things), others which have different languages (but share other things). In other words, we often come to intercultural philosophy with an unexamined set of categories which incline our modes of understanding in one way or another.

At its best, hermeneutic philosophy should raise all these categories to question. Even among hermeneutic thinkers, though, this can be a blind spot. In an interview in 1985–6, Gadamer addresses the question about hermeneutics in a non-European cultural setting:

QUESTION: Could one say that your hermeneutics is a European hermeneutics, that one cannot think about hermeneutics in the same way when one teaches the classics in Salt Lake City or Winnipeg?

GADAMER: … This isn't how I experienced my presence as a teacher in North America, where I also feel that I am well understood now, when I speak English. But I think of the interest in Heidegger among the Japanese who come to study with us in Germany … The way Heidegger has made the Christian history of the Occident go up in smoke, so to speak, so that there is only this vague talk of the divine, of a God, or of Gods, all this suits them. But then I wondered why there wasn't an interest in my work. It is because they confused the category of historically effective consciousness with the real content of effective history in the Occident. Thus it was not understood that when I make use of Augustine's trinitarian speculations, (the theme of "verbum"), I am not defending Christian claims, but identifying their categorical significance.

(Gadamer 1992: 69)

It is noteworthy that Gadamer did not consider the possibility that he was, in fact, understood by the Japanese scholars, and that the reason that his thought was not found as useful as Heidegger's was that Heidegger enabled them to ask questions relevant to their culture, whereas Gadamer (on the surface at least) did not. It may not be that the Japanese didn't understand the "categorical significance" as much as that they were unable to see hermeneutic theory as applicable to their own history. The strangeness of the fact that Heidegger's work was accepted in Japan while Gadamer's was not, could have been the opportunity to ask whether he was mis-understanding something about the Japanese, but instead it underscored the limita-tions of the questioning that was available to Gadamer. It was them, not he, who misunderstood, and it doesn't even occur to him that he might misunderstand.

Would Gadamer have had this reaction to someone from the West who did not use his work? He did not react this way in the debate with Derrida, although the discussion was different in that case. The only point to make here is that the terms of the intercultural often come with unexamined baggage, and as with any categor-ization, it can both cover over and uncover understanding.

African philosophy and hermeneutics

Hermeneutics has had a recurring presence in African philosophy, and exhibits many of the forms already mentioned in this chapter. Here, I will expand on some of the significant work in this area, to illustrate the range of hermeneutic engagement, but also to set the stage for a further discussion on the prospects of hermeneutics in intercultural understanding more broadly. The thinkers I mention here will not be all who work on hermeneutics within Africa, but these should give a sense as to how hermeneutics is used there, and what it has to do with intercultural understanding.

In *African Philosophy: A Historico-Hermeneutical Investigation of the Conditions of its Possibility*, Theophilus Okere presents one of the earliest conscious efforts within African philosophy to apply hermeneutics to an African life-world. His hermeneu-tics are intercultural only in that his theoretical frame of reference is the European tradition of hermeneutic thought – the point is not to set up a dialogue with another culture, but to understand the roots of his own. He is not interested in thinking about a "collective" philosophy (in fact, he dismisses that as a "false route" to Afri-can philosophy in his first chapter). The usefulness of hermeneutics is to provide a mediation between philosophy and the non-philosophical features of lived experi-ence and its expression, whether that be religion, culture, or even just the irration-ality of other presuppositions. Hermeneutic philosophy is both the interpretive tool and the result of mediating and rationalizing lived experience. Okere is somewhat unclear about the nature of non-philosophy; sometimes, it is the irrational, some-times the prerational, sometimes the transcendent. The philosophical and hermeneutic moment is the appropriation or repetition of these non-philosophical roots without negating them.

The appeal of hermeneutics to Okere is that he wants to ensure that African philosophy has a unique starting point, since it is rooted in a particular tradition of non-philosophy. This means that African philosophy can be unique, not reducible to other philosophical systems, and at the same time make use of all the rational tools that any other philosophical tradition assumes as essential. In other words, hermeneutics allows the ontological moment of self-understanding to emerge through repetition for African philosophy. Okere's use of hermeneutics is largely limited to being a method for uncovering meanings that are latent within the patterns of objectification a culture employs. As such, there are limits to how much his method can reflect on itself so as to foreground its own prejudices, as well as to how well it can deal with meanings that are not simply there to be uncovered, but are the result of some violence that does not want itself to be named.

Tsenay Serequeberhan's work is not a direct response to Okere, but he does address the question of violence, and he extends hermeneutics past an attempt to uncover unspoken content within a culture. *The Hermeneutics of African Philosophy: Horizon and Discourse* works out a version of African hermeneutics that is more sophisticated and more pointed than Okere's. His work appropriates key insights from Heidegger and Gadamer to fashion a philosophy "born of struggle" that can lay bare patterns of oppression and de-centering, without resorting to the cynicism of a Foucauldian critique of power or a Lacanian archaeology of desire. This is an approach that has a chance of bearing positive fruit as Africa tries to rethink the meanings that have accrued to it over the past several hundred years.

Serequeberhan has grasped a central fact that Okere overlooked – that hermeneutics itself has, to use Gadamer's term, an effective-history (*Wirkungsgeschichte*). While Okere gives an overview of the development of hermeneutics in the West, Serequeberhan recognizes that this history is relevant to the nature of hermeneutics itself. The fact that hermeneutics itself has a history, however, does not rule it out as a useful way of interrogating a particular kind of being. Rather, it means that we need to take seriously the history of the kinds of questions that hermeneutics has been designed to address. In the West, those questions have revolved around science's claim to universal knowledge, and the resultant limitation of all human meaning to that which is examinable in scientific categories. In African history, in Serequeberhan's Eritrea and elsewhere, the hermeneutic was one built on an encounter with a "foreign and aggressive piety." These are not the questions that need to be addressed now. The salient issue is the crisis resulting from the colonial project of Europe.

Serequeberhan follows both Heidegger and Gadamer here, in seeing hermeneutics as occurring in a failure of some sort, either a Heideggerian disruption that leads to reflection or a Gadamerian sense of misunderstanding that is made manifest in the act of dialogue. Serequeberhan recognizes that failures of understanding must be defined in encounter, not in some essentialized manner. It is not, for example, that Africa does not "work," that there is slow economic or technological progress, which brings us to reflective thought. While Heidegger does spend a great deal of time talking about the way technology "enframes" (a word Serequeberhan picks up) the world and produces a certain kind of non-critical, derivative understanding, he is mostly concerned with a product of European rationality and the kinds of questions it poses. It is an encounter, for him, between ourselves and our interaction with the milieu around us.

So, the failure at stake here is one which has enframed discourse about Africa, both by Africans and by the rest of the world, and has led to certain kinds of quasi-metaphysical assertions being made. The encounter has set the stage for a certain kind of alienated self-understanding; this is interpreted metaphysically by some, as a statement about "the way Africans are." Serequeberhan wants to define the issue as one of interpretation, not essence, and he wants to see that as emerging from encounter. Hermeneutics, in other words, makes apparent the misunderstandings about Africans while at the same time suggesting a path forward, both among and between African cultures, and between Africans and non-Africans. Serequeberhan tends to isolate a single kind of dialogue (that is, colonialism) as determinative of African experience, but the basic hermeneutic insight is valid.

Serequeberhan continues in later work (e.g., Serequeberhan 2000) to think about the emancipatory potential of hermeneutics (see also Mbembe 2001 on this). The central question is that of how existence might be exercised in the face of pervasive violence. The crucial element in answering this question is the notion of heritage, a concept that has its lineage, for Serequeberhan, in Gadamer's effective-history. Early in the book he even puts it in platial terms:

> This (non)identity, this in-between, is the ambiguity of our heritage. For we are the ones – in one way or another – who live and have experienced this "ambiguous adventure" and feel, in the very depth of our being, the unnerving experience of being two in one, Europe and non-Europe.
>
> (Serequeberhan 2000: 2)

It is an "in-between," specifically in-between two places which themselves have coherence and identity, but this is not simply an alienated space. It is a place in its own right. Existence happens here, and it does not owe its integrity to the oppression which produced the in-between in the first place (17). African culture does not owe its integrity to the racism which hems it in.

The strength of *Our Heritage* is that it recognizes that hermeneutics is not a foreign methodology imposed from the outside, but can be a way of theorizing expressions of life within Africa. This version of hermeneutics has the elements we expect – dialogue, a sense of tradition, an interpretive approach to subjectivity which avoids the tendency of many to essentialize African existence. At the same time, it also diverges from European versions of hermeneutics in that its central questions are different.

A third approach to hermeneutics in African philosophy can be seen in Raphael Okechukwu Madu's *African Symbols, Proverbs and Myths: The Hermeneutics of Destiny*. Madu is interested in the relative disdain that philosophers have had for symbols, the belief that symbols were pre-rational and thus not worthy of philosophical attention. He wants to rehabilitate symbolic, proverbial, and mythological thought as relevant to philosophy by showing that it need not merely lead to anonymously held world-views, or deep structures. The goal, then, is to establish that symbols are *philosophically* relevant, not simply *culturally* relevant, and that hermeneutics is the best method for extracting the philosophical content. In this, he is reacting to thinkers such as Paulin Hountondji, who argued that Africa's symbolic and mythological past was largely irrelevant to philosophy, as it was a set of beliefs held anonymously and uncritically by a large group of people (which he called "ethnophilosophy"). Madu wishes to rehabilitate these forms as philosophically important without reducing them to ethnophilosophy.

Madu begins by asking what kind of hermeneutics is appropriate for African philosophy. It must be recognized that this question is crucial, and overlooked by most thinkers who make use of hermeneutic theory. He sets up the question as a choice between existential hermeneutics, represented by Heidegger and Gadamer, and methodological hermeneutics, represented by Ricoeur. Ricoeur, Madu argues, moves to a reliance on symbols precisely because phenomenology does not suggest a method. While Ricoeur is more complex than Madu allows here, the important issue is that he seems to want to use hermeneutics as a tool for the excavation of philosophical thought within culture. In itself this may not be a problem, but it is not clear that it is something which can be found in Ricoeur. However, what can be drawn from Ricoeur is the commitment to symbols and metaphors, and the need to connect this with human existence, rather than simply an abstract structure or set of functions. The key, for Madu, is in the use he makes of hermeneutics. And the key to understanding that is the term "destiny."

The subtitle of his book, "The Hermeneutics of Destiny," is significant but not immediately clear. As with the term "hermeneutics," Madu gives an overview of Western thought on the matter. He interprets destiny as fate, and as the issue of one's state after death, and then briefly outlines the various metaphysical options in Western thought. And, as with the outline of Western hermeneutics, this is not just done for the intellectual exercise. Although he does not explicitly say so, it seems clear that the list of options amounts to a set of beliefs and arguments about the afterlife. As beliefs and arguments, these are metaphysical. In contrast, Madu delves into Igbo cultural life for another way of understanding destiny. While he sketches a very different set of beliefs to those offered by Western thought, what really matters is not the difference in the beliefs but the fact that hermeneutics allows access to meaning or significance in Igbo culture.

Madu's typical pattern in the second half of the book is to analyze an aspect of Igbo culture in a "metaphysical" manner, by trying to isolate and define a concept. Then, he applies his hermeneutic method in order to overcome contradictions or paradoxes that arose in the metaphysical analysis. For instance, in his discussion of Chi ("Igbo Symbolic Forms on the Human Destiny as Language-Bound," chapter 8), he points out that the term is ambiguous. It can refer both to destiny, and the "dispenser of destiny," both one's fate and the divine spark within that directs that fate (Madu 1992: 180). Madu's way of reconciling the ambiguity is to consider the language used to express the concept. It is possible, he says, that the language used when speaking of Chi is metonymical, in that effect and cause can stand in for each other. As well, the religious aspect has to be remembered. Chi may also be understood as an intermediary between the divine and the human, that which determines or describes the relationship between God(s) and the human. And thirdly, it is possible that the seeming ambiguity in the understanding of Chi really points to the many ways in which people's lives find expression. The "Chi" points to the truth of a person's life, which may not be the same as another's truth, but nevertheless has an integrity.

It is important to recognize what Madu contributes in his specific analysis here. In moving beyond the metaphysical, that is, the notion that our words are about things and it is our task to get those things right, he has recognized that there are forms of life that can be explicated in their own terms. Destiny plays a real part in people's lives. It matters to them, and the strength of hermeneutics is to give access to what matters, to those for whom it matters, and hopefully others who might be willing to listen. Understanding Chi does not require a structuralist/functionalist analysis; that account could not matter to those who hold Chi as significant. It only fits into the discourse of a distant academy, and only answers foreign questions.

So, we have three ways of engaging African culture hermeneutically. All blur the boundary between inter- and intra-cultural understanding. Okere asks about non-philosophy, and as he develops his way of dealing with his own culture, he provides an insight on how other cultures might ask about their own non-philosophy. Serequeberhan addresses the fundamentally perverse dialogue of colonialism, and uses the resources of hermeneutics to reset the intercultural conversation. And Madu uses hermeneutics to mine the symbolic resources of his own culture, and in the process renders his own culture to be a text, a horizon for discourse.

The potential of intercultural hermeneutics

This account of intercultural hermeneutics might have been told using other cultures as the focal point. The sites for hermeneutics would bear similarities with what has been described here, at least in some cases, and no doubt would differ in some. Hermeneutics offers some potential for intercultural understanding, especially in light of problematic versions of encounter that exist in the past and present. There are, to be sure, issues, and potential pitfalls, but also hope.

Bibliography

Elias Bongmba, "Toward a Hermeneutic of Wimbum *Tfu*" *African Studies Review* 41:3 (December 1998): 165–91.

Thomas B. Ellis, "On the Death of the Pilgrim: The Postcolonial Hermeneutics of Jarava Lal Mehta" in P. Bilimoria and A. B. Irvine, eds., *Postcolonial Philosophy of Religion*. Springer, 2009: 105–19.

Hans-Georg Gadamer, *Truth and Method, 2nd Revised Edition*. New York: The Crossroad Publishing Company, 1989.

——, "Interview: Writing and the Living Voice" in Dieter Misgeld and Graeme Nicholson, eds., *Hans-Georg Gadamer on Education, Poetry, and History: Applied Hermeneutics*. New York: SUNY Press, 1992: 63–71.

Armin Geertz, "Ethnohermeneutics and Worldview Analysis in the Study of Hopi Indian Religion" *Numen* 50 (2003): 309–48.

David L. Hall, "Just How Provincial *is* Western Philosophy? 'Truth' in Comparative Context" *Social Epistemology* 15:4 (2001): 285–97.

David Couzens Hoy, "Is Hermeneutics Ethnocentric?" in David R. Hiley, James F. Bohman and Richard Shusterman, eds., *The Interpretive Turn: Philosophy, Science, Culture*. Ithaca, NY: Cornell University Press, 1991: 155–75.

Bruce B. Janz, *Philosophy in an African Place*. Lanham, MD: Lexington Books, 2009.

Jay Lampert, "Gadamer and Cross-Cultural Hermeneutics" *The Philosophical Forum* 28:4; 29:1 (Summer/Fall 1997): 351–68.

Kenneth Liberman, "The Hermeneutics of Intercultural Communication" *Anthropological Linguistics* 26 (1984): 53–83.

Raphael Okechukwu Madu, *African Symbols, Proverbs and Myths: The Hermeneutics of Destiny*. New York and Frankfurt a.M.: Peter Lang, 1992. Reprinted by Owerri, Nigeria: Assumpta Press, 1996.

Ram Adhar Mall, *Intercultural Philosophy*. Lanham, MD: Rowman and Littlefield Publishers, 2000.

Achille Mbembe, *On the Postcolony*. Oakland, CA: University of California Press, 2001.

Diane P. Michelfelder and Richard E. Palmer, eds., *Dialogue and Deconstruction: The Gadamer–Derrida Encounter*. Albany, NY: SUNY Press, 1989.

Barry Michrina and Cherylanne Richards, *Person to Person: Fieldwork, Dialogue and the Hermeneutic Method*. Albany, NY: SUNY Press, 1996.

V.Y. Mudimbe, *The Invention of Africa*. Bloomington and Indianapolis, IN: Indiana University Press, 1988.

Peter Ogom Nwosu, "Understanding Africans' Conceptualizations of Intercultural Competence" in Darla K. Deardorff, ed., *The SAGE Handbook of Intercultural Competence*. Thousand Oaks, CA: Sage publications, 2009: 158–78.

Theophilus Okere, *African Philosophy: A Historico-Hermeneutical Investigation of the Conditions of its Possibility*. Lanham, MD: University Press of America, 1983.

Kolowole A. Owolabi, "The Quest for Method in African Philosophy: A Defense of the Hermeneutic-Narrative Approach" *The Philosophical Forum* 32:2 (Summer 2001): 147–63.

Nirmala Pillay, "The Significance of Gadamer's Hermeneutics for Cross-Cultural Understanding" *South African Journal of Philosophy* 21:4 (2002): 330–44.

Tsenay Serequeberhan, *The Hermeneutics of African Philosophy: Horizon and Discourse*. New York, NY: Routledge, 1994.

——, *Our Heritage: The Past in the Present of African-American and African Experience*. Lanham, MD: Rowman and Littlefield, 2000.

Chibueze C. Udeani, "Cultural Diversity and Globalisation: An Intercultural Hermeneutical (African) Perspective" in *International Review of Information Ethics* 7 (September 2007): 2–4.

Tetsuro Watsuji, *Fudo*. Translated as *Climate and Culture: A Philosophical Study*. Tokyo: The Hokuseido Press, 1961.

Kwasi Wiredu, *Cultural Universals and Particulars*. Bloomington: Indiana University Press, 1996.

Kathleen Wright, "On What We Have In Common: The Universality of Philosophical Hermeneutics" *Renascence: Essays on Values in Literature* 56:4 (Summer 2004): 235–55.

39

HERMENEUTICS AND THE SOCIAL SCIENCES

William Outhwaite

The complex interactions between hermeneutics and the social sciences can be simplified historically into two anti-positivist waves: one in the mid-nineteenth century, running into the early twentieth, and the other in the mid-to-late twentieth. This is the case at least in Europe; in North America, the pragmatist tradition which fed into symbolic interactionism was both more continuous across the two centuries and also less preoccupied with anti-positivism and what has been called 'methodological dualism': the insistence on the differences between natural and social science (Bernstein 1992; Helle 2005; Aiken 2006).

The story, like the term 'sociology' (the most prominent of the emergent social sciences in this connection) begins essentially with Comte (1798–1857). Comte's positivism, like the twentieth-century version, had a model of the unity of the sciences but, unlike later positivism, was not reductionist. However, sociology, the queen of the sciences for Comte and the last to ascend to the positive stage, was, like the other sciences, oriented to prediction and control: 'savoir pour prévoir, afin de pouvoir'. Early hermeneutic approaches to history and the (other) social sciences took shape in opposition to positivism.

Schleiermacher's consolidation of hermeneutics in a systematic form established the term understanding (*Verstehen*), which has survived as standard usage in English-language social science discourse, and made it central to interpretation – understood as a more systematic activity. Schleiermacher's contribution was made the central and culminating point of the account of 'the rise of hermeneutics' given by Wilhelm Dilthey (1833–1911), with whom hermeneutics becomes central to the self-definition of what he called the human sciences or *Geisteswissenschaften*. In these sciences, as Dilthey put it, the mental activity of humans and of some other animals, and its products, can be understood. Dilthey and his contemporary, the philosopher of history J.G. Droysen (1808–84) developed what we would now call a research programme for history and the other human sciences based on the distinctiveness of human psychic expressions and the understanding of those expressions. In a move which was to become a definitional feature of later interpretive social science, Dilthey, like Schleiermacher, emphasised the continuity between everyday understanding and more formal processes of interpretation. His distinction between the natural and human sciences was developed in large part in opposition to Comtean positivism, which had become influential, even in the German-speaking countries, by the middle of the nineteenth century.

In a parallel but more methodological formulation, two other neo-Kantian thinkers, Wilhelm Windelband and Heinrich Rickert, argued that the study of culture is essentially concerned with individual processes and relating them to shared human values, whereas the natural sciences are concerned with general laws about objects which are essentially remote from questions of value. We are interested, for example, in the French Revolution not just as a member of a class of revolutions exhibiting certain common features (this would be, for Rickert, a natural-scientific mode of approaching it), but as a unique event embodying, and perhaps also violating, certain crucial human values.[1]

In the background were the broader processes described by two great intellectual historians, Stuart Hughes (1958) and John Burrow (2000), in which a confidence about scientific knowledge which in the UK tends to be called 'Victorian' was coming into question. Max Weber (1864–1920) felt these tensions acutely. Along with Georg Simmel (1858–1918), whose attitude to the 'crisis of reason' was somewhat more relaxed, he worked out a relatively stable synthesis which incorporated hermeneutic insights without, he thought, compromising the scientificity of sociology and the other social sciences. The first sentence of Weber's posthumously published masterpiece, *Economy and Society*, links understanding with causal explanation: 'Sociology is a science which aims at the interpretative understanding of action in order thereby to understand its course and its effects.'

Whether by this Weber means that explanatory understanding is itself a form of causal explanation, or merely a complementary preliminary to it, the crucial point for him is that explanations of social phenomena must be both 'causally adequate' and 'meaningfully adequate'. Thus, for example, in his famous analysis of 'The Protestant Ethic and the "Spirit" of Capitalism', we need to know both that ascetic Protestants *were* economically innovative in early modern Europe, and that it 'makes sense' that someone concerned about their salvation should seek reassurance from their methodical and hopefully successful pursuit of their vocation.

Weber had tried to combine two mutually antagonistic conceptions of social science, with neo-Kantians on both sides.[2] In North America, pragmatist philosophers, most prominently represented in the social sciences by the social psychologist George Herbert Mead, had worked out an easier accommodation. Mead had studied at Harvard and then at Leipzig, with the psychologist Wilhelm Wundt (1832–1920), and with Dilthey in Berlin. Dilthey had been much concerned to differentiate between what he called an analytic and a descriptive psychology, with the latter seen as a humanistic science based on understanding as opposed to causal analysis. Mead disagreed, stressing instead the continuity between natural and social science, even while he distinguished between physiological and social psychology, as he did in an essay of 1909.

This is the crucial difference between interpretive sociology in Germany, with its methodological dualism, and North American pragmatism as represented by Mead. Symbolic interactionism in the mid-twentieth century, as we shall see in a moment, differentiates itself from positivistic social science and also from the then dominant structural functionalism – though a minority current of interactionism, the so-called Iowa School, was positivistic in its approach.

By this time the dominant form of positivism was what we associate with the logical empiricism of the Vienna Circle, though in North America it seems to have been more home-grown (Platt 1996). Logical empiricism was reductionist in its assertion that the language of all the sciences should be ultimately reducible to material-object language or to the language of physics. And whereas for Comte scientific diagnosis led directly to prognosis and prescription, logical empiricism proclaimed a sharp separation between facts and value-judgements – the latter being analysed as mere expressions of taste. Verstehen, Otto Neurath wrote, might help the researcher, but no more than a good cup of coffee (Neurath 1973: 357).

From the other direction, another Austrian, Alfred Schutz (1899–1959), brought phenomenology into the philosophy of social science and the practice of sociology.[3] Phenomenology, as Edmund Husserl (1859–1938), developed it in the early years of the twentieth century, means an approach to knowledge which focuses on our experience of things, bracketing out the issue of whether or not they really exist or are optical or other illusions, and what they are made of. Thus a phenomenological approach to time, for example, will not be concerned with its intrinsic nature so much as with our experience or awareness of it.

It is this dimension of our social experience that Schutz felt had been overlooked in conventional sociology, even when, as in Weber's case, it purported to be concerned with understanding the intended meaning of human actions. In a book published in Vienna in 1932 with the title *Der sinnhafte Aufbau der sozialen Welt* (The Meaningful Constitution of the Social World), Schutz argued that the problem with Weber's ideal types was not that they were insufficiently scientific (as some empiricists in the US had argued), but precisely the opposite: Weber was too quick to impose them on the phenomena he described, paying insufficient attention to their grounding in acts of typification performed by ordinary members of society. For Schutz (1962: 59), the social scientist is merely constructing second-order typifications based on those already carried out in the lifeworld. Facts, as Nietzsche and Dilthey had stressed, are always interpreted facts (Endress 1999: 345; Schutz 1971: 5; see also Welz 1996; Barber 2006).

Schutz, who emigrated to the US in 1939, was well placed to mediate between European and North American pragmatism and phenomenology, and also between interpretive sociology as it was understood in Europe and symbolic interactionism.[4] He even made unsuccessful overtures to the structural functionalist Talcott Parsons (Grathoff 1978). Peter Berger and Thomas Luckmann (1966), who studied with Schutz, introduced the idea of 'social construction', again reworking pragmatism and phenomenology into a sociology of (commonsense) knowledge.

Schutz's essays of the 1950s coincided with yet another Viennese influence: the later work of Ludwig Wittgenstein. Beginning on the margins of the logical empiricist Vienna Circle, Wittgenstein had come to abandon the simple conception of a picturing relation (*abbildende Beziehung*) between propositions and the world, and was drawn into a more sensitive and holistic analysis of the practicalities of 'language-games' based on implicit rules and embedded in what he enigmatically called 'forms of life' (Wittgenstein 1953). In a religious language-game and form of life, for example, words like prayer, sacred, holy, salvation and so on have a specific meaning which is given to them only by and in this context (Schatzki 1983).

An important book by the Wittgensteinian philosopher Peter Winch (1958) drew the consequences of Wittgenstein's concepts of language-game and 'form of life' for social theory, using Max Weber, as Schutz had done, as one of the foils for his argument. For Winch, knowing a society meant learning the way it is conceptualised by its members. He thus revived the central principle of nineteenth-century German historicism, according to which every age must be understood in its own terms (Winch 1958: vii). Winch directly identified himself with the German idealist tradition by further insisting that social relations are 'like' logical relations between propositions (1958: 126) as well as, more concretely, with an ethnographic field-work approach (Winch 1964). While some Wittgensteinians have questioned Winch's use of Wittgenstein, Karl-Otto Apel (1967) brought out the similarities between this development in analytic philosophy of language and the German tradition of the human sciences or *Geisteswissenschaften*. Other thinkers have contrasted this descriptivist approach with a more critical hermeneutic one.

Around the same time as Apel's book, Rom Harré and Paul Secord (1972) developed a philosophy for social psychology based on the work of the later Wittgenstein and the analytic philosophy of language practised at Oxford by J.L. Austin. Ordinary language, they argued, is better suited to the description of the mental processes of social actors than apparently more scientific artificial terminology, and they drew attention to models of research practice of this kind in the work of Erving Goffman, Harold Garfinkel and others. Harré has continued this social constructionist programme with unflagging energy into the present.

Analytic philosophy of language was also drawn on by the anthropologist Clifford Geertz (1973) in his very influential defence of what, following the English philosopher Gilbert Ryle (1949), he called 'thick description'. For Ryle, a thick description is one which can, for example, differentiate between the twitch of an eyelid and a wink, with all its complex contextual and cultural connotations. Geertz's classic account of cock-fighting in Bali exemplifies this approach, moving from a sensitive description of the practice to a consideration of its cultural significance. This relatively informal research strategy, which has affinities with what Glaser and Strauss (1967) called 'grounded theory', can be contrasted with more formal approaches such as functionalism and structuralism. It is sometimes framed in terms of the use of 'emic' (actors') as opposed to 'etic' (observers') categories, terms based on the linguistic distinction between phonemic and phonetic (Pike 1966). Geertz himself deprecated this usage, as well as that of 'Verstehen': an 'actor-oriented' anthropological interpretation is 'usually too casually referred to as "seeing things from the actor's point of view", too bookishly as "the verstehen approach", or too technically as "emic analysis"' (Geertz 1973: 14).

Hermeneutic theory itself took a new turn with Gadamer's 'philosophical hermeneutics'. Here, understanding is not just a matter of immersing oneself imaginatively in the world of the historical actor or text, but a more reflective and practical process which operates with an awareness of the temporal and conceptual distance between text and interpreter and of the ways in which the text has been and continues to be reinterpreted and to exercise an influence over us. This effective history (*Wirkungsgeschichte*), which traditional historicist hermeneutics tends to see as an obstacle, is for Gadamer an essential element which links us to the text. Our pre-judgements or prejudices are what make understanding possible. As Charles Taylor (2002: 130, 134) puts it:

> Our account of the decline of the Roman Empire will not and cannot be the same as that put forward in eighteenth century England, or those that will be offered in twenty-fifth century China, or twenty-second century Brazil … this will not be because what we can identify as the same propositions will have different truth values. The difference will be rather that different questions will be asked, different issues raised, different features will stand out as remarkable, and so forth.[5]

The alternative conception of the human sciences or *Geisteswissenschaften* put forward in Gadamer's work also made it central to Jürgen Habermas' reformulation of the *Logic of the Social Sciences*. Habermas (1967, 1968) welcomed Gadamer's critique of hermeneutic objectivism, which he saw as the equivalent of positivism in the philosophy of the natural sciences, and also his stress on the totalising character of understanding. For Habermas, however, Gadamer's insistence on the fundamental nature of language, expressed in his claim that 'Being that can be understood is language', amounted to a form of linguistic idealism. Together with Gadamer's stress on the importance of tradition and his rehabilitation of the category of prejudice, this suggested an ultimately conservative approach which was unable to deal with the systematic distortion of communicative processes by relations of power and domination.

Habermas and Gadamer debated these issues in the late 1960s and early 1970s (see Apel, *Theorie-Diskussion* 1971; Bleicher 1980). There are also echoes in Habermas' position of the earlier critical theorist Theodor Adorno's defence of an objective and contextualising hermeneutics; this in turn has been carried forward by Ulrich Oevermann (Oevermann et al. 1987; Müller-Doohm 2006). Recent theorists have tended to stress the compatibility of hermeneutics and critical theory in a conception of critical hermeneutics (Thompson 1981; Outhwaite 1987; Kögler 1996a, 1996b; see also Kögler 2006). Gadamer also engaged briefly with the French deconstructionist philosopher Jacques Derrida, whose conception of interpretation was more sceptical (Michelfelder and Palmer 1989; Bernstein 2008). Another major French philosopher, Paul Ricoeur (1913–2005), engaged more directly with hermeneutic issues in the social sciences, in his 1965 book on Freud, in which he formulated his concept of a 'hermeneutics of suspicion', in his response to the Habermas–Gadamer debate and in a large number of other essays (Ricoeur 1981a, 1981b, 1991, 2010). He addressed in particular the question of analysing action in textual terms (Ricoeur 1973).

The term hermeneutics, then, has come to be used loosely in English-language social science to refer to all interpretive approaches, without the kinds of opposition between phenomenological and 'objective hermeneutic' approaches found in Germany (Jung and Müller-Doohm 1993; Grathoff 1989: 193 n.31). Thomas Luckmann (1978: 13) described the connections between symbolic interactionism or cognitive anthropology on the one hand and 'phenomenological sociology' and 'ethnomethodology' on the other as 'an elective affinity between intellectual traditions of dissimilar origin'. As Horst Helle (1992: 87) pointed out, Mead's posthumously published essay of 1936 on the selectivity of attention puts forward an essentially hermeneutic position, in which the specific object of concern is understood by locating it in a broader background. More generally, Blumer's distinction between descriptive and 'sensitizing' concepts, where the latter do not refer to a precisely delimited set of objects but rather suggest a framework in which to conceptualise a complex reality, develops familiar themes of neo-Kantian hermeneutics. Most broadly of all, the theme of the knowledge process as an active engagement between subject and object, which may transform the subject of knowledge as well as his or her account of the object domain, is something which can be found even in early twentieth-century positivism (Lübbe 1978) and is taken up in a more radical form in phenomenology and Gadamerian hermeneutics.

A crude but possibly helpful way of thinking about these relations is to take the example of music. An approach which we might call positivistic would translate the musical score as accurately as possible into notes as played; a hermeneutic approach would raise more complex questions about the composer's intentions or the cultural significance of the music, while a phenomenological approach would focus on the activity of playing the music and the audience's experience of it. As it happens, a classic essay by Schutz (1951) is on 'Making Music Together'. Here he addresses in particular the communication between players, but he also refers (Schutz 1951: 83) to the possibility of the automatic performance of music (something which of course has now become commonplace with computer technology) and to the essentially hermeneutic theme of the players' background knowledge or, in Schutz's well-known formulation, 'stock of knowledge at hand'.

One reference-point for the interpenetration of these perspectives in contemporary work is the 'sociology of everyday life'; another is the theme of 'social construction'. There are further connections to post-modern or 'post-structuralist' theory, despite its suspicion of mainstream hermeneutics as instanced in the Gadamer–Derrida debate discussed above, and narrative theory.

Habermas' version of 'critical theory' can be seen, along with critical realism and Anthony Giddens' structuration theory, as one of three particularly influential attempts in the final third of the twentieth century to reconcile, as Max Weber had done at the beginning of the century, the rival claims of explanation and understanding in the social sciences. Habermas, along with his close collaborator Karl-Otto Apel, argued for the complementarity between an empirical-analytic approach oriented to the explanation, prediction and control of objectified processes and a hermeneutic approach concerned with the extension of understanding. These could combine in an emancipatory model of critical social science, instantiated by psychoanalysis and the marxist critique of ideology, which aims at the removal of causal obstacles to understanding. Much of this remains in his more recent theories of reconstructive science and communicative action (Outhwaite 1994, 2000).

Whereas critical theory tends towards a dualism of natural and social science, but in an increasingly muted form, the assumption that opposition to positivism also entailed dualism or antinaturalism was however also put in question in the late 1960s and early 1970s by the realist metatheory of science developed by Rom Harré and Roy Bhaskar. Both Harré and Bhaskar, like Habermas, were substantially motivated by the desire to undermine positivistic theories and approaches in the social sciences. They were interested in giving a more adequate account of science as a whole, in a world composed of relatively enduring structures and mechanisms. Some of these could be isolated in scientific experimentation, given the contingent existence of Homo sapiens and Homo scientificus. An important aspect of the realist programme developed by Harré, Bhaskar and others was a conception of explanation as involving not a semantic reduction of causal *statements* to general laws but a reference to the causal powers of entities, structures and mechanisms. Causal tendencies might or might not be outweighed by countervailing tendencies, and two causal tendencies may neutralise one another, as do the centrifugal force of the Earth's rotation and its gravitational attraction, with the convenient consequence that human beings and other animals are safely anchored to the Earth's surface.

This and other features of realism meant that the whole issue of naturalism could be rethought. Human beings could be seen as having causal powers and liabilities, just like other entities; it no longer mattered if their relations rarely sustained any universal generalisations of an interesting kind, but only sets of tendencies regular enough to be worth exploring. The fact that many of the entities accorded causal force in social scientific explanations were necessarily unobservable was not, as it was for empiricism, a problem of principle. And the understanding of meaning could, as Bhaskar (1979: 58–9) put it, be seen as in some ways equivalent to measurement in the natural sciences. Finally, it seemed natural to include among the causes of human action the agents' reasons for acting – reasons which must be understood as far as possible.

The realist critique of traditional epistemology found an echo in social theory, notably in the work of Anthony Giddens, who had become similarly impatient with the residues of positivist social science as well as the more extreme contentions of social constructionism. Giddens' conception of the 'duality of structure' was designed to replace the traditional dichotomies between theories of social structure and social change, the micro–macro divide and between interpretive and more structural approaches. Approaches like these which aim to mediate between pure hermeneutics and more naturalistic conceptions of social science coexist, in the early twenty-first century, with more explicitly hermeneutic or phenomenological conceptions (Soeffner 1989; Jung and Müller-Doohm 1993). Hermeneutics in a broader sense continues to exist as a major research tradition in the humanities, as well as a minority one in the social sciences (Shapiro and Sica 1984). More importantly perhaps, social scientists who would not sign up to an explicitly hermeneutic programme have at least accepted the importance of hermeneutic issues.

In particular, as Habermas (1967) showed, symbolic interactionism and phenomenological sociology can be enriched by a closer attention to language; 'ethnomethodology' in the work of Garfinkel, Aaron Cicourel and others, attending to the production of social order by communicative acts in everyday life, is a major example of this enrichment and has linked sociology with linguistics. Similarly, Gadamer's notion of the fusion of horizons, the intermediation between competing perspectives, forms a useful correction to Winch's radical relativism. Finally, as suggested in the discussion above of Habermas and Giddens, it may be useful to complement interpretive approaches as a whole with more structural perspectives drawn from critical theory, structuration theory, Pierre Bourdieu's reflexive sociology (see Bourdieu 1996) or realism. Some interpretive theorists would deny the need for this, just as some empiricists, functionalists or rational choice theorists would deny the need to pay any attention to hermeneutic issues.

So far this chapter has focused mainly on social theory, and particularly on sociology and social anthropology, but hermeneutic issues have also played a central part in the history of political thought, notably in that of the so-called 'Cambridge School'. Of its leading figures, Quentin Skinner and J.G.A. Pocock represent the traditional polarisation of hermeneutic theory, with Skinner emphasising the need to understand an author's *intention* in 'speech acts' of argumentation and Pocock stressing the diversity of political *languages*, conceived in more holistic terms. Their responses to the German strand of intellectual history in the later twentieth century focusing on the history of concepts (*Begriffsgeschichte* – see Richter 2001) differ accordingly. Skinner, having earlier claimed that 'there can be no histories of concepts; there can only be histories of their uses in argument' (Tully 1988: 283; cited in Richter 2010: 109), has come to 'welcome' them, while still preferring the formulation above (Skinner 2002: 59–60; cited in Richter 2010: 113). For Pocock (1996: 51; cited in Richter 2010: 108), by contrast, 'A discourse or language ... is a complex and living entity, a system, or even an organism.' Any history of concepts is 'ancilliary to the history of multiple discourses and to the people who have used and been used by them'. As Melvin Richter suggests in his masterly overview, these approaches should probably be seen as complementary, with different language communities, with their different histories, using concepts in ways which repay comparative study (see also Richter 1995, 2001).

An approach on the borders of social science and linguistics known as 'discourse analysis' has been developed in a variant, more concerned with social and political issues, of 'critical discourse analysis', which identifies itself with a hermeneutic methodology (Wodak and Meyer 2009: 22–3, 28; see also Wodak 2013). As Wodak and Meyer (2009: 22–3) note, however, 'the specifics of the hermeneutic interpretation process are not made completely transparent in many CDA-oriented studies.'

Hermeneutic questions have also been prominent, though usually not explicitly addressed as such, in comparative political research. To take an early example, the classic five-nation study of *The Civic Culture* by Gabriel Almond and Sidney Verba (1963: 57–68) addressed issues about translatability and interpretation of interview material.

Finally, one of the best introductory discussions of the place of a hermeneutic approach in the social sciences focuses in particular on international relations. Martin Hollis and Steve Smith (1991) focus on the difference between 'understanding' and 'explaining', but this distinction intersects with that between individualism and structural holism. There may be, as Max Weber (2012: 273–300) insisted, an affinity between individualistic approaches and understanding, but it is also possible to take individual behaviour as the mere outcome of causal influences (as in behaviourism) or, conversely, to give primacy to large structures of ideas which have to be understood from the inside (Hollis and Smith 1991: 4–5).

Here, then, we are back with familiar controversies over the place of sociology and the other social sciences 'between literature and science' (Lepenies 1988). In some, such as history and social anthropology, an interpretive approach may be accepted more or less automatically; in others, such as economics, it will seem very exotic and eccentric. But what I think the debates throughout the past century have shown is that interpretation, as theorised by hermeneutics, is not just an option in social theory; it is the way in which we get access to the social world.

Notes

1 Karl Mannheim, in an early essay, emphasises the value of Dilthey's contribution, while criticising that of Windelband and Rickert (Mannheim 1980: 176–8).
2 On neo-Kantianism in social science, see Rose 1981, chapter 1.
3 An earlier contribution, not mentioned by Schutz, is a short book by Siegfried Kracauer (1922). For discussions, see Mülder-Bach 1985; Koch 2000.
4 Schutz (1972: 240) does not mention hermeneutics explicitly and has only one substantive, and ridiculously dismissive, reference to Dilthey: 'We must never cease reiterating that the method of Weber's sociology is a rational one and that the position of interpretive sociology should in no way be confused with that of Dilthey, who opposes to rational science another, so-called "interpretive" science based on metaphysical presuppositions and incorrigible "intuition".' On Schutz's relation to Husserl, see Schutz 2009.
5 This is very similar to Max Weber's well-known sentence: 'Some time or other the colour changes, the light of the great cultural problems moves on' (Weber 2012: 138).

Bibliography

Aiken, S. (2006) 'Pragmatism, Naturalism, and Phenomenology', *Human Studies* 29: 317–40.
Almond, G. and Verba, S. (1963) *The Civic Culture. Political Attitudes and Democracy in Five Nations*, Princeton: Princeton University Press.
Apel, K-O. (1967) *Analytic Philosophy of Language and the Geisteswissenschaften*, Dordrecht: Reidel.
Apel, K-O. et al. (1971) *Theorie-Diskussion: Hermeneutik und Ideologiekritik*. Contributions by Apel, Borman, Bubner, Gadamer, Giegel, Habermas. Frankfurt: Suhrkamp.
Barber, M. (2006) 'Philosophy and reflection: A critique of Frank Welz's sociological and "processual" criticism of Husserl and Schutz', *Human Studies* 29: 141–57.
Berger, P. and Luckmann, T. 1966 *The Social Construction of Reality*, London: Allen Lane.
Bernstein, R.J. (1992) 'The Resurgence of Pragmatism', *Social Research* 59, 4: 813–40.
——(2008) 'The Conversation That Never Happened (Gadamer/Derrida)', *Review of Metaphysics* 61, 3: 577–603.
Bhaskar, R. (1979) *The Possibility of Naturalism*, Brighton: Harvester.
Bleicher, J. (1980) *Contemporary Hermeneutics*, London: Routledge.
Bourdieu, P. (1996) 'Understanding', *Theory, Culture and Society* 13, 2: 17–37.
Burrow, J. W. (2000) The Crisis of Reason: European Thought, 1848–1914, New Haven and London: Yale University Press.
Dallmayr, F. and McCarthy, T. (1977) *Understanding and Social Inquiry*, Notre Dame, IN: Notre Dame University Press.
Dostal, Robert J. (ed.) (2002) *The Cambridge Companion to Gadamer*, New York: Cambridge University Press.
Endress, Martin (1999) 'Alfred Schütz (1899–1959)', in Dirk Kaesler (ed.), Klassiker der Soziologie. Bd. I: Von Auguste Comte bis Norbert Elias, München: Beck, pp. 334–52.

Endress, M., Psathas, G. and Nasu, H. (eds) (2005) *Explorations of the life-world: continuing dialogues with Alfred Schutz*, Dordrecht: Springer.

Gadamer, H-G. (1960) *Wahrheit und Methode*, Mohr: Tübingen [1975 *Truth and Method*. New York: Sheed and Ward].

Garfinkel, H. (1967) *Studies in Ethnomethodology*, Upper Saddle River, NJ: Prentice-Hall.

Geertz, C. (1973) *The Interpretation of Cultures*, New York: Basic Books.

Glaser, B. and Strauss, A. (1967) *The Discovery of Grounded Theory: Strategies for Qualitative Research*, Chicago: Aldine.

Goffman, E. (1959) *The Presentation of Self in Everyday Life*, New York: Doubleday.

Grathoff, R. (1978) *The Theory of Social Action: The Correspondence of Alfred Schutz and Talcott Parsons*, Bloomington and London: Indiana University Press.

——(1989) *Milieu und Lebenswelt. Einführung in die phänomenologische Soziologie und die sozialphänomenologische Forschung*, Frankfurt am Main: Suhrkamp.

Habermas, J. ([1967] 1988) *On the Logic of the Social Sciences*, Cambridge: Polity.

——([1968] 1978) *Knowledge and Human Interests*, London: Heinemann.

Harré, R. and Secord, P. (1972) *The Explanation of Social Behaviour*, Oxford: Blackwell.

Helle, H.J. (1992) *Verstehende Soziologie und Theorie der Symbolischen Interaktion*, 2nd edn, Stuttgart: Teubner.

——(2005) *Symbolic Interaction and Verstehen*, Frankfurt am Main/New York: Peter Lang.

Hollis, M. and Smith, S. (1991) *Explaining and Understanding International Relations*, Oxford: Oxford University Press.

Hughes, H.S. (1958) *Consciousness and Society: The Reorientation of European Social Thought*, Cambridge, MA: Harvard University Press.

Joas, H. (1996) *The Creativity Of Action*, Cambridge: Polity.

Jung, T. and Müller-Doohm, S. (eds) (1993) *Wirklichkeit im Deutungsprozeß*, Frankfurt: Suhrkamp.

Koch, Gertrud (2000) *Siegfried Kracauer: An Introduction*, trans. Jeremy Gaines, Princeton: Princeton University Press.

Kögler, H-H. (1996a) *The Power of Dialog. Critical Hermeneutics after Gadamer and Foucault*, Cambridge, MA and London: MIT Press.

——(1996b) 'The Self-empowered Subject: Habermas, Foucault and Hermeneutic Reflexivity', *Philosophy and Social Criticism* 22, 4: 13–44.

——(2006) 'Hermeneutics, phenomenology and philosophical anthropology', in G. Delanty (ed.), *Handbook of Contemporary European Social Theory*, Abingdon: Routledge, pp. 203–17.

Kracauer, S. (1922) *Soziologie als Wissenschaft. Eine erkenntnistheoretische Untersuchung*, Dresden: Sibyllen-Verlag.

Lepenies, W. (1988) *Between literature and science: the rise of sociology*, trans. R.J. Hollingdale, Cambridge: Cambridge University Press.

Lübbe, H. (1978)[1960] 'Positivism and Phenomenology: Mach and Husserl', in T. Luckmann (ed.), *Phenomenology and Sociology*, Harmondsworth: Penguin, pp. 90–118.

Luckmann, T. (ed.) (1978) *Phenomenology and Sociology*, Harmondsworth: Penguin.

Mannheim, K. (1980) 'Eine soziologische Theorie der Kultur und ihrer Erkennbarkeit', in Mannheim (eds David Kettler, Volker Meja and Nico Stehr), *Strukturen des Denkens*. Frankfurt: Suhrkamp, pp. 155–303; trans. as *Structures of Thinking* by J.J. Shapiro and S.W. Nicholsen, London and Boston: Routledge and Kegan Paul, 1982, pp. 141–288.

Michelfelder, D.P. and Palmer, R. (1989) *Dialogue and Deconstruction: The Gadamer–Derrida Encounter*, Albany, NY: SUNY Press.

Mueller-Vollmer, K. (1986) *The Hermeneutics Reader*, Oxford: Blackwell.

Mülder-Bach, Inka (1985) *Siegfried Kracauer, Grenzgänger zwischen Theorie und Literatur: seine Frühe Schriften*, Stuttgart: J.B. Metzler.

Müller-Doohm, Stefan (2006) 'How to criticize? Convergent and divergent paths in critical theories of society', in Gerard Delanty (ed.), *Handbook of Contemporary European Social Theory*, Abingdon: Routledge, pp. 171–84.

Neurath, O. (1973) *Empiricism and Sociology*. Edited by M. Neurath and R.S. Cohen, Dordrecht: Reidel.

Oevermann, U., Tilman, A., Konau, E. and Krambeck, J. (1987) 'Structures of meaning and objective Hermeneutics', in V. Meja, D. Misgeld and N. Stehr (eds), *Modern German Sociology*, New York: Columbia University Press, pp. 436–47.

Outhwaite, W. (1987) *New Philosophies of Social Science*, London: Macmillan.

——(1994) *Habermas. A Critical Introduction*, Cambridge: Polity, 2nd edn 2009.

——(2000) 'Reconstructive Science and Methodological Dualism in the Work of Jürgen Habermas', *Philosophical Inquiry*, Vol. 37, No 1-2, Winter - Spring 2014, pp.2–18.

Pike, K.L. (1966) 'Etic and emic standpoints for the description of behavior' in A.G. Smith (ed.), *Communication and Culture*, New York: Holt, Rinehart and Winston, pp. 152–63.

Platt, J. (1996) *A History of Sociological Research Methods in America, 1920–1960*, Cambridge: Cambridge University Press.

Pocock, J. (1987) 'The concept of a language and the *métier d'historien*: some considerations on practice', in A. Pagden (ed.), *The Languages of Political Theory in Early-Modern Europe*, Cambridge: Cambridge University Press, pp. 19–38.

——(1996) 'Concepts and Discourses: A Difference in Culture?', in H. Lehmann and M. Richter (eds), *The Meaning of Historical Terms and Concepts: New Studies on Begriffsgeschichte*, Washington, D.C.: German Historical Institute, pp. 47–58.

Richter, M. (1995) *The History of Political and Social Concepts. A Critical Introduction*, New York: Oxford University Press.

——(2001) 'A German version of the "linguistic turn": Reinhart Koselleck and the history of political and social concepts', in D. Castiglione and I. Hampshire-Monk (eds), *The History of Political Thought in National Contexts*, Cambridge: Cambridge University Press, pp. 58–79.

——(2010) 'Towards a Lexicon of European Political and Legal Concepts: A Comparison of Begriffsgeschichte and the "Cambridge School"', *Critical Review of International Social and Political Philosophy*, 6, 2: 91–120.

Ricoeur, P. (1970 [1965]) *Freud and Philosophy: An Essay on Interpretation*, New Haven: Yale University Press.

——(1973) 'The Model of the Text: Meaningful Action Considered as a Text', *New Literary History*, 5, 1, What Is Literature? (Autumn): 91–117.

——(1975) *The Conflict of Interpretations: Essays in Hermeneutics*, Evanston: Northwestern University Press.

——(1981a) *Hermeneutics and the Human Sciences*, Cambridge: Cambridge University Press.

——(1981b) *Lectures on Ideology and Utopia*, New York: Cambridge University Press.

——(1991) *From Text to Action: Essays in Hermeneutics II*, Evanston: Northwestern University Press.

——(2010) *Écrits et conférences 2: Herméneutique*, Paris: Seuil.

Rose, Gillian (1981) *Hegel Contra Sociology*, London: Athlone.

Ryle, Gilbert (1949) *The Concept of Mind*, London: Hutchinson.

Schatzki, T. (1983) 'The Prescription is Description: Wittgenstein's View of the Human Sciences', in S. Mitchell and M. Rosen (eds), *The Need for Interpretation. Contemporary Conceptions of the Philosopher's Task*, London: Athlone, pp. 118–40.

Schutz, A. (1932) *Der sinnhafte Aufbau der sozialen Welt*, Vienna: Springer [1972 *The Phenomenology of the Social World*, London: Heinemann].

——(1951) 'Making Music Together – A Study in Social Relationship', *Social Research* 18, 1: 76–97.

——(1962) *Collected Papers I: The Problem of Social Reality*. Edited by M.A. Natanson and H.L. van Breda, Dordrecht: Martinus Nijhoff.

——(1971) *Gesammelte Aufsätze 1*, Den Haag: M. Nijhoff.

——(1972) *The Phenomenology of the Social World*. Heinemann: London.

——(2009) *Philosophisch-phänomenologische Schriften 1. Zur Kritik der Phänomenologie Edmund Husserls*. Werkausgabe 3/1 Eds. G. Sebald, R. Grathoff, and M. Thomas, Konstanz: UVK.

Shapiro, G. and Sica, A. (1984) *Hermeneutics: Questions and Prospects*, Amherst: University of Massachusetts Press.

Skinner, Q. (2002) 'Interview with Quentin Skinner', *Finnish Yearbook of Political Thought*, 6: 34–63.

Soeffner, H-G. (1989) *Auslegung des Alltags – Der Alltag der Auslegung*, Frankfurt: Suhrkamp.

Taylor, C. (2002) 'Gadamer on the Human Sciences', in R.J. Dostal (ed.), *The Cambridge Companion To Gadamer*, New York: Cambridge University Press, pp. 126–42.

Thompson, J.B. (1981) *Critical Hermeneutics*, Cambridge: Cambridge University Press.

Tully, J. (1988) *Meaning and Context. Quentin Skinner and his Critics*, Princeton: Princeton University Press / Cambridge: Polity.

Weber, M. (2012) *Max Weber: Collected Methodological Writings*. Eds H.H. Bruun and S. Whimster, Abingdon: Routledge.

Welz, F. (1996) *Kritik der Lebenswelt. Eine soziologische Auseinandersetzung mit Edmund Husserl und Alfred Schütz*, Opladen: Westdeutscher Verlag.

Winch, P. (1958) *The Idea of a Social Science and its Relation to Philosophy*, London: Routledge, 2nd edn 1990.

——(1964) 'Understanding a Primitive Society', *American Philosophical Quarterly*, I: pp. 307–24.

Wittgenstein, L. (1953) *Philosophical Investigations*. Trans. G.E.M. Anscombe, Oxford: Blackwell.

Wodak, R. (ed.) (2013) *Critical Discourse Analysis – Challenges and Perspectives*, London: Sage.

Wodak, R. and Meyer, M. (eds) (2009) *Methods for Critical Discourse Analysis*, London: Sage (2nd edition).

Further reading

Bleicher, J. (1980) *Contemporary Hermeneutics*, London: Routledge.

Dallmayr, F. and McCarthy, T. (eds) (1977). *Understanding and Social Inquiry*, Notre Dame, IN: Notre Dame University Press.

40

HERMENEUTICS, RACE AND GENDER

Tina Fernandes Botts

Introduction

This chapter takes place within the context of debates in late twentieth century and early twenty-first century Anglo-American philosophy over whether or to what extent the human categories of race and gender are "real." It is meant to contribute to these debates, as well as to the growing body of work that uses insights from hermeneutic ontology to address matters of pressing social concern by examining the deeper, more fundamental question of whether there are better ways of thinking about existence than in the classical modern way; ways, in other words, that do not involve classical metaphysical starting points like substance. According to hermeneutic ontology, a better way to think about existence involves a shift in focus away from what metaphysicians call "reality" toward what Heidegger called "being." It is important that this recommended shift in focus is not semantic, but symbolic of a rejection of both metaphysical essentialism and epistemological foundationalism in favor of identifying *interpretation* as central to what we take things to be or mean.

The key hermeneutical insight is that there is a fundamental connection between what we take to exist and what we take things to mean; and that both are determined by the way human beings interact with the world around them and with each other. Hermeneutics can be understood to provide, in other words, a philosophically sophisticated account of the idea that meaning and existence (or what we call "reality") are created by social forces and lacking in the kind of foundationalist and essentialist content they are often thought to have. From a hermeneutical point of view, in other words, all things, including race and gender, can be understood to have a meaning and existence that is interpretive, context-dependent, collectively generated, and changeable rather than autonomous, absolute, ultimate, fixed or spatiotemporally independent (sometimes called "atomistic").

The idea that meaning is lacking in foundationalist content finds support in the field of social epistemology (Kukla 2000; Kuhn 1970; Mathiesen 2006), the central concept of which is that epistemology is not limited to the study of the nature of knowledge and justified belief, but also includes "the study of knowers and believers as subjects who are positioned within a particular social and historical context"

(Steup 2008: 509). The idea that being or existence is lacking in essentialist content has gained much traction within the field of feminist metaphysics: in discussions about what sort of metaphysical framework (e.g, Aristotelian, Cartesian) works best to further feminist projects (Bordo 1987; Young 1990; Schiebinger 2000; Witt 2010), in discussions about the degree to which the concept of a "natural" world is code for a world as conceived by men (Frye 1983; Haslanger 1993; Butler 1993; Warren 1997), in discussions about foundationalist epistemological assumptions in traditional meta-physics (Fraser and Nicholson 1990), and particularly in discussions surrounding the existence or meaning of gender (Delphy 1984; MacKinnon 1989; Wittig 1992).

The chapter's primary aim is to provide an account of the relationship between hermeneutics, race and gender by examining these phenomena through the lens of hermeneutic ontology; that is, from the vantage point of the hermeneutics of facticity (*Faktizität*) developed by Martin Heidegger, as modified and enhanced by Hans-Georg Gadamer. More specifically, the questions *What is race?* and *What is gender?* will be addressed within the context of the ways in which Heidegger and Gadamer asked and answered the deeper questions, *What does it mean for anything to be?*, *What is the meaning of being itself?* and *What is the relationship between being and understanding?* Heidegger's key insight was that what exists and what things mean are both a function of what human beings take to exist or mean within a given socio-historical context, system of intelligibility, or Heidegerrian *world*; and what human beings take to exist or mean within a given system of intelligibility is a function of the ways in which human beings interact with each other and with that world. Gadamer added to this insight that correct understanding of anything (1) is generated by agreement between competing interpretations achieved through dialogue (2) is measured by the degree to which competing interpretations overlap or "fuse" and (3) is guided by self-reflexivity and a critical yet responsibly held gaze.

Critics of hermeneutic ontology as described above come from two main camps. The first camp worries that the seed in Heidegger's work that hints at a path toward correct understanding grows and expands to such an extent in Gadamer's thought (primarily in importance placed on the concept of *tradition*) that hermeneutic ontology ends up as committed to the metaphysics of presence as the modern philosophy it claims to critique (Derrida 1979, 1993; Foucault 1985). The second camp finds a troubling relativism in hermeneutic ontology, according to which its claims of providing a path to correct understanding are found lacking and in need of supple-mentation (Habermas 1980, 1984, 1990; Ricoeur 1991). The position taken in this chapter is that neither of these opposing vantage points accurately depicts hermeneutic ontology. Instead, hermeneutic ontology takes a position orthogonal to both camps by stepping outside of modern philosophy's mind/body problem. For the hermeneuticist, in other words, the question is not how mind and body (human beings and the world) interact, but why philosophy ever came to mistakenly believe that mind and body were separate, isolated, autonomous entities in the first place. Mind and body are not separate, nor isolated, nor autonomous from a hermeneutical point of view. Instead, mind and body exist in a relationship of mutual interdependence in which human beings affect the world and the world affects human beings; both in terms of what human beings and things in the world *are* and in terms of what they *mean*. Correct understanding, on this view, is not some sort of one-on-one correspondence between mind and body (or thoughts and world), but a recognition that mind and body mutually inform one another in an ongoing relationship that changes with time and space.

In response to those who worry that hermeneutic ontology is committed to a metaphysics of presence, hermeneutic ontology is able to reply that Gadamer's concept of *tradition* is merely an articulation of the very basic hermeneutic principle that all interpretation starts within a given, established system of intelligibility; that is, within a factical situatedness that discloses possibilities. At first blush, the concept of *tradition* appears to limit the scope of available interpretations of a given phenomenon and to simultaneously limit the possible ways of being. However, upon closer examination, there are resources within the Gadamerian concept of *tradition* that allow for it to be modified over time to make room for the inclusion of novel interpretations and novel ways of being. For this reason, an examination of race and gender through the lens of hermeneutic ontology does not generate fixed, essentialist or foundationalist interpretations of these phenomena but an understanding that the meaning and existence of these phenomena changes with time, place and context. In other words, hermeneutic ontology can be understood to not subscribe to the metaphysics of presence.

In response to those worried that hermeneutic ontology is troublingly relativistic, one reply of hermeneutic ontology is that the extreme relativism some find in hermeneutics fails to account for the fact that the goal of all hermeneutic inquiry is correct understanding. This correct understanding, while decidedly situated, can be achieved nonetheless, particularly if achievement of correct understanding is guided by self-reflection and a deliberately critical gaze; that is, by an awareness of oneself as both an object of interpretation and an interpreter of meaning. In this way, while it may be the case that hermeneutic ontology does not aim toward perfect, timeless understanding or a universally applicable grasp on some sort of external reality or absolute truth, what it does aim toward is the best interpretation possible in a given interpretive moment. Of course, from the vantage point of hermeneutic ontology, neither perfect, timeless understanding, absolute truth, external reality nor universally applicable grasps on reality or truth exist in the first place. Instead, meaning and being inhabit a distinctively middle ground between particularity and universality – a location that might be called *situated understanding* or *situated being* – that has a noticeably pragmatic air about it. In this way, hermeneutic ontology can escape the charge of relativism. Instead, what things are and what they mean exist in a relationship of identity. Existence is interpretation, "all the way down."

Adopting the position that Heidegger's and Gadamer's hermeneutic ontology constitutes a useful way of understanding the meaning and being of the phenomena of race and gender,[1] the chapter will proceed as follows. First, a description of the salient features of hermeneutic ontology will be explicated. After that, the hermeneutic ontology explicated will be placed into dialogue with the question of whether the phenomena of race and gender have meaning and/or being. The results will show that from the vantage point of hermeneutic ontology as explicated in the chapter, race and gender, while changeable, nonetheless have being and meaning within the socio-historical context of a given time and place, including as of this writing, although this will likely change over time. The final substantive section of the chapter will be an inquiry into contemporary scholarship bearing on the relationship between hermeneutics, race and gender, after which the chapter will close with concluding remarks.

I. Hermeneutic ontology

a. To be is to be interpreted

Martin Heidegger's hermeneutic ontology is a statement on the intimate relationship Heidegger believed existed between meaning and being. For Heidegger, to be is to be interpreted. What this rather cryptic statement is meant to convey is that, for Heidegger, things have neither meaning nor existence in the philosophical void. Things come into being always and already within at least one system of intelligibility or *world*. In other words, as things come into being, they also acquire meaning. This description of the being and meaning of things emerging up out of a given factical context is meant to counteract the view – emerging from a more scientific vantage point – that things can and do have an essential kind of existence or meaning. For Heidegger, nothing could be further from the truth. Although Heidegger adopts phenomenology as the method through which human beings can strip away the layers of externally created meaning and being in order to get closer to the way things are on a deeper level, what is found after hermeneutical phenomenological reduction is applied to a given phenomenon is not Husserlian essence but the fact that all things, including the human way of being, are interpretation "all the way down."

b. Hermeneutic phenomenology

In *Ontology – The Hermeneutics of Facticity*, an early collection of lecture notes from a summer course in 1923, Heidegger sets out to transform the study of ontology from a discipline in which objects are understood to exist separate and apart from subjects, and whose being can be determined from afar, into a framework within which it is possible to come to understand the key role that human beings play in the determination of meaning (1999). It is the human way of being, or what Heidegger calls *Dasein* that is at the center of a proper understanding of ontology, according to Heidegger (1999: 5). Translated literally as *being there*, the word *Dasein* is also meant to express Heidegger's view that existence is always some*where*; that is, within some context, some system of intelligibility, in what Heidegger calls a *world* (ibid.). Heidegger emphasizes the context-dependent nature of the human way of being by using the neologism *being-in-the-world* interchangeably with the word *Dasein* and by using the word *facticity* instead of *ontology* to refer to the study of being. Heidegger says that *facticity* is another word for *Dasein's* particular *mode* of being, which is having an awareness of one's own being (ibid.). There is something about being itself, Heidegger is saying in these lecture notes, that roots it in the human way of being. Since human beings are always some*where* at some *time*, being is similarly context-dependent. To be anywhere at any time (for a person, an object, a concept or anything else) means to be interpreted within that time and place and vice versa.

Heidegger makes this point more forcefully by stating that the way to understand anything is to first understand *Dasein* (1999: 12). To do this, one must seek, as a preliminary matter, what *Dasein* is in its "average everydayness" and then engage in Heidegger's own version of phenomenological reduction to arrive at a fuller, richer understanding (*Verstehen*) of *Dasein* (1999: 53). Unlike Husserl's phenomenological reduction, which Heidegger considered overly mathematical, Heidegger's phenomenology is hermeneutic, or interpretive (1999: 60). For Heidegger, to say that his phenomenology is hermeneutic or interpretive is to say that his phenomenology is concerned primarily with discovering *Dasein*'s "authentic" "mode" of being (1999: 58).

In Heidegger's words, hermeneutic ontology requires that *Dasein* confront itself and reveal itself as it is in itself. In its *average everydayness*, *Dasein* covers over itself, and covers over its authentic mode of being (1999: 60). In ordinary life, in other words, the human way of being is defined by what Heidegger calls *the they*, or the externally derived systems of intelligibility, world views or ideological value systems in which *Dasein* finds itself. *Dasein* uncovered, however, or *Dasein* revealed, *Dasein* after phenomenological reduction, or *authentic Dasein*, on the other hand, is discovered through exposing the *they self* as *inauthentic*.

The path away from the *they self* to a more *authentic* self, for *Dasein*, is through what Heidegger called *formal indication*, a kind of mediate stage between the experiences of the *they self* and authentic experiences (1999: 61). A *formal indication* can be understood as a guiding light between average, everyday understanding and authentic understanding. *Formal indications* show *Dasein* the way to a deeper understanding of itself. *Formal indications* are often misinterpreted as universal truths from which deductions can then be made, according to Heidegger (1999: 62). But, there are no universal truths and deductions cannot be made. Instead, *formal indications* merely lead *Dasein* from the conclusions of *the they* (also known as *forehaving*) to correct understanding, the most fundamental idea of which is that *Dasein* is interpretation "all the way down."

What we learn about *Dasein* in these lecture notes from the summer course in 1923 then, is that, for Heidegger, the human way of being operates on two levels. On the first level, *Dasein* understands itself in terms of the systems of intelligibility (or Heideggarian *worlds*) in which it finds itself. These systems are largely determined by *the they* or everyone around us. On the second level, and with the aid of *formal indication*, *Dasein* can uncover a deeper, more authentic understanding of itself. This more authentic understanding is that *Dasein* is interpretive in nature. Heidegger elaborates on his idea that the human way of being is interpretative in his masterpiece, *Being and Time*.

c. Forestructures of understanding

In *Being and Time*, Heidegger distinguishes further between the less authentic level of being and the more authentic by labeling the levels, respectively, as the *ontic* and the *ontological* levels of being (1962: 32). On the *ontic* level, the world is composed of objects separate and apart from human beings. On the *ontic* level, we have adopted and internalized the scientific mindset that subjects can be distinguished from objects, and that objects (and other subjects, for that matter) can be described and understood at arm's length. On the *ontological* level, however, the world is revealed as interconnected and dynamic and the things within it are understood best not as objects but in terms of the way they are useful to and used by *Dasein*. Moreover, when Heideggerian hermeneutic phenomenology is working well, things reveal themselves as what they are on a deeper level (that is, as *Dasein* most fundamentally encounters them) through the uses to which they are put (1962: 96). What's more, all things in *Dasein*'s system of intelligibility (in a given *world* in which *Dasein* dwells) make up a system of interconnected reference (ibid.). Things only make sense in relation to the other things. Hermeneutic ontology's radical move is that not only do things only have meaning within a given system of intelligibility, they also only have being, or existence, there (1962: 99).

Elaborating upon this framework, in *Being and Time* Heidegger defines truth as unconcealing, uncovering or revealing (*aletheia*) (1962: 261). If hermeneutic phenomenology is performed well, for Heidegger, things will be unconcealed, uncovered or revealed as what they are on a deeper level. To carry out a program of hermeneutic ontology, one must look to what Heidegger called *forestructures of understanding* or simply *forestructure* (*Vorstruktur*) (1962: 190–2). These *forestructures – fore-having* (*Vorhabe*), *fore-sight* (*Vorsicht*) and *fore-conception* (*Vorgriff*) – are always present when anyone is attempting to understand anything. *Fore-having* is simply one's intention, or what is already understood; *fore-sight* is a fixed perspective carefully chosen; and *fore-conception* is simply previously grasped concepts (1962: 191). According to Heidegger, the more careful attention is paid to these *forestructures of understanding*, the greater the degree of unconcealment of the things to be understood, the higher the likelihood that the meaning of the phenomenon in question will be authentic or accurate, and the closer one gets to the truth as unconcealing (*aletheia*).[2] Heidegger writes, "The being-true (*truth*) of [a statement] must be understood as *being-uncovering*. Being-true as *being-uncovering* is in turn ontologically possible only on the basis of being-in-the-world" (1962: 261).

d. Language as the house of being

In Heidegger's later work, including *Poetry, Language, and Thought*, Heidegger places more emphasis on the role of language in the connection he sees between meaning and being (1971). In this work, Heidegger emphasizes his view that language articulates understanding or meaning. In the essay, "Language," Heidegger repeatedly states that language speaks, not man; meaning that what meaning (or being, for that matter) there is, is contained in language. Outside of language, there is no being and the concept of meaning is nonsensical. Translated into more descriptive language, Heidegger can be understood to be saying in this essay, at a minimum, that the highly contingent and interpretative nature of both being and meaning are well articulated using the metaphor of language. But, Heidegger seems to be saying much more than this as well. Specifically, he seems to be making the bold point that things actually *come into being* through language. In his "Letter on Humanism," Heidegger explains that language is the "house of being" because it is the medium through which human beings interact to bring things into being (1993: 217).

e. Historicity

Key to Heidegger's hermeneutic ontology is an awareness of the historicity (*Geschichtlichkeit*) of the human way of being. *Dasein's* historicity is not a statement that human beings each exist at some point in time or along some sort of spatio-temporal axis, but rather a statement that we all exist within a historical context that is situated. Another way to put this is to say that *Dasein* dwells within historical life. On this view, human beings have histories and relate to themselves as having histories. They also all share death as a feature of their future existence. The more *Dasein* confronts that death is its future – the more *Dasein* exists in what Heidegger calls "being-towards-death" – the more human beings are dislodged from our *they selves* and opened up to the myriad possibilities available to us. This confrontation with death "allows the interpreter to recover the past as a restorative for future action" (Davey 2008: 710) and results in the "conscious pursuit of the past's unrealized possibilities" (ibid.). Authentic understanding of any phenomenon, then, involves an awareness of its mutability and potential for change grounded in an awareness of the past.

f. Authentic understanding

Heidegger's hermeneutic ontology, then, provides a very pragmatic account of meaning and being. What things are/what existence they have, Heidegger is saying, is a function of the uses to which they are put. The *meaning* of things is defined in the same way, as a function of the uses to which they are put. Things have no existence or meaning outside of the spatio-temporal or historical context in which they are utilized by human beings. This existence/meaning can be authentic or it can be inauthentic, with the degree of authenticity in either case being measured by the extent to which the existence/meaning uncovered (by a phenomenological reduction guided by keeping the human way of being front and center at all times) is commensurate with the things themselves. Heidegger's message seems to be that although we can never escape the systems of intelligibility or worlds in which we dwell to determine the being or meaning of anything in the philosophical void, we can increase the likelihood that the conclusions we draw about the meaning or being of anything are authentic to the extent that we are self-reflexive about the preconceived notions we all bring to the table when we attempt to *understand* something, and to the extent that we are able to consciously pursue the past's unrealized possibilities.

g. Legitimate and illegitimate pre-judgments

In developing what he called "philosophical hermeneutics" in his classic, *Truth and Method*, Gadamer fully accepts Heidegger's hermeneutic ontology as an accurate description of the near identity relationship between meaning and being, also known as the interpretive nature of being (1993). However, Gadamer adds some important and helpful enhancements, elucidations and extrapolations to Heidegger's account. For example, what Heidegger calls *forestructures of understanding* Gadamer calls *pre-judgments* (*Vorurteile*) (1993: 270). And like Heidegger's *forestructures of understanding*, Gadamer's *pre-judgments* are neither good nor bad.

Gadamer writes, "Thus 'pre-judgment' certainly does not necessarily mean a false judgment, but part of the idea is that it can have either a positive or a negative value" (ibid.). In this way, *Vorurteile* is not unjustifed bias that might cloud understanding but merely one or more aspects of the hermeneutical situatedness in which the process of understanding always unfolds. Gadamer adds nuance and depth to Heidegger's description of these aspects of hermeneutical situatedness by distinguishing between *legitimate* and *illegitimate* pre-judgments. *Illegitimate pre-judgments* (analogous to the conclusions drawn by Heidegger's *the they*) are a barrier to understanding and meaning but *legitimate pre-judgments* actually help us in achieving it through the disclosure of the original set of possibilities within which a given understanding takes place.

For Gadamer, in other words, it can be argued that all understanding begins within a set of preconceived notions that are taken to have meaning. It is in this sense that *pre-judgments* are structural. Along this line of thinking, there is no universal vantage point from which objective understanding can be ascertained or determined. On the way to understanding, everyone begins from a predetermined concept of the whole subject matter to be understood, then moves into an investigation into the parts (the specific details of the matter at issue), and then moves back out into a fuller conception of the whole subject matter. This is the hermeneutic circle of understanding at work. Lawrence Schmidt writes, "Understanding transpires within the hermeneutic circle. In interpreting a text [or a situation or a concept or a phenomenon] the interpreter moves from a projected meaning for the whole to the parts and then returns to the whole" (2006: 103). Rather than a statement on the inevitable circularity of meaning and being, however, it can be argued that the concept of the hermeneutic circle merely makes explicit that the path to understanding must always be entered from some*where* by some*one*, and is necessarily informed and led by a given question that arises out of a particular set of circumstances.

h. Horizons and traditions

Together, a set of *pre-judgments* amounts to what Gadamer calls an *historical horizon* within which every attempt at understanding begins (1993: 302). Gadamer defines a *horizon* as "the way in which thought is tied to its finite determinacy, and the way one's range of vision is gradually expanded" (ibid.). Included within a given *historical horizon* are all of the largely unarticulated assumptions and so-called facts that each of us has integrated into our conception of who we are and what we value and hold dear. An *historical horizon* includes everything one thinks one knows, both consciously and subconsciously. What is correct within a given *historical horizon* is a *legitimate pre-judgment*. What is incorrect is an *illegitimate pre-judgment*.

A Gadamerian *tradition* is a vehicle through which *legitimate pre-judgments* survive over time and *illegitimate pre-judgments* fall away. A *tradition* involves "the historical process of preservation that, through constantly proving itself, allows something true to come into being" (1993: 287). In other words, in the process of understanding, one first makes an assessment of the correctness of a given interpretation on the basis of the degree to which it fits in with the other *pre-judgments* of a given *tradition*. If the interpretation does fit in with the other *pre-judgments*, its *legitimacy* is justified. In Gadamer's words, the next step is to determine what the text has to say to us, today, in our current situation or circumstances. Gadamer writes, "new sources of understanding are continually emerging that reveal unsuspected elements of meaning" (1993: 298). What this means is that *correct understanding* of anything is never finished. "[I]t is in fact an infinite process" (ibid.). Gadamer writes, "Understanding is, essentially, a historically effected event" (1993: 300). Nicholas Davey explains:

> That the meaningfulness of a new perspective depends upon its relation to other networks of meaning implies that any alteration in the related field will alter the meaningfulness of that perspective. In short, philosophical hermeneutics recognizes that it is the very instability and uncertainty of meaning that enables the emergence of the meaningful.
>
> (2006: 143)

i. The importance of application

Meaning or understanding is also always and necessarily affected by application, for Gadamer. We come to understand things through application. Gadamer writes, "we consider application to be just as integral a part of the hermeneutical process as are understanding and interpretation" (1993: 308). Like Aristotle's *phronesis* in ethical decision-making, all attempts at meaning, writes Gadamer, require deliberation within the confines of particular, concrete circumstances (1993: 312–24). Just as for Aristotle the application of an ethical principle to facts is just not how ethical deliberation occurs, meaning determinations are simply not made by the application of so-called universal truths about the world onto new things to be understood. Instead, in the process of understanding, the *horizon* of the thing to be understood (a text, a concept, a so-called object) is projected onto the new concrete situation before us. In this way, understanding is a dialogical exchange between previous interpretations and the specific context at issue. In this process, hermeneutic integrity is preserved over time to the extent that *legitimate* (or accurate) aspects of prior understandings are preserved and *illegitimate* (or inaccurate) understandings drop out of the realm of consideration. Correct understanding, then, evolves over time, as the distinction between *legitimate* and *illegitimate pre-judgments* becomes apparent.

j. Hermeneutic truth

Gadamer's conception of (hermeneutic) truth differs from Heidegger's. While Heidegger understands truth as the uncovering (*aletheia*) of how things are *in-the-world* (i.e., as how they interact with *Dasein* and vice versa), Gadamer defines (hermeneutic) truth as the *fusion of horizons* between the text (or the phenomenon to be understood) and the interpreter, or between two or more interpreters. Gadamer writes, "In the process of understanding, a real fusing of horizons occurs – which means that as the historical horizon is projected, it is simultaneously superseded" (1993: 307). Some describe this progress as follows: When the fusion of horizons is achieved, a word arises up out of a given language. At the same moment in time, the being of the subject matter, the text, the concept or object to be understood is revealed. In other words, correct understanding of a thing and its being or existence occur simultaneously and as a function of the fusion of two or more *historical horizons*. Notably, however, there is no end point, no final stop on the hermeneutic journey, on this view. It can never be justifiably said that a timeless, definitive understanding has been obtained. Instead, Gadamer's hermeneutic truth is always situated within a specific time and place and for a particular application.

In Gadamer's *Truth and Method*, then, Heidegger's insight that truth as *aletheia* (or uncovering) reveals that meaning and being are one and the same, is developed into an account of truth as a *fusion of horizons* that more explicitly involves the role of others. While Heidegger's truth involves others in the sense that everyone who participates in a given *world* contributes to the creation of the system of intelligibility that obtains there, Gadamer's truth requires active dialogical interchange between different interpreters or interpretations. For Heidegger, truth (*aletheia*) is revealed after hermeneutical phenomenological reduction is performed on a given phenomenon. The awareness generated in the wake of the uncovering is meant to, in some sense, free the interpreter up to envision new and different ways to understand the phenomenon in question. New possibilities for the meaning and being of the phenomenon are disclosed. Gadamerian truth highlights that this process, this journey toward understanding, necessarily entails dialogical exchange between at least two interpretations or interpreters.

Central principles of Gadamer's account are that (1) every attempt at understanding is an act of interpretation; (2) every interpretation begins within a particular schema of intelligibility; (3) a given schema of intelligibility is made articulate through language; (4) every schema of intelligibility contains assumptions, some of which are legitimate (true to the things themselves) and some of which are not; (5) correct understanding – or hermeneutic truth – arises up out of a dialogue between interpreter and text (or between previous interpreter(s) and current interpreter); (6) all interpretation takes place within a *tradition*, which operates as a basis upon which to discern legitimate pre-judgments from illegitimate ones; (7) *traditions* are not static but evolve over time as new pre-judgments are legitimized and others are delegitimized through dialogue; and (8) correct understanding can be had, but is situated.

II. Hermeneutic ontology and the phenomenon of race[3]

There is a branch of late twentieth and early twenty-first century philosophy of race that has spent a significant amount of time debating whether race is "real." One strand of this branch of philosophy – often called the "eliminativist" position – has involved bringing into the philosophical mainstream evidence (available since at least the 1950s) to the effect that race as it is commonly understood to exist (i.e., as having a basis in biology) is not supported by scientific evidence (Zack 1993, 2002, 2010; Appiah 1993; Piper 1992, 1992–3). For the eliminativist, belief in the existence of biological race is thought to be the core misconception driving racial oppression. This is because, for the eliminativist, a belief in biological race carries with it at least two related beliefs: (1) the belief that there is a correlation between somatic traits (like hair texture, eye shape, or skin color) and character or personality traits (like intelligence or trustworthiness); and (2) the belief in a kind of natural racial hierarchy according to which some races are superior to other races. The assumption behind the eliminativist position is that once racial hierarchy is exposed as lacking in scientific support, those holding racist views and engaging in racially oppressive practices will suddenly stop the offending practices. For the eliminativist, then, in order to end racial oppression, we should eliminate "race talk" or "race thinking" because continuing to speak of race or think about race at all perpetuates the misconception that race has a biological basis, to the detriment of efforts to curb racism.

Building upon the evidence that biological race is unsupported by scientific evidence but acknowledging nonetheless that race operates very powerfully in our lives, another strand of contemporary philosophy of race emphasizes the *social* – as opposed to the biological – existence of race. Often called "social constructionism," on this view concepts of race "are the products of the socio-historical practices, behaviors, conventions and institutions that give rise to them" (Atkin 2012: 47) providing race with an ontological status that is significant, if not fixed or unchangeable (Taylor 2003; Shelby 2005).

Some have argued that social constructionism comes in both *weak* and *strong* forms (see, e.g., Atkin 2012). According to this argument, the strong form holds that social forces are actually *reality-conferring* whereas the weak form falls short of making this claim. The distinction is thought to turn on whether race is intended to capture some underlying physical reality about the world. Upon closer inspection, however, it can be argued that so-called strong social constructionism is not social constructionism at all but is instead a version of metaphysical essentialism dressed in the emperor's new clothes. In other words, if social constructionism is meant to describe the ways in which social forces generate and affect *what we take to be real* rather than to generate or affect what is *actually real*, then the only social constructionism deserving of the name is so-called weak social constructionism, a core tenet of which is that metaphysical essentialism is fundamentally wrong-headed.

An interesting twist on social constructionism – sometimes called "reconstructionism" – incorporates what is known as "racial realism" or a concession to the permanence of racism (Bell 1995) as a key aspect of the philosophical examination of the phenomenon of race. For the racial realist, it is of no moment whether race exists biologically, socially or any other way since regardless of the outcome of that inquiry, racism is alive and well. The racial realist disentangles the problem of racial oppression from the question of whether or not race is "real" to focus instead on improving conditions for racialized minority groups (ibid.). The racial reconstructionist adds to the (weak) social constructionist position a recommendation that the concept of race should be used to actually improve conditions for members of racialized minority groups rather than used in the service of oppressing them.

In alignment with (weak) social constructionism, Heideggerian hermeneutic ontology can be understood to lead to the conclusion that race has both meaning and being but still falls short of being "real" in a traditional metaphysical sense. Certainly on Heidegger's ontic level, people take the concept of human racial categories seriously and interact with each other and the systems of intelligibility in which they dwell as if race has both meaning and being. However, on Heidegger's ontological level (the level of understanding reached through phenomenological reduction in the hermeneutical sense), *Dasein* has "formal indications" or hints all around to the effect that race has neither being nor meaning. For some time, there has been widespread, although not undisputed, acceptance in the scientific community, for example, to the effect that race has no genetic basis (Montagu 1942; UNESCO 1951; Livingstone 1962; Lewontin 1972; Hubbard 1999; Graves 2001). Nevertheless, these scientific revelations do not seem to have had a significant effect on the fact that race still operates very meaningfully in our lives. Moreover, words denoting different racial categories do not seem to have dropped out of existence. Our culture and our language still operate as if race exists and has meaning, so in an important sense, race still exists and has meaning despite the scientific discoveries that there is no scientific basis for the phenomenon.[4]

At the same time, however, the meaning and being of race, like all phenomena, is contingent from a Heideggerian point of view. Authentic interpretation of anything is not static but open to future possibilities. An authentic attempt to understand the phenomenon of race, then, would involve acknowledging that whatever concept of race we may hold today is subject to change in the future. To gain a glimpse of the possibilities for alternative understandings of race, we must look to the array of possibilities that are disclosed to us by our past and by our current situation, and then open ourselves up to alternative meaning possibilities as disclosed by a confrontation with our own finitude. So, while the meaning and being of the phenomenon of race may be alive and well within contemporary western cultural hegemony, from a Heideggerian point of view, race is both an inauthentic and contingent concept.

A Gadamerian analysis of race does not seem to differ much from the Heideggerian analysis. From a Gadamerian standpoint, the competing pre-judgments or interpretations are (1) that race is based in biology and has meaning and being, and (2) that race is not based in biology and has little or no meaning or being. The first is the commonly held view. The second is the view of those who have generated the scientific data indicating that race is not based in biology. Recall that Gadamer's method for distinguishing legitimate (accurate) pre-judgments from illegitimate (false) ones is to place them into dialogue. This dialogue begins by placing a given pre-judgment within a tradition to determine the extent to which the pre-judgment fits into that tradition. If it fits in with all of the other pre-judgments of the tradition (i.e., those that have withstood the test of time), it is legitimate. If it does not fit in, the interpreter is called upon to engage in self-reflexivity and apply a critical gaze to the pre-judgment.

The pre-judgment that race is not based in biology (the new pre-judgment up for interpretation) does not seem to fit in with the western tradition going back at least to Kant that race is based in biology (Kant 1775).[5] Because of this dissonance – this disconnect between the new pre-judgment up for interpretation and the tradition at issue – it is incumbent upon the interpreter to investigate more deeply into the question of whether race has being or meaning. The scientific evidence referenced above will be consulted, as will the philosophical debates on the topic. Certainly, any sociological evidence will be consulted, as well as any more deeply held viewpoints held by racial minority groups on the topic. Gadamer's philosophical hermeneutics suggests that if there is enough contrary evidence available to the interpreter of meaning to successfully challenge the western tradition that race is based in biology, eventually the tradition (western socio-cultural or socio-political ideology) will change to accommodate the new pre-judgment (that race is created by social forces instead). And if the new pre-judgment is sound or legitimate, it will remain a part of the tradition over time with at least two possible concomitant results: Either the words we use to denote (biological) races will simply drop out of common usage or the words will come to be associated with race understood as the product of socio-historical forces rather than biological ones.

III. Hermeneutic ontology and the phenomenon of gender

Simone de Beauvoir famously wrote, "One is not born, but rather becomes a woman" (1949). At the core of feminist theorizing regarding women's condition in society, their bodies, their access to educational, political, cultural and social goods, and their relationship to institutions and structures of knowledge and power is an investigation into what it means to be a woman, what it means to have a gender, and what gender is as a first order of business. Contemporary feminist theory understands gender as a social institution, a "process of creating distin-guishable social statuses for the assignment of rights and responsibilities" (Lorber 1994). Gender creates, on this view, the social differences that separate what we call a "man" from what we call a "woman" (ibid.). The gender roles "man" and "woman" occur, in other words, within a complex system of social stratification (patriarchy) according to which the equality statuses of those gendered "male" and those gendered "female" are quite different. Within this system is contained the cultural belief that this difference in equality status is somehow natural such that normality becomes a function of the degree to which one performs or displays the gender role linked to their biological sex (Rubin 1976). Feminist metaphysics interrogates this cultural sense of gender difference through an examination of the extent to which society's values are embedded in the categories and descriptions with which reality is customarily cognized (Delphy 1984; MacKinnon 1989; Butler 1990; Haslanger 1995, 2000).

In "Hermeneutics and Constructed Identities," Georgia Warnke writes that the Gadamerian concept of a fusion of *horizons* is helpful when thinking about gender and gender identity (2003). While contemporary feminist theorists have identified at least two important problems with the category "woman" – specifically, that it is either too general to include all women, or that it is harmfully essentializing – if the category of "woman" is thrown out altogether, there is left no "subject for whom feminism struggles" (Warnke 2003: 57). Warnke suggests that (Gadamer's) herme-neutics may provide a way out of this problem, through rejecting essentialism while retaining a gendered identity created through the socialization into a particular interpretive tradition.

Feminist standpoint theory is hermeneutic in flavor as well, allowing for the (social) construction of the category "women" as a subject of study as well as an epistemologically cognizable and credible knowledge source rooted in the experi-ences of women (Benhabib 1995; Fraser 1997; Hartstock 1983).

IV. Recent scholarship on hermeneutics, race and gender

a. Race and gender

The hermeneutic insight that race and gender are situated, culturally derived phenomena from which particularized experiences and approaches to understanding are located has been adopted by many contemporary theorists of race and gender. In *Visible Identities: Race, Gender, and the Self,* Linda Martín Alcoff draws on the insights of hermeneutic ontology to develop the idea that race and gender are social identities that function as interpretive horizons (Alcoff 2006). They are the locations from which each of us understands and experiences the world, including the experience of interacting with others. Race and gender are embodied and situated, in other words, and operate as Heideggerian *worlds* or Gadamerian *historical horizons* in the sense that they are systems of intelligibility within which understanding and meaning generation take place.

Alcoff translates these insights into epistemological terms in "Gadamer's Feminist Epistemology" (2003). Describing Gadamer's account of justification and truth as offering us a way to characterize the reality of situated knowing not as a negative, but as simply a necessary condition for knowledge, Alcoff identifies as feminist the fact that Gadamer gives "relatedness ontological primacy" (2003: 232). She identifies four specific features of Gadamer's hermeneutics that are useful for feminism: (1) openness to alterity; (2) a move from knowledge to understanding; (3) holism in justification; and (4) immanent realism. Contemporary body theory, according to which the body is seen as a kind of canvas upon which systems of intelligibility (or cultures or ideologies) paint what they will, is hermeneutic in this way as well (Foucault 1990; Cixous 1981).

Lorenzo Simpson grapples with the question of whether hermeneutics can legitimize the kind of particularized meaning thought to come out of the experience of being a race or gender in "On Habermas and Particularity: Is there Room for Race and Gender on the Glassy Plains of Ideal Discourse?" (Simpson 1986). In this article, Simpson situates the question of the relationship between hermeneutics, race and gender within classical philosophical debates about universality vs. particularity, objectivism vs. relativism, and ultimately about transcendental-universalist vs. historicist philosophical strategies. Simpson's position is that Habermas's concept of ideology critique renders his hermeneutics useful to questions of race and gender. Under conditions of Habermasian ideal dialogue, for Simpson, to the extent that particular interests are generalizable, they amount to an accepted critique of the reigning ideology and are then incorporated into the consensus that counts as truth.

b. Race

In contemporary critical philosophy of race, much has been made of the question of whether the universalist theories advocated by certain canonical thinkers in the history of philosophy can be separated from the apparent racism of these philosophers. For example, Charles Mills has argued that social contract theory cannot be saved from its racist origins (Mills 1997); Emmanuel Eze and Robert Bernasconi have argued that Immanuel Kant's racist views, particularly on the correlation he thought existed between race and the ability to reason, cast doubt on the legitimacy of his moral theory (Eze 1997; Bernasconi 2001, 2003). Claims to the universal applicability of one's theories in the history of philosophy, these thinkers say, often correlate with deeply held racist views that exempt those racialized as non-white from the full array of rights or considerations afforded to whites. Universal applicability of a theory, in other words, for these thinkers, is code (at least in modern philosophy) for applicability to whites only. This proposition is a question for hermeneutic ontology because it engages the issues of the situatedness of these theories and the degree to which the theories can be abstracted out of context. Matthew Bruenig has recently built upon the work of Mills, Eze and Bernasconi in this area to argue that the principle of "atomistic individualism" central to modern political theory (or the idea that each human being is an isolated, unique, lone entity in the world) is in fact highly racialized, "making group-based justice claims impossible" (Bruenig 2011). Moreover, Bernasconi has recently argued that a phenomenological approach to race should be supplemented by a "hermeneutics of racialization" (or an inquiry into the historical origins of the concept of race) in the fight against "current racisms" (Bernasconi 2012).

c. Gender

In *Epistemic Injustice: Power and the Ethics of Knowing*, Miranda Fricker defines "hermeneutical injustice" as the injustice of having some significant area of one's social experience obscured from collective understanding (Fricker 2007). She argues that there is a "collective hermeneutical resource" at work at any given time that contains tools to help us understand our experiences in the world. This "collective hermeneutical resource" is akin to a Heideggerian *world* or a Gadamerian *historical horizon*. It is the system of intelligibility in which we find ourselves when we are attempting to understand anything. Where that collective hermeneutical resource contains no tools to process an experience, the experience is left unincorporated into the epistemic framework at issue. So, for example, before the phrase "sexual harassment" came onto the scene, there was no way for a victim of sexual harassment to come to grips with experiences that we now come to understand as examples of sexual harassment. There was no way for the victim to *understand* what happened at the time because the collective hermeneutical resource was lacking.

In "Feminist Social Theory and Hermeneutics: An Empowering Dialectic," Eloise A. Buker argues that philosophical hermeneutics, in the Gadamerian sense, is good for feminist theory in that it accounts for a social reality that allows women-centered research to make claims to legitimacy (Buker 1990). Feminist theory, in turn, is also good for hermeneutics, for Buker, in that it can give hermeneutics social and political substance.[6]

Concluding remarks

Nicholas Davey has described hermeneutic philosophy as a "dialogical *modus operandi*" with a "disposition towards openness" that enables hermeneutics "not merely to prepare for the other but to allow the other to be the other" (2008: 693). Hermeneutics prepares for the other through acknowledging the degree to which meaning and being are collectively generated. Hermeneutics allows the other to be the other through the active inclusion of situated vantage points in the production of correct understanding. At the same time, hermeneutics is a critique of the tendency to essentialize and reify situated difference. Race and gender, from the vantage point of hermeneutics, in other words, are not fixed entities in a static world, but are instead mutable and changeable categorical labels placed on groups of persons in society through the manner in which certain people interact with other people, and interact with the world around them. Put another way, hermeneutics explicitly acknowledges that the meaning and being of race and gender are collectively generated and changeable. But, the story does not end there. From the vantage point of hermeneutics, the fact that race and gender are collectively generated and changeable does not in any way diminish the fact that these phenomena have existence in the sense that they operate meaningfully in the lives of human beings, affecting both the life possibilities available to one, as well as one's perceptions about those life possibilities.

From the hermeneutical point of view taken in this chapter, then, that is, from the vantage point of the hermeneutic ontology developed by Martin Heidegger, as enhanced and developed by Hans-Georg Gadamer, the question of whether race and gender are "real" is translated into the question of whether these phenomena have meaning or being. From a hermeneutical point of view based in hermeneutic ontology, this question is answered in the same way as the answer to the question of whether *anything* has meaning or being and that is that these phenomena have meaning and being *to the extent that the way we react to these phenomena generates meaning and being for them*, where "we" refers to the participants in the system of intelligibility (the culture, the language, the value system) in which the question is being asked at the time and place where the question is being asked.

Notes

1 It should be noted that the assumption made in this chapter to the effect that Gadamer's thinking can be construed as largely a continuation of Heidegger's is not without its critics – see, for example, Kiefer 2013.

2 Clarification of Heidegger's concept of *forestructure* can be found in Ka-wing Leung's "Heidegger's Concept of Fore-structure and Textual Interpretation" (Leung 2011).

3 The focus of this section is an examination of the phenomenon of race through the lens of hermeneutic ontology. Regarding those aspects of hermeneutic ontology based in Heidegger's thought, the reader should be aware that Heidegger was affiliated for a time with National Socialism (Nazism). I raise this point because I feel a responsibility to make readers aware that the originator of hermeneutic ontology is known to have said things at times that many would consider racist. For some, this may mean a specter of suspicion is raised surrounding anything Heidegger or his philosophy may have to say about the meaning or being of the phenomenon of race. I am sympathetic to this view to the extent that I believe that attempts to lop off philosophical ideas from the political or personal views of their creators should be handled with care and attention. However, I also find Heidegger's concept of *being-in-the-world* to have a high degree of explanatory power. In any event, for me, at this point in my own hermeneutical dialogue with Heidegger's thought and life, I am comfortable working with Heidegger's thought on its own terms. This may

not be true for others, and if not, I understand why. The reader should note that scholars disagree about the exact nature of Heidegger's affiliation with National Socialism as well as about the extent to which Heidegger's political convictions or personal views may have affected his philosophy of being. While for some, Heidegger's notion of *historicity*, for example, problematically operated as the driving force behind the racial purity fueling national socialism (Sheehan 1993), others focus on the fact that Heidegger invited his contemporaries to rethink the phenomenon of race so as to reject biological reductionism, in keeping with Heidegger's general project of overcoming western metaphysics (Bernasconi 2010). Additional information on Heidegger's relationship with National Socialism can be found in Farias 1989; Sheehan 1993; Radloff 2007; Safranski 1998; Young 1998; and Fritsche 2012.

4 Whether it is biological race or sociohistorical race that survives in the face of the scientific evidence, however, is unclear.

5 It is important that the selection of a tradition against which to measure a given pre-judgment is not particularly outcome determinative, for Gadamer, because, for him, the tradition within which understanding begins is simply the point at which the interpreter enters the hermeneutic circle. Once within the circle of understanding, the interpreter is called upon to responsibly investigate and test the legitimacy of each existing pre-judgment within the tradition that does not cohere with the new pre-judgment, for the purpose of re-assessing the legitimacy of that pre-judgment, and ultimately, of the tradition itself.

6 Diane Elam disagrees with Buker's characterization of the relationship between hermeneutics and feminist theory being harmonious, arguing instead that after Heidegger, hermeneutics "contains within it the litter of phallocentric tradition that refuses point blank to acknowledge the significance of gender differentiation" (Elam 1991: 2).

Bibliography

Alcoff, Linda Martín (2006) *Visible Identities: Race, Gender, and the Self*. Oxford: Oxford University Press.

——(2003) "Gadamer's Feminist Epistemology," in *Feminist Interpretations of Hans-Georg Gadamer*. University Park, PA: Pennsylvania State University Press.

Appiah, K. Anthony (1993) *In My Father's House*. Oxford: Oxford University Press.

Atkin, Albert (2012) *The Philosophy of Race*. Durham, England: Acumen Publishing.

de Beauvoir, Simone (1949) The Second Sex, trans. H. M. Parshley. New York: Vintage Books.

Beeby, Laura (2011) "A Critique of Hermeneutical Injustice," *Proceedings of the Aristotelian Society*, 111, Part 3, 479–86.

Bell, Derrick (1995) "Racial Realism," in *Critical Race Theory: The Key Writings that Formed the Movement*, eds. Kimberlé Crenshaw, Neil Gotanda, Garry Petter, and Kendall Thomas, 302–12. New York: The New Press.

Benhabib, S. (1995) *Feminist Contentions*. New York: Routledge.

Bernasconi, Robert (2001) "Who Invented the Concept of Race? Kant's Role in the Enlightenment Construction of Race," in *Race*, ed. Robert Bernasconi, 9–36. Oxford: Blackwell.

——(2003) "Will the Real Kant Please Stand Up: The Challenge of Enlightenment Racism to the Study of the History of Philosophy," *Radical Philosophy* 117, 13–22.

——(2010) "Race and Earth in Heidegger's Thinking During the Late 1930s," *The Southern Journal of Philosophy*, 48(1), 49–66.

——(2012) "Crossed Lines in the Racialization Process: Race as a Border Concept," *Research in Phenomenology*, 42(2), 206–28.

Bordo, Susan (1987) *The Flight to Objectivity: Essays on Cartesianism and Culture*. Albany: SUNY Press.

Bruenig, Matthew (2011) "Atomistic Individualism and the Hermeneutics of Racist Philosophy," *APA Newsletter on Philosophy and the Black Experience*, 11(1), 28–33.

Buker, Eloise (1990) "Feminist Social Theory and Hermeneutics: An Empowering Dialectic?," *Social Epistemology*, 4(1), 23–39.

Butler, Judith (1990) *Gender Trouble: Feminism and the Subversion of Identity*. New York: Routledge.

——(1993) *Bodies That Matter: On the Discursive Limits of Sex*. New York: Routledge.

Cixous, Hélène (1981) "The Laugh of the Medusa," in *New French Feminisms*, eds. Elaine Marks and Isabelle de Courtivron, 254–68. New York: Schocken Books.

Davey, Nicholas (2006) *Unquiet Understanding. Gadamer's Philosophical Hermeneutics*. Albany. State University of New York Press.

——(2008) "Twentieth-Century Hermeneutics," in *The Routledge Companion to Twentieth Century Philosophy*, ed. Dermot Moran, 693–735. London and New York: Routledge.

Delphy, Christine (1984) *Close to Home: A Materialist Analysis of Women's Oppression*. Amherst, MA: University of Massachusetts Press.

Derrida, Jacques (1979) *Spurs: Nietzsche's Styles*. Chicago: University of Chicago Press.

——(1993) "Structure, Sign, and Play in the Discourse of the Human Sciences," in *A Postmodern Reader*, ed. Joseph Natoli and Linda Hutcheon, 223–42. Albany: SUNY Press.

Elam, Diane (1991) "Is Feminism the Saving Grace of Hermeneutics?," *Social Epistemology*, 5(4), 349–60.

Eze, Emmanuel C. (1997) "The Color of Reason: The Idea of 'Race' in Kant's Anthropology," in *Postcolonial African Philosophy: A Critical Reader*, ed. Emmanuel C. Eze, 103–40. Cambridge: Blackwell.

Farias, Victor (1989) *Heidegger et le nazisme*, trans. Myriam Benarroch and Jean-Baptiste Grasset. Lagrass: Verdier.

Foucault, Michel (1985) *The Order of Things*. London: Tavistock.

——(1990) *The Use of Pleasure*, Vol. 2, *The History of Sexuality*, trans. Robert Hurley. New York: Vintage Books.

Fraser, Nancy (1997) *Justice Interruptus*. New York: Routledge.

Fraser, Nancy and Linda Nicholson (1990) "Social Criticism without Philosophy: An Encounter Between Feminism and Post-modernism," in *Feminism/Postmodernism*, ed. L. Nicholson, 19–38. New York: Routledge.

Fricker, Miranda (2007) *Epistemic Injustice: Power and the Ethics of Knowing*. Oxford: Oxford University Press.

Fritsche, Johannes (2012) "Heidegger's 'Being and Time' and National Socialism," *Philosophy Today*, 56(3), 255–84.

Frye, Marilyn (1983) *The Politics of Reality: Essays in Feminist Theory*. New York: The Crossing Press.

Gadamer, H-G. (1993) *Truth and Method*, 2nd rev. edn., trans. Joel Weisenheimer and Donald G. Marshall. New York: Continuum.

Graves, Joseph L., Jr. (2001) *The Emperor's New Clothes: Biological Theories of Race at the Millennium*. New Brunswick, NJ: Rutgers University Press.

Habermas, Jürgen (1980) "The Hermeneutic Claim to Universality," in *Contemporary Hermeneutics: Hermeneutics as Method, Philosophy and Critique*, ed. J. Bleicher. London: Routledge.

——(1984) *The Theory of Communicative Action*, vol. 1, trans. Thomas McCarthy. Boston, MA: Beacon Press.

——(1990) "A Review of Gadamer's *Truth and Method*," in *The Hermeneutic Tradition: From Ast to Ricoeur*, eds. Gayle L. Ormiston and Alan D. Schrift. Albany: State University of New York.

Hartstock, N. (1983) *Money, Sex and Power*. New York: Longman.

Haslanger, Sally (1993) "On Being Objective and Being Objectified," in *A Mind of One's Own*, eds. L. Antony and C. Witt, 85–125. Boulder, CO: Westview.

——(1995) "Ontology and Social Construction," *Philosophical Topics*, 23(2) (Fall), 95–125.

——(2000) "Feminism and Metaphysics: Unmasking Hidden Ontologies," *APA Newsletter on Feminism and Philosophy*, 99(2) (Spring), 192–6.

Heidegger, M. (1962) *Being and Time*, trans. J. Macquarrie and E. Robinson. New York: Harper & Row.

——(1971) *Poetry, Language, and Thought*, trans. Albert Hofstadter. New York: Harper & Row.

——(1993) "Letter on Humanism," in *Basic Writings*, 2nd rev. and expanded edn., ed. David F. Krell, 213–66. New York: HarperCollins.

——(1999) *Ontology: Hermeneutics of Facticity*, trans. John van Buren. Bloomington: Indiana University Press.

Hubbard, Ruth (1999) *Exploding the Gene Myth: How Genetic Information is Produced and Manipulated by Scientists, Physicians, Employers, Insurance Companies, Educators, and Law Enforcers*, 3rd edn. Boston: Beacon Press.

Kant, Immanuel (1775) "Von den verschiedenen Racen der Menschen," *Gesammelte Schriften*. Berlin: Walter de Gruyter, 1902, 429–43; revised and expanded in 1777. English translation: (2000) "Of the Different Human Races," in *The Idea of Race*, eds. Robert Bernasconi and Tommy Lott 8–22. Indianapolis: Hackett.

Kiefer, Thomas (2013) "Hermeneutical Understanding as the Disclosure of Truth: Hans-Georg Gadamer's Distinctive Understanding of Truth," *Philosophy Today*, 57(1), 42–60.

Kuhn, Tomas (1970) *The Structure of Scientific Revolutions*, 2nd edn. Chicago: University of Chicago Press.

Kukla, Andre (2000) *Social Construction and the Philosophy of Science*. London: Routledge.

Leung, Ka-wing (2011) "Heidegger's Concept of Fore-structure and Textual Interpretation," *Phainomena: Journal of the Phenomenological Society of Ljubljana*, 20(79), 23–40.

Lewontin, R.C. (1972) "The Apportionment of Human Diversity," *Evolutionary Biology*, 6, 381–98.

Livingstone, F. (1962) "On the Nonexistence of Human Races," *Current Anthropology*, 3, 279–81.

Lorber, Judith (1994) "Night to His Day: The Social Construction of Gender," in *Paradoxes of Gender*, 13–15, 32–36. New Haven, CT: Yale University Press.

MacKinnon, Catharine (1989) *Toward a Feminist Theory of the State*. Cambridge, MA: Harvard University Press.

Mathiesen, Kay (2006) "The Epistemic Features of Group Belief," *Episteme: A Journal of Social Epistemology*, 2(3), 161–75.

Mills, Charles W. (1997) *The Racial Contract*. Ithaca, NY: Cornell University Press.

——(1998) *Blackness Visible: Essays on Philosophy and Race*. Ithaca, NY: Cornell University Press.

Montagu, M.F.A. (1942) *Man's Most Dangerous Myth: The Fallacy of Race*. New York: Columbia University Press.

Nietzsche, F. (1968) *The Will to Power*, trans. W. Kaufman and R.J. Hollingdale. London: Weidenfeld & Nicolson.

Piper, Adrian M.S. (1992) "Passing for White, Passing for Black," *Transition*, 58, 5–32.

——(1992–93) "Xenophobia and Kantian Rationalism," *Philosophical Forum*, 24(1–3) (Fall–Spring), 188–232.

Radloff, Bernhard (2007) *Heidegger and the Question of National Socialism: Disclosure and Gestalt*. Toronto: University of Toronto Press.

Ricoeur, Paul (1991) "The Task of Hermeneutics," in *From Text to Action: Essays in Hermeneutics, II*, trans. John B. Thompson, 53–74. Evanston, IL: Northwestern University Press.

Rubin, Gayle (1976) "The Traffic in Women," in *Toward an Anthropology of Women*, ed. Rayna R. Reiter, 159. New York: Monthly Review Press.

Safranski, Rüdiger (1998) *Martin Heidegger: Between Good and Evil*, trans. Ewald Osers. Cambridge, MA: Harvard University Press.

Schiebinger, Linda, ed. (2000) *Feminism and the Body*. Oxford: Oxford University Press.

Schmidt, Lawrence (2006) *Understanding Hermeneutics*. Stocksfield, England: Acumen.

Sheehan, Thomas (1993) "Reading a Life: Heidegger and Hard Times," in *The Cambridge Companion to Heidegger*, ed. Charles Guigon, 70–96. Cambridge: Cambridge University Press.

Shelby, Tommie (2005) *We Who Are Dark*. Cambridge, MA: Belknap Press of Harvard University Press.

Simpson, Lorenzo C. (1986) "On Habermas and Particularity: Is there Room for Race and Gender on the Glassy Plains of Ideal Discourse?," *Praxis International*, 6, 328–40.

Steup, Matthias (2008) "Epistemology in the Twentieth Century," *The Routledge Companion to Twentieth Century Philosophy*. New York: Routledge.

Taylor, Paul C. (2003) *Race: A Philosophical Introduction*. Cambridge: Polity Press.

UNESCO (1951) *Race and Science: The Race Question in Modern Science*. New York: Columbia University Press.

Warnke, Georgia (2003) "Hermeneutics and Constructed Identities," in *Feminist Interpretations of Hans-Georg Gadamer*. University Park: Pennsylvania State University Press.

——(2008) *After Identity: Rethinking Race, Sex, and Gender*. Cambridge: Cambridge University Press.

Warren, Karen (1997) *Ecofeminism: Women, Culture, Nature*. Indianapolis: Indiana University Press.

Witt, Charlotte, ed. (2010) *Feminist Metaphysics: Explorations in the Ontology of Sex, Gender, and the Self*. Dordrecht: Springer.

Wittig, Monique (1992) *The Straight Mind*. Boston: Beacon Press.

Young, Iris M. (1990) *Throwing Like a Girl and Other Essays in Feminist Philosophy and Social Theory*. Indianapolis: Indiana University Press.

Young, Julian (1998) *Heidegger, Philosophy, Nazism*. Cambridge: Cambridge University Press.

Zack, Naomi (1993) *Race and Mixed Race*. Philadelphia: Temple University Press.

——(2002) *Philosophy of Science and Race*. New York: Routledge.

——(2010) "The Fluid Symbol of Mixed Race," *Hypatia*, 25th Anniversary Issue, 25(4), 875–90.

Further reading

Apel, K-O. (1967) *Analytic Philosophy of Language and the Geisteswissenschaften*. Dordecht: Reidel.

Caputo, J.D. (1987) *Radical Hermeneutics, Repetition, Deconstruction and the Hermeneutic Project*. Bloomington: Indiana University Press.

——(2000) *More Radical Hermeneutics*. Bloomington: Indiana University Press.

Clark, T.C. (2005) *The Counter-Culturalist Turn in Heidegger, Derrida, Blanchot and the later Gadamer*. Edinburgh: Edinburgh University Press.

Cunningham, V. (2002) *Reading After Theory*. Oxford: Blackwell.

Davidson, D. (1984) "Truth and Meaning," in *Inquiries into Truth and Meaning*. Oxford: Clarendon Press.

Derrida, J. (1997) *Limited Inc*. Evanston, IL: Northwestern University Press.

Dilthey, W. (1976) *Selected Writings*, ed. H.P. Rickman. New York: Cambridge University Press.

Dostal, R., ed. (2001) *The Cambridge Companion to Gadamer*. Cambridge: Cambridge University Press.

Dreyfus, Hubert L. (1991) *Being-in-the-World: A Commentary on Heidegger's Being and Time, Division I.* Cambridge and London: MIT Press.

Eagleton, T. (2003) *After Theory.* Harmondsworth: Penguin.

Eco, U. (1994) *The Limits of Interpretation.* Bloomington: Indiana University Press.

Gadamer, Hans-Georg (1976) *Philosophical Hermeneutics.* Berkeley: University of California Press.

Grondin, J. (1995) *Introduction to Philosophical Hermeneutics.* New Haven, CT: Yale University Press.

——(1996) *Sources of Hermeneutics.* Albany: State University of New York Press.

Hahn, L.E. (1993) *The Philosophy of Hans-Georg Gadamer.* Chicago: Open Court.

Hoy, David Couzens (1993) "Heidegger and the Hermeneutic Turn," in *The Cambridge Companion to Heidegger,* ed. Charles Guignon, 170–94. Cambridge: Cambridge University Press.

Kögler, H.H. (1996) *The Power of Dialogue: Critical Hermeneutics after Gadamer and Foucault.* Cambridge, MA: MIT Press.

Lafont, C. (1999) *The Linguistic Turn in Hermeneutic Philosophy.* Camgridge, MA: MIT Press.

Murray, M., ed. (1978) *Heidegger and Modern Philosophy.* New Haven, CT: Yale University Press.

Ormiston, G.L. and A.D. Schrift, eds. (1990) *The Hermeneutic Tradition.* Albany: State University of New York Press.

Ricoeur, Paul (1974) *The Conflict of Interpretations.* Evanston, IL: Northwestern University Press.

——(1981) *Hermeneutics and the Human Sciences,* ed. J.B. Thompson. Cambridge: Cambridge University Press.

——(1983) "On Interpretation," in *Philosophy in France Today,* ed. A. Montefiore, 175–97. Cambridge: Cambridge University Press.

Schatzki, T.R., K.K. Cetina and E. von Savigny (eds.) (2001) *The Practice Turn in Contemporary Theory.* London: Routledge.

Schleiermacher, F. (1998) *Hermeneutics and Criticism and Other Writings,* trans. A. Bowie. Cambridge: Cambridge University Press.

Silverman, H., ed. (1991) *Gadamer and Hermeneutics.* London: Routledge.

Szondi, P. (1995) *Introduction to Literary Hermeneutics.* Cambridge: Cambridge University Press.

Vattimo, G. (1997) *Beyond Interpretation.* London: Polity.

Wachterhauser, B. (1999) *Beyond Being: Gadamer's Post-Platonic Hermeneutic Ontology.* Evanston, IL: Northwestern University Press.

Weinsheimer, J. (1991) *Philosophical Hermeneutics and Literary Theory.* New Haven, CT: Yale University Press.

41
HERMENEUTICS, AESTHETICS AND THE ARTS

Beata Sirowy

Is it really the case that a work of art, which comes out of a past or alien life-world and is transferred into our historically educated world, becomes a mere object of aesthetic-historical enjoyment and says nothing more of what it originally had to say? ... This question gives us access to the real problematic dimension of the theme "aesthetics and hermeneutics".

(Gadamer, "Aesthetics and Hermeneutics")

The discipline of aesthetics is relatively new, but philosophical inquiry into art and beauty is by no means a recent phenomenon. In classic writings we may find allusions to now lost works of Democritus dealing with poetry. He maintained that a work of poetry is truly beautiful if composed with passion (*enthusiasmos*) and "sacred spirit" (*hieron pneuma*) (Boitani 2008: 125). Works of Plato and Aristotle provide a more systematic reflection on art, and set the boundaries for most of the further art discourse until the early eighteenth century. At that time modern aesthetics emerged – a new branch of philosophy focused on the study of beauty and taste. It fundamentally departed from the classical view of aesthetic experience as a form of cognition of truth, towards its conceptualization as a free play of mental faculties. Kant's theory has been here most influential; it directed much of the subsequent aesthetic discourse and guided a variety of styles and art movements. Hermeneutic discourse on art has developed in polemics with modern aesthetics – addressing its limitations, particularly marginalization of art as a source of knowledge.

Distancing itself from the tradition of modern aesthetics, hermeneutics incorporates many elements of classical theories of art, as expressed by Plato and Aristotle. Art is for hermeneutic thinkers, like it was for classical authors, a "statement of truth" (Gadamer 2007: 195). This truth is not accessed from without, through disengaged intellect, but rather from within, through our intuitive engagement with the world; it is a part of our experience of the world. In this perspective the experience of art is not a distinct, non-cognitive, aesthetic type of experience; it rather represents the essence of experience per se (Gadamer 2004: 60).

The experience of art has a relevance that goes far beyond the domain of aesthetics. As Gadamer argues, art gives us clues as to the mode of experience defining human sciences. It also helps us to legitimate their claim to truth – a claim that does not admit verification. In this sense, "arts, taken as a whole, quietly govern the metaphysical heritage of our Western tradition" (Gadamer 2007: 195).

Hermeneutics does not provide a theory of art in a conventional sense. It is neither aimed at a systematic exploration and categorization of art-related concepts, nor particularly interested in differences among specific types of art. It rather "transforms the systematic problem of *aesthetics* into the question of the experience of *art*" (Gadamer 2007: 126) and is primarily concerned with the role art plays in forming our culture, its meaning in communal and individual lives (Gadamer 2007: 195). Above all, hermeneutics is a practical philosophy that helps us "to understand the meaning of what [a work of art] says and make it clear to ourselves and others", and to integrate these meanings into our self-understanding (Gadamer 2008: 100).

In the following sections, in order to grasp the distinctiveness of the hermeneutic view of art, we will look at two traditions that constitute the essential setting for its development: the tradition of modern aesthetics and the early Greek view of art. As Heidegger and Gadamer teach us, such a return to the past is the essential part of hermeneutic practice. There we can find invaluable resources for understanding the present condition. Against this background, we will examine the major themes in hermeneutic discourse on art: the element of truth in art, the nature of artistic creation, and the character of the experience of art.

A radical subjectivization of the experience of art: modern aesthetics and its hermeneutic critique

The term "aesthetics" is derived from the Greek word *aisthetikos* referring to that which is given through sense perception. Alexander Gottlieb Baumgarten reintroduced this term to modern philosophical discourse and gave it a new meaning in his 1735 master thesis, where he defined aesthetics (*epistêmê aisthetikê*) as the science of what is sensed and imagined, delimiting it from the domain of reason. His basic assertion was that "things known are to be known by the superior faculty as the object of logic; things perceived are to be known by the inferior faculty as the objects of science of perception or aesthetics" (Baumgarten 1735, quoted in Vesely 2004: 372). In his 1750 *Aesthetica* he writes: "Aesthetics (as the theory of the liberal arts, as inferior cognition, as the art of beautiful thinking and as the art of thinking analogous to reason) is the science of sensual cognition" (Baumgarten, quoted in Guyer 2007). Aesthetics is here understood both as a theory of art and a theory of sensual cognition.

Leibniz's distinction between clear and confused cognition was an important source of inspiration for Baumgarten. Confused cognition is rich, complex, emotionally engaged. "We sometimes comprehend in a clear manner without any doubt whether a poem or a picture is well made or not, because there is an I-don't-know-what (je ne sais quoi) that satisfies or repels us" (Leibniz, quoted in Hammermeister 2002: 6). In this perspective beauty may be considered a result of human imperfection, incompleteness of human cognition. Baumgarten, however, was convinced that "confused perceptions" are not exclusively an inferior kind of cognition, but a distinctive, rich and complex, but non-cognitive mode of understanding, which needs to be appreciated and investigated in a more systematic way.

Baumgarten's major focus was the study of good and bad taste, and a deduction of the principles of artistic or natural beauty from an individual taste. In *Metaphysic* (1739), § 451, he defines taste as the ability to judge according to the senses, instead of according to the intellect, and argues that a judgement of taste is based on feelings of pleasure or displeasure (Guyer 2007). It was a radical departure from earlier theories of art, based on the understanding of aesthetic experience as a form of *cognition* of truth. In other words, the novelty of modern aesthetics was in assigning the aesthetic experience a fundamentally autonomous status. In earlier theories, the experience of art shared the general dynamics of human experience of the world. Accordingly, it contributed to knowledge and enriched understanding. Modern aesthetics eliminated this cognitive dimension.

Baumgarten initiated modern aesthetic discourse, but it is Immanuel Kant who has been most influential within this domain. As Scruton (1982: 79) asserts, without the first part of the *Critique of Judgement* (1790) "aesthetics would not exist in its modern form". Kant established Baumgarten's assumption as to the inherently non-cognitive character of aesthetic judgements: "The judgment of taste is ... not a judgment of cognition, and is consequently not logical but aesthetical, by which we understand that whose determining ground can be no other than subjective" (Kant 1951: 37).

The major challenge for Kant is to find the basis on which we can argue that the judgement of taste is legitimate – an *a priori* element which would constitute the universal validity of aesthetic judgements. This element is, according to Kant, based on the universality of human mental faculties. Judging a work of art as beautiful we refer to a specific feeling of pleasure it invokes. This feeling is grounded on the fact that the form of a work of art is suited to our cognitive faculties, it stimulates a free play of our faculties that gives us a pleasant sensation. As Gadamer (2004: 38) explains, "[t]his suitedness to the subject is in principle the same for all – i.e., it is universally communicable and thus grounds the claim that the judgement of taste possesses universal validity."

An inherently subjective character of aesthetic judgement necessarily induces a departure from the classical understanding of beauty, denoting integral properties of an object, and follows an understanding that was earlier expressed by Hume (1985: 229): "Beauty is no quality in things themselves: It exists merely in the mind which contemplates them." Beauty does not have here any objective references, it only stands for a subjective feeling – this feeling is not the effect but the very origin of beauty.

From this perspective, the essential feature of the judgement on the beautiful is its disinterestedness. The fact that an object serves some purpose or invokes conceptual associations limits the aesthetic pleasure it can give; these aspects disturb the free play of mental faculties. Free beauty of nature and – in the sphere of art – ornament are considered by Kant as "the beauty proper", for these are "beautiful in themselves". Whenever a conceptual element is brought in – for instance, in the case of representational art – we are dealing with "dependent beauty," an inferior form of beauty.

The non-cognitive, autonomous character of a judgement of taste demands a corresponding view of artistic creation. In this context Kant introduces the concept of genius. Art in its proper sense is the art of genius. Genius intuitively discovers something that cannot be found through learning, methodological work or conceptual reflection. Genius *invents* aesthetic ideas – unconsciously creating forms that appeal to our mental faculties. The lack of any conceptual element behind the origins of a work of art confirms that there is no other principle of judgement than the feeling of pleasure it gives a cultivated observer. In Gadamer's view, "[i]t is the concept of genius ... , and not the 'free beauty' of ornament, that actually forms the basis of Kant's theory of art" (Gadamer 2002: 97).

Summing up, the tradition of modern aesthetics does not permit a philosophy of art in the broadest sense, it only justifies the claim to aesthetic judgement. As Gadamer comments, "[i]n taste nothing is known of the objects judged to be beautiful, but it is stated only that there is a feeling of pleasure connected with them ... in the subjective consciousness" (Gadamer 2004: 38). In this perspective, fine art neither says anything about reality, nor confronts us with moral issues.[1]

In order to do justice to Kant, it has to be noted however, that his understanding of the domain of aesthetics, as presented in the *Critique of Judgment*, is not limited to the judgements on the beautiful (natural or artistic), but includes also the judgement on the sublime, which is a type of experience linked to Kant's moral theory.[2] Nevertheless, the subsequent appropriations of Kant within aesthetics leave behind the concept of the sublime. Modern aesthetics therefore cannot be seen as a transposition of Kant's philosophy; it rather "takes the form of a one-side reading of Kant" (Bernasconi in Gadamer 2002). Kant himself encouraged this understanding, suggesting that the sublime in principle does not belong to the domain of fine art, but is experienced in the encounter with "crude nature". In the essay "Intuition and vividness" Gadamer (2002: 167) suggests that the concept of the sublime can be integrated into the theory of art in a way Kant did not fully accomplish himself.

As Harries (2009: 3) points out, the approach of modern aesthetics "betrays the promise of art". The concept of beauty as a disinterested pleasure directly inspires a formalist view, an "art for art's sake" perspective, disconnecting art from historical, cultural and social realities. Furthermore, the subjectivization of modern aesthetics directly influenced the subjectivization of human sciences – inducing a view that human sciences with their specific methods and approaches do not deal with true knowledge, but only with subjective expressions. In a search for legitimacy, the inquiry in human sciences had been subordinated to models and evaluation criteria transferred from natural sciences (Gadamer 2002).

Hermeneutics is not alone in its dissatisfaction with the perspective of modern aesthetics. Already Hegel (1835) in his *Lectures on Aesthetics*, criticized its limited scope: "The science here referred to does not investigate beauty in its general signification, but the beauty of art pure and simple" (Hegel 1964: 382). In this context he points at the lost aspect of truth:

> Art no longer counts for us as the highest manner in which truth obtains existence for itself. One may well hope that art will continue to advance and perfect itself, but its form has ceased to be the highest need of the spirit. In all these relationships art is and remains for us, on the side of its highest vocation, something past.
>
> (Hegel, quoted in Heidegger 1971: 80)

Art "on the side of its highest vocation" is for Hegel an alternative mode of pursuing the truth, a way to express a different kind of truth than implied in the rational, conceptual model of science, but not inferior to it. Art, understood in this way, reveals what truly matters, it addresses "the profoundest interests of mankind and spiritual truths of a widest range" (Hegel 1964: 388). In this, it is related to philosophy and religion.

Heidegger (1971) follows Hegel's line of thinking when he calls on art to regain interest in ideas he believes have been overshadowed by the instrumental rationality of the modern world. Criticizing the approach of modern aesthetics, he points at the relevance of early Greek insights on art. Also Gadamer on numerous occasions refers to classical philosophers, emphasizing that "our return to the Greek beginnings in Western thinking ... is of central importance for hermeneutic philosophy" (Gadamer 2007: 203). In many respects hermeneutics seems to be indeed a continuation of the early Greek discourse on art, rather than a part of the modern aesthetic debate. For both classical and hermeneutic authors the assumption is central that aesthetic experience has a cognitive dimension – it results in knowledge, it enriches our understanding of reality, and contributes to a better self-understanding and moral development.

The early Greek concepts and their relevance for hermeneutics

The following sections examine elements of Plato's and Aristotle's views on art. We will particularly focus on the themes of *mimesis* (imitation) and truth, that is, on the nature of artistic creation and the character of knowledge that is given in an encounter with art – these aspects have been of major importance for hermeneutic thinkers. Discussing truth in art, we will also address the ancient understanding of beauty. The reciprocal relationship of the true, the beautiful and the good has been lost in modern aesthetics, but it has been revived by hermeneutic authors.

It is worth noting that the Ancients did not have a separate category for fine arts, which were situated in the broad domain of productive (poetical) sciences, a realm of crafts and skills concerned with producing an end result. There belong also shoemaking, shipbuilding, rhetoric and so on. The ideal of productive sciences is *poiesis*, a reasoned state or capacity to make an artifact. It is not just a tacit "know-how", but refers to a practice that involves theoretical understanding, here "the knowledge ... *guides* the making" (Gadamer 2007: 2002). In this way of making, the result reflects the given context. As Vesely (2004: 387) explains, "what characterizes a way of making as poetic is the situatedness of the results in the communicative space of culture". Such a way of thinking stands in clear contrast with the autonomous approach of modern aesthetics as well as modern technology.

Mimesis and knowledge

The concepts of mimesis and knowledge in relation to art are closely interconnected. Mimesis describes a mode of artistic creation that results in knowledge on the side of the spectator. Accordingly, both mimesis and knowledge point here towards the truth of the world, rather than to the reality of the artist's mind, that is, Kantian aesthetic ideas. Both Plato and Aristotle share this understanding, yet their different views of reality lead them to different conclusions as to the appreciated form of artistic imitation.

Plato considers the changing physical world accessible by senses as a deficient copy of a perfect, rational and immutable sphere of Ideas. Individual objects are always inferior in relation to the idea that forms them. Yet, we mistakenly consider the world we see as the "real" one. We are like chained prisoners that can only see the shadows of objects that appear on a wall in front of them – but since they do not know any other reality, they assume that they see the things as they are. What is the role of art here? It can either strengthen our false beliefs, or help us to transcend the illusion. Consequently, Plato is very critical about certain forms of art, but admits that some forms of art can have a positive effect. In both cases, the value of art is being evaluated from the perspective of knowledge.

In book X of *The Republic* Plato addresses the nature of artistic imitation referring to examples of everyday objects. Behind many particular instances of tables, there exists the idea of a table. This idea is the origin of any particular table: the carpenter "makes a table for our use, in accordance with the idea"; he reproduces the universal idea of a table in a concrete object (Plato 2000: 253). The painter who in turn makes an image of that table may be described as "the imitator of that which the others make", and is therefore removed from the original idea further than the carpenter.

Which is the art of painting designed to be – an imitation of things as they are, or as they appear – of appearance of reality?
– Of appearance.
Then the imitator ... is a long way off the truth.

(Plato 2000: 255)

Art providing an imitation of an already imperfect world draws us far from the truth towards an illusion. The more skilled the artist is, the more deceptive the illusion he creates. This is not only the case for painting. Particularly dangerous, in Plato's view is imitative poetry, that is, poetry that imitates the actions of men – a skilled poet can easily give the impression that he knows "all things human, virtue as well as vice, and divine things too", while he is only creating appealing, deceitful images (Plato 2000: 256). Not only a cognitive, but an ethical dimension of art is important here: in Plato's theory the good and the true are intimately connected; virtue and true knowledge are two sides of the same coin.

Accordingly, imitative arts drawing us into illusion as to the nature of reality also impact our moral development. The poets "are guilty of making the gravest misstatements when they tell us that wicked men are often happy, and the good miserable; and that injustice is profitable when undetected" (Plato 2000: 63). In this, imitative arts corrupt human character. These reasons led Plato to ban imitative arts from the ideal state he envisioned in *The Republic*.

> At all events we are well aware that poetry, being such as we have described, is not to be regarded seriously as attaining to the truth; and he who listens to her, fearing for the safety of the city which is within him, should be on his guard against her seductions and make our words his law.
>
> (Plato 2000: 282)

Plato is very critical about imitative art, but he is far from condemning art in general. He admits that certain types of art can have a positive potential, directing the spectator towards philosophical knowledge and a noble way of life. In book III of *The Republic* Plato appreciates art that shows the essences of things: "Let our artists rather be those who are gifted to discern the true nature of the beautiful and graceful" (Plato 2000: 73). How is such art possible? As Plato suggests in *Ion*, great works of art (he refers here particularly to poetry) do not originate in the imperfect world of appearances, but in the divine source. "God takes away the minds of poets, and uses them as his ministers, as he also uses diviners and holy prophets ... and ... through them he is conversing with us." Poets are here "the interpreters of the gods" (Plato 1871). We may assume that Plato's divine source is coterminous with the realm of Ideas. The element of imitation may be still traced here: the inspired poet *imitates* the realm of Ideas, and in this he is involved with truth on much the same level as the philosopher – both of them transcend the changeable, perceptible reality and deal with essences.

The idea of the artist as divinely inspired, or even possessed, has exerted influence on many subsequent theories. It may be also traced in Kant's concept of genius. Unlike for Kant, however, here artistic "madness" is not associated with idiosyncrasy – an inspired artist does not *invent* ideas, but rather *transmits* them, giving us access to the domain of eternal forms.

Raphael's fresco *The School of Athens* (1511) portrays Plato and Aristotle as though they were discussing their philosophies. Plato is pointing upwards to that which is beyond appearances, to his theory of Ideas, knowable only through reason. Aristotle, by contrast, indicating earth displays his primary concern with concrete particulars, including both form and matter, knowable through both experience and reason. This difference in conceptualization of reality and knowledge is reflected in the approaches to art of these two philosophers. Accordingly, while for Plato artistic imitation of the sensuous world had a negative role distancing us from the true reality, for Aristotle it is a way towards knowledge.

In *Poetics* Aristotle (2008a: 12) argues that the concept of mimesis is central for all types of fine art. The imitation, not "the verse" (i.e. the formal characteristics), is at the core of any work of art. The differences among particular arts (music, poetry, epics) are basically the differences in respect to the medium of imitation. Unlike for Plato, however, for Aristotle imitation is not just a slavish reflection of reality. It has a productive, discursive element. This may be confirmed by Aristotle's assertion that music is a typical imitative art. It reproduces human emotions through a variety of rhythms and tones (Marshall 1953: 230). This is also the case for a dramatic form. The artist does not only depict a given state of art, but also interprets, generalizes, draws consequences. Artistic imitation in this perspective "does not imply a reference to an original as something other than itself, but means that something meaningful is there as itself" (Gadamer 2002: 121). Yet, it is not an idiosyncratic form of interpretation, which is more a self-expression of an artist than a reflection of reality. The concept of imitation gives the priority to the phenomena, not to artistic consciousness. As Gadamer (2002: 99) explains, for Artistotle "the essence of imitation consists precisely in the recognition of the represented in the representation". Recognizing means seeing things "in terms of what is permanent and essential in them". Imitating phenomena, art is revealing their essences; in this it is related to philosophy. Aristotle (2008a: 17) famously states, "Poetry ... is a more philosophical and a higher thing than history: for poetry tends to express the universal, history the particular." In this perspective, art clearly contributes to knowledge.

In *Metaphysics* Aristotle (2008b: 126–7) claims that all knowledge (*dianoia*) is either practical, poetical (productive) or theoretical (speculative).[3] It seems that knowledge given in an encounter with art primarily belongs to the realm of human practice; here art contributes to *phronesis*, practical wisdom, showing what is good in terms of human action and contributing to moral development. Unlike Plato, Aristotle is far from equating moral and theoretic knowledge. As the very name "ethics" indicates, he bases virtue on practice and "ethos", the sphere of human institutions and modes of behaviour (Gadamer 2004: 311). Art assists us in grasping the essences of concrete situations in life, and in this it helps us to direct our actions. Here emerges what Harries (2009) calls the "ethical function" of art.

Art may also contribute to theoretic understanding – for example, imitating the order and symmetry of nature, it gives us an intuitive insight as to the nature of reality. In addition, in Aristotle's view art also has a transformative, therapeutic role. It helps to release, purify repressed emotions (*catharsis*), reproducing them in a dramatic or a musical form.

The beautiful and its links

In early Greek thought, discussions of beauty and art are only to some extent overlapping. Although beauty (*kalon*) can be attributed to some works of art, and have sensuous character, it is more fundamentally an ethical and a metaphysical concept, irrevocably associated with the ideas of the good and the true. The mutual relationship of the beautiful and the good (*agathos*) is evident in the term *kalos k'agathos* used by classical Greek writers to describe an ideal of personal conduct, a perfect man.[4] An interplay of the physical and the spiritual, the unity of form and meaning is here essential. This understanding radically departs from the Kantian conceptualization of beauty as disinterested pleasure.

According to Plato, the beauty we can find in physical form is a lesser, deficient manifestation of the ideal beauty, but it still has some value – as far as it engages the soul and draws it toward thoughts of the ideal. In *Symposium* Plato (1993: 32–3) describes progress toward ever-purer beauty, from the appreciation of beautiful bodies, through beautiful souls, and branches of knowledge, to arrive at beauty itself.[5] Sensuous beauty is here by no means the aim in itself, it is rather a way to direct our personal development and enhance understanding. This may be also understood as the task of art.

Similarly to Plato, Aristotle situates the beautiful, the good and the true in close relationship. "The good and the beautiful are the beginning of both knowledge and the movement of things" (Aristotle, quoted in Marshall 1953: 229). For this reason, *Poetics* alone does not provide a full insight into Aristotle's philosophy of art (as we define it today) – it has to be supplemented by Aristotle's writings on metaphysics and ethics. In *Metaphysics* (2008b: 297) he emphasizes the mathematical attributes of beauty, such as order, symmetry and definiteness.[6] In *Nicomachean Ethics* he associates beauty with virtue. For example, discussing courage he argues that it is always "for the sake of the beautiful, for this is the end of virtue" (Aristotle, quoted in Sachs n.d.). Here the beautiful is related to the noble, the admirable, the excellent; it belongs to the domain of human action and has a clear ethical dimension. In addition, there may also be traced an understanding of beauty related to productive sciences. It is based on the concept of appropriateness, elaborated by Aristotle earlier in the context of nature: nature exemplifies the appropriate. A way to attain beauty in the domain of productive sciences would be to embrace the appropriate in created objects. Here, understanding of beauty depends upon given circumstances; for example, "[b]eauty varies with the time of life" (Aristotle 2010: 19).

Summing up, in spite of differences between Plato and Aristotle, we can identify many common traits. Both thinkers see the essence of art in mimesis, assuming that art contributes in knowledge not through *expression* of the individual feelings of an artist, but through *imitation* of reality. Even though Plato is critical about imitative art, he seems to employ the idea of imitation in the case of inspired art – which imitates the domain of eternal forms in an artistic medium, and in this it contributes to knowledge. Accordingly, it seems that Plato is not critical about mimesis as such, but only of the forms of imitation that distance us from the true reality. Aristotle's more affirmative approach towards mimesis reflects his affirmative approach towards perceptible reality.

Both thinkers evaluate art in the perspective of knowledge. Formal, sensuous aspects have here secondary importance, a beautiful form is not the aim in itself, but a means to direct our attention towards moral or philosophic truth. Beauty is more essentially an ethical or metaphysical concept, rather than a concept of the productive sciences where fine arts belong.

Hermeneutic revival of the Greek concepts: mimesis, truth and beauty in modern art

The examination of the Greek view of art makes it clear that hermeneutics is much more related to this tradition than to the discourse of modern aesthetics. Hermeneutic thinkers themselves emphasize this connection. In the essay "Poetry and mimesis" Gadamer (2002: 122) states: "anyone who thinks that art can no longer be adequately grasped using Greek concepts is not thinking in a sufficiently Greek way."

Both Heidegger and Gadamer conceive the truth dimension as central for art. Art is "the creative preservation of truth in the work" (Heidegger 2002: 49). "The fact that through a work of art a truth is experienced that we cannot attain in any other way constitutes the philosophic importance of art" (Gadamer 2004: xxi). In this context, hermeneutic authors lament the modern loss of the original connections of the beautiful, the true and the good, which resulted, on the one hand, in radical subjectivization of the notion of beauty, and on the other hand, in subordinating the good and the true to standards of rationality detached from the lived world. The history of Western art, according to Heidegger, reflects the transformation of the essence of truth (Heidegger 1971).

What kind of truth is experienced in art? Heidegger frequently refers here to the early Greek concept of *aletheia*.[7] It denotes a state of not being hidden, a disclosure of reality, the unconcealment of being.

> The truth of which we have spoken does not coincide with what is generally recognized under its name – that which is assigned to knowledge and science as a quality to be distinguished from the beautiful and the good, terms which function as the values of non-theoretical activities. Truth is the unconcealment of beings as beings. Truth is the truth of beings.
>
> (Heidegger 2002: 51–2)

In this understanding truth has ontological character – it is largely coterminous with reality. This view differs essentially from later conceptualizations of truth in episte-mological terms: as a correspondence between a statement and a given state of affairs, where the "locus" of truth is not the reality, but an assertion (judgement). For the early Greek philosophers the opposite was the case: only the disclosed reality could be a basis for a true judgement. Heidegger, following the Greek tradition, claims that we have to understand reality in a non-reductive way, as it reveals itself in all its complexity, in order to be able to provide adequate judgements about it. In this sense *aletheia* provides a basis, an "opening", for a true assertion.[8] This under-standing of truth can be also identified behind the original Greek usage of the word *theoria*, which differs essentially from our today's understanding of theory. As Nightingale (2004: 40) points out, *theoria* originally had a non-conceptual dimension, it was closely related to contemplation. It was "a venerable cultural practice char-acterized by a journey abroad for the sake of witnessing an event of spectacle". In the journeys of *theoria*, "the pilgrim or *thereos* traveled away from home ... to learn something about the outside world, thus confronting foreign peoples and places", witnessing "the spectacle of truth" (Nightingale 2004: 40). The attitude of *theoria* exemplifies a non-reductionist approach to reality.

In *The Origin of a Work of Art* (1935/37) Heidegger discusses a Greek temple and Van Gogh's painting *A pair of shoes* (1886), explaining the essence of art in terms of its capacity to reveal the truth. In both cases, the work of art "makes publicly known something other than itself, it manifests something other" (Heidegger 2002: 3). The temple manifests material and spiritual aspects of Greek culture and articulates a specific place.[9] Van Gogh's painting lets us know what the shoes in their essence are, revealing the world of their owner – a peasant woman.

> A pair of the peasant shoes and nothing more. And yet. From the dark opening of the worn insides of the shoes the toilsome tread of the worker stares forth. In the stiffly rugged heaviness of the shoes there is the

accumulated tenacity of her slow trudge through the far-spreading and ever-uniform furrows of the field swept by a raw wind. On the leather lie the dampness and richness of the soil. Under the soles slides the loneliness of the field-path as evening falls. In the shoes vibrates the silent call of the earth, its quiet gift of the ripening grain and its unexplained self-refusal in the fallow desolation of the wintry field. This equipment is pervaded by uncomplaining anxiety as to the certainty of bread, the wordless joy of having once more withstood want, the trembling before the impending childbed and shivering at the surrounding menace of death.

(Heidegger 1977: 159)

The picture reveals what it means to use shoes as a piece of everyday equipment. It also gives insights into the reality of the owner. As Heidegger explains, "Van Gogh's painting is the disclosure of what … the pair of peasant shoes, in truth *is*. … The unconcealment of beings is what the Greeks called *aletheia*" (Heidegger 2002: 16).

Encountering the painting we experience not only its truth, but also its beauty. Yet, contrary to the claims of modern aesthetics, beauty in great works of art "does not exist merely relative to pleasure, and purely as its object" (Heidegger 2002: 52). Heidegger follows classical thinkers arguing that beauty is never autonomous; it never appears on its own, but is always associated with truth. There is an essential convergence of beauty and truth: the appearing of truth in a work of art constitutes its beauty, and truth manifests itself through beauty. "*Beauty is one way in which truth as unconcealment comes to presence*" (Heidegger 2002: 32). Further, Heidegger (2002: 52) explains: "Beauty … appears when truth sets itself into the work. This appearing (as this being of truth in the work and as the work) is beauty. Thus beauty belongs to the advent of truth."

Seeing truth as a fundamental element of a work of art, Heidegger refutes the view of artistic creation as a self-expression of an artist, as well as a slavish imitation of reality. In this respect he shares Aristotle's view of art as an expression of the essences:

Do we mean that the painting takes a likeness from the real and transposes it into an artistic production? By no means. The work, then, is not concerned with the reproduction of a particular being … Rather, it is concerned to reproduce the general essence of things.

(Heidegger 2002: 16)

This reproduction of the essences of things in an aesthetic medium is the common denominator of all types of art. In this context Heidegger introduces the concept of poetry expressing the fundamental character of art. "*All art*, as the letting happen of the advent of the truth of beings, is, *in essence, poetry*" (Heidegger 2002: 44). Heidegger's understanding of poetry is not limited to verbal arts. Poetry denotes the very nature of any type of art, its capacity to reveal truth. This view is based on the Greek understanding of poetical (productive) sciences, and their ideal of *poiesis*. As already noted, the domain of productive sciences neither designates the technical in the modern sense, nor is coterminous with today's understanding of fine arts or crafts. It includes both a way of knowing and an activity of making. The creation process is here not guided by blindly applied rules of handicraft, it is also far from being an autonomous self-expression. Rather, the knowledge and skills of the maker are here subordinated to considerations of use – the user of the product and his context determines what is to be made. As in the well-known Platonic example "it is the ship's master who determines what the shipbuilder is to build" (Gadamer 2002: 13). Accordingly, the concept of *poiesis* points toward the sphere of common understanding and communication.

What distinguishes fine arts from other types of productive, *poetic* activity? A work of art has no "real" use. It is also not "real" in the same manner as what it represents. Its very essence is in the imitation of reality. In this understanding, the artist "brings *forth* what is present, as such, *out of* concealment, specifically *into* the unconcealment of their appearance" (Heidegger 2002: 35). Imitating reality a work of art opens up for us, articulates, different aspects of reality in an artistic medium. As Simone Weil (1968: 62) put it, the great works of art "give us, in the guise of fiction, something equivalent to the actual density of the real, that density which life offers us every day but which we are unable to grasp because we are amusing ourselves with lies". These works of art are a result of attention paid to the world, and they "have the power to awaken us to the truth" (1968: 162).

The concept of imitation has been on numerous occasions discussed by Gadamer. While Heidegger primarily focuses on the great traditional art of the past, Gadamer seeks for a perspective that can also cover the art of modern times. "For although modern art is opposed to traditional art, it is also true that it has been stimulated and nourished by it" (Gadamer 2002: 9). Furthermore, "[i]t can hardly be over-emphasized that anyone who believes modern art to be degenerate will not be able to understand the great art of the past properly either" (Gadamer 2002: 48).

In the essay "Art and imitation" Gadamer (2002: 97) suggests that the idea of mimesis seems broad enough to help us to understand the phenomenon of contemporary, even nonobjective art: "For when it is correctly understood, Aristotle's fundamental concept of mimesis has an elementary validity." It is however "a disturbing question whether modern painting can possibly contribute to the task of ... self-recognition" in the sense that earlier art did, imitating human reality (2002: 100). In the Greek world, as well as in subsequent centuries until Baroque, myth and religion provided a common background for artistic representation. "Recognition, as understood by Aristotle, presupposes the continuing existence of a binding tradition that is intelligible to all and in which we can encounter ourselves" (Gadamer 2002: 100). Such a tradition is a basis of what Dalibor Vesely (2004) refers to as a "participatory" mode of representation. Today, in the world of disjointed traditions, the act of recognition is still possible, but incomplete. "Even in most modern pictures, we can still recognize something we understand – if only fragmentary gestures rather than stories once rich in meaning" (Gadamer 2002: 100). This fragmentary understanding is far from being satisfactory. At the end, we seem to encounter the rejection of meaning rather than its expression (Gadamer 2002: 101).

Gadamer comes to the conclusion that mimesis today cannot be understood in terms of recognition based on continuity of a cultural tradition. The modern world in which we live does not allow for such understanding. It not only banished all forms of myth to the margins of life, but also destroyed "things" as meaningful objects, replacing them with mass-produced articles that can be at any time thrown away and replaced (Gadamer 2002: 102). In this context, it is worthwhile to refer to Gadamer's essay "What is practice?" (1974) where he argues that in the pre-modern period the human relation to making and shaping was primarily directed by a certain openness, a reciprocal intimacy and care. The challenging and ordering of the world was not as important as the attitude of "letting be", letting the world show itself in its own forms. Accordingly, in crafts the user's needs and choices were the main criteria for the standard of what was made. This was the ideal of *poiesis*. Modern technology, however, first makes the things, and then creates the needs, building "a consumer awakening and need-stimulating industry" around us (Gadamer 1981: 71). The standards are not set by the users, but rather imposed on them. According to Gadamer, what happened was "the degeneration of practice into technique" and its "general decline into social irrationality" (Gadamer 1981: 74).

Gadamer (2002: 103) is well aware that today there is no return to the pre-industrial reality, it would be therefore meaningless to demand such a return from art:

> Can any thinking person expect the visual arts of today to give us the opportunity of recognizing things that are no longer real, that we can no longer encounter around us, that mean nothing to us, as if that could deepen familiarity with our world?

We have to accept this stance, and seek a different understanding of artistic imitation. One possibility is an understanding of mimesis as a presentation of order: "Mimesis reveals the miracle of order that we call the *kosmos*" (Gadamer 2002: 101). This view seems to be more related to Pythagoras and Plato than to Aristotle. What does it mean in today's context? According to Gadamer:

> art is present whenever a work succeeds in elevating what it is or represents to a new configuration, a new world of its own in miniature, a new order of unity and tension. ... Testifying to order, mimesis seems as valid now as it was then, insofar as every work of art, even in our own increasingly standardized world of mass production, still testifies to that spiritual ordering energy that makes our life what it is.
>
> (Gadamer 2002: 103)

Art in this understanding "transforms our fleeting experience into the stable and lasting form of an independent and internally coherent creation" (Gadamer 2002: 53). In this, it manifests the most fundamental characteristic of human existence: the continuous effort of building and maintaining a world. In this ever-changing reality, a work of art stands out as a promise of order, revealing one of our most essential needs – the need of a stable system of references. As Gadamer (2002: 104) concludes, "[p]erhaps our capacity to preserve and maintain, the capacity that supports human culture, rests in turn upon the fact that we must always order anew what threatens to dissolve before us."

Besides, works of art can help us to experience what things once were – individually made objects, created with the attitude of attention. Through them we "experience the presence of what is essentially irreplaceable" (Gadamer 2002: 103). This uniqueness and irreplaceability Walter Benjamin called the aura of the work of art. In this context it is of minor relevance whether an artist produces objective or nonobjective art. "The only relevant thing is whether we encounter a spiritual and ordering energy in the work, or whether we are simply reminded of some cultural motif or the peculiarities of this or that particular artist" (Gadamer 2002: 103). In the latter case, we can speak rather about "production" than about true creativity.

The experience of art: an event of understanding

A work of art worthy of its name has a capacity to address us in a direct way: it "speaks to us across all temporal distance" (Gadamer 2007: 196); it makes a claim on us. In this, a work of art is always contemporaneous (*Gleichzeitig*) with its time; its message is never out of date: "In comparison with all other linguistic and non-linguistic tradition, the work of art is the absolute present for each particular present, and at the same time holds its word in readiness for every future" (Gadamer 2008: 104).

Yet, we do not always succeed in grasping the message the work of art communicates; "in the experience of art we must learn how to dwell upon the work in a specific way" (Gadamer 2002: 42). We have to realize "that every work of art only begins to speak when we have already learned to decipher and read it" (Gadamer 2002: 48). One of the major aims of hermeneutics, which defines itself as a practical philosophy, is to assist us in the encounter with art, enhancing our experience of art. As Nietzsche (1873) declares in relation to history "we need it for life and action, not for a comfortable turning away from life and action" (Nietzsche 2010: 3). This is also the case for the hermeneutic art discourse.

The experience of art does not have a special, non-cognitive status in the hermeneutic perspective, as it has in Kantian aesthetics. Confronting a work of art we confront meanings, the experience of art is thus considered as a particular instance of the general dynamics of human understanding: "In any case, when we say that a work of art *says* something to us and that it thus belongs to the matrix of things we have to understand, our assertion is not a metaphor, but has a valid demonstrable meaning. Thus the work of art is an object of hermeneutics" (Gadamer 2008: 98).

Understanding is for hermeneutic thinkers not something derived from abstract knowledge. As Heidegger (1996: 134) argues, understanding is "a fundamental mode of *being* of Dasein". It is an intuitive way in which we relate to the world, inseparable from the historical and temporal horizon of human being.[10] Understanding involves both fore-understanding (based on individual experience, conceptual knowledge, cultural heritage, tradition, etc.) and projecting (we make sense of things in terms of particular possibilities they raise for our existence). In this perspective, understanding is ultimately a self-understanding, "a person who understands, understands himself (*sich versteht*), projecting himself upon his possibilities" (Gadamer 2004: 25). In *Truth and Method* (1960) Gadamer describes this dynamics as the "fusion of horizons":

> The horizon of the present cannot be formed without the past. There is no more an isolated horizon of the present itself than there are historical

horizons which have to be acquired. *Rather, understanding is always the fusion of these horizons supposedly existing by themselves.*

(Gadamer 2004: 305)

This is also the case for a work of art: "the encounter with art belongs within the process of integration that is involved in all human life that stands within traditions" (Gadamer 2008: 96). The experience of art is a hermeneutic situation in which meanings are mediated and an understanding emerges. A work of art is here not a self-enclosed, sealed, static entity, but a dynamic outcome of a process, that integrates both the horizon of the past and the horizon of the future of the spectator.[11] Being engaged with a work of art we project ourselves into its universe. This projecting as a modality/possibility of our existence belongs to the horizon of the future. The way we see the future, however, to a large extent depends upon the horizon of the past – on our previous experiences, on our cultural and social background, on the traditions in which we stand.

This type of experience Gadamer refers to as *Erfahrung*, contrasting it with *Erlebnis*, a mode of experience defining modern aesthetics. *Erleben* means primarily "to be still alive when something happens"; accordingly, the word *Erlebnis* suggests "the immediacy with which something real is grasped", an individual, momentary, isolated experience (Gadamer 2004: 53). *Erfahrung*, on the other hand, is used to indicate the experience as ongoing and cumulative. The experiencing individual participates here in an "event of understanding", an event in which one involves one's own horizon and through which this horizon is widened.

> The appeal to immediacy, to the instantaneous flash of genius, to the significance of "experiences" (*Erlebnisse*), cannot withstand the claim of human existence to continuity and unity of self-understanding. The binding quality of the experience (*Erfahrung*) of art must not be disintegrated by aesthetic consciousness. This negative insight, positively expressed, is that art is knowledge and experiencing an artwork means sharing that knowledge.
>
> (Gadamer 2004: 84)

Discussing the experience of art Gadamer introduces the concept of play. Play is one of the elementary functions of human life. It is not limited to leisure activities, but can be also traced behind cultic and religious practices. It is therefore a fundamental element of culture. The concept of play can be also applied to the mode of being of a work of art. Gadamer follows here Schiller's *Letters on Aesthetic Education*, according to which artworks are dramatic in that they *place something in play* (Davey 2007). Aesthetic consciousness is here drawn into something much larger than it is aware of; it becomes a part of a bigger event that goes far beyond the subjectivity of the spectator or the intentions of the artist. Gadamer emphasizes the primacy of the play over the subjectivity of players: "all playing is being played. The attraction of a game ... consists precisely in the fact that the game masters the players" (Gadamer 2004: 106).

Even though every instance of play is different, it has its own fundamental nature independent of the consciousness of those who play. Yet, it reaches presentation (*Darstellung*) only through players (2004: 103). Similarly, a work of art is realized in interpretation. Interpretation is the execution (*Vollzug*) of the work of art (Gadamer 2007: 217). What follows is that a work of art is never complete, never finished – it remains open for future interpretations. Like play, it includes a form of constant movement. "The movement of playing has no goal that brings it to an end; rather, it renews itself in constant repetition" (Gadamer 2004: 104). In this context Gadamer recalls Aristotle's term *"energeia"* – the energy of a person or animal being alive. The experience of art has also certain "aliveness", contemporaneousness. Trying to limit the understanding of a work of art to its original context or to the intentions of the artist, we miss the message it carries. A work of art invites an observer to a hermeneutic conversation, which like any genuine dialogue, involves reciprocity of partners. The meaning of a work of art, as the meaning of any hermeneutic "text", can be considered as a collection of sedimented significations (*Bedeutungen*) continuously emerging from new interpretations. It then follows that meaning is never complete; it is open for sedimentations that may come from future perspectives. "Not just occasionally but always, the meaning of a text goes beyond its author. That is why understanding is not merely a reproductive but always a productive activity as well" (Gadamer 2004: 296).

A person who intends to evaluate a work of art in a disengaged, objective manner, like an art critic, misses the real experience of art. In this sense, "[t]he connoisseur represents the opposite extreme of kitsch" (Gadamer 2002: 52). In order to access a work of art in the context of a living conversation, we have to assume that its meaning is not what the author originally said, but "what he would have wanted to say to me if I had been his original partner in conversation" (Gadamer 2007: 186). Every return to a living context of a work of art is a return "to what is to be accepted as identical in meaning to what was originally announced" (2007: 173). In order to preserve the original meaning, an interpretation requires a "translation" – an expression of the meanings in a contemporary way, meaningful for the observer. A genuine understanding brings the author's speaking back to life again (2007: 236). As the German theologian Gerhard Ebeling argues:

> Actually, both factors, identity and variability, belong inseparably together and are linked to one another in the process of interpretation, whose very nature is to say the same thing in a different way and, precisely by virtue of saying it in a different way, to say the same thing.
>
> (Ebeling 1967: 26, quoted in Gadamer 2008: xxvi)

Following Roman Ingarden's *The Literary Work of Art* (1926), Gadamer suggests that in the encounter with a work of art a synthetic act is required in which we must unite and bring together many different aspects of an artwork.

> It was not Cubist painting that first set us this task, though it did so in a drastically radical manner by demanding that we successively superimpose upon one another the various facets or aspects of the same thing, to produce finally on the canvas the thing depicted in all its facets and thus in a new colorful plasticity. It is not only when confronted by Picasso and Braque ... that we have to "read" the picture. It is always like this.
>
> (Gadamer 2002: 27)

Such an experience of art demands a profound engagement. As Gadamer explains, the players are aware that play is not serious – that is why they play. Yet, play contains its own seriousness. "Play fulfills its purpose only if the player loses himself in play" (Gadamer 2004: 103). Without such seriousness, the play is spoiled. Not only the players, but also the spectators engage themselves substantially. "The spectator is manifestly more than just an observer who sees what is happening in front of him, but rather one who is a part of it insofar as he literally takes part" (Gadamer 2002: 28). In this sense, everyone involved in play is a participant – there is no radical separation between the work of art and the audience.

According to Gadamer, "this desire to transform the distance of the onlooker into the involvement of the participant can be discerned in every form of modern experimentation in the arts" (2002: 24). In this context many contemporary artists and critics argue that the work of art itself no longer exists, being co-constituted by the audience in limitless ways. Yet, "[i]t is quite wrong to think that the unity of the work implies that the work is closed off from the person who turns to it or is affected by it" (Gadamer 2002: 25). Rather, this openness toward the audience is a part of the closedness of the play (Gadamer 2004: 109). In other words, the identity of a work of art resembles the identity of play: it is inviolable. The inclusion of the spectator does not disturb it. On the contrary, it is an essential part of a work of art to engage the audience into a dialogue, "the genuine reception and experience of a work of art can exist only for one who 'plays along,' that is, one who performs in an active way himself" (2002: 26). Just as there is no play without an authentic engagement, there is also no true experience of art.

An authentic experience of art transforms us: we are not left with exactly the same feeling about life we had before we entered a museum, listened to a concert or read a poem. "If we really had a genuine experience of art, then the world has become both brighter and less burdensome" (Gadamer 2002: 26). Such an experience of art has an ability to challenge our customary expectations and to reveal the limitations of our cultural perspective.

In the hermeneutic perspective art not only enhances our understanding and self-understanding, but also has an important intersubjective dimension. It grounds a communal experience, establishing a shared realm among individuals of different backgrounds. Gadamer explains this aspect of art by referring to the idea of festival. In a festive celebration – any recurrent event of cultural or religious significance – we are not separated, but gathered together; a festival unites everyone. "A festival is an experience of community and represents community in its most perfect form" (Gadamer 2002: 39). The unifying character of a festival is related to its temporal character: in a festival we transcend our own, individual, pragmatic time viewed as a resource to be planned and spent, subordinating it to something that happens in its own time, like for instance Easter or Christmas celebration. In contrast with the "empty" time that needs to be filled, Gadamer (2002: 42) calls this type of time "fulfilled" or "autonomous" time. "It is the nature of the festival that it should proffer time, arresting it and allowing it to tarry." A festival does not dissolve in separate moments, but fulfills every moment of its duration – we experience here the continuity of time, and this is what draws us together. A work of art has a similar, autonomous temporality, it imposes its temporality upon us, unifying us and establishing communication. As Davey (2007) observes, "[t]he art work *festivises*: it reveals our personal indebtedness to past and future communities of meaning." Referring to theatre, Gadamer (2002: 65) writes: "The genuine experience of the enduring festive character of the theater seems to me to lie in the immediate communal experience of what we are and how things stand with us in the vital exchange between player and onlooker." The communal character of the experience of art is evident not only in the case of high culture, but also in the events of popular culture such as modern adaptations of classical operas. Accordingly, Gadamer (2002: 51) is far from condemning popular culture as such: "It is a profound mistake to think that our art is simply that of the ruling class." Certain events of popular culture "have a capacity to establish communication in a way that reaches people of every class and educational background". This communal aspect of the experience of art is missing in modern aesthetics, focused on a solitary, personal response to an artwork.

Summing up, in the hermeneutic perspective a work of art "is taken seriously in its claim to truth" (Gadamer 2004: 296). The meaning of a work of art is neither once and for all determined by the author and waiting to be deciphered, nor freely constructed by the observer. It is rather negotiated between the observer and the work of art; it thus has a dialogical, discursive character. Here, "interpretation is an insertion [Einlegen] of meaning and not a discovery [Finden] of it" (Gadamer 2007: 181).

In *Pharmakon* Plato addresses the contradictory nature of writing – while it helps us to remember things, it also poses a risk of misunderstanding, separating the meanings from their original context of living conversation. This is also the case for art – encountering works of art in exhibitions, in museums, we often conceive them as documents of the past, and miss their message. In the hermeneutic perspective the purposes and meanings that artists originally ascribe to their works have a minor importance. Rather, something bigger is at play here – an event encompassing cultural, social, historical realities, and the individual perspectives of the spectators. As Gadamer emphasizes, "we understand in a *different* way, *if we understand at all*" (Gadamer 2004: 269).

Hermeneutic art discourse assists the observer in the encounter with art, but also provides some clues for the artist, making her more aware of the dynamics of understanding that operate behind the observer's perception of an artwork, and facilitating a more successful communication with the audience. As Heidegger argues:

> Such reflection cannot compel art in its coming-to-be. But this reflective knowledge is the preliminary and therefore indispensable preparation for the coming-to-be of art. Only such knowledge prepares, for art, the space, for creators, the path, and for preservers the location.
>
> (Heidegger 2002: 49)

One of the lessons that is given by hermeneutics is that the artists have to anticipate that the progress of time may bring out new aspects of their artworks, and leave some openness, so as to provide space for a fruitful dialogue with the future.

Concluding remarks

What is the role of art for hermeneutic thinkers? Answering Hölderlin's question, "what are poets for in a destitute time?", Heidegger (1971) argues that the task of art in our technologically oriented, "destitute" era is to assist us in establishing a meaningful relation with the world, to help us to see the true possibilities of our existence, to define ourselves in regard to the traditions we stand in. In his later essays, Heidegger uses the notion of dwelling in this context. Art enables and facilitates human dwelling – an authentic way of being, directed not by instrumental values, but founded on a meaningful engagement with cultural heritage, fellow human beings, and the environing world. Two major dimensions of the experience of art may be distinguished here: an individual and a communal one.

On the individual level, art enhances our understanding, allowing us to grasp human reality in a non-reductive way. Reality reveals itself, opens up, through a work of art. At the same time, a work of art confronts us with ourselves, enhancing our self-understanding. In this, it has a transformative role. It helps individuals to identify and develop their true possibilities, to adopt a more reflective and resolute stance towards their lives. Accordingly, "the significance of the art ... depends on the fact that it speaks to us, that it confronts man with himself in his morally determined existence" (Gadamer 2004: 45). Through this experience artworks "have an effect on the quality of (our) way of living" (Gadamer 2007: 222).

On the intersubjective level, art connects the sphere of individual experience with the larger sphere of common meanings, providing grounds for the community's self-understanding and social interactions. This is a challenging task in today's fragmented realities. As Gadamer (2002: 9) contends, "the poetry of our time has reached the limits of intelligible meaning and perhaps the greatest achievements of the greatest writers are themselves marked by tragic speechlessness in the face of the unsayable." Still, art represents an effort to find essences in human reality, to express in the particular the universal human condition, and to name the order of things.

Notes

1 Beauty of nature however, unlike any kind of artistic beauty, can arouse moral interest. Nature gives us an idea as to the character of our being, "the unintentional consonance of nature with our wholly disinterested pleasure ... points to us as to the ultimate purpose of creation" (Gadamer 2004: 44). Fine art, in Kant's view, does not have this ability. As a consequence, "the nature of art proper emerges badly from the contrast with natural beauty" (Gadamer 2004: 46).

2 The sublime refers to a type of experience where we feel overwhelmed by the size or force of the phenomenon we face – Kant particularly emphasizes here nature, for example violent storms, great mountains. Yet, the overwhelming phenomenon is not the real object of the sublime. What we confront here are ideas of reason: the ideas of absolute totality or absolute freedom. As Burnham (n.d.) observes, the sublime feeling is a two-layered experience, a kind of "rapid alternation" between the fear of the overwhelming and the specific pleasure of seeing that overwhelming overwhelmed.

> Now, in the immensity of nature ... we find our own limitation; although at the same time in our rational faculty we find a different, non-sensuous standard, which has that infinity itself under it as a unit, and in comparison with which everything in nature is small. Thus in our mind we find a superiority to nature even in its immensity. ... Thus, humanity in our person remains unhumiliated, though the individual might have to submit to this dominion.
>
> (Kant 1951: 101)

Accordingly, the discussion of the sublime is closely related to Kant's moral theory.

3 The *theoretical sciences* are concerned with that which can be described by exact laws. This is where domains such as physics, mathematics and metaphysics belong. The ideal of theoretical science is theoretical (or philosophic) wisdom, *sophia*. It is scientific knowledge combined with intuitive reason. The *practical sciences* are concerned with human good and the principles of right conduct. Here Aristotle situates politics and ethics. The ideal of the practical sciences is practical wisdom, *phronesis*, that unlike theoretical wisdom is always context-dependent, and requires an extensive experience of particulars, which is typically gained throughout the years of life. The *poetical or productive sciences* (technê) are concerned with producing an end result. This is the domain of crafts and skills, including artistic production. The central term here is *poiesis*, a reasoned state or capacity to make an artifact.

4 The ideal of *kalos k'agathos* is closely associated with the concept of *paideia*. Werner Jaeger in his book *Paideia, the Ideals of Greek Culture* (1967: xxiii) describes *paideia* as "the process of educating man into his true form, the real and genuine human nature." In this context, *kalos k'agathos* can be understood as "the chivalrous ideal of a complete human personality, harmonious in mind and body, foursquare in battle and speech, song and action" (1967: 62).

5 And the true order of going ... is to begin from the beauties of earth and mount upwards for the sake of that other beauty, using these as steps only, and from one going on to two, and from two to all fair forms, and from fair forms to fair practices, and from fair practices to fair notions, until from fair notions he arrives at the notion of absolute beauty, and at last knows what the essence of beauty is.

(Plato 1993: 33)

6 [T]hose who assert that the mathematical sciences say nothing of the beautiful or the good are in error. For these sciences say and prove a great deal about them ... The chief forms of beauty are order and symmetry and definiteness, which the mathematical sciences demonstrate in a special degree. And since these (e.g. order and definiteness) are obviously causes of many things, evidently these sciences must treat this sort of causative principle also (i.e. the beautiful) as in some sense a cause.

(Aristotle, *Metaphysics* 1078b, quoted in Hofstadter and Kuhns, 1964: 93)

7 Even though Heidegger (1998: 155–82) blames Plato for the departure from conceptualization of truth as *aletheia*, numerous authors point at the affinity of the Heideggerian and Platonic conceptions of truth. Heidegger himself in one of his later essays "The End of Philosophy and the Task of Thinking" (1964) admits that "the assertion about the essential transformation of truth [in Plato] ... from unconcealment to correctness is ... untenable" (Heidegger 1964; quoted in Dostal 1985: 71).

8 In his later works, Heidegger contends that *aletheia* is not equal to truth, but defines the background for truth, it is "the opening" for truth. "*Aletheia*, disclosure thought of as the opening of presence, is not yet truth. Is *aletheia* then less than truth? Or is it more because it first grants truth as *adequatio* and *certitudo*, because there can be no presence and presenting outside of the realm of the opening?" (Heidegger 1972: 69).

9 Christian Norberg-Schulz, referring to Heidegger, argues that the role of architecture is to assist us in establishing a meaningful relation with the world, to help us to interpret and understand the world.

The meaning of a work of architecture ... consists in its gathering the world in a general typical sense, in a local particular sense, in a temporal historical sense, and, finally, as something, that is, as the figural manifestation of a mode of dwelling between earth and sky. A work of architecture does not exist in a vacuum, but in the world of things and human beings, and reveals this world as what it is.

(Norberg-Schulz 1985: 30)

10 This fundamental mode of understanding has to be distinguished from the most common view of understanding as "one possible kind of cognition among others" which is a "derivative of the primary understanding which constitutes the being of there in general" (Heidegger 1996: 134).

11 As Gadamer (2007: 198) explains, the German word for present, *Gegenwart* (warten – waiting) points at the horizon of the future. "The future, as what is coming, is the present that 'waits' for us, and that we await. All expectation of the future as such, however, rests on experience. Therefore, in every present moment not only is a horizon of the future opened up, but also the horizon of the past is in play."

Bibliography

Aristotle (2010) *Rhetoric*. New York: Cosimo.

——(2008a) [335 BC] *Poetics*. New York: Cosimo.

——(2008b) *Metaphysics*. New York: Cosimo.

——(1998) [350 BC] *Nicomachean Ethics*. New York: Dover Thrift Editions.

Aristotle (2010) Rhetoric. New York: Cosimo.

Baumgarten, A. (1735) *Metaphysics*. In: E. Watkins, ed. (2009) *Kant's Critique of pure Reason: Background Source Materials*. Cambridge: Cambridge University Press.

Boitani, P. (2008) "The Folly of Poetry". In: *Comparative Critical Studies* Vol. 5, Iss. 2–3: 125–40.

Burnham, D. (n.d.) "Immanuel Kant: Aesthetics". In: *Internet Encyclopedia of Philosophy*. Available on-line: www.iep.utm.edu/kantaest/ Retrieved: 17.03.2013.

Davey, N. (2007) "Gadamer's Aesthetics". *The Stanford Encyclopedia of Philosophy*. Winter 2011 Edition. Available on-line: http://plato.stanford.edu/entries/gadamer-aesthetics/ Retrieved: 30.07.2014.

Dostal, Robert J. 1985. "Beyond Being: Heidegger's Plato". In: *Journal of The History of Philosophy* No. 23: 71–98.

Ebeling, G. (1967) *The Problem of Historicity*. Philadelphia: Fortress Press.

Gadamer, H.-G. (2008) *Philosophical Hermeneutics*. Berkeley: University of California Press.

——(2007)*The Gadamer Reader. A Bouquet of the Later Writings*. Evanston, IL: Northwestern University Press.

——(2004) [1960]. *Truth and Method*. London and New York: Continuum.

——(2002) *The Relevance of the Beautiful and Other Essays*. Cambridge: Cambridge University Press.

——(1981). *Reason in the Age of Science*. Cambridge, MA: MIT Press.

Guyer, P. (2007) "18th Century German Aesthetics". In: *Stanford Encyclopedia of Philosophy*. Available on-line: http://plato.stanford.edu/entries/aesthetics-18th-german/ Retrieved: 17.09.2013.

Hammermeister, K. (2002) *The German Aesthetic Tradition*. Cambridge: Cambridge University Press.

Harries, K. (2009) *Art Matters: A Critical Commentary on Heidegger's* The Origin of the Work of Art. New York: Springer.

Hegel, G.W.F. (1964) [1835] "The Philosophy of Fine Art" (Introduction to *Aesthetics. Lectures on Fine Art*). In: A. Hofstadter, R. Kuhns, eds. *Philosophies of Art and Beauty. Selected Readings in Aesthetics*. Chicago: The University of Chicago Press.

Heidegger, M. (2002) *Off the Beaten Track*. Cambridge: Cambridge University Press.

——(1998) *Pathmarks*. Cambridge: Cambridge University Press.

——(1996) [1927] *Being and Time*. New York: State University of New York Press.

——(1977) *Basic Writings*. London: Routledge.

——(1972) *On Time and Being*. New York: Harper and Row

——(1971) *Poetry, Language, Thought*. New York: Harper & Row.

Hofstadter, A., Kuhns, R., eds (1964) *Philosophies of Art and Beauty. Selected Readings in Aesthetics.* Chicago: The University of Chicago Press.

Hume, D. (1985) [1757] "Of the Standard of Taste". In: E. Miller, ed. *Essays: Moral, Political and Literary.* Indianapolis: Liberty.

Jaeger, W. (1967) [1939] *Paideia: the Ideals of Greek Culture.* Oxford: Oxford University Press.

Kant, I. (1951) [1790] *Critique of Judgment.* New York: Hafner Press.

Marshall, J.S. (1953) "Art and Aesthetics in Aristotle". In: *The Journal of Aesthetics and Art Criticism.* Vol. 12, No. 2: 228–31.

Nietzsche, F. (2010) [1873] "On the Advantage and Disadvantage of History for Life". Available on-line: www.scribd.com/doc/12728754 Retrieved: 12.11.2013.

Nightingale, A. (2004) *Spectacles of Truth in Classical Greek Philosophy. Theoria in its Cultural Context.* Cambridge: Cambridge University Press.

Norberg-Schulz, C. (1985). *The Concept of Dwelling. On the way to figurative architecture.* New York: Rizzoli.

Pérez-Gómez, A. (2006) *Built upon Love. Architectural Longing after Ethics and Aesthetics.* London and Cambridge, MA: MIT Press.

Plato (2000) [380 BC] *The Republic.* New York: Dover Thrift Editions.

——(1993) [385–80 BC] *Symposium and Phaedrus.* New York: Dover Thrift Editions.

——(1871) [380 BC] *Ion.* Available on-line: http://classics.mit.edu/Plato/ion.html Retrieved: 30/07/2014.

Sachs, J. (n.d.) "Aristotle: Poetics". In: *Internet Encyclopedia of Philosophy.* Available on-line: www.iep.utm.edu/aris-poe Retrieved: 14.09.2012.

Scruton, R. (1982) *Kant: A Very Short Introduction.* Oxford: Oxford University Press.

Vesely, D. (2004) *Architecture in the Age of Divided Representation. The Question of Creativity in the Shadow of Production.* Cambridge, MA: MIT Press.

Weil, S. (1968) *On Science, Necessity and the Love of God: Essays.* Oxford: Oxford University Press.

Further reading

Arthos, J. (2013) *Gadamer's Poetics: A Critique of Modern Aesthetics.* London: Bloomsbury Academic.

Davey, N. (2013) *Unfinished Worlds. Hermeneutics, Aesthetics and Gadamer.* Edinburgh: Edinburgh University Press.

Vattimo, G. (2008) *Art's Claim to Truth.* New York: Columbia University Press.

Young, J. (2001) *Heidegger's Philosophy of Art.* Cambridge: Cambridge University Press.

42
HERMENEUTICS AND EDUCATION

Paul Fairfield

It will not be surprising that philosophical hermeneutics carries implications for education given the centrality in Hans-Georg Gadamer's writings not only of understanding and interpretation but of dialogue and *Bildung* as well. While Gadamer never put forward a fully elaborated philosophy of education, he did remark upon several important ideas which it would profit theorists in this field to consider or perhaps reconsider, especially those who seek an alternative to the kind of corporate scientism that currently reigns in a good part of the discourse of education. Educational thinkers who want to hold onto the idea that the university is neither a set of professional schools nor a corporation but a fundamentally different kind of institution with a logic and a spirit that is unique to it require a way of conceptualizing this that transcends the order of the empirical and the economic. It is here that hermeneutics may be of service, not as a mere reminder of ideals of old but as a phenomenologically rich way of thinking about the nature of a university education and the aims that belong to it. What is it to be educated in the most fundamental sense? It is to have received a certain kind of learning, but of what kind, by what means, and to what if any end?

Of the themes in Gadamer's writings that carry consequences for education, three stand out in importance. These are dialogue, *Bildung*, and what Gadamer, following Wilhelm von Humboldt in the nineteenth century, called "living with ideas," each of which I shall discuss, however briefly, in what follows. There are further ideas in the literature of hermeneutics that have implications for education, and of course there is far more to say about these three themes than I can undertake here, but perhaps this will suffice as an overview.

Dialogue

While it is in *Truth and Method* that the concept of dialogue has received its most adequate phenomenological treatment, the idea itself in one form or another has been awarded a central place over the last few decades by a growing number of thinkers, including some philosophers of education. Paulo Freire's *Pedagogy of the Oppressed* and Nicholas Burbules' *Dialogue in Teaching* in particular stand out among attempts to identify the educational implications of dialogue, where this is conceived not as any straightforward bestowing of information but as a reciprocal practice modeled more or less roughly on Platonic dialectic (see Freire 2004 and Burbules 1993). Neither thinker nor the movement of critical pedagogy of which they are a part, however, incorporates Gadamer's analysis in the thoroughgoing way for which hermeneutical thinkers might wish. The word itself has become decidedly popular in educational circles, although, as is generally the case with popular conceptions, a notable lack of clarity clings to it. What is the dialogical model as it pertains to what happens, or might happen, in the university classroom? Can what takes place there be appropriately described as dialogue, given both the inequality that traditionally and perhaps necessarily prevails between educators and students as well as other institutional realities that are far removed from, if not antithetical to, the art of conversation as either Socrates practiced it or Gadamer described it?

What is the meaning of dialogue as it pertains to education? For Gadamer, the salient facts about conversation are fundamentally two: reciprocity and openness. All education, hermeneutically conceived, is an education in thinking, where this is conceived not in terms of the straightforward mastery of information but more fundamentally as an affair of language:

> We think with words. To think is to think something with oneself; and to think something with oneself is to say something to oneself. Plato was, I believe, quite correct to call the essence of thought the interior dialogue of the soul with itself. This dialogue, in doubt and objection, is a constant going beyond oneself and a return to oneself, one's own opinions and one's own points of view.
>
> (Gadamer 2006: 547)

Human thought itself is "this infinite dialogue with ourselves," and an education in it may be spoken of as a gradual process of "growing up in the midst of this interior conversation with ourselves, which is always simultaneously the anticipation of conversation with others and the introduction of others into the conversation with ourselves" (Gadamer 2006: 547). It is in this conversation that "the world begins to open up and achieve order in all the domains of experience," in which meanings are understood and truths are discerned (Gadamer 2006: 547). No technique governs this art; no empirical or "evidence-based" pedagogy tells us how it is done or how to measure success, however, as is the case with any art and any skill, practice and habit-formation are imperative. In education students become habituated not only to acquiring facts but to raising questions and pursuing them with patience and persistence, to listening and discerning, to judging, criticizing, imagining, and other cognitive skills that resist our efforts at quantification and formalization. Dialogue itself is an art that no method governs but the dialectic of question and answer. Gadamer emphasized the priority in this art of the questioning act since it is this that brings the object that is to be known into the open and that is also inseparable from the event of insight. "The real nature of the sudden idea," he noted, "is perhaps less that a solution occurs to us like an answer to a riddle than that a question occurs to us that breaks through into the open and thereby makes an answer possible. Every sudden idea has the structure of a question" (Gadamer 2006: 361). The art of thinking is nothing else than the art of questioning, of learning both to discern what is questionable and to formulate the question that brings the matter into the open.

What Gadamer spoke of as the play structure of language refers to the back-and-forth of question and answer which characterizes knowledge in general. "Knowledge is dialectical from the ground up," he noted, in the sense that it emerges from the movement of statement and reply which belongs to all genuine conversation (Gadamer 2006: 359). Reciprocity and equality fundamentally characterize the relation between speakers in a process over which no one altogether presides, including, in an educational context, the professor. While their role includes the important matter of informing the students of certain matters, it is not to play the expert but to inquire, as John Dewey often put it, with the students into a given problem or question. The professor, from this point of view, is less "professing" what they know than guiding the conversation in a direction that is productive and education-ally worthwhile. The equality between speakers is not an equality of knowledge but one in which professors and students are free to question and to assert anything they wish as well as obliged to defend their answers.

The concept of dialogue becomes a false idealization when it is either overtly politicized, as one may well say of Freire, or turned into an empty catchword. Conversation as Gadamer conceived it is neither an exercise in Marxian consciousness-raising nor a rationalist's utopia, and its institutional setting is no ideal speech situation but the classroom of the modern university. This is a site, let us not forget, of a conflict that is multifaceted – the conflict of ideas most obviously, but also at times between students themselves (among many of whom the notion of a competition for grades continues to be deeply rooted), between the grader and the graded, as well as a conflict within the student's own experience between that which is being formed and that which is doing the forming. *Bildung* itself is not a process that is devoid of conflict and struggle, and the same may be said of dialogue. When Jean-François Lyotard asserted that "to speak is to fight," his point was that advancing an idea is hazarding a move within a Wittgensteinian language game, and that if the aim in so doing is not exactly to win then it is to win over an interlocutor or conversational adversary (Lyotard 1984: 10). Dialogue is a site of struggle, and if Lyotard somewhat overemphasized the point and Gadamer perhaps underemphasized it, it remains a fundamental aspect of the practice whether it happens within the classroom or without it. To think is to participate in the conversation that is a given field of knowledge and to play in a sense of the word that connotes not aimlessness but dialectical reciprocity.

Let us briefly consider the practice of the classroom discussion which has long been thought an invaluable part of a university education in any field of the human sciences, and perhaps not only there. The standard practice of many an educator is to attempt to preserve some class time for discussion after the period of formal lecturing ends, perhaps with a smallish grade assigned to it. The quantity of time is usually moderate – depending in the main on whether it is a lecture course or a seminar – and it is engaged in only when the essential matter of "getting through the material" has been accomplished. Often it takes the form of a simple question and answer period, but sometimes it approximates actual conversation – or so, at any rate, the professor hopes. This hope is disappointed when students either do not perceive the value of dialogue, are too numerous, or are overcome by inhibition, or when educators themselves do not encourage it by expecting it and themselves practicing it in questioning the texts or ideas that they are teaching and the students no less. One learns to participate in dialogue by participating in dialogue and by seeing it done by the professor, and neither is a straightforward matter. There is no pedagogical technique and no learning technology that instills dialogical competence, but practice helps.

The conditions of such dialogue are several. They include, first, an intellectual environment in which students and professors are maximally free to pursue whatever topics they choose and to proffer opinions, criticisms, and questions without fear of censure, including especially when those opinions are at odds with intellectual fashion. Second, dialogue in the classroom requires that the number of students not be so high that they adopt a posture, by a seemingly inevitable process, of spectatorship. Third, it presupposes that professors demonstrate by their own example how to comport oneself in the realm of ideas and to exhibit intellectual virtues of open-mindedness, reasonableness, rigor, and related values. Fourth, it presupposes that students are taught to see the value of dialogue and that the will to communicate in a richer sense of the word be cultivated thereby. This last condition warrants emphasis given that the will to communicate, which importantly includes the will to listen no less than to speak, does not appear to enjoy a happy existence in the educational and cultural conditions that we now face. It is an elementary fact, but one that nonetheless bears noting, that listening is a necessary precondition of having something intelligent to say, and ours, if I may venture an observation, is not a society of listeners. There are further conditions of dialogical education, of course, but let this suffice as a short list.

Bildung

Part of Gadamer's project in Part One of *Truth and Method* was to rehabilitate for the human sciences several guiding concepts of the humanist tradition, including one whose implications for education are not far to seek. Originating in medieval mysticism, *Bildung* (culture) is an idea that found its way into modern German idealism in the writings of Johann Gottfried Herder, Wilhelm von Humboldt, and G. W. F. Hegel in particular before undergoing something of a deterioration in the early part of the twentieth century. The disrepute into which this idea fell was owing to its association in many minds with a kind of cultural and intellectual snobbery. *Bildung*, many came to believe, belongs to the affluent and the elite, although this is not what the term meant in the humanist tradition and it is not at all what was intended by the philosophers just listed. The word refers to a life task that belongs to every human being, and while it occurs both within and without educational institutions it has special importance for what happens within them. In *Bildung* we are not pursuing a particular end-state, a condition of "being cultured" or "sophisticated," but are, as Herder expressed it, "rising up to humanity through culture" (cited in Gadamer 2006: 9). The word connotes a process rather than an end, and while it aims at the transformation of the self it does not proceed in any single direction but toward a general cultivation not only of given talents but of capacities of mind that take one beyond the immediacy of the self and toward some conception of the universal. In Humboldt's words, "when in our language we say *Bildung*, we mean something both higher and more inward, namely the disposition of mind which, from the knowledge and the feeling of the total intellectual and moral endeavor, flows harmoniously into sensibility and character" (cited in Gadamer 2006: 9). One contemporary scholar speaks of this as "a condition of acquired maturity which exhibits itself in both a receptive and reflective disposition to the lifelong challenge of experience," one that is "formed from an engagement with the world and its concerns and maintained in the continuing movement that openness to experience requires" (Davey 2011: 46). *Bildung* in this sense is a way of being that has no goal outside of itself and that is nourished by exposure to what is different.

Gadamer cited with approval Hegel's notion of *Bildung* as a break from human naturalness and immediacy in order to cultivate higher capacities of thought: "In this sphere he is not, by nature, 'what he should be' – and hence he needs *Bildung*" (Gadamer 2006: 11). "What he should be," for Hegel, is to be understood in terms of "rising to the universal," where this refers to a life process of transcending the self in its immediate circumstances and taking up an idea that partakes of a higher universality. This is accomplished, to take Hegel's example, in work; this form of activity finds one becoming disciplined in a fashion in view of the task at hand and is formed in so doing. "Whoever abandons himself to his particularity," as Gadamer put it:

> is ungebildet ("unformed") – e.g., if someone gives way to blind anger without measure or sense of proportion. Hegel shows that basically such a man is lacking in the power of abstraction. He cannot turn his gaze from himself towards something universal, from which his own particular being is determined in measure and proportion.
>
> (Gadamer 2006: 11)

Work cultivates a capacity for abstraction in the sense that in laboring upon an object one is forming it in light of an idea at the same time that one is forming the self. Work requires a self-forgetfulness and a self-overcoming in order to accomplish a task, a cultivation of sensibilities that transform the individual and impart a sense of oneself. In being initiated into a profession, for instance, students are developing a range of skills and habits that take them out of the immediacy of interest and desire and transform them in light of what it means to be a professional in a given field. Becoming a historian is a rising to the universal in this sense; the student develops a general conception of what a historian is, what form of work is involved and what it takes to accomplish it, what capacities of thought, work habits, and so on, require cultivation, the effect of which is to become a different self. One becomes a servant of a kind and makes oneself answerable to the demands that every profession makes, yet not in a sense that intimates mere conformity. One makes one's profession one's own as we learn to find our way about a language or any dimension of a lifeworld; we become ourselves in the same gesture that has us learning to serve something beyond ourselves.

Bildung requires a distancing from the given, an orientation toward the universal, and that one make oneself at home in a world that is initially unfamiliar. Hegel referred to this process as "the basic movement of spirit" or the fundamental orientation of the mind. In Gadamer's words, "to recognize one's own in the alien, to become at home in it, is the basic movement of spirit, whose being consists only in returning to itself from what is other" (Gadamer 2006: 13). The same process of "getting beyond his naturalness" characterizes the acquisition of language and culture, this universal life task of becoming at home in a world in the same process in which one is formed by it (Gadamer 2006: 13). It is a process of ascending not only from ignorance to knowledge but from particularity to universality, nature to culture, and immaturity to maturity. It is a formation that happens through habit formation, broadening horizons, and becoming exposed and receptive to ideas whatever their source. In this process it is not only our reason narrowly conceived that is cultivated but a range of capacities that Gadamer referred to as senses. Thus "someone who has an aesthetic sense knows how to distinguish between the beautiful and the ugly, high and low quality," much as the student of philosophy develops a facility with concepts, a sense of whether an idea is plausible and worth pursuing or whether it may be left aside (Gadamer 2006: 15). Common sense as well consists not in any mere possession of information but in a practical sensibility and a judgment that is broadly shared by members of a historical community and a sense of what that community holds in common. "Thus," as Gadamer put it, the educated or "cultivated consciousness has in fact more the character of a sense" – of how to do things, how to see what is required, form distinctions and judgments, and respond to whatever situations we encounter (Gadamer 2006: 16). It is a consciousness that is "active in all directions," and accordingly is a "universal and common sense" (Gadamer 2006: 16). One may say that the basic structure of *Bildung* is the dialectic of venture and return. Learning is a venturing toward the unknown and strange, an undertaking that involves risk and in which another can play at most a supporting role. It is followed by a return to the familiar, but no longer as the self whom one was. Education is transformative in this sense; it forms the self in a process that is dialectical and lifelong, and is little different from what Dewey called growth (see especially Dewey 1980).

A conception of education that places *Bildung* in the center has far-reaching implications. What matters most in education is not the acquisition of information or any other tangible outcome but the art of questioning. If no pedagogical technique teaches how to ask questions – not any and all questions but the productive question, that which brings the things themselves into the open – how is this learned? The answer is through practice or by engaging with ideas habitually. We learn to ask questions, in short, by asking questions. We learn by doing, and it is harder than we may imagine. It is nourished by exposure to the unfamiliar and the exacting task of coming to critical terms with it, becoming familiar with it, and making oneself at home in it.

Living with ideas

The fundamental aim of the university, Gadamer maintained, is to create an environment in which professors and students may "live with ideas" in the sense that Humboldt gave to this phrase. For Humboldt, it is research that defines the university's mission more than any doctrinal or utilitarian consideration, and it is a mission in which students are involved no less than their educators. It was Humboldt's view, as Gadamer noted in "The Idea of the University – Yesterday, Today, Tomorrow" that "freedom, the struggle for which has constituted the world-historical fate of humanity, was supposed to especially become possible by this 'living with ideas' at the university" (Gadamer 1992: 48). While career preparation is of an importance that is obvious to all, the university's mission is not limited to this but is "to discover a balance between the duty to prepare students for a profession and the duty to educate which lies in the essence and activity of research" (Gadamer 1992: 49). Some distance from practical life is the vital matter, the love of ideas and the search for understanding for their own sake. The meaning of this is readily seen in the case of professors. Their role in the institution and in the broader culture is not only to teach but to contribute to a given field of knowledge through research, and it is a practice in which students as well may be expected to offer something of their own or to prepare to do so. The student's task, as Gadamer expressed it, is to "find his free space" in the sense of discovering an environment in which one may think for oneself and pursue questions that vitally concern one in association with one's peers (Gadamer 1992: 59). The heart and soul of a university education, he believed, is to become at home in the realm of ideas.

Let us think this matter through a bit more. What is it to "live with" ideas, or with anything? That with which we live is familiar not only in the sense of being well known in an informational sense but that it is familial, of a piece with what we are. To be at home in a particular place is to dwell in a profound, ontological sense in a realm of meanings that are shared with particular others who are not associates but intimates. Home is a site of shared significations, shared knowledge, and shared conflict, and while it is well known that such conflicts can be the most divisive, beneath the division one normally observes a commonality of spirit that is profound and mutually constitutive. Even when estranged, apples and the trees from which they fall are seldom strangers in a genuine sense. That with which we live forms us; to say that it is us is an exaggeration, but the exaggeration is more slight than we sometimes imagine. Living with ideas, whether we are speaking of a practice that takes place in the university or beyond it, is inseparable from *Bildung*. The ideas with which we live, the questions we habitually pursue, and the truth that we seek all form the soul in some fashion. Since so much of what we are is governed by habits of thought, feeling, and action, educators and students alike might give serious consideration to what habits of mind the contemporary university is fostering – whether it is emboldening minds, widening horizons, and fostering freethinking or allowing new forms of orthodoxy to replace the orthodoxies of the past.

Jean Grondin illustrates the point by relating a story from Gadamer's own student days:

Gadamer met his most influential teacher, Martin Heidegger, already a well-known figure, during the fall semester at the University of Freiburg in 1923, and in the following summer, Heidegger would invite Gadamer and his wife to spend four weeks at his private hut in the Black Forest and hold private seminars on Aristotle with him. This form of teaching was by no means exceptional in the old German university: aside from their formal teaching duties, all university professors would form private reading and discussion groups to which they would invite their most gifted students. Gadamer took part in many such groups, where he surely learned more than in the classes (learning, he would restate in 1999, does not only come from the teachers, but also from the class mates), and would himself form such circles when he would become a professor.

(Grondin 2011: 7–8)

While living with ideas no longer takes such a personal form, of course, the idea that professors and students might inquire on a common basis in the "free space" that is the university remains the animating principle of this institution. It is a principle that stands opposed to the narrowing influence of managerialism and instrumentalism, and enjoins us to keep the horizon of education broad so that the life of the mind may be as free as the realities of institutional life allow. The obstacle that such realities constitute is formidable and includes everything from the scale and bureaucratic nature of the university to the ratio of students to professors, the colonizing of education by a logic of the marketplace, and institutional inanities of a great many kinds. There is no practice that is more susceptible to what one might call meddling – by government, social and economic trends, and so on – than education, yet in spite of this it remains both a possibility and an imperative to resist many of the pressures that come to bear on the university and the kind of inquiry that takes place there. To learn, this most fundamental aim of students, means to become at home in the realm of ideas, or whatever ideas prevail in the field of research that one chooses. It is to learn to listen to ideas, where this means more than being informed but capable of discerning layers of significance and responding in an intelligent way to what we hear. To become at home in the study of history, for instance, is to listen to history and to acquire a sense of it, an understanding not only of "what happened" but of how things stood in a given era, what was possible within it, and what things meant for its inhabitants. The student of history gains an understanding of what was at stake in a given time and place, a sense of what living in that time was like and of who these people were. It is a sense acquired through not only information but habituation – habitual questioning, reading, and writing about a particular age in association with one's peers. From the student's point of view, finding one's free space here means finding a degree program, professors, and fellow students all of which allow for this kind of *Bildung* to take place. What "learning outcomes" result from this is an afterthought and rather often is beside the point if we mean by this expression any tangible and measurable results which may be carried over into the marketplace. Whether a sense of history or the capacity to listen to ideas qualifies as an "outcome" is doubtful, but it is also fundamental to what the student of history must cultivate if they are to be educated in this field. One would say nothing different about the student of philosophy, whose education also includes a great deal of information about the great thinkers of the past and present but also, and more essentially, a cultivated capacity to listen to ideas and to pursue philosophical questions thoroughly and habitually. The student here is at home in the realm of concepts, is able to discern which arguments are not only valid and invalid in a technical sense but persuasive and unpersuasive, and to exercise judgment and inventiveness in this field of knowledge. Whether anything results from this in the resolutely empirical and economic sense that is currently the fashion is unlikely, but the aim of living with ideas in a discipline such as this is to develop an educated capacity to question and to think beyond the boundaries of the useful.

"We need," as Gadamer expressed it, "to think through the continual opposition between the educational task of the university and the practical utility which society and the state expect from it" (Gadamer 1992: 49). It is an opposition that is fraught with economic and ideological considerations that tilt the scale away from the intellectual virtues of which hermeneutics speaks and away in general from the intangibles of education which make it the practice that it is. Philosophical hermeneutics gives us a way of thinking through this tension in a way that might preserve it rather than overcome it in any simple reversal of educational values. The university remains a social institution and what happens there is not divorced from the life of the society and the practical realities of human lives. It is not any banishment of the practical that is to be hoped for, but that this does not exhaust the mission of the institution. What hermeneutics reminds us of is that while there is no unbridgeable divide between education and practical life, there is a distance there that must be preserved, that there is such a thing as the love of ideas for its own sake and the search for understanding as an end in itself. If professors pursue this in their research, it is the student's task as well to live with ideas by finding an environment in which to question their world and inquire into the matters that most vitally concern them.

Bibliography

Burbules, N. 1993. *Dialogue in Teaching: Theory and Practice.* New York: Teacher's College Press.

Davey, N. 2011. "Philosophical Hermeneutics: An Education for all Seasons?" In *Education, Dialogue and Hermeneutics*, ed. Paul Fairfield. New York: Continuum.

Dewey, J. 1980. *Democracy and Education.* Middle Works Volume 9: 1916, ed. Jo Ann Boydston. Carbondale: Southern Illinois University Press.

Freire, P. 2004. *Pedagogy of the Oppressed.* Trans. M. Ramos. New York: Continuum.

Gadamer, H.-G. 2006. *Truth and Method.* Second revised edition. Trans. J. Weinsheimer and D. G. Marshall. New York: Continuum.

——1992. "The Idea of the University – Yesterday, Today, Tomorrow." In *Hans-Georg Gadamer on Education, Poetry, and History: Applied Hermeneutics*, eds. Dieter Misgeld and Graeme Nicholson. Trans. L. Schmidt and M. Reuss. Albany: State University of New York Press.

Grondin, J. 2011. "Gadamer's Experience and Theory of Education: Learning that the Other May Be Right." In *Education, Dialogue and Hermeneutics*, ed. Paul Fairfield. New York: Continuum.

Lyotard, J.-F. 1984. *The Postmodern Condition: A Report on Knowledge.* Trans. G. Bennington and B. Massumi. Minneapolis: University of Minnesota Press.

43

HERMENEUTICS, HEALTH AND MEDICINE

Fredrik Svenaeus

Introduction

In what way can medicine be considered to be a form of hermeneutics? Even if we assume doctors and other health care professionals to be *interpreting* what patients say, how the body looks and feels, as well as the results of diagnostic investigations, are these interpretations not fundamentally different from the ones we find in the humanities? Can medical practice be claimed to be a form of hermeneutics in a similar way as the reading of a literary or historical text is so? In this chapter I will explore questions pertaining to medical hermeneutics with the help of Hans-Georg Gadamer's philosophy, paying particular attention to his late publication *The Enigma of Health* (1996). In this collection of essays, the earliest of which date back to the 1960s, Gadamer develops a kind of outline of how to think about the subject of medicine and hermeneutics, and I will try to fill in his arguments and make them more explicit and comprehensive as we go along. But allow me to start with some preparatory remarks.

Hermeneutics and phenomenology

In the beginning of the nineteenth century, at the same time as modern scientific medicine took its first tottering steps, the theologian Friedrich Schleiermacher set himself the goal of developing what he called a *general* hermeneutics – that is, a hermeneutics that would not be limited to a certain discipline or doctrine, but would rather provide the general rules for all forms of possible interpretations. Schleiermacher focused upon what he called the capacity for "*Einfühlung*", generally translated as "empathy". According to Schleiermacher, in the attempts to find out what the author of a historical document meant by his words, one not only has to learn his language and culture, one must also imagine oneself in his position, striving to embody his intentions. Wilhelm Dilthey, writing towards the end of the nineteenth century, attempted to reformulate this general hermeneutics of Schleiermacher as providing the methods of the humanities in contrast to the methods of the natural sciences, then emerging as the new powerful research paradigm. Understanding the meaning expressed by artefacts and explaining the causal laws of nature were designated by Dilthey as distinct and different methodologies of the humanities and the natural sciences, respectively. As medicine is generally considered to belong to the natural sciences this division threatens to leave medicine out of hermeneutic reach.

The idea of hermeneutics as a method peculiar to the humanities in contrast to the natural sciences was used in the twentieth century as a theoretical basis to develop interpretive manuals for uncovering the meanings of texts and other kinds of artefacts. The term hermeneutics consequently came to take on the meaning of a collection of *methodological principles* used in order to uncover more or less hidden meanings in artefacts. Before we go any further, let me say that this is *not* the kind of hermeneutics I will claim to be essential to medical practice in this chapter. Patients are not works of literature, although, as we will see, they share some important ontological characteristics with texts. This similarity is in fact the reason why doctors can learn and hone their clinical skills through the reading of novels and poetry. However, the knowledge they gain from this reading is not primarily knowledge of how texts work, but rather knowledge about how human beings work in their attempts to make themselves at home in the world (Downie and Macnaughton 2007).

The kind of hermeneutics I will claim to be essential to medicine is the *phenomenological* hermeneutics that Martin Heidegger first developed in his main work from 1927, *Being and Time* (1996), and which, as we will see, Gadamer has developed further. According to such a hermeneutic view, medical practice is a particular form of understanding activity, which is identical with neither explanation in the sciences nor interpretation in the humanities. Medical knowledge includes applied biology – scientific explanations of what happens in the diseased body – but it is not limited to this scientific approach. The hub of medical hermeneutics is the dialogue between health care professional and patient that represents a particular form of understanding in and by itself by which all forms of particular scientific investigations are guided (or, at least, should be guided). I will now try to make this hermeneutics of medicine visible with the aid of Heidegger and Gadamer.

Phenomenological hermeneutics, as we find it in Heidegger, is an ontological endeavour, not the application of a method, since hermeneutics in phenomenology is taken to be a basic aspect of human life. Human beings, according to Heidegger, understand themselves by being placed in a context of meaning-relations referred to as their "being-in-the-world" (1996: 53 ff.). This being-in-the-world of human existence (or "*Dasein*" as Heidegger calls it), is primarily constituted by our practical doings, but our understanding activities also include the processes of articulation, according to Heidegger (1996: 61). When we are building a house together, for example, I will hand you the hammer or ask for it by way of showing you my open hand in a situation calling for a hammer to strike nails. Articulation in its more explicit form then takes on the mode of being of language: "give me the hammer". Yet a step is taken when dialogues (and monologues) are fixated by way of signs as texts, which may then be read and interpreted in various ways, as spelled out in the hermeneutics of Schleiermacher and Dilthey. Understanding in these cases takes on a rather indirect form as compared to the more immediate understanding of everyday practical activities, but the activity of reading is still tied to the same kind of worldly meaning relations (hammers used to build houses, etc.) as the ones found in other practices. Hermeneutics is thus not only and not primarily a methodology for text reading, but a basic aspect of life. To be – to exist as a human being – means to understand (Ricoeur 1992; Wierciński 2005).

Gadamer and the hermeneutics of medicine

At first sight Gadamer's *magnum opus*, published originally in 1960, *Truth and Method* (Gadamer 1994), might seem rather remote from the phenomenology of being-in-the-world that Heidegger presents in *Being and Time*. Gadamer's book is divided into three parts; the first and second parts, which are by far the most extensive, deal with the work of art and with interpretation in the humanities, respectively. The third part of the book deals with the ontology of language and can be read as an articulation of the special pattern of understanding, which Gadamer has found to be present in these disciplines. As Gadamer acknowledges himself, however, and as I will attempt to elucidate further, *Truth and Method* is most accurately read as an extension of the phenomenological hermeneutics of *Being and Time* (Gadamer 1994: 254 ff.).

As many readers have remarked, the title of Gadamer's book should properly read "Truth or Method" and not "Truth and Method", since it is precisely the methodological conceptualization of hermeneutics, formulated by Schleiermacher and Dilthey, that Gadamer is trying to go beyond. Truth in *Truth and Method* is meant as a basic experience of being together with others in and through language and not as a criterion for the correct interpretation of texts. This conception of truth is completely in line with Heidegger's interpretation of the concept as "*a-letheia*" in *Being and Time*; that is, truth as the openness or disclosedness of *Dasein* to the world of meaning in which things can be found and articulated *as* such and such things (as hammers, for instance) (Heidegger 1996: 213 ff.). Thus, for a sentence to describe, to correspond to, a state of the world – as, for example, in: "the hammer is heavy" – this prior dismantling of the world as meaningful – a place where hammers can be too heavy – is necessary. Truth in Gadamer's philosophy, however, is to be understood primarily as openness to *the other* and *his* world and not only to *my own* world. The difference, from Heidegger's point of view, would not be decisive, because the world of the other is also mine – we share the same world in our being-together. Still, human understanding is to a much greater extent a shared experience in Gadamer's hermeneutics than in Heidegger's philosophy.

Language is emphasized by Gadamer as the key mode of human existence in being together with others. The form of language he concentrates his analysis upon in *Truth and Method* is not, however, the spoken dialogue, but rather the reading of literature and other texts of the past. Historical texts are separated from us by a temporal distance, which makes the meaning incarnated in them more difficult to dismantle. Indeed, what does it mean to uncover the meaning of such a text? When we try to understand a historical document, our world – our horizon of meaning – is not identical with the world of the author of the document. Nevertheless, our horizons are not totally separated, but distantly united through the "*Wirkungsgeschichte*" – the history of effects – of the document (Gadamer 1994: 300 ff.). It is consequently possible to bring the horizons closer together and reach an understanding of the document through that which Gadamer here calls a "merging of horizons".

The medical encounter can be viewed as such a coming-together of the two different attitudes and worlds of health care professional and patient – in the language of Gadamer, of their different horizons of understanding – aimed at establishing a mutual understanding, which can benefit the health of the ill party (Svenaeus 2000). Doctors (as well as representatives of other health care professions) are thus not first and foremost scientists who apply biological knowledge, but rather interpreters – hermeneuts of health and illness. Biological explanations and therapies can only be applied *within* the dialogical meeting, guided by the clinical understanding attained in service of the patient and his health. Gadamer's philosophy of hermeneutical understanding, which has mainly been taken to be a general description of the pattern of knowledge found in the humanities, might thus be expanded to cover the activities of health care.

Gadamer's late work *The Enigma of Health*, supports this interpretation, addressing the area of medicine and health care in a more direct way than the philosopher's earlier works. Medicine is here characterized as a dialogue and discussion (*Gespräch*) by which the doctor and patient together try to reach an understanding of why the patient is ill:

> It is the disruption of health that necessitates treatment by a doctor. An important part of the treatment is that the patient actually discusses his or her illness with the doctor. This element of discussion is vital to all the different areas of medical competence, not just that of the psychiatrist. Dialogue and discussion serve to humanize the fundamentally unequal relationship that prevails between doctor and patient.
>
> (Gadamer 1996: 112)

What is particularly obvious in the medical meeting is the *asymmetrical* relation between the parties. The patient is ill and seeks help, whereas the doctor is at home – in control by virtue of his knowledge and experience of disease and illness. This asymmetry necessitates empathy on the part of the doctor (Halpern 2001). He must try to understand the patient, not exclusively from his own point of view, but through trying to put himself in the patient's situation. Consequently, that the doctor attempts to reach a new, productive understanding of the patient's illness in no way implies that he should avoid empathy. It is only through empathy that the doctor can reach an independent understanding that is truly productive in the sense of being shared, *and* novel in the sense of offering new perspectives on the patient's health problems.

At this point we may return to Gadamer's model of textual interpretation in *Truth and Method* (something Gadamer does not do himself in *The Enigma of Health*) to understand more in detail how clinical understanding is developed. It is first and foremost the doctor who is the "reader" and the patient who is the "text". But since the meeting is dialogic, the reading is also a reciprocal process of questions and answers. The distance between the two parties is not a time-related distance as in the case of the reading of a historical text; it is rather a distance between two *lifeworld* horizons – the doctor's medical expertise of diseases and the patient's lived experience of illness – which can be narrowed down through the dialogue. This narrowing-down, this "merging of the horizons" of doctor and patient in the medical meeting, means that the horizons are brought into contact with each other, but nevertheless preserve their identities as the separate horizons of two different attitudes and life-worlds (Svenaeus 2000).

Hermeneutics and medical ethics

As several commentators have pointed out, Gadamer's project in *Truth and Method* is deeply indebted to the practical philosophy of Aristotle (Berti 2003). Indeed, a discussion of "The Hermeneutic Relevance of Aristotle" is at the centre of the chapter devoted to the problem of application (*Anwendung*) in the second part of the book (Gadamer 1994: 312 ff.). When Gadamer chooses to continue his analysis of hermeneutic practice by turning to Aristotle and the *Nicomachean Ethics* (2002), he does so in order to underline the *normative* aspect of hermeneutics:

> To summarize, if we relate Aristotle's description of the ethical phenomenon and especially the virtue of moral knowledge to our own investigation, we find that his analysis in fact offers a kind of *model of the problems of hermeneutics*. We too determined that application is neither a subsequent nor merely an occasional part of the phenomenon of understanding, but codetermines it as a whole from the beginning.
>
> (Gadamer 1994: 324)

The Greek concept rendered as "the virtue of moral knowledge" by Gadamer in the quote above, is "*phronesis*", often translated as "practical wisdom". Among the last books to be published by Gadamer before his death in 2002 was his own annotated translation of Book VI of the *Nicomachean Ethics* – that is, precisely the book that deals with *phronesis* (Gadamer 1998). This fact is yet another sign of the importance of the concept for Gadamer's philosophy. It is thus clear that Gadamer intended his hermeneutics to be a practical philosophy in the Aristotelian sense, and it is also clear that practical, phronetic wisdom is to be considered a hermeneutical virtue. Accordingly, *phronesis* is the mark of the good hermeneut, and maybe, in particular, the good medical hermeneut – the doctor (Svenaeus 2003). What does this mean in this context? And what conclusions can we draw, in the case of medicine, from such a strong link between Aristotle's concept of practical, moral wisdom and Gadamer's hermeneutics?

Phronesis for Aristotle is not a particular moral virtue, in the manner of fidelity, compassion, justice, courage, temperance or integrity. It is rather an intellectual ability; however, as such, it informs the moral virtues in specific situations, allowing the possessor of these virtues to make moral judgements. *Phronesis* is therefore in a sense a moral ability – despite being counted among the intellectual virtues by Aristotle – since it deals with practical decisions in situations in which not only abstract truths but also the concrete good are the matter at hand. The *phronimos* – the wise man – knows the right and good thing to do in *this* specific situation; in the case of medicine we would say that he knows the right and good thing to do for this specific patient at this specific time. This cannot be learned merely by applying universal, scientific truths, but only through long experience in concrete, practical matters of life.

Let us now connect the concept of *phronesis* to hermeneutics in the way that Gadamer envisages, and by extension to medical hermeneutics. The first thing worth noting is that the reference to *phronesis* by Gadamer makes clear that applied hermeneutics does not mean application of universal rules. Medical hermeneutics is thus not applicative in the sense that universal, methodological rules are applied to the concrete situation. Rather, the hermeneutics of medicine is grounded in the *meeting* between health care professional and patient – a meeting in which the two different horizons of medical knowledge and lived illness are brought together in an interpretative dialogue for the purpose of determining why the patient is ill and how he can be treated (Svenaeus 2000). This was one of the main points above: medical practice is not applied science, but rather interpretation through dialogue in service of the patient's health. Within this interpretative pattern science is made use of in various ways, but the pattern itself is not deductively (or inductively) nomologic in the natural-scientific sense.

The appropriation of *phronesis* at the heart of (medical) hermeneutics can also be viewed as a critique of applied (medical) ethics. The idea that ethical principles can somehow be applied to the clinical situation by health care personnel is strongly countered by the reference to *phronesis*, since Aristotle's main purpose in developing this concept is that the application of abstract principles in the field of practical, ethical knowledge is insufficient (Svenaeus 2003). Indeed, the appropriation of *phronesis* can be taken as a critique of the idea that the profession of medical ethics is at all possible, if "medical ethicist" is taken to mean a person who has specialized, theoretical knowledge in medical ethics – knowledge that is not based on practical experience. Medical ethics cannot only be "epistemic"; it must also be "phronetic" (Pellegrino and Thomasma 1993).

Phenomenology of health and illness

How does Gadamer himself address the issues of medical ethics in *The Enigma of Health* (1996)? I would say that he does so in at least two separate yet interconnected ways, neither of which bears much resemblance to mainstream work on the contemporary medical ethics scene.

The first of these approaches consists precisely in going back to ancient philosophy and Aristotle. His discussions of Aristotelian themes and concepts are very similar to those we find in *Truth and Method* and other works of his, except for one thing: he now explicitly addresses *medical* practice (*Heilkunst*), and not only practice in general. Gadamer makes the point that medical practice – in its ancient as well as in its contemporary form – never "makes" anything, but rather helps to *re-establish* a healthy balance which has been lost. Health is a self-restoring balance, and what the doctor does is to provide the means by which a state of equilibrium can re-establish itself by its own powers. Gadamer's strategy in *The Enigma of Health* is to investigate the ancient philosophy of medicine in order to find guidance for contemporary medical practice. This is not (only) a nostalgic appeal for a premodern, "humane" medicine, which was not dominated and controlled by technoscience, but rather a strategy that rests on Gadamer's insistence upon the importance of Greek philosophy for our contemporary thinking and our contemporary way of life. We need to address and make explicit this influence in order to elucidate the structure and goals of contemporary medical practice, just as we need to do so in order to elucidate the structure and goals of the humanities.

The second way chosen by Gadamer in *The Enigma of Health* to address medical practice philosophically is via phenomenology. Phenomena central to clinical practice, such as death, life, the relationship between the body and the soul, anxiety, freedom and health are analysed by Gadamer, for the most part according to the phenomenological framework developed by Heidegger in *Being and Time*. We have already confirmed the importance of Heidegger's philosophy for Gadamer in *Truth and Method*, and the same holds for *The Enigma of Health*. Since the phenomenological hermeneutics of Heidegger and Gadamer is itself firmly rooted in Aristotelian patterns of thought, the marriage between the historical, philological approach and the phenomenological attitude in the latter work should come as no surprise (Figal 1995). What might be more surprising is that Gadamer relies to such a small extent on the pattern of understanding developed in *Truth and Method* when he analyses the dialogue essential to medical practice. Instead he focuses upon the phenomenon that is central to the *goal* of medical practice: health. Since this goal is what distinguishes medicine from other hermeneutical activities, which have other goals, it seems in many ways a promising way to go. It is also an original way to approach questions of medical ethics, which are seldom related to health theory in any substantive way.

Central to Gadamer's analysis of the concept of health is the thought that health is not simply synonymous with the absence of diseases (i.e., pathological states or processes affecting the biological organism). Health has a phenomenological structure in itself, as a certain way of being-in-the-world:

> So what genuine possibilities stand before us when we are considering the question of health? Without doubt it is part of our nature as living beings that our conscious self-awareness remains largely in the background so that our enjoyment of good health is constantly concealed from us. Yet despite its hidden character health none the less manifests itself in a general feeling of well-being. It shows itself above all where such a feeling of well-being means we are open to new things, ready to embark on new enterprises and, forgetful of ourselves, scarcely notice the demands and strains which are put on us. ... Health is not a condition that one introspectively feels in oneself. Rather, it is a condition of being involved, of being-in-the-world, of being together with one's fellow human beings, of active and rewarding engagement in one's everyday tasks.
>
> (Gadamer 1996: 112–13)

In many ways the phenomenon of illness seems to be far more concrete and easy to get hold of than the phenomenon of health. When we are ill, life is often penetrated by feelings of meaninglessness, helplessness, pain, nausea, fear, dizziness or dis-ability. Health, in contrast, effaces itself in an enigmatic way (the dual meaning of the German *Verborgenheit* in the original title of the book). It seems to be the absence of every feeling of illness, the state or process which we are in when everything is flowing smoothly, running the usual way without hindrance.

The conceptual background for Gadamer's analysis of health here is undoubtedly Heidegger's phenomenology of everyday human existence found in the first division of *Being and Time*, although Heidegger himself never addresses health and illness there. Gadamer's approach to health is not tied to the humourist theories found in ancient Greek thought; rather, it thematizes the notion of a self-establishing healthy equilibrium in a phenomenological manner. That is, it seeks to analyse health and illness by investigating the experiences of these states in everyday life, and not by invoking biology or physiology (in either their ancient or their modern forms). Thus the analysis of health is placed on a lifeworld level and takes into account not only the absence of detectable biological diseases, but also the embodied being-in-the-world of the patient, which includes thoughts, feelings and actions (Aho and Aho 2008; Carel 2008; Svenaeus 2011).

In what way does a phenomenological analysis of health bring us closer to *phron-esis* as a key concept for medical ethics? In other words, in what way do the two roads travelled by Gadamer in *The Enigma of Health* meet? Precisely by defining the goal of clinical practice as something dependent on the *individual* patient. If health is to be understood in terms of embodied being-in-the-world, and not only in terms of biomedical data, then the doctor needs to develop an understanding of the patient's thoughts, feelings and lifeworld predicaments, in order to carry out his profession. He needs to address the questions of the good (enough) life and of the meaning of life for this particular person. This is food for thought for medical ethics. To emphasize the hermeneutic structure and essence of medical practice will bring a focus upon narratives in medical ethics to excavate the embodied suffering of indi-viduals (Charon 2006; Frank 2013; Zaner 2004).

The past and future of medical hermeneutics

Gadamer is hardly the first philosopher in the phenomenological-hermeneutic tradi-tion to approach issues of health and illness. But the other attempts made for developing theories of health and illness on a phenomenological basis have most often been restricted to the areas of psychiatry and psychology; somatic ailments have either been seen as the territory of biology and physiology, or they have been treated as psychosomatic symptoms by the phenomenologically inspired psychia-trists. That the university of Heidelberg, the place where Gadamer spent the second half of his long life, has hosted some of the most prominent figures of this tradition of phenomenological psychiatry, such as Karl Jaspers, Viktor von Weizsäcker and Wolfgang Blankenburg, is no doubt one of the reasons why Gadamer began approaching the themes of medicine and health in the 1960s (see Gadamer 1977). Jaspers, Weizsäcker and Blankenburg are mentioned by Gadamer in *The Enigma of Health*, but without doubt he also knew the works of Ludwig Binswanger, Medard

Boss and other key figures of this tradition, such as F. J. J. Buytendijk and Erwin Straus, who are not mentioned in his book (Spiegelberg 1972; Toombs 2001).

The thesis that medical practice is a hermeneutical activity in the Gadamerian sense of a dialogical encounter between reader (doctor or other health care professional) and text (patient) on the way to truth (about the person and his lacking health), tends to expose itself to exactly the same of kind of critical questions that were put to Gadamer by Jürgen Habermas and others, following the publication of *Truth and Method* in the 1960s (Habermas 1971). How does medical hermeneutics take into account the embeddedness of medicine and health care in a political context? The question asks for a study of the interconnection between the more specific meaning patterns of medical practice and the socio-political pattern of, for example, the organization of health care and medical science. Interestingly, as we have seen above, Gadamer nurtures such a critical perspective by his roots in a Heideggerian phenomenology, which can be (and has been) developed as a critique of modern technology.

In the essay *The Question Concerning Technology*, published in 1954, Heidegger claims that modern technology has decisively changed the meaning patterns of the lifeworld, which traditionally has involved a number of different features constitutive of human practices (like building, reading, healing, etc.) (Heidegger 1977). His point is also that modern technology has done so in a way that we should find problematic and strive to move beyond because it severely limits what we are able to see, think and do in the world. The idea is not that we should abstain from all use of scientific technology and try to live a premodern life. Heidegger's thesis is instead that the essence of technology has developed into a danger of becoming the *dominating* and, most often also taken for granted and therefore *barely visible*, world view of the modern age. We must live a life "enframed" (*Ge-stell* is the German concept Heidegger is using) by modern technology, since there is no other way to live today, but we can strive to make this meaning pattern of modern technology and science visible through a philosophical analysis, and take measures to prevent it from becoming the all-encompassing pattern of our being-in-the-world (Ruin 2010).

Reflecting upon the meaning and significance of *medical* technology (something that Heidegger never did in a systematic way himself) is actually a good way to save Heidegger's analysis from falling into traps of romantic anti-scientism (Svenaeus 2013). Heidegger could hardly deny that inventions such as X-ray, the medical laboratory, the artificial kidney or antibiotics do more and better things to us than exposing us to a life in the "*Ge-stell*". Therefore, it would be wrong, I think, to forge a necessary and immediate link between the use of modern technology and the domination of a technological world view. To facilitate the health of a patient with the help of medical technology need not be identical to enforcing a "framework" of technology on him, a new way of defining, shaping and producing health and life under the reign of medical science, provided the doctor is aware that he is first and foremost encountering a human being. But it is a constant *risk*. Gadamer articulates this risk well in *The Enigma of Health*:

> In medical science we encounter the dissolution of personhood when the
> patient is objectified in terms of a mere multiplicity of data. In a clinical

investigation all the information about a person is treated as if it could be adequately collated on a card index. If this is done in a correct way, then the data (*Werte*) all belong to the person. But the question is nevertheless whether the unique value of the individual (*Eigenwert*) is properly recognized in this process.

(Gadamer 1996: 81)

The hermeneutics of medicine needs to be developed beyond Heidegger's and Gadamer's interests by carefully analysing the implications of new medical research findings and health care developments from the point of view of the lifeworld and its different patterns of human understanding. There are many topics in contemporary medicine and biomedical ethics that could profit from such a hermeneutical-phenomenological analysis. They concern, for example, issues of diagnosis, the concepts of health and disability, the status of human body parts, the beginning and ending of life, so-called "patient centred care", and the concept of suffering. I have already mentioned so called "narrative bioethics" as one field which is particularly hospitable to hermeneutic philosophy (Charon 2006; Frank 2013; Zaner 2004). Other important examples of fields in medical ethics in which phenomenology and hermeneutics are gaining ground are feminist bioethics (Zeiler and Käll 2014), disability bioethics (Scully 2008) and culturally based bioethics (Rehmann-Sutter et al. 2008). The common denominator seems to be a need to give voice to marginalized or oppressed parties and to dismantle the relations of power that keep the positions in place. Hermeneutics is thus expanded to provide an analysis not only of the medical encounter, but of other meetings between health care and suffering parties in our society today.

Bibliography

Aho, J. and Aho, K. (2008) *Body Matters: A Phenomenology of Sickness, Disease, and Illness*, Lanham, MD: Lexington Books.

Aristotle (2002) *Nicomachean Ethics*, trans. C. Rowe, Oxford: Oxford University Press.

Berti, E. (2003) "The Reception of Aristotle's Intellectual Virtues in Gadamer and the Hermeneutic Philosophy", in R. Pozzo (ed.), *The Impact of Aristotelianism on Modern Philosophy*, Washington D.C.: The Catholic University of America Press.

Carel, H. (2008) *Illness: The Cry of the Flesh*, Stocksfield, UK: Acumen Publishing.

Charon, R. (2006) *Narrative Medicine: Honoring the Stories of Illness*, Oxford: Oxford University Press.

Downie, R. S. and Macnaughton, J. (2007) *Bioethics and the Humanities: Attitudes and Perceptions*, London: Routledge.

Figal, G. (1995) "*Phronesis* as Understanding: Situating Philosophical Hermeneutics", in L. K. Schmidt (ed.), *The Specter of Relativism: Truth, Dialogue and Phronesis in Philosophical Hermeneutics*, Evanston, IL: Northwestern University Press.

Frank, A. (2013) *The Wounded Storyteller: Body, Illlness, & Ethics*, 2nd edn, Chicago: University of Chicago Press.

Gadamer, H-G. (1977) *Philosophische Lehrjahre: Eine Rückschau*, Frankfurt am Main: Suhrkamp Verlag.

——(1994) *Truth and Method* (2nd rev. edn), trans. J. Weinsheimer and D. G. Marshall, New York: Continuum Publishing (original published in 1960).

———(1996) *The Enigma of Health: The Art of Healing in a Scientific Age*, trans. J. Gaiger and N. Walker, Stanford CA: Stanford University Press (original published in 1993).

———(1998) *Aristoteles, Nikomachische Ethik VI: Herausgegeben und übersetzt von Hans-Georg Gadamer*, Frankfurt am Main: V. Klostermann.

Gordijn, B. and Chadwick, R. (eds) (2008) *Medical Enhancement and Posthumanity*, Dordrecht: Springer.

Habermas, J. (1971) *Hermeneutik und Ideologiekritik*, Frankfurt am Main: Suhrkamp Verlag.

Halpern, J. (2001) *From Detached Concern to Empathy: Humanizing Medical Practice*, Oxford: Oxford University Press.

Heidegger, M. (1977) *The Question Concerning Technology and Other Essays*, trans. W. Lovitt, New York: Harper & Row (original published in 1954).

———(1996) *Being and Time*, trans. J. Stambaugh, Albany: State University of New York Press (original published in 1927, page references are to the German original found in the margins of the English translation).

Pellegrino, E. D. and Thomasma, D. C. (1993) *The Virtues in Medical Practice*, Oxford: Oxford University Press.

Rehmann-Sutter, C., Düwell, M. and Mieth, D. (eds) (2008) *Bioethics in Cultural Contexts: Reflections on Methods and Finitudes*, Dordrecht: Springer.

Ricoeur, P. (1992) *Oneself as Another*, trans. K Blamey, Chicago: University of Chicago Press (original published in 1990).

Ruin, H. (2010) "*Ge-stell*: Enframing as the Essence of Technology", in B. W. Davis (ed.), *Martin Heidegger, Key Concepts*, Durham, UK: Acumen Publishing.

Scully, J. L. (2008) *Disability Bioethics: Moral Bodies, Moral Difference*, Plymouth, UK: Rowman & Littlefield Publishers.

Spiegelberg, H. (1972) *Phenomenology in Psychology and Psychiatry: A Historical Introduction*, Evanston, IL: Northwestern University Press.

Svenaeus, F. (2000) *The Hermeneutics of Medicine and the Phenomenology of Health: Steps towards a Philosophy of Medical Practice*, Dordrecht: Kluwer.

———(2003) "Hermeneutics of Medicine in the Wake of Gadamer: The Issue of *Phronesis*", *Theoretical Medicine and Bioethics* 24: 407–31.

———(2011) "Illness as Unhomelike Being-in-the-World: Heidegger and the Phenomenology of Medicine", *Medicine, Health Care and Philosophy* 14: 333–43.

———(2013) "The Relevance of Heidegger's Philosophy of Technology for Biomedical Ethics", *Theoretical Medicine and Bioethics* 34: 1–16.

Toombs, S. K. (ed.) (2001) *Handbook of Phenomenology and Medicine*, Dordrecht: Kluwer.

Wierciński, A. (ed.) (2005) *Between Description and Interpretation: The Hermeneutic Turn in Phenomenology*, Toronto: The Hermeneutic Press.

Zaner, R. (2004) *Conversations on the Edge: Narratives of Ethics and Illness*, Washington D.C: Georgetown University Press.

Zeiler, K., and Käll, L. (eds) (2014) *Feminist Phenomenology and Medicine*, New York: SUNY Press.

44
HERMENEUTICS, ARCHITECTURE AND DESIGN

Richard Coyne

The reception of architecture

There's a space at the front of most buildings known as "the reception area". That's an entry porch, foyer or other welcoming space, where visitors leave behind the dust and rain of the street as they enter into the recesses of the house, hospital, museum or hotel – the inside spaces. The reception area may also have a desk, a place for people to meet, security checkpoints, prominent signs, the company logo and other devices to prepare visitors for the building they are entering. As it happens, this simple idea of being received into a building helps to introduce some of the main themes of hermeneutics. When I lecture on architectural theory I find it helpful to introduce such philosophical themes by referring to everyday elements of architecture, such as *the reception area.*

Buildings don't receive everyone. The design and organisation of buildings discriminate. Whereas museums are welcoming to families, busloads of school children and respectful tourists, they generally discourage groups of sports fans in celebratory mode, hen or stag parties, or people who want somewhere to set up for a picnic or bed down for the night. Buildings inevitably welcome some people and their activities but they discourage others.

The reverse is also the case. Building users receive buildings. People form opinions about the building as they enter it. In this sense buildings get received by their occupants. Reception is an evaluative process, and inevitably involves interpretation. We make judgements about places, but also events. Entering a building is an event, and building owners, sponsors and authors organise events around the opening of a new building, the launch of a film or the publication of a book. Artists receive awards, lavish events receive guests, audiences receive speeches and dinner guests receive what's on their plates. Reception operates in diverse ways and constitutes an important area of study in the arts and humanities, that have spawned a field of study known as "reception theory" or "reception aesthetics". These fields address how a work of art, literature or a building is received, and how or why this reception varies over time (Wilson 1993; Jones 2000).

How do we receive architecture? The question is similar to asking, "how is architecture evaluated?" Opinions about architecture flow freely in casual conversation, and professional critics provide reviews in journals and the media. A recent edition of a journal for architects in Scotland carried an article by historian Ian Wall who asserted: "The great majority of new buildings are at best bearable but normally poor, with the odd leavening of 'Starchitect' sculptures, the most recent of these in Scotland being Glasgow's Transport Museum by Zaha Hadid, certainly the most expensive warehouse ever built in Scotland" (Wall 2013: 19).

In the age of mass consumption and social media it's also easy to adopt numbers as indicators of how services and entertainments are being received: received well, badly or with indifference. Arts reviewers sometimes even report on the numbers of tweets for and against a particular television programme. A practice has also emerged whereby audiences comment on a TV show, sports events or any other major event while it is happening. Tweets are there to be mined for opinion, representative or otherwise. Twitter supplements other readily available reception indicators such as BARB's (Broadcasters' Audience Research Board) viewing figures.

The reception of architecture is not so susceptible to numerical assessment. Buildings are one-off interventions or impositions rather than services or consumer goods of choice. If building users don't like a building then they can't change the channel. Unlike bad comedy, people have to accommodate the architecture they are served. Architecture also operates with large time periods, and buildings get altered over time. There are many buildings that were badly received 50 years ago that now appear on heritage listings and so are now well received. Some buildings thought highly innovative in their day and received well by critics and users might now get torn down. People's values change. Often cited examples include those residential tower blocks built in the 1960s and once thought efficient and pleasant places to live. We think differently now. The main point of reception theory is that reception varies over time, and according to circumstances. Reception is historically situated.

This is one of the philosopher Hans-Georg Gadamer's key points about interpretation (Gadamer 2004). Reception involves the way people evaluate, interpret and understand a building, and reception is historical. As described elsewhere in this volume, he calls this historical contingency of reception *Wirkungsgeschichte*, sometimes translated as "history of effect": "Understanding is, essentially, a historically effected event" (Gadamer 2004: 299).

If reception is not static, and varies over time, and according to historical contingencies then it's also something that depends on repetition. Like the role of the reception area in a restaurant, hotel, office building, theatre or home, it depends on and supports comings and goings, and repeat visits. The reception of a built work of architecture is not decided once and for all. Like all interpretation it feeds off the repeat visit. The encounter changes as our horizon changes. Gadamer describes the process of interpretation as a movement that "has no goal which brings it to an end; rather it renews itself in constant repetition" (Gadamer 2004: 104). Opinions about a film get summarised and fixed on opinion aggregators such as rottentomatoes.com, but the summation of opinion is never the end of the matter. Recognising this point provides consolation for the not yet recognised or acknowledged, in other words the makers of inconspicuous, everyday and "immaterial" architecture (Coyne 1991; Karandinou 2013). The reception of art and architecture is more subtle than star ratings can supply.

As Adrian Snodgrass and I have argued elsewhere, the repetitive process of interpretation and reception also sounds like what happens during the design process, as a cycle of renewal, an iterative process, a to-and-fro dialogue with a set of circumstances and an interpretation. Hermeneutics in architecture is a matter both of reception of what exists and of the creation of objects there to be interpreted, that is, the design of buildings (Snodgrass and Coyne 2006). Snodgrass and I expand on the idea of design as a hermeneutical process in our book *Interpretation in Architecture*. In this we draw on Gadamer's concepts of play and dialogue, and Donald Schön's ideas about design as "reflection-in-action" in which the designer is engaged in "a reflective conversation with the situation". As if echoing the hermeneutical project he says: "The principle is that you work simultaneously from the unit and from the total and then go in cycles – back and forth, back and forth." We designers "begin with a discipline, even if it is arbitrary", which is the projection of a pre-understanding. This projected discipline is a "what if" to be adopted in order to discover its consequences, and can always "be broken open later". So the designer begins the design task by shaping the situation in accordance with an initial judgement. The situation then "talks back" and the designer responds to the situation's back talk by reflecting-in-action on the construction of the problem, the strategies of action, or the model of the phenomena. The process then develops in a circle, "back and forth, back and forth". Each move draws out the implications of earlier moves that affect later moves, creating new problems to be described and solved. In this way the designer plays out "a web of moves, consequences, implications, appreciations and further moves" (Schön 1983: 78).

The language of hermeneutics is coincident with the language of design as a dialogical process. Of course, this dialogical process resides not only with a singular designer, but in the context of a hermeneutical community (Fish 1989), which brings me to the matter of how the architectural community has received hermeneutics.

Architecture's reception of hermeneutics

Have architects and architectural theorists embraced ideas about hermeneutics? Architecture is a multifaceted discipline, but it has something of a fixed reference point in what actually gets built, or at least designed and published. Architecture is invariably a team project, but is wedded to the idea of the singular project, the iconic building, and the sole author. Not only might an architect claim authorship of a particular building as head of a firm or key designer, but she might also write books and appear in the media. Those texts and pronouncements might also indicate affinity with a particular philosopher. If the building is well received, then so might the architect's writing, ideas and affinities be received well. The architect Peter Zumthor provides a handy example. He won the commission for and designed the public spa bath facility in the town of Vals in Switzerland. The building has received much acclaim and won awards. Zumthor also wrote a book in which he attributes much of his design thinking to the philosopher Martin Heidegger (Zumthor 2006). Heidegger wrote about building (Heidegger 1971), and his ideas were already in circulation amongst architectural theorists (Norberg-Schulz 1971). No doubt much depends on the content and quality of Zumthor's writing, but even just the association increases the reception of Heidegger, the philosopher and others who have developed his ideas in architecture (Sharr 2007). Psychologists have described the way such threads, themes and attributes gain legitimacy by association as "the halo effect" (Thorndike 1920; Kahneman 2011). We like the building so we'll look favourably on the ideas the designer attributes to it. From a hermeneutical point of view, the inheritance and transmission of legitimacy is one of the ways that pre-judgment, that is prejudice, operates. Architects and architectural theorists seem to look for this kind of endorsement of philosophical ideas by celebrated architects before giving those philosophical ideas serious attention.

Another example of how architecture adopts philosophy is the way that Jacques Derrida's ideas were developed by the writer-architect Peter Eisenman. Eisenman had already earned fame through a series of writings and buildings (Eisenman 1982). He then befriended Derrida and they worked on an architectural project together (Kipnis and Leeser 1997). Architects brought Derrida into their fold, and his philosophy of *deconstruction* became a catchword in architecture for a couple of decades. Scholars do not necessarily adopt the philosophical ideas on the philosopher's own terms, but the ideas become the focus of a particular discursive practice, and a focus for agreement and disagreement (Papadakis et al. 1989; Broadbent and Glusberg 1991). In thinking too about architecture as a hermeneutical community, there's substantial wriggle room in the career of an architect or architectural scholar for toying with ideas, and support for an acquisitive and cavalier approach to ideas and methods. The way hermeneutical communities operate (Fish 1989) has a lot to say about the way architects work and legitimate their ideas.

History attests that architects have a particular affinity with writing and publishing, but the scenarios I've described here are similar in the fine arts in general. At its best architecture is aspirational and experimental. I do not mean to suggest that architecture is therefore different from philosophy (Wigley 1995). Architectural scholarship simply manifests what goes on elsewhere, though perhaps some of its attributes manifest the nature of hermeneutical communities in exaggerated form.

No doubt I've overstated the case for what counts as legitimate study in architecture, but my case serves as a working hypothesis to explain why hermeneutics has not yet enjoyed the same currency in architecture as some other philosophical terms and some other philosophers. At best, hermeneutics is subsumed within more conspicuous themes, such as deconstruction, phenomenology, structuralism, critical theory, system theory, posthumanism and digital studies. Hermeneutics is subsumed within the reception of prominent and well-received thinkers such as Martin Heidegger, Michel Foucault, Giles Deleuze and Jean Baudrillard. Hans-Georg Gadamer, as the champion of hermeneutics, didn't establish as strong an association with architecture in his writing as did some other philosophers. Nor have prominent architects as yet associated their work with his, at least in a conspicuous and compelling way.

The game of architectural scholarship is changing. Many architectural scholars are interested in writings outside the mainstream. They resort to online publication outlets, and the availability of publications from different disciplines, looking for new sources. The open access publication initiative (Finch 2012) and other developments expose architecture to a wider range of thinking, and even the generation of its own innovations in thought. Philosophers might one day cite the work of architectural scholars as part of the philosophical canon.

The philosopher Paul Kidder (2013) provides a recent account of architectural writers who have picked up on the theme of hermeneutics. My own foray into hermeneutics began during discussions with my friend Adrian Snodgrass with whom I worked at the University of Sydney in the late 1980s. At the time he was steeped in translation work, examining Japanese art texts. I had just finished a PhD on applications of logic programming, knowledge engineering and artificial intelligence (AI) to architectural design, an overtly rationalist approach to architecture. This rationalism was assailed on three sides. One assault came from Adrian's enthusiastic revelations over lunch of his discoveries as he read deeper into theories of translation and interpretation. The second came from the shifting mood amongst the computer fraternity that after all AI wasn't delivering on its promises. I read Terry Winograd and Fernando Flores' short book in which they explained the problem with recourse to Gadamerian hermeneutics (Winograd and Flores 1986). They showed that it was acceptable for people interested in computers and programming to venture into philosophy of the kind discussed in the humanities, as opposed to the limited fare of the Positivists, a view later confirmed by a detailed study of Hubert Dreyfus' commentary on *Heidegger's Being and Time* (Dreyfus 1991). The third assault came from the mood of postmodernism which we were just catching up on, and which we discovered was not really a style of nostalgic architecture but a way of thinking that challenged the scientism of the time. We ran some reading groups that branded us as "intellectuals" during a period when, apart from some well known Schools in the USA and Europe, architecture departments were pervaded by a no-nonsense practical approach to their craft, and with much emphasis on the design studio, served perhaps by some history, environmental psychology and technical subjects. I think this is a profile that has changed radically since the early 1990s, certainly in the Anglo tradition and as academic architects have responded to the pressure to do research and to publish. Architecture has since positioned itself more firmly in the humanities, referencing literary studies, cultural theory and philosophy.

In the early 1990s I had two sabbatical periods at Cambridge University, connected with the Martin Centre and the Architecture Department. There I was introduced to Dalibor Vesely and his seminars, and the tradition of hermeneutical reflection that exercised its influence more in the design studio and a flow of influential academics and practitioners than in publications. In 2004 Vesely produced his book *Architecture in the Age of Divided Representation*. From my understanding, the tradition here of dealing with hermeneutics was mentored initially by the architectural historian and critic Joseph Rykwert who worked at the Universities of Essex, Cambridge and Pennsylvania. His influence on a number of scholars is extensive, including Alberto Pérez-Gómez at McGill University in

Montreal (Pérez-Gómez 1994). There are other strands to the hermeneutical project in architecture, notably from the area of phenomenology (Mugerauer 1994, 1995). Robert Mugerauer has worked at the University of Washington. An early book on interpretation in architecture by Juan Pablo Bonta references the historical aspect of the hermeneutical project as expounded by Gadamer (Bonta 1979), but without the language of contemporary hermeneutics (horizon, prejudice, part-whole).

Though overt allegiance to hermeneutics is not widespread in architecture, hermeneutics has exerted covert influence. Developments in architectural thinking draw on similar sources to developments in hermeneutics. I gave an account of the development of architectural hermeneutics in the Introduction to *Interpretation in Architecture*. There I aligned developments in hermeneutics with those of *historicism* in architecture, a concern with the peculiarities of the time and place in which events unfold, and with the character of a community. Freidrich Schleiermacher (1768–1834) contributed to this tradition, that was largely attributable to an emerging German idealism as outlined elsewhere in this volume. Historicism promoted a view that the historian must penetrate the essential spirit of a country or period. Interpretation under historicism is evident in contemporary architectural writing. For Karsten Harries, the main task of architecture "is the interpretation of a way of life valid for our period" (Harries 1997: 11), a view he also ascribes with approval to Sigfried Giedion (1888–1968), one of the first systematic historians of modernism. Historicism is also promoted by Giedion's protégé, Christian Norberg-Schulz, for whom "Modern architecture came into existence to help man feel at home in a new world" (Norberg-Schulz 2000: 9). Commonly, historicism requires of the architect a sensitivity to place: "primarily it means to identify with a physical and social environment" (Norberg-Schulz 2000: 9). The historicist legacy resonates with the idea of a receptive kind of architecture with which I began this chapter. Good architecture is welcoming and homely. The hermeneutical project offers hope to those disaffected by the unwelcoming face of modernism, particularly as manifested in the construction of impersonal tower blocks and those grim left-over, interstitial, wind-swept non-places between.

Architecture also shares themes with the founders of hermeneutics. For the ancient architectural theorist, all was to succumb to a unity, and the elements of architecture had to be related to form a unified whole, within the building and in connection with the universe (Vitruvius 1960; McEwen 2003). Classical architecture's appeal to unity drew on concepts of coherence. The relationship between the parts and the whole is a theme in hermeneutics, that aligns with the pre-modern and the early modern canon of architecture, through concepts of symmetry, ratio and coherence.

Whether or not it is recognised as such, hermeneutical themes operate at least as a subcurrent within architectural theory. Hermeneutics also provides an excellent way of situating various architectural discourses, not least the role of the creator in architecture.

Reception of the architect

I began the previous section with reference to the architect as author of the building. Hermeneutical theory presents a challenge to the idea of authorship as the source of authority in the interpretation of a building or work of art. Does the author of the words in a text know any more than the reader? The same question applies to all creative production. Can you ever know the mind of the artist, writer, designer, architect or originator of a creative idea or product?

Paul Kidder's book *Gadamer for Architects* explains the problem from a hermeneutical perspective (Kidder 2013). There are at least three responses to the problem of an author's meaning. One is to try to get back to the author, scrutinise their interviews, diaries, articles, books, and if they are still alive then ask them what they meant by their creation, as if their opinion settles the matter. Scholars may debate what the author *really* meant, but somewhere there's an original meaning that can be ascribed to the author-creator.

The second approach is to put any commentary an author may have about their own work to one side and presume that we know more than they do. In looking back at an author we may well, with the benefit of hindsight, be better able than they are to situate their work, and in any case we'll know more about the effect their work has had, its long-term reception. But (third) from a hermeneutical perspective it's more important to note that we know *differently* rather than know *better* or *more*. As discussed in this volume, this is the nature of interpretation, to approach any interpretive task from a different *horizon*. This difference may be the product of the difference in time, being in a different place, culture, educational context or social context. This is what keeps the interpretive process alive. The other two approaches tend to close off discussion or at least take it in the direction of *originality* and *authenticity*.

As everyone knows, no matter how we ascribe authorship in any particular case, the fact remains that architectural inventions, like works of literature, are of their time and the products of many minds. As the author Chuck Palahniuk writes, "Nothing of me is original. I am the combined effort of everyone I've ever known" (Palahniuk 2011: 104). The persistence of authorial intention so often deprecates the social dimension of any particular achievement. It also diminishes the shared and communal nature of architecture's reception at any particular time.

There are sound arguments against a reliance on the authority of authorship in the way we receive a work of art or architecture, even from the discipline of behavioural economics. The economist Daniel Kahneman provides sobering and unsettling evidence that we really are very unreliable when it comes to reporting our own state of knowledge (Kahneman 2011). So there are many experts who claim they knew about the 2008 financial crisis before it happened. Similarly, an architectural employee might claim they knew the firm would lose the competition, that the design would not be well received. In fact the evidence shows that our knowledge about what we *knew* gets skewed according to what we *now* know – or think we know now. Kahneman sees this as a weakness in human reasoning. But from a hermeneutical perspective such "unreliability" and forgetfulness indicates yet again how indebted we are to the shifting horizons within which we find ourselves – and by which we are enabled. We can't think otherwise. In any case, people to whom we ascribe authorship are as prone as their readers to their own shifting horizons and points of view. So hermeneutics has much to say about the authorship of a building, and the relationship between the building and its designer.

Radical reception

I began this chapter with a discussion of the reception area of a building as a particular space. It relates to the ordinary concept of a *receptacle*. Reception is also a philosophical term. Plato in *Timaeus* (Plato 1997) refers to *hypodoche*, the receptacle of all being that prefigures the Intelligible and the Sensible, and from which the Intelligible and the Sensible emerge, a term on which Jacques Derrida makes play in his essay "Chora" (Derrida 1997), and then relates to architecture in his work with Peter Eisenman (Kipnis and Leeser 1997). Derrida makes much of the problems that inhere within the use of the term by Plato, and the contradictions and paradoxes it entails. How can there be anything that prefigures the Intelligible and the Sensible, and that has the properties of both or neither?

In the more prosaic realm of architecture, it's the case too that a reception area is a more specific instance of a threshold, dividing the interior from the street. Thresholds are objects of fascination for architects (Norberg-Schulz 1980: 170). The threshold is the stone step where the cook in the household would sit and thresh the wheat, and where there's a chance that the wind would carry away the chaff and keep it from getting inside the house. It then came to mean simply the entrance way to a building or city. There's a depth to a threshold depending on the depth of the wall, and it may have extra covering, as in a porch, or thickening around the lintels. Entrances may involve a series of transitions across different thresholds. The threshold is a place of spatial ambiguity, where you are neither inside nor outside the space. It's also the gate of the city. The idea of the threshold has direct relevance to hermeneutics through the etymology of the word "hermeneutics". The generalised architectural feature of the threshold is also where Hermes the trickster god resides.

As this volume has pointed out many times, it's from the name Hermes that the term hermeneutics derives. Plato said, "the name 'Hermes' seems to have something to do with speech: he is an interpreter (*hermeneus*), a messenger, a thief and a deceiver in words, a wheeler-dealer – and all these activities involve the power of speech" (Plato 1997: 408a, 126). Language is tricky, and so is interpretation. After all, people can be lulled, deceived and persuaded against their better judgement by mere words. The literary theorist Lewis Hyde positions Hermes at the threshold, as "a wily boy, flattering and cunning, a robber and a cattle thief, a bringer of dreams, awake all night, waiting by the gates of the city" (Hyde 1998: 317). Hyde provides a compelling description of this trickster function in spatial terms:

> In short, trickster is a boundary-crosser. Every group has its edge, its sense of in and out, and trickster is always there, at the gates of the city and the gates of life, making sure there is commerce. He also attends the internal boundaries by which groups articulate their social life. We constantly distinguish – right and wrong, sacred and profane, clean and dirty, male and female, young and old, living and dead – and in every case trickster will cross the line and confuse the distinction. Trickster is the creative idiot, therefore, the wise fool, the gray-haired baby, the crossdresser, the speaker of sacred profanities. ... Trickster is the mythic

embodiment of ambiguity and ambivalence, doubleness and duplicity, contradiction and paradox.

(Hyde 1998: 7)

This tricky aspect of hermeneutics enables me to make sense of what goes on in much contemporary architecture. Architectural innovation occurs at the boundaries between the inside and the outside of a building, and between spaces. It also occurs at the boundaries between categories. Bookshops become coffee shops with books. Airports are also shopping complexes, and have supermarkets. Buildings now tend to be multi-use and multi-functional. Architecture also merges with the city and with landscapes, such that at times we don't know where one ends and the other begins. Is Melbourne's well-received Federation Square a building or a public square? Most architectural projects for students in the advanced years of an architecture degree course involve an exploration of a city or a landscape. Architecture also merges into film making.

Un-built, avant-garde paper architecture also presents challenges and provocations. In his criticism of the designs emerging from architecture schools, and that win RIBA awards, critic Patrik Schumacher laments that the student designs, and attendant films, digital animations and narratives are "provocation at best", but "are not designs of spaces intended to frame social life". Rather, they are merely "narratives and messages pushed by evocative imagery" (Schumacher 2012). Contrary to this conservatism, architect and educator Bernard Tschumi says of the process of designing a building that "the ultimate pleasure of architecture lies in the most forbidden parts of the architectural act; where limits are perverted, and prohibitions are transgressed. The starting point of architecture is distortion" (Tschumi 1994: 91). As an educator he set up projects in which his students would read works of literary fiction, watch films and be tasked with designing something like a nightclub in a graveyard. It was Tschumi who designed the Parc de la Villette in Paris as a series of red follies apparently without function, interwoven with paths inspired by the idea of filmic narratives. Tschumi introduced Derrida to Eisenman.

There's something pedagogically edifying about setting yourself a challenge, even if such a project is never encountered in practice. But in any case, designers are on the lookout for new ways of tackling a problem, and new problem definitions. According to architect and architectural writer Rem Koolhaas, design is not about "meticulous definition, the imposition of limits, but about expanding notions, denying boundaries, not about separating and identifying entities, but about discovering unnameable hybrids" (Koolhaas and Mau 1997: 969). Lest we think that some ideas and metaphors are out of bounds for the designer, he coins the notion of "junkspace", which is a "fuzzy empire of blur, it fuses high and low, public and private, straight and bent, bloated and starved to offer a seamless patchwork of the permanently disjointed" (Koolhaas 2004: 163). This stirring language and provocative architecture speaks of the redaction of boundaries, or at least their reconfiguration.

This brand of architectural recklessness accords with Jacques Derrida's radical brand of hermeneutics, where he takes issue with Gadamer (Derrida 1989). Instead of anticipation, we encounter surprises. A "radical hermeneutics" supports a restoration of the "trickster" in favour of a transgressive, deconstructive approach to architecture.

Exit

In this chapter I've attempted to position architecture within the spectrum of hermeneutical discourse. I introduced the theme of hermeneutics by referring to an ordinary building element, namely the reception area, porch or entrance way to a building. This identification provided a way of talking about how buildings receive building users, but in turn how users receive the architecture they inhabit. Users, tourists, visitors and critics also have opinions about particular works of architecture, that vary over time. This is in the nature of interpretation, to vary as our horizons shift and we adapt to new encounters and experiences. I alluded to interpretation as a dialogical, play-like and reflective process that also accords with understandings of the design process.

So hermeneutics is ubiquitous in architecture, from the way we interpret, use and understand a building to the way buildings get designed. Hermeneutics also provides a way of positioning the processes by which communities receive philosophical concepts – such as hermeneutics. I elaborated on the reception of hermeneutics by the architectural community, and offered a brief account of my own historical understanding. The way ideas are received in architecture seems to rely substantially on how they are promoted by leading architects and theorists. The dissemination of authority and authorship is a major issue in architecture, and ideas from hermeneutics provide interesting challenges to the conventional notion of authorship on which architecture seems to rely. Finally, I returned to the idea of the reception area as threshold, that is after all the site of duplicity and "doubleness", a place of reckless invention, in keeping with the character of hermeneutics' name sake Hermes the trickster god.

Bibliography

Bonta, J.P. (1979) *Architecture and its Interpretation: A Study of Expressive Systems in Architecture*, London: Lund Humphries.

Broadbent, G. and J. Glusberg (eds) (1991) *Deconstruction: A Student Guide*, London: Academy Press.

Coyne, R. (1991) "Inconspicuous architecture", in R. Coyne, A. Snodgrass, T. Fry and P. Redding (eds), *Gadamer, Action and Reason: Proc. Conference on the Application of the Hermeneutical Philosophy of Hans-Georg Gadamer within the Human Sciences*, Sydney: University of Sydney, pp.62–70.

Derrida, J. (1989) "Three questions to Hans-Georg Gadamer", in D.P. Michelfelder and R.E. Palmer (eds), *Dialogue and Deconstruction: The Gadamer–Derrida Encounter*, Albany, NY: SUNY Press, pp.52–54.

——(1997) "Chora", in J. Kipnis and T. Leeser (eds), *Chora L Works*, New York: Monacelli Press, pp.15–32.

Dreyfus, H.L. (1991) *Being-in-the-world: A Commentary on Heidegger's Being and Time, Division I*, Cambridge, MA: MIT Press.

Eisenman, P. (1982) *House X*, New York: Rizzoli.

Finch, J. (2012) *Accessibility, sustainability, excellence: How to expand access to research publications (Report of the Working Group on Expanding Access to Published Research Findings)*, http://www.researchinfonet.org/wp-content/uploads/2012/06/Finch-Group-report-FINAL-VERSION.pdf (accessed 30 July 2014).

Fish, S. (1989) *Doing What Comes Naturally: Change, Rhetoric, and the Practice of Theory in Literary and Legal Studies*, Durham, NC: Duke University Press.

Gadamer, H.-G. (2004) *Truth and Method*, trans. J. Weinsheimer and D.G. Marshall, New York: Continuum.

Harries, K. (1997 [1971]) *The Ethical Function of Architecture*, Cambridge, MA: MIT Press.

Heidegger, M. (1971) "Building, dwelling, thinking", *Poetry, Language, Thought*, New York: Harper and Rowe, pp.143–61.

Hyde, L. (1998) *Trickster Makes This World: Mischief, Myth and Art*, New York: North Point Press.

Jones, L. (2000) *The Hermeneutics of Sacred Architecture: Experience, Interpretation, Comparison, Volume Two: Hermeneutical Calisthenics: A Morphology of Ritual-Architectural Priorities*, Cambridge MA: Harvard University Press.

Kahneman, D. (2011) *Thinking, Fast and Slow*, London: Penguin.

Karandinou, A. (2013) *No-matter: Theories and Practices of the Ephemeral in Architecture*, London: Ashgate.

Kidder, P. (2013) *Gadamer for Architects*, Abingdon, England: Routledge.

Kipnis, J. and T. Leeser (eds) (1997) *Chora L Works: Jacques Derrida and Peter Eisenman*, New York: Monacelli Press.

Koolhaas, R. (2004) "Junk space", in R. Koolhaas, AMO and OMA (eds), *Content*, Köln: Taschen, pp. 162–71.

Koolhaas, R. and B. Mau (1997) "What ever happened to urbanism?", in R. Koolhaas and B. Mau (eds), *S, M, L, XL*, Rotterdam: 010 Publishers, pp. 959–71.

McEwen, I. (2003) *Vitruvius: Writing the Body of Architecture*, Cambridge, MA: MIT Press.

Mugerauer, R. (1994) *Interpretations on Behalf of Place: Environmental Displacements and Alternative Responses*, Albany, NY: SUNY Press.

——(1995) *Interpreting Environments: Tradition, Deconstruction, Hermeneutics*, Austin, TX: University of Texas Press.

Norberg-Schulz, C. (1971) *Existence, Space and Architecture*, London: Studio Vista London.

——(1980) *Genius Loci: Towards a Phenomenology of Architecture*, New York: Rizzoli.

——(2000) *Principles of Modern Architecture*, London: Andreas Papadakis.

Palahniuk, C. (2011) *Invisible Monsters*, London: Vintage Books.

Papadakis, A., C. Cooke and A. Benjamin (eds) (1989) *Deconstruction: Omnibus Volume*, London: Academy Editions.

Pérez-Gómez, A. (1994) 'Chora: The space of architectural representation', in A. Pérez-Gómez and S. Parcell (eds), *Chora 1: Intervals in the Philosophy of Architecture*, Montreal, Canada: McGill-Queen's University Press, pp.1–34.

Plato (1997) *Complete Works*, ed. J.M. Cooper, Indianapolis, IN: Hackett.

Schön, D.A. (1983) *Reflective Practitioner: How Professionals Think in Action*, London: Temple Smith.

Schumacher, P. (2012) "Schumacher slams British architectural Education", *The Architectural Review*, 31 January: http://www.architectural-review.com/folio/schumacher-slams-british-architectural-education/8625659.article (accessed 30 July 2014).

Sharr, A. (2007) *Heidegger for Architects*, London: Routledge.

Snodgrass, A. and R. Coyne (2006) *Interpretation in Architecture: Design as a Way of Thinking*, London: Routledge.

Thorndike, E.L. (1920) "A constant error in psychological ratings", *Journal of Applied Psychology*, 4: 25–29.

Tschumi, B. (1994) *Architecture and Disjunction*, Cambridge, MA: MIT Press.

Vitruvius, P. (1960) *Vitruvius: The Ten Books on Architecture*, trans. M.H. Morgan, New York: Dover Publications.

Wall, I. (2013) "The demise of architecture?", *Quarterly Journal of the Royal Incorporation of Architects in Scotland*, Autumn, 15: 18–24.

Wigley, M. (1995) *The Architecture of Deconstruction: Derrida's Haunt*, Cambridge, MA: MIT Press.

Wilson, T. (1993) *Watching Television: Hermeneutics, Reception and Popular Culture*, Cambridge: Polity.

Winograd, T. and F. Flores (1986) *Understanding Computers and Cognition: A New Foundation for Design*, Reading, MA: Addison Wesley.

Zumthor, P. (2006) *Atmospheres: Architectural Environments – Surrounding Objects*, Basel: Birkhäuser.

Part V

HERMENEUTIC CHALLENGES AND DIALOGUES

45

HERMENEUTICS AND PHENOMENOLOGY

Robert Dostal

The relationship of hermeneutics to phenomenology is much contested. The history of the development of philosophical hermeneutics in the twentieth century has led some to see phenomenology and hermeneutics in opposition to one another. This opposition might most obviously be seen in the mutual criticisms and recriminations of Edmund Husserl and Martin Heidegger. The subsequent development of philosophical hermeneutics, most notably by Hans-Georg Gadamer and Paul Ricoeur, both accepts Heidegger's critique of Husserl's phenomenology and appears to rely little on Husserl's accomplishments. This too suggests a distance and an independence of hermeneutics from phenomenology. Yet, Heidegger in *Being and Time* proclaimed that phenomenology is hermeneutical. In this seminal work he was the first to bring together the age-old tradition of hermeneutics with phenomenology. The phenomenology of Heidegger thus is both indebted to the phenomenology of Husserl and takes some distance from it. The situation is further complicated by the fact that Heidegger abandoned the project of *Being and Time* and almost entirely foregoes any explicit reference to hermeneutics in the work after 1929. The philosophical hermeneutics of Gadamer and Ricoeur rely importantly on the hermeneutical phenomenology of *Being and Time*, but also adopt much from what might be called the post-hermeneutical "later" Heidegger. Thus any consideration of the relation of phenomenology and hermeneutics must consider the phenomenology of Husserl, the hermeneutical phenomenology of *Being and Time*, and the development of philosophical hermeneutics by Gadamer and Ricoeur and the relation of their work to that of Husserl and Heidegger.

Yet there is quite another way to approach this question of the relation of hermeneutics and phenomenology. It is possible to provide a phenomenology of hermeneutics, that is, a phenomenology of the practice of interpretation. Thomas Seebohm has attempted to do just this in a recent book, *Hermeneutics: Method and Methodology* (Seebohm 2004). We will attend to this approach in addition to the consideration of the relation of philosophical hermeneutics to the phenomenology of Heidegger and Husserl. This chapter thus has three parts: first, the hermeneutic phenomenology of *Being and Time* and its relation to Husserlian phenomenology;

second, the philosophical hermeneutics of Ricoeur and, especially, Gadamer; and, third, Seebohm's phenomenology of hermeneutics.

Let's begin with a consideration of Heidegger's *Being and Time* where phenomenology and hermeneutics are first brought together.

Heidegger's hermeneutical phenomenology in *Being and Time*

The question for Heidegger in *Being and Time* is, as everyone knows, the question of Being. Accordingly, this work is a work of fundamental ontology. He tells us in *Being and Time* and elsewhere in the publications of the 1920s that the proper method of philosophy is phenomenology.[1] He sets for himself the task of pursuing the question of Being phenomenologically. Phenomenology is, at the same time, hermeneutics, since the task is to understand being *qua* being and all understanding is interpretive. In sum, Heidegger identifies phenomenology, fundamental ontology, and hermeneutics. Seen historically, this triadic fusion situates Heidegger's work, or at least the Heidegger of *Being and Time*, between the phenomenology of Husserl and the philosophical hermeneutics of Gadamer and Ricoeur. Husserl's phenomenology does not focus on the question of Being (Husserl's ontology is a "formal" ontology) and the philosophical hermeneutics of Gadamer and Ricoeur neither directly appeal to the method of phenomenology nor directly address the question of Being. Let us briefly consider Heidegger's hermeneutical phenomenology in its own terms and then consider its relation to Husserl's phenomenology and to the subsequent development of philosophical hermeneutics by Gadamer and Ricoeur.

The part of Heidegger's project of fundamental ontology that was published as *Being and Time* consists only in the first two divisions of what was projected to be a six division book. This published portion provides an "analytic of *Dasein*," because, according to Heidegger, we need first to consider 'there' where the question of Being gets raised. And the 'there' is *Dasein* (there-being). This analytic of *Dasein* attempts to provide an interpretation of who *Dasein* is. This account would show that understanding (*Verstehen*), attunement (*Befindlichkeit*), and discourse (*Rede*) are constitutive of *Dasein*. Understanding, on this account, always has an "as" structure. To take something to be something (S is p) is to take something "as" something. This taking or "grasping" may be explicit in language, that is, thematized, as an assertion or proposition whose terms are concepts. But Heidegger is particularly interested in our pre-thematic and pre-conceptual grasp of our world. Accordingly, he distinguishes between the thematic "assertoric 'as'" and the pre-thematic "hermeneutic 'as'" in his treatment of understanding. The assertion is secondary and derivative. Heidegger would resist the "fetishizing of assertion," as Bernard Williams has called it (Williams 2002: 100).

There are at least three important aspects of this account of understanding for our purposes here. The first is that understanding is always a matter of interpretation; the hermeneutic 'as' has primacy. The second is the priority given to our direct contact with things in intuition and perception. Heidegger uses the language of "ecstasy" and "transcendence" to render in his own terms the Husserlian notion of intentionality.[2] Alva Noë has expressed this more simply by saying that we are "out of our heads" (Noë 2009). In the introductory discussion of *logos* Heidegger approvingly points to the priority of *aesthesis* over *logos* for the Greeks.[3] At the same time, he does not wish to give a grounding status to a version of intuition that is disengaged, a mere 'looking' or 'observing.'[4] The third follows from this. Closely related to this demotion of the propositional and the conceptual is the primacy Heidegger gives to our involvement and engagement with others and things in the world over the disengaged theoretical approach to what confronts us in our experience. We are to understand ourselves as beings-in-the-world who are engaged and involved in our world and experience ourselves and our world as purposive, teleological. Hubert Dreyfus has usefully discussed this idea as "skillful" or "absorbed" "coping."[5]

Through this account of interpretive understanding Heidegger attempts to overcome both the primacy of the disengaged theoretical ego (the Cartesian ego) and the representationalism of so much of modern and contemporary philosophy. By representationalism I mean simply the view that we come to terms with the world of our experience by way of representations that provide an inner depiction of an outer reality.[6] Locke called these representational inner depictions 'ideas' and Kant thought of them as '*Vorstellungen*' – 'representations.' For these thinkers representations are the stuff of consciousness. We are inevitably left with the central modern epistemological problem of ascertaining whether our representations are correct. If all we have are our representations and there is no "getting out of our heads" to compare the representation with whatever it represents, we are left with skepticism or the Kantian distinction of appearances and things in themselves. The phenomenological starting point for Heidegger is not the Cartesian starting point – the representations of consciousness – but rather the recognition that we live "in the truth." And Heidegger asks in *Being and Time* what are the conditions of possibility for our truthfulness.

Heidegger explicitly acknowledges his reliance on the phenomenology of Husserl especially with regard to three very basic tenets of his hermeneutical phenomenology:

1. the understanding that philosophy is concerned with the *a priori*;
2. Husserl's notion of a categorial intuition; and
3. the concept of intentionality.

(Bernet 1990)

The first of these is equivalent to saying that phenomenology is transcendental philosophy.[7] In addition, Heidegger's conception of temporality that is fundamental to his early project rests on Husserl's treatment of time and temporality.[8] Most importantly Heidegger adopts Husserl's account of the extended or thick 'now' in which there is a kind of unity of past, present, and future and rejects as inadequate what he calls "clock-time." Furthermore, we find Heidegger in *Being and Time* using a number of important concepts and distinctions borrowed from Husserl, such as 'horizon,' '*das Man*,' and the distinction of the ready-to-hand (or handy – *Zuhandenheit*) and the present-at-hand (or 'objectively present' – *Vorhandenheit*).[9]

Heidegger's resistance to Husserlian phenomenology is complex and multiple – and has been much discussed. Perhaps the simplest way to locate the key aspect of this resistance is to recognize that Husserl's project is a phenomenology of consciousness which he also refers to as "transcendental subjectivity." Though the

Cartesian starting point may serve as a way into phenomenology according to Husserl, phenomenology on this same account soon leaves Descartes behind.[10] Heidegger argues that Husserlian phenomenology does not and cannot overcome this starting point. One way this objection takes shape in the secondary literature concerns the status of the *noema*. Husserl calls for a phenomenological description of both the subjective, or 'noetic' side, and the objective, or 'noematic' side, of the experience of consciousness. Inasmuch as the noema is "within" consciousness, Husserlian phenomenology seems to render everything internal to consciousness. There is no outside. Gadamer and others have referred to this as the problem of phenomenological immanence.[11] Husserl's declaration of his view as idealistic might seem to settle the matter. For Heidegger this is a continuation of (or lapse back into) representationalism. The noema, on this view, mediates between the thing or matter at hand and the subject as a representation of the matter at hand. The phenomenological insight of the early Husserl concerning intentionality in the *Logical Investigations* is lost in the idealism of the *Ideas*. Against this interpretation of Husserl, others have argued that Husserl successfully broke with representationalism and maintained this break. The noema should not be taken to be an entity of consciousness; it is not meaning or *Sinn* in a Fregean sense. The noema is just the consciousness of the object in the context of the reduction.[12]

It follows from this concern about the possible lapse back into representationalism and subjectivism, that Heidegger rejects or avoids various aspects of Husserl's phenomenology. He avoids, for example, talk of the method of reduction that is so important for Husserl. He rejects the language of "consciousness" which is omnipresent in Husserl and the characterization of time as "inner."[13] One can make much of the abandonment of the language of inner and outer and the avoidance of the language of consciousness and the subject. Heidegger is clearly more interested than Husserl in our practical involvement in our world, but the critics of Husserl in this regard ignore how much Husserl sees our coming to terms with our world as an activity and a practical matter. It is understandable that it has become commonplace to speak of the primacy of the practical in Heidegger, but we should recognize that Heidegger objects to what he takes to be the standard distinction of the theoretical and the practical. He is keen to point out that practice has its theory and theory has its practice.[14]

Given these arguable differences and given the explicit criticisms of Husserl by Heidegger and Heidegger by Husserl, some commentators see a radical break between their two ways of phenomenology.[15] Others have argued that there is a fundamental commonality of the project of phenomenology that is philosophically more significant than the differences and that both Husserl and Heidegger, each for his own reasons, exaggerated the differences.[16] A relatively early and important commentator on the relation between their phenomenologies, Merleau-Ponty in the Preface to his *Phenomenology of Perception*, writes: "yet the whole of *Sein und Zeit* springs from an indication given by Husserl and amounts to no more than an explicit account of the '*naturlicher Weltbegriff*' or the '*Lebenswelt*' which Husserl, towards the end of his life, identified as the central theme of phenomenology" (Merleau-Ponty 1962: vii).[17]

In response, those who would urge the radical difference between them (and the superiority of Heidegger) have sometimes argued that the similarities of Husserl with

Heidegger, especially the later Husserl of genetic phenomenology and the *Krisis*, show that Husserl learned from Heidegger. This question is difficult, perhaps impossible to untangle.[18] But few deny the proximity of the work of the late Husserl and Heidegger's work contemporary with it. This proximity has primarily to do with the 'life-world' (or ordinary experience) and the taking seriously of the historical character of human experience. We can find, for example, Husserl in his "Phenomenology and Anthropology" lecture of 1931 acknowledging that a genuine analysis of consciousness can be called "a hermeneutic of the life of consciousness" (Husserl 1997. 497).[19] I find it implausible (but not impossible) that the developments in the thought of the later Husserl should be accorded to Heidegger. There were systematic issues in Husserl's work that propelled his development. For the significance of the differences we should not be too taken by Heidegger's own account, for it seems natural he would wish to exaggerate his differences with his teacher to create a space for his own work and career.[20] This difficult historical and philosophical question of their relation cannot be explored further here.

The question of the relation of phenomenology and hermeneutics may be located in the debate about the relation of Husserlian and Heideggerian phenomenology, as I have just indicated. But this question also can be located within the project of *Being and Time*. Some, like William Blattner, find an irresolvable tension, an *aporia*, between the descriptive task of phenomenology and the interpretive task of hermeneutics.[21] He ties this to Heidegger's abandonment of the project. Rather than pursue this question in the context of the phenomenological project of *Being and Time* and Heidegger's subsequent development, let us turn to the philosophical hermeneutics of Ricoeur and Gadamer whose roots are to be found in Heidegger and *Being and Time* but who follow Heidegger's turn to language and embrace his later work. Before we do, we should note that there is almost no mention of hermeneutics in any of Heidegger's writings after the publication of *Being and Time*. Heidegger himself writes in the 1950s in "A Dialogue on Language," that he has abandoned the term: "It can hardly have escaped you that in my later writings I no longer employ the term 'hermeneutics'" (Heidegger 1971: 12). There is little said in this "dialogue" to explain why he abandons the term except that he had "left an earlier standpoint" (Heidegger 1971: 12). This suggests that hermeneutics for Heidegger was part of the warp and woof of the project of the incomplete *Being and Time* – a project in transcendental phenomenology. As he leaves this project behind, he leaves behind hermeneutics.[22]

Philosophical hermeneutics and phenomenology: Ricoeur and Gadamer

Long after Heidegger apparently abandons both phenomenology and hermeneutics, Gadamer published what is perhaps the most important single text in philosophical hermeneutics, *Truth and Method* (1960). The work has surprisingly little to say about either 'truth' or 'method.' With regard to the latter, Gadamer is critical of the methodologism of much of modern and contemporary thought including methodological hermeneutics. He would replace method with 'discipline.' The work is not transparent with regard to its own 'method,' the critics pointed out. Gadamer responded in the forward to the second edition by explaining that the work is "phenomenological in its method" (Gadamer 1989: xxxvi). What can this mean? I would suggest that there are two important aspects of this claim: first, that the work is descriptive and not normative; and, second, that the work relies importantly on the phenomenological account of understanding as it was presented in *Being and Time*. With regard to the first, Gadamer writes that "my real concern was and is philosophic: not what we do or what we ought to do, but what happens to us over and above our wanting and doing" (Gadamer 1989: xxviii).[23] In other words, the work means to provide a description of the event of understanding, the central theme of the book. And Gadamer's description of the "phenomenon of understanding" (as he names his topic in the second sentence of the Introduction) relies importantly on Heidegger's account in *Being and Time*. The first half of the work is primarily historical and leads us from Kant through Schleiermacher, among others, to Dilthey and then Heidegger. Gadamer writes that with Heidegger "the problem of hermeneutics gains a universal framework, even a new dimension, through his transcendental interpretation of understanding. ... so we shall start by following Heidegger" (Gadamer 1989: 264). The book concludes with a discussion of 'hermeneutic ontology.' Gadamer's project, like that of Heidegger, brings together phenomenology, hermeneutics, and ontology.

Gadamer's phenomenology, like that of the Heidegger of *Being and Time*, abjures the absolute, does not work toward a final foundation (*Letztbegründung*), makes no mention of the method of reduction, and avoids any talk of the subject or transcendental ego – all aspects of Husserl's phenomenology. We have already noted his reference to what he calls the "problem of phenomenological immanence" by which he is clearly referring to Husserl and his idealism.

However much the frame for Gadamer's project and much of the substance of his account relies on Heidegger, there is much in Gadamer's phenomenology of the understanding that does not have Heidegger as its source – for example, the rehabilitation of authority and tradition, the reliance on the hermeneutical circle (an age-old hermeneutical concept that Heidegger also took up), the importance of the concept of 'play,' the concepts of the effective-historical consciousness and the fusion of horizons. Important and central to Gadamer's account of understanding is the Heideggerian concept of truth that is closely tied to a conception of human finitude. In short, truth is presented as a revealing; and every revealing is at the same time a concealing. Gadamer's hermeneutics and his phenomenology of understanding brings with it a contextualism and a perspectivism. Gadamer relies on an aspect of Husserl's phenomenology of perception, particularly vision, to illustrate the finite and perspectival character of any understanding. On this account we cannot assume a god-like point of view, a "view from nowhere" as Thomas Nagel has phrased it. We always have a point of view, a view from somewhere. We ineluctably only have a perspective on things. This perspectivism, however, does not entail a strong relativism, since it does not follow from the perspectival character of perception that the perception is not true. We may only see one side of a thing, but we may see it quite well. As we move around something and examine it, we come to know it better. The understanding of the setting, current and historical, and of the possible use of the thing among other things is important. This contextualism of the understanding takes on a circular character – the hermeneutical circle.

This understanding of understanding as finite, circular, perspectival, and historically situated is also at the same time anti-representationalist in much the same way as Husserl and Heidegger. Gadamer, like his two phenomenological predecessors, is committed to the notion that there is but one world that we share, act in, and talk about: "the world is the common ground, trodden by none and recognized by all, uniting all who speak with one another" (Gadamer 1989: 404). Gadamer here too appeals to an argument from Husserl. There is no 'world in itself' that lies beyond language and beyond our experience of it. He writes that:

> the infinite perfectibility of the human experience of the world means that, whatever language we use, we never achieve anything but an ever more extended aspect, a 'view' of the world. Those views of the world are not relative in the sense that one could set them against the 'world in itself,' as if the right view from some possible position outside the human, linguistic world could discover it in its being-in-itself. No one questions that the world can exist without man and perhaps will do so. … The variety of these views of the world does not involve any relativization of the 'world.' Rather, what the world is is not different from the views in which it presents itself. The relationship is the same with the perception of things. Seen phenomenologically, the 'thing-in-itself' is, as Husserl has shown, nothing other than the continuity with which the perspectival profiles of perceptible objects pass into one another.
>
> (Gadamer 1989, 405–6)

This way of talking about 'views of the world' and our common world, allows Gadamer to make sense of the significant differences between individuals and cultures but at the same time to insist that, in principle, cultures and views are not incommensurable, however difficult the achievement of a mutual understanding and agreement may be.

Another aspect of Gadamer's hermeneutics that agrees with and develops a theme in *Being and Time* is the "practical" character of the understanding. Gadamer develops this theme, in part, by turning to and relying on the Aristotelian concept of practical judgment (*phronesis*).[24]

Yet another central theme in Gadamer's hermeneutics that follows Heidegger is the linguisticality of understanding. This aspect of Gadamer's treatment of understanding relies not on *Being and Time* but on the work of the later Heidegger, the Heidegger who left behind his early project and who stopped speaking of hermeneutics. Commenting on his efforts in *Truth and Method*, Gadamer later writes that the work was "to make it accessible in a new way" (Gadamer 1997: 46–7). "It" is the work of the later Heidegger. Gadamer's work thus establishes a hermeneutics that brings together the early and the later Heidegger. For Gadamer, understanding is always a matter of language. His hermeneutical ontology culminates in the much discussed assertion: "Being that can be understood is language" (Gadamer 1989: 474). Charged with linguistic idealism by Habermas and others, Gadamer responded by saying that this claim only means that our understanding is linguistic, not that Being is linguistic. This claim is less metaphorical than Heidegger's "language is the house of Being" (Heidegger 1977: 193).

What markedly distinguishes Gadamer's hermeneutics from Heidegger, early and late, is that the language of our understanding is always a matter of conversation. *Being and Time*'s account of *Dasein* shows it to be thoroughly 'social,' though Heidegger's account does not develop this theme.[25] Gadamer's hermeneutics attempt to make good on this by showing, to cite Hölderlin, that we are a conversation. Gadamer is concerned as to how the I–Thou relation can find an agreement and become a 'we' of solidarity. Additionally, we might note that there are other features that give Gadamer some distance from Heidegger. These include his humanism and his rejection of Heidegger's claim that the language of the tradition is inevitably 'metaphysical.'

Paul Ricoeur comes to adopt a position of philosophical hermeneutics that is very like the position of Gadamer (Ricoeur 1981). In his work, he explores a wide variety of questions and themes from the viewpoint of hermeneutics: what is text, the relation of hermeneutics to the critique of ideology, metaphor, truth and history, time and narrative, and so on. Later in his life he wrote extensively on issues in ethics and politics; justice is a central theme. It is not for us to consider his extensive contributions here, but it is relevant here to consider Ricoeur's articulation of the relation of phenomenology and hermeneutics (Ricoeur 1981). He acknowledges his "dependence ... on Heidegger and above all on Gadamer," and he writes that "what is at stake is the possibility of continuing to do philosophy with them and after them – without forgetting Husserl" (Ricouer 1981: 101). Ricoeur distinguishes phenomenology from the idealistic interpretation that Husserl provides. That is, Husserl does not provide the best interpretation of his own accomplishment. It is the "idealism" to which Ricoeur objects. Characteristics of this idealism, according to Ricoeur, are its location in subjectivity, its "scientificity," and its appeal to unmediated intuition. Ricoeur contrasts these three characteristics with the following three characteristics of hermeneutics: the turn to the world (not to subjectivity), finitude (not scientific certitude), and interpretation (not unmediated intuition). In sum, hermeneutics rejects the idealistic interpretation of phenomenology. Second, Ricoeur argues both that "phenomenology remains the unsurpassable presupposition of hermeneutics," and that "phenomenology cannot constitute itself without a hermeneutical presupposition." That is, these two mutually belong to one another. He points particularly to the role of the pre-predicative (or pre-thematic) in Husserlian phenomenology and Heideggerian hermeneutics and also to the fundamental significance of historical experience to both of these. He also points to the way that the Husserl of the *Logical Investigations* refers to his work there as an *Auslegung* and a *Deutung* – an explication and an interpretation. In conclusion, Ricoeur argues that evidence of phenomenology must be explicated hermeneutically. He reconciles them by rejecting idealism and showing how they mutually implicate one another. It is an affirmation of the hermeneutical phenomenology of *Being and Time*.

Seebohm's phenomenology of hermeneutics

Thomas Seebohm has approached the question of phenomenology and hermeneutics in quite a different way. He is concerned with providing a phenomenological critique of methodological hermeneutics. His critique is not a rejection of methodology (à la Gadamer) but a "clarification and justification of the basic concepts of methodology" (Seebohm 2004: 1).[26] Seebohm expressly relies on Husserl's phenomenological approach but acknowledges that Husserl scarcely dealt with the methodology of the human sciences. Seebohm attempts to do that work, in part with the help of Dilthey whose descriptive work in this regard, Seebohm points out, was recognized as phenomenological by Husserl.

Though Seebohm is negatively critical of Gadamer's hermeneutics on some aspects, he does not see his work to be in opposition to the ontological hermeneutics of Heidegger and Gadamer. These two approaches are working on different levels and are concerned with different things. Most notably, the concept and understanding of truth is central for Gadamerian hermeneutics, while Seebohm is not concerned with truth so much as validity. As noted above, Heidegger distinguishes the thematic from the pre-thematic, the 'hermeneutic as' from the 'apophantic as.' The truth of assertion is 'derivative' from the former. Seebohm is concerned with the latter – something that receives almost no treatment in Heidegger or Gadamer. It is a misreading of Heidegger and Gadamer to take their work to be anti-science. Yet they give little attention to the sciences and their methods. This is what Seebohm attempts to provide – a phenomenological approach to the human sciences.

Though Seebohm does not object to the phenomenological and ontological approach of Gadamerian hermeneutics, he does see as inadequate the overly simple alternative that Gadamer seems to leave us with: either the methodologism of positivism (the more recent heir of Cartesianism) or his hermeneutics of the understanding which does not address the question of method in the human sciences and leaves the impression that there is no place for method, while, in fact, the Gadamerian account of interpretation presupposes a valid interpretation.

The appropriate method, for Seebohm, insures validity. It does not provide a warrant for truth but for falsification. The methodological approach to the interpretation of the text would ask that the interpreter bracket truth claims. This bracketing supports one of the traditional principles of hermeneutical methodology – the distinction of understanding and application. Gadamer rejects this principle and famously claims that application is integral to understanding; to understand is to apply. Seebohm does not simply reject the relevance of application for interpretation. He rather says that any consideration of what a text means requires the consideration of how it would be applied. Placing the application in the subjunctive places both the truth of the claims of the text and its application in brackets. It provides a certain 'objectivity' to the enterprise.

Seebohm provides an extensive discussion of another traditional principle of hermeneutics: circularity. He relies, in part, on Husserl's account of whole and parts. He claims that this principle is not so much a methodological principle as a heuristic. He points out that some circles are vicious and others are not and discusses how we might distinguish these kinds of circularity. For Seebohm, like Gadamer, interpretation is always situational and contextual. Method does not rescue us from our situation, but it does assist in coming to terms with the text, however strange it might be.

Seebohm situates his account of hermeneutical methodology within an account of the understanding. We cannot provide the details of his account here but there are levels of understanding, and hermeneutical methods are appropriate not to every level but to a certain one. Within hermeneutic methods there are similarly a variety of levels of approach, including grammar, syntax, historical references, style, and genre – to name a few. He provides a rich and nuanced account that situates itself in relation to the history of hermeneutics, but especially nineteenth–century methodological hermeneutics, the philosophical hermeneutics of the twentieth century, and developments in the human and social sciences.

Conclusion

The tradition of hermeneutics, of considering how we read and interpret texts, begins presumably when there first were texts. There is a long and well-established tradition that, in the West, goes back to the Greeks. The question of interpretation found a focus in the late classical period with the interpretation of sacred scripture. These questions become heightened in the Renaissance and Reformation. They assume a 'scientific' posture in the nineteenth century as the historical and social sciences (the human sciences) try to adopt the methods of the modern natural sciences. Hermeneutics, which traditionally always had a focus on the text, becomes identified in the first part of the twentieth century with the basic philosophical enterprise of providing an account of understanding in the early work of Martin Heidegger, most notably in *Being and Time*. Heidegger does this in the context of the new movement of phenomenology inaugurated by Husserl to escape the modern epistemological predicament of representationalism and the dead ends of scientism, skepticism, world-views, and Neo-Kantianism. Heidegger's bringing phenomenology and hermeneutics together provides the basis for most of the subsequent developments in hermeneutics – most importantly the philosophical hermeneutics of Gadamer and Ricoeur. The relationship between phenomenology and hermeneutics remains contested. And the concern for a closer account of how we encounter the text and provide defensible interpretations also remains.

Notes

1 Heidegger identifies philosophy with phenomenology in both the introduction and the conclusion of *Being and Time* where he writes straightforwardly: "philosophy is universal phenomenological ontology" (Heidegger 2010: 413). See also Heidegger 1982, which is a set of lectures Heidegger gave in Marburg (Summer 1927) in the same year that *Being and Time* was published. In these lectures Heidegger clearly and unequivocally identifies philosophy with phenomenology – phenomenology is the method for philosophy and this method is "scientific" (*wissenschaftlich*).

2 In a footnote late in the text (Heidegger 2010: 346), Heidegger tells the reader that the next division (never published) of the work will show how the "intentionality of 'consciousness' is *grounded* in the ecstatic temporality of Dasein."

3 This is a difficult matter in *Being and Time*. Heidegger here wishes to make *logos* and linguistic expression secondary to what he calls the pre-thematic. Though an obvious candidate for that which is prior to thematization is perception, Heidegger does not wish to endorse the primacy of perception. See his comment that "the closest kind of dealing is not mere perceptual cognition, but, rather, a handling, using, and taking care" (Heidegger 2010: 67). He is suggesting that Husserl's phenomenology is too much oriented on perception as 'mere looking.'

4 See Heidegger's comments (2010: 142–3) where he negatively refers to "mere intuition" in a way to prepare for a critique both of Husserlian phenomenology and Greek metaphysics and epistemology.

5 See Dreyfus' commentary on *Being and Time* (Dreyfus 1991). Attention to this aspect of Heidegger's account has led to a pragmatist reading of the text. Perhaps the most notable pragmatist appropriation of the text is that by Richard Rorty. The priority of the handy over the objectively observed has led Dreyfus to challenge John McDowell's understanding of the conceptuality of experience. The ensuing debate with commentary from other prominent philosophers can be found in Schear 2013.

6 This formulation is close to that of Charles Taylor (1995). See also Taylor's more recent consideration of this, "Retrieving Realism" in Schear 2013: 61–90.

7 Stephen Crowell (2001, 2013) provides an excellent discussion of the transcendental character of phenomenology for Husserl and Heidegger. See also his edited volume with Jeff Malpas (2007) in which Dermot Moran directly addresses the relation of the transcendental phenomenological projects of Husserl and Heidegger.

8 The precise character of how it 'rests' on Husserl's account is contested. See Dostal 1993 and Neumann 2012.

9 The concept of horizon can be found in many of Husserl's works. The concept of *das Man* ('the one' – poorly translated as 'the they') and the distinction of the *zuhanden* and *vorhanden* can be found in Husserl's *Ideen II*, with which Husserl provided Heidegger as an unpublished manuscript and which Heidegger explicitly refers to in *Being and Time* and in his lectures of that period. See the comment in the "Introduction" to *Being and Time* in which Heidegger refers to Husserl's interpretation of personality and footnotes the fact that the work has "not yet been published"(Heidegger 2010: 46). See Rudolf Bernet's discussion (Bernet 2009) of Heidegger's reception of *Ideen II*.

10 In both the *Cartesian Meditations* and *The Crisis of the European Sciences and Transcendental Phenomenology* Husserl discusses how the Cartesian starting point might provide a starting point for transcendental phenomenology, but also in both texts he shows the inadequacy of Cartesianism.

11 Gadamer 1989: xxxvi.

12 For interpretations of the noema as an intermediate third between the subject and the object, see Dreyfus and Hall 1982; see especially the contributions by Dreyfus and Dagfinn Føllesdal. Robert Sokolowski (2000), J.N. Mohanty (1997), and John Drummond (1990) are among those that oppose this view.

13 At the time of the publication of *Being and Time* Heidegger edited the publication of Husserl's early lectures on time: *Toward a Phenomenology of Internal Time Consciousness*.

14 Heidegger 2010: 341: "And just as praxis has its own specific sight ('theory'), theoretical research is not without its own praxis."

15 Taylor Carmen (2003) writes about the "abyss" between these two thinkers and argues that Heidegger's break with and criticisms of Husserl are fundamental. Dreyfus also sees the differences as basic.

16 Some of the many commentators who have emphasized the continuity of Heideggerian phenomenology with Husserlian phenomenology include Steven Crowell, Daniel Dahlstrom, Jacques Taminaux, and Rudolf Bernet. See the contributions of these last three in Kisiel and van Buren 1994.

17 Oskar Becker, a close colleague of Husserl's and Heidegger's in the 1920s, writes in 1929 of hermeneutical phenomenology that it is the "further concretization of the transcendental-idealistic position of the *Ideas*" (in Gadamer 1976: 157).

18 Gadamer, who studied with both Heidegger and Husserl in the 1920s, writes of the convergence of Husserl's doctrine of the life-world and Heidegger's account of world and concludes by saying that the question as to who was the initiator and who the follower "remains undecided" (Gadamer 1976: 156).

19 Here the later Husserl claims hermeneutics for his project, if only by way of a brief mention. In the 1930s Heidegger makes a reference to "pre-hermeneutical phenomenology" by which he is clearly referring to Husserl's phenomenology and thereby identifying his own particular phenomenological approach as hermeneutical. See Heidegger 1989: 188.

20 See Dahlstrom 1994 and Prufer 1993. It should also be noted that there were others, like Eugen Fink and Ludwig Landgrebe, who may have influenced Husserl's development.

21 Blattner 2007: 239. Others like Nicholas H. Smith (2002: 42) do not see a problem here: "I take hermeneutic reflection to be continuous with phenomenological description."

22 Some commentators take Heidegger at his word; that is, that Heidegger abandons hermeneutics. Others claim that Heidegger's work remains hermeneutical, though he abandons the label. Claudius Strube (1993) and Hubert Dreyfus (1984) are among those that take him at his word. Those who argue that Heidegger's *opus* is hermeneutical throughout include Otto Pöggeler (1983) and Jean Grondin (2003). By "hermeneutical" they mean the central importance of history and historicity. For a good overview of this question see Zaborowski 2011.

23 The exclusion of "what we do" is the exclusion of the empirical and demarcates what is properly philosophical from the empirical. The exclusion of "what we ought to do" is the exclusion of the methodological. The reference to "what happens to us" is an appropriation of the Heideggerian concept of an 'event' (*Ereignis*).

24 Though this theme pervades Gadamer's work, two essays (in Gadamer 1981) devoted to the practical character of hermeneutics are "Hermeneutics as Practical Philosophy" and "Hermeneutics as a Theoretical and Practical Task."

25 'Communal' might be a better word here than 'social.' The word 'social' never appears in *Being and Time* but 'being-with' is a basic existentialia or characteristic of *Dasein*. The word 'community' appears once as an important aspect of authentic *Dasein* (Heidegger 2010: 366).

26 For a somewhat more detailed account of Seebohm's hermeneutics in relation to Gadamer, see Dostal (2004), and Seebohm's response in the same issue.

Bibliography

Bernet, R. (1990) "Husserl and Heidegger on Intentionality and Being," *Journal of the British Society for Phenomenology* 21: 136–52.

——(2009) "Leiblichkeit bei Husserl und Heidegger," *Heidegger und Husserl: Neue Perspektiven*, Frankfurt a.M.: Vittorio Klosterman, 43–72.

Blattner, W. (2007) "Ontology, the A Priori, and the Primacy of Practice," in S. Crowell & J. Malpas, eds., *Transcendental Heidegger*, Stanford: Stanford University Press, 10–27.

Carmen, T. (2003) *Heidegger's Analytic*, New York: Cambridge University Press.

Crowell, S. (2001) *Husserl, Heidegger and the Space of Meaning: Paths Toward Transcendental Phenomenology*, Evanston: Northwestern University Press.

——(2013) *Normativity and Phenomenology in Husserl and Heidegger*, New York: Cambridge University Press.

Crowell, S. & Malpas, J., eds. (2007) *Transcendental Heidegger*, Stanford: Stanford University Press.

Dahlstrom, D. (1994) "Heidegger's Critique of Husserl," *Reading Heidegger from the Start*, Albany: SUNY Press.

Dostal, R. (1993) "Time and Phenomenology in Husserl and Heidegger," in C. Guignon, ed., *The Cambridge Companion to Heidegger*, New York: Cambridge University Press, 135–50.

——(2004) "Seebohm's Hermeneutics and Gadamer," *International Journal of Philosophical Studies* 16: 719–29.

Dreyfus, H. (1984) "Beyond Hermeneutics: Interpretation in Late Heidegger and Recent Foucault," *Hermeneutics: Questions and Prospects*, Amherst: University of Massachusetts Press.

——(1991) *Being-in-the-World*, Cambridge, Mass: MIT Press.

Dreyfus, H. & Hall, H., eds. (1982) *Husserl, Intentionality and Cognitive Science*, Cambridge, Mass.: MIT Press.

Drummond, J. (1990) *Husserlian Intentionality and Non-Foundational Realism: Noema and Object*, Boston: Kluwer.

Gadamer, H-G. (1976) "The Phenomenological Movement," *Philosophical Hermeneutics*, Berkeley: University of California Press.

——(1981) *Reason in the Age of Science*, trans. F. Lawrence, Cambridge, Mass.: MIT Press.

——(1989) *Truth and Method*, New York: Continuum.

——(1997) "Reflections on My Philosophical Journey," in L. Hahn, *The Philosophy of Hans-Georg Gadamer*, Chicago: Open Court, 46–7.

Grondin, J. (2003) "Stichwort: Hermeneutik. Selbstauslegung und Seinsverstehen," in D. Thoma, ed., *Heidegger-Handbuch*, Stuttgart: J.B. Metzler, 47–51.

Guignon, C., ed. (1993) *The Cambridge Companion to Heidegger*, New York: Cambridge University Press.

Hahn, L. (1997) *The Philosophy of Hans-Georg Gadamer*, Chicago: Open Court.

Heidegger, M. (1971) *On the Way to Language*, New York: Harper & Row.

——(1977) *Basic Writings*, ed. D. Krell, New York: Harper & Row.

——(1982) *The Basic Problems of Phenomenology*, Bloomington: Indiana University Press.

——(1989) *Beiträge zur Philosophie, Gesamtausgabe 65*, Frankfurt a.M.: Vittorio Klosterman.

——(2010) *Being and Time*, trans. J. Stambaugh, Albany: SUNY.

Husserl, E. (1997) "Phenomenology and Anthropology," *Collected Works VI: Psychological and Transcencental Phenomenology and the Confrotnation with Heidegger*, trans. & ed. T. Sheehan & R. Palmer, Boston: Kluwer.

Kisiel, T. & van Buren, J., eds. (1994) *Reading Heidegger From the Start*, Albany: SUNY Press.

Merleau-Ponty, M. (1962) *The Phenomenology of Perception*, trans. Colin Smith, New York: Humanities Press.

Mohanty, J. (1997) *Between Essentialism and Transcendental Philosophy*, Evanston: Northwestern University Press.

Moran, D. (2007) "Heidegger's Transcendental Phenomenology in Light of Husserl's Project of First Philosophy," in S. Crowell & J. Malpas, eds., *Transcendental Heidegger*, Stanford: Stanford University Press, 135–50.

Neumann, G. (2012) "Phänomenologie der Zeit und der Zeitlichkeit bei Husserl und Heidegger," in R. Bernet, A. Denker, & H. Zaborowski, eds., *Heidegger Jahrbuch 6: Heidegger und Husserl*, Freiburg: Karl Alber, 153–86.

Noë, A. (2009) *Out of Our Heads*, New York: Hill and Wang.

Pöggeler, O. (1983) *Heidegger und die hermeneutische Philosophie*, Freiburg: Karl Alber.

Prufer, T. (1993) "Husserl, Heidegger, Early and Late, and Aquinas," *Recapitulations*, Washington, D.C.: The Catholic University of America Press.

Ricoeur, P. (1981) *Hermeneutics and the Human Sciences*, ed. J. Thompson, New York: Cambridge University Press.

Schear, J., ed. (2013) *Mind, Reason, and Being-in-the-World: The McDowell–Dreyfus Debate*, New York: Routledge.

Seebohm, T. (2004) *Hermeneutics: Method and Methodology*, Boston: Kluwer.

Williams, B. (2002) *Truth and Truthfulness*, Princeton: Princeton University Press.

Sokolowski, R. (2000) *Introduction to Phenomenology*, New York: Cambridge University Press.

Smith, N. (2002) "Overcoming Representationalism," *Perspectives on the Philosophy of Charles Taylor*, ed. A. Laitenen & N. Smith, Helsinki: Societas Philosophica Fennica.

Strube, C. (1993) *Zur Vorgeschichte der hermeneutische Philosophie*, Würzburg: Königshausen & Neumann.

Taylor, C. (1995) "Overcoming Epistemology," *Philosophical Arguments*, Cambridge, Mass.: Harvard University Press, 1–19.

Zaborowski, H. (2011) "Heidegger's Hermeneutics: Towards a New Practice of Understanding," in D. Dahlstrom, ed., *Interpreting Heidegger: Critical Essays*, New York: Cambridge University Press, 15–41.

46

HERMENEUTICS AND DECONSTRUCTION

Donatella Di Cesare

The first meeting between Gadamer and Derrida took place from April 25 to 27 in 1981, in the "Goethe Institut" in Paris. The aim was a public debate between the main representatives of continental philosophy. But both participants and witnesses were unanimous in speaking of the event as a conversation between deaf people, and the essays published a little later in Germany and France seem to confirm this impression (Forget 1984). Nevertheless this "unlikely debate" – as Philippe Forget described it – was epoch-making. The 1989 American edition, entitled *Dialogue and Deconstruction: The Gadamer-Derrida-Encounter*, contains new essays by philosophers from both parties (see Michelfelder and Palmer 1989).[1]

The legitimate question of the difference between hermeneutics and deconstruction was left open, even after the Paris meeting. It is not by chance that the debate continued primarily in North America, where the proximity of both philosophical streams led to doubts on the possibility of identifying different positions behind the two different labels (see Silverman and Ihde 1985; Caputo, Nehamas and Silverman 1986: 678–92; see also Nicholson 1986: 263–74; Behler 1987: 201–23; Froman 1991: 136–48; Grondin 1999: 5–16).

On the other hand, the common provenance of hermeneutics and deconstruction appears clear (see Kimmerle 1991: 223–35; Tholen 1999; Gasche 2000a: 137–50; Feldman 2000: 51–70; see also Bertram 2002: 9–23, 219–21; Störmer 2002; Jankovic 2003; Angehrn 2003). Both have followed the way opened by Heidegger's philosophical turn. Both refer to another philosopher whose presence, in both camps, is still rarely discussed, namely Hegel. Both, albeit on different paths, go back to Greek philosophy in which they find an inexhaustible source – a trait that is not obvious in the contemporary panorama. Their historical-philosophical as well as philosophical-theoretical proximity is reflected in the themes they share. It is sufficient to think of the importance of art, and above all of literature and poetry (see Di Cesare 2012: 137–84; 2013: 202 ff.).

But the question is more complex. These two principle streams of contemporary European philosophy, so close to each other as to be confused for two aspects of the same project, represent different philosophical options and therefore demand to carefully clarify and weigh this difference.

Thus the question raised in the North American context in the 1980s has still lost none of its relevance: *how hermeneutic is deconstruction and how deconstructive is hermeneutics?*

The two protagonists, Gadamer and Derrida, profiling their position the one in relation to the other, have thus confirmed during the time both the legitimacy and the need of the dialogue. But neither of them has actually brought it to the end. Indeed, the dialogue has failed from the start.

It seems that the debate at first leaves deeper traces in Gadamer's thinking, since he accepts Derrida's challenge and changes his position, or makes it more detailed and explicit, in several essays (see especially Michelfelder and Palmer 1989; also Gadamer 2006: 372–406). Gadamer clearly expresses, in these essays, how seriously he takes the debate and reveals, above all, his esteem for the French philosopher. In Derrida he recognizes one of the most important names he encountered after the publication of *Truth and Method*:

> Back in the 1960s, when I had finished up my own project in philosophical hermeneutics and offered it to the public, I paused to take a look at the world around me. At that time, two important things struck me, in addition to the works of the later Wittgenstein. The first of these was that I met the poet Paul Celan, in whose late works I began to immerse myself. The other was the fact that Derrida's essay, "Ousia et Grammé," published in the *Festschrift for Beaufret*, came into my hands, followed later by the several important books that Derrida published in 1967 which I immediately began to study.
>
> (Gadamer 2006: 377)

For his part, Derrida only occasionally engaged hermeneutics, and when he did it was especially to emphasize the difference between deconstruction and hermeneutics (see Gasche 1994). But one year after Gadamer's death, on February 15, 2003, Derrida gave a memorial address in Heidelberg entitled "Rams: Uninterrupted Dialogue between Two Infinities, the Poem" (Derrida 2005: 135–64).

From the "strange interruption" of that time, in Paris, Derrida takes up again the "uninterrupted dialogue," that "encounter" or "clash" between two rams, alluding to the thread of the poem that has joined them. He welcomes the word "dialogue" in his vocabulary in order to announce an unexpected interpretation: that "improbable debate" has been "successful," contrary to what most believed – and precisely because of the interruption, which has not been an "originary misunderstanding," but an "*epoché* that made one hold one's breath, without judgment or conclusion" (Derrida 2005: 136). Thus it has left behind a living and provocative trace, promised more than one future. By taking up again the uninterrupted dialogue Derrida relaunches the topic of "interruption," which had already emerged in the Paris encounter, but which had afterwards remained in the shadows. Thus he indicates, even if just indirectly, less in the proverbial opposition between orality and writing and more in the *question of understanding*, that motif which had guided the debate and which could still illuminate the distance and the proximity between both philosophies. For in the topics the understanding becomes clear how hermeneutics moves from unity and how deconstruction proceeds from difference.

When Gadamer holds his opening address in Paris, which was published later with the title "Text und Interpretation," he seems most concerned to take distance from French philosophy in general and deconstruction in particular through the conception of the "text" (Gadamer 2006: 156–91). He advocates the need to give voice to the text, in order to highlight its "unity of sense" and to lead it back to the dialogue from which it originally springs (Gadamer 1986–95: 2, 355). His unquestionable reversions to the "language of metaphysics" – Gadamer speaks for example of the "task of understanding" – must have sounded like a provocation to Derrida's ears. Gadamer reaches the limit when he speaks of the "goodwill to try to understand one another," and with these words provokes the discussion (Gadamer 2006: 174).[2]

It is not surprising that Derrida responds on the next day with three short questions that aim to put in question the entire hermeneutics and that converge to a single goal. Behind the efforts of hermeneutics to understand the other, behind its "appeal to goodwill," lies Nietzsche's "will to power."[3] Already with his first question, Derrida charges hermeneutics with a relapse into metaphysics. The will to understand, which precedes every concrete interaction between speakers, shows for Derrida the outlines of an ethical axiom that would equate Gadamer's good will to understand with Kant's "good will." Would not the good will to understand, which is as axiomatic and unconditioned as the "absolute value" of Kant's will, be simply a new version of metaphysical "subjectivity," which would be ready, following Heidegger's expressed suspicions, to dominate the Being?

With the second question Derrida appeals to psychoanalysis, which is of course a borderline case, but nevertheless paradigmatic for abandoning "good will" and so bears witness to the failure of the "living dialogue." Habermas had already recognized a problematic limit in psychoanalysis and expressed his doubts about the possibility to integrate it into a general hermeneutics. For his part, Derrida emphasizes that the psychoanalytic discourse lets the widest interpretative context explode that Gadamer suggests. Therefore he requires a kind of productive interpretation that would at first occur through a "rupture."

It is around the concept of rupture, or better, of interruption that Derrida's third, philosophically decisive question turns. In question here is what Gadamer calls *Verstehen*, "understanding." One would have to ask, according to Derrida, whether the condition of understanding would not be the limitless readiness for dialogue, the continuous relation to the other, but instead "the interruption of rapport, a certain rapport of interruption, the suspending of all mediation" (Derrida, in Forget 1984: 58). The suspicion of deconstruction overtakes the hermeneutic dialogue. Deconstruction seems to offer an alternative view, because it prefers the interruption, maintains dissonance, preserves the difference and the otherness of the other, which cannot be appropriated, as well as the impossibility of understanding.

Gadamer answers with an equally brief paper entitled "Und dennoch: Macht des guten Willens" (Gadamer, in Forget 1984: 59–61; 55–7). He lets the contradictions in Derrida's position appear by using the classic argument against the skeptics: "I am finding it difficult to understand these questions that have been addressed to me. But I will make an effort, as anyone would do who wants to understand the another or be understood by the other" (Gadamer, in Michelfelder and Palmer 1989: 55).

However, this "effort" has nothing to do with metaphysics or with Kant's "good will." Gadamer would much rather draw on the Platonic Socrates, who explains in the *Gorgias* (458a) that it would be better to be refuted than to refute. This principle, in which hermeneutics recognizes itself, is however not an ethical instance. "Even immoral beings try to understand one another" (Gadamer, in Michelfelder and Palmer 1989: 55). Thus it is a matter of a phenomenological position describing the everyday practices of speaking and understanding. Whoever opens their mouth to speak would like to be understood – unless the speaker wants to hide something. Derrida and Nietzsche do not constitute exceptions: "both speak and write in order to be understood" (Gadamer, in Michelfelder and Palmer 1989: 57).[4] But this in no way means that non-understanding and misunderstanding could be eliminated. Gadamer agrees with Derrida, that there is no unbroken understanding. The psychoanalytic dialogue, which aims to understand not what the speaker wants to say, but what the speaker does not want to say, is an extreme manifestation of such a *rupture*, of such a break.

Philosophical hermeneutics has often been misunderstood in its attempt to raise the question of understanding within philosophy. According to hermeneutics, understanding would be an appropriation of the other. Animated by a "fury of understanding", hermeneutics seems to claim that it could and should understand all in a complete and perfect way (see Hörisch 1988). From this perspective, understanding would be obvious. If this were so, however, hermeneutics would have no reason to exist, since if it exists, it is in order to raise the philosophical question about understanding.

According to Heidegger understanding is the originary way in which the Dasein succeeds. Gadamer maintains, on his turn, that *agreement ... is more primordial than misunderstanding.*"[5] This "agreement" is neither a matter of glib optimism nor of simply adopting an ethical task. On the contrary, with this thesis Gadamer describes in phenomenological terms the practice of speaking and understanding. For a *more originary understanding* is nothing else than the consent of the shared language that communalizes. Whoever speaks in a historical language – and in doing so speaks for the other and with the other – assents, even before any consent, by being ready to attune one's own voice to the voice of the other, articulating oneself in the meaningful sounds of the common language. In short, whoever speaks has already agreed to share what is common and communicable with the speakers of that language, has already agreed with the other, even before himself. It is in this sense that Gadamer interprets the *syntheke* of Aristotle: "the concept of 'syntheke,' of mutual agreement, suggests in the first place the view that language forms itself in the being with one another (LL 12 / Gadamer 1986–95: 8, 354 – see Aristotle 1961: 16a 19). The assent is the *prelude of language*, and sets in motion every further play of agreement and disagreement. This prelude cannot be avoided: every speaker must enter into the play of language, accepting the originary communality that language assures. To speak means, then, to re-articulate the commonalities of the world articulated in language. This is the reality of human communication, that is, of dialogue.

Yet the flow of dialogue can be interrupted and agreement can also turn into disagreement. In this context Gadamer speaks of a "stumbling block" (Gadamer 1994: 270). Almost completely overlooked by the reception, the "stumbling block" is a key concept for hermeneutics, because it clarifies the movement of understanding (Gadamer 2006: 93). Without it, one might assume that understanding is self-generated. In order to delineate the concept of a stumbling block more precisely, Gadamer returns to Greek philosophy:

> The Greeks had a very beautiful word for what brings our understanding to a standstill, they called it the *atopon*. That actually means: the unplaceable, whatever cannot be brought into the schematism of our horizon of understanding and therefore causes us to halt.
>
> (Gadamer 2006: 93)

The *atopon* is whatever provokes uneasiness and irritation, what seems strange, uncanny and alien. In the Platonic dialogues it is Socrates who is *atopos*, the philosopher who, being out of place, puts into question the order of the *polis* and points to an *ou-topos*, a place to come. For hermeneutics the *atopon* is the incomprehensible that breaks in on what was once understood, and almost entirely forgotten, has been taken for granted as self-evident. Thus the *atopon* strikes language's apparent familiarity, puts suddenly in question the commonality of the words. The non-understandable, which has still not taken place, gives rise to both non-understanding and misunderstanding. This does not, however, prevent attempts to continue to interpret in order to seek agreement again – without excluding disagreement.

Where, then, does the distance lie between Gadamer and Derrida, if not in the need for the interruption? For hermeneutics interruption is not fundamental and originary, because the prelude of language always takes precedence. Thus interruption is already inscribed in the constellation of language, since it is the difference that engraves that unity. Here hermeneutics shows its proximity to the critique of ideology (see Habermas 1987: 198). A still greater distance from deconstruction is shown in the conception of the rupture. Even where the rupture is more noticeable and the collision more violent, as in the work of art and above all in the poetic text, hermeneutics takes up this collision but doesn't strengthen it, just as it also does not deepen it. Rather it acts in the reverse way: for hermeneutics the interruption opens the conversation, but does not close it off. Though it may know that the rupture never heals, that non-understanding is never eliminated, hermeneutics itself is destined to an infinite dialogue. This is, by the way, the position that Gadamer also takes up in the debate with Derrida. One year after the encounter in Paris, Gadamer writes: "Whoever wants me to take deconstruction to heart and insists on difference stands at the beginning of a conversation, not at its end" (Gadamer, in Michelfelder and Palmer 1989: 113).

The distance between hermeneutics and deconstruction, in other words, does not lie in the good will to understand, but in understanding itself, in the way in which understanding follows from either the *unity of the uninterrupted dialogue* or from the *difference of the interruption*. For Gadamer, the one perspective points to the other. After Heidegger's attempt to dismantle the language of metaphysics there are for Gadamer only two ways, or perhaps one common path, which could still lead into the openness of philosophical experience: the path of hermeneutics, which goes from dialectics back to dialogue, and the path of deconstruction, which in *écriture* provokes the laceration of metaphysics (Michelfelder and Palmer 1989: 108).

Gadamer's *Truth and Method* carries out the turn to language following the model of writing rather than that of orality. Though he will claim the opposite, Gadamer starts from the interpretation of the text in order to go back to dialogue and to then reach the universality of language (Gadamer 1994: 383–9). This path is unavoidable, because history is transmitted in the "medium" of language; in other words, language is the happening of history. Here the linguistic character of understanding emerges, which is "*the concretion of historically effected consciousness*" (Gadamer 1994: 389). It is true that there are "fragments of the past"; but what tradition hands down to us as spoken, or better, written language is quite another matter (Gadamer 1986–95: 8, 260). In as much as what is written goes beyond all finite particularity, it allows anybody to participate in the transmission of the past. Historically effective consciousness is a reading consciousness (Gadamer 1994: 389–95).

But what is the relationship between orality and writing? What is the place of the voice? And what role does the text play? Gadamer's complex position on these questions has changed over the years as a result of his debate with Derrida. This also led Gadamer to distance himself from Plato. His position can be summarized in the thesis of an inseparable connection between orality and writing: "In truth there is no real opposition. What is written must be read and therefore all that is written is 'subordinated to the voice'" (Gadamer 1997: 403–4).

Gadamer does not share Plato's "one-sided" condemnation of writing in the *Phaedrus* (274b–278e) and in the excursus of the *Seventh Letter* (Gadamer 1986–95: 7, 228–69). He takes Plato's argument about the peculiar "weakness" of all written language to be an "ironic exaggeration." Nor does he accept the thought, expressed in the *Protagoras*, that written language is resistant to dialogue (Gadamer 1994: 393). For Gadamer the text *speaks* in responding to the questions a reader puts to it. Gadamer does not give up the idea that the text is a partner in a dialogue. Hermeneutics itself is just this "coming into conversation with the text" (Gadamer 1994: 368). Without ignoring the asymmetry between a written and an oral dialogue, when an embodied other is present, Gadamer nevertheless emphasizes the *continuity* between the oral and the written. The boundaries are fluid: what is written is voice-like and can at any time become oral again; what is oral, insofar as it is language, can always potentially be written, or is always "destined for writing," as Gadamer argues in his 1983 essay, "Unterwegs zur Schrift?" (Gadamer 1986–95: 7, 258–69). In other words: orality is potentially always already given in writing, and writing is potentially always already given in orality.

The transition from the oral to the written occurs through *reading*. Here the distance from Derrida emerges clearly. *Lécture*, reading, becomes a paradigm that is implicitly opposed to *écriture*, writing. And it is not by chance that the paradigm of reading, which is described as letting-speak or giving-voice-to, is ultimately expanded so far that it coincides with hermeneutics. "What is writing, if it is not read?" (Michelfelder and Palmer 1989: 97). Gadamer poses this question to Derrida. "Writing is a phenomenon of language only insofar as it is read" (Gadamer 1986–95: 8, 264). Writing is just as voice-like (*stimmlich*) as speech is potentially writing (*schriftfähig*). How can one avoid vocalizing the writing while reading or articulating it with the voice?

In 1981 Gadamer published an essay with the programmatic and significant title, "Voice and Language" (Gadamer 1986–95: 8, 258–70). Here he answers Derrida's objections and develops his own conception of the *voice*, which therefore comes to play a key role in the debate between hermeneutics and deconstruction. The voice is, in a certain sense, a bridge launched to the *écriture*. If writing is not an "image of the voice," then the voice is not an image of writing (Gadamer 2006: 388). But what do articulated writing and voice have in common?

Plato had already asked this question in a passage of the *Philebus* (14c–18d) which will be decisive for dialectics, because it concerns the relation between the one and the many. Both the sounds articulated by the voice and the letters of the alphabet are given as examples. In the end, however, it becomes clear that both, far from being mere examples, are precisely what reveal the unity of the many and the multiplicity of the one in the *lógos*. The voice reveals our incompleteness and finitude, because we cannot master it and we are thus referred back to the *méson*, to what is in the "middle," that is to those "elements," articulated sounds and written signs, that mark the limits in the phonic continuum and so enable us to speak *and* to write. Both are constants that open up a "field of play" (*Spielraum*) which is bound nevertheless to the *articuli*, to the limits carved into the boundlessness of phonic and graphic material (Gadamer 1986–95: 8, 259). Articulation is therefore the reciprocal link between voice and writing, a link that sheds light on the passage accomplished by reading. In contrast to every natural form of expression, speaking and writing are in fact an assenting in what is held in common, starting with the shared fields of play both of the letters and articulated sounds in any language.

Yet the voice for Gadamer has "both the first and the last word," and here lies his distance from Derrida (LL 34 / Gadamer 1986–95: 8, 419). But this does not mean that the voice, for Gadamer, has superiority. The voice is the continuous unity of speaking, whereas writing is characterized by the difference of interruption. It is "a phase in the event of understanding," which is fixed in the text (Michelfelder and Palmer 1989: 21–51, 30). This fixity is, however, not definitive, and the text becomes that "between" which interrupts the continuity of the voice (see Risser 1991, 93–105, 102–5). This finds an echo in the figure of the reader, who as *inter-pres* is the interlocutor. The "eminent text" of literature is no exception (Michelfelder and Palmer 1989: 40). It demands to achieve a voice again. In the circular continuity of the voice the text traces the discontinuity. Since hermeneutics is a philosophy which emphasizes unity over difference, continuity over discontinuity, it favors the voice.

If it is impossible, after Derrida, to rethink writing, that which remains problematic is the voice. In the 1960s Gadamer was powerfully impressed, as he himself pointed out, not only by *Ousia and grammé*, but above all by the little book *Speech and Phenomena* (Gadamer 2006: 377). Derrida had "rightfully criticized Husserl in this book," by putting into question the self-conscious *cogito* that presumes it can think without signs (LL 33). Gadamer does not put into question Derrida's critique of Western metaphysics – the critique based on the supposed logocentrism (though it might better be called the "monologocentrism") of metaphysics. His doubts concern rather Derrida's condemnation of the voice and, more precisely, the link that Derrida claims to find between the *voice* and the *self-presence* of consciousness (Michelfelder and Palmer 1989: 112). Even though Gadamer has never advanced a thorough critique, his objection to Derrida is easy to summarize. Voice, so readily denounced for its presumed metaphysics of presence, is the phenomenological voice, the "spiritual flesh" that hears itself in the absence of world (Derrida 1973: 59). But it is not clear why this should be so, both for the voice in its physicality and in its relation to articulation, that is, to writing. This voice should indeed be a form of exile no less than writing. In other words, for hermeneutics, difference also engraves the voice. The possibility that what is evoked may regain a voice in no way eliminates the reference to its absence (Michelfelder and Palmer 1989: 112–13). This reference is the space of difference in the voice. On the other hand, the hermeneutic voice is first of all the voice of the other, the voice I hear before I hear my own. This voice carries the difference of the other, that is, of the you, into what would only be the identity of a self-presence. Nor should it be forgotten that presence is also simultaneously an absence, both for hermeneutics and for deconstruction; it is never a pure, full and perfect presence which could suddenly occur without past or future. It is the presence of an absence that is spoken by the voice or testified by the writing.

It remains an open question whether the hermeneutic voice can be accused of relying on the metaphysics of presence, or whether, by contrast, deconstruction, with its critique of phenomenology, on its turn succumbs to an objectivistic conception of presence understood mainly as permanence. Certainly, Gadamer has been moved, after Derrida, by the aim to let the voice reemerge from its concealment, that is, not in order to restore its central position, but to emphasize the co-belonging of voice and writing through articulation.

There are other points in which Gadamer's later hermeneutics appears almost to overlap with Derrida's deconstruction. In the last subsection of *Truth and Method*, which concerns the universal aspect of hermeneutics, Gadamer addressed the meaning of "the turn" from being to language with one of his most famous and widely cited passages: *"Being that can be understood is language"* (Gadamer 1994: 474). This is also, however, among Gadamer's most misunderstood statements, because it has been read as an identification of being with language. Yet Gadamer never argues such identification. It is not by chance that Heidegger's famous metaphor of language as the "house of Being" does not appear in his work. More than the house of Being, language is for Gadamer that human dwelling that is often a cramped shell. The mother tongue, for Gadamer, is the most familiar being-by-oneself, but starting from an even more fundamental uncanniness (Gadamer 1986–95: 8, 366–72). For language appears so "uncannily near" (*unheimlich nahe*) that it belongs among the "most mysterious questions that man ponders" (Gadamer 1994: 378). The most well known version of hermeneutics is the most urbanized one, which emphasizes the familiar. But to this should be added the more disquieting version, which emphasizes the unfamiliar, the uncanny. The fleeting and ephemeral home that language offers us can be achieved every time from that homelessness which defines our finitude in the language, even before our finitude in the world.

"Language is dialogue" (Gadamer 1986–95: 8, 369). Gadamer formulates this thesis as early as *Plato's Dialectical Ethics*, returns to it in *Truth and Method*, and takes it up again in his late works (PDE 35–65 / Gadamer 1986–95: 5, 27–48; Gadamer 1994: 446, Gadamer 1986–95: 1, 449; Gadamer 1986–95: 2, 207; Gadamer 1986–95: 8, 360). The hermeneutics of language unfolds as hermeneutics of dialogue. If language arises from the openness of a historical language and realizes itself as individual speech, which for its part is always a speaking for or with the other, then the existence of language lies in dialogue. This is the secret core of Gadamer's philosophy which, both in its theoretical aspiration and in its practical aim, is a philosophy of dialogue.

At the basis of this thesis there lies, however, a philosophical motivation that should not be overlooked. Gadamer offers here a radical interpretation of Hölderlin's verse: "Since we have been a conversation ... " (Hölderlin 1992: 1, 341). We don't simply participate in a dialogue. We are always already in dialogue and we speak from that infinite flow, in that infinite flow. Even more: we are dialogue. Not only are each of us in a dialogue, but on our turn we are, in our most intimate nature, dialogue. For dialogue is our *ubi consistam*; it is the hermeneutic universe in which we breathe, in which we live.

But what does it mean that dialogue is an infinite flow? Every word (*Wort*) opens up to an endless number of possible further words (*Antworte*), of answers that it calls for (Gadamer 1986–95: 8, 38). Since it speculatively reflects the unspoken, every spoken word cannot be the last word. Because of this virtuality, every word points toward that openness in which we continue to speak. Thus it can be said that "speaking proceeds from dialogue" (Gadamer 1986–95: 2, 198). The endlessness opened by the virtuality of the word is the endlessness of the dialogue. Hence dialogue has "an inner endlessness and no end" (Gadamer 1986–95: 2, 152).

Certainly, the dialogue can be interrupted for many reasons: one might have nothing more to say, become irritated or not want to continue speaking. But for hermeneutics the interruption is only a suspension, the prelude to the restart of dialogue. An interruption from outside might occur, but it in no way undermines that endless openness. According to Gadamer, even the limit-case of the soul's inner dialogue with itself is endless (Gadamer 1994: 547–8). This is one of the most significant points of dissonance between hermeneutics and deconstruction: whereas Derrida underlines the creativity of the interruption, Gadamer invokes and solicits – beyond all interruption – the endless, or better, the uninterrupted dialogue. This adjective, "uninterrupted," suggested by Derrida, seems to be the right one to designate Gadamer's dialogue. Even if the process of dialogue continues endlessly, it is discontinuous, that is, both ending and endless. Rather than endless, we might say from the perspective of interruption that dialogue is *un-interrupted*.

Hence the unlimited readiness for dialogue which characterizes hermeneutics and which is philosophically justified by the trust in language and its ability to establish community. This does not mean that dialogue will always succeed. On the contrary, agreement is never certain and understanding is never perfect. The dialogue cannot succeed, if success means conclusion, ending in a wordless, ultimate agreement. Dialogue never closes. Of course this does not mean that dialogue in its potential infinity does not reach a successful unity. But when can one then say that a dialogue has succeeded? Not certainly when we have learned something new, but rather when we come across the other to something new that we have not met before in our experience of the world. This something new changes and transforms us. Dialogue has a "transformative power" (Gadamer 1986–95: 2, 211). It is not a surplus of information. Important in the dialogue is the encounter with the you. Dialogue thus succeeds when the I has changed through the you, and the you has changed because of the other. "Conversation transforms both" (Gadamer 1986–95: 2, 188). After the dialogue one is no longer the same person as before. Paradoxically, a dialogue succeeds all the more, the less it comes to a close: the more the disagreements come to light, the more misunderstandings and non-understandings reemerge. Hence, the dialogue does not conclude, if the word, which the I addresses to the you and the you to the I, leads to a new openness, from which, through new questions and answers, the dialogue can go further (Gadamer 2006: 393). Even after death. Insofar as it itself is destined to an infinite dialogue, it is not surprising that hermeneutics, also, in its eschatological aspiration, declines itself in the word and conjugates itself in the dialogue.

In his memorial speech, "Béliers," Derrida again takes up the topic of interruption, which this time refers to a final interruption, the separation of life and death. What will become of the dialogue, after death has stamped its seal on it? Will there still be a dialogue after death? The dialogue continues, according to Derrida, and follows the traces in those who survive, who in the future will bring the voice of the dead friend to be heard. The promise and the obligation find their expression in the verse of the poet who brought the two philosophers together: Paul Celan. "The world is gone, I must carry you" (Celan 1986: 97). The topic of death is interweaved here with the topic of dialogue, but also with the topic of the poem. Two works by Gadamer stand in the background: *Poem and Conversation* and *Who am I and Who are You?* The death of the other is "the world after the end of the world" (Derrida 2005: 140). The surviving one remains alone, robbed of the world of the other, remains in the world outside of the world, responsible alone and thereby determined to carry both the other and her/his world further. As Heidegger had pointed to the nearness of "thinking" (*Denken*) to "thanking" (*Danken*), Derrida draws together "thinking" (*penser*) and "weighing" (*peser*). In order to think and to weigh, also in the sense of bearing a weight, one must therefore carry; carry within oneself and on oneself. Yet:

> to carry now no longer has the meaning of "to comprise" (*comporter*), to include, to comprehend in the self, but rather to carry oneself for bear oneself toward (*se porter vers*) the infinite inappropriability of the other, toward the encounter with its absolute transcendence in the very inside of me, that it to say, in me outside of me.
>
> (Derrida 2005: 161)

It means, above all, to transmit and translate what is untranslatable, what will remain as such, as an irreducible surplus, if that remainder of "unreadability" (*illegibilité*) will be preserved which hermeneutics has made possible and which makes hermeneutics possible. The commitment of deconstruction thus consists of *carrying* hermeneutics, and in the process of perceiving what is common to them and preserving the remainder of the difference. Unity and difference, difference and unity, offer in return the uncanny secret of their elusive reference. Between both infinities, Celan is the *tertium datur*, more than the point of convergence between them, a point of new orientation.

Notes

1 The volume includes essays by Fred Dallmayr, Josef Simon, James Risser, Charles Shepherdson, Gary B. Madison, Herman Rapaport, Donald G. Marshall, Richard Shusterman, David F. Krell, Robert Bernasconi, John Sallis, John D. Caputo, Neal Oxenhandler, and Gabe Eisenstein.

2 Originally in Forget 1984: 24–55. It is important to emphasize here that, in the entire oeuvre of Gadamer's writings, this expression only appears this once. What remained neglected in the discussion, however, is among other issues the concept of the "text," which is interpreted differently by Gadamer and Derrida, since Gadamer proceeds from the unity of the text. Derrida takes aim at precisely this presupposed unity – see Gasche 1989: 278–80.

3 Derrida's last statement in the Paris meeting circled around Nietzsche – see Forget 1984: 62–77. The target of Derrida's polemic is Heidegger's interpretation, according to which Nietzsche would be the last metaphysician. For Derrida it was, on the contrary, Heidegger who remained chained to a logocentric metaphysics, because he consistently asked about Being and about the meaning of Being. Heidegger thus presumed to be able to hold Being in a *logos*.

4 But Gadamer's attempt to derive Derrida's position form Nietzsche's is questionable. Gasché correctly warns of this (see Gasche 2000b: 183–93).

5 This thesis, which also appears in *Truth and Method*, is subsequently developed in Gadamer 2006: 96; Gadamer 1986–95: 2, 187; Gadamer 1986–95: 8, 354.

Bibliography

Angehrn, E. (2003), *Interpretation und Dekonstruktion. Untersuchungen zur Hermeneutik*, Verbrück: Weilerswist.

Aristotle (1961), *Aristotle's Categories and De Interpretatione*, trans. and ed. J. L. Ackrill, Clarendon Aristotle Series. Oxford: Clarendon Press.

Behler, E. (1987), "Deconstruction versus Hermeneutics: Derrida and Gadamer on Text and Interpretation," *Southern Humanities Review* 21: 201–23;

Bertram, G.W. (2002), *Hermeneutik und Dekonstruktion. Konturen einer Auseinandersetzung der Gegenwartsphilosophie*, München: Fink.

Caputo, J. D., A. Nehamas and H. Silverman (1986), "Symposium: Hermeneutics and Deconstruction," *Journal of Philosophy* 83: 678–92.

Celan, P. (1986), *Gesammelte Werke*, ed. Beda Allemann and Stefan Reichert with Rolf Bücher, Frankfurt: Suhrkamp.

Derrida, J. (1973), *Speech and Phenomena. An Essay on the Problem of the Sign in Husserl's Philosophy*, trans. David B. Allison, Evanston: Northwestern University Press.

——(2005), *Sovereignties in Question: The Poetics of Paul Celan*, trans. Thomas Dutoit and Out Pasanen, New York: Fordham University Press.

Di Cesare, D. (2012), *Utopia of Understanding: Between Babel and Auschwitz*, trans. Niall Keane, Albany: SUNY Press.

——(2013), *Gadamer: A Philosophical Portrait*, trans. Niall Keane, Bloomington: Indiana University.

Feldman, S. (2000), "Made For Each Other: The Interdependence of Deconstruction and Philosophical Hermeneutics," *Philosophy and Social Criticism* 26: 51–70.

Forget, Phillipe (ed.) (1984), *Text und Interpretation. Deutsch-französische Debatte mit Beiträgen von Jacques Derrida, Philippe Forget, Manfred Frank, Hans-Georg Gadamer, Jean Greisch und Francois Laruelle*, München: Fink UTB.

Froman, W.J. (1991) "L'Ecriture and Philosophical Hermeneutics," in *Gadamer and Hermeneutics*, ed. Hugh J. Silverman, pp.136–48, New York and London: Routledge.

Gadamer, Hans-Georg (1986–95) *Gesammelte Werke*, Tübingen: J. B. C. Mohr.

——(1994) *Truth and Method*, trans. Joel Weinsheimer and Donald G. Marshall, New York: Continuum.

——(1997), *The Philosophy of Hans-Georg Gadamer*, ed. Lewis E. Hahn, Chicago and La Salle: Open Court.

——(2006), *The Gadamer Reader: A Bouquet of the Later Writings*, ed. Richard Palmer, Evanston: Northwestern University Press.

Gasche, R. (1989), *The Tain of the Mirror*, Cambridge, MA: Harvard University Press.

——(1994), *Inventions of Difference. On Jacques Derrida*, Cambridge, MA: Harvard University Press.

——(2000a), "Deconstruction and Hermeneutics," in *Deconstructions. A User's Guide*, ed. Nicholas Royle, Houndmills: Palgrave, pp.137–50.

——(2000b), "Specters of Nietzsche," in *The Proceedings of the Twentieth World Congress of Philosophy*, vol. 8, *Contemporary Philosophy*, ed. Daniel O. Dahlstrom, Bowling Green: Philosophy Documentation Center, pp.183–93.

Grondin, J. (1999), "La définition derridienne de la deconstruction. Contribution au rapprochement de l'hermeneutique et de la deconstruction," *Archives de Philosophie* 62: 5–16.

Habermas, J. (1987), *The Philosophical Discorse of Modernity: Twelve Lectures*, trans. Frederick G. Lawrence, Cambridge, MA: MIT Press.

Hölderlin, F. (1992), *Saemtliche Werke und Briefe*, ed. Jochen Schmidt, Frankfurt/M: Deutscher Klassiker Verlag.

Hörisch, J. (1988), *Die Wut des Verstehens: Zur Kritik der Hermeneutik*, Frankfurt: Suhrkamp.

Jankovic, Z. (2003), *Au-dela du signe: Gadamer et Derrida. Le depassement hermeneutique et deconstructiviste du Dasein*, Paris: L'Harmattan.

Kimmerle, H. (1991), "Gadamer, Derrida und kein Ende," *Allgemeine Zeitschrift für Philosophie* 16: 223–35.

Michelfelder, D.P. and R.E. Palmer (eds.) (1989), *Dialogue and Deconstruction: The Gadamer-Derrida-Encounter*, Albany: SUNY Press.

Nicholson, G. (1986), "Deconstruction or Dialogue," *Man and World* 19: 263–74.

Risser, J. (1991), "Reading the Text," in *Gadamer and Hermeneutics*, ed. Hugh, J. Silverman, pp.93–105, New York and London: Routledge.

Silverman, H.J. and D. Ihde (eds.) (1985) *Hermeneutics and Deconstruction*, Albany: SUNY Press.

Störmer, F. (2002), *Hermeneutik und Dekonstruktion der Erinnerung. Über Gadamer, Derrida und Hölderlin*, München: Fink.

Tholen, T. (1999) *Erfahrung und Interpretation. Der Streit zwischen Hermeneutik und Dekonstruktion*, Heidelberg: Winter.

47

HERMENEUTICS AND CRITICAL THEORY

Nicholas H. Smith

One of the achievements of Hans-Georg Gadamer's *Truth and Method* was to make plausible the idea that hermeneutics constitutes a distinct body of thought, an intellectual tradition whose history of successes, stalemates, and defeats, heroes and villains, could be recounted in a single coherent narrative (Gadamer 1993). But the popularity of this idea, both in the sense of the number of people who came to accept it and the number who came to identify with the hermeneutic tradition itself, was due as much to a number of books published in the decades following the appearance of *Truth and Method* which either re-staged the central episodes of this history by way of the reproduction of canonical texts, or defended the newly reconstructed tradition against rival contemporary ones (Bleicher 1980; Hoy 1978; Mueller-Vollmer 1986; Ormiston and Schrift 1990; Thompson 1981; Warnke 1987). Indeed, the popularizing anthologies of the hermeneutic tradition typically left off where the more systematic defences of hermeneutics typically began: namely, with the sketches for a critical theory of society then being outlined by Jürgen Habermas and Karl-Otto Apel. These pieces were read either as the opening up of a new, politically progressive chapter in the history of hermeneutics – as the dawning of a 'critical hermeneutics', no less – or as representing a fundamental challenge to hermeneutics by exposing fatal flaws in its capacity to orient genuinely critical reflection. Either way, Habermas's and Apel's responses to *Truth and Method*, and Gadamer's subsequent rejoinders to them, made it seem obvious to many intellectuals in the 1960s and 1970s that the self-understandings of philosophical hermeneutics and the critical theory of society were intimately bound up with each other.[1]

That connection is not so obvious today. What has changed? If we restrict ourselves to considerations internal to the self-understanding of hermeneutics and critical theory, perhaps the most striking difference is that now there are many conceptions of how hermeneutics can perform a critical function, or serve progressive political purposes, just as there are many conceptions of how a critical theory of society can integrate the basic insights of hermeneutics. Given the degree of differentiation that has taken place within the traditions of hermeneutics and critical theory over the past three decades or so, it might seem more appropriate to uncouple their self-images. On the side of hermeneutics, there are, for example, those who credit its critical function and progressive nature to its insistent opposition to 'metaphysics', to its thoroughgoing anti-foundationalism and anti-essentialism (Rorty 1979; Caputo 1987; Vattimo 1988; Vattimo and Zabala 2011). For others, its critical dimension arises more from its focus on local, context-bound applications of norms (Walzer 1987). For others again, it is the framework hermeneutics provides for thinking about identity politics that supplies its radical edge (Warnke 2002).[2] On the critical theory side, Habermas himself came to rely less and less on the moment of hermeneutic reflection in his efforts to ground critical theory in a theory of communicative action; a trend that has been continued by others concerned to retain the universalist features of the ethics and politics associated with the theory (Cooke 2006; Forst 2013). Others have urged a return to the orientation developed in Adorno's work, with its focus on the problematic of 'identity-thinking' and the task of overcoming it (Bernstein 1995). And the most systematic attempt at rebuilding the foundations of critical theory in recent years, the theory of recognition developed above all by Axel Honneth, is aimed precisely *against* the 'linguistic turn' taken by Habermas and Apel – the turn, that is, inspired by their reading of Gadamer – and at first sight seems barely related to philosophical hermeneutics at all (Honneth 1995, 2007, 2009).

In light of such considerations, the special relationship enjoyed between hermeneutics and critical theory at the time of Habermas's debate with Gadamer seems to belong to the distant past; indeed, one might wonder if they still have anything particular to say to each other. Yet the appearance of distance between potential conversation-partners itself affords an excellent opportunity for hermeneutic reflection. And in the spirit of such reflection, I shall consider in what follows how the conversation between hermeneutics and critical theory might be productively continued today. My discussion will be divided into two parts. In the first part, I shall glance back at the Gadamer–Habermas debate in order to determine more precisely how their initial conversation came to a stop. In the second part, I shall suggest that an unfortunate legacy of the debate was an overly restricted conception of the hermeneutic field, a restriction operative but not always acknowledged in Habermas's and Gadamer's own stated views. Once this restriction is made explicit and overcome, so I argue in the remainder of the chapter, new possibilities for the simultaneous renewal of hermeneutics and critical theory open up, suggesting ways in which productive interaction between these traditions may resume.

As my main purpose here is to identify the precise points at which Gadamer's debate with Habermas came to a halt, for now I shall leave to one side the features of Gadamer's hermeneutics that Habermas sought to integrate into critical theory and shall address directly their fundamental points of disagreement.

Habermas's critique of Gadamer boils down to two core objections, plus a third one which is a consequence of these two, which lead him to the conclusion that the critical reflection that properly belongs to a critical theory of society departs decisively from hermeneutic reflection as Gadamer conceived it (Habermas 1980, 1983, 1988).

The first objection, which has since become something of a nostrum amongst scholars ill-disposed towards Gadamer's hermeneutics, is that Gadamer's hermeneutics leaves no room for genuinely *rational* reflection. This thought is provoked by Gadamer's description of the 'hermeneutic situation' and elements of his account of 'hermeneutic experience' (Gadamer 1993). In brief, the situation of the interpreter, according to Gadamer, is that of an agent oriented to reaching an understanding about a subject-matter, by way of anticipations and pre-conceptions which Gadamer chose to call 'prejudices' (*Vorurteil*), of which the agent is never fully aware. When the interpretation goes well – that is, when understanding is reached – the tradition in which the interpreter and the interpreted text stand broadens and corrects itself, in an 'event' which the agent participates in but is not wholly in command of or responsible for. The interpretation carries authority only in the context of a tradition, and it is only by acknowledging such authority that the interpreter both acquires and maintains her competence and status as an interpreter. Thus excellence by way of interpretation, or put otherwise, success in the process of reaching understanding, 'is more being than consciousness' (Gadamer 1976: 38), and there is no structure more fundamental than the hermeneutic situation to which the process of reaching understanding that prevails within it can be brought to account.

There are several strands to Habermas's worry that this renders the rationality inherent in processes of reaching an understanding unintelligible, and that it effectively robs the process of reaching an understanding of its properly rational form. One of these strands has to do with Gadamer's apparent reluctance to open up the process of reaching an understanding to *scientific* reflection, as if the 'truth-event' that characterizes the hermeneutic situation was in principle, and therefore irrationally, opposed to the methodologically rigorous standpoint of 'science'. Like many of his contemporaries, and others since, Habermas detects a scent of irrationalism in the apparent disjunction between 'truth' and 'method' announced in the title of Gadamer's great work. A second strand concerns the role attributed to the concepts of tradition, authority, and prejudice. One can acknowledge the ever-presence of pre-formed opinions, background assumptions, presumptions of authority, and so forth in attempts at reaching understanding, but the capacity to reflect on the *validity* of any pre-verbalized claim to authority is an essential feature of genuine acts of *understanding*, so Habermas argues. The capacity to interrupt the transmission of a tradition with a 'no' or a 'why?' regarding the presumption of its validity, Habermas continues, points unmistakeably to the conclusion that tradition and authority are never *self-authenticating*. Tradition and authority are thus accountable to standards that lie beyond them; namely, *rational* standards. Furthermore, the concept of a rational standard, Habermas continues, is bound up with the idea of the *individual subject* taking ownership and responsibility for his or her thought. This, presumably, is the 'permanent legacy bequeathed to us by German Idealism' that Habermas invokes against Gadamer – a formidable authority indeed (Habermas 1988: 170).[3] By subordinating the power of judgement of the individual subject to the anonymous happening of the tradition-event, by falsely lending authority and tradition a self-authenticating power, and by dogmatically insisting on the scientific inscrutability of the hermeneutic situation, Gadamer's hermeneutics fails to make sense of the rationality of the process of reaching an understanding and in doing so betrays its own fundamental irrationalism.

Habermas's first objection could be put in terms of there being a force internal to language – the force of communicative reason at play in all genuine processes of reaching an understanding – which Gadamer's hermeneutics effectively renders invisible. His second objection is that there are also forces outside language, though manifest indirectly within it, that go missing in Gadamer's account. In neglecting these *supra*-linguistic forces, Habermas contends, Gadamer's hermeneutics is guilty of a naïve *linguistic idealism*. The charge, of course, is not that hermeneutics is idealist in the sense that Kant, Fichte, and Hegel used that term, but in the sense that Marx gave it: namely, a doctrine or outlook that failed to make sense of, or accord due importance to, *material* reality.

The criticism that hermeneutics suffers from a crippling linguistic idealism has become as familiar as the objection that it is fundamentally irrationalist, but it is worth reminding ourselves of the exact way in which Habermas initially formulated the charge. The objection rests on a series of distinctions Habermas insists must be drawn between cognitive attitudes, methods of enquiry, and object-domains (Habermas 1983). Deploying these distinctions, Habermas describes the cognitive attitude of hermeneutics as reaching understanding, using methods of interpretation that involve the adoption of the standpoint of a participant in a dialogue, the object-domain of which are the *meanings* it participates in. Much, but by no means the 'totality', of the human world can and ought to be subject to such hermeneutic reflection. For the human world is amenable to explanation as well as understanding, explanation that requires the adoption of the standpoint of an outside, neutral observer, using concepts fit for describing *material* reality *rather than meanings*. The crucial point Habermas insists upon is that the latter object-domain, the realm of the material, is governed by 'non-normative forces' (Habermas 1988: 173); that consequently it is amenable to explanation in naturalistic terms, and in particular in terms of those objective forces that determine how a system is able to maintain and reproduce itself in interaction with its environment. The human species, as a whole, materially maintains and reproduces itself by way of *social labour*. The system of social labour, the functional reproduction of which is the material condition of processes of reaching understanding, in turn shapes and is shaped by systems of power that affect other social relations. Hence, in Habermas's view, social labour and power mark the limiting points of hermeneutic reflection. They do so on account of constituting a realm of 'law' or 'force' rather than 'meaning', of having an intelligibility graspable by descriptive-explanatory concepts rather than normative ones. But it is not just the *reach* of hermeneutic reflection that is affected by theoretical reflection on social labour and power; the very content of that reflection is affected too. For processes of reaching understanding in language are now revealed as sharing 'an objective context' given not just by tradition (as proposed in Gadamer's hermeneutics), but also by potentially distorting and corrupting systems of social labour and domination.[4]

A critical theory of society, Habermas insists, must be able to explain the material reproduction of society through social labour as well as understand its symbolic reproduction through cultural traditions. Moreover, it must be able to reflect on any given cultural tradition in a way that discloses the function the tradition serves in reproducing the distribution of power embedded in the system of social labour and other social relations. In other words, it must be alert to the *ideological* function of tradition and be capable of undertaking a critique of ideology. In prosecuting such critique, a critical theory aims at *emancipation* from sources of domination, and in particular those that are legitimated and made to seem 'natural' by just those 'prejudices' and 'authorities' that structure the hermeneutic situation. It follows, then, that hermeneutic reflection must fall short as a model of critical reflection, since it is constitutively blind to potential sources of domination embedded in hermeneutic reflection itself. The inadequacy of hermeneutic reflection in this regard is only compounded by the first of Habermas's objections considered above, namely that it fails to subject itself, and the concepts of 'authority', 'prejudice', and 'tradition' it seeks to 'rehabilitate', to properly rational criticism. By cocooning authority and tradition from rational scrutiny, and by ignoring how they function under ideological veils, hermeneutic reflection falls short both as justification and explanation, and thereby as reflection worthy of a *critical theory* of society.

Habermas actually drew not on a case of ideology-critique, but Lorenzer's account of psychoanalysis, to illustrate how understanding and explanation, driven by a 'passion for critique', could be combined in reflection to fulfil an 'emancipatory interest' (Habermas 1972). And the implausible analogy between the situation of the critical theorist reflecting on the ideologies of a society and that of the psychoanalyst interpreting the symptoms of a patient suggested by this example was pressed home by Gadamer in his response to Habermas (Gadamer 1990). In Gadamer's view, this was one of several respects in which Habermas exaggerated the power of methodically grounded theory. It is the theorist's conceit, Gadamer reasonably pointed out, to presume that the healthy course of human history as a whole can be known like the conditions for the healthy course of an individual human life. Habermas took Gadamer's criticism on board and soon dropped the idea that a critical theory of society could satisfy an emancipatory interest by way of theoretically mediated reflection on the disturbed self-formative process of the human species.[5] But Habermas would be less ready to give up other features of his model of critical theory that Gadamer considered epistemologically and metaphysically extravagant, if not politically dangerous. Habermas's claim that authority and tradition were accountable to an independent standard of reason, for example, implied that a form of theoretical self-consciousness potentially existed in which the human life-form would become transparent to itself and manipulable according to rational standards of means–ends efficiency. Similarly, the idea that reflection, when properly critical, is oriented to emancipation *from* tradition, authority, and prejudice, is not only problematically abstract in conception, but likely to end up in the service of tyranny, as traditional practices and beliefs are denigrated and dismantled in the name of universal reason. In these respects, then, the model of critique Habermas opposes to hermeneutic reflection overreaches itself and indeed regresses back to a kind of Enlightenment fundamentalism.[6]

But Gadamer's issue with Habermas was not just that his alternative to hermeneutics could not deliver on its promises; it was also that hermeneutic reflection was broader in scope and more fundamental in depth than Habermas gave it credit for. In reply to Habermas's first objection, namely the putative rational deficits of hermeneutic reflection, Gadamer re-iterated that hermeneutic reflection at its best has a self-transformative, practical character, in which the *self-correction* of tradition takes place or traditions *advance* by way of a 'fusion of horizons'. The whole point of hermeneutic reflection, Gadamer insists, is self-transformation through practical *insight*; it is just that expressions like 'fusion of horizons' are needed to avoid subjectivist self-misunderstandings of what such insight consists in. Gadamer could also point to the centrality of Aristotle's conception of practical wisdom (*phronesis*) for the account of hermeneutic experience presented in *Truth and Method*. No one would suppose that the *phronemos*, the person of practical wisdom, was irrational, but the *phronemos* manages without a method or procedure for guaranteeing validity claims and thereby shows what hermeneutic reflection on its own can achieve. In reply to Habermas's second objection, the alleged linguistic idealism of hermeneutic reflection, Gadamer just shrugs it off, insisting that the material world patently lies within its reach: 'From the hermeneutical standpoint, rightly understood, it is absolutely absurd to regard the concrete factors of work and politics as outside the scope of hermeneutics' (Gadamer 1976: 31). Finally, Gadamer could plausibly claim that his model of hermeneutic reflection is perfectly consistent with psychoanalytical conceptions of therapeutic, emancipatory reflection, insofar as it conceives of such reflection as the resumption through insight of a blocked process of self-formation.

Of course it is one thing to avow a position, another to entitle oneself to it. And although Gadamer's responses to Habermas's objections seem quite reasonable, they are not always supported by further argument. While Gadamer replies to the 'irrationalism' objection in some detail, his denial of the 'linguistic idealism' attributed to his hermeneutics is abrupt, tantamount to a dismissal of the charge rather than a refutation of it. So, for example, his rebuke that it would be absurd to regard 'concrete factors of work and politics' as outside the scope of hermeneutic reflection is not supported by a consideration of how those phenomena *do* feature within hermeneutics. Nor is *Truth and Method* much help in this regard. This is no small matter from the standpoint of a critical theory of society. Indeed, from that standpoint, oriented crucially by Marx, the mere inattentiveness to the material reality of social labour in Gadamer's hermeneutics would itself be sufficient to warrant the charge of idealism.[7]

In any case the issue goes deeper than that. Consider again Habermas's proposal for overcoming hermeneutic idealism. The basic idea is that whatever 'meanings' human beings find in things, whatever they reach understanding about and transmit through cultures and traditions, they must also maintain and reproduce the material basis of their existence, a process for which social labour is responsible. The mechanisms by which this function is met, Habermas supposes, are analytically independent of the processes by which cultural traditions are maintained and reproduced. The system responsible for this function – to use the vocabulary Habermas was later to draw upon for shoring up the materialist credentials of his critical theory of society – has a logic of its own, a logic which can be reconstructed without appeal to the kind of norms on which cultures and traditions depend. For purposes of analysis and social explanation, Habermas maintains, it is thus incumbent on the critical theorist to adopt the standpoint of the observer of a *norm-free* sphere; only in this way will the unfolding of history as it is conditioned by the requirements of material reproduction come to light. And the idea that those requirements decisively condition the unfolding of history is the primary, and in Habermas's view incontrovertible, insight of *historical materialism*. By positing social labour as a distinct determinant of the 'objective context' of social action – distinct, that is, from language – a critical theory of society is thus able to absorb the emancipatory potential of hermeneutic reflection without forfeiting Marx's fundamental insight about the material basis of historical change.

But the idea that social labour is 'norm-free', that it constitutes a sphere or system intelligible independently of the meanings it expresses, is very far removed from the *lived reality* of work. The activity of working – be it the making of bread, the manufacture of bricks, the teaching of children, or anything else required for the material reproduction of society – is saturated with norms about how it ought to be done. These norms relate not just to the quality of the product or the activity (enabling distinctions to be drawn between well-made and badly made products, or well or badly provided services), but also to what is acceptable by way of interaction with other workers, what is acceptable within a profession, an organization, and so on. That the activity of working is redolent with norms and 'meanings' should be obvious to anyone who reflects upon the matter with an unprejudiced mind. How, then, could work come to be construed by Habermas as 'norm-free'? What is the source of this idea?

It is none other than Gadamer himself, along with Arendt. More specifically, Habermas owes the idea to Aristotle's distinction between productive action (*poiesis*) and moral action (*praxis*) and the associated distinction between technique (*techne*) and practical wisdom (*phronesis*) presented in the central section of *Truth and Method* on the hermeneutic relevance of Aristotle and as adapted by Arendt in the distinction she draws between labour, work, and action in *The Human Condition* (Arendt 1958).[8] Habermas follows Gadamer (and Arendt) in conceiving productive action as *instrumental* action, rational solely to the extent that it is efficient as the means to an end (the product made, or indirectly, material self-preservation), which is external to the subjectivity or 'self' of the actor, and which accordingly lacks any normative (in the sense of moral) content. Furthermore, this contrast between the techniques of work, the excellences of which are shown in efficient production, and moral insight, which at its best delivers practical self-knowledge and even practical self-transformation, is crucial to Gadamer's *general* conception of hermeneutics. For it is on this basis that 'truth' is distinguished from 'method' in the sense invoked by the title of Gadamer's masterpiece. The central claim advanced in that text, and throughout Gadamer's metaphilosophical writings on hermeneutics, is that there is no 'technique' or 'art' to hermeneutic reflection, no teachable or learnable skill involved in it, no rules that can be automatically applied for the sake of reaching its goal, the disclosure of 'truth'.

But if the concrete world of work is conceived in this way, namely as the realm of *poiesis* or instrumental action governed by the requirements of *techne* or technically efficient production, then one might wonder how exactly Gadamer envisages it as falling within the scope of hermeneutics. And it is precisely because Habermas *shares* this conception of work that he can legitimately raise the objection of linguistic idealism against Gadamer's claim regarding the universality of hermeneutic reflection. For unless there is some *other* form of reflection available – a form, that is, outside the scope of hermeneutics – then the world of work does seem to disappear, however absurd this conclusion must seem to any sane mind.

The suspicion that there may be more to the charge of linguistic idealism than Gadamer is prepared to concede is reinforced by a further consideration. This is that for all the reassurance Gadamer gives that the 'concrete factors of work and politics' are within the hermeneutic purview, he does not give many actual examples of how they fit the hermeneutic situation. There is no doubt that the paradigm case of the hermeneutic situation for Gadamer, the case to which his description of the hermeneutic situation is best suited, is that of the interpreter of classical texts. Likewise, the primary context in which hermeneutic reflection is called for is the transmission and renewal of cultural tradition through reading and writing. That activities of working, of making useful things or providing useful services, are not themselves contextualized within a hermeneutic situation – that they are for the most part simply presumed not to share in that structure – suggests that Gadamer's description of the hermeneutic situation may indeed be idealistically skewed. Certainly, the material contexts in which acts of interpretation take place do not feature at all prominently in Gadamer's hermeneutics.

If the previous remarks are sound, then Gadamer's hermeneutics does stand in need of 'materialist' correction. But the correction proposed by Habermas arrives, as it were, too late. For Habermas's historical-materialist alternative to hermeneutics presupposes the very conceptual repertoire that gives rise to Gadamer's problematic linguistic idealism in the first place: namely, the categories of *poiesis* and *praxis* and their associated forms of rationality. The way to overcome hermeneutic idealism is not to complement a communication-theoretic account of meaning-transmission with a system-theoretic account of material reproduction, as Habermas's version of historical materialism intends to do. Rather, the problem must be tackled at its conceptual source: namely, *the separation of meaning and materiality embedded in the distinction between poiesis and praxis.*

Another way of making this point would be to say that the idealist (in the sense of insufficiently materialist) appearance of hermeneutics is best corrected from within. And a decisive step that could be taken in that direction would be to take seriously the thought that the human encounter with material reality, which is most pressing, most insistent, and least forgiving in working activity, typically bears the features of a hermeneutic situation. To take seriously this thought would be to take a sustained look at work as the locus of 'hermeneutical problems', which, as Ricoeur once put it, are problems 'about concealed meaning' (Ricoeur 1991: 38). The concealed meanings which hermeneutic reflection on work would seek to uncover would include the personally indexed knowledge expressed in work situations that is invisible to outsiders; the values that shape the ethos of professions and trade organizations which are integrated more or less self-consciously into the self-conceptions of their members; the singular power of judgement that must come into play whenever the demands of a task depart from the prescribed rules for performing it; contributions to the performance of tasks which defy standardization, categorization, and transparent means of measurement; social relations of trust and cooperation with others; and so forth. In other words, it would seek to uncover the concealed *praxis* of *poiesis*. But the hermeneutics of work, so conceived, would not just be a hermeneutics of 'belonging'; a reminder and retrieval of the moral, more than merely instrumental, meaning of work. It would also attend to the hidden suffering experienced at work; to barely articulable experiences of failure and humiliation; to the pre-verbal, inchoate sense of being duped by the false promises of employers; to the gut-level feeling of dissatisfaction with a culture of individual performance and achievement. In short, it would also be a hermeneutics of 'suspicion', alert to the systematically distorted communication that corrupts the modern work situation, to the ideological self-understanding that surrounds it, and ready to undertake a critique of that ideology.

The critical hermeneutics envisaged here would return both hermeneutics and critical theory to their roots in phenomenology and philosophical anthropology. Both the hermeneutic and critical theory traditions take their departure, after all, from falsely dualistic conceptions of human reality that 'hold us captive' in spite of their falsity. The dominance of these conceptions, which infiltrate much modern philosophy and which reflect actual oppositions or 'contradictions' in the modern world, is such that we continually need to be reminded of the fundamental wholeness of the human being and the irreducible meaning-content of lived experience. While neither Gadamer nor Habermas ultimately lose sight of this task, their shared focus on reaching an understanding in language has the unfortunate consequence of neglecting the ways in which meaning is experienced in material, non-linguistic form. This is a serious defect in their formulations of hermeneutics and critical theory, because the fact of human embodiment, and the consequent vulnerability of the human life form, makes the material (and not just linguistic) expression of meaning quite basic from a phenomenological and anthropological point of view. In the critical theory tradition, Axel Honneth has done much to correct the phenomenological impoverishment and anthropological one-sidedness of Habermas's critical theory. To that extent, he has re-aligned critical theory with the phenomenological and anthropological stands of hermeneutics, without, as I observed at the beginning of the chapter, explicitly aligning his theory with philosophical hermeneutics as such.[9] In the hermeneutic tradition itself, the return to phenomenological and anthropological themes and foundations has been less prominent. While Ricoeur did once outline a bold programme of synthesis of phenomenology and philosophical anthropology, the critical animus of which became evident in his influential commentary on the Gadamer–Habermas debate, neither he nor anyone else was really able to pull it off. What progress there has been along these lines, it seems to me, has come principally from critically oriented hermeneuticists within the human sciences, for example in the ethnography and social anthropology of capitalism and the psychodynamics of work (Huspek 1991; Sennett 2008; Dejours 2012).[10]

Such efforts are needed if hermeneutics is to exorcize once and for all the spectre of linguistic idealism. But would they help to dispel the appearance of irrationalism that also haunts hermeneutics? Would they remain faithful to the interest in emancipation which, for critical theory, cannot be satisfied except through a correction of the deficits in rationality, or 'pathologies of reason', that permeate modern society? (Honneth 2009). These are fundamental questions for a critical, non-idealist (in the sense of sufficiently materialist) hermeneutics to address, though I have not been able to address them here. But let me conclude with the thought that a hermeneutics aiming at the retrieval of materially expressed meaning-contents and the material mediation of the hermeneutic situation has *prima facie* good democratic credentials, and it is, after all, the rationality implicit in the concept of democracy that critical theorists, Habermasian or otherwise, want to see more of. For *everyone* has some stake in the free expression and proper recognition of their practical intelligence – which we should recall is always an amalgam of *techne* and *phronesis* – and hence in the material contexts in which that intelligence is exercised. As Habermas wryly observed, 'Hermeneutics is not reserved for the noble and the unconventional' (Habermas 1983: 269): it is for all rational animals in their messy, material diversity.

Notes

1 The Gadamer–Habermas–Apel debate has received massive commentary from hermeneutic, critical theory, and other perspectives. This can be gleaned from the bibliographies in Holub 1991 and How 1995.

2 Michael Marder explores further possibilities along these lines in his contribution to this volume.

3 Habermas's complaint about Gadamer betraying the rationalist legacy of German Idealism has since become commonplace. See for example Pippin 2002 and Gjesdal 2009.

4 To quote Habermas in full: '*The objective context in terms of which alone social systems can be understood is constituted conjointly by language, labour, and domination*' (Habermas 1988: 174). The emphasis is Habermas's and indicates the central importance he attached to this point in his review of *Truth and Method* as a whole.

5 As Habermas would reflect thirty years later, 'Such a form of argumentation belongs unambiguously to the past' (as cited in Honneth 2009: 20).

6 'Enlightenment fundamentalism', a deliberately paradoxical term coined by Ernest Gellner, acknowledges the ultimately dogmatic basis to its opposition to dogma, and provides a useful counterpoint to all varieties of hermeneutics. See Smith 1997.

7 Gadamer did sometimes assert the anthropological co-centrality of work (alongside language) (e.g. Gadamer 1981: 75); he refers to 'traditions' of tool use and craftsmanship (Gadamer 1976: 99); and he was capable of biting criticism of the division of labour in modern societies (e.g. Gadamer 1998). But these are occasional remarks and, more to the point, they are at odds with other features of his hermeneutics, as I go on to explain. For more extended analysis, see Smith 2011.

8 'The study of H. Arendt's important investigation [*The Human Condition*] and of H. G. Gadamer's *Wahrheit und Methode* … have called my attention to the fundamental significance of the Aristotelian distinction between *techne* and *praxis*' (Habermas 1974: 286, note 4).

9 The importance of philosophical anthropology for Honneth is evident from his first writings (e.g. Honneth and Joas 1988). The underlying affinity between his recognition-theoretic recasting of critical theory and phenomenology, but also a certain ambivalence towards Gadamer's hermeneutics, comes to the surface in some of his more recent work, for example his account of reification (Honneth 2003, 2008).

10 I should mention that a compelling philosophical case for moving beyond the critical paradigms presented by both Gadamer and Habermas, for the reason that they are deformed by the dichotomy between *poiesis* and *praxis*, was put some time ago by Gyorgy Markus (1982). Alas, Markus left the task of developing a superior paradigm to us.

Bibliography

Arendt, Hannah (1958), *The Human Condition*, Chicago, University of Chicago Press.

Bernstein, Jay (1995), *Recovering Ethical Life: Jürgen Habermas and the Future of Critical Theory*, London, Routledge.

Bleicher, Josef ed. (1980), *Contemporary Hermeneutics: Hermeneutics as Method, Philosophy and Critique*, London, Routledge & Kegan Paul.

Caputo, John D. (1987), *Radical Hermeneutics: Repetition, Deconstruction and the Hermeneutic Project*, Bloomington, Indiana University Press.

Cooke, Maeve (2006), *Re-Presenting the Good Society*, Cambridge MA, MIT Press.

Dejours, Christophe (2012), 'From the Psychopathology to the Psychodynamics of Work', in Nicholas H. Smith and Jean-Philippe Deranty eds, *New Philosophies of Labour*, Boston, Brill, pp. 209–50.

Gadamer, Hans-Georg (1976), *Philosophical Hermeneutics*, tr. David E. Linge, Berkeley, University of California Press.

——(1981), 'What is Practice? The Conditions of Social Reason,' in Gadamer, *Reason in the Age of Science*, trans. Frederick G. Lawrence, Cambridge MA, MIT Press.

——(1990) 'Reply to My Critics', in D. Ormiston and A. Schrift eds, *The Hermeneutic Tradition*, Albany NY, SUNY Press, pp. 273–97.

——(1993), *Truth and Method*, second revised edition, tr. Joel Weinsheimer and Donald G. Marshall, London, Sheed and Ward.

——(1998), 'Isolation as a Symptom of Self-Alienation', in Gadamer, *Praise of Theory*, tr. Chris Dawson, New Haven, Yale University Press.

Gjesdal, Kirstin (2009), *Gadamer and the Legacy of German Idealism*, Cambridge, Cambridge University Press.

Forst, Rainer (2013) *Justification and Critique: Towards a Critical Theory of Politics*, Cambridge, Polity.

Habermas, Jürgen (1972), *Knowledge and Human Interests*, tr. Jeremy L. Shapiro, London, Heinemann.

——(1974), *Theory and Practice*, tr. John Viertel, London, Heinemann.

——(1980), 'The Hermeneutic Claim to Universality', in J. Bleicher ed., *Contemporary Hermeneutics: Hermeneutics as Method, Philosophy and Critique*, London, Routledge & Kegan Paul, pp. 181–211.

——(1983), 'Interpretive Social Science vs Hermeneuticism', in Norma Haan et als eds, *Social Science as Moral Inquiry*, New York, Columbia University Press, pp. 250–69.

——(1988), *On the Logic of the Social Sciences*, Cambridge, Polity.

Holub, Robert C. (1991), *Jürgen Habermas: Critic in the Public Sphere*, London, Routledge.

Honneth, Axel (1995), *Struggle for Recognition*, tr. Joel Anderson, Cambridge, Polity.

——(2003), 'On the Destructive Power of the Third: Gadamer's and Heidegger's Doctrine of Intersubjectivity', *Philosophy and Social Criticism*, 29:1, 5–21.

——(2007), *Disrespect: The Normative Foundations of Critical Theory*, Cambridge, Polity.

——(2008), *Reification. A New Look at an Old Idea*, Oxford, Oxford University Press.

——(2009) *Pathologies of Reason: On the Legacy of Critical Theory*, tr. James Ingram, New York, Columbia University Press.

Honneth, Axel and Joas, Hans (1988), *Social Action and Human Nature*, Cambridge, Cambridge University Press.

How, Alan (1995), *The Habermas–Gadamer Debate and the Nature of the Social*, Ipswich, Avebury.

Hoy, David Couzens (1978), *The Critical Circle: Literature, History and Philosophical Hermeneutics*, Berkeley, University of California Press.

Huspek, Michael (1991), 'Taking Aim on Habermas's Critical Theory: On the Road toward a Critical Hermeneutics', *Communication Monographs*, 58, 225–33.

Markus, Gyorgy (1986), 'Beyond the Dichotomy: Praxis and Poiesis', *Thesis Eleven*, 15, 30–47.

Mueller-Vollmer, Kurt ed. (1986), *The Hermeneutics Reader*, Oxford, Blackwell.

Ormiston, Dayle L. and Schrift, Alan D. eds (1990), *The Hermeneutic Tradition*, Albany NY: SUNY Press.

Pippin, Robert (2002), 'Gadamer's Hegel', in J. Malpas et al. eds, *Gadamer's Century: Essays in Honor of Hans-Georg Gadamer*, Cambridge MA, MIT Press, pp. 217–38.

Ricoeur, Paul (1991) *From Text to Action. Essays in Hermeneutics II*, tr. Kathleen Blamey and John B. Thompson, Evanston, Northwestern University Press.

Rorty, Richard (1979), *Philosophy and the Mirror of Nature*, Princeton, Princeton University Press.

Sennett, Richard (2008), *The Craftsman*, New Haven and London, Yale University Press.

Smith, Nicholas H. (1997), *Strong Hermeneutics: Contingency and Moral Identity*, London, Routledge.

——(2011), 'Language, Work and Hermeneutics', in Andrzej Wiercinski ed., *Gadamer's Hermeneutics and the Art of Conversation, International Studies in Hermeneutics and Phenomenology* Vol. 2, Berlin, LIT Verlag, pp. 201–20.

Thompson, John B. (1981), *Critical Hermeneutics and the Human Sciences*, Cambridge, Cambridge University Press.

Vattimo, Gianni (1988), *The End of Modernity: Nihilism and Hermeneutics in Post-Modern Culture*, tr. Jon R. Snyder, Cambridge, Polity.

Vattimo, Gianni, and Zabala, Santiago (2011), *Hermeneutic Communism: from Heidegger to Marx*, New York, Columbia University Press

Walzer, Michael (1987), *Interpretation and Social Criticism*, Cambridge MA, Harvard University Press.

Warnke, Georgia (1987) *Gadamer: Hermeneutics, Tradition and Reason*, Stanford, Stanford University Press.

——(2002) 'Social Identity as Interpretation', in J. Malpas et al. eds, *Gadamer's Century*, Cambridge MA, MIT Press, pp. 307–28.

Further reading

Gadamer, Hans-Georg (1976), *Philosophical Hermeneutics*, tr. David E. Linge, Berkeley, University of California Press.

Habermas, Jürgen (1988), *On the Logic of the Social Sciences*, Cambridge, Polity.

Honneth, Axel (2007), *Disrespect: The Normative Foundations of Critical Theory*, Cambridge, Polity.

Ormiston, Dayle L. and Schrift, Alan D. eds (1990), *The Hermeneutic Tradition*, Albany NY: SUNY Press.

Ricoeur, Paul (1991) *From Text to Action. Essays in Hermeneutics II*, tr. Kathleen Blamey and John B. Thompson, Evanston, Northwestern University Press.

Smith, Nicholas H. (1997), *Strong Hermeneutics: Contingency and Moral Identity*, London, Routledge.

48

HERMENEUTICS AND PRAGMATISM

Endre Begby

At a first glance, hermeneutics and pragmatism will seem the oddest of pairings, about as different as two philosophical traditions can be. Lightly caricatured, hermeneutics is staid and solemn, historically allied with theology, focused on the highly intellectualized discipline of textual interpretation and exegesis. Pragmatism, on the other hand, is mercurial and iconoclastic, largely oriented toward the sciences, and looking to develop a thoroughly naturalistic picture of the human being and its capacities. Nonetheless, hermeneutics and pragmatism have crossed paths at several points in the history of twentieth-century philosophy. While we would likely look in vain for the prospect of a merger, a final confluence, the interaction between the two schools of thought has always produced striking and interesting results.

Section 1 of this chapter charts some of the distinctive doctrines of the early (or "classical") pragmatists. In section 2, we turn to Heidegger's ambitious reconceptualization (Heidegger 1927) of the hermeneutic problem, from an issue arising within theology and philology to one that purports to capture a fundamental dimension of mankind's orientation to the world. As many have argued, several distinctively pragmatic themes in hermeneutics are foregrounded as a result of Heidegger's contribution. In section 3, we look at Richard Rorty's neo-pragmatist treatise *Philosophy and the Mirror of Nature* (Rorty 1979). Here, Rorty explicitly turns to hermeneutics in order to outline a positive self-conception for philosophy once the tradition following Descartes and Kant has run its course. Finally, section 4 looks at criticisms that have been levied against Rorty's ideas from both hermeneutic and pragmatist camps. These criticisms not only display the difficulties of doing constructive philosophy at the intersection of hermeneutics and pragmatism, but may also serve to shed some light on complexities and tensions within each tradition of thought.

1. Pragmatism

Pragmatism is, in origin and essence, a distinctively American product. It is common to pick out the trio of Charles Sanders Peirce (1839–1914), William James (1842–1910), and John Dewey (1859–1952) as its earliest and most influential expositors. Though quite different in terms of intellectual temperament and philosophical focus, their work overlaps in substantial and interesting ways which allows us to say, at least to a first approximation, what pragmatism as a philosophical orientation is all about.

Pragmatism, as a coinage and a rallying-cry, traces back to what is sometimes referred to as Peirce's "pragmatist maxim," a methodological precept for philosophical reflection which counsels us to analyze our philosophical concepts and commitments in terms of their "practical bearings" (Peirce 1878: 132). Accordingly, pragmatism was, from its earliest beginnings, driven by the idea that philosophy should focus on the human situation: "Philosophy is a science based upon everyday experience," wrote Peirce; accordingly, "we must not begin by talking of pure ideas," but rather with "men and their conversation" (Peirce n.d.: 112).

The early pragmatists recognized the tremendous progressive potential of scientific inquiry and argued that we should view philosophy – or at any rate, *good* philosophy – as fundamentally continuous with science. Thus, the pragmatic maxim joins with the scientific conception of philosophy to produce a robust anti-metaphysical stance: pragmatism, James argued, is a corrective against philosophy's tendency to get entangled in interminable metaphysical disputes. Unless their resolution can be shown to make some difference to our practical affairs, philosophical questions should simply be cast aside, rather than be honored with reverence and dedicated study.

Nonetheless, the pragmatists' attempt to bring philosophy into register with scientific inquiry at large was never done in a spirit of reductionism. Not only would such reductionism be at odds with the deep-rooted humanism of the pragmatist project. It would also run counter to the grounding spirit of the pragmatist maxim itself: for the point of expanding the domain of scientific inquiry is the *practical aim* of improving the human condition. By contrast, reductionism is driven by a *metaphysical agenda* of just the sort that pragmatists abjure, namely that of showing how the ontology of science (or some preferred branch of science) can account for all there is.

So on the one hand, it is distinctive of pragmatists that they considered scientific inquiry in the broadest possible sense, and would pay particular attention to the then nascent disciplines of biology and psychology. But they were also explicitly concerned with reconciling "the scientific loyalty to facts" with "the old confidence in human values" (James 1907: 495). Here they drew inspiration from a number of previous efforts, such as David Hume's *A Treatise of Human Nature* (1739–40), Auguste Comte's *Course de Philosophie Positive* (1832–40) and John Stuart Mill's *A System of Logic* (1843).

This foregrounding of practical concerns within philosophy and science can be seen quite clearly in pragmatist epistemology. Most immediately, pragmatist epistemology can be characterized as *fallibilist* but *anti-Cartesian* (Hookway 2013). It is fallibilist insofar as it holds that none of our beliefs could ever be immune from the possibility of error, and in particular, that no amount of rational reflection could ever ensure us of its infallibility. Yet their position is anti-Cartesian in holding that Descartes reasoned illicitly from the fact of human fallibility to the relevance of radical skepticism. On the one hand, Cartesian skepticism presumes the cogency of a subject that is alienated from its environment in a particular way, such that it could even be in the position to deploy its rational capacities at the same time as it casts doubt on all its worldly beliefs. Pragmatists deny that this Cartesian picture of the detached rational cognizer is even cogent. But less obviously, Cartesian skepticism also presumes that we could not be warranted in holding any belief unless we could cite positive evidence in its favor. Instead, pragmatism counsels us to embrace the consequences of fallibilism more fully: inquiry must start in the thick of things, within a concrete context defined by the beliefs and the practical concerns that brought us to where we are. These beliefs can have a positive epistemic status in spite of the fact that they may well be wrong, and in spite of the fact that we are (currently) unable to cite any evidence for them.

With their critique of Descartes, pragmatists clearly signaled their allegiance to empiricism. But, their admiration of Hume notwithstanding, it is also important to recognize within their epistemology an important corrective to traditional empiricist thought. Thus, pragmatists were empiricists insofar as they believed that any claim to knowledge must prove its mettle with respect to experience. But simultaneously, they chastised Hume (and other empiricists) for holding on to a narrow and reductionist conception of experience. Traditional empiricists held that knowledge must be traced back to immediate sensory experience. Pragmatists, by contrast, believed there was no such thing as a sensory "given." On their view, all experience is richly suffused with human conceptualization and shaped by our practical concerns. John Dewey, in particular, denounced what he called the "spectator theory of knowledge," which he saw as a shared sin of both rationalism and empiricism. Instead, Dewey's account of experience revolves around the notion of a "situation" arising from "the intercourse of a living being with its physical and social environment" (Dewey 1917: 47). This situational approach thematizes experience in terms of its practical significance first and foremost, leading Dewey to define pragmatism as such in terms of the view that reality itself possesses a "practical character" (Dewey 1908: 126).

With their combination of a fallibilist epistemology and an unflinching focus on human concerns, pragmatists were never going to have an easy time with the concept of truth. Pragmatists were united in the negative claim that certain received accounts of truth – such as the notion that truth consists in the "correspondence" between belief and reality – were hopelessly muddled. Nonetheless, the positive accounts of truth on offer in pragmatism can be seen to pull in contrary directions: on the one hand, toward realism, with the belief that truth is transcendent and independent of human concerns, and on the other hand, toward idealism, with the belief that truth is indexed to human belief. This is clearly an uncomfortable position for pragmatists to find themselves in, insofar as the dispute between realism and idealism is precisely the sort of metaphysical baggage that they would have hoped to dispense with.

A famous passage from Peirce may be seen to illustrate both tendencies at once. Peirce writes: "the opinion which is fated to be ultimately agreed by all who investigate, is what we mean by truth, and the object represented in this opinion is real" (Peirce 1878: 139). On the one hand, this view seems to flirt with idealism insofar as it makes appeal to agreement among "those who investigate." But on the other hand, it tries to soften this appeal and pull in the direction of realism by stipulating that we are talking not about what is agreed to *now* by a specific set of investigators, but rather about what is "fated" to be agreed by all investigators. Thus, Peirce's view of truth is sometimes also cashed out in terms of what would be believed by an ideal scientific community at the end of inquiry.

It is fair to say that Peirce's account of truth never fully satisfied even his fellow pragmatists. (See, e.g., Misak 2013: 36–7.) By contrast, James's most famous exposition of the concept of truth draws an analogy with the place of goodness in the ethical realm: truth is simply what is "good in the way of belief" (James 1907: 520). James seems to cash this out in terms of a notion of "instrumental truth," leaving it open, perhaps, whether there could be any other form. Thus: "any idea that will carry us prosperously from any one part of our experience to any other part, linking things satisfactorily, working securely, saving labor; is true for just so much, true in so far forth, *true instrumentally*" (James 1907: 512). Dewey's most notable contribution introduces the notion of "warranted assertibility" (e.g., Dewey 1938), that is, the question of what justifies our claims to knowledge in a social context. This is surely a question that pragmatists ought to focus on. But it remains controversial whether it could take the place previously assumed by the concept of truth, or whether it simply amounts to letting go of that concept altogether. (On this, see Dewey 1941.) At any rate, the question of truth was sharply contested among the early pragmatists, with Peirce, in particular, chiding what he saw as the irrationalist and relativist tendencies of James and Dewey. And as we shall see later, it remains a bone of contention to the present day, with the battle over the legacy of pragmatism largely divided by those who side with Peirce, on the one hand, and those who side with James and Dewey on the other.

2. Heidegger's hermeneutics

Throughout most of its history, hermeneutics had been devoted to the study of textual interpretation – paradigmatically, scriptural interpretation. Even though hermeneutics would seek to apply itself more broadly as philology gained a foothold in various academic disciplines, it would remain, within the context of German philosophy at large, but an eddy within the larger streams of thought following from Kant and Hegel.

But there were signs indicating that a more fundamental shift of perspective was coming on: among the trailblazers were Schleiermacher, who championed a view of hermeneutics as dealing with all linguistically mediated understanding, not just with textual interpretation, and Dilthey, who advocated hermeneutics as the canonical method for the human sciences as such. Martin Heidegger would build on these developments, radicalizing them even further. On his development, "hermeneutics" comes to denote, first and foremost, not an epistemological method or procedure that individuals can apply to come to grips with a particular problem, as would still appear to be the case with Schleiermacher and Dilthey. Rather, with Heidegger hermeneutics takes an *ontological* turn, aiming to reveal the fundamental structure of Dasein's being-in-the-world.

Heidegger's *Being and Time* (1927), in particular, is a work that resonates deeply with pragmatist themes, even though it is cast in a terminology and style of argumentation that would have been quite unfamiliar to the early pragmatists. We can only speculate whether this is an instance of actual influence or just happy convergence: it is likely that Heidegger would at least have been exposed to American pragmatism through his teacher Emil Lask, who was a well-known early exponent of pragmatism in German academia. (See Dreyfus 1990: 6; Kisiel 1995: 25–8; Joas 1993: 105–6.) And over the last decades, there has emerged an impressive body of work reading Heidegger in a way that puts his thinking into register with themes in American philosophy in general, and with pragmatic themes in American philosophy in particular (e.g., Okrent 1988; Dreyfus 1990; Blattner 1992; Carman 2003; Wrathall 2010; Haugeland 2013).

Heidegger remained deeply skeptical of pragmatism's infatuation with science, and specifically with the idea that science holds the key to social progress. Nonetheless, he is in deep agreement with the pragmatists' view that mankind's orientation to the world is engaged and practical first and foremost, and only derivatively detached and theoretical. There is nothing wrong or disingenuous about the theoretical stance as such: on its own terms, it is an important and entirely valid stance. But philosophy loses track of itself and the human condition when this stance is elevated and seen as fundamental in the way that it is, for instance, in Cartesian epistemology. Cartesian epistemology invites us to think of a detached and perhaps even disembodied cognitive subject which is faced with the task of building up its relation to the world piece by piece by way of intellectual operations. Heidegger believes, very much in line with the pragmatist critique above, that this picture entirely distorts our situation. The world is not given to us as a collection of facts or entities whose nature and interconnections it is our task to sort out (see, e.g., Ramberg and Gjesdal 2005). Instead, our way of inhabiting our world is characterized by what Heidegger terms "understanding" (*Verstehen*) (see, e.g., Heidegger 1927: ch. 5).

In using this term, Heidegger certainly means to connect his inquiry with the hermeneutics of Schleiermacher and Dilthey. But his deployment of the term also suggests the point at which he breaks with his predecessors. For in traditional hermeneutics, understanding is precisely thought of in epistemological terms, as the concerted effort to overcome an initial state of confusion and bewilderment so as to make sense of the text or phenomenon that confronts us. On Heidegger's deployment of the term, to the contrary, "understanding" bespeaks familiarity rather than estrangement and denotes our pre-reflective way of inhabiting the world. Understanding, then, is not best thought of as something that we can seek, cultivate, be better or worse at, as traditional hermeneutics would have it. Rather, it is the fundamental and distinctive aspect of our being-in-the-world. It is this form of familiarity which in turn makes possible the more distanced, empirical, objectivizing modes of knowledge that are characteristic of the sciences and other forms of methodical inquiry. With this emphasis on the practical orientation over the detached observer perspective, Heidegger's ontological turn in hermeneutics displays a clear affinity with themes from pragmatism.

But it is not just the anti-Cartesian stance that suggests interesting overlaps with pragmatism. Like the pragmatists, Heidegger asserts that inquiry – even the more refined inquiries of natural science – must start in the middle of things, with our day-to-day routines and purposes. Moreover, inquiry cannot confront facts and objects one by one, but always operates within a given structure of significance, "a relational whole" (*Bewandtnisganzheit*) (see, e.g., Heidegger 1927: chs. 15, 18). Perhaps the clearest illustration of this pragmatic strand in Heidegger's thinking comes in the form of his famous notion of the "ready-to-hand" (*Zuhandenheit*) (Heidegger 1927: chs. 15–16). Ready-to-handness is the property that objects have insofar as we engage them in an immediate and unreflective manner in order to carry out our everyday projects. Heidegger draws an analogy with tools to illustrate this property: our way of engaging with, say, a hammer, is not qua inert object. Rather, we *use* it, and are scarcely more aware of it qua object than we are of our own bodily appendages. It is only when the tool breaks or otherwise fails to serve its purpose that explicit attention is brought to it as such. This mode of ready-to-handness is to be contrasted with that of the present-to-hand (*Vorhandenheit*), where things are encountered simply or primarily as objects of observation and inquiry, as they are in science. Of the early pragmatists, it is perhaps Dewey, with his explicit emphasis on the distinction between propositional and practical knowledge, and with his assertion that reality itself has a "practical structure" which is closest in spirit to Heidegger's hermeneutic program in *Being and Time*.

3. Rorty and the resurgence of pragmatism

By the 1930s, the influence of pragmatism on American philosophy was on the wane, as logical positivism came to prominence, aided by the influx of émigré scholars such as Rudolf Carnap, Hans Reichenbach, and Carl Gustav Hempel. Logical positivism was a school of comparable sweep and ambition to pragmatism, and similarly committed to a naturalistic and scientific conception of philosophy. But it was driven by a much more rigorous methodological program, and had little patience with pragmatism's pluralism and anti-reductionism. Even though it is common – in retrospect – to recognize distinctive pragmatist themes in many of the leading American analytic philosophers during the period, such as W.V.O. Quine, Wilfrid Sellars, and Nelson Goodman, there can be little doubt that pragmatism was effectively marginalized in the decades flanking World War II.

If any one person is to be credited with the resurgence of interest in pragmatism, it is arguably Richard Rorty. Though immersed in contemporary analytic philosophy, Rorty was deeply dissatisfied with the direction it had taken, and turned to pragmatism to frame his critique. Much of his 1979 book *Philosophy and the Mirror of Nature*, while extremely polemical, nonetheless follows along relatively familiar pragmatist tracks. What might have seemed more surprising – certainly so to his contemporaries – was the fact that Rorty also explicitly and self-consciously turned to hermeneutics to frame both the critical and the constructive aspects of his work.

While Heidegger was certainly instrumental to Rorty's turn toward hermeneutics (see, e.g., Rorty 1976), it is the work of Heidegger's student Hans-Georg Gadamer which provides the scaffolding for the final and perhaps most important part of *Philosophy and the Mirror of Nature*. While deeply inspired by Heidegger's ontological turn in hermeneutics, Gadamer's magnum opus *Truth and Method* (Gadamer 1960) has none of the self-conscious revolutionary zeal that marks out Heidegger's work. Instead, Gadamer's work constitutes a subtle and careful rumination on the quest for knowledge in the human sciences. Among its central ideas is the positive epistemic significance of prejudice (*Vorurteile*) and the indispensable role played by tradition in mediating truth and knowledge. One may certainly wonder what appeal a work building on such premises might have held to a self-styled pragmatist renegade such as Richard Rorty.

Rorty's appropriation of Gadamer is certainly tendentious and agenda-driven. But at the same time, it does pick up an important strand in Gadamer's work. As noted above, Rorty's primary engagement with Gadamer takes place in the third and final section of his book, in which philosophy itself becomes the subject matter of critical reflection. The overarching aim of the book is to throw critical light on a certain conception of the task of philosophy, especially entrenched since Descartes and Kant, according to which philosophy stands as the adjudicator of knowledge-claims in the various disciplines of inquiry, a role that it can claim in virtue of its "special understanding of the nature of knowledge and of mind" (Rorty 1979: 3). In order to unmask the conceit behind this self-conception, Rorty aims to "historicize" a selection of central and distinctive philosophical problems, with the aim of showing that they are not the "perennial problems" that philosophy likes to claim as its own, and on whose solution would hang insights into the deepest structures of reality and the human mind. Instead, they are historically transient problems – pseudo-problems, even – that arise as a consequence of philosophy coming to take up specific conceptual tools and vocabularies at specific times. These problems will not be solved, so much as simply abandoned whenever philosophy reaches its next conceptual crossroads. Here, Rorty was clearly drawing inspiration from Kuhn's account of scientific progress as occurring by way of wholesale switches from one theoretical paradigm to another, where each paradigm sets its own agenda for what are the problems worth solving (Kuhn 1962). (Kuhn himself would occasionally invoke hermeneutics to describe an important dimension of his account (see, e.g., Kuhn 1977: xv).) Accordingly, the first two parts of Rorty's book apply this procedure, respectively, to the problem of mind and body and to the problem of epistemology. The third and final part of the book looks to philosophy itself. And here is where Gadamer's work becomes central to Rorty's thinking.

The final part of Rorty's work is entitled "From Epistemology to Hermeneutics." Rorty wants to make clear from the outset, however, that hermeneutics is not being put forward as a "successor subject" to epistemology, some alternative agenda for pursuing the theory of knowledge. Instead, Rorty claims to use "hermeneutics" as a "polemical term" (Rorty 1979: 357), in particular, as "an expression of hope that the cultural space left by the demise of epistemology will not be filled" (Rorty 1979: 315).

On Rorty's analysis, traditional epistemology proceeds on the assumption that all contributions to discourse – all knowledge-claims – are "commensurable" (borrowing terminology from Kuhn), such that disputes can be brought under a single set of rules – a decision procedure – which would allow us, at least in principle, to adjudicate which claim is right. According to the tradition from Descartes and Kant, it is the job of philosophy to clarify these rules and to serve as custodians of the decision procedure.

Rorty believes there can be no such rules, and accordingly, that philosophy's self-conception rests on a mirage. As a counterpoint, Rorty draws on Gadamer's idea that knowledge-seeking should be thought of in terms of a conversation in which different points of view are expressed, and through which, when all goes well, we may hope to transcend the cognitive limitations of either of the original contributions (what Gadamer (1960: 305) called a "fusion of horizons"). But as we embrace this picture, we also come to realize that this moment of transcendence is not a resting point in which we can claim final knowledge. Rather, it is simply the starting point for yet more conversation. Moreover, on this dialogical picture of knowledge-seeking, there is no way to disentangle the "substantive" points of agreement and disagreement from those that concern the question of how disagreements should be resolved. These matters are inextricably linked, and both under scrutiny.

Instead of Knowledge (with a capital K, as conceived of in traditional epistemology), Rorty argues that philosophers should seek to cultivate what Gadamer (e.g., 1960: 8–16) calls *Bildung* (roughly, learning or edification). Unlike Knowledge, *Bildung* does not imply a final product, but rather a personal attitude: rather than despair of the loss of a single all-encompassing decision procedure for adjudicating knowledge-claims, a person possessing *Bildung* will cultivate an openness to new and enriching experiences, constantly seeking to integrate a diversity of perspectives. Thus, Rorty turns to hermeneutics, in no small part, for therapeutic counsel: to adjust ourselves to this post-epistemological conception of philosophy is for us to come to terms with the fact that our knowledge-seeking practices can never finally transcend the limitations of the human situation. Even though we may never find a decision procedure that will enforce agreement among all rational parties (or else allow us to dismiss as irrational those who do not agree), Gadamer's dialogical model of understanding reminds us that "the hope of agreement is never lost so long as the conversation lasts" (Rorty 1979: 318).

But Rorty is clear that conversational agreement is no substitute for truth. Just as hermeneutics is not the name of a successor discipline to epistemology, so Rorty's focus on agreement is not tantamount to putting forward a "consensus theory of truth" to substitute for traditional epistemology's correspondence theory. Rorty's pragmatism makes no claim that truth and agreement are conceptually connected. Nonetheless, the focus on agreement is a good thing, in that it serves to remind us that insofar as our pursuit of knowledge is governed by norms – knowledge claims must, after all, be backed by justification – the norms in question pertain primarily to our relationship to our fellow human beings, not to the relation between the individual inquirer and the world.

Nonetheless, it is important to note that Rorty's appropriation of hermeneutics is not without critical intent. Many leading hermeneuticists – Heidegger and Gadamer not least – display strong anti-scientistic tendencies, and they seek to entrench their anti-scientism in the form of a firm and principled distinction between two domains of inquiry: on the one hand, that which concerns human beings and their situation, and, on the other hand, that which concerns the rest of the physical universe. The truths of hermeneutics, then, are meant in part to serve as a bulwark against the intrusion of natural scientific modes of inquiry on the human domain.

On Rorty's pragmatist approach, this distinction can only be provisional: hermeneutics is guilty of fashioning metaphysics from conceptual baggage which may be unceremoniously abandoned at the next crossroads in science or philosophy. Rorty does not mean to dispute the distinction between the natural and the human sciences *within our current scheme of inquiry*. The distinction is real, but its significance may have nothing to do with its tracing a fundamental cleavage in the fabric of the universe. On Rorty's view, the virtue of *Bildung* described above requires precisely that we remain open to the possibility that such a distinction – fundamental though it may seem to us now – may simply reflect a hang-up in our current way of thinking.

4. Reactions to Rorty

If Rorty's book was meant to provoke, it was an immediate success. *Philosophy and the Mirror of Nature* would quickly garner scorching criticism from virtually all quarters of philosophy. One persistent and vocal critic has been Susan Haack, who argues that Rorty's attempt to reroute the course of contemporary philosophy "masks a cynicism which would undermine not only epistemology, not only 'systematic' philosophy, but inquiry generally" (Haack 1993: 182–3).

Haack's challenge is important in its own right, but is doubly noteworthy for the fact that it also concerns Rorty's appropriation of the label "pragmatism." She derides Rorty's appropriation as "vulgar pragmatism," one that steals the name but shamelessly abandons the constructive project that once animated it. Similar thoughts are echoed by Nicholas Rescher (e.g., Rescher 2000) and, most recently, by Cheryl Misak in her important book *The American Pragmatists* (Misak 2013). In an important sense, though, Rorty is not the sole target of criticism here. Rorty was always explicit that his pragmatism is that of James and Dewey, not that of Peirce (see, e.g., Rorty 1993). And what unites these critics is precisely a deep admiration of Peirce, and a sense that the history of pragmatism is one of decline ever since. To this extent, the controversy over Rorty's neo-pragmatism bears testimony to deep tensions within pragmatism itself. As we saw above, the crux of the rift between Peirce and subsequent pragmatists was precisely the concept of truth (and cognate concepts such as evidence, justification, and objectivity). What would be vulgar about Rorty's pragmatism is simply his self-conscious abandonment of any vestige of the Peircean heritage, and in particular, the abandonment of any substantive account of the role of truth in guiding inquiry.

From the standpoint of this criticism, it is tempting to think that Rorty's flirtation with hermeneutics and other forms of "continental philosophy" is just another symptom of his reckless disregard for truth. Accordingly, it is important to note that similar concerns have also been voiced by hermeneuticists protesting against Rorty's appropriation of Gadamer. Thus, for instance, Charles Guignon (1982: 366), Georgia Warnke (1987: ch. 5), and Brice Wachterhauser (1994) all argue that Rorty's appropriation of hermeneutics misses the central role of truth in Gadamer's work. Even though Gadamer insists that no cognitive procedure would ever allow us to finally transcend our historical finitude, he remains firm in his conviction that it is truth which comes to light through these conversational encounters. In Wachterhauser's words:

> Only by seeing our conversation as ultimately governed by the norm of truth do our many attempts to make a point in a conversation become

something more than the utterance of a series of sounds which we hope will affect the behavior of our interlocutor for our own advantage. Only the sincere search for truth adequately distinguishes rational inquiry from mere sophistry.

(Wachterhauser 1994: 3)

This suggests, interestingly enough, a second and very different perspective on the convergence between hermeneutics and pragmatism, namely a convergence in resistance to Rorty's disregard for the concept of truth. From this perspective, Rorty emerges as a vulgarizer of hermeneutics no less than of pragmatism: one who coopts the surface rhetoric, while letting go of the subtler ideas lying underneath. This is certainly not a trifling matter. But Rorty's challenge remains: how might one connect, in a useful and substantive way, this notion of truth with a notion of inquiry strongly centered, as both pragmatism and hermeneutics is, on the human situation? It is one thing to assert that without appeal to the concept of truth, our conversational interactions will reduce to manipulation and inquiry will grind to a halt. It is quite another thing to say, in concrete practical terms, what the invocation of truth contributes above and beyond that of being justified in the eyes of one's peers. On Rorty's view, once one has come properly to terms with fallibilism and with the irreducibly social character of epistemic justification, then invoking the concept of truth does nothing more than pander to vestigial philosophical scruples which should be ruthlessly abandoned rather than indulged.

Bibliography

Blattner, W.D. (1992) "Existential Temporality in *Being and Time* (Why Heidegger is not a Pragmatist)," in H.L. Drefyus and H. Hall (eds.), *Heidegger: A Critical Reader*, Oxford: Blackwell, pp. 99–129.

Carman, T. (2003) *Heidegger's Analytic: Interpretation, Discourse and Authenticity in Being and Time*, Cambridge: Cambridge University Press.

Dewey, J. (1908) "Does Reality Possess Practical Character?" reprinted in L.M. Hickman and T.M. Alexander (eds.), *The Essential Dewey*, Vol. 1, Bloomington: Indiana University Press, 1998, pp. 124–33.

——(1917) "The Need for a Recovery of Philosophy," reprinted in L.M. Hickman and T.M. Alexander (eds.), *The Essential Dewey*, Vol. 1, Bloomington: Indiana University Press, 1998, pp. 46–70.

——(1938) *Logic: The Theory of Inquiry*, New York: Henry Holt and Co.

——(1941) "Propositions, Warranted Assertibility, and Truth," in *The Journal of Philosophy* 38 (7), pp. 169–86.

Dreyfus, H.L. (1990) *Being-in-the-World: A Commentary on Heidegger's Being and Time, Division I*, Cambridge, MA: The MIT Press.

Gadamer, H.G. (1960) *Truth and Method*, translated by J. Weinsheimer and D.G. Marshall, London: Continuum Publishing, 1989.

Guignon, C.B. (1982) "Saving the Differences: Gadamer and Rorty," in *PSA: Proceedings of the Biennial Meeting of the Philosophy of Science Association*, pp. 360–67

Haack, S. (1993) *Evidence and Inquiry: Towards Reconstruction in Rpistemology*, Oxford: Blackwell.

Haugeland, J. (2013) *Dasein Disclosed: John Haugeland's Heidegger*, edited by Joseph Rouse, Cambridge, MA: Harvard University Press.

Heidegger, M. (1927) *Being and Time*, translated by J. Stambaugh, Albany, NY: SUNY Press, 1996.

Hookway, C. (2013) "Pragmatism," in E. Zalta (ed.), The Stanford Encyclopedia of Philosophy (Winter 2013 Edition), Stanford, CA: CSLI Publications.

James, W. (1907) *Pragmatism: A New Name for Some Old Ways of Thinking*, reprinted in *Writings 1902–1910*, New York: Library of America, pp. 479–624.

Joas, H. (1993) *Pragmatism and Social Theory*, Chicago, IL: University of Chicago Press.

Kisiel, T.J. (1995) *The Genesis of Heidegger's "Being and Time"*, Berkeley: University of California Press.

Kuhn, T.S. (1962) *The Structure of Scientific Revolutions*, Chicago, IL: University of Chicago Press.

——(1977) *The Essential Tension. Selected Studies in Scientific Tradition and Change*, Chicago, IL: University of Chicago Press.

Misak, C. (2013) *The American Pragmatists*, Oxford: Oxford University Press.

Okrent, M. (1988) *Heidegger's Pragmatism: Understanding, Being, and the Critique of Metaphysics*, Ithaca, NY: Cornell University Press.

Peirce, C.S. (1878) "How to Make Our Ideas Clear," reprinted in N. Hauser and C. Kloesel (eds.), *The Essential Peirce: Selected Philosophical Writings*, Vol 1, Bloomington: Indiana University Press, 1992, pp. 124–41.

——(n.d.) "Review of Josiah Royce, *The World and the Individual*," reprinted in A.W. Burks (ed.), *The Collected Papers of Charles Sanders Peirce*, Vol. VIII, Cambridge, MA: Harvard University Press, 1958, pp. 100–131.

Ramberg, B. and Gjesdal, K. (2005) "Hermeneutics," in E. Zalta (ed.), The Stanford Encyclopedia of Philosophy (Winter 2005 Edition).

Rescher, N. (2000) *Realistic Pragmatism: An Introduction to Pragmatic Philosophy*, Albany, NY: SUNY Press.

Rorty, R. (1976) "Overcoming the Tradition: Heidegger and Dewey," in *The Review of Metaphysics* 30 (2), pp. 280–305.

——(1979) *Philosophy and the Mirror of Nature*, Princeton, NJ: Princeton University Press.

——(1993) "Hilary Putnam and the Relativist Menace," in *The Journal of Philosophy* 90 (9), pp. 443–61.

Wachterhauser, B.R. (1994) "Introduction: Is there Truth after Interpretation?" in B.R. Wachterhauser (ed.), *Hermeneutics and Truth*, Evanston, IL: Northwestern University Press, pp. 1–23.

Warnke, G. (1987) *Gadamer: Hermeneutics, Tradition, and Reason*, Palo Alto, CA: Stanford University Press.

Wrathall, M.A. (2010) *Heidegger and Unconcealment: Truth, Language, and History*, Cambridge: Cambridge University Press.

Further reading

Bernstein, R.J. (1983) *Beyond Objectivism and Relativism: Hermeneutics, Praxis, and Science*, Philadelphia: University of Pennsylvania Press.

——(2010) *The Pragmatic Turn*, Malden, MA: Polity Press.

Brandom, R.B. (2002) *Tales of the Mighty Dead. Historical Essays in the Metaphysics of Intentionality*, Cambridge, MA: Harvard University Press.

McDowell, J. (1994) *Mind and World*, Cambridge, MA: Harvard University Press.

Ramberg, B.T. (1989) *Donald Davidson's Philosophy of Language: An Introduction*, Oxford: Basil Blackwell.

49

HERMENEUTICS AND PSYCHOANALYSIS

Philippe Cabestan

Sigmund Freud (1856–1939) is known as the founding father of psychoanalysis and we are used to identifying psychoanalysis with his thinking. But we have to remember that psychoanalysis today carries on a rich and eventful history made right from the beginning, of impassioned relationships, conflicts, splits and quite unusual reconciliations, which partly depend on personalities and their own contribution to the psychoanalytical research. For example, in 1912, Alfred Adler and Wilhelm Steckel quit the International Psychoanalytical Association (IPA), founded in 1910. Two years later, C. G. Jung resigns as president of the association. After Freud's death, the psychoanalytical "community" divides up into different groups and leading figures like Freud's well-known daughter Anna Freud, Melanie Klein, Wilfred Bion, Donald Winnicott, Daniel Lagache without forgetting Jacques Lacan. But even if it sounds a little bit artificial, this study is not going to take account of the internal debates of the movement. For it seems more effective to focus the reflection on Freud's thought and his way of interpreting psychological phenomena. We are therefore going to proceed as if psychoanalysis was the work of a single man: Sigmund Freud.

In two articles for an encyclopedia, Freud himself gives a definition of psycho-analysis:

> psycho-analysis is the name (1) of a procedure for the investigation of mental processes which are almost inaccessible in any other way, (2) of a method (based upon that investigation) for the treatment of neurotic disorders and (3) of a collection of psychological information obtained along those lines, which is gradually being accumulated into a new scientific discipline.
>
> (Freud 1920–22)

At first sight, psychoanalysis has nothing to do with hermeneutics. Freud is a scientist and a physician, animated by a scientific and therapeutic ambition. He sometimes compares the work of the analyst with that of the chemist. For instance, explaining the way he constructed the word psycho-analysis, Freud sets off this analogy:

> the patient's symptoms and pathological manifestations, like all his mental activities, are of a highly composite kind; the elements of this compound are at bottom motives, instinctual impulses. But the patient knows nothing of these elementary motives or not nearly enough. We teach him to understand the way in which these highly complicated mental formations are compounded ... , just as a chemist isolates the fundamental substance, the chemical "element", out of the salt in which it had been combined with other elements and in which it was unrecognizable.
>
> (Freud 1918)

If we remember Dilthey's famous distinction between natural sciences (*Naturwissenschaften*) and spiritual sciences (*Geisteswissenschaften*), psychoanalysis apparently belongs to the former.

But these first explanations ought not to hide the deep ambiguity of Freud's way of thinking and the tight connection between psychoanalysis and hermeneutics. It is commonly said that hermeneutics is the theory of text interpretation, especially the interpretation of biblical texts. Philosophical hermeneutics however is a little bit different. It refers to the theory of knowledge and, according to Dilthey (1833–1911), to the idea that exploration of human phenomena has nothing to do with the natural sciences, which seek to explain (*erklären*) natural processes in terms of cause and effect. On the contrary, human phenomena are a matter of human sciences, which seek to understand (*verstehen*) human behaviour (Dilthey 2010). Besides, Freud says that understanding or comprehension is not based on empathy, which would suppose a direct identification with the other, but can only be attained by interpretation. In fact, when Freud writes, as quoted before, that "psychoanalysis is the name of a procedure for the investigation of mental processes which are almost inaccessible in any other way", he wants to emphasize that the main part of these mental processes is unconscious – according to Freud's iceberg model of the mind, only 10 per cent are visible or conscious whereas the other 90 per cent are beneath the water or unconscious – and can be neither immediately observed nor biologically explained. Because they are unconscious, their meaning has actually to be discovered through another way, that is to say through interpretation. It is thus not surprising that Freud himself presents psychoanalysis as an "interpretive art" (Freud 1922).

It follows that we have two or three issues to consider. First of all, since psychoanalysis, also called "depth psychology" or "psychology of the deeper layers" (Freud 1920), is concerned with the unconscious meaning of dreams, slips and mistakes, neurotic symptoms, perversions, it necessary to examine how it interprets these psychological phenomena. Second, because psychoanalysis claims to be also a hermeneutics of the human condition and Freud a doctor of our modern civilization, we must examine its interpretations of phenomena like religion, artistic production, culture. But, third, the crucial and difficult question is obviously to evaluate what kind of hermeneutics the Freudian psychoanalysis is and to consider the conflicts of interpretations.

Freud and the birth of psychoanalysis

Given our topic, it's worth noticing a few preliminary things about Freud's biography. Freud's father, Jacob Freud (1815–96), was a Jew and even if he had moved away from the tradition he came to be known for his Torah study. Freud himself isn't religious and considers religion as an illusion. In his book, *The Future of an Illusion*, he assimilates religion to a neurosis of humanity (Freud 1927). Nevertheless he claims to be Jewish and declares at the very beginning of his autobiography: "I was born on May 6th, 1856, at Freiberg in Moravia, a small town in what is now Czechoslovakia. My parents were Jews, and I have remained a Jew myself" (Freud 1925). Among others things, it means that he had, of course, to suffer from anti-Semitism and to escape the Nazi barbarity with his family in 1938 but also that he knew the holy writ and was used to hermeneutics in the way of biblical exegesis.

However, Freud doesn't begin his work in this hermeneutical direction. He is first of all a neurologist, qualified as a doctor of medicine at the University of Vienna in 1881, and then carries out research into cerebral palsy (cerebral paralysis), aphasia and neuroanatomy at the Vienna General Hospital. In 1885, Freud goes to Paris and meets Jean-Martin Charcot, a renowned neurologist who is conducting scientific research into hypnosis and hysteria in the hospital La Salpêtrière. From this time, Freud turns himself toward the practice of medical psychopathology. With his friend and collaborator Joseph Breuer (1842–1925), he begins using hypnosis in his clinical work. But the very beginning of psychoanalysis coincides with giving up hypnosis (and the cathartic method) and adopting the rule of encouraging patients to talk freely about whatever ideas or memories occurred to them. Hence arises the fundamental technical rule of "free association", which has from that time on been maintained in psychoanalytic work. It means that the patient is required to put himself in the position of a self-observer and to give up the whole of his critical attitude. The material which is thus brought to light, is to be used for the purpose of uncovering unconscious connections.

All the difficulty lies in the gap between what is conscious and unconscious, and the necessity to overcome the repression that prevents awareness of unconscious conflicts in which, according to Freud, neuroses such as psychoses or perversions are deeply rooted. Here psychoanalysis becomes an interpretive art that enables patients, with the help of the physician, to become aware of unconscious conflicts dominating their mental lives. For Freud is convinced, according to the principle of determination of natural phenomena in modern science, that all mental events are strictly determined, in other words that everything that occurred to a patient setting out from a particular starting-point must also stand in an internal connection with that starting-point. In addition Freud believes that psychoanalysis ought to set itself the task of carrying deeper the first of Breuer's great discoveries – namely, that neurotic symptoms are significant substitutes for other mental acts, which have been omitted. Freud writes: "it was now a question of regarding the material produced by the patients' associations as though it hinted at a hidden meaning and of discovering that meaning from it" (Freud 1922).

The best way to give an idea of Freud's interpretive art is to take an example among Freud's famous and numerous cases. But first it is worth saying that giving a meaning to insignificant events like slips of the tongue, random movements and actions, forgetting words (parapraxis), which aren't usually noticed and interpreted, is typical of Freud's method. For example, the *Psychopathology of Everyday Life* begins with a chapter, entitled "Forgetting of proper names", in which Freud studies the reasons for the escape of the name Signorelli. During a trip through Bosnia-Herzegovina, Freud had a conversation with a friend and couldn't recall the name of the painter of the Orvieto frescos in Italy. Instead of Signorelli, he produced as substitutes the names of two painters: Botticelli and Boltraffio. Freud tries to find out the associative processes that linked Signorelli to Botticelli and Boltraffio as substitutes. The understanding of this involuntary forgetting supposes knowledge of a few events, which belong to Freud's life and are indicated by Freud himself during his analysis. One important ingredient is the name of a North-Italian village, Trafoï, where he received the message of the suicide of one of his patients, struggling with sexual problems. According to Freud, there is an obvious connection between Trafoï and Boltraffio and the metamorphosis of the name Trafoï is explained by repression, that is to say by the repressed link to the theme of death and sexuality, which occurred in the conversation Freud had with his friend during the trip through Bosnia-Herzegovina.

The second important ingredient in Freud's analysis is the extraction of an Italian word *signor* from the forgotten name Signorelli. *Herr*, the German counterpart of *Signor*, is then linked to *Herzegovina*, to Bosnia-Herzegovina and to a stream of thoughts concerning sexuality and the custom of the Turks in Bosnia. It isn't possible here to expose all the ingredients on which Freud's interpretation is based, but these few are enough to suggest how Freud proceeds to find out the associative processes. According to Freud, the name Signorelli was thus divided into two parts. One pair of syllables (elli) returned unchanged in one of the substitutions (Bottic*elli*), while the other (Signor) had gained through its translation (sir, Herr) many and diverse relations to the names (*Herzegovina* and *Bosnia*) contained in the repressed theme (death and sexuality), but was lost through it in the reproduction. Its substitution (*Botticelli*) was formed in a way to suggest that a displacement took place along the same associations – "Herzegovina and *Bosnia*" – regardless of the sense and acoustic demarcation. On may not be convinced by such an explanation but the point is to understand that the names are treated in this process "like the written pictures of a sentence (rebus)" (Freud 1901). Generally speaking, forgetting is motivated by repression and the substitutions are compromise-formations or symptoms, that is manifestations of unconscious thoughts and impulses *versus* repression. Discovering these unconscious thoughts and impulses is therefore the task of an interpretive art.

How to interpret dreams

Although it took many years to sell out the first 600 copies, the most famous book of the history of psychoanalysis is certainly *The Interpretation of Dreams* (*Die Traumdeutung*), published in 1900. In Freud's eyes, this book is fundamental as far as – and the sentence is very well-known – "interpretation of dreams is in fact the *via regia* (royal road) to the interpretation of the unconscious" (Freud 1910). In other words, interpretation of dreams allows for privileged accessibility to parts of the mind that are inaccessible through conscious thought. From that point of view, Freud adds a little bit further: "if I were asked how one could become a psychoanalyst, I should answer through the study of his own dreams". Freud regrets that the opponents of the psychoanalytic theory pass over dream-interpretation with the most superficial objections, when they are not going to assimilate dreams with the irregular twitchings of St. Vitus' Dance. On the contrary, Freud pleads for sharing the prejudice of the ancients and the common people and pretends nothing but to follow "in the footsteps of the ancient dream interpreters" (Freud 1915–17). For a dream, according to the ancients and then to Freud, has a hidden meaning, and interpreting one, like the interpretation of a parapraxis, means finding out its hidden meaning.

We have therefore to distinguish when we are dreaming between the manifest and the latent content of the dream. The former is the dream itself as it is remembered; the latter is nothing but the hidden meaning. To uncover it is possible by dream analysis, which begins with the search for irruptive ideas that arise through free association from each separate dream element. From this material the latent dream thoughts may be discovered and the real sense of the dream appears as the fulfilling of an unsatisfied wish. Here is Freud's main thesis about dreams: "the manifest dream, which we remember after waking, may be described as a disguised fulfillment of repressed wishes" (Freud 1910). What are these repressed wishes? Essentially, all the wishes that are connected with the sexual life of the dreamer, like sadism, masochism, exhibitionism, voyeurism but first of all wishes linked to the Œdipus complex, that is desire to replace the father (or the mother) and to possess sexually the parent of the opposite sex. Freud calls dream-work the processes that have "brought about the distortion of the unconscious dream-thoughts into the manifest content of the dream". Among these psychic processes, those of condensation (one dream object stands for several associations and ideas) and displacement (a dream object's emotional significance is separated from its real object or content and attached to an entirely different one that does not raise the censor's suspicions) are especially noticeable. But better known is the symbolism: the unconscious makes use of a sort of symbolism, especially in the presentation of sexual complexes. For example, oblong objects like cucumbers or sticks can symbolize the penis; riding a horse, because of the analogy with sexual behaviour, might express *coitus*; all action that separates a part from the whole like losing a tooth can signify castration, and so on.

But Freud himself warns us against what he calls the "harmful error" of overestimating the meaning of symbols and underestimating the technique of free association to the dream elements. In his *Introduction to Psychoanalysis*, Freud gives this very simple example that allows us to understand dream interpretation a little bit better. The dream of a Munich physician in the year 1910 goes to show how it is usually impossible to understand a dream before the dreamer has given information about it.

> On July 13, 1910, toward morning, I dreamed that I was bicycling down a street in Tübingen, when a brown Dachshund tore after me and caught me by the heel. A bit further on I get off, seat myself on a step and begin to beat the beast, which has clenched is teeth tight … . Then I wake up and, as so

often happens to me, the whole dream becomes perfectly clear to me in this moment of transition to the waking state.

According to Freud's comment, symbols are of little use in this case and one doesn't immediately think of castration because of the biting. The dreamer gives besides some important information: "I lately fell in love with a girl, just from seeing her on the street, but had no means of becoming acquainted with her. The most pleasant means might have been the Dachshund, since I am a great lover of animals." He also adds that this particular dog always accompanied the girl. In fact the girl was disregarded in the manifest dream and there remained only the dog that he associates with her.

From neurotic symptoms to civilization

As a physician, Freud applies the same hermeneutical rules to neurotic or psychotic symptoms, which are interpreted as compromise-formations, and therefore as involving unconscious meanings. Let's take for example Anna O. (Bertha Pappen-heim), the famous hysteric who was at first treated by doctor J. Breuer – who fell in love with her.

Anna O. developed a series of physical and psychological disturbances (hysterical conversion). She suffered from a rigid paralysis, accompanied by loss of sensation, of both extremities on the right side of her body; and the same trouble from time to time affected her on her left side. She had, among other disturbances, a severe nervous cough. She had an aversion to taking nourishment and on one occasion she was for several weeks unable to drink in spite of tormenting thirst. Finally, she was subject to conditions of "absence", of confusion, of delirium, and of alteration of her whole personality (Freud 1910). How to interpret such a series of neurotic symptoms? Are they connected? Is it possible to bring out their general meaning? Freud's first thesis is that hysterics suffer from reminiscences. In other words, hysterics are haunted by intolerable wishes of which repression was a failure: they have been driven out of consciousness and out of memory but continue to exist in the unconscious. Freud's second thesis is that symptom is a substitute or surrogate for the repressed idea. As well as the interpretation of latent content from manifest content of dreams, the interpretation of the hysterical symptom consists in finding out its repressed meaning under its disguise and in tracing the paths along which the substitution was effected in the course of the patient's psychoanalytic treatment.

But psychoanalysis is not only a way of interpreting individual phenomena like dreams or neurotic symptoms. It also claims to develop a hermeneutics of human history and civilization. In 1930 Freud published *Civilization and its Discontents*. The father of psychoanalysis compares cultural development and libidinal development in an individual. In both cases Freud uncovers a process that is "usually identical with what we know so well as sublimation (of the aim of an instinct)" (Freud 1930). This means that our sexual instincts or drives (as it is phrased in updated translations) are deflected into acts of higher social valuation and that sublimation is what makes it possible for higher psychical activities, scientific, artistic or ideological, to play such an important part in civilized life. But, as a physician of our civilized world, Freud warns us against repressing too much our natural instincts. From this point of view he relates an old German tale about a town called Schilda. The citizens of Schilda had a horse against whom they had only one grudge, that he consumed so many expensive oats. They concluded that by good management they would break him of this bad habit, by cutting down his rations each day. One day the horse was found dead. The citizens could not understand why he had died. Freud concludes that he is inclined to believe that the animal has starved and that without a certain ration of oats no work would be expected from a horse. The same is true of humanity and it is no wonder that sexual frustration causes a feeling of discontent among civilians (Freud 1910).

Freud's interpretation of civilization and its discontents is connected with another tale or hypothesis, which comes from Darwin, about the very beginning of human culture. In *Totem and Taboo*, Freud aims to uncover the roots of the repression of all the incestuous instincts the Œdipus complex is made up of, but also the origin of Law, Morality and Religion. Freud imagines the beginning of humanity in the form of a primal and patriarchal horde, with a father who owned several wives and who drove away his sons to keep his wives for himself out of jealousy. But one day the brothers came together and killed their father. Cannibal savages as they were, they devoured their victim after killing him. From this point of view, the totem meal, which was perhaps mankind's earliest festival and the starting point of religion, would thus be a repetition and a commemoration of this memorable deed. But the dead became stronger than the living had been. What the father's presence had formerly prevented they themselves now prohibited "in the psychic situation of subsequent obedience, which we know so well from psychoanalysis" (Freud 1913–14). The brothers undid their deed by declaring that the killing of the father substitute, the totem, was not allowed, and renounced the fruits of their deed by denying themselves the liberated women. Thus they created the two fundamental taboos of totemism that correspond with the two repressed wishes of the Œdipus complex.

The conflicts of interpretations: Freud, Ricœur, Sartre

Before criticizing Freud's hermeneutics, it is worth studying how he evaluates his own interpretations of human phenomena such as dream, neurotic symptom, religion or civilization. We will see afterwards two other interpretations of Freud's hermeneutics.

We have to notice first that Freud's thinking is partly ruled by a kind of empiricism or even of positivism. Freud actually distinguishes among his work between on one hand scientific theories that he considers as empirical research grounded on what it is called experience, that is, all that occurs in the frame of the psychoanalytical relationship, and on the other hand unscientific theories that belong to speculation, philosophy or poetry. No wonder therefore that in his book, *Group Psychology and Analysis of the Ego*, Freud characterizes his unverifiable hypothesis about the primitive form of the human society as "a Just-So Story" although he considers at the same time that "it is creditable to such a hypothesis if it proves able to bring coherence and understanding into more and more new regions" (Freud 1921). In the same way, asking himself about his speculations from biology concerning *Eros*, the erotic instincts or drives, which seek to combine more and more living substance into ever greater unities, and *Thanatos*, the death instincts, which oppose this effort and lead what is living back into an inorganic state, Freud writes in his *New Introductory Lectures on Psycho-analysis* (1932) that "the theory of the instincts is so to say our mythology. Instincts are mythical entities, magnificent in their indefiniteness. In our work we cannot for a moment disregard them, yet we are never sure that we are seeing them clearly" (Freud 1932).

These statements don't mean that the whole theory of instinct is lacking scientific bases. Freud simply considers that the speculative part of his theory can't claim the same certainty as, for example, the extending of the conception of sexuality or the establishing of narcissism. For these latter innovations, according to Freud, rest on observed material and are direct translations of observation into theory, whereas the former is worked out by combining facts with pure imagination and thereby departing far from observation (Freud 1920). However it is quite easy to find out the weakness of the argument and the kind of vicious circle it is based on: what pretends to be founded on experience is actually made up from very questionable interpretations of what occurs in the therapeutic relationship between the analyst and his patient. In other words, Freudian interpretations claim to be confirmed by previous interpretations of the experience. And paradoxically, although psychoanalysis keeps interpreting individual as well as collective phenomena, although Freud himself, as already seen, presents psychoanalysis as an "interpretive art", he maintains at the same time that psychoanalysis proceeds like any empirical science following the pattern of experimental physics as if psychoanalysis was a "natural science" (as Dilthey uses this phrase).

The following quotation is certainly going to increase the trouble concerning Freud's ambiguous thinking about science:

> Were we to appraise our speculations upon the life and death-instincts it would disturb us but little that so many processes go on which are surprising and hard to picture ... . This comes only from our being obliged to operate with scientific terms, i.e. with the metaphorical expressions (*bilde Sprache*) peculiar to psychology ... . Otherwise we should not be able to describe the corresponding processes at all, nor in fact even have remarked them. The shortcomings of our description would probably disappear if for the psychological terms we could substitute physiological or chemical ones. These too only constitute a metaphorical language (*Bildersprache*), but one familiar to us for a much longer time and perhaps also simpler.
>
> (Freud 1920)

In other words, it appears that every science uses an improper language as if the proper scientific expression of the phenomena was an impossible scientific dream. Freud considers his own vocabulary to be metaphorical and a substitute for physiological or chemical vocabulary. But it doesn't follow that psychoanalytic language is more metaphorical and less scientific than the others. We are indubitably far from any kind of positivism. Does it mean that every science is an interpretative one based on a specific and improper language?

Among the hermeneutical tradition, Paul Ricœur (1913–2005) is perhaps one of the most open philosophers towards psychoanalysis, even if Ricœur's hermeneutics of meaning contrasts with Freud's energetics of drives (instincts). In his important work, *Freud and Philosophy: An Essay on Interpretation* (1965), Ricœur undertakes one of the most extensive examinations to date of psychoanalysis. Ricœur supports the basic thesis that psychoanalysis is and has to be – in accordance with the double nature of the psychological life – a mixed discourse partly energetic, partly hermeneutical; that is, like a natural science, psychoanalysis reduces psychological phenomena to forces and play of forces, and like a human science, it seeks to uncover their meaning (Embree 1997: 571). But Ricœur's interest in Freud's work also finds its roots in his reflection about evil and the symbolism of evil. For, according to Ricœur, evil is never described literally and is always spoken of symbolically or metaphorically, for example, in terms of stain, burden, errance or captivity. These symbols as double-meaning terms demand a specific method of interpretation, which is somehow brought into play by Freud when he tries to find out the secret meaning of human behaviour patterns. In his book, Ricœur develops a very useful distinction between two ways of interpretation, that match with, on the one hand, symbolic language as a revelation of the sacred and, on the other hand, symbolic language as a distortion or mask that promotes an illusion. Freud as well as Marx and Nietzsche belong to this kind of legitimate hermeneutics (Ricœur 1970).

Whereas Ricœur points out the double nature of psychoanalysis and welcomes Freud's depth psychology in his way, Jean-Paul Sartre (1905–80) definitively rejects the idea of unconscious mental processes or of an unconscious region of the mind – even if one should note that Sartre's suspicion of Freudian psychoanalysis becomes quite nuanced in his later years. Generally speaking, the French philosopher opposes an existential psychoanalysis to Freudian psychoanalysis, as a hermeneutic method that would interpret the concrete behaviour of the person, thanks to his original project, that is, the free choice of himself in a determined situation. This kind of psychoanalysis is grounded on a theory of consciousness as well as on an ontological phenomenology of freedom that Sartre sets out in *Being and Nothingness* (1943). In this text, he supports the idea that the human being isn't divided between reason and passions or between conscious and unconscious drives but is a totality, expressed completely through his conduct. From this point of view, "there is not a taste, a mannerism, or a human act which is not revealing" (Sartre 2003: 568). For any conduct expresses in various ways the basic choice of the individual subject, which can be unveiled and revealed as Sartre himself attempts to do with his study of Baudelaire (1947).

But after *Search for a Method* (1957) and *Critique of Dialectical Reason* (1960), Sartre enlarges his conception of existential psychoanalysis and begins to write his massive three volume study of Gustave Flaubert: *The Family Idiot* (1970–2) which remains unfinished. In this "true novel", Sartre intends to understand dialectically Flaubert's interiority and exteriority. In this way of thinking, existential psychoanalysis aims to understand Flaubert's internalization of exteriority; that is, how Flaubert's interiority refers on the one hand to objective structures: the social and economic organization of society, which are commanded by material conditions, and on the other hand to the action upon our adult life of "the childhood we never wholly surpass". In *Search for a Method*, Sartre writes:

> Today psychoanalysis alone enables us to study the process by which a child, groping in the dark, is going to attempt to play, without understanding it, the social role which adults impose upon him. Only psychoanalysis will show us whether he stifles in his role, whether he seeks to escape it, or is entirely assimilated into it. Psychoanalysis allows us to discover the whole man in the adult; that is, not only his present determinations but also the weight of his history.
>
> (Sartre 1963: 60)

Conclusion

It is commonly thought that Freudian psychoanalysis is the only way – the *via regia* – to understand dreams, psychopathology of everyday life, neurotic symptoms, sexuality, perversions, delusion, and so on. In fact, Freud's *Interpretation of Dreams* and other works try to develop a huge hermeneutics of human life and of its psychological pathologies. As we have seen, even if Freud doesn't refer in his own research to hermeneutics, we can consider his psychoanalysis, with Paul Ricœur, as a very specific hermeneutics based on the hypothesis of a secret, unconscious meaning of psychological phenomena. But it's worth noticing that other hermeneutics are possible and that Freudian interpretation can be ontologically criticized insofar as it is partly based on a questionable reification of the human being and a negation of his freedom.

Bibliography

Works by Freud

Freud, S. (1900–1) *The Interpretation of Dreams*, Standard Edition, first part and second part, vols 4–5.
——(1901) *The Psychopathology of Everyday Life*, Standard Edition, vol. 6.
——(1910) *Five Lectures on Psycho-Analysis, Leonardo da Vinci and Other Works*, Standard Edition, vol. 11.
——(1913-1914), *Totem and Taboo and Other Works*, Standard Edition, vol. 13.
——(1915–17) *Introductory Lectures on Psycho-Analysis*, Standard Edition, vols 15–16.
——(1918) *An infantile Neurosis and Other Works*, Standard Edition, vol. 17.
——(1920–22) *Beyond the Pleasure Principle, Group Psychology and other Works*, Standard Edition, vol. 18.
——(1925) *An Autobiographical Study, Inhibitions, Symptoms and Anxiety, The Question of Lay Analysis and Other Works*, Standard Edition, vol. 20.
——(1927–31) *The Future of an Illusion, Civilization and its Discontents, and Other Works*, Standard Edition, vol. 21.
——(1932–36) *New Introductory Lectures on Psycho-analysis and Other Works*, Standard Edition, vol. 22.

Other works

Dilthey, W. (2010) *The Understanding of Other Persons and Their Manifestations of Life, Selected Paper, vol. III, The formation of the historical world in the human sciences*, Princeton: Princeton University Press.

Embree, L. (ed.) (1997) *Encyclopedia of Phenomenology*, Dordrecht: Kluwer Academic Publishers.

Ricœur, P. (1970) *Freud and Philosophy: An Essay on Interpretation*, London: Yale University Press

Sartre, J. P. (1963) *Search for a Method*. Trans Hazel E Barnes. New York: Knopf.

——(2003) *Being and nothingness*, New York: Philosophical Library.

50

HERMENEUTICS AND LANGUAGE PHILOSOPHY

Lee Braver

If hermeneutics is the philosophical study of interpretation, then it is hardly the exclusive province of continental philosophy. For much of its history, analytic philosophy has also studied the nature of interpretation, primarily by way of language. If we examine the world of thought or logic through the lens of language, or if we are just interested in the nature of language itself, then the question of how we are able to understand it seems thrust upon us. The philosopher most responsible for turning analytic philosophy to language, and arguably the greatest figure in that tradition, is Ludwig Wittgenstein. After largely ignoring the interpretation in his early work, he makes it the center of his later thought. I will argue that many of the most prominent topics of his later work – naming, pictures, private languages, and rule following – can all be understood as hermeneutic in that they all demonstrate the need for interpretation where we might not suspect its presence, and teach us about its nature. If I am right, Wittgenstein should be included among the great hermeneutic philosophers of the twentieth century.

While analytic philosophy is often associated with the study of language today, its founders – Frege, Moore, and Russell – were relatively uninterested in the subject. It was Wittgenstein who, in his 1921 *Tractatus Logico-Philosophicus*, turned decisively towards it, arguing that "all philosophy is a 'critique of language'" (Wittgenstein 2001a: 4.0031). The Kantian term is no accident. Like Kant, Wittgenstein wanted "to draw a limit to thought" (Wittgenstein 2001a: 3) but he found that drawing such a limit directly would require us to think about what lies on the far side of it which, *ex hypothesi*, is unthinkable. Whereas we cannot think the unthinkable, we can in a sense say the unspeakable; it just comes out as nonsense. This allows us to plot the border between sense and nonsense, thus setting a limit to sensible language and, if thought is intrinsically linguistic, this will reveal the outermost boundary of thought as well without requiring us to cross it.

Wittgenstein seeks this border by determining the essence of language, which is to describe reality. The most basic linguistic unit will be the simplest piece of language that does this – elementary propositions which are made of names arranged in a certain way. Names get their meaning by being correlated with simple objects, the ultimate building blocks of reality. When names are arranged properly, the elementary proposition asserts or denies the existence of a state of affairs: a set of objects in the world arranged the same way. A proposition therefore represents a state of affairs in the world by picturing it, that is, by having its own linguistic components (names) mirror the state's worldly components (objects). For instance, if you want to say that the cat is on the mat, your proposition must have names standing in for the cat and the mat, and the names must be related in the proposition in a way that corresponds to the "oneness" that obtains between the two entities in the world. This isn't quite accurate since Wittgenstein's objects are far simpler than macroscopic entities like cats and mats, but it gives you the idea.

Since all other propositions are made up of logical combinations of elementary propositions, all linguistic meaning derives ultimately from the connection forged between names and objects. Wittgenstein describes his early conception of meaning:

> the concept of meaning I adopted in my philosophical discussions originates in a primitive philosophy of language. The German word for "meaning" is derived from the German word for "pointing". When Augustine talks about the learning of language he talks about how we attach names to things, or understand the names of things. *Naming* here appears as the foundation, the be all and end all of language.
>
> (Wittgenstein, 2005, 56)

Understanding how language represents the world ultimately devolves on explaining how names represent simple objects.

But this Wittgenstein does not do. He never even identifies what simple objects are, much less how we access them and tag them with names. As suggested by the connection between the German words for meaning and pointing, he was almost certainly thinking of the act of naming as a form of ostensive definition, that is, pointing at things and giving them a name. This is how mature adults learn new words, after all, so we tend to read this way of acquisition back into the origin of language itself, as Augustine does in his account of the way he initially learned to speak as a baby in the quote that opens the *Philosophical Investigations* (Wittgenstein 2009).

This Tractarian picture of language as made up of names that get attached to objects by means of ostensive definitions becomes one of the main targets of Wittgenstein's later work. Although we do often ostensively define words without problems, he now realizes that this apparently simple act is actually quite complex, with many factors needing to be in place for it to succeed. He had already had intimations of these complications in his early work, but he repressed them. The fact that we must construct arbitrary signs to represent the world brings in interpretation, for how am I to know what a particular sign is meant to indicate? I must listen to a great deal of your speech and watch your behavior in order to align the signs you are saying with the symbols and matters of fact they stand for.

This is no simple matter since signs can link up with the world in all sorts of ways. Indeed, the possibility of negation means that a picture of something could actually mean its prohibition or denial. Thus a sign must not only possess certain logical properties to represent a state of affairs successfully but it must also be taken the right way to function as that sign, and this way of taking it cannot be included in it since any such instructions on how to take it would themselves have to be taken correctly. This is where the messiness of daily human life seeps into the immaculate translucent structure of logic since "everyday language is a part of the human organism and is no less complicated than it" (Wittgenstein 2001a: 4.002). Although Wittgenstein constructs a perfectly pristine realm where all is lucidly logical, he cannot simply bypass the ad hoc hurly-burly of words and acts and things and people. These form what Derrida calls a necessary detour; that is, something that is actually necessary even though philosophers dismiss it as accidental.

Wittgenstein later acknowledges this tension in the *Tractatus*: "the more closely we examine actual language, the greater becomes the conflict between it and our requirement. (For the crystalline purity of logic was, of course, not something I had *discovered*; it was a requirement)" (Wittgenstein 2009: §107). Instead of looking through everyday language for the pure essence at its core, he now tells us to accept it as language's true nature: "we're talking about the spatial and temporal phenomenon of language, not about some non-spatial, atemporal non-entity" (Wittgenstein 2009: 52). His later work asks about what actually happens when we speak instead of reading in what must be the case based on assumptions. And perhaps the main phenomenon he finds which had been lacking in his earlier account of language is interpretation.

First, let's reexamine naming, the foundation of all meaning in the Tractarian picture of language. To point to what you mean in order to name it is actually a rather complex and sophisticated operation since anything you can point to has numerous, even innumerable qualities. If I point at a pencil, am I indicating its being a pencil, or its color, size, number, function … ? No matter how clearly I feel like I am pointing to one aspect, "an ostensive definition can be variously interpreted in *every* case" (Wittgenstein 2009: §28). We don't notice the endless ways of, literally, missing the point because we are so used to taking it in certain ways, and we have the linguistic resources to correct the occasional miscommunications: "no, I'm not talking the number; I'm talking about the color." But the finger cannot indicate the relevant meaning by itself.

What picks out the relevant aspect and thus ensures successful communication is the context, what Wittgenstein comes to call its language-game. "An ostensive definition explains the use – the meaning – of a word if the role the word is supposed to play in the language is already clear. … One has already to know (or be able to do) something before one can ask what something is called" (Wittgenstein 2009: §30). I have to grasp "colors" as a group of associated qualities to understand someone indicating the color of something or teaching me a new color; this cannot be the way I grasp the group "color" in the first place. To use one of Wittgenstein's favorite examples, under certain circumstances I can perfectly well teach you chess by, among other things, pointing at a piece and saying, "This is the king." But for you to grasp the significance of this, you need to have a sense of what board games are, that different pieces often play different roles in games, and so on. Although this seems obvious to the point of self-evidence, that's only because we are so familiar with it. I could be passing an encoded message to a spy by uttering that sentence while pointing to a particular piece on the board, or fomenting a very peculiar form of revolution, or

I could simply be fond of naming small objects in my vicinity: "This carved piece of wood is the king; that bit of tin over there is Larry; my belt buckle is Hortense."

The significance of naming the chess piece is determined by what I intend you to do with that information and with the standard ways of reacting to this kind of naming. Meaning is not *identified* with use, as is sometimes suggested, but meaning cannot be extricated from use. "How does pointing to its colour differ from pointing to its shape? … The difference, one might say, does not lie in the act of demonstration, but rather in the surrounding of that act in the use of the language" (Wittgenstein 1969: 80). You cannot understand the meaning of a word until you grasp what it is being used for because different uses give the apparently simple act of naming different significance. The gap between definition and understanding is rarely noticeable because we usually do get the point effortlessly. This success is due neither to rationality nor exceptional pointing skills, but rather to one of those immensely important but inconspicuous-because-ubiquitous facts about humans, namely, that "pointing is used and understood in a particular way – that people react to it in a particular way. … One only has to point to something and say, 'This is so-and-so', and everyone who has been through a certain preliminary training will react in the same way" (Wittgenstein 1976: 182).

What applies to the most basic Tractarian level of connecting names to objects also applies at the next level up: the correlation of propositions or pictures to states of affairs. A picture's method of projection, that is, the way we connect shapes or scratches on paper to the things they represent, is so natural to us that it becomes invisible, as if it automatically referred to its subject. Picturing seems to take care of itself by apparently being intrinsically, transparently related to what it pictures. But as with names, understanding the significance of a picture is a learned skill, and one that can change depending on the circumstances. Therefore, as Wittgenstein already realized in his early *Notebooks*, we only know a picture's meaning if we know its method of projection. "The way of representing determines how the reality has to be compared with the picture. … The same picture will agree or fail to agree with reality according to how it is supposed to represent. … The method of comparison must be given me before I can make the comparison" (Wittgenstein 1961: 22–3). As with the ostensive definitions, if I hand you a picture, even if you have a sense of what it depicts, you cannot understand its meaning until you see why I have given it to you. Is it an instruction to be followed, or a warning to be avoided? Or a piece of art to be admired? Or a birthday card, to be briefly kept and then thrown away? Or an example deftly illustrating a philosophical point?

The point Wittgenstein is making for both names and pictures is that by themselves they cannot fix their referent or meaning. No matter how obvious a certain understanding of a name or picture appears to be, it can always be understood differently. Every apparently rock-solid, self-evident understanding papers over innumerable other possible interpretations. While many of these may seem bizarre to us, that's only because we're used to the typical reading, not because of some intrinsic intelligibility in the sign that forces us to read it one way rather than any other.

> Is there a picture, or something like a picture, that forces a particular application on us … ? We're at most under a psychological, not a logical,

compulsion. ... Our belief that the picture forced a particular application upon us consisted in the fact that only the one case and no other occurred to us.

(Wittgenstein 2009: §140)

His conclusion is that "you can't give any picture which can't be misinterpreted" (Wittgenstein 1993: 59), what I have called elsewhere the Thesis of Inescapable Ambiguity (Braver 2012: 121–5). No matter how self-evident its standard application appears, a picture or name can always be understood otherwise by someone sincerely trying to comprehend it correctly.

What is sometimes known as the Private Language Argument is an example of ostensive definitions' inability to nail down precise meanings by themselves. A private language is a language that no one else can understand since no one else has access to the referents of the words: you can't feel my pain so you can't know exactly what I mean by "pain." In keeping with the Tractarian picture of language that forms the target of his later criticisms, Wittgenstein frames the problem in terms of naming: "how do words *refer* to sensations? ... How is the connection between the name and the thing named set up?" (Wittgenstein 2009: §244). We imagine that we simply give ourselves an internal ostensive definition just as others give us external ones by pointing to an object. In fact, it seems that we have no other choice in the case of naming something completely private like a pain; no one else has access to my pains in order to point at them and label them with words. This seems like a realm in which teaching is neither necessary nor possible. Surely I know what my pain feels like so I know how to talk about it; attaching a word to it lets the intrinsic nature of pain drive the grammar of what I say about it. "'But I can (inwardly) undertake to call THIS 'pain' in the future. ... Once you know *what* the word stands for, you understand it, you know its whole use" (Wittgenstein 2009: §§263–4).

Wittgenstein demolishes this picture piece by piece. Our "inner" sensations are not radically closed off from others; much of the time I can tell perfectly well what you're feeling. If you hit your thumb with a hammer and it starts to bleed while you hop up and down cursing and tearing up, only a philosopher in thrall to a picture would say that I cannot be sure what you are feeling (Wittgenstein 2009: §246). We are disproportionately impressed by moments of pretense, forgetting how rare they are as well as the fact that even pretense requires the proper surroundings to count as such. For it to make sense that someone is faking pain, some of the factors associated with subterfuge must be present: a motive, effort in keeping the deception going, times when the person drops the mask, and so on. "Lying is a language-game that needs to be learned like any other one" (Wittgenstein 2009: §249). This is why Wittgenstein says that some indefinite but recognizable set of qualities must accompany any being we can coherently ascribe pain to.

Although sensations seem completely private, it is from public language-games that we learn of internal feelings in the first place; they set up what was called in the *Tractatus* the idea's logical space, grammar in the later works. This isn't just labeling a fully fleshed-out object, but establishing what *kind* of object it is, which then sets up the appropriate ways to think and talk about it. Public language-games are not accidental verbal appendages that simply direct our attention to intrinsically meaningful items; according to Wittgenstein, language-games *constitute* meaning in the sense of creating and sustaining it, albeit inconspicuously. "*Essence* is expressed in grammar. ... Grammar tells what kind of object anything is" (Wittgenstein 2009: §371, §373). Talking about pain is a socially determined practice, like talking sensibly about anything else. Naming a feeling "pain" no more settles matters than naming a piece of wood "king."

> When one says "He gave a name to his sensation", one forgets that much must be prepared in the language for mere naming it to make sense. And if we speak of someone's giving a name to a pain, the grammar of the word "pain" is what has been prepared here; it indicates the post where the new word is stationed.
>
> (Wittgenstein 2009: §257)

What seem like simple immediate encounters with private entities clandestinely rely on this publically learned grammar in order to make sense, even to ourselves. "Would I know that pain, etc., etc., is something inner if I weren't told so?" (Wittgenstein 1980: §643). It does not happen spontaneously through direct contact with a sensation that just means what it means without the need for interpretation. Even their privacy is something I learn publically. "The sentence 'Sensations are private' is comparable to 'One plays patience by oneself'" (Wittgenstein 2009: §248).

What we have learned is that, despite the feeling that names and pictures and sensations are intrinsically meaningful, in fact they all need interpretation to do the work that they do. The hermeneutic upshot of this is that interpretation is to be found in all sorts of places where it appears to be absent. However, we need to be careful about what we mean by interpretation. If Wittgenstein argues on the one hand against the idea that we simply follow what intrinsically meaningful pictures and sensations tell us to do, he is equally opposed to the notion that we consciously think about these matters. In fact, it is usually only when we stop to think that Inescapable Ambiguities arise.

Because of how easily and naturally we follow signs most of the time, we tend to think that interpretation plays no role here; we're just following what the sign obviously says.

> We are extraordinarily affected by the way in which we do in fact react to a sign. The result is that certain ideas stand to us for certain uses because that is how we usually apply them. We therefore think that those ideas have that most usual use *in* them, though they could perfectly well be imagined to have another use.
>
> (Wittgenstein 2001b: 88–9)

However, any picture, regardless of medium or apparent legibility, underdetermines its interpretation. The same goes for ostensive definitions: just pointing at something and saying "this is X" cannot by itself convey which aspect of the thing one is naming or under what description or in what context, and so on. And for sensations that seem to determine how we talk about them.

And for rules. Wittgenstein notes that rules are meant to apply to indefinitely many cases and yet, of necessity we only get instructed in applying them to a limited number of cases. A rule such as "X * 2" allows any number in the "X" slot even though in learning the rule we only see it applied to a small number of examples. The teacher shows the student how to multiply 1 by 2, 2 by 2, 10 by 2, 150 by 2, and at some point says something like, "continue applying the rule the same way for all inputs," or just, "and so on." Wittgenstein questions how this "and so on" – so crucial to the very meaning of rules – works. The student must apply the rule to new circumstances in which she was not specifically taught what to do. She's supposed to carry on in the same way, but what does "same" mean? Sometimes a change in circumstances legitimately affects how the rule is to be applied, such as when we input negative numbers or fractions. These circumstances are relevant to changing how we multiply, whereas others – such as going above 1,000 – aren't, but how is the student supposed to know which differences make a difference? In principle, the teacher cannot anticipate all possible circumstances; he must stop instructing at some point, confident that the student has caught on. Where does the student get this sense of relevance? How does she learn how to continue past where instruction leaves off? Multiplying by 3 after 1,000 and 4 after 10,000 is equally compatible with the examples given as continuing to multiply by 2, as Nelson Goodman and Saul Kripke have shown. If the student does start multiplying by 3 the teacher will say that she needs to continue the rule the same way, but the student will respond that it is the teacher who is changing the rule by multiplying by 2 after 1,000. Both ways of carrying on are compatible with all the examples that have been given since they are all under 1,000. As in the other cases, we run up against Inescapable Ambiguity: it is "possible to derive anything from anything according to some rule or other – nay, according to *any* rule with a suitable interpretation" (Wittgenstein 1983: 389).

Rather than resorting to conscious acts of reasoning to escape this ambiguity, Wittgenstein's conclusion is that this traditional conception of thinking is the source of the problem. The futility of the disengaged reasoner's search for the "right" interpretation amidst a pullulating sea of alternatives represents a *reduction ad absurdum* of the idea that we actually are faced with such an array from which we must choose.

> It is felt to be a difficulty that a rule should be given in signs which do not themselves contain their use, so that a gap exists between a rule and its application. But this is not a problem but a mental cramp. ... We are only troubled when we look at a rule in a particularly queer way. ... In ordinary life one is never troubled by a gap between the sign and its application.
> (Wittgenstein 2001b: 90)

Here Wittgenstein is close to Heidegger's definition of our usual way of carrying on as a "non-thematic circumspective absorption" which does not take up bare objects or sensations in order to interpret them, but interacts knowingly with them without explicit thought (Heidegger 1962: 107/76 – see also Braver 2012). At the root of this line of thought is the idea that what we are doing in these situations is interpreting:

This was our paradox: no course of action could be determined by a rule, because every course of action can be brought into accord with the rule. ... That there is a misunderstanding here is shown by the mere fact that in this chain of reasoning we place one interpretation behind another, as if each one contented us at least for a moment, until we thought of yet another lying behind it. For what we thereby show is that there is a way of grasping a rule which is *not* an interpretation, but which, from case to case of application, is exhibited in what we call "following the rule" and "going against it".

(Wittgenstein 2009: §201)

We're tempted to think of the rule as mechanistically determining how we follow it but Wittgenstein has revealed that we must take the rule in a particular way for it to guide our actions correctly. This way of taking it is not a matter of explicit thought, but unthinking reaction:

"All the steps are really already taken" means: I no longer have any choice. The rule, once stamped with a particular meaning, traces the lines along which it is to be followed through the whole of space. ... No ... – I should say: *This is how it strikes me.* ... I follow the rule *blindly.*

(Wittgenstein 2009: §219)

It is not thematic thought that leads me to the right application because explicit thought can always find indefinitely many alternate ways to follow the rule. What happens the vast majority of the time is an immediate reaction that has been formed by years of training which conditions us to simply react a certain way, the same way as pretty much everyone else. "These misunderstandings only immensely rarely arise – although my words might have been taken either way. This is because we have all been trained from childhood to use such phrases ... in one way rather than another" (Wittgenstein 1976: 20). Wittgenstein rejects the traditional philosophical emphasis on overt reasoning. Such acts occur rarely, and if they were our guide we would never know how to continue; we certainly wouldn't have the tremendous, easy agreement that we have.

Therefore, in one sense, interpretation is ubiquitous. Nothing by itself – no picture, name, sensation, or rule – can determine how we understand or apply it. No matter how clearly the world seems to take us by the hand and lead us, it is always up to us to recognize its authority and interpret its commands; neither past usage nor reality forces us to go on in one particular way. "There is no such thing here as, so to say, a wheel that he is to catch hold of, the right machine which, once chosen, will carry him on automatically" (Wittgenstein 1970: §304). We will never get to the other side of the ellipsis of "and so on ... ," not because of our all-too-human limitations but because there is no other side; that's the point of an ellipsis. However, it is training that conditions our reactions to take names, pictures, pointing, sensations, and rules the same way.

The child learns this language from the grown-ups by being trained to its use. I am using the word "trained" in a way strictly analogous to that in which we talk of an animal being trained to do certain things. It is done by means of example, reward, punishment, and suchlike.

(Wittgenstein 1969: 77)

We almost never sit and think about which way to follow, say, an arrow; we take it in at a glance and simply go the direction it points. Thus, in one sense, interpretation is everywhere; in another sense, virtually nowhere. Explanations only work if one reliably reacts in certain ways: finding certain similarities similar and relevant and others not, looking at what ostensive definitions point to, reading pictures and taking rules certain ways, and so on. Once these tendencies are in place, the student can learn more sophisticated rules and can do so in more explicit ways, just as ostensive definitions are a perfectly good way to learn new words after one has mastered the skill of looking at what is being pointed out and associating it with the word. "Doubtless the ostensive teaching helped to bring this about; but only together with a particular training. With different training the same ostensive teaching of these words would have effected a quite different understanding" (Wittgenstein 2009: §6).

Wittgenstein wants to get rid of both the idea of a self-applying rule and the idea that we examine various interpretations of a rule before deciding on the right one. Much early analytic philosophy chose the first option. Logic promised to turn messy everyday language into an impersonal procedure which can be mechanically computed, purified of all the vagueness and vagaries of the world and the messy mind of man. Logic was supposed to tell us exactly what to do in all circumstances, operating with the perfect consistency of a machine. It removed human subjectivity from the equation – what Frege feared as "psychologism" – ensuring the absolute Platonic objectivity of truth. Russell was not far off when he said of the *Tractatus* that, "a perfect notation would be a substitute for thought" (Wittgenstein 2001a: xix). Along with the linguistic turn, later Wittgenstein can be credited with what has been called an anthropological turn, meaning that humans cannot be taken out of the equation since we are the ones who run these logic machines and determine when they've been applied correctly. "If calculating looks to us like the action of a machine, it is *the human being* doing the calculation that is the machine" (Wittgenstein 1983: 234). Logic cannot replace hermeneutics because logic itself requires a certain kind of interpretation.

Bibliography

Braver, Lee. 2012. *Groundless Grounds: A Study of Wittgenstein and Heidegger*. Cambridge: MIT Press.

Heidegger, Martin. 1962. *Being and Time*. Trans. John Macquarrie and Edward Robinson. San Francisco: HarperSanFrancisco.

Wittgenstein, Ludwig. 1961. *Notebooks, 1914–1916*. Trans. G.E.M. Anscombe. Oxford: Blackwell.

——. 1969. *The Blue and Brown Books: Preliminary Studies for the 'Philosophical Investigations'*. Madsen: Blackwell.

——. 1970. *Zettel*. Ed. G. E. M. Anscombe and G. H. von Wright. Trans. G. E. M. Anscombe. Berkeley: University of California Press.

——. 1976. *Wittgenstein's Lectures on the Foundations of Mathematics: Cambridge 1939.* Ed. Cora Diamond. Chicago: University of Chicago Press.

——. 1980. *Remarks on the Philosophy of Psychology, Volume II.* Ed. G. H. von Wright and Heikki Nyman. Trans. C. G. Luckhardt and Maximilian A. E. Aue. Chicago: University of Chicago Press.

——. 1983. *Remarks on the Foundations of Mathematics.* Rev. ed. Ed. G. H. von Wright, R. Rhees, and G. E. M. Anscombe. Cambridge, MA: MIT Press.

——. 1993. *Philosophical Occasions, 1912–1951.* Ed. James Klagge and Alfred Nordmann. Indianapolis: Hackett.

——. 2001a. *Tractatus Logico-Philosophicus.* Trans. D. F. Pears and B. F. McGuinness. New York: Routledge.

——. 2001b. *Wittgenstein's Lectures: Cambridge, 1932–1935.* Ed. Alice Ambrose. Amherst, NY: Prometheus Books.

——. 2005. *Philosophical Grammar.* Ed. Rush Rhees. Berkeley: University of California Press.

——. 2009. *Philosophical Investigations.* 4th ed., rev. P.M.S. Hacker and Joachim Schulte. Trans. G. E. M. Anscombe, P.M.S. Hacker, and Joachim Schulte. Malden, MA: Wiley-Blackwell.

Further reading

Kripke, S. 1982. *Wittgenstein on Rules and Private Language: An Elementary Exposition.* Oxford: Blackwell.

Baker, G. P., and P. M. S. Hacker. 1985. *Wittgenstein: Rules, Grammar and Necessity, Volume 2 of an Analytical Commentary on the Philosophical Investigations.* Oxford: Blackwell (2nd extensively revised edition 2009).

Williams, Meredith. 2002. *Wittgenstein, Mind and Meaning: Towards a Social Conception of Mind.* London: Routledge.

51
HERMENEUTICS AND FEMINISM

Georgia Warnke

For the most part, feminists have not had much use for the German tradition of hermeneutics in general or with Gadamer's philosophical hermeneutics in particular. Despite Heidegger's Nazi affiliations, his contributions to the tradition are of more interest to some feminists because Derrida was interested in his work and because some feminists are interested in Derrida. Yet in her introduction to *Feminist Interpretations of Hans-Georg Gadamer* Lorraine Code lists some of the problems Gadamer's hermeneutics causes for feminists: his 'quietistic ... pursuit of scholarship during World War II,' his 'silence on questions of political ferment and social-political change during the latter half of the twentieth century' and the male intellectual world he depicts in his autobiographical writings (Code 2003: 3). Other feminist scholars have pointed to his disregard for issues of embodiment, his neglect of the effects of power relations and his attempt to rehabilitate prejudice and tradition. What is the point of feminism if not a challenge to the sexist (as well as the racist, classist, nationalist, ableist and homophobic etc.) prejudices of a tradition? In its commitment to the social, economic and political equality of all, has feminism not had to upend 'traditions regarding women's roles in marriage, families, public spaces, and religious practices,' as Linda Martin Alcoff points out (Alcoff 2003: 251)? Does Gadamer's hermeneutics therefore not 'contain within it' as Diane Elam insists 'the litter of phallocentric tradition' (Elam 1991: 350).

Alcoff's reference to upended traditions notwithstanding, she finds much of value for feminists in Gadamer's hermeneutics, in particular, his 'openness to alterity, the move from knowledge to understanding, holism in justification and immanent realism' (Alcoff 2003: 256). Susan-Judith Hoffman also maintains that many of Gadamer's ideas and perspectives 'point toward a hermeneutics that is in solidarity with feminist theorizing.' Her list includes his:

> account of the importance of difference, his notion of understanding as an inclusive dialogue, his account of prejudices as positive conditions of an understanding that must always remain provisional, his account of tradition

as not only the foundation that carries us but as that which is transformed by our reflection, and his account of language as an on going project.

(Hoffman 2003: 103)

In this chapter, I want to follow up on this list by re-examining Gadamer's rehabilitation of prejudice and tradition and by focusing on what remains a sore-point for feminists, namely Gadamer's alleged neglect of power.

Prejudice and tradition

To be sure, Gadamer's starting point for rehabilitating the status of prejudice and tradition is far afield of political and social issues, never mind feminist social and political issues. He begins with our understanding of texts and with the projections of meaning this understanding requires. As we begin to read a book we form expectations about what kind of book it is, what its themes are, who its interlocutors are and so on. Its opening pages may encourage us to think it is a psychological thriller such as *The Talented Mr. Ripley* or a text in feminist epistemology such as Alcoff's and Elizabeth Potter's edited collection, *Feminist Epistemologies*. These initial projections provide us with an orientation to the rest of the text by providing a context within which to situate what we read. As such, Gadamer maintains, they are indispensable. By offering us a notion of what the whole of the text is, they supply a framework within which to place the particular part of the text we are reading. 'A person who is trying to understand a text is always projecting,' he insists. 'He projects a meaning for the text as a whole as soon as some initial meaning emerges in the text' (Gadamer 1989: 267).

Nevertheless, projections of meaning do not begin only after the point at which we start to see meaning in a text. Rather, the 'initial meaning' that sparks projections about that whole is itself the result of projections. Hence, Gadamer continues his thought about 'the person who is trying to understand a text' by declaring that 'the initial meaning emerges only because he is reading the text with particular expectations with regard to a certain meaning' (Gadamer 1989: 267). Before we begin to read, we already possess expectations about the text. We pick up *The Talented Mr. Ripley* because we have heard about the author, Patricia Highsmith and anticipate that the book will be a riveting read. We start a book on feminist epistemologies because we have certain ideas about feminism and epistemology and expect an informed analysis of issues at their intersection. At work here is what, following Heidegger, Gadamer calls the fore-structure of understanding. Heidegger emphasizes the pre-existing engagements we have with aspects of our world. We are immersed in a structure of pre-formed meanings and are always anticipating the possibilities these meanings create. We understand a glass as the receptacle for the iced tea we want to pour or a desk as a structure that will support the computer we are thinking of buying. Our projections of meaning are our way of being in the world. We are always anticipating meanings that illuminate our world for us as a field of possible actions and interventions.

For his part, Gadamer emphasizes the historical character of these anticipations. The meanings we project do not come from nowhere but are rather parts of our

645

heritage. They embody the experiences and conceptions of those who came before us and comprise the set of resources they hand down to us for making sense out of our world. In short, they constitute our tradition. We not only have ideas about *The Talented Mr. Ripley*; we know what books are before taking up this particular one to read and we possess genre headings under which we approach them – *The Talented Mr. Ripley* as a psychological thriller, for example. We also inherit particular shared understandings – for example, understandings of what war, personal freedom or education is – and we inherit norms and values that define the significance things have for us – war as justified or terrible, personal freedom as a right or a privilege and so on. The totality of these understandings and valuations constitutes our historical tradition. To the extent that members of the same tradition can differ in their values and understand significances differently and to the extent that we can group meanings under different headings – political, literary, cultural and the like – we can speak of traditions in the plural. Gadamer's point, however, is that because our projections and anticipations of meaning are rooted in these traditions, they are prejudices, pre-established meanings that are bequeathed to us and that help us make sense out of our world. Indeed, without the context they provide we would have no way of approaching or situating the contents of our world at all.

Gadamer draws two implications from this analysis. First, prejudices are not necessarily illegitimate. Instead, they can be justified or unjustified: our further reading of a text or exploration of an issue may confirm or refute them. We may be justified in our initial supposition that a text is a psychological thriller or proved wrong as further reading fails to bear out this supposition. We may be so oriented as to shrink from the prospect of war and find that its ensuing gruesomeness confirms our prejudice. As Gadamer puts his point, 'That the prejudices determining what I think are due to my own partiality is a judgment based on the standpoint of their having been dissolved and enlightened, and it holds only for unjustified prejudices' (Gadamer 1989: 279–80). There can be justified prejudices, however, expectations that work out and that turn out to have appropriately directed us to the meaning of a text or what he might call a text-analogue such as an event, action, institution or practice.

Second, the Enlightenment demand that we eliminate all prejudice is impossible to meet. If the ways we understand subsequent events or chapters of a text bear out certain of our prejudices, they do so only because they conform to other of our prejudices. The same holds for the understandings that dissolve and enlighten certain prejudices; they do so only on the basis of others that, at least for the present, hold firm. We determine that a text is a psychological thriller because it conforms to our expectations about what psychological thrillers are; we decide the book on feminist epistemologies is not a contribution to feminism because it fails to take the contributions of those we consider prominent feminists into account. These standards are assumptions we have about the categories of psychological thriller and contributions to feminism, assumptions that themselves do not come from nowhere but are rooted in the literary and philosophical traditions to which we belong. Justifying or rejecting prejudices, our 'enlightenment' about our prejudices, thus depends upon other prejudices. Gadamer declares:

The overcoming of all prejudice, this global demand of the Enlightenment, will itself prove to be a prejudice, and removing it opens the way to an appropriate understanding of the finitude that dominates not only our humanity but also our historical consciousness.

(Gadamer 1989: 276)

Indeed, because we are historical creatures, because we find ourselves in a world we have inherited rather than in one we can create from scratch, 'The prejudices of the individual, far more than his judgments, constitute the historical reality of his being' (Gadamer 1989: 276–7).

Gadamer's critics, including his feminist ones, do not as much dispute these conclusions as wonder at his apparent sanguinity with regard to them. On the one hand, Gadamer's rehabilitation of prejudice and tradition is more benign than his provocative terminology may initially suggest: tradition signals simply the shared understandings history bequeaths to us while prejudices reflect the pre-orientations it offers us. We cannot deny our participation in history. Rather, we come to our projects and activities *in media res* as it were: within a world we did not create and that has already formed interpretations of its possibilities and limits. We can intervene in, rethink and modify these interpretations but we cannot begin anew and the resources we have to appeal to in our interventions are also ones we inherit rather than create. We are therefore inevitably prejudiced, where prejudiced means historically situated and always already directed towards that which we are trying to understand. On the other hand, our historical traditions are clearly not themselves benign. Even if history represents more than the 'catastrophe which keeps piling wreckage upon wreckage' that Walter Benjamin sees in Klee's *Angelus Novus* painting (Benjamin 1968: 257–8), history and the traditions of its interpretation are surely at least partly that. Gadamer focuses on the riches with which our history endows us: ideals to which to aspire, values and norms worth preserving and classical texts that trace the varieties and contours of human experience. In one of the few examples *Truth and Method* offers he notes that Descartes, despite his intention to start knowledge over on a firm basis, 'excluded morality from the total reconstruction of all truths by reason' (Gadamer 1989: 279). Yet, our historical traditions also include racism, sexism, homophobia and a plethora of other horrors. Should we not focus as much on these and on the means for overcoming them as on the historical wealth our traditions bequeath to us? Albrecht Wellmer insists that 'The context of tradition as a locus of possible truth … is, at the same time, the locus of factual untruth and continued force' (Wellmer 1974: 47). Similarly, Jürgen Habermas asks us not to forget that 'the background consensus of established traditions … can be a consciousness forged of compulsions, a result of pseudo-communication, not only in the pathologically isolated case of disturbed familial systems, but in entire social systems as well' (Habermas 1977: 358–5). Surely to remain indifferent to the pernicious biases in our collective understandings is to perpetuate relations of power that distort expressions of needs and misdirect goals and aspirations.

Miranda Fricker's *Epistemic Injustice: Power and Ethics of Knowing* provides ample support for these concerns and does so with particular relevance to feminists (Fricker 2007). Before asking whether Gadamer's work is as indifferent to the distortions of historical tradition as it is often accused of being, I want to use Fricker's work to elaborate on them.

Hermeneutical injustice

Fricker is interested in what she sees as gaps or lacunae in the tradition, or in what she views as the collective hermeneutical resources available to individuals and groups to articulate important areas of their experience, including women's experience. These resources are either not adequate for expressing some areas of experience at all or, where they do provide the means for expressing them, they do so in inadequate or misleading ways. This failure or inadequacy is unjust, Fricker argues, because it affects people differentially. Take the case of Carmita Wood. In 1975, Wood served as an administrative assistant in a university department where she was continually hounded by a senior professor who liked to jiggle his crotch when he stood at her desk and to find ways of brushing against her breasts. After a Christmas party during which he trapped her in an elevator and accosted her with unwanted kisses, she started to take the stairs and requested a transfer to another department. When her request was denied, she abruptly quit and subsequently applied for unemployment benefits. Her application was rejected because she was not able to cite anything other than personal reasons for leaving her job.

Fricker attributes Wood's difficulty in explaining why she quit to the absence of a collective understanding of the kind of oppression she and other women were experiencing. The hermeneutical resources available to Wood, and to those considering her request for a transfer and unemployment benefits, possessed a hole where an understanding of sexual harassment should have been. Wood was not alleging any standard ills that were codified in the existing hermeneutical repertoire. She did not claim that she had been physically assaulted, denied a promotion or subjected to pay inequities. She may have been embarrassed but was not embarrassment precisely a personal matter and not subject to compensation or redress? Under prevailing conceptions of the professor's behavior, it was a form of harmless flirting. Ought not Wood simply to have learned to tolerate it and even developed a sense of humor with regard to it? While the hermeneutical lacuna here that was eventually filled by an understanding of sexual harassment cost Wood her job, it did not affect the senior professor. Indeed, the absence was conceivably a boon to him since it left him free to engage in his behavior without the sort of shame he might have felt had the behavior been understood differently.

Fricker thinks it would be a mistake to see this gap in the collective hermeneutic resources as merely bad timing, as might be the case if one suffered from a disease that had not yet been diagnosed or understood. Rather, because the inadequacy affected Wood and the senior professor differentially it led to an injustice. Moreover, it derived from one. Fricker argues that the hermeneutical gap was the result of 'unequal hermeneutical participation' in which women were left out of or barred from engaging in the formation of the relevant collective understandings (Fricker 2007: 152). In a social world in which men have more power than women, men also have more say over defining what experiences mean. Fricker therefore thinks it is no accident that much of early second-wave feminism centered on the exclusionary practices of professions such as journalism, politics, academia and the law since these are the fields that are centrally involved in generating collective under-standings. If women are not part of these fields, they are also not contributing to the description and definition of what certain important experiences mean, experiences, furthermore, that it may be particularly important for them to describe and define.

Fricker's term for this exclusion from participating in the generation of collective understandings is hermeneutical marginalization. One can be marginalized more or less systematically, she thinks, that is, with regard to all or some of one's social experience. Indeed, because social identities are complex, one can be marginalized in contexts pertaining to one aspect of one's identity, say being female, and not in contexts pertaining to others, say being white and middle class. Generally, Fricker argues, marginalization results from a combination of two forms of power: material power, in that one occupies a relatively low socio-economic position in the society, and what she calls 'identity power,' in that one's identity is the object of damaging stereotypes, including those disfavoring women and minority groups. The effect of this marginalization, she says, is to render 'the collective hermeneutical resource structurally prejudiced' (Fricker 2007: 154–5). Here the ways a tradition offers for understanding meaning are not simply preliminary projections or prejudices that may be either warranted or unwarranted, as Gadamer argues. Rather, like Wellmer and Habermas, Fricker suggests that if we go behind the understandings we have inherited to consider the conditions of their generation, we can appreciate the way they are skewed to the advantage of some and the disadvantage of others. They not only understand unsolicited sexual advances in the workplace as flirting, but also, for example, forced intercourse with one's husband as non-rape and a disinclination to work family-unfriendly hours as a lack of professionalism. Because this structural bias derives from one group and disproportionately affects less powerful groups and because these less powerful groups are less powerful in part because of damaging stereotypes about their identity, Fricker thinks we can call the bias 'structural iden-tity prejudice.' The upshot is her full definition of systematic hermeneutical injus-tice: 'The injustice of having some significant area of one's social experience obscured from collective understanding owing to a structural identity prejudice in the collective hermeneutical resource' (Fricker 2007: 155).

Fricker thinks matters can get even worse. Hermeneutical injustice can connect up with what she calls testimonial injustice in which the structural identity prejudices under which certain individuals and groups operate affect their credibility as speak-ers and conveyors of knowledge. Suppose, for example, that Wood tries to articu-late the way the professor's behavior affects her. Because women were largely absent from the process of forming the relevant collective understanding of the behavior, the collective hermeneutical resource fails to contain the appropriate vocabulary to communicate her experience and her attempts to articulate it will likely be confused or halting. She cannot make use of the standard interpretation of the behavior as flirting and no other interpretation is available. Furthermore, because she is a woman and probably possesses a lower socio-economic status than the academic staff in her department or those reviewing her case, she probably suffers from prejudicial stereotypes about her identity. Consequently, the problems in her expression will likely be understood, not as gaps in the collective hermeneutical resources, but as an ineptness and over-emotionalism indicative of her class and sex. In this connection, Fricker refers to the way in the screenplay of *The Talented Mr. Ripley*, Marge Sherwood is unable to communicate her suspicions about Ripley because of the identity prejudices against her: 'Marge,' Herbert Greenleaf says, 'there's female intuition, and then there are facts' (in Fricker 2007: 88). Greenleaf regards Sherwood as a woman and as such apt to respond emotionally instead of rationally to a situation. His attitude here operates by way of 'identity power,' downgrading Sherwood's credibility because of prejudicial stereotypes that Greenleaf, a man of the 1950s, uncritically maintains. In the Wood scenario, this same sort of testimonial injustice compounds the hermeneutical injustice from which she already suffers.

If we follow Fricker, then, we can fault Gadamer's attempt to rehabilitate prejudice and tradition for ignoring the sort of damaging prejudices that marginalize certain groups and prevent them from contributing to the tradition and its projections of meaning that he wants to rehabilitate. The tradition to which we belong is not only a productive collective hermeneutic resource but also a heritage created by and still shot through with power, exclusion and misrepresentation. It depends upon the marginalization of certain groups and prolongs that marginalization by continuing to project stereotyping identity prejudices. These prejudices are not merely pre-orientations that may or may not work out but inherited and dogmatic ideas of who people are and of what they are or are not capable. To the extent that Gadamer ignores this underside of our heritage in favor of its undeniable riches, it appears that he can offer no tools for uncovering these injustices or mitigating their effects.

Yet it is not clear that Gadamer is as indifferent to the distortions they contain as this conclusion suggests. Indeed, as Richard Bernstein points out, in the course of their discussions, it became clear to Gadamer and Habermas that their positions were much closer than either of them had initially supposed (Bernstein 1982: 335). More to the point, a great deal of Gadamer's work is concerned precisely with possibilities for going beyond our hermeneutic limits and assumptions. Indeed, he suggests that the key to going beyond them is a renunciation of precisely the kind of epistemic power relations that Fricker describes. In order to begin to sketch out his argument, I start with his notion of the fore-conception of completeness.

The fore-conception of completeness

In describing the prejudices or projections of meaning we make in trying to understand a text or text-analogue, Gadamer appeals to the hermeneutic circle of whole and part. We project the meaning of a whole of a text as the context within which we can understand its initial parts. At the same time, our understanding of the following parts of the text may require us to revise our projection of the whole and, if so, we then use this new projection as the context for re-reading the initial parts. We engage in this circle of projections and revisions until we can integrate all the parts and the whole into a coherent unity of meaning. As Schleiermacher uses it, this hermeneutic circle describes a method for ensuring correct understanding. We fully understand a text when we can understand a word in terms of the sentence to which it belongs, the sentence in terms of the paragraph, the paragraph in terms of the text as a whole and the text as a whole in terms of the totality of the writer's work as well as each of these wholes in terms of their parts. Schleiermacher also applies the hermeneutic circle to understand the text as a part of the writer's inner or subjective life and that life in terms of the text.

Gadamer objects to the methodological direction of this analysis. For him, as he says for Heidegger, the hermeneutic circle is not a method for understanding a text but rather a description of what we do whenever we understand. Nor does the circle offer us a uniquely correct understanding of the text. Rather, we can piece its meaning together in different ways depending upon what our interest in it is and the perspective we take on it. Fricker, for example, offers an illuminating interpretation of *The Talented Mr. Ripley* but it is undeniably one that looks at it from a particular vantage point, that of its importance for exploring testimonial injustice. Her interpretation, then, is not one that can claim to understand the text in the only way it can be understood but rather one that looks at it from a specific horizon. Moreover, insofar as texts take part in history, they will always connect up with new and different issues as well as new and different texts so that our understanding of them, even when illuminating and internally coherent, will always be an understanding from a particular historical position or horizon. Indeed, insofar as any historical position will allow for different culturally influenced interests and include different ways of connecting texts up to different additional texts and events, no textual understanding can be uniquely correct.

Of equal significance for Gadamer as the implications the hermeneutic circle posesses is what it presupposes: namely, 'the fore-conception of completeness' (Gadamer 1989: 293–4). If we are to tie the acceptability (if not the unique correctness) of our understanding of a text to its success in integrating part and whole into a coherent unity of meaning, then we must presume that part and whole actually compose a coherent unity of meaning. But why should we make this presumption? Are the insights of deconstruction, for example, not premised on precisely the opposite, that the coherence and unity of a text are only apparent and that we should look for meaning along its fault lines, where, say, form and content work against one another to reveal a previously hidden sense? Gadamer concedes that the fore-conception of completeness is precisely that: a fore-conception or prejudice. Nevertheless, he thinks it is a necessary one if we are to possess any way of monitoring the meanings we project. His point is easy to see with regard to our practical engagements or ability to cope with the world that Heidegger emphasizes. If we are to function in that world at all, we have to assume that it fits together in a coherent way. We can rely on our understandings of meaning because we presume that they integrate with others so that the world we inhabit is an intelligible one. Assuming its unity supplies us with a standard against which we can assess our projections of the meaning of particular aspects of that world and correct them if they lead us astray. Gadamer transfers this reasoning to our understanding of texts. Unless we assume that a text composes a complete whole, we have no way of uncovering glitches or mis-directions in our understanding of its parts. Our understanding of one part will have no consequences for our understanding of another and our inability to integrate them into a unity of meaning will have no implications for their invalidity. Only if we suppose the coherence of the whole can we assess whether our projections of the meanings of the parts are justified or not.

Yet how can the conformity of parts and whole be enough to ensure validity? After all, the understanding Herbert Greenleaf has of Marge Sherwood is internally consistent. He thinks she is led by her emotions rather than reason and every suspicion she raises about Ripley confirms the validity of this understanding for him. In fact, as Fricker points out, Sherwood's inability to make herself heard contributes to making her emotional and upset, so that she becomes what Greenleaf and the other men she must deal with already think she is. Greenleaf thus imposes his internally consistent understanding on her to make her into what he already supposes she is. All the same, his is an understanding distorted by sexism while hers is an understanding that plumbs the depths of Ripley's crime. As elucidated thus far, the foreconception of completeness looks only to internal coherence and does not resolve the question of whether the way we achieve that coherence can be deformed by power relations, identity prejudices and the like. As the example of Herbert Greenleaf indicates, however, the hermeneutical resources we possess can allow for coherence in the way we understand our texts and text-analogues and yet be warped by inherited but pernicious assumptions.

Gadamer suggests a way out of this predicament. In a 1975 article, he relates a conversation he had with Heidegger in 1943 about the hermeneutic significance of others in which he proposed that 'the very strengthening of the Other against myself would, for the first time, allow me to open up the real possibility of understanding' (Gadamer 2000: 284). In *Truth and Method*, he makes a similar claim: 'Not only does the reader assume an immanent unity of meaning, but his understanding is likewise guided by the constant transcendent expectations of meaning that proceed from the relation to the truth of what is being said' (Gadamer 1989: 294). Or, as he also puts his point, 'The prejudice of completeness ... implies not only this formal element – that a text should completely express its meaning – but also that what it says should be the complete truth' (Gadamer 1989: 294). Part of the point here is the same as it is in the case of a prejudice in favor of the coherence of a text or text-analogue. If we are to be able to test the validity of our projections of its meaning, we must assume that they make formal sense in that they fit with other aspects of the text or text-analogue. With respect to the written tradition or what another says to us, however, we can also ask for what we might call substantive sense in that their integration with other parts of the text or statement amounts to a claim that is possibly true. On the face of it, of course, this prejudice seems ripe for dogmatic misuse. If we must suppose, at least initially, that what texts or other people say is not only formally coherent but also substantively true, will we not be prone to shifting their meaning until they say something with which we can agree? Hence, will we not foist our own prejudices upon them so that they end up making a claim to the truth to which we already subscribe? The context of Gadamer's remark indicates that he means just the opposite:

Just as we believe the news reported by a correspondent because he was present or is better informed, so too are we fundamentally open to the possibility that the writer of a transmitted text is better informed than we are, with our prior opinion.

(Gadamer 1989: 294)

In other words, to presuppose the truth of a text or what another person says is not to foist our beliefs upon it or her but to assume that the text or person knows better than we do.

How does this aspect of the fore-conception of completeness compensate for the possibility of distortions in our understanding? In her own attempt to deal with testimonial and hermeneutical injustice, Fricker appeals to a 'neutralization of prejudice in our credibility judgements' (Fricker 2010: 165). But Gadamer denies that we need either to neutralize or to rise above our prejudices. Rather, he insists that it is by supposing the truth of what we read or what another person says that we can first see what our prejudices are. They come to light because they are suddenly challenged, and thereby brought to the fore, by what we take to be the truth of another's claim. By supposing the truth of what we read or what another person says we therefore put our prejudices in play. Moreover, in supposing that a text or another person might know better than we do, we concede that the prejudices thus illuminated may be inadequate. In Gadamer's terms, we thereby acquire the wisdom of Socrates; that is, we know that we do not know. Knowing that we do not know allows us to ask – hence the significance of Socrates's questions. Gadamer maintains that a good question is open-ended in that it does not presume to know the answer in advance or slant itself to favor one sort of answer over another. At the same time, a good question is motivated in that it reveals the set of premises that orient it. In acknowledging our ignorance and allowing for the possible truth of what we hear or read, we put our prejudices in play and ask questions that allow those prejudices to be confirmed, rejected or revised.

Nor are we the only ones to ask questions. Rather in asking motivated open-ended questions, we elicit questions about the premises we reveal and, in turn, our interlocutors' questions or the questions the text poses to us reveal premises we can question. The result is a dialogue. To the extent that its partners take one another's claims as possibly true, each remains open to the other and neither tries to dominate the conversation or move it in one direction or another. Rather, the dialogue tracks the development of the subject matter under discussion. As Gadamer puts the point:

> The maieutic productivity of the Socratic dialogue, the art of using words as a midwife, is certainly directed toward the people who are the partners in the dialogue, but it is concerned merely with the opinions they express, the immanent logic of the subject matter that is unfolded in the dialogue. What emerges in its truth is the logos, which is neither mine nor yours and hence so far transcends the interlocutors' subjective opinions that even the person leading the conversation knows that he does not know.
>
> (Gadamer 1989: 237)

Alcoff compares this account of dialogue to the account Donald Davidson gives of radical interpretation, by which he means the situation in which a linguist must try to understand a speaker with a language no part of which is intelligible to the linguist and all he or she knows is 'what sentences a speaker holds true.' Davidson begins with the polar opposite of the fore-conception of completeness, with the assumption that he thinks the linguist must have according to which what the speaker holds true conforms to what the linguist already believes. While this strategy might be plausible in such a radical case, Alcoff notes that it allows for no reflexive awareness on the part of the linguist that what he or she holds true may be problematic. 'And thus there is no counsel given to be open to the alterity of the other and to the possibility that the other has access to some truth beyond what we might consider initially, plausible, rational, or even sane' (Alcoff 2003: 237). In fact, according to Alcoff:

> Davidson's view might easily be read as a form of imperialist anthropology in which 'we' take ourselves to be the civilized, enlightened culture whose own belief system has been exhaustively put to the test of reason and is thus entirely rational, and who will therefore accept only those beliefs of other cultures that fundamentally conform to our own.
>
> (Alcoff 2003: 238)

Whether or not we accept this assessment of Davidson's view, the Socratic *docta ignorantia* that Gadamer adopts is quite different. Because we are historical creatures, we not only accept orientations bequeathed to us from the past but must also concede that we are ignorant with regard to the future. We project meanings in order to understand at all but if we are sensitive to the conditions of our historical existence, we will begin our encounters with all others, including those very different from ourselves, with a Socratic attitude. We will see our encounters with them as opportunities to question and to learn and we will refrain from making them into occasions for imposing our own views, as Alcoff thinks Davidson does. For, unless we conceive of our encounters with others and with texts as opportunities to learn, unless we enter them presupposing their superiority to us in that their claims might be true, we cannot hope, Gadamer thinks, to overcome our prejudices. As he writes in recalling his 1943 conversation with Heidegger, 'To allow the Other to be valid against oneself ... is not only to recognize in principle the limitation of one's own framework but is also to allow one to go beyond one's own possibilities ... in a dialogic, communicative process' (Gadamer 2000: 284).

Fricker makes close to the same point in asking how Herbert Greenleaf might avoid treating Marge Sherwood unjustly. According to Fricker, Greenleaf would have to be aware of the impact of prejudicial stereotypes in two directions: on both his reaction to Sherwood and on his own judgment of his own position. In other words, he would have to take account of the difference it made to her perceived credibility not only that she was a woman and but also that he was a man. Such reflexive critical awareness would permit him to correct for his prejudice by revising her credibility upwards. 'The guiding idea is to neutralize any negative impact of prejudice in one's credibility judgements by compensating upwards to reach the degree of credibility that would have been given were it not for the prejudice' (Fricker 2007: 91–2). Of course, Fricker assumes we can neutralize the effect of our prejudices on our judgments, whereas Gadamer thinks we can, at best, put them in play. Fricker also implies that we know what degree of credibility we would give a speaker were it not for our prejudices. Yet if prejudices have the negative impact on our judgments she thinks they do, it is difficult to see how we could simply peel them off our judgments to see what those judgements would look like without the prejudices. Nonetheless, in trying to eliminate the impact that the disparity in social status has on hearers such as Greenleaf, Fricker attempts to achieve the same goal as Gadamer's force-conception of completeness does. Rather than allowing our identity prejudices against a speaker to run unchecked, we revise his or her credibility upward, or as Gadamer more plausibly suggests, we simply assume that what they say is true and we proceed from there in asking questions, comparing their beliefs to ours and so on.

Fricker thinks a form of critical awareness can compensate for hermeneutical injustice as well as testimonial injustice. In this case, we are to allow for possible gaps in the hermeneutical resources that may make speakers appear hesitant and incoherent and, if we have time, we are to initiate a kind of dialogue with them in which we are 'more pro-active and more socially aware' than we are in normal conversations (Fricker 2007: 171). In these cases, we should also listen to what is not said, Fricker says, as well as to what is said, and we should look for corroborating evidence for their somewhat inchoate claims. When we do not have sufficient time for this sort of dialogue, she recommends that we reserve judgment and keep an open mind as to the speaker's credibility. In this case:

> What the virtuous hearer brings to the conversation is a background social 'theory' that is informed by the possibility of hermeneutical injustice, with the result that she may avoid resting content with an unduly low judgement of credibility, and such a 'theory' may often tell her little more than that she should be suspicious of her initial spontaneous credibility judgements when it comes to speakers like this on a subject matter like that.
>
> (Fricker 2007: 172)

By theory here and by cordoning the term off with scare quotes, Fricker means only the insight we have that the collective hermeneutical resource is skewed in distorting ways and that the speaker's apparent inarticulateness is at least potentially a consequence of this skewing rather than his or her own rhetorical deficiencies. If we ignore Fricker's interest in neutrality, her point again – with regard to hermeneutical as well as testimonial injustice – comes close to accomplishing the same re-calibrating of the relationship between speaker and hearer as Gadamer's *docta ignorantia*. Recourse to 'theory' and the *docta ignorantia* both subvert power relations and by doing so allow us to listen to others.

In this regard, Fricker and Gadamer conceive of listening to the other as equally a virtue and an epistemic demand. In refusing to listen to Marge Sherwood, Herbert Greenwood not only treats her unjustly, he fails to discover what happened to his son. In contrast, a corrective anti-prejudicial revision of her credibility upward on his part would have allowed him both to avert a testimonial injustice and to satisfy his own interest in the truth. Similarly, what Gadamer conceives of as openness to the other has not only an epistemic side in providing us with a corrective to our own prejudices but an ethical side as well. In fact, he notes two ways in which hearers can fail to treat speakers ethically. They can objectify them and try to explain their statements as symptoms or effects of some underlying cause: instead of listening to Marge Sherwood's claims about Ripley, Greenwood explains them as indices of her gender. Alternatively, hearers can patronize speakers and claim to know what they are saying better than they know it themselves: here, Greenwood maintains that what Marge is really expressing is her dismay at how little she knew his son, her fiancé. In objectifying another, one looks for ways of predicting his or her behavior and thus treats him or her as a means, Gadamer says, contradicting 'the moral definition of man' (Gadamer 1989: 358). In patronizing him or her one 'robs his claims of their legitimacy' (Gadamer 1989: 360).

Fricker elides these two ethical failures. In distinguishing them Gadamer better articulates, I suspect, two different ways in which women can suffer from testimonial injustice: in some cases, they are reduced to the stereotypical characteristics of their gender, conceived of, for example, as emotional rather than rational thinkers; in other cases, women are told that what they are really saying is something different from what they think they are saying: in Wood's case, perhaps not that she has been treated unjustly but that she has no sense of humor with regard to innocent flirting. In any case, Gadamer conceives of the openness to the other that allows us to listen to him or her as the only way of relating ethically to him or her. In objectifying or patronizing others we reflect out of a relationship to them. We hold ourselves apart from the relationship and deny any reciprocity between others and ourselves. In effect, we pull rank. The effect is not only to fail to leave ourselves open to what we might learn. We also perpetuate relations of power. As Gadamer puts the point, 'Without … openness to one another there is no genuine bond' (Gadamer 1989: 361). Refusing to allow for the validity of another's claim is an ethical failing.

Strikingly, Fricker limits virtuous listening. She notes a proposal that Louise Antony makes for dealing with the low credibility judgments that can be afforded to women and members of minority groups. Antony recommends that men or those not subject to prejudicial stereotypes adopt 'a kind of epistemic affirmative action' with regard to women or those who are so subject. In other words, when a woman says 'something anomalous' men should simply assume that 'it's they who don't understand, not that it is the woman who is nuts' (in Fricker 2007: 170). Yet Fricker rejects the blanket application of this recommendation because she thinks it fails to account for the complexity of social identities. A white middle-class woman may be perfectly able to articulate her experience in one context, where her being white and middle-class is most salient, even though she is not in another, where her being a woman is the issue. In the first case, Fricker says, 'If she seems nuts, well maybe she is' (Fricker 2007: 171). The necessity of virtuous listening, then, applies only to those in situations which we know to be suspicious of our 'initial spontaneous credibility judgements' because they involve 'speakers like this on a subject matter like that.'

Nevertheless, in limiting virtuous listening in this way, Fricker restricts its efficacy to situations we already know to be fraught, situations, in other words, that are already part of our critical self-awareness. On this analysis, it is not clear, as Fricker admits, that we can expect anything better of Herbert Greenleaf than the injustice with which he treats Sherwood. In the 1950s world in which he lives, sexism is not yet part of the critical hermeneutical repertory. Therefore Fricker thinks that the injustice with which he treats Sherwood is of a 'non-culpable' sort (Fricker 2007: 100). Yet, whether culpable or not, limiting virtuous listening surely limits his ability to learn – not only about what happened to his son but also about women's equal capacities for discernment to his own and women's equality in general. Gadamer thus moves beyond Fricker, both ethically and epistemically. Ethically, Gadamer suggests that conceiving of a person as 'nuts' or as over-emotional is a form of reflecting out of the relationship. Instead of relating to the other as a particular other with his or her own particular claims, instead of letting him or her 'really say something to us,' we dominate the other, either reducing him or her to presumed generalizations about human behavior the way Greenleaf reduces Sherwood or insisting that we know better than he or she does what he or she is trying to say. Gadamer concludes, 'Whoever reflects him or herself out of the mutuality of … a relationship alters this relationship and destroys its ethical bond' (Gadamer 1989: 360). Epistemically, in relation to a speaker who appears to be nuts or over-emotional, as in relation to a difficult text, Gadamer places the initial burden on the hearer or interpreter to piece together both what is being said and its possible truth. Only when our efforts to do so fail are we forced to look for causes for the claims in a person's history or psychology. Conversely, to presume from the outset that we know better than the text or other person is to give up on the possibility of our own education. If we are to learn, we must always assume that what we read or hear is 'the complete truth,' and not just in relation to certain speakers on certain subjects with regard to which our credibility judgments should be revised upward. Otherwise, we retard our efforts to recognize new aspects of the distortions history has bequeathed us.

Conclusion

It has been a consistent theme for those criticizing Gadamer's hermeneutics that he ignores the effects of power. To be sure, he takes his task to be that of clarifying 'the conditions under which understanding takes place' (Gadamer 1989: 295), not that of explaining the conditions that impede it. Nonetheless, he uses conditions in two senses: in the sense of the historical conditions from which understandings of meaning necessarily begin and in the sense of the enabling conditions that can lead to what he calls genuine understanding. His hermeneutics is often associated only with the first sense of conditions, conditions he rests on prejudices indebted to the languages and practices of the traditions to which we belong. Because understanding is historical in this way, it is also horizonal, as Gadamer puts it. Its purview is limited by the past it inherits and a future it cannot know. Yet horizons can broaden and Gadamer is just as interested in the way our understanding can expand as he is in the historical limits under which it operates.

Gadamer is also aware that expanding our understanding often requires re-aligning the power relations that inhibit it. In Fricker's terms, it often requires overcoming hermeneutical and testimonial injustice. For Fricker, then, these forms of epistemic injustice involve structural identity prejudices that impede our understanding of important areas of experience and undermine the credibility of marginalized speakers and interpreters. Yet Fricker limits the culpability of some of those prey to such prejudices – where their circumstances appear to make critical self-reflection impossible, as in the case of Herbert Greenleaf. In contrast, Gadamer writes critical reflection into all our attempts to understand. To understand is to take seriously the possible truth of the claims we read or hear. In doing so we set our prejudices into bold relief and give ourselves the opportunity to go beyond them. Those like Herbert Greenleaf who dogmatically refuse to do so not only fail to treat others as equals but miss out on their own edification.

Bibliography

Alcoff, L. M. (2003) 'Gadamer's Feminist Epistemology' in L. Code (ed.) *Feminist Interpretations of Hans-Georg Gadamer*, University Park, PA: Penn State University Press.

Benjamin, W. (1968) 'Theses on the Philosophy of History' in W. Benjamin, *Illuminations*, trans. H. Zohn, New York: Schocken Books.

Bernstein, R. (1982) 'What is the Difference that Makes a Difference: Gadamer, Habermas and Rorty,' *Proceedings of the Biennial Meeting of the Philosophy of Sciences Association 2*.

Code, L. (2003) 'Introduction: Why Feminists Do Not Read Gadamer' in L. Code (ed.) *Feminist Interpretations of Hans-Georg Gadamer*, University Park, PA: Penn State University Press.

Elam, D. (1991) 'Is Feminism the Saving Grace of Hermeneutics?' *Social Epistemology* 5: 349–60.

Fricker, M. (2007) *Epistemic Injustice: Power and Ethics of Knowing*, Oxford: Oxford University Press.

——(2010) 'Replies to Alcoff, Goldberg, and Hookway on Epistemic Injustice,' *Episteme* 7: 164–78.

Gadamer, H-G. (1960 2nd revised edn 1989) *Wahrheit und Methode*, trans. Joel Weinsheimer and Donald G. Marshall as *Truth and Method*, New York: Crossroads Publishing Co.

——(2000) 'Subjectivity and Intersubjectivity, Subject and Person,' trans. P. Adamson and D. Vessey, *Continental Philosophy Review* 33: 275–87.

Habermas, J. (1977) 'A Review of Truth and Method' in F. Dallmar and T. McCarthy (eds.) *Understanding and Social Inquiry*, Notre Dame, IN: The University of Notre Dame Press.

Hoffman, S-J. (2003) 'Gadamer's Philosophical Hermeneutics and Feminist Projects' in L. Code (ed.) *Feminist Interpretations of Hans-Georg Gadamer*, University Park, PA: Penn State University Press.

Wellmer, A. (1969, trans. 1974) *Kritische Gesellshaftstheorie und Positivismus*; trans. John Cumming as *Critical Theory of Society*, New York: Seabury Press.

Further reading

Alcoff, L. M. (2005) *Visible Identities: Race, Gender, and the Self*, New York: Oxford University Press.

Alcoff, L. M. et al. (2010) 'Book Symposium: Miranda Fricker's *Epistemic Injustice: Power and the Ethics of Knowing*,' *Episteme* 7.2: 128–78.

Code, L. (ed.) (2003) *Feminist Interpretations of Hans-Georg Gadamer*, University Park, PA: Penn State University Press.

Hekman, S. J. (1997) 'Truth and Method: Standpoint Theory Revisited,' *Signs* Winter: 1–17.

O'Neill, L. (2007) 'Embodied Hermeneutics: Gadamer Meets Woolf In A Room Of One's Own,' *Educational Theory* 57: 325–37.

Warnke, G. (2007) *After Identity: Rethinking Race, Sex and Gender*, Cambridge: Cambridge University Press.

Wisnewski, J. J. (ed.) (2012) *Review Journal of Political Philosophy* Volume 10: *Georgia Warnke's After Identity*.

52

HERMENEUTICS, STRUCTURALISM AND POST-STRUCTURALISM

Nicholas Davey

1. A path to language

Paul Ricoeur's (1913–2005) titular triad "Structure, Word and Event" alludes to the intricate ontological and conceptual relationships between hermeneutics, structuralism and post-structuralism (Ricoeur 2004: 77–96). However, these relations are asymmetric. Though the "event" that is word – its ability to bring worlds of meaning into play – manifests the presence of language's syntactical structures – those formal structures cannot be readily translated into the semantic relations they underwrite. Ricoeur's triad illuminates tensions between language conceived as structure (linguistics), word (semantics) and event (the address of meaning). It usefully charts the differences that characterise hermeneutical, structuralist and post-structuralist approaches to language.

Any evocation of the "word" (*Sprachlichkeit* – linguisticality, a term absolutely key to philosophical hermeneutics) makes little sense without a recognition of the formal linguistic structures underpinning every linguistic utterance. Such structures pre-occupied much early structuralist thought. However, Gadamer's concept of *Sprachlichkeit* cannot easily be divided into Saussure's distinction between *langue* (formal lingustics) and *parole* (everyday conversation). Structuralists ascribe logical priority to *langue* over *parole*: *langue* constitutes the formal region of objective linguistic relations whereas *parole* constitutes the (secondary) world of subjective opinions and utterances. In contrast, hermeneutical thinkers like Heidegger and Gadamer attribute ontic priority to *Sprache*: the world-revealing power of everyday language is primary and not the formal abstractions of linguistics which derive from language's secondary power of objectifications.

Structuralism is less fearful than hermeneutics about challenging the role of a subject's intentionality in the expression of meaning. For Roland Barthes (1915–80), the author is not so much dead as an epiphenomenon: a medium through which "the rustle of language" speaks (Barthes 1989: 76). In its celebration of the "word", philosophical hermeneutics too emphasises the eventual or performative aspects of language. For Heidegger, in its "speaking", language brings a world into effective being. But the question for Gadamer and Ricoeur is whether and to what extent first person experiences of meaning (the interrogative address of the text) can be reduced exclusively to the play of linguistic structures. The notion of a *disclosive* event implies an element of involvement or participation (it may disclose itself but as a dialogical event it discloses itself *to* an interlocutor). Yet, this sits unhappily with post-structuralist emphasis on the autonomous subsumptive operation of social and political structures within language. Ricoeur's conceptual triad in which structure, word and event overlap, interlock, attract and repel each other, identifies the *Spannungsfeld* (field of tension) which characterises the uneasy but nevertheless revealing contrasts between structuralism, hermeneutics and post-structuralism.

To a degree, the field on which hermeneutics, structuralism and its successors contest and probe each other is delineated by fault lines which define the rift between explanation and understanding. Whereas Wilhelm Dilthey (1833–1911) doubted whether the explanatory frameworks of science offered an adequate insight into the external expressions of a subject's consciousness, his peer Friedrich Nietzsche (1844–1900) doubted whether a study of consciousness could lead to an understanding of action at all. Nietzsche rather than Dilthey illuminates the difference between hermeneutics and structuralism; indeed, structuralism is part of Nietzsche's effective heritage.

Nietzsche combines a "genealogical hermeneutics" with a "hermeneutics of suspicion". Both are the consequence of his embrace of Schopenhauerian phenomenalism which treats consciousness as the phenomenal effect of a noumenal will. Nietzsche's genealogical hermeneutics rests upon that interdictive negation of the concept of Being which is implicit in his affirmation of Becoming as the sole actuality. If Being is excluded from a world of Becoming, then, for Nietzsche one must ask how the illusion of such a Being could arise (Nietzsche 1968b: Section 708). The answer lies not in the self-understanding of the dialogical subject but in grasping objectively the semiotics of consciousness; that is, the fact that it is a sign-language of the assimilating and simplifying powers that underlie language (Nietzsche 1968a: 38).

From Nietzsche's metaphysical amputation, a hermeneutics of suspicion arises which serves as the basis for a critique of Being and of epistemological legitimacy of the concepts of subject, consciousness, identity and thing. Post-structuralist denials of (1) fixed "natural" structures in language, (2) the identity of the text and (3) the unity of institutions, have their roots in Nietzsche's interdictive negation of Being and its derivative modes. For the post-structuralist, the things of which we speak do not exist in themselves but are spoken into being by language. Language refers not to the "world" but to a speech-created world (*Sprachsgeschaffene Welt*) all too easily mistaken for the "world". Indeed, Nietzsche's *Interpretationsphilosophie* with its refusal of fixed meaning, sets the framework for the contest between hermeneutical and structuralist approaches to the reconstruction and deconstruction of meaning. His claim that the products of consciousness are a sign-language for the formal powers that shape it, opens a conceptual door to structuralism. If we can understand the deep formative powers operating within language – the need to operate, for instance, with a subject–object schema – then we might gain an insight into how language compels us to think about (what appears to us as) our world.

Nietzsche's genealogical hermeneutic subsequently developed by Michel Foucault concerns the consequences of doubting the veracity of consciousness's conceptual representation of the world in terms of the grammatical schema of things and subjects. How does the illusion of Being and its association with truth arise? Nietzsche replies that "a type of Becoming must itself have created the illusion of beings". Nietzsche's genealogical hermeneutics or what he also calls "a history of an error" considers how it is that something untrue comes to be believed true. The fact that Nietzsche's hermeneutics presciently deploys oppositional relations – being–becoming, truth–untruth, strength–weakness, health–sickness – is not presently significant. It is the gap he opens between conscious phenomena and the noumenal forces that underlie their production which proves crucial to the way structuralism and post-structuralism subsequently develop. This differential space raises the following question: to what degree can conscious phenomena be regarded as the expression of an underlying objectifying power? Ironically, in seeking for such a foundation, Nietzsche was perceived by his peer Dilthey as guilty of the subjectivism that his own *Verstehens*-methodology endeavoured to escape. Yet it is clear that Nietzsche's genealogical hermeneutics struggles to escape the isolation and illusions of subjectivity by revealing it as the objectification (effect) of underlying forces.

These introductory remarks indicate why the triad "Structure, Word and Event" concerns a set of asymmetric relations with regard to language. For Nietzsche and his structuralist successors there is a straightforward opposition between a primary objective sub-conscious world of linguistic forms, psychological drives and wills to power and the secondary derivative subjective world of meanings, intentions and surface understandings. Heidegger, Ricoeur and Gadamer certainly recognise that in the language-event, meanings that are not my own burst forth from my words. Nuances, articulations and associations characteristic of a tradition or form of life spontaneously erupt into my expression. In other words, the objective structures of language are not distinct, separable and, in a logical sense, opposed to the contents of individual expression. To the contrary and contrary to the suppositions of structuralism, inter-subjective linguistic expressions have their own objectivities which are continually sustained and moderated by individual expression. This chapter will now explore how the differential gap opened by Nietzsche's hermeneutics of suspicion between what language as a schema of representation represents and what is re-presented or revealed about language in its representations, is widened by the structuralists and post-structuralists in their attack upon hermeneutical approaches to meaning. What should also be considered is how Heidegger, Gadamer and Ricoeur (who are anxious to defend concepts of meaning and action from the reductivist approaches of post-structuralist argument) also utilise the differential gaps in language between what speaks, what is spoken about and how what is spoken about is spoken about. Debating the critical contrasts between these three dispositions of twentieth century thought requires us then to think critically about the philosophical issues at stake in Ricoeur's distinction between structure, word and event.

2. Meaning's truth

The fractious controversies that drive the history of philosophy are fuelled in large part by disputes concerning the grounds of truth. Whereas empiricism sought legitimacy for its truth-claims in experience itself, rationalism claimed justification for its epistemological propositions in (alleged) indubitable orders of *a priori* ideas. The "language-turn" of twentieth-century philosophy raised an analogous set of questions about the relationship of language and truth. If language is the medium through which truth-claims about the world are made, how does language structure them? Is it the case, as Wittgenstein believed, that what is expressible in language marks the limits of what is expressible about the world? Furthermore, as language is also the medium through which assertions of meaning are made and if such meaningfulness is dependent on sets of syntactical and semantic relationships, what guarantees the truth of those relationships?

The form of these questions is distinctly epistemological: what can a cognitive subject grasp of the substantive operations of language and how do they influence our knowledge of the world? For the most part, the questions of structuralism are framed in this form. The supposition of Levi Strauss is that the social world can be studied scientifically, *as if* it were a set of linguistic relations. The assumption is not that language enables the social world to be studied as the object of a *Geisteswissenschaft* (as an object of embodied meanings) but as a *Naturwissenschaft* (as a body of observable, and, therefore, confirmable linguistic relations). The dispute between post-Heideggerian hermeneutics and structuralism hinges on what Hans-Georg Gadamer and Paul Ricoeur regard as the questionable scientism of the structuralist movement. The language-world is not, they would claim, something that the cognitive subject can stand beyond and assess as an autonomous object. This strikes at the heart of structuralism: language cannot be theorised. If so, language's veracity as a medium for representing the world escapes appraisal. Hermeneutic ontology challenges not just structuralism but any general epistemological approach to language: it displaces the epistemic question of truth with an ontological evaluation of the question of meaning. The argument is as follows.

If the language world is something the subject participates in, the subject's relation to that world will inevitably be perspectival. No claim about that world can be regarded as complete. Nor can the adequacy of its epistemic representations be assessed. Within post-Heideggerian hermeneutics the language-turn in philosophy bids farewell to the epistemic concern with truth. The question of truth is displaced by that of meaning. When Heidegger and Gadamer continue to talk in terms of the "working of truth" or of the "truth" of the artwork, we must be sensitive to what this (understated) transition implies.

Any departure from prioritising questions of epistemic truth does not imply that nihilism and/or relativism are the inevitable consequences of asserting the phenomenological primacy of meaning. For Heidegger that which *is* (Being) displays its truth as an endless "showing" or process of appearing. It is not *that which* appears but the actuality of the *appearing* itself. The "truth" of Being is eventual, performative and as such "is evident in itself" (Gadamer 1989a: 485). This for Gadamer decisively links language and Being: "Being is self-presentation" (Gadamer 1989a: 484) and the essence of language is presentational: "Being that can be understood is language" (Gadamer 1989a: 474). For both Heidegger and Gadamer, just as Being reveals itself, so it also hides itself. What Being *is* cannot be asserted: it can only be shown through what the word "Being" manifests as *word*. As a word, its meaning simultaneously comes forth and falls into opaqueness always leaving something further to be said. However, as word, that is, as an annunciative event which reveals the simultaneity of withholding and disclosure, it *shows* what Being is (or, rather, *does*). The "irruption of language is simply Being itself formed into word" (Richardson 1963: 292). This is perhaps what Gadamer means when he describes, "Being as the word in which truth happens" (Gadamer 2007: 137). The word as annunciative event *does* what Being is; it is an ever present waxing and waning of disclosure (Davey 2009: 251). What are the practical consequences of this characterisation for the performative nature of language?

Following Heidegger's neologism *der Sprache spricht*, Gadamer insists that it is more correct to say that language speaks us, rather than we speak it. Insofar as humanity's fundamental experience of the world is linguistic, that experience is one of being *addressed*: texts, artworks, situations speak directly to us. Gadamer insists that "no matter how much a work of art may appear to be a historical datum ... it is always the case that the work says something to us, and it does so in such a way that its statement can never be exhaustively expressed in a concept." Part of the hermeneutic task is to "*Begreifen, was uns ergreift*" – "To grasp something that takes hold of *us*" (Gadamer 2007: 61). The *experience* of meaning is indubitably primary though the *meaning* experienced remains dubitable. What is meaningful asserts itself as such, without invoking the aim of occasional knowledge (Gadamer 1989a: 469). An epiphany of meaning is, phenomenologically speaking, an autonomous occasion: it is detached from subjective opinion and does not point back to some "primordial act of oral utterance" (Gadamer 2007: 181): it *says* something that seems to originate in-itself.

What experience presents as indubitably meaningful commits Gadamer neither to essentialism, nor to subjectivist reduction. (1) What discloses itself as meaningful is necessarily (as a singular appearance) perspectival, a finite and limited aspect of the self-revealing subject-matter. It is never complete. (2) Nor is what discloses as meaningful a subjective re-construction. What discloses itself as meaningful does so only on the condition that it is *already* connected to a pre-established infinity of meaning which can never be "explicated and laid out" (Gadamer 1989a: 458). That infinite horizon constitutes a "whole" whose parts differently address the language speakers who participate in its etymological and conceptual reach. Emerging from, belonging to and being cognitively enabled to reach into an infinity of past and future configurations of meaning constitutes humanity's linguistic being. The ontology of language therefore pre-figures the ontology of tradition. The indubitable experience of linguistic meaningfulness does not, as stated, pre-suppose acquaintance with any essential meaning. What presents itself phenomenologically as singularly meaningful remains, logically and historically, but one configuration of that meaning or subject-matter. Gadamer, like Derrida, openly acknowledges that any thing expressed in words "can never stop consisting of meanings that arise out of th(ose) words, or parts of them" (Gadamer 2007: 147).

Gadamer is openly committed to a dual thesis which (1) recognises the indubitable primacy of language addressing us and (2) proclaims that the meaning experienced is (because of its linguistic nature) subject within reflection to endless re-configurations. What (2) articulates – the infinite capacity of *parole* (everyday spoken language) to generate instabilities of meaning – convinces structuralist thinkers that it is only in the autonomous operations of what underlies *parole*, namely, language (*langue*), that objective insight into the conditioning agencies of social exchange can be found. This reveals parallels between the structuralist perspective and Gadamer's own. (1) Both concur that what is said is less significant than the prior existence of enabling language structures (or horizons) which enable the said to be said. (2) Meaning does not reside in subjective intentionality but beyond it, namely, in the relational structures of significance which antedate individual consciousness and yet inform human expression. As Nietzsche remarks: "The isolation of the individual ought not to deceive us: something flows on underneath individuals" (Nietzsche 1968b: Section 686). Gadamer observes: "In language, the reality beyond every individual consciousness becomes visible" (Gadamer 1989a: 449). The dispute between hermeneutics and structuralism concerns how the reality beyond every individual linguistic consciousness is to be grasped. Structuralism opts for a parallelist view (the linguistic world of signs exists autonomously and is prior to individual articulation) whilst hermeneutics elects an immanentist stance (the historical and cultural structures that enable and yet transcend individual expression, emerge from within and do not exist apart from the language world).

Gadamer is sceptical of structuralism's attempt to think language (*langue*) as an autonomous order of signs; a system of internal linguistic dependencies which operates systematically behind every individual utterance. He argues:

> nor does comparative linguistics, which studies the structure of languages, have any one linguistic point of view from which we could know the in-itself quality of what exists and for which the various forms of the linguistic experience of the world could be reconstructed, as a schematised selection, from what exists in itself.
>
> (Gadamer 1989a: 411)

Structuralism represents a fundamental alienation from what both Heidegger and Gadamer hold as the primacy of humanity's language orientation to the world, namely, the world "addresses" us. To assert an autonomous system of signs which antedates the possibility of individual articulation, is to succumb to the simplifying illusions of apophantic language. What is given in the aletheic experience of language (the primacy of disclosure) is beyond formal capture. Heidegger and Gadamer readily acknowledge that statemental language schematises in a variety of ways the complexities of what is given in evidentiary experience, that is, the occasion of language's address. However, what are objectified in statemental language as linguistic structures, structures that are logically secondary to language's address and which, furthermore, evolved as a way of simplifying that address, are then projected back on to that address as its formal cause. The effect is muddled with the cause. We are, Gadamer insists, as incapable of objectifying the rules of our own linguistic system without employing particular pre-understanding of meanings, as we are of dealing objectively with the contents of our own tradition. As Hans Herbert Kögler puts it, we can never recover the substantial horizon of meaning that resonates in our understanding of language (Kögler 1996: 41).

Gadamer insists that there are enabling structures antedating individual experience of the world. These are identified as life-horizons, history and tradition. Though each of these frameworks transcends any individual's experience of language, they do not transcend language itself and are given to the individual only in and through language. Whereas thinkers such as Wilhelm Dilthey defended the distinction between the *Naturwissenschaften* and the *Geisteswissenschaften* by appealing to menta-listic terms such as empathy and *nacherleben* (to re-construct and re-experience), structuralism, as Paul Ricoeur discerns, endeavours to displace humanistic with sci-entific knowledge:

> the triumph of the structural point of view is at the same time a triumph of the scientific enterprise. By constituting the linguistic object as an autono-mous object, linguistics constitutes as science ... *the act of speaking is exclu-ded not only as exterior execution, as individual performance, but as free combination, as producing new utterances.*
>
> (Ricoeur 2004: 81, emphasis added)

The ontological parallelism of structuralism forces it to impose an opposition between *langue* and *parole* whereas the immanentist ontology of hermeneutics pre-sents the formalisations of *Sprache* (*langue*) as secondary and dependent on our being in the world, that is, on our being in a *Sprachswelt*. Gadamer remarks:

> Language is not just one of man's possessions in the world; rather, on it depends the fact that man has a world at all ... This world is verbal in nature ... Not only is the world *world* only insofar as it comes into language, but language has its real being only in the fact that the world is presented in it.
>
> (Gadamer 1989a: 180)

Gadamer accepts the structuralist argument that there are linguistic structures which antedate individual expression but the decisive difference between the two modes of thought is made clear in the passage:

> To be sure what comes into language is something different from the spoken word itself. But the word is a word only because of what comes into lan-guage in it. Its own physical being exists only because of what comes into language in it. Its own physical being exists only in order to disappear into what is said. Likewise, that which comes into language is not something pre-given before language, rather, the word gives its own determinateness.
>
> (Gadamer 1989a: 469, 475)

In conclusion, whereas for structuralism formal linguistic structures antedate indivi-dual expression, for hermeneutics they arise with the expression of meaning. For hermeneutics, the truth of meaning (disclosure) is not independent of its expression but arises from it.

3. Languages of scepticism

Structuralism, post-structuralism and hermeneutics *all* emphasise different degrees of scepticism with regard to how assertions of meaning are to be understood. Structuralism tends simply to disregard "the subjectivity of the act of speech". understanding has nothing to do with the recovery of meaning but with discerning the ahistorical codes, linguistic conventions and binary sign relationships implicit in what is said. The constitution of meaning is grasped as a sign-immanent process determined solely through the internal differences between linguistic signs (Kögler 1996: 188). Subjective intention and reference to actual objects are displaced by the play of signifiers and signified. Speaking is rendered a law-like form of socio-linguistic behaviour. In this respect, Michel Foucault was severe in his criticism of structuralism. Dreyfus argues that Foucault "sought to avoid the structuralist analysis which eliminates notions of meaning altogether and substitutes a formal model of human behaviour as rule-governed transformations of meaningless elements" (Dreyfus 1982: xix). For Foucault there was no "deep meaning" in humanistic discourses. To believe that there is a fundamental meaning to human discourses "dooms us to an endless task ... [because it] rests on the postulate that speech is an act of translation ... an exegesis which listens ... to the Word of God ... For centuries we have waited in vain for the decision of the Word" (Dreyfus 1982: xix). The quest for hidden meaning or deep grammar is for Foucault a symptom of the very problem. Through the temptations of their practices and disciplines, religious and political powers offer the individual the illusion of redemption or liberation only to ensnare the disciple in the perpetuation of its ends. Humanistic discourses are not about the communication of meaning (*forces of institution*) but concern the remorseless jostling of competing power structures. Jacques Derrida (1930–2004) is not concerned with what underlies language but with the restless play of language itself. Derrida agrees with Heidegger that (ontologically speaking) language is the medium through which beings are brought to presence but only on the basis of continuous displacement. Derrida develops an idea that is central to contemporary hermeneutics. In language, subject and world continually differentiate themselves. Derrida contends that "language does not show a being as it is, but always in displacement. This displacement is due to the fact that language is supplementary: it is added to a being in order to let this being appear" (Heiden 2008: 101). Derrida regards this doubling of language as evidence for its *iterability*. This repeatability concerns not the repeatability of same meaning but the fact that whenever a meaning is repeated it endlessly differentiates itself from previous articulations. "The same expression can be used in a different context, and in this different context it may present something else ... No linguistic expression can coincide with the being (or meaning) it presents" (Heiden 2008: 101). As we shall see, Gadamer too deploys a version of this hermeneutical differential. Derrida's deployment of tactical terms such as "the over-abundance of the signifier", difference, supplementarity and repetition contribute to his understanding of the language world as "a world of signs without fault, without truth, and without origin", a constant play "without security", the "seminal adventure of the trace" (Derrida 1978: 369). The "play" of language is the disruption of presence: the presence of an element is always a signifying and substitutive reference inscribed in a system of differences and the movement of a chain. Play is always a play of absence and presence (Derrida 1978: 369). Whereas Barthes insisted on the death of the author (Barthes 1989: 49–55), for Derrida any attempt by interpretation to seize authorial meaning will, because of language's supplementarity, only defer that meaning, never arriving "at the reassuring foundation, the origin and the end of play" (Derrida 1978: 370). The political thrust of Derrida's deconstructive approach to language concerns those who would halt its play by claiming an authorative arrival at *the* meaning of a text. Derrida is for Gadamer the culmination of that new Nietzschean:

> path of thinking that rests on a doubt about the assertions made in one's consciousness ... In Nietzsche, this doubt resulted in a change in his sense of truth as such, so that interpretation as a process becomes an expression of one's will to power and with this step interpretation acquires an ontological significance.
>
> (Gadamer 2007: 56)

Gadamer is, in certain respects, just as sceptical as Barthes and Derrida about the weight given to the authorial in interpretation: "we have seen that the words that express an object are themselves known as a speculative event. Their truth lies in what is said in them; and not in a meaning locked in the impotence of subjective particularity" (Gadamer 1989a: 445). However, it is one thing to deny that the truth of a text lies in authorial intention but quite another to deny it on the grounds of truth lying in what words state independently of their author. The argument would seem to directly oppose the post-modernist stance that claims that there is no intrinsic truth to any text. Here the difference between Gadamer and Derrida becomes plain but the difference is not what it initially appears. Gadamer, like Derrida but for different reasons, insists the truth of a text will never be arrived at because: (1) the finitude of mind prevents it from grasping the historical totality of what a text has been and will become and (2) language can only infer never state the fullness of a text's meaning. There is for Gadamer no final word which conclusively reveals the truth of a text. Mechanisms in Gadamer's hermeneutics suggest that the truth of a text will never be arrived at precisely because of the nature of the hermeneutic operation itself.

In the address of a text a subject-matter (*Sache*) addresses us. The disclosure of that address will be incomplete for various reasons. (1) A subject-matter can be presented in a variety of registers or forms: literary, poetic, philosophical or musical. (2) No subject-matter can be completely disclosed: what can be conveyed by music or dance about rhythm cannot captured by poetry in the same way. An excess will remain for exploration. (3) A given literary disclosure may have the transformative force of an evidentiary experience but as a specific disclosure it remains but one of many possible configurations of a subject-matter's meaning. For Gadamer, there is no original and no final meaning attached to subject-matter: its field of meaning is continuous in play. In this, Gadamer and Derrida agree but for different reasons. Derrida sees efforts to close the play of difference in language as attempts at closure, to colonise and gain authority over a region of meaning. Derrida's deconstructive reading stratagems challenge any attempt at hypostasising the meaning of a text by keeping it in continual play. Indeed, it has been suggested that Derrida's attempts to keep fields of meaning in continuous play is indicative of a fear of death (Pickstock 1998: 103–6).

In contrast to Derrida's playfulness, Gadamer's tactics appear stalwartly conservative but this is, nevertheless, to seriously misunderstand the ambition of his operation. Foucault insists that hermeneutics is committed to the belief that its inquiries can lead to "the final word" or *the* decisive interpretation. Gadamer insists that "the meaning of a word resides not just in the language and in the context: rather, this 'standing in a context' means at the same time that the word is never completely separated from the multiple meanings it possesses" (Gadamer 2007: 107). Gadamer will always seek as sharp, well defined and persuasive an interpretation of a text as possible. His anticipation of an "ideal unity of meaning" is always provisional, a way of bringing a particular configuration of meaning forward, not to lay claim to a definitive interpretation of that meaning but to heighten the difference between its horizon of meaning and the horizon of meaning from which we approach that text's concern. The aim is to bring the horizon of the text into play with our own and thereby generate and magnify the differences between the two. If we understand at all, we come to understand differently (*Andersverstehen*). The aim of understanding as conceived in philosophical hermeneutics is to *move on* (Gadamer 1989b: 96).

Wolfgang Iser sees how the practice of interpreting subject-matters proliferates rather than closes hermeneutic possibilities (Iser 2000: 158). To interpret a subject-matter is to select one determination of meaning as opposed to another. A differential gap is opened between what that subject-matter is presently taken to mean and what it could yet come to mean. The uncovering of new determinations of meaning potentially challenge how we presently understand that subject-matter, transforming our understanding of both it and ourselves. Whereas Derrida wishes to keep meaning-in-play to avoid semantic atrophy, Gadamer utilises that play not as a means to a continuous dispersal and weakening of meaning but as a procedure to magnify and transform hermeneutic possibilities. Whereas for Derrida the play of meanings signifies a falling away from a trace of a (non-original) meaning, Gadamer's hermeneutics expands the range of play on the grounds that a temporal accumulation of additional meanings surrounding a subject-matter allows it to become "more what" it is. The openness of linguistic meaning is conceptually bound in Gadamer's thought to a reworking of the classical notion of *mimesis* as future orientated: a subject-matter establishes and increases its effective identity over time (*Bildung*). The language orientation of philosophical hermeneutics establishes it (unlike the hermeneutics of suspicion) as a philosophy of hope. Within the temporal horizon of language, language's own indeterminacy keeps open the possibility that a given alignment of meaning can be transformed.

The transformative aspect of meaning returns us to the question of subjectivity and its relation of the "word" as event. The annunciative capacity of the word to bring a world of meaning into being is not a matter of just adding to a range of possible meanings. The transformative nature of such an event speaks necessarily of an effect upon a horizon of meaning. The "event" which is the word brings about a re-alignment of meanings, commitments and concerns; an orientation is changed. It is not necessary to return to the language of the subject but it is, as Gadamer and Ricoeur grasp, impossible to speak about language, meaning and understanding without invoking a notion of subjectivity. Understanding as a transformative event demands it.

4. Understanding and language: Being as being-subject to subjectivities

Ricoeur and Gadamer concur in a number of observations. As a study of semiological functions, structuralism excludes the notion of a subject: it makes no sense to ask who is speaking as the semiological function of language provides a system without a subject (Ricoeur 2004: 253). But then, as Ricoeur argues: "how does an autonomous system of signs, postulated without a speaking subject, enter into operations, evolve towards new states, or lend itself to usage or to history?" (Ricoeur 2004: 245). He observes that semantic functions make no sense without a subject that organises them (Ricoeur 2004: 246). Gadamer makes a similar point: "Artificial signs and symbols alike do not … *acquire* their functional significance from their own content but must be taken as signs or symbols … Signs only have a sign function *when they are taken* as a sign" (Gadamer 1989a: 137, emphasis added). An agency is implied. Furthermore, in a field of indeterminacy, establishing new or alternative meanings does not make sense without the invention of an active horizon of meaning capable of responding to and re-forming those it encounters. Ricoeur contends that in the absence of any final meaning, the process of recovering new meanings from available ones requires some notion of subjective agency. This does not have to be conceived of as a transcendental subject (Ricoeur 2004: 244). All that is required is a cluster of interdependent interests (a horizon or alignment of loosely unified concerns) which *act* together as if they were a subject. Gadamer of course insists that hermeneutic engagement is dialogical, which is another way of saying that it is an interactive occasion in which one horizon of meanings (the reader's) is re-arranged by exposure to another (the text's). The horizon of meaning which constitutes a given subjectivity holds within itself loyalties to given alignments of meaning which embody its primary concerns, be they religious, cultural or existential. These constitute the orientation of its tradition. This is, in other words, to admit that a way of life – a given hermeneutic – has its vulnerabilities, that alignments of concern establish it as an interactive subjectivity that is both subject to other alignments of meaning and capable of subjecting them to its norms. For humans, *being* is being subject to subjectivity. Iser offers an insightful account of how such interaction can be described in terms of semantic exchange.

Iser's invocation of the hermeneutic differential reveals the gap between what a subject-matter has been taken to mean and what it might yet mean. Not only does the process of interpretation open this space, but (transformational) understanding requires the instabilities of meaning that the space generates. Subject-matters denote the central pre-occupations of practice whether political, artistic or academic. Their indeterminacy of meaning dictates that they can never be fully but always better articulated. Indeed, when subject-matters such as openness, justice, integrity or transparency acquire normative status in a practice, commitment to them will always demand better articulation and grasp of what can by definition only be partially understood. Such "immeasurables" prompt a proliferation of interpretation "each of which must give way to another because of its inherent limitations" (Iser 2000: 141). Whereas Derrida contends that it is *différance per se* which renders any herme-neutic object (text) ungraspable, for Iser it is the process of interpretation that for-ever proliferates fleeting figurations of meaning, each of which "is either modified or cancelled by what is to follow" (Iser 2000: 158.) Any attempt of the hermeneutic subject to grasp its object only serves to disperse it once again. However, under-standing does not have to be understood as the impossible quest for *the* meaning of a text or artwork. It can also be understood transformatively, that is, as a process whereby in coming to think differently (though never definitively) about a text our understanding of both that text and ourselves "moves on".

Subject matters which ground the practices of a "form of life" indicate fields of normative vulnerability. Since they shape and form our practices, we are clearly sensitive to possible changes in their meaning. Interpretation, that is, pursuing how an "immeasurable" at the root of one of our practices might be developed, "is basi-cally performative in character. It makes something happen, and what arises out of this performance are emergent phenomena" (Iser 2000: 153), that is, interpretation can prompt and bring about new and unexpected determinations of a subject-mat-ter's meaning. What requires stressing is that interpretation is performative because it is interactive: it involves the inter-action between the horizons of meaning attached to a text or body of work and those of the reader, spectator or disciple. Both horizons of meaning can embrace a shared subject-matter but configure it quite differently according to tradition and historical perspective. The subject-matter operates as a place-holder between both alignments of meaning, allowing each alignment to be transposed. The connection between vulnerability and transfor-mation becomes clear.

Precisely because of its normative commitment to a subject-matter, a life form will seek out in other and strange alignments of cultural meaning new determinations of its principal meanings (concerns). Interpretive engagement with other literary or his-torical forms of that subject can generate unexpected determinations of meaning. This fission of hermeneutic horizons exposes that life-form to unforeseen re-align-ments of its constituent values. It is the position of a subject-matter as a placeholder between two horizons of meaning that allows the alignment of meaning around the subject-matter in one perspective to infuse counter-part alignment, transforming its initial understanding of the subject-matter in question. The transformed horizon has not grasped *the* meaning of the subject-matter but has, as a result of the interaction, acquired a different grasp of it, exposing the limitations of its previous suppositions. Its understanding has not achieved closure, but movement. Ricoeur offers a helpful remark at this juncture.

In the essay 'The Question of the Subject: the Challenge of Semiology', Ricoeur remarks: "Language is no more a foundation than it is an object; it is mediation, 'milieu' in which and through which the subject posits himself and the world shows itself" (Ricoeur 2004: 250). This throws an informative light on Iser's argument concerning transformative engagement. In his criticism of structuralism's exclusion of the subject from its analysis of *langue*, Ricoeur notes that "what is admirable is that language is organised in such a way that it allows each speaker to appropriate the entire language by designating himself as the *I*" (Ricoeur 2004: 248). In Iser's terms the "I" is an "immeasurable", that is, the ground from which we spring is not fully available to us. This is not for Ricoeur a negative conclusion. When in language the subject posits him or her self as "I", the entire speech-created world (the life of embodied meaning) also appears. *In principium erat verbum* implies for both Ricoeur and Gadamer, the co-determinacy of the subject and the speech-created world. Gadamer insists that language is a medium where "I" and "world" meet or manifest their original belonging together (see Gadamer 1989a: 442). In Gadamer's *Sprachlichkeit* the two are inseparable. As an "I", I am grounded in a formative tradition which lies ahead of me. Both Ricoeur and Gadamer contend that when we speak of ourselves we do not speak in terms of interior noumenal spaces but in the language of beings *already* related to the world they are in. This confirms the mutuality between the language of self and the language of (the speech-created) world. The grounding of the "I" in tradition implies that first-person descriptions will always contain an implicit understanding and, hence, relation to third person descriptions of the world. Conversely, and precisely because of that relationality, changes in world descriptions can imply changes in self-descriptions. Since *Sprachlichkeit* entails for Gadamer an infinity of potential meaning configurations, it follows that the totality of possible self-descriptions is implicitly held within everything that can be said about the world, hence Gadamer's affirmation of the dialogical inseparability of "I" and "world". Who I am reveals me to be an endless conversation. However such an "I" or subject grasps itself, it will be within a determinate set of incomplete self-descriptions. As an "immeasurable" however, it will seek to extend its self-understanding. The quest will always threaten to put that self-understanding at risk. Furthermore, as we have seen in our discussion of subject-matters as placeholders, a language-being in a speech-created world will be exposed to and be vulnerable to alignments of meaning other than its own capable of challenging and transforming its initial understanding. This is where Derrida completely misunderstands Gadamer's hermeneutic "good will" (Michelfelder and Palmer 1989: 21–74). Openness to the other is not a matter of drawing the other into dialogue on one's own terms alone. It concerns a dialogical recognition that in both the other and in the otherness of the speech-created-world lie waiting unrealised determinations of meaning capable of transforming both my self-understanding and my understanding of the world: "if we understand, we understand differently" (Gadamer 1989a: 297). The openness of Gadamerian dialogue is not a surreptitious power stratagem, as Derrida's and Foucault's arguments suggest, but involves a kenotic attentiveness to the other subjectivity as holding a key to the unrealised possibilities of understanding within my horizon. Because of language, the extent to which I can find myself in the world, and find the world in me, is infinite. The meanings I associate with my own self-descriptions are constantly challenged by variations of those meanings found in texts and artefacts. It is, indeed, in and through language that human beings find, lose and produce themselves. The word is the medium of understanding's movement, a movement discernible only to a subjectivity whose being is rooted in language. In this respect, hermeneutics and its philosophy of language offer a deeply plausible challenge to both structuralism and post-structuralism.

Bibliography

Barthes, Roland, 1989. *The Rustle of Language*. Berkeley: University of California Press.

Davey, Nicholas, 2009. "Lest we Forget: The Question of Being and Philosophical Hermeneutics". *Journal of the British Society for Phenomenology*, 40(3), pp. 239–54.

Derrida, Jacques, 1978. *Writing and Difference*. London: Routledge.

Dreyfus, H. L., 1982. *Michel Foucault: Beyond Structuralism and Hermeneutics*. Brighton: Harvester Press.

Gadamer, Hans-Georg, 1989a. *Truth and Method*. London: Sheed and Ward.

——, 1989b. "Letter to Dallmayr". In Diane P. Michelfelder and Richard E. Palmer, eds. *Dialogue and Deconstruction*. Albany: State University Press of New York. pp. 93–101.

——, 2007. *The Gadamer Reader*, ed. by Richard E. Palmer. Evanston: Illinois University Press.

Heiden, Gert-Jan van der, 2008. *Disclosure and Displacement*. Nijmegen: University of Nijmegen Press.

Hemming, Laurence Paul, 1999. "Nihilism: Heidegger and the grounds of redemption". In John Milbank, Catherine Pickstock and Graham Ward, eds. *Radical Orthodoxy: A New Theology*. London: Routledge. pp. 91–108.

Iser, Wolfgang, 2000. *The Range of Interpretation*. Columbia: Columbia University Press.

Kögler, Hans-Herbert, 1996. *The Power of Dialogue*. Cambridge, MA: MIT Press.

Michelfelder, Diane P. and Palmer, Richard E., eds, 1989. *Dialogue and Deconstruction*. Albany: State University Press of New York.

Nietzsche, Friedrich, 1968a. *Twilight of the Idols*. London: Penguin.

——, 1968b. *The Will to Power*. London: Weidenfeld and Nicolson.

Pickstock, Catherine, 1998. *After Writing: On the Liturgical Consummation of Philosophy*. London: Blackwell Publishing.

Richardson, William J., 1963. *Heidegger: Through Phenomenology to Thought*. The Hague: Nijhoff.

Ricoeur, Paul, 2004. *The Conflict of Interpretations*. London: Continuum.

53

HERMENEUTICS AND CONFUCIANISM

Kathleen Wright

In reflecting on his long life and philosophical journey, Hans-Georg Gadamer (1900–2002) recalls the effect on him as a young student of reading Theodor Lessing's *Europe und Asia*. For "the first time in my experience the *all-encompassing horizon* which I had grown into through birth, education, schooling, and, indeed, the whole world around me, was *relativized*. And so for me something like *thinking* began" (Gadamer 1997: 3–4: emphases added). Gadamer's insight is that when we confront another way of thinking that relates to our customary way of thinking yet also at the same time differs from and challenges it, we recognize that the conceptions that we take for granted as "universal" are rather preconceptions and that our horizon that we take to be "all-encompassing" is instead *finite*, that is, "for or related to us."[1] For Gadamer, the task of "knowing ourselves" in Plato's sense of exposing ourselves in and through dialogue to our limits and the limitations of what we believe we know becomes the task of a hermeneutical thinking that is philosophical.[2] However, although greatly indebted to Hegel and his dialectical thinking, hermeneutical thinking, Gadamer insists, never ends in the all-encompassing horizon of a knowledge that is or at least claims to be absolute.

Even though Gadamer did not bring philosophical hermeneutics to bear on the culturally different and temporally distant texts of China, scholars writing on China's "classical learning" (*jingxue*) from around the world often acknowledge the help of Gadamer's theory of philosophical hermeneutics in their books and articles.[3] Chinese "classical learning" came to be identified primarily with the "teachings of Confucius" (*Kongjiao*) and designated, simply and misleadingly, as "Confucianism" (*Ruxue*) by thinkers in the West starting late in the nineteenth century even though classical learning includes not just the thought of Confucius (and Confucians such as Mengzi and Xunzi) but also the thought of others such as the Daoists, Laozi and Zhuangzi, and the Song-Ming dynasty literati such as Zhu Xi and Wang Yangming.[4] The "Confucianism" (*Ruxue*) this chapter is about that is related to Gadamer's philosophical hermeneutics is more properly called "New Confucianism" (*Xin ruxue*).[5] New Confucianism is a multifaceted philosophical movement that arose within China in the first half of the twentieth century to defend Confucianism when it was under attack during the Republic of China prior to 1949. New Confucianism moved to the "borderlands"[6] outside "mainland" China after the Chinese Revolution in 1949 and also emerged "overseas" in North America after the Cultural Revolution (1966–76). When Gadamer's *Truth and Method* appeared in English in 1975, what appealed immediately to New Confucians working "overseas" in Canada and the USA, including Hawaii, was Gadamer's concept of *tradition*, which they however mistook to be an "all-encompassing horizon" comparable to the *Dao* of Confucius that is normative, "all-embracing and thus absolute" (Chan 1984: 430).

Simplifying the complicated history of twentieth century New Confucianism, we can say that "borderland" New Confucians such as Mou Zongsan and Tang Junyi seek to transform "Confucianism" by way of Kant and Hegel respectively starting in the 1950s in order to *create* a "modern Confucianism" for "mainland" China as an alternative to Mao Zedong's Chinese version of Marxism. Later and in reaction to Mao's attempt to eliminate any and all vestiges of "traditional Confucianism" during the Cultural Revolution, "overseas" New Confucians such as On-Cho Ng and Alan K. L. Chan try to *preserve* "traditional Confucianism" by way of Gadamer's hermeneutics, starting in the 1980s. Wang Ban has this to say about what motivates the hermeneutic turn to Gadamer in particular:

> Hans-Georg Gadamer's historical hermeneutics recognizes disruptive forces in history that shatter tradition as a continuous stream of meaning and value. What prompts the hermeneutic attitude [in general and in particular in modern China] is that texts from the past become alien, estranged objects [like a "foreign country"] at risk of being forgotten or waiting to be recharged with new interpretations. In modern China the very notion of tradition itself is indicative of the culture's attempt to both distance from and reconnect with the past.
>
> (Wang 2005: 244)

When *Zhen li yu fang fa*, the Chinese translation of Gadamer's *Truth and Method*, was published in Taiwan in 1993 (parts I and II) and in 1995 (part III) and then in Shanghai in 1999, Gadamer's hermeneutics, mediated by its reception by "overseas" New Confucians, became part of a debate within China about how postsocialist China should understand China's "Confucian tradition" and whether the stand it should take toward tradition should be to conserve it or to reform it. This on-going debate is framed in various ways, one of which is to ask – as New Confucians do – how Confucius himself understood the tradition handed down to him and whether the stand he took toward tradition was to conserve or to reform it. Since "overseas" New Confucians initially identified Confucius's stance toward tradition with Gadamer's stance toward tradition, the debate within China became a debate that was as much about Gadamer's relation to tradition as about Confucius's.

After some background on past debates about Confucius, we shall examine two essays by Ng and Chan, both published in 2000, that reach diametrically opposed conclusions about how Gadamer and Confucius stand toward tradition. On the one hand, Ng will maintain – as Chan had earlier in 1984 – that Gadamer's hermeneutics is like contemporary "orthodox" New Confucian hermeneutics in being profoundly culturally conservative about "tradition," which Ng takes (mistakes) to be like the *Dao* of Confucius. On the other hand, Chan uses the 1976 Gadamer–Habermas debate to frame a Gadamerian defense of the capacity within "conservative" New Confucianism to reform itself by criticizing from within what has been traditionally systematically distorted by ideology, namely, gender relations.[7] Whereas Chan recognizes by 2000 that it was a mistake in 1984 for him to identify "tradition" in Gadamer with the *Dao* of Confucius, an "all-encompassing horizon" that is absolute, Ng comes to realize this same mistake in an essay published five years later in 2005 when he mounts what has now become the standard "orthodox" New Confucian critique of Gadamer for not being conservative enough.

I. Recent history of the debate in China

Who is Confucius (551–479 BCE)? D. C. Lau answers this complex question in the following way:

> Behind Confucius' pursuit of the ideal moral character lies the unspoken, and therefore, unquestioned, assumption that the only purpose a man can have and also the only worthwhile thing a man can do is to become as good a man as possible.
>
> (Lau cited in Chan 1984: 245–6)[8]

From the *Analects*, we know that Confucius was concerned with "tradition," that is, with the life-world handed down to him that consisted of (1) *rituals or social conventions*, along with (2) *institutions*, for example, marriage, that are based on ritual speech acts such as promising.[9] For Confucius, however, "it was not enough simply to carry out the appropriate … [ritual action or ritual speech-act] correctly; it was necessary also to live up to the right moral standard" (Goldin 2011: 8) when performing them. This meant thinking for oneself; hence Confucius emphasized life-long learning and moral self-cultivation.[10] One other thing we know is that for Confucius himself "tradition" did not yet consist (3) of a set of *canonical classical texts*[11] that were to be studied "religiously," for Confucius lived at a time and in a society where communication was primarily oral (Goldin 2011: 9). However knowing that Confucius was concerned with tradition does not yet tell us how Confucius stood toward tradition.

The essays published in 2000 by Ng and Chan discussed below continue a debate that began in China late in the Qing dynasty (1644–1911) about Confucius's stance toward tradition, a debate that is in many ways similar to Habermas's debate with Gadamer about his stance toward tradition. At issue in the Gadamer–Habermas debate was whether the hermeneutical understanding of tradition that Gadamer proposed in *Truth and Method* in terms of a fusion of horizons admits of the possibility of thinking critically about, taking a stand against, and actively reforming traditional ways of thinking and traditional life-practices that are systematically distorted by ideology. Something like the Gadamer–Habermas debate arose in China late in the eighteenth century when an ancient but hitherto unorthodox form of Confucianism, Gongyang Confucianism, that took Confucius and Confucianism to be essentially about the *reform of tradition*, began to challenge the orthodox picture of Confucius and Confucianism as dedicated to the *preservation of tradition*.

The philosophical debate about Confucius's stance toward tradition that started in the Qing dynasty and that continues in the essays by Ng and Chan is not just important from an academic standpoint. That the debate also matters historically becomes clear when we consider different outcomes of the debate in relation to China's recent history.[12] First of all, Kang Youwei's conclusion in 1897, that Confucius was a "reformer," lent support to the forces that brought the Qing dynasty to an end. Then Mei Ssu-ping's answer in 1930, that Confucius was a "counter-revolutionary" and "reactionary," invited Marxist theorists to take over the terms of the debate, thereby insuring a hearing for Marxism in China. Subsequently Kuo Mo-jo's claim in 1945 that Confucius was a "revolutionary" in siding with the people and a "selective traditionalist" lent the authority of Confucius to the popular forces that brought about the Chinese Revolution in 1949. Finally Mao Zedong's assessment that Confucius was a "counter-revolutionary" brought about the Cultural Revolution (1966–76) aimed at annihilating any and all vestiges of Confucianism.

II. Gadamer's hermeneutics and Confucian hermeneutics: profound cultural conservatism?

[M]any "borderland" students of Chinese philosophy increasingly rally around Gadamer's profound cultural conservatism as the means to reinvent China's classical hermeneutics ... as the basis for the postsocialist future of New Confucianism.

(Elman 2002: 544)

Elman's perception that Gadamer's cultural conservatism is "profound" is based on Gadamer's reception by "borderland" students and professors of Chinese philosophy such as On-cho Ng, originally from Hong Kong and now Professor of History, Asian Studies, and Philosophy at the Pennsylvania State University.[13] In this section, we will examine Ng's essay on Gadamerian and Confucian hermeneutics, "Negotiating the Boundary between Hermeneutics and Philosophy in Early Ch'ing Ch'eng-Chu[14] Confucianism" (2000). The essay connects Gadamer's hermeneutics and the hermeneutics of the seventeenth century Confucian, Li Guangdi (1642–1718), "the most important figure in the formulation of the official orthodoxy of the Qing [dynasty]" (Wm. Theodore de Bary, quoted by Ng 2000: 166). Right from the start then, Ng relates Gadamer's hermeneutics to the "orthodox" hermeneutics of the most culturally conservative Confucian interpreter in the Qing dynasty. Although Ng mentions two other forms of Confucian hermeneutics during the Qing dynasty, namely, "political statecraft" and "evidential studies" (Ng 2000: 166), he fails to mention that these other forms of "Confucian hermeneutics" allow the Confucian interpreter to take a critical stand toward and even reform the Confucian tradition. Instead Ng universalizes Li's seventeenth century "orthodox" Confucian hermeneutics and equates it with "Confucian hermeneutics" as a whole, including the twelfth century neo-Confucian hermeneutics of Zhu Xi and the twentieth and twenty-first century hermeneutics of his own New Confucianism. This then is the "Confucian hermeneutics" that Ng likens to Gadamer's twentieth century, Western hermeneutics. What then does Ng claim is characteristic of Li's "Confucian hermeneutics" and what about it, according to Ng, is comparable to Gadamer's hermeneutics?

The figure Ng selects to represent "Confucian hermeneutics," Li Guangdi (1642–1718), has the "illustrious role" of being "the imperial interpreter of orthodoxy, devoted to consolidating and promoting the *daotong* (lineage of the Way) as defined by Zhu Xi" (Ng 2000: 166). It is clear from this job description that Li was not hired to think critically about or to challenge the Confucian teachings (the *daotong*) of the neo-Confucian sage, Zhu Xi (1130–1200 CE). For Li is convinced, despite his rhetorical question, that:

> Because nature is constant, the Way [*Dao*] is constant, without the caprice of fads. Is it not true that the sages' teachings, which established the ultimate for human living and which resist changes in the ten thousand generations, are based on this?
>
> (Li quoted by Ng 2000: 182)

According to Ng, the task of Li's "Confucian hermeneutics" is twofold. First and foremost, Li has to "promote" Zhu Xi's neo-Confucian "orthodox interpretation" of the *Dao* or Way of Confucius written during the Song dynasty (960–1279). Li's own interpretation is expected to differ initially from Zhu Xi's "orthodox interpretation" because Li's views reflect a later historical time, the Qing dynasty. Li, it turns out, disagrees with Zhu Xi's commentaries on two classical Confucian books, the *Doctrine of the Mean* and the *Great Learning*. Li's second task, therefore, is to "consolidate" or "harmonize" his own diverging interpretations with Zhu Xi's "orthodox interpretations" of these two classical texts. Li's profoundly culturally conservative "Confucian hermeneutics" makes it impossible therefore to question orthodox Confucian doctrines let alone reform them.

According to Ng's presentation of "Confucian hermeneutics" via Li Guangdi, the "classical texts" are the primary repository of "tradition":

> [T]he ultimate universality of the values embodied in the classics was taken for granted, not subject to questioning in relativistic terms. Thus, although individual authorial imprints and historicocultural conditions did yield interpretive latitude, the timeless authority of the classical texts themselves furnished the *unshakeable bedrock* of the hermeneutic order.
>
> (Ng 2000: 167; emphasis added)

Critical thinking on the part of a Confucian interpreter such as Li occurs only when evaluating sources for Zhu Xi's "orthodox" commentary on the *Doctrine of the Mean* but criticism cannot extend to the content of the text being commentated upon, here the *Doctrine of the Mean*. According to Ng, therefore, the Five Classics and the Four Books present an all-encompassing horizon, the "Way [*Dao*] of Heaven," for a Confucian interpreter. So long as the overall and all-encompassing horizon remains intact, there is room within this horizon for different views that arise because the interpreter is situated later in history. However we do not find in this "Confucian hermeneutics," as Ng has represented it, any position within this all-encompassing horizon from which the Confucian interpreter could, to refer back to Habermas's charge against Gadamer's hermeneutics, critically question whether the classical texts and commentaries by the sages were themselves systematically distorted by ideology.

What is the basis for Ng's claim that Gadamer's philosophical hermeneutics is comparable to a "Confucian hermeneutics" such as the profoundly culturally conservative one that Ng presents? Ng maintains that there are the following "five commonalities":

[1] Both conceive the understanding of particular phenomena in terms of a *larger overarching framework*. [2] Both strive for understanding the classics' words *through dialogic communication*. [3] Both, notwithstanding their acceptance of the classics' cultural function as the preservation of truths, *subject these truth-bearing texts to constant interrogation*. [4] *Both make no assault* on the classics' claim to ultimate value, [5] but they dissect the particular ways in which the classics served as the vessels of ancient sages' pleas and teachings in finite historical moments.

(Ng 2000: 181; emphases added)

Gadamer's philosophical hermeneutics can only be "profoundly culturally conservative" (Elman) if these five points of comparison prove to be true. In regard to point one, let us question Ng's grasp of Gadamer's concept of "tradition," in respect to point four, Ng's characterization of the ultimate value of the classics for Gadamer, and finally, in regard to points two, three, and five, Ng's conception of what Gadamer refers to as the fusion of horizons. First of all, is "tradition" for Gadamer a "larger overarching framework" like the "Way [*Dao*] of Heaven"? To be sure Gadamer does say that we always stand within a tradition and that those who claim to be unaffected by tradition are most prone to being led astray by preconceptions and prejudgments that have been handed down to them. However Gadamer does not say that "tradition" is a "larger overarching [and "all-encompassing"] framework" but rather that tradition is what makes us finite; it is what we become conscious of being affected by when we realize that our horizon is *not* all encompassing. The first point of comparison is based therefore on Ng's misunderstanding of Gadamer's concept of "tradition" which Ng compares mistakenly with the "Way [*Dao*] of Heaven" that does provide a "larger overarching framework" for the kind of "Confucian hermeneutics" that Ng presents.

Ng makes this same mistake when he claims in point four that the ultimate value of classical texts is the same for a Gadamerian interpreter as for a Confucian interpreter:

A Confucian such as Zhu Xi or Li Guangdi, like a Hebrew theologian [Martin Buber], a Christian [systematic theological] thinker [David Tracy] or a contemporary philosopher of the interpretive enterprise [Gadamer], all play the role of Hermes ... the messenger of the gods ... The messages of the "gods" and "the Lord" are canonical and scriptural texts, or in other words, the classics that ineluctably impart a sense of the sacral.

(Ng 2000: 179–80)

If we unpack this comparison, we discover two things. The first is that Ng takes the canonical texts of Confucius and subsequent Confucian sages to be like "religious texts," namely, like the scriptural texts of Judaism and Christianity that "ineluctably impart a sense of the sacral." Thus this first part of the fourth comparison likens the "Way [Dao] of Heaven" to "the will of God" in Judaism and Christianity. The second discovery is that Ng mistakenly compares Gadamer's classical texts that are secular with "sacred texts" whose ultimate authority is a priori unassailable. However Gadamer's point about the "timeless" quality of the "classic" is that a text will only continue to prove to be a classic if it continues, when challenged, to pass the test of time. Ng's fourth comparison seriously misconstrues Gadamer's *Truth and Method* by turning it into "religious hermeneutics" and, in effect, eliminating the qualifier "philosophical" from Gadamer's "philosophical hermeneutics."

Ng's misconception of what Gadamer means by a "fusion of horizons" follows from these other two misunderstandings. Ng cites Gadamer's statement that "[h]ermeneutic experience is concerned with *tradition*. ... But tradition is not simply a process that experience teaches us to know and govern; it is *language* – that is, it expresses itself like a Thou" (Gadamer cited in Ng 2000: 183). He ignores other I–Thou relationships more central to Gadamer's concept of dialogue such as the I–Thou relationship that exists between two friends in book eight of Aristotle's *Nichomachean Ethics* and concludes instead that "Thou" for Gadamer refers to Martin Buber's 1923 book, *I and Thou*, in which the "Thou" that speaks to one through another Thou's words (the sacred text) is ultimately the "Lord" (Ng 2000: 183–4).[15] Ng mistakenly substitutes Buber's "Eternal Thou" for Gadamer's "tradition that speaks to us as a Thou" when he compares the fusion of horizons in Gadamer's philosophical hermeneutics with the fusion of horizons in "Confucian hermeneutics." In the case of "Confucian hermeneutics," the "dissection" of a canonical text by recourse to "dialogic communication" and "constant interrogation" (points five, two, and three) leads to the interpreter's ultimately "being *in tune with* the minds of the sages" (cited by Ng 2000: 183; emphasis added), starting with Confucius, whose minds have already become attuned to the "Way [Dao] of Heaven" that is constant (Li quoted by Ng 2000: 182). Whereas the fusion of horizons in Gadamer's hermeneutics starts and ends in experiencing more consciously that one is *affected by tradition* (*wirkungsgeschichtliches Bewußtsein*) and *finite*, the fusion of horizons or attunement in "Confucian hermeneutics" claims to transcend history and the limits of any and all traditions by *becoming of one mind via the words of the sages with the "Way [Dao] of Heaven"* that is constantly one and the same.

In 2000, Ng's essay on Gadamer and Li Guangdi, the "imperial interpreter of orthodoxy" in pre-modern Qing dynasty China, promotes a misunderstanding of Gadamer's philosophical hermeneutics among "borderland" Chinese (Elman).[16] According to this misunderstanding, Gadamer's philosophical hermeneutics is as "profoundly culturally conservative" as Ng's version of "orthodox" Confucian hermeneutics. We have seen, however, that Ng's comparison rests on "five commonalities" that do not withstand further scrutiny, as Ng himself admits five years later in "Affinity and Aporia: A Confucian Engagement with Gadamer's Hermeneutics."[17] What we have learned, however, by questioning Ng's comparisons is that both Ng and Elman are wrong about Gadamer's cultural conservatism being profound, but John Makeham is right about Ng's New Confucianism: "New Confucianism has emerged as a neo-conservative philosophical movement, *with religious overtones*, which claims to be the legitimate *transmitter and representative* of orthodox Confucian values" (Makeham 2003: 2; emphases added).[18] As we turn now to Chan's essay from 2000 in which he reaches quite different conclusions, it is important to keep in mind that when Ng writes about "the Confucian act of reading" or exegesis, what he means specifically is one kind of "Confucian hermeneutics" that he claims is "orthodox" for any hermeneutics that can call itself "Confucian," be it the hermeneutics of Zhu Xi, of Li Guangdi, or of New Confucians such as himself. This kind of "Confucian hermeneutics" presupposes that Confucius can only be a "transmitter" of tradition and cannot also be a "reformer" of tradition. What Chan's "Gadamer–Habermas debate" about Confucius is all about, however, is whether there is not also another kind of "Confucian hermeneutics" that allows Confucius (and Confucians) to be both transmitters and reformers of tradition.

III. Gadamer's hermeneutics and Confucian hermeneutics: the critique of ideology?

At the end of the twentieth century and beginning of the twenty-first, there is probably no philosophical position that, in view of its lasting and indeed increasing effective power and central role, would need less defense than that position elaborated in *Truth and Method*.

(Honneth 2003: 7)

When one so closely connected with Jürgen Habermas as Axel Honneth speaks of Gadamer's "increasing power and central role" in the beginning of the twenty-first century, he probably did not have in mind Gadamer's reception among those concerned about the future of Confucian thought in general and specifically in China. Yet what Honneth says holds true for China, as we shall see, and not just because the Chinese translation of *Truth and Method* was published in Shanghai in 1999. We turn now to an essay by Alan K. L. Chan, Professor of Philosophy and Dean of the Humanities, Arts, and Social Sciences at Nanyang Technological University in Singapore.[19] Where Ng's concern in 2000 is to advance a profoundly culturally conservative New Confucianism in the Chinese speaking world with the help of Gadamer's hermeneutics (and later without it), Chan's "Confucian Ethics and the Critique of Ideology" (2000) aims to further a dialogue with the West about Confucian philosophy. Chan takes Gadamer's response to Habermas to frame Confucius's answer for those in the West who ask "To what extent can a conservative Confucian be a critic of tradition if tradition is systematically distorted by ideology?" Chan, we should note, uses – with one notable exception – the terms "Confucian" and even "Confucius" to "refer no more than to what can be gleaned" from the *Analects* (Chan 2000: 259, fn. 4), thus he does not generalize about "the entire Confucian tradition" based only on the *Analects* as he did in his 1984 essay.[20] Furthermore the argument Chan makes in his "Gadamerian" defense of Confucius against the "Habermasian" charge of "conservatism" in this essay no longer makes tradition depend on anything transcendent such as "the Way of Heaven" as it did in his essay in 1984.[21]

Chan's essay focuses specifically on Confucius's concept of tradition as ritual (*li*), a concept that Gadamer wrote about late in his life. According to Gadamer's biographer, Jean Grondin, "the concept of the ritual ... would then replace tradition in Gadamer's philosophy and would at the same time make the concept of tradition more able to be understood" (Grondin 2001: 49).[22] Ritual has emerged in Confucian studies thanks to Herbert Fingarette's *Confucius – The Secular as Sacred* that argues that Confucius is not concerned in the *Analects* with individual moral agency so much as with ritual performances (ritual acts and ritual speech-acts). Ritual (*li*) then refers to the "web of social conventions within which we live" in our being in the world with others. Analytic philosophers, we are told, conceive of rituals as "the intelligent practice of learned conventions and language" (Fingarette 1972: 16). This web of *learned* social conventions and language is "in the first place inherited from tradition" (Graham 1989: 23). We have, for example, traditional ritual acts and speech-acts associated with being a family[23] when we celebrate birthdays, weddings, and funerals as well as traditional ritual practices around everyday ways of being together socially with those unfamiliar to us. For example, those entering a building or a room will let those inside exit before entering or a driver will yield to the driver on the left in intersections. Because they are learned, these social conventions can also be revised and relearned. An American driving in England will learn to yield to the driver on the right. Gay marriage as a traditional ritual act associated with the family is increasingly being recognized in the United States and around the world.

In Chan's essay, the "Confucian ethics" that Confucius teaches in the *Analects* concerns something that has until recently been of only peripheral interest to ethicists in the West, namely, how "to think ourselves inside the [for us up until now] unnoticed context of ritualised [social] behaviour" where agents spontaneously perform ritual acts "influencing [other persons] through interrelations which the agents do not [at first] analyse" (Graham 1989: 25). Musical performance as a social performance,[24] specifically chamber music performance, is an apt analogue for the kind of ritual performance Confucius is concerned about in the *Analects*.[25] The objective in playing together in a chamber music group is not to be individually "outstanding" but to be in "harmony with others" so that one performs one's best as an individual player by enabling the other players to also perform their best. To make a chamber music performance "better" requires each player to *attend critically* to how they are playing while *listening attentively* to the others with whom they are playing.

Confucius, according to Chan, has a Gadamerian concept of tradition (Chan 1984). Tradition thought of in terms of traditional rituals continues to exist only as long as it is renewed, but in being renewed tradition either "refines itself or deteriorates with the creative fluidity or sterile rigidity of performance" (Graham 1989: 23). Confucius, who lived in a period of war and cultural decline, recognized that rituals have a history and that they had *evolved* during the course of the three dynasties prior to the time of decline in which he lived. Thus when Confucius expresses his preference in *Analects* 3, 14 for the [Western] Zhou dynasty (1046–1771 BCE), this is not a preference for the rituals of an archaic "golden past" before dynastic history but rather a preference for the rituals that were performed during the most cultivated of the three dynasties that preceded his own: "The Master said, 'The Yin [i.e. Shang dynasty] built on the rites of the Xia. The additions and abridgments can be *known*. The Zhou built on the rites of the Yin. The additions and abridgments can be *known*" (*Analects* 2, 23 quoted by Chan 2000: 247; emphases added). Knowledge, then, of tradition, that is, of the history of ritual in the past three dynasties, provides Confucius with two things: an ideal for his society to measure back up to and tools for critically assessing what to "abridge" and what to "add" that will enhance the performance of a ritual.

Chan, a modern day Confucian, is left therefore with the need to answer two questions about a Confucian's stance toward traditional Confucian rituals and practices. First, how does a modern Confucian appropriate the Confucian tradition and traditional rituals critically and thereby "conserve" them? Second, is it possible for a modern conservative Confucian to criticize the Confucian tradition if it is systematically distorted by ideology? Chan chooses the gender relations of those related by marriage as an example of a critical appropriation of a traditional Confucian ritual or practice. His example for the second question has to do with Confucius's hierarchical ordering of those superior in moral cultivation above their inferiors who are less able or inclined to morally cultivate themselves through what Confucius himself characterizes as a traditional practice (*li*), namely, the "attentive questioning" of past traditional ritual practices (*Analects* 3, 15).

Chan's example of critically appropriating traditional rituals related to gender relations stems from Mencius, the second most important Confucian thinker and the second source of what has come to be called in Western terms "Confucian ethics."[26] In Mencius (4A. 17), "tradition prescribes that it would be contrary to *li* for a male person to physically touch his sister-in-law." Confucius and Mencius would hold, however, that "*ethical reflection* would demand that the ritual 'taboo' be overruled" if she were drowning (Chan 2000: 257; emphasis added) because *li* or ritual belongs together in Confucian thought with *ren* or benevolence (also translated as humanity). Indeed, what makes Confucius "a great cultural innovator" (Fingarette cited in Chan 1984: 428) rather than a conservative and traditionalist is that the Confucian approach to *li* necessitates on-going ethical "reflection that brings to light the ethical [*ren*] content of *li* and the need to critically assess *li* performance" (Chan 2000: 250–1). A brother-in-law's extending his hand and assisting his drowning sister-in-law is, upon ethical reflection, benevolent and the right ("humane") thing to do and not therefore a case of the potentially sexual touching that is and still remains traditionally taboo. While the case Chan gives us is admittedly exceptional, for such life–death situations are not everyday occurrences, the ethical reflection it describes highlights Confucius's requirement that one think critically for oneself about what interaction (*li*) is best (*ren*) while attending to the perspective of the other (in this case, the sister-in-law) when performing ritual practices.

Chan's answer to the first question about how a modern Confucian can critically appropriate and thereby "conserve" traditional Confucian practices is "Gadamerian"

(Chan 2000: 246). Gadamer, we know, insisted in *Truth and Method* that "The important thing is to be aware of one's own bias (*Voreingenommenheit*), so that the text [or text-like action] can present itself in all its otherness and thus assert its own truth against one's own fore-meanings" (Gadamer 2004: 271–2). If, as in this example, preconceptions of appropriate gender relations prescribe traditional gender-related practices ("not-touching"), critical ethical reflection upon these preconceptions can "add to" or, as in this case, "abridge" the performance of a traditional Confucian ritual practice.

> [E]thical judgment follows directly from the Confucian claim that *li* performance must be informed by the right attitudes and motivations. They do not exhaust the meaning of ethical judgment, but highlight how the Confucian conservative approach to tradition, in its advocacy of *li*, harbours a "built-in" [immanent] critical component. It is of course possible that one may judge wrongly. This only renders more poignant the need to devote oneself to *[Confucian] learning – to understand fully the teachings of the ancient sages and to reflect critically upon one's own experiences* [*Analects*] (2.15) – on which ethical judgment ultimately depends.
>
> (Chan 2000: 251; emphasis added)

Let us look at Chan's "Gadamerian" answer to the second and Habermasian question about the possibility for a critique of ideology from *within* the Confucian tradition.

Chan's argument is initially startling given our "democratic prejudice" (Nietzsche) for Chan assumes along with, he claims, Confucius in the *Analects* that there are four distinct "kinds" of individuals based on their "[Confucian] learning," that is, based on their "attentive questioning of past practices" while reflecting critically upon their own social performance when acting together with others. Since Confucius in *Analects* 3, 15 takes "learning as attentive questioning" of past practices to be itself a practice (*li*), Confucius is in effect discriminating between four kinds of individual performers based on their *performances of "[ethical] learning."* At one extreme of the "human spectrum," there is the "sage" (*shengren*) whose spontaneous performance presents to all the highest ethical ideal (*Analects* 7, 25) (Chan 2000: 255); at the other, there are those who Confucius, using the language of his agrarian society, likens to "'a piece of rotten wood' or a 'wall of dried dung'" in *Analects* 5, 10, "of whom little can be expected in terms of ethical accomplishments [ethical performances]. Though perhaps not as rare as sages," Chan points out, "this group is presumably small" (Chan 2000: 255–6). Neither of these kinds of individuals contributes, however, to the "gradual, evolutionary change" that can change tradition from within to a more perfect order. In regard to our case, namely, traditional Confucian gender relations that discriminate against women starting with girl babies, neither kind of individual can eliminate or diminish gender discrimination.

Confucius, Chan argues, distinguishes two other kinds of individuals between these two extremes: "[T]he *junzi* or gentlemen, who represent the main, accessible ethical ideal[27] in the *Lunyu* [*Analects*]. Opposite to the *junzi* are the *xiaoren*, ethically inferior and unworthy, small-minded, mean or petty persons … The main ethical battle in the *Lunyu* is fought between these two groups" (Chan 2000: 256).[28] Let us pause for a moment to clear up any possible misunderstandings about what Chan is saying about these two kinds of individuals where the difference is ethical and not a difference in social class. Brooks and Brooks inform us that the distinction between an individual who is a *junzi* and one who is a *xiaoren* was originally a distinction made by members *within* the warrior class about each other.[29] The older warrior code of honor required assessing the performance of warriors and so developed the capacity to discriminate between those whose performances were worthy of honor (*junzi*) and those whose performances were unworthy of honor because they were only for their own personal glory or advantage (*xiao*). Confucius turned this capacity to discriminate between what was honorable and what was not honorable but instead shameful into an ethical judgment about the "attitudes and motivation" informing a ritual performance. Ethical judgment became the capacity to assess one's own attitudes and motivation as to whether they were honorable (*junzi*) or not, and if they were shameful (*xiao*), of criticizing them and *learning from this experience*. The example of Lance Armstrong can help to make the distinction between a *junzi* performance and a *xiaoren* performance clearer and Chan's "Gadamerian" argument less suspicious and more compelling.

We can say that Armstrong, leader of Team America in the Tour de France, was initially a *junzi* and subsequently a *xiaoren*. Armstrong, a cancer survivor, was judged to be a superior moral role model, a *junzi*, because of his outstanding performances as the team leader of a winning American bike-racing team and because of the success of the philanthropic organization, Livestrong, that he founded to benefit other cancer victims. Young and old proudly wore yellow Livestrong bracelets throughout America and beyond. Armstrong's athletic performance became inferior and shameful (*xiao*) when it became evident that he had cheated by doping. However Lance Armstrong's performance as an individual person became ethically inferior and shameful (*xiaoren*) by his lying to himself and to others when he continued to deny that he had been doping. What ultimately made Lance Armstrong into a *xiaoren* was not just that his performance as a bicycle team leader and a philanthropist were for his own personal glory and advantage. It was his resistance to "Confucian learning from experience," that is, his resistance to critically assessing his own attitudes and motivations and thereby cultivating his ethical judgment after his mistakes were exposed that revealed him to others to be a *xiaoren*.

Chan's "Gadamerian" answer to the possibility for a critique of ideology from within the conservative New Confucian tradition is based on the possibility of "Confucian learning" overcoming such "resistance to learning from experience" and thereby transforming an individual from being one kind of human being, the morally inferior *xiaoren*, into the another kind of human being, the morally superior *junzi*:

> To confront the possibility of systematic corruption, a conservative Confucian would have to argue, first of all, that the *junzi* can effect significant change within tradition ... [and in addition] that a sufficient number of individuals – relative to population and other socio-political variables – can be transformed into morally significant human beings [i.e., *junzi*] ... Granted

that the *junzi* and the *xiaoren* represent two opposing kinds of individuals, this does not rule out the possibility of the latter becoming the former in the ethical sense, or the possibility of an ethical transformation by small steps and degrees.

(Chan 2000: 256)

Chan's "Gadamerian" argument depends then on the transformational power of *Confucian learning*, that is in this case on the ability to attentively question the gender-related preconceptions (*Vormeinungen*) or prejudices (*Vorurteile*) about ourselves and about others that inform the attitudes and motivation we bring to our social interactions and traditional practices where gender plays a role.

According to Chan's account, Confucian learning leading to individual moral self-cultivation starts when girls and boys are young and takes place anytime, indeed is lifelong. The effect of encouraging more Confucian learning will be to decrease the number of individuals who are *xiaoren* by increasing the "community of *junzi* [who are capable of] leading in the process of [the] reform [of society]":

[S]tructurally ethical judgment is able to challenge particular *li* acts governing, in this instance, gender relations. Over time and with the community of *junzi* leading in the process of reform, it is conceivable that gender relations could be so fundamentally realigned that older standards of propriety would become all but forgotten.

(Chan 2000: 257)

Although Chan does not highlight this here in concluding his Gadamerian defense of a conservative New Confucian's capacity to critique ideology, it must follow that the "community of *junzi*," once reserved for men ("gentlemen") only, would now include women.

In this chapter on "Hermeneutics and Confucianism," we have examined two essays that relate Gadamer's hermeneutics to Confucianism at the start of the twenty-first century. Although their authors, Ng and Chan, may not be writing with each other in mind, the views of Gadamer and Confucius that they present have parallels in the 1976 debate between Gadamer and Habermas. Ng's conclusion in 2000 (retracted in 2005) that Gadamer's hermeneutics is just like "orthodox" New Confucian hermeneutics in being profoundly culturally conservative echoes Habermas's original charge against Gadamer's hermeneutics in this debate. Chan, who held a similar view about Gadamer's hermeneutics and about Confucius sixteen years earlier, argues instead in 2000 that there is a capacity within "conservative" Confucianism to critique ideologies and reform for example gender relations from within the Confucian tradition. The model for this argument is Gadamer's argument in response to Habermas's criticism of philosophical hermeneutics in the 1976 Gadamer–Habermas debate. Where does this comparison of Gadamer's hermeneutics with Ng's and Chan's two forms of Confucianism leave Confucians and where does it leave Gadamerians?

We have seen that the debate in China about Confucius's stance toward tradition preceded the essays by Ng and Chan by more than a century and that the debate is developed further in 2000 in these essays when Confucius and Confucian hermeneutics are compared to Gadamer and Gadamerian hermeneutics within the framework of the Gadamer–Habermas debate. Since the debate about Confucius's stance toward tradition has had historical consequences in and for China in the twentieth century, what might we expect of twentieth-first century New Confucianism after the contributions Ng and Chan made to this debate in 2000?

In criticizing Ng's New Confucianism and, related to it, Ng's concept of Gadamer's hermeneutics, for "profound cultural conservatism" in his essay on "rethinking Confucianism" in 2002, Elman writes, we can infer, without knowledge of Chan's essay in 2000 that is framed in terms of the Gadamer–Habermas debate.[30] Elman is fundamentally concerned about the *reinvention* of "New Confucianism in [postsocialist] China for the twenty-first century," given "the social inequalities of rampant capitalism" that have arisen after "the failure of messianic socialism" (Elman 2002: 536). Elman contrasts the New Confucians in the Chinese "borderlands" (and "overseas") with their "post-Maoist counterparts in China" (Elman 2002: 536). What New Confucians outside of China such as Ng ignore and the post-Maoists reinventing New Confucianism within China have to confront is, he maintains, that "the failure of communism [in China] ... has bequeathed irrevocable political and gender revolutions that accompanied the rise and fall of militant Chinese socialism, 1915–76, and that have survived the fall of Maoism as Chinese Communist Party orthodoxy" (Elman 2002: 534). Elman rejects Ng's New Confucianism and, related to it, Gadamer's hermeneutics as Ng understands it, for twenty-first century China because it is unprepared to "ameliorate the dual legacies of capitalism and socialism" (Elman 2002: 534) by virtue of its profound cultural conservatism. We have shown, however, that both Elman and Ng are wrong to identify Gadamer's hermeneutics with a profoundly culturally conservative and "orthodox" form of New Confucianism. We have also found that Chan is right to relate Gadamer's hermeneutics instead to a modern "conservative" Confucianism that *develops within itself the capacity to critique ideology* and to reform and transform itself from within by attentively questioning the preconceptions and prejudices that inform the canonical texts and traditional ritual practices (*li*) of Confucianism. The New Confucianism that we are left with thanks to Chan's understanding of Confucius *and of Gadamer* is a Confucianism that is in a better position to "ameliorate the dual legacies of capitalism and socialism" in twenty-first century China.

We have seen where this comparison of hermeneutics and Confucianism leaves twenty-first century Confucians reinventing New Confucianism in China but where does it leave twenty-first century Gadamerians? Insofar as Chan's rethinking of Confucianism has also involved a "rethinking of Gadamerian hermeneutics" in terms of ritual, and in particular of the ritual practice (*li*) of *Confucian learning and moral self-cultivation*, this comparison of hermeneutics and Confucianism leaves Gadamerians in a better position to ameliorate the social inequalities that Jonathan Kozol calls "*savage*" that have also been the legacy of "rampant capitalism" in America and in the West.

Notes

1 Becoming conscious of one's finitude is not to be confused with relativism for it is an experience that consciousness makes about itself rather than an experience that consciousness has of an object.

2 Hegel's concept of "experience" as "determinate negation" also involves exposing limits and limitations. Gadamer rejects, however, Hegel's goal of "absolute knowing." See Gadamer 2004: 348–51.

3 For example, Steven van Zoeren (USA), Zhang Longxi (China), Rudolf Wagner (Germany), and John Makeham (Australia).

4 I have found Benjamin A. Elman's essay in "Rethinking Confucianism: Past and Present in China, Japan, Korea, and Vietnam" (2002) particularly helpful in clarifying the terminological issues pertaining to the differences between "Confucianism," "New Confucianism," and "New New Confucianism" (also called "Post-New Confucianism"). See Elman 2002: 524–30. See also Makeham 2003.

5 For more on New Confucianism, see Makeham 2003 and 2008.

6 Elman notes that "This notion of 'borderlands' is sinocentric and should not be applied uncritically to Japan, or Vietnam, since it represents Chinese tributary conceits toward them" (2002: 524, fn. 20).

7 The cause for gender inequality and the oppression of women in traditional, premodern China may be other or more than the systematic distortion of gender relations by ideology, here by "Confucianism as a state ideology." Li-Hsiang Lisa Rosenlee, for example, argues that the "institution of the family" rather than "Confucianism as a state ideology" is the cause of "women's oppression in premodern China," starting with the preference for boy babies and male heirs that insure the "continuity of the family name," "ancestor worship," and the "familial virtue of filial piety." The Chinese preference for boy babies has led to [1] the over two thousand year old practice of the infanticide and abandonment of "excess female babies," [2] the "child-bride/servant, [3] concubinage, [4] widowhood, and [5] footbinding" (Rosenlee 2006: 9). It is telling that although the Republic of China as well as the People's Republic of China outlawed all five forms of women's oppression in modern twentieth century China, the practice of female infanticide and the abandonment of girl babies was halted only briefly by Mao in the 1950s and continues to this day under another state ideology, that of the Chinese Communist Party.

8 For a richly rewarding introduction to the many faces of Confucius, see Nylan and Wilson 2010.

9 Confucius famously describes himself as "transmitting but not originating, trusting in and loving the ancients" in *Analects* 7, 1 (Graham 1989: 10).

10 Confucius warns that "To learn without thinking is stultifying, to think without learning is dangerous" in *Analects* 2, 15 (Graham 1989: 10). See also Goldin 2011: 9 on *Analects* 7, 8.

11 The canonical Confucian texts include the "Five Classics" (the *Odes*, the *Documents*, the *Three Rites Canons*, the *Book of Changes*, and the *Spring and Autumn Annals*) and the "Four Books" (the *Analects*, the *Mencius*, the "*Great Learning*," and the "*Doctrine of the Mean*"). A lost work on music is sometimes included as a sixth "Classic."

12 I am grateful to Chan for pointing out the history of this debate. See Chan 1984: 426 and 434 fn. 15.

13 See Elman 2002: 547.

14 With the exception of proper names and titles of publications, I have converted Wade-Giles Romanization into pinyin wherever possible.

15 Buber is never mentioned in *Truth and Method*.

16 Ng also published a Chinese version of this essay in Taiwan in 2000.

17 In this 2005 essay, Ng maintains that there are three fundamental differences between Gadamerian and Confucian hermeneutics. First, he points out that according to Gadamer there is "an insurmountable 'barrier that separates us from the divine'" (Gadamer cited by Ng 2005: 302), whereas for New Confucians there is not. Second, the interpreter for Gadamer is inevitably historically effected (*wirkungsgeschichtliches Bewußtsein*), whereas the orthodox New Confucian interpreter of the classical texts of the sages is capable of

"ultimately transcending history" (Ng 2005: 307). Finally, "while the Confucian classics, as embodiment of the *dao*, are sacral, Gadamer in the end sees the classics, even the scriptural ones, as texts. A classic-qua-text does not make the sort of truth-claim that a Confucian classic does, which seeks to define and embody the very being of the reader" (Ng 2005: 307).

18 Ng's "New Confucianism" is but one of many. For more on New Confucianism, see Makeham 2003 and 2008. For more on Gadamer's hermeneutics in relation to the "onto-hermeneutics" of the New Confucian, Cheng Chung-ying, Ng's teacher and mentor, see Wright 2011.

19 Chan's 1984 essay, "Philosophical hermeneutics and the *Analects*: The paradigm of 'tradition'," was written when he was a graduate student in Religious Studies at the University of Toronto. Thus he was initially an "overseas" New Confucian.

20 Ng, we recall, generalized about the whole Confucian tradition based on Li Guangdi, the most conservative Confucian interpreter in the Qing dynasty.

21 Chan states that "There is no need to impute a theory of human nature to Confucius, or to appeal to a transcendent 'Way of Heaven'" (Chan 2000: 255).

22 See also Palmer 2000: 385–8 on Gadamer and ritual. Palmer has also compared Gadamer and Confucius in Pfister 2006.

23 These traditional ritual practices may also be religious practices if they include baptism, a church wedding, or burial in a sanctified burial ground.

24 See Lisa McCormick, "Music as Social Performance" (McCormick 2006).

25 See Karyn Lai, "Confucian Moral Cultivation: Some Parallels with Music Training" (Lai 2003).

26 This is the one "notable exception" I referred to above to Chan's rule of using the terms "Confucius" and "Confucian" to refer to "no more than what can be gleaned" from the *Analects*.

27 Chan does not read Confucius or the *Analects* to support the idea that everyone can become a sage.

28 How this order of ranking differs from the rankings "good and bad" and "good and evil" discussed by Nietzsche in *On the Genealogy of Morality* is important but beyond the scope of this chapter.

29 Court service had probably been a monopoly of the chariot-driving elite. Their military values are here [in *Analects* 4, 7] civilized, but retain links to a military ethos. The … [ren] man has the traits of an ideal comrade-in-arms: strength, courage, steadfastness in crisis, consideration for others, capacity for self-sacrifice … It may help to remember the connotations of the Western term '*honor*.'

(Brooks and Brooks 1998: 15; emphasis added).

30 "Indeed those who cite Gadamer usually make no mention of Habermas" (Elman 2002: 549).

Bibliography

Brooks, E. Bruce and Brooks, A. Taeko (1998) *The Original Analects: Sayings of Confucius and His Successors*, New York: Columbia.

Chan, Alan K. L. (1984) "Philosophical hermeneutics and the *Analects*: The paradigm of 'tradition'," in *Philosophy East and West*, 34, 4: 421–36.

——(2000) "Confucian Ethics and Critique of Ideology," in *Asian Philosophy: An International Journal of the Philosophical Traditions of the East*, 10, 3: 245–61.

Elman, Benjamin A. (2002) "Rethinking 'Confucianism' and 'Neo-Confucianism' in Modern Chinese History," in *Rethinking Confucianism: Past and Present in China, Japan, Korea, and Vietnam*, eds Benjamin A. Elman, John B. Duncan, and Herman Ooms, Los Angeles: University of California Press, 518–54.

Gadamer, Hans-Georg (1997) "Reflections on my Philosophical Journey," trans. Richard E. Palmer in *The Philosophy of Hans-Georg Gadamer*, ed. Lewis Edwin Hahn, Chicago and La Salle, IL: Open Court, 3–63.

——(1999) *Zhen li yu fang fa* (*Truth and Method*), trans. Hong Handing, 2 vols, Shanghai: Shanghai yi wen chu ban she (Shanghai Translation Publishers).

——(2004) *Truth and Method*, 2nd rev. edn, trans. Joel Weinsheimer and Donald G. Marshall, London: Continuum.

Fingarette, Herbert (1972) *Confucius: The Secular as Sacred*, New York: Harper Torchbooks.

Goldin, Paul R. (2011) *Confucianism*, Berkeley and Los Angeles: University of California.

Graham, A. C. (1989) *Disputers of the Tao: Philosophical Argument in Ancient China*, La Salle, IL: Open Court.

Grondin, Jean (2001) "Play, Festival, and Ritual in Gadamer: On the theme of the immemorial in his later works," in *Language and Linguisticality in Gadamer's Hermeneutics*, ed. L. K. Schmidt, Lanham, MD: Lexington Books, 43–50.

Honneth, Axel (2003) "On the Destructive Power of the Third: Gadamer and Heidegger's doctrine of intersubjectivity," in *Philosophy and Social Criticism*, 29, 1: 5–21.

Kozol, Jonathan (1991) *Savage Inequalities: Children in America's Schools*, New York: Crown.

Lai, Karyn (2003) "Confucian Moral Cultivation: Some Parallels with Musical Training," in *The Moral Circle and the Self: Chinese and Western Perspectives*, eds Kim-Chong Chong, Sor-Han Tan, and C. L. Ten, La Salle, IL: Open Court, 107–39.

Makeham, John, ed. (2003) *New Confucianism: A Critical Examination*, New York: Palgrave Macmillan.

——(2008) *Lost Soul: "Confucianism" in Contemporary Chinese Academic Discourse*, Cambridge, MA and London: Harvard University Press.

McCormick, Lisa (2006) "Music as Social Performance," in *Myth, Meaning, and Performance: Toward a New Cultural Sociology of the Arts*, eds Ron Eyerman and Lisa McCormick, Boulder, CO and London: Paragon, 121–44.

Ng, On-cho (2000) "Negotiating the Boundary between Hermeneutics and Philosophy in Early Ch'ing Ch'eng-Chu Confucianism: Li Kuang-ti's (1642–1718) Study of the *Doctrine of the Mean* (Chung-yung) and *Great Learning* (Ta-shueh)," in *Imagining Boundaries: Changing Confucian Doctrines, Texts, and Hermeneutics*, eds Kai-wing Chow, On-cho Ng, and John B. Henderson, Albany: State University of New York Press, 165–93.

——(2001) *Cheng-Zhu Confucianism in the Early Qing: Li Guangdi (1642–1718) and Qing Learning*, Albany: State University of New York Press.

——(2005) "Affinity and Aporia: A Confucian Engagement with Gadamer's Hermeneutics," in *Interpretation and Intellectual Change: Chinese Hermeneutics in Historical Perspective*, ed. Ching-I Tu, New Brunswick, NJ and London: Transaction, 297–310.

——(ed.) (2008) *The Imperative of Understanding: Chinese Philosophy, Comparative Philosophy, and Onto-Hermeneutics*, New York: Global Scholarly Publications.

Nylan, Michael and Wilson, Thomas (2010) *Lives of Confucius: Civilization's Greatest Sage Through the Ages*, New York: Doubleday.

Palmer, R. E. (2000) "Gadamer's recent work on language and philosophy: On 'Zur Phänomenologie von Ritual und Sprache'," in *Continental Philosophy Review*, 33: 381–93.

——(2006) "Gadamer and Confucius: Some Possible Affinities," in *Journal of Chinese Philosophy* Supplement 1 *Hermeneutical Thinking in Chinese Philosophy*, ed. L. Pfister (December), 33: 81–93.

Pfister, Lauren (ed.) (2006) *Journal of Chinese Philosophy* Supplement 1 *Hermeneutical Thinking in Chinese Philosophy* (December), 33.

Rosenlee, Li-Hsiang Lisa (2006) *Confucianism and Women: A Philosophical Interpretation*, Albany: State University of New York Press.

Wang, Ban (2005) "Tradition, Modernity, and Critical Historical Consciousness," in *Chinese Hermeneutics in Historical Perspective: Interpretation and Intellectual Change*, ed. Ching-I Tu, New Brunswick, NJ and London: Transaction, 241–56.

Wright, Kathleen (2011) "Gadamer's Philosophical Hermeneutics and New Confucianism," in *Gadamer and Ricoeur: Critical Horizons for Contemporary Hermeneutics*, eds Francis J. Mootz III and George H. Taylor, New York: Continuum, 241–64.

54

HERMENEUTICS AND JUDAIC THOUGHT

Andrew Benjamin

> Do and practice, then, the things I have always recommended to you, holding them to
> be the stairway to a beautiful life. First, believe that god is a blissful, immortal being,
> as is commonly held.
>
> Epicurus, Letter to Menoecus

1. Hermeneutics, if only as a beginning, can be defined by a relation to texts. Once a definition of this generality can be assumed then two particular questions are posed. The first concerns the conception of text at work within the project of interpretation while the second concerns the differing ways in which the nature of the text generates the possibilities of approaches to it and then the way those approaches reflect the time(s) of interpretation. Within this generalized setting Jewish hermeneutics cannot be differentiated, at least initially, from the commentary and exegesis the history of which forms an integral part of any definition of Judaism. In sum, it can be argued that Judaism is a uniquely hermeneutic exercise, even if the introduction of Midrash contains the potential to question, from within the field of interpretation, certain conceptions of the hermeneutic.[1] While the presence of Judaism as a locus of interpretive conflict is a possibility that can always be recovered from a concentration on the history of interpretations within Judaism, it is also a position that emerges from the differing though ultimately interconnected ways in which the *Christian Bible* stages its necessary differentiation from firstly the Hebrew bible (Torah), and then, secondly, from its accompanying sacred texts and then finally from the hermeneutic projects that will continue to measure the latters' presence.

The affirmation of Judaism as a hermeneutic undertaking and then the provision of the grounds for the subsequent project of Christianity's differentiation from its conception of the Judaic and thus its construction of what can be called the *figure* of Judaism are both announced in the opening lines of the *Gospel of St John* in the *Christian Bible* (see Benjamin 2010a).[2] The use of the term 'logos' within these lines stages initially a relation to the history of Greek philosophy in which 'logos' refers as much to an 'account' as it does to 'reason', whilst also evoking an abstract ontological category in which 'logos' can be taken to name a thinking of Being.[3] Whatever position is maintained and thus whatever understanding of 'logos' prevails, what has to be assumed is that as far as lines 1.2–3 of the *Gospel of St John* are concerned, the term 'logos', as it appears within them, is held apart from the Christological.[4] Indeed, as will be suggested below, the rhetorical force of *John* 1.14, in which the Christological appears, demands that this is the case. The opening lines of the Gospel itself read as follows: Ἐν ἀρχῇ ἦν ὁ λόγος, καὶ ὁ λόγος ἦν πρὸς τὸν θεόν, καὶ θεὸς ἦν ὁ λόγος ('In the beginning was the word, the word was with God, and God was the logos'). The term 'beginning' (ἀρχῇ) stages a complex structure of time. Within the context of this line it suggests a temporality of that which always was. It allows for a form of continuity. Within that continuity the 'logos' is identified firstly as 'with' (πρὸς) God and then, secondly, an identity is established insofar as God is identified with the 'logos'. This separation between 'with God' and then God as the 'logos' is of fundamental importance. It sets up a twofold possibility. The first is to retain a conception of 'logos' as 'account' or as that which is compatible with 'book' and thus with Torah and then with the incorporation of God into a setting defined in those terms. Within such a setting there would not be a clear differentiation between God and 'logos'/Torah/book (the latter formulation – 'logos'/Torah/book – marks the inherent confluence that these terms stage). Here not only is the Christological unnecessary, more significantly the space in which it would be thought is itself absent. The second possibility, which is the undoing of the already present relation between God and 'logos'/Torah/book, begins with the radical transformation of 'logos'. 'Logos' becomes Christ. This transformation is not a mere repositioning. More is at stake, since it involves the overcoming of the setting defined, as noted above, by the interplay of God and 'logos'/Torah/book. That overcoming occurs systematically in the *Christian Bible*. It is clear, for example, in Paul's argument for the 'suspension' (καταργειν) of the Jewish law; a suspension that is predicated upon a twofold move in which, firstly, the law is literalized in order for it then to be differentiated from life, such that, secondly, the law now literalized continues with its radical separation from life.[5] (And this would be the condition of the law being able to continue.) This 'suspension' is the opening up and thus the systematic separation of the nexus comprised of God and 'logos'/Torah/book; a nexus in which God would have been defined in the terms that were created by the nexus itself. As a result of that nexus having been broken up God is redefined. The suspension of the law, which is the undoing of this set of complex interconnections, necessitates not the abandoning of 'logos' but its reconfiguration; 'logos' is retained though only in its reconfiguration. Reconfigured as Christ. This provides the claim in *Galatians* 3.13 that 'Christ redeemed us from the curse of the law' with its force. The 'suspension' of the law yields the law as both a literal presence and as a 'curse'. (Luther's translation underscores the figure of Christ as the 'redeemer' locating that from which this redemption occurs as the 'law', where this law's literalization will always have named Judaism – *Christus aber hat uns erlöst von dem Fluch des Gesetzes* – Luther 1984.) Within the *Christian Bible* Judaism reconfigured as the 'law' endures therefore as a 'curse' (one which it is possible to overcome, though it would be true that the Jews themselves could not overcome this 'curse').[6]

In the context of *John* the repositioning of 'logos' with its fundamental ensuing consequences takes place in 1.14: Καὶ ὁ λόγος σὰρξ ἐγένετο ('And the logos became flesh'). It should be noted here that the use of ἐγένετο (became) is already to evoke the terminology of creation in terms of a form of genesis rather than with the complex beginning that the Hebrew Bible states and that *John* 1.2–3 sets up in order then to overturn. The Hebrew בְּרֵאשִׁית בָּרָא אֱלֹהִים ('In the beginning of God's creating ... ') allows for a form of identification between בְּרֵאשִׁית and εν ἀρχῇ to be established insofar as they both announce a modality of beginning (see also De' Rossi 2001).[7] However, the Hebrew allows for the possibility of a beginning within the process of creating. In other words, the line can be read as suggesting that God's activity was a continuity of acting in which there was a beginning. While there are other possibilities and thus other translations, to insist on God's action as bound up with a form of continuity links God to the continuity of actions such that this continuity then comes to be articulated within and as 'logos'. The emphasis on continuity demands therefore a definition of God that is compatible with an emphasis on activity. Moreover, the insistence on continuity is also there in *Deuteronomy* 17.19. Here the relation to 'logos'/Torah/book, a connection that has already located both instruction and law within a locus defined by the necessary presence of a 'book' (*sefer*) is formulated in the following terms:

> It is to remain with him, and he is to read in it every day, as long as he lives; so that he will learn to fear his God and keep all the words of this *Torah* [אֶת־כָּל־דִּבְרֵי הַתּוֹרָה] and these laws and do them [לַעֲשֹׂתָם].

Whatever may be argued in connection to the nature of 'law' that this setting entails, not only does that 'law' have an already present instructive force, it is defined in relation to the 'book' where both involve modalities of continuity. It is also the case that within this setting there cannot be any easy way of effecting a separation of law and life. There is a continuity in which there would be a continual state of being 'on the way' to the law (Rosenzweig 1955: 74). As a result 'law' could not be set in opposition to life (and this will be the case even if the law/life relation is itself the site of contestation). And yet, there is of course an inherent fragility within this structure. It is always possible to literalize a text. What a literalization of the law entails (and this needs to be understood within Judaism as the Pauline legacy), once coupled to the repositioning of 'logos' from the domain of the textual to the bodily that occurs in *John*, is the refusal of a form of mediacy that necessitates both the deferring of any sense of finality, on the one hand, and consequently the distancing of the inscribed necessity of interpretation on the other. Mediacy, understood in this context therefore as the interarticulation of interpretation's necessity with the impossibility of finality, necessitates a locus of activity; that locus is the placed presence of being-in-common, that is, the place where community is defined by the continuity of the nexus between God and 'logos'/Torah/book.[8] The impossibility of finality is of course a position predicated upon defying continually any text's literalization as well as the equation of the allegorical or symbolic with the literal. Again it is worth noting the response in the *Christian Bible* to such a possibility. In a remarkable formulation in *Galatians* 5.4 the position is that the retention of the law, moreover the attempt to retain either *logos* or *nomos* in its written, and therefore inherently interpretive form, will bring about what is described as 'an estrangement from Christ'. Here, in an extraordinary usage of the term, the verb καταργειν now takes on the form of suspending a relation to Christ and thus the refusal of 'grace' through an attempt to use 'law' as that through which identity would have been secured and justified. The full passage is the following: 'You have suspended our relation to Christ [κατηργηθητε απο του χριστου], you who attempted to be justified by law [εν νομω].'[9]

The move from *John* 1.2–3 to 1.14 is not a simple occurrence. It stages nothing other than the overcoming of 'logos' by the 'flesh'. Text cedes its place to the body. The presence of 'flesh' is clear, for example, in the argumentation of Tyconius in his *Liber Regularum* (Tyconius 1989). The latter demands both that the body be present and that the body have a doubled determination. In the first instance it is the literal body, and then in the second, it is the body as the body of the Church, or the Church as the embodiment of the law (Tyconius 1989: 15–21). The latter sense of the body is defined in terms of a specific sense of continuity. The continuity of law which is the continuity of the nexus of God and 'logos'/Torah/book within and as life, which is a continuity where the discontinuous always remains a real possibility, has been transposed to become the continuity of Christ's doubled body. This is the context in which to understand the fourth rule of the *Liber Regularum* – *De promissis et lege* – in which Tyconius argues in relation to the 'just' (*iustos*) that:

> They have God's favor and do the law without any law [*legem sine lege faciunt*]: they serve God freely [*liberi*] and live according to the image and likeness of God and of Christ [*ad imaginem et similitudinem Dei et Christi vivunt*].
>
> (Tyconius 1989: 45)

The second law, the absent law, is only absent as a result of its literalization. That the law is retained 'without any law' (*sine lege*) means nothing other than the transference of the law to God. Law acquires the status of mystery and as such demands of its 'servants' and its 'brethren' that they are subjects of God not of the law. Life continues structured by an image not by law. The latter is only possible because of radical disjunction between law and life. The text therefore has been subdued by God. Love replaces law and thus the place in which the possibility of justice would have been thought has been emptied. Replaced by the individual's relation to God. Universality in regard to the latter is the universality of love.

2. Standing opposed to the literalization of the law, which is a move within a hermeneutics in which the ascription of rigidity and redundancy to a text renders it inoperative, does not mean that the only plausible counter-claim is to argue for a text – or conception of text – with greater semantic depth and openness. These elements must be in play. However there would need to be more. The possibility of the inherently interpretable text therefore must have greater extension than a text whose 'gates' remain open. This openness has to do as much with the status of the text as it does to God's relation to that text. The move from 'logos' to 'flesh' is the abandoning of the text. The centrality of writing is overcome as a result of having acknowledged the ineliminability of the effective presence of the Christological. To retain the interpretable text as the locus of investigation demands therefore a double move. The first is a configuration of God that refuses the triune structure demanded by the effacing of *logos* and therefore is a conception of God that is inherently

compatible with the retained centrality of the text. The second element is of course the text as defined by the continuity of its openness. There has to be a return therefore to the question of the text. Here the way in to both God and text and then the complex interknitting of their relation is provided by the formulation of the *Bracha* that occurs prior to the reading of *Torah*. The source is the *Babylonian Talmud: Tractate Berakhot 11b*. The central component of the *Bracha* in this instance is found in the line: 'Blessed art Thou, O Lord, who gives the Torah' (*notein haTorah*). What has to be argued here is that the act of giving does not occur once. The 'gift' therefore is what it is in the continuity if its being given (by the giver). In other words, it is not as though the Torah having been given announces the withdrawal of God. Indeed it is possible to go further and evoke *Genesis Rabbah* 1.1 'The Torah was to God, when He created the world, what the plan is to an architect when he erects a building.'[10] As a result not only is the Torah there as held within an always already present relation to God, there is a different sense of giving and thus continuity at work such that the thinking of one is the thinking of the other.

In both instances what is essential is the definition of God. God is present as that which cannot be thought independently of *Torah*. There is only *logos*, where logos is not the 'logos' of logocentrism necessarily.[11] Rather 'logos' in this context marks the retained centrality of the text. At work here therefore, rather than the presence of the logocentric impulse, is a text defined in terms of an infinite state of self-realization. This is the other possibility for continuity. God is there in the continual giving of *Torah*. Hence the question that arises concerns whether it would be possible to allocate to God a status that is independent of the continuity of the giving of *Torah*. As an attempt to address this question the approach taken here involves staying with this early tradition of commentary and exegesis. Moreover, in this instance, it will involve evoking a set of texts and an author whose impact on the interpretive tradition and thus on the history of Jewish hermeneutics was by no means great; nonetheless, these texts were one of the first to take up an allegorical interpretation of Torah from within Greek philosophical tradition. That interpretation was part of the development of Philo's own philosophical and theological project.[12]

The importance of Philo in this context is twofold. In the first instance the body of his writings were was probably completed 50 years before the final redaction of *John* (approximately 90 CE) and therefore allows for a Greek engagement with the Hebrew Bible that owes a great deal to Plato but little or nothing to Christianity. Secondly, there is the presence within the interpretation of translations of significant passages from Torah. In this instance of particular importance is his translation of *Genesis* 2.4 in the *Legum Allegoria*. The text in Philo's Greek is: Αυτη η βιβλος γενεσως ουρανου και γης οτε εγεντο ('The book is that of the origin of heaven and earth, when it came into being').[13] Philo is translating תּוֹלְדוֹת (account) as 'η βιβλος (book).[14] Even though this is a possible translation it could also be the case that he has interpolated *Genesis* 5.1. In the latter text there is a similar formulation though with the presence of the word סֵפֶר (book). What is significant about the positioning is the identification of the 'account' with a 'book'. (A position that could be justified by reference to 'logos' in Heraclitus DK 1.) Hence the interpretation that follows is of the 'book'. The force of Philo's text is that there is a continual movement between the philosophical and the interpretive. The presence of one mediates the presence of the other. A clear instance of the latter is the way in which a Platonic distinction between the 'mind' (την νους) in the first instance and 'sense-perception' (της αισθησεως) in the second, is incorporated into the interpretation of the creation of the earth and objects in it.[15] Indeed, both the text's interpretation and the philosophical are worked out together. In an extraordinary passage in the *Legum Allegoria* that could be taken as a formulation of a Philovian hermenutics, insofar as it allows for the literal whilst locating both another level of meaning and then the mind's capacity to attain it, Philo states the following:

> whenever we wish to get an accurate understanding of a subject we hurry off to a lonely spot; we close our eyes; we stop our ears; we say 'good bye' to our peceptive faculties [ταις αισθησιω]. So then, we see that, when the mind is astir and awake, the power of perception is supressed.
>
> (II.VII. 25)

This capacity for differentiation is essential. Levels of meanings are always there. In *De Abrahamo* (88:1) literal meaning is defined in relation to the human and thus to the senses while the level of meaning that is located deeper in the text – a level of meaning identified throughout Philo's corpus by the term υπονοια (hyponoia) – is linked, for the most part, to the soul. Philo interprets *Deuteronomy* 23.13, in which reference is made to Moses carrying a 'shovel', with the claim that the term 'shovel' is used 'symbolically' as it unearths 'hidden matters' (τα κρυμμενα των πραγματων).[16] The relation between a particular philosophical anthropology and the nature of the text continues. One works with the other.

In Philo, as suggested, the relation between surface and depth may correspond to a similar structure within the nature of human being. However, it is precisely the care that is needed to establish and maintain these differing but connected distinctions that marks the inscription of forms of instability within them. Difficulties arise. In the first instance, this relation no matter how it may be reconfigured will always be able to allow for the literalization of the truth. In other words, it could be conjectured that the 'deeper meaning' and thus allegory may only ever point to one possible referent. In *De vita contemplativa* (78:2) Philo argues that, 'The exposition of the sacred scriptures treats the inner meaning conveyed by allegory' (αι δε εξηγησεις των ιερων γραμματων γινονται δι'υπονοιων εν αλληγοριαις)[17] (9.161). Similar formulations are found throughout his writings. In *De fuga et inventione* 75:3 for example, the claim is: 'Let us have recourse to the scientific modes of interpretation which look for the hidden meaning of the literal words' (το απορον ουν και δυσαπολογητον αποδρασμεθα της δι'υπονοιων) (4:69).

Once these general claims are set in relation to specific interpretations of verses of Torah then the full nature of the hermeneutic enterprise emerges. For example there is the argument in *Quis rerum divinarum heres sit* (288:3) made in regard to *Genesis* 12.10, which claims that if a turn is made to the '*hyponia*' contained by these words in this passage, then there is evidence of the meaning of 'peace' rather than 'stress'. This means that Philo's position still allows for the possibility that there is a truth, one that is hidden such that in its having been recovered, the 'hidden meaning' can then become commensurate with *the* meaning. Even if this possibility is allowed it still brings two attendant problems into play. The first is that the very presence of the 'deeper', 'allegorical', 'hidden' or 'inner meaning' complicates in advance the identification of an interpretive singularity. The presence of a domain of meaning that demands an interpretive practice that depends upon the presence of depth always retains the possibility of the continuity of its opening up and thus yielding further depths. This amounts to the claim that the hidden resists its equation with a 'surface'. Were such an equation to occur this would entail that the 'surface' would have been equated with the 'hidden' such that the 'hidden' would have been trans- formed into the actual or literal meaning. Resisting this equation indicates that what cannot be effaced is the necessity of further elements of the 'hidden' being identified and then recovered. There would be therefore the continuity of a process which because it allows for conflict positions discontinuity at the centre of continuity such that the discontinuous defines the nature of continuity itself. It will be essential to return to this point when the move from the purely hermeneutic to Midrash occurs.

The second element that complicates any possible equation of the 'hidden' with the singularization of meaning and which allows for a repositioning of Philo beyond the limits established by his conception of the hermeneutic project resides in one of the direct implications at work with the identification of God as the 'giver of Torah', namely the continuity of the object of interpretation is the continuity of its being given; that continuity has already been identified as the nexus of God and 'logos'/ Torah/book. To be given, to continue to be given, is to continue to be received. Even allowing for different modalities of acceptance once acceptance can be under- stood as the construction of a tradition, then what is presupposed is a place of reception. Continuity therefore has to bring with it the question of place. As has already been noted continuity necessitates a locus of activity. Consequently what this necessity underscores is what can be described as the essential placedness of human being.[18] What this means in broader terms is that a philosophical anthro- pology cannot be thought other than in relation to the assumed centrality of place. Here, the place in which there is the continuity of giving, the place to which Torah is given, is the world. A setting that finds one of its most succinct formulations in *Deuteronomy* 30.12. The force of the verse is the positioning of the law. While it is defined in the negative, insofar as the place of law is 'not in heaven' (לֹא בַשָּׁמַיִם) the force of the claim is that the locus in which law pertains cannot be separated from what it means to live a life.[19] Being-in-place therefore incorporates law with it.[20] This accounts for why Paul's overcoming of Judaism, his 'suspension' of the law, has to separate law from life. This separation could only have occurred as the result of the latter's literalization. To the extent that law remains part of life then its relation to life is such that the law/life relation involves an inherent adaptability. Although the detail would need to be pursued it can be noted that one of Philo's evocations of *Deuteronomy* 30.12, in this instance in *De Mutatione Nominum*, argues that Moses' 'exhortation' is that the 'acquisition of the good' is a possibility in the here and now. The good (αγαθον) attends this life. And moreover all the elements of which it is comprised when taken together make up 'human happiness' (την ανθρωπινην ευδαι- μονιαν).[21] Philo's further interpretation of the import of *Deuteronomy* 30.12ff is that it leads to the development of a sense of being-in-common. His argument is that the 'good' leads to a situation of living 'with our fellow citizens in peace and law observance'. The point that needs to be emphasized here is that this is not a moral or political claim made *in vacuo*. The contrary is the case. It is an interpretation of *Deuteronomy* 30.12ff. Therefore it is a position held within a general interpretive project. Even if the ostensibly social nature of Philo's concerns are distanced such that the presence of the law and thus God's presence – God as the continuous giving of Torah such that God *is*, is what it is, in Torah's being given – is not taken as central, what remains essential is a prevailing sense of community. Community names the collectivity of those accounted for in terms of being-in-place.

The notion of community cannot be generalized. As a term it refers as much to a sense of place as it does to commonality. It is also the case that commonality as a locus in which 'human happiness' pertains should not be naturalized. *Eudaimonia* is not a necessity. Indeed, precisely because of the absence of its own necessity, 'happiness' has to be understood as a potentiality for human being. The identification of a link between a modality of well being and potentiality is further evidence of an interarticulation of law and life. The sense of continuity that this interarticulation generates not only provides elements integral to an understanding of being-in-common and being-in-place, it also has important implications. For example, within this context, *Psalm 89* can be interpreted as defining community in terms of the 'holy' (*cadoshim*). While the term 'holy' can be read with a sense of exclusivity, it can equally be understood as naming a potentiality within human being for 'holiness'. Moreover, precisely because the term is in the plural, what it identifies is a sense of being-in-common that is originally plural (Benjamin 1997 and 2015). This form of plurality would refuse the possibility that the 'holy' could be reduced to that which had only regional, ethnic or chronological exclusivity. Once 'holiness' is located within a generalized philosophical anthropology it names a potentiality for human being and as such it becomes similar to the realization of 'human happiness' and thus can be linked to the relationship between the 'highest good' and the 'good life' as it appears in both Aristotle and Epicurus and then continues within Roman stoicism.[22] Again what comes to the fore is the way in which law is present within life and it is present as a continual locus of interpretation and adaptation. Law as a locus of interpretation will always be more than its 'author'.

Moreover, to the extent that it can be assumed that God is the giver of Torah and that God cannot be thought as a consequence independently of the nexus God and 'logos'/Torah/book then the continuity of the critique of Moses and law that is found, for example, in Spinoza, is premised upon a misunderstanding of God's relation to law. Spinoza argues that once the law had been received by the 'Hebrews' they then, 'gave to Moses the sovereign right of command [*jus summum imperandi*], and he alone possessed the authority of instituting and abrogating the laws in the name of God [*leges Dei nomie*]'.[23] Even if this were only a historical claim, and thus one that depended upon a specific evidential basis, it would remain the case that as a claim concerning the nexus of God and 'logos'/Torah/book it fails systematically to address the specificity that arises from law as a province of interpretation. Spinoza imports a conception of Moses' relation to the law, that while evident in the Renaissance especially in Machiavelli, bears a lineage that more likely runs from Paul than it does from the tradition's own engagement with already present understandings of the connection between God and 'logos'/Torah/book.[24] In part this is because Spinoza's God, one which is thought in terms of 'substance', is commensurate with the activity of nature itself. Thus this God has an arbitrary relation to the presence of 'logos'/Torah/book. God, for Spinoza, as the 'giver' of Torah becomes a purely historical claim and thus one with mere parochial force. As a result the 'logos'/Torah/book becomes no more than a historical document. What would then become otiose would be claims made on the basis of the after life of the text.

For Spinoza God as substance is pure activity. However activity in this instance may demand an account that began to identify nature with its law, but what is thereby precluded is nature as a locus of interpretive conflict in which that conflict and its history become the history of a tradition. The full force of Spinoza's misunderstanding of the God of the 'Hebrews' can be found in his failure to recognize that once law is established as a locus of interpretation and then once law can only be thought in terms of its interarticulation with life, God's necessity is equally the non-necessity of God given the presence of 'logos'/Torah/book. The necessity of God gives way to the necessity of the 'logos'/Torah/book as defining a locus of interpretation where the concerns that regulate interpretation are not located in 'heaven' but are defined by the placedness of human being. Being-in-place names that which is staged by the formulation 'not heaven'.

3. How, within this context, is the move to Midrash to be understood?[25] In part the move has to do with the position taken by the text within the setting created by the complex sense of continuity that has been noted above and which comes to define what is meant more broadly by the text's iterability. Midrash holds open the possibility of that which while at work in the texts and thus is other than a literal interpretation cannot be thought in terms of depth. In a way it can be argued that Midrash is both the possibility of the text's iterability and that which *comes from the outside*, that is, the place that is 'not heaven', namely the worldliness of the world. However, what has to be sustained is the text. What lives on within Midrash is the text itself. If hermeneutics is ultimately defined by the relationship between surface and depth then Midrash is the possibility that attends that opposition whilst functioning, at the same time, as its deconstruction. Midrash is therefore the potentiality that was always at work once the distinction between surface and depth is allowed.

Within the tradition the structure of interpretation that stages in more detail the relationship between surface and depth is provided by the acronym *PaRDeS*.[26] The term is a combination of the different levels of interpretation, *Peshat*, *Remez*, *Derash* and *Sod*. *Peshat* can be understood as the literal; after which comes *Remez* or the allegorical; *Derash* the exegetical dimension incorporates what can be described as both the moral as well as the social aspects of the text. This is also the level, it might be agued, in which a certain understanding of Midrash might enter insofar as it opens up the possibility for the registration of a sense of time that is external to the text. Finally, *Sod*, which is the mystical dimension of the text. These levels of interpretation are at work whether or not acts of interpretation are occurring within or outside the mystical or Kabbalistic traditions.[27] The difficulty that emerges here is attempting to establish a clear distinction between the history of exegesis and interpretation on the one hand and the possibility on the other hand that the nexus God and 'logos'/Torah/book defines a locus of interpretation in its own right such that what is brought to the text becomes the relation that determines the interpretive. In other words, the move would be from the study of the history of interpretations to the possibility of adding to interpretation. Midrash conceived as *coming from the outside*. That addition, were it to be an actual addition, would necessitate a relation between internality and externality. Once the relationship defines a specific locus then what is tied together is firstly, the nexus God and 'logos'/Torah/book and then secondly *being-in-place*. The latter – 'logos'/Torah/book – is demanded by the necessity that the nexus is placed 'not in heaven' but in the place of human life. While the former – God – pertains because of a definition in which necessity becomes the necessity of Torah. However the necessity of Torah while allowing for the possibility of an interpretation in which the hidden and the literal coincided because of an equation of meaning with the singular will equally always resist that possibility. Mediation is the continuity of the text's being given. More significantly once the text as gift is itself mediated by the necessity of the external (the 'not in heaven') then what counts as necessity – Torah's necessity – will have been transformed.

And yet, even within such a setting – one marked by ineliminability of processes of mediation – there needs to be the presence of a form of constraint. The limit is already there within the history of interpretation. It has a number of different forms. In this instance one of the most significant is the concept of *haggadot shel dofi*. In strict terms it is intended to delimit interpretations by excluding those 'designed to mock or malign the teachings or teachers of Scripture' (Fishbane 1998: 21). The source for this conception of constraint is *Sanhedrin* 99b. What is interesting about this as pact of Talmud is that the one who acts this way has a specific name, that is, '*Epikoros*'. That Epicurus figures within *Babylonian Talmud* in ways that are similar to the presence of the 'same' name in Kant's *Critique of Practical Reason* is a point worth noting even if it cannot be pursued.[28] To ask what the text means by an '*Epikoros*' is already to ask an interpretive question. Moreover *Sanhedrin* 99b is itself concerned with an attempt to answer the question: what is an *Epikoros*? The question concerns a limit. Equally it concerns an attitude to both the scholar and the text. It might be the case that '*Epikoros*' names the threat that is always there within processes of interpretation. Even though it is advanced as part of a historical claim Boyarin argues that 'midrash came about within rabbinic culture as the product of a complex politics of resistance to logocentric thinking' (Boyarin 2005: 133). If logocentrism here means that conception of interpretation that is defined in terms of abstract universals then Midrash can be understood as part of a process of particularization. The text becomes a locus of multiplicities. '*Epikoros*' names therefore that which will always attend this resistance. It is the system's attempt to secure itself while allowing for its own openness. That move however is never purely textual. Hence there is an undoing of the logocentric that occurs by interarticulating the continuity of giving that is the nexus of God and 'logos'/Torah/book in the first instance and the 'not heaven', that is, being-in-place in the second. One of the great ironies is that the setting that this establishes, namely one in which both law and life are defined by an already present imbrication, bears the name Epicurean. In other words, the problem staged by *Sanhedrin* 99b is the problem of Midrash itself. What counts therefore both as *haggadot shel dofi* and the possibility of its avoidance is itself a question of interpretation for which Midrashim need to be written and adduced.

What this means therefore is that the threat to interpretation named as '*Epikoros*' – more generally the term for an apostate – is what allows for interpretation in the first place. Interpretation unless it is determined in advance in terms of outcomes always runs the risk of 'mockery'. This is the risk that is inherent to creativity; equally it is the sense of exposure that occurs once the oscillation between the figural and the literal is displaced. Such a displacement however does not mean that what is then sanctioned is a disruption in which the continuity of Torah is refused. Rather the displacement occasions the registration of the mediating presence of being-in-place. What registers therefore can be understood as the affirmation of the continuity of the interarticulation of law and life. Philosophically a way of naming that setting is by invoking the names of Aristotle and Epicurus. In this context it involves recognizing that once life exercises control then Torah's mediation is the continuity of its being conditioned. This is the opening that the move to Midrash as a source of invention has to allow.

Notes

1 This project works within the opening created by Michael Fagenblatt's conception of Midrash. His position concerning Midrash is the following:

> the method of Judaism is called Midrash. Much more than an exegetical tradition Midrash is the way Jewish thinkers have reread the tradition in order to reconceive their world. The *modus operandi* of Jewish thought is such that it reconfigures its ever-changing boundaries and populates them with new thoughts woven of old texts.
>
> (Fagenblatt 2010: 19–20)

This chapter needs to be read therefore as a contribution to this project. Moreover it continues work I have undertaken on Midrash as Jewish Thought (see Benjamin 2013). In addition, this larger project sets up a conception of Midrash, again following Fagenblatt, that insists on an open-ended tradition rather than identification of Midrash with the forms and functions it has taken historically. The latter position is evident, for example, in the treatment of Midrash in Stern (1991). Equally it departs from Boyarin's original encounter with Midrash that was defined by the internality of texts (see Boyarin 1990). In addition it should not be thought that the tradition is without attempts to divest interpretation of the need for the hermeneutic via an insistence on the complete transparency of the original text: for example, Uriel da Costa in his *Exame das tradiçoes pharises* (first published in 1624) argued as part of an interpretation that:

> there is no room left for any explanation or tradition apart from what is written down in the Law. Besides it stands to reason that any explanation indispensible to the law would have been written down at the same time as the Law itself if the law was incomprehensible without it.
>
> (da Costa 1993: 272)

2 A compelling and important interpretation of *John* that begins with the same set of concerns though which differs in orientation because of the way the body's insistence is understood here is the one that has been provided by Boyarin (2004). It needs to be noted that the brilliance of Boyarin's work demands far more than can be offered in the context of this chapter.

3 See in this regard the use of 'logos' in Heraclitus DK 1 and DK 50 in which, from one perspective, 'logos' can be read both as an 'account' and a 'true account' (see Diels and Kranz 1951).

4 All references to the *Christian Bible*, the *Revised Standard Version*. At times translations have been modified.

5 See in addition: *Corinthians* 15.24: 'Then comes the end, when He delivers the kingdom to God the Father, when He puts an end to all rule and all authority and power' (ειτα το τελος οταν παραδω την βασιλειαν τω θεω και πατρι οταν καταργηση πασαν αρχην και πασαν εξουσιαν και δυναμιν). Clearly the current interest in this aspect of Paul's work within contemporary philosophy comes from the work of Agamben (2005). I have discussed Agamben's Paul interpretation in Benjamin 2010b. In broader terms it can be noted that contemporary philosophical accounts that seem to move from logos to flesh as the beginning of a material(ist) account of life also efface the inscription within life of law (see e.g. Henry 2000: 323–39).

6 I have analysed this particular structure as it pertains to the relationship between Jews, diseases and animality in Hegel. Judaism becomes a disease from which it is possible to be cured. The cost of the cure is of course the effacing – perhaps 'suspension' – of Judaism (Judaism structured as that which could be suspended) – see Benjamin 2010a: 95–112).

7 The opening lines of *Genesis* are given an interpretive translation that makes a decision in relation to how בְּרֵאשִׁית is understood. The translation reads: 'In former times, in days of old, when there was a beginning of existence, God created', 367. The extraordinary translation in *The Zohar* needs to be noted. 'With beginning – created God'. For a discussion of this translation see the footnote in *The Zohar* 2003: 110.

8 Continuity also means continuity through time. Within the tradition this can be understood as already prefigured within the formulation *ladorvador* (from generation to generation) or more specifically *ladorvativim* (throughout your generation). The latter is interpreted in the *Mekhilta de-Rabbi Ishmael* as that which occurs 'forever'. However the problem is how 'forever' is to be understood. Is it the continuity of the always the same or is it the continuity of the same's continual self-transformation? See *Mekhilta de-Rabbi Ishmael* 2004: *Tractate Pisha* 7. 126–8.

9 Indeed it is passages such as this that would complicate Boyarin's attempt to set up a rapprochement between the hermeneutic project of Origen and the study of Torah (see Boyarin 2010: 52).

10 For a discussion of the connection to Philo, see Niehoff 2008.

11 For the most important attempt to establish a compatibility between developments in contemporary European philosophy and the interpretive tradition within Judaism, see Handleman (1982).

12 The most significant introduction to Philo is still Wolfson (1947). For Philo's place within the general tradition of Jewish Philosophy, see Benussan 2003: 21–64. All references to Philo are to the Loeb editions.

13 The traditional English translation of *Genesis* is: 'This is the account of the heavens and the earth when they were created.'

14 See also *Legum Allegoraria* I.19 in which 'book' is described by Philo as the name for 'the reason of God' (του τον θεου λογον).

15 The influence of Platonic and Neoplatonic formulation of the relationship between the 'mind' and the 'body within the history of Jewish thought is clearly not confined to Philo. For an eleventh century example see Ibn Pakuda 1993: 441.

16 There is an important correlate here to an occurrence of a cognate term in Heraclitus. DK 123 states: φυσις κρυπτεθαι φιλει ('The nature of things is accustomed to hiding itself'). The surface or the surface as the literal does not present the truth. It needs to be uncovered.

17 The use of the term υπονοια is central to the development of Philo's hermeneutic project. An earlier and instructive use of the term occurs in Xenophon's *Banquet* in which, in a passage mirroring Plato, Socrates says of the poets that they 'did not know the inner meaning of the poem' (τας υπονοιας ουκ επιστανται) (III.6). Moreover as Runia (1991) has argued,

meaning in the Mosaic text 'is located at various levels', 'Philo is above all concerned with the deeper "philosophical" meaning of the text' (IV 237) (see also Fishbane 1992: 39).

18 For one of the founding texts opening up place as a dominant question within philosophy, see Malpas 1999.

19 While there are a number of important formulations of this position within the history of philosophy, one of the most acute is found in Arendt's summation of the 'first half of Kant's *Critique of Judgment*'. She wrote: 'Men = earth bound creatures, living in communities, endowed with common sense, *sensus communis*, a community sense; not autonomous, needing each other's company even for thinking ("freedom of the pen") = first part of the *Critique of Judgment*: aesthetic judgment' (Arendt 1982: 27).

20 See in addition the way this line from *Deuteronomy* is deployed to argue for a similar position in *Babylonian Talmud: Tractate Baba Mezi'a 59b*.

21 Philo's use of the term 'eudaimonia' opens up a way of investigating the tensions within Philo's work. As much as he is a Platonist in terms of the hermeneutic project that obtains within his writings, his use of a term that will recall both a certain Aristotelianism and the Epicurean tradition locates his thinking within a domain in which a concern with 'life' and thus the 'good life' will have a great importance. It is this concern with life that defines his presence as a philosopher within a Judaic tradition. There is important secondary literature attesting to the link between Stocism, Epicureanism and Philo (see e.g. Graver 1999). What will complicate this position is the misunderstanding of Epicurus that occurs in the Talmud and then is repeated by Kant in the *Critique of Practical Reason*. This is a topic that will need to be treated elsewhere.

22 See for example Seneca, *Ad Lucilium Epistulae Morales*, 9.1 and 66.45. The additional point that needs to be made (its relevance will be clear by the end of this chapter) is that Seneca's evocation of the 'greatest good' is always linked to the name Epicurus.

23 Spinoza 1999: XVIII. 5–7.

24 See for example the discussion of Moses in which he is linked to Solon in Machiavelli's work on Livy (Machiavelli 1998: 75). There are also important references to Moses in *Il Principe*. The link between Machiavelli and Spinoza is developed in Del Lucchese (2011). In the *De Monarchia* Liber 1. XIV, Dante will move from the recognition of Moses writing the law (*Moyses in lege conscribit*) to the argument that what this indicates is the position in which 'it is better for mankind to be ruled by one person rather than several'. (*Ergo melius est humanum genus per unum regi quam per plura*). What occurs therefore is conflation of law with 'law maker'.

25 For another formulation of the project of Midrash see Zvi 2013: 143.

26 Pivotal studies of *PaRDeS* can be found in Halivini (1991) and Fishbane (1992).

27 According to Wolfson (1994: 36) from 'the perspective of the kabbalist, these four levels – including the literal or contextual sense – comprise four distinct hermeneutical postures that collectively make up the Oral Torah'.

28 It should be added immediately that the name Epicurus within both provides a compelling case to rethink the position of Epicurus and thus to rethink the extent to which his work is in fact antithetical to both Kant and Jewish thought.

Bibliography

Agamben, Giorgio, 2005. *The Time That Remains: A Commentary on the Letter to the Romans.* Translated by Patricia Dailey. Stanford: Stanford University Press.

Arendt, Hannah, 1982. *Lectures on Kant's Political Philosophy.* Chicago: University of Chicago Press.

Benjamin, Andrew, 1997. *The Plural Event.* London. Routledge.

——, 2010a. *Of Jews and Animals.* Edinburgh: Edinburgh University Press.

——, 2010b. *Place, Commonality and Judgment: Continental Philosophy and the Ancient Greeks.* London: Continuum Books.

———, 2013 'Recovering holiness and the place of others: Notes on *Vayikra* 19:34'. *Parralax* No. 26, pp. 36–48.

———, 2015. *Towards a Relational Ontology*. Albany: SUNY Press.

Benussan, Gérard, 2003. *Qu'est-ce quela philosophie juive?* Paris: Desclée de Brouwer.

Boyarin, Daniel, 1990. *Intertextuality and the Reading of Midrash*. Bloomington: Indiana University Press.

———, 2004. 'The Crucifixion of the Logos: The Prologue to John as a Jewish Midrash'. In *Borderlines. The Partition of Judaeo-Christianity*. Philadelphia: University of Pennsylvania Press. pp. 89–142.

———, 2005. 'Midrash and the "Magic Language": Reading without Logocentrism'. In *Derrida and Religion. Other Testaments*. Edited by Yvonne Sherwood and K. Hart. New York. Routledge. pp. 131–9.

———, 2010. 'Origen as theorist of allegory. Alexandrian contexts'. In *The Cambridge Companion to Allegory*. Edited by Rita Copeland and Peter T. Struck. Cambridge: Cambridge University Press.

da Costa, Uriel, 1993. *Examination of Pharisaic Traditions. Exame das tradições phariseas. Facsimile of the Unique Copy in the Royal Library of Copenhagen*. Translation, Notes and Introduction by H.P. Salomon and I.S.D Sasson. Leiden: E.J. Brill.

Dante, 2012. *De Monarchia: Parallel Text Latin – English*. CreatSpace Independent Publishing Platform.

Diels, H. and Kranz, W., 1951. *Die Fragmente der Vorsokratiker*. Berlin: Weidmann.

Fagenblatt, Michael, 2010. *A Covenant of Creatures. Levinas's Philosophy of Judaism*. Stanford: Stanford University Press.

Fishbane, Michael, 1992. *The Garments of Torah. Essays in Biblical Hermeneutics*. Bloomington: Indiana University Press.

———, 1998. *The Exegetical Imagination. On Jewish Thought and Theology*. Bloomington: Indiana University Press.

Graver, Margaret, 1999. 'Philo of Alexandria and the Origins of the Stoic ?'. *Phronesis* Vol. 44, No. 4, pp. 300–25.

Handleman, Susan, 1982. *The Slayers of Moses. The Emergence of Rabbinic Interpretation in Modern Literary Theory*. Albany: SUNY Press.

Henry, Michel, 2000. *Incarnation. Une philosophie de la chair*. Paris: Éditions de Seuil.

Del Lucchese, Filippo, 2011. *Conflict, Power, and Multitude in Machiavelli and Spinoza: Tumult and Indignation*. London: Continuum.

Luther, Martin (1984) *Die Bibel nach der Übersetzung Martin Luthers. Standardausgabe mit Apokryphen*, Stuttgart: Deutsche Bibelgesellschaft.

Machiavelli, 1998. *Tutte le opera*. Firenze: Newton.

Malpas, Jeff, 1999. *Place and Experience: A Philosophical Topography*. Cambridge: Cambridge University Press.

Mekhilta de-Rabbi Ishmael, 2004. Translated by Jacob Z. Lauterbach. Philadelphia: Jewish Publication Society.

Midrash Rabbah: Genesis, 1939. Translated by H. Freedman and Maurice Simon, Vols. 1–2. London: Soncino Press.

Niehoff, Maren R., 2008. 'Questions and Answers in Philo and Genesis Rabbah'. *Journal for the Study of Judaism* Vol. 39, pp. 337–66.

Ibn Pakuda, Bahya ben Josef, 1993. *The Book of Direction to the Duties of the Heart*. London: Routledge and Kegan Paul.

Philo in Ten Volumes, 1929–34. Translations by F. H. Colson and Rev. G. H. Whitaker. Cambridge, MA: Harvard University Press.

Rosenzweig, Franz, 1955. *On Jewish Learning*. New York: Schocken Books.

De' Rossi, Azariah, 2001. *The Light of The Eyes*. Translated and Edited by Joanna Weinberg. Yale Judaica Series (Book 31). New Haven: Yale University Press.

Runia, David T., 1991. *Exegesis and Philosophy. Studies on Philo of Alexandria*. Aldershot: Variorum.

Spinoza, 1999. *Tractatus Theologico-Politicus*. Paris: Presses Universitaires de France.

Stern, David, 1991. *Parables in Midrash. Narrative and Exegesis in Rabbinic Literature*. Cambridge, MA: Harvard University Press.

Tyconius, 1989. *The Book of Rules. (Liber Regularum)*. Translated, with an Introduction by William S. Babcock. Atlanta: Scholars Press.

Halivini, David Weiss, 1991. *Peshat & Derash. Plain and Applied Meaning in Rabbinic Exegesis*. Oxford: Oxford University Press.

Wolfson, Elliot, 1994. *Through a Speculum that Shines. Vision and Imagination in Medieval Jewish Mysticism*. Princeton: Princeton University Press.

Wolfson, Harry Austyn, 1947. *Philo: Foundations of Religious Philosophy in Judaism, Christianity and Islam*. Cambridge, MA: Harvard University Press.

The Zohar. Volume 1, 2003. Translation and Commentary by Daniel C. Mitt. Stanford: Stanford University Press.

Zvi, Ron, 2013. 'The book of Jubilees and the Midrash on the early chapters of Genesis'. *Jewish Bible Quarterly*, Vol. 41, Issue 3.

55

ARABIC AND ISLAMIC HERMENEUTICS

Ebrahim Moosa

Introduction

Arabic and Islamic hermeneutics have an ancient and a more recent history. The hermeneutical enterprise in each epoch played very different roles and fulfilled discrete purposes. Yet, it is not easy to separate the ancient and the modern hermeneutical traditions because they share overlapping vocabularies. However, the meaning, purpose and intention of hermeneutics in each epoch has also undergone radical change.

Hermeneutics in the modern period is at the center of searing and often controversial debates advancing Islamic reform and reinterpreting tradition; newer forms of hermeneutics are resisted by varieties of Muslim orthodoxies among both Sunni and Shi'a Muslims. Why do such polarizing debates occur on the stage of hermeneutics in Islam? Part of the answer is that Islam has no church: the equivalent of a church is the elaborate discursive tradition constructed and curated by religious scholars (ulama) over the centuries. The religious scholars have cultivated distinctive hermeneutical methods in order to make alterations to the canonical tradition in the mainstream Sunni and Shi'a interpretations. The orthodox hermeneutical tradition in its Sunni guise takes the Prophet and the Companions as the central paradigm of righteousness whereas for the Shi'as it would be the Prophet and a select number of Companions, but most importantly the exemplary role of the descendants of the Prophet. These are the vital paradigms shaped by the politics at the beginning of Islam, which has also impacted the hermeneutical tradition. As an example, for an orthodox Sunni interpreter an authentic received opinion issued by a Companion or for a Shi'a by a member of the Prophet's household would have more weight, even if it contradicted reason. Of course, interpreters will often try to reconcile received opinion with reason, but if the two are not reconcilable, then received opinion will triumph. In most cases interpreters are adept at making even implausible received opinion look plausible. In addition orthodox interpretations either affirm patriarchal interpretations of religious texts or espouse reformed versions of patriarchy. The interpretations of texts are subject to canonical hermeneutical strictures. Only tolerable change within the broad parameters of their hermeneutical paradigm is acceptable, although some orthodox scholars can on occasion issue surprisingly progressive interpretations. Yet, one has to note that the hermeneutical battle in modern Islam is waged against orthodox practitioners. Orthodoxy fiercely guards against all those who might violate their approved protocols of interpretation, ranging from wayward insiders to subversive outsiders.

Philosophical hermeneutics are intimately tied to debates on religion. From a historical perspective, philosophy in the Islamic tradition viewed itself as the cousin of religion. Philosophy took pride in its ability to articulate the purpose and values of religion in more universal terms. In the modern period, those Muslim thinkers who do engage with contemporary hermeneutical philosophy as constructionists still see their role as enhancing and evolving the discursive capacity of Islam as a religio-philosophical tradition in order to deal with the modern world and its challenges with greater integrity and efficiency. Needless to say, some, if not most, orthodox religious authorities see this offer from largely secular trained intellectuals to assist in the updating of tradition as a gratuitous, if not a malevolent gesture. Most orthodox religious thinkers view modern philosophy with suspicion; they see it as a subversive move to secularize Islam in a bid to undo its religious foundations. Therefore, the battle lines are explicitly drawn between religious scholars and more radical voices among academic philosophers. Yet the most dramatic developments in hermeneutics in modern Islam have occurred in the realm of Islamic political thought, feminism, gender and sexuality. Vigorous hermeneutical debates have opened up new horizons of possibility for Muslims of different stripes who prefer to explore alternative modes of thinking as opposed to orthodox traditions.

Hermeneutics in early Islam

Philosophical hermeneutics in Islam is organically connected to the questions of faith and doctrine. The hermeneutical template goes back to the need of early Muslim communities to understand the meaning and intentions of the teachings of the Prophet Muhammad and the scripture he brought in the form of the Qur'an. While he and his companions lived in the world, they were the living interpreters of the tradition; once they left the world, according to tradition, the need to follow in their footsteps and develop the interpretative tradition became a major preoccupation.

Instead of exclusively using the term hermeneutics, called *ta'wil* (pronounced ta-weel) in Arabic, Muslim jurist-theologians interpreted foundational texts in the light of reason and their social experiences using the rubric of "intellectual effort" or "independent thinking," called *ijtihad*. *Ijtihad* was possibly the most common generic term for a range of hermeneutical practices in the Islamic tradition. There are different modalities of *ijtihad*-type interpretations, ranging from those who stick closely to the literal meanings (*zahir*) of words to those who put the "text" (*nass*) in a larger conversation with the world (*ta'wil*), knowledge of the times and modalities of reasoning.

Scholars devised specialized vocabularies where semiotics blurred into their discrete hermeneutical strategies. Even when the primary teachings were in the form of oral traditions they required elaboration. Thus, whatever the Prophet said or any action he took, often needed some kind of "surface/superficial explanation" or "gloss" (*sharh*) in order for the text to be understandable to multiple audiences. At times the coherence and reasoning of the teachings in the form of texts and reports required more "detailed explication" (*bayan*), which often was shorthand for a method of inter-textual explication. Sometimes, a reader might steer a set of passages in one of many possible interpretative directions in order for the material to make sense. Such an interpretation is called an "actively guided" or "steered interpretation" (*tawjih*). But when an interpreter moved away from the literal meaning of a text and attempted to connect the dots to other materials or other sources of information then it resulted in an "expansive interpretation" (*ta'wil*), what most people would regard today as hermeneutics proper.

Explication and expansive interpretation are the most common forms of Arabic–Islamic hermeneutics frequently deployed in discursive practices related to theology, law, Qur'an exegesis, studies of prophetic literary traditions, language and grammar. The gradual monopoly of the Muslim jurist-theologians over interpretative authority gave this emerging hermeneutics enduring power and naturalized it at different times as part of the specialized toolkit of an internally diverse Islamic orthodoxy and traditionalism. Over time orthodoxy constituted itself as a closed hermeneutical circle because it sought to only reinforce and justify the discursive authority of orthodoxy instead of being open to new interpretative horizons.

Sure, the hermeneutical traditions in both the Sunni and Shi'a traditions might represent different styles of reasoning, yet each discursive tradition neatly articulates the coherence of power and authority at a particular instant in history. In Islamic history institutional authority was robustly cultivated through a hermeneutical tradition sustained by a republic of letters. Islam's consecrated hermeneutical tradition provides its authors and defenders a narrative to secure adherence to its orthodox authority and to defeat all competitors. To challenge the hermeneutical tradition and its authors, therefore, was tantamount to questioning Islam itself. Yet, over time, the critical interrogation of the hermeneutical tradition itself created an opportunity for orthodoxy to grow and become internally diversified.

The modern period

Muslim encounters with the West introduced non-indigenous knowledge traditions. This not only generated further epistemological diversity within Muslim societies but also created new ways of imagining life and existence. Competition between native and foreign knowledge systems generated a politics of knowledge and many a contestation as to who had the power to decide what is right and wrong, true and false, especially in matters of faith, values, ethics, law and cultural practices. In order to deal with new and altering political and social realities, the indigenous Muslim hermeneutical traditions also underwent change through alteration, borrowing and hybridity. Some actors firmly resisted and withstood the modern knowledge tradition by tenaciously holding on to tradition and promoted indigenous knowledge systems through religious institutions such as seminaries (*madrasas*) and specially designated Islamic universities. Others, especially those at modern universities embraced the modern knowledge tradition and after some time attempted to reconcile the multiple knowledge traditions at work in Muslim societies. The key question that stalked thinkers was this: how to deal with the past tradition (*turath*) and reconcile it with the renewal (*tajdid*) of knowledge traditions? Contemporary Arab and Islamic thinkers at modern universities largely pursued this endeavor.

Yet, it is important to note that in Muslim majority societies the hermeneutical debates occurred not in the realm of philosophy as much as it occurred in new readings of history, ethics/law theology and moral philosophy. Yes, Western philosophical influences were palpable through colonial educational systems in many countries but the manifestation of influence occurred not in the academic halls but in the lives of people, communities: they impacted religious institutions. Philosophical questions became manifest in debates centered on conceptions of gender, personhood, self and community, authority and tradition. Often Western influences were indirect, in so far as Muslim intelligentsia began to re-read and re-understand their tradition in an age of science, technology and the rise of the nation-state and which had very different outcomes than before. Because so much was at stake for lived communities, therefore the hermeneutical debates also became a highly combustible terrain of theological dispute where divisive charges of heresy and excommunication were traded between adversaries.

Hermeneutics in reformist religious thought

The late nineteenth century marked a great moment of hermeneutical fervor in the Muslim world, sparking a momentum that continued for most of the twentieth century (Johnston 2008: 168). An emergent Muslim reform movement, known as the salafiyya, based in Egypt under the auspices of Jamaluddin Afghani (d. 1897) and his disciple Muhammad 'Abduh (d. 1905) along with others initiated a movement of re-reading the Muslim discursive tradition in order to find ways of upgrading their tradition to meet the demands of new contexts. 'Abduh and his colleagues specifically addressed questions of theology, moral thought and what is generally called Islamic law or *Shari'a* debates. Muslims were adopting European cultural practices around the world as a result of greater contact with Europe: was it was advisable for Muslims to adopt new practices?

In terms of Qur'an exegesis, it was 'Abduh and his disciple Rashid Rida (d. 1935) who broached an intertextual hermeneutical approach. Rida echoed 'Abduh's views in a popular exegesis of the Qur'an where the notion of intertextuality meant that some parts of the Qur'an provided an exposition of other sections of the Qur'an in a more focused manner. The 'Abduh–Rida alliance of reformists differed from more canonical and traditionalist readings of the Qur'an in two fundamental ways. The reformists, firstly, no longer accepted some of the presuppositions adopted by early orthodox theologies that were foregrounded in exegesis; and secondly, they did not allow the prophetic tradition, the practice, the sunna derived from *hadith*, to fundamentally alter a Qur'anic teaching or value. Yes, they would adopt prophetic reports that were consistent with the teachings of the Qur'an or if prophetic report constructively elaborated a Qur'anic teaching. But the notion that a prophetic report could limit or abrogate a Qur'anic teaching was no longer acceptable.

This was a major hermeneutical shift in the hegemonic Sunni tradition. In traditional and canonical teachings the authority of the Qur'an and the authority of the prophetic tradition were derived from prophetic reports (hadith pl. ahadith). While the Qur'an was uncompromisingly viewed as revelation, orthodoxy treated the utterings and teachings of the Prophet also as revelation. The only difference was that the Qur'an was a liturgical revelation whereas the prophetic tradition did not qualify for liturgical purposes, but otherwise they were of equal knowledge-value (epistemological value). In modern Islam this changed. Self-educated Muslims as well as those who did not subscribe to canonical tradition re-contextualized and re-interpreted the Qur'an as exclusively God's word. They viewed the Prophet reverentially but only as a deliverer of God's message and a living exemplar.

But for Rida and 'Abduh the shift to the exclusive "authority of the Qur'an on the lives of those who understand it and its effect on the hearts of those who truly recite it" was a definitive move; in their words, "no other speech can share in that task" (Rida n.d.: 1, 19–20) And the Qur'an was viewed as the permanent authority (hujja) while "its wisdom and learning had yet to be unveiled" (Rida n.d.: 20). A saying attributed to the Prophet sealed the argument for Rida, for the Qur'an was "either a favorable authority or your adversary" (Rida n.d.: 20).

Canonical teachings argued that the teachings of especially the Qur'an could not be interpreted by way of personal opinion or without authorized scholarship that relied on the teachings of the early Muslim community who witnessed the Qur'an. Rida downplays that teaching arguing that the early Muslim community was not privileged because of their personal preeminence, but because they were "individual human beings" whom the Qur'an addressed thus: "Oh people show reverence for your Sustainer" (Qur'an 4:1; Rida n.d.: 1, 20). "Is it reasonable that we be asked to surrender to the claim that we should not seek to understand this speech of God, but that we rather agree with the opinion of someone else who made the inquiry and studied [the Qur'an]?" Rida asked rhetorically. The truth of the matter was that "no revelation mandated us to follow the Qur'an in summary form and in detail" (Rida n.d.: 1, 20). Rida staked his own position against the mainstream Sunni tradition and boldly claimed: "Never! It is mandatory for every human being that they understand the verses of the Book according to their capacity without discriminating between a learned and an unlearned person" (Rida n.d.: 20).

Each individual would understand the Qur'an according to their wits, he explained, even in their own language. He justified this position, for in his view each person will encounter the Qur'an to the extent that they are drawn to the notion of "the good." While to the more democratically minded this might sound like an innocuous statement, for a reform-minded traditionalist, Rida's push in the direction of individualism was quite courageous and unique. Rida pressed what Michael Fishbane would call the "deposit of tradition" (traditium) into the service of an ongoing and unfolding tradition. But Rida also torqued the tradition in order for it to be more responsive to the needs of the individual and lessened the communitarian control over the meaning of the Qur'an. The 'Abduh–Rida school's hermeneutics was to modernize Islamic theology by grounding it in rational and natural discourses.

'Abduh in particular drew on the work of the medieval Mu'tazilites, a theological tradition in early Islam that prized a rational discourse. For example, the Qur'an attributes the defeat of Muslims in the Battle of Uhud in 625 between Muhammad and his Meccan foes to the fact that "Satan caused them to fail," stating the reason as: "because of some evil they had done" (Qur'an 3:155). This refers to a group of archers who were given strict instructions by the Prophet Muhammad not to leave their positions in the battle. Traditional commentators explained that only "some" of the archers left their battlefield positions because they concluded that their enemies would not return and hence they went in pursuit of booty and treasure. How did Satan mislead them? The standard traditional explanation was that some of the fighters had committed sins in the past (Ibn Kathir and al-Sabuni 1402/1981: 1, 330). The traditional hermeneutic aimed at protecting the reputation of the Companions of Muhammad from any negative aspersion in keeping with Sunnism's strictures.

While 'Abduh and Rida did not deny the standard explanation they provided an additional interpretation consistent with their hermeneutical stress on reason and justice. They elucidated what could be called a golden rule of how God operated in the world with reference to the character of humans. Sin, they explained, had psychic consequences on people (Rida n.d.: 4, 192). The weakened mental attitudes of the people as a result of sin had social manifestations which became evident in the morale of the fighters at the Battle of Uhud, explained Muhammad Asad, who closely followed their reformist line of interpretation (Asad 2003: 107 n.117).

While the 'Abduh–Rida hermeneutical toolkit focused on issues of theology and moral philosophy, there were others who were giving greater attention to history and literary criticism that would impact the religious imaginary of twentieth century Muslims. The pursuit of reasoned debate as a defense of Islamic theological teachings was the crowning achievement of Islam historically speaking, many traditional theologians and philosophers claimed. Any project in philosophical hermeneutics invariably began with the theological debates of the past. That was because theology did indeed borrow extensively from the playbook of philosophy. If Muslim theology represented a discourse of being (*wijdan*) in the world, then Muslim philosophy was an attempt to make that being relevant to the world in which Muslims live (Fayduh 2005: 199). Hermeneutics thus became the narrative and vehicle to reconcile "reason" and "received opinion."

There were both positive and negative receptions of hermeneutics in modern Islam. The pre-partition Indian poet-philosopher Muhammad Iqbal had a good sense of the importance of hermeneutics. Iqbal showed an awareness of how religious consciousness differed from one era to another. He petitioned for an intellectual language that would be able to deal with multiple forms of human experience from the mystical to the empirical. But he was also aware that a new moment required a new metaphysics. Hence Iqbal explicitly stated that old Muslim theological systems draped in "dead metaphysics" could be of no help to modern Muslims whom he described as "possess[ing] a different intellectual background" (Iqbal 1960: 97). He was acutely aware of the need for a hermeneutics that would renew the reasoning of the past and empty it as a resource but not a solution into the present (Fayduh 2005: 43). In Iqbal's words: "The task of the modern Muslim is therefore immense. He has to rethink the whole system of Islam without completely breaking with the past" (Iqbal 1960: 97). He also believed that intellectuals who had "deep insight into the inner meaning of the history of Muslim thought and life" who also engendered a broad understanding of human experience were in the best position to accomplish the task of rethinking. "The only course open to us is to approach modern knowledge with a respectful but independent attitude and appreciate the teachings of Islam in the light of that knowledge," Iqbal wrote, "even though we may be led to differ from those who have gone before us" (Iqbal 1960: 97).

Iqbal himself only alluded to the hermeneutical possibilities by gesturing to the fruitful possibilities of a re-engagement with Muslim thinkers of the past as well as with modern Western thinkers from Hegel and Nietzsche to Bergson. In fact, at times Iqbal's cunning irony in a colonial milieu could give the superficial reader the impression that he was against hermeneutics and modernity if one were not aware that he was an ardent advocate for the reconstruction of religious thought in Islam. Yet, in a poem entitled "The Psychology of Slavery" he ends in a mocking tone:

> Slaves are easily persuaded to accept their slavery
> By making the interpretation of issues a pretext.

> (Iqbal 2000: 773)

In another poem he praises innovation and extols how time honors those who innovate, but then darkly warns:

> I fear this cry for modernism
> Is but a ruse to make the East subservient to the West.

> (Iqbal 2000: 798)

Iqbal's clear-eyed assessment of the hermeneutical challenges Islamic thought faced on the one hand, if read together with his agnosticism towards Western political power and modernity on the other, neatly encapsulated the agonism (strenuous struggling) Muslim modernists experienced, desiring progress with authenticity. Painful ambivalence and searing self-criticism marked the philosophical hermeneutics of modern Arabic and Islamic thought and was perhaps the reason why present-day Muslim philosophy was a hobbled enterprise while less complex theologies triumphed.

Hermeneutical turn in literature

Contemporaneous to Iqbal in the first half of the twentieth century Egyptian intellectuals like Taha Husayn, Amin al-Khuli and 'A'isha 'Abd al-Rahman, better known as Bint al-Shati, shaped Arabic–Islamic philosophical hermeneutics via language debates. 'Abd al-Rahman (d. 1998) was the first to take a complex Arabic poem of Abul 'Ala al-Ma'arri (d. 1057) called "The Epistle of Forgiveness" and read it not as a Dantesque journey into the afterworld, but rather as the blind poet experiencing another possible earthly world ('Abd al-Rahman, 1970). Ma'arri delved into literary and grammatical puzzles all the while talking to poets and grammarians of the past in an imagined world. 'Abd al-Rahman read his poetry with empathy as re-living the other's experience. While she thought of his poem as a potential play she admitted that the historical reason embedded in Ma'arri's poem might not be fully captured by moderns.

Taha Husayn (d. 1973) was perhaps the most visible literary scholar who enjoyed both a traditional education in Egypt and also studied in France. In a controversial book Husayn unleashed his skepticism on aspects of the Arabic–Islamic literary tradition by drawing on the skepticism of his eleventh century hero, Ma'arri, coupled with a Cartesian strategy of interrogation. He breached the orthodox boundary placed around the discursive paradigm and the acceptable hermeneutical frame by asking the unthinkable. "I wish to create for literature the philosophical method innovated by Descartes in order to investigate the truth of things," he wrote (Husayn 1997: 23). This can only be understood in the context of the following back story. Northern Arabia, the region of Yemen was the place where the original Arabs and speakers of the language came from. But the area that became known as Islam's heartland, known as the Hijaz, only Arabized later. Scientific discoveries revealed that the northern dialects were much closer to Ethiopian languages; yet, the conventional history attributed to the northerners a dialect that was similar to the dialect of South Arabia. The archive of this early Northern dialect was the pre-Islamic poetry, known as the Jahiliyya period. Husayn questioned this conventional history amidst great controversy and proposed that the Jahiliyya poetry was an invention and a forgery of post-Islamic developments for ideological reasons linked to the work of grammarians, story-tellers or the invention of Qur'an commentators, reporters of prophetic teachings and theologians who wanted to create some seamless, less complex and authentic genealogy for Islam. Knowledge, especially theology, but also philosophy, Husayn argued, resonated with the material conditions of particular times and places. Egypt's orthodox Muslim circles, including a few philosophers, were scandalized by his claims, and it took a court case to vindicate Husayn from blasphemy charges and wrongdoing.

In Arabic thought the literary scholar was known as an *adib* (erudite person), a word that is a correlate to the term *adab*, "literature." Literary figures were well read in philosophy and erudite in questions of wisdom (*hikma*), an older term for philosophy (*falsafa*). Thus, Ahmad Muhammad Khalafallah (d. 1983), also an Egyptian literary scholar, caused an outcry with his dissertation on the "Art of Story-telling in the Noble Qur'an" that was later published. He argued that the multiple stories in the Qur'an performed an aesthetic function, while their more important goal was to articulate a moral narrative. The literalness of the stories, their historical accuracy and factual veracity, in his view, were less important concerns. Through his extensive reading of the classical sources, Khalafallah showed that some early Muslim scholars held similar views. The structured plot of the stories of the Qur'an were shaped by the goals of the telling. However, Khalafallah's non-literal hermeneutical readings of the Qur'anic stories caused an outrage. His advisor, an enlightened traditional scholar and legal authority Shaykh Amin al-Khuli (d. 1966) suffered blame and was marginalized by the Egyptian clerical establishment.

Nasr Hamid Abu Zayd (d. 2010) was a professor of Arabic literature at Cairo University's Arabic Department. One of his earliest works was a *Critique of Religious Discourse*. In it he questioned the modes of religious discourse of political Islam that were prevalent in Egypt in the 1980s. Abu Zayd showed that Egyptian activists like Sayyid

Qutb, the revolutionary ideologue of the Muslim Brotherhood, executed in 1966, often turned the views of classical scholars and figures of the past into authoritative texts (*nass*) to which readers had to unhesitatingly submit (Abu Zayd 1992: 31). Abu Zayd indicted modern Islamic thought for refusing to concede that authoritative "texts" were human constructions. Most thinkers failed to appreciate that even the most divine of revelations had an earthly and human aspect, a feature that even classical authorities admitted; yet, modern authors resisted such acknowledgment.

Supporters of authentic and ahistorical religious discourses in contemporary Islam, he argued, often proclaimed the sovereignty of God in politics and with it the sovereignty of the text. They held up their political and hermeneutical models as antidotes to arbitrary governance, and condemned secular rule as the oppression of humans by fellow humans. Despite this claim, Abu Zayd showed that in practical terms political Islam was just another kind of tyranny. What was at stake, he pointed out, was that a certain class of humans, meaning the religious scholars and the ideologues of political Islam, monopolized "the right to understand, comment, do exegesis and interpretation, as if they alone could transmit from God" (Abu Zayd 1992: 56). This kind of hermeneutically informed meta-critical evaluation of analysis earned Abu Zayd the ire of political Islamists and the clergy. His more detailed and insightful analysis of Arabic–Islamic hermeneutics have yet to enjoy proper attention. His readings of the hermeneutics of premodern thinkers like Ibn 'Arabi (d. 1240) as well as other prominent classical Islamic thinkers show that the mutation in language and embedded notions of ambivalence, multivocality in signification coupled with the politics of reading in the past were lessons that modern Islamic hermeneutics have ignored.

Not the Muslim clerics but ironically fellow religiously committed academics on a Cairo university committee denied him promotion. Critics claimed that he espoused a Marxist materialist hermeneutical analysis of Islam, a charge the left-aligned Abu Zayd would not deny. As the battles in the university hit the Egyptian public sphere a case of blasphemy and heresy was made against him. Abu Zayd was not as lucky as Taha Husayn or Khalafallah and Egypt's courts declared him a non-Muslim for holding views that amounted to denying Islam's *a priori* theological doctrines. In other words, he was tried for espousing positions arrived at by interpretation that challenged mainstream paradigms of Muslim orthodoxy and political Islam. Since a Muslim woman was not allowed to marry a non-Muslim man, his marriage to his wife was declared void. Abu Zayd went into self-imposed exile in the Netherlands.

Philosophical hermeneutics

The Cairo and French-trained Hasan Hanafi energetically took the hermeneutical project seriously as a philosopher. Like other philosophers and constructionists, Hanafi viewed the engagement with the past Muslim legacy of intellectual production and thought (*turath*) as an object of study. For him the need was to study the Islamic past in order to have a renewed engagement with it as a resource for the present. Hermeneutics, especially Husserlian phenomenology was Hanafi's main ally (Hanafi 2004: 11). Hanafi's elaborate and ambitious historical hermeneutical program in multiple volumes involved designing an interpretative analysis of the multiple disciplines developed within Muslim civilization. He provided readings of legal theory, law, theology, exegesis, philosophy and mysticism. In each reading he tried to decipher the synthesis that occurred between the exogenous and the indigenous elements in thought and how new hybridities were established. His goal was to take a broad look at the translation of Greek and other currents of thought and the reception of these ideas into an Islamicate grammar.

Hanafi's project was to read the Muslim tradition in a transformative manner. If the emphasis in the past was placed on detailed discussions of dogma, then he believed the shift in the present should be in the direction of a revolution in thought. Instead of a preoccupation about debates dealing with the afterlife he argued for how religion could deal with reviving human life and conditions in the present. In other words, for him religion was about how to live in the world and had an instrumental function. Hermeneutics in Hanafi's view fulfilled an epistemological function: to find theoretical concord between the self and the world; a conjunction between a knowing subject and an object of knowing. Hence, hermeneutics built the "knowledge bridges" between subject and object in order for the world to be known and so that the subject could exist in the world and engage it. Since the "text" mediated between the subject and the world there was a necessity to engage the text in its two sided mirror: the text reflected the infinite desires of the subject and his or her mental conceptions just as it reflected the reality of the world, its limits and possibilities (Hanafi 2006: 298). For Hanafi hermeneutics became the vehicle for innovation in religious thought that would bring philosophy together with religion, just as hermeneutics attempted to bring sapience (sapientia/hikma) together with revealed norms (Shari‘a). He proposed a hermeneutical method in order to "reconstruct a discipline in accordance with the conditions of the time, in its own terminology, language, instruments of analysis … which is at the heart of ijtihad," he wrote (Hanafi 2006: 299).

‘Ali Harb, a Lebanese philosopher also made a compelling case in favor of hermeneutics. The interpreter sought out an unknown dimension of a text in order to find what other readers missed, he wrote. For indeed, such a reader, Harb said, discovered the unknown from the known. To discover things from the already known, he pointed out, was not knowledge but was rather properly called pedagogy. When the interpreter read the text anew from the vantage point of his or her experience then a genuine hermeneutical enterprise was born (Harb 2007: 14). In modern Muslim discourses of hermeneutics the return to reason and the renewal of multiple forms of reason were important features of the hermeneutical revival point on which both Harb and Hanafi would agree.

One area where contemporary Muslim hermeneutics created a common discourse between orthodox traditionalists and non-traditionalist intellectuals was in their discovery of a fourteenth century thinker from Muslim Spain, Abu Ishaq al-Shatibi (d. 1388). Modern advocates of Shatibi's ideas included the previously mentioned Muhammad ‘Abduh and his student Rashid Rida. ‘Abduh found Tunisian scholars were teaching Shatibi's text al-Muwafaqat at the famous Zaytunah mosque-university during a visit there. Once Shatibi's text was published in Egypt it gained a significantly larger pan-Islamic audience. Shatibi advocated what could be called the "big picture version of the Shari'a." The moral teachings of Islam, Shatibi argued, focused on preserving major values; they included the goal to preserve religion, life, reason, property and offspring.

History and the philosophy of ideas

Philosophers at Muhammad V University in the city of Rabat, Morocco have for nearly two decades pursued a spirited debate on the reconstruction of Muslim thought, especially the philosophical, historical and religious dimensions of a complex past Muslim intellectual legacy. Their efforts yielded uncanny insights and sparked earnest debates in scholarly circles around the Arab and Islamic worlds. Yet, Shatibi's reception among contemporary Muslim philosophers and their analysis of Shatibi's ideas were less well studied. Muhammad 'Abid al-Jabiri (1936–2010), trained at Muhammad V University, was a philosopher and critic whose writings have spawned a minor canon of literature. His influential books include titles such as the *Construction of the Arabic Reason* (*Binyat al-'aql al-'arabi*), *Critique of Arabic Reason* (*Naqd al-'aql al-'arabi*), *Arab Ethical Reasoning* (*al-'Aql al-akhlaqi al-'arabi*) among many others.

Jabiri was for a long time the premier pan-Arab intellectual interlocutor who relentlessly argued that the Arabs missed the opportunity to author their own enlightenment as a result of some unfortunate events that occurred in the twelfth century. What were those developments centuries ago? Arabic–Islamic thought was contaminated by a very bad strain of Persian gnostism, Jabiri argued, that dampened and fatally wounded the rational content of Islamic thought. The man Jabiri incredulously blamed for undermining reason was the influential polymath Abu Hamid al-Ghazali (d. 1111). Instead of a serious analysis, Jabiri in my view, made Ghazali a scapegoat responsible for the crippling of Arabic–Islamic thought. Ghazali became Jabiri's bête noir because the twelfth-century Persian thinker validated the authority of mystical intuition and defended orthodox Muslim theological propositions by launching a scathing critique of three philosophical propositions advanced by medieval Muslim philosophers. Ghazali in an unfortunate turn accused the philosophers of heresy when their views clashed with theology on three issues.

More deserving an exemplar in Jabiri's view, was Abu al-Walid Ibn Rushd (d. 1198), better known in the West as Averroes. Ibn Rushd provided solid rational grounds for religious thought but his project was sidelined by mainstream Muslim thought, Jabiri argued. Despite his flawed historiography, Jabiri's hermeneutical readings and writings about large issues in the tradition did indeed gain him many admirers.

The Andalusian polymath, noted for his writings on law and an exponent of the phenomenological or Zahiri school Abu Muhammad Ibn Hazm, in his view, was the protagonist of demonstrative reason (*burhan*).

It was the impact of Ibn Hazm and Ibn Rushd that produced jurists like Shatibi who effectively brought about a mini-revolution in modern Muslim ethical and moral hermeneutics. Taha 'Abd al-Rahman, also a leading Moroccan philosopher of language and ethics had challenged some of Jabiri's ideas. However, he too viewed

Shatibi as a vital ally and refined Shatibi's ideas in order to propose a paradigm of virtue ethics.

The Pakistani thinker Fazlur Rahman (d. 1988) also derived inspiration from Shatibi for his double-movement hermeneutics. Fazlur Rahman found Gadamer's hermeneutics too subjective but found common cause with the Italian jurist, Emilio Betti. However, for Fazlur Rahman the Qur'an was the principle hermeneutical resource. His first step was to study the "meaning of the Qur'an as a whole," including its historical theater. From this body of learning he elicited general principles in order to construe a systematic framework of values and principles. His second step was to apply these principles and values to a new context in the present. Such a hermeneutics, he argued, required a careful study of the present in order to change the present to the extent that change was necessary (Rahman 1982: 6–7). It involved both the skills of an historian, the instrumentality of a social scientist and the engineering of an ethicist. For Fazlur Rahman "the process of questioning and changing a tradition – in the interests of preserving or restoring its normative quality in the case of its normative elements – can continue indefinitely and that there is no fixed or privileged point at which the predetermining effective history is immune from such questioning and then being consciously confirmed or consciously changed" (Rahman 1982: 11).

Gender debates

Islamic feminism clearly generated the most productive and far-reaching conversations in Islamic hermeneutics. A cross-section of scholars in Muslim majority countries, including those writing in European languages in minority contexts, did close readings of Muslim religious and historical documents in order to combat interpretations that cemented patriarchal practices in Islamic law, politics, theology and society reading. Suffice to mention prominent names like Qasim Amin (d. 1908), Tahir al-Haddad (d. 1935), Huda Sharaawi (d. 1947), Nazira Zeiniddine (d. 1976), Zaynab al-Ghazali (d. 2005) and Nawaal el-Saadaawi (b. 1931) among others, who actively petitioned for Muslim women's rights in the Middle East amidst polarizing controversy. Pioneering Muslim voices in the West included Amina Wadud who did a theological reading of certain Qur'anic passages against the grain of patriarchy in order to find a hermeneutic of justice and equality for women. Wadud sought a "female inclusive exegesis" (Wadud 1999: xii). To reach that goal she proposed "a hermeneutics of *tawhid* [unity]" in order to demonstrate how "the unity of the Qur'an permeates all its parts" (Wadud 1999). Moroccan sociologist, Fatima Mernissi interrogated the prophetic reports regarding women with a hermeneutic of suspicion. In her reading of the tradition she found that politics in early Islam generated certain misogynistic threads in a context that was saturated with patriarchy and resulted in the exclusion of women. In her view the main impetus for this was the resentment of the male elites towards influential and knowledgeable women at the very inception of Islam in Arabia (Mernissi 1991). A number of scholars have followed the legacies of Wadud and Mernissi and others in order to explore new possibilities in retrieving the feminine in Muslim history and Islamic texts or in order to critique the text.

Conclusion

Some of the most dynamic developments in Arabic and Islamic hermeneutics have occurred in the modern period. Orthodox traditionalists by definition subscribe to an ontology of community and assert an operation of hermeneutics from the word in the direction of the world. While this is not entirely true for even orthodoxy, most orthodox advocates will assert the proposition of the capacity of the text to change the world in its image, namely the image of the text. Reformists and those favoring the reconstruction of the tradition would say it is the state of affairs of the world that asserts itself with extraordinary force and thus determines the revealed and authoritative narrative of tradition in unforeseen ways. Both parties would see the hand of Providence as either operating through revelation and prophecy or reason and history or mixtures thereof as the ingredients that shape the world.

Bibliography

Abú Zayd, Naṣr Hámid. 1992. *al-Khiṭāb al-dīnī:ruʾyah naqdīyah-nahwa intāj wa ʾyʾilmī bi-dalālat al-nuṣūṣ al-dīnīyah*. 1. ed. Beirut: Dār al-Muntakhab al-ʿArabī li al-Dirāsāt wa al-Nashr wa al-Tawzīʿ.

ʿAbd al-Raḥmán, ʿĀʾishah Bint al-Sháṭi; Abú al-ʿAlá', al Maʿarrī. 1970. *Qirāʾah jadīdah fī Risālat al-ghufrān, naṣṣ masraḥī min al-qarn al-khāmis al-hijrī*. Cairo: Maʿhad al-Buḥūth wa al-Dirāsāt al-ʿArabīya.

Asad, Muhammad. 2003. *The message of the Qurʾan*. Bitton, England: Book Foundation.

Faydúḥ, ʿAbd al-Qádir. 2005. *Naẓarīyat al-taʾwīl fī al-falsafah al-ʿArabīyah al-Islāmīyah*. Damascus: al-Awāʾil.

Ḥanafī, ḥasan. 2004. *Min al-naṣṣ ilá al-wāqiʿ*. 1. ed. Cairo: Markaz al-Kitāb lil-Nashr.

——2006. *Ḥiṣār al-zaman: al-māḍī wa-al-mustaqbal: ʿulūm*. Cairo: Markaz al-Kitāb lil-Nashr.

Ḥarb, ʿAlī. 2007. *al-Taʾwīl wa-al-ḥaqīqah: qirāʾāt taʾwīliyah fī al-thaqāfah al-ʿArabīyah*. 1. ed. Beirut: Dār al-Tanwīr.

Ḥusayn, Ṭáhá. 1997. *Fī al-shiʿr al-jāhilī*. Súsa-Tunis: Dār al-Maʿárif li al-Ṭibáʿah wa al-Nashr.

Ibn Kathír, Abú al-Fidá Ismáʿil & Ṣábúní, Muḥammad ʿAlī. 1402/1981. *Mukhtaṣar Tafsír Ibn Kathír*. Beirut: Dār al-Qurʾān al-Karím.

Iqbal, Muhammad. 1960. *The Reconstruction of Religious Thought in Islam*. Lahore: Shaikh Muhammad Ashraf.

——2000. *Ásán Kulliyát-i Iqbál*. Islamabad: Alhamra Publishing.

Johnston, David L. 2008. *Earth, Empire and Sacred Text: Muslims and Christians as Trustees of Creation*. London; Oakville Conn.: Equinox Pub.

Mernissi, Fatima. 1991. *Women and Islam: An Historical and Theological Enquiry*. Oxford: Basil Blackwell.

Rahman, Fazlur. 1982. *Islam and Modernity: Transformation of an Intellectual Tradition*. Chicago: University of Chicago Press.

Ridá, Ridá Muḥammad. n.d. *Tafsír al-Qurʾān al-ḥakím al-shahír bi tafsír al-manár*. Beirut: Dār al-Maʿrifa.

Wadud, Amina. 1999. *Qurʾan and Woman : Rereading the Sacred Text from a Woman's Perspective*. 2nd ed. New York: Oxford University Press.

Zarkashí, Badr al-Dín Muḥammad ibn Bahádur b. ʿAbd Alláh. 1421/2000. *al-Baḥr al-muḥíṭ fī uṣúl al-fiqh*. Ed. Muḥammad Muḥammad Támir, Beirut: Manshúrát Muḥammad ʿAlī Baydún, Dār al-Kutub al-ʾIlmíya.

Further reading

Barlas, Asma. 2002. *"Believing Women" in Islam: Unreading Patriarchal Interpretations of the Qur'an.* Austin: University of Texas Press.

Boullata, Issa J. 1990. *Trends and Issues in Contemporary Arab Thought.* Albany: State University of New York Press.

Chaudhry, Ayesha S. (2006) "The Problems of Conscience and Hermeneutics: A Few Contemporary Approaches," *Comparative Islamic Studies,* 2: 157–70.

CONCLUSION: THE FUTURE OF HERMENEUTICS

Gianni Vattimo
Translated by Faustino Fraisopi

As we can see from many of the essays in this volume, it is impossible to consider hermeneutics as if it were only one philosophical discipline among others – such as ethics or aesthetics – but it is impossible, at the same time, to consider it merely as if it were a philosophical school or movement – such as positivism, historicism or any school of that sort. It seems quite plausible to think that the future of hermeneutics, whose traits we are seeking to define, will be constituted – even if not exclusively – by the dialectical relationship between these two meanings of 'hermeneutics', in a sort of oscillation that will never be completely resolved one way or the other. Yet it is also possible to identify the future of hermeneutics as lying precisely in the progressive convergence between these two meanings: so the real future of hermeneutics as a philosophical discipline will depend on the recognition of hermeneutics as a general philosophical perspective or movement and not as a single 'part' of philosophy. It is just such a view of hermeneutics (as specific discipline *and* general perspective taken together) that characterizes the modern history of hermeneutics from Schleiermacher onwards. Beginning with the modern origins of hermeneutics, the question concerning a rationally grounded understanding of texts has progressively tended towards the thinking of a general ontology. The traditional maxim that was already leading Schleiermacher's thought, according to which we must understand a text as well as and better than the author, cannot be considered a frivolity or joke – every text has its own life, rooted in the historical fabric wherein the author as well as the reader (even if centuries after) are rooted.

One cannot treat Gadamer's idea of 'effective history' (*Wirkungsgeschichte*) as just a matter of the historical success or 'good fortune' of a text. In other words, the episodes in the history of a text's effects, the stories of its reception, and the interpretations it generates, cannot be reduced to the specificities of a single and determinate 'history'; the historical effectedness of the text consists in its being open to history in general – open to what Heidegger called the 'history of being', and nothing less than this. On this basis, the history of hermeneutics as a specific philosophical 'discipline' does indeed appear as the progressive transformation of the philosophy of interpretation into a general ontology. Consequently, in asking after the future of hermeneutics what we must also ask is the following: what new paths await hermeneutics after it has assumed – with Heidegger, Pareyson, Ricoeur, Gadamer and Rorty – the form of the only possible ontology?

Following on from this, we also need to consider another question contained under the general title 'the future of hermeneutics': not just the question as to what hermeneutics as theory will produce in its disciplinary future – what different insights, ideas and methods of interpretation – but what is the future towards which hermeneutics thinks, how does the future appear from a hermeneutical perspective? As ontology, hermeneutics implies a certain philosophy of history – it projects such a philosophy and such a history and so provides its own interpretation of the history in which it is itself implicated. Yet renouncing, as any philosophy of interpretation must do, any metaphysics of eternal essences, hermeneutics is also brought to the announcing of a sort of eschatology – the announcing of a certain ending of history understood *metaphysically*. The classical text of hermeneutics in the twentieth century, Gadamer's *Truth and Method* (Gadamer 1992), prudently tries to avoid any commitment to a philosophy of history of the usual (metaphysical) sort. Similarly, with respect to his own central thesis – '*Being that can be understood is language*' (Gadamer 1992: 474) – Gadamer showed the same anti-metaphysical prudence, and always refused any extreme or metaphysical understanding of the thesis (see Vattimo 2002: 299–306).

Until the end of his life, Gadamer still complied, even if only implicitly, with the classical distinction between the *Geisteswissenschaften* (the 'human' or 'moral' sciences) and the *Naturwissenschaften* (the natural sciences).[1] The being that is language is what can be understood, and this 'being' is not being 'in its entirety'. Yet even given such a cautious qualification – in my view required by academic prudence – our 'founding father' did not bring to an end the process of the 'ontologization' of hermeneutics that, as I have noted already, characterizes the entire history of the idea of interpretation from Schleiermacher to Heidegger and to Gadamer himself (see Zabala 2009).

It may be that what will happen to hermeneutics in the future – to hermeneutics as an ensemble of texts, as a body of theoretical speculation, also as a community of scholars – will be a further step in this process of 'ontologization'. The battle of ideas about interpretation from its beginnings to the present – including debates such as that over Kuhn's idea of the 'paradigm' or the more recent controversies concerning the question of 'realism' (see Vattimo 2012) – can only move onwards inasmuch as the hermeneutical commitment takes the form of a *political*, or at least *existential* commitment. Such a development is unavoidable for those who take hermeneutics seriously and dedicate themselves to its practice (it is a commitment outlined in Vattimo and Zabala 2011).

The history of modern hermeneutics, and, so far as we can imagine, also its future, is a history of 'excess' – of the transgression of limits, or, to use another idiom, the history of a continuous 'overflowing'. From its origins as an inquiry into the understanding of the texts of the past, it developed into a general philosophy of existence, and then into the only possibly ontology: '*Being that can be understood is language*'. But where does this lead? Does it mean that hermeneutics must be understood more and more in idealist terms? Can we come to identify hermeneutics with an idealistic metaphysics? Does 'being' become 'language'? If we are not to sever

Gadamer from his Heideggerian roots, then we have to reaffirm that the 'is' that is said of being in this sentence of Gadamer's does not have a meaning that would allow that sentence to be construed metaphysically. The language in which being consists (the language that being *is*) is the language of *Gespräch* – of dialogue or conversation. This conversation is what we all are. It is the *Ereignis* – the event – that happens without being.

The future of hermeneutics must take the form of the transformation of hermeneutics into a practical philosophy or philosophy of *praxis*. That does not mean that hermeneutics, as philosophy of interpretation, somehow progresses in a positive sense through its increasing realization of its character as a philosophy of praxis. There is no object proper to hermeneutical thought that is better understood, described or represented, through the progressive development of hermeneutics into an explicit philosophy of praxis. At this point, we may have reached a moment like that of St Paul speaking at the Areopagus – the moment at which, incredulous and outraged by the absurdity of what is said, the audience gets up and leaves. The intolerance of any form of radical hermeneutics within academic philosophy is more or less a reaction in an 'Areopagus' style. Hermeneutics is forbidden from transgressing the proper limits of academic 'good manners', limits that are essentially those of 'descriptive' metaphysics: there is a thing in front of me, 'the world out here', I describe it, I analyse it; I also judge it and condemn it (as absurd, false, morally unacceptable ...); limits that depend always on assuming the validity of the distinction between subject and object – the very distinction which does not hold within the *Geisteswissenschaften*, the human sciences, and whose rejection gives rise to the 'excess' of hermeneutics – an excess that has an impact like that of a 'terrorist' attack, even if an attack of ideas. Recognizing this, we can better understand how little an exaggeration it was when Nietzsche – a poor professor of Ancient Greek at Basel and prematurely retired – described himself in *Ecce Homo* (Nietzsche 1989) as a 'mortal danger' for the world. If we dare, for a moment, to imitate Nietzsche, we can propose a 'terrorist' vocation for hermeneutics. The adoption of such a vocation becomes more and more a demand, the more the metaphysical integration of the world increases – '*The desert grows!*' (Nietzsche 1978: IV: 76.1). In our late metaphysical world, determined by the triumph of technology and the technical, science and power reciprocally sustain themselves (see Horkheimer and Adorno 2002 – in which scientists appear as respected officers perfectly integrated in a total *Verwaltung* or administrative/organizational system), and science, or what presents itself as science, itself becomes an instrument of oppression. Such a world can consider only as terrorists those who think, as Nietzsche did, that 'there are no facts, only interpretations', and who thereby threaten to unmask the complicity of metaphysical scientism and coercive power.

We are experiencing the transformation of the most 'innocent' of crafts (see Heidegger 2000) – so hermeneutics has often portrayed itself – into a sort of terrorist network constantly subjected to policing and attempts at control. Here 'policing' takes many different forms: the 'policing' of thought (notably the proponents of analytic epistemology), the 'policing' of the leading classes (consider the 'neo-realism' of the major academic journals, as well as of the international 'mainstream' media), the 'policing' of governments (in the form, for instance, of cultural policies 'compliant with the current order', 'neutral' audit and assurance exercises and processes, or 'objective' evaluation of scientific productivity – the latter, starting from the privilege of English, represent a continuation of old imperialist and colonialist policies by other means).

The transformation of hermeneutics into a dangerous praxis – and philosophy of praxis – goes hand in hand with what Heidegger taught us to recognize as the culmination of metaphysics in the form of what he called *Gestell* – 'enframing' or 'framework' – which is to say, in the total reduction of being (operating through different modes of 'setting' or 'positing' – *Stellen* – see Heidegger 1977: 15ff; see also Malpas 2012: 99–105) to that which is calculable and manipulable – allowing its appearance only within that 'frame'. Through the progressive marginalization and obscuration – the *forgetting* – of what is *not* calculable or manipulable, *Gestell* reduces the world to *itself* – to *Gestell*. Maybe we can find here one meaning of Heidegger's ambiguous statement, to the effect that in the *Gestell* there is 'a first flashing of Ereignis' (Heidegger 2006: 47; see Vattimo 1988: 26) – a sort of *hapax legomenon* in his work (something spoken only once) that can be seen as an optimistic opening consistent with Hölderlin's motto: 'But where danger is, grows/The saving power also' (quoted in Heidegger 1977: 42). In the same pages of *Identity and Difference* where Heidegger alludes to this 'first flashing', he also suggests an explanation of its occurrence: in *Gestell* man and world lose their metaphysical character, more specifically, they lose their character as subject and object. This explanation still leaves open, however, many different readings. On the one hand, one might suggest that Heidegger thinks of *Gestell* as the place of the overcoming of humanism – and so of the overcoming of the subject, of the oppositions of consciousness-thing, *Geist-Natur* and so on ('Zen' readings of Heidegger are particularly significant here – see e.g. Nishitana 1983). On the other hand, we can also interpret the matter as follows: *Dasein*, just as naked of its *humanitas* and reduced to a mere calculable entity, wakes up to the memory (of the oblivion) of being. In either case, the progressive reduction to calculation and technical manipulation appears as preparatory to the overcoming of metaphysics. This is not to be understood merely as an objective 'happening' in the world (how could such 'happening' configure itself?), but is instead a change in the conditions of being – it is something that happens to *Dasein* under the reign of *Gestell*.

Can we suppose that *Gestell* simultaneously brings a *pathos* or suffering that wakes human being to the memory of the oblivion into which *Gestell* throws it?[2] In the origins of Heidegger's *Being and Time*, as it stands in proximity to the spirit of the avant-garde of the beginning of the twentieth century, and already in the debate over the relation between the *Geistes-* and *Naturwissenschaften*, a revolt was underway against the dehumanization of existence, especially as that was evident in the 'rationalization' of work (exemplified by the application of new modes of production and industrial organization in firms such as Fiat and Ford). Hermeneutics, so much taken up with a historical spirit (as *historisch*), so deeply linked to the memories of the past, has become more fully aware of its own 'subversive' inspiration as the *Naturwissenschaften* have themselves been increasingly integrated into the global *Verwaltung*. Consider, for example, education policies as they are operative in schools and universities in most Western industrialized countries today – and especially the difficulty in defending the space of the humanities in teaching programmes and in the distribution of research funds. It is no exaggeration to say that hermeneutics is now the expression of a mode of intellectual life and activity that has been progressively marginalized within contemporary academic hierarchies, and in being so marginalized, politically as well as intellectually, is thereby pushed together with many other similarly marginalized groups (see Vattimo 2012: 208–16).

The latter remark would be quite inconceivable, however, within the frame of philosophy conceived merely as a 'scientific discipline' – philosophy as the 'science of being' whether in the Aristotelian sense or in the sense of Kantian 'critique' (and so as answering to critical questions about knowledge, action and hope). If we compare hermeneutics with those two classical ways of doing philosophy, the distance (an abysmal one) is abundantly clear. It is true that the fundamental problems with which classical philosophy began were often presented as *pathē* – as modes of 'suffering' or 'illness' that required a cure – and the work of the philosopher was presented as a response to those *pathē*. The liberation from the suffering, the discovery of the cure for the illness, was always imagined in terms of the discovery of some incontrovertible *given* – some principle, authority or evidence – even when presented in the form of an Other understood as a person (the God of Augustine). Yet the particular *pathos* that preoccupied Heidegger in *Being and Time* – that of anxiety or *Angst* – cannot be countered through any such 'given', since it is precisely the givenness that is the source of anxiety (our anxiety arises out of our being). And such givenness disturbs us even more unbearably as it objectivizes itself in a world progressively dominated by calculus and manipulation. To put the matter in slightly different terms: at the beginning of the twentieth century the revolt of the 'humanistic spirit' against the self-imposition of social rationalization could still show the traits of an aesthetic revolution – the revolution of the artistic avant-garde and of a theological or philosophical existentialism, but during the past century such forms of 'humanistic' resistance have appeared ever weaker and more partial. Here is part of what is at issue in the *Kehre*, the 'turning', associated with Heidegger's thought – one of the most damaging effects of which was to bring him (even if perhaps temporarily) to Nazism.

The demand for authenticity that emanates from *Dasein's* own being cannot be restricted just to the existentialist perspective of *Being and Time*: the world as anonymous speech was the primary sign of inauthenticity in that work, but the same inauthenticity is even more clearly evident in the world of the great capitalistic organization of industrial work that belongs to *Gestell*. Similarly, Gadamer's critique – albeit respectful and polite – of the hegemonic scientism of the philosophy of his time (including that of neo-Kantianism) could not be contained within the limits of that academic debate alone, but extends to all domains, as does hermeneutics itself. At the same time, it has to be acknowledged that Heidegger's Nazi 'misadventure' can also be seen as the effect of the transformation of hermeneutics into praxis and its philosophy. Yet whatever the dangers, it is impossible to practice an anti-metaphysical mode of thinking by purporting to maintain the position of a neutral observer – of holding to 'a view from nowhere'. The hermeneuticist, if they are to become serious, must also become, fatally, a militant – the question is: for which cause?

Now we can consider the question concerning the future of hermeneutics in the second sense identified earlier. Not only because hermeneutics stands opposed to metaphysics, but also, and above all, because hermeneutics must measure itself against the future, hermeneutics has no world 'outside' to take as its own 'given', not even as a norm written into being (which is nothing but event). Of course, talk of *Gestell* may seem to imply something, some 'phenomenon', that is indeed 'outside' and autonomous. But not for nothing were we led to speak earlier of the possibility that Gestell may itself be accompanied by a certain pathos or suffering. What helps us here is Foucault's notion of *ontologie de l'actualité* (see Foucault 1997) – 'ontology of the present' – which I have tried elsewhere to reinterpret from Heidegger's point of view (see Vattimo 2004: 3–4): remembering being can refer only to the attempt to understand how being gives itself to us in this moment, in the event that properly concerns us and in which we are caught up – it can refer only to the attempt to understand what it means 'to be' today. The terms in which Foucault introduces this notion of an 'ontology of the present', which he contrasts with an 'analytics of truth' (see Foucault 1997: 99–100), originally seemed to me to be overly psychologizing – as if such an 'ontology' concerned nothing more than a certain mode of biographical-historical consciousness. I recognize now that such a reservation can lead to an overlooking of that crucial element of *pathos* or suffering: it is this element, and only this, that allows hermeneutics to be a philosophy of history without being at the same time an objectivistic metaphysics. *Gestell* is thus described only from the perspective of its effect *on us*, and so in terms of the *pathos* that it brings, and not from the perspective of some panoramic view – giving a particular significance, in this content, to the Greek phrase '*pathei mathos*' ('suffer and learn').

But someone could ask: will the militant hermeneuticist undertake some sort of historic action – look to some sort of transformation of the world – on the basis only of their *personal* suffering and what happens to them alone? The frequently repeated demand for an ethics based on universal principles appears here in all its (metaphysical) force. How can the principle of one's own action – as Kant asks – be legislated as universally valid, if the starting point is one's own individual situation and individual *pathos*? Here it should be remarked – although it may seem outrageous – that Heidegger refused to formulate an ethics since to do so would have forced him to develop a metaphysical discourse. Moreover, the Kantian imperative, which is absolutely uncontaminated by any purpose external to it (it is categorical not hypothetical), is a fact of reason – we may also say it is a 'given' – and as such it is something that is indeed metaphysical from Heidegger's point of view. Consequently, if hermeneutics 'has' a future (or an 'image' of it), this can only ever appear as a *project*, and never as something 'given' (as a categorical imperative, for instance, or a natural essence from which norms of actions are derived). What Benjamin says of the revolutionary in his *Theses on the Philosophy of History* (see Benjamin 1969) seems here to be especially apt: the revolutionary who fights for change in the world is not inspired by the image of a new order ahead, but by the memory of the horror of what is past. Here we can add a thesis advanced by Emmanuel Lévinas: ethics rises only by listening and responding to the request for help that the other addresses to me, and not from any rational awareness of what 'is' good or bad (see e.g. Lévinas 1969). 'Until we are a dialogue … ' Hölderlin would say: truth happens only when we are and we still remain in a dialogue. The foundation of a hermeneutical ethics constitutes itself when we are doing something with others – reacting to a *pathos* or suffering that we discover as common, and that gives 'content' to the dialogue itself. Such suffering is not only the suffering that is experienced in the moment, but also the memory of the suffering of those who have gone before – the memory of a history as it constitutes itself and as we are constituted by it.

Can such a project be a 'project' for a world? Reduced to their essential terms, the considerations at issue here recall not only Benjamin and his philosophy of history but, more radically, the passages in the Gospels in which Jesus refuses to answer the questions of his disciples regarding the means by which the Messiah may be identified on the day of *parousia* (see *Matthew* 24:3). There Jesus warns against those who will say 'that is him, the Messiah' at the same time as he nevertheless refuses to provide any positive indications – refuses to provide the objective 'signs' of the sort that may be demanded by the metaphysician. In these Gospel passages are the roots of the ontological difference. The undoubtedly 'apophatic' tone (the tone of *denial* or *negation* – from the Greek *apophēmi*, meaning 'to deny') that is present throughout Heidegger's thought is at the same time a characteristic tone within hermeneutics. That is something that can be found in some of the most important decisive pages of *Being and Time*, in the passage from the existential analytics to the ontology. In §44, at the end of a long excursus on truth, Heidegger writes: 'Being (not entities) is something which "there is" only in so far as truth is. And truth *is* only in so far and as long as Dasein is' (Heidegger 1962: H230). Such a sentence cannot be taken merely as the concluding synthesis of previous analyses. Instead it must be interpreted as intending a programme – a project. The endeavour to remember being against the oblivion of metaphysics – not to forget the ontological difference – aims at letting being be through attending to singular beings. Yet the happening of truth, as this occurs in the conversation or dialogue that we are, is not a matter of bringing those beings to appearance merely as 'true', as 'given', or as fully 'present'. The happening of truth places the singular being in the light of the true precisely because it staves it off – it places it, also and especially, in the background.

We could say, at this point, that the future of hermeneutics does not appear only in terms of some prediction as to what we think will happen to the theory of interpretation in the years to come. What is said here assumes the meaning of a radical subjective genitive: the future will belong to hermeneutics – or it will not be at all. The world of the future – as seen by hermeneutics, as searched for by hermeneutics – is a world where the 'objective' constraints, the 'principle of reality' (which is increasingly indistinguishable from the laws of corporate capitalism) must increasingly be challenged by the world of dialogue and conversation, by the world of the truth-event, by the world of a progressive symbolization in which objects move into the background as that which supports the engagement between subjects and in which the violence of immediacy is also thereby reduced. What is at issue is nothing less than a reformation of the world. A reformation that must be undertaken by a militant hermeneutics with all the tools of the humanities at its disposal – philosophy, theology, fine arts, law, politics – and that will draw the world ever closer to being what for Hegel (and afterwards for Marx) is the place of the spirit, where the spirit feels itself finally (but never thoroughly) at home.

Notes

1 That compliance was expressed in more nuanced fashion in private conversation with me and Richard Rorty in Heidelberg on the day of his hundredth birthday.
2 This idea has been suggested to me by G. Chiurazzi in the seminar he conducted at the University of Turin on 28 March 2014.

Bibliography

Benjamin, Walter (1969) 'Theses on the Philosophy of History', in Illuminations, ed. Hannah Arendt, trans. Harry Zohn, New York: Schocken Books, pp.253–64.

Foucault, Michel (1997) The Politics of Truth, ed. Sylvère Lotringer, New York: Semiotext(e).

Gadamer, H.-G. (1992) Truth and Method, trans. Joel Weinsheimer and Donald G. Marshall, 2nd rev. edn, New York: Crossroad.

Heidegger, Martin (1962) Being and Time, trans. J. Macquariue and Edward Robinson, New York: Harper and Row.

——(1977) The Question Concerning Technology and Other Essays, trans. William Lovitt, New York: Garland.

——(2000) Elucidations of Hölderlin's Poetry, trans. K. Hoeller, New York: Humanity Books.

——(2006) Identität und Differenz, Gesamtausgabe v.11, Frankfurt: Vittorio Klostermann.

Horkheimer, Max and Theodor W. Adorno (2002) Dialectic of Enlightenment: Philosophical Fragments, ed. and trans. Gunzelin Schmid Noerr, Stanford: Stanford University Press.

Lévinas, Emmanuel (1969) Totality and Infinity: An Essay on Exteriority, trans. Alphonso Lingis, Pittsburgh, PA: Duquesne University Press.

Malpas, Jeff (2012) Heidegger and the Thinking of Place, Cambridge, Mass.: MIT Press.

Nietzsche, Friedrich (1978) Thus Spoke Zarathustra, trans. Walter Kaufmann, Harmondsworth: Penguin.

——(1989) Ecce Homo, in The Genealogy of Morals/Ecce Homo, trans. Walter Kaufmann, New York: Vintage.

Nishitana, Keiji (1983) Religion and Nothingness, trans. Jan Van Bragt, Berkeley: University of California Press.

Vattimo, Gianni (1988) The End of Modernity: Nihilism and Hermeneutics in Postmodern Culture, trans. J. R. Snyder, Baltimore: Johns Hopkins University Press.

——(2002) 'Gadamer and the Problem of Ontology', in Gadamer's Century, ed. J. Malpas, U. Arnswald and J. Kertscher, Cambridge, Mass.: MIT Press, pp. 299–306.

——(2004) Nihilism and Emancipation: Ethics, Politics, and Law, ed. S. Zabala, trans. William McCuaig, New York: Columbia University Press.

——(2012) Della Realtà, Milan: Garzanti (translation forthcoming with Columbia University Press).

Vattimo, Gianni and Santiago Zabala (2011) Hermeneutic Communism: From Marx to Heidegger, New York: Columbia University Press.

Zabala, Santiago (2009) The Remains of Being: Hermeneutic Ontology after Metaphysics, New York: Columbia University Press.

INDEX

Please note that page numbers relating to Notes will contain the letter "n" followed by note number. Publications by authors can be found under their specific titles.

Made in United States
North Haven, CT
21 August 2023

40577273R00428